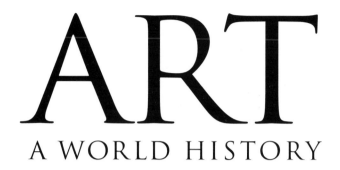

ART

A WORLD HISTORY

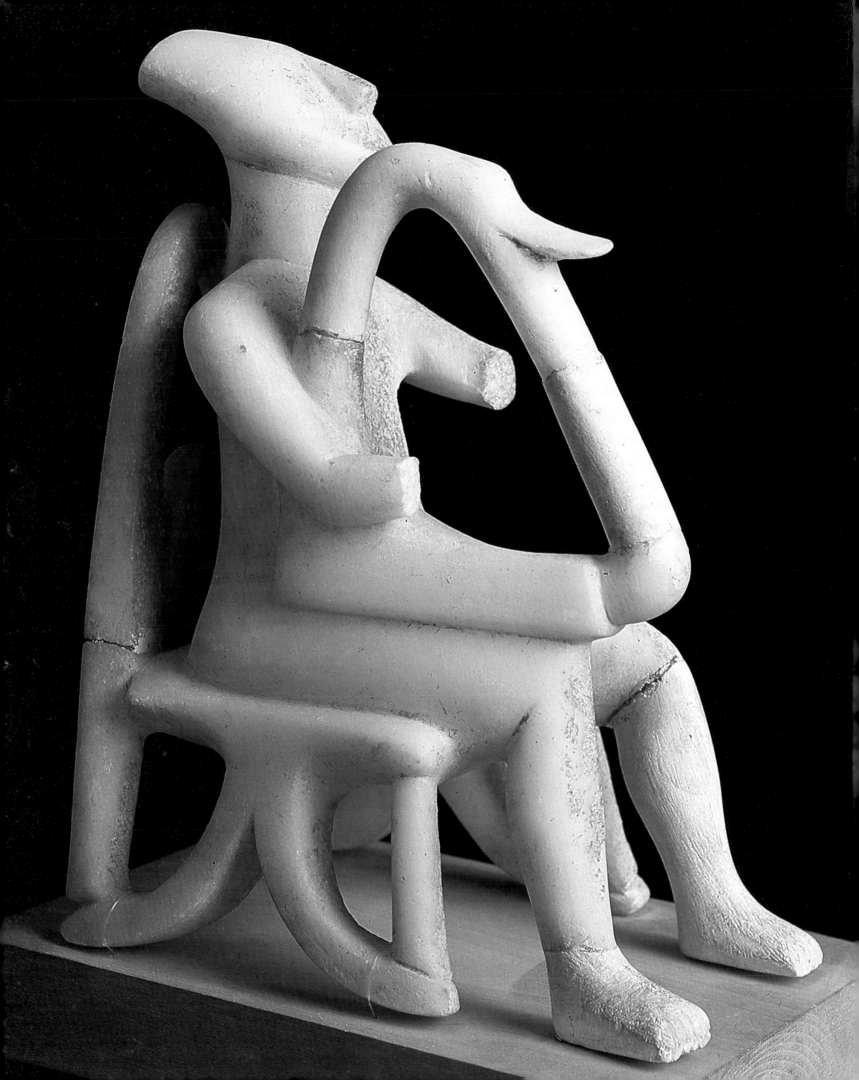

ART

A WORLD HISTORY

DK PUBLISHING, INC.

www.dk.com

A DK PUBLISHING BOOK
www.dk.com

Project editor Jo Marceau
Senior editor Louise Candlish
Editors Fergus Day, David Williams
Assistant editor David Sinden
Coordinating editor Anna Bennett

Art editor Simon Murrell
Senior art editor Heather McCarry
Managing editor Anna Kruger
Deputy art director Tina Vaughan

US editor Ray Rogers

First American Edition 1998
2 4 6 8 10 9 7 5 3
Published in the United States by
DK Publishing, Inc., 95 Madison Avenue,
New York, New York 10016

Library of Congress Cataloging-in-Publication Data

Arte storia universale. English.
    Art: a world history. — 1st American ed.
        p. cm.
    Includes index.
    ISBN 0-7894-2382-0
    1. Art—History. I. Title.
N5300.A69513 1998
709—DC21   97-20234
                                                     CIP

Printed and bound in Spain by Artes Gráficas Toledo. S.A.
D.L. TO: 1416-1999

Page 2:
Lyre Player, from Amorgos,
2400–2200BC. National
Archaeological Museum, Athens.

CONSULTANTS

Dr. Noël Adams, *British Museum*
Tanya Barson,
  Tate Gallery, London
Sarah Blount, *University of
  East Anglia*
Iain Borden, *University
  College London*
David Buckton, *British Museum*
Miranda Bruce-Mitford,
  *School of Oriental and
  African Studies, London*
Warren Carter, *University
  College London*
Amanda Claridge, *Institute of
  Archaeology, University of
  Oxford*
Richard Clay, *University
  College London*
Dominique Collon,
  *Department of Western Asiatic
  Antiquities, British Museum*
Jill Cook, *British Museum*
Christopher Entwhistle,
  British Museum
Don Evely, *University of Oxford*
Claudia Ghetu, *University College
  London*
Robin Hamlyn, *Tate Gallery,
  London*
Colin Harding, *National Museum
  of Photography, Film and
  Television, Bradford*
Louise Hesketh, *University of
  East Anglia*
Joyce Holliday, *University of
  East Anglia*
Dennis Kelly, *University of
  East London*
Julia Kelly, *Courtauld Institute
  Galleries*
Bryony Llewelyn, *University of
  Cambridge*

Ann Menpes, *University of
  East London*
Dr. Oliver Moore, *Sinological
  Institute, Leiden University,
  the Netherlands*
Jim Mower, *School of Oriental and
  African Studies, London*
Susan Owens, *University College
  London*
Michela Parkin, *Tate Gallery, London*
John Pickton, *School of Oriental and
  African Studies, London*
Dr. Paul Roberts, *Department of
  Greek and Roman Antiquities,
  British Museum*
Louise Schofield, *Department of
  Greek and Roman Antiquities,
  British Museum*
John Taylor, *Department of Egyptian
  Antiquities, British Museum*
Helen Thomas, *University College
  London*
Dr. Judith Toms, *Institute of
  Archaeology, University of Oxford*
Cleo Witt, *Holbourne Museum, Bath*
Philippa Baker
Rachel Bean
Helen Castle
Claire O'Mahony
Lynda Stephens

TRANSLATION

John Gilbert
Chrissa Woodhouse
Sara Harris
Ardèle Dejey

AUTHORS
(ITALY)

Enrico Annoscia
Marco Biscione
Rossana Bossaglia
Alessandra Cardelli Antinori
Claudio Cavatrunci
Nicoletta Celli
Cinzia Cingolani
Egidio Cossa
Vittoria Crespi Morbio
Gillo Dorfles
Enrico Leonardo Fagone
Chiara Fagone Bozzi
Silvia Ferrari
Lilli Ghio Vallarino
Alexia Latini
Paolo Moreno
Carlo Pirovano
Federica Romagnoli
Alessandro Rovetta
Evelina Schatz
Erich Steingräber
Giorgio Taborelli
Valerio Terraroli
Silvia Vesco
Susanna Zatti

CONSULTANTS & EDITORS
(ITALY)

Rossana Bossaglia
  *Western modern and
  contemporary art*

Gian Carlo Calza
  Oriental and Islamic art

Maria Antonietta
Fugazzola Delpino
  *African, Pre-Columbian,
  and Oceanic art*

Maria Luisa Gatti Perer
  Medieval and Renaissance art

Paolo Moreno
  *Art of the ancient
  Mediterranean*

Giorgio Taborelli
  Coordinator

CONTRIBUTORS

Alessia Devitini
  Timelines

Antonia Garavelli
Pietro Nimis
  Painting analyses

Particular thanks are due to Flavio
Ermini, Giorgio Seppi,
and Luigi Sterzi for their
contribution to planning this book.

Further thanks are due to Simona
Bartolena, Elisa Dal Canto,
Monica Dalla Pasqua, Giovanna
D'Amia, Natalia Grilli, Ornella
Marcolongo, Alessandra Oleotti,
Giovanni Torresan, and Studio
Editoriale Menabò, Como.

ART
A WORLD HISTORY

THIS BOOK IS INTENDED FOR INTERESTED *readers everywhere as a guide to world art, taking special account of the most up-to-date investigations, discoveries, and opinions to appear in recently published works. In terms of new disciplines and technical innovations in the field of research, plus the opportunities afforded by the mounting of numerous exhibitions throughout the world, art history today is arguably more challenging and exciting – both in form and content – than at any time in the past.*

According to modern thinking, art is the living production of people and cultures, the expression of social realities and ideals – material, economic, and cultural – and a synthesis of the deeper thoughts, emotions, needs, fears, and hopes that are common to people of all periods and all places.

In this world survey, we can identify three fundamental notions that are today generally agreed on by scholars and students alike: that there is no basic difference in the aesthetic quality of the artistic expression of diverse civilizations and periods; that there is no difference in value between the products of the fine arts and the so-called lesser or applied arts; and that it is easier to acquire an intimate knowledge of art through the study of works that are relatively close to us in time.

Consequently, we have combined the art of the Old, New, and developing worlds into a continuous narrative, beginning with prehistory. We have treated all forms of art together; and we have devoted the greatest amount of space (proportionately) to modern and contemporary art.

Pride of place necessarily goes to pictorial art, simply because a painting or drawing lends itself better to photographic reproduction than sculpture or architecture. A good photograph can provide an accurate idea of, say, a two-dimensional watercolor. A photograph of a statue or the exterior of a palace, on the other hand, can convey only a partial aspect of the whole, although obviously it can and does focus upon many eloquent and expressive details.

It is, of course, possible to adopt the conventional approach to art history by considering the life and work of exceptional artists and describing outstanding masterpieces. The latter cannot be ignored because they reflect wide-ranging and profound expressions of mental attitude, taste, and creative intelligence. Insofar as it is possible to make a distinction, we have attempted to consider forms, trends, personalities, and movements that are of a wide cultural as well as aesthetic importance. This will be clear from the list of contents.

Although we have aimed throughout for clarity, we have tried to avoid the obvious and to take particular account of the latest debates in the world of art. In the field of classical antiquity, for example, we have tried to follow original lines of inquiry, mentioning major artists who are little known, suggesting alternative attributions, and illustrating innovative approaches to certain aspects of art that, even at the distance of many centuries, appear strikingly modern. In our survey of the long and complex Renaissance period, we have preferred to place more emphasis on the strand of creativity that can be traced throughout central Europe than on the incontestably important, but all too familiar, period of central Italian achievement. These are just two examples, but they may serve to underline the freedom our authors have enjoyed in presenting their given material in the way they see fit, though mindful of the critical opinions and attitudes toward art history that prevail today.

This is a collective work that bears the distinctive signature of each and every author. It is they who have organized their subject matter into separate though occasionally overlapping sections, selected the salient points, and contributed to the graphic presentation. The authors of the longer essays and shorter articles in boxes include acknowledged experts and younger researchers. Their assembled work has gradually been shaped and integrated by an experienced team of editors, designers, consultants, and, not least, translators into several languages. Cooperation has therefore been very important; the impact of words and pictures in the book derives from the effective combination of the creative skills of everyone concerned in its production.

The need to follow a pattern, to maintain a chronological order, has not been allowed to impose limitations on the treatment of a subject which, if necessary, is amplified by others in a different context. Thus the cultural cross-references between literature, the visual arts, and music are clearly defined. Such associations are enriching in that they stimulate the personal urge to make other discoveries. Moreover, the opinions and arguments of different authors are of value in helping to formulate one's own thoughts and ideas.

This is not a cold, scholarly history of art. What we are trying to do is to share with the reader our love of art , to reflect on its past splendor, its present vitality, and its future potential. In the spirit of relaxed discourse rather than formal lecture, we hope to be able to communicate something of our own experience, to stress what we consider to be important, to pass on a little of what we ourselves have learned from our teachers and, very often, from our pupils. We have endeavored to present our subject in a lively, informative manner, focusing on mainstream trends, exploring interesting byways, pausing to sum up and consolidate information, pointing the way toward independent study. Nothing, however, has been left to chance. The overall structure is orderly – long essays interspersed with extended boxes of subsidiary information, detailed examination and dissection of particular paintings, brief surveys of key personalities and works, and timelines showing comparative and associated art forms. Everywhere, we have looked for links and continuity.

Readers can use this work in any way they choose. They can read it all the way through from start to finish, like a novel – after all, the story of art is an unending novel and our version merely a digest of it. Alternatively, they can simply enjoy it as a book to be dipped into for reference or pleasure. They can begin with those that are of greatest interest and with which they are perhaps most familiar, or they can be more adventurous and explore unknown territory that may lead to fresh insights. They can decide for themselves whether we have been tempted to overvalue the work, say, of Goya or Cézanne, or they can weigh up the pros and cons of the current view of Picasso. They can turn to a page where a Caravaggio painting is analyzed or to one that compares the respective treatment of the same subject by Velázquez and Bacon. They can decide whether they agree with the views offered or whether, on closer examination of the picture, they are inclined to draw different conclusions.

No matter how familiar our readers are with the topics under discussion, we hope that they will be sufficiently stimulated by the combination of words and images to formulate their individual ideas and opinions and, just as importantly, to derive pleasure from the contents. If, on closing the pages, they feel impelled to go out and visit a gallery or a museum, to see art with their own eyes and not just through ours, we, the authors and publishers, will feel amply rewarded.

CONTENTS

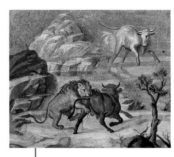

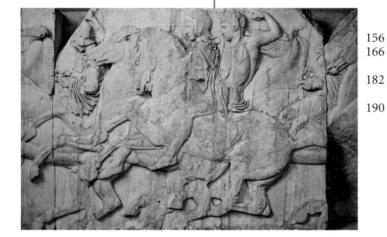

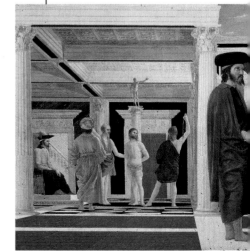

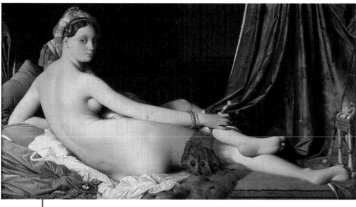

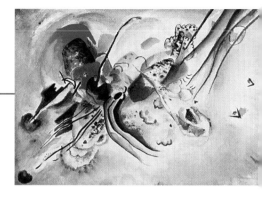

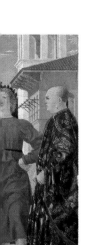

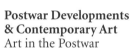

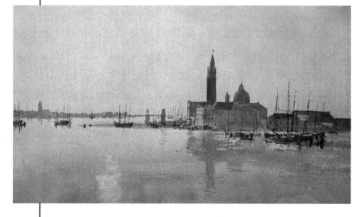

Erich Steingräber

WHAT IS ART TODAY?

IN OUR PLURALISTIC SOCIETY, *we can no longer answer this question unequivocally. When, in 1913, Marcel Duchamp denied the formal creative act by promoting his "Ready-mades," he lodged a provocative protest against the traditional thinking of public museums, which placed art on a pedestal. Since that moment, no one can doubt the fact that art, and the way we respond to it, has undergone a radical change. It was Dada that decisively refuted the old, all-embracing claim of the work of art as both guide and influence.*

Until the end of the *ancien régime*, wiped out in the French Revolution in 1789, the individual arts were part of a greater, total work of art that aspired to be absolute. It was the sensitive expression of order based on religion, accepted in Europe both by the Church and the monarchy, but equally by the political regimes that controlled the ancient cultures of pre-Columbian America, the Near East, and the Far East.

In pre-industrial civilizations, artists did not enjoy much freedom of individual expression. They were wholly dependent on the person or organization commissioning the work in question. During more than five millennia of world art history, artistic freedom was possible for the first time only after the "secularization" of the absolutist European states. From the late 18th century onward, there developed in Europe and the United States a liberal model of state constitution founded upon the concept of democracy. The hitherto unchallenged unitarian image of the world based on Christian values began to crumble and dissolved with the emergence of the independent concepts of Church, State, Arts, and Science. Aesthetics proclaimed the absolute autonomy of the artistic sphere. As an increasingly secular society cast off its constricting shackles, the newly independent artist was now eager to confront social issues and problems.

The stylistic authenticity of history, nurtured on the substance of past ages, already harbored the seeds of future development. The pretence of "art for art's sake," which culminated in Impressionism and which imposed criteria of aesthetic finality, stripped the work of art of virtually any function. The choice of theme became irrelevant. In delighting the eye, the painting served only for personal pleasure.

Nineteenth-century middle-class European art had, like Janus, two faces. It already prefigured the arrival of modernity, but, by breaking radically with the past, it led only to the avant-garde movements of the early 20th century. In different ways and in different European countries, Fauves, Expressionists, Futurists, Cubists, Dadaists, Surrealists, and metaphysical painters reacted like seismographs to the profound upheavals provoked by World War I and to the new ideas engendered by the natural sciences after the revolution in traditional physics brought about by atomic physics.

The object in painting was progressively dissolved. In 1913, Wassily Kandinsky painted his first nonfigurative works. At the same time, other artists sought new principles of composition along the path of geometrical abstraction. Today's European art is derived from the epoch-making innovations of Braque, Picasso, Boccioni, Kandinsky, Marc, Malevich, Mondrian, Klee, Duchamp, De Chirico, Ernst, and Dalí.

In 20th-century architecture, the school that had the greatest following was that of the Bauhaus, founded by Gropius in 1919 at Weimar. "Pure architecture," dominated by geometry and freed from painting, sculpture, and decoration, conquered the force of gravity by placing itself at the service of the constantly growing needs of the mass societies of the great cities. Nevertheless, 20th-century architects have also developed forms based on Abstract Expressionism. Highly evolved forms of abstract and technical art mingle with modern architecture to create a universal language comprehensible everywhere. After World War II, with the development of "heroic" action painting and the subsequent reaction of Pop art, the United States, until then largely influenced by European art, assumed for the first time in history a dominant role that would continue for over thirty years. Paris had finally lost its position of unchallenged supremacy.

Quotations taken almost literally from comic strips, with riotous colors from an imaginary world, rapidly assumed an iconic role in art, proclaiming the American way of life – the dream of wealth, fame, and glamour. In a consumer society, Pop art, with its parallels in punk and pornography, had no high intellectual or visionary pretensions, adopting the slogan of "everything is beautiful" – even cans of Campbell's soup stacked tightly together. It was this that constituted the point of convergence between Pop art and Dada.

In contrast to the optimism of the American artistic scene, European art of the 1960s onward seemed to be sucked increasingly into the area of political and social tensions, finding its own most powerful expression in the revolutionary student protests that erupted in Paris in 1968. Paris, Berlin, Frankfurt, Milan, Rome, and London were the fulcrums of the "New Culture." Dada, which had provided weapons for the artists who supported a cultural revolution, offered fertile stimuli to the neo-avant-garde art scene, which continued to assail artistic barriers in every category, creating a definite effect of *déjà vu*.

The interpretation of Duchamp's equation "Art=Nature and Life" became the central question of Tachism, arte povera, Op art, Body art, Fluxus, and conceptual art or "happenings," which aimed to transform the observer and art lover into an active participant in the creative process. Joseph Beuys declared: "Every human being is an artist," paraphrasing the broad concept of art matured in the field of social therapy.

Because art proved incapable of fulfilling the revolutionary mandate of bringing about a radical change of existing society, silence descended upon the politically active avant-garde and its Marxist interpreters of the Frankfurt School. Years previously, Sartre had written: "Who can believe that the bloodbath of *Guernica*, that masterpiece, recruited even a single person to the Spanish cause?" Today, when there are no longer any taboos, there are not even pretexts for "direct action," what the Spanish philosopher and critic Ortega y Gasset called the "Magna Carta of the barbarians." Those who still pursue the principles of an avant-garde appear hopelessly outdated, sadly convinced that theirs is the path to progress and determined to impose their views on others. One hopes, nevertheless, that we have seen an end to the worldwide manipulation of art practice by unscrupulous lobbies composed of cultural politicians, museum directors, and gallery owners hidebound by ideology, not to mention journalists intent upon pursuing the *Zeitgeist*. Artistic management too commonly adopts an overt marketing strategy, operating autonomously and reaping huge profits from its activities.

At the end of the 1970s, there was a switch of interest away from social theory and back to history. The Postmodern artist was no longer prepared to take on political responsibilities that he or she could not honor. There was a reaction against the oppressive claim of the avant-garde to a monopoly of opinion and action. In 1980, Bonito Oliva coined the more significant term "Trans-avant-garde." The complex relationship between Postmodernism and tradition is one of many factors that determine the myriad forms of artistic expression, including the obvious risk of noncommittal superficiality. Jean-François Lyotard was the philosophical mouthpiece in France.

In this context, the most open, impartial, and tolerant discussion comes from America. For example, the US-based British artist David Hockney, much admired also as a stage designer, brought Tristan, in the Oseberg Viking ship, onto the stage of the Dorothy Chandler Pavilion in Los Angeles. Back in 1975, at age 38, he had said: "We should not forget that many figurative artists are admired: yet the idea of abstract art also deserves to be fully appreciated, even if many do not consider it to be more interesting (and indeed I subscribe to the latter view)." He was saying that even present-day modernism recognizes an essential characteristic of European art and thought, namely the dialectic principle, the reconciliation of extremes. In its free relationship with the past, the Postmodern work of art, even in its most outrageous manifestations, acknowledges the evocative impact of history rather than an absolute respect for historic tradition.

Looking back in time arouses nostalgic, sad emotion, by reason of the fact that the beauty of our world, as manifest in examples of, or references to, past art, is transitory. The ancient theme of *vanitas* carried similar poetic and emotional connotations. However, the coziness of such visions, not without irony, rules out any rhetoric, any excessive display of sentiment.

Although, in the 1970s, the sensational staging of politically inspired multimedia happenings met with the widespread incomprehension of most people – the gap between art and public had never been so great – art in the last twenty years has met with considerable success. The predictions of the left-wing Hegelians, who believed art might be dying, have not come to pass.

Belief that there are no substitutes for original works of art has not been abandoned, even in the age of technical reproduction. Everywhere in the world new galleries of modern art are opening. The Pompidou Centre in Paris – built over two decades ago by Richard Rogers and Renzo Piano – is an impressive multimedia cultural machine conceived as an antimuseum. With its daily figure of some 24,000 visitors, it is among the world's major public attractions.

In the era of mass tourism, looking at art is undoubtedly one of our favorite pastimes.

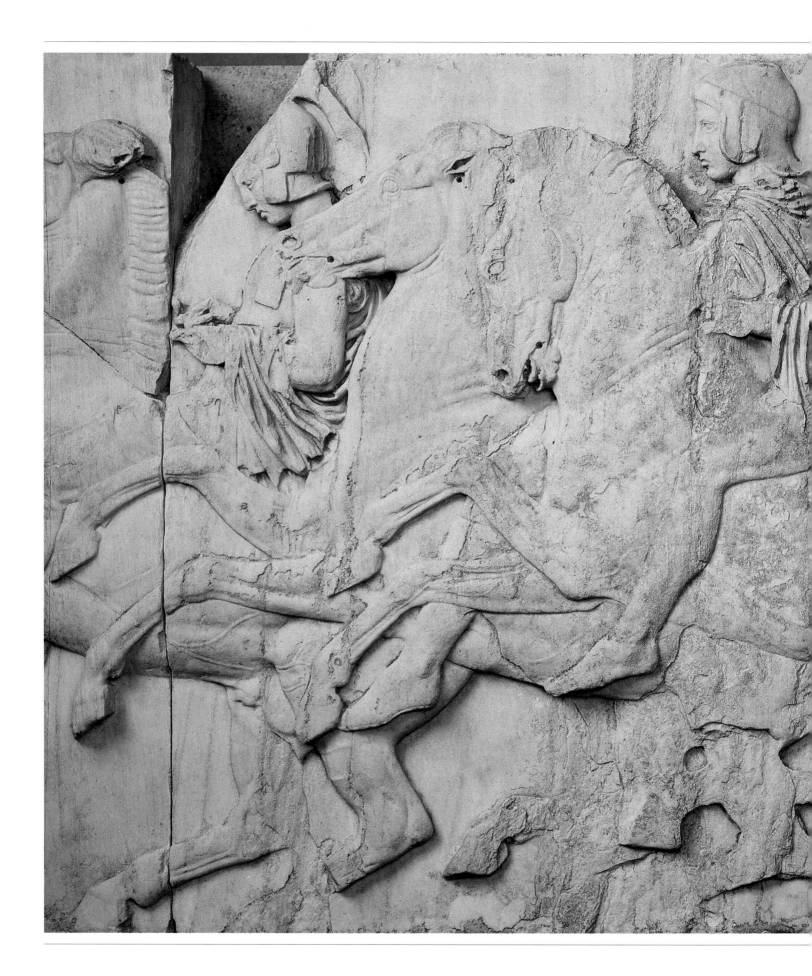

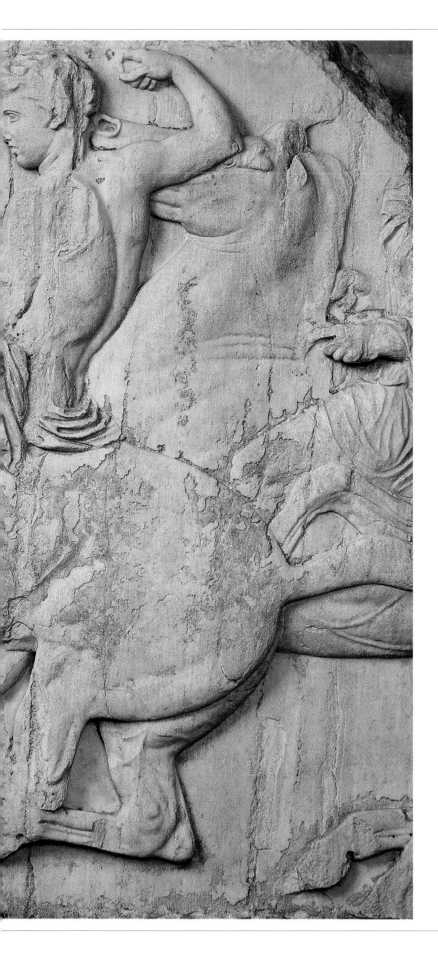

PREHISTORIC & ANCIENT ART

From the Paleolithic Age to the Pre-Classical Civilizations

Prehistoric Art
The Art of the Ancient Kingdoms
The Art of the Ancient East
Ancient Aegean Art

Hellenic & Italic Civilizations

The Art of the Greeks
Italic Art

Phidias, detail of a group of horsemen,
frieze from the Parthenon. British Museum, London.

PREHISTORIC ART

Prehistoric people often represented their world – and perhaps their beliefs – through visual images. Art emerged with the appearance and dispersion of fully modern people through Africa, Europe, Asia, Australasia, and the Americas. Paintings, sculptures, engravings, and, later, pottery reveal not only a quest for beauty but also complex social systems and spiritual concepts.

The first art that we can recognize appears in association with the remains of fully modern people. These people were just like us, although their lifestyles depended on hunting and foraging for food or, later, on pastoralism and subsistence agriculture. It is possible that earlier peoples might have decorated their bodies and clothes or marked trees or features in the landscape but, if they did, evidence of their art has not survived. Recognizable art dates from at least 38,000BC in Europe, Africa, and Australia. There are also controversial claims for rock art of similar age in

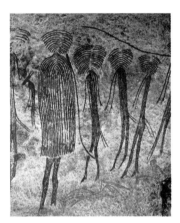

Cave painting of procession of stylized human figures officiating at a rite, Kondoa region, Irangi, South Africa, Latest Stone Age (fifth to first millennium BC).

South America. Works of this early period are not simple. They do not show development in the manner of a child's drawing, that is, gaining competence and accuracy in realistic representation before perhaps achieving a more mature confidence for abstraction. Rather, the oldest known works of art, including paintings, sculptures, and engravings, seem to show all these qualities at once. They are the products of minds as intellectually capable and sophisticated as our own. In Europe and Africa, early works of art depict animals and humans and include

symbols. The former may be drawn or sculpted realistically or represented by the clever emphasis of a distinctive characteristic, such as the tusks of the mammoth or the horn of a rhinoceros. Paintings, low relief sculptures, and engravings adorned areas of caves and rock shelters where hunter-foragers lived. They also covered dark caverns and less frequently visited recesses where light from fires and lamps illuminated occasions which probably had special social and spiritual significance.

With the spread of farming as a way of life, people began

TOPOGRAPHICAL COMPOSITIONS

Early farming communities depicted their view of the area in which they lived. So-called topographical compositions include animal pens and "maps" of villages and, later, towns. In Valcamonica, several of these constitute the most ancient maps known in Europe,

Schematic relief of the Bedolina Map, cave engraving from Valcamonica, Italian Alps, Bronze Age (third to first millennium BC).

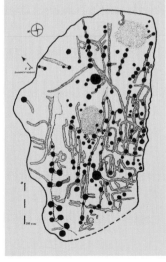

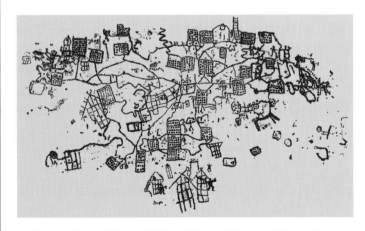

Schematic relief of the engraving of the Topographical Stone of Jebel Amud, Jordan, fourth to third millennium BC. The stone is about 54 square feet (five square meters) in width.

such as the Bedolina Map. It is possible to make out cultivated fields, access paths, houses, and other topographical details. One large composition found at Okladni-kov on Lake Baikal (Siberia) includes human figures and areas filled with squares or circles in solid or dotted lines, which are suggestive of a harvest scene. The Wall-map of Çatal Hüyük (Turkey) is unique, showing an urban settlement with an erupting volcano, the oldest documentation of such an occurrence. The Topographical Stone of Jebel Amud in the Jordanian desert, reproduces the layout of a zone comprising 150 settlements (indicated by various shapes) joined to one another by engraved paths.

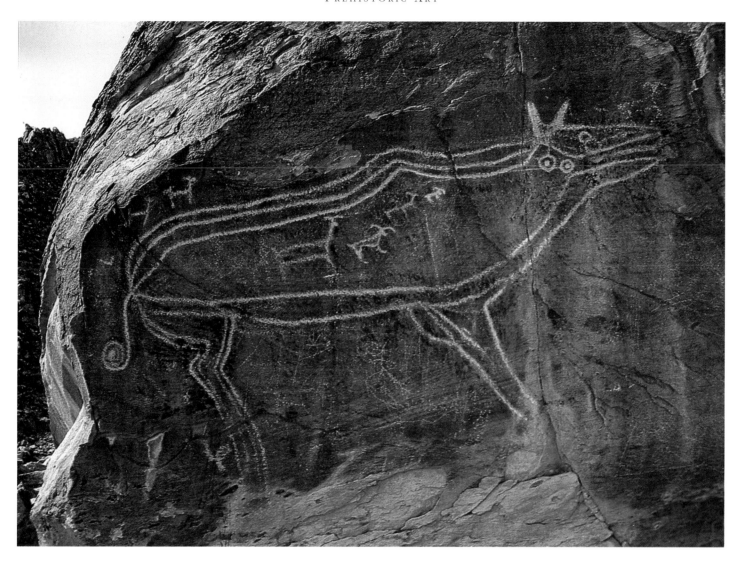

Cave engraving with figure of mythical beast, Mount Helan, Ningzia, China, Archaic hunter period (12th–10th millennium BC).

Cave painting relief showing cattle, deer, ibex, and hunters, Cueva de la Veja, Spain, tenth to sixth millennium BC.

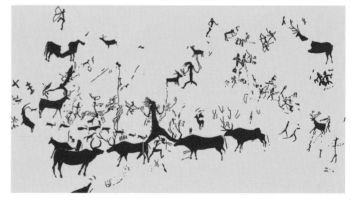

A SENSE OF CONTINUITY

In temples dating from historic times, structures and images may be superimposed over one another. The same

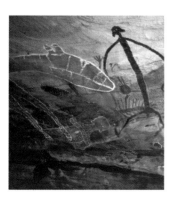

Ten layers of painting from the 20th millennium BC to the present day, Giant Horse cave, Cape York Peninsula, Australia.

happened over periods of thousands of years with inscriptions and paintings on rocks in the open air or deep in caves. This may signify a spiritual need to establish a sense of continuity. In many sites, there are examples of multiple superimpositions dating from prehistory to modern times. They range from Valcamonica in Italy to sites in Australia, where ancient compositions are worshiped to this day and sometimes "freshened up" for new ceremonies.

to settle in villages and territories were defined. Drawings like maps and landscapes appeared, along with domesticated animals and more human figures. Changing styles of decorated pottery became the designer labels of successive generations of prehistoric peoples.

Of all the known prehistoric

works of art, some 70 percent may be attributed to hunter-foragers, 13 percent to herders and stock raisers, and 17 percent to people with an organized economy (farmers, livestock breeders, and the like). The cave art of all social groups consists of five principal motifs: human figures, animals, tools and

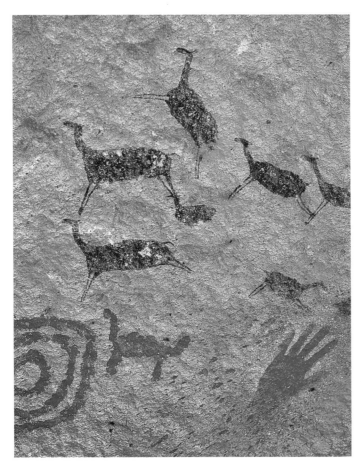

Cave painting with camels and hands (pictograms) and concentric circles (ideograms), Chubut, Patagonia, Toldense culture (tenth millennium BC).

throughout. Animal associations vary, but compositions including particular pairs of animals, such as bison and horses in Europe or elephants and giraffes in Africa, are known. On both continents, mythical beasts including half animal, half human creatures are occasionally depicted. Portraits of people are rare, and landscapes, plants, fruit, and flowers are unknown.

In Africa, south of the Sahara, and in present-day Tanzania (Kondoa and Singida in the Rift Valley), ancient hunters left black and yellow paintings and graffiti in granite caves and sandstone galleries. Later polychrome works are also found here, including ideograms, paintings, handprints, and rare human figures, together with the traditional association of elephants and giraffes. In densely inhabited North Africa, art is found on rock walls at the foot of mountain massifs such as Tibesti and Tassili, now surrounded by vast deserts.

In Europe, some 200 caves and rock shelters are known to contain art. The majority occur in France and Spain, with a few in Italy, Portugal, Romania, and Russia. The oldest sites are attributed to the Aurignacian period (36,000–30,000BC). It is notable that paintings and figurines of this phase often depict dangerous animals such as lions, bears, hyenas, and woolly rhinoceroses, as well as humans and horses and other food animals. Handprints and dot motifs also appear. The colors used were produced from ochre (reds and yellows), manganese dioxide (violet and black), and charcoal (black). These minerals were pulverized on stone palettes and mixed with animal fat to moisten them before they were applied with the fingers, bone spatulas, or brushes. Stone engraving tools known as burins were used to engrave and carve portable works. In the later European periods of the Solutrean-Magdalenian (24,000–12,000BC), large low relief sculpture, engravings, clay modeling, and big compositions including many animals are characteristic at sites such as Roc-de-Sers, Lascaux, and Niaux in France.

weapons, rudimentary local maps, and symbols or ideograms. These motifs occur on portable objects (engraved, sculpted, or clay-modeled) and immovable surfaces (rock paintings and engravings).

EUROPEAN CAVE AND ROCK ART

The cave and rock art of the later Old Stone Age or Upper Paleolithic (which ended in about 10,000BC) is especially famous and has certain particular characteristics. In these older sites, large pictures of animals are only rarely associated with human figures, whereas in more recent paintings animals are smaller and people more numerous. Within sites, one animal may be more frequently represented than others. Some animals may be restricted to certains parts of the cave; others may occur

ANIMAL IMAGES

Animals are to be found everywhere in prehistoric art, being the favorite subjects of hunters, herdsmen, and breeders. We can recognize species and breeds that still exist today. These pictures also furnish us with precious contemporary documents of animals now extinct from the region of the paintings, such as the cave lion, bear, saber-toothed tiger, mammoth, *Homoicerus* (large-horned buffalo), and giant deer. There are elaborate paintings of animals in the cave "sanctuaries" of France and Spain and in open-air shelters all over the world. In Europe, the animals most often depicted were horses, bison, mammoths, reindeer, aurochs, wild boars, fish, eels, birds, and other animals

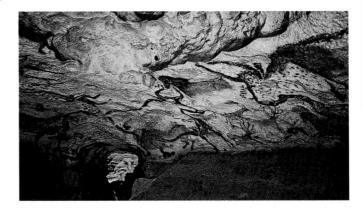

Rock painting of bison, deer, and horses, France, Upper Paleolithic (13,500BC).

valued for food and raw materials such as fur, leather, antlers, and ivory. In Tassili and Tibesti in Africa the teeming fauna of rivers and lakes (hippopotami, crocodiles, fish, and birds), the plains (cattle, goats, and sheep), and the savanna (elephants, giraffes, and rhinoceroses) are brought to life on rock walls.

Among the most prized animal images are those at Altamira, near Santander in northern Spain. There are life-size images of bison as well as naturalistic portrayals of stags, wild boar, and wild horses.

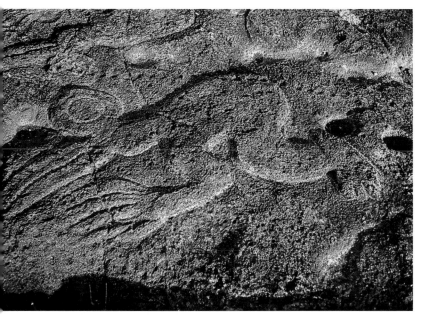

In some sites like Altamira in Spain (the first example of cave art to be discovered), wooden scaffolding must have been used to paint the remarkable friezes on high walls and ceilings.

In the Near and Middle East, Paleolithic art made its first appearance prior to 12,000BC. Archaic hunter-foragers of central Arabia left art in the form of shallow to deep engravings, while, in India, some of the rock paintings of the Vindihya Hills may date from about 14,000BC. However, many of the earliest

High relief pictograph on stone of a bird man, Easter Island, Laura culture (fourth millennium BC).

depictions drawn in yellow have been painted over with scenes in red dating from the Bronze Age and white historical pictures. The red paint was obtained from plant stems and leaves.

THE MOTIFS OF ROCK ART

In Australia, the Murray culture (20,000–8,000BC) and the Panaramitee culture (10,000–3,000BC) produced notable ideographic engravings. In Patagonia (the southernmost region of South America), the "Toldense" people covered their caves

---

DECORATED VASES

Vase decoration is a typically Neolithic art form. The first, fairly simple buff-colored terracotta vases date from the Peiligang culture of China (seventh to sixth millennium BC). Later findings from the Yang-Shao culture (fifth to fourth millennium BC) include vases decorated with fish and other animals and tripodal vessels shaped like owls. The figures not only had symbolic significance but also modified the appearance of the vase by focusing attention on the decoration, the background color contrasts, and the rhythm of the outlines. The motifs shown, although the same as those used for mural art, also assumed other meanings. By the third millennium BC, the variety of form and ornamentation of pottery was already well developed. Goblets, bowls, and

covered dishes had now come into existence.

In the Near and Middle East, the production of ceramics had begun by the sixth millennium BC. Simple, rough, burnished or reddish-colored wares were made, the mouths of which formed holes. They were decorated with impressed or rolled shells and geometric and figurative motifs.

In Africa, the oldest known pottery has been found in Egypt at Merimda and then Faiyum (fifth millennium BC), whereas in southern Europe it dates from the seventh millennium BC. The latter was often well finished and painted with red or black geometric designs. By the sixth millennium BC, banded pottery known as *Bandkeramik* had appeared across central Europe from France to the Ukraine. It was decorated with incised parallel lines, often filled in with dots or cross-hatching.

Sall guan vase in painted terracotta with stylized animal shapes, Miadigou, Henan province, China, Chinese Neolithic, Yang-shao culture (fifth to fourth millennium BC).

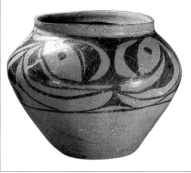

This chart, which shows the most important ceramic types from the Old World Neolithic, follows Müller-Karpe, History of the Stone Age, plate 13. The shapes pertain to the Mesopotamian, Anatolian, Persian, and Egyptian Neolithic (sixth to third millennium BC).

MAIN OLD WORLD NEOLITHIC CERAMIC FORMS

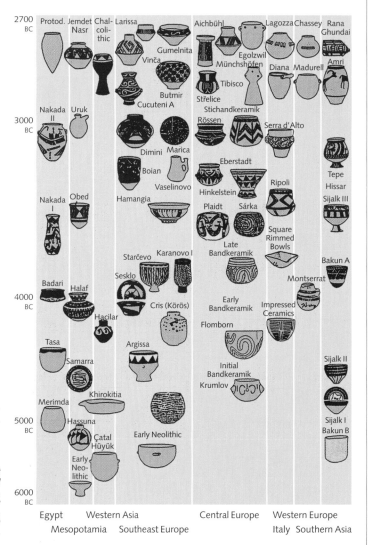

THE DAWN OF ABSTRACT ART: SEXUAL SYMBOLS

Sexual symbols occur frequently in prehistoric art in conjunction with animals. These include phalluses and vulvas, and perhaps the breasts and pudenda of the female figurines. In 1968, Leroi-Gourhan suggested that the horse and deer of Africa and ibex of Europe were male symbols, and that the giraffe of Africa and bison, cattle, and mammoths of Europe were female symbols.

Male symbols also included long, narrow signs such as rows of dots, parallel lines, feathers, sticks, and rods. Female symbols were "broad" signs such as rectangles, triangles, ovals, parentheses, and empty bodies. "Narrow" male symbols can be found deep inside and at the entrance of caves, together with "male" animals, whereas the "broad" female symbols are located in the central areas alongside the "female" animals.

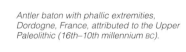

Antler baton with phallic extremities, Dordogne, France, attributed to the Upper Paleolithic (16th–10th millennium BC).

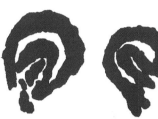

Carved reliefs of two vulva symbols from a much larger series, Helan Shan, Ningzia region, China, Archaic hunter period (12th–10th millennium BC)

Cave engravings of stylized vulva and phallus symbols, Muleje cave, San Borjita Sierra, Baja California, Mexico, Archaic hunter period (before the eighth millennium BC).

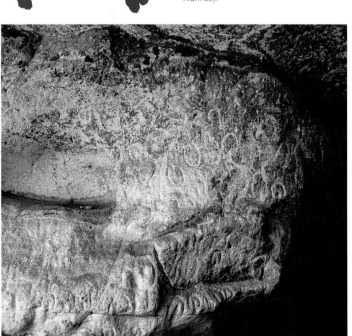

hands are of children (for example, at Gargas, Les Combarelles, and Le Postel in France and Altamira in Spain) or of babies (Lascaux in France). Interpretations vary: they may be symbols of possession or marks of rituals and ceremonies. Handprints dating from the early Neolithic have been found at Çatal Hüyük in Turkey.

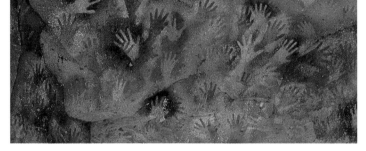

HANDPRINTS

Hands are frequently encountered in Upper Paleolithic cave art. Prints were obtained either in "positive," by pressing the hands, smeared with red, white, or black, over the wall surface; in "negative," by outlining the hands in color; or in "pseudo-positive," by outlining the hands in one color and pressing them against the wall, which was painted with a different color. They are almost always left hands (the right hand was used for painting) and often female (for example, at Patagonia), with the fingers sometimes appearing mutilated (Laussel and Gargas in France, El Castillo in Spain) or confined to the nails at the end of a long arm (for example, Santian in Spain). At times, the

Cave painting with negative and positive handprints of female left hands, Rio Pinturas, Chubut, Patagonia, Toldense culture (tenth millennium BC).

ABSTRACT SYMBOLS

In all cave art, from the Aurignacian onward, abstract motifs are found alongside human and animal figures and are given equal prominence. Abstraction arose from the need to represent, in a sign, an idea with a meaning unknown to outsiders, and it was achieved either simply or symbolically. Paleolithic people practiced abstraction in the form of repetitive symbols, which represented primitive logical constants that were widely shared and diffused. These included schematic figures of

and shelters with handprints. After about 12,000BC, a new style (derived from Africa and depicting numerous humans and smaller animals) appears in the Spanish Levant and Italy. This coincides with a phase known in Europe as the Mesolithic, a period sometimes regarded as transitional between Paleolithic hunting and foraging and the earliest phases of farming

referred to as Neolithic. Scandanavian pictures of this period and the Neolithic include depictions of boats and skis.
In North Africa, the period 12,000–6000BC also sees the introduction of branches, fruit, and leaves into paintings with people and animals. Drawings changed to reflect the change of environment, which caused the spread of

the desert and the extinction from these areas of elephants, giraffes, lions, rhinoceroses, and crocodiles. They also show the introduction of domesticated dogs, cattle, sheep, and goats as the hunter-forager economies were replaced. South of the Sahara between 5,000 and 1,000BC, images became more naturalistic and identifiable. The outlines are particularly

precise and expressive, but the figures of elephants, deer, giraffes, and other wild animals still represent archetypes rather than particular individuals of the species. As part of an unbroken artistic tradition, rock art in sub–Saharan Africa continued into comparatively recent times. The tradition has also persisted in Australia, where it still fulfills important social

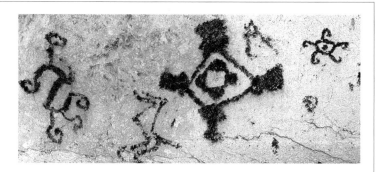

Cave pictograms, Porto Badisco, Apulia, Italy, sixth to third millennium BC.

animals, signs of vulvas and phalluses, handprints, series of dots and notches, which possibly had a numeric significance, and the occasional stylized anthropomorphic symbol. Other representations were grouped in similarly associated sequences. These take various forms: pictograms, mythograms, schematic figures,

or barely indicated figures of humans and animals, ideograms, abstract repetitive signs – such as arrows, sticks, tree shapes, disks, crosses and "V" shapes, parallel lines, series of dots – and psychograms, signs that have no obvious reference to objects or symbols.

Cave engravings of ideograms, Panaramitee, southern Australia, 12th–5th millennium BC. These ideograms are considered sacred to this day.

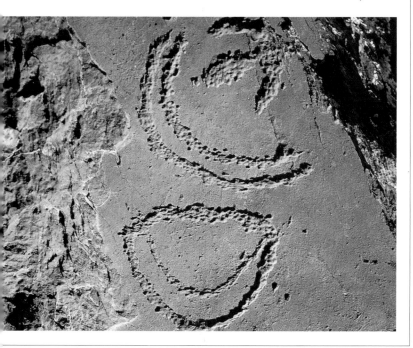

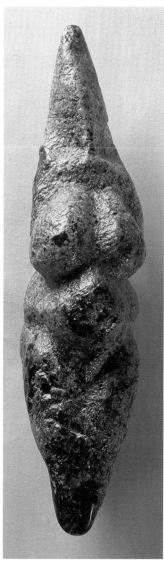

The Venus of Savignano, Modena, Italy, 18th–8th millennium BC. Pigorini Museum, Rome.

PORTABLE ART

The oldest portable art from Russia and central and western Europe includes carvings of animals such as bears, lions, and mammoths, as well as remarkable human figures, including one with a lion's head from Hohlensteinstadel, Germany. These figures were made from bone, antler, ivory, and stone.

Spearthrowers were the most effective hunting devices before the development of the bow, and carved and decorated examples of these have been found. The technique of working in these materials gradually became more refined. Simple incised and dot decoration began to appear on equipment and personal ornaments, such as pins and pendants, which began to appear more often. The period between 30,000 and 20,000BC is most noted for images of women. Generally characterized by large breasts, stomachs, buttocks, thighs, and exaggerated pudenda, these figures represent women in all stages of life: pubescence, pregnancy, childbirth, and the obesity of later life.

Bison carved in bone, La Madeleine, Dordogne, France, 13th millennium BC.

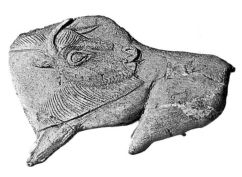

and spiritual functions. Prehistoric art, in general, can be seen as the representation of a symbolic system that is an integral part of the culture that creates it. It is therefore not readily intelligible to other cultures. The symbols often appear ambiguous, and it is likely that they have also changed in meaning within the same culture that originally produced them.

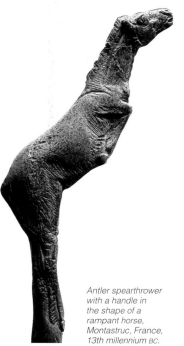

Antler spearthrower with a handle in the shape of a rampant horse, Montastruc, France, 13th millennium BC.

Only rarely do they have faces, as in the lovely portrait head on the Brassempouy "Venus" found in France, although they often show individual touches in their hairstyles and jewelry. "Venuses," as archeologists have called the more detailed female sculptures, are more common outside France, especially across Russia, and some particularly fine examples have also been found in Germany and Italy.

Later portable art is noted for its more naturalistic representations of animals on items of everyday equipment and personal ornaments.

THE ART OF THE ANCIENT KINGDOMS

*From the end of the fourth millennium BC, civilizations of farmers
living along the Nile, the Euphrates, and the Tigris and between
the Caspian and Mediterranean Seas created highly developed social
systems and sophisticated artistic cultures. Much of this
remains at the root of art today.*

Between 3100 and 3000BC, the kingdoms of Upper and Lower Egypt were united by a king named Narmer, who founded the first dynasty. This was effectively the first great state, with numerous cities including Memphis, where the king resided.

For the Egyptians, art was associated with the creative process of the universe. According to religious tradition, Khnum, the potter god with a ram's head, fashioned the world and modeled every living form on his potter's wheel. The Egyptians were also deeply influenced by magic and faith in transcendental forces, which needed to be humored or appeased in order to counteract their negative effects.

Wooden tomb model showing cattle census, 11th dynasty. Egyptian Museum, Cairo.

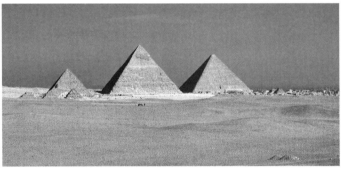

Pyramids of King Khufu, Khafre, and Menkaure, Giza.

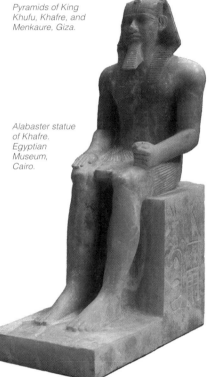

Alabaster statue of Khafre. Egyptian Museum, Cairo.

EGYPTIAN ART

Testimony to the intense cultural activity that characterized the predynastic period (c.5000–3100BC) exists in the form of "palettes." These slate slabs, often decorated in relief, are thought to have been used originally for grinding pigments for eyepaint. By the Late Predynastic period, they had taken on a celebratory, official character, and their decoration was inspired by specific historical events. The palette of Narmer was a symbol of power and may have commemorated the unification of Upper and Lower Egypt. Its creation heralded the beginning of the historical age, subdivided traditionally into dynasties, in which the pharaoh was the emblem of political and religious power. The compositional elements found in the palette of Narmer were to remain constant in Egyptian art: the division of the background into registers, the greater dimensions given to the figure of the sovereign, and the pictorial value of certain images. The falcon is the personification of the king seizing the Nile Delta (Lower Egypt), which is represented by a papyrus with a human head. Objects are presented as they are conceived, not as they are seen. The Egyptian artist aimed to reflect social and religious hierarchies in the composition and to assign proportions to the figures and objects whose relationships to one another were constant. For example, the pharaoh-god was greater than man and therefore had to be shown as such.

The age of the first and second dynasties (c.2850–2650BC) saw the birth of monumental architecture, including the first mastabas – flat-topped tombs with sloping sides – and pyramids. During this period, the pharaohs had two royal cemeteries, one at Abydos, the other at Memphis; architectural elements from both sites have survived. From these seeds developed the awe-inspiring art of the Old Kingdom (third to sixth dynasties, c.2650–2150BC).

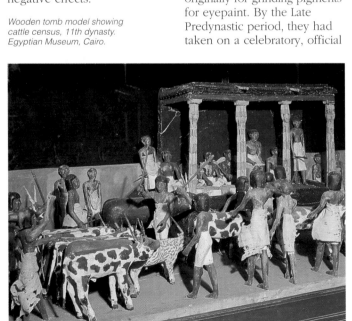

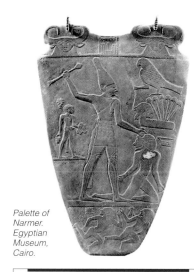

Palette of Narmer. Egyptian Museum, Cairo.

THE PYRAMIDS

It was a pharaoh of the third dynasty, Djoser, and his royal official Imhotep who created the complex of Saqqara. This was a vast area enclosed by a white limestone wall, inside which stood the Step Pyramid and several smaller structures. The project was impressive in its unprecedented use of calcareous stone instead of perishable materials, such as the bricks and wood that had been common in the preceding age.

During the fourth dynasty, stepped structures, such as the rhomboidal pyramid of King Sneferu at Meidum, gave way to the uniformly smooth-walled pyramids of King Khufu, Khafre, and Menkaure in the necropolis of Giza, near Cairo. Erected between 2550 and 2470BC, they were listed by the Greeks as one of the Seven Wonders of the World. The grandiose dimensions of these funerary monuments, built to preserve the bodies of the dead kings for eternity, conveyed a sense of timelessness and immutability. In this, they were like the circumpolar stars toward which the pyramid sites were oriented and to which the pharaohs, departed from this Earth, would return as gods to take their place among the divinities. The pyramids form part of a large complex, including mortuary temples and mastabas, the burial places of priests, nobles, and high ranking officials.

DAILY LIFE IN EGYPTIAN TOMB ART

Scenes of everyday life are depicted in bas-reliefs and paintings in tombs and mastabas from all periods of Egyptian history. Carved or painted on sepulchre walls, figurative scenes re-create scenes of activity from the earthly life, with the aim of ensuring their continuation in the afterlife. Until the time of the New Kingdom, these did not portray specific events but were naturalistic renderings of generalized communal activities such as plowing, harvesting, breeding birds and livestock, hunting animals and birds, and fishing.

However, subject matter became increasingly varied during the New Kingdom (c.1550–1070BC). While daily life had previously been portrayed in a continuous succession of typical events, tomb paintings now included imagery evoking personal aspects of past life, with the aim of extolling the status of the tomb's owner. The wall painting from the tomb of Nakht in Thebes, for example, is a good example of this kind of personal observation: here, we see detailed scenes of grape harvesting, winemaking, and the storage of wine in amphorae. Nakht, a noble and royal astronomer, was also the keeper of the king's vineyards.

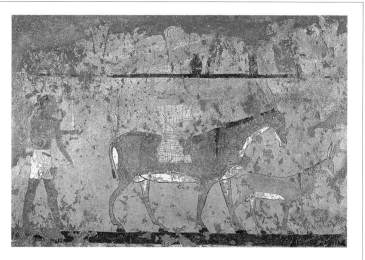

Wall painting of an ass transporting grain, from the Tomb of Iti, Gebelein, First Intermediate Period. Egyptian Museum, Turin.

Wall painting of the harvesting of grapes, from the Tomb of Nakht, Thebes, 18th dynasty.

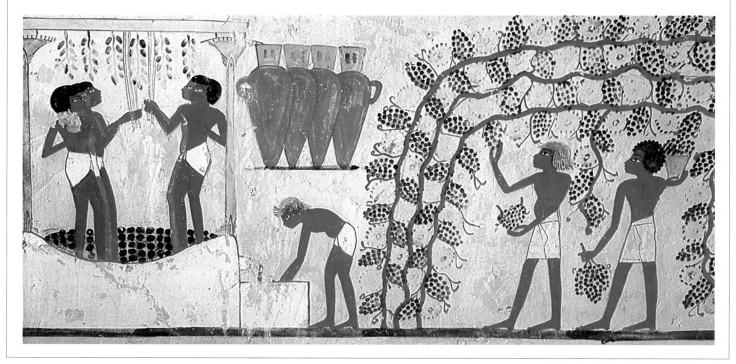

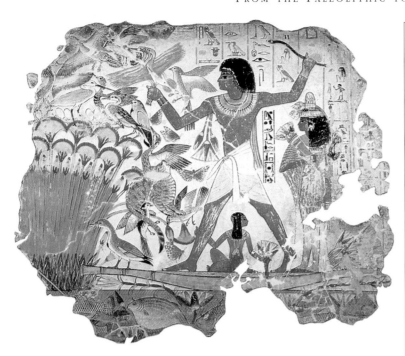

Wall painting showing Nebamun hunting, from Thebes. British Museum, London.

PAINTING AND SCULPTURE

The most important paintings and sculptures of the Old Kingdom come from the mastabas. The frieze of geese in the tomb of Itet at Meidum was the lower part of a huge painting depicting the hunting of birds with nets and is perhaps the oldest surviving wall painting on stucco. The function of bas-reliefs and paintings was to furnish the tomb with enduring pictures that imitated, transcended, and re-created nature. The need to guarantee the survival of the dead, and to assemble in one single figure or object the fundamental elements for their magical reanimation, lies at

the root of the Egyptian iconographical repertory. The desire to show all the essential characteristics of the human figure in a single image led the Egyptian artists to present it in an unnatural way. The face was shown in profile with the eye to the front; shoulders and chest were viewed from the front, showing the juncture of the arms; and the legs were shown in profile to indicate the direction of movement. Each part was exhibited from its most characteristic angle in order to present the whole figure on the flat surface. Similar conventions governed the plastic arts. Enclosed in its cubic structure, the funerary effigy of Khafre is the proto-type of pharaonic statues, with its immobile, hieratic, imper-turbable pose – the very

THE BOOK OF THE DEAD

The Egyptians considered earthly life to be a fleeting moment, the prelude to eternal happiness. Man, absolved of all his sins after death, would continue to live among the blessed in the Fields of Ialu, identified symbolically with the god Osiris. At the end of the Old Kingdom, this privilege, once reserved for the pharaohs, became the prerogative of all. Essential elements of the death ritual were mummification, the "opening of the mouth," and the protection of the corpse. To assist the dead person in his or her transition before the tribunal of Osiris was the *Book of the Dead*, a roll of papyrus containing religious and magical texts. It included the representation of the tribunal of Osiris and answers to the questions posed by the 42 deities sitting in judgment. In order to verify the "negative confession," the heart of the dead person was placed on one pan of a scale, under the supervision of the god Anubis, while on the other was placed an ostrich feather, symbol of Maat, the goddess of truth.

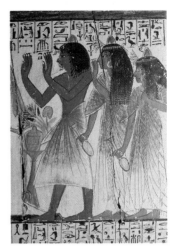

Painting from the tomb of Sennedjem at Deir el-Medina, c.1250BC.

The sarcophagus preserved the mortal remains, which were necessary for eternal life. In the Old Kingdom this was decorated with brief texts and, occasionally, paneled decora-tion. In the period of the Middle and New Kingdoms, it was covered in magical reli-gious inscriptions and images of the protecting divinities.

Papyrus from Book of the Dead of the Scribe Hunefer *(detail), 19th dynasty. British Museum, London.*

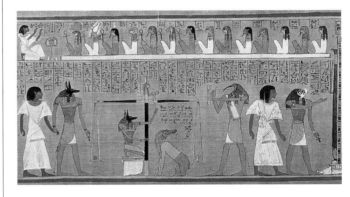

essence of royalty. Standing or seated, in wood or in stone, such figures, in spite of their rigid attitudes, are indepen-dent and vivid entities that immortalize the individual. At Saqqara, the statue of Djoser was positioned inside a stone-built chamber next to the Step

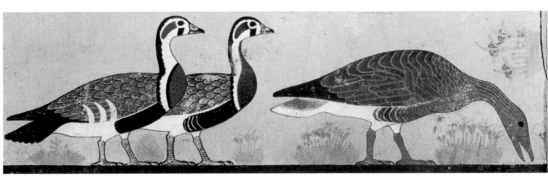

Wall painting of geese, from the Tomb of Itet at Meidum. Egyptian Museum, Cairo.

Pyramid, where it could "watch" the performance of rituals for the dead through tiny apertures in the walls. In the First Intermediate Period (7th–11th dynasties, c.2200– 2040BC), with the collapse of the equilibrium of the preceding age, authority was gradually decentralized, and the power of the provincial states increased. There was little activity in the visual arts at this time, and it is only with national reunification in the 11th dynasty and the beginning of the Middle Kingdom (11th– 12th dynasties, c.2040–1778BC) that there is evidence of an artistic revival in the spirit of the Old Kingdom. The architecture of the Middle Kingdom is repre-

sented by the unique temple of Mentuhotep at Deir el-Bahri. While it cannot compare to the Great Pyramids in monumentality, its sculpture and painting reveal great clarity and compositional rigor. Typical of Middle Kingdom royal statuary are the colossal red granite sculptures of Sesostris III and the maned sphinxes of Amenemhet III, which personify the pharaoh and his power. Freer of the conventions of official art are the small sculptures in painted wood in which the artists skillfully and naturalistically capture aspects of everyday life. The Second Intermediate Period (13th–17th dynasties, c.1778–1570BC) witnessed much internal unrest and the waning

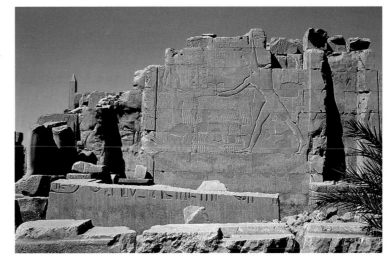

of centralized power. Virtually defenseless against the incursions of the Hyksos from Western Asia, Egypt was

Relief of Tuthmosis III, from the Temple of Amun, Karnak, 18th dynasty (1550–1295BC) It was at this time that the largest temples and statues were built.

JEWELRY

Egyptian jewelers were highly skilled in the working of gold and *electrum* (a natural alloy of gold and silver). Mines in Nubia, the southern deserts of Egypt, and Punt were the source of these materials. Having no knowledge of gemstones, they made jewelry from semiprecious stones

chosen for their brilliant colors. Gold signified the flesh of divinity, and the three basic colors for mounting – red, green, and azure – represented life-giving blood, the sense of renewal, and the dominion of the gods. Jewels were important indications of wealth and social standing, but they also served as instruments of protection. Magical charms, worn on

necklaces and bracelets, could be used to ward off evil if the right materials were used and a significant message incorporated within the composition. During the Middle Kingdom, forms became increasingly refined and original. In the pectoral ornament of Amenemhet III, the king (who represents order) is depicted subduing the enemies of Egypt (who represent chaos). Above them is the vulture goddess with outspread wings, subject matter that would reappear on similar jewels from the New Kingdom.

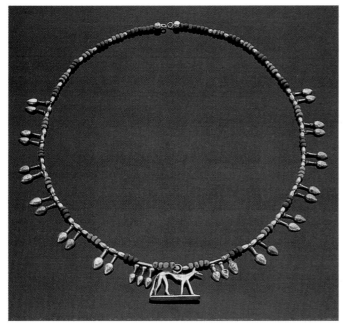

Necklace in electrum, 18th dynasty. Egyptian Museum, Cairo.

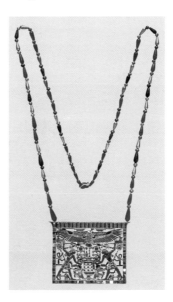

Pectoral ornament with name of Amenemhet III, 12th dynasty. Egyptian Museum, Cairo.

IMHOTEP

The name Imhotep is inscribed on the base of a statue of the pharaoh Djoser, found at Saqqara in 1926. Physician, seer, architect, and royal official, Imhotep is credited with directing the construction of Djoser's pyramid and the impressive complex around it. Living in about 2700BC, he was the first architect whose name is known and may have been the first to build in hewn stone. From 525BC, he was worshiped as the god of medicine in Egypt and in Greece.

nonetheless to rise phoenix-like from the ashes to enter its most splendid period of artistic achievement – the 18th dynasty.

THE GOLDEN AGE

With the reestablishment by the Theban princes of pharaonic authority and the tradition of the king's divine descendancy, Thebes became the magnificent capital of the New Kingdom (18th–20th dynasties, c.1570– 1069BC). The splendor and extravagance of the art of this period is exemplified in an exceptional variety of pictorial and plastic forms. The descriptive realism that had marked the configurations of the Middle Kingdom was revived, particularly in funerary painting, which now depicted naturalistic scenes of

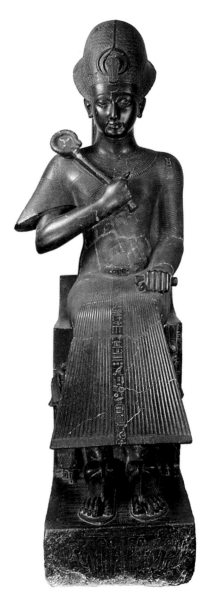

Statue of Ramesses II. Egyptian Museum, Turin.

the oldest surviving monumental relief – on the south wall of the seventh pylon of Karnak. The classic scene of the victorious pharaoh defeating the many enemies of Egypt is treated here on a gigantic scale, ascending the full height of the pylon. Carved in relief, the group of Asiatics, whom the king is dragging by the hair, is structured in an ordered, almost graphic manner, with some heads shown in profile

and others frontally. Courtiers, plants, and sacred animals appear alongside religious symbols and hieroglyphs in the polychrome reliefs of the chapel of Tuthmosis III, dedicated to the goddess Hathor. Typical of the decoration of such sanctuaries, it places repeated emphasis on ritual sacrifices offered by the king to the gods.

After the political and religious revolution that characterized the age of Amenhotep IV

(ruled 1379–1362BC) and the ensuing restoration under Tutankhamun, the Ramesside pharaohs (19th–20th dynasties) moved the capital to Pi-Ramesse in Lower Egypt. They nonetheless continued to erect temples and sanctuaries in the region of Thebes and Nubia. Building activity was intense during this period: at Abydos, the city sacred to Osiris, Seti I began the construction of a vast temple complex, which was completed by his son,

THE THEBAN TOMBS

The pharaohs of the 18th dynasty, originating from Thebes, chose the left bank of the Nile as their heavenly resting place. Beyond the long line of funerary temples, which extend to the edges of the cultivated land, is the winding Valley of the Kings, with its tombs of the sovereigns of the New Kingdom cut into the cliffs. While the plan of the early tombs was asymmetrical, that of later tombs was symmetrical – best exemplified by the tomb of Seti I. The room where the sarcophagus was placed was originally painted in yellow, with the mummy housed in a gold coffin – the unalterable nature of the metal was believed to guarantee the incorruptibility of the mummy. In the square, columnar hall, were placed the royal chariot and funerary

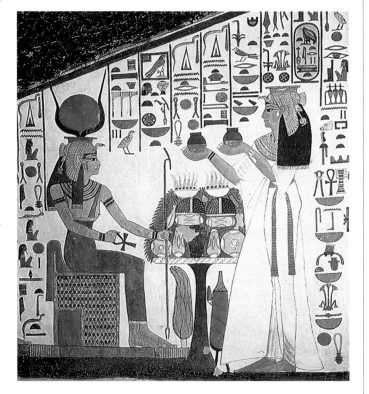

Tomb of Nefertari, Valley of the Queens, Thebes.

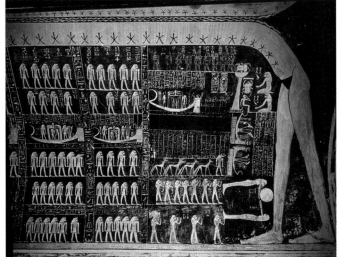

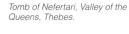

equipment. Walls and pillars were decorated with texts and scenes symbolizing the transformation of the dead king into the sun and the transmission of power to his successor. To the south of the Valley of the Kings lies the Valley of the Queens, resting place of queens and other members of the royal family; a large private necropolis accommodates the tombs of the nobles.

Star-studded vault, Tomb of Seti I, Valley of the Kings, Thebes, 19th dynasty.

daily life. Although still inspired by the traditional style, figures were released from their ancient static rigidity and painted more freely than ever before. The portrayal of the land of Punt (an area on the coast of eastern Africa) in the funerary temple of Queen Hatshepsut at Deir el-Bahri devotes minute attention to the plants, homes, and people of Punt, sealing forever the memory of the expedition to that exotic place.

Scenes and reliefs of an official and commemorative nature are much more conventional. From the reign of Hatshepsut's successor, Tuthmosis III, is the

THE AGE OF AMENHOTEP IV–AKHENATEN

Artistic production acquired new strength during the brief 17-year reign of Amenhotep IV, following the death of his father, Amenhotep III, in about 1379BC. In his fifth year of rule, Amenhotep IV changed his name to Akhenaten to accord with the religious changes that he initiated. He was a heretical monotheist who eliminated the cult of the god Amun, recognizing the solar disk of Aten as the supreme divinity and establishing Akhetaten (present-day Tell el-Amarna) as the new capital. The secularization imposed by the sovereign resulted in a new realism of artistic representation, evident both in statuary and carvings. Figures were

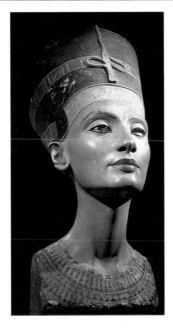

Painted limestone portrait of Nefertiti. Staatliche Museen, Berlin.

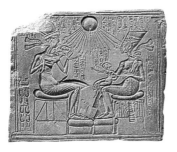

Relief showing Akhenaten, Nefertiti, and the princesses under the rays of Aten. Painted limestone. Staatliche Museen, Berlin.

rendered with extreme naturalism, and individual features were emphasized. In relief carving and paintings, artists depicted tender scenes of domesticity, showing the king with his wife Nefertiti or bouncing his daughter on his knee. The delicately rendered portrait of Queen Nefertiti, found during excavations at Amarna in 1912, is arguably the most memorable work of art from New Kingdom Egypt.

TUTANKHAMUN

In 1922, the English archaeologist Howard Carter discovered in the Valley of the Kings the tomb of the boy pharaoh, Tutankhamun, complete with its fabulous hoard of treasure. The royal mummy, its face covered by a mask of gold, was placed inside three priceless coffins in a burial chamber adorned with paintings. In an adjoining room were golden statuettes, necklaces, and jeweled coffers. The furnishings were of a richness that exceeded anything displayed in tomb and chapel decoration since the end of the fourth dynasty. Chairs, beds, and couches exhibited a wealth of magic symbolism: the legs of these pieces, sometimes inlaid with gold and ivory, were carved in the form of animal feet,

intended to serve the dead person as a celestial vehicle for eternity. The throne of Tutankhamun is a work of masterly refinement, covered with gold, silver, and vitreous paste. The backrest is adorned with figures of the young royal couple, and the armrests are protected by a winged uraeus (the sacred cobra symbol). The reign of Tutankhamun, who succeeded Akhenaten and restored the cult of Amun, represented a transitional phase in ancient Egypt, and this is evident in the repertory of figures and choice of subjects. Alongside the tender discourse of the royal pair on the throne is a coffer with battle scenes that depict the pharaoh fighting the Asiatic and Nubian foes.

Wooden coffer from the Tomb of Tutankhamun (detail of battle scene). Egyptian Museum, Cairo.

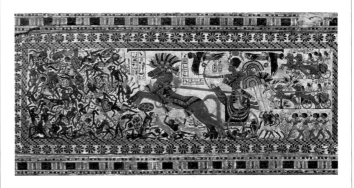

Ramesses II. There, for the last time, space was given on the interior wall decorations to bas-reliefs; this would soon be replaced by less costly sunk

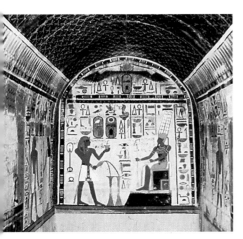

Painted relief from the Hathor chapel decorated by Tuthmosis III, Deir el-Bahri. Egyptian Museum, Cairo.

reliefs. Ramesses II, the greatest builder of the New Kingdom, was responsible for the forest of columns in the hypostyle hall of Karnak, the Ramesseum at Thebes, and the temples of Abu Simbel – works that are still breathtaking to visitors for their sheer majesty. The reliefs that cover the walls represent an entirely new concept in Egyptian art: they deal with historically identifiable events in which the king, no longer portrayed as a generic ritual figure, acts in a specific context. Statuary of the time

Throne of Tutankhamun. Gilded and painted wood. Egyptian Museum, Cairo.

is also notable for its monumental proportions. Perhaps the most impressive piece is the seated effigy in black granite of Ramesses II, with his wife Nefertari and eldest son carved on a smaller scale. Stories of the battle with the "Sea Peoples" (who tried to invade Egypt from the north) are recounted in the temple of Medinet Habu, near Thebes, built by Ramesses III, the last powerful ruler of the New Kingdom. This complex, which appears as an impregnable fortress, marks the ideal conclusion to the first cycle of Egyptian art.

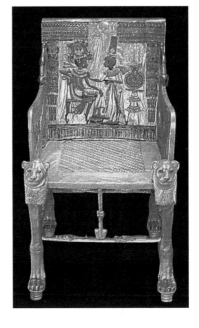

THE ROYAL CEMETERY OF UR

The objects recovered from the royal tombs of Ur testify to the richness of Sumerian decorative arts. In Mesopotamia, the afterlife inspired only dread and anguish, as revealed in sources such as the Gilgamesh epic, one of the best-known works of ancient literature. The resting places of the dead were less important than palaces or temples, and tombs were built only in underground hypogea. However, the wish to demonstrate the power in life of the dead monarch is evident in such works as the celebrated standard of peace and war, inlaid with lapis lazuli, shell, and limestone. Among the other important treasures is the funerary

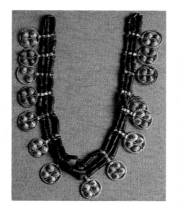

Necklace of Queen Puabi of Ur. Iraq Museum, Baghdad.

hoard of Queen Puabi (2600–2500BC), including diadems and earrings, testimony to the technical skill of craftsmen working with precious metals.

presence within the temple. The hands clasped against the chest, the rapt expression, and the large attentive eyes outlined in bitumen all proclaim a close relationship with the god in an attitude of humble reverence. The generally small dimensions, far removed from the colossal size of Egyptian effigies, are explained partly by the fact that such durable material as stone was hard to obtain and partly because of different religious beliefs: the power of the monarch was conveyed by the monumental nature of the overall architectural and decorative design.

The Sumerians also made a number of seals, which are examplary of their inventive fantasy, narrative flair, and lively realism. The seals were enlivened by rams and oxen and scenes of fighting animals.

pink sandstone stele that celebrates the victories of Naram-Sin, Sargon's grandson, bears figures that are freely arranged in a pyramidal design, breaking the monotony of the subdivided registers characteristic of Sumerian reliefs. The monarch, protected by three stars, keeps watch over his warriors; his figure is larger than those of the soldiers to emphasize the importance of his position. Animals and domestic scenes are represented with great realism on the seals that were used to mark property and authenticate contracts.

Stele of Naram-Sin, King of Akkad. Louvre, Paris.

SUMER

The cradle of homogenous yet diverse cultures, Mesopotamia nurtured a wealth of native art forms that cast their influence well beyond the country's geographical boundaries.
The city-states of Ur, Lagash,

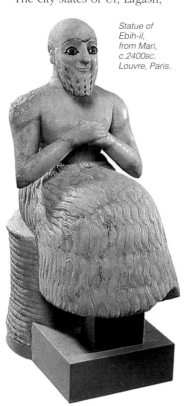

Statue of Ebih-il, from Mari, c.2400BC. Louvre, Paris.

and Mari were established after the long protohistorical phase of the fourth millennium, during the Early Dynastic period (2800–2350BC). The theocratic organization of Sumerian (Southern Mesopotamian) society affected every aspect of artistic activity. Architecture found its principal outlet in temples and sanctuaries. The temple, constructed of brick, was the city's religious and economic center: adjacent to it were storerooms, workrooms, and administrative offices. A central courtyard, as in the temple of Sin at Khafajeh, was reached through a monumental entrance and up an imposing staircase. Plastic art gave pride of place to the figure of the worshipper. Craftsmen produced statuettes in limestone, alabaster, and terracotta, endlessly repeating the image of a traditional, anonymous model. Ranging from small statues of gods, priests, and the faithful as found at Tell Asmar, to the naturalistic seated figure of the temple superintendent Ebih-il, statuary portrayed the act of dedication, symbol of the perpetual honor that must be paid to the divinity, thereby guaranteeing the eternal

AKKAD

In about 2335BC, Sargon united the entire region of Sumer under his rule, extending his kingdom toward Elam and Syria and choosing the city of Akkad as his new capital. His reign heralded a period of Semitic predominance in the region (c.2350–2150BC) and, for the first time in Mesopotamia, embodied the notion of universal monarchy ruled by a deified sovereign.
The new concept of royalty and the retreat from the formal abstraction associated with preceding tradition are exemplified by a majestically severe copper head from Nineveh; this may perpetuate the features of Sargon himself. In carvings, a greater sense of freedom alleviates the rigidity of typical Sumerian compositions. For example, the

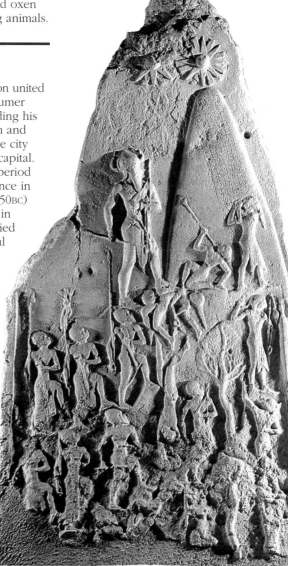

THE UR STANDARD

The Ur standard, now in the British Museum, London, is a masterpiece of the Early Dynastic period, dating from the third millennium BC. Probably displayed in a palace or temple, it consists of two rectangular panels of wood joined by trapezoidal ends. The two sides are ornamented in mosaic with limestone, shell, and lapis lazuli, set in black bitumen paste. On each panel historical figures are depicted in three rows, or registers: one side shows peaceful activities, the other scenes of war. The registers are divided and framed with colored friezes that enliven the surfaces. The standard was discovered by the English archaeologist Sir Leonard Woolley, who excavated Ur during the 1920s and '30s. He identifed, among other things, the tombs of the city's early rulers. Ur (*Genesis* 11:31) was the land of Abraham, founder of the Hebrew race.

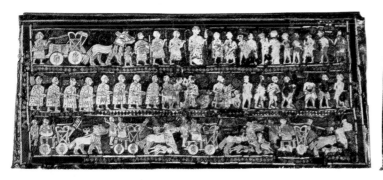

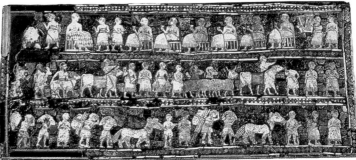

▼ 1. "War" side. Following the line of figures from left to right and bottom to top, we see a war chariot drawn by a team of four onagers (wild asses) and driven by the king with his groom. The three chariots in front on the same register are drawn by onagers, respectively walking, trotting, and galloping. The action becomes increasingly urgent, and the corpses of the defeated enemy fall to the ground. The pictorial narrative is organized from left to right on the middle and lower registers and from both directions on the top register.

▼ 3. "Peace" side. This panel shows a line of servants or conquered foreigners bringing tribute to the king (depicted with his court in the upper register of the panel). Sitting on solidly built seats, they wear the typical sheepskin skirts, their heads and faces are shaved, and they are bare-chested. The king, positioned on the far left, is larger in size than the other figures; he looks to his right at the courtiers who face him. At both ends stand attendants, including a lyre player on the right, whose instrument is adorned with a bull's head.

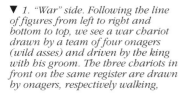

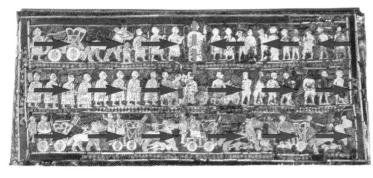

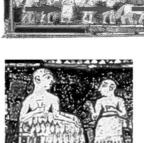

▼ 2. "War" side. The chariots have four wheels, solid rather than spoked and constructed from two linked sections. These are vehicles better for transportation than warfare, and their number demonstrates the king's power. In the second register, the infantry advances from the left. The soldiers wear copper helmets and leather cloaks with metal studs. They hold their lances horizontally in order to drive their prisoners ahead of them. In the upper register, the figure of the king, taller than the rest, is positioned in the center. Two processions converge toward him. From the left proceeds a royal chariot with the groom and a page; from the right the soldiers bring prisoners and booty.

◀ 4. "Peace" side. On both panels, the figure of the king appears in a comparatively static context, while other scenes are full of movement and action. Here he is seated among his attendants; his posture is upright and solemn, and, like the other seated figures in the register, he holds a cup in his right hand. His clothing is austere: he wears his sheepskin skirt with the wool on the outside.

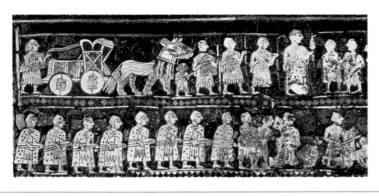

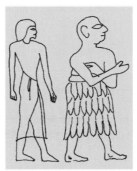

◀ 5. The two drawn silhouettes depict one figure derived from the Egyptian *Book of Gates* and one from the upper register of the "Peace" side of the Ur standard. The figures have much in common: legs and head are presented in profile, and the torso is turned to the front. However, the features of the Sumerian figure are larger than life, and the ankles and tufts of wool are rendered in a more naturalistic fashion. The taller Egyptian figure is more obviously stylized, with delicately rendered clothing and a graceful rhythm to the lines of the legs and arms.

NEO-SUMERIAN PERIOD

Akkadian rule ended with the invasion of the Guti (c.2150BC). Order was restored by the kings of the Third Dynasty of Ur, and central power returned to the south (c.2112–2004BC). Neo-Sumerian artistic activity consisted mainly of monumental religious architecture. One notable example was the impressive ziggurat of Ur-Nammu, which consisted of a system of superimposed terraces, at the top of which stood the temple dedicated to Nanna, god of the moon. Religious statuary, too, enjoyed a renaissance, recovering the strength and imaginative power of earlier Sumerian art. The effigies of Gudea, governor of Lagash, in the garb of a worshiper, seated or standing, are finely modeled in green or black diorite, a naturally smooth, shiny material. The conquest of Sumer by the Amorites led to the formation of a series of independent states, whose history is documented in the royal archives of Mari.

THE PALACE OF MARI

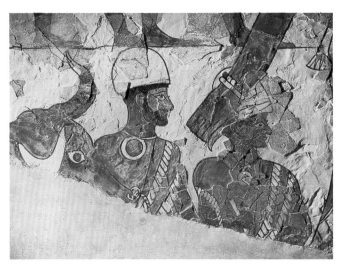

Prosperous from local agriculture and traffic control on the Euphrates River, the Mesopotamians built their temples and palaces with rows of rooms opening onto one or more inner courtyards. The only difference between the two was that the temple accommodated an altar. Particularly impressive was the enormous residence of the reigning dynasty at Mari during the period that followed Akkadian rule. This was added to by successive rulers, the last of which was King Zimri-Lim. Built mainly of mud brick, it was arranged around two courtyards and contained 300 rooms. It was 650 feet (200 meters) long and 390 feet (120 meters) wide and covered an

Fresco of sacrificial scene from the palace at Mari (detail), c.1800BC. Aleppo Museum, Syria.

area of six acres (two and a half hectares). The rooms in the palace included the private apartments of the king and his queens, domestic quarters, and diplomatic record offices. The existing fragments of the wall decorations provide testimoniy to both style and subject in Mesopotamian painting. Among the identifiable subjects are sacrificial scenes and Zimri-Lim's investiture at Mari by the goddess Ishtar. There are also geometric compositions, glimpses of landscape, and lively representations of contemporary society, dress, and customs.

BABYLONIA AND ASSYRIA

After his conquest of Mari, Larsa, and Eshnunna, Hammurabi, king of Babylon, reunited the whole of Mesopotamia and proclaimed himself universal monarch. The art of the Old Babylonian period (c.1900–1595BC) retained Neo-Sumerian motifs and styles, including a wealth of fantastic animals, bulls, and lions, posted as guards to the palaces and temples. In sculpture, repetition of compositional structure and subject are revealed in the relief carved at the top of the stele inscribed with the code of Hammurabi. The king stands in worship before the seated god of the sun and justice, Shamash. Around 1595BC, the political geography of the Near East was once again thrown into confusion as the kingdom of Babylon crumbled under the onslaught of the invading Hittites from Anatolia. In the first millennium BC, Assyrian might was reflected in the creation of an immense

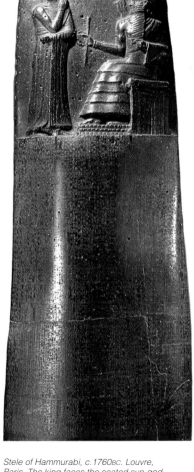

Stele of Hammurabi, c.1760BC. Louvre, Paris. The king faces the seated sun-god Shamash. The stele is carved front and back in cuneiform script with Hammurabi's law code.

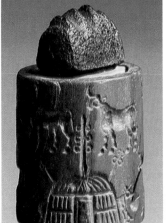

empire. Assyrian art, for the most part secular, found expression in the narrative reliefs that once adorned the walls of their palaces. These bas-reliefs provide visual evidence of conquests, with scenes that illustrate military techniques and the exploits of

Cylindrical seal with antelope design, Uruk period. The seal was rolled along wet clay to leave an impression

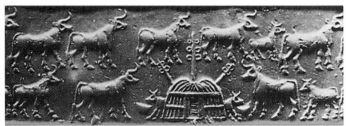

THE PALACE OF ASHURBANIPAL

Nowhere are the descriptive and symbolic intents of Neo-Assyrian relief carvers better exemplified than in the decorations of the palace of Ashurbanipal (669–626BC) at Nineveh. The depictions of the exploits and everyday occupations of the king had the double effect of extolling the glory of the sovereign and of astonishing the

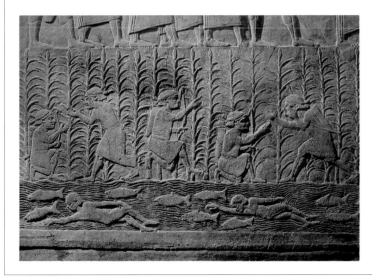

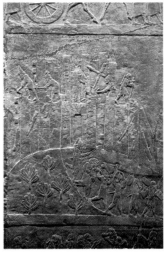

Sacking and Demolition of the City of Hamanu, *relief from the palace of Ashurbanipal at Nineveh, c.650BC. British Museum, London. A characteristic image of Assyrian art.*

Elamite Enemies Hiding in the Reeds, *relief from the southwest palace at Nineveh. British Museum, London.*

observer. This art is fresh and lively, and the spirit of the landscape is impressively conveyed. Traditional hunting scenes are animated by realistic and dramatic episodes in which wild beasts leap up at the king's chariot or fall wounded by his arrows. Men and animals are strongly portrayed: the artist is eager to emphasize the powerful physique of the monarch and his warriors, and his rendering of animals is also exceptionally naturalistic. The war scenes are crowded with people: accounts of military activity include the army crossing rivers and attacking fortresses. There are also episodes of minor significance: daily life in camp, a horseman calling to his companions who have climbed a hill, and an Elamite noble who, handed over to the enemy, spits in the face of his own king.

---

the king, as valiant in his hunting of wild beasts as on the battlefield. Ashurnasirpal II (883–859BC) was the first Assyrian monarch to decorate the lower part of the throne room and other areas of his palace at Nimrud with a frieze in relief on hundreds of white limestone slabs. The narrative, which depicts chiefly mythological scenes and images of fertility rites, is told in juxtaposed episodes that build up

Human-headed bull. *Louvre, Paris.*

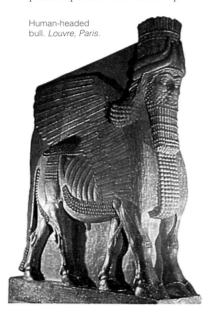

independently toward a climactic event not shown. In the reign of Shalmaneser III (858–824BC), the gates of his royal palace at Balawat were decorated with bas-reliefs on bronze sheets. The gigantic palace of Sargon II (721–705BC) in the city of Khorsabad was encircled by massive walls. Figures of bulls with human heads, designed to ward off evil spirits, stood guard at the entrance gates. The use of five feet for the winged monster made it possible for the spectator to see the bull either as immobile (when viewed from the front) or in movement (when viewed from the side). After the fall of Nineveh in 612BC, the revival in southern Mesopotamia was marked principally by its architecture. During the reign of the Neo-Babylonian king Nebuchadnezzar II, this was exemplified in temples, imposing palaces with hanging gardens, and ziggurats standing more than 330 feet (100 meters) high – inspiration for the biblical Tower of Babel. In 539BC, Babylonia was taken by Cyrus and became part of the vast Persian Empire.

THE GATE OF ISHTAR

The Greek historian Herodotus (fifth century BC) describes with admiration the new Babylon created by King Nebuchadnezzar II: "Apart from its size, its beauty is unequaled by any other city we know."

The seven-terraced ziggurat, dedicated to Marduk, god of Babylon, dominated the city and was entered by way of a long processional street that began at the gate of Ishtar, goddess of love and war. The gate, the most splendid of all Mesopotamia's monuments, opened in the center of walls so massive that, according to Herodotus, a four-horse chariot could turn on them. The enormous gate is a fine example of the technique of brick construction prevalent in ancient Mesopotamia. On a blue enameled background were relief decorations of bulls, dragons, lions, and stylized symbolic images. The marvelous reconstruction of the gate in the Staatliche Museen, Berlin, gives an idea of its colossal dimensions and the colorful effect of the original bricks. The decorative art of relief on enameled bricks was widespread in the East, one example being the palace of Darius at Susa.

Detail of Gate of Ishtar, glazed bricks, from Babylon. Staatliche Museen, Berlin.

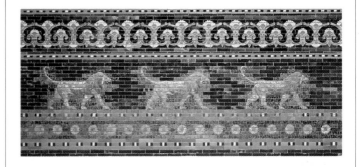

SYRIAN AND PALESTINIAN ART

Bordered at one end by Anatolia and Mesopotamia and at the other by Egypt is a Mediterranean coastal strip that acts as a center of lines of communication linking three continents. The geographical situation helps to explain its enduring political fragmentation. From as early as the third millennium BC, successive Semitic-speaking populations – known as Canaanites by the

Statue of King Idrimi of Alalakh, c.1500BC. British Museum, London.

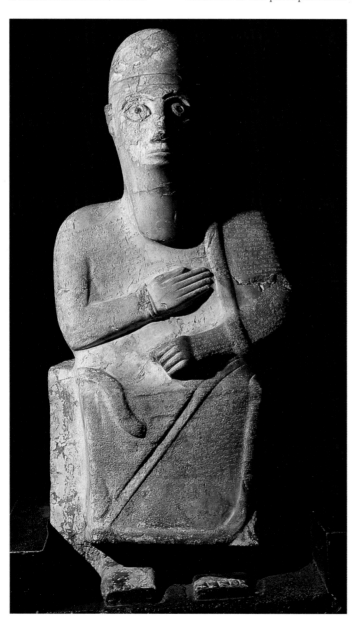

Hebrews who had followed them to the Promised Land – fell under the sway of powerful neighboring states. Architecture from the third millennium onward provides evidence of sophisticated levels of urban civilization, notably in the palaces of Ebla (royal palace G) and Alalakh (level VII).

The palace of Yarim-Lim at Alalakh (18th century BC) shows similar originality in its design. It was built on three successive floors, the lowest of which was designed for public use, with orthostats in basalt, similar to those that appeared later in Anatolia and Assyria. Entrance to the principal room was through a smaller room with an opening supported by columns, anticipating the *bit hilani*, the princely dwelling that was to appear in the first millennium.

In the realm of figurative art, originality appears in designs on the seals used in royal correspondence. Formal sculpture, too, was of a high quality, as represented by the head of King Yarim-Lim. The palace was destroyed by the Hittites, but the fortunes of the city revived under Idrimi in about 1500BC, although his statue is less sophisticated than that of his predecessor. Decorated with hunting scenes and bulls, gold bowls from the nearby city of Ugarit are the precursors of Phoenician bowls of the first millennium BC.

EBLA

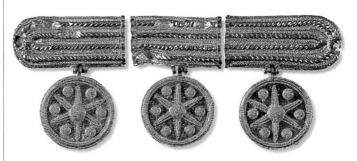

Pieces of a necklace with disk-shaped pendants, c.1750BC. Aleppo Museum, Syria.

An important urban center in northern Syria, Ebla (modern Tell Mardikh) flourished in the third millennium BC and may have extended its rule into Mesopotamia. Destroyed by Sargon I after a phase of decline, Ebla was rebuilt during the first decades of the second millennium. Protected by massive ramparts of up to 66 feet (22 meters) high, with a ring of stones and jagged rocks at the base, the city's most important buildings were the temples, including that of Ishtar, and the royal palace E. Temple D consisted of three successive rooms, axial in plan, built along lines that were later to be developed by the Phoenicians in

Ritual basin carved with sacred banquet, from Ebla, c.1800BC. Aleppo Museum, Syria.

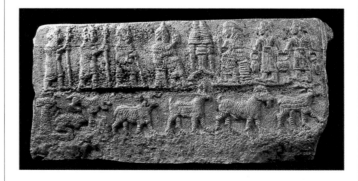

their construction of the temple of Solomon in Jerusalem.

In the lower city was the royal necropolis (18th–17th century BC): of the three hypogea excavated, the tombs of the Lord of the Goats and of the Princess contained vessels, jewelry, bronze weapons, and ivory amulets. Finds of ritual basins, rectangular in shape and consisting of two sections, proved important for their stone carvings. They testify, both in their form and subject matter – banqueting scenes and animals shown from side and front views – to considerable autonomy in the treatment of common models derived from Mesopotamia.

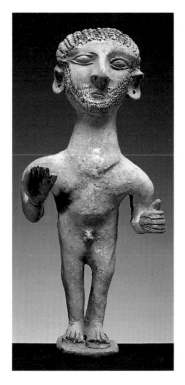

Phoenician terracotta statue of male with punctured earlobes, from Ibiza, 4th century BC. National Archaeological Museum, Madrid.

Both Alalakh and Ugarit were destroyed during the invasion of the "Sea Peoples" (c.1200BC), leading to massive migrations. The influx of Hebrews from the south and Arameaens from the north left only the coastal strip to its former inhabitants. The Phoenician city-states, as they should now be called, sought new trading outlets and established Punic colonies throughout the Mediterranean. They are renowned for the manufacture of glass, metal bowls, carved ivories, and jewelry. The Phoenicians were eclectic artists who were open to cultural influences. They borrowed motifs from both East and West, skillfully incorporating them into their own designs. They were thus able to combine the Mesopotamian love of symmetry and the Aegean taste for galloping animals with the Syrian taste for groups of fighting animals – not to mention the sphinxes

and griffins of Levantine origin. Production of small bronzes, which had Syrian precedents, were also revived in the first millennium BC. Evidence of Egyptian influence can be found in the statuette of Heracles-Melqart (shown in the typical pose of the "warrior

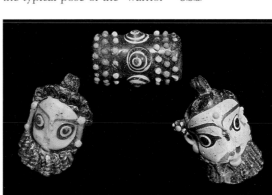

god"), most notably in the short skirt and headgear. The vitality of the Phoenician merchants did not cease with the conquest of their territory by the armies of Persia: the

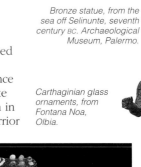

Bronze statue, from the sea off Selinunte, seventh century BC. Archaeological Museum, Palermo.

Carthaginian glass ornaments, from Fontana Noa, Olbia.

Punic colonies they founded on the coasts of the western Mediterranean and, above all, the city of Carthage, would keep their heritage alive for centuries to come.

IVORY

Precious because of its scarcity, ivory has always been a symbol of a high social status, making it a suitable material for both ritual

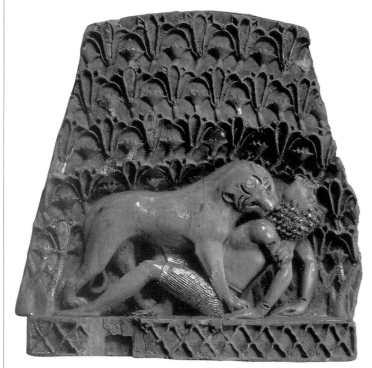

and private use. From the second millennium BC, there were flourishing schools of ivory engravers across the Syrian-Palestinian region. Particularly famous are the spoons, combs, boxes, and

Lioness Attacking an Ethiopian in a Papyrus Grove, ivory plaque with gold overlay, revealing Egyptian influence, ninth to eighth century BC. British Museum, London.

Cow Feeding her Calf, ivory plaque with Phoenician-style decoration, found at Nimrud. Iraq Museum, Baghdad.

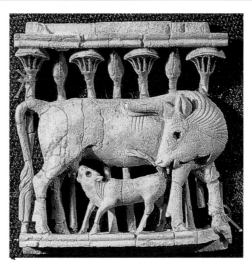

decorative plaques for furniture from Megiddo (12th century BC). These traditions were revived by the Phoenicians and Syrians in the first millennium BC. Ivories were produced in a series of workshops in a variety of styles, and letters incised on the backs of some indicate that they belonged to palaces. The Assyrians plundered the cities of the Levant and seized craftsmen, who produced ivories

for their new masters. The storerooms excavated at Nimrud were full of ivories and others have been found in wells, where they were thrown during the sack of the city in 612BC. When the wells were excavated in the 1950s, the ivory depicting the *Lioness Attacking an Ethiopian* was found. In addition to the gold leaf decoration, the work was inlaid with pieces of lapis lazuli and carnelian.

SUSA

The political, diplomatic, and administrative capital of the Persian Empire, the city of Susa enjoyed its period of greatest splendor during the reign of Darius I. The king was responsible for the construction of all the Achaemenid buildings in the city, and he employed workmen from far and wide. The royal palace, built on raised ground, was similar in style to the Babylonian palaces, with its three large inner courtyards surrounded by offices and residential quarters. Next to the palace was the *apadana* (audience chamber) with 72 columns, almost 64 feet (20 meters) tall, supporting the ceiling. These columns were the pride of Achaemenid architecture; more slender than their Greek prototypes and adorned with capitals featuring the foreparts of animals, they seemed to multiply until they merged with the side walls. The full length of the walls was taken up by a procession of soldiers flanked by benevolent spirits in the guise of winged lions and bulls: these were the so-called "Immortals," faithful guards of the king's person who formed a symbolic garrison.

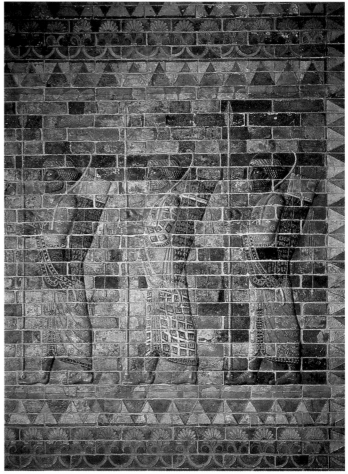

Three of the Immortals, detail of the decoration at the palace of Darius. Louvre, Paris.

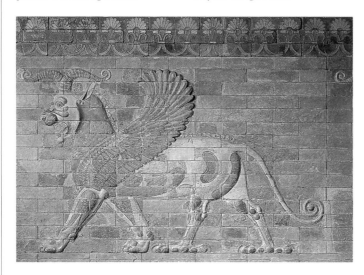

Winged griffin, detail of the decoration in glazed bricks from the palace of Darius at Susa. Louvre, Paris.

PERSIAN ART

When Alexander the Great invaded Persian territory in 331BC, he was captivated by the grand scale of the Achaemenid palaces and their decoration. In the southwest region of the Persian plateau, the Elamite civilization, with its capital of Susa, had flourished since the fourth millennium BC, when its handmade ceramics were decorated with geometrical patterns (triangles, lozenges, crosses, concentric circles, and swastikas) and animal and plant motifs. Human figures were rarer and, although stylized, displayed a lively naturalism. In the second half of the third millennium BC, the kings of Elam went to war against Sumer and Akkad, and the influence of Mesopotamian culture is clearly visible in the statue of the goddess Innin (analogous to the Babylonian Ishtar) and in the production of stelae. A new phase of cultural autonomy marked the rise of the Elamite state (13th–12th century BC). The gracefully monumental bronze statue of Napir-Asu, wife of King Untash-Khuban of Susa; the ziggurat of Choga Zanbil; and the reliefs of Kurangan, which herald the figurations of the Achaemenid palace, are all significant manifestations of art from this period.

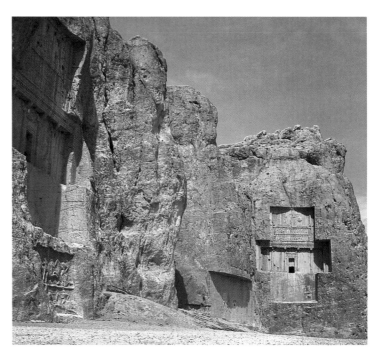

Rock tombs of the Achaemenids, at Naqsh-i Rustam. In the background stands the tomb of Darius I.

During the first millennium BC, the expansion of Iranian-speaking Mede and Persian peoples altered the political aspect of the region. The ephemeral Median Kingdom, with its capital of Ectabana founded in 722BC, was overthrown by Cyrus II the Great and came under Persian rule

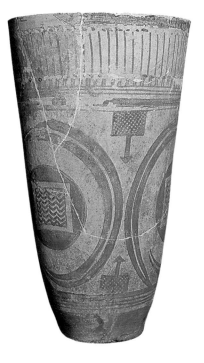

Ceramic beaker from Susa, fourth millennium BC. Louvre, Paris. This example of Susa I style features decoration with stylized ibixes, hounds, and birds.

THE OXUS TREASURE

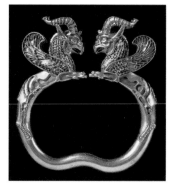

Gold bracelet with griffin motif. British Museum, London.

Discovered in 1877 at Kuad, near the Amu Dariya (Oxus) river, the Oxus treasure consists of rings, vases, necklaces, bracelets, pendants, ornamental stones, and figures, including a complete *quadriga* (two-wheeled chariot drawn by four horses harnessed abreast). Almost all of the treasures are made of gold and date from the fifth to fourth century BC. One large armlet (one of a pair) is richly decorated with the figures of winged griffins with ibex horns. It incorporates a favorite motif of Persian art,

that of two animals confronting each other. The griffins were originally inlaid with semi-precious stones, only one of which remains. More modest is a silver statuette, perhaps of a sovereign, which has a simple elegance that is also present in the relief work. Animal subjects provided the opportunity for Persian artists to display their most delicate decorative skills: for example, the nimble ibex forms the base of a silver *rhyton* (drinking vessel or horn) from Erzincan. In fact, animal art had earlier been a feature of the pre-Achaemenid period, best exemplified by the mysterious bronzes of Luristan, with their horse trappings, weapons, and belts bearing lively representations of fantastic creatures.

Small golden quadriga with charioteer and warrior. British Museum, London.

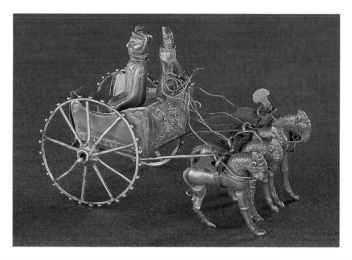

Procession of nobles and dignitaries, Palace of Darius, Persepolis. Situated on the northern stairway of the apadana, the reliefs show the official life of the great king's court in about 500BC.

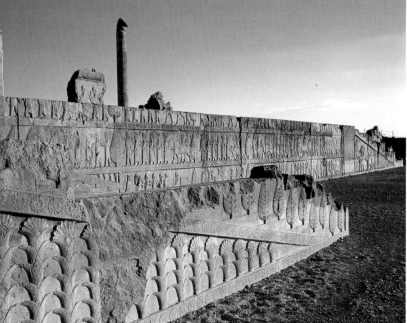

in 539BC. Cyrus, having overthrown Astyages, king of the Medes, laid the foundations of his future empire, the boundaries of which would extend from the Nile to the Indus. Persian art continued in the great Mesopotamian tradition, inheriting its fundamental characteristics. Cyrus, Darius, Xerxes, and other Persian kings vied with the magnificence of Babylonian king Nebuchadnezzar in the embellishment of their main cities: Pasargadae, Susa, and Persepolis. The gates of the palaces were protected by statues of animals like those found in Mesopotamia, while Persian sculptors derived the bas-relief from Assyrian art. In 518BC, Darius I initiated the building of Persepolis, which was to become the hub of the Persian empire. Conceived as the symbol of universality, the focal point where heaven and earth met, the palace of

Persepolis was decorated with reliefs and monuments proclaiming the power of the dynasty. The spacious throne room and reception rooms boasted parallel rows of fluted columns more than 64 feet (20 meters) high. The axial plan was continued throughout the palace, the pivot of which was the columned *apadana*, or audience chamber. Processions of dignitaries and nobles decorated the staircase that led to the great hall. The Persians had succeeded in transforming the dramatic force of their Mesopotamian models into a serene magnificence that was to be the hallmark of their art. In 331BC, Alexander the Great, following his victory over the last of the Achaemenid kings, Darius III, decreed the end of the empire and opened a new chapter in history: for the first time East and West were united under the rule of a single overlord.

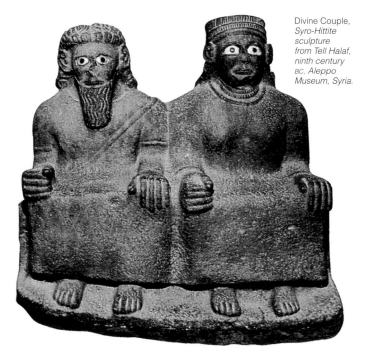

Divine Couple, Syro-Hittite sculpture from Tell Halaf, ninth century BC. Aleppo Museum, Syria.

ANATOLIAN ART

Often classified as peripheral to Mesopotamian culture, the art of Anatolia exhibits original features that have their roots in the pre-Hittite period. An initial burst of artistic activity saw modeling in gold, silver, and bronze, evincing a high level of workmanship from as long ago as the second half of the third millennium. The advanced state of urban development is shown by the city of Beycesultan on the Maeander River. The lower part of the imposing palace (mid-19th century BC) was constructed of stone and the upper part of mud reinforced with wooden beams. The palace, with its painted deco-

rations, consisted of a series of courtyards flanked by rooms. The advance of the Hittites, an Indo-European people, altered the appearance of the region. The Hittite state had a strong central structure, at least in its second imperial phase (1450–1200BC), and this was reflected in the supremacy of Hattusas (present-day Boğazköy) over the other cities. Capital of the empire and center of military and political power, its palaces and walls reflect the Hittite ambition for power and the urge to glorify the king. A double fortification with towers encircled the city, following the contours of the hillside, and the monumental arched gates, often compared to that at Mycenae, were guarded not only by sphinxes

THE SANCTUARY OF YAZILIKAYA

Dating from the 13th century BC, the carved figures of the rock sanctuary of Yazılıkaya near the Hattusas, the capital of the Hittite Empire, are an enduring source of mystery and fascination. Processions of male and female divinities converge on the wall of Chamber A. The depiction of the Storm-god facing the goddess of love testifies to the originality of Hittite carving, expressed just as vividly on orthostats as on the rock face. The divinities would have been recognizable by their ritual functions, and close attention is given to their individual configuration and personalities, adding a rhythmical variety to the

processions. The gods, who wear pointed hats, move from the left and are shown with their torsos in frontal view, while the goddesses move from the right, their bodies shown in profile; they wear conical hats. The major divinities appear taller and are raised up. Special meaning is also attached to the 12 gods – possibly divinities of the under-world – who bring up the rear of the male procession. Their forms are also repeated on the wall of inner Chamber B.

Dagger-god, relief on the eastern wall, chamber B, rock sanctuary at Yazilikaya, 13th century BC.

Procession of the Twelve Gods, relief on the western wall, chamber B, rock sanctuary at Yazilikaya, 13th century BC.

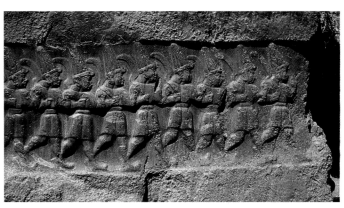

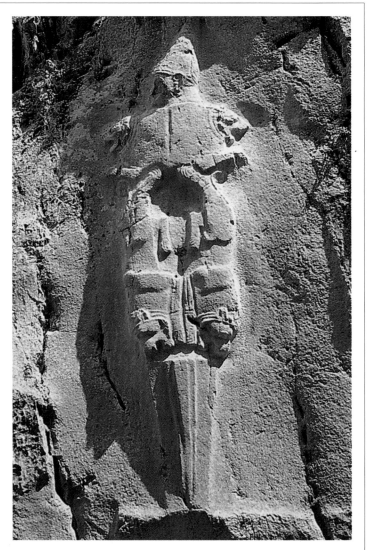

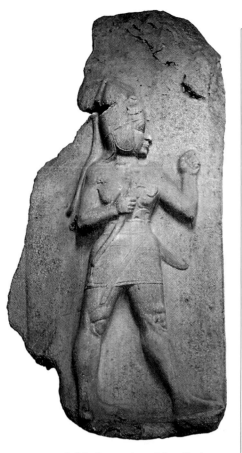

Relief with a warrior-god, from King's Gate at Hattusas, 13th century BC. Archaeological Museum, Ankara.

"PRIAM'S TREASURE"

Pioneer of the discovery of Mycenean civilization, the German archaeologist Heinrich Schliemann identified and excavated the site of Troy. A dedicated reader of Homer, he explored the places described in the *Iliad* and the *Odyssey*. He was convinced that the objects in gold, silver, and amber found in the second level of Troy were associated with the legendary King Priam. Attributable to the middle of the third millennium BC, the jewels are nevertheless of an earlier date than that which Greek historians give for the Achaean expedition led by Agamemnon. (The dating of Troy VIIa, to which the Homeric account of the war

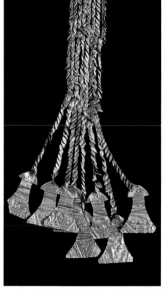

Gold earrings with leaf decoration, from "Priam's Treasure," c.2300BC. Pushkin Museum, Moscow.

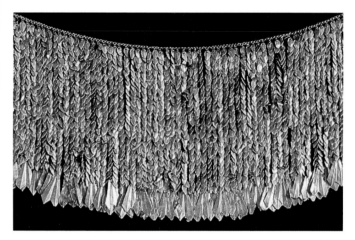

may refer, is believed to be between 1300 and 1230BC.) In any event, the jewels testify to the culture and prosperity of Troy, a fortified city.

Large diadem with pendant decoration (detail), from "Priam's Treasure," c. 2300BC. Pushkin Museum, Moscow.

and lions, as in the Babylonian temples, but also by an armed divinity. On the north side of the King's Gate, the orthostat with the god perfectly demonstrates the link between sculpture and architecture. Special importance was attached by the Hittites to monumental carving, as seen on the walls of the major cities. The Hittite relief was essentially a form of commemorative art in which, in contrast to the friezes in Mesopotamian palaces and Egyptian temples, the artist did not try to tell a story. The ostentation and affirmation of power were conveyed not in a historical description of warlike events but in the representation of divinity and the ritual ceremonies, in which the king was the protagonist.

At the end of the second millennium, the invasion of the "Sea Peoples" overthrew the Hittite empire (c.1200 BC), and the colonies established in Syria were all that remained of

Indo-European power. A new cultural and artistic phase now originated with the fusion of Hittite and Semitic traditions. On the Hittite relief illustrated below, for instance, the king wears a Hittite robe and carries a curved stick as his royal insignia. He faces the Syrian version of the Storm-god, who, characteristically, has his hair in a long curl, wears a kilt with a curved sword in his belt, brandishes a weapon, and holds lightning. However, his kilt, with its curved hem and his tall, horned headdress, is Hittite in style, and the Storm-god in the chariot behind him also derives from Hittite tradition. Sphinxes and lions continued to guard the city gates, but the sphinxes often betray the Egyptian influence that was widespread in the Levant. The Assyrians campaigning in Syria in the ninth century BC saw these figures and reliefs and created their own versions to decorate their palaces. In the late eighth century BC, the Assyrians annexed the city-states of Syria and imposed their own art and architecture.

King Sulumeli Offering a Libation Before the Storm-god, gateway relief from Malatya, c.1150BC. Archaeological Museum, Ankara.

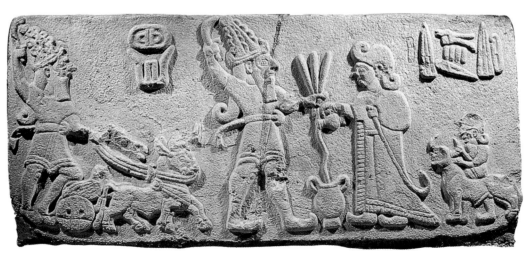

THE ART OF THE ANCIENT EAST

In the fourth and third millennia BC, the first civilizations took shape on the vast swaths of land surrounding the great rivers of India and China. These civilizations consisted of highly developed and independent cultures, which, over the centuries, would produce important works of art and technological innovations quite distinct from those of more Western civilizations.

THE INDUS VALLEY CITIES

The ancient cities of Harappa and Mohenjo-daro (now in Pakistan), were the main centers of the urban civilization that developed along the Indus river, which flows from the Himalayas through Kashmir and Pakistan to the Arabian Sea. Formality and rationality governed the development of these cities in their early stages, the major sites being made up of individual rectangular areas measuring some 650 x 1,300 feet (200 x 400 meters). Straight thoroughfares ran from north to south and from east to west, with smaller streets branching off to the sides, and a walled acropolis overlooking the cities. Wealth and power were expressed in the overall structure and appearance of the city itself rather than in individual buildings. In fact, there is no archaeological evidence of the temples, grand palaces, or royal tombs that are so characteristic of Mesopotamian and Egyptian civilizations. There were, however, private houses made of baked brick and wood based on a central courtyard giving access to rooms, baths, and other areas. Sensible use of the land and a constant struggle against the implacable force of the rivers, so vital to life, enabled the civilization of the Indus valley to develop over a long period (third to second millennium BC). With the help of an effec-

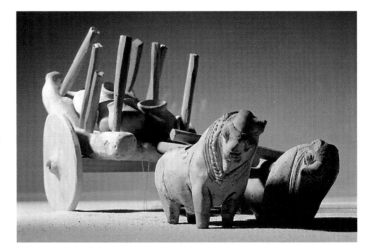

Ceramic sculpture of a small cart with vases and tools pulled by oxen, from Mohenjo-daro.

tive irrigation system, farmers harvested wheat and cotton and raised livestock. Improved hydraulic techniques made it possible to create drains, pipes for drinking water, dikes, and brick wells that were shared by groups of houses. The quality of life, materially, culturally, and intellectually, was unusually advanced for its time. There was cultural and ideological unity, with unified systems of measurement and writing, and a centralized structure of political organization.

ART OF THE INDUS

Evidence of the artistic output of the Indus valley reveals great skill. Pottery worked on the lathe was of an exceptionally high standard. The rounded vases were decorated mainly in black on a red background or in polychrome on a lighter background. Geometrical motifs, rows of parallel lines, and checkered, circular, and spiral designs were joined with

INDUS JEWELS

Excavations of Indus jewelry reveal a high level of craftsmanship in their working of precious metals and stones. These small ornaments may be of seemingly little importance when compared with the wealth of treasures piled up in Egyptian and Mesopotamian tombs; however, they possess intrinsic value because of the sophisticated technology required to produce them. As well as gold, semiprecious stones such as jasper, serpentine, alabaster, and steatite were frequently used. A deep interest in artistic

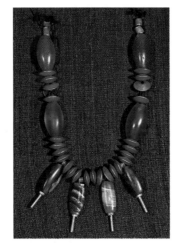

Necklace in gold and semiprecious stones, from Mohenjo-Daro. National Museum, New Delhi.

creation is revealed in the manipulation of raw materials through the use of chemical processes. Thus, agate was heated to obtain carnelian, and an elaborate production system was developed in order to obtain the desired form of stoneware.

Valuable objects such as jewels were undoubtedly handed down through generations, but they have rarely been found in funerary furnishings. In fact, very few personal ornaments have been recovered, which indicates an attitude toward death that was quite different from those of other ancient urban cultures.

naturalistic subjects; stylized plants and animal or human figures were often combined to fill available space.

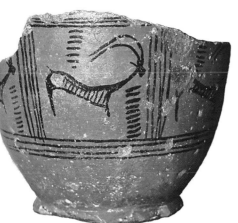

Fragmentary vase with ibex decoration, from Mohenjo-Daro. National Museum, Karachi.

Typical of the Indus culture were seals molded in steatite. Square in shape and with a raised surface, their subjects were repetitive in pattern and based exclusively on the animal kingdom. Elephants, buffaloes, rhinoceroses, antelopes, zebras, and unicorns are the most frequent images. These animals are depicted standing before particular objects, the functions of which are sometimes unclear. Above

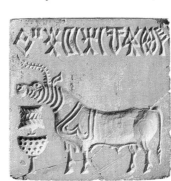

Seal in steatite with unicorn figure and vessel. National Museum, New Delhi.

them is a short inscription of four or five signs. The unicorn, a fantastical creature with a equine body, is always shown opposite a vessel consisting of a stem, a bowl, and another vertical piece. There are also a few specimens of bronzes,

statuettes, and stone carvings. The latter are best exemplified by a splendidly expressive votive portrait of a priest from Mohenjo-daro, with its

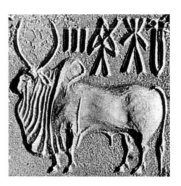

Seal in steatite with buffalo and writing, (emblem of the city of Harappa).

TERRACOTTA STATUETTES

Among the most original products of the Indus civilization are the lively and exuberant terracotta statuettes. The subjects most often represented, on seals of steatite in particular, include animals such as tigers, buffaloes, and oxen, which are shown either alone or yoked to small carts. Molded with great realism, these articles may have been used as toys. Small, everyday scenes – for example, a bird escaping a snare or a mother suckling her baby – were also captured with refreshing naturalism. The heads of female statuettes are characterized by their richly elaborate and varied hairstyles. Wrapped only in a short skirt, their bodies are adorned with necklaces. It is believed they were intended to portray the Mother Goddess. Mastery of three-dimensional modeling and a shrewd observation of anatomy are features of all Indus sculpture. These skills can be seen to great effect in the artists' application of pieces of clay to depict the fine details of the face and body.

Four terracotta figurines from Mohenjo-daro, mid-third millennium BC. National Museum, New Delhi. Clockwise from left: small cage with a bird at the door; bull; female figurine (perhaps representing the Mother Goddess); and toy animal with wheels and sheep's head.

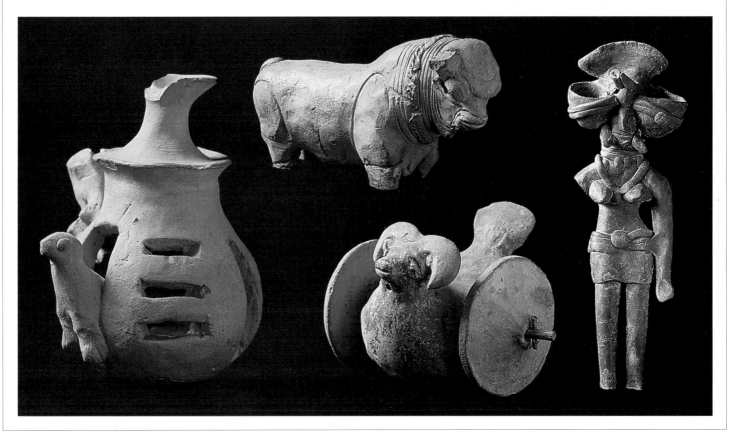

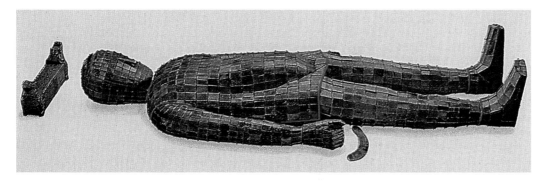

power, and the exercise of both by a priestly class, meant that the sovereign was responsible for the rites of worship and relations with the supernatural. They believed that earthly order had to be reflected in heavenly order, control of the world of magic,

Jade funeral garment of Prince Liu Sheng. Museum of Chinese History, Peking.

detailed rendering of the beard, delicate molding of the face, and slight incline of the head.

The Indus civilization collapsed in the 16th century BC, and the cities of Harappa and Mohenjo-daro were abandoned for rural villages. However, the Harappan style of pottery was to live on.

ANCIENT CHINESE ART

Although the Neolithic culture of China dates from the seventh millennium BC, according to ancient written tradition it was not until the 21st century BC that the Hsia (Xia) founded the first of the Chinese dynasties.

While little is known of the art of the Hsia, art found its most perfect expression in ritual bronzes under the rule of the Shang dynasty (1700– 1025BC). Designed for the presentation of offerings and sacred libations, there was a variety of different vessel types. The decoration consisted of idealized animal forms that may have had a totemic function: the *t'ao-t'ie* (mask of the glutton seeking to devour man), the dragon, the phoenix, birds, and fantastic monsters often stand out in relief from a background of ornamental motifs, such as meanders, intermingled triangles and parallel lines, clouds, and spirals. The imprisonment of the animal effigy or totemic creature in a ritual object may have been to harness its power and transfer its control to the shaman. The link between political and religious

THE INLAID STYLE

The technique of inlaying gold and silver, as distinct from that of gold-leaf application, was developed in the Warring States period (475–221BC). Originally

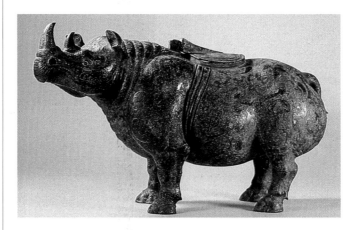

Rhinoceros in bronze from the King of Zhongshan's tomb, late third century BC. Museum of Chinese History, Peking.

executed by forcing cold strips of gold, silver, or other precious metals (iron at an early stage) into the body of the object, craftsmen then elaborated this new technique. They adapted inlaying to the age-old methods of mold-casting by preparing the cavities where the inlay was to be inserted ahead of casting. In the case of the winged monster from Pingshan, the silver decoration helps to emphasize the ferocity and power of the animal figure with its gaping mouth and sharp claws. A rhinoceros-shaped wine jug from the steppes achieves a synthesis of the inlaid and animal styles. The body is sprinkled with cloudlike shapes and spiral patterns, and the inlaid threads of gold and silver wire imitate its thick bristles; on the back is a small lid, and on the right side of the mouth is a long, thin copper tube for pouring the wine.

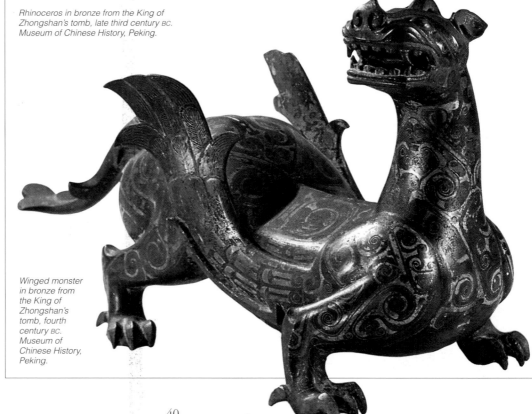

Winged monster in bronze from the King of Zhongshan's tomb, fourth century BC. Museum of Chinese History, Peking.

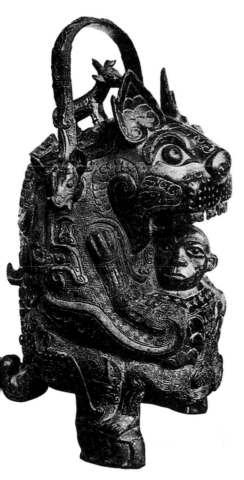

anthropomorphic earthenware statuettes full of vivacity and movement were created to accompany the dead to the next world. Bronzes gradually lost their function of transmitting magical and divine forces, and their decoration became more abstract in style. The metal surfaces were covered with long inscriptions, perhaps to celebrate an event exalting a family or clan or to honor ancestors. A new ornamental element that consisted of interlacing dragons became widespread in the "Spring and Autumn" period (c.770–476BC), during which the state took on an increasingly feudal character, and nobles often rebelled against the central power. Civil wars led to a crisis in Chou authority and brought the subsequent restoration of order in the Ch'in (Qin) dynasty (c.221–206BC), followed by the Han dynasty (206BC–AD220). There were notable achievements in science, agriculture, and craftsmanship, and commerce was revived thanks to Chinese control of the Silk Route. Small bronzes were produced in the form of fully rounded figures of animals. Their physical features are barely sketched but reveal an acute sense of observation in their lively poses and expressions. The same characteristics were evident in many terracotta pieces – statuettes of animals or people continued the tradition of the small funerary images that characterized the Chou period. Among the most notable are the hollow brick slabs of the tombs featuring relief decoration of hunting scenes. An exceptional find from one tomb was the funeral garment of the prince Liu Sheng, made of 2,498 pieces of jade held together by 2½ lb (1.1kg) of gold thread. The corpse was wrapped in the jade, a material that is both precious and enduring, to ensure that the body and spirit should be preserved for all eternity.

Zoomorphic example of a yu, a ritual wine vessel, Shang dynasty. Cernuschi Museum, Paris.

and the harmony of cosmic forces were essential for good government.

When the Chou (Zhou) (1025–221BC) succeeded the Shang, the social and political conditions of the state underwent considerable change, and philosophical and religious systems such as Confucianism appeared. Art objects of jade, bone, and ivory, and

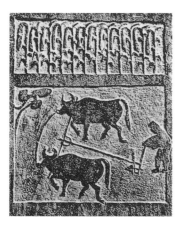

Terracotta tile with bulls pulling plow, Han dynasty.

THE TERRACOTTA ARMY

The naturalistic, artistic impulses of the Ch'in era are best revealed in the terracotta statues of soldiers that were discovered in 1974 on the site

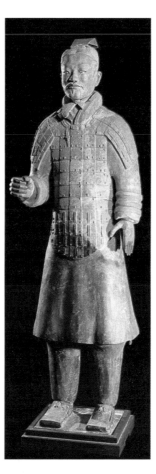

of the mausoleum of Ch'in Shih-huang-ti (Qin Shihnangdi) at Lintong in Shaanxi province. The 10,000 warriors, which have individual faces, represent every rank in the army and numerous racial types. The army is equipped with complete military outfits: archers, infantrymen, charioteers, and horsemen carry sharp-bladed weapons of the finest material. The height of each figure varies from 6 to 6½ feet (1.75 to 1.97 meters), and the foot soldiers are flanked by more than 130 wooden chariots and 500 horsemen. The various body parts of the figures, produced in series, are of different colors. The terracotta army represents the power of the great Ch'in dynasty, whose founder, King Cheng, created the first centralized and multinational empire. In celebration of this accomplishment, he adopted the name Ch'in Shih-huang-ti, the First Emperor. He also initiated the building of the great monument of Chinese unity, the Great Wall, which extends 1,240 miles (2,000 km) from the China Sea to the northwest border of the country.

Terracotta soldier in armor, 220–210BC. Museum of Chinese History, Peking.

Terracotta battle horse, 220–210BC. Museum of Chinese History, Peking.

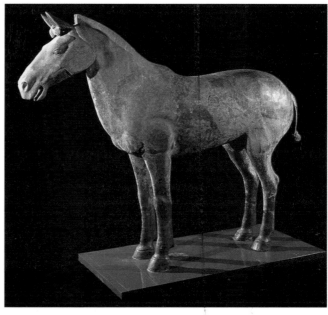

ANCIENT AEGEAN ART

*Toward the end of the third millennium BC, a flourishing civilization
with a vast potential for expansion – thanks to its maritime trade links –
developed on the island of Crete and in the Cycladic islands to the north.
The highly original works of art produced in this area were to become
models for the Mycenaean culture a few centuries later.*

AEGEAN ART

The Aegean Sea, with its many islands, was the cradle of pre-Hellenic civilization. A widely diffused culture had appeared in the Cycladic archipelago by the middle of the third millennium BC. This early phase of Cycladic art was characterized by ceramics decorated with zigzags, running spirals, and ship motifs that symbolized the marine activity of the region. The islands abounded in marble, which provided the ideal material for the sculpture of vases and of idols, the most typical of which were female figures (possibly fertility goddesses). Also known are *kouratrophoi* (women with babies in their arms), musicians (lyre and pipe players) and hunter-warriors. These figures varied both in size – from a few inches to a yard or so in height – and in type. Examples include schematic figures, violin-shaped or with a rounded lower body, and even the more naturalistic ones have the head reduced to a plane surface relieved only by the nose. The artists worked to a canon of proportions: all features are formalized, faces (nose, eyes, and mouth) at best simply delineated, though details were also picked out in paint.

In the course of the second millennium, Crete, to the south of the Cyclades, became dominant in the Aegean Sea and its islands. The prosperity of this

THE PALACE OF KNOSSOS

A catastrophic earthquake in about 1700BC left the magnificent palace at Knossos in ruins. However, impressive and extensive reconstruction work produced an even more glamorous successor. This second palace was built on the terraced mound around a central court, with the surrounding quarters – up to four stories high in places – spreading out in a design more concerned with practicality than symmetry. Among many imposing features were monumental entrances, staircases, colonnaded halls, light-wells, lustral basins and extensive storage facilities. Lavish use was made of wooden columns, tapered

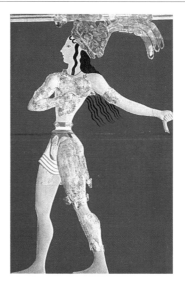

The Lily-Prince, *painted relief plaster from the palace at Knossos, c.1425BC. Archaeological Museum, Heraklion, Crete.*

at the base, which contributed to the light, airy atmosphere. The frescoes took much of their inspiration from nature: flowers and animals mingle with humans in symbolically charged settings. Colors were bright, if not always strictly realistic; species were at times combined; and human anatomy was carefully portrayed. Occasional scenes of court life exist, such as ritual dances, as well as sporting events, such as bull-leaping. After about 1450BC, development toward a more static and formalized style (found also in pottery) is evident in friezes, such as the *Campstool* and *Cup-Bearer* frescoes; reliefs such as the *Lily-Prince* retain the older, naturalistic style.

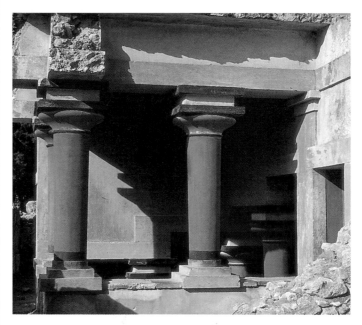

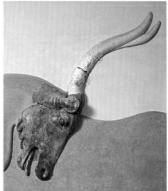

Head of a charging bull, *detail of painted relief from Knossos, c.1600BC. Archaeological Museum, Heraklion, Crete.*

Remains (extensively restored) *of a lustral basin from the palace at Knossos.*

civilization, named Minoan after the legendary King Minos, is evident in the construction of the palaces at Knossos, Phaistos and Mallia. These first palaces were all damaged in about 1700BC, and were at once rebuilt. Surviving art shows the development of original forms and styles with an interest in nature. This is manifested by items such as the precious metalwork and carved stone vases of the second palaces. Some of these are decorated with bull and

lion heads, from which liquids were poured at ritual occasions. Even much earlier, decorative vitality was illustrated in the mottled surface colorings of Vasilki ware (the result of skillful painting and kiln control), and also in the seals enlivened by linear plant and animal motifs.

A large number of high-quality ceramics were produced during the time of the first palaces (2000–1700BC). The Kamares style involved often refined wares in a variety of

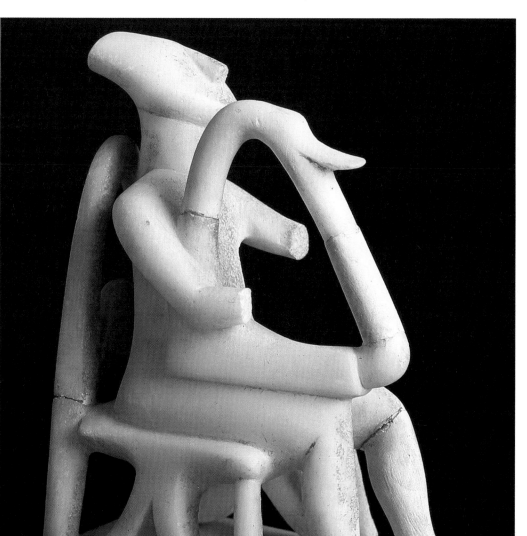

Snake Goddess, *faience statuette from Knossos, c.1600BC. Archaeological Museum, Heraklion, Crete. The goddess carries a panther or a leopard on her headdress.*

Seated Harpist, *marble statue from Keros, Cyclades, c.2300BC. National Museum, Athens. The cleanness of line in this and other pieces has influenced artists in modern times.*

forms, featuring designs of white and polychrome patterning on a dark background, often complex in the ordering of both geometric and natural motifs.

After 1700BC, magnificent new palaces arose in urban settings, and an extensive building program took place in the countryside. The pottery of this period developed slowly: simple, formalized renditions of flowers (daisies, delicate lilies, branches of foliage) and animals (leaping dolphins) were featured in white on a brown-black ground. They were developed from Kamares wares but had some original features. Soon, natural

THE PAINTINGS OF AKROTIRI

At some point between 1620BC and 1500BC (scholarly opinion differs), a terrible volcanic eruption devastated the island of Thera (modern-day Santorini). The disappearance of part of the island possibly inspired Plato's myth of Atlantis, his utopian island that was swallowed by the sea. On Thera, the marvelous wall paintings of the great city at Akrotiri have survived in the rock and ash. Geometric patterns and marbled stones exist, as do plant motifs, such as crocuses, lilies, and myrtles; animal motifs, such as monkeys, swallows, antelopes, lions, and dolphins; and scenes of life in town and countryside, which range from images of marching soldiers to peaceful cattle. Painted on plaster, all are represented in a simple yet meticulous manner, and the artists have paid close attention to color. Episodes of a single, apparently continuous narrative appear in the miniature frieze of the West House. The detailed topography has persuaded some that the frieze portrays an actual event associated with the house's occupant – possibly a sea voyage, via Crete, to North Africa.

Detail of frieze, West House, Akrotiri, Thera, Greece, c.1550BC.

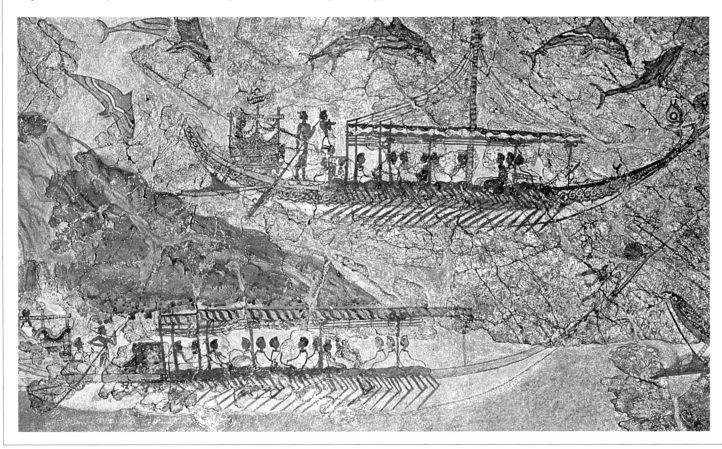

elements abounded, depicted in black set against a beige ground and greatly inspired by floral and marine subjects. Swimming octopi with clutching tentacles covered the surfaces of vases, interspersed with argonauts, starfish, corals, shells, and jagged rocks. The technical brilliance of Minoan art is best seen in its products in miniature. Bronze cast figurines show male votaries wearing loincloths and the women wearing long skirts and open bodices that expose their breasts. The statuette of the snake goddess is more elaborate, typical of the Minoan faience, or highly

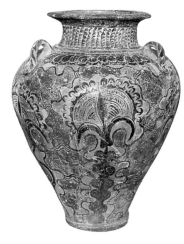

Jar with floral decoration, Knossos, 1450–1400BC. Archaeological Museum, Heraklion, Crete.

colored earthenware. An attentive observation of nature is clearly evident in images in frescoes and on vases made of a variety of materials (many of a serpentine-related matter, others in obsidian, rock-crystal, and porphyry). Among those portrayed is the bull captured at full speed in its charge. The stone vases, with their relief carvings, are deservedly famous: one pear-shaped *rhyton* (horn-shaped drinking vessel) shows a bustling procession of reapers with pitchforks led by a priest wearing a scaled jacket, and four singers, one playing a *sistrum* (a rattle of Egyptian origin). The artisan conveys depth by superimposing bodies and crossing the forks; the narrow waists of the figures minimize the contrast of the frontal view of the torso and the side view of the legs. Even with the more stylized models of domestic animals, such as bulls, sheep, wild goats, and birds, this interest is maintained. Bulls are especially prominent, since they are enshrined in the legend of the Minotaur, a monster with the body of a man and the head of a bull. This compositional exuberance and freedom is contrasted with the tense formality that increasingly

CRETAN MASTERS: "BULL-LEAPING"

15th century BC; wall painting on lime plaster; Archeological Museum, Heraklion, Crete.

This work, part of the Taureador fresco from the east side of the Palace at Knossos, shows a sport involving three figures and a bull. From Persia to Egypt, the bull was an important animal in ancient symbolism and was often ritually sacrificed. In Crete, contests pitting bull against athletes (in a ritual activity termed

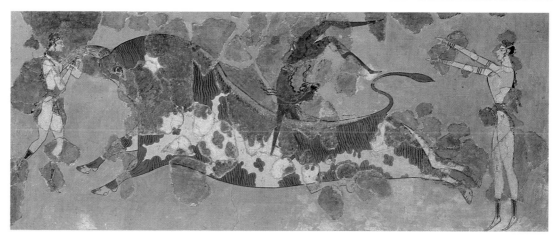

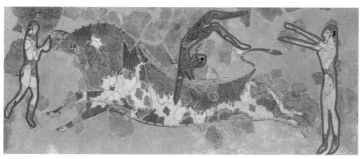

taurokathapsia, or bull-leaping) are portrayed in various media: this painting, made with pigments on lime plaster, features a beautiful palette of subdued colors, including ochre and blue. Like many of the works found by Sir Arthur Evans at Knossos, the fresco was badly damaged and in need of restoration.

▲ *1. A strong contrast is created between the mass of the bull's body and the slightness and gracefulness of the athletes. The animal's body, with its neck curving majestically to the left, stretches across three quarters of the picture length. From right to left, the body shape develops with fluidity, and both the bull and the human figures seem to float in the air.*

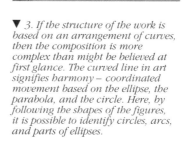

◄ *4. The detail on the left shows the human figure confronting the bull, having run at it in order to grasp the animal's horns and achieve the necessary impetus for the vault. Bull-leaping was a game that demanded strength, timing, skill, and grace, but never violence. It is possible that young girls may also have been active in this sport.*

▼ *3. If the structure of the work is based on an arrangement of curves, then the composition is more complex than might be believed at first glance. The curved line in art signifies harmony – coordinated movement based on the ellipse, the parabola, and the circle. Here, by following the shapes of the figures, it is possible to identify circles, arcs, and parts of ellipses.*

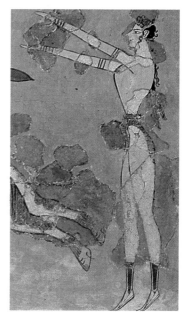

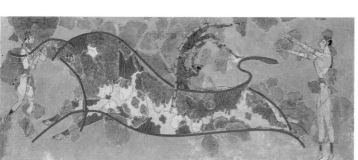

▲ *2. The lines that describe the figures and bull are interconnected in a system of curves, continuous for the bull and interrupted for the humans. The skin of two of the athletes is white, a color used by the Minoans to represent women, while that of the third is brown, a color used for men. Here, this coloring system could be intended to signify two youths and an adult male. The three figures may be demonstrating three successive phases of an exercise that involves vaulting on and off the creature's back.*

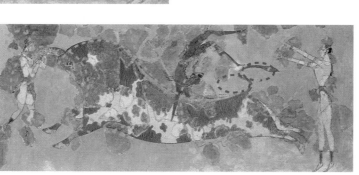

▲ *5. The figure behind the tail of the bull, dressed in a loincloth, is standing with arms already raised. Perhaps he has been captured at the moment of landing after leaping off the bull's back – he stands on the tips of his toes – or is preparing to catch the vaulting figure. If so, Cretan perceptions may anticipate those of the Greeks, representing movement by introducing the dimension of time into figurative art.*

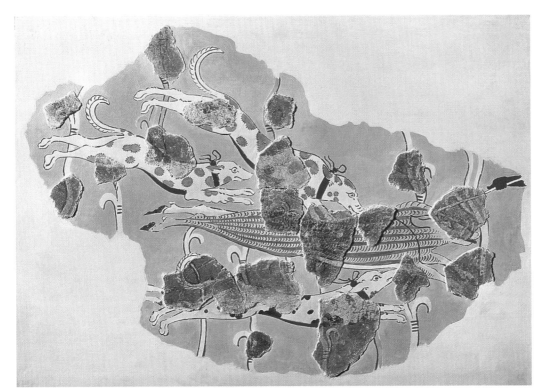

Fresco fragment with hunting scene, from the palace at Tiryns, c.1250BC. National Museum, Athens.

immense, Cyclopean walls. Those at the citadel of Tiryns range in thickness between 16 and 55 feet (5 and 17 meters). Towers may have strengthened the walls, and water supplies on the outside were reached by underground passages. The majestic Lion Gate of Mycenae was built of simple, massive blocks. The two lions, created in heraldic pose, are positioned over the lintel, guarding the entrance; they are among the earliest examples of monumental sculpture on the Greek mainland.

The heart of each royal seat was the palace, centered on the enclosed *megaron*, a reception area surrounded by storage rooms, living quarters, and courts; it was smaller than

pervades portrayals after about 1450BC – following the arrival of the Mycenaean overlords in Crete. These mainlanders, whose local culture in central and southern Greece had been transformed under the spur of Minoan culture, now took advantage of Cretan weakness to establish control first there and then through-out the Aegean.

Such stylistic changes are readily observed in the processional frescoes that adorn the palace of Knossos, as well as the limestone sarcophagus from Hagia Triada, dating from about 1400BC, which is decorated with religious scenes of sacrifice and worship. They are also evident in the ceramics: for example, the octopus is now placed vertically, while surviving floral and marine motifs are arranged stiffly and symmetrically.

The social organization of places like Mycenae, Tiryns, and Orchomenos revolved around a class of military leaders, often identified with the legendary Achaeans, celebrated by Homer. They built their palaces on elevated positions, later protecting them with

THE BULL AND THE OCTOPUS

Aegean art, from its earliest days on Crete and the Cyclades, only seldom featured grandiose or overtly royal figures – more the norm in the Near East. However, mythological, symbolic, and ritual concepts permeated every aspect of daily life. One regularly depicted symbol was the bull – featured in the abduction of Europa by Zeus, and as the father of the Minotaur on Pasiphaë, queen to Minos. The animal may have stood for the more remote figure of the god-king, its horns used to mark out the sacredness of a place.

In later Greek myth, the Titaness Metis (or Counsel) assisted Zeus in administering the potion by which Cronos was made to disgorge Zeus' siblings. Zeus dethroned his father and took Metis as his consort. Alarmed by a prophecy that a second, male child would depose him, Zeus

swallowed the pregnant Metis by trickery. Eventually, his daughter Athene was born fully formed. The octopus, being apparently a large head with many arms and being able to change color at will, became a symbol for the divine wisdom of the two goddesses and stood for clear thinking.

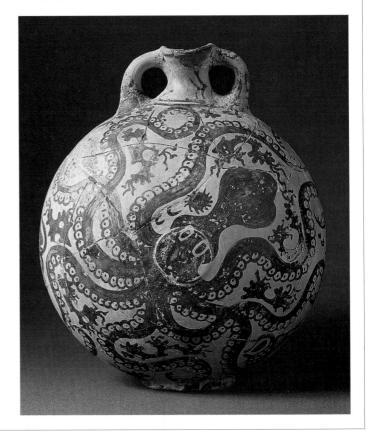

Flask with octopus decoration, c.1450BC. Archaeological Museum, Heraklion, Crete.

its Cretan counterpart, with its open central courts.

Just as Mycenean architecture borrowed from Cretan but diverged from it, so the artistic styles developed along their own paths. Frescoes depicting ritual scenes, as well as more violent pursuits such as battles, adorn the walls. Stone vases, metal weaponry, and jewelry all produced new forms. The decoration of ceramics grew progressively more stylized and simple, with banded zones reducing the patterned area; however, a pictorial element remained.

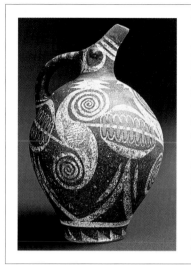

THE KAMARES STYLE

Named after the cave sanctuary on Crete's Mount Ida, where the first substantial amounts of Kamares pottery were found, such wares combined refined technique and creative flair. It is believed this style of pottery was produced for the first palace centers of Knossos and Phaistos between the 20th and 19th century BC. Decoration of

Kamares vase, Phaistos, c.1800BC. Archaeological Museum, Heraklion, Crete.

the vases consisted of balanced and often repeating patterns of linear and spiral-based motifs, with many naturalistic motifs as well as stylized humans, all painted in white, yellow, orange, red, and crimson-mauve on a metallic-looking black or brownish ground. Stamped motifs, such as shells and flowers, added relief elements. Such shapes decorated all sorts of plates, fruit stands, jugs, jars, bowls, and cups – some with walls as thin as eggshell, others quite heavy.

THE TOMBS OF MYCENAE

Following his earlier excavations at Troy, Heinrich Schliemann, the romantically minded archaeologist, turned his attention to Mycenae, the city of the legendary King Agamemnon, who was murdered by his wife and her lover. He believed that he had found the remains of the unfortunate king and gave the royal name to a magnificent gold mask, found in one of a group of shaft graves that had been encircled by a stone perimeter and enclosed within the later citadel walls. The strong features and accentuated lines of the mask, together with the retold

story by such figures as the Greek travel-writer Pausanias, evoke the memory of the tragedy. The mask did not actually belong to Agamemnon, but the funeral trappings and the profusion of gold indicate that the graves did contain royalty. As well as the masks, there were vessels of metal, stone, and clay; smaller personal items of metal, ivory, and stone; vases of faience; and many metal weapons, some with intricate inlay. Chief of these are the dagger blades, set with heavily Minoanized scenes of the hunt and of animals and flowers; these are all carefully built up from individually prepared stamps of gold, silver, and copper.

Gold Agamemnon mask, Mycenae, c.1500BC. National Museum, Athens.

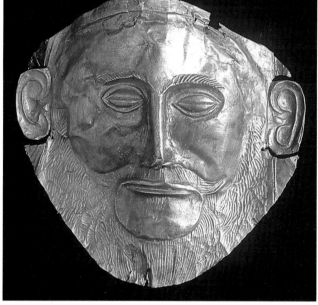

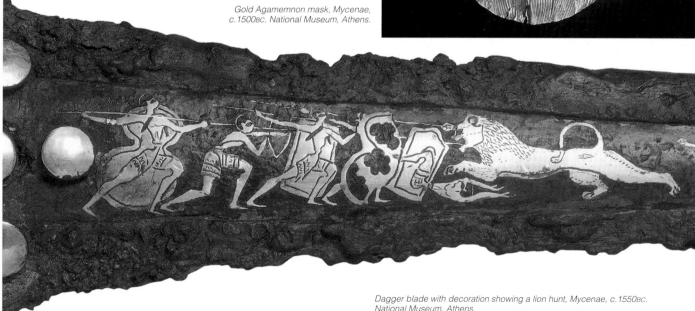

Dagger blade with decoration showing a lion hunt, Mycenae, c.1550BC. National Museum, Athens.

PREHISTORIC ART

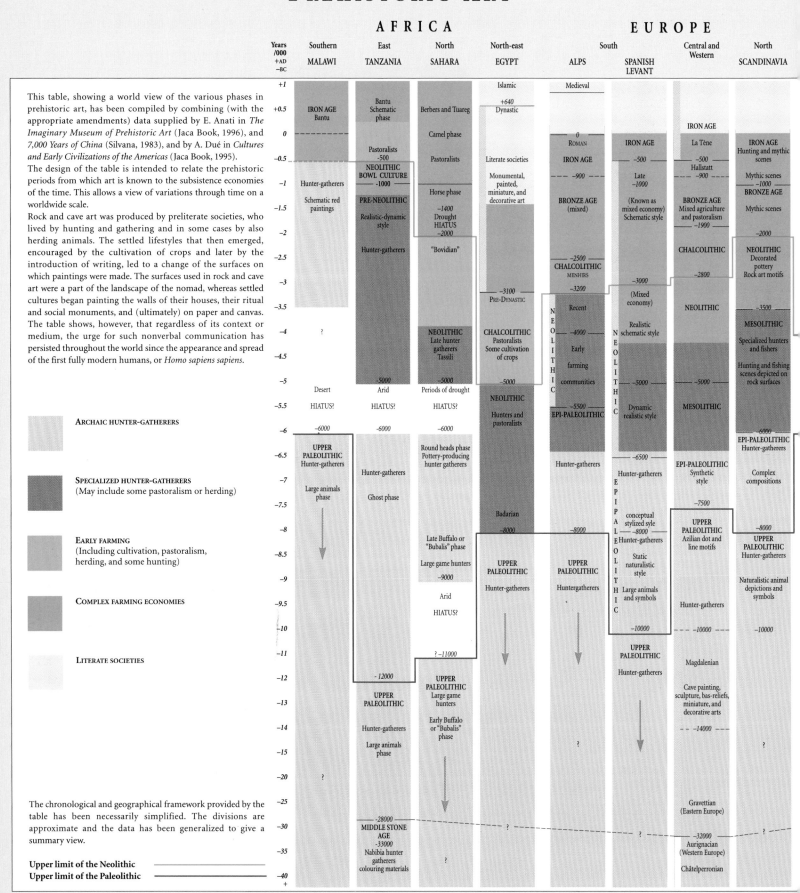

AFRICA   EUROPE

Years /000 +AD −BC	Southern MALAWI	East TANZANIA	North SAHARA	North-east EGYPT	South ALPS	SPANISH LEVANT	Central and Western	North SCANDINAVIA

This table, showing a world view of the various phases in prehistoric art, has been compiled by combining (with the appropriate amendments) data supplied by E. Anati in *The Imaginary Museum of Prehistoric Art* (Jaca Book, 1996), and *7,000 Years of China* (Silvana, 1983), and by A. Dué in *Cultures and Early Civilizations of the Americas* (Jaca Book, 1995).

The design of the table is intended to relate the prehistoric periods from which art is known to the subsistence economies of the time. This allows a view of variations through time on a worldwide scale.

Rock and cave art was produced by preliterate societies, who lived by hunting and gathering and in some cases by also herding animals. The settled lifestyles that then emerged, encouraged by the cultivation of crops and later by the introduction of writing, led to a change of the surfaces on which paintings were made. The surfaces used in rock and cave art were a part of the landscape of the nomad, whereas settled cultures began painting the walls of their houses, their ritual and social monuments, and (ultimately) on paper and canvas. The table shows, however, that regardless of its context or medium, the urge for such nonverbal communication has persisted throughout the world since the appearance and spread of the first fully modern humans, or *Homo sapiens sapiens*.

ARCHAIC HUNTER-GATHERERS

SPECIALIZED HUNTER-GATHERERS
(May include some pastoralism or herding)

EARLY FARMING
(Including cultivation, pastoralism, herding, and some hunting)

COMPLEX FARMING ECONOMIES

LITERATE SOCIETIES

The chronological and geographical framework provided by the table has been necessarily simplified. The divisions are approximate and the data has been generalized to give a summary view.

Upper limit of the Neolithic ⸻
Upper limit of the Paleolithic ⸻

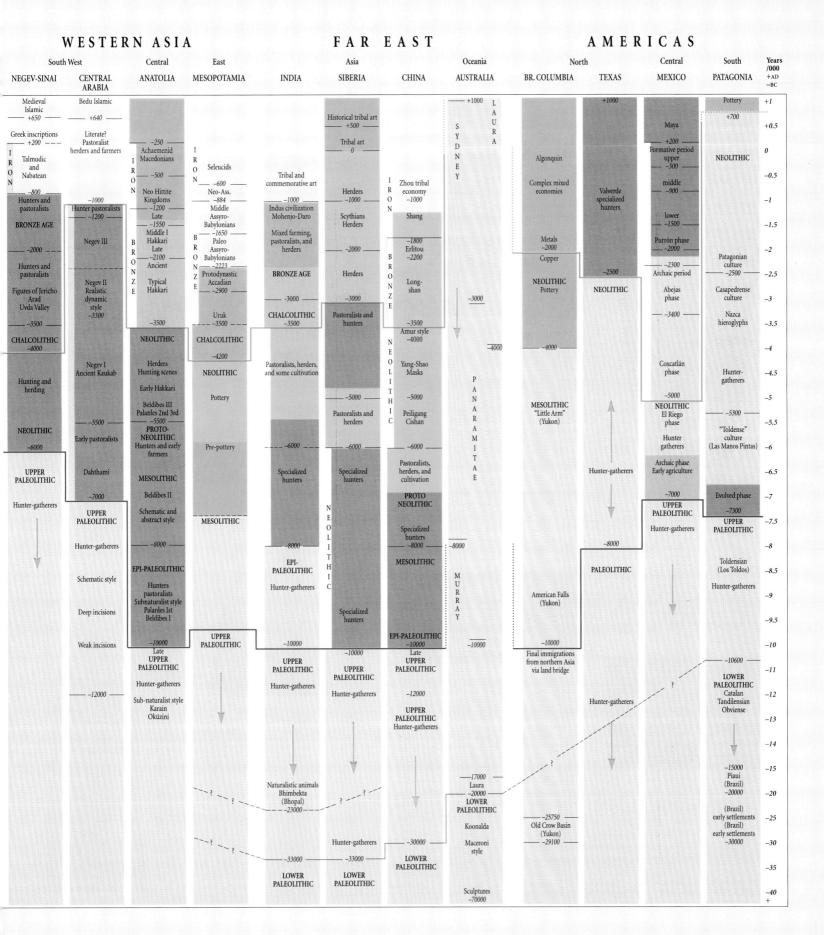

WESTERN ASIA

South West		Central	East
NEGEV-SINAI	CENTRAL ARABIA	ANATOLIA	MESOPOTAMIA

FAR EAST

Asia		
INDIA	SIBERIA	CHINA
		Oceania
		AUSTRALIA

AMERICAS

North		Central	South
BR. COLUMBIA	TEXAS	MEXICO	PATAGONIA

Years /000 +AD −BC

NEGEV-SINAI
Medieval Islamic +650
Greek inscriptions +200
IRON
Talmudic and Nabatean −800
Hunters and pastoralists
BRONZE AGE −2000
Hunters and pastoralists
Figures of Jericho Arad Uvda Valley −3500
CHALCOLITHIC −4000
Hunting and herding
NEOLITHIC −6000
UPPER PALEOLITHIC −7000
Hunter-gatherers

CENTRAL ARABIA
Bedu Islamic +640
Literate? Pastoralist herders and farmers −1000
Hunter pastoralists −1200
Negev III −2000
Negev II Realistic dynamic style −3300
Negev I Ancient Kaukab
Early pastorals −5500
PROTO-NEOLITHIC Hunters and early farmers
Dahthami −7000
UPPER PALEOLITHIC
Hunter-gatherers
Schematic style
Deep incisions
Weak incisions −10000
Late UPPER PALEOLITHIC
Hunter-gatherers −12000
Sub-naturalist style Karain Oküzini

ANATOLIA
−250 Achaemenid Macedonians
IRON −500
Neo Hittite Kingdoms −1200
Late −1550
Middle I Hakkari Late −2100
Ancient
BRONZE
Typical Hakkari −3500
NEOLITHIC
Herders Hunting scenes
Early Hakkari
Beldibes III Palanles 2nd 3rd −5500
MESOLITHIC
Beldibes II
Schematic and abstract style −8000
EPI-PALEOLITHIC
Hunters pastoralists Subnaturalist style Palanles 1st Beldibes I −10000

MESOPOTAMIA
IRON
Seleucids −600
Neo-Ass. −884
Middle Assyro-Babylonians −1650
Paleo Assyro-Babylonians −2223
BRONZE
Protodynastic Accadian −2900
Uruk −3500
CHALCOLITHIC −4200
NEOLITHIC
Pottery
Pre-pottery
MESOLITHIC
UPPER PALEOLITHIC

INDIA
Tribal and commemorative art −1000
Indus civilization Mohenjo-Daro
Mixed farming, pastoralists, and herders
BRONZE AGE
CHALCOLITHIC −3500
Pastoralists, herders, and some cultivation
−6000
Specialized hunters −8000
EPI-PALEOLITHIC
Hunter-gatherers −10000
UPPER PALEOLITHIC
Hunter-gatherers
Naturalistic animals Bhimbekta (Bhopal) −23000
? ?
? ?
−33000
LOWER PALEOLITHIC

SIBERIA
Historical tribal art +500
Tribal art 0
Herders −1000
Scythians Herders
Herders −2000
−3000
Pastoralists and hunters −3500
Yang-Shao Masks
−5000
Pastoralists and herders −6000
Specialized hunters
N E O L I T H I C
Specialized hunters −8000
Hunter-gatherers
Specialized hunters
−10000
UPPER PALEOLITHIC
Hunter-gatherers −12000
Hunter-gatherers −30000
LOWER PALEOLITHIC −33000

CHINA
IRON
Zhou tribal economy −1000
BRONZE
Shang
−1800 Erlitou −2200
Long-shan −3500
Amur style −4000
Yang-Shao Masks −5000
Peiligang Cishan −6000
PROTO NEOLITHIC
Specialized hunters −8000
MESOLITHIC
EPI-PALEOLITHIC −10000
Late UPPER PALEOLITHIC −12000
UPPER PALEOLITHIC Hunter-gatherers −30000
LOWER PALEOLITHIC

AUSTRALIA
+1000
S Y D N E Y
L A U R A
−3000
−4000
P A N A R A M I T A E
−8000
M U R R A Y
−10000
−17000 Laura −20000
LOWER PALEOLITHIC
Koonalda
Maceroni style −30000
Sculptures −70000

BR. COLUMBIA
Algonquin
Complex mixed economies
Metals −2000
Copper
NEOLITHIC Pottery
−4000
MESOLITHIC "Little Arm" (Yukon)
American Falls (Yukon)
Final immigrations from northern Asia via land bridge −10000
?
Old Crow Basin (Yukon) −25750

TEXAS
+1000
Valverde specialized hunters
−2500
NEOLITHIC
Hunter-gatherers
−8000
PALEOLITHIC
Hunter-gatherers

MEXICO
Maya
+200 Formative period upper −300
middle −900
lower −1500
Purrón phase −2000
−2300 Archaic period
Abejas phase
−3400
Coxcatlán phase
−5000
NEOLITHIC El Riego phase
Hunter gatherers
Archaic phase Early agriculture −7000
UPPER PALEOLITHIC
Hunter-gatherers
−8000
Hunter-gatherers
?

PATAGONIA
Pottery
+700
NEOLITHIC
Patagonian culture −2500
Casapedrense culture
Nazca hieroglyphs
Hunter-gatherers
−5300
"Toldense" culture (Las Manos Pintas)
Evolved phase −7300
UPPER PALEOLITHIC
Toldensian (Los Toldos)
Hunter-gatherers
−10600
LOWER PALEOLITHIC Catalan Tandilensian Ohviense
−15000 Piaui (Brazil) −20000
(Brazil) early settlements (Brazil) early settlements −30000

Years /000 +AD −BC
+1
+0.5
0
−0.5
−1
−1.5
−2
−2.5
−3
−3.5
−4
−4.5
−5
−5.5
−6
−6.5
−7
−7.5
−8
−8.5
−9
−9.5
−10
−11
−12
−13
−14
−15
−20
−25
−30
−35
−40
+

PRE-CLASSICAL CIVILIZATIONS

3000BC: tablets from Uruk in Sumer attest to the invention of cuneiform writing. **c.3000BC:** Narmer unites Egypt under a single pharaoh. **2500BC:** oldest civilization in the Indus valley

flourishes in northern India; in Egypt, papyrus and ink are used for writing. **2400BC:** literature in the local Semitic language develops at Ebla in Syria. **2000BC:** Crete affirms her supremacy

in the Aegean Sea. **c.1894BC:** Babylon ("Gate of Gods") is founded on the banks of the Euphrates. **c.1700BC:** verified use in Crete of the still undeciphered linear A script. **1600BC:**

earliest urban civilization established in China under the Shang Dynasty. **c.1350BC:** early example of writing, with 30 characters, at Ugarit, in Syria. **1402BC:** under Amenophis III, Egypt

4000BC – 2800BC | **2800BC – 2400BC** | **2400BC – 2000BC** | **2000BC – 1600BC**

▼ SUSA

Elamite civilization flourished in 4000BC, and ceramics were produced with decorative plant and animal motifs against geometric background patterns.

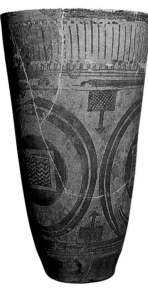

Ceramic beaker from Susa, fourth millennium BC. Musée du Louvre, Paris.

▼ INDIA

In 2500BC, Harappa and Mohenjo-Daro were centers of the thriving and technically advanced civilization of the Indus valley. Typical products were steatite seals with figures of animals and lively statuettes in terracotta.

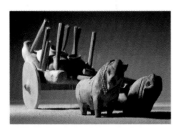

Ceramic sculpture of a small cart with vases and tools pulled by oxen, from Mohenjo-daro.

▼ SUMER

With the growth of the city-states of Ur, Lagash, and Mari (2800-2500BC), the construction of fortified walls and brick temples on high platforms took place. Art forms included sculpture in the round and mosaic decoration.

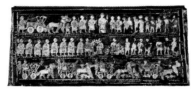

The Ur standard, third millennium BC. British Museum, London.

ANATOLIA

In about 2300BC, beautifully worked gold, silver, and amber objects were produced, such as parts of "Priam's Treasure," found in the second level of Troy.

▼ EGYPT

Under the pharaohs of the Fourth Dynasty (2723-2536BC), the smooth-faced, triangular pyramid replaced the stepped pyramid. There was a marked development of polychrome-relief painting, with a repertory of iconography drawn from daily life.

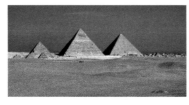

Pyramids of King Khufu, Khafre, and Menkaure, Giza.

SYRIA

From 2400BC, in the north of the country, an advanced, original urban culture developed at Ebla. There was a rich production of pottery, jewelry, bronze weapons, and ivory amulets. Typical utensils included rectangular stone cult basins divided into two sections, lavishly carved on three sides.

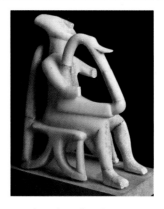

Lyre player, from Amorgos (2400–2200BC). National Archaeological Museum, Athens.

▲ AEGEAN

Cycladic culture was established in about 2400BC. Vases with spiral-shaped decoration and abstract marble carvings of idols and figures of musicians were produced.

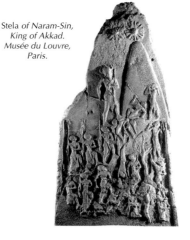

Stela of Naram-Sin, King of Akkad. Musée du Louvre, Paris.

▲ AKKAD

Cultural ferment was linked with the foundation of the first Mesopotamian empire (2350-2150BC). Sculptural reliefs were marked by compositional freedom and a lively naturalism.

▼ CRETE

The earliest appearance of a complex urban civilization occurred in about 2000BC. Royal palaces were constructed at Phaistos, and the refined Kamares style in ceramics spread.

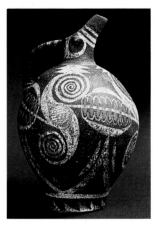

Kamares vase, Phaistos, c.1800BC. Archaeological Museum, Heraklion, Crete.

▼ BABYLONIA

There was notable artistic development under Hammurabi (1792-1750BC), with the reinterpretation of Neo-Sumerian motifs.

Stela of Hammurabi, c.1760BC. Musée du Louvre, Paris.

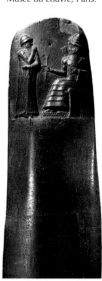

attains its utmost splendor. **1347BC:** Tutankhamun abolishes the cult of Aten (the Sun), introduced by Akhnaton and his wife Nefertiti, and restores the traditional worship of Amun. **1200BC:** the Veda, the most important collection of Sanskrit religious texts, is completed in India; first migrations of the Dorian people into Greece occur, heralding the end of Mycenaean civilization. **1100BC:** the practice of horseriding and use of the saddle spreads through the Near East. **667BC:** Assyrian kingdom achieves its maximum expansion under Assurbanipal. **c.770BC:** Chinese empire splits into numerous small kingdoms. **550BC:** Cyrus the Great of Persia defeats the Medes, conquering Asia Minor, Babylonia, Syria, and Palestine.

1600BC–1200BC   1200BC–800BC   800BC–400BC   400BC–200BC

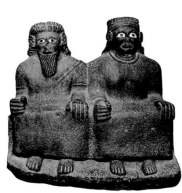

Zoomorphic example of a yu, a ritual wine vessel, Shang dynasty. Cernuschi Museum, Paris.

▲ CHINA
There was pronounced artistic development under the Shang Dynasty (1770–1025BC), including a particularly rich production of ritual bronze vases decorated with forms of animals (dragons, fantastic monsters, and phoenixes) on a geometrical background. Highly elaborate techniques of casting with molds were used.

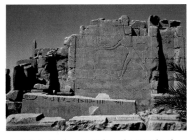

Relief of Tuthmosis III from the Temple of Amon, Karnak, 18th dynasty (1550–1295BC).

▲ EGYPT
In the New Kingdom (c.1550–1069BC), the colossal pyramid form was abandoned. The Temple of Amon was built at Karnak under Thuthmosis I (1505–1493) and Thuthmosis III (1490–1436), and a peak of splendor and magnificence was reached under Amenophis III (1402–1364), builder of Temple of Luxor.

▼ ANATOLIA
The invasion of the "Sea Peoples" (1200BC) overthrew the Hittite empire and its stately capital of Hattusas. Art production, with a blend of Semitic, Hittite, and gradual Assyrian influence, occurred in the Hittite colonies of Syria.

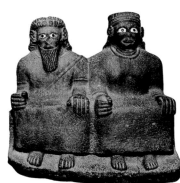

Syro-Hittite sculpture of divine couple, Tell Halaf, ninth century BC. Aleppo Museum, Syria.

▼ AEGEAN
There was a decline, in about 1100BC, of Mycenaean culture, paramount since 1425BC in succession to Minoan tradition. Frescoes of the palace of Tiryns, with scenes of hunting and warfare, date from the 12th century BC.

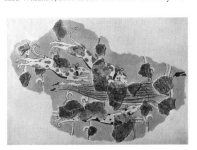

Fresco fragment with hunting scene, from the palace at Tiryns, c.1250BC. National Museum, Athens.

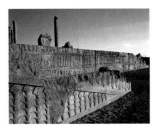

Sacking and Demolition of the City of Hamanu, relief from the palace of Ashurbanipal at Nineveh, c.650BC. British Museum, London.

▲ ASSYRIA
Between 880 and 539BC, secular art celebrated the war exploits of the kings. Assyrian bas-reliefs constitute some of the finest narrative cycles in art history.

Procession of Nobles and Dignitaries, Palace of Darius, Persepolis.

▲ IRAN
The building of Persepolis began under Darius I (518BC), exemplifying monumental architecture with a mixture of Assyrian (decorations with celebratory reliefs), Sumerian (severity and stylization), and Achaemenid (columnar halls) elements.

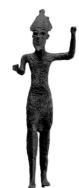

Bronze statue from the sea off Selinunte, seventh century BC. Archaeological Museum, Palermo.

▲ PHOENICIAN CITY-STATE
Between 900 and 570BC, eclectic art forms appeared, including highly original bronze and terracotta statuettes.

▼ CHINA
During the Warring States period (475–221BC), there was a flourishing production of bronze animals richly worked in inlaid style. A revival of naturalism in terracotta statuary occurred under the Ch'in Dynasty (221–206BC). The Great Wall was built.

Terracotta soldier in armor, 220–210BC. Museum of Chinese History, Peking.

Hellenic & Italic Civilizations

THE ART OF THE GREEKS

Greek art, the foundation and inspiration of Western artistic culture, was responsible for the invention of forms that embody the ideal of beauty. The vast output, emanating from centers located throughout the Greek empire, comprised works of fundamental importance created by artists of extraordinary talent.

For a period of more than a thousand years, the Hellenic peoples of mainland Greece, Sicily, Magna Graecia (the Greek colonies in southern Italy) as well as those of the islands of the Aegean and Ionian Seas, created a wealth of sculpture, painting, and architecture whose types, forms, and values lie at the very heart of Western aesthetics. Recently, new archaeological discoveries, combined with new studies and cultural concepts, have brought a historical reality to the

Amphora, early Geometric period. National Archaeological Museum, Athens.

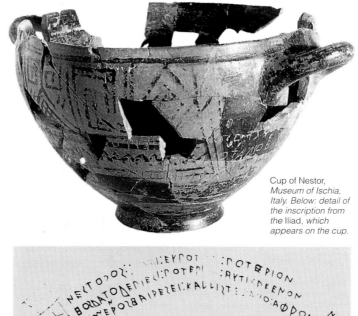

Cup of Nestor, *Museum of Ischia, Italy. Below: detail of the inscription from the* Iliad, *which appears on the cup.*

Torso of female figure, Eleutherna, Crete. Archaeological Museum of Heraklion.

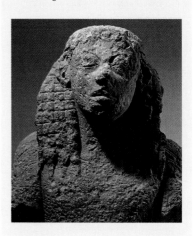

personalities of artists who were previously shrouded in legend. As a result, the artistic culture of the ancient Greeks is appreciated for its breadth and influence, from the earliest days through its absorption into the heart of Roman imperial art, and from there into the mainstream of European culture.

Greek art can be seen in the art of the Byzantine period, as well as pre-Romanesque and Romanesque art and in the modern and artistic cultures of Europe and farther afield. The thinkers of ancient Greece are still regarded as the source of modern aesthetic philosophy.

THE GEOMETRIC PERIOD

The appearance of pottery that was decorated with regular, circular motifs drawn with a pair of compasses marked the start of a new era of artistic creativity in Greek art. Liberated from the direct influence of natural shapes, this style gave expression to intellectually based compositions. The addition of graphic designs – zigzags, triangles, and meandering lines – established the so-called Geometric style, which visualized and was able to

express force, opposition, tension, and balance. It reached its peak during the eighth century BC (Late Geometric), coinciding with the transformation of the

BUILDING INNOVATIONS

In Greek building techniques, walls were traditionally erected by applying clay directly to a wooden framework, and the building design was dominated by an apselike curve at the ends. However, the use of sun-dried bricks was introduced during the Geometric era, and it then became easier to create right angles. Houses took on a square shape, and an elongated rectangular space was used as a place of worship. With the introduction of terracotta tiles in 675BC, it became easier to make a roof waterproof. However, this also increased its weight, leading to a complete reorganization of the network of beams and roof trusses. It was at this time that the word *architekton* ("chief carpenter") acquired its modern meaning, referring to the person responsible for the plans of a building.

As stone gradually replaced wood, the Doric style of classical Greek architecture evolved. This, the oldest and simplest of architectural styles, consisted of heavy, fluted columns, plain, saucer-shaped capitals, a bold, simple cornice, architraves, and friezes. A perspective modification of the horizontals and verticals in buildings was first introduced in the Temple of Apollo at Corinth (c.540BC), built at a time when painters were first aware of foreshortening. Optical corrections remained a unique feature of Doric architecture, which in mainland and colonial Greece retained the concept of buildings as geometric solids (except in the Ionic temples of Asia Minor, where it would have been incompatible with the double row of pillars around the *cella*, or inner room of the temple). As an anti-earthquake device, monolithic columns – such as those at Corinth – were replaced by columns of super-imposed blocks of stone held together by flexible lengths of wood, or pegs.

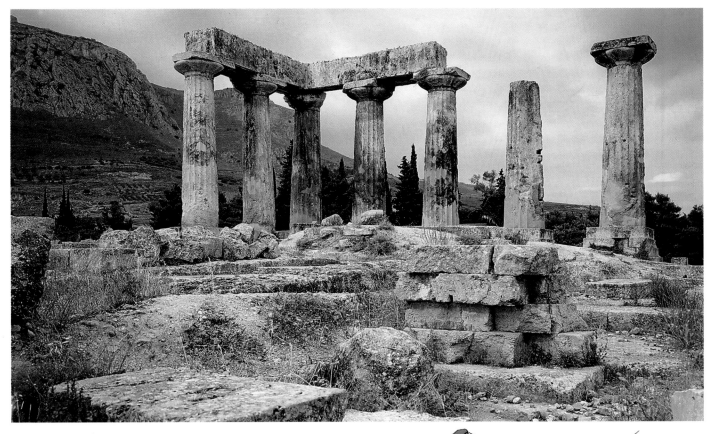

Temple of Apollo, Corinth, Greece, c.540BC.

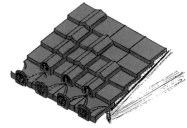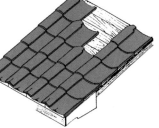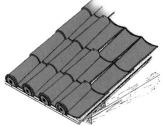

Illustration of the roof construction of an Archaic house. The combination of flat and curved tiles was a Hellenic invention. One notable characteristic was the antefix, a form of decoration that covered the end of a series of semicircular tiles.

complex system of tribes into the organism of the city-state (*polis*). In the same way that citizens took control of their own community, public craftsmen, called *demiourgoi,* became responsible for the way in which objects were shaped and decorated. A strong sense of public spirit guided craftsmen and politicians alike toward the ideals of order, restraint, and harmony.

The Greek colonial system meant that designs spread quickly to the provinces. The earliest known signature of a potter appears on a *krater*, or two-handled bowl, from Pithecusae, on the Italian island of Ischia, dating from about 720BC. A *skyphos* (cup) from the same site bears the

SHADOW PAINTING

The Greeks had a word to indicate the origins of painting: *skiagraphia* ("shadow drawing"). Saurias of Samos is said to have been the first man to trace the outline of a horse from its shadow cast on a wall, although the same process is attributed to the anonymous pioneers of painting at Sicyon and Corinth. In pottery designs from the Geometric era, the dark silhouettes of people and animals gradually become elongated, with bodies and heads growing smaller and legs and hooves extended. The last of the Geometric wares made use of a technique that the writer Pliny (AD23–79)

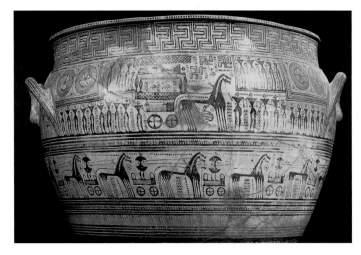

attributed to Aridices of Corinth and Telephanes of Sicyon, who filled in the outlines of the silhouetted figures. Pliny's

Geometric-style pottery, Necropolis of Dipylon, Athens. National Archaeological Museum, Athens. The central strip of such pottery often showed funeral rites; here, it is the laying-out and chariot procession.

knowledge of monumental painting during that remote age led him to attribute a painting of a battle scene by Boularchus, active in Ionia, to the "time of Romulus." In the sanctuary at Isthmia, near the Corinth Canal, fragments of wall decoration have been discovered that belong to the Temple of Poseidon (700BC). It was during this period that the technique of black-figure painting, the final successor to *skiagraphia*, was introduced in Corinth. The names of the characters depicted on the vases were added, a union of symbols and images echoed during the modern era in Braque's Cubist collages.

first lines known to come from the *Iliad*. In narrative scenes on pottery – the laying-out of the dead, processions, shipwrecks – the "shadow" of the human figure gives the impression of movement in the limbs and head in relation to the torso. The shape of all vessels was significant, representing the physical unity of the human body into a powerful allegory: the krater became a "sign" of male burials, while slender amphorae became a mark of female ones. Even today, the different parts of a vase are described in human terms, such as foot, shoulder, neck, mouth, and lip.

ORIENTALIZING PERIOD

In the Cyclades during the seventh century BC, the so-called Orientalizing period, human figures were sculpted from marble found on the islands, a practice dating from the Bronze Age. Egyptian influence increased following the founding of the trading port of Naucratis on the Nile Delta and after

THE CHIGI VASE

The Chigi Vase, a masterpiece of the Corinthian polychrome style (c.635BC), has a decoration of banded friezes (in keeping with Oriental style) depicting carefully alternated subject matter. The one mythological scene, *The Judgment of Paris*, has been placed below the handle. The rest of the decoration relates to life and nature: the hunting of hares and foxes, a procession of warriors with a chariot, a lion hunt, hounds chasing wild animals, and a battle scene. To

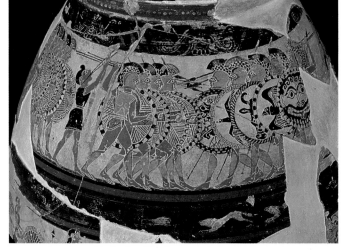

Ekphantos Painter, Warriors, detail of the Chigi Vase, Veio. Museo Nazionale di Villa Giulia, Rome.

Ekphantos Painter, Chigi Vase, Veio. Museo Nazionale di Villa Giulia, Rome.

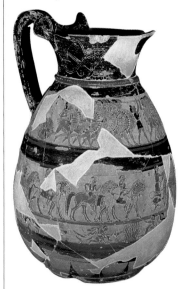

display the devices on the shields, the painter has depicted fewer warriors on the right but densely overlapped the *hoplites*, or infantrymen, to the left – only the backs of their shields are visible. In so doing, he provided space for the flutist, shown vigorously blowing on his flute. The music is to accompany the soldiers who advance in a

rhythmic fashion, and the change from fast steps to a steady march can be seen in the figures of the last men joining the fray. The portrayal of movement blends with a sophisticated representation of space; the ranks converge at the center, where the shields are already colliding and the spears are clashing in mortal combat. The artist was clearly not content merely to decorate the surface for the casual delight of the observer, instead wanting to create an elaborate interplay of figures and ornamentation that demanded detailed study.

THE FRANÇOIS VASE

Kleitias owes his fame to the decoration of the largest and most impressive vase known from the Archaic period, modeled by Ergotimos in about 570BC. The piece was found at Chiusi by Alessandro François in 1844. The base, body, and neck are decorated with bands of differing widths, a device that creates a great sense of movement. Although most of the vase is decorated with solemn or dramatic episodes, its base bears a comic fight scene. Above this is a band of decorative animals, a band portraying Achilles'

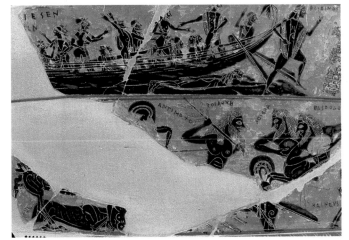

François Vase, Chiusi, c.570BC. Archaeological Museum, Florence.

ambush of Troilus beneath the walls of Troy, and, finally, the return of Hephaestos to Olympos. On the broadest part of the vase is a procession of the gods at the wedding of Peleos and Thetis. The lower neck shows the chariot race in memory of Patroclos and the fight between the Lapiths and Centaurs, while the upper section depicts the hunt for the Kalydonian boar and the dance of the young people rescued by Theseos from the Minotaur. The principal narrative of the decoration is drawn from the life of Achilles, from the mythical marriage of his parents

François Vase, Chiusi, c.570BC. Archaeological Museum, Florence. Kleitias' decoraton of Ergotimos' vase shows the return of Theseos as victor over the Minotaur at Delos.

to his killing of Priam's son on hallowed ground and the loss of his beloved companion. The vase handles portray the removal of the corpse. The painting uses all the techniques that Pliny attributes to various ancient masters: the accurate distinction between male and female figures, which turn without stiffness, and the use of superimposition and foreshortening. The wild animal at the center of the hunting scene dominates the wounded dog and man, while at the sides, heroes grouped in pairs at an angle to the background create the illusion that the action takes place within a defined space.

ARCHAIC PERIOD

The Archaic period of Greek history (600–480BC) began in Athens when the statesman Solon codified the privileged position of the wealthy, while at the same time giving jurisdiction to the people (594–591BC). The aristocracy gloried in colossal *kouroi* (statues of nude youths), erected at Cape Sounion (590–580BC). Emerging from the isolation of the Daedalic Vision, these figures appeared as a *perikalles agalma*, "an image of great beauty" (for the pleasure of the gods and the contemplation of mortals). In Corinth, one of the Seven Sages, Periander, succeeded Cypselus (his father) and maintained a court of poets, musicians, and artists. Between 600 and 560BC, he encouraged the production of the middle Corinthian wares, which dominated Western markets. In Athens, the first known master of the black-figure technique was Sophilos. He signed a vivid, epic scene of the games held in honor of Patroclos before Achilles and a crowd of Achaeans in about 580BC. The François Vase, made slightly later by Ergotimos and Kleitias, was commissioned in about 570BC by an Etruscan lord. A second generation of *kouroi* can be seen in the statue from Volamandra

visits by Greek mercenaries to the Nile valley. Through the late seventh century BC, stone sculpture on the island of Crete during the highly inventive Daedalic period was a form in which craftsmen attempted to encapsulate the essence of life. Areas of uniform color were used in painting, as a result of Eastern influences that arrived via Corinth. The Corinthians traded with the Phoenicians, Khalcideans, and Rhodians, and with peoples of the East via the port of Al Mina on the

Orontes River (730–640BC). The work of the innovative Corinthian Ekphantos Painter, to whom the Chigi Vase is credited, inspired the technique devised by Athenian potters of black figures on a red clay ground. Most black-figure wares are decorated with beasts or mythological scenes, arranged with a greater feeling of space than in Corinthian pottery.

Fragment of an Attic black-figure bowl, 580BC. This illustrates funeral games given in honor of Patroclos. National Archaeological Museum, Athens.

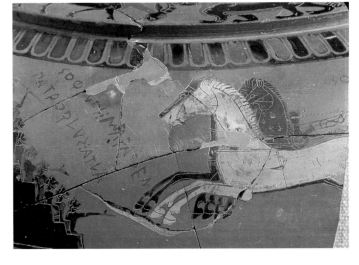

from about 565BC. The way in which the triangular stomach joins with the legs creates an effective sense of harmony. The skin is stretched tautly over the muscles, and the figure's mouth turns up in a smile. During the late Corinthian period (from 560BC), Corinth lost its monopoly on exports

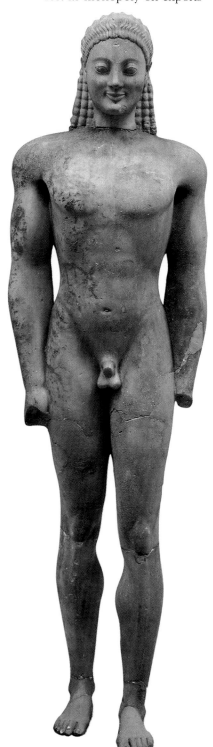

Kouros, *Volomandra*, 565BC. National Archaeological Museum, Athens.

ARISTODIKOS MASTER: "KOUROS" AND "KORE"

At the end of Pisistratid rule, shortly before an edict was issued in 510BC curbing lavish burials, the funerary monument of Aristodikos was erected near Athens. In contrast to the powerful athleticism of the preceding generation of *kouroi*, this figure is slender, with a strong sense of inner tension and smooth, expressively modeled skin. The long legs barely betray their underlying structure as shin, knee, and thighs flow into each other in a single sweep. The forward movement of the left leg is reflected in the asymmetry of the pelvis and in the musculature of the abdomen, which is modeled in sections and bounded by chest muscles. The hollow at the base of the neck below the collarbone is clearly visible, and the head inclines to the left, in keeping with early studies into the way weight is distributed on the legs. The mouth has a strong lateral quality, and the skin stretches tightly over the chin and full cheeks. The broad, curving forehead holds back the short hair that replaces the heavy wig of earlier figures. A later *kore* (statue of draped female figure) by the same hand also forms part of the monument.

Aristodikos Master, kore, 520–510BC. Acropolis Museum, Athens.

Aristodikos Master, kouros. National Archaeological Museum, Athens.

to Athens, where, from 561 to 555BC and from 546 to 528BC, the tyrant Pisistratos fostered a policy of economic expansion. Here, the representations of myths began to include the relationship between man, heroes, and gods. Later *kouroi* showed a more athletic musculature, as in the statue of the youth buried at Anavysos (c.540BC). He stands on a large, stepped plinth inscribed: "Stop and grieve at the tomb of the dead Kroisos, slain by wild Ares in the front rank of battle." The arms, linked to the pectoral muscles, no longer touch the body, while the face reveals a realistically modeled lower jaw and slightly parted lips.

From 528 to 510BC, Endoios remained the favorite artist of the sons of Pisistratos. He is credited with having created the pediment on the Acropolis that shows Athena defeating the giants. This was probably a dedication by Hippias to make up for a conspiracy by Aristogeiton and Harmodios that resulted in the death of Hipparchos (514BC). For a century, the *kouros* was skillfully used by sculptors as a way of investigating the reality of different social and religious circumstances. The subject was portrayed as a bringer of offerings, a dead man, a hero, and even a god, as in the advancing bronze figure of Apollo from Piraeus (c.525BC). The carving of the female figures (*korai*) on the

ATHENS: THE CITY OF IMAGES

The technique of black-figure painting on pottery was superseded by a reversal of the process, in which the figures were outlined in red clay and the background was filled in in black. One of the first red-figure artists was Andokides, working in about 520BC. It was no longer necessary to incise details, since these were now painted using light strokes of diluted black or pale brown, a technique that allowed for softer modeling, in keeping with advances in other forms of painting. After the expulsion of Hippias and the birth of the democratic order (510–507BC), much pottery art depicted beautiful youths – often described with the word *kalos* – and athletes in training or bearing arms. Military service, which was compulsory for all citizens, is shown in scenes of divination and departure or return from war.

From about 490BC, painting lost its static quality and began to show an awareness by the artists of their surroundings. Athenian vase painters depicted increasingly fluid scenes on their cups, jugs, amphorae, and other vessels commonly used by all contemporary citizens at banquets, for display in homes, and for burials. These objects were carefully decorated with scenes that included hunting, athletic contests, weddings, ritual Dionysiac drinking, sacrifices, feasts, and funerals. Every aspect of the city's life is revealed on such pieces, just as it was in the theater and literature of the day. The export of such products brought the culture they depicted to both the Greek colonies of southern Italy and Sicily, and the Etruscans, Italic tribes, and other Western peoples. Attic pottery (from Athens) frequently formed part of grave goods.

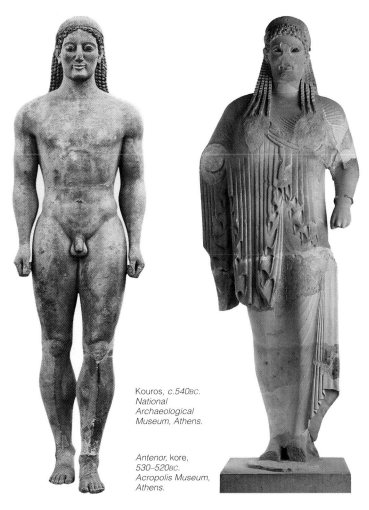

Kouros, c.540BC.
National
Archaeological
Museum, Athens.

Antenor, kore,
530–520BC.
Acropolis Museum,
Athens.

Acropolis employs the use of circular bases to dictate the form of the whole figure. The sun plays on the curved surfaces of the marble, penetrating its crystals, and the light seems to suggest an extra dimension to the stone. During the same period, the exiled Alkmaeonid clan employed the sculptor Antenor to work on the pediment of the temple of Apollo at Delphi. A statue of a goddess there has the same structure as the *kore* on the Acropolis, which was completed by the artist on his return to Athens after the expulsion of Hippias. Circular bases were soon replaced by rectangular plinths to accommodate the increasingly extroverted gestures of the figures. When Kleisthenes, an Athenian statesman of the Alkmaeonid clan, introduced his democratic reforms between 509 and 507BC, Antenor created a bronze monument in memory of the unsuccessful tyrannicides Harmodios and Aristogeiton.

ARISTION AND THE SCHOOL OF PAROS

The school of Paros, which made use of the island's ancient marble quarries, achieved its finest expression between 550 and 540BC in the work of Aristion. His statue *Phrasikleia*, found at Merenda (ancient Mirrhynos) on the east coast of Attica, bears the bitter lament: "For ever I shall be called *kore*. In place of marriage I have received this name as my lot from the gods." The monumental quality of this virginal figure flows from the embroidered band that closes her dress at the front and is clear in the stately fall of the overlapping folds, which hint at the shape of her leg beneath. The drapery of her floor-length woollen *chiton* falls in Ionic waves at the sides. Aristion's influence and style spread to Attica, Boeotia, and Delos, and can be seen in a *kore* from Cyrene.

Aristion, Phrasikleia, *Merenda (Mirrhynos)*.
National Archaeological Museum, Athens.

THE SIPHNIAN TREASURY

In ancient times, to demonstrate their power, major cities erected richly decorated *thesauroi* inside their shrines. These buildings housed the finest and costliest offerings of private individuals, and, as a result, the original meaning of the word "storehouse" gradually changed to "treasury." A frieze of the marble *thesauros*, built in Ionic style in about 525BC by the inhabitants of the island of Siphnos (in the Cyclades) with proceeds from their silver and gold mines, can still be seen at Delphi. The entrance was in the western facade, adorned with two karyatids (supporting

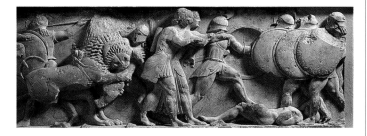

Gigantomachia. *Archaeological Museum, Delphi.*

columns crafted in the form of women). The west frieze showed Athena, Hera, and Aphrodite arriving in their chariots for the judgment of Paris. The southern relief depicted the capture of Helen by Theseos and Pirithoos, and a procession of horsemen. Carved in strong outline, the design followed the grain of the marble. The eastern and northern friezes are by a different hand. The former shows the fight between

Achilles and Memnon under the watchful eye of the gods, as they weighed the contestants' souls to decide the winner. The latter depicts a *gigantomachia* (a war between giants and gods). The artist's signature was originally incised on the shield of one of the giants, but the stone has since disintegrated. He was a member of the Parian school and belonged to the generation following Aristion.

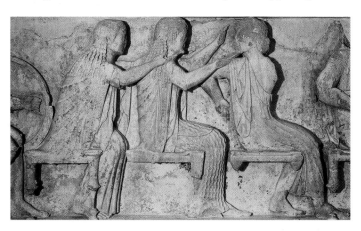

Detail of frieze. *Archaeological Museum, Delphi.*

THE FIRST REALISM

In 479BC, the Athenians reestablished their territorial security with a victory over the Persians at Plataea. Fragments of statues left in ruins by the Persians were religiously gathered up and buried on the Acropolis. Fire had completely destroyed paintings by the "primitives," which had for so long provided the models for the portrayal of gods and heroes. The resultant need for the Athenians to rethink their institutions combined with their victory meant that they were able to plan the future of their city with confidence. For the first time, artists depicted their subjects in realistic situations and characterized them according to surrounding events.

THE SEVERE STYLE

In sculpture, the transition to realism can be seen in the works of Kritios, Nesiotes, and Egia in Athens, and Agelades at Argos. Using dynamic, fluid outlines, Micon and Myron rejected the solidity of the work of Polygnotos and Kalamis, and in painting, Micon developed spatial concepts, depicting the area

Discus Thrower, *copy after Myron. Museo Nazionale Romano, Rome.*

MYRON

An influential sculptor from Eleutherae in Boeotia, Myron (c.480–455BC) was a student of Agelades of Argos. The dynamic linear style of his work in bronze contrasted with the solidity of Kalamis' work. His *Timanthes*, *Ladas*, and *Discus Thrower* are thought to date from the early Peloponnesian period, and his *Lycinos at Olympia* from a later phase. The group of *Zeus, Athena, and Herakles* was sculpted at Samos, while his *Perseos*, *Erechtheos*, *Athena,* and *Marsyas* groups, and *Theseos and the Minotaur*, were made in Athens. His famous cow was reproduced as a bronze statuette.

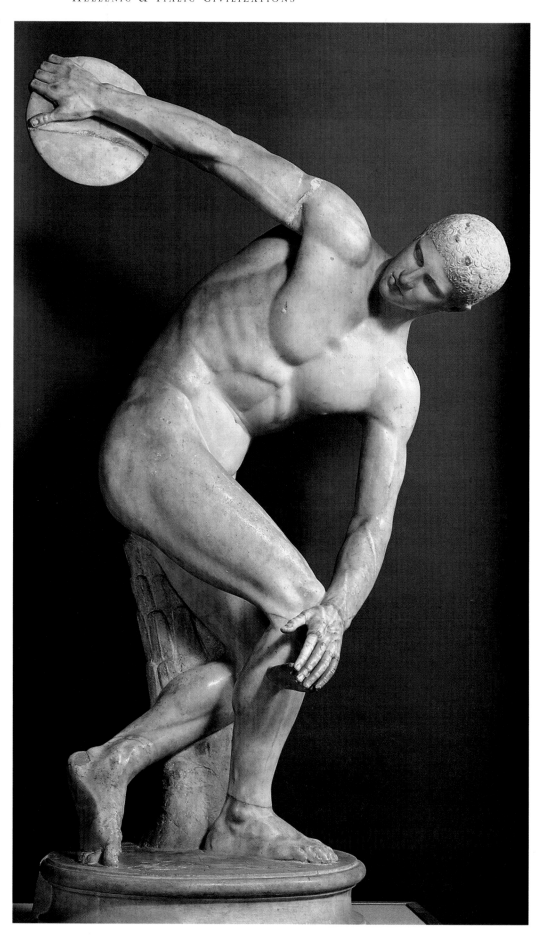

THE TEMPLE OF ZEUS

Agelades dominated the decorative program of the Temple of Zeus at Olympia (471–456BC), and it is his statues that adorned the east front of the temple. Under the eye of the gods, Oenomaos prepares for sacrifice in the presence of his wife Sterope and his daughter Hippodamia, at whose side stands Pelops, destined for victory and kingship. An old man seated on the ground surveys the scene with the eye of a seer. Samples of clay used in casting taken from the statue of Tydeos (*Bronze A*) reveal that it was created in Agelades' workshop at Argos. Resembling the Olympian statue of Zeus in its

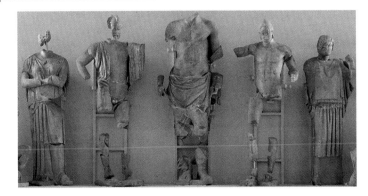

Sterope, Oenomaos, Zeus, Pelops, and Hippodamia, *from the east front of the Temple of Zeus, Olympia. Archaeological Museum, Olympia.*

Lateral figures on the east front of the Temple of Zeus.

Surviving statues of the entire front of the Temple of Zeus.

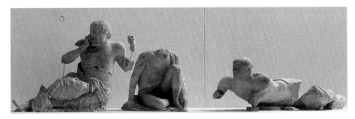

structural style, the bronze is still archaic with a strong sense of directness. The left foot advances aggressively, the body twists threateningly, and the muscles convey pent-up strength. Agelades' marvelous statues were an inspiration for his pupils: Myron learned to portray "breath enclosed in bronze," Phidias how to instill a feeling of life, and Polycleitos how to create the illusion of energy and movement.

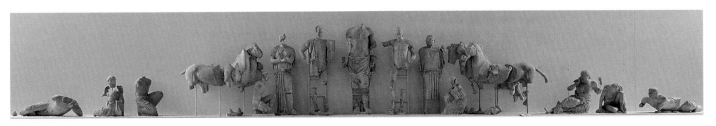

between figures and landscape, lifelike gestures and movements, and the tangled tumult of battle. In Myron's statue of *Ladas at Olympia* (460BC), the runner looks as though he is about to leap off his pedestal; his *Timanthes* (456BC) raises his arms to his head to fasten his leather cap; and the legs and torso of his *Discus Thrower* (c.450BC) are long,

the body lean and tense, and the muscles taut. The head echoes the oval shape of the *Bronze A*, one of two bronze warriors found off Riace, in southern Italy. The pose and physique of Myron's colossal statue of Zeus, on Samos, imitate the work of Agelades. Influenced in Athens by the imagery of the theater, Myron arranged his

sculptures like paintings, using the type of layout that culminated in his group *Apollo and Marsyas*.

Attributed to Agelades, Tydeos (better known as Bronze A), from the sea at Riace, southern Italy. National Museum, Reggio Calabria.

Niobid Painter, Slaughter of the Niobids, detail on an Attic vase showing Apollo and Artemis with bows and arrows. Musée du Louvre, Paris.

POLYGNOTOS

The painter Polygnotos (c.510–460BC) came from Thasos. He freed art from the craft tradition and rivaled the poets in reviving mythology as a basis for aristocratic virtues. His *Punishment of the Suitors at Plataea* (479BC) was followed by *Odysseos* and then *Achilles in Skyros* (475BC), painted in Athens while in the political entourage of Kimon. He also began the decoration of the *Stoá Poikile*, which may have remained unfinished until the introduction of democracy (462–461BC). His *Destruction of Troy* and *Odysseos Visiting Hades* adorned the large "meeting room" at Delphi.

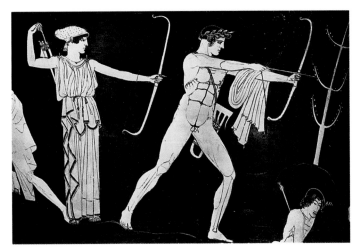

VOYAGE TO ETERNITY

As Greek expansion continued with the defeat of the Persians at Salamis, the victory over the Carthaginians at Himera in Sicily, and the rout of the Etruscan fleet at Cumae by the Syracusans in 474BC, the quality of life in Greece improved. The power of Athens was consolidating, Persia was collapsing as a serious threat, and a new level of comfort and sophistication had been achieved. Paintings on the ceiling and slab of the Tomb of the Diver at Poseidonia (as the city of Paestum was then known) reflect these improvements. Guests recline in front of tables decorated with foliage, with a wine-krater at the center. A naked boy offers drinks with a long ladle, as drunkenness spreads through the crowd; one man sings, another plays the flute, others talk. An old man arrives, preceded by a flutist and followed by his son, who carries his stick. As in contemporary paintings by Polygnotos, the narrative element of the decoration engages the spectator with its depth of meaning. This is a parting with no return. The youth following his father is the same figure that reappears in the painting on the ceiling – there, amid the tree branches, he dives into the rolling sea. His athletic glory highlights the destiny of the departed, whose soul will cross the sea to reach the Isles of the Blessed.

Diver, painting from the slab of the Tomb of the Diver, Paestum. National Archaeological Museum, Paestum, Italy.

Flutist, Dancer, and Deceased, painting from the lateral slab of the Tomb of the Diver. National Archaeological Museum, Paestum, Italy.

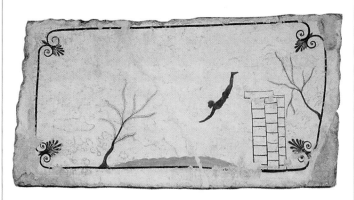

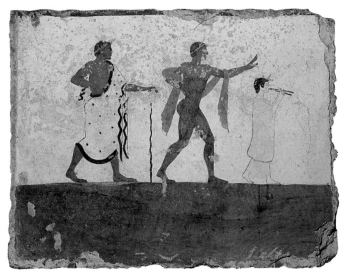

THE ART OF ATHENS

After the Doric phase of the Severe style, the vigorous Athenian style became even more firmly established with Phidias, who portrayed the gods in open communication with the city that they protected. His *Apollo* (Kassel version) differs from Kalamis' *Apollo Alexikakos* in the broad structure of the body and the crisp outline. Compared to the oblong heads of Myron's statues, the forehead has a rectangular quality, and a sense of forward motion creates a powerful effect of immediacy.

Whereas Kalamis interpreted the ideals of Kimon, Phidias followed the democratic path of Perikles, who gave him the post of superintendent of new monuments.

Apollo Alexikakos, copy after Kalamis. National Archaeological Museum, Athens.

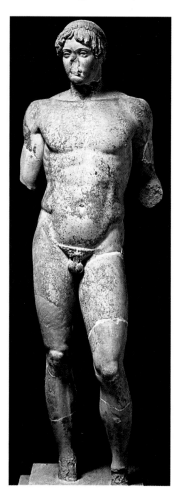

ANONYMOUS MASTER: "SYMPOSIUM SCENE"

470BC, painting on a slab on the southern side of the Tomb of the Diver, National Archaeological Museum, Paestum, Italy.

This tomb offers a rare example of Hellenic painting, decorated as it is with scenes of a funeral banquet held in honor of the departed. On the interior and exterior of the lid of the tomb is a depiction of the diver after whom the tomb is named. This part of the slab portrays a section of the banquet chamber and shows a row of three banquet couches, with arm supports on the right, each of which has a low serving table in front of it.

Five figures are shown reclining on the couches. To the right is a singer, who is performing with a youth who accompanies him on the flute. In the center, a bearded man and another youth are talking, each holding a goblet in his hand, and on the third couch, to the left, a lyre player has stopped playing and is resting the instrument on his lap and has turned to face his companions who are listening to the song. The scene is skillfully composed and animated by the artist. Each figure is involved in an activity that relates him both to another figure and to the overall action taking place. There are no women in the picture. Instead, this is a world of relationships between the old and young, a society of men gathered together in private solidarity.

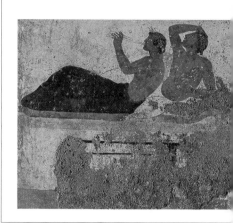

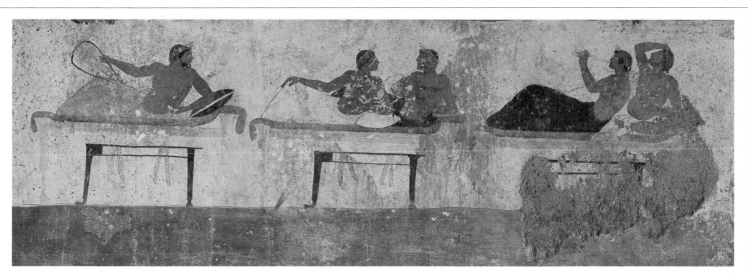

▲ 1. Olive branches decorate the tables, there are crowns of olive leaves on the heads of the guests, and two varieties of the plant appear on the tomb's ceiling – one wild, the other cultivated. The plant symbolizes both nature and the order imposed by man. The symbolism of the painting's color scheme is equally strong, reflecting that of the world. All four colors of classical theory, which refer to the four elements in nature, are here: white, the symbol for water, on the background plaster; black, the color of the night sky, in the goblets; pure red, a metaphor for fire, on the men's lips and some of the cushions; and ochre, an earth color, for the wood of the couches and the fabric. Also present are pale blue, a symbol for the daytime sky, and brown.

▶ 2. The fact that these figures were drawn before they were painted gives a clue to their age. The drawing technique links the work to later Macedonian paintings, although a pencil with a slightly blunt tip has been used. The use of a preliminary outline was abandoned at Paestum following the Lucanian invasion, as can be seen in a later series of quick funerary decorations. Some running of the colors betrays the fact that this work was intended to survive only for the short duration of the funerary ceremony.

The drawing stands out against the luminous background, which gives the figures an atmospheric vibrancy. The various ages and characters of the participants are clearly portrayed, and the objects included are easily identifiable: light furniture, thin covers, soft cushions, heavy winter cloaks, metal vases, and elegant musical instruments. Leisure and wealth are clearly conveyed in this depiction of an aristocratic society with its traditional and simple privileges.

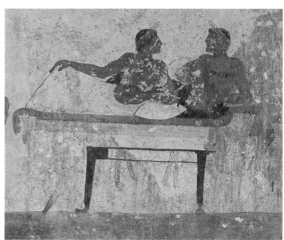

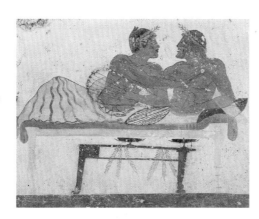

◀ 3. The delicately arranged tables and couches impose a rhythm on the work that is picked up in the line of the raised knees and clothing. The mass created by these draperies is at its highest in the lyre of the musician on the left and the raised arm of the singer on the right. The heads of the central figures are lower. Similarly, the tension evident in the turning body of the lyre player and in those singing and playing is less between the two conversing drinkers. The significance of music in the life of the deceased and the ritual of burial is confirmed by the presence of a tortoiseshell lyre in the tomb, complete with metal tuning keys. It matches the two shown here (another is on the northern side). Music was an important element in Orphism, an ancient Greek mystic religion from the sixth century BC that merged pre-Hellenic beliefs and the cult of Dionysos.

◀ 4. The figures on the right-hand couch are carefully composed. The young flutist is in profile, the curve of his back in the space created by the raised arm of the man behind him. Propped up on his elbow, the latter's head is also in profile, but his bare torso faces the viewer, powerfully rendered in lines of varying thickness to portray the anatomy. His legs and hips, enveloped in white fabric, are hidden from his companion, whose red-brown cover is the strongest mass of color in the entire scene. A delicate chiaroscuro enlivens the bearded face as song emerges from the half-open mouth through perfectly foreshortened lips. The hand, raised to the head, conveys rapture.

◀ 5. This detail from the northern side of the tomb, painted in slightly larger proportions, appears almost as an extension of the enthusiasm of the singer and the flutist on the opposite side. Here, too, there is a musician, a lyre player like the one on the left-hand couch on the southern side. The youth has just broken off his performance (it seems almost as if he were playing in unison with the flutist) and still holds the instrument in his left hand while he returns the embrace of the man stretched out on the same couch. Some of the details used here recall the vase painting of Campania in Italy, although this work amounts to more than an ornamental painted background. Indeed, the portrayal of the passion with which one lover draws toward him the head of the other is unique in ceramic painting. The immediacy and the intensity of the portrayal elevate the realism of the narrative to new heights.

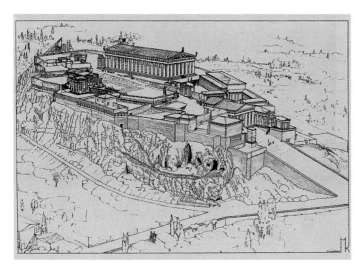

Drawing of the Acropolis, Athens, from the Hellenistic age.

The building of the Acropolis gave rise to the style of dynamic narration that lies at the heart of European figurative language. The hierarchy of the subjects, progressively enlivened with color, is revealed by their different levels above the ground: the Panathenaic festival on the frieze around the inner temple, rising to the mythological and epic subjects on the metopes, and culminating in the pediments. The sacred element increases from west to east, the direction taken by visitors arriving from the Propylaea. In the metopes to the west and south, there are no deities. Some appear on the northern side, while in the *gigantomachia* on the facade of the Parthenon

there is an Olympian god for each metope. Similarly, the frieze contains deities on the eastern side only. The western pediment is peopled by heroes, with just two deities – Poseidon and Athena – shown competing for the ownership of Attica; the eastern pediment contains Zeus and the birth of Athena as well as the divine court.

The architectural narrative of the Parthenon progresses from isolated episodes in the metopes to the processional continuity of the frieze and the heavy mythology of the pediments; the *cella* once held a colossal gold and ivory statue of Athena. The Parthenon, a monument to democratic coexistence, combines the Doric style with Ionic elements. It celebrates the coming together of citizens ruled by different political systems,

Attributed to Alcamenes, Hero in Arms (better known as Bronze B), from the sea off Riace, southern Italy. National Museum, Reggio Calabria, Italy.

PHIDIAS

The great artist of the classical age, the Athenian sculptor Phidias (c.490–430BC) was the one most copied by the Romans. After studying bronze-working with Aegios in Athens and Agelades in Argos, he was the probable creator of *The Apollo Parnopios* (Kassel version). He was commissioned by Perikles to supervise work on the Acropolis and the Parthenon to plans by the architects Ictinus and Callicrates. He designed (and may have partly executed) the Parthenon's 92 metopes of mythical battles, a frieze measuring 522 feet (159 meters) of the Great Panathenaea (the most important Athenian religious festival), sculptures for the pediments, and the 40-foot (12-meter) gold and ivory *Athena Parthenos* (447–438BC). *The Wounded Amazon* (Mattei version) and *The Aphrodite Urania* (Doria Pamphili) then followed. After being put on trial for misappropriating gold and for impiety, Phidias moved to the Peloponnese, where he created a new *Urania* at Elis. He also set up a workshop at Olympia, where he made a colossal 45-foot (14-meter) gold and ivory statue of *Zeus* and *The Anadoumenos*. The originals from the Parthenon, largely kept in the British Museum, London, were an inspiration for European Neoclassical art.

BEAUTY

For the Greeks, beauty was not simply a cultural ideal connected with art and the gods but was also a personal pursuit. This is clearly demonstrated in the decoration of many artifacts, including this oil jar.

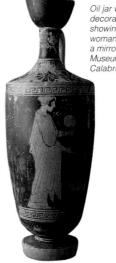

Oil jar with decoration showing a woman holding a mirror. National Museum, Reggio Calabria, Italy.

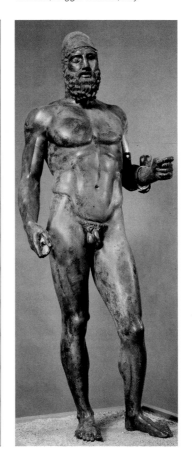

THE SMITING GOD

At the colony of Motya, on the far western tip of Sicily, the cult of Melqart of Tyre was practiced by the ruling Carthaginians. Melqart, a Phoenician tutelary god, was generally associated with Herakles in Hellenic times (c.450BC). This statue of Melqart-Herakles is evidence of the maturity of the artist, who was also responsible for the metopes on the Temple of Hera at Selinus (c.465BC). There, his Carthaginian employer allowed him to Hellenize his Eastern subject. As in other statues of Melqart-Herakles discovered on Cyprus, this figure was originally clothed in a lionskin (in this case, made of bronze), although it was later removed by Syracusans during the sack of Motya in 397BC. A club in the hero's right hand was raised behind his head, but this threatening pose was softened by the nonchalance of the other hand, which rested on his hip. The sculptor Lysippos, in Alexander's retinue when the sanctuary at Tyre was rebuilt (331BC), was influenced by this statue; his later work of *Herakles Overcoming the Lion for Cassander* (314BC) included the original image of the vanquished animal held in the left hand.

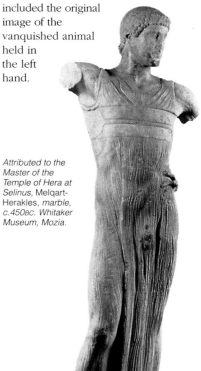

Attributed to the Master of the Temple of Hera at Selinus, Melqart-Herakles, marble, c.450BC. Whitaker Museum, Mozia.

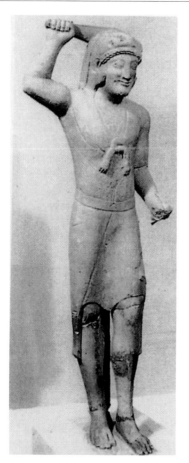

Melqart-Herakles, *limestone.*
Nicosia Museum, Cyprus.

Nicola Pisano, Strength, *allegorical*
figure from the pulpit of the Baptistry,
Pisa, Italy, c.1260.

Hercules Overcoming the Lion *(detail from*
the Labors of Hercules*), after Lysippos.*
Pillared sarcophagus, Via Cassia, Rome.
Museo Nazionale Romano, Rome.

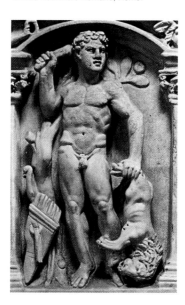

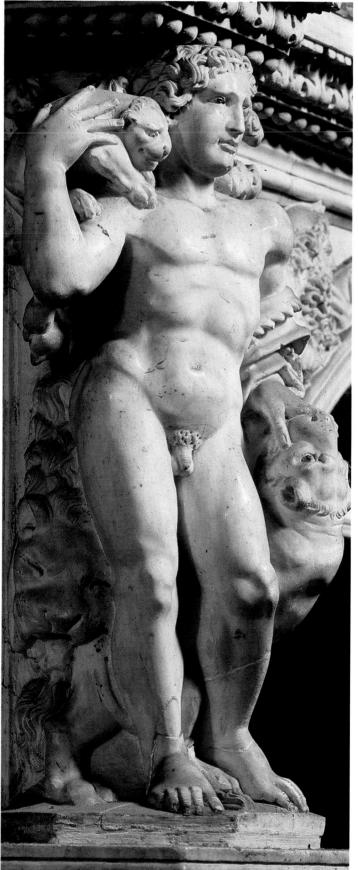

and it brings together mortals, heroes, and deities. The decoration of the metopes alludes to the threat posed by the constant struggle between Greeks and barbarians. The hand of the Lemnian sculptor Alcamenes can be seen on the slab in the eastern frieze. Poseidon's flowing hair has the same softness found in the *Bronze B,* one of the two statues of warriors found off Riace, and the wide, staring eyes are also familiar. A similar use of drapery can be seen in Alcamenes' marble group of the mythological *Procne and Itys* on the Acropolis.

POLYCLEITOS' CANON

Whereas Myron captured the transient and the fortuitous, Polycleitos inherited Kritios' and Kalamis' interest in volume and metrical rhythm. A native of Argos like Agelades, he investigated the possibilities of illustrating movement in standing figures. The distribution of weight in his *Discophoros* echoes the Riace *Bronze A.* In his *Achilles* or *Doryphoros,* unlike Phidias' *Apollo,* Polycleitos paid great attention to the distribution of weight and strength in the limbs, and he created a

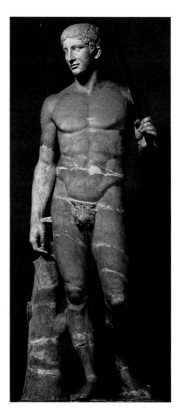

Doryphoros, *copy after Polycleitos. Vatican Museum, Vatican City.*

canon derived from Pythagoras' research into mathematical proportion. The asymmetrical position of the feet is counterbalanced by an intersection of force lines (*chiasmos*) through the body. The curls of the hair provide the finishing touch to a perfectly balanced work composed of many disparate elements. In about 440BC, Polycleitos moved to Athens and challenged the dominance of Phidias. The influence of Polycleitos' rhythmic style proved decisive and came to exemplify the classical period.

ZEUXIS THE PAINTER

The best-known works of the painter Zeuxis (c.455–97BC) include *Helen* in the sanctuary of Hera Lacinia (Croton), *Crowned with Roses*, *The Centaur*, and *Pan*. Born in Heraclea, Sicily, he taught in Athens, seeking to sever official links with the city so he could practice art for art's sake. His style is reflected in the ceramics of the Meidias Painter.

THE RISE OF INDIVIDUALISM

The arrival in Athens from Sicily of the painter Zeuxis was as important as that of the philosopher Gorgias, also from Sicily, who influenced the birth of rhetoric. However, during the Peloponnesian War (431–404BC), Athens was not the only artistic center. Parrhasios was painting at Ephesos (as was his father, Evenor), as was Timanthes at Kythnos, in the Cyclades. Although attracted to Athens, these masters preferred to travel through Greece and the surrounding dominions: Zeuxis worked in southern Italy, Ephesos, Macedonia, Olympia, and Samos, and Parrhasios in Lindos, Rhodes, Samos, Corinth, and Delos. Theirs was "art for art's sake," to be appreciated by other experts, and so technically self-assured that its exponents believed they had found perfection – Parrhasios in his mastery of line and Zeuxis in his brilliant chiaroscuro. This boast was founded more on creative freedom than the secrets of the workshop. The climax of classical art amid the crisis of war, the radicalism of the Athenian

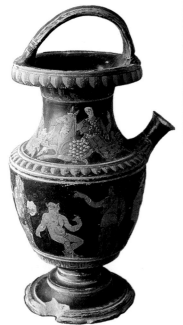

Red-figured situla, *from the school of Meidias. National Museum, Reggio Calabria, Italy.*

THE PAINTING AND SCULPTURE OF EUPHRANOR

Among the *typoi*, or reliefs, that Pliny attributed to Euphranor is a funerary tablet (c.340BC) showing an aged parent who resembles the dismayed ambassadors in his *Madness of Odysseos*. In a marble in Athens' National Archaeological Museum, the dead are represented by a naked man who faces the viewer, shown in torment as he contemplates the scene. Beside him crouches a young boy, who has fallen asleep weeping, his head cradled in his arms. The dead appear to the boy as a dreamlike vision.

Euphranor's bronze of Paris, son of the king Priam and his wife Hecuba, is designed to embody

Theseos with the Children Rescued from the Minotaur, *fresco, copy of original by Euphranor from Herculaneum, first century BC. National Archaeological Museum, Naples.*

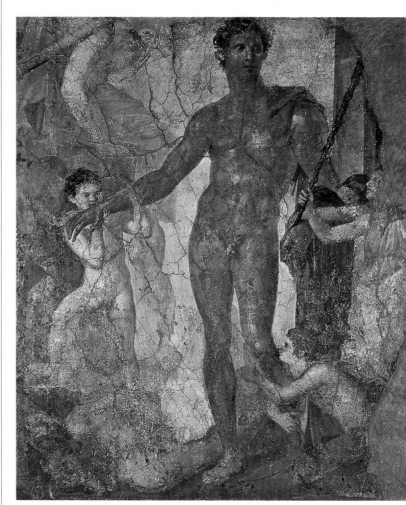

general Alkibiades, and the impatience of the new intellectuals saw the creation of an extrovert painting style. Stating that he would rather paint for the future than for the city, Zeuxis portrayed a range of everyday subjects for a circle of independent art lovers, which suggests that genre painting was popular with individual enthusiasts.

The fall of Athens (404BC) marked the end of art as a means of existential knowledge. The city's artists had lost their gift for seeing nature in terms of the human form, and it also lost

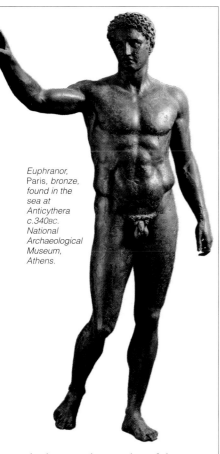

Euphranor, Paris, *bronze*, found in the sea at Anticythera c.340BC. National Archaeological Museum, Athens.

faith in reproducing reality according to recognized rules: form was no longer governed by a feeling of certainty. Most of the works produced before the death of Alexander the Great in 323BC had highly original creators, who were working in exceptional circumstances. As the dominant role of the city diminished in the arts, and references to democracy grew fewer, artists became more aware of their independence. Following in the steps of Zeuxis, freedom from public directives encouraged them to replace representational objectivity with a personal agenda. The sculptors Euphranor, Silanion, and Lysippos all experimented with their own systems of representing the human body.

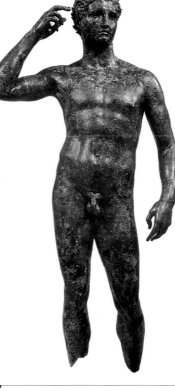

Lysippos, Crowned Athlete, *bronze*, found in the Adriatic Sea. J. Paul Getty Museum, Malibu, California. This splendid statue has recently been added to the catalog of works by Lysippos.

THE PERFECT BALANCE

The work of Leochares (c.390–325BC) shows how he maintained a delicate balance in his sculpture between the different contemporary trends. The lightness of his *Apollo Belvedere* matches the attenuated proportions of the warriors carved by him on the Mausoleum. Because he has not concentrated the tension in one specific limb, the figure's weight is distributed equally between the two legs, while the bending of the left knee fills the whole body with energy. The undulating contours reflect a feeling of life and physical mobility that is enhanced by the formal vibrancy of the modeling, more so than in the work of Phidias. Apollo rises up from some remote depth, a supreme example of *parousia* ("presence"). It is generally accepted that he was an archer, his left hand grasping the bow from which he has just unleashed an arrow. In the enigmatic language used by Leochares, the god represents a perfect balance between the pitiless archer and the lord of the sun.

Apollo Belvedere, *Roman copy from the original by Leochares. Museo Pio-Clementino, Vatican City.*

the hero's role as judge of the goddesses, husband of Helen, and the killer of Achilles. Euphranor portrayed the dignity of heroes and preferred a muscular, physically robust look – he himself referred to his Theseos as "beef-fed," as opposed to the richer and more elegant "rose-fed" Theseos of Parrhasios. His painting showed Theseos freed from the Minotaur, and it is known today from a copy completed in the first century BC. His critics often remarked on the comparatively large heads of his figures.

MAUSOLEUM

Whereas the Parthenon frieze, the work of many different artists, was unified by its design, the *Amazonomachia* on the tomb of Mausolos, begun at Halicarnassos in about 360BC, shows avid desire by the craftsmen to assert their individual characteristics. The reliefs on the four sides of the tomb were seen as an opportunity to compare the work of the different artists – Timotheos, Skopas, Leochares, and Bryaxis – and to discuss their relative values. Pliny writes that after the death of Artemisia (351BC), who had taken over the building project from Mausolos, "the

four men did not stop work until it was finished because they realized it would stand as a monument to their talent and their glory, and the contest between them is still undecided today." The faces of Timotheos' soldiers show a classical composure – the calm determination of the ancient heroes – while the aggressiveness in Skopas' sculptures separates them from aristocratic sensibilities: the naked figures are violent, their mouths half-opened, their nostrils flared, and their eyes flashing beneath frowning foreheads.

Timotheos, Amazonomachia, *from Halicarnassos. British Museum, London.*

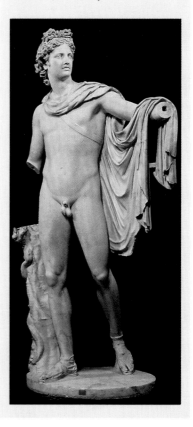

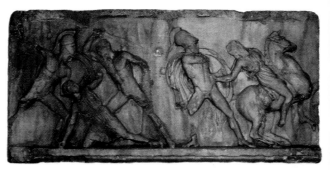

SKOPAS OF PAROS

A sculptor and architect from Paros, Skopas (c.395–325BC) was active in Continental Greece, in the Peloponnese, and in Asia Minor. His original works survive in the Mausoleum of Halicarnassos (360–350BC), and his *Aphrodite on a Goat*, the *Pothos*, the *Meleager*, and the *Maenad* are also known from copies. He was noted for his vigorous and forcefully realistic style.

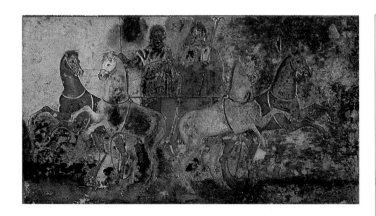

Hades and Persephone in the Chariot, detail from the back of a throne. Tomb of Queen Eurydice, Vergina, Greece.

PHILOSOPHY IN ART

Individual spiritualism was upheld through belief in the "mysteries" which, unaffected by social and political change, promised personal salvation. The paintings of Eleusian mysteries, as seen on Attic pottery, had a metaphysical quality and seduced initiates with their vision of benevolent beings in the afterlife. At Vergina, decoration on the marble throne of Eurydice, mother of King Philip, shows the scepter and Persephone's ornaments in gilded relief, a technique also used on contemporary Attic pottery from Panticapaeum (Kerch). The use of gold led to the discovery of what Pliny calls *splendor*, a reflection that masks the original color through the intervention of sunlight. Philosophy encouraged people to aspire to abstract thought: Plato urged an escape to a higher awareness, and Praxiteles followed his example, returning to ideal models.

PRAXITELES AT THEBES

From 364 to 361BC, Praxiteles was commissioned to decorate the pediments on the Temple of Herakles at Thebes with a scene depicting his 12 labors. The sculptures were soon removed to Rome, however, where they adorned the imperial residences on the Esquiline hill. It was there that the figure of Herakles fighting the mythical queen Hippolyta was unearthed. She was on horseback but was grabbed by her hair by Herakles' left hand, while his right brandished a bronze club. Herakles' stance is similar to that of a warrior armed with a sword shown attacking an Amazon in a relief on the Temple of Apollo at Bassae (c.400BC). The tree-trunk and plinth of the Herakles, now in the Palazzo dei Conservatori, Rome, is modern but incorporates the ancient outlines beneath each of the feet, which were crossed by bronze clamps. This system was also used by Skopas to attach his figures to the pediments of the temple at Tegea. The distorted quality of the bust and face reflects the

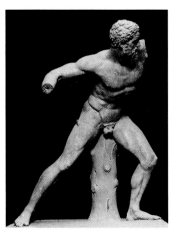

Praxiteles, Herakles Fighting, from the Esquiline. Palazzo dei Conservatori, Rome.

fact that they were originally intended to be viewed from below. The torso, as it is now, is excessively broad and the two halves of the face are unequal, but both features were originally compensated for by foreshortening when the group occupied the pediment of the temple. The sculpture was carved out of a single block of marble from Mount Pentelikon, the material favored by Athenian artists. The dynamics of the modeling follow the unbroken tension of the limbs, and, as usual, Praxiteles has given a sense of immediacy to the actions of the figure. The raw aggression of Herakles was tempered by later sculptors such as Antisthenes, who represented him as meditative and melancholic.

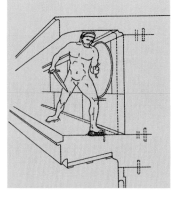

Reconstruction of the method used by Skopas to attach a statue to the pediment of Tegea.

Amazonomachia, detail from the Temple of Bassae. British Museum, London.

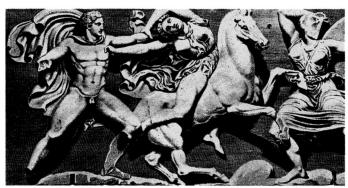

Attic vase by Naples Painter 3245, showing the divinities of Eleusis, from Piedimonte d'Alife. National Archaeological Museum, Naples.

APOLLODOROS

Apollodoros was called a "painter of shadows" (*skiagraphos*) in accordance with a concept that had evolved in the Geometric period. In time, it became clear how apt the term was, for the artist "was the first to discover shading and the thickening of shadows" (Plutarch). This technical skill gave rise to the comment that he was a "painter of appearances." His contemporary Democritos said that it is not the object that strikes the organs of sense – and is thus able to be represented – but an insubstantial image emanating from the atoms of which matter is composed. According to Pliny, Apollodoros was a painter of "illusory appearances." The importance of Apollodoros was fully recognized in the ancient world, and this concept of illusionistic painting was referred to by Plato in opposition to his notion of universal forms. This idea of imitating appearances signaled the birth of painting with a full array of perspective, chromatic, and luministic devices. Centuries later, it was taken up by the Impressionists ("...it is not the object that must be portrayed but the semblance of the object," Eugène Delacroix).

PRAXITELES

The sculptor Praxiteles was the greatest Athenian exponent of the "beautiful" style (c.395–326BC); his sculptures are characterized by soft, full contours and deep-set eyes. His father was Kephisodotos, also a sculptor. His statues of *Eros* (Centocelle version), *Phryne and Aphrodite* (c.370BC), the *Twelve Gods* (copy in relief, Ostia), and the group of *Latona, Apollo, and Artemis* (Dresden version) were carried out for the city of Megara. He acknowledged Dionysos in his *Pouring Satyr* (366–65BC), and his *Draped Aphrodite* was found on the island of Kos. The Knidian *Aphrodite* (364–61BC) was followed by *Aphrodite with a Necklace*, *Resting Satyr* (360–50BC), and *Apollo Killing a Lizard* (c.350BC). *Eros Being Crowned* (Chigi-Dresden version, c.343BC) is among the last of his many known works.

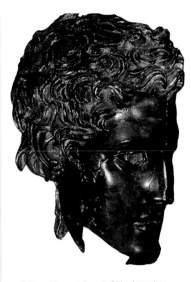

Colossal bronze head of Hephaestion, c.324BC. Prado Museum, Madrid.

reincarnation. His naked *Aphrodite of Knidos* is a fitting representation of the goddess of love, beauty, and fertility; it was described by Pliny as "The finest statue not only of Praxiteles but in the whole world...." Silanion, also within the orbit of the Academy, examined the concept of "divine madness" with his bronze *Portrait of Apollodoros*, the subject of which was a follower of Socrates and a sculptor himself. Silanion captured the disdain with which Apollodoros, who was popularly called Manikos, smashed his own statues whenever they failed to achieve perfection. Lysippos, too, explored new aspects of the artistic experience, with the difference that he and other Sikyonian artists did not shrink from physical experience because they were actively involved in new historical developments. From the domination of Thebes (371–323BC), Lysippos took it upon himself to express the experience of living in the midst of incredible change. He interpreted the social upheavals in emotional, ephemeral terms.

The era of art as a medium for visual knowledge was

His statues give tangible form to qualities that were hidden to the naked eye, and women assumed a definitive role in art for the first time. Phryne, a courtesan and Praxiteles' mistress, was his model for a memorial to the absolute beauty contemplated by the spirit prior to

THE STAG HUNT

Pamphilos, a native of Amphipolis on the Macedonian coast and successor to Eupompos as head of the Sikyonian school of painting, encouraged the invitation of his pupil Apelles to Philip II's court. Apelles' *Stag Hunt by Alexander and Hephaestion* was painted between 343 and 340BC, the years when the prince was educated by Aristotle. Hephaestion became a friend of Alexander's during childhood and remained his closest companion. His face can be recognized from a colossal bronze in the Prado Museum, Madrid, a later work commissioned by Alexander. The dominant feature of the painting, reproduced in a mosaic in Pella, Greece, was the balanced relationship between the figures. The careful use of shadows gives a three-dimensional effect to the work, with the different figures on different planes. The foreshortened angle of the dog is contrasted against the flat, solid figures of the heroes, placed either side of the central axis. The feeling of emergent mass and convergent depth, and the illusion of space in the work, are the result of the positioning of regular shapes, as found in the teachings of Pamphilos. The entire group is contained within an ideal circle, and the gap between the hunters and their prey is evoked by the space around and at the center of the picture. The action of the figures is frozen in suspended gestures, while the rhythm of movement is translated into monumental harmony. The bodies are placed within a mathematical symmetry. A shaft of light from the top left-hand corner illuminates all the figures in the center but casts no shadows: "artists, when placing many figures together in a painting, distinguish them by means of spaces in such a way that shadows do not fall upon the bodies" (Quintilian). The large, clearly defined layout is matched by the narrow tonal range, in accordance with the use of only four colors, as espoused by Apelles. An effect of realism is created by muted tones and subtle shades, rather than with strong, separate colors.

Stag Hunt by Alexander and Hephaestion, *pebble mosaic, copy after Apelles. Peristyle Houses, Pella, Greece.*

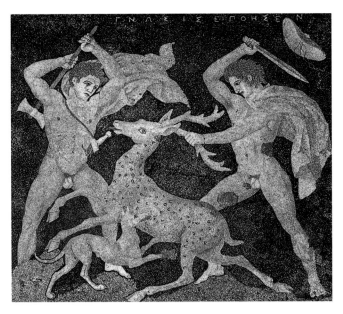

brought to an end by the aesthetic philosophy of Aristotle. As the *polis* grew weaker, communication was transferred to the individual, unleashing the doctrine of expressive freedom preached by the philosopher. Life was portrayed at the "critical moment," represented by Kairos, the deity whom Lysippos popularized

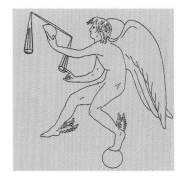

in sculptural form. As the phenomenal influenced the physical, and reality became fragmented into countless facets, statues reflected the influence of myriad events on the personality and perceptions of the artist.

Illustration of Lysippos' Kairos.

THE BRONZES OF LYSIPPOS

Lysippos was aware of the "antithetical" system that embodied the Pythagorean theory of contrasts: right and left, rest and movement, straight and curved, light and shade. This can be seen in the ascending spiral of the figure of a runner crowning himself with the Olympic olive branch, which is typical of the rotating movements often portrayed in Lysippos' statues. On the surface of the original, now in the J. Paul Getty Museum, Malibu, there is an excellent

interplay between light and shade. Wax imprints on the inside of the statue reveal that the figure's youthful proportions were altered during its making to convey a sense of courage: the neck was lengthened and the right arm forced aloft. There is a feeling of tautness on the right side of the body, with the right leg bearing the weight, in contrast with the relaxed left side, its leg free and arm resting on a palm frond (now lost). Lysippos' ability to express social and political problems through striking sculptural statements in a way that language was unable to do

meant that he was soon working for the dynastic propaganda machine of the Macedonians, producing his *Alexander with a Lance*. His plinth depicting the stories of Polydamas was intended to support a seated figure, such as the bronze *Boxer*, now in Rome's national museum. The statue was thought to possess curative powers, and its foot was worn away by the constant touching of devotees. Lysippos' talent and meticulous technique are evident in the fingers that appear to be sheathed in skin so thin that the joints show through, and also in the

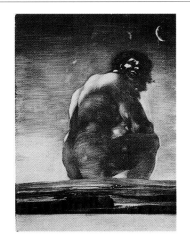

Francisco Goya, The Giant, aquatint. Metropolitan Museum of Art, New York.

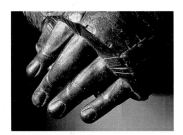

Lysippos, Boxer, bronze. From the Baths of Constantine, Rome. Museo Nazionale Romano, Rome.

fingertips with chiseled nails. On the wristbands, the dense series of dots is reminiscent of stitching. Visual immediacy is conveyed by the patches of red bronze damascening on the leg and the right arm – drops of blood that have fallen from the boxer's face as he turns his head – and the loss of the top teeth has deformed his lip. His breath emerges beneath a splayed moustache, and there is a bruise under his eye, created with a separately applied lump of dark alloy. Lysippos was famous for his references to deafness; damage to the ear and poor hearing is implicit in this work, along with a feeling of tiredness, suggested by the abrupt turn of the boxer's head. Centuries later, Goya, himself deaf, recreated the movement of the *Boxer* in his terrifying image *The Giant*.

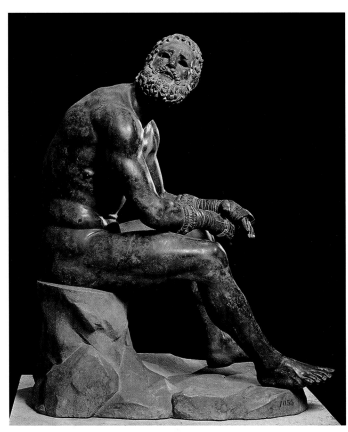

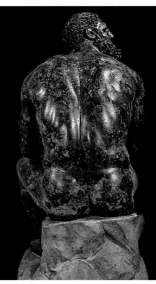

THE ARRIVAL OF HELLENISM

In about 324BC, a furious debate on the destiny of art broke out at the Babylonian court of Alexander the Great, which had attracted every sort of artist and craftsman. When the most highly regarded exponents of the Athenian and Sicyonion schools attempted to capture the royal likeness, Stasicrates, a native of Bithynia, described their efforts as "wretched and dishonorable." He declared that man was now capable of putting his own imprint on nature, a reference to a plan to carve the features of Zeus onto Mount Athos, a project that was never carried out. In Macedonia, Alexander's eastern expeditions had expanded the palette of artists, introducing long-lasting and vibrant natural colors: black and ochre, shades of glowing yellow, green from malachite, and bright red from the precious mineral cinnabar. In the decoration of a tomb from Aineia, a fresco inside one stone chest shows the women's quarters of a house. Falling shadow gives a feeling of solidity to the far wall, an illusory boundary for objects hanging or resting on the cornice. In both influence and technique the role of the artist was clearly changing.

THE TRUE FACE OF ALEXANDER

King of Macedonia before he was twenty years of age, Alexander the Great (356–323BC) spread Greek culture far beyond its geographical boundaries. Taught by Aristotle, he was a great scholar and helped promote knowledge and learning. Any attempt to glean the true appearance and character of Alexander from contemporary paintings and sculptures is problematic. Busts of the king give a vague impression of his features, but they differ from written reports that are considered to be reliable; these give fuller details about Alexander's facial features.

Lysippos played a decisive role in transforming the Macedonian leader's image from sullen adolescent to sublime hero. His practice of imbuing the composition of Alexander's features with a powerful sense of harmony was continued by a number of sculptors wishing to elevate the emperor to superhuman status, including Euphranor, Leochares, and their successors at the Hellenistic courts. It was generally the

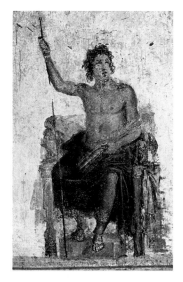

Alexander-Zeus, *fresco, copy after Apelles. House of the Vettii, Pompeii. The monarch is shown as Zeus, seated on his throne and grasping thunderbolts in his hand.*

Battle of Issus Between Alexander and Darius III, *detail from Apulian vase by the Darius Painter, Ruvo di Puglia. National Archaeological Museum, Naples.*

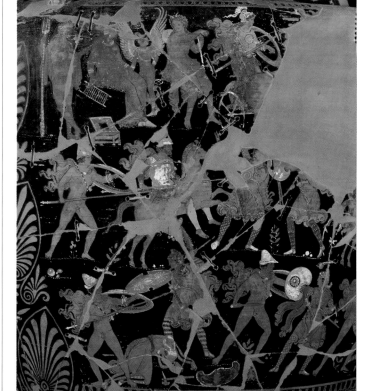

romantic image of Alexander as explorer of the unknown and exceptional leader and statesman that led to depictions of him as godlike and super-human.

Painting was the one medium in which this practice gave way to a realistic style. Apelles, for example, was happy to bestow the throne and thunderbolts of Zeus on Alexander, yet did not allow himself to be overly influenced by mythical context in his search for individual truth. In works discovered at Pompeii, Alexander is depicted as short in stature, with irregular features. Such images were often copied from originals by masters living close to the city. Other portrayals of Alexander that suggest a less than godlike appearance include a fresco based on Aetion's *Wedding of Alexander and Roxana*, the mosaic of the *Battle of Issus* attributed to Philoxenus, and the *Marriage of Alexander and Statira as Ares and Aphrodite*. In the latter, the wife is taller than her husband, who possesses a head with rather heavy features. The full beard, erroneously added in many other depictions of Alexander (such as the Darius Painter vases found in Apulia, southern Italy), is missing here. Such evidence suggests that documentary realism was of more importance to many artists than the more symbolic, traditional portrayal of nobility.

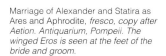

Marriage of Alexander and Statira as Ares and Aphrodite, *fresco, copy after Aetion. Antiquarium, Pompeii. The winged Eros is seen at the feet of the bride and groom.*

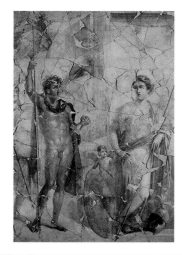

ANONYMOUS MASTER: "THE LION HUNT OF ALEXANDER AND HEPHAESTION"

320–310BC; pebble mosaic; Archaeological Museum, Pella, Greece.

This mosaic is from one of the peristyle houses erected in Pella, Alexander the Great's native city, after his death. The custom of paving courtyards with pebble decoration dates from the Minoan civilization and continues to this day in the Mediterranean region. Strictly speaking, this work is not a mosaic, because the pieces used

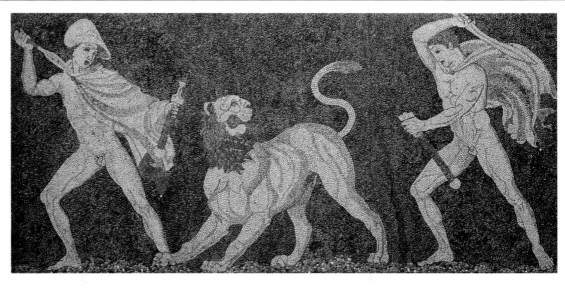

were not previously cut into even shapes. However, the technique was frequently used in Greece for the decoration of interiors from classical times up to the third century BC, after which mosaics were produced using uniform, square pieces. This scene, together with the *Stag Hunt by Alexander and Hephaestion*, is from one of ten floors found in private homes in Pella that are decorated with

geometrical motifs or paving stones. *The Lion Hunt of Alexander and Hephaestion* is a copy of an earlier statue group from about 343–340BC. The statue does not easily translate into mosaic: its border cuts through the handle of Alexander's spear, and the two boys and the beast are awkwardly arranged along a system of parallel lines.

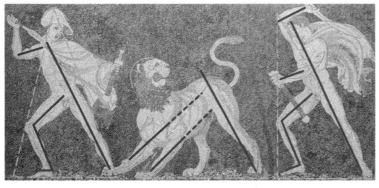

▲ *1. The positioning of the figures side by side as if on the base of a statue emphasizes the similarity with Lysippos' group statue. The overlapping of the limbs, which is very complex in Apelles' Stag Hunt, is here restricted to one of the lion's paws, positioned near Alexander's foot. The gestures and expressions of the figures convey the drama of the occasion, their outlines from legs to trunk identically positioned. Thus, the prince's withdrawal accentuates the rhythm of the assault. Alexander's face still shows a youthful softness under the shade of the petasos (the headdress often found in images of the Macedonian kings), and his cloak protects his left arm. The lion is distracted by the attack of Hephaestion who has his sword drawn and raised.*

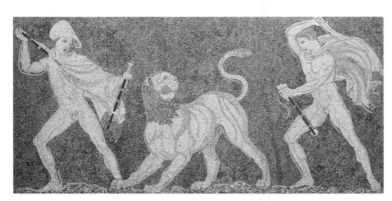

▲ *2. The dynamic outline of the figures has a three-dimensional feel that is suggested by the use of chiaroscuro. To translate the statue group into a picture, the mosaic artist has employed a dark background – in keeping with Aristotle's observation that when a rainbow is in front of a black cloud, colors appear in contrast. This is useful in paved decoration since the pieces are restricted to the four colors commonly used in the classical period and prehistoric times: white, black, red, and yellow.*

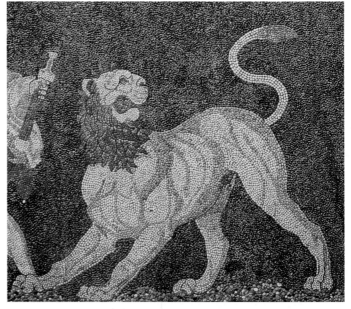

▲ *3. The boys' youth is emphasized by the size of the lion. The animal, its paws on the ground and its tail coiled, abruptly turns its head from Alexander toward Hephaestion. The absence of dogs in the scene suggests a convincing alternative interpretation: this is not the end of a hunt, but a casual attack by a lion (a beast commonly found in Macedonia) on two wanderers in a park. Alexander may have been surprised, which would explain why his sword remains in its hilt.*

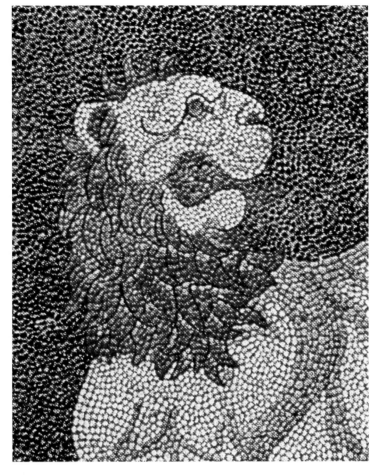

The three centuries between the death of Alexander the Great in 323BC and the Battle of Actium (31BC, when Octavian defeated Egypt, home to the last monarchy of Macedonian origin) saw the rise of Hellenistic culture. This term is used equally to refer to artistic developments and political events; its roots lie in the ancient Greek verb *hellenizo*, which refers to the ability of that culture to impose itself on others. During the complex Hellenistic period, which had several different phases, Greek language and custom were dominant.

Up until the battle of Ipsus (323–301BC), the *diadochi* (direct heirs of Alexander), ensured the survival of the classical tradition. Lysippos, the only one of the great contemporary sculptors to survive at Macedon, was especially important. He created some 1,500 bronzes throughout a huge area, from the Peloponnese to Macedonia, Athens to Acarnania, and as far afield as Magna Graecia; no artist of the time has been recorded as traveling farther. His sons and pupils – who helped perpetuate his work – and the pupils of other great masters were the last survivors of a bygone era. Kephisodotos and Timarchos, sons of Praxiteles, worked on the sarcophagus of Abdalonymos, the King of Sidon; a portrait of the dramatist Menander;

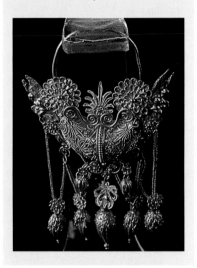

and a group of the first Epicureans. The sculptor Silanion trained Zeuxiades, who created a likeness of the Athenian statesman Hyperides. Euphranor's spirit lived on in the painting and bronze sculpture of Sostratos. These tenacious survivors promoted the classical ideal in funerary *stelae*, or tablets, the production of which

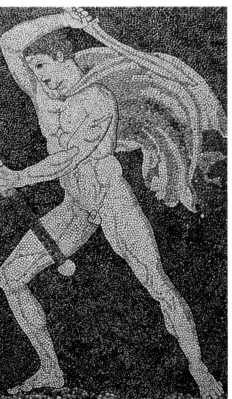

▲ *4. The above detail shows the extraordinary techniques used in mosaic-making at this time. At Pella, the uniformly small and simple gravel pieces came from a river deposit and were fixed with a grout inserted with minimum regular spaces. The lifelike quality and movement is achieved by adapting the pieces to the shape of the images. Terracotta outlines that sharpen the anatomical detail emphasize contours provided by the chiaroscuro. The subjects of pebble mosaics, still found in Mediterranean terraces or courtyards today, are mostly floral or geometric. Lead outlines are not used.*

◀ *5. The figure of Hephaestion seems to evoke qualities of art forms other than mosaic-making, such as sculpture and mural painting. In Hellenistic culture, the creators of all of these art forms, and others, such as dance and music, shared common criteria and aesthetic aims – underlining the impressive unity and coherence of Greek art.*

Altar of Zeus, Pergamum. Staatliche Museen, Berlin.

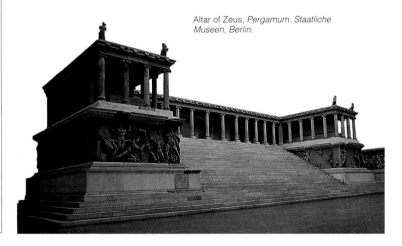

LYSIPPOS AFTER ALEXANDER

Following Alexander's death, Lysippos sided with the Greek cities striving for independence. His statue of *Chilon* at Olympia was a homage to the Achaean League (a confederation of Greek and Achaean cities), and the athlete who fell beneath the walls of Lamia (322BC). At Sikyon, his statue of *Praxillas* commemorated a literary and musical figure at a time when local glories were celebrated following liberation from Macedonian rule. The twisting of the flutist's body matches that of the *Apoxyomenos*, in which the projected right arm accentuates the feeling of movement. Following the fall of Sikyon to Kassander, Lysippos returned to the Macedonian fold (317–314BC). His *Silenus with the Infant Dionysos* matches the *Herakles at Rest*, while the pose of Hermes, loosening his sandal as Zeus summons him, reappeared in Caravaggio's portrayal of St. Matthew turning at the sound of the angel's message. Until the Byzantine Middle Ages, the colossal *Herakles at Rest* taken from Tarentum to Rome and Constantinople was attributed to Lysippos, the last artist of the classical tradition. In the *Satyricon*, Petronius quipped that Lysippos starved himself to death while working on the statue.

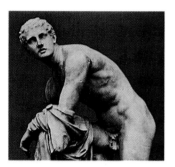

Hermes Loosening His Sandal (detail), Rome. Ny Carlsberg Glyptotek, Copenhagen.

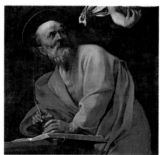

Caravaggio, Saint Matthew and the Angel *(detail), 1599. San Luigi dei Francesi, Rome.*

FROM LYSIPPOS TO MICHELANGELO

The sense of movement in Lysippos' final works was revived by Michelangelo, whose debt to the Greek sculptor has only recently been recognized. Since the divinities of polytheism have been repeatedly used in Christian imagery, it is hard to identify the original models used by Michelangelo, especially since his desire for originality was matched by a need to conceal his original inspiration because of the risk of censorship. The figure of John the Baptist from his *Last Judgment*, in the Sistine Chapel, is clearly derived from the *Herakles at Rest* now in the Pitti Palace, Florence, which bears the inscription "Work of Lysippos." Michelangelo had ambitions to create a monument akin to the huge *Zeus* of Lysippos described by Pliny. To those who asked whose follower he was, he would reply that his "master" had been the *Belvedere Torso* (Pio-Clementino collection), although it is unlikely he realized that this torso reproduced a Hellenistic bronze inspired by Lysippos' *Meditating Hercules*. His reply suggests that he knew of

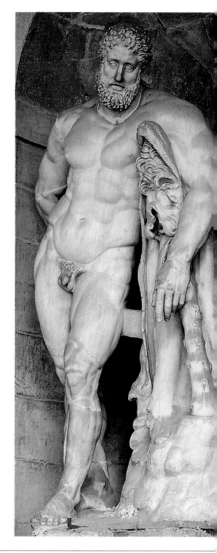

Herakles at Rest, Roman copy inscribed with the name of Lysippos, Rome. Palazzo Pitti, Florence.

was halted by Demetrios Phalereos, governor of Athens from 317BC to 307BC. Vergina was the site of one of the greatest monuments created by Alexander's successors – the tomb of his son Alexander IV, who reigned until 310BC, when he and his mother Roxana were killed by Kassander (King of Macedonia, 301–297BC). Inside the tomb, the painted frieze of a chariot race shows a strong Attic influence. The race unfolds on uneven ground against a blue sky; both chariots are fore-shortened in different ways as they overtake each other. A skillful use of shadow increases the sense of depth, and long brown brushstrokes on the charioteers' robes give a sense of chiaroscuro.

Chariot race, detail of frieze from the tomb of Alexander IV, Vergina, Greece.

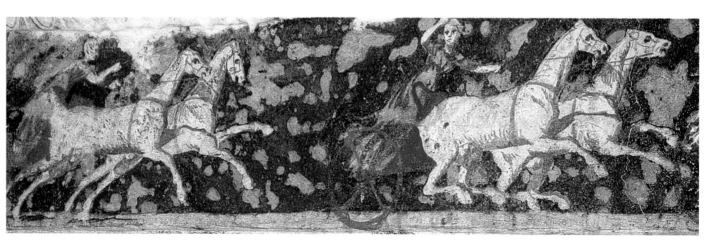

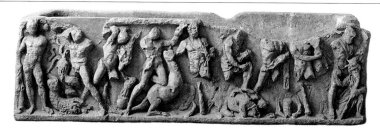

Lysippos' response to the same question, as reported by Cicero, that his "master" was the *Doryphoros*, another sculptural masterpiece that lay at the root of the "Manneristic" style that preceded the Hellenistic "Baroque" style. Decorations on a sarcophagus showing the *Labors of Herakles* are similar to a cycle created by Lysippos in bronze at Alizia in 314BC and then taken to Rome; the same likeness of

Detail from sarcophagus showing the Labors of Herakles. *Palazzo Corsini, Rome.*

Herakles is constantly repeated in the *Last Judgment* by Michelangelo. The figure of St. Peter repeats the three-dimensionalism of Herakles wrestling with the Cretan bull, which in turn reflects the *Apoxyomenos*. Most remarkable among the resurrected figures taken up to heaven is the one

whose bent knee, twisted torso, and raised arm echo Herakles kneeling over the Arcadian Stag. The ascending nude, hands clasped behind his back and head turned in the opposite direction, combines two other images of Herakles: the hero slaying the Stymphalian Birds, and walking away after the cleaning of the Augean Stables. There are also references to Herakles in the blessed figure raising up two devotees who are clutching a rosary (similar to Herakles bending over the body of Hippolyta), and the mystical crown, which evokes the girdle seized from the Amazon.

Detail from sarcophagus showing the Labors of Herakles. *Boboli Gardens, Florence.*

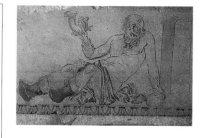

Silenos, fresco on the tomb at Potidae, *c.300BC. Archaeological Museum, Salonika, Greece.*

eye of the beholder – later mirrored in the divisionist technique practiced by 20th-century Neo-Impressionists. The most striking features of the *Silenos* painted on a tomb from Potidae in Macedonia (c.300BC) are the disheveled beard that frames the subtly malicious expression of the man's face, and the red leather boots. The lines have a thin, sketchy quality, while the shadow in the pink cloth around his hips is created by means of thicker brushstrokes in the same color. The complexity of Asiatic painting is further revealed in the Tomb of the Judgment, which dates from the reign of Demetrios Poliorcetes (294–288BC). It is the work of Theon of Samos, from the eastern Aegean, who was commissioned by the son of Antigonos I. In another tomb, that of Lison and Kallikles (brothers

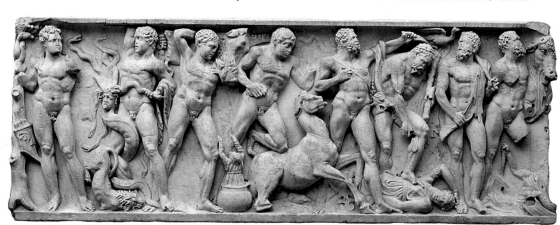

HELLENISTIC BAROQUE

Independence, as advocated by Lysippos, encouraged every artist to plow his own furrow, to change canons and conventions, and to establish a new, relative truth. The real creativity of Hellenistic art lies in representing the world according to the transient effect of the particular moment. Awareness of the distance and difference from the classical period ushered in a time of radical artistic experimentation that ended with the Battle of Pydna (300–168BC). In some senses, the Hellenistic "Baroque" era

is similar to that of late 20th-century Western societies; both saw a transition from totality to plurality, from coherence to variety. In the late 20th century, sovereign states existed, but they shared a style of civilization, just as the inhabitants of the Hellenistic kingdoms followed the collective Greek culture. Aristotle sensed that realism and possibility, the authentic and the fictitious, could all exist simultaneously. In both Greek and modern cultures, art responded to a vast and sophisticated public and needed to address a variety of events and ideas that went beyond the realms of traditional style. Painting no longer entailed "applying the appropriate

color to each part," as Plato had stated. Shape now emerged from the outlines created by a juxtaposition of minute brushstrokes of different, unmixed colors. Synthesis occurred in the

Tomb of Lison and Kallikles, lunette painted with weapons, Lefkadia, Greece.

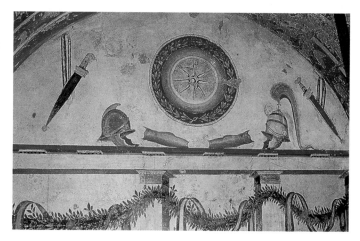

killed during the battle of Kynoscephalae in 197BC), their weapons adorn the lunettes (semicircular openings to admit light) of the chamber, enhancing the illusionistic layout. The painter has used impasto and shading, paying close attention to plastic effects, color contrasts, and the brilliant light, to progress from the stark outline of the

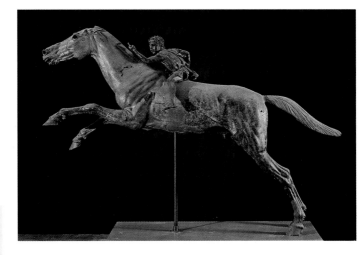

THEATRICAL SCENES

One striking aspect of Hellenistic art was that of deep introspection. Once under the control of monarchic states, individuals were forced to live in an environment that offered fewer guarantees of democratic independence. The people's need to defend themselves and give meaning to their existence led, on the one hand, to philosophical attempts at clarifying the distinction between the private and public personas of individuals, and on the other to a theatrical ambiguity between existence and appearance. Menander's comedies were a source of inspiration for Kalates' small paintings, known from numerous replicas. One of two mosaics at Pompeii signed by Dioscurides of Samos is taken from Kalates' *Women at Dinner,* a popular subject in Italy; a similar scene occurred in *Cistellaria,* by the Roman playwright Plautus. In the mosaic, beams of light enter a dining room from the left, the old procuress and her prostitute daughter sit next to the young woman who has invited them, with a maid at the side. Chiaroscuro provides a contrast between figures and background, a deceptive suggestion of shadows, and the "shot" effect of the silk in the clothing and cushions.

Mosaic signed by Dioscorides of Samos, copy after Kalates, Villa di Cicero, Pompeii. National Archaeological Museum, Naples. The work was inspired by a scene from a play by Menander.

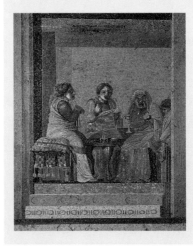

metal artifacts to the soft quality of the plumes on the gilded helmet.

The kingdoms established in Egypt and Anatolia by the first generation of *epigoni,* who succeeded the *diadochi,* competed to outdo each other's monumental projects. Immediately after Lysippos died, his followers moved to Rhodes, taking with them the skills they had developed at Tarentum. Chares of Lindos doubled the height of his master's *Zeus* with his 150-foot (32-meter) *Colossus* (304–293BC). This bronze effigy accentuated the movement of the subject in every direction, marking the birth of an art open to the world, a visual translation of an infinite vastness. At the sanctuary of the sun god, there was a sculpture of a worshiper by Boithos in a

Horseman, bronze, Cape Artemision. National Archaeological Museum, Athens.

pose often adopted in the presence of the gods. Similar to this was Euboulides' ecstatic figure of the *Mulier Admirans.* Euboulides' signature is scratched on the base of a beaker discovered in the founding pits at the foot of the Acropolis at Rhodes. These pits, with thin brick cladding and efficient drainage channels for the wax, were used to create works up to nine feet (three meters) tall. The statue of *Tyche, Good Fortune,* by Lysippos' son Eutychides (300BC), was commissioned

Epigonos, Ludovisi Gaul, Roman copy. Capitoline Museum, Rome.

Epigonos, Dying Gaul, Roman copy. Capitoline Museum, Rome.

by Seleucus I to symbolize Antioch and was even more complicated than the *Meditating Herakles,* another colossus from Tarentum.

A local style asserted itself in Pergamum after 282BC, when its ruler, Philetaerus, achieved political independence. This was characterized by eccentric shapes, irregular gestures, and figures that had no central anchorage and seemed to embrace the void. Space became a challenge, an opportunity to capture the onlooker. Work produced during the evolutionary period, which elsewhere preceded the liberation of sculpture from the earlier "Mannerist"

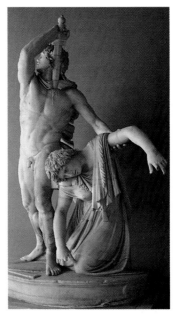

school, was concentrated at the court of Eumenes I (263–241BC) by exponents of the two main schools of the classical era – the Athenian and the Sikyonian. The sculptors Phyromachos, Niceratos, and Xenocrates were responsible for the rapid maturity of Pergamene sculpture and for creating the "Baroque" style, destined to achieve universal and lasting success. Advances in knowledge of anatomy were demonstrated in the powerful modeling of

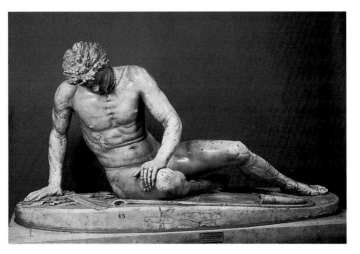

BAROQUE ANCIENT AND MODERN

Although this marble statue was once attributed to Myron by Pliny, it has since become clear that this attribution arose from a confusion over the name of the subject, Maronis. The original description was: "Maronis, an old Jewish woman, at Smyrna, one of the most famous works." It was made famous in about 250BC by Leonidas of Tarentum, the first man to write of this indulgent personification of an old woman's drunkenness: "the lover of wine, the wringer of jars, lies here, an old woman. An Attic cup rests on her tomb.

Maronis, *Roman copy of an Asiatic original, Via Nomentana, Rome. Capitoline Museum, Rome.*

And she moans underground, not for her children, not for her husband whom she left in penury, not for any of this, but because her cup is empty." A century later, Antipater of Sidon returned to the subject: "This is the tomb of the white-haired Maronis, a lover of undiluted wine and always talkative." Her age, her love of drink suggested by the prominence of her throat, her garrulousness expressed by her open mouth, and the jug of undiluted wine are all recurring features of Roman copies of the Maronis sculpture. The mystical interpretation is that she has forgotten her earthly family in order to embrace god in the guise of wine: the flagon is crowned with ivy, like the infant Dionysos. The way her head is

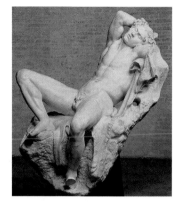

Barberini Faun, *Roman copy of an original from Pergamum, Castel Sant'Angelo, Rome. Glyptothek, Munich.*

thrown back gives her the appearance of a *maenad* (a female member of the orgiastic cult of Dionysos), while her skeletal body reveals how close she is to death. Her ecstatic smile reflects the transcendental joy, the link between physical decay and the flowering of the spirit, and thus death with rebirth: her tomb will be hallowed by the cup of the gods.

In the 17th century, the Italian sculptor Gian Lorenzo Bernini worked on the restoration of a statue of a sleeping satyr known as the *Barberini Faun*, dating from the second century BC. He went on to recreate the drunken pose of the satyr in his sculpture *Ecstasy of Saint Theresa*, in Santa Maria della Vittoria, Rome.

Gian Lorenzo Bernini, Ecstasy of Saint Theresa, *Santa Maria della Vittoria, Rome, 1644–52.*

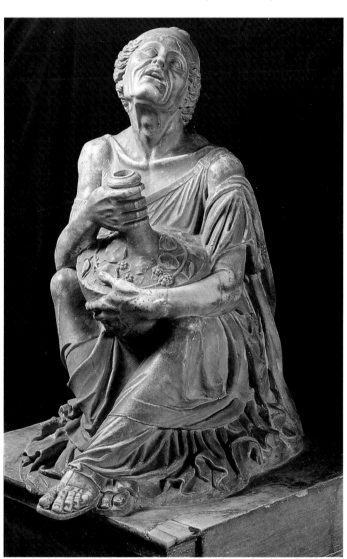

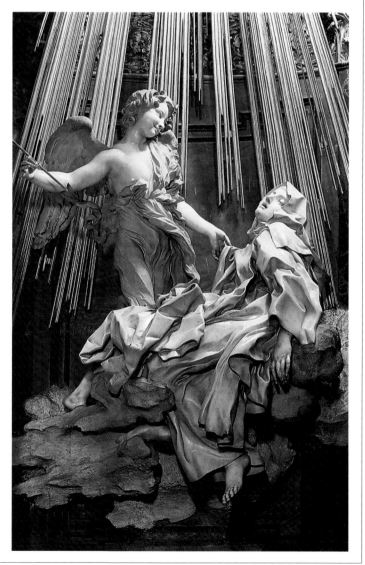

THE FARNESE TAZZA

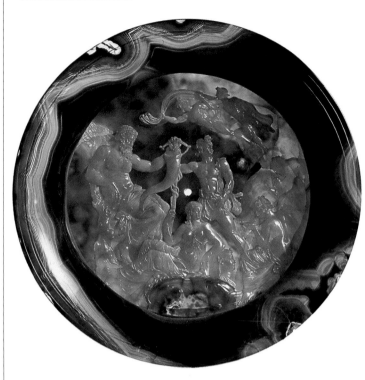

The Farnese Tazza is one of the largest known pieces of sardonyx. Since ancient times, it has passed from court to court, through the castles of Federico, the treasury of Lorenzo the Magnificent, the Farnese collection, and, finally, to the Naples Museum, where it resides today. The *tazza* (shallow cup) was created for the offerings of Nile water made every year by the Ptolemies at the start of the floods. The brown and white veins of the

Allegory of Egypt, base of the sardonyx cup known as the Farnese Tazza. National Archaeological Museum, Naples.

crystal were incorporated in a fascinating engraving of nature, history, and myth. The cup seems to embody Egypt itself, the unformed crystal mass symbolizing the stability and security of the country. The king is represented as the Pharaohs once were – as a sphinx with a lion's body and a human head adorned with the

royal regalia – and the stoutness of Ptolemy VIII (145–116BC) is in keeping with the majesty of the gods. Lying on the sphinx is the figure of the queen, Cleopatra III, whose diadem crowning her curly hair is typical of Demeter, Greek goddess of fertility. The old seated man, his arm resting on a sycamore trunk, represents the Nile, and two young girls on the opposite side are allegories for the main seasons of agricultural Egypt. At the side flies Wind, while above, the airy curve of the robe worn by Sky matches the roundness of the sphinx and crowns the microcosm contained within the *tazza*. At the center, a young man grips the yoke of a plow; a sack of seed hangs from his arm and his hand grasps a sickle, a compendium of the farming cycle, from plowing to sowing to harvesting. In Greek mythology, he is Triptolemus (patron of agriculture), but could equally represent the Horus (falcon-god) of Egyptian tradition. Clear symbolism links the ears of wheat of the woman, the cornucopia of the old man, and the plow of the youth. All are aligned with each other, indicating that the fortunes of the country depend on the fertility of the Nile and

on the work of man. The farmer is the incarnation of the Egyptian people, those rural workers who were favored by Ptolemy VIII over the citizens of Alexandria.

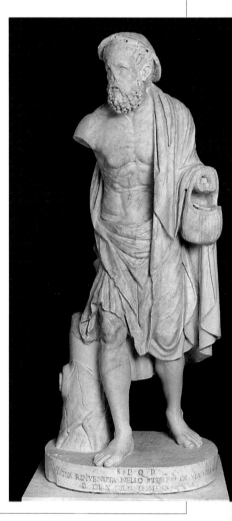

Old Fisherman, Roman copy of an Alexandrian original, the Esquiline, Rome. Palazzo dei Conservatori, Rome.

musculature and bones, exemplified by the *Artemision Horse*, the *Artemision Jockey*, and the *Fighting Man of Delos*. The sculptor Epigonos gave new prominence to the peripheral in his series of statues known as the *Dying Gauls* (c.235BC), whose figures seem to challenge the boundary between art and life by invading the space occupied by the onlooker. Signatures found on the base of statues in Rhodes distinguish the designers of the base from the modelers, revealing a

specialization that encouraged mass production. Barter was replaced by credit and a banking system, which increased the flow of goods, now represented by numerical amounts that everyone understood. Cities were now being planned on a grand scale, and sculptors favored a style in which figures were set against a

Drunkenness of Polyphemus, fragmentary Roman copy of the group of the Rhodian sculptors Agesander, Athenodoros, and Polidoro from the Grotto of Tiberius at Sperlonga, first century BC. National Archaeological Museum, Sperlonga, Italy.

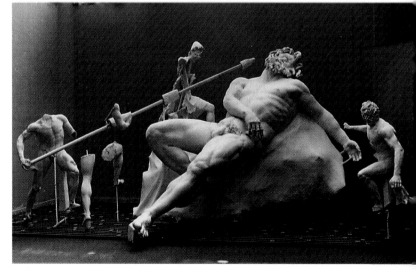

deep background, with perspective used to portray distant objects. For the artists of Rhodes, space was inseparable from distance. The background was no longer the city, such as Pergamum, with its porticoed squares, but rocks, caves, water, greenery, and sky. In the Stoic philosophy, morality was the "fruit of a garden," and nymphaea (grottoes, temples, or sanctuaries) became filled with images conducive to meditation, involving punishments meted out by the gods to reestablish the divine equilibrium and symbolic representations of human courage. In Epigonos' disturbingly powerful *Torment of Dirce,* the subject lies with her head turned away, gazing into the

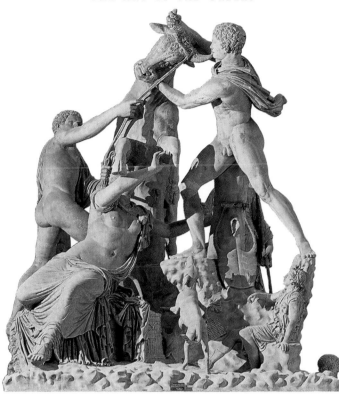

terrifying eye of the bull rearing over her. Sculptural groups became increasingly complicated and less and less linked to everyday life, almost as though they were governed by the most primitive laws of mankind. To understand them, the viewer must recapture the primeval fascination that the artist drew on in order to endow each of his creations with their own strength and impact. The dense fog that Menander tried to pierce with his gaze, the darkness that concealed the flight of Ulysses and Diomedes, the spring welling up at the feet of Dirce, and the ancestral

Torment of Dirce, *fragmentary Roman copy of a Rhodian original, from the Baths of Caracalla, Rome. National Archaeological Museum, Naples. The sculpture is positioned near a jet of water, in memory of the spring named after Dirce at Thebes.*

PERGAMUM AND THE ACROPOLIS

The *stoa* (covered walkway) at the Acropolis, given by Attalus II of Pergamum in c.145BC, celebrates the mythical and historical victories of order over chaos. The passage of time is

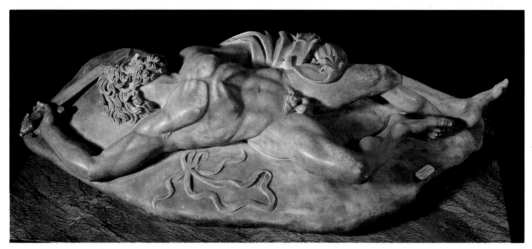

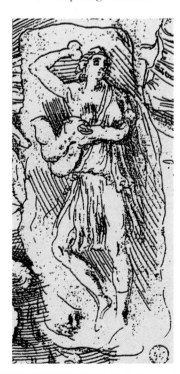

Fallen Giant, *Baths of Alexander Severus, Rome. National Archaeological Museum, Naples.*

Hippolyta Dying with the Young Theseos, *drawing made before the restoration of a group statue in the National Archaeological Museum, Naples. Kupferstichkabinett, Basel, Switzerland.*

depicted in the victims' agony – for example, a horse collapsed under a falling Amazon, a child stroking its still warm mother – marking the relentless approach of the death that will destroy the aggressors. The sense of disquiet conveyed by these fragments

springs from the contrasting values of form and composition that each figure preserves from the overall design, like snatches of an epic poem. The isolated copies now on pedestals in museums have lost their original coherence, for it was the serial nature of the scenes of slaughter, the disjointed bodies that looked as if they had been violently pushed in a frantic scuffle, that endowed the works with a feeling of metaphysical truth. The result was to present the vanquished in a primitive, idealized light, which gave the

drama a sense of totality that had been lost when the classical ideal was abandoned. The clearly defined figures of giants, Amazons, Persians, and Gauls stand out against the dazzling background, with no evidence of physical authenticity. Each episode is a pretext for the reinvention of the battle, in which the character of the combatants is filtered through an imaginary veil that binds them all together in a spell, freezes them in static poses, astonished by their wounds, and rendered motionless by death.

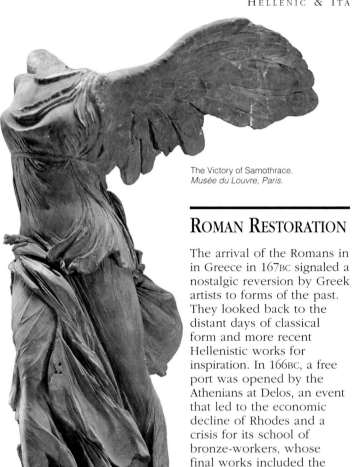

The Victory of Samothrace.
Musée du Louvre, Paris.

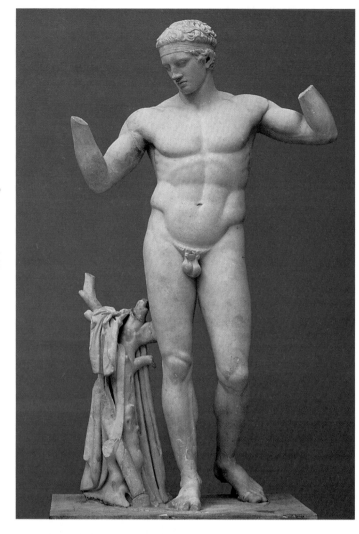

ROMAN RESTORATION

The arrival of the Romans in in Greece in 167BC signaled a nostalgic reversion by Greek artists to forms of the past. They looked back to the distant days of classical form and more recent Hellenistic works for inspiration. In 166BC, a free port was opened by the Athenians at Delos, an event that led to the economic decline of Rhodes and a crisis for its school of bronze-workers, whose final works included the mournful groups of *Scylla* and *Laocoon*. Thanks to commissions from the Roman ruling class, work produced by families of

cavern of the Cyclops all create different excitements and fears in the viewer as he or she contemplates the work. Similarly, the Palladium torn from its shrine, the *thyrsus* (staff) of Dirce, the hapless bacchant abandoned on the rock, the banquet cup bloodied by the Cyclops and thrown on the ground – each image evokes previously buried emotions and sensations.

The marble statue of the *Victory of Samothrace* and the *Altar of Zeus* (189–182BC) erected in Pergamum commemorate the victories at Rhodes, Pergamum, and of their Roman allies over Antiochus III of Syria. The giants writhe alongside the steps of the altar in a magnificent frieze depicting a battle between gods and giants.

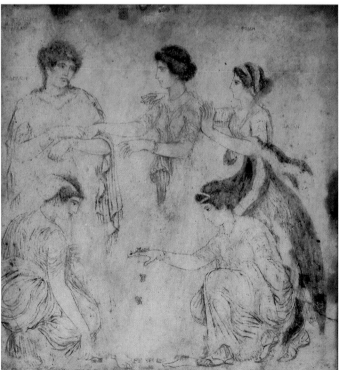

Diadumenos, *copy by a Neo-Attic artist after Polycleitos, Delos. National Archaeological Museum, Athens.*

Girls Playing Knucklebones, *painting on marble signed by the Athenian Alexander, copy after Zeuxis, Herculaneum. National Archaeological Museum, Naples.*

traditional Athenian sculptors was revived. Likenesses of Italic merchants at Delos were placed on statues carved in the old aristocratic style. A small painting on marble from the city of Herculaneum, *Girls Playing Knucklebones* (derived from a work by Zeuxis and signed by Alexander as copyist) was delicately colored according to classical rules.

At Pergamum, Rhodes, and Antioch, the importance of the space around a sculpture diminished in deference to the Athenian style, while a Neo-Egyptian style appeared at the court of the Ptolemies, giving visual form to the religious reconciliation foisted on Egypt by their Macedonian invaders. The realistic style used to raise social awareness by earlier generations was exaggerated in the realism of Alexandrine artists. The result verged on the romantic, but was a reminder of and a comment on social injustices. It marked the slide from Utopian ideals to disenchantment, and the beginnings of civilization on a mass scale.

THE OASIS PAINTER

By marrying his half-sister Arsinoë in 278BC, Ptolemy II established the Egyptian cult of rulers known as *Theoi Adelphoi*. It was their love for each other that inspired the name Philadelphia, given to the colony founded in the Fayum oasis as part of a far-reaching agrarian policy under the supervision of Zeno of Kaunos. The papyri in Zeno's archive detail the care taken by the Alexandrine Greeks to create an environment in keeping with their civic aspirations. In 256BC, Zeno commissioned Theodorus, an Alexandrine painter, to decorate the houses according to strict specifications. The following year, Theodorus tackled the house of Diothimus, the "vice-administrator" of Philadelphia. The decoration consisted of large areas of different color with a broader central band, the same format that appears in some Alexandrine tombs, with the master undertaking to decorate the ceiling of the main room in accordance with the agreed model. The papyri also reveal that the artist made panel paintings: mention is made of "strong" sinope red, suitable for use on wood, as well as wax and glue from Busiris (an ancient city of Lower Egypt), technical elements that were later used in funerary portraits from the same Fayum region. For his encaustic paintings (using paint mixed with soft wax) Theodorus used a heated metal spatula.
His last letter to Zeno reveals a yearning for his Alexandrine workshop: "Since the commission from you is finished and there is no more work, I have no money. If you still have some paintings that need to be done, please be so kind as to give me the job so that I may have enough to live on. If you cannot offer me any work, please send me money for traveling expenses so that I can return to my brothers in the city."

PORTRAITS OF THE CYNICS

The best way to appreciate fully the many different variations in Greek painting style is to compare portraits of the same person executed at different times. An original effigy of Antisthenes, the philosopher and founder of the Cynic sect, was molded in Athens shortly after his death (366BC). However, he can also be seen in more recent copies by Phyromachus (c.290–245BC), another Athenian who worked at the court at Pergamum. Phyromachus' dynamic contrasts and

Antisthenes, *bronze attributed to Silanion, from the sea at Punta del Serrone. Provincial Museum, Brindisi, Italy.*

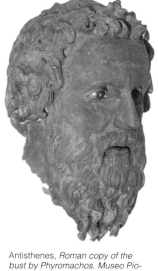

Antisthenes, *Roman copy of the bust by Phyromachos. Museo Pio-Clementino, Vatican City.*

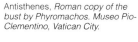

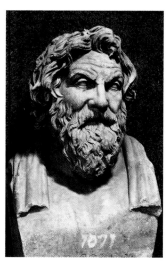

chiaroscuro unshackle the figure's polemical spirit – his very name indicated an attitude of obstinate opposition. He was a sullen old man, according to Lucian, the Greek rhetorician and satirist, "with his unkempt beard and furrowed eyebrows, his Titan's glare and ruffled hair at the front." Of Diogenes, the most famous Cynic philosopher, there are replicas both of the portrait dedicated in Athens during his life (he died in about 325BC) and of a statuette conceived in Alexandria as an ornament for the Library (120–100BC). The more ancient busts of these thinkers reveal an affinity with portraits of Socrates.

Diogenes, *statuette from Rome. Metropolitan Museum of Art, New York.*

Diogenes, *Roman copy. Museo Nazionale Romano, Rome.*

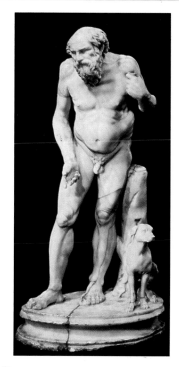

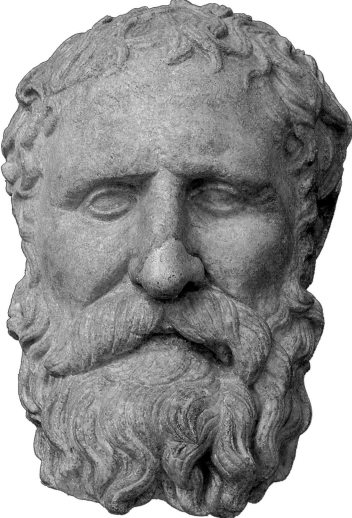

ITALIC ART

Complex civilizations of many races and languages developed in the Italian region from the early centuries of the first millennium BC. Of the various artistic cultures of Italy, the most prominent were those of the Etruscans and the Romans, each with their own individual characteristics.

Various peoples occupied Italy during the first millennium BC: the main groups in the Alps were the Ligurians in the west, the Veneti to the east, and the Protocelts to the north.

The Po valley and Etruria were occupied by the Villanovan group, which developed into the historical Etruscan civilization. South of Etruria were the Latins, who founded Rome; farther south, to the east, and in the islands were various populations of different provenances, some of whom, like the Sardi, or the Elymi of Sicily, evolved highly original cultures. From this rich diversity of peoples, and with the addition of Greek (Magna Graecia and Sicily) and Punic (Sardinia and western Sicily) colonies, evolved the ancient art of Italy.

THE DAUNIAN DYNASTIES

Daunian *stelae* (commemorative slabs or pillars) were cut from the soft stone of the Gargano promontory in Apulia. Initially white, this stone tended to darken as it aged. The *stelae* were painted in red and black, as was contemporary pottery (seventh to sixth century BC). Across Apulia, from Sipontum to Arpi, to Canosa, and as far as Melfitano, the ruling families

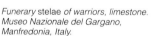

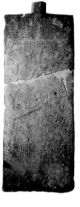

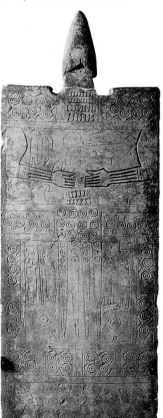

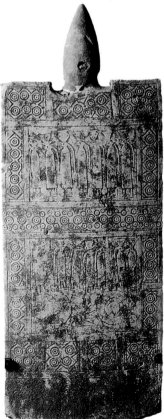

honored their dead in this monumental form. The figures, mostly female, are heavily stylized and contained within the rectangular form, with just the faintest sign of chiseling in places to create the almost imperceptible effect of bas-relief details. The body, long garments, jewels, and other personal objects are very stylized. So too is the head, which is often rendered as a smooth, featureless oval with a conical headdress for women or a sectioned helmet for men. The arms are folded across the torso, and the feet are not included. Instead, the rectangle becomes a space that is filled with delicate and intricate decoration, combining geometric patterns with a variety of figurative scenes – travel, hunting, fishing, navigation, milling and weaving, lovers, banquets and ritual games, domesticated animals, monsters, and mythical figures. The sculptors were precise in their rendering of detail, since they were convinced of the power of symbols and of the significance of human existence within the cosmic design.

Funerary stelae of warriors, limestone. Museo Nazionale del Gargano, Manfredonia, Italy.

Funerary stelae of women, limestone. Museo Nazionale del Gargano, Manfredonia, Italy.

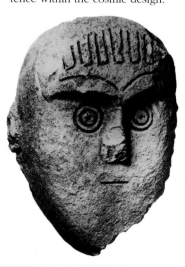

Head from a stela, Sipontum. Museo Nazionale del Gargano, Manfredonia, Italy.

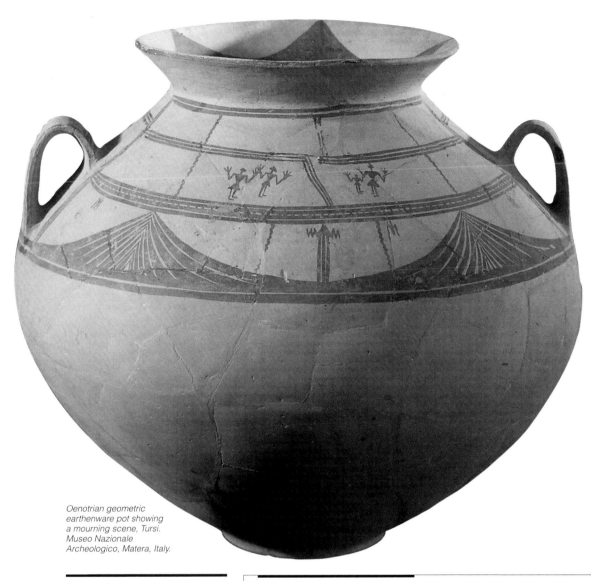

Oenotrian geometric earthenware pot showing a mourning scene, Tursi. Museo Nazionale Archeologico, Matera, Italy.

first millennium BC, there had been profound changes in society, with the development of complex social stratification; this was reflected in art in the erection of memorials to eminent people and other public monuments. In the Gargano area of the Italian peninsula and in Sardinia, stone sculpture was produced from the end of the Bronze Age. The Myceneans, who had reached southern Italy earlier in the Bronze Age, introduced the use of refined clay as a substitute for the rougher impasto materials. Painted decoration on pottery began with the protogeometric style of the Iapygian peoples in Apulia (11th–9th century BC), followed by the Oenotrian style found from Basilicata to the Tyrrhenian coast. Then, in the late ninth and eighth centuries BC, Phoenicians and Greeks arrived in Italy and Sardinia, resulting in the adoption of new pottery techniques for some forms in Central Italy: the use of the wheel, refined clay, and painted decoration. During the Orientalizing period (seventh century BC) and Archaic period (sixth and earlier fifth centuries BC), there was increased cultural

THE ITALICS

Despite the diversity of the peoples and regions, artistic production in the Italian peninsula was united by a readiness to embrace existing forms. From early prehistory, the need to express beliefs and experiences – magical, religious, and funerary – was manifested in personal adornment and in the production of cult and votive objects. It was also evident in other artistic endeavors, such as the great series of rock carvings in the Alpine foothills of northern Italy, which depict scenes of hunting, plowing, and combat and seem to include both human and supernatural figures. By the end of the

THE CAUDINE FORKS

A painting at Paestum from the tomb of a survivor of the battle of the Caudine Forks commemorates this Samnite victory over the Romans at a time when the Lucanians, rulers of Paestum, were their allies (321BC). The painting conforms to the historical narrative style of ancient Greece. In the background are a mountain and four cattle, which are drawn to a larger scale than the human figures. These animals are seen in similar circumstances in a painting by the Greek artist Euphranor of the confrontation preceding the battle of Mantinea (362BC). Also related to Euphranor's painting of the Stoa of Zeus at Athens is the

contrast between the marching Romans, carrying spears and shields, and the deployment of their enemies, hidden by the terrain. The helmeted commander, who stands on the rise, threatens the legions that have fallen into the ambush. A

Battle of the Caudine Forks, tomb painting from Andriuolo. Museo Nazionale Archeologico, Paestum, Italy.

fresco from a tomb in Rome shows the counterpart to this scene, with episodes from the Samnite wars as seen by the Romans in the style of Fabius Pictor. *Quirites* (Roman citizens) with large shields also appear in the polychrome decoration of vases from Arpi, the Daunian city allied with Rome against the Samnites.

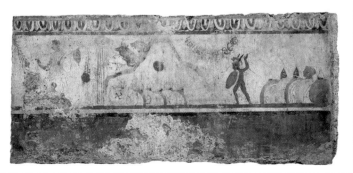

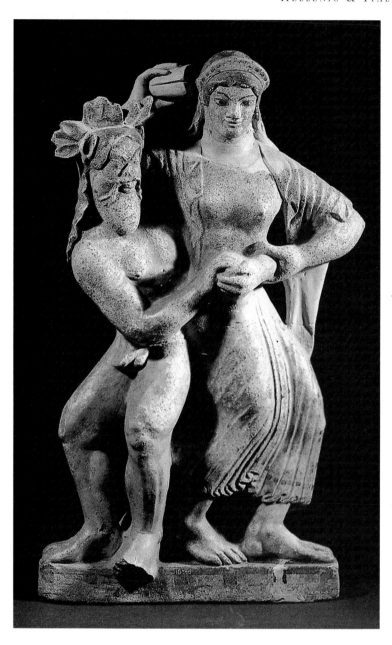

adopted Greek forms of worship, and developed monumental architecture. Etruscan influence prevailed in Campania as a result of their direct dominance as far as the valley of the River Sele. By the end of the fifth century BC, the use of both painted terracotta decorations for the eaves of buildings and terracotta votives was widespread in southern Italy. The influence of the Greek colony at Cumae extended from Capua to Teanum, Minturnae, and Satricum and as far as Rome and Caere. With the Sabellian conquest of Capua in 423BC, production of sculpture in tufa began, a parallel practice to the Etruscan limestone carving at Chiusi.

From about 400BC, when the Lucanians took control of Poseidonia (Paestum), until the foundation of the Latin colony in 273BC, funerary painting became popular in this area, though it had started in the Orientalizing period in Etruria. The subjects were mainly funerary scenes depicting musicians, games, and offerings. The red, black, and yellow on a white ground (blue and green were rare) conformed to the four-color convention observed by the great Greek painter Apelles (360–315BC). In Italy, the color was painted on a layer of lime plaster applied to the rock. This contrasted with the Greek

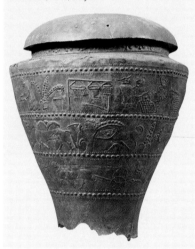

Benvenuti situla, bronze. Museo Nazionale Atestino, Este, Italy.

Silenus and Maenad Dancing, terracotta antefix, Satricum. Museo Nazionale di Villa Giulia, Rome.

Male funerary stele, limestone, Bigliolo (Aulla, Val di Magra). Museo Civico, Pontremoli, Italy.

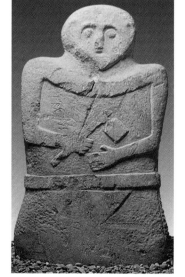

exchange over ancient land routes or by way of new sea lanes along the Adriatic and Tyrrhenian coastlines. The Orientalizing period is named after the wealth of luxury goods imported from the Near East and the Aegean, including vessels of gold, silver, glass, and fine pottery, as well as ivories and ostrich eggs, many decorated with figured scenes. The Daunians controlled the mouth of the Ofanto from Canusium, as well as trade with groups across the

Adriatic. The geometric tradition of the Iapygians provided the basis for a regulated decorative style, which, in pottery, resisted outside influence. The princely tombs of Noicattaro and Conversano in Peucetia reveal an accumulation of imported merchandise rather than the products of a purely local tradition. The Messapians, who were in close contact with the Greeks, imitated the use of the Black-Figure technique in ceramics,

tradition, in which stucco was used to simulate marble as a support for the color.

The Sabines were influenced by a style that spread beyond the Apennines from Etruria and the Faliscan area; it featured animals and an original treatment of monster images. In Umbria, during the fifth century BC, small bronzes of stylized warrior men and gods, elongated to the point of deformation, were dedicated at sanctuaries. The stelae statues from Luna represented a late development of megalithic sculpture among this warrior community. Of interest are their anthropomorphic figures, which arose from contact with northern Etruria (610–600BC). Paleo-Venetian art adopted Orientalizing elements to depict the life of the upper classes. Later, the theme was used in the thriving local bronze-working industry and revealed Etruscan influence. The art of the Siculi and Elymi in Sicily developed independently of Greek and Punic art.

At a very early stage they used monumental forms for dwellings and sanctuaries, as at Mendolito, Sabucina, and Monte Adranone (late sixth century BC).

The exploits of Alexander the Great inspired the western campaigns of Alexander of Epirus and Pyrrhus, and the ensuing period was dominated by Hellenistic innovations.

DAUGHTERS OF LAVINIA

Lavinium was a sacred city linked with the origins of Rome. According to legend, Lavinium was founded by Aeneas in honor of his wife Lavinia, daughter of King Latinus. For centuries the magistrates of Rome came to Lavinium to offer

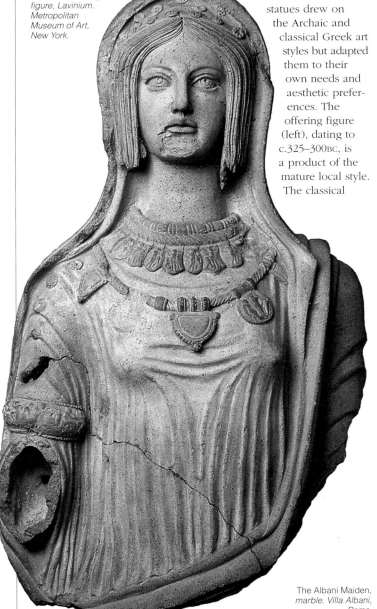

Terracotta offering figure, Lavinium. Metropolitan Museum of Art, New York.

sacrifices when taking office. The city had links with the Hellenic shrines, Magna Graecia, and Etruria, the art styles of which would have been familiar. Painted terracotta sculpture was common to Etruria, Latium, and Campania and, like other artistic products, had distinct local styles. The sculptors at Lavinium who made the series of fine terracotta votive statues drew on the Archaic and classical Greek art styles but adapted them to their own needs and aesthetic preferences. The offering figure (left), dating to c.325–300BC, is a product of the mature local style. The classical

Greek influence is clear in the heavy rounded jaw, the pouting, slightly downturned mouth, and the clothing (a long tunic of fine linen and a woollen cloak); while the frontal pose and lavish jewelry are reminiscent of the sixth-century Archaic Greek *korai* (young women). However, the overall effect is non-Greek. This

and the second figure have a powerful presence and are the work of skilled craftsmen with a long tradition behind them. They have exploited the plastic qualities of the terracotta to the full, with the pose giving solemnity and intensity, and the various details and textures adding a sense of vitality. The

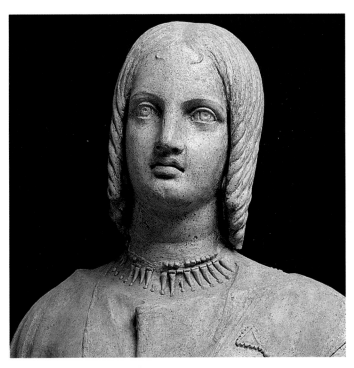

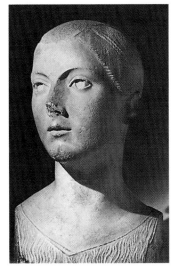

The Albani Maiden, marble. Villa Albani, Rome.

Head of maiden, terracotta, Lavinium. Soprintendenza Archeologica per il Lazio, Rome.

necklaces, armring, and diadem have been copied from life – examples in gold, silver, semiprecious stones, glass, and amber have been found in contemporary central Italian tombs. These are wealthy, aristocratic figures, or possibly goddesses, and would have carried clear messages about religious beliefs and the organization of society, easily understood by contemporary viewers. Their calm dignity is also seen later in sculptures such as *The Albani Maiden.*

THE ETRUSCANS

The Etruscans developed a sophisticated civilization in the first millenium BC in Central Italy – between the Tiber and Arno rivers – with outposts in the Po valley and Campania. They adopted an alphabet from the Greeks to write inscriptions in their own language, which was unlike any other in Italy. For them, the religious aspect

BEYOND THE GRAVE

In the Villanovan and earlier Etruscan periods, highly abstract renderings of the body accompanied some dead to the grave. Villanovan biconical cinerary urns may be interpreted as a replacement for the body destroyed by cremation. This body reference later became more explicit: at Vulci, the head was rendered as an anonymous sphere on a cylindrical neck (680–670BC). At Chiusi, in the seventh and sixth centuries BC, there was a flourishing production of anthropomorphic cinerary urns featuring heads with eyes, nose, mouth, and ears and often decorated with bronze elements such as earrings. The urns sometimes have arms and may be seated on bronze or pottery chairs.
Later, a widespread practice developed of sculpting one or more human figures on the lid of a sarcophagus or ash chest. For example, the painted terracotta Sarcophagus of the Married Couple from Cerveteri carries exquisitely modeled, life-size figures of a man and woman, reclining as if on a banqueting couch.

Stylized bronze head, Vulci. Museo Nazionale di Villa Giulia, Rome.

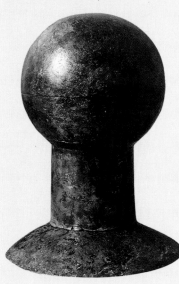

THE CHIMAERA

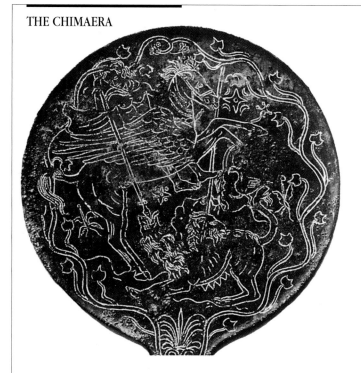

Bellerophon on Pegasus defeating the chimaera, back of a mirror, bronze, Palestrina. Metropolitan Museum of Art, New York.

The chimaera is a mythical beast, part lion, part goat, and part snake, which was killed by the hero Bellerophon. In Etruscan art, it occurs on mirrors, painted pottery, and private seals. Most famous is the *Chimaera of Arezzo*, a magnificent life-size bronze statue, made in the early fourth century BC and found during building work in 1553 near the Porta San Lorenzo, Arezzo. Although wounded in the leg and goat's head, the cornered beast crouches as if about to spring at its attacker and snarls ferociously. An Etruscan votive inscription on its right foreleg,

Full view and detail of the Chimaera of Arezzo. Museo Archeologico, Florence.

added to the wax model before casting, indicates that this sculpture was made in a North Etrurian workshop. The tail is a restoration of 1785. The powerful body is modeled naturalistically, in sharp contrast with the stylized muzzle and the stiff petal-shaped tufts of the ruff and mane. On the mirror from Palestrina, dating from about 330BC, Bellerophon riding Pegasus deals the mortal blow to the chimaera. The goat's head has already been speared, but the animal fights to the last. The turmoil of bodies enclosed within the circle of the mirror enhances the sense of drama.

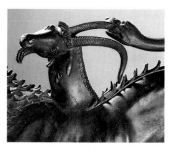

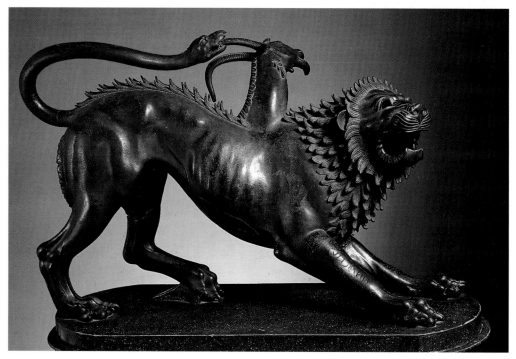

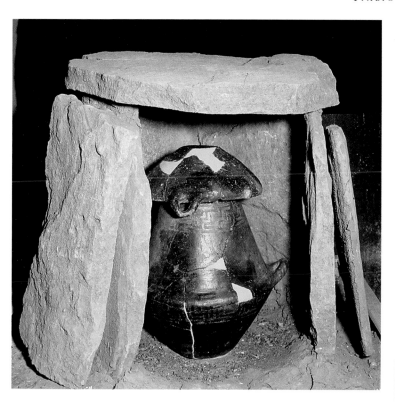

Villanovan ossuary with bowl-shaped lid, impasto, ninth–eighth century BC, San Vitale. Museo Civico Archeologico, Bologna.

of life was all-embracing, ritual pervaded everyday life, images of death took on natural guises, and women enjoyed undisputed privileges.

The people who became the historical Etruscans are recognizable in the Proto-Villanovan (12th–10th century BC) and Villanovan (ninth to eighth century BC) archaeological cultures. They found self-expression in the production of bronzes by specialized craftsmen and handmade pots that were incised and impressed with complex geometric patterns. Some also had tiny figures of humans and animals on handles, rims, and lids. They exploited extensive iron, copper, and lead deposits in Etruria to form the foundations of a thriving economy. Trading contacts with the eastern Mediterranean began in the late ninth century and were soon enhanced by the establishment of Greek and Phoenician trading stations in southern Italy, Sicily, and Sardinia. The local Italian groups adopted

new techniques, such as wheel-throwing and painting pottery, and precious metal-working techniques. The elites who controlled trade were increasingly interested in acquiring exotic luxury items and in adopting eastern aristocratic behavior such as wine drinking and banqueting as indicators of rank. From the seventh century, the Etruscans promoted representational art, drawing on eastern Mediterranean models. Etruscan potters became specialized, producing their own versions of Greek figured pottery (Corinthian, Black-, and Red-Figure), and also inventing the elegant black pottery known as *bucchero* (c.670BC), and soon traded across the Mediterranean. From early times, the Etruscans were skilled seafarers, and for centuries dominated the Tyrrhenian sea. The new skills were introduced partly by foreign craftsmen. Greeks living in western Turkey were driven out by the Persians in the sixth and early fifth centuries BC, and many of them settled in the west. Etruscan art at this time was especially influenced by the Ionian Greek art, and it is

THE HUMAN CONDITION

These elongated votive figures may be male or female, children or adults, nude or clothed, with arms at their sides or with one forearm extended in a gesture of offering. One figure of a naked boy stands one and a half feet (half a meter) high. The face, toes, fingers, genitals, navel, and buttocks are naturalistically modeled, drawing ultimately on Greek art. The spectral elongation of the large figure shown – referred to by one romantic author as "The Evening Shadow" – came out of a very different artistic and cultural tradition rooted in popular Italic and Etruscan cult. This tradition continued to produce wooden ex-votos of boardlike form and simple stylized figures in sheet and cast bronze with nonclassical proportions throughout the first millennium BC. The figures have attracted much attention by their strange form and powerful presence. The similarly elongated figures by the 20th-century Italian sculptor Giacometti suggest a direct influence, although they are differently modeled.

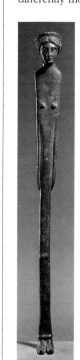

Votive figure, bronze, Sanctuary of Diana Nemorensis, Nemi. Musée du Louvre, Paris.

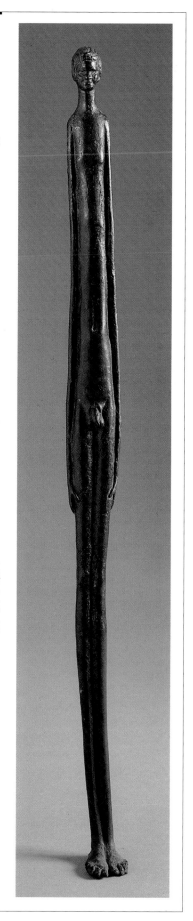

Votive figure, bronze, second–first century BC, from Volterra. Museo Etrusco Guarnacci, Volterra, Italy.

ANONYMOUS MASTER "DANCING COUPLE"

Circa 520BC; detail of a wall-painting from the Tomb of the Lionesses, Monterozzi necropolis, Tarquinia, Italy.

Tomb paintings were rare and the privilege of an elite few in Etruscan society. Only a section of the society was buried in chamber tombs, and only one or two percent of these tombs was decorated with paintings. A recurrent theme is that of the banquet, in which couples recline on couches and are attended by servants, dancers, and musicians. This detail comes from the back wall of the Tomb of the Lionesses, which has a pair of lionesses in the gable space, a high dado of dolphins and birds above a dark sea, and a decorative upper border of lotus and palmette. Between the gable and the dado is the main scene of dancers and musicians flanking a great bronze krater – a vessel used for mixing wine and water. Along the side walls, four men recline against cushions. The scenes are divided by slender columns, and banqueting and funeral garlands are painted as if hanging from iron nails.

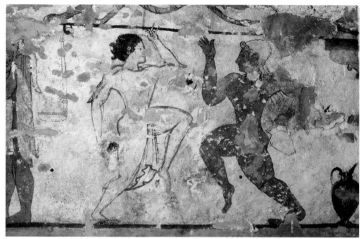

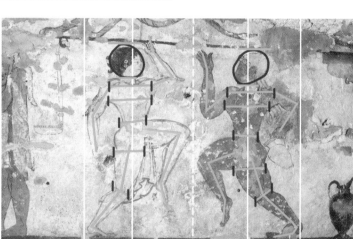

▶ *3. In preparation for painting, a lime plaster was applied to the smoothed rock surface. In the damp underground conditions of these tombs, the plaster often never completely dries – one reason for the wonderful freshness of color after 2,500 years. Dry plaster will not fuse with paint, and so plaster can be applied above ground only to the area an artist can paint in one day. However in Etruscan tombs the artist could approach the wall as a single canvas. Cartoons were not used; instead, the main lines of the composition were incised or sketched on the plaster, with some minor elements added freehand. The combination of the rich, vivid colors and the pale creamy background is very striking.*

▼ *1. The bodies of the dancers, particularly that of the man, are short in stature and rather heavy, but their movements appear supple and lively. The two figures mirror each other: their bent and extended arms and legs occupy complementary positions. They are also painted in contrasting colors, as was the convention, the female figure with pale skin and the male with red. The curving main lines and the fresh colors express the energy and vitality of an impetuous dance. This enthusiasm is characteristic of the festive and joyous atmosphere of these Archaic Etruscan tomb paintings. Despite the inherent grief and fear of death, the accent was on rejoicing in honor of the dead, on sumptuous feasting, dances, and gymnastic games.*

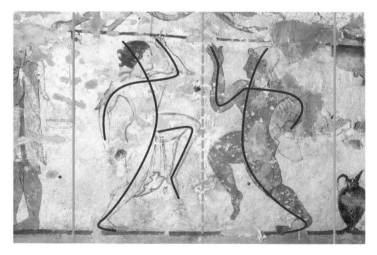

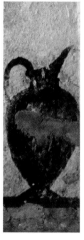 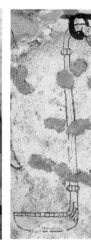

▲ *2. The two figures are arranged inside a square, the middle line of which passes between their two bent knees. They have slightly different proportions: the woman is slimmer, which, together with the color and delicacy of her clothing, conveys a sense of grace and lightness in comparison with the more robust male figure. These are muscular, youthful bodies of trained dancers and athletes and are typical of the body type portrayed in contemporary Greek art. Formal conventions for depicting the body were drawn largely from Archaic Greece, which, in turn, drew on the great tradition of Egyptian figurative art. The feet, legs, and heads are shown from the side, while the shoulders and torso are seen from the front.*

likely that Ionian craftsmen and artists came to work in Etruscan cities: Cerveteri was the home of the Master of the Hydriae (water vases) and the Micali Painter, and Tarquinia has a concentration of fine tomb paintings depicting banquets, funeral dances, and games.

At Veii, the sculptors of the fine terracottas decorating the roof of the Portonaccio Temple (510–490BC) worked in the Ionic tradition, but the final products are nonetheless distinctively Etruscan. Most striking are the full-size painted terracotta statues of Apollo and Herakles confronting each other over a hind, watched by Hermes and Apollo's mother Leto. These powerfully modeled figures stood on the roof ridge and, with the other figured and floral terracottas protecting the eaves, would have made a great display. Contact with the merchants of Aegina (510BC) and relations with Magna Graecia and Sicily followed. The maritime supremacy gained by Syracuse after the Greeks won the battle of Cumae (474BC) interrupted the importation of Greek goods

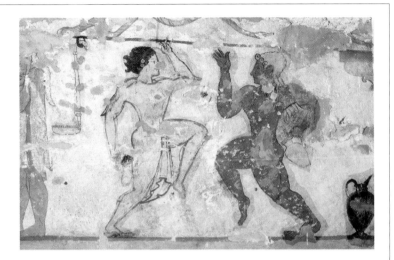

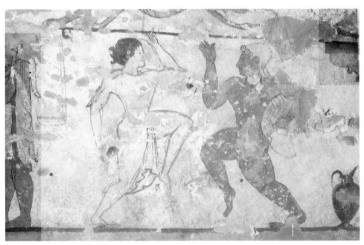

give expression to Attic forms and decorative styles in the great temples of the late fifth century BC. Local bronze-workers made the almost life-size statue of Mars (400BC), found at Todi, for an Umbrian client, displaying skillful artistic license compared with the classical Greek tradition.

The fifth century BC also saw conflict with the growing power of Rome. The great city of Veii finally fell in 396BC, and some other cities remained independent only via treaties and alliances with Rome. Conflict with the Greeks of Magna Graecia continued: for example, the Syracusans sacked the port of Pyrgi and captured Caere. In Etruscan tomb painting the banquet scene was often now set in Hades and accompanied by demons and spirits of the underworld, producing a more somber vision of death.

Temple terracottas continued to be important. At Falerii, which remained the bulwark of the

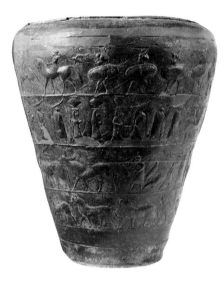

Bronze situla *from Bologna, Certosa. Museo Civico Archeologico, Bologna.*

Etruscan area after Tarquinia's war with Rome (358–335BC), the Temple of Lo Scasato I, dedicated to Apollo, has fine sculptures in the pediment zone, including one of Apollo leaping into his chariot. Artists from Volsinii may have worked

◀ *4. Attention to detail is demonstrated in the fine drapery of the woman's dress, her earrings, and the* crotali *(castanets) she holds. Also precisely drawn is the metal wine strainer or ladle hanging by a ring, with the handle terminating in a bird's head and the stem and lip elaborated with embossed decoration. The elegant* oinochoe *(wine jug) on the floor has a slender spout, perfectly shaped body, and narrow foot. The Etruscan wine-drinking equipment depicted in this tomb is closely observed from life, as examples found in Etruscan tombs and elsewhere testify. Along with other Etruscan household bronzes, these were admired in antiquity and sought after in the Mediterranean and also in Celtic lands.*

▲ *5. The decoration of Etruscan tombs as if they were houses is a common feature: the Tomb of the Reliefs has details in stone and painted stucco, and other tombs at Cerveteri have furniture and architectural details carved from the bedrock. In the Archaic tomb paintings, the gable spaces are painted with a midpost flanked by opposing figures – in the case of this tomb the back leg and tail of a lioness can be seen above the figures. The junction between the walls and roof is always marked, generally by a group of colored bands, which might refer to a wooden beam supporting the roof. In the Tomb of the Lionesses, this junction is only a single, narrow black line which, together with the thin columns, might suggest a lighter structure such as a tent.*

into the ports of Etruria. Gradually, some trade was rerouted via the Adriatic and the Etruscan site of Spina on the Po delta. The northern inland cities such as Clusium (Chiusi) and Arretium (Arezzo) continued to thrive, and industries developed from the import of ceramics

from Athens via Spina (450–440BC). The new Greek classical style is clearly reflected in the tradition of stone sculpture at Chiusi, especially in the fine limestone *stelae* with scenes of banqueting and funeral games. The sculptors of Volsinii (Orvieto) used terracotta to

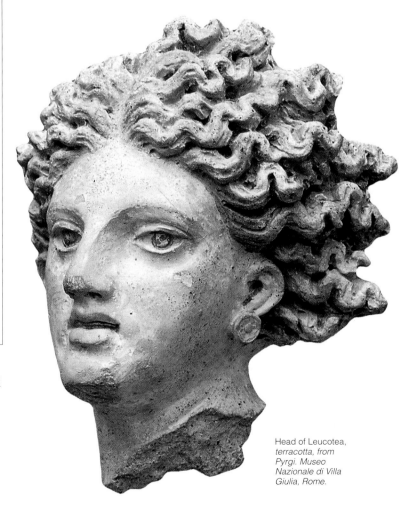

Head of Leucotea, *terracotta, from Pyrgi. Museo Nazionale di Villa Giulia, Rome.*

At a time when a classicizing style was current in Greece (323–301BC) and Greek influence was uppermost, the character of Etruscan art contrasted ever more strongly in its content. The limestone sarcophagus of the Amazons at Tarquinia (c.320BC) has a finely painted scene of Greeks fighting Amazons. The grimaces on the warriors' faces and the shape of some of the helmets recall the south Italian pottery by the Darius Painter. Like the murals of the Greek porticoes, the scenes are framed by pilasters and architraves, but the architectural design is local. The Amazons' victory over the Greeks is an Etruscan theme, symbolizing hostility toward the Greek colonies in southern Italy and Sicily. Non-Greek features are the nudity of one of the combatants, the red footwear, and the decorative collars on some of the horses. Etruscan autonomy is also evident in the *Amazonomachia* painted on the sarcophagus of the Priest, where the figure of a Lasa, an Etruscan death companion, appears with the fallen warriors.

Detail from the sarcophagus of the Amazons, painted limestone, Tarquinia. Museo Archeologico, Florence.

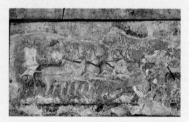

THE ETRUSCAN HOUSE

References to the house are common in the shape and decoration of tombs belonging to leading Etruscan families. The Tomb of the Reliefs (late fourth century BC) at Cerveteri is a rock-cut underground chamber, with 13 niches for burials and more marked in the floor, and a pair of supporting pillars. It belonged to the aristocratic Matuna family and is unique in being decorated with realistically modeled and painted stuccos of armor and weapons; household, prestige, and cult objects; and real and fantastic creatures. Actual examples of many of these objects are known from contemporary tombs and cult deposits. On the left pillar (right) are a *lituus* (ceremonial horn), two staffs, a leather belt, a wine jug, a wine cup with leaf decoration, a baton, an ax, a large knife, coiled rope, a piece of folding furniture (possibly a crib), a bag, a goose, and a beech-marten (probably a household pet). The main burial niche (below) is carved to represent a *kline* (banquet couch). Underneath are a low footstool and two figures from the underworld:

Details of the Tomb of the Reliefs at Cerveteri, Italy.

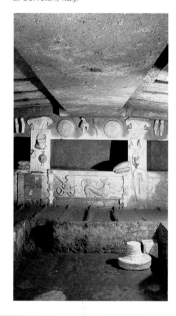

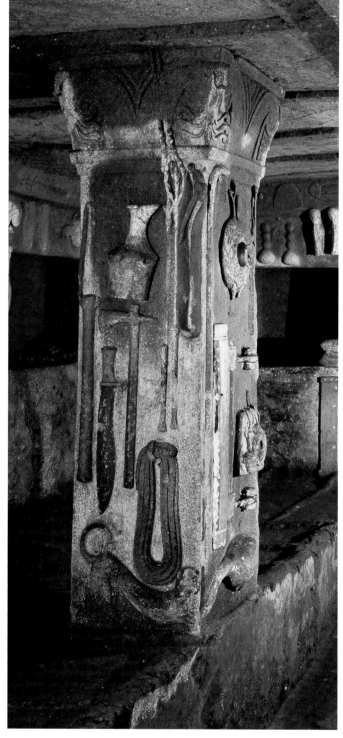

in Tarquinia on the "Ara della Regina" temple. Remaining from the pediment is a pair of splendidly modeled winged horses pawing the ground as if about to take flight. Also important are the terracottas of Temple A at Pyrgi, with late classical features again in an Etruscan formulation.
Etruscan bronzes – especially votive figures and household items, such as mirrors, candelabras, and incense burners – were famed in antiquity. Also important was the production of sarcophagi and ash chests in terracotta and stone from the sixth to the first centuries BC, with varied local traditions and specialties. For example, in the later period, the northern city of Volterra produced chests in local alabaster with complex high-relief scenes from myth and history on the front.

the three-headed dog Cerberus and the Scylla, who is half man and half serpent. A frieze of weapons and armor runs along the top of the wall. The pilasters bear two busts (now faceless), possibly of underworld deities, and objects expressing the elite status of the family: the woman's fan, a staff, and the wine cup and jug used in aristocratic banquets. The wood and ivory chest is of the type used for household papers or linen and has two folded cloths on top.

ROME – FROM MONARCHY TO REPUBLIC

In order to understand the art of a particular place, it is necessary to look at the artistic output of its earliest period. Rome seems to have begun life as a series of Iron Age villages of huts on the Palatine Hill and elsewhere (ninth century BC). The great Roman Empire had its roots in a society of warrior-farmers

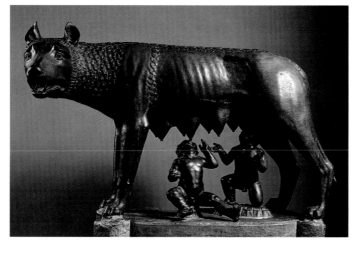

The Capitoline Wolf, *bronze, c.500–480BC. Museo del Palazzo dei Conservatori, Rome.*

who furnished their tombs with personal ornaments and weapons signifying social role and rank. Where the Tiber island formed a convenient river crossing, an important port on the left bank grew up (beside the later *Forum Boarium,* or cattle market). Out of the cultural mixing of goods and ideas arriving in Rome over the following centuries, an independent art style gradually emerged. A familiarity with Greek art helped determine choice, and from early on Rome shared many aspects of artistic production with Etruria and Campania. From the time of Tarquinius Priscus to that of Tarquinius Superbus (616–509BC), Rome was ruled by an Etruscan dynasty. Direct inspiration also came from the colonies of southern Italy and Sicily.

TEMPLES

Temple architecture in Italy developed differently from that in the Greek world. The Roman architect Vitruvius, writing at the time of Augustus, described what he called the Tuscan temple type, and many of the features characteristic of Etruscan temples also occur in their Roman counterparts. There is a high *podium* (platform); the columns could be widely spaced because the architraves were of wood; and the *pronaos* (front porch) was as deep as the *cella* (enclosed chamber). In the Temple of Capitoline Jupiter, the division into three *cellae* repeated the Etruscan tradition, as did the sculptures decorating the roof, which tradition holds were executed by Vulca, a sculptor of the Etruscan city of Veii. Begun by the kings, it was finished under the new Republic (est. 509BC). In 494BC, artists from Sicily came to work on the Temple of Ceres Liber and Libera. The Temple of Portunus shows how the Greek Ionic *peripteros* (with columns on all sides) was adapted to Roman taste, emphasizing the front: the columns of the *pronaos* continue along the *cella* walls in the form of *pseudoperipteros* (half-columns) attached to the wall.

Temple of Portunus, Rome, first century BC.

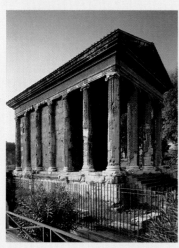

ARCHITECTURE AND LANDSCAPE

Macedonia had a significant influence on Roman wall-painting. One house at Amphipolis has frescoes of both the First and Second Pompeiian styles of wall-painting. The pavilion of the tomb of Lyson and Callicles at Lefkadia is a masterpiece of bold architectural illusion. The Macedonian painter Heraclides, who moved to Athens after the defeat of King Perseus at Pydna (168BC), was one of many

Landscapes of the Odyssey: Ulysses in the Land of the Lestrygonians, *fresco, 50–40BC, the Esquiline, Rome. Biblioteca Vaticana, Vatican City.*

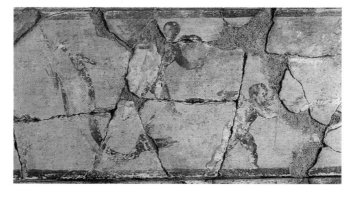

artists to introduce Hellenistic traditions to the Romanized Western world. Iaias of Cysicum, who migrated from Pergamum when the kingdom collapsed in 133BC, became a successful portrait painter. A marine fresco with cupids survives in a house

Marine fresco with cupids. Archaeological Museum, Rhodes.

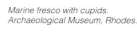

on Rhodes. The figures, against a pale background, were first traced in gray outline and their forms then modeled with shadows and touches of light. This technique was also used in the *Landscapes of the Odyssey* fresco series in a house on the Esquiline in Rome, but with reddish brown outlines. The frescoes were inspired by a cycle of Rhodian panels, from a period when the island's sculptors were reproducing bronze groups showing the adventures of Ulysses for Roman commissions. In the painting, the hero and his crew appear as tiny figures acting on the world's stage. In a metaphor of life, the Odyssey is enacted amid perilous seas, towering rocks, and shadows from the afterlife.

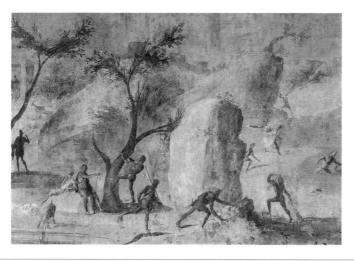

The Roman Republic was created after the expulsion of the Tarquinian dynasty in 509BC. At the outset, sculptors made statues in bronze, such as the cult figure of the goddess Diana in Aricia. *The Capitoline Wolf* (c.500–480BC) – which has long been interpreted as the she-wolf who suckled Romulus, the mythical founder of Rome, and his twin

Remus – is similar in style and quality to the great Etruscan bronzes like the *Chimaera of Arezzo* but may also have been produced in Rome. The twins were added in the 15th century AD. Aristocratic laws against excessive public spending and private luxury led to a decline in artistic production. From 366BC, plebeians were eligible for the consulship. The

peaceful resolution of plebeian conflict with the patricians (339BC), in fact, consolidated the domination of the wealthy, regardless of family background. The economic influence of the eastern world, as experienced during the period of Alexander the Great (334–323BC), helped expand the internal economy, and in Rome, as elsewhere, art was

commissioned as a sign of social status. Classicizing (323–301BC) and Hellenistic Baroque styles characterized the revival of architectural and votive decoration terracottas. Trade and war brought fine artworks to Rome. The conquest of Syracuse (212BC), when the Romans removed a number of pictures, statues, and decorative objects from

GREEK SCULPTORS AND ROMAN CLIENTS

The Roman generals who led the armies of conquest in the eastern Mediterranean from 200 to 60BC were quick to adopt the Greek art of sculpture, especially individual portraiture. Many commissioned statues of themselves in bronze and marble from the best Greek sculptors of the day, shipping the results back to be displayed

in Rome. In style and technique, the Roman portraits closely resemble those of contemporary Hellenistic kings, with powerfully modeled features of heroic cast, but they do not wear royal diadems and often sport the short beard of the campaigning soldier. In time, by force or of their own accord, many Greek artists moved to Rome, importing the marble from their homelands. Throughout the later Roman Empire, Greece and the Greek East continued to supply much of the marble and most of the craftsmen employed in the West.

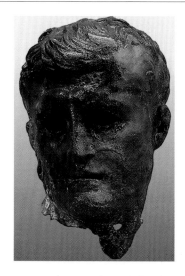

In about 50BC, major new marble quarries were opened in Italy (Carrara), which greatly increased supplies. However, the last two centuries BC saw many statues made from several smaller blocks joined together, in lieu of a single block sufficiently large to carve a work in one piece. For example, the statue of a general found at Tivoli, dating from about 70BC, was constructed from at least seven separate

Roman general with beard, bronze, by an Asiatic artist, from the Punta del Serrone off the Brindisi coast. Museo Archeologico Provinciale F. Ribezzo, Brindisi.

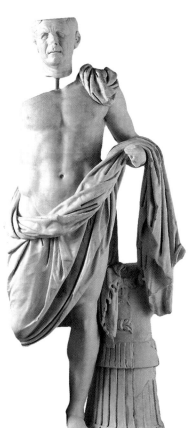

The Tivoli General, marble, by a Greek sculptor, Sanctuary of Hercules Victor at Tivoli. Museo Nazionale Romano, Rome.

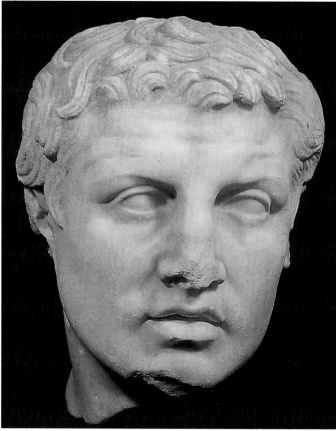

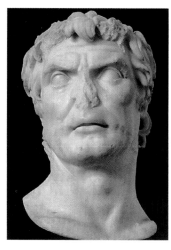

Roman general, marble, Rome. Glyptothek, Munich.

pieces. His face is highly individual in the Roman manner, while the body is an ideal type taken from the earlier Greek repertoire, partially draped in a military cloak to suit Roman tastes.

Roman general, marble, Apollonia. Archaeological Museum, Tiranë, Albania.

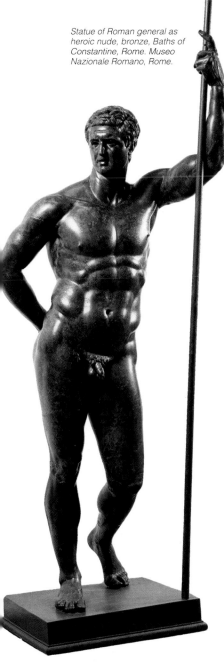

Statue of Roman general as heroic nude, bronze, Baths of Constantine, Rome. Museo Nazionale Romano, Rome.

at will and the chance to see them in a new setting stimulated a fresh approach to figurative art. From the subject matter and styles of another people came a new form of artistic production. The images served to venerate both the traditional gods and those taken over from the Mediterranean pantheon. They portrayed private individuals as votives in sanctuaries; they also celebrated triumphant generals to describe their exploits and to commemorate the dead.

THE LATE REPUBLIC

After the second Macedonian war (200–197BC), more importance was given to the notion of *otium* (private leisure) as opposed to *negotium* (public service). Greater interest was shown in beautiful objects for everyday use and in wall

the city, brought about another unforseeable and definitive change in attitude toward Greek art forms. Imports included masterpieces of art from various periods. These were displayed in temples, porticoes, and private homes, regardless of their original provenance and purpose. They were all brought together at the whim of the conquerors as booty, expressions of aristocratic taste, and symbols of public benefaction. Distancing works from their source in this way meant that their original meanings could be manipulated

paintings for home decoration, exemplifying the taste for refinement and luxury, against which Cato the Censor (Marcius Porcius Cato, died 149BC) had raged in vain. During the period of the Late Republic (100–31BC), complete Roman control of the Mediterranean stimulated a flourishing trade in luxury merchandise. Whether at work in their lands of origin or as immigrants to the city of Rome, artists from Attica, Asia, and Rhodes turned out faithful marble copies of the famous bronzes of classical (Neo-Attic) or Baroque (Neo-Hellenistic) art. To satisfy the growing fashion for furnishings, they produced statues in smaller forms such as *herms* (bust-bearing pillars with four sides) and a wide range of decorative objects, which included large stone vases. Private collections often reflected the interests of

POMPEY

After the Social War (89BC), current political events in Rome were reflected in its portraiture. Replicas exist of the statue that the general and statesman Pompey installed at the height of his power in the room where the Senate met. The sculptor carefully modeled his forelocks in a manner reminiscent of the styles of Alexander and Aemilius Paulus, and reproduced his caring expression. The work reflected Pompey's dual nature – aristocrat and demagogue. The plump cheeks, soft lines around the mouth, nearsighted eyes, and raised eyebrows that wrinkle the forehead: all are captured in an expression that suggests both the reserve of the high-ranking diplomat and the charisma of a man who was the idol of the people. (Compared with the harsh Sulla, in whose service he had begun his career, the affable young Pompey had completely won

over the ordinary citizens.) This image of Pompey was the enigmatic witness to the killing of his great rival, Julius Caesar (44BC). The dictator was stabbed to death at the foot of the statue, which had been re-erected after the inconstant populace had pulled it down. Pompey himself had been stabbed to death in 48BC, having fled to Egypt after being defeated in battle by Pharsalus.

Portrait head of Pompey, Licinii Tomb, Rome. Ny Carlsberg Glyptotek, Copenhagen.

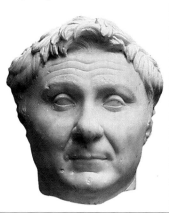

PASITELES

The great Greek-Italian sculptor Pasiteles, born in southern Italy, grew up during the civil wars – an age when military commanders were noted for their revolutionary ideas. Cosmopolitan and adventurous, he wrote a five-volume book on "the famous works throughout the world," which in terms of history and criticism was as significant a landmark for its age as Winckelmann's *History of Ancient Art* was for the 18th century. For the first time, the Greek artworks in Rome were listed with locations and descriptions. This was an immense museum, which contemporary and later artists could use freely for reference and imitation, expanding upon the past in their choice of models, the novel ways in which they were combined, and technical virtuosity. It was the theoretical equivalent of the Roman scholar Varro's approach to language. Attic purity was the sign of an excessively bigoted code of ethics, whereas Asiatic license reflected moral laxity. The path indicated by Pasiteles exemplified the balanced outlook of the Roman citizen. Varro adopted the same principle in the encyclopedic classification that would later serve to revive learning and custom under Caesar and Augustus. Pasiteles became a Roman citizen in 89BC and made a significant contribution to a nation just emerging from civil war. The example he gave the city was not derived from Athens or the East but from the Greek colonies of Italy, which for centuries had nourished Roman culture. A technical innovator, he perpetuated the figurative art of the Greek world in his sculpture and metalwork and founded a school that in its copies of classical masterpieces formed a new chapter in the history of Italian and European art.

the owner, and among the prized contents of villas were busts of philosophers, orators, military leaders, and athletes. The galleries of famous Greeks were counterparts to the family portraits found in traditional Roman houses. Pride of place went to the *maiores*, the ancestors who represented the highest moral virtues and guaranteed continuity, meriting emulation and personifying (like the philosophers) the wisdom of the past. Ancestors explained names and gave meaning to the cults and activities of the family. The family tree represented an archive of likenesses whereby the legitimacy of descendants

ALEXANDRIAN MASTER
"NILE LANDSCAPE"

120–100BC; floor mosaic;
199 x 242 in (506 x 615 cm);
Museo Nazionale Archeologico,
Palestrina, Italy.

This mosaic is from the floor of the apse of a public hall, facing the forum of Praeneste (now Palestrina), and predates the setting up of the colony by Sulla in 82BC. The structure, with its wall decorations, was built at the same time as the Temple of Fortune during a period of prosperity for Praeneste brought about by the opening of the free port of Delos (166BC) and the increased presence of Italian merchants in the Aegean. The mosaic was laid with a slight depression in the center and may have been covered with a thin film of water, which would have brought out the vivid coloring. It is a unique example of such detailed representation: the scene includes a wide range of rocks and minerals, plants and animals, and depicts activities from the daily life of the people who lived on the plain and in the marshes of Alexandria.

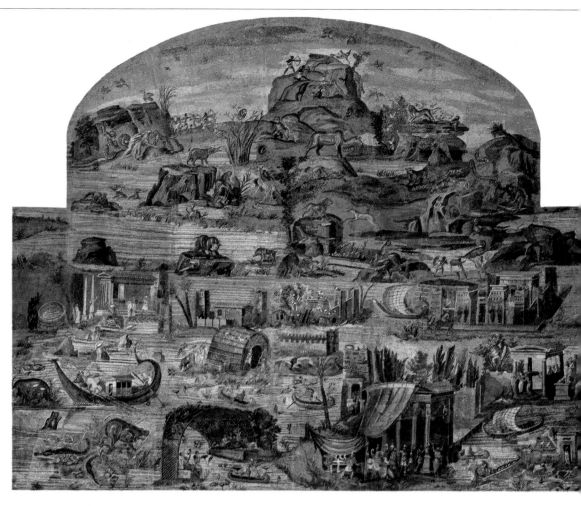

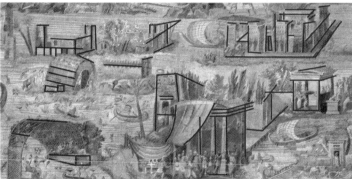

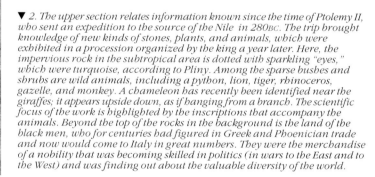

▼ *2. The upper section relates information known since the time of Ptolemy II, who sent an expedition to the source of the Nile in 280BC. The trip brought knowledge of new kinds of stones, plants, and animals, which were exhibited in a procession organized by the king a year later. Here, the impervious rock in the subtropical area is dotted with sparkling "eyes," which were turquoise, according to Pliny. Among the sparse bushes and shrubs are wild animals, including a python, lion, tiger, rhinoceros, gazelle, and monkey. A chameleon has recently been identified near the giraffes; it appears upside down, as if hanging from a branch. The scientific focus of the work is highlighted by the inscriptions that accompany the animals. Beyond the top of the rocks in the background is the land of the black men, who for centuries had figured in Greek and Phoenician trade and now would come to Italy in great numbers. They were the merchandise of a nobility that was becoming skilled in politics (in wars to the East and to the West) and was finding out about the valuable diversity of the world.*

▲ *1. The mosaic, composed of tiny, regularly-shaped pieces of colored stone (tesserae), shows the Nile at high water in a panorama that runs from the river's upper reaches to the delta. The image is accompanied by illustrated treatises on geology ("lapidaries," according to the medieval term), botany ("herbals"), and zoology ("bestiaries"). The nature of the terrain ranges from the rocky landscape at the top down to the alluvial plain in the foreground. The flora changes from dry savannah to cultivated crops, and the fauna progresses from wild beasts to domestic animals. The presence of humans becomes more pronounced as the river approaches its mouth. In a bird's eye perspective, the subjects are depicted vertically, with little overlapping, in order for as much as possible to be included. This was typical of the method used in Rome by the Alexandrian painter Demetrios (c.165BC). The individual scenes have realistic settings and colors, which change from reddish brown to ochre, from grays to a dull green, and from dark to light blue. The suffused light creates a mellow atmosphere of a river environment enlivened with points of light on the waves and most prominent forms.*

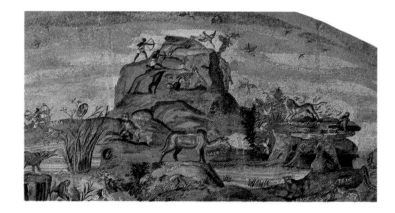

▶ *3. In this detail, between the river and the rocks around the valley, there is a flight of herons. Only the bird right at the top is original: the others were added by the restorer Giovanni Battista Calandra, master mosaicist at St. Peter's in Rome. The floor was intact when discovered in 1614 but was later damaged.*

▼ *4. The last rocks refer to the cataracts of the Nile at Aswan, where the Thebaid commences. A sailing boat travels the river while the adjacent flat, grassy land nourishes palms and other tall trees. There are huts and farms with pigeon coops and defense towers, a Greek-style votive chapel, and a temple monument in the Egyptian style. The rendering of building techniques, in rough mud bricks, stone, or marble, is well observed.*

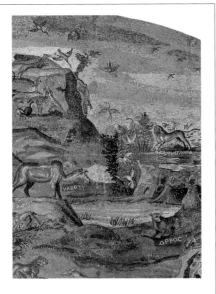

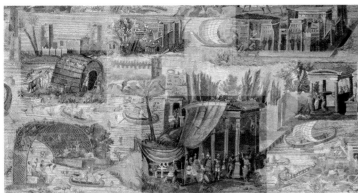

▼ *5. In the lower course of the Nile, there are lotus and papyrus plants and waterlilies. The fact that the hippopotami and the crocodiles (familiar to the Egyptians but not the Italians) are not labeled by inscriptions suggests that they the mosaic corresponds to an Alexandrian design. A large variety of vessels sail the waves. Alexandria is marked by the royal pavilion on the right, in which a ceremony is taking place in the presence of soldiers. The Canopus is represented by the canal passing under the pergola, with a banquet in progress. On one side, there is a flutist with a double flute and, on the other, a player of a transverse flute. Great attention to detail has been paid to the trellis, drapes, festoons, and other furnishings. It is an image of life comparable to that witnessed by the Romans, when an embassy led by Scipio Africanus visited Egypt in 139BC: "...the beauty of the country, the importance of the Nile, the large number of cities, the multitude of people, the ease of defense, in sum, all the privileges of a land that can guarantee the security of a great empire." Egypt was later to guarantee provisions for Rome, and the cult of the Egyptian goddess Isis became very popular in Rome and throughout the Empire.*

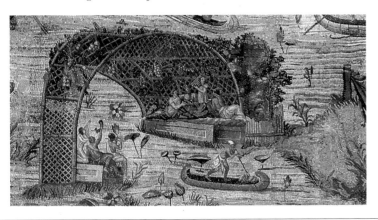

ROME'S GARDEN VILLAS

In the first century BC, the aristocracy in Rome began to develop into luxury garden villas what had previously been *horti* (vegetable plots) in the hills around the city. Dining pavilions, bath houses, and private theaters of exotic architectural design, richly ornamented with paintings, mosaics, and colored stones, were set in landscaped parks of colonnaded garden courts, artificial lakes, and fountains. The buildings were filled with niches and other specially made settings for bronze and marble statuary of great variety. The collections included older Greek works, antiques of the fifth to third centuries BC brought to Rome as war booty or later purchased on the Mediterranean art market. Some complemented the genuine antiques with close replicas made by famous Greek artists. Most, however, were new productions by contemporary sculptors adapting Late Hellenistic traditions to an increasingly discriminating Roman clientele. This statue of a maidenly Venus, goddess of fertility, beauty, and love, was found on one of the *horti* on the Esquiline hill, where it may have adorned a bath house. The goddess is shown in preparation for a bath. Beside her is a tall vase standing on a cosmetic box, over which she has draped a towel. The cobra entwined around the vase and the roses on the box are attributes associated with the Egyptian goddess Isis, whom Romans identified with Venus. Carved in translucent white marble from the Greek island of Paros, the brilliance of which is emphasized by the high polish on the flesh, the statue echoes figures of Venus' Greek equivalent Aphrodite. However, the sweet expression, small breasts, and slightly boyish figure are very much to Roman taste.

Esquiline Venus, Lamiani, Rome. Palazzo dei Conservatori, Rome.

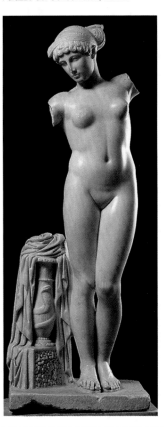

could be confirmed. In the symbolic sense, the resemblance to Alexander the Great claimed by Pompey (106–48BC) could be backed up by the long-standing exercise of military powers. In due course, wax masks based on the facial features of ancestors were carried in processions through the streets. The Greek historian Polybius wrote: "When an illustrious member of the family dies, he is carried to his funeral by men who resemble him in stature and general appearance. If the deceased was a consul or praetor, they wear a toga edged with purple, if he was a censor, they wear an all-purple toga, and if he was a triumphator, they wear a gold-bordered toga. They proceed in chariots, preceded by *fasciae*, axes, and whatever other insignia may be appropriate for magistrates, according to the status that the deceased enjoyed in life among his fellow citizens."

THE ART OF THE GREEKS

1050–900BC: production begins of proto-Geometric style pottery decorated with patterns and motifs. **c.900–800BC:** with the continued penetration of the Doric peoples into Greece, Sparta evolves from the settlement of Lacedaemon. **776BC:** the first Olympic Games are held. **c.730–700BC:** the first Greek colonies in southern Italy are founded. **624BC:** Thales, the father of Hellenic philosophy, is born in Miletus. **c.600BC:** knowledge of the *Iliad* and *Odyssey* spreads through the Hellenic world. **510–507BC:** Clisthenes gives Athens a democratic constitution. **472BC:** Aeschylus composes his tradegy, *The Persians*. **460–429BC:** Athens begins its period of greatest democracy under Perikles. **c.447–438BC:** The architect Ictinus builds the Parthenon. **431BC:** the

1200BC–700BC   700BC–500BC   500BC–400BC

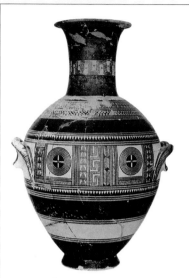

Amphora, early Geometric period.
National Archaeological Museum, Athens.

▲ GREECE

The proto-Geometric style became widespread between 1050 and 900BC: pottery was decorated with circular motifs as well as triangles, zigzags, and meanders.

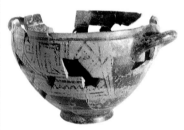

Cup of Nestor, Museum of Ischia, Italy.

▲ ISLAND OF ISCHIA

At Pythecuse, the most ancient city in Magna Graecia, the signature of a potter appears for the first time in 720BC, on a Geometric-style vase.

▼ CORINTH

The Chigi Vase is a masterpiece of the Corinthian polychrome style (c.635BC).

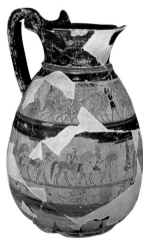

Ekphantos Painter, Chigi Vase, Veio.
Museo Nazionale di Villa Giulia,
Rome.

▼ ARISTION
(active c.550-540BC)

The sculptor Aristion is regarded as the most important figure in the school of Paros.

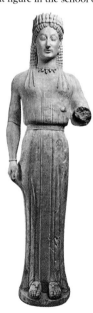

Aristion, Phrasikleia, Merenda
(Mirrhynos). National Archaeological
Museum, Athens.

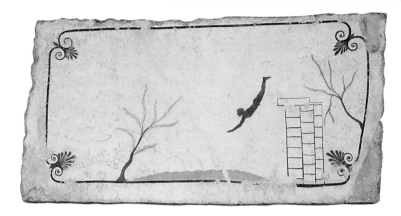

Slab from the Tomb of the Diver.
National Archaeological Museum, Paestum.

▲ PAESTUM

The paintings that decorate the Tomb of the Diver describe the rich lifestyle enjoyed by the aristocracy in Magna Graecia.

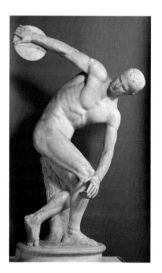

Discus Thrower, *copy after Myron.*
Museo Nazionale Romano, Rome.

▲ MYRON
(c.480-420BC)

Work by the sculptor from Eleuthera, Boetia, can be linked to the Severe style, its dynamism contrasting with the firm volumes of Calamides.

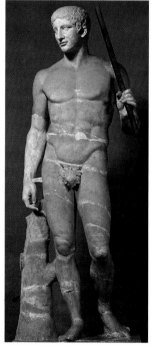

Doryphoros, *copy after Polycleitos.*
Vatican Museums, Vatican City.

▲ POLYCLEITOS
(c.480-c.420BC)

A pupil of Agelades, this sculptor from Argos created work that expressed his research into the harmony of proportion and the juxtaposition of force lines – theories he included in his famous canon.

Peloponnesian War breaks out, lasting 30 years and leading to the collapse of Athenian power. **399BC:** Socrates is tried and condemned to death. **387BC:** Plato's Academy is founded in Athens. **351BC:** Demosthenes composes the first Phillipic, an appeal to the Greek states for solidarity against the Macedonian threat. **338BC:** battle of Cheronea: the Macedonian hegemony over Greece begins. **336BC:** Alexander the Great becomes King of Macedonia. **290BC:** the Library at Alexandria is created, the first in the ancient world. **168BC:** with the defeat of Pidna, Macedonia becomes a Roman province. **c.150BC:** *Venus* is sculpted, attributed to Milo. **86BC:** Athens is occupied and sacked by the Roman army led by Scilla. **27BC:** the province of Achaea is created.

400 BC – 300 BC   300 BC – 200 BC   200 BC – 1 BC

▼ PRAXITELES
(c. 395-326BC)
The foremost exponent in Athens of the "beautiful" style, Praxiteles sought ideal beauty in figures with forms that attained perfection.

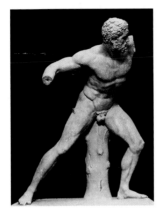

Praxiteles, Herakles Fighting, from the Esquiline. Palazzo dei Conservatori, Rome.

SKOPAS
(c. 395-325BC)
Sculptor and architect from Paros, active in Continental Greece, the Peloponnese, and Asia Minor. He concentrated mainly on expressive research, creating an intense language full of pathos.

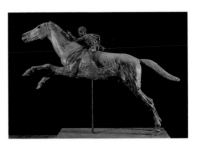

The Stag Hunt by Alexander and Hephaestion, pebble mosaic, copy after Apelles. Peristyle Houses, Pella, Greece.

▲ APELLES
(c.375-305BC)
A painter from Colophon, Apelles learned his craft at Ephesus and Scion. He is regarded as one of the greatest artists of antiquity, sadly known to us only through pottery and copies of his work.

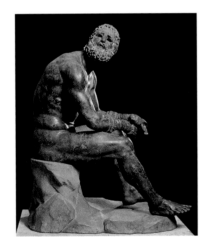

Lysippos, Boxer, bronze, from the Baths of Constantine, Rome. Museo Nazionale Romano, Rome.

▲ LYSIPPOS
(born c. 370BC)
This sculptor from Scion was favored by Alexander the Great. He substituted Polycleitos' canon for one based on the contrast between individual parts, which gave his bronzes an extraordinary charge of tension and elasticity.

▼ ATHENS
The vitality of the galloping bronze horse, ridden by a man stretching forward, epitomizes Hellenistic Baroque. It is now housed in the Archaeological Museum in Athens.

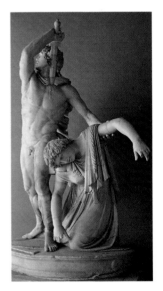

Horseman, bronze, Cape Artemision. National Archaeological Museum, Athens.

▼ PERGAMUM
The stoa of Attalus I celebrating the victory over the Galatians was decorated by many artists, including Epigonos. The leader of the Pergamum sculptors, he arranged his dying Gauls (c. 235BC) according to a spectacular conception of space.

Epigonos, Ludovisi Gaul, Roman copy. Capitoline Museum, Rome.

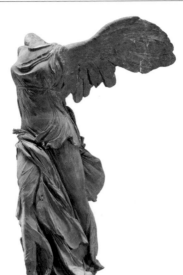

The Victory of Samothrace. Musée du Louvre, Paris.

▲ SAMOTHRACE
The chief importance of the island of Samothrace lay in the mysterious cult of its twin gods, the Cabeiri. This cult attained a wide vogue in the Hellenistic age, and a Victory was created, standing on the prow of a ship. The left wing, right breast, and square pedestal are modern.

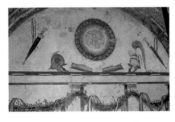

Tomb of Lison and Kallikles, lunette painted with weapons, Lefkadia, Greece.

▲ LEFKADIA
The paintings of the tomb of Lyson and Kallikles, showing the arms of the brothers killed in 197BC, create the illusion that the room is widening. Such effects are typical of Hellenistic Baroque.

ITALIC ART

1000–800BC: various local geometric styles in pottery and bronzework develop in the Early Iron Age. c.850BC: Sardinian Nuragic civilization reaches its greatest splendor. 753BC: according to legend, Romulus founds a village called Rome on the Palatine Hill. c.600BC: parts of Italy participate in Greek art styles. 540BC: after a period of dispute, the Etruscans are victorious over the Greeks in a sea battle off Corsica. 509BC: the last king of Rome, Tarquin the Proud, is ejected from Rome and the republican period begins. 474BC: after the battle of Cuma, the Greeks become dominant in the Tyrrhenian Sea. 450–400BC: large quantities of Greek Attic pottery are imported into Etruria; large-scale votive bronzes are produced in

1100 BC – 600 BC

▼ BOLOGNA

This was a major site of the Early Iron Age Villanovan cultural group, located in Etruria and the Po valley. It is notable for bronze jewelry and dark, hand-modeled pottery with impressed and incised geometric decoration.

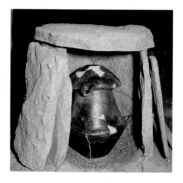

Villanovan ossuary with bowl-shaped lid, impasto, ninth–eighth century bc, San Vitale, near Bologna. Museo Civico Archeologico, Bologna.

▼ ESTE

Este was an important Venetic center for the production of *situlae*. Here, for the first time, in the Benvenuti *situla* (c.600BC), themes connected with the Homeric poems appeared.

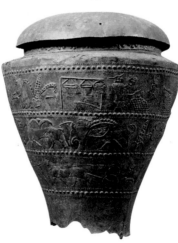

Benvenuti situla, bronze. Museo Nazionale Atestino, Este, Italy.

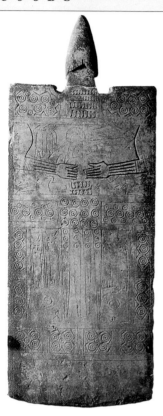

Funerary stelae of women, limestone. Museo Nazionale del Gargano, Manfredonia, Italy.

▲ GARGANO

From the seventh to the sixth century BC, *stelae* were produced in this area of southern Italy, commissioned by the Daunian dynasties to celebrate their dead. Square, monumental figures, mostly female, with tapered, narrow heads, are carved within the rectangular dimensions of the plates and subsequently decorated in light relief.

LUNIGIANA

In about the seventh or sixth century BC, statue *stelae* were produced in this coastline area (roughly between Nice and Genoa). They were still linked to megalithic sculpture, but revealed a comparatively more realistic representation of the human figure, owing to the influence of nearby northern Etruria.

600 BC – 400 BC

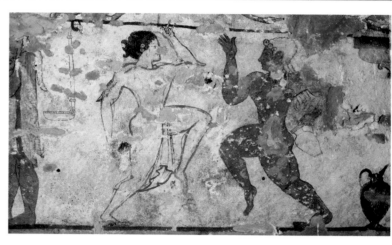

Anonymous master, Dancing Couple, detail of a wall-painting from the Tomb of the Lionesses, Monterozzi necropolis, Tarquinia, Italy, c. 520BC.

▼ CENTRAL AND SOUTHERN ITALY

In the sixth century BC, the tiled-roofing system of houses and temples, possibly derived from Greece but much developed in Italy, included modeled and painted plaques to protect the ends of the roof beams (antefixes and simas), and three-dimensional figures decorating the ridge pole and gables.

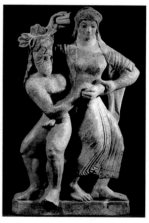

Silenus and Maenad Dancing, terracotta antefix, Satricum. Museo Nazionale di Villa Giulia, Rome.

▲ TARQUINIA

This important Etrurian center has many painted tombs that date from the sixth century BC onwards. The most famous include the tombs of the Augurs, the Jugglers, and the Lionesses. The latter, dating from about 520BC, show a lively banquet with dynamic dancers above a dado with waves, dolphins, and birds.

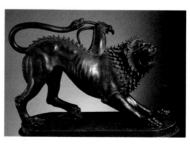

The Chimaera of Arezzo. Museo Archeologico, Florence.

▲ AREZZO

Attributed to an artist from North Etruria and dating from the late fifth century BC, the *Chimaera of Arezzo* expresses the vitality and tension that permeates the Etruscan sculpture of this period.

Etruria. **c.400BC:** the Lucanians take Posidonia (Paestum). **396BC:** Veio is destroyed by Marcus Furius Camillus; thus begins the Roman subjugation of the Etruscan world. **312BC:** the Appian Way is laid out. **290BC:** the third Samnite war ends in Roman triumph. **212BC:** Syracuse is conquered by the Romans. **133BC:** Iaia of Cyzicus comes to Italy, where she gains fame for her portrait paintings. **106BC:** birth of Marcus Tullius Cicero, orator, politician, and philosopher. **89BC:** the sculptor Pasiteles, originally from Magna Graecia and the creator of a five-volume catalogue devoted to the most beautiful statues ever made, is granted Roman citizenship. **44BC:** fear of the sovereign power of Julius Caesar prompts his assassination.

400BC–200BC

200BC–100BC

100BC–1BC

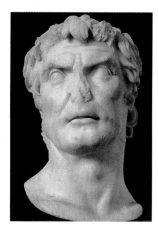

Terracotta offering figure, Lavinium. Metropolitan Museum of Art, New York.

▲ ROME

A spectacular series of statues from Latium, including Lavinium, continue the tradition of sculpting in terracotta. Although drawing on Greek models, the artists developed a distinctive local style and made figures that are both beautiful and impressive.

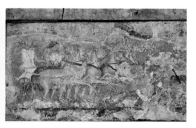

Detail from the sarcophagus of the Amazons, painted limestone, Tarquinia. Museo Archeologico, Florence.

▲ TARQUINIA

In the late classical and Hellenistic periods, Etruscan artists increasingly participated in international Greek art styles.

▼ ROME

Following the conquest of Syracuse (212BC), there was a new relationship with Hellenic art. Many works were transported to Rome and used as source material. The use of Greek forms from different periods came to be adapted within a different range of subject matter. Roman clients frequently turned to Hellenic sculptors throughout the second century BC.

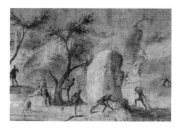

Roman general, marble, Rome. Glyptothek, Munich.

▼ PALESTRINA

The famous mosaic showing a Nile landscape, which dates from the second century BC was found at the sanctuary site of Praeneste, southeast of Rome.

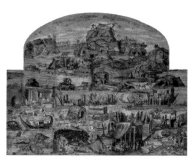

Alexandrian master, Nile Landscape, floor mosaic, 120–100BC. Museo Nazionale Archeologico, Palestrina, Italy.

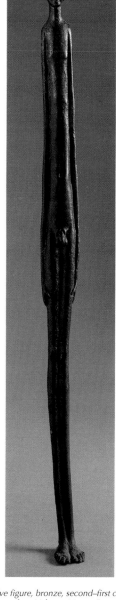

Votive figure, bronze, second–first century BC, from Volterra. Museo Etrusco Guarnacci, Volterra, Italy.

▲ VOLTERRA

Highly stylized statuettes of human figures are typical in Etruscan production. Two thousand years later, the work of Giacometti recalled their striking, elongated forms.

▼ ROME

The cycle of frescoes from the Esquiline provides some of the most important evidence of Roman landscape painting: small, brownish pink silhouettes are arranged in evocative, naturalistic settings.

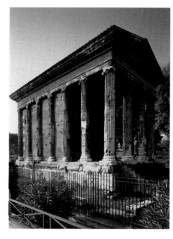

Landscapes of the Odyssey: Ulysses in the Land of the Lestrygonians, fresco, the Esquiline, Rome, 50–40BC. Biblioteca Vaticana, Vatican City.

▼ ROME

Religious Roman architecture borrowed elements of Etruscan building, including the use of a high podium and the division into three cellas (Temple of Jove Capitoline). In the Temple of Portunus, Greek elements are adapted to Roman needs: some columns are set into the wall of the cella, thus maintaining the frontal approach.

Temple of Portunus, Rome, first century BC.

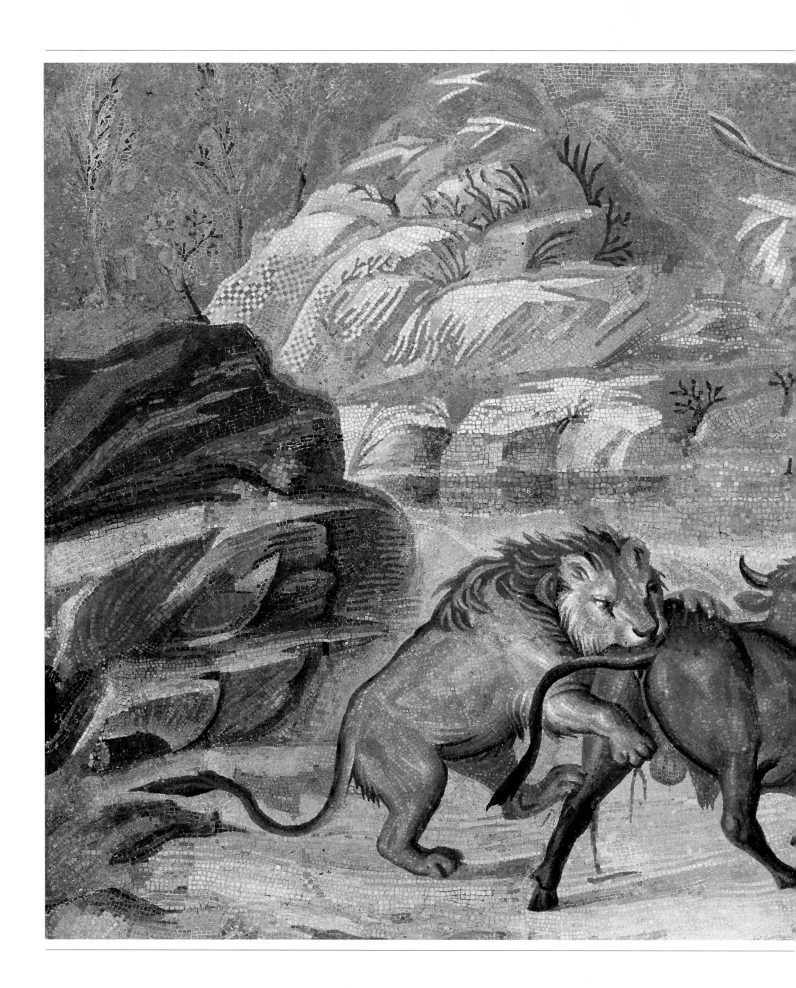

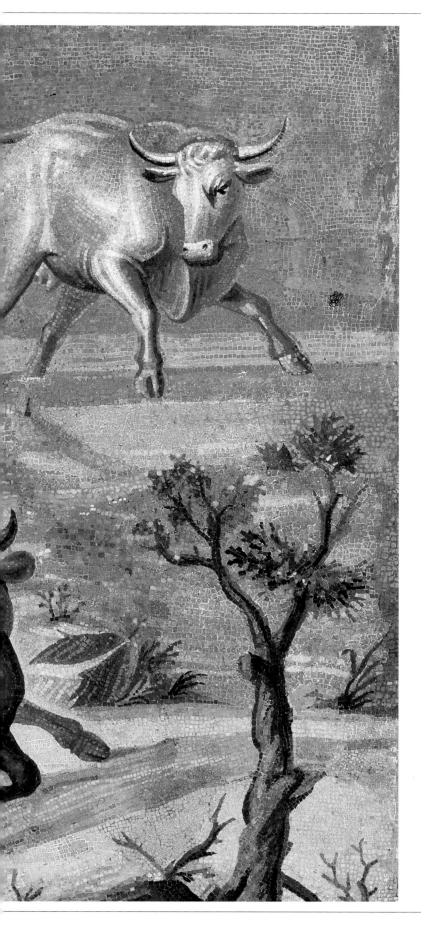

THE ANCIENT WORLD FROM THE ROMAN EMPIRE TO THE FOURTH CRUSADE

An Art for Europe, Asia, & Africa
Art of the Roman Empire

From Late Antiquity to the Romanesque
The Early Christians & their Art
Barbarian Art
Byzantine Art
From Carolingian to Romanesque Art

The Artistic Cultures of Asia & Africa
Persian & Islamic Art
The Indian Region & the Far East
Classical Art of sub-Saharan Africa

Bulls Attacked by a Lion, *mosaic.*
Museo Pio-Clementino, Vatican City.

An Art for Europe, Asia, & Africa

ART OF THE ROMAN EMPIRE

Under Augustus, arts of Hellenic tradition were adapted to proclaim the permanence and universality of Roman power. Artists and craftsmen from Alexandria, Athens, and Asia Minor flocked to the imperial court to create models that celebrated the best of all possible worlds. During the crisis years of the reign of Commodus, artists developed the independent artistic language that led to the remarkable works of late antiquity.

The enduring image of Rome represents one of mankind's greatest collective achievements. Reflected in imperial art from the accession of the first Roman emperor, Octavian (31BC), to the deposition of the last, Romulus Augustus (AD476), it was continued by the Byzantine dynasties ("emperors of the Romans" until 1453) and revived at intervals in the medieval and modern Western world. During the reign of Augustus (31BC–AD14), imperial art – whether in the context of public celebration or in the form of portraits of the sovereign – was promoted at every social and economic level and exported to the most distant regions of the empire. This mood of ideological fervor permeated the art of the entire imperial era.

AN EMPIRE OF SYMBOLS

Undaunted by any challenge, the Romans built arches, bridges, aqueducts, roads, walled cities, and frontier fortresses. These constructions were the conscious symbols of a mighty empire, the lasting and immutable traces of which may still be seen today from Europe and North Africa to what was once Mesopotamia.

At the heart of the continued reverence by so many generations of the ideal of the empire was the long-standing religious concern of the Romans to guarantee the survival and good fortune of their community through the scrupulous observance of divine will. Superstitious

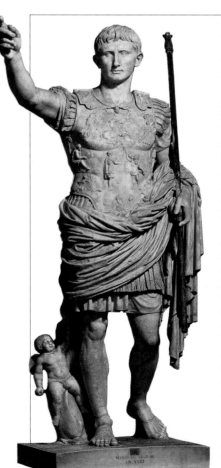

Statue of Augustus, Prima Porta, Rome. Museo Chiaramonti, Vatican City.

AUGUSTUS

Certain motifs from the Hellenistic-style imagery of Octavian remain in official portraiture created after 27BC, when he was honored with the title of Augustus. However, these Greek influences are tempered by the Roman preference for specific detail in portraiture. This is typified in the impressive marble statue of Augustus from Prima Porta, dating from after 17BC, which, although based on a classical model, has been modified in order to capture the actual features of the emperor. In Greece, among the many conventional images, there is an extraordinary bronze statue depicting Augustus on horseback with military and religious attributes. Among these can be seen the sheath of his sword and the *lituus* (a staff used for divination) of the augurs on the mount of his ring – Augustus was appointed Chief Pontiff in

12BC. His neck is long and the fringe of hair is typically forked above the brow as in the earlier portraits. The body is thin under the mantle, the face is bony, and the skull irregularly broad. An air of defiance is suggested by the prominent chin, the lips pursed by the nervous contraction of the cheeks, and the tension in the eyes. The memory of youth contrasts with the harsh truth of a man in advanced age. The principal representation of Augustus and other images of him are cast aside by the artist, who shows the disturbing truth, far removed from the image favored for propaganda purposes – the signs of an unhappy adolescence and the mental turmoil of an aging man who, behind the mask of power, never reached full maturity.

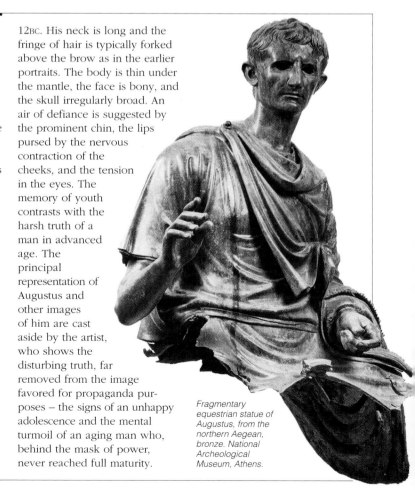

Fragmentary equestrian statue of Augustus, from the northern Aegean, bronze. National Archeological Museum, Athens.

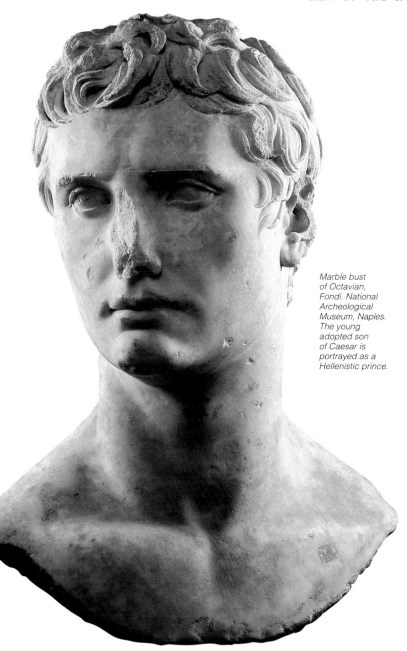

Marble bust of Octavian, Fondi. National Archeological Museum, Naples. The young adopted son of Caesar is portrayed as a Hellenistic prince.

Romans in accordance with the will of providence. In reviving the forms of worship necessary for the maintenance of the state, the leading personage of the governing class evoked the moral aspect of ancient religious zeal, adapting it to popular philosophical attitudes. The portraits of Augustus embody the heroic and the divine aspects of the "actions" (*res gestae*) of the man who performed them. Crossing the "city of marble" from the Palatine to the Capitol and the Campus Martius, one is surrounded by buildings and monuments that culminate in the Mausoleum of Augustus, where the apotheosis of the Emperor fulfilled the legend

THE HOUSE OF AUGUSTUS

Octavian, renamed Augustus in 27BC, originally lived near the Forum but later moved to the Palatine, where he bought the house that belonged to the orator Hortensius. After the victory over Sextus Pompeius (36BC), he purchased nearby buildings and had them demolished, donating the land to the state for the Temple of Apollo. On the ground floor of his house, in the western sector that was intended for private use, the decorative paintings of the so-called Room of the Masks still appear remarkably fresh and bright. The walls represent, by means of skillful illusion, the outlines of a theater stage. The structure appears superimposed on the permanent background of stone, which is enlivened by recesses and projections. The central area reproduces the painted fabric curtain covering the door to the stage, with a reference to the work being performed. On the western wall is a sacred landscape that alludes to a satirical play. The horizontal lines, which in reality come toward the foreground, converge at a vanishing point set at the eye level of anyone entering the room, in accordance with the theory of geometric perspective outlined by the Greek philosopher Democritus in *Aktinographia*. Equally rigorous rules applied to the depiction of shadows. In this "second style" decoration of the House of Augustus, perspective of what was much later termed the Brunelleschi type was generally superseded by a system of different viewpoints for the three horizontal sections (plinth, central fascia, and cornice) of the wall. In the Room of the Masks, adherence to the theoretical model is attributed to a painter from the court of Cleopatra, who followed the victorious Octavian from Alexandria (28BC).

Wall-painting of theater scene, from the Room of the Masks, House of Augustus, Rome.

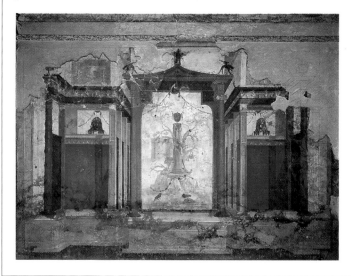

practices, threatened by the popularity in Italy of Epicurean doctrine, were modified for future centuries by Augustus, who translated them into loyal adherence to the images of the new regime. Of the mythology inherited from eastern Greece, which had caused so much embarrassment to the rationalists, a few elements were retained sufficient to trace the essential historical origins of Rome and to rechannel traditional beliefs toward the new structures of imperial rule. These included the descent of the Julians from the goddess Venus Genitrix; the role of Mars from the birth of Romulus to the avenging of the murder of Caesar; and the protection of Diana and Apollo in the battles that ended the civil wars. The task of the Chief Pontiff, charged with religious functions, was to preserve on the basis of these beliefs the "reciprocal link" (religion) with the gods rather than to expound the nature of the divinities. The past was reinterpreted as the forerunner of the history of Rome by writers such as Livy, who began with Aeneas and continued with the achievements of the

THE ARA PACIS

During the period from Sulla to Caesar (c.90–40BC), artists in Rome from the Greek cities of southern Italy and Sicily had concentrated on the revival of parts of ancient Greek culture. This trend culminated in the Ara Pacis, or Altar of the Augustan Peace, erected in 13BC to celebrate the era of prosperity and security during the rule of Augustus. The sculpture, which blends Hellenistic influence with the universal message of Periklean Athens, is an Italic-style realistic record of the consecration ceremony and was dedicated on January 30, 9BC. It shares the same formal treatment as Phidias' Panathenaic processional frieze in the Parthenon. On the northern face is a procession, perfectly ordered by family and rank, of the principal figures: priests, augurs, *lictors* (attendants), Octavian, *flamens* (priests), Agrippa, the young Caius Caesar, Livia, Tiberius, Antonia Minor and Drusus with their son Germanicus, Domitia and Domitius Ahenobarbus, and Maecenas. For many centuries to come, this composition typified dynastic propaganda. The arrangement of acanthus scrolls crowded with small animals beneath the figures brings together patrician traditions and the new order of the principate. On the eastern face of the monument, Aeneas is shown as the founding father, whose family tree is traced by the tendrils. These were the noble branches of an ancestry rooted in custom. The hypnotic rhythm of the plant spirals changes for the sudden halt of the procession at the entrance to the enclosure, enabling the participants to gather up their robes or turn around, while a cloaked figure in the background, a symbol of winter, places his finger to his lips to impose holy silence.

Relief depicting the consecration ceremony, with Augustus, members of his family, priests, and officials. Ara Pacis, Rome.

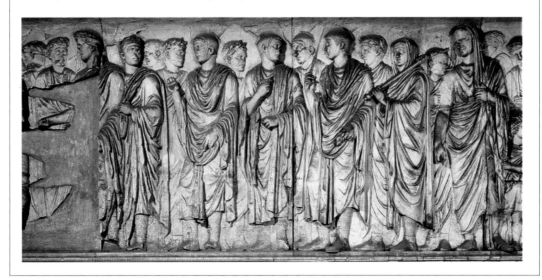

of Athenian sculptors were recruited to provide copies of the most famous originals by Greek sculptors such as Myron and Lysippos. This became the most popular way to furnish a house or villa. Some artists moved to Italy and supplied a wide range of casts, a selection of which were added to Rome's growing collections. The most famous masterpieces of the moment were copied, although it was hard to capture the poetic spirit of the original; the final result depended on the ability of the artist to imbue his copy with some of the original's vitality and energy. At Baiae, one workshop possessed the molds of dozens of famous works from Athens, from which it turned out statues and bronze herms, monuments with a square shaft bearing a bust. Many of these statues were found in the Villa of the Papyri at Herculaneum where, along

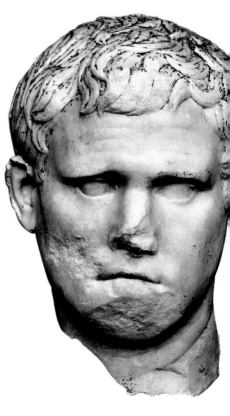

Marcus Vipsanius Agrippa (son-in-law of Augustus). Capitoline Museum, Rome. From humble origins, Agrippa became Augustus' most competent general and admiral. As aedile, he played an important role in the embellishment of Rome.

of his origins: the entrance to the mound was in line with the Pantheon, the place where Quirinus, at Rome's beginning, ascended to the skies. Virgil's *Aeneid* projects the message into the future. The Ara Pacis, the altar set up to commemorate the rule of Augustus, transmits the tidings of messianic investiture and discloses the eternity of Rome, as do the *Carmen Saeculare* (a choral lyric) of Horace and the fourth *Eclogue* of Virgil. Henceforth, no public monument would fail to reflect (in either the actions of the heroes being portrayed or in its allegorical decoration) faith in the sacred, everlasting essence of Rome.

CLASSICISM

Augustus entrusted the continuity of his ideas to forms of unquestionable beauty. Since Rome appears as the magnified projection of the predominant Greek city-state, its archetype was the Athens of Perikles. The Hellenic figurative tradition was acknowledged most of all in the decoration of civic and religious buildings in Rome. A law was even proposed (but not approved) by Agrippa, Augustus' son-in-law, whereby all original Greek works of art transferred to Italy would be exhibited in public places. Appreciation of Rome's heritage was guaranteed by classicism, which tempered the acceptance of Hellenic experiments. With craftsmen working to specific models, they were conforming to a single will, taking pride in being part of a collective enterprise, the allegorical transformation of Rome, which conferred upon Augustus the character of Supreme Being. In the official portrait of the *princeps*, to which the title of Augustus was added in 27BC, the facial features were adapted to meet the rules of classical statuary and the hairstyle made to resemble those of the heroes of Polykleitos. For the court and the citizens in outlying estates and provincial cities who were following the example of Rome, workshops

PUBLIC BATHS

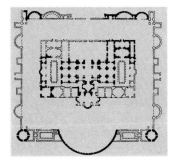

During the imperial period, the popularity of the public baths signaled a reversal of the trend of the late republican age, when privacy had prevailed. The *lavatrina*, a small room for private ablutions in houses, was replaced by communal establishments. The *balaneia*, or public baths, which originated in Sicily and Greece, offered hot water and steam baths, using a system of hot air passed through underground pipes (*hyperkausterion*). The hygiene value of this system was emphasized in the sanctuary of Epidaurus, where the original Greek system was supplemented by new structures in the Roman age. Initially, the public baths built in Rome were known as *balnea* (third century BC), and then *thermae*, still of Greek derivation (*thermos* meaning "warm"). The baths were regularly inspected for cleanliness and temperature; later, the

inspectors were called *curatores thermarum*. The Romans were inspired by the Greek combination of baths (*loutra*) with gymnasiums and soon had special areas for physical exercise. The Baths of Agrippa (19BC) were built on a monumental scale, complete with a park and a vast swimming pool.

Plan of the Baths of Diocletian, Rome. The central part of the baths now forms the Church of Santa Maria degli Angeli.

Baths of Trajan, detail of the model of ancient Rome. Museo della Civiltà Romana, Rome.

The Central Baths of Pompeii (still incomplete in AD79) were based on the precepts of Vitruvius, the military engineer and author of *De architectura*. One of Nero's architects introduced the axial and symmetrical plan (AD62), later developed by Apollodorus of Damascus in the Baths of Trajan, where a separate section was provided for cultural activities with Latin and Greek libraries and rooms (*auditoria*) for lectures and conferences. This plan became even larger in the subsequent urban complexes of Caracalla

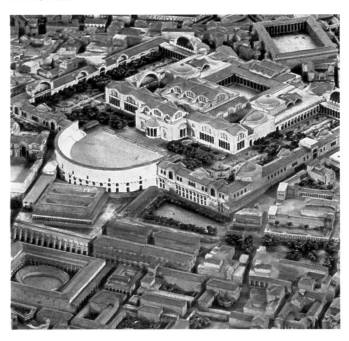

and Diocletian. As visitors followed the ritual sequence of changing room, gymnasium, *caldarium* (hot room), *tepidarium* (warm room), and *frigidarium* (cold room), they could enjoy the statuary and decoration, which included all manner of subjects: athletes, nymphs, the Bacchic dance, Venus rising from the water, and the beneficent divinities. In the words of an anonymous epigram: "Baths, wine, and love corrupt our bodies. But they are life."

Contemporary view of the Baths of Diocletian, Rome. The modern semicircular building has the same diameter as the original edifice, built between AD298 and AD306.

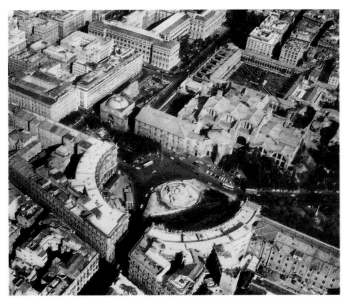

with images of the owner, the heads of philosophers stood side by side with the busts of warriors and the likenesses of heroes, such as Achilles and Pentesilea, and divinities including Minerva, Apollo, Diana, Hermes, Bacchus, and Herakles. In wall-paintings, known as the "second style" (according to the four Pompeian "styles"), architectural forms created an illusion of space, at the center of which were reproductions of Hellenistic masterpieces showing mythological scenes.

ALEXANDER AND AUGUSTUS

The dissemination of the imperial message was reminiscent of the reign of Alexander the Great (356–323BC). The conquests of Rome rivaled those of Macedon in terms of territorial gain, promising even greater stability. The link was made by the consecration of the bronze supports of the tent that Alexander had taken on his campaigns in the temple of Mars Ultor. However, it was made clear that the Roman Empire shared nothing, nor bore comparison, with any Greek monarchy: this illusion had been dispelled by Caesar. When the young Octavian visited the founder's tomb in Alexandria, he refused to look at the remains of King Ptolemy, declaring that he had come to see a king, not a corpse. Rome had subdued the kingdom of Macedonia (and all the others derived from it) in order to reassume the universal destiny of Alexander.

The long-established strategy of forming contacts was replaced by annexation, an integral form of rule in which Augustus' image was replicated everywhere, as that of Alexander had been, as the living embodiment of the all-embracing empire. Artists, with their responsibility for perpetuating heroic human faces and deeds, were part of culture and as necessary as lawyers, doctors, and state officials in safeguarding humanity. One outcome of the Roman vision was that Greco-Latin culture was made tangible and lasting in the form of monuments. Architecture, painting, and sculpture took on a role comparable in society to that attributed to Greek philosophy. Aristotle held that logic was the foundation of reason and central to all discourse, even if the conversation turned from fact to persuasion; in Roman treatises it was the practical outcome of eloquence that became the highest expression of intellectual activity. Artistic production was a "demonstrative discourse," entrusted to specialists whose task was to immortalize collective functions and ceremonies or individual services.

PUBLIC ART

The end of the class struggle and the civil war helped bring a new sense of cohesion to society. From the time of the early kings to the middle of the republican period, conflicts among patricians and plebeians had emphasized the contrast between native art and works intended for an aristocracy that was cautiously receptive of Hellenic models. Now it was difficult to isolate "plebeian" art in the historical sense of that social class. By the time of Augustus, Rome had already established an equilibrium between both factions, resulting in a more uniform structure of government. Augustus chose to revive the title of "tribune of the people," which would render inviolable his own

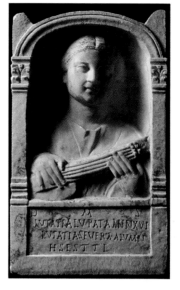

Funerary stela of Lutatia Lupata, portrayed as a lute player, first century AD, Augusta Emerita. Museo Arqueológico, Merida, Spain. The portrayal of the dead person was a privilege now extended to the middle classes.

vary in form according to the public level of cultural sophistication. The new factor, as compared with the traditional social structure of republican times, was that Rome now ruled over a cosmopolitan population such as Alexander had only dreamed of in his final years, when he encouraged Macedonian men to marry Persian women. Ever since the Hellenic age, Greeks had been amazed at the custom of the *quirites* (Roman citizens) of granting citizenship to freed slaves and of allowing the sons of such slaves access to the magistracy. The father of the family could likewise free his foreign servant to make him his equal. Every Roman could thus create new citizens, investing them with prestige and power, and helping to formulate a mass culture more complex and comprehensive than that of Alexandria. The multitudes, with their basic representative needs – votive offerings, portraits, and funerary monuments – were allotted that element of Greek culture which had already permeated Italic culture and plebeian art: socialist realism. This was not so much promoted by the people as offered to them like "bread

ANTONIA

Antonia Minor, daughter of Mark Antony and Octavia (sister of Augustus), married Drusus Minor (second son of Livia), by whom she bore Claudius. As emperor, Claudius dedicated coins inscribed "Antonia Augusta" to her after she died in AD37, their image corresponding to that of the large bust known as the *Ludovisi Juno*. The woollen band, adorned with pearls and beading that surrounds the diadem of Juno, is appropriate to her role as priestess to the Divine Augustus. Hellenic queens were often exalted in this ambiguous manner, both as priestesses and divinities. A perfect example is provided by this courtly sculpture in Neo-Attic style. Compared with models of the classical age, the effect of light and shade in the coiffure becomes more prominent here, and charming ringlets appear behind the ears and trail down the neck, alluding to the style introduced by Agrippina the Elder. The head, inclined slightly to the left, was inserted into the

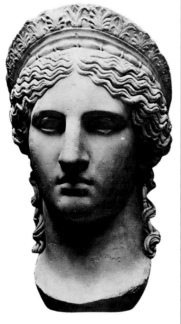

Antonia Minor. Museo Nazionale Romano, Rome (formerly Ludovisi Collection).

drapery of a colossal statue of the imperial cult. As Seneca declared in his *Apocolocynthosis* ("The Pumpkinification of Claudius," an irreverent comment on the deification of the late Emperor), "the step from the sublime to the ridiculous is a small one."

person and his right to pass laws. Restoration of internal peace after the final defeat of Mark Antony had removed the most serious threat to Roman unity. Official planning gradually yielded to private patronage, the living standards of the middle class improved, and purchasing power mushroomed. The general mood was one of harmonious celebration. Romans had always found reassurance in the purpose and content of their monuments, which tended to

Detail of a relief commemorating the Dacian Wars showing a soldier with mule loaded with booty, Trajan's Column, Rome. The natural setting of this scene is typical of Hellenistic art.

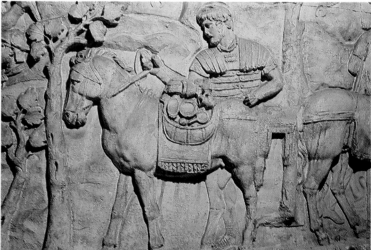

and circuses." The combination of simplicity and Greek influence can be seen in the figurative decoration of commemorative monuments, a form of public art implemented by the state. Originally, there had been the triumphal painting of the republican age on huge canvases, illustrating the actions of victorious heroes. These were much more likely to influence the collective mind than any easel painting, rather in the manner of modern-day billboards. In the celebratory relief of the imperial age, state policy still indulged the popular partiality for storytelling, combining clear narrative with spectacular rediscovered Hellenistic devices. Over time, the Roman manner of depicting history became so entrenched in the social imagination that, up until the age of medieval Christianity, it came to be seen as the only way of presentation and was almost second nature, part of the visual experience of Western civilization. No matter how Roman citizens of every extraction might differ privately in the choice of other forms of art, they were united in their positive reaction to the omnipresent propaganda of the Empire.

THE TOMBS OF THE FREEDMEN

Characteristic of the Roman world, *clientes* (or freedmen) were literally the plebeian followers of the patricians, who gave service and loyalty in return for protection. The career of a rising politician depended on the number of *clientes* he had, so maintaining them was regarded as an economic investment along with property. The freed slaves became citizens and remained followers of their *patronus* (manumitter). Even in death, they continued to enhance the patrician's prestige, with their funerary monuments that lined the roads outside the city and

inside a window: from the tomb toward life. Family members were placed close together or shown in embrace. Customs governing the public image were once again controlled by rules that had been blurred at the tempestuous conclusion of the republic. Augustus ordered the wearing of an unusually large toga as a sign of a *civis romanus*, and this style found avid acceptance among the freedmen who could thus assert the privileges they had won. Children born of a freedman after his manumission were free of all special restrictions, and the son of a freedman gained the right to join the army. Alongside representations of toga-wearing men and

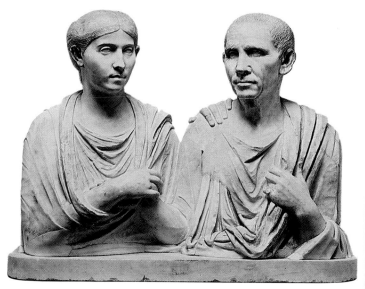

women wrapped in mantles were the citizens in arms, in the heroically naked pose of Greek derivation. The number of individuals represented (including those still living) and the size of the monument constituted a metaphor of pride and hope for the growing family. The figures vary greatly: each one has a story to tell; it is a record of the past and a model for the future.

Gratidii group, restored relief. Museo Pio-Clementino, Vatican City (formerly Mattei Collection).

For example, the gestures of the married couple in the Gratidii group tell a love story. The static representation of individual faces derives from Italic tradition, but the overall composition has elements of both classical nobility and Greek sentiment.

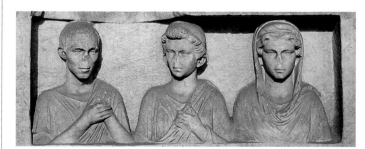

Portraits of freedmen. Museo Nazionale Romano, Rome (formerly Mattei Collection).

Rabirii group, Via Appia, Rome. Museo Nazionale Romano, Rome.

bore inscriptions proclaiming the bonds made through manumission. During the time of Augustus, Luni marble replaced travertine stone for these sculpted portraits. Cutting off the figure at the base of the chest was a legacy of the Etruscan tradition. Busts were sculpted in deep frames, as if they were facing outward from

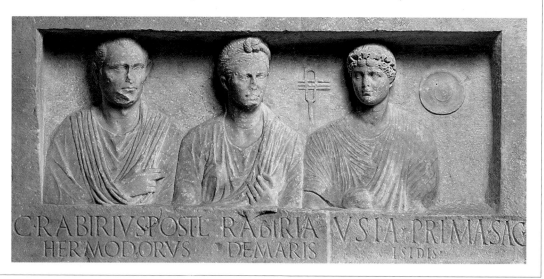

TITUS FLAVIUS VESPANIUS

From the reign of Augustus, the wearing of the toga became increasingly popular. The *balteus*, the sweep across the chest, became looser with a tuck in it (*umbo*); another fold of material (*sinus*) hung at knee level. In the marble statue of Titus (AD79–81),

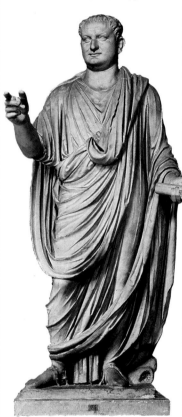

which came from the Lateran Palace, the line of the drapery runs from the right foot to the left shoulder, over which the end (*lacinia*) falls. The shadows are so dense and the folds so fine that it resembles a work in bronze. The artist has combined the emperor's coarse features with an elegance achieved through the delicate carving, which in the skillfully rendered folds reveals the pose of the body beneath. The large head is modeled with incredibly light touches. The small, rather disquieting eyes are surrounded by tiny wrinkles and framed by a square face. The smile on the prominent mouth suggests both sensuality and amiable optimism. Near the left foot lies a wasp nest; this is a reference to Titus' grandmother Vespasia Polla, who derived her name from the insect, *vespa* (wasp), and from his father's surname Vespasian. The log, inside which is a honeycomb (*favus*, another phonetic allusion to the family name Flavius), serves, therefore, not merely as a physical prop: it is his family tree.

Marble statue of Titus Flavius Vespanius, Lateran Palace, Rome. Museo Chiaramonti, Vatican City.

types of facing were used for concrete walls. Ordinary stonemasonry (*opus quadratum*) gradually gave way to walls of mass concrete in which the mixture was poured into a casing constructed with two sides of small stone blocks. The pieces were initially irregular in shape (*opus incertum*), and work proceeded slowly because they had to be held together; the concrete pieces were then made into a more standard form in the shape of small pyramids with square bases (*opus reticulatum*), which were quicker to assemble. Under Augustus, true bricks came to be used widely and were produced in vast quantities. Only a few experts were needed to supervise the large workforces engaged in extracting, refining, and mixing the clay; molding the bricks; drying and firing them in kilns; letting them stand; and eventually transporting them. The economy of the whole process, guaranteed by seals stamped on the bricks, was the monopoly of the emperor. He gave his personal blessing to finished works, using his name on the dedicatory inscription for perpetuity, as public benefactor.

Pantheon, Rome. This splendid edifice was originally constructed by Agrippa in 27BC.

THE GAZE OF ROME

The Roman mood of confidence and resolution, which proclaimed itself heir to the Hellenic tradition and asserted its authority, can also be seen in portraits of individuals. In the words of Virgil (*Aeneid*, vi. 847–53): "Others…shall hammer forth more delicately a breathing likeness out of bronze, coax living faces from the marble…. But you, Roman, must remember that you need to guide the nations by your authority, for this is to be your skill, to graft tradition into peace, to show mercy to the conquered, and to wage war until the haughty are brought low."
Whether from the faces of those who managed the system, such as the Emperor or the magistrates, or ordinary men and women, Rome's gaze follows us. Allegorical statues and portraiture depicted a distinctive Roman face wearing a proud look that in ancient Greece denoted respect for particular schools, traditions, and institutions. Rome was a veritable museum of styles, where models from any period in the past could be assembled. Public monuments and celebratory portraits combined to reflect the taste and aspirations of each imperial dynasty.

PUBLIC BUILDING

Vitruvius resorted to Greek architectural models to offer families homes that were attractive and comfortable, to provide the public with arcades and basilicas, and to dedicate to the gods temples that were both decorous and well-proportioned. During Augustus' reign, the construction of public utilities assumed an importance that had previously been unknown in Mediterranean countries. Technical advancement and the testing of original inventions were the responsibility of the town magistracies, the public works offices, and the curators or commissioners of the various areas of production. Motivated by contractors who were conscious of their civic and electoral responsibilities, architects from Asia (such as Quintus Mutius) developed the techniques that enabled works to be mass-produced, including the stone arch based on reusable wooden frames, concrete vaulting, and paved roads over uniform drainage beds. The organizational skills of the Latins were applied to a slave economy. Specialized manual work was reduced to a minimum, and unlimited scope was given to general construction work. Different

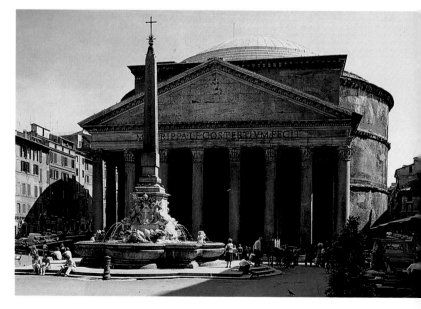

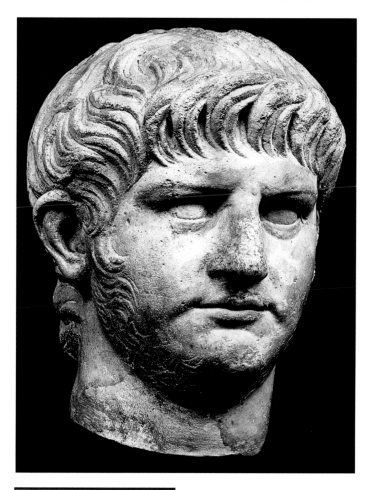

Portrait of Nero with beard inspired by Greek philosophers. Galleria degli Uffizi, Florence.

components of Roman culture. In one work, he harks back to the early foreign kings – Numa Pompilius was a Sabine, while Tarquinius Priscus was the son of the Corinthian Demaratus and an

Etruscan mother; Servius Tullius, who rose to be king, was the son of a prisoner. Portraits of Claudius echo the manner of the first heirs of Alexander in their monumentality.

From the outset, Nero (AD54–68) abandoned the simple, arid sculptural tradition of the Augustan age.

THE JULIO-CLAUDIAN DYNASTY

Portraits of the Emperor Tiberius (AD14–37), who succeeded his father-in-law, Augustus, retain the classicizing features favored by his predecessor, while those of Caligula (AD37–41) show a certain delicacy in the shading of the cheeks and the soft light in the eyes. Claudius (AD41–54), who had studied Italian and Etruscan antiquity, reflected on the

"DOMUS AUREA"

The fire that devastated Rome in the tenth year of Nero's reign (AD64) affected a large part of the emperor's *Domus Transitoria* ("temporary home"), which occupied the imperial lands of the Palatine and Esquiline hills, and from which the emperor watched the conflagration. His sumptuous new residence, the *Domus Aurea* (Golden House), was planned on a grand scale rivaling Greek or Oriental counterparts, with natural parks, country villas, and a huge network of luxurious buildings

for accommodating and entertaining guests. The plan was subsequently copied in Domitian's uncompleted villa situated in the Alban Hills and in Hadrian's Villa built at Tivoli. One of the domestic wings, buried below the Baths of Trajan, was rediscovered at the end of the 15th century. The decoration of the vaults of what

had become grottoes inspired and gave its name to the "grotesque" style that emerged during the Renaissance. The decoration was the work of Fabullus, a painter noted for the color and splendor of his gilded stuccowork. The ceilings and walls were adorned with lively mythological frescoes in the so-called "fourth style."

Plan of a residential quarter of Nero's Domus Aurea *in Rome.*

Imaginary architectural scene in a frescoe from the House of the Vettii, Pompeii.

He wears a beard modeled on the Greek philosophers, his face is soft and fleshy, and his eyes are deep-set and with shadows, suggesting a restless personality.

The so-called "fourth style" was adopted for wall-paintings such as those in the House of the Vettii at Pompeii, which predate the earthquake of AD62. The composition is still symmetrical in the theatrical tradition of the "second style," but with a wholly new type of landscaped architectural background that opens up the entire wall to the viewer. The figures, which stand out from the decorative surroundings, lend a spiritual atmosphere. The design is executed with consummate skill, the perspective is sharp, and the quality of the painting is very high. An increased depth of space creates more tension between foreground and background, while slender, entwined garlands link the colonnades with the cross-beams of the airy loggias that stand out against the clear sky. A vital element of the scene is the light, which graduates gently from the dense luminosity of the realistic still-life subjects in the foreground to the transparent shadows that soften the details of the distant landscape.

After upheavals in the economy and in Nero's dealings with the Senate (AD64), his policies took on a Hellenistic tendency: in his portraits, the beard and hair-style become curly, the cheeks plump, and the lower lip fleshy and protruding; his eyes look upward, like those of Alexander. At the entrance to the *Domus Aurea* (the Golden House, the residence built by Nero after the great fire of AD64 had destroyed much of Rome), the bronzeworker Zenodoros erected a colossal statue of Nero wearing the radiant crown of the sun. The design of the palace was faithful to Hellenistic landscape architecture.

THE FLAVIAN DYNASTY

The intermixing of Hellenic and Roman elements in imperial art is evident in the portraits of Nero's successor Vespasian (AD69–79). Those designed for private appreciation placed emphasis on past republican realism, evoking the emperor's military background, while those for public consumption show a harder face with classical features. The theories behind

HIPPOLYTUS

The myth of Hippolytus, the innocent and tragic son of Theseus, was a popular subject that frequently appeared in the decoration of funeral monuments.

In the absence of Theseus, Hippolytus' lustful stepmother, Phaedra, made advances toward him, which he rejected. She then hanged herself, leaving for her husband a letter in which she accused the prince of raping her. On Theseus' return, he banished his son and used one of three wishes given to him by Poseidon to dispose of the alleged culprit and restore the family honor. While Hippolytus was driving his

This scene from the same sarcophagus shows the departure of Hippolytus.

Rear face of the sarcophagus, illustrating Hippolytus trampled by the horses and killed by the bull of Poseidon, seen in the background with the trident.

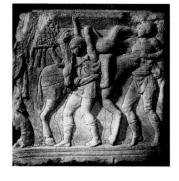

Detail showing the transportation of a dead hind from a sarcophagus depicting the myth of Hippolytus. Museo Arqueo-lógico Provincial, Tarragona, Spain.

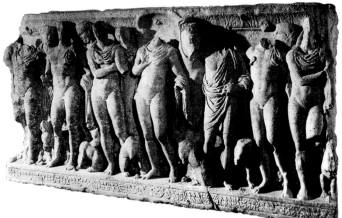

chariot along the seashore, a bull emerged from the water and terrified the horses; Hippolytus was thrown from the chariot and trampled to death by his horses. Theseus later learned the truth from Artemis. Based on a painting by Antiphilus, a sarcophagus made in Athens (c.AD230) and exported to Tarragona illustrates the whole story. The cruel climax is powerfully depicted on the rear of the tomb in a surprisingly modern style. The modeling stands out

from the background in slight relief, and the complex composition is made striking by its stark realization. The interplay of the elements of the myth – the sea personified as Thalassa startled by the bull; the foreshortened chariot; the god heedlessly dispensing justice; the messenger in the presence of Theseus – creates a choral lament for the victim and sharply reminds us of our fate.

the wall-paintings of Nero's reign found wider practical application in stucco decoration, which was ideally suited to the subtle realism of the "fourth style." In the decoration of a villa at Stabiae, incomplete at the time of the eruption of Mount Vesuvius (AD79), a portrait of Narcissus with architectural details and skillful depiction of the young man's delight at his reflection in the water reveals the artist's virtuosity. A feeling of transience pervades the work:

the foliage, the soft feathers of the cupid's wing, and the blaze of the torch. The changing quality of the light lends definition to the angles of the youth's body and the strong lines of his face and hair. The varying effects of daylight, sometimes sharp and focused, at other times diffused or flickering, as if drawn from the flow of the stucco, enliven the images, creating abstractions of light and shade that were to become the ghost of the

Detail of relief showing the victory of Titus, Arch of Titus, Rome. Here, the spoils from the Temple of Jerusalem are displayed in a triumphal procession.

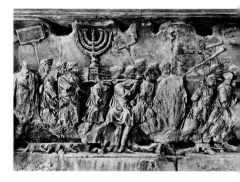

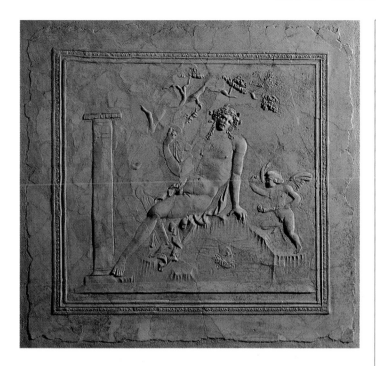

The myth of Narcissus, stucco relief, Stabiae. Antiquarium, Castellammare di Stabia, Italy.

classical form, evoked with an independence of expression that would not be seen again until the Renaissance bas-reliefs of Donatello.

On a monumental scale, the freedom of Flavian art is evident in the Arch of Titus, erected by Domitian (AD81–96) on his accession. Its purpose was to illustrate, in a symbolic sense, the victory over Judea, which had been celebrated a decade earlier by his brother Titus and their father Vespasian. On the northern panel, the figure of Titus is shown alone in his triumphal chariot, flanked by Victory who crowns him, while the horses are led by the goddess Roma. They are followed by personifications of the Senate and the Roman people. The rods and axes (known as *fasces*) carried by the *lictors* (attendants) as symbols of their authority are angled to the background, conveying the depth of the scene. The other frieze deals with documented history, specifically the episode that marked the achievement of the age. We witness the transportation of the sacred

objects looted from the Temple of Jerusalem: the seven-branched candelabrum and the Ark of the Covenant with the trumpets of Jericho; the tablets held aloft contain information about conquered cities. Whereas the procession represented on the Ara Pacis follows a straight line, in this work both scenes follow a curve, giving prominence to the central section where the sculpture juts out in relation to the bas-relief of the heads in the distance. Passion breaks through the surface in dramatic contrasts of light and shade, and the formality of the structure is overshadowed by the content, with its passionate celebration of Rome and its people. In reviving the epic ardor of Hellenism, the artist makes a deliberate display of expressionism to convey a sense of excitement and turmoil. The horses rear up in the air, and the rhythmical movements of the bearers create an atmosphere of frenzied fervor, which can still be witnessed today, in some Mediterranean countries, during Catholic processions in which sacred objects are borne. There is a strong internal structure to the composition. The chariot is the unifying element of the design and

ANTINOUS

No other classicizing tendency of the ancient or modern world was as intent on recognizing itself in archetype as the world of Hadrian (AD117–138). In expressing their personal vision of the emperor, the great Hellenic masters of the age seemed united in their adaptation of classical models to the realities of modern life. Antinous, a beautiful youth from Bithynia, was the beloved favorite of the Emperor Hadrian. When he died in Egypt in AD130, his image inspired artists to follow in the footsteps of the great Greek sculptors Calamis, Phidias, and Praxiteles, reverting to the ancient figurative tradition in order to portray contemporary power in aesthetic, philosophical, and religious terms. Perfect models were to be found in mythology, from which portraits of Antinous assumed the body and attitudes of heroes and deities. The relief carved in Rome by Antonianus of Aphrodisias is original in its elevation of the ordinary to the devine. Wearing a pine crown, like Silvanus, the god of forests and uncultivated land, Antinous

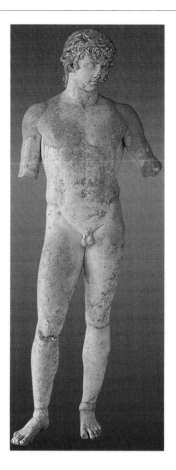

Fragmentary statue of Antinous. Archeological Museum, Delphi.

is shown as a typical forester with his short tunic and billhook. The dog standing at the side of Antinous emphasizes the funereal nature of the image of Silvanus, reinforced by analogy with Attic *stelae*. In this sacred, Alexandrian-style landscape, the grape vine alludes to Bacchus. The Greek signature of the scuptor has been placed at the side of an altar, which is surmounted by fruits from the bloodless offering. If the position of the arms is reversed, the figure of Antinous recalls the *Doryphorus* of Polykleitos, while the face reflects the sadness of a period of uncertainty: it draws on Attic dogma, while retaining contemporary reactions and feelings.

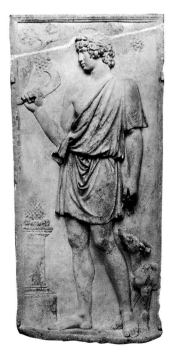

Antonianus of Aphrodisias, relief of Antinous as Silvanus, Torre del Padiglione, between ancient Lanuvium and Antium. Private Collection, Rome.

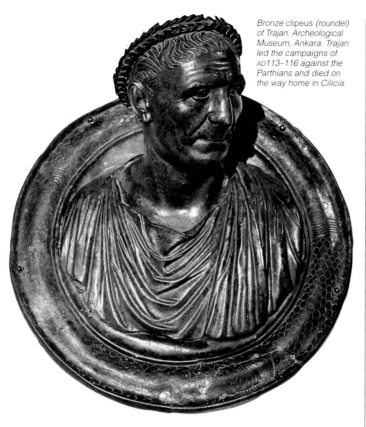

Bronze clipeus *(roundel) of Trajan. Archeological Museum, Ankara. Trajan led the campaigns of AD113–116 against the Parthians and died on the way home in Cilicia.*

ANONYMOUS MASTER: "PORTRAIT OF A MAN AND WOMAN"

First century AD; frescoe from Pompeii; 19 x 19¼ in (48 x 49 cm); National Archeological Museum, Naples.

This fragment from a composition in the "fourth style" shows the portraits of a man and woman viewed in the Etruscan-style pose. The man, with his markedly Mediterranean features, is thought by some to be the lawyer Terentius Neus. Others believe him to be an unknown magistrate dressed in his white toga and clutching a scroll, but it is widely held that he is Paquius Proculus, a baker, whose shop lay adjacent to the house containing the painting. The elevated quality of life of the couple, which we could call upper middle class, is shown in the refined dress and elegant hairstyle of the woman, who has a stylus in her right hand and a two-leafed wax tablet on which to write. According to long-standing convention, the skin of the male is tanned while that of the woman is lighter.

▶ *1. The structure of the composition is simple: the woman is placed in the foreground with the man at her shoulder. The man is foreshortened, lessening the difference in height between the two, as seen in the dancers of the Tomb of the Lionesses at Tarquirlia. The line of the scroll is continued strongly in the man's face, while those of the pen and tablet converge at the top of the woman's head. The bodies converge at the center of the picture, but the heads are turned out to face the viewer full-on. The couple are part of their family history; in their harmony, they are perfect ancestors for their descendants to use in a family tree. Like those that adorned the atria of patrician dwellings. During Nero's later reign, the emperor's despotic style of rule had rocked the security of many noble families in Italy. The middle classes, on the other hand, enjoyed a period of prosperity, reflected in the appearance of new families and dynasties. In AD64 monetary reforms brought about a reduction in the weight of silver and, more significantly, gold, to the advantage of the humbler classes. It was against this background that the portrait of the couple was painted.*

holds together the twisting mass around it, bringing the tumult of the action into a single, organic whole. The notion of an internal impetus exploding throughout the work is reminiscent of the powerful *Gigantomachia* on the Pergamum altar. By positioning a splendid group of animals in the center of the work, the artist again conveys the message of a triumphant, immutable destiny.

The few images of Domitian that survived the destruction of the statues decreed by the Senate's *damnatio memoriae* after his assassination symbolize, in their variety, the entire imperial experiment, derived from a mixture of the realism imposed by Vespasian and the adherence to various phases of Hellenic art.

TRAJAN

Nerva (AD96–98), an elderly senator and the first of the Antonine Emperors, introduced the system of adoption into the imperial succession. This emperor had an aristocratic,

asymmetrical elegance to his face, an "inimitable" quality for which the last Ptolemies of Egypt had striven in their portraits. His adopted successor, Trajan (AD98–117) – who, born in southern Spain, was the first emperor born outside Italy – went to the opposite extreme of the ambiguous iconography of Domitian. His preference for solid, monumental realism suggests the deep determination of this military leader in its strict formal equilibrium. The Roman historian Tacitus observed that innumerable descendants of freed slaves were among the noblemen and senators living in the reign of Trajan. After a century of victories and crises, the government embarked with renewed vigor on a variety of enterprises whereby Rome was embodied, publicly and privately – whether by the state, the emperor, or individual citizens – in the form of a warrior. The military fringe haircut was encouraged, and every artistic representation was geared to promote the sense of power.

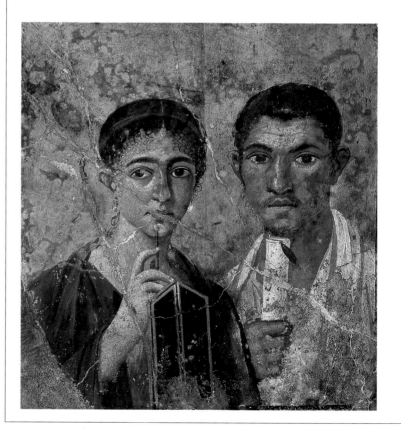

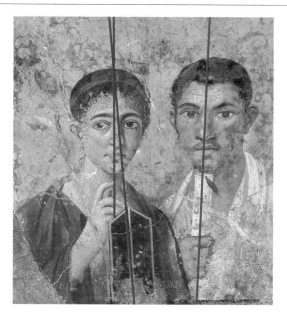

▶ 3. The light falls from the left, creating a delicate chiaroscuro, emphasized on raised areas by touches of brilliant white applied with the tip of the brush. The shading in parallel strokes (shown in black in this image) has been executed in brown earth colors, according to the classical technique. It is a method that, along with other aspects, elevates these veristic portraits to a higher plane, placing them on a par with figures from legend – figures that in other paintings on the same wall are themselves modified by the influences of everyday life. The extraordinary ability of the Pompeian painters makes us feel we are being watched by the faces which are timeless, and in which myth and history fuse to produce a perfect image of individual life.

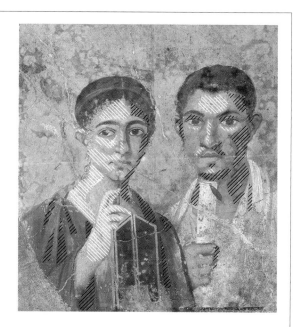

▼ 2. The outlines of the figures are soft and flowing. Solid forms are limited to the writing materials. The solid cylinder of the scroll reflects the stability and security of the man who presses it to his chin. It holds complex texts which could be preserved and transmitted for the common good. The wax tablet holds less momentous words. Held in the woman's left hand, it is angled toward her pensive face, against which rests her pen, held in the half-opened fingers of her right hand. The tablet, turned away from the viewer, may indicate the woman's involvement in the family business and may therefore contain notes and accounts. However, it could also suggest literary activity – outlines, rough drafts, or poetry. The similarity to the encaustic mummy portraits of the Roman period is explained by the common dependency on Hellenistic painting styles. The place of portrait painting in Campania was affirmed by the arrival of the Pergamene paintress Iaia of Cyzicus, who worked in Naples (as well as Rome) in tempera and encaustic. She commanded prices higher than those of Sopolis and Dionysius "whose works fill the galleries" (Pliny).

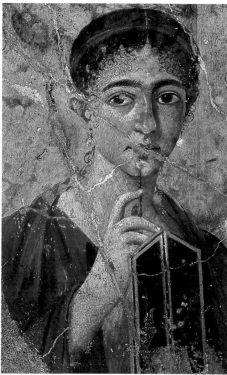

▼ 5. The character study deepens and intensifies in the different identities of the two. A gentle asymmetry is contained in the man's face, with its intense brushstrokes, his strong chin, fleshy lips, high cheekbones, irregular nose, and large expressive eyes. His ears recall the relief portraits of the Republican period. His sensibility is emphasized by his furrowed brow – the sign of a pensive character. The beard has been painted with light strokes, while the thick hair frames the head. The face is clearly Mediterranean in type, but it is impossible to say whether he is Greek, Samnite, Roman, or Levantine.

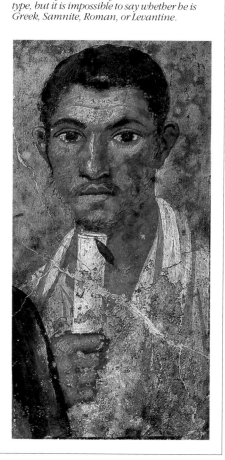

▲ 4. The woman's fingers are slender and refined, in contrast to the strong hand of her husband. Her feminine grace, seen in her elegant neck and smooth, oval face, is set off by her pearl earrings. Her personality is suggested in the line of her cheeks, her arched eyebrows, and her large, dark eyes, which gaze out from the shaded lids. Her brown hair, centrally parted and held by a red band, gently covers her nape and brow in long ringlets, a fashion introduced by Agrippina, the mother of Nero. Like her husband, the woman has a pronounced nose and ears and large eyes set wide apart.

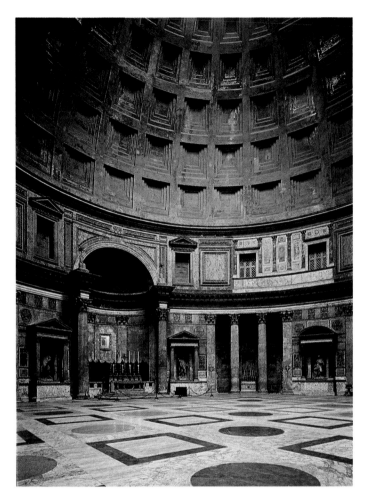

Trajan's Forum (AD107–113) represented the marble heart of the eternal city, an immense fortified encampment, the outpost of an aggressive military machine. The basilica was positioned as the *principis* (headquarters) of the *castrum* (fort), the libraries as the archives of the legions, and the Column marked the site in the parade ground where the standards were venerated. The decorative scheme of the Column was charged with metaphor, with commanders alternating with shields on the exterior, a triumphal chariot over the entrance, a colossal equestrian statue of Trajan in the center of the square, and around him crowds of chained barbarians, stunned witnesses and victims of this great glory. The column, in a human touch, brings in its recounting of the two Dacian wars a certain sense of compassion for the victims.

Interior of the Pantheon, Rome. Originally erected by order of Agrippa, the Pantheon, so-called because it was a temple dedicated to many deities, was rebuilt by Hadrian in AD130. In 609, it became a Christian church.

HADRIAN

The supposed architect of Trajan's Forum, Apollodorus of Damascus fell from grace under Hadrian (AD117–138) for his severe criticism of the emperor's plan for the Temple of Venus in Rome. The double building, with colossal proportions, explicitly linked the sanctity of Rome to the goddess whom Caesar and Augustus claimed presided over the city's fortunes. Hadrian's other lasting tribute to Rome's immortality was the rebuilding of the Pantheon, with its marvelous dome. The massive circular interior (spanned by a dome with an opening in the center) was punctuated by the "houses" of

TRAJAN'S COLUMN

The column was erected as the centerpiece of the Forum of Trajan, between the Basilica Ulpia and the Greek and Latin libraries (AD110–113). The recess in its base housed a golden urn containing the ashes of the emperor. The parian marble frieze of the column exceeds 650 feet (200 meters) in length and follows a spiral course around the column, which is about 100 feet (30 meters) high. Recounting the two wars against the Dacians (AD101–106), which on the Column are separated by the image of Victory writing on a shield, the narrative is based upon contemporary sketches made to reconstruct the campaign in triumphal paintings. Just as Alexander had his court artists, Trajan had a military engineer, Apollodorus of Damascus, who used his avid eye for details of landscape, animals, clothing, and weapons to document with technical precision boats, engines of war, watchtowers, forts, city buildings, and encampments. The events begin at the bottom of the column with the signals of the sentries on the Danube. The tranquility is suddenly shattered by the peasant tumbling from his mule in front of the emperor; it is

Detail of Trajan's Column, Rome. This depicts the battle at Tapae during the First Dacian War.

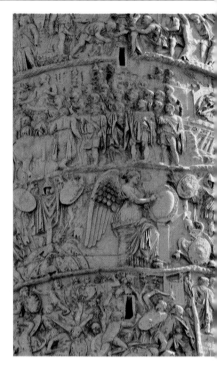

Detail of Trajan's Column, Rome. Here, Victory writes on a shield following the First Dacian War.

perhaps an omen, the meaning of which is lost because the *Commentaries of the Dacian War*, compiled by Trajan himself, have not survived, but this does not detract from the satisfying effect. According to the ancient Greek style of historic illustration, the different races, both among the Roman auxiliaries and the allies

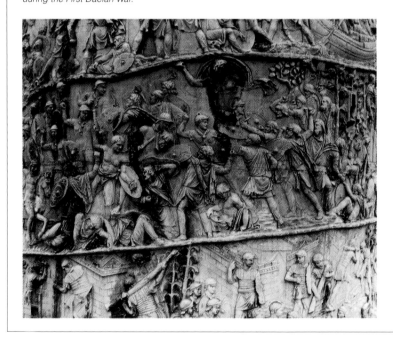

of the Dacians, are scrupulously characterized. Jove, armed with a thunderbolt, intervenes in support of his favorites at the first battle of Tapae, just as Zeus does in a statuary group of Alexander at Sagalassus (Turkey). The glory of the victors is dampened in this narrative by the cruelty of the massacre: for example, an auxiliary grips the hair on the head of a decapitated enemy between his teeth.

Numerous scenes illustrate troops on the move, addresses to the soldiers, field battles, infantry and cavalry actions in various types of terrain, and sieges. Each of them ends with the flight of the enemy and the capture or surrender of its leaders. Various exemplary actions of the emperor are also depicted, punctuated by ritual deeds that invite the observer to look beyond the detail and recognize the reassuring values of the event and

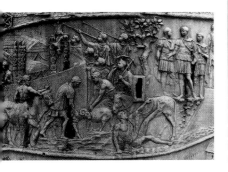

Detail of Trajan's Column, Rome. This detail shows a peasant falling from his mule in front of the emperor during the First Dacian War.

the strength of the political structure behind it. The narrative concludes at the top of the column with a flock of sheep passively pushed on by the deported population; these animals vanish in the last spiral of the frieze where the fluting of the huge column reappears.

The idyllic naturalism of the style of Alexandria is realistically interpreted to provide a setting for contemporary history in a show of inexorable might. Objective portrayal and epic vision unite to produce an emotional atmosphere that is shared by the artist, the figures, and, ultimately, the observers themselves in its implication that the rule of Rome is rooted in the permanent reality of nature.

THE ANTONINE COLUMN

During the reign of the Antonines, society was more prosperous and content than ever before. In particular, the reign of Marcus Aurelius marked the peak of ancient civilization as well as the beginning of its end. The orator Aelius Aristides commented on the universal benefits brought about by Roman rule yet sought in vain a vestige of personal happiness through mystical remedies. The government's authoritarian actions, though far-sighted and efficient, left a spiritual void. In the reliefs on the Antonine Column, begun by Commodus after his father's death in AD180, the Romans continued their disciplined offensive against the world, but they were troubled by the irrational. Faith in the Olympian divinities was questioned. In comparison with Trajan's Column, fewer and shorter sacrificial scenes are shown. In the former, the appearance of Jupiter was enough to encourage the army. Now the earthly results of divine intervention must be shown – such as the thunderbolt that sets on fire a war engine close to the fort sheltering the emperor. When the thirsty Romans were saved by a

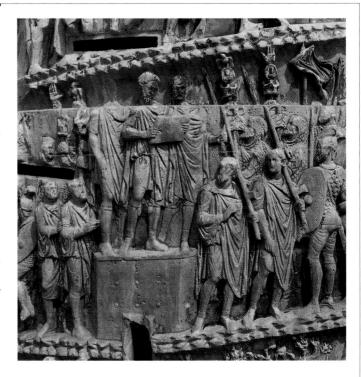

rainstorm, the cloud assumed the guise of a terrifying old man who stretched his enormous wings over the enemy hosts to wash them away. Such a miracle could be attributed to the prayers of the Christians, many of whom now marched with the legions. In addressing the troops, the Emperor stands on a tall

Detail of the Antonine Column, Rome. In this section, German nobles are decapitated in the presence of the army.

Detail of the Antonine Column, Rome. Here, Marcus Aurelius addresses the army during the war against the Quadi.

podium between two generals. Crushed by the repetitive burdens of service, the figures of soldiers lack variety in individual features and spontaneous gestures. The same faces are seen in the marches of soldiers fatigued by the constant readiness for battle. Whereas the frieze on the Trajan Column held minute details that could be read from surrounding balconies, everything on the Antonine column had to be viewed from below, so the illustrated narrative band was larger, the separation of the episodes was clearly defined, and the figures were taller and stood out against the landscape, which was no more than conventional map markings. There was no more place for mercy toward an enemy. Hence, countless images appear of defeated, humiliated, and slain barbarians with the spears, swords, and even the feet of the Romans immobilizing the barbarians in an effort to exorcise their growing threat.

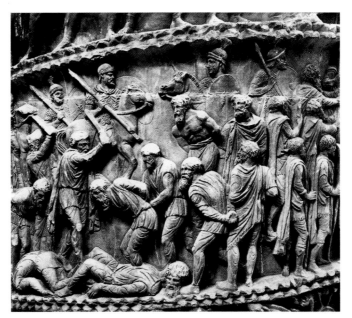

Publius Aelius Hadrianus (AD76–138), successor to Trajan, was an intellectual who, during his 20 years of government, expressed his personal vision as writer, architect, and artist. With the technical assistance of Decrianus (Demetrianus), he moved the Colossus of Nero and built the Temple of Venus and Roma in its place. He also rebuilt the Pantheon and designed his own funerary mausoleum (now the Castel Sant'Angelo). In Britain, Hadrian planned the 75-mile (120-kilometer) wall that bears his name. His villa at Tivoli perfectly embodied the imperial dream, evoking idyllic places such as the Nile and the Vale of Tempe. It was a lavishly decorated complex, made up of living quarters with reception rooms, porticos, baths, a theater, grottoes, vistas, and underground storerooms. He also recreated parts of famous buildings such as the Erechtheum at Athens and the Temple of Aphrodite at Cnidos. Hadrian fell ill in about AD137 and moved to Baiae, where he died.

The personality of Hadrian has been imaginatively encapsulated in *Memoirs of Hadrian* by Marguerite Yourcenar (1951), a modern "autobiography" ostensibly written by the emperor for his adopted grandson Marcus Aurelius. Hadrian's enlightened cultural policy, particularly in restoration, is reflected in a letter written to him by the historian Arrian, then governor of Cappadocia, at the end of a journey of inspection along the coast of the Black Sea (c.AD130): "We arrived at Trapezus (Trebizond), the Greek city of which Xenophon once spoke, and I was moved to see the Euxine Bridge from the spot where Xenophon, and you yourself, looked down on it. The altars are still there, but the stone is so rough that the letters are no longer distinct, and the Greek inscription was engraved with several errors by the barbarians: so I decided to rebuild them in white marble and to provide them with a new epigraph in clear letters. The situation of your statue, facing the sea, is fine, but it does not look like you nor is it well executed. Arrange to send a statue worthy of your name, in the same pose. The spot is absolutely right for a lasting memorial."

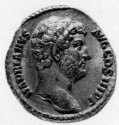

Gold coin (aureus) *depicting Hadrian in profile. Museo Civico Archeologico, Bologna.*

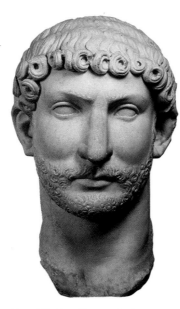

Bust of Hadrian. Museo Archeologico Nazionale, Ostia. The bust is from the early years of Hadrian's rule when he was little over 40 years old.

the planetary deities, and the pediment, with the bronze eagle inside a crown, combined the symbols of *Aiôn* (eternity). Naturally, grandiose monuments such as these advertised the prestige of Rome, but the emperor (like Trajan, of Iberian origin) also enhanced its reputation by his frequent travels and his desire to bring unity to his dominions. As the emperor's image became more familiar, it developed in the many lines of coinage with different representations according to each province. The highest expressions of these personifications are in the reliefs surrounding the Roman temple at Rome dedicated to Hadrian after his death by his successor Antoninus Pius (AD138–161).

MARCUS AURELIUS

Rome's system of adoption, which produced the most enlightened rulers the Western world has ever seen, was celebrated by Marcus Aurelius (AD161–180) in the frieze of the Parthian monument built at Ephesus in memory of Lucius Verus, who died prematurely in AD169. One panel portrays

three generations of the family, with Hadrian on the right, Antoninus Pius in the center (with his hand on the shoulder of the young Lucius Verus), and, at left, Marcus Aurelius. Hadrian's Neo-Hellenic features are reminiscent of the sad funerary groups of Attic *stelae*, which were used to bring humanity to the imperial message. In a

display of theoretical speculation allied to Roman pragmatism, the philosopher-emperor Marcus Aurelius combined meditation with military action, defending the Danubian frontiers in person. Equally, the figurative art in carvings that illustrate his ritual activities (such as those kept in the Palazzo dei Conservatori

ANTONINUS AND FAUSTINA

Upon the death of Antoninus Pius (AD161), his sons Marcus Aurelius and Lucius Verus dedicated a column to him. The shaft was a monolith of granite measuring almost 50 feet (15 meters) in height, surmounted by a statue of the divine Emperor. All that remains of the column is the carved base with the inscription and scene of the apotheosis. The scene is set by the goddess Roma, who wears a helmet and is sitting by a pile of weapons, and opposite the personification of the Roman people, significantly linked by the left arm to the obelisk of Octavian from the Campus Martius – the place where the funeral pyre was set and where the column itself would be raised. Gathered together in memory of the first Augustus who was buried there, the inhabitants of Rome pay their last respects to

the dead emperor. The people look forward, as if to their glorious and lasting destiny, to *Aiôn* (eternity), which in the form of a winged guardian spirit bears Antoninus and his wife Faustina (died AD141) up to heaven. The flying figure, associated with the revival of the Golden Age, assumes the guise of a cosmic deity. The spirit of the world is represented by the sphere in the youth's left hand and symbolizes the universality of imperial rule. As was funerary custom, only the busts of the two rulers are shown, seated side by side with their scepters; this detail would have made the solemn deification scene familiar to the eyes of the citizens. A pair of eagles in flight complete the work.

Apotheosis of Antoninus and Faustina, from the base of the Column of Antoninus in the Campus Martius (now Piazza di Montecitorio), Rome. Museo Pio-Clementino, Vatican City.

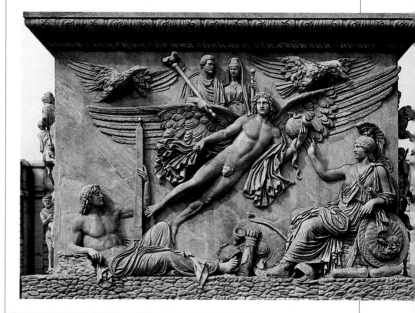

MARCUS AURELIUS

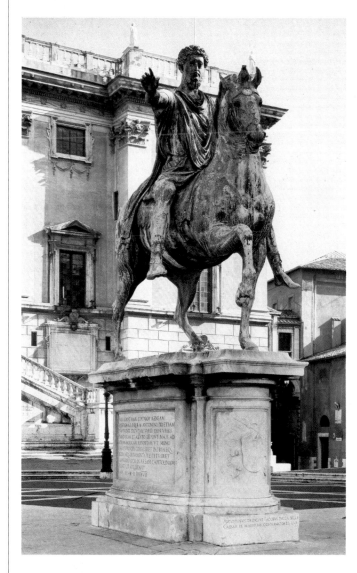

In this bronze statue of Marcus Aurelius, the emperor's features powerfully convey his strong personality and his disposition for abstract thought. The face is elongated, making him resemble his son Commodus, who was represented together with his father in the equestrian group on the latter's death in AD180. The maker of the statue used the bold, simplifying technique that is commonly found on tombs: rounded, juxtaposed geometric forms and regular planes, taking inspiration from Greek models. Hellenic influence is also evident in the beard, which radiates evenly from the clean shape of the

Equestrian statue of Marcus Aurelius (before restoration), bronze. Piazza del Campidoglio, Rome.

face. A solid, archaic structure emphasized the sanctity of the subject. The impassioned tone of the images of the Antonines is also felt in the dynamic tension. The facial features are defined by light. Preserved for eternity in his philosophical pose (*êthos*), he returns to the living world to extend his hand to his son who rode alongside. Marcus Aurelius is now remembered particularly for his twelve books of *Meditations*, in which he records his Stoic views on life.

and others reused in the Arch of Constantine) reveal a variety of subjects illustrating Roman custom: merciful treatment of the defeated enemy, triumph and sacrifice to the gods, return from war, purification of the army, investiture of a foreign prince, address to the troops, presentation of prisoners, surrender of barbarian chiefs, donation of gifts to the people, and departure of a new expedition. These are the peaceable images of the twilight of the dynasty.

COMMODUS

Marcus was succeeded by his son Commodus, whose reign (AD180–192) saw the empire drop its offensive policy in favor of a defensive stance. The philosophical soliloquies of Marcus Aurelius ended the period of rational search for truth. Art now broke the structural bonds of classical composition as humanity entrusted itself increasingly to mysticism. Until then, Rome had borne the banner of Greek tradition, remaining faithful to the models of classicism and Hellenism. After the Danubian wars and the plague that killed the emperor, the new avant-garde threw off the fetters of convention and embarked on a course of ideological discovery that would bring about radical changes in culture and customs and hasten the end of Greek influence.

Allegorical group representing imperial succession through adoption, from the Parthian Monument, Ephesus. From right: Hadrian, Lucius Verus, Antoninus, and Marcus Aurelius. Kunsthistorisches Museum, Vienna.

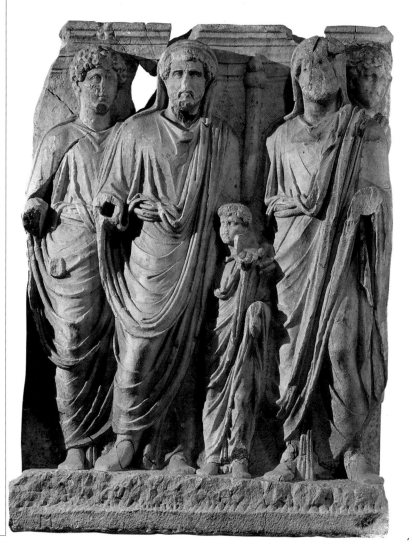

THE ROMAN HERCULES

Compared with the equestrian figure of Marcus Aurelius in the Piazza del Campidoglio, the portraits of Commodus are more human and intimate. The harmony

Commodus as Hercules, bust from the Esquiline. Palazzo dei Conservatori, Rome.

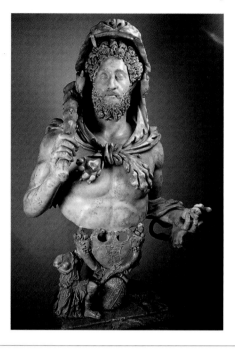

of naturalism and formal style is nowhere better evident than in the final bust of the emperor (AD192), which is displayed in the Palazzo dei Conservatori. Never have the signs of alcoholism been portrayed in so noble a setting: the wasted cheeks, bags under the eyes, and heavy eyelids partly hiding the watery, unfocused eyes.

Detail of the bust of Hercules showing the marble decoration that masks the plinth of the bust.

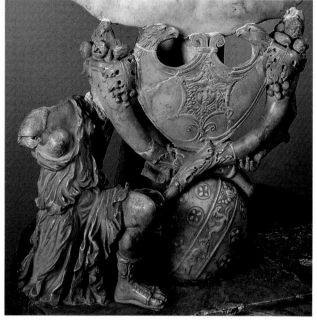

In *Storia Augusta*, one senatorial historian described the emperor as having the stupid face of a drunkard, but, in fact, these features are allusions to the watery gaze of Alexander and to Dionysian inebriation. The

individual depicted no longer shows any distinction between the human and the divine, the solidity of sculpture and the light of painting. The beard and hair, ruffled by shadows, encircle the smooth skin of the face set in its waxy pallor. The various attributes of the bust differ in their treatment. Commodus, the "Roman Hercules" like his Macedonian predecessor, is dressed in the hide of the Nemean lion – Alexander the Great had also been depicted as Herakles. Drapery billows around the emperor's head, lending it flashes of light and shade. The bust stands on a plinth, concealed at the front by carved marble decoration. The whole work balances on the heavenly sphere (another reminder of the ideology of Alexander), on which sits the *pelta*, the characteristic shield of the Asiatic people, and the double horn of plenty, a symbol of prosperity in the Ptolemaic kingdom, and thus a reminder of Africa. The western boundary of the empire is represented by the apples of the Hesperides (mythical islands at the western extreme of the world) in the sovereign's left hand.

SEPTIMIUS SEVERUS

Helvius Pertinax, successor to Commodus, was killed by the Praetorian Guard after a reign of three months; he was, in turn, succeeded by Septimius Severus (AD193–211). Of African origin, Septimius added foreign gods to the Olympian divinities, even identifying himself with the Egyptian Serapis. Most portraits of him show the curly hair of the deity flowing down over his forehead. In Leptis Magna, where Septimius was born, a four-sided arch decorated with reliefs launched the dynastic program that was to substitute continuity for adoption. The monument owes its coherence to the work of sculptors from Aphrodisias. The surface is covered with ornate decoration in the same techniques as the narrative

panels, namely with deeply drilled holes and grooves. Two sections show the procession staged for the ten-year celebration of the reign, while the others show the agreement between the father and the sons (Caracalla and Geta) designated to assume power, and the religious devotion of the family in a sacrificial scene.

Caracalla, House of the Vestal Virgins in Rome. Museo Nazionale Romano, Rome.

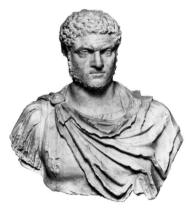

CARACALLA AND THE LAST OF THE SEVERANS

Rome's independence from the Hellenic world led to a bewildering modernity and experimentation.
In contrast to the almost mystic ambiguity of his father, Caracalla (AD211–217) saw himself in terms of an earthy solidity, which led to a new definition of heroism. Just as the tide of classicism swept away the distinctive features of the emperors, so it charged everyone with their own destiny – Caracalla's most famous measure, the Constitutio Antoniniana de Civitate introduced in AD212, had given Roman citizenship to all inhabitants of the empire. The new sense of universality surged irrationally

from the depths of the individual, almost in denial of the ideal of virtue. As innovations in style renounced traditional aesthetic sensibilities, so they tended to acclaim violence. The signs of mental disturbance, which in the youthful portraits of Caracalla (who killed his brother Geta in AD212) were masked by convention, later became dramatically evident. Biographers claimed that the representation of the emperor with his neck twisted to the left was an intentional reference to Alexander the Great, with whom Caracalla strongly identified, but in some surviving sculptures this movement distorts the subject in a way that is unprecedented in such images of power. The severity of the features banishes any hint of spirituality, while the contraction of the facial muscles and the

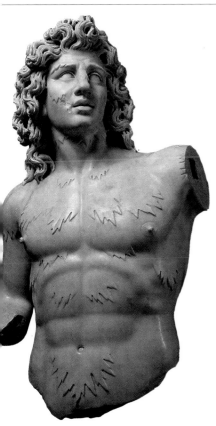

Triton, side figure of a group with Commodus as Hercules, from the Esquiline. Palazzo dei Conservatori, Rome.

Carrying a club on his shoulder, the hero who has completed his deeds introduces mankind to the "Commodian" golden age. The Amazons flanking the trophy illustrate the epithet *Amazonius*, adopted by the Emperor. It was as an Amazon that he dressed his lover Marcia, who now plotted his death.

Commodus, head affixed in ancient times to the statue of Hercules Resting, copy of the Lysippos statue, from the Palatine in Rome. Palazzo Pitti, Florence.

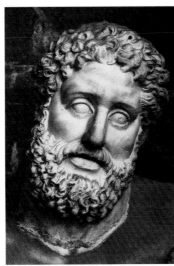

portrayal of heroes of the age. The *venatores* (hunters) of Hadrumetum vary in age and model different hairstyles; the figures wear a variety of richly embroidered tunics and carry an assortment of weapons. The medium of the mosaic translated the glowing naturalism of a painting into solid materials and served to perpetuate the solid presence of the empire. In funerary sculpture every detail of a face was carefully reproduced, as were the objects or symbols that defined the personality or status of the dead individual. Death exceeded the aspirations of life, offering a freedom that extended beyond the realms of public activity. Recorded in images and inscriptions on

luxurious tombs and modest *stelae* are the achievements of countless unknown citizens, whether bride or widow, drinker or sage, teacher, scholar, musician, or struggling poet. Tomb portraits were often characterized by symbolic and mythical motifs, which registered the social import-ance of the departed rather than just the individual nature, addressing the dilemma of human existence at the moment of its extinction. Document of a people and mirror of a society, the cold stone revealed the epic stories of everyday life, the activities of the innumerable farmers, artisans, merchants, and soldiers who helped run the eternal empire.

brow seen in later examples combine to produce a surly and forbidding expression, which seems to probe the very depths of the brutality of fratricide. In this "new Romulus" there is a feeling of menace that could be generated at will toward internal and external enemies of the regime. Such emotional intensity, veering from light to shadowy darkness, was never attained by classical sculptors. Under Caracalla and his successors, the reliance on inner feelings, alternated with irrational outbursts, became characteristic in both art and politics. For many, actions were valued more than words, and experiences counted more than a yearning for the ideal. This was reflected in sculpture and painting, which adopted forms, expressions, and styles drawn directly from reality. During the reigns of Caracalla,

Elagabalus (AD218–222), and Alexander Severus (AD222–225), the art of floor mosaics, produced by master craftsmen and generally in polychrome, was extended to the African regions. In place of mytho-logical themes, emphasis was now placed on contemporary life, with scenes from the amphitheater and the circus, and of hunts in natural surroundings. Interest in the subject arose from the econo-mic importance to North Africa of the export of wild animals destined for the circuses of Rome and other cities. Man's struggle with the forces of nature was revived from antiquity via Oriental cultures. In a mosaic from Hadrumetum (modern-day Sousse in Tunisia), four *bestiarii* (gladiators) bring down deer, ostriches, antelopes, and wild horses. The desire for realism extended to the authentic

SOLDIER AND FARMER

Having successfully command-ed armies all over the empire in his youth, Probus – born at Sirmio in Pannonia (Balkans) – was proclaimed emperor in AD276. An important aspect of his policy was to increase agricultural production, and he made use of legionaries for reclamation work and civil duties. When announcing his plan to assimilate barbarians into the empire, Probus declared, "Soon there will

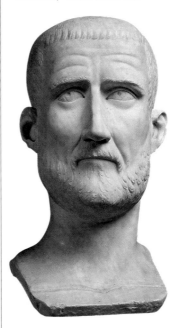

be no need for soldiers." A colossal head in the Capitoline Museum shows the upright posture and direct gaze of a man "worthy of the name he bears" (*Storia Augusta*). The symmetrical wrinkles on his forehead, the sunken eyes, sharp nose, and pursed mouth with furrows on either side are sculpted simply, as if on a wooden mask; neat, separate incisions are used for the short haircut. The realism of the asymmetric eyebrows stands out in the solemn squareness of the face. Lines take precedence over modeling, while contours compress volume. The calm, steadfast expression suggests that the imperial crisis has abated – a short-lived dream – and that all anxieties are now dispelled. The emperor conformed to the ancient model of farmer and settler and planted grapes with his own hands when he return-ed with his army to his home-land. The bust perpetuates the story of the soldier from the frontier who rose to be emperor. His policy, based on the need for justice and peace, became a program of universal government.

Probus. Capitoline Museum, Rome (formerly Albani Collection).

Gordian

During the reign of Gordian III (AD238–244), the city offices of works created sarcophagi of high quality and originality. The relaxed articulation of space progressed after a brief interval during Caracalla's rule. New techniques heralded a break with academic tradition. The anatomy of heroic figures surpassed that of Greek models, expressionism took on visionary proportions, and drapes and inanimate objects increased in number and significance. The stylization of the obsessively carved detail gave the whole work a meta-physical coherence: the manes of the horses tamed by Castor and Pollux on one sarcophagus from the Appian Way might have inspired the steeds of the 20th-century Italian painter Giorgio de Chirico. In April AD248, Philip the Arabian (AD244–249) celebrated the first millennium of Rome.

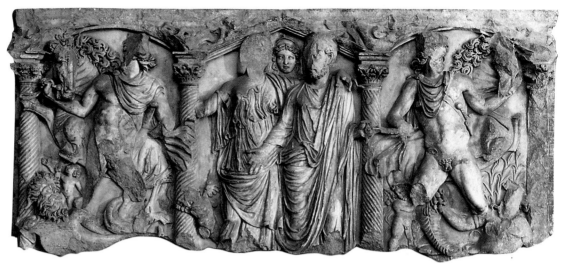

Sarcophagus with column decoration depicting a married couple, with Castor and Pollux at the sides taming horses, Via Appia. Museo Nazionale Romano, Rome.

THE LUDOVISI BATTLE

Carved from an exceptionally large single block, the Ludovisi Sarcophagus measures 9 feet (2.75 meters) wide, 5 feet (1.55 meters) high, and 4½ feet (1.4 meters) deep. The monument honors Erennius Etruscus, who died with his father Decius at the battle of Abritto (modern-day Razgrad in Bulgaria) against the Goths (AD251). The image of the general is known from coins and portraits, one of which, in the Capitoline Museum, has the mark of an initiate of the Mithras cult. Judging by the female bust on the lid, his mother Etruscilla was also laid in the sarcophagus. The dense carving of the relief and the extension to all four sides of the tomb of the battle scene, which teems so thickly with figures as to negate the background, are without precedent. The manner in which the frieze develops upward, as seen on the panels of the arch constructed by Septimius Severus, reveals an affinity with triumphal paintings. The same method was also used by the Baroque painter

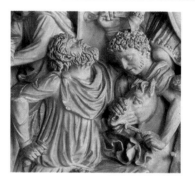

Pietro da Cortona in his painting of Constantine at the Milvian Bridge (Palazzo dei Conservatori).

The figures are arranged along a diagonal line running from the lower left-hand corner, thus separating the two military formations. Rooted in the Stoic acceptance of the passions that disturb the world's equilibrium, universal Greek art and public Roman art are combined in a stirring vision of individual destiny. The clash of opposing armies reflects the duels of classical tradition, but here it is disfigured by cruelty, as testified by the wounded. The single combatants and the soldiers in their formations are portrayed with unsparing realism and yet assume symbolic value: the two large foot soldiers in the left foreground declare the solidity of the Roman front which has broken the enemy onslaught. In the triangle on the right-hand side, the horde of defeated barbarians have been trampled by the victors into a small space, their distorted limbs locked together in agony. Their drapery seems to shudder in unison with the writhing bodies, and their faces resemble theatrical masks of terror and suffering. Above, the line of horses from the left flank advances on the exposed

Front and details of the Ludovisi Sarcophagus, showing a battle between the barbarians and the Romans under the command of Erennius Etruscus, son of the Emperor Decius, outside Porta San Lorenzo, Rome. Museo Nazionale Romano, Rome.

GALLIENUS

Portraits of the Emperor Gallienus (AD260–268) show great mastery. In his final years, the image of the Emperor lost the descriptive detail and nervous contraction of the face. The new image had a Hellenic element, introduced by artists from Athens who had immigrated to Rome after the city was sacked by the Goths in AD267. Tonal nuances were achieved by the contrast of diffused light on the skin, with the rough beard in a rare effect of abstraction quite in contrast to the faces of Hadrian and the Antonines. The upward glance, with the

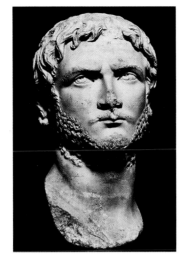

Gallienus, from the House of the Vestal Virgins, Rome. Museo Nazionale Romano, Rome.

iris partly covered by the eyelid, expresses the mystical side of power and suggests the influence of the philosopher and teacher Plotinus and Neo-Platonist philosophy, which stimulated the desire for religious and moral reforms.

AURELIAN

Aurelian (AD270–275) restored the unity of the empire, which had been threatened by widespread uprisings in both the West and East. He eliminated the remaining powers of the Senate and invested himself as god and lord (*deus et dominus*) of the universe. The destruction of Athens led him to use the military-style architecture of the border provinces for Rome. The city, which in the time of Augustus had expanded in the knowledge that it was secure, was now encircled by turreted brick walls that still remain impressive to this day.

DIOCLETIAN

As architecture reached dizzy heights of grandeur, allegorical ornamentation reflected the apparent stability of the empire. Diocletian's reforms brought new respectability to the administrative, political, and moral institutions of the state. They transformed citizens into subjects who were bound by strict discipline, and taxes were introduced to fund the army, repairs to public works, and the construction of grand public buildings. The pyramid of power set up by the Tetrarchy (the rule by four emperors), reproduced the court of Rome in its new centers of residence: Treviri, Nicomedia, Sirmio, and Milan. The provinces were divided and then grouped into dioceses, and this system was extended to Italy itself. Diocletian (AD285–305), building upon the theocratic ideas of Aurelian, explicitly incorporated within the immense walls of his new monuments signs of the divine power with which he believed the empire to be invested. The largest baths ever built in Rome were dedicated to Jupiter, king of the gods and guardian deity of Diocletian – who adopted the divine surname Jovius. In Milan, the baths took the name of Hercules by order of Maximian to commemorate his protector. The colossus of Hercules at rest (a fragment of which survives in the Archaeological Museum in Milan) was the centerpiece of the decoration. Diocletian retired to a magnificent palace at Salona, on the edge of the Adriatic (modern-day Split in Croatia), built like a military camp with polygonal gate towers, which served as the model for the castle of the Mount of Frederick II on the opposite shore of the Adriatic.

MAXENTIUS AND CONSTANTINE

Struggles for the succession brought about the dissolution of the system of the Tetrarchy. Maxentius (AD306–312) revived the myth of Rome's foundation and restored the city as the central seat of power. He enlarged the House of Augustus on the Palatine (and was the last emperor to live there) and built on the Appian Way a dynastic complex consisting of palace, circus, and the mausoleum of his son Romulus, which in its Pantheon-like form celebrates the immortal memory of Rome's founder. Constantine the Great (AD306–337), who defeated Maxentius at the gates of Rome, had his dreams of a universal monarchy fulfilled in AD313 through the grace of the Christian God – he was the first Roman emperor to embrace Christianity. In the colossal head from the Basilica Nova (built by Maxentius) his despotic nature is underlined in the strong chin, furrowed cheeks, and irregular nose.

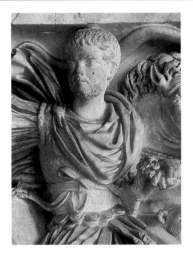

trophies, and yet another delivers the *coup de grace* to a fallen foe. Amid the frenzy of slaughter and barbarian despair, the light moves rhythmically, giving shape to forms and distances, coordinating events, sending a vibrant wave across the heap of corpses, and announcing the turbulent advance of the horsemen. Roman sculpture and relief was generally colored, and this scene would have been even more stunning when the trumpets, weapons, and armor glittered among the purple and blue cloaks. The young hero stands bareheaded and alone in the center; with an imperial gesture and distant gaze, he contemplates his destiny as the eternal conquerer. Transcending everything is the pervading idea of victory as the reason for this dark slaughter.

flank to capture the survivors. The battle is over, and prisoners are being taken. A legionary drags a bound old man by the beard, while two more at the sides raise

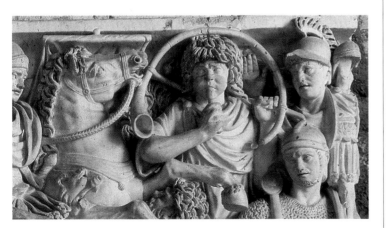

THE TETRARCHS

The statues of Tetrarchs (c.AD300) – now immured in St. Mark's basilica in Venice – added a new dimension to the traditional working of porphryry, mined in Egypt at Mons Porphyrites and worked at Alexandria. In the classical style, stone was used exclusively for images of gods or rulers, and the St. Mark's sculptures combine the two privileged subject types in a metaphor of theocracy. This very hard rock symbolized the primordial essence of sculpture. The three-dimensional mass retains its original weight and character and embraces the rounded figures in a symmetrical, compact group. The faces, aligned vertically, wear the same stiff expression, with a touch of abstraction that prevents any natural variety. The divine nature of the emperors has transformed them into icons with the same surreal look: the gaze is fixed, with prominent eyes, surrounded by a curve accentuated by the brows. Yet for all the facial impassivity and cool formality of the military dress, there is a sense of warm solidarity in the unusual, embracing poses of these imperial figures. Diocletian, Maximianus, Constantius Chlorus, and Galerius stand side by side in their would-be concordlike pillars of a living tetrapylon. The Tetrarchs affirm the natural beauty of the four elements, the four seasons, and the division of the heavens. In this indestructible block, material and form, structure and function, are rooted in the belief that the divine manifests itself on Earth through dynastic rulers. The arrival of the Augusti in Milan (AD290) was hailed as the "visible and present" manifestation of Jove; Herakles was no longer a stranger in Italy, being embodied by Maximianus. The emperor, "born of god," was, in his turn, the "creator of gods" through his creation of a Caesar. He belonged to a superior world, where harmony reigned and where reforms could bring transcendent order to worldly confusion.

The Tetrarchs, *exterior of St. Mark's basilica, Venice.*

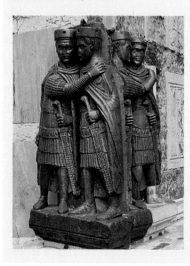

LOVE AND DEATH

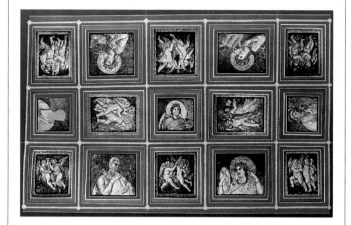

Crispus, later renamed Caesar by his father, Constantine, lived at Treviri from AD316 until AD326, when his villa was razed to the ground to make way for the construction of a church. Fragments of a ceiling fresco from a reception room, painted in about AD321, have been retrieved, carefully restored, and are displayed in the Diocesan museum of Treviri. The church was erected in atonement after Crispus was exiled to Pola for committing incest with his stepmother Fausta, who was killed soon afterward. The coffers in the fresco contain pairs of cupids who are playing with symbols of power (a prophetic allusion). These figures alternate with portraits of two pedagogues (one of whom may be Lattantius, the Christian writer

Painted ceiling from the palace of Crispus at Treviri depicting princes of the second Flavian dynasty, relations of Constantine. Museo Diocesano, Treviri.

of African origin) and of the imperial women, who are distinguished by a circular halo of light. Constantia, half-sister of Constantine, takes a pearl necklace from a jewelry box; Helena, wife of Crispus, plays the lyre as a Muse; Flavia Helena, Constantine's mother, in the center of the fresco, is represented as Juno, holding a golden bowl in her left hand and raising a veil with her right hand; finally, Maxima Fausta, wife of Constantine and instigator of the fatal love affair, is depicted as Aphrodite gazing at herself in a mirror. The face of Crispus himself is removed as part of his "*damnatio memoriae.*"

In contrast to the portraits of Caracalla, Constantine's heroism attains divine majesty in an image that is marked by pride, solemnity, and detachment. The eyes are abnormally large, and the wrinkled forehead denotes fixed concentration. The fringe of hair, reminiscent of Trajan's military haircut, is more compact, tracing the line of the weighty crown worn by the emperor. The victory of Constantine over Licinius in Thrace (AD324) was represented allegorically through the death of Lycurgus,

the avowed enemy of Dionysius. The scene is shown on a glass cup in the British Museum, with Lycurgus being overcome by grapevine shoots. The addition of small quantities of gold and silver to the glass produces a transformation, from green to red, in the transparent color of the vessel when light shines through it. The achievement of bright colors on such a thick medium implies workmanship of great virtuosity and suggests that this traditional material was deliberately chosen by the emperor. From the birth of the

empire, the technique of glass-blowing made it possible to produce glass that was absolutely pure, easy to handle, capable of being molded with maximum speed into a variety of shapes, and which lent itself to engraved decoration. The cost-effective production, with an organization that paralleled modern industry, meant that glassware was widely exported and came to characterize material culture. From the capitals of the Tetrarchy to Cologne, Alexandria, and Syria spread techniques of glass manufacture originally used in cameos, namely exquisitely carved "cage cups" (*diatreta vasa*). In recognition of the need to free his policies from class-ridden conservatism and to pave the way toward a new Europe, Constantine took the following measures: he founded Constantinople, or "New Rome" (AD325); he was

Colossal head of Constantine, Basilica of Maxentius, Rome. Capitoline Museum, Rome.

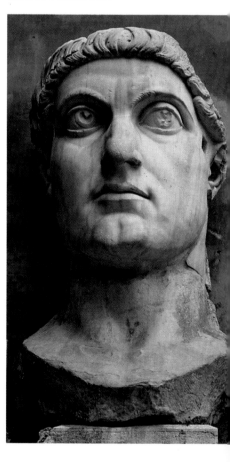

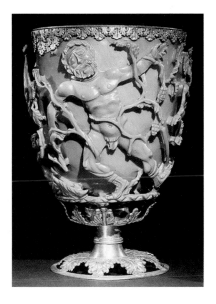

Glass cup depicting the death of Lycurgus. British Museum, London (formerly Rothschild Collection).

emperor's entry into Rome (AD357): "He stared ahead so fixedly that he seemed to be wearing an iron collar around his neck, moving his head neither to the right nor the left, so that he appeared not so much a person as an icon." In a colossal bronze of the emperor, now in the Palazzo dei Conservatori, Rome, the forehead is concealed by an archaic skullcap of hair. The reign of Julian (AD361–363) was marked by a desperate attempt by the senatorial class to revive the cult of polytheism. A portrait statue in Paris shows the emperor wearing a sheathed beard and cloak, resembling a Greek scholar. The link between imperial authority and the army was reinforced by Jovian (AD363–364) and the two succeeding Augusti who co-ruled the empire, Valentinian I (AD364–375, west) and Valens (AD364–378, east). Gratian (AD367–383), son of Valentinian, shared office with his father and uncle during part of his reign. A portrait, discovered at Trevisi, shows a return to the vision of the Christian emperor and to the figures of Constantine's descendants, with a revival of former motifs from Caracalla to the Tetrarchs. This retrospective trend prevailed in luxury items such as ivory diptychs and jewelry produced for the court. The base of the obelisk erected by Theodosius (AD379–395) in the hippodrome of Constantinople shows the imperial family surrounded by high dignitaries in the presence of the public, while the barbarians prostrate themselves in submission. On the death of Theodosius, his sons Arcadius and Honorius formally divided the kingdom into east and west. It was a total partition without either claiming supremacy; it proved definitive because both empires hereafter pursued a separate and independent course.

THE CHRISTIAN EMPIRE

The monogram of Christ was the ultimate unifying symbol of the empire, which pursued its course with renewed faith in its eternal future. The dynastic role was exaggerated by Constantine's son, Constantine II (AD337–361), who isolated himself from his subjects in a court that was indifferent to the pressing needs of the moment. Ammianus Marcellinus described the

present as Emperor at the Council of Nicea (which earned him the description of the "thirteenth apostle"); he reformed the coinage with Christian symbols; he undertook to tie farmers to the land; he permitted the large-scale entry of barbarians into the army; and he accorded privileges to the army under the direct control of the sovereign (*comitatentes*) in comparison with the border troops (*limitanei*).

Relief portraying Constantine's speech in the Roman Forum, Arch of Constantine, Rome. The arch was built in AD313 in honor of the emperor after victory over his rival Maxentius at the Milvian Bridge.

THE LEGACY OF ROMAN ART

In the frontier regions, away from the city with its elegant busts, artists produced powerful portraits, modifying the Hellenistic interpretation of the classical style and providing models for later European art. A particular form of 15th-century Flemish painting, for example, derived inspiration from the art of the Roman provinces. Jan van Eyck's *Portrait of a Boy* exhibits certain features – the cutting off of the bust, the inscription, the scroll in the hand, and a kind of fluted drapery – that show a clear link with Rhenish *stelae* of the imperial age. For a thousand years, the incomplete dream of the empire continued to find expression, not so much on an official level, convulsed by military defeat, economic collapse, and invasions, but in lesser parts of society. The variation between the Italic-provincial style and the centralized form of propaganda art was reflected during the medieval age in the contrast of "everyday" art and the aristocratic art that was typical of the intermittent phases of revival (Carolingian, Ottonian, Frederican, and Burgundian). In the Roman imperial age, the most truly authentic art had from the start been found in the provinces, where it did not have to suffer comparison with courtly models, and where, both in the colonial settlements and the army, the plebeian class was in the majority. The quantity and durability of Roman provincial artifacts inspired the architecture and decorative arts of Christian Europe in its many forms, from Romanesque to Gothic, culminating in the Renaissance. Many of the elements that contributed to these styles and that appeared to be novelties in Italy were actually born from these peripheral aspects of Italic art. The so-called "French" style was, in fact, "antique" in that

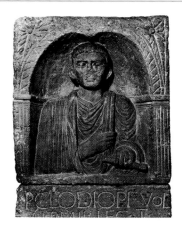

Funerary stela of Publius Clodius. Rheinisches Landesmuseum, Bonn.

it was a steady uninterrupted development of the popular art of the Roman age, but from beyond the Alps. It differs from the antique style of the Italian Renaissance, which was modeled on a revival of Roman urban art, similar to the styles that evolved around the centers of royal power during the previous periods of cultural renaissance.

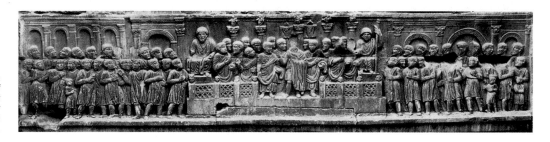

ART OF THE ROMAN EMPIRE

27BC: Octavian receives the title of Augustus; birth of the Roman Empire; during the Augustan period, Vitruvius composes his famous treatise on architecture. **19BC:** death of Virgil, one of the greatest poets of all time. **AD14:** on the death of Augustus, Tiberius becomes emperor. **AD49:** Jews and Christians are driven out of Rome following an edict by Claudius. **AD64:** Rome is devastated by a terrible fire. **AD70:** Titus razes the Temple of Jerusalem to the ground and conquers the city. **AD79:** the eruption of Vesuvius destroys Pompeii, Herculaneum, and Stabia; Pliny the Elder, author of *Naturalis Historia*, perishes in the disaster. **AD96–98:** Nerva introduces the principle of adoption into the imperial succession. **AD107:** after Trajan's successful military campaigns, Dacia becomes a Roman

31 BC – AD 14

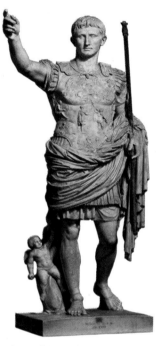

Statue of Augustus, Prima Porta, Rome. Museo Chiaramonti, Vatican City.

▲ ROME

The official portrait of Augustus, with idealized features, is memorably handed down to us through the statue from Prima Porta (after 17BC).

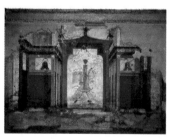

Wall-painting of theater scene, from the Room of the Masks, House of Augustus, Rome.

▲ ROME

Exemplifying the "second style" are the frescoes of the house of Augustus (28BC), where false architectural vistas are rendered in *trompe l'oeil* through the use of complex perspectives.

15 – 68

▼ ROME

In the Julius-Claudian period the classicizing trend of the Augustan age continued: portraits such as that of Antonia (c.37), however, reveal the use of chiaroscuro and details that are extraneous to classical models.

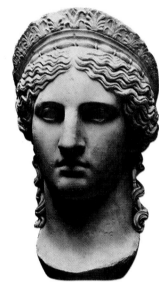

Antonia Minor. Museo Nazionale Romano, Rome (formerly Ludovisi Collection).

▼ POMPEII

The paintings in the house of the Vettii (before 62) are in the "fourth style": architectural illusion continued, amplified by the introduction of airy landscapes and enriched by ornament.

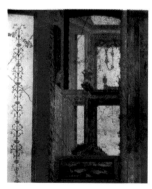

Imaginary architecture in a fresco from the House of the Vettii, Pompeii.

69 – 117

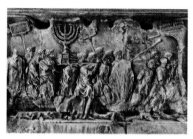

Detail of relief showing the victory of Titus, Arch of Titus, Rome. Here, booty from the Temple of Jerusalem is displayed in a triumphal procession.

▲ ROME

The Arch of Titus, erected by his brother Domitian (81–96) is decorated with reliefs that reveal an illusionist concept of space, achieved through the arrangement of the figures along a curved line.

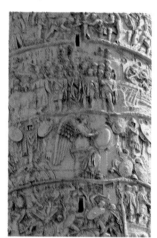

Detail from Trajan's Column, Rome. Here, Victory writes on a shield following the First Dacian War.

▲ ROME

Trajan's Column, erected between 110 and 113 in celebration of the emperor's victories, is decorated with a continuous spiral relief that closely records events during his wars.

118 – 180

▼ APHRODISIAS

The relief of Antinous reveals the essential characteristics of Hadrianic sculpture (117–138): influenced mainly by the sculptors of Aphrodisias, the Greek classical models were taken up again, but with a melancholy air.

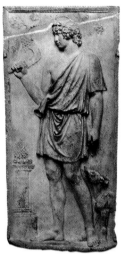

Antonianus of Aphrodisias, relief of Antinous as Silvanus, Torre del Padiglione, between ancient Lanuvium and Antium. Private Collection, Rome.

▼ ROME

Dating from the time of Marcus Aurelius (161–180), this statue later inspired artists of the Roman Renaissance.

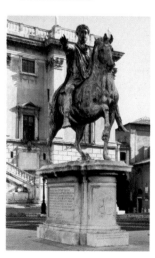

Equestrian statue of Marcus Aurelius, (before restoration), bronze. Piazza del Campidoglio, Rome.

province; Trajan's Forum is built by the architect Apollodorus of Damascus. **AD122:** the building of Hadrian's Wall begins in Britannia. **AD193:** the army of Illiria proclaims Septimus Severus, of African origin, emperor. **AD212:** Roman citizenship is granted to all free citizens of the empire. **AD248:** Philip the Arab celebrates the first millennium of foundation of Rome. **AD271:** on the orders of Aurelian, Rome is surrounded by protective walls. **AD285–305:** Diocletian institutes a system, known as the Tetrarchy, to organize the empire. **AD324–330:** Constantine, having become the sole Augustus after the defeat at Maxentius, founds Constantinople. **AD395:** with the death of Theodosius, the empire is definitively divided into two parts by his sons.

1 8 1 – 2 1 7   2 1 8 – 2 7 5   2 7 6 – 3 9 5

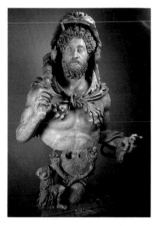

Commodus as Hercules, bust from the Esquiline. Palazzo dei Conservatori, Rome.

▲ ROME

During the rule of Commodus (180-192), a technique of strong chiaroscuro prevailed, as can be seen in the bust of Commodus as Hercules.

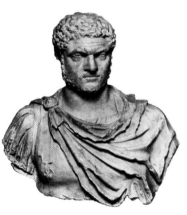

Caracalla, House of the Vestal Virgins in Rome. Museo Nazionale Romano, Rome.

▲ ROME

Under the rule of Caracalla (180-192), classicism underwent a crisis. Sculpture distanced itself from the classical idealization and elements of reality were introduced, until a sense of brutality was expressed in portraits of the emperor.

▼ ROME

The production of marble sarcophagi was widespread in the third century, becoming more sumptuous after 250. The Ludovisi Sarcophagus (251) presents agitated forms and an almost obsessive attention to detail.

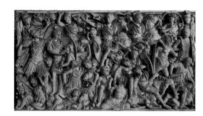

Front of the Ludovisi Sarcophagus, outside Porta San Lorenzo, Rome. Museo Nazionale Romano, Rome.

▼ ROME

The portraits of Gallienus (260-268) reveal a new Hellenic effect, due to the influx of craftsmen from Athens into Rome.

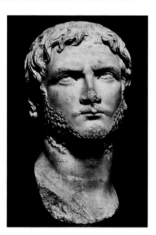

Gallienus, from the House of the Vestal Virgins, Rome. Museo Nazionale Romano, Rome.

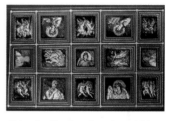

Contemporary view of the Baths of Diocletian, Rome.

▲ ROME

The period of Diocletian (285-305) was characterized by a vast program of restoration and building of public works, both in Rome and in the provinces. The Roman baths of Diocletian constitute the largest complex of this type ever. It may have been a way for Diocletian to stress the symbolic presence of the emperor in his capital city, at a time when wars frequently kept the emperor away from Rome.

The Tetrarchs, exterior of St. Mark's basilica, Venice.

▲ ALEXANDRIA

The abstract symmetry and elementary compactness of the porphyry group showing the Tetrarchs (c.300), sculpted in Alexandria, effectively spread the message of the divine meaning behind the earthly actions of rulers.

▼ TREVIRI

Chosen as the imperial seat by Diocletian in 287, Treviri enjoyed an artistic flowering during the rule of Constantine. Valuable evidence of the style of painting of the time, the fresco in the residence of Crispus Caesar reveals a return to classicism.

Painted ceiling from the palace of Crispus at Treviri depicting princes of the second Flavian dynasty, relations of Constantine. Museo Diocesano, Treviri.

CONSTANTINOPLE

Under Theodosius (379-395), Constantinople was enriched by urban and monumental additions, with the aim of equaling the splendor of Rome: for example, a vast Forum was built and an obelisk was erected in the hippodrome, its base lavishly decorated with sculptures.

EARLY CHRISTIANS AND THEIR ART

As iconography became an increasingly powerful tool for those religions with creeds based on the idea of salvation, so imperial images became more important for inspiration. Christians in particular displayed conspicuous skill in placing monotheism within the classical tradition, and they also assimilated barbarian traditions to influence the medieval artistic expression.

The Christians differed from the various religious sects of the Jewish people – the Sadducees, the Pharisees, the Essenes, and the Qumran community – in three ways. First, they believed that the Scriptures were completed with the coming of the Messiah. Second, they accepted women as participants in common prayer. Third, they followed the policy of attempting to convert Gentiles. Within the multicultural arena of the Roman Empire, they found points of reference with other religious beliefs: the monotheism of the Stoics, who believed in the spiritual majesty of the Greek God Zeus; the individual salvation promised by the mysteries of Demeter and Dionysus, whose symbols – ears of corn and wine – came to indicate the bread and wine of the Eucharist; the cult of Isis (a similar figure to Mary), the mother who offers comfort, represented on her throne with the young Harpocrates; and spiritual motifs in Orphic and Pythagorean practices. It was to take centuries, however, before this adaptable religion found favor in a wider realm.

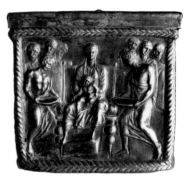

Adoration of the Magi, detail of the silver reliquary of the Saints Celsus and Nazarius, fourth century. Museo del Tesoro del Duomo, Milan.

MITHRAS

The sepulchre of Antiochus I of Commagene (34BC) on the peak of Nemrud Dagh in Turkey depicts the Persian god Mithras with Greek and Hindu divinities. The meeting of these cultures gave birth to an elaborate initiation rite that established itself in the imperial age. It tied in well with the Syrian cult of the Sun God, which the emperor Aurelian had assumed as the official state religion, inaugurating the grandiose Temple of the Unconquered Sun on the Quirinal (AD274), one of the seven hills of Rome. Diocletian considered Mithras to be the "protector of the empire." The mysteries of Mithraism were enacted in underground crypts, representing the grotto (symbol of the heavenly vault) where the god had been born from the rock (emblem of the earth). However, the exclusion of women deprived the cult of the popular support that was afforded to the Christian faith. This involvement of the whole family unit laid the foundation of the social system on which the success of the religion ultimately depended. Though in Western Europe the name of Mithras can now only be found buried beneath the churches and in shrines, the name lives on in the branches of Zoroastrianism in Iran and India. Present-day knowledge helps provide an astrological explanation for the animals that appear in the paintings and carvings of many Mithraic shrines featuring the sacrifice of the Bull. The Crow, Scorpion, Snake, Lion, and Dog all represent constellations in depictions of the night sky, together with the personifications of the Sun and the Moon. In the fresco pictured here, Mithras is flanked by Cautes and Cautopates, whose torches – symbols of life and death – are raised and lowered respectively.

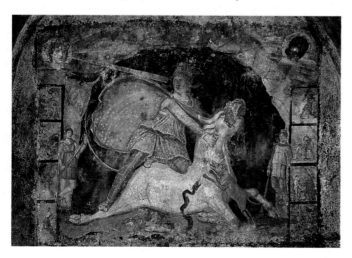

Fresco from the Shrine of Mithras, Marino, Rome, third century.

THE CHRISTIANS IN THE ROMAN EMPIRE

In AD35, shortly after the crucifixion of Jesus, the Emperor Tiberius (ruled AD14–37) ordered the senate to recognize Christianity. The assembly opposed it, and the senatorial decree prohibiting the cult – *non licet esse christianos* – initiated a campaign of persecution. It was during the reign of Claudius (41–54), that the apostle Peter went to Rome. One of his letters in later years confirmed the decision of Claudius' successor Nero (54–68) to incriminate the Christians for "illicit superstition" prior to the fire in AD64. Flavius Clemens, cousin of the emperor Domitian (81–96), was the first Christian to become consul, but in AD95 he was put to death for being guilty of "atheism." Hostility to Christians waned under Nerva (96–98),

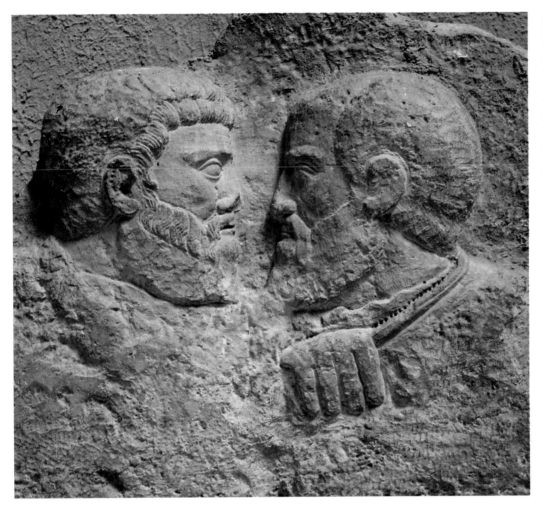

anarchy and the behavior of the Christian majority. They were accused in general of "outright opposition." The emperor Commodus (180–192) generally assimilated the Christians into the empire. During his rule, for example, underground cemeteries were established. There was keen interest in religious matters at the court of Septimus Severus (193–211), and the obsession of the empress Julia Domna with the cult of the Sun God struck a monotheistic note. There was an image of Jesus in the *lararium* (a shrine to the spirits protecting a place) of Alexander Severus. Christians now began to participate in political life, and the duty of administering the catacombs

St. Peter and St. Paul, relief, fourth to fifth century. Museo Paleocristiano Nazionale, Aquileia.

Christ the Teacher and Shepherd of a Flock, fresco, mid third century. Ipogeo degli Aureli, Rome.

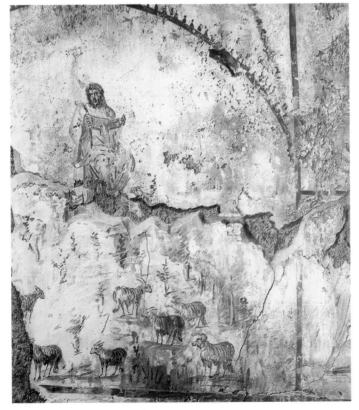

and Trajan (98–117) tried to find a compromise between the protective policies of his predecessor and the oppressive designs of Domitian. He put a stop to persecution but ordered action to be taken against anyone who, when called before the court, refused to offer sacrifice to the gods. Hadrian (117–138) decreed that Christians should be punished only if they actually broke the law. Under Marcus Aurelius (161–180), the situation was again ambiguous. Montanist heretics, opposed to the belief that Jesus Christ was the Son of God, damaged temples and statues of divinities, but the emperor failed to distinguish between this radical

EARLY CHRISTIAN FINDINGS

Today, strange signs and symbols testifying to the message of the apostles have come to light. A fragment of papyrus relating to St. Mark's Gospel, found in the caves of Qumran, dates from before AD68, and extracts of St. Matthew's Gospel (Oxford) date from about AD60. The novel *Satyricon* contains a satirical account of the facts related by St. Mark. The story, set just outside Naples and Pozzuoli, was written by a companion of Nero, Gaius Petronius, who was driven to suicide in AD65 by the hostility of Tigellinus. In the region of Campania, other pieces of evidence precede the eruption of Vesuvius in AD79. The "magic square" of Pompeii conceals the words *Pater noster*, while at Oplontis, outside Naples, there is a reference to the persecution of the Christians in the villa of Nero's wife Poppaea, who died in AD65. In a graffito reading *mnesthêi Béryllos* –"Berillus, take care!"– the letter "Rho" has a horizontal line across it, making it the oldest known *chrismón* – monogram of Christ – ever found (a letter from Paul in AD63 indicates that there were Christians in court). The writer of the graffiti is warning Nero's secretary that someone is aware of his spiritual leanings and is plotting his downfall.

Ancient graffiti with the monogram of Christ inserted in the word Béryllos, the name of Nero's secretary. It was found in the Villa of Poppaea at Oplontis, outside Naples.

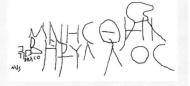

was given to organized funeral associations. In the early stages of Christian decorative art, the tone was one of harsh dogmatism, as exemplified in the writings of Tertullian (active between 197 and 220), and symbolism revolved around the concepts of holiness and salvation. Motifs were based on narrative episodes from the Old and New Testaments.

Philip the Arabian (244–249) was arguably the first Christian emperor, and sarcophagi inspired by the new faith are dated to his rule. Images of philosophers and scholars represented the intellectual qualities of the dead, and agricultural and pastoral scenes derived from Virgil were interpreted as a vision of paradise. Gradually, the Hellenistic tradition was abandoned. In

THE CATACOMBS

Peter and Paul were buried after their martyrdom in the communal necropolises situated respectively in the Via Cornelia on the Vatican Hill and on the Ostiense. So too were other Christians until the donations of land by adherents of the faith led to the building of *coemeteria,* or "resting places," where the deceased could await resurrection. In the Middle Ages, the name "catacombs," derived from a sign under the basilica of San Sebastiano on the Appian Way, was applied to these underground cemeteries. More than 60 such catacombs were built in locations around Rome, each consisting of mile upon mile of galleries in tufa, a form of lime-stone. Starting from old caves or wells, they descended to a depth of up to five levels. Branching off the galleries were innumerable burial niches (*loculi*), arched recesses (*arcosolia*), and chapels to accommodate the more important tombs. In the time of Theodosius, the diggers who carried out the work belonged to an organization and handled the sale of plots.

Gallery with burial niches and arched recesses, first level of the Priscilla catacombs, Rome, second to third century.

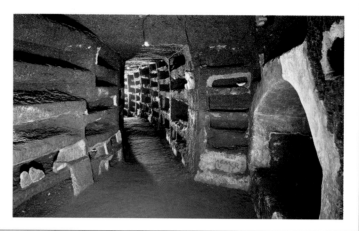

SARCOPHAGUS OF JUNIUS BASSUS

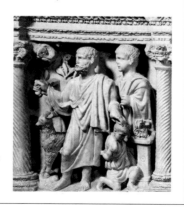

Detail from the Sarcophagus of Junius Bassus. Treasury of St Peter's, Vatican City.

Junius Bassus, prefect of Rome, had recently been converted when he died in AD359. His sarcophagus was a masterpiece of technique and inventiveness. Its subject matter and style spanned two ages, blending elements of both classical and Christian art. The work was arranged on two layers, the lower level with arched sections and the upper with lintels. The entry of Christ into Jerusalem mirrors the arrival of the emperors. The three central scenes of the upper panel are static and solemn, in contrast to the narrative vivacity of the others; this recalls the contrast between the symbolic appearances of the emperor and the depiction of the military activities on the column of Marcus Aurelius. In the center, the sovereignty of Christ is supported by the personification of Heaven. The arrest of Peter (on the left) is placed on the same footing as that of Jesus (on the right), in consideration of the fact that St. Peter's basilica was chosen as the site for the monument. The hand of God appears in the upper left corner to halt Abraham as he prepares to sacrifice his son: the direction of the gesture makes a diagonal line across the sculpted surface, which concludes with Paul being led to his martyrdom, facing outward like Abraham. The two extremes of the other diagonal, however, arrive at the seated, inward-facing figures of Pilate (above), and Job (below). On one side of Christ's entry the Fall of Man is shown, and Daniel in the lions' den is shown on the other.

Detail from Sarcophagus of Junius Bassus. Treasury of St. Peter's, Vatican City.

sculpture, incorporeal forms were lost in space and shadow, with emphasis instead on the symbolism of a few selected objects. The sarcophagus of the Via Salaria (Museo Pio Cristiano) blends the rustic motif of rams with groups of people reading, two disciples, and the deceased's wife with her servants. In the center is the Good Shepherd, allegory of Christ. The increasing power of Christianity troubled its opponents. Decius (249–251) ordered all citizens to worship the gods, and, in an empire scourged by pestilence and famine, Valerian (253–260) renewed general persecution. He issued edicts against the clergy in an attempt to dismantle the entire structure of the Church. Decorative art was influenced by the thinking of some of the individuals who were subjected to persecution: Cyprian of Carthage, bishop and martyr, a moralist who developed the philosophy (based on Lucretius) of a world that had grown old and tired, and Novatian, who initiated theological speculation. The authority of the bishops, recognized by Valerian, provided an excuse for

POPULAR ART OF THE CATACOMBS

In order to avoid an elitist form of decoration, the burial niches of the catacombs developed an artistic style that was neither technically nor economically demanding. Besides the paintings on the ceilings and walls, the rectangular sepulchres, hemmed in by areas of marble and brick, provided a great opportunity for artistic experimentation. Here, the ideas of the faithful were concentrated within a confined space, surrounded by the natural frame of the tufa.

Initially, the space was left undecorated, as was customary in the expectation of the imminent return of Christ. But attention to the deceased persons increased as hope for the reincarnation faded. In some cases, the name of the person was inscribed in the mortar. The illiterate tried to reproduce the evocative and protective value of inscriptions by using sequences of enigmatic signs. Articles buried in the tomb were chosen not so much as comfort for the deceased but as souvenirs of past lives and relationships. Set into the plaster were items of nostalgia such as bracelets,

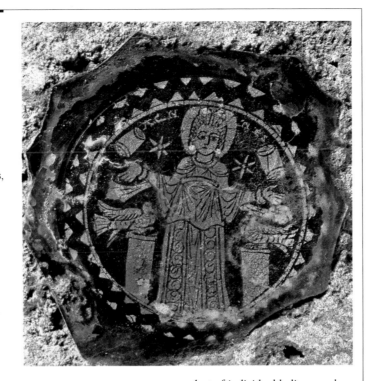

Saint Agnes between columns and doves, stars, and scrolls of the law, gilded base of a glass vase inserted into the plaster of a burial niche, third century. Catacombs of Panfilo, Rome.

necklaces, dolls, ivory statuettes, and small domestic items such as buttons, pins, and coins. These objects were of no great symbolic significance and had meaning only for the family of the deceased. Catacomb decoration was not the work of a particular school of artists

but of individual believers who, by assembling and reconverting humble belongings, managed to express themselves in a spontaneous and intimate way. From a means of giving recognition to anonymous tombs, this custom went on to kindle new styles. The addition of bright materials, shells, pieces of glass, and colored marbles meant that these subterranean creations came to life in the light of the blazing lanterns.

destroying churches, burning scriptures, and convicting adherents. In AD306, peace returned to Italy with Maxentius and to the western provinces with Constantine (306–337), who defeated Maxentius in AD312, bearing the monogram of Christ on his soldiers' shields. The following year, he issued the edict of tolerance. The church soon made an impact on cities with its new ceremonial buildings, climaxing with the building of St. Peter's basilica (AD319–24).

THE JEWS OF ROME

Under Greek rule, the Jews had struggled to retain their identity as a people, but the Romans recognized their religious practices as lawful. The destruction of Jerusalem by the Roman emperor Titus (AD70) led to a widespread *diáspora* ("dispersal"), with large-scale immigration to Italy, where the Jews were permitted to observe their rites. Excavations at Pompeii uncovered the writing on the wall of a member of the Jewish community, who, during the catastrophic eruption of Vesuvius (AD79), had scribbled "Sodom and Gomorrah." During the reign of Hadrian, the Jewish rising in Palestine (AD132–135) widened the rift with the Christian community of Jerusalem, which was loyal to the Romans. In Rome, there were at least 12 synagogues, one fine example surviving to this day at Ostia. The inscriptions in the Jewish catacombs were initially in Aramaic and Greek but then superseded by Latin. Alongside these writings, other features of Jewish rituals were found in the architecture of synagogues, or on ceramics and gilded glass vases, for example the seven-branched candelabrum (menorah), the dove, the palm, and the ampulla of oil. All these symbols became associated with the conventional funeral repertory but sometimes contained within a narrative influenced by local styles. In one painting from the Jewish cemetery of Vigna Randanini, for example, the mythical singer Orpheus merges with the psalmist David, and the background contains liturgical subjects.

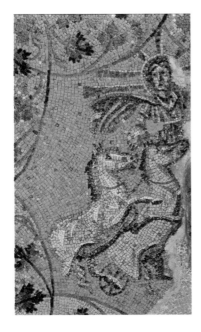

Christ with a radiating crown, wall mosaic, third–fourth century. Mausoleum of the Julii, Vatican Tombs, Vatican City.

Gallienus (260–268) to revoke the notion of the primacy of the bishop of Rome and establish the jurisdictional rights of individual Christian communities. Christianity was the *religio licita* ("permitted religion"), and Christian officials were relieved of the obligation to worship idols. In painting, the subject of salvation was supplemented by deeper issues. Extreme human conditions were examined in the disobedience of Adam and Eve, the patience of Job, and the dedication of Abraham. The principle of a guiding

providence was celebrated in the story of David armed with a sling, Tobias with the fish that restored his father's sight, and Jonah rescued from the belly of the whale and spared to convert the city of Nineveh. The last is the only prophet with whom Christ compares himself and his mission during his sermons (Matthew 12: 39–41). He is depicted as a teacher as well as a central figure in the ranks of the apostles.

Diocletian (284–305) returned to the original belief in the sacred nature of the empire and excluded Christians from the army in AD297. Galerius (305–311) extended Valerian's policy of extermination,

Stone slab that closed the burial niche of a baby, with Hebrew symbols and the Greek inscription "Judas, aged seven months, lies here," catacombs of Via Portuense, fourth century. Museum of Hebrew Inscriptions, Vatican City.

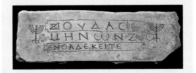

BARBARIAN ART

The term "barbarian" loosely defines a broad range of peoples and art styles that existed alongside the "civilized" cultures of the Mediterranean, China, and the Near East. "Barbaros" is Greek for "foreign" but literally means "stammering," after the unfamilar sound of tongues other than Greek. Because barbarian cultures were fundamentally nonliterate, we know them primarily through their rich material culture and art.

The influence and exchange of ideas and art styles between "barbarian" and "civilized" cultures was a continual process. The Greeks and the Etruscans were in contact with three primary groups of "barbarians" – the Celts, Scythians, and Thracians. Modern knowledge of these cultures is derived largely from archaeological investigations, although one literary source – Herodotus, the Greek geographer and historian writing in the mid-fifth century BC – vividly describes Scythian culture. The vast Roman Empire dealt with different groups of "barbarians" that superseded the above – the later Celtic populations, the Sarmatians, and groups of Germanic-speaking peoples who had migrated from the north to southern Russia and Eastern Europe. In the late fourth century AD, Hunnic tribes from Inner Asia, the "ultimate barbarians," arrived in southern Russia. This forced the Germanic and Sarmatian populations west and initiated the historical process known as the Migration Period, which transformed the Roman Empire into medieval Europe.

THE CELTS

The "Keltoi" to the Greeks or "Galli" to the Romans were Indo-European speaking peoples whose culture spread from the upper Danube and eastern France south to northern Italy, the Iberian peninsula,

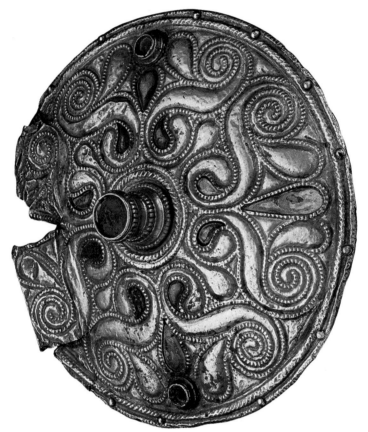

Bronze disk covered with embossed gold sheet inlaid with coral and enamel, Auvers-sur-Oise, early fourth century. Bibliothèque Nationale, Paris.

and North Africa; west to the Low Countries and the British Isles; and east to the Balkans and Asia Minor. The first manifestation of Celtic art appears on the objects found in more than a thousand graves excavated at Halstatt, a salt-mining settlement in the Alps, near Salzburg in Austria. In this Bronze Age phase, which began in the late second

millennium and continued until the mid-sixth century BC, the "art" consisted largely of functional but highly sophist-icated metalwork designed for personal adornment and to embellish weapons, and horse and chariot fittings. It was probably produced under princely patronage and is chiefly geometric and non-representational in nature. The second (Iron Age) phase lasted from about 500BC to the Roman conquests in the late second and early first century BC and is called La Tène, after a settle-

ment and votive deposit on the shores of Lake Neuchâtel in France. Early La Tène styles derive from classical decorative and plant motifs such as palmettes and scrolls, but these still incorporate animal figures and human heads into their curvilinear structure. Depending on the region, these styles evolved in different ways with the representational elements often becoming more cryptic and abstract and the continu-ous geometric designs more fluid, often underpinned by complex, compass-based patterns. Some stylistic variants were completely linear, engraved on flat surfaces, while others were more plastic and naturalistic. The artists still worked primarily in metal, favoring gold, copper alloys, and iron, sometimes adding

Gold torc from the chariot burial of a princess, Waldalgesheim, Germany, second half of the fourth century BC. Rheinisches Landesmuseum, Bonn.

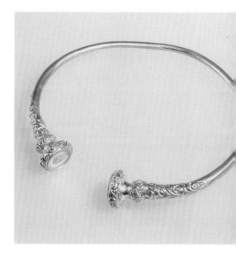

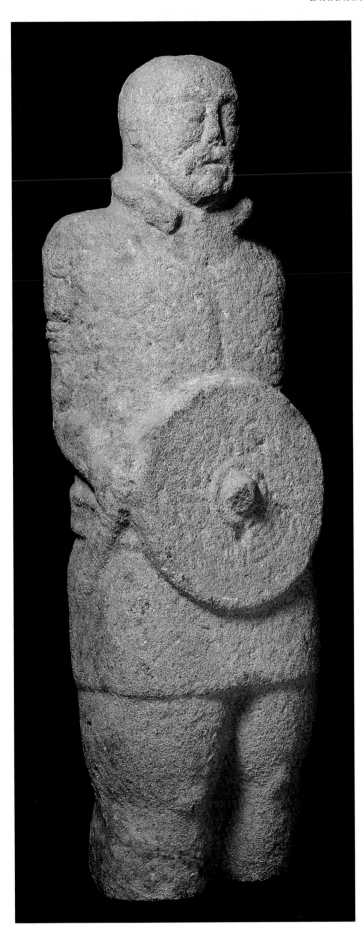

Stone statue of a warrior wearing a torc, Castro do Lezenho, Boticas, Portugal, first century BC to first century AD. Museu Nacional de Arqueológia e Etnológia, Lisbon.

inlays of coral, amber, or enamel. Personal jewelry for both men and women, arms, armor, and horse trappings were elaborately decorated, as were everyday articles such as mirrors and vessel fittings. Torcs, or neck rings, were status symbols in many Celtic societies, which together with long hair, beards, and trousers, came to signify "barbarian" in Greek and Roman representations. Celtic artists also worked in wood and stone, producing large representational sculptures of both humans and animals; many of these appear to have been used in cult temples or as grave markers. After the Roman conquest, abstract variants of the Celtic style survived primarily in the remote British Isles, to be invested with new vigor by artisans in the second half of the first millennium AD.

CLASSICAL AND BARBARIAN IMPULSES

The territories beyond the Greek cities around the Black Sea were occupied by Thracians in the west and Scythians to the north and east. The latter traded wheat, fur, slaves, gold, and amber from the north. Scythian burial mounds in southern Russia were storehouses of everyday Greek pottery, buried side by side with breathtaking gold jewelry, vessels, and fittings reflecting both classical and barbarian traditions. Some items, such as necklaces, earrings, and ritual vessels, were purely Greek in both style and function; other ornaments, such as large pectorals and combs, were Scythian forms decorated in Greek style; yet other objects were purely Scythian in both decoration and function. Some objects in the second category,

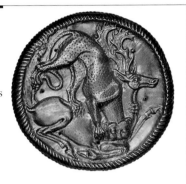

Gold phalera with a feline attacking a stag, Ol'gino Mound, fifth century BC. Museum of Archaeology at the Ukraine National Academy of Science, Kiev.

which must have been made by Greek craftsmen for Scythian clients, bear naturalistic images of the Scythians themselves, engaged in battle, milking mares, and shoeing horses. These contrast with abstract and stylized representations of animals used to decorate horse harnesses and with representations of animal combat, which derive ultimately from ancient Near Eastern sources. A similar mixture of Greek, Persian, and barbarian traditions also characterizes the objects from Thracian tombs on the western shores of the Black Sea in present-day Bulgaria. In contrast to the Scythian finds, many of these were fashioned in silver, probably obtained from mines in the Carpathians. The sheer quantity of precious metals and their exuberant decoration may have reflected "barbarian" taste, but in general the decoration of all of these luxury goods is of the highest standard.

Gold comb showing a battle, Solokha kurgan, Ukraine, early fourth century BC. The State Hermitage Museum, St. Petersburg.

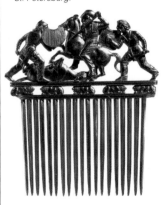

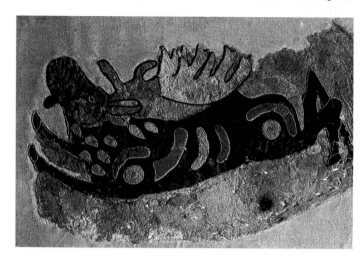

Felt saddle cover with appliqué depicting an elk, Kurgan 2, Pazyryk, Altai, Siberia, fourth century BC. The State Hermitage Museum, St. Petersburg. The arcs enclosing dots used on the haunches are a typical steppe motif derived from Iranian art.

THE ART OF THE STEPPES

The steppe, the vast grasslands that stretch across Eurasia, was in ancient times, as it is now, home to nomadic and semi-nomadic pastoral peoples of both Caucasian and Mongolian stock. They were in contact, both peacefully and aggressively, with the great settled civilizations of the ancient world – the Assyrians and Persians, the Greeks and Romans, and the Indians and Chinese – and their art was a rich blend of their own cultural symbols with those classical traditions. Much of the art they produced was small, portable metalwork and wood carving, suited to their lifestyle and stylistically conservative for many centuries. The primary tribes with which the Western civilizations were acquainted were the Scythians, their successors the Sarmatians, and, finally, in the early medieval period, the Huns. The Iranian-speaking Scythians are first mentioned in Assyrian sources around the middle of the seventh century BC. Within two centuries, their territories stretched from the Danube to the Don and north to the boundary between the forest

and steppe, but their cultural sway extended southeast into the Caucasus and west to the Dobruja with a far eastern branch in Siberia. Herodotus described the everyday life of the Scythians, who drank mare's milk and interred their dead beneath massive earthen mounds, accompanied by human and animal sacrifices. His observations have been borne out by excavations of these mounds, or *kurgans*, the underground chambers of which were filled not only with sacrifices but splendid golden grave goods. In the east, a spectacular group of Scythian burials in wooden chambers was discovered in the Altai mountains in Siberia. The permafrost preserved human bodies, including one entirely tattooed man, and

Large gold stag plaque from a shield, Kostromskaja kurgan, Krasnodar region, late seventh or early sixth century BC. The State Hermitage Museum, St. Petersburg.

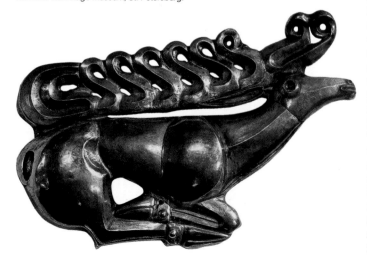

horses still wearing their elaborate wooden bridles and headgear. Colorful felt textiles, such as three-dimensional stuffed swans designed to hang from the top of a tent, illustrate the richness of the nomadic lifestyle, while a knotted woollen rug, the oldest one known, testifies to long-distance trading contacts between the Scythians and Achaemenid Persians. The animal style developed by the Scythians was powerful and stylized, depicting animals and birds with their most important attributes (horns, paws, and beaks) exaggerated. It was applied to horse trappings, personal status symbols such as belt buckles, and weaponry such as *akinakes* (short swords), battle axes, and bow cases.

The Iranian Sarmatians continued a stylized version of this animal ornament, often executed in repoussé gold sheet accented with turquoise inlays. Ornaments in this style have been found across a large region stretching from Afghanistan to the Caucasus and across southern Russia. These artifacts span a long period from the first century BC to the fourth century AD. Dating from the Roman period, graffiti of mounted Sarmatians depict them carrying long spears and with both themselves and their

"BOETHIUS IMPRISONED"

Severinus Boethius (c.AD480-525), a Roman of noble birth, was a philosopher and translator of classical Greek who served as consul to Theodoric, the Ostrogothic ruler of Italy. Accused of siding with the Byzantines against the Ostrogoths, he was condemned to death. Before his execution, he was imprisoned at Pavia, where he wrote *De Consolatione Philosophiae* (*The Consolation of Philosophy*). Various early Romanesque manuscripts illuminated in Germany, France, and England depict the imprisonment of Boethius. He is shown suffering at the hands of the guards, as in this image, but also consoled by Philosophy and the Muses in others. He became a key figure in later medieval schools of thought and education. His work forms the basis of the *Quadrivium*, the four mathematical branches of the seven liberal arts – arithmetic, geometry, astronomy, and music.

Boethius in prison, De Consolatione Philosophiae, 11th century (cod. Paris, Lat. 6041, fo. 13v). Bibliothèque Nationale, Paris

horses encased in suits of armor. Like the Scythians, their leaders were buried beneath massive mounds. Recent excavations in Ukraine at sites such as Porogi have unearthed large quantities of gold ornaments and vessels studded with semi-precious stones in a polychromatic style that influenced later Migration Period art.

The Huns, who appeared without warning at the Sea of Azov in AD369, were traditionally regarded as the most brutal and physically ugly of all barbarians. They probably spoke a proto-Turkish tongue, and, although their origins remain obscure, there can be

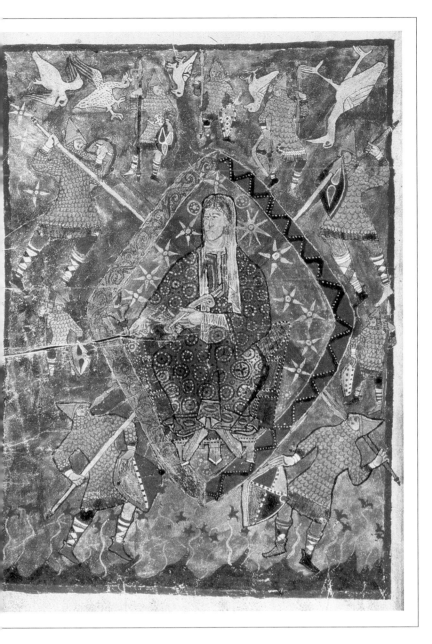

THE GOTHS

Historical sources combined with archaeological evidence suggest that the Goths originally lived around the Baltic Sea on the islands off the coast of Sweden and in modern Poland. Sometime in the second century AD, these Germanic-speaking tribes began to move southward into Ukraine, where they amalgamated with the local agrarian peoples. These were known as the Chernyakov culture, and their artifacts are characterized by humpbacked bone combs and bow fibulae with flat semicircular heads and long footplates. The Goths established themselves along the northern shores of the Black Sea and gradually expanded south and west into the province of Dacia, abandoned by the Romans. In the fourth century, they were converted to the Arian form of Christianity by Ulfilas, a missionary who translated the Bible into Gothic. Two primary groups of Goths were known to the Romans in the fourth and fifth centuries – the Visigoths (eastern Goths) and Ostrogoths (western Goths). When Hunnic tribes from Inner Asia moved into the Crimean penninsula in the 370s, the Goths fled, along with other tribes, crossing the Danube in 376. Allied with Huns and Alani (a Sarmatian tribe), they defeated the Roman Empire in a decisive battle at Adrianople in 378, killing the Roman emperor Valens. Visigoths were settled in Thrace and the Ostrogoths, Huns, and Alns in Pannonia Secunda (roughly the Carpathian Basin in Hungary). Discontented Visigoths under Alaric invaded Italy in 401, sacking Rome in 410. The Visigoths were allowed to settle in southern Gaul and eventually took control of the Iberian peninsula. The Ostrogoths, under their leader Theodoric, marched to Italy, where he was proclaimed King

and allowed to govern the Western Empire. The later fourth and fifth centuries, before these kingdoms were established, are known as the Migration Period, and the distinctive art produced by the Goths at this time consists largely of portable personal possessions such as weapons, jewelry, and horse trappings. The wealthiest examples of these were fashioned of gold decorated with garnet cloisonné; like the Franks, their leaders probably had access to such gold and gemstones as a result of their close relationship with the Eastern Roman government in Constantinople. The everyday material culture of the Ostrogoths in Italy, revealed largely by female grave goods, is closely similar to that produced while they occupied Pannonia – the women secured their garments with large bow fibulae and wore rings and earrings in the classical manner. Unfortunately, their stable government and patronage of the arts was cut short by the reconquest of Italy by Justinian, finalized by 555. Visigothic culture, on the other hand, developed steadily in southern France and the Iberian peninsula and is particularly well represented by grave goods from large cemeteries dating from the sixth to the eighth century. Large plate fibulae continued to be worn by women, along with earrings and distinctive square buckles. The latter were decorated initially with semi-precious stones and then increasingly with glass. Eventually, they were made solely of copper alloy, engraved with scenes derived from early Christian iconography borrowed, in turn, from the Byzantine empire. The Visigoths officially converted to Catholicism under Reccared in AD589. A group of splendid votive hanging crowns, regal offerings to the Church of Toledo in the first half of the seventh century, was found at Guarazzar, near Toledo. Fashioned of gold embellished

no question that their primary vessels – large bronze cauldrons with projecting ring handles – can be traced with them across the steppe from the northern borders of China. In the late fourth and early fifth centuries, they formed alliances with Sarmatian and Germanic tribes and often fought with the Romans against other barbarians. They succeeded in extracting large subsidies in gold from the Roman government, both in payment for their services and to keep them at bay. Once their power base was established in Pannonia, the Hunnic federation under Attila

(died AD452) began plundering and raiding farther to the west, remaining undefeated until a disastrous battle at the Catalunian Fields in France, where the allied Huns, Ostrogoths, and Burgundians suffered heavy losses. We almost know more about them from historical sources than from archaeology, since they cremated their dead and founded no settlements. Their most splendid ornaments were fashioned of gold sheet studded with cabochon garnets. Many of these took nonclassical forms, such as diadems, temple pendants, and whip handles.

OSTROGOTHIC ARCHITECTURE

Theodoric built in the grand Roman manner at Ravenna, the capital of the Western Empire, in the fifth century AD. A nave mosaic at Sant'Apollinaire Nuovo depicts his palatium (imperial residence) with a triple arched entrance projecting from a colonnaded facade. Each arch originally contained a figure below a hanging crown of laurel leaves – Theodoric in the center, flanked by his wife, family, and court. The portraits were replaced by curtains after Justinian's reconquest of Italy. Theodoric's tomb, probably

begun the year before he died in AD526, is the only monument in Ravenna to be built of dressed limestone blocks. The building is decagonal in plan, with a lower story of ten arched niches and a complex, unfinished upper story. The ground floor was cross-shaped and groin-vaulted, while the upper floor was circular and topped with a monolithic shallow dome weighing more than 233 tons. The dome is encircled by 12 pierced spurs, each inscribed with the name of an apostle.

Nave mosaic depicting the palatium of Theodoric, before AD526. Sant'Apollinare Nuovo, Ravenna, Italy.

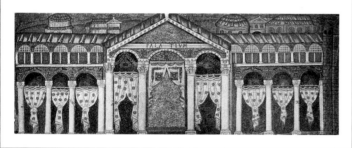

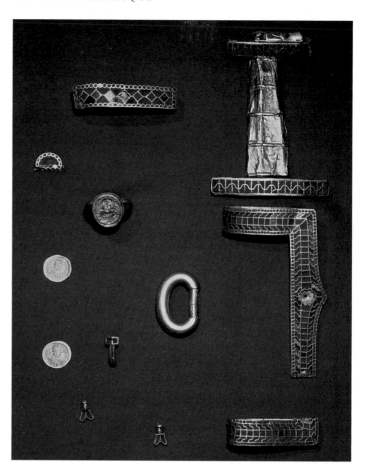

Objects from the burial of Childeric, including gold and garnet cloisonné sword fittings, buckles, coins, and a copy of his signet ring. Bibliothèque Nationale, Paris.

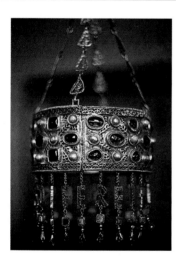

Votive crown with hanging pendants spelling the latinized name of Recceswinth (ruled AD653–72), gold with sapphires, pearls, and garnets. Museo Arqueológico Nacional, Madrid.

with semiprecious stones, their form derives from a fusion of imperial and sacred traditions. The excellent preservation of a few seventh-century churches in northern Spain testifies to a tradition of high-quality building and sculptural ornamentation that

prefigures the Romanesque. The invasions of the Arabs in 711 overwhelmed all of southern Spain, but a reduced Visigothic kingdom survived in Asturias and southern France into the ninth and tenth centuries.

THE FRANKS

The Franks were a political amalgamation of many smaller Germanic tribes who lived between the Weser and Rhine rivers. From the second to the fourth century AD, in exchange for the defense of the northern frontier, they were allowed by the Roman Empire to cultivate fallow lands in the heartland of Gaul. Their gradual infiltration ensured that provincial Roman industries, such as glassmaking, pottery, and metalworking, continued without interruption. These crafts are well preserved in burials in large Frankish cemeteries known as row-grave

cemeteries. Weaponry and belt sets in male graves reflect late Roman army styles, while female ornaments are closer to native Germanic traditions. One of the most important finds of the early medieval period is a burial mound, discovered in 1685, outside Tournai in Belgium. A signet ring in the grave was inscribed with the name of the Frankish ruler Childeric, who was succeeded by his son, Clovis, in about 481. Many of the finds were later stolen, but a gold crossbow brooch and garnet cloisonné ornaments suggest that Childeric served in the Roman militia, the civil and military bureaucracy in the provinces. The Merovingian dynasty he founded takes its name from his semilegendary father, Merovech. From the sixth to the eighth century, the Merovingians ruled the Low

Countries, northern Germany, and most of France, with their dominions divided into two kingdoms, Austrasia and Neustria. In the sixth and seventh centuries, their buckles, brooches, and weaponry were decorated with garnet cloisonné and Christian imagery. This mixture of Germanic and classical traditions continued in the decoration of manuscripts and reliquaries from the seventh to the ninth century. The Merovingians maintained a monetary economy, investing their wealth in the construction of churches, monasteries, and abbeys, thereby preserving the heritage of stone carving and architecture. Key monuments that survive from this period are the Baptistry of St. Jean at Poitiers and the crypt at the Abbey of Jourre, founded by the daughter of a barbarian noble, which still holds the elaborate stone and plaster sarcophaghi of its abbesses. In 751, Pepin, mayor of Austrasia, deposed Childeric III to found the Carolingian dynasty.

ANGLO-SAXON AND HIBERNO-SAXON ART

Accounts of the settlement of England by different Germanic tribes given by the Venerable Bede, an early eighth-century monk, have been largely borne out by modern archaeology. Comparison of metalwork and pottery found in England with Continental types suggests that the Saxons came from between the Elbe and Weser rivers in Lower Saxony, the Angles from Angeln (modern Schleswig-Holstein), and the Jutes from the Jutland peninsula and perhaps southern Scandinavia. The causes and nature of the arrival of these tribes in the fourth and fifth centuries is complex – some served as mercenaries for the Roman army, but the majority probably came as invaders to a land that was ill-defended by the later Roman Empire. Saxon sea pirates had been raiding the

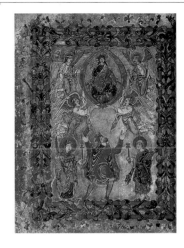

King Edgar, Christ, the Virgin Mary, and St. Peter in the Statute of Winchester, *AD966. British Library, London.*

Carpet page introducing St. John's Gospel, The Lindisfarne Gospels, *c.AD698 (Cotton MS Nero D.iv). British Library, London.*

southern coasts of England since the third century; eventually, in the fifth century, considerable numbers of immigrants colonized large areas of England. By the sixth and seventh centuries, the Saxons, the Angles, and the Jutes had evolved distinctive regional variations of dress and art. As with other Germanic tribes, we

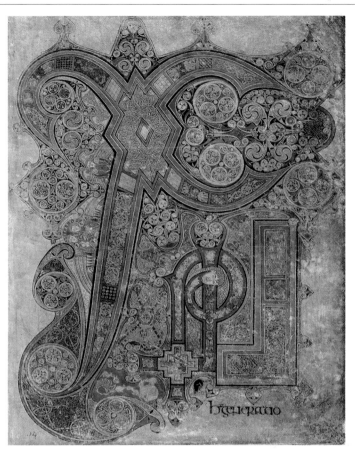

Chi-Rho monogram from The Gospels of Matthew, The Book of Kells, *c.AD800 (fo. 34r). Trinity College Library, Dublin.*

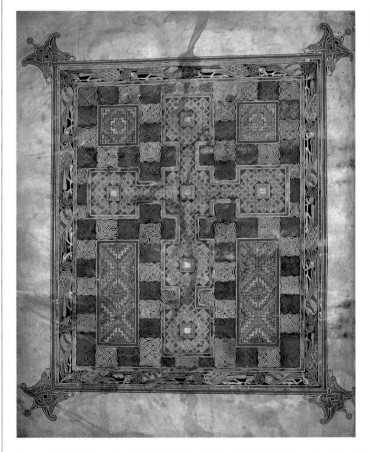

understand their art primarily from their grave goods. The women wore either large bow brooches with square heads, or circular brooches of various forms. These were decorated with abstract human and animal figures in a style known as "chip-carving." In areas such as Kent, which had close trading links with the Franks, the brooches were often decorated with garnet inlays. One of the most outstanding finds of the entire early medieval period is the grave of an Anglian chieftain buried in a large sailing ship beneath a mound at Sutton Hoo in Suffolk, East Anglia. He was interred with a full set of regalia and weaponry, much of it decorated with gold and garnet cloisonné; silver tableware imported from Byzantium; and symbols of his authority such as a standard and scepter. Gold coins in his waistpurse, each representing a different Frankish

mint, suggest that he was buried sometime in the late 620s. Although his style of burial was purely pagan, by that time the process of Christianization was well advanced in England. By the middle of the seventh century, the practice of inhumation with grave goods ceased, and our knowledge of Anglo-Saxon art is based upon splendid illuminated manuscripts from monasteries in Northumbria. Some early examples of these, such as the carpet pages from the *Lindisfarne Gospels*, still bore animal interlace and geometric patterns derived directly from metal prototypes, mixed with classical motifs from the Mediterranean world. These styles were further developed in monastic scriptoria in Ireland, where native Celtic impulses produced intricate linear patterns underpinned by complex geometric compass work. Some of these interlaced patterns were translated into stone carving, where they appear on large stone crosses dating from the seventh to the ninth century.

MONASTERIES

It was politically advantageous for the aristocracy of the Germanic tribes to convert to Christianity, so the Christian church grew immensely wealthy from donations in the sixth and seventh centuries. Two hundred monasteries existed south of the Loire when St. Columba, an Irish missionary, arrived in Europe in 585, and by the end of the seventh century, over four hundred flourished in the Merovingian kingdom alone. Monastic foundations served as the springboard for the conversion of the pagan Germanic peoples, with missionaries traveling widely across Europe. Monastic scriptoria played a key role in the transmission of the Latin language and classical culture, copying and illuminating not only religious texts but also medical and scientific treatises from the ancient world. The *Codex Amiatinus* was copied from a Vulgate version of St. Jerome brought from Rome to England in 678; the large Anglo-Saxon copy was being taken back to Rome by Ceolfrid, abbot of the twin monasteries of Jarrow and Monkwearmouth in Northumbria, when he died at Langres in 716.

The prophet Ezra as a scribe, from the Codex Amiatinus, an Anglo-Saxon manuscript illuminated in Italo-Byzantine style, before AD716 (Amiatinus I, fol. Vr). Biblioteca Medicea-Laurenziana, Florence.

Marble panels from a presbyterial enclosure, eighth century. Abbey of San Pietro in Valle, Ferentillo.

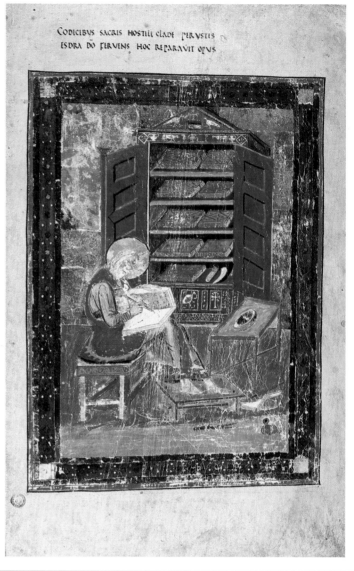

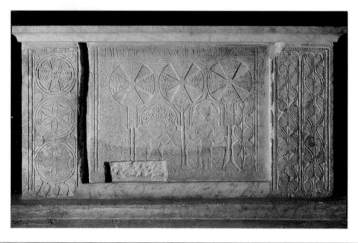

THE LOMBARDS

The Langobards (literally long-beards), or Lombards, as they became known, lived around the Elbe river in the first and second centuries AD. Contemporary Roman accounts describe them as warlike, and they were responsible for many raids into the Roman provinces of Pannonia. They eventually moved into lower Austria and settled south of the great bend of the Danube in the Carpathian Basin, alongside the native population and another Germanic tribe called the Gepids. With Byzantine aid, the Lombards defeated the Gepids in the mid-sixth century and in 568 occupied northern Italy, where they founded the last "barbarian" kingdom in the region that still bears their name. They established their capital at Pavia, and, although they never took Ravenna or Rome, autonomous Lombardic kingdoms were founded at Spoleto near Rome and at Benevento near Naples. Prior to their migration into Italy, we know their culture primarily from excavated inhumation graves in Hungary. These reveal that they shared many key aspects of material culture with neighboring Germanic tribes such as the Franks, Alamanni, and even with the Anglo-Saxons, who had been their neighbors in the north. Men were buried with belt sets and weaponry, often decorated in animal style, while women wore radiate bow fibulae decorated with animal heads and geometric motifs in cast "chip-carving" and sometimes with garnet inlay. In the first phase of their occupation of Italy, these cultural traditions remained unchanged. By the early seventh century, however, female jewelry shifted almost entirely to Byzantine style, while the decoration of male

Gilt-bronze plaque, possibly from a helmet, identified by an inscription as belonging to King Agilulf (AD591–615) enthroned between attendants and acolytes, Val de Nievole, near Lucca, Italy. Museo Nazionale del Bargello, Florence.

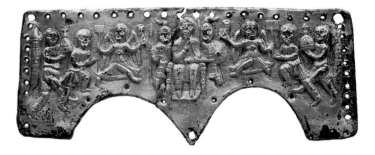

belt sets remained closely related to contemporary Germanic styles to the north. Unlike the Ostrogoths, the Lombards were converts from Arianism to Catholicism, and their graves often contained distinctive stamped gold crosses. They became patrons of Christianity, erecting both grand basilicas and small cross-plan churches and monasteries. The rich ornamentations in marble, stucco, and fresco have been preserved in the interiors of some of these buildings. Some, such as the famous relief panel depicting the Adoration of the Magi at Cividale, are uniquely Lombardic in their very stylized and linear treatment of figures surrounded by interlace. The marble panels at San Pietro in Valle, dedicated by Ilderico II, Duke of Spoleto from AD739 to 740, depict a

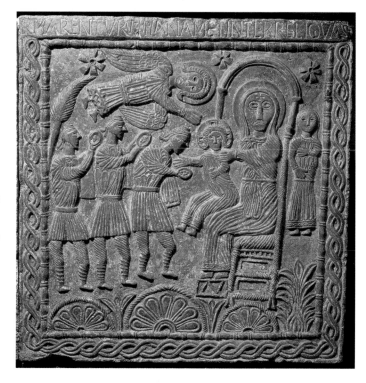

Adoration of the Magi *from the altar of the Duke of Ratchis, San Martino, Cividale, c.740. Christian Museum and Cathedral Treasury, Cividale del Friuli.*

figure holding a chisel labeled "URSUS MAG-ESTER FECIT", a rare and early instance where a medieval artisan has signed his work. Other carvings reflect Byzantine carving styles or, as in the case of the seventh and eighth century frescoes at Santa Maria Antiqua in Rome and Castelseprio, classical painting styles. Both of these form a critical link between the ancient world and the styles that evolved in the Romanesque and Gothic periods. The Lombards in the north were defeated by the Franks under Charlemagne, while the lesser southern principalities survived until the conquests of the Normans in the 11th century.

THE VIKINGS

"Viking" is a generic name applied to the seafaring raiders from Scandinavia whose invasions terrorized Britain and Europe from the ninth to the eleventh century AD. They were the last true pagans, perceived as such by the Christianized Germanic kingdoms, and their extensive oral sagas, written

Box brooch made of partially gilt bronze, covered with silver and gold decorated with niello, filigree, and granulation, Mårtens, Grötlingbo, Gotland, Sweden, eleventh century. Statens Historiska Museum, Stockholm.

Rock carving depicting warriors and ships, Vitlycke, Bohuslän, Sweden, Bronze Age.

down in the high Middle Ages, were sources of pagan myths and social traditions for the early medieval period. Although the Norse were settled agricultural peoples, their primary means of communication was by sea. Improvements in shipbuilding in the early medieval period meant that long-distance travel and trade became increasingly practical. The raids by Norsemen from across Scandinavia, which began in the late eighth century, were not coordinated in any overall fashion but had as their initial goal the acquisition of precious metals to be used as bullion in a nonmonetary economy. Many hoards of gold and silver ornaments, often cut up for melting down, survive from the early Viking period. Lightning raids,

particularly of the treasuries of wealthy monasteries, were often followed by settlement. A network of trading stations was established in the Baltic, along the rivers of Russia, in Iceland, Greenland, Ireland, northeast England, and northern France. Superb Viking metalwork, executed with complex animal interlace in various styles, was mirrored in wooden carvings such as those found in a burial at Oseberg, Norway, which include elaborately decorated carts, sledges, and a ship. They also erected large standing stones decorated with carved, narrative figural scenes and/or runes, the native alphabet.

BYZANTINE ART

As the Roman power base shifted to the city of Constantinople (previously Byzantium), Byzantine art spread through eastern Europe. There was also a great influence from the Near East and from barbarian art and Persian culture. The common language, or Koine, *spoken throughout the Roman world faded, and Greek became the language of the empire.*

The emperor Constantine founded Constantinople in AD324, dedicating the new city to the Virgin Mary. Gradually, in the centuries that followed, Roman culture became influenced by the East and the "barbarian" cultures of northern Europe. Respect for tradition was passed down without question or criticism, evident in the fact that the Greek language of a fifth-century writer is virtually indistinguishable from that written in the 12th century. Byzantine art displayed the same constancy: in the fifth and sixth centuries, it developed a formal expression that was manifested in thousands of works of art that came to be regarded as sacred and immutable. This survived the eighth and early ninth centuries (when those who venerated graven images were terrorized by the iconoclasts) and was revived in the late ninth century.

FEATURES OF BYZANTINE ART

Byzantine art is a stylized, religious art form, distinguished by its naturalism and by a rejection of the ordinary in favor of the extraordinary. The wide social gulf between lay and church leaders on the one hand and the people on the other was evident in Byzantine art. Intricate aesthetic detail is paramount: in architecture, outer walls are made to look like thin curtains and topped by a dome (an emblem of perfection), while interior walls are lavishly encrusted

Marble capital with horses, San Vitale, Ravenna, Italy, sixth century. Typical Byzantine capitals such as this gradually developed from the earlier Hellenistic-Roman designs. The characteristic abstract surface design is achieved by a combination of fretwork and the repetitive patterns of the acanthus leaves.

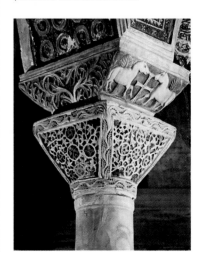

ARMENIAN ARCHITECTURE

The Armenian people enjoyed a long period of prosperity between their conversion to Christianity and the Mongol invasion of the 13th century. Throughout Armenia and neighboring Georgia there was much important and original architecture, with historical links to the traditions of the peoples who had long dominated the region – the Persians and Romans – and with the Byzantine *koinè* from the fifth century. By the tenth century, Armenian architecture was developing along independent lines. Advanced building techniques, notably the use of concrete domes and vaults on stone walls, led to many remarkable monuments that still survive, despite earthquakes and wartime destruction. Earlier than in other regions, Armenian church architects employed the basic plan of a central dome on a square base, a theme that was elaborated on many times. The dome, set on a circular or

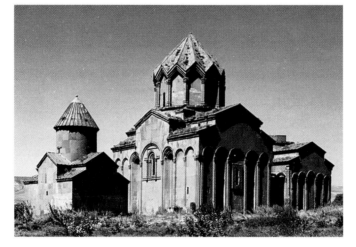

Monastery of Marmashen, 10th–13th century. Following the decline of Armenian power, monastic buildings gained in importance and became the places where culture was preserved. The building next to the church, the gavit, was used not just for worship but also for assemblies and meetings.

polygonal drum, is often supported by four pilasters, and the interior contains pilasters with arches and niches. In many cases, the plans of the buildings are quite complex, such as those of the church of Kazkh. Those that follow the Greek cross type sometimes have terminal apses and corner pieces between the arms. The fascinating ruins of the old Armenian capital, Ani, include rectangular, domed, and polygonal churches. There are also castellated monastic complexes. Much of the ornamentation was carved from stone and in some cases was inlaid in a style incorporating Persian, Arabic, Syrian, and Byzantine elements. Armenian architecture had a lasting influence on later styles in the Caucasian region.

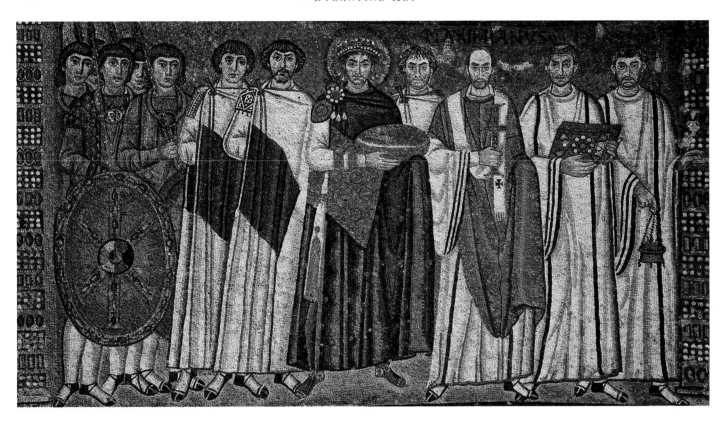

Wall mosaic, Justinian and His Attendants, *San Vitale, Ravenna, Italy, c.546–47. Suspended in a golden space and identical in posture, the figures are individualized by their faces. The emperor is identified by emblems of rank, including the red footwear, the three-pendant fibula, the diadem, and the halo. There are also strips of purple amethyst in the clothing of other dignitaries.*

with marble and gold. Byzantine aesthetics exemplify a culture based on the unchanging laws of a Christian universe, always with an attention to detail and ornamental finery. The greatest monument of Byzantine architecture is the Hagia Sophia, or Church of Divine Wisdom, in Constantinople. Built between AD532-537, under the rule of Justinian, it replaced a more modest church that was destroyed by fire. The sixth century was seen as the first "Golden Age" of Byzantine art. At this time, mathematics was regarded as the highest of the sciences, and one of the architects of the Hagia Sophia, Anthemius of Tralles, described architecture as the "application of geometry to solid matter." The interior of the church shows a rejection

COPTIC ART

Another important late antique and high medieval culture that continued with little change until the ninth century was Coptic art, produced by Christians in the Nile valley area of Egypt and stretching in some cases to modern Ethiopia. However, there was no influence of ancient Egyptian art, since Alexander had all but annihilated the dynastic cultures. The principal points of reference in the ancient world were the cities of Constantinople and Alexandria, and their influence extended to this region. Byzantine styles and themes can be seen in many small objects of

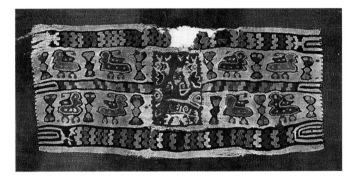

Decorative tunic sleeve border, ninth to tenth century. Museo Nazionale di Antichità, Ravenna, Italy. The polychrome wool border stands out against the cobalt blue fabric.

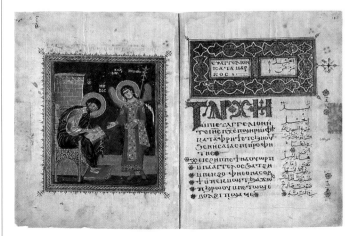

Two pages from the Gospels, 1204–05. Biblioteca Apostolica Vaticana, Vatican City. This Coptic and Arabic manuscript was produced in Cairo. It shows St. Mark and, in imperial dress, St. Michael.

Coptic art. These include linen textiles decorated with medallions that bear colored figures – these were used both for burial and ecclesiastical clothing – as well as many small paintings on wood, a variety of inlaid woods, and finely worked miniatures of sacred books. The influence of Coptic art was to last beyond the Islamic conquest of Egypt.

of homogeneity and, in its place, a luxurious, exotic diversity. It contains columns of green marble (from the temple of Artemis at Ephesus), of porphyry (possibly from the temple of Zeus at Baalbek), and of granite (from Egypt), and the walls are lined with colored marble. A lively mosaic of the figures of Justinian and Constantine adds to the splendor conjured up by the play of sunlight on the interior. The vastness of this imperial, mystical building contrasts with the more sober buildings of public worship in Rome. Constantine VII, himself a sculptor and writer, came to power in 945 and was emperor of the Byzantine Empire at the height of its glory. In his *De Ceremoniis* he describes court life and gives an idea of what the

TORCELLO

Churches on Torcello, in Venice, are remnants of the Byzantine "cities of silence," which were tantamount to museums in the declining Byzantine culture of the ninth century. Buildings of brick, the most typical material of Byzantine architecture, rise up from the gray waters of the lagoon, the brick interspersed with thin layers of stone or decorated with marble-lined openings. The cathedral of Santa Maria Assunta, founded in 639 and rebuilt in 1008, has a 9th-century portal and a crypt with an 11th-century architrave and bell tower, all of which are constructed of marble. Inside, there are columns with 11th-century capitals and a huge mosaic, *The Last Judgment* (late 11th to 12th century), on the west wall. In the apse, which dates from the original church, other mosaics from the same period include the *Twelve Apostles* and the *Virgin and Child*. Another church, Santa Fosca, has a floor plan in the shape of a Greek cross.

The Last Judgment, *wall mosaic, Torcello Cathedral, Venice, late 11th–12th century.*

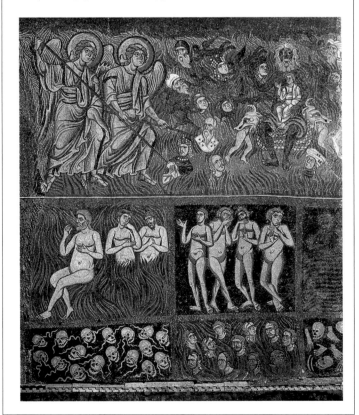

ANONYMOUS MASTER: "JESUS OF NAZARETH AS CHRISTUS IMPERATOR"
Circa 494–520; mosaic; Cappella Arcivescovile, Ravenna, Italy.

This mosaic is in the lunette of the small atrium leading to the chapel, above the door. The rooms are among the few that survived from the original palace, which was built at the time of Archbishop Peter II (491–519). Portrayals of Jesus as universal sovereign or victorious hero were favored in areas influenced first by the culture of the imperial court, and then by Byzantine art. This mosaic shows Jesus standing in a hilly landscape. He wears the military garb of the emperor, carries a cross and a book, and is standing on a lion and a serpent. The few gaps in the original mosaic are finished in tempera.

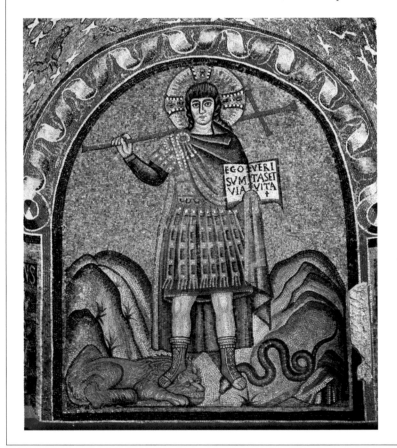

ancient imperial palace looked like. It bore no resemblance to the great residences of Rome, which consisted of one building with gardens and pavilions, but was a complex of buildings of every kind – religious and secular – with its own harbor and courts. It was influenced by Eastern palace designs. The many rooms were notable more for their furnishings and ornament-ation than for their structure. However, the palace did contain mosaics that continued the classical tradition, portraying pastoral, nonreligious scenes. From Constantinople, Byzantine art spread through northern Europe. The Vikings, or "Rus," who ruled the people of Russia and traded with the Byzantine Empire by ship, took Byzantine art with them when they returned to their lands, the influence lasting there until today.
The frescoes and mosaics of true Byzantine art show a break with the classical tradition, as does the painting. The individual elements are suggested by

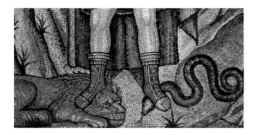

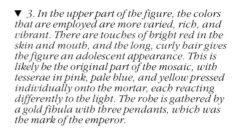

▼ *2. The viewer's eye is drawn to the color variations in the mosaic, the lighter pieces suggesting reflective light. The Christ figure, which is defined by a strong brown outline, appears to be inspired by the great statues of emperors from late antiquity – it is almost a graphic reinterpretation of these. There is no movement implied by the position of the arms: the right one bears the cross, while the left one is concealed by the robe, its cloth-covered hand holding the book, with its message of redemption.*

▼ *3. In the upper part of the figure, the colors that are employed are more varied, rich, and vibrant. There are touches of bright red in the skin and mouth, and the long, curly hair gives the figure an adolescent appearance. This is likely be the original part of the mosaic, with tesserae in pink, pale blue, and yellow pressed individually onto the mortar, each reacting differently to the light. The robe is gathered by a gold fibula with three pendants, which was the mark of the emperor.*

▲ *1. The artist uses the serpent and lion as symbols of vanquished enemies tamed by Christ. There are complex references here to a variety of groups and themes: the Roman senatorial classes, who were still pagan at this time; the heretic barbarian kings; heresy in general; and to Satan (symbolized by the serpent), humiliated by the Son of God. The basileus, or head of the church, had to pay meticulous attention to his clothing, dictated by his different functions, festivities, and rituals. Jesus' red footwear is a reflection of this, as well as a symbol of power.*

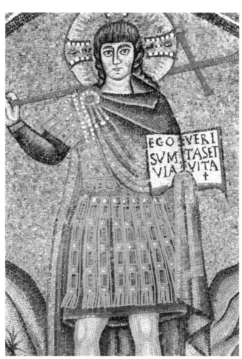

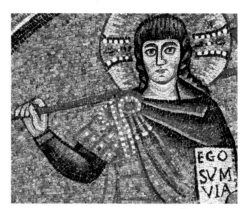

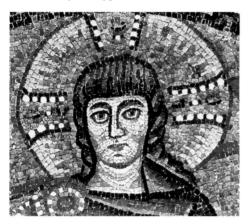

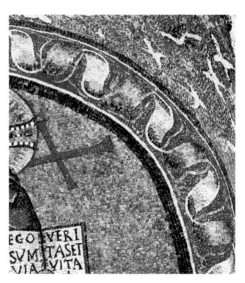

▲ *4. Christ's face is beardless and is like the images of Jesus as the Good Shepherd by early Christian artists. Behind the head, the thin rays of the imperial halo suggest the sun as inspiration for this iconographic element; it is achieved with turquoise mandorlas and white, ochre, gray, red, and black tesserae. Minute tesserae with touches of cream and orange enrich the face, in which black eyes under powerful eyebrows express a balance between a real presence and a distant abstraction.*

▶ *5. Many European mosaics from late Antiquity to the 15th century have the same gold background, which continued to be used even later in orthodox countries. It is not uniform in color, however; the gold sparkles with various slightly lighter and darker shades, which give an impression of dappled sunlight to the surface of the work. The "background" is therefore ambiguous, both part of the landscape and an indication of the divine.*

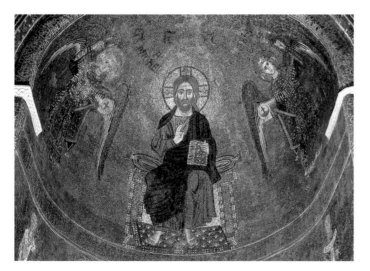

shapes that are almost hieroglyphic. Scenes are usually shown without perspective, there is a code of repetitive poses and gestures (figures and forms are often stylistic or ritualistic), and the emphasis on outlines echoes the "barbarian" taste for linear definition. Areas of empty space are often represented

Christ in Majesty between the Archangels Michael and Gabriel, *mosaic in the vault of the chapel's apse, Torcello Cathedral, Venice, 13th century. The island of Torcello was the spiritual center and bishopric of the lagoon before Rialto-Venice.*

in gold. Unlike the Christ of Western art, the Christ of Byzantine art is portrayed as awesome and is similar to the Jehovah of the Old Testament. The golden circle adopted from the sun kings of the East was transferred to Christ and became the medieval halo. In 1204, the Crusaders left the city of Constantinople in ruins. The glorious Eastern Empire of the Romans dwindled, but its influence remained in the art of the region for centuries to come.

ITALIAN BYZANTINE ART

The most important center of Byzantine art in Italy was that of the exarchate of Ravenna, part of the territory ruled from Constantinople by Justinian from 527 to 565. There, the church of Sant'Apollinare – from the early sixth century – was inspired by examples from Constantinople and the Pantheon of Rome, and decorated by Justinian's finest mosaicists. The Orthodox baptistry (early fifth century), the Arian baptistry (early sixth century), and the San Vitale baptistry (mid-sixth century) are also variations on the Pantheon, with wonderful effects of light in relation to the domes, which were built of very pale terracotta. Fretwork in the sculpture of the capitals and the low partitions and barriers show a rejection of sheer mass in favor of a more delicate, graphic treatment. The vigorous and sensitive moulding on fifth-century Ravenna tombs became more austere in the following century, relying on contrasts of light between solid and hollow panels rather than figurative elements. The unrivaled complexity of form, wealth of detail, and visionary expression in the Ravenna mosaics make them the finest examples of Byzantine art from the middle of the

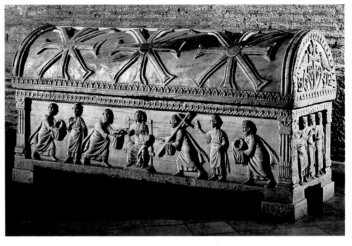

Sarcophagus of the "Twelve Apostles," Jesus Giving the Scriptures to Paul, Peter, and four other Apostles, fifth century. Sant'Apollinare in Classe, Ravenna. The series of sarcophagi in the side naves of this church provides interesting clues to the development from late Roman to late Byzantine art.

fifth century (the so-called Mausoleum of Galla Placidia built at this time still had Roman traits) to the late sixth century (Saints and Virgins in Sant'Apollinare Nuovo). In the Adriatic region, both new and established settlements flourished among the Venetian lagoons and were proud of their political autonomy. Although they paid lip service to the sovereignty of Byzantium, they never came under its rule. The fifth-century basilica of Aquileia, for example, was rebuilt in the Romanesque style in the 11th century. The whole area is notable for its important Roman mosaics from fourth-century religious buildings, some of later date in the cathedral presbytery, and another fine floor mosaic in the remains of the baptistry of the hamlet of Monastero. The floor mosaic of the baptistry of Grado dates from the sixth century, and the local great basilica of Sant'Eufemia, consecrated in AD579, contains other late-antique mosaics. On the island of Torcello, the cathedral of the Assumption

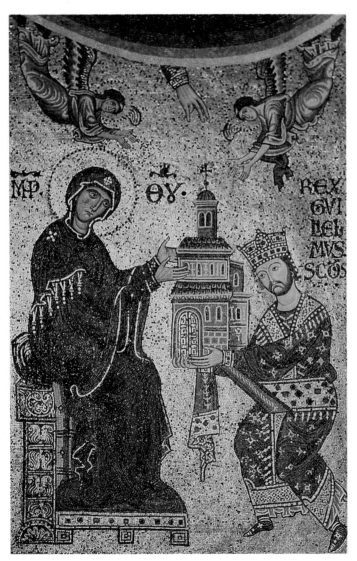

Mosaic, William of Sicily offers the Church to the Mother of God, 1180–94. Cathedral of Monreale, Sicily. This is one of an extraordinary series of mosaics executed between the 12th and the 13th centuries by local craftsmen as well as Venetians, and possibly also Greek-Macedonians. During the Norman reign, Greek, Muslim, and Latin masters devoted themselves to the arts; works bear scripts in all three alphabets, and also in Hebrew.

has a beautiful iconostasis (the screen dividing the sanctuary from the main body of the church). The Byzantine pre-Romanesque and Romanesque style of this area can also be seen in the church of Santi Maria e Donato on the island of Murano; there, a splendid mosaic of the Mother of God from the 13th century bears a strong Greek influence. In Sicily, mosaics from the Norman period betray a similar influence. In the royal country residences of Cuba and Zisa, outside Palermo, the Altavilla family lavished money on buildings of rare charm and remarkable complexity while retaining an outward appearance of consummate simplicity. Islamic, Byzantine, and Latin craftsmen decorated and built these residences, using a variety of techniques and styles. Similarly, many sacred buildings in southern Italy can be defined as Byzantine pre-Romanesque and Romanesque, including the church of San Pietro in Otranto, with its fine tenth-century frescoes, Santa Filumena at Santa Severina, and San Marco at Rossano.

ANONYMOUS MASTER: "THE ARCHANGEL MICHAEL"

Tenth century; framed icon; Treasury of San Marco, Venice.

This is a beautiful example of Byzantine goldwork, executed with extreme precision. The icon is made of embossed gold leaf and colored enamel. The figure of the archangel is shown from the front, clad in armor, with wings and a halo. In his left hand he carries the orb and the cross, symbols of Christ's authority, and in his right a drawn sword. At the top of the frame are three round plaques, with Christ at the center. Saints feature in the four elliptical plaques at the sides. The interstices are richly decorated with jewels. Such a refined, detailed work is likely to have come from the court workshops in Byzantium.

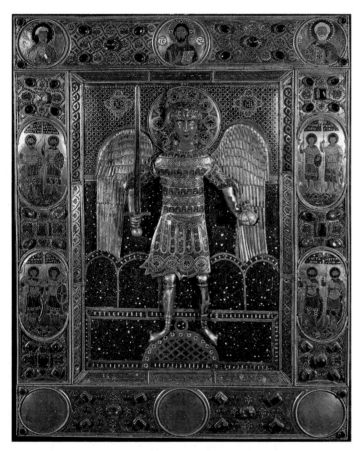

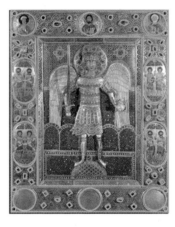

▲ *1. The composition of icons was determined by iconographic rules on the placing of figures, their clothing, emblematic objects, and geometrical relations between the parts. Two geometrical grids were used here, one for the background and general proportions, the other for the figure of the archangel.*

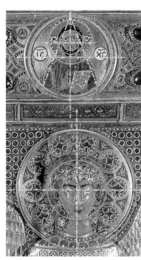

▼ *2. In some icons not created in relief, the orb, a symbol commonly held by saints and representing the world and God's authority over it, is replaced by a disk bearing the initials or the image of Christ. Images of St. Michael are common in Byzantine art. He was the prince of the angelic horde that hurled Satan and his devilish entourage into hell. As a symbol of righteousness, he was protector of the Byzantine army. He was also the weigher of the souls of the dead before Christ. He is often shown as a grand, magestic figure, sometimes wearing classical robes, but by the tenth century his representation was less realistic and more imaginative.*

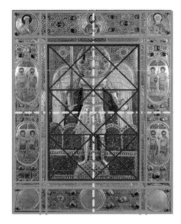

◀ *3. The frame, richly decorated with 54 gemstones, is rendered even more "holy" by the figures on the plaques. To the right of Christ is the apostle Peter in prayer. To the left of Christ is the martyr St. Menas, with the cross, and below are four pairs of warrior saints, all of whom were venerated by the Eastern church.*

▶ *4. The half-length figure of Christ merits particular attention. Though images of the suffering Jesus are rare in the East, the iconography employed is usually constant and restricted. Here, by contrast, the iconography is varied and complex. This figure is the Sotèr, or Saviour, blessing with his right hand as his left holds the Bible. Originally, the head of the archangel was thought to be made of onyx but it is in fact enameled in the round. This is particularly interesting, as this enameling process was previously thought to have been developed in the West in the 12th century.*

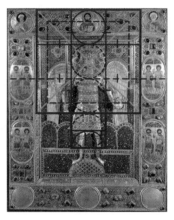

▶ *5. The wide range of Byzantine artistic skills is revealed in the background and frame of the icon. The predominant technique, enameling, fused vitrifiable paste onto embossed or honeycombed metal sheets. The cooling glass was retained in the cells. Here, the technique was done on such a small scale that the enamel seems almost immaterial, like a delicate touch of pigment. The even-toned background is meant to symbolize an earthly paradise. Persian influences are evident behind the legs of the saint (the colonnade topped by arches or a pergola) and in the rectangle inside the hemisphere on which the feet rest, which is bordered with a design reminiscent of a carpet or a mosaic.*

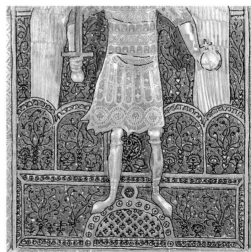

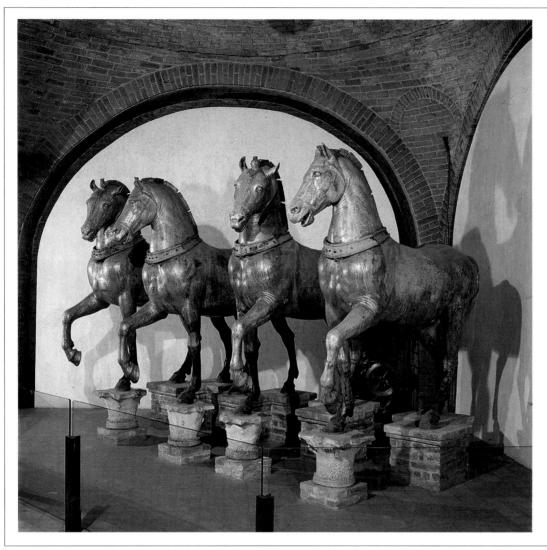

THE TREASURY OF ST. MARK'S

St. Mark's basilica in Venice was consecrated in 832 as the chapel of the body of St. Mark and was for centuries the chapel of the court of the doges. Although a succession of other architectural styles – Romanesque, Gothic, and Renaissance – left their mark on the basilica, it never lost its essentially Byzantine character. Its remarkable collection of icons, alongside other artistic genres, make it a great example of Byzantine artistic culture in the West. The celebrated bronze horses arrived in Venice in 1204, looted by the Doge Enrico Dandolo from the hippodrome of Constantinople during the Fourth Crusade. Some regard the horses as Greek works from the fourth or third century BC, while others see them as Roman masterpieces from the age of Constantine (fourth century AD). There is also an astonishing variety of art works – Egyptian, Roman, Persian, and, above all, Byzantine – in St. Mark's Treasury, next to the museum.

Bronze horses, St. Mark's basilica, Venice.

GREEK ART

Continental Greece was declining by the fourth century, and the once-glorious city of Athens was losing its tolerence – non-Christian philosophers were persecuted. However, Greek culture was still a major force in Constantinople, and in medieval times the empire itself was often described as Greek. In the Byzantine age, the most influential city was Thessalonica (Salonika), known for its magnificent art and splendid monuments, even during the years of Turkish domination. The reconstructed basilica of Hagia Sophia, complete with vaults and dome, was dedicated in the sixth century, and the Boeotian church of the Koimesis at Skripou (AD873–74), with its domed cruciform plan, is also notable for its fine decoration. In the 11th and 12th centuries, a number of cruciform churches were built, their domes supported by four columns or by two columns and two pilasters. Other important churches were constructed on an octagonal plan, such as the 11th-century Sotera Lykodimou in Athens and those at Chios and Daphni. Churches on the inscribed-cross model, with a central dome and four smaller domes at the tips of the arms, were built as far afield as Epirus and Macedonia. Wall paintings in churches at Salonika, Nikopoli, and Lesbos are reminders of Alexandrian influence in the sixth century, while wall paintings in the monasteries of Mount Athos, dating from about the 14th century, are more rigidly Byzantine.

There is little evidence of Latin influence, although there is some interesting Latin architecture in the Holy Land, including the fortress of St. Jean d'Acre at the port of Acre.

Panagía ton Chalkeon, or "bronzesmiths' church," Salonika, Greece, 1028. A masterpiece of late Byzantine art, the church is laid out in the shape of a Greek cross with an apse, one central dome, and two on the narthex. Its red brick exterior with round arches and projecting cornices houses 11th- and 14th-century frescoes.

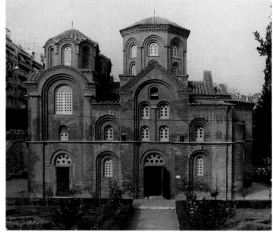

SLAV ART

Although Byzantine art had a profound influence on that of eastern Slavs (Russians, Bielo-Russians, and Ukrainians) and southern Slavs (Bulgars, Croats, Macedonians, Serbs, and Slovenes) over a long period, the individual contribution of these ethnic groups was equally important – hence the differences between the major schools: Bulgar, Serb, and Russian. The Slavs built temples of wood, decorating them with sculptures and paintings, and their beauty was noted first in the the tenth century by the Arabic geographer al-Masudi and then in the 11th century by Bishop Thietmar of

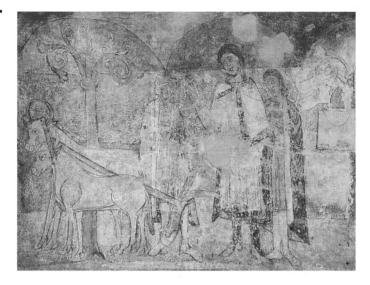

The Ploughman Premysl is Summoned to Court, *mural, 12th century. Rotunda, Znojmo, Czech Republic. Premysl was the founder of the Slav dynasty which united the Czech populations and led to the founding of the kingdom of Bohemia.*

Merseburg. It is probable that the mysterious decorations of the 12th-century stone church of Vladimir and Suzdal originate in the *kontine*, the

sacred buildings of the Slavs that were painted outside in bright, almost indelible colours, and decorated inside with carvings of wild beasts and birds. Sculptures of idols in wood or stone, and gods with gold and silver inlay, confirm the influence of ancient Slav art on stone architecture, which became widespread after the conversion of the Slavs to Christianity. This influence is evident in the churches of the Rus in Kiev, where Russian art flourished from the tenth century until the age of Peter the Great (1672–1725). When the Tartars invaded, the art centers shifted from Kiev toward the north, initially to Novgorod and Pskov and later to Moscow.

RUSSIAN ICONS

Russian iconic art dates back to 988, the year when Vladimir, Grand Duke of Kievan Russia, married a Byzantine princess and converted to Christianity. It took its cultural and spiritual inspiration wholly from Greek sources and became the art of the clergy, deliberately creating a wide gulf between itself and the secular world.

As art flourished in cities and monasteries, identifiable schools appeared in Vladimir, Suzdal, Rostov, Yaroslavl, Kiev, and Novgorod. From the outset, the Russians showed a predilection for icons rather than large-scale

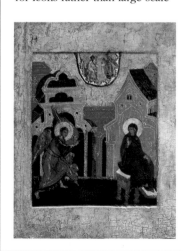

frescoes. Large panels painted in wax were installed on a screen separating the sanctuary from the main body of the church (the iconostasis), sometimes forming an entire wall of icons. The icon's spiritual significance lay in the arrangement, position, and gradual revelation of its image. Layers of color become progressively more luminous, set off by thin lines of white lead, and there is no depth, no perspective, and no conscious stylistic evolution to compare with that of the West.

In Russia, Greece, and the Peloponnese, iconographic art is the art of variations on a theme, combining a simple language with a highly complex content, both in small domestic pictures and in large, awe-inspiring panels. The figure of the Mother of God, the gospel narrative, the figures of the warrior saints (favorite of all imperial Byzantine art subjects), and significant prophets, patriarchs, holy bishops, and monks are all recurring images.

Moscow School, The Annunciation, *late 16th century. Ambroveneto Collection.*

Constantinople School, The Vladimir Virgin, *12th century. State Tretyakov Gallery, Moscow.*

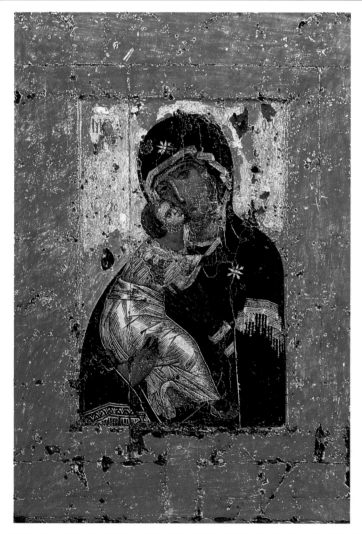

FROM CAROLINGIAN TO ROMANESQUE ART

Late antique forms were revived under Charlemagne and continued in the art of the Ottonian empire, which incorporated many Byzantine traditions. However, it was not until the 11th century, when the influence of the monasteries at Cluny and Monte Cassino spread along the pilgrimage routes, that a truly new style – the Romanesque – developed.

The history of the Carolingian dynasty is inextricably linked to the evolution of early medieval civilization in western Europe. Inaugurated by the coronation of Pepin the Short in AD751, the dynasty was eventually sent into decline by the division of the empire following the death of Charlemagne (AD742–814), whose aim of reestablishing a Roman empire involved a revival of the classical styles. With the lack of a central influence, the migrations of barbarian people brought a panorama of cultural change and a confusion of styles. However, as they gradually came under the influence of the burgeoning Christian culture, so this confusion of styles was gradually replaced by a trend toward unity and harmony, the like of which had not been experienced since the golden age of the Roman Empire.

CAROLINGIAN ART

The relationship between the Carolingian Empire and the Church was of great significance and proved to have a decisive effect on the development of artistic and architectural styles. During the course of the eighth century, the Church became involved in settling the regular clergy in monastic institutions. These monasteries were the subject of new architectural norms, often sanctioned and funded directly by those in power. This policy helped create a close bond between sacred worship, imperial ceremony, architectural design, and religious furnishings. It aimed to communicate the idea that earthly events and imperial guidance were linked with historical destiny. One such example of this is the apocalyptic image of the Heavenly Jerusalem – the exemplary image of human history being redeemed by Christ – which was modeled onto silver incense burners (censers). It was also a dominant feature of the crown of the Holy Roman Empire and appeared on the pages of illuminated manuscripts, written in the clear, elegant Carolingian miniscule script.
The most important innovations of Carolingian church architecture were clearly influenced by the idea of joining church and empire in a single enterprise. The most notable examples were the westworks: these fortresslike towers found at the west end of Carolingian churches were designed partly to accommodate the emperor when he attended solemn religious functions.
The importance of the

Lothair Cross, late tenth century. Cathedral Treasury, Aachen, Germany. The treasury also contains an ivory diptych from about AD800.

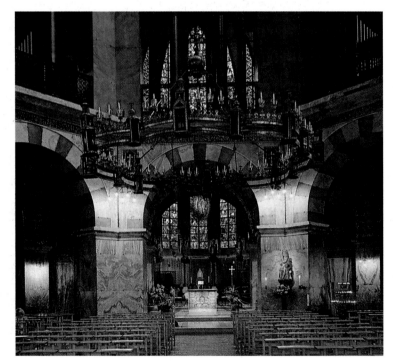

Odo of Metz, Palatine Chapel, Aachen, Germany, AD796–805.

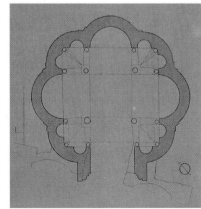

Plan of the votive chapel of San Satiro, Bishopric of Ansperto, Milan, c. AD868–81.

crypt also increased, chiefly as a result of the growth of the cult of saints. This underground chamber was where relics were often kept, and it was used as both burial place and place of worship. Architectural space was apportioned in both square and circular forms, the latter echoing the Anastasis Rotunda (or Church of the Holy Sepulchre) in Jerusalem. It is found in Saint Riquier at Centula, the votive chapel of San Satiro, Milan, and the Palatine Chapel of Aachen

(although this last was most strongly influenced by the octagonal plan of the San Vitale in Ravenna). The sheer scale of the Carolingian vision had much in common with the ambitions of grandeur that dominated the Roman world. Indeed, Charlemagne's decision to restore the imagery of the Roman Empire at all levels was a striking feature of the

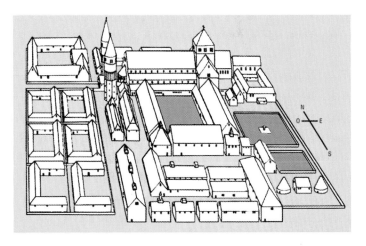

Plan of the abbey of St. Gallen. Stiftsbibliothek, St. Gallen, Switzerland.

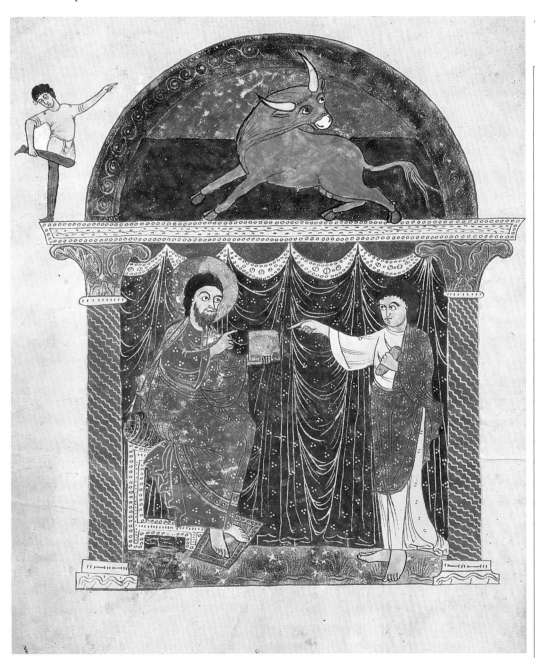

Apocalypse of Saint Sever, Christ hands the Gospel to Luke, Albigensian School, 1028–1072. Bibliothèque Nationale, Paris.

WESTWORKS

Taken from the German word *Westwerk*, a westwork was a monumental tower or combination of towers built at the western end of a Carolingian church. Containing an entrance, vestibule, chapel, and galleries, it was distinctive for its 12 windows, or porticos, mirroring the 12 gates of the Heavenly Jerusalem. At the abbey of Corvey, and St. Michael's, Hildesheim, the westworks duplicate the presbytery area at the opposite end and give the churches a bipolar aspect. The westwork was to remain an important feature of Germanic Romanesque architecture; later versions included a transept and a crossing tower.

Westwork of the abbey of Corvey, Germany.

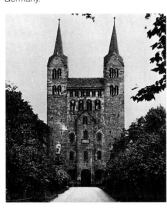

was a striking feature of the new culture, and several works attest to the way in which classical forms permeated the new religious and imperial ideals. These include the reliquary of Einhard, Charlemagne's biographer and minister, in the form of a triumphal arch; the Corinthian capitals of the abbey of Lorch; the transepts of Aachen; and the architecture portrayed in

paintings in the *Grandval Bible* (British Library, London). In fact, chronicles actually report that items of classical origin were brought directly from Ravenna to Aachen (Aix-la-Chapelle), Charlemagne's capital and the coronation city of German kings (936–1531). Whereas Irish and Merovingian illuminated manuscripts had previously contained material of deliberate fantasy and abstraction – as exemplified by the *Book of Durrow* (Trinity College, Dublin) and the *Codex Aureus* (Canterbury) – the art of Charlemagne's court veered toward a style of classical, realistic represent-ation. This style was used to adorn walls and to commemorate past events rather than encourage spiritual feelings. The classical mood

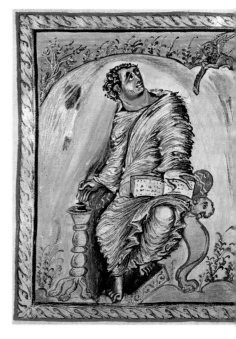

Ebbo Gospels: St. Mark, *ninth century.* Municipal Library, Epernay.

was strongly evoked in the *Gospel Book of St. Médard of Soissons* (Bibliothèque Nationale, Paris) and in that of Lothiar (emperor of the Holy Roman Empire AD840–55). A lively narrative spirit infuses the crowds of characters in the pages of the *Utrecht Psalter* (University Library, Utrecht) – the greatest example of early medieval drawing – and the *Bible of Charles the Bald* (San Paolo Fuori le Mura, Rome). The atmosphere of the court was such that it was clearly receptive to new ideas and initiatives. Works such as the *Coronation Gospels* and the *Ebbo Gospels* (Municipal Library, Epernay) from the important Rheims School provide evidence that, by the

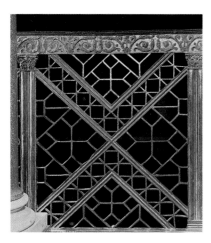

Bronze grating, *c. AD800. Palatine Chapel, Aachen, Germany.*

Adam and Eve *from the* Bible of Charles the Bald. *San Paolo Fuori le Mura, Rome.*

Gospel Book of St. Médard of Soissons, the Source of Life. *Bibliothèque Nationale, Paris.*

first decades of the ninth century, access to classical painting was paving the way for a vibrant and powerfully expressive form of graphic art. The break with the Byzantine world, which was attributed to

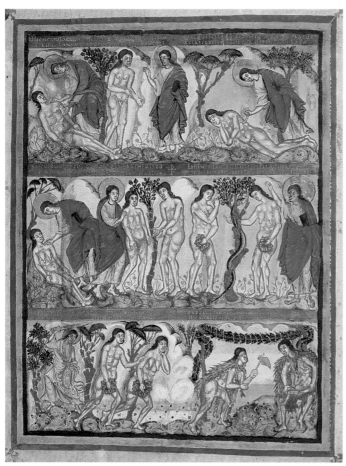

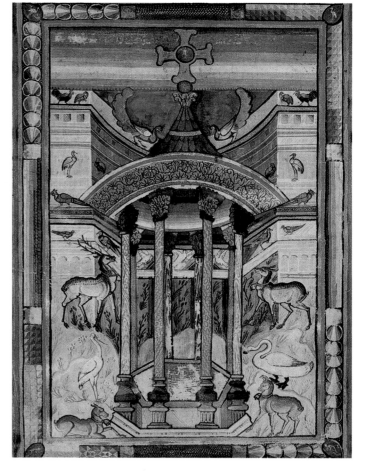

FRESCO CYCLES

The destruction of the fresco cycles from the monastery of Monte Cassino, Italy, (founded in 1071) in an aerial bombardment during World War II, is compensated for by the pictorial decoration that remains in Sant'Angelo in Formis, southern Italy. This monastery was established by the abbot Desiderius in about

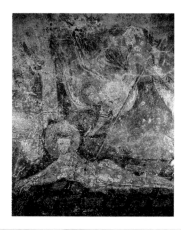

Martyrdom of San Lorenzo, *San Vincenzo al Volturno, Isernia, Italy*, AD824–42.

1072 before his election to the papacy. The glorious apse, dominated by the figure of Christ and the triarchy of archangels, provides the background for the detailed narrative of the Life of Christ illustrated on the walls of the central nave. This is, in turn, linked by figures of the prophets to the Old Testament cycle in the aisles.

The cycles, which revive early Christian subjects, are completed by one of the oldest versions of the Last Judgement on the back wall. It was the Christian experience, with its capacity to communicate and its mission to understand the complete history of humankind, that produced the vitality of these works.

The same culture is to be discovered in central-southern Italy in the *Exultet* scrolls and

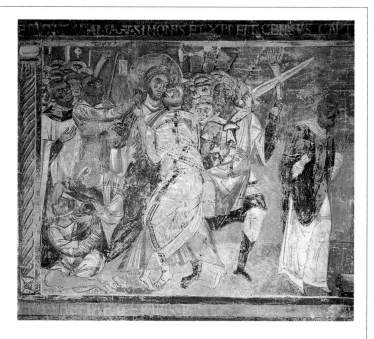

the fragmentary mosaics that remain in Salerno cathedral. The most significant example is provided by the abbey of San Vincenzo al Volturno; here, its theophanic cycle

The Kiss of Judas, *Sant'Angelo, Formis, Capua, Italy, second half of 11th century.*

from the crypt of San Lorenzo is again dominated by the angelic hosts.

THE FRESCOES OF MÜSTAIR AND MALLES VENOSTA

Of the few surviving frescoes from the Carolingian age, the fragments in St. Germain d'Auxerre and St. Maximian in Trier and the more complete examples of St. John in Müstair and St. Benedict in Malles Venosta (both in northern Italy) tend to be monumental compositions of great simplicity, highly figurative and deeply expressive, with a flair for bright, warm colors. The paintings in San Procolo in Naturno, though, are more closely linked to Lombard or Irish tradition and reveal the typical barbarian taste for precious materials and manual skills. These styles survive in various monuments, notably in the decorative sculpture of the ancient temple of Santa Maria in Valle in Cividale del Friuli and in San Salvatore, Brescia.

Detail of one of the frescoes of San Benedetto, Malles Venosta, Italy, c. AD800.

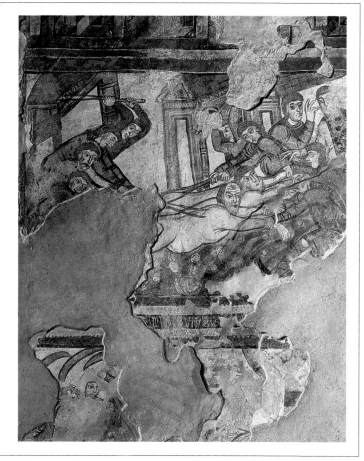

Charlemagne's imperial claims, proved only temporary when, in AD827, the fourth- or fifth-century mystical writings of Dionysius the Areopagite, a Syrian monk, influenced the court of Louis the Pious. These works, later translated into Latin by Johannes Scotus Erigena, introduced Neo-Platonic ideas, which stated that visible form is not fashioned for its own sake but intended as an image of invisible beauty. This principle was to have a lasting effect on the aesthetics of the medieval Christian world.

The tendency towards a narrative style also influenced wall-painting and transformed the fresco cycles into painted sermons with the introduction of instructive titles and captions. There were also secular cycles and allegorical representations, as seen in the villa of Theodulf of Orleans and in the palace at Aachen. Some evidence has shown that Greek fresco painters also contributed to these works, perhaps as a

THE MOSAICS OF SANTA PRASSEDE AND SANTA CECILIA IN ROME

The move toward a revival of the Roman Empire held special meaning for Rome. Constantine's concept of historical renewal became evident in the revival of Palaeo-Christian art. This is attested by the presence of the model of St. Peter's in the foundation of the Santa Prassede basilica and the rebirth of the mosaic and its iconographic emphasis again in Santa Prassede and in Santa Cecilia and St. Mark's, Venice. Reciprocal influences between

Rome and other cities of the empire led to many important artistic achievements. The abbey of Fulda was modeled on the Vatican basilica, and Roman influence was evident in *The Psalter of Charles the Bald* and in St. Peter's throne. The throne was decorated in an antiquarian style, which, with its symbolic ramifications, shows the earliest signs of commitment to the Pseudo-Dionysian aesthetic that was to influence the period.

Saints Praxedes and Paul, *Santa Prassede, Rome, AD930–40.*

The Saviour and the Saints, *Santa Cecilia, Trastevere, Rome, AD817–24.*

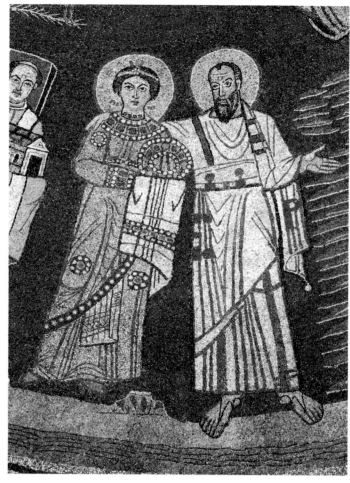

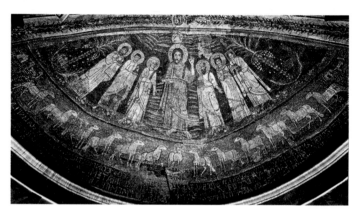

result of the traffic of trade in the Adriatic.

The barbarian taste for precious materials and technical skills managed to survive and be incorporated

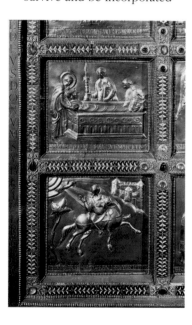

Gold altar, *two Stories of the Saint, Sant'Ambrogio, Milan, AD824–859.*

in Carolingian art; this resulted in the creation of masterpieces of gold and ivory work. The liturgical reforms proved profitable for artists and their pupils, who were now more responsive to both classical ideas and the practicalities of their art. The golden altar of Sant'Ambrogio in Milan, "signed" by Vuolvinius and commissioned by Angilbert II, bears astonishing testimony to the power with which the metallic splendor of gold could enhance a narrative. The precious mounting of filigree and enamel relates the iconographic messages perfectly. Similar comments could apply to the ivory covers of *The Psalter of Charles the Bald* (Bibliothèque Nationale, Paris), the *Lorsch Gospel Book* (Vatican Library,

Rome), the *"Pax" of Chiavenna*, Italy, and the amazing "Lothair crystal," now in the British Museum.

OTTONIAN ART

The Norman invasions and the anarchic kingdoms that were set up after the dissolution of the Carolingian empire were to hinder advances in art for decades. However, two important historical events then signaled a new leap forward: the first was the foundation of the abbey of Cluny in Burgundy, France, in AD910, which activated a major religious revival, and the second was the AD936 coronation at Aachen of Otto I, who promised a revival of the imperial initiative that had begun so successfully under Charlemagne.

The dynasty of the Saxon

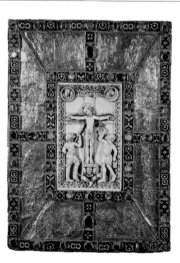

Cover of the Codex Aureus of Echternach, *AD983. Germanisches Nationalmuseum, Nuremberg.*

emperors, and the powerful bishops who supported them in their rule of the German lands during the 10th and 11th centuries, looked back to the past glories of the Carolingians

A BRIEF PENITENTIAL JOURNEY

The decoration in the apse of the church of San Vincenzo in Galliano, Lombardy, depicts Christ between the prophets Jeremiah and Ezekiel. This cycle was commissioned by Ariberto d'Intimiano, the future bishop of Milan who had ordered the renovation of the church. The iconography is Byzantine in style and shows the influence of the Ottonian miniature.

This merging of different trends can also be seen in the foothills of the Alps in Lombardy in the cycles at the churches of San Calocero al Piano and San Pietro al Monte in Civate. A penitential, and possibly baptismal, route existed between the two churches, forming a miniature version of the great European pilgrimages. At San Calocero al Piano, pilgrims studied the episodes of the Old and New Testaments in the 11th-century frescos and then climbed to the other church, San Pietro al Monte, to see the images of Pope Marcellus and Pope Gregory at the church entrance and the Heavenly Jerusalem on the vault inside. Other apocalyptic scenes completed this fresco cycle, which culminated in the *Defeat of the Dragon*, a fresco that served as a warning to pilgrims on leaving the church.

Defeat of the Dragon, San Pietro al Monte, Civate, Italy, 11th–12th century.

Sacramentary), and Cologne (*Gospel Book of the Abbess Hilda*). The style of drawing in these works is powerfully graphic, and the color is full of tonal variety. Also evident are associations with Byzantine culture and the aesthetic symbolism derived from the works of Dionysius the Areopagite. The influence of the Levant is also obvious in the most important cycle of frescos in northern Italy during that time, namely the frescoes in Santa Maria Foris Portas, Castelseprio, which were possibly executed by an artist from Greece.

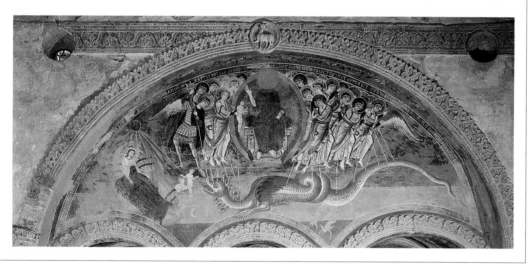

and forward to renewed contact with Byzantine culture, particularly after the marriage of Otto II (AD955–83) to the princess Theophano in AD972. Contemporary architecture and figurative art both developed

Miniature from the Gospel Book of the Abbess Hilda, early 11th century. Darmstadt, Germany.

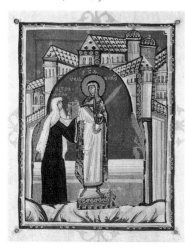

from the Carolingian models, with additional emphasis on ceremonial and spiritual values. While the monumental churches, such as St. Michael's, Hildesheim, Germany, were being constructed, the extraordinary skills of goldsmiths and engravers were producing masterpieces such as the *Lothiar Cross* (Cathedral Treasury, Aachen), the portable altar of Henry II, the cover of the *Codex Aureus of Echternach* (Germanisches Nationalmuseum, Nuremberg), and the Trier diptych (Staatliche Museen, Berlin). Each of these works passed through workshops, schools, and masters, the most well-known of which were in Trier, Cologne, Bamberg, Ratisbon, and Reichenau. Some significant monumental sculptures have survived, such as the doors at Hildesheim and Mainz and the ciborium reliefs

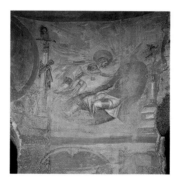

Frescos of Santa Maria Foris Portas (detail), Castelseprio, Italy.

of Sant'Ambrogio, Milan. These works point to a formal, strongly gestural, and deeply spiritual style of composition through the representations of the sculpted figures. The same applies to wall paintings and miniature works, which were predominantly made by the schools of Reichenau (*Gospel Book of Henry II*), Echternach (*Codex Aureus*), Trier (*Lorsch*

THE COSMIC ORDER

Apart from the cathedral of St. James at Compostela, the final destination for the pilgrims, the most impressive churches on the road to Santiago de Compostela were those of Saint Sernin of Toulouse and Sainte Madeleine of Vézelay. In these places of worship, pilgrims could wander freely through the broad naves, transepts, apsidal ambulatories, and upper galleries, pray at the altars, admire the lofty columns and soaring vaults, and study the extraordinary figures carved on the portals and capitals. The figurative sculpture of the 11th and 12th centuries was powerfully iconographic, reflecting the more outward nature of Christian worship, which was no longer restricted to closed monastic communities. The *Mystic Wine Press* carved on one of the capitals at Vézelay, the signs of the zodiac at Toulouse, the huge, angular pillars bearing reliefs of the apostles St. Paul and St. Jeremiah at Moissac, and many other examples of imagination and creativity on the part of religious architects and artists were designed to extol the providential cosmic order of the world created by God and redeemed by Christ.

Capital of the Mystic Wine Press, Sainte Madeleine, Vézelay, France, 12th century.

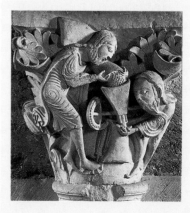

ANONYMOUS MASTER: "ANNUNCIATION TO THE SHEPHERDS"

Mid-12th century; fresco on the vault of the Pantheon of the Kings, Church of San Isidoro, León, Spain.

The fresco decorates the royal chapel of the ancient Spanish kingdom of Asturias, which was absorbed by the kings of Castile in 1230. The roof of the three-naved chapel (previously the narthex of the older church) has six elaborate cross vaults.

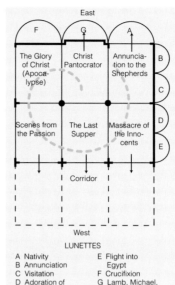

The decoration covers the six bays and lunettes and also the south and east walls, developing the narrative in a spiral, from the *Annunciation* in the southeast corner to *Christ Pantocrator* on the ancient main door. The dating has recently been established by a new interpretation of the figures at the foot of the cross. One of the most expressive parts of the entire cycle, the *Annunciation*, shows a peaceful scene with shepherds and domestic animals. The announcing angel points to the incomplete *Nativity* fresco in the east lunette, Mary and Joseph, a donkey and ox, and in the background a portal with a column in the middle and decorated with drapes.

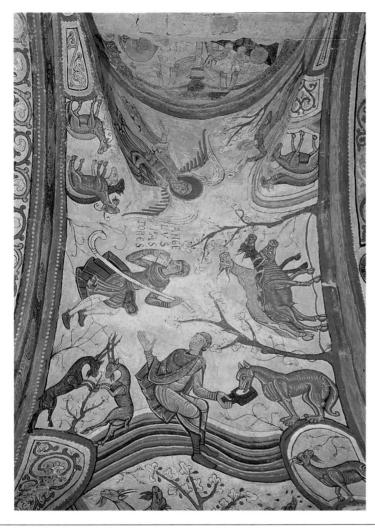

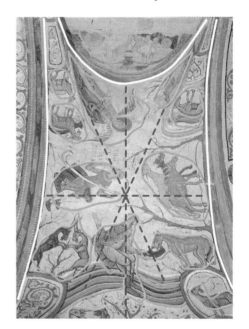

▶ *1. The figures are freely distributed within the space without precise symmetry or arrangement, as indicated by the superimposed diagonal and median lines. However, the artist has obtained a good balance between filled and empty spaces. The figures occupy about half of the available space and are either isolated, like the angel and two of the shepherds, or positioned in small groups, in some cases near trees. Areas that could appear too empty have been filled with further drawings by the artist. The light background holds the scene together while keeping the individual sections quite distinct from each other when observed from below.*

ROMANESQUE ART

The teachings of Cluny were already well established by the year 1000 and now spread to southwest Europe. They prompted the concepts of pilgrimage and monasticism throughout medieval society, which in itself placed a great deal of emphasis on human destiny and communal life. The Benedictine abbey of Cluny, which was exclusively dependent on the pope and so immune to the excessive power of feudal lords, was rebuilt twice in the course of a century, thanks to the initiative of the abbots Odilo and Hugh. The order continued to flourish, and the artistic achievements it encouraged were enthusiastically recorded by the Cluniac monk Rudolf. He wrote, "In all the world, but particularly in Gaul and Italy, churches were built and enlarged as if the world, discarding its old look, was dressing itself in white church vestments." The Cluniac order controlled the main monastic foundations on the pilgrimage routes to Rome and Santiago de Compostela, the latter particularly notable for ancient churches that had been renovated and enlarged. Many of these buildings were extensions on the basic basilica plan but with much more emphasis placed on the use of interior space. Church design was based on the symbolic shapes of the square

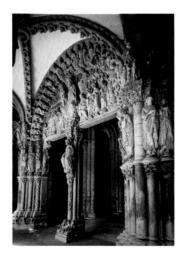

Master Mateo, portal of the Portico of Glory, Santiago de Compostela Cathedral, Spain, 1183.

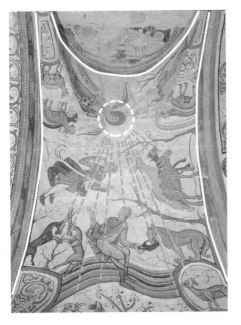

◄ *2. In this vision of idyllic serenity, the Annunciation makes a strong impact, even though there is no dynamic sense of movement. The figures, who have been surprised by the angel, interrupt their work: one shepherd has pushed away his panpipe, another has removed the horn from his pursed lips, and the third holds a milk jug at an awkward angle. The two butting goats and other animals also seem to have come to a halt and stand motionless. Their looks and gestures are directed at the angel, who appears from the corner and flies, with wings spread, toward the center of the picture.*

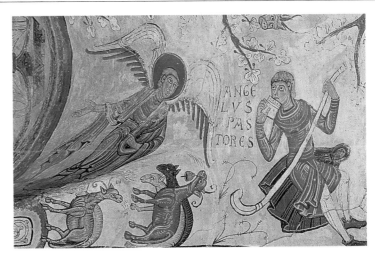

▲ *3. The artist has used a limited but harmonious palette of blue-gray, yellow-ochre, and soft pink, punctuated by flecks of deeper gray. Human figures, trees, and branches share the same tone, while the angel's red-fringed wings are painted in white on a base of parchment color. Details of the figures are sketched in with incisive, compact strokes.*

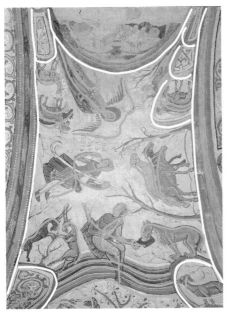

◄ *4. The shapes are constructed decisively and achieve a complex harmony despite the absence of regular rhythmical structure. The predominance of curved lines creates a feeling of light, movement, and spaciousness. It imposes an overall organic rhythm, giving the effect of a meadow, with figures instead of vegetation. The angel's curved shape has a particular tension that makes it stands out. With its echoes of Irish illumination, Byzantine graphic art, and Islamic arabesque art, this powerful and original work expresses the religious fervor of the Christian reconquest in a region of Spain that had never succumbed to Moorish influence.*

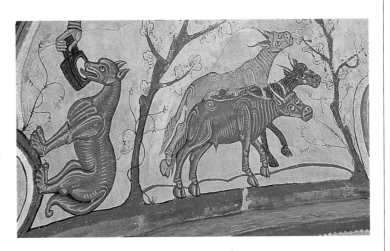

▲ *5. The artist is familiar with the pastoral life in the kingdom of León and depicts the animals fondly. Sheep, rams, goats, kids, oxen, and cows are all painted with great care. Wearing fine clothes, the seated shepherd feeds milk to a large dog, while neighboring oxen graze on acorns. The angel's Annunciation is received by a serene-looking world that is elegantly painted and affectionately described, a typically medieval interpretation.*

and the circle. Walls were made of square stone slabs (*lapides quadri*), and columns were gradually replaced by pilasters that could support a system of vaulted roofs. The image of the Transfiguration, placed intentionally on the portal of Santiago, seemed to animate this desire to transform material into spatial arrangements that were both functional and symbolic. The development of Romanesque architecture was closely linked with the buildings' natural surroundings. This is best demonstrated by the abbey of Mont-St.-Michel in Normandy, which is suspended between land and sea; the basilica of Sainte-Foy of Conques, set on a steep slope in the Auvergne; and the church of San Pietro al Monte, which sits on the summit of a foothill in Civate in the Italian Alps.

Equally significant in the development of Romanesque style was the role of monumental sculpture. Historical and religious scenes were created in the form of reliefs on capitals and doors, one of the best examples of which can be found in the cloisters at the Monastery of Santo Domingo de Silos. Here, intricately sculpted capitals depict events from the Bible and the lives of the saints, reflecting the increase in learning that was taking place at the time. In terms of painting, unfortunately very little has survived from this

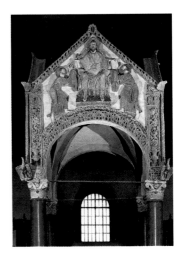

Ciborium with stuccowork depicting Christ and Saints Peter and Paul, Sant'Ambrogio, Milan, mid-12th century.

OTTONIAN CHURCH DESIGN

Considered to be the great Ottonian churches, St. Michael at Hildesheim, St. Pantaleon in Cologne, St. Bartholomew in Paderborn, Sainte Gertrude in Nivelle, and the collegiate church of Essen collectively broadened the scope of church design. The Carolingian style of juxtaposition was transformed into new systems and layouts that created a unified monumental structure.
Lateral naves, double transepts, crypts, and galleries all provided the necessary scenario for the richness and complexity of liturgical ceremony. This was accentuated by the extraordinary variety of religious furnishings: most notably crucifixes such as those of Gero in Cologne and Otto in

Interior of St. Michael's, Hildesheim, Germany. Though originally dating from c.1186, it was rebuilt after World War II.

Essen; ante-pendiums (altar frontals), such as the ivory example thought to have once been in the Magdeburg Abbey of Hildesheim and one of Henry II in Basle; and reliquaries, including the masterpiece of miniature architecture commissioned by the abbess Theophanu.

Cross of the Archbishop Gero, Cologne Cathedral, Germany, pre-AD976.

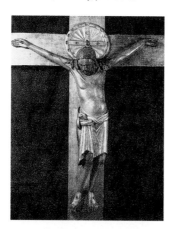

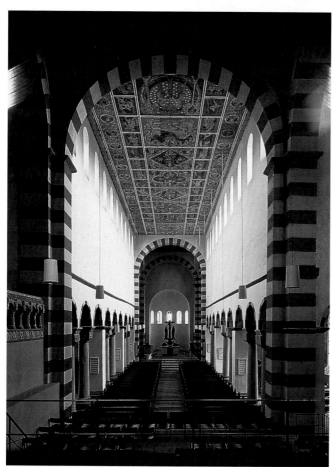

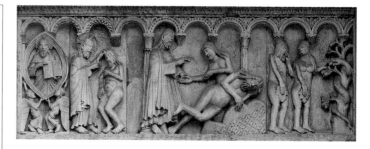

Wiligelmo, Stories from Genesis, Cathedral facade, Modena, Italy, c.1099–1106. Shown here are God the Father, the creation of Adam and Eve, and Adam and Eve tempted by the serpent.

period, even though they once covered countless church walls. While much of the most impressive Romanesque architecture is to be found in France, the artistic styles in Italy were extremely diverse: the splendid Lombardic architecture was exemplified in Sant'Ambrogio in Milan, San Michele in Pavia, and in the cathedrals of Piacenza, Parma, and Modena, all situated on the pilgrimage route to Rome. Decorative Romanesque

WILIGELMO AND BENEDETTO ANTELAMI

A special characteristic of Modena cathedral, unusual for the Romanesque period, is that the names of its first architect, Lanfranc, and its even more important sculptor, Wiligelmo, are known. Their work testifies to the professional competition that must have existed between architects and sculptors. The reliefs on the facade narrate episodes from Genesis, which were the subject of the earliest sacred drama performances. Wiligelmo successfully combined expressive vitality and extraordinary plastic strength, embracing both the realism and classicism of Byzantine icons as well as the calligraphic tendency evident in French sculpture.
While Wiligelmo's carvings can be dated from the early 12th century, the *Deposition* in

Parma Cathedral was signed and dated by Benedetto Antelami in 1178. One of the great masters of engraving and mural painting, Antelami made important contributions to Romanesque art. While he seemed to be most responsive to the rhythms of Provençal plastic art, in other respects he displayed the vast energy that is so characteristic of artists from Emilia and Lombardy. Toward the end of the 12th century, Antelami undertook the sculptural decoration at Parma cathedral, where his *Months* communicates the dignity of human labor through the passing of the seasons. The great iconic reliefs of the portals reflect the cultural depth and richness that medieval thought had attained.

Benedetto Antelami, Deposition, Parma Cathedral, Italy, 1178.

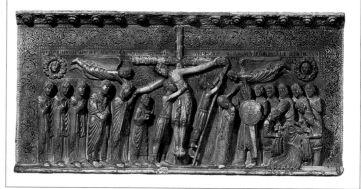

FRENCH ROMANESQUE FRESCOS

The maturity of French Romanesque painting in the mid-11th century can be seen in the frescos of Le Puy Cathedral. These are dominated by the figure of the archangel Michael, the iconography of which reveals the Byzantine influences that were active in southern France, especially around Cluny. The opening years of the 12th century saw an enrichment of the pictorial and ornamental repertory, as exemplified by the huge decorative landscape in the Benedictine church of Saint-Savin-sur-Gartempe (Poitou), with its astonishing color

Fresco of St. Michael, Notre-Dame, Le Puy, France, 11th century.

Stories of Saint Theophilus, *Abbey church, Souillac, France, late 12th century.*

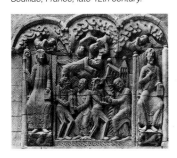

contrasts and iconographic variety. Farther north, a feel for calligraphy was more common, with luminous and graceful compositions that reflected the religious serenity. The fresco

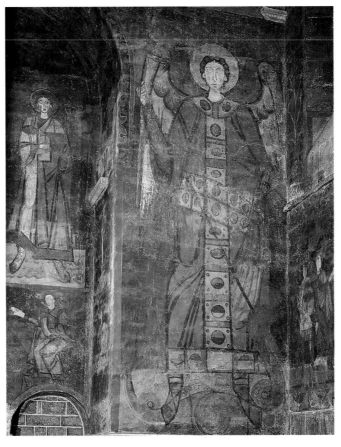

figures in the chapel of St. Gilles Priory at Montoire-sur-le-Loire and the portal reliefs of Souillac both dance and vibrate with soft light and color.

Lunette with Crucifixion and Saints, *Notre-Dame, Le Puy, France, 11th century. This cathedral in the Auvergne, built between the 11th and 12th centuries, is one of the most important monuments in French Romanesque art.*

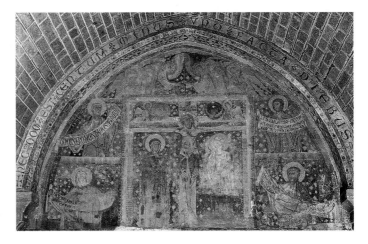

more difficult. This can be seen, for example, in the clashes with the compositional stiffness and strong graphic emphasis of Germanic culture in the church of Lambach. Western culture exhibited a much wider, more complex range of iconography in the marriage of its narrative style and symbolism. This was particularly true in Rome, where, partly due to the great reforming zeal of Pope Gregory VII, Romanesque pictorial art was gloriously represented, for example in the cycle of San Clemente and the triptych of Tivoli cathedral, with its typically graphic treatment of drapery.

The frescos in the chapel of Berzé-la-Ville, just outside Cluny, also reflect the courtly compromise between Byzantium and Rome. Cluniac illuminated miniature art was still based on Germanic models, as in the *Cluny Lectionary,* though a second wave of Byzantine culture soon appeared to stimulate masterpieces such as the *Souvigny Bible* and the *Transfiguration* in the cathedral of Le Puy. The most pronounced opposition to Byzantine influence, however, was to be found in the British Isles, Spain, and Aquitaine (the ancient province of southwest France). In the *Lambeth Palace Bible*, for example, traditional linear decoration totally overwhelmed the formal harmony of the Italian-Greek motifs that were displayed in the *St Albans Psalter.*

sculpture flourished from the Lombardy region to Emilia-Romagna, and examples ranged from the capitals of Sant'Ambrogio to the facade of San Michele. The style reached its peak during the early 12th century in the work of the sculptor Wiligelmo of Modena, whose great figures carved for the reliefs in Modena cathedral combined classical simplicity with dramatic force.

The movements based on the journeys of pilgrims and the Cluniac monasteries created a cultural network that linked distant areas and resulted in notable achievements in painting. Over the same period, often for political reasons, styles became increasingly

diversified. In countries such as Germany and Italy, for example, the Byzantine influence persisted well beyond the 12th century, whereas in France and Italy there was a much quicker progression toward the Gothic. The impact of Greek culture was felt in Venice and Rome by the 11th century and reached Sicily the following century. Art historians and critics continue to debate the direction of these exchanges and, consequently, the extent of reciprocal influences.

The near-illusionist quality of Byzantine painting needed to contend with other traditional elements from elsewhere in Europe. In some cases, the exchange of these was trouble-free, while in others it was

FROM LATE ANTIQUITY TO THE ROMANESQUE

c.400BC: the wholly Celtic La Tène civilization becomes established in the region of the Middle Rhine, Champagne, and the Marne. **c.300BC:** the Scythians occupy part of the lowlands between the Don and the Danube. **c.100BC:** the Goths settle along the Baltic coasts of present-day Poland. **AD64:** persecutions of Christians begin. **313:** Emperor Constantine, together with Licinius, issues an edict of tolerance toward the Christian religion. **432–440:** construction in Rome of Basilica of Santa Maria Maggiore, the first of papal rather than imperial foundation. **476:** deposition of Romulus Augustulus signals fall of the western Roman Empire. **507:** Clovis, king of the Franks and founder of the Merovingian dynasty, defeats the Visigoths; Paris

400BC–AD100   200–400   400–600   600–700

▼ EURASIATIC STEPPES

Medieval bestiaries were anticipated in the Scythian art of the Eurasiatic Steppes.

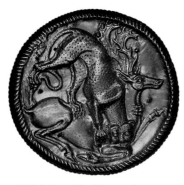

Gold phalera with a feline attacking a stag, Ol'gino Mound, fifth century BC. Museum of Archaeology at the Ukraine National Academy of Science, Kiev.

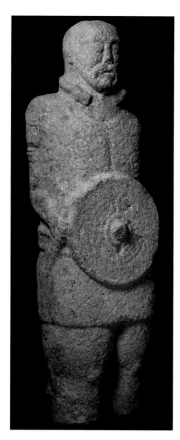

Stone statue of a warrior wearing a torc, Castro do Lezenho, Boticas, Portugal, first century BC to first century AD. Museu Nacional de Arqueología e Etnológia, Lisbon.

▼ ROME

During the third century, Christian iconography permeated painting and mosaic decoration. Myths and allegories were adapted to the spirit of the new faith.

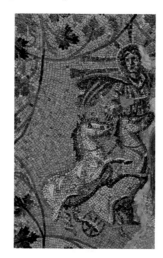

Wall mosaic showing Christ with a radiating crown, Mausoleum of the Julii, Vatican Tombs, Vatican City, third to fourth century.

▼ ROME

During the fourth century the "aligned text" form of sarcophagus was superseded by that of superimposed registers, in response to a revival of formal courtly models.

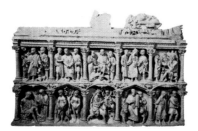

Detail from the Sarcophagus of Junius Bassus. Treasury of St. Peter's, Vatican City.

KINGDOM OF ITALY

Known as the Migration Period, the later fourth and fifth centuries saw striking cultural and artistic development under the Ostrogoth Theodoric (493-526), particularly in Rome and Ravenna. The art produced by the Goths at this time consisted largely of portable personal possessions, such as weapons and jewelry.

CONSTANTINOPLE

The Church of Hagia Sophia was rebuilt between 532 and 537, under the rule of Justinian. With its sumptuous decoration and coordinated spaces, it is one of the undisputed masterpieces of the sixth century, a period viewed as the first "Golden Age" of Byzantine art.

PANNONIA

In the late fourth and fifth centuries, the Huns concentrated their power base in Pannonia. Although their origins remain obscure, one of their primary artifacts – large footed bronze cauldrons with loop handles – can be traced across the steppe to the northern borders of China. Other Hun artifacts include splendid ornaments fashioned of gold sheet and studded with cabochon garnets. Many of these took non-classical forms, such as diadems, temple pendants, and whip handles.

▼ RAVENNA

The basilica of San Vitale (532-547), with its original fusion of Oriental and traditional Western models, constitutes one of the loftiest expressions of Justinian art. The intricate mosaic decoration is rich in symbolic value.

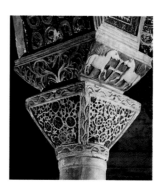

Marble capital with horses, San Vitale, Ravenna, Italy, sixth century.

▼ ENGLAND AND IRELAND

There was a rich production of illuminated codices in the seventh and eighth centuries. Importance was placed on the ornamental motif applicable both to initial letters and, in the case of the "carpet page," to the whole sheet.

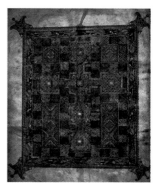

Carpet page introducing St. John's Gospel, The Lindisfarne Gospels, c.AD698 (Cotton MS Nero D.iv). British Library, London.

▼ KINGDOM OF ITALY

During the Lombard period (568-774), the ornamental tradition of Barbarian art was challenged by Western models, with highly original results in architecture, goldwork, and sculpture.

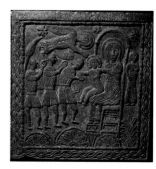

Adoration of the Magi from the altar of the Duke of Ratchis, San Martino, Cividale, c.740. Christian Museum and Cathedral Treasury, Cividale del Friuli, Italy.

becomes capital of kingdom. **568:** the Lombards, led by their king Audoin, settle in Italy. **614:** Irish monk St. Columba founds monastery of Bobbio. **726:** Byzantine emperor Leo III the

Isaurian condemns the cult of images. **800:** Charlemagne, king of France and conqueror of the Lombards, crowned emperor of the West by Pope Leo III. **820–830:** illumination of Utrecht

Psalter, supreme masterpiece of Carolingian art. **972:** following the marriage of Otto II and the Greek princess Theophano, the empire is influenced by Byzantine culture. **1059:**

consecration of the baptistry of Florence, an extraordinary example of Tuscan Romanesque architecture. **c.1107:** the goldsmith Rainer of Huy works in Liège.

800 – 900   1000   1100

▼ AACHEN
The Palatine Chapel, referring to classical and Ravenna-style models in its proclamation of the new imperial ideals, synthesized the tendency toward a programmatic revival of antiquity that typified Carolingian culture.

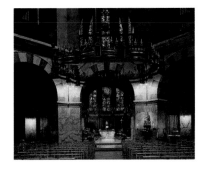

Odo of Metz, Palatine Chapel, Aachen, Germany, 796–805.

MILAN
Testimony to the importance of Milan as a Carolingian cultural center in Italy exists in the Golden Altar (824–859) in the basilica of St. Ambrogio. This is one of the greatest accomplishments of medieval goldwork.

REICHENAU
It is believed that there was an important and influential scriptorium here in the second half of the tenth century.

▼ VENETIAN AREA
Throughout the Middle Ages, Byzantium was the main source of cultural and artistic influence in this region.

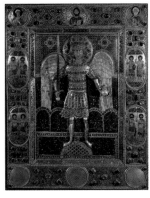

Anonymous Master, The Archangel Michael, tenth century, framed icon, Treasury of San Marco, Venice.

▼ THESSALONICA
In the 11th century, Thessalonica (Salonika) was a flourishing center of Byzantine culture.

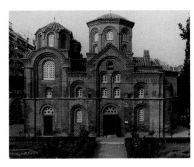

Panagía ton Chalkeon, or "bronzesmiths' church," Salonika, Greece, 1028.

FRANCE
The frescoes of Le Puy Cathedral (mid-11th century) represent some of the most interesting examples of French Romanesque painting.

SPEYER
In the rebuilding of the imperial cathedral in Speyer, some structural elements of the Norman and Anglo-Norman architecture are Romanesque in style.

▼ MODENA
Employed in the cathedral workshop, directed by the architect Lanfranc, was Wiligelmo (active c.1099–1106). He was the greatest interpreter of the vividly realistic style of Romanesque sculpture in the Po valley.

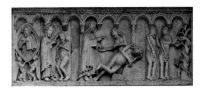

Wiligelmo, Stories from Genesis, Cathedral facade, Modena, Italy, c.1099–1106.

SICILY
The artistic achievements of the Normans in architecture, mosaic work, and ornamentation showed an original fusion of Islamic, Byzantine, and Western elements.

▼ FRANCE
The rich and complex sculptural decoration of the churches of Sainte-Madeleine at Vézelay (c.1122) and Saint-Lazare at Autun, where the unmistakable hand of Giselbertus (active c.1120–1135) is evident, provides important testimony to the quality of Romanesque plastic art in Burgundy.

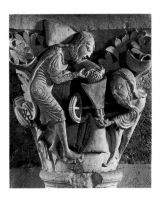

Capital of the Mystic Wine Press, Sainte Madeleine, Vézelay, France, 12th century.

▼ HILDESHEIM
Romanesque art in Germany found its highest expression in the Benedictine church of St. Michael in Hildesheim (rebuilt in 1186).

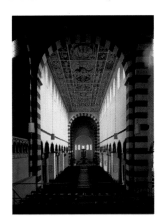

Interior of St. Michael's, Hildesheim, Germany. Originally dating from c.1186, St. Michael's was rebuilt after World War II.

PO VALLEY REGION
In the Po valley, during the second half of the 12th century, the works of the architect and sculptor Benedetto Antelami marked a period of transition between Romanesque and Gothic forms.

ENGLAND
The English school of illuminated manuscripts was particularly productive in the 12th century, notably in the scriptoria of Canterbury Cathedral and the abbeys of Winchester and St. Albans.

SLAV REGION
The decorations of the stone churches of Vladimir and Suzdal date from the 12th century, possibly inspired by the *kontine*, sacred buildings adorned with carved animals and lively paintings.

▼ RUSSIA
Production of icons remains the most enduring and important expression of Russian art and Slav sensibility.

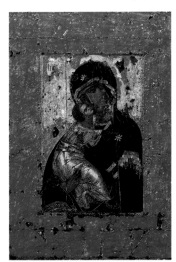

Constantinople School, The Vladimir Virgin, 12th century. State Tretyakov Gallery, Moscow.

The Artistic Cultures of Asia & Africa

PERSIAN & ISLAMIC ART

The artistic tradition of Persia (modern Iran) dates from ancient times and continued throughout the medieval period. During these centuries, Islamic art reached its peak, spreading throughout the Mediterranean, Asia, and parts of Africa, and employing various regional languages to express a unique aesthetic culture.

The Persian region exemplifies a culture that was already mature in the ancient Achaemenid age (the dynasty of Persian kings from 559 to 331BC), and it shares certain features with the Seleucid civilization. This dynasty brought about the fall of the Achaemenid empire, but was in turn conquered by the Parthians, or Arsacids, in the mid-second century BC. The Arsacids and Sassanids, both ruling nomadic tribes of the region, reinforced and evolved their separate identities before dispersing their most enduring art forms throughout the Islamic world.

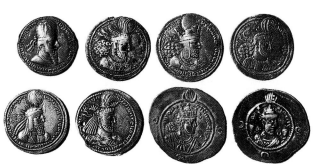

Coins from Sassanid Persia. Cabinet des Médailles, Bibliothèque Nationale, Paris. From left to right, the coins show the following kings: Ardashir I, Bahram II, Shapur I, Bahram III, Bahram I, Narsete, Ardashir III, and Kosroe I.

THE PALACE OF ARDASHIR AT FIRUZABAD

One of the oldest buildings of the Sassanid era is the Atishqadeh, the garden palace commissioned by King Ardashir at Firuzabad in about AD224: an imposing two-story structure of freestone cemented with lime. The front part of the palace was a public and official thoroughfare that faced a pool fed by a natural spring, which at one time presumably watered the entire garden. It consisted of a spacious *iwan* hall flanked by two small rooms opening into three larger domed rooms. These in turn led to the rear of the palace, consisting of numerous private apartments arranged around a central courtyard in the traditional style of a Persian residence. This palace is regarded as particularly important in the history of Persian architecture because it is one of the oldest, if not the oldest, in which the problem of building a circular dome over a square or rectangular structure was resolved by forming a transition with pendentives (small triangular segments of vaulting that fill the empty areas between the base and the roof). This system later became widespread throughout the Muslim world and also in Europe. In terms of decoration, the palace shows several significant innovations compared with the opulent architectural ornamentation of the late Parthian age. While the exterior owed its only decorative effect to the interplay of light and shade created by the regular series of buttresses, the interior reveals a covering in plaster with niches surmounted by "Egyptian-style" curved molding motifs. These are reminiscent of the Achaemenid palaces of Persepolis.

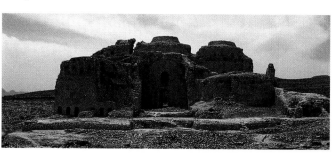

The ruins of the palace of Atishqadeh, built in about AD224 by the Sassanid king Ardashir.

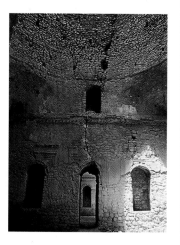

Interior of Ardashir's palace at Firuzabad, southern Iran.

ARSACID PERSIA

After the Parthian conquest of Seleucid Persia (250BC), there were major changes in artistic production. The Parthians, or Arsacids (their empire was named after its founder, Arsaces), were a nomadic people from the eastern Steppes. Since the reign of Mithridates II (123–87BC), they had blended their ancient traditions with the Hellenistic conventions that had permeated Persian art after the conquest of Alexander the Great, eventually combining them in an original, artistic language of their own. The territory influenced by the Parthians was vast and extended from Mesopotamia and the Iranian plateau to the Punjab and northern areas of Afghanistan. Most of the artworks that have survived from this region are essentially monuments and statues. Coins displaying various monarchs provide vital information as to dates and, in some cases, are a key to other contemporary art products. An original feature of Arsacid architecture was the

THE IMPORTANCE OF ROCK CARVINGS

The practice of rock carving as a form of artistic expression, already known in ancient Persia, found a new and splendid lease on life during the Sassanid period. These carvings are notable not only for their great number but also for their enormous dimensions and compositional excellence. The most popular themes, found in almost all the images, were those associated with the sovereign, principally scenes of investiture or victory. A famous example is the rock monument of Naqsh-i Rustam that glorifies King Shapur's victories over the Roman emperors Philip the Arabian and Philip the Valerian. The carvings can be accurately dated and identified, and are of great iconographic and historical importance because some of them bear inscriptions with the name of the king, sometimes written in three languages. Details of the individual's clothing, headgear, and hairstyle provide valuable information concerning many aspects of court life, such as the use of weapons and musical instruments. Furthermore, they constitute an invaluable source of reference for the study and analysis of the iconographic motifs of Sassanid art.

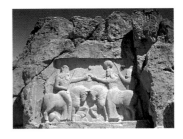

Bas-relief showing the investiture of Ardashir I (AD224–41), the valley of Naqsh-i Rustam. Ardashir, who founded the Sassanid dynasty, was of Persian stock and a follower of the Zoroastrian religion.

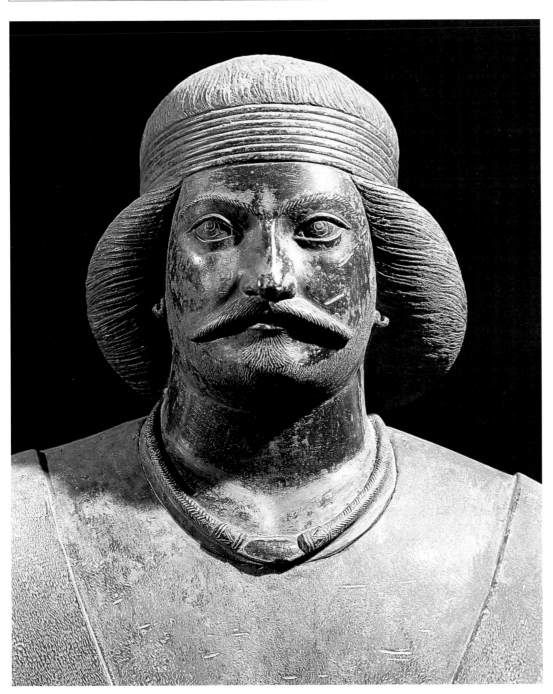

Parthian warrior, first century AD. Archaeological Museum, Tehran.

introduction of the *iwan*, a hall generally covered by a vault, enclosed on three sides by walls and open on the fourth. The *iwan* was to become an important element in the centuries to come, particularly during the Islamic period. In the applied arts, the aspect that most notably distinguished the Parthian from the classical Hellenistic style was the treatment of the human figure. The Arsacid artist revived the ancient, indigenous tradition of the frontal pose, both in painting and in the plastic arts. The portrait was of great importance, the definition of detail (both of the face and the body) being characteristic of a form of artistic realism far removed from the Hellenistic spirit of idealizing the individual represented. Details of clothing and hairstyle reveal the social status of the subject portrayed and often incorporate ornate architectonic motifs (swastikas and merlons). These were frequently executed in stucco, an easily molded material ideally suited to the sometimes dense and exuberant style typical of the Parthian decorative repertory. It is hard to establish whether these new orientations were a deliberate attempt to differentiate cultures or merely a signal of a change in tastes, but certainly it would not be inaccurate to define the Arsacid period as a turning point in the history of Persian art.

SASSANID SILVERWARE

Some of the most attractive pieces of Sassanid decorative art are the beautiful objects of silverware, many of which can be seen in museums and private collections all over the world. Used as luxury tableware at the Persian court, they were also given as expensive diplomatic gifts or exchanged as items of barter. This is probably why they have been so widely found. Many items have been recovered from excavation sites in certain parts of Russia, a country that frequently supplied the Sassanid empire with precious stones and furs. The most important collection of these silver objects is housed in the State Hermitage Museum in St. Petersburg.

Silverware production reached its peak around the fourth century AD, although later imitations and copies also exist. The classic forms are trays, cups, semicircular or boat-shaped bowls, and jugs. The most common decorative motif is the portrayal – and the glorification – of the monarch, where he is shown hunting, in battle, or simply in scenes of everyday life. The technique consisted of working the individual parts of the ornamentation before gilding and welding them onto the object. Only in a few instances were the products embossed and incised, and it is only in the later silverware that the decoration was simply engraved onto the item.

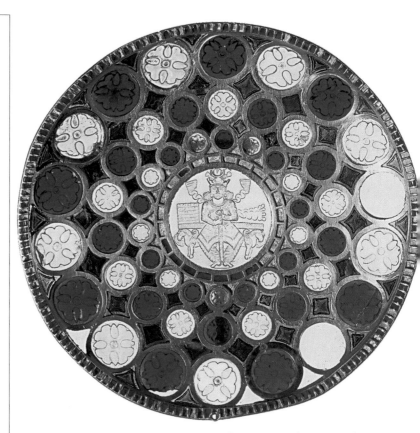

Kosroe bowl. Cabinet des Médailles, Bibliothèque Nationale, Paris.

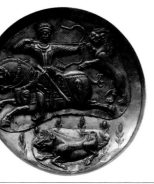

Sassanid silver-gilt plate featuring a mounted huntsman with bow and arrow and sword. The State Hermitage Museum, St. Petersburg.

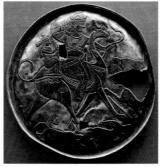

Sassanid silver-gilt plate portraying Bahran Gur with Azadè. The State Hermitage Museum, St. Petersburg. In poorer condition than the one on the left.

SASSANID PERSIA

When the Sassanid prince Ardashir defeated the last Arsacid king in about AD224, he became lord of an empire that controlled an immense territory, the frontiers of which, though not precisely defined, extended from China to Byzantium.

The size of the territory and the duration of the dynasty, which ended only with the Muslim conquest of AD636, make it difficult to trace the history of Sassanid art. However, coins (providing precise and accurate dates) and rock carvings are of some

assistance. Some experts have chosen to define the body of Sassanid work as a new form of Persian art, in which Achaemenid and Parthian styles are merged with elements of Hellenistic and Roman traditions. One example to support this theory is the new manner of representing divinity: the god, in accordance with the tenets of Western classical tradition, is depicted as human. His size, demeanor, mount, and clothing are not substantially different from those of the king, alongside whom he stands in the scenes of investiture. Similarly, the palace of Bishapur, although typically

Persian in design (a square central courtyard surmounted by a dome and enclosed by four iwan halls) is decorated in a recognizably Western style. Fretwork, grapevines, and painted acanthus leaves adorn the rooms, while brightly colored mosaics showing court scenes decorate a number of the floors. Sassanid architecture develops themes already tested in Parthian iwan halls, vaults, and

cupolas. At Ctesiphon, capital of the Parthians and then of the Sassanids, there are the ruins of a large iwan that formed part of the palace of Taq-i Kisra, dating to the second half of the third century AD. Once a building of impressive dimensions, a large part of it has sadly since been lost. The decorative material most

Remains of the small palace of Bahram V (AD420–40). Sarvestan. Although not as well known as some of the larger palaces, this monument still displays all the typical features of Sassanid architecture.

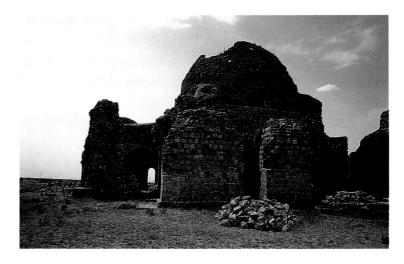

frequently used in Sassanid architecture was stucco, a material that was widely used from the fifth century onward. Both the arches and walls of *iwan* halls were ornamented in stucco, but, in contrast to Parthian and later Muslim techniques, Sassanid stucco was molded rather than carved. This enabled the artist to produce panels similar to tiles for decorating surfaces of almost any breadth and height. The motifs were often derived from nature: grape-vines, flowers, leaves, and fruit. There were also a few animal figures, sometimes set in circular medallions. Typical of Sassanid art, although of course inherited from a very ancient tradition, were the rock carvings, invaluable works of art excavated both in the province of Fars during the first hundred years of Sassanid rule and, toward the fourth century, from the

Taq-i Bustan site near the city of Kirmanshah. Textile manufacture and gold work were also significant features of the decorative arts of the period. Sassanid textile production, much appreciated in Europe, was closely linked with, and owed its success to, the silk trade between China and the West. Part of the trappings of king and court were the elaborate and refined jewels, also apparent from the figures depicted in rock carvings. The celebrated Kosroe bowl, dating from the sixth century AD and now in the Biblio-thèque Nationale, Paris, is a work of great value that apparently arrived in Europe in the eighth century AD as a gift from the caliph Harun Al-Rashid to the emperor Charlemagne. The image of King Kosroe, inlaid in a rock crystal medallion, is framed in colored glass. However, this was an uncommon technique,

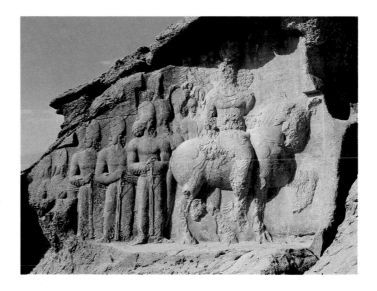

Bas-relief portraying Shapur I (AD241–72) being escorted by noblemen and soldiers at Naqsh-i Radjab. This king defeated and captured the Roman emperor Valerian.

as the medium most frequently used by the Sassanids was silver with gold reliefs. Glass production was widespread, especially in the workshops of Susa. Enamels were also

produced, perhaps influenced by Chinese enameling, earthenware, and engraved gems. Sassanid art was therefore codified, characterized by a clear and definite language

SASSANID TEXTILES

Thanks to the prominent role played by Sassanid Persia in the raw silk trade from the Far East to the Mediterranean, a flourishing native silk-weaving

industry developed, with Persian-manufactured goods being exported widely to the West. The textiles were remarkable for their exquisite quality and elegant designs, often serving as models for the

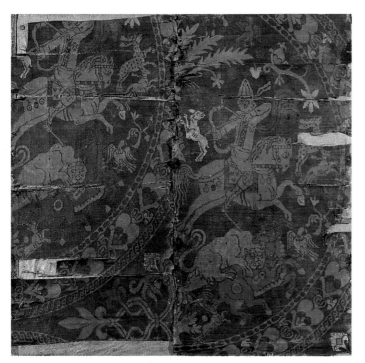

Silk cloth from the altar of the Basilica of Sant' Ambrogio, Milan. This design depicts a hunting scene, one of the recurrent themes in Sassanid art.

prestigious workshops of the cities of Constantinople and Antinoöpolis, which proceeded to rework and reproduce them at least until the early medieval period. The sheer quantity of imitation textiles, coupled with their excellent quality, has sometimes led, in the case of certain styles, to serious problems of attribution. However, the textiles sent to the West to be used as protective coverings for the reliquaries of saints have been preserved in many European church treasuries and are almost certainly Persian.

The most frequent decorative motifs found in Sassanid textiles are symbolic hunting scenes and figurations of animals, both real and fantastic, either singly or in facing pairs, in which case they are depicted beside a more or less stylized tree, perhaps the so-called Tree of Life. Sometimes the subject is set in a circle or oval, adorned with rows of pearls. This richly imaginative

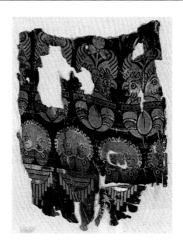

Sassanid silk cloth. Museum of the History of Textiles, Lyons. Although badly torn, the stylized, naturalistic design of this rare example of Sassanid silk can still be appreciated.

repertory of subjects also constitutes the colorful themes found in the rock carvings of Persepolis and Taq-i Bustan, and in the decorations of silver-gilt plates, typical of Sassanid art production.

MOSAIC DECORATION

The use of mosaic as a form of decoration was very shortlived in the Muslim world (if we exclude the mosaic pavements and walls in colored marble or ceramics). It was, however, the most sacred and important buildings of Islam that adopted the decorative technique of mosaic in glass paste. The Dome of the Rock in Jerusalem (AD687–91), the Umayyad Great Mosque of Damascus (AD705–15), and the Great Mosque of Cordoba in Spain (AD785–987)

best exemplify the application of this technique. It is interesting to note that such decoration often reverted to classical and, most markedly, Byzantine motifs, suggesting that Christian artists were probably involved in making the panels. In spite of restorations, the mosaic that decorates the portico of the Great Mosque of Damascus is of the highest quality, its

Mosaic of the Tree of Life, Great Mosque, Damascus. The mosque was built by the Umayyad caliphs at the beginning of the eighth century.

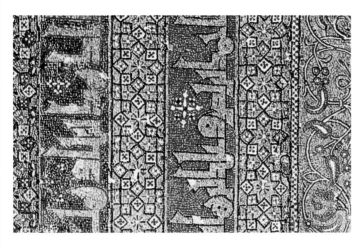

Detail of the mosaic arch, Great Mosque Cordoba. This was built by the Umayyad caliphs of Spain in the tenth century. The mosaic arch is to the right of the mihrab.

Detail of the mosaics in the Dome of the Rock, Jerusalem. Built by the Umayyads, the Dome of the Rock was embellished by Sultan Suleiman in the 16th century.

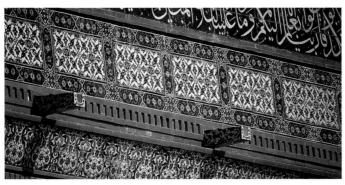

detailed architectural features alternating with motifs of plants and trees set in gardens with bridges and pools. This opulent setting, created by the brilliant sequence of images on a gold

background, has been interpreted as a representation of the Muslim conception of Paradise, or as the cities conquered by the armies of early Islam.

that was applicable to any type of material within the vast territory of the empire. Evident traces of it remain not only in the repertory of Islamic art, at least of the earliest period, but also in the styles of certain works of medieval Europe and central Asia.

IMPERIAL ISLAMIC ART

The Muslim era began officially in AD622, the year of the prophet Muhammad's flight from Mecca to Medina. The rapid expansion of the new faith led to Arab armies conquering vast areas of

territory, already occupied by advanced civilizations, within a span of barely a hundred years. The celebrated battle of Poitiers (AD732), on the southern borders of France, occurred a century after the Prophet's death and halted the Muslim advance into Europe. Eastward expansion was

equally swift; by AD711 the adherents of the new faith already controlled part of central Asia and had reached the northern frontiers of India. The art that they developed was borrowed from established cultures – notably Byzantine to the west and Sassanid to the east – but such exchanges

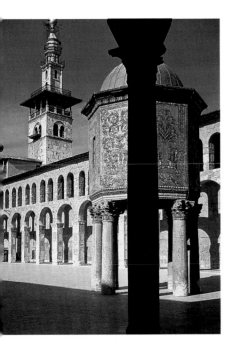

The treasury, court-yard, and minaret of the Great Mosque of Damascus. This was built by the Umayyads over a former Byzantine church, which had previously been a pagan temple and was destroyed by al-Walid in AD705. It is considered to be one of the finest examples anywhere of Islamic art.

quickly led to the elaboration of a recognizably original and individual artistic language. Because the Islamic artist was a man of faith, analysis of his means of expression exclusively in terms of aesthetics would be misleading. His relationship to divinity prevented him from committing the sin of pride – only the Omnipotent could create and inspire life. Man was the servant of God (the Arabic word *Islam* means "submission"), and therefore needed to avoid creating a finished, perfect representation of nature, but instead merely suggest a fragmentary interpretation. It was not uncommon, therefore, for there to be more than one perspective in the construction of a miniature and for this to be irregular, for a drawing to go outside its borders, or for the design of a composition (on a carpet or panel) to be interrupted by a border or frame, as if to suggest that the work continued and

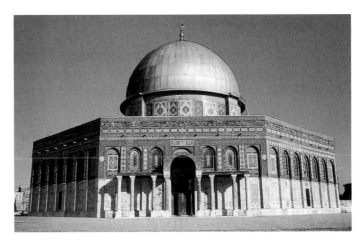

The Dome of the Rock, Jerusalem. The name is taken from the rock from which Muhammad is believed to have ascended to Heaven. Completed in AD691, the Dome of the Rock is the oldest surviving masterpiece of Islamic art.

could only be partially shown. Muslim ornamentation avoided representations of humans or animals (at least in works designed for public view) and adopted calligraphic, geometrical, or abstract floral

(arabesque) motifs. The results were highly imaginative and varied compositions, which, in the case of geometric ornamentation, have been likened to the fantastic images achieved by a kaleidoscope. Motifs using the arabesque, on the other hand, seem to have been inspired directly by reality. As for calligraphy, the fundamental importance given to Arabic (the language of the

THE KORAN AND THE ART OF WRITING

The sacred book of the Muslims is the Koran, revealed by God to the Prophet Muhammad, who in turn recited its verses to the faithful. Oral tradition is highly valued in Islam; it was only after the death of Muhammad in AD632

Page of the Koran in Kufic script, eighth to ninth century. Biblioteca Ambrosiana, Milan. Although incomplete, it is one of the oldest in existence.

that, in order to avoid misunderstandings and violations, it was decided to gather together all the written sections of the Koran that were already in circulation. Given that the Koran is in Arabic and signifies the "divine word," the importance of Arab script (Semitic, with a 28-symbol alphabet) was considerable in art as well as literature. Of such elegance as to enable the creation of a wide variety of graphic forms and styles, it

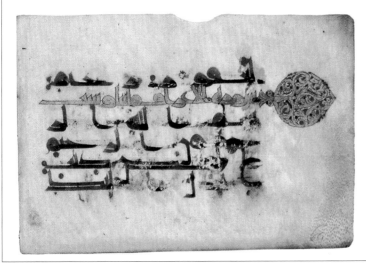

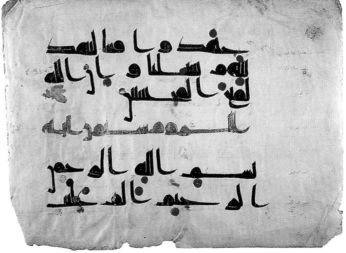

was used by every Muslim community. The manuscript format was so sacred that it was not until 1787 that the first printed Koran appeared, in St. Petersburg. Indeed, religion plays such an important role in everyday life – and is often represented by writing rather than images, which are forbidden in public – that the veritable iconography of the Muslim world is the highly decorative

Page of the Koran in Kufic script, probably ninth century. Russian Academy of Science, St. Petersburg. The gold, red, and black color and the elegance of the text attest to the importance of the sacred book.

script of calligraphy. Over the centuries, numerous styles were developed, from Kufic, the Arabic alphabet used to write the original Koran in the time of Muhammad, to various cursive scripts.

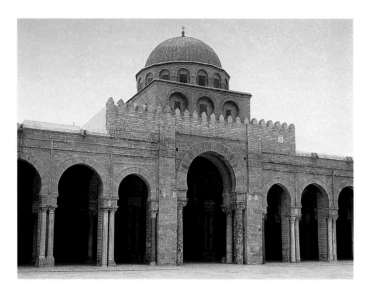

The Great Mosque of Kairouan, Tunisia. Built by the Aghlabid emirs in the ninth century, the mosque's structure has remained intact. It is the oldest in the Western world.

Koran) was manifested in the detailed study and development of styles of writing – from the cursive to the Kufic – and the script of the earliest Koran manuscripts.

Jerusalem and Damascus were the main centers of an art style that would acquire a deep sense of awareness and identity in the years of Muslim expansion. Damascus was chosen as the capital of the new empire ruled by the

subsequently became almost completely neglected by Islamic artists), and the palaces for their stuccowork and paintings.

ABBASID ART

The year AD750 signaled the accession of the Abbasid dynasty and the shift of central imperial power to Mesopotamia. In AD762, Baghdad was chosen as the new capital by Caliph al-Mansur. Although nothing has survived of the foundations of the circular city on the Tigris,

DESERT CASTLES

Among the earliest architectural achievements of the Muslim conquerors who had settled in Palestine and Syria was a series of buildings known as the "desert castles." These were fortified camps, palaces, hunting pavilions, citadels, and workshops, scattered over vast areas of what is now desert in Syria, Jordan, and Israel. Dating from the end of the Umayyad period, in about AD750, these buildings show how the late antique models of Byzantine edifices were adapted to the changing needs and demands of Islamic society. A striking example is the pavilion, with adjacent bathhouse, of the palace of Qusayr Amra (AD724–43) in the Jordanian desert. The exterior of the stone building is very compact, with three domed

chambers. The interior consists of a large reception hall with an apse where the caliph sat, flanked by two alcoves. The decorations on all the walls are tempera paintings (the fresco technique was unknown), showing the coronation of the monarch (depicting the six great sovereigns of antiquity), hunting scenes, baths, acrobats, and female dancers. The style is provincial Byzantine with Coptic features. Entrance to the bathhouse is via a small, domed room adorned with paintings of the night sky. The importance of the pavilion derives from the variety and rarity of its decoration, for once artistic theory was codified, Islamic wall paintings were to become scarce.

Wall-painting from the palace of Qusayr Amra, Jordan.

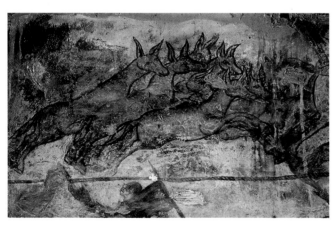

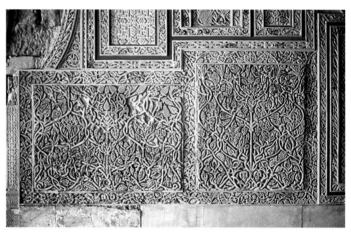

Stuccowork in the Ambassadors' Room of the colossal palace of Medina Zahara in Cordoba, Spain. Built in AD936 by Caliph Abd er-Rahman III, it was destroyed in 1010, but was later partially reconstructed.

hereditary Umayyad dynasty (AD661–750). Little is known about the art objects from this period, but a few religious and secular monuments survive, the most significant of which are the Dome of the Rock (AD687–91) and the al-Aqsa Mosque in Jerusalem, the Great Mosque in Damascus (AD705–15), several fortresses, and a group of palaces built in the Syrian-Israeli desert. Despite the reconstruction and restoration work that have taken place over the centuries, these structures remain important monuments: the mosques for their individual architecture and decoration, which includes glass-paste mosaics (a technique that

a series of monuments and artifacts have been excavated that demonstrate the opulence of contemporary Muslim art. The Great Mosque at Samarra, built in AD847, exhibits a design common to other religious constructions of the time: its large, open, central courtyard is surrounded by an arcade and a prayer hall, with many columns supporting the roof and divided into aisles. The adjacent minaret is virtually unique in its design. Based on an ancient ziggurat, a Sumerian temple in the shape of a pyramidal tower with an ascent around the outside of the structure, it has a circular base and an exterior ramp climbing in a spiral to the top. It was the inspiration for the minaret of the Ibn Tulun Mosque in Cairo (AD876–79), although here the base is square. Cairo, culturally close to the heart of the empire but

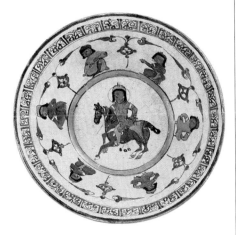

Seljuk bowl from Persia, glazed painted earthenware, late 12th–early 13th century. Al-Sabah Collection, Kuwait.

MOSQUES, BATHS, AND PALACES

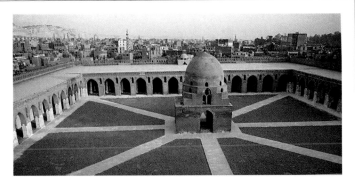

Great Mosque of Ibn-Tulun, Cairo. Besides the prayer hall, a mosque complex will also include a fountain for ritual cleansing prior to worship, a women's prayer area, and perhaps a portico, school, hospital, and hostel.

Every civilization has its own particular architectural nuances and clues as to how its society functioned. Islam, as an all-embracing faith that organizes and controls every activity of the individual's life, has its own characteristic features. The center of the populated area (whether a village, a town, a city, or a neighborhood) is the mosque, place of prayer and at the same time of political assembly. As a rule, the mosque consists of a spacious courtyard surrounded on three sides by an arcade and on the fourth by the prayer hall that faces the direction of Mecca. The buildings may vary slightly

effectively independent of the Abbasid caliphate from the Tulunid dynasty onward (AD868), was to be the hub of an enduring artistic culture. When Samarra, the seat of the early Abbasid caliphs, was abandoned, the court was permanently transferred to Baghdad, seat of power until the city was sacked and destroyed by the Mongols in 1258, ending the caliphate itself as an institution. Archaeological excavations have not yet brought to light any quantity of monuments or objects that could compare with the finds of the previous period. What is certain, however, is that from the year 1000 and for at least three centuries more, Baghdad, together with Mosul and probably Basra and Kufa, would give rise to a school of miniatures that was to produce works of extraordinary refinement. Some were of a religious nature (the most famous being the Koran produced in Baghdad and now in the Chester Beatty Library, Dublin) and others secular.

PERSIAN AND SELJUK ISLAM

Persia occupied quite a different position to that of Mesopotamia, Syria, and Egypt in the panorama of the early centuries of Islam. The

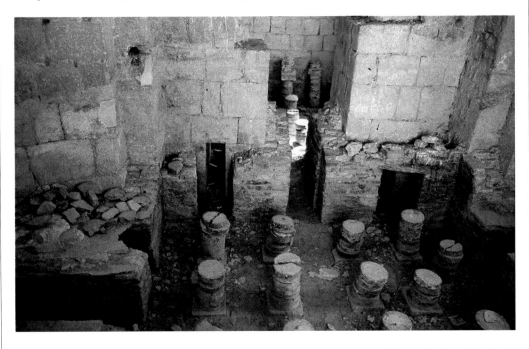

Remains of Hammam al-Hallabat. Baths were a Roman-Byzantine structure popular in Turkey and inherited by Islam.

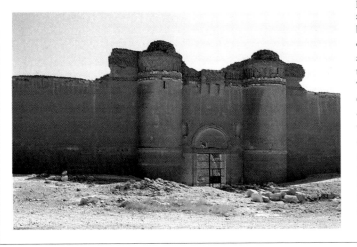

Qasr ak Khayr al-Shargi. A qasr (from the Latin castrum, meaning fortress) is a fort or a palace where the sovereign could reside.

according to the lay of the land or other local restrictions, but they generally adhere to this plan. The faithful pray in a state of ritual purity achieved by means of ablutions so, consequently, in earlier times, an essential building was the *hammam* (public baths). Today, too, the *suk* or *bazar* (market) remains an important center of commercial activity, with buildings allocated to different arts and crafts, as in medieval times. The sovereign's palace, on the other hand, was of minor importance, partly because of the nomadic origins of many sultans.

inhabitants of the region were non-Arabic and the country was, in fact, more closely linked to the regions to the north, Turan, and to the east, central Asia, and was heir to the Sassanid culture and tradition. Furthermore, the land was broken up into a number of separate kingdoms ruled by independent dynasties, at least until the Seljuk conquest of Khurasan in 1040.

ROCK CRYSTAL

Rock crystal is a transparent, colorless quartz that in antiquity was one of the most sought-after semiprecious materials. The skill needed to work such a hard mineral, combined with the exceptional beauty and shine of the finished product, gave it a value even higher than gold. The amounts produced were considerable (sources mention thousands of pieces) but restricted to the Fatimid period in Egypt (late 10th and 11th century). Favorite objects were brooches, bottles, and small flasks for cosmetics and perfumes. Many of the surviving examples, numbering fewer than two hundred, form part of the treasuries of European cathedrals, such as St. Mark's in Venice and the Abbey of St.-Denis outside Paris. For Christians their transparent purity symbolized divine grace, and the fact that Arabic inscriptions frequently appeared on them did not diminish their worth: many, indeed, became reliquaries. Their arrival in the West, as a result of barter or as booty from the Crusades, helped to feed the myths of a wealthy and exotic Orient.

Rock crystal jug with flower and bird decoration and an inscription dating it to between AD992 and 1011. Museum of Silverware, Palazzo Pitti, Florence.

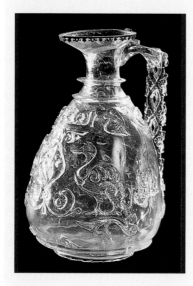

METALLIC LUSTERWARE

The ancient Egyptians had already introduced a technique of metallic luster painting on glass, but the application of this form of decoration to earthenware was also characteristic of the Islamic world. From the ninth century onward, the Muslims of Egypt, Syria, Persia, and Spain were able to produce pottery with an iridescent metallic decoration ranging in color from brilliant golden yellow to dark brown. This was obtained by means of a double firing in special kilns. The results of this complex process produced lusterware in the form of vases, bowls, and tiles, highly prized both in the East and the West. Examples include those from

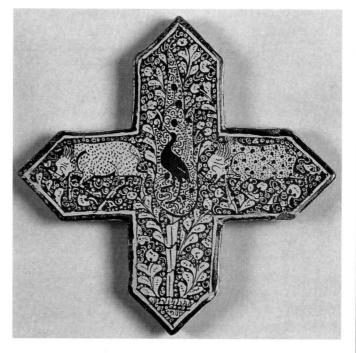

Persian metallic luster tile, intended for use with others of a similar shape. Al-Sabah Collection, Kuwait.

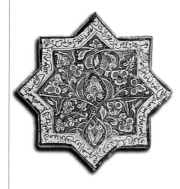

Persian metallic luster tile in the shape of an eight-point star, with floral decoration and Koranic script, Kashan, 13th–14th century. Al-Sabah Collection, Kuwait.

the ninth-century mosques of Kairouan and Samarra and the 13th–14th-century Mosque of Kashan, in Iran. Spanish products (from Malaga, Manises, and Paterna), including Alhambra vases and majolica jars and dishes, greatly influenced contemporary Italian pottery.

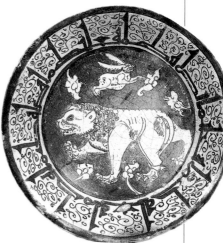

Metallic luster bowl with animal and calligraphic designs. Al-Sabah Collection, Kuwait.

The Seljuks were a seminomadic Turkish dynasty from central Asia. They were skilled builders, and their original, baked-brick monuments form an important part of Persian art history. The Seljuks built domes of extreme elegance, both in their exterior and interior proportions and their decorative design. The brick ornamentation of the domes of the Masjid-i-Jami in Isfahan (1088) is regarded as one of the most glorious examples of architecture, not only in Persia, but all over the world. On some buildings the brick is covered by a layer of stucco or ceramic, a material in which

local artists excelled, both in terms of variety of technique and in the quality of the finished product. Not much metalwork has survived from the Seljuk period, however, although known specimens, particularly the bronzes of Mosul, show a highly refined technique that was probably influenced by objects produced in eastern Persia. The construction of a fairly large group of buildings is attributed to the Seljuks of Rum, a branch of the dynasty whose advance westward was triggered by its defeat of the Byzantines in 1071 at Manzikert. They settled in

Anatolia, creating a state that was destined to last until the beginning of the 14th century. The buildings in question were mostly built of stone, using a technique inherited from the local Christians, and decorated with rich, elaborate inlays or, less frequently, with ceramic coating. They were mainly Koranic schools and mosques but also caravanserais, or *hans*, which were used as resthouses for those traveling along the major highways. A network of well-preserved *hans* from the Seljuk period can still be seen today at intervals on the road from Kayseri to Konya in Turkey.

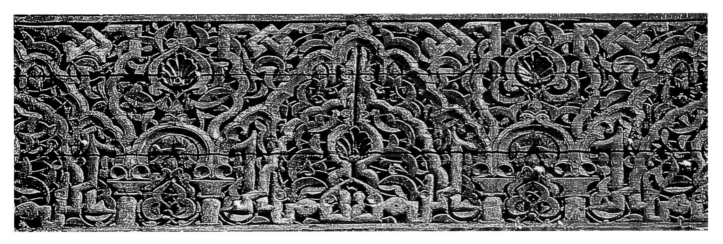

WESTERN ISLAM

In the West, the swift advance of the Muslim army was eventually halted on the frontiers of France and Spain. The Iberian peninsula was to provide the stage for the development of a totally original form of Islamic art and culture that has accurately been described as Hispano-Moorish.

In Cordoba, capital of the Andalusian kingdom, work began on the Great Mosque in AD785. Today it survives as a glowing example of the use of the Moorish, horseshoe-shaped arch. Typical of Hispano-Moorish decoration was colored stucco, which was a cheap but effective substitute for marble. Another characteristic art form was the fine, woven textiles produced in all the major Andalusian towns. However, the most noted product of Hispano-Moorish art was inlaid ivory.

In these early centuries of the Abbasid caliphate, the whole coastal belt of North Africa enjoyed relative autonomy. The main cities, although recognizing the overall authority of the sovereign in Baghdad, were ruled by local dynasties. Kairouan, capital of the Aghlabids in Tunisia, was an important city, judging by its many splendid monuments and mosques, especially the Great Mosque founded by Hisham in AD724. By AD902 the Tunisian dynasty had conquered Sicily, which became an extremely active centre for the manufacture of textiles and ivory. After the Norman conquest, products still remained typically Islamic in style. For example, the ceiling paintings of the Cappella Palatina in Palermo, executed in 1154, a century after the end of Arab rule on the island, are very similar to the art works of the Fatimids. This dynasty governed Egypt for two centuries

(AD969–1171), and founded Cairo as their capital, where their fortifications and religious buildings, such as the al-Azhar Mosque (founded AD970) and the al-Hakim Mosque (AD990–1013) can still be seen today.

Detail of decoration in wood from the medersa, or school, of Misbahiya, mid-14th century. Fez, Morocco.

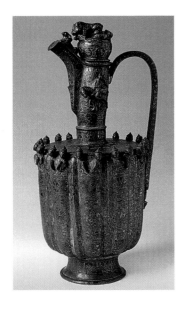

Brass jug from Khorasan, embossed with silver and copper inlay. Galleria Estense, Modena, Italy. The body of the jug is multifoiled and decorated in high relief with nine couples of harpies. The neck bears a couple of falconers, and the lid is topped by a lioness and her cubs.

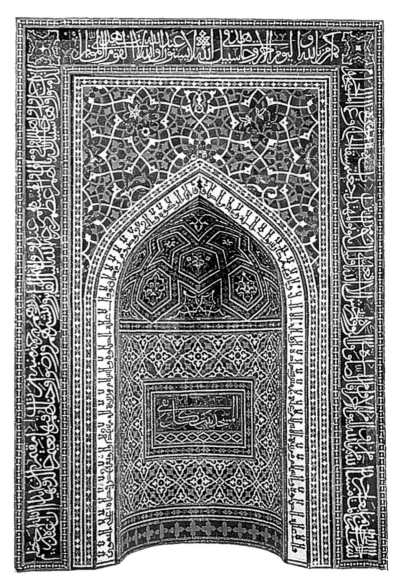

Mihrab of the Medersa Imami, Isfahan, 1325. Mosaic in glass-paste tiles. Metropolitan Museum of Art, New York.

THE INDIAN REGION & THE FAR EAST

Between the ancient and modern eras, sophisticated civilizations were developing or already in existence in places as distant as India, Java, and Japan. Inspired by differing – and sometimes overlapping – forms of religious thought and life, these cultures produced a varied array of art and architecture.

In Asia, the cultures of India and China have developed rich artistic traditions over thousands of years. Both have had a profound and widespread influence upon the cultures of surrounding peoples, often developing in tandem with the existing local cultures.

INDIAN ART FROM THE MAURYA TO THE GUPTA

During its long development, Indian art has reflected the constant endeavor to give artistic shape to the divine. The principles of this pursuit remained unchanged over the centuries, but the style of expression took different forms. The preclassical age is exemplified by the artistic activity of the Maurya (4th–2nd century BC) and Śunga (2nd–1st century BC) periods, and later in the art of the important city of Mathura in the Kushan period (first–third century AD). The powerful molding of Maurya figurative sculpture in polished sandstone and the frontal forms of the Śunga figures at Bharhut and Sañchi were the stylistic examples for the typical Kushan statuary. During the early centuries AD, the abundant production of statues using local pink sandstone provided the foundations for the development of sculpture and the rich Hindu and Buddhist iconography of

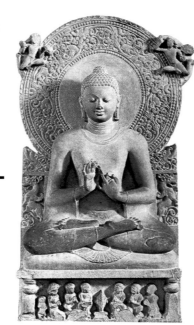

Sandstone statue of preaching Buddha, fifth century AD. Archaeological Museum, Sarnath. An example of Gupta art of the Sarnath school, this sculpture is decorated with great elegance. The contours of the Buddha are smooth and express a great sense of concentration.

future years. Some of the most typical images of the Indian world are found at Bharhut and Sañchi; these are the *yaksa* and *yaksini* – male and female nature spirits associated with trees and fertility. The male figures are usually in a rigid standing position with a round face and spherical eyes. Female figures reveal characteristic features of Indian grace and beauty: the supple body bent in the *tribhanga* posture with the weight on one leg, the sensual shape of the hips and breasts, and

the expressive details in the face. There are stupas (domed edifices) and reliquaries dating to the Śunga period, the earliest of which contain the remains of the Buddha and act as the true focal point of Buddhist culture. These buildings were characterized by an ancient hemispherical shape.

On the top of this, a square wall surrounded a pole that passed through the stupa and came out through two or more parasols. The monument was bordered by a circular balustrade, with four gate walls, or *toranas*, facing the four cardinal points. Stupa 2 at Sañchi was decorated with low

KUSHAN SCULPTURE

In the early centuries of the first millennium AD, during the reign of the Kushan sovereigns, two important schools of art developed in the regions of Gandhara in the northwest of modern Pakistan and Mathura in Uttar Pradesh, India. Both centers inherited an ancient artistic tradition, which was manifested in the formulation of well-defined sculptural styles. These two major art schools developed different formal solutions to the anthropomorphic representation of the Buddha. Characterized by an original artistic language enriched by various contributions from other cultures, including the Romano-Hellenist, the Gandharan style can be seen in the production of schist statues of Buddha and narrative reliefs inspired by the Master's life. On the other hand, the sandstone images of the Buddha from Mathura are based solely on Indian tradition.

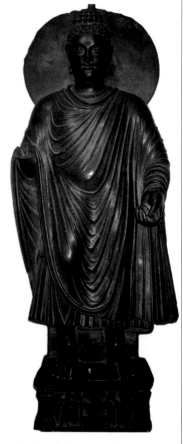

Gandharan schist statue of a standing Buddha, second century. National Museum, New Delhi.

THE ORIGINS OF THE INDIAN TEMPLE

True Indian temple architecture dates from the Gupta period. Prior to this, there had been centuries of religious activity associated with sanctuaries hewn from rock walls, particularly in central western India. Among the most famous examples of cave temples are the Buddhist grottoes of Ajanta, which were entirely cut out of the rock. In the Gupta period, the format of many Indian temples followed a standardized plan that was to remain the blueprint for later temples. The heart of the building was the cubical cella where the divine image was placed. Raised slightly on a low platform, it was situated inside a square room with an antechamber. A passage surrounded the shrine for the ritual walk around the sacred image. The architraves and jambs of the entrance portal were often richly decorated with plant motifs and the male and female figures of the temple protectors. Images of the Hindu deities also adorned the walls.

Temple of Vishnu, Deogarh, Uttar Pradesh, second half of the fifth century. This temple represents the standard design of temples in the formative Gupta period.

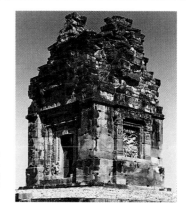

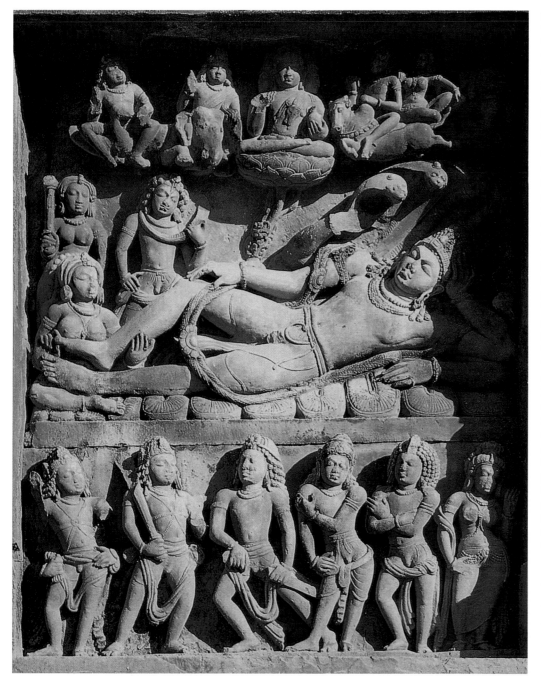

relief, as were the four gateways at Bharhut. Amaravati was another artistic center, which existed at the same time as Mathura, and its sculpture is distinguishable by an image of the Buddha with delicate and elongated features, his robe falling in heavy folds. The Gupta period (AD370–550) was an important part of the classical phase of Indian art. It embodied all Indian aesthetic ideals and formulated the rules for the representation and iconography of Hindu and Buddhist divinities. It was also the period when the shape of the Hindu temple was defined and a formal mode of expression was developed in the arts. The more localized styles of artistic production, which had typified the earlier periods, were replaced by a more unified style. This was first elaborated in Mathura and later exemplified by the school of Sarnath, which established itself as the principal artistic center of the fifth century. Achieving a balance of form and decoration was both the goal and culmination of Gupta art. However, political, religious, and social changes in the sixth century were to bring distinct changes to the forms of art in medieval times.

Relief showing Vishnu Anantasayana, Vishnu Temple, Deogarh, Uttar Pradesh. The thick and animated network of figures on a variety of levels and the luminosity and sensuality of the high-relief sculpture are very striking. Perhaps less obvious to the Western observer is the theological content of this sacred work of art.

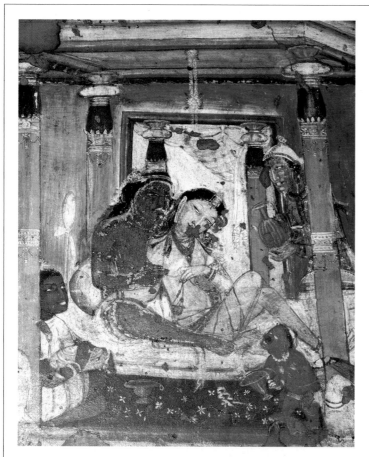

ANONYMOUS MASTER: "COURT LIFE SCENE"

Fifth century; detail from the wall paintings in Cave XVII of Ajanta, Maharashtra, India.

The rock-cut temples and "cave" paintings of Ajanta are religious in character and inspired by sacred texts. This particular painting refers to the *Vishvantara Jataka*, a work narrating the life of Buddha.

It shows part of an episode in which the prince tells his wife of his wish to renounce the pleasures of court life and become a monk in his new life as Buddha. Seated on a bed, the princely couple converse, surrounded by three figures. The four columns of the bed and the eyelines of the three figures frame the couple, highlighting them as the subjects of the painting.

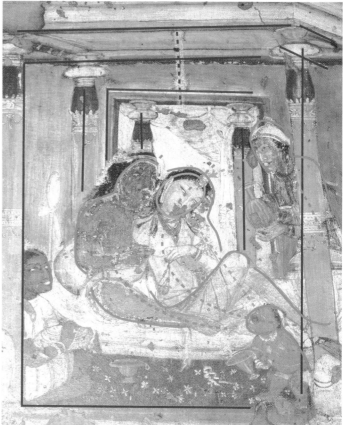

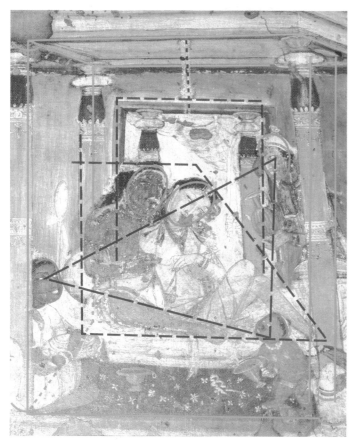

◀ *1. The couple is contained in a cubic space defined by the columns that support the top of the bed. The sense of volume is heightened by the garland of flowers suspended in the area above the woman's head. Within this space, the figures are composed two-dimensionally, following the plan of a rectangular trapezium. The eyes of the three secondary figures may be linked to form a triangle that intersects the trapezium. In the background, a rectangular opening throws light on the main figures. Together, the three polygons, the cylindrical columns, and the cube constitute a very precise spatial and compositional structure.*

▲ *2. The lines that define the architectural spaces are straight and therefore emphasize the dimensions of the scene. Curved lines define the forms of the main figures; the female figure, painted lighter according to convention, is particularly graceful and delicate. Her face is in the center of the scene and is gazed at by the secondary figures. The grace and light coloration of her presence serves to intensify the figure of the prince, whose limbs, body, and head seem to envelop and protect her.*

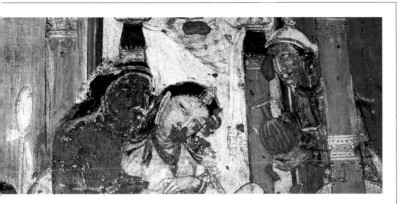

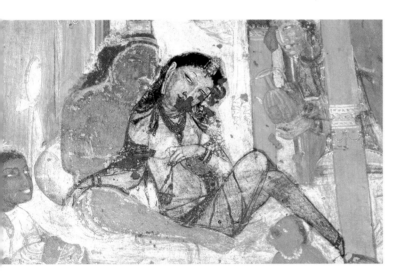

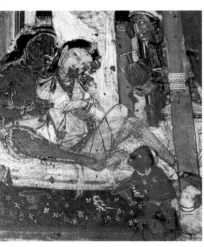

▲ 3. The colors in the composition consist mainly of white and a variety of burnt tints. There are slight touches of blue in the fabric of the bed, black in the capitals, and blue-green in the clothing of the rear figure, contrasting with the burnished color of the background. The application of color is fragmented, into small areas varying little in tone, thus enhancing the picture surface. The delicate brushstrokes seem to bring a sense of vibration to the scene.

▼ 4. Both principal male and female figures are depicted with great vigor. The woman, wearing a dress of fine material, leans delicately against the body of her husband. Her attitude suggests confidence in her powers of seduction, an effect reinforced by her expression. The graceful hand, full breasts, and slender waist convey a sense of sexual power that encapsulates the delights of the life that the future Buddha wishes to abandon.

◄ 5. The male body is athletic and firmly structured. Rich ornamentation indicates the rank of the prince and reminds us of the luxurious worldly pleasures that he will now have the strength to leave behind. The story is in no sense weighed down by the rich decoration. The fasciae on the columns, drawn in gold with the tip of the brush against a burnt background, do not detract from the impression of a cylindrical shape. The small white flowers scattered over the carpet and painted from a frontal angle add to the sense of depth as the carpet "continues" beneath the bed.

SINHALESE ART

The art of Sri Lanka (previously known as Ceylon) from the fourth century BC to the tenth century AD is best seen in the regions of the ancient capitals of Anuradhapura and Polonnaruwa. The art was inspired mainly by the form of Buddhism that was introduced to the island in the third century BC. Among the most

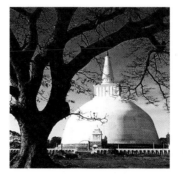

Stupa of Ruanveli, Sri Lanka, Anuradhapura period.

typical monuments are the stupas, such as those of Thuparama and Ruanveli at Anuradhapura, which follow the famous Indian example of Amaravati but without the narrative reliefs that decorate its body and balustrade. Also typical are the monasteries and the characteristic *bodhighara* – sanctuaries erected around the sacred *bodhi* ("illumination") tree. The sculpture in stone and bronze, also influenced by the Amaravati style, consists of statues of the Buddha, clad in a tightly pleated cloak with his right shoulder uncovered. A new, refined sensibility is evident in the carvings of the "moon stones" – engraved slabs situated at the base of the entrance steps to the Buddhist temples. During the last centuries of Anuradhapura's dominance, Sinhalese sculpture reveals the influence of other Indian schools, such as the classical Gupta style and the Pallava

HINDU AND BUDDHIST IMAGERY

The representation of the human figure, which occupies a central position in Indian art, is not concerned with the achievement of realism or individuality. The artists did not seek to illustrate any notion of empirical reality, but chose to represent the spiritual in human form. This is reflected in the bodies of the Hindu gods (rarely defined with anatomical accuracy in order to ensure a harmony of the whole); in the serene and controlled expression of their faces (portraying celestial sovereignty and dominion over the passions); in the multiplication of limbs (sign of divine omnipotence); and in attributes that identify supernatural power. Similarly, the Buddha's image is conveyed through the rapt gaze, the gestures of his hands, and the characteristics that mark him out as a superior being – protruberant skull, open hand, and the symbol of

the wheel on the soles of his feet. These sum up the whole spiritual experience as lived and transmitted to his disciples.

Statue of Vishnu. The deity's expression evokes harmony and serenity.

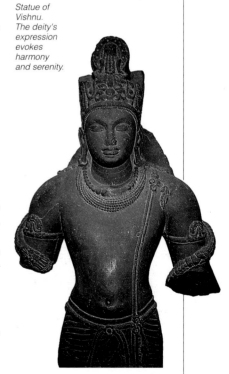

THE WALL-PAINTINGS OF AJANTA AND SIGIRIYA

Some compensation for the absence of ancient Indian painting is afforded by the wall-paintings of Ajanta in Maharashtra, India, and Sigiriya in Sri Lanka, both dating from the fifth century AD. Painted in watercolors on dry plaster on the walls of the rock-carved rooms and galleries, both show the influence of classical Gupta art, albeit interpreted in differing fashions. The Ajanta paintings, drawn freely and confidently along conventional lines, illustrate Buddhist narratives, with crowded scenes of people in palaces and gardens. The full, sensual forms of the figures are created by the soft lines of

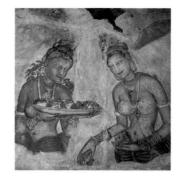

Wall-painting from Sigiriya, Sri Lanka, last quarter of the fifth century.

Wall-painting from the first cave, Ajanta, India, fifth century.

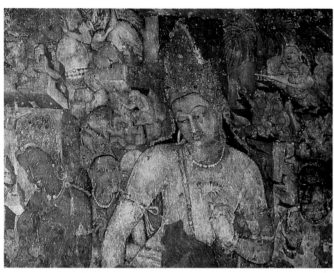

the contours and by the interplay of color, light, and shade, which accentuates the shapes and creates subtle effects in the expressions of the people. In the figures from Sigiriya, however, there is a sense of greater simplicity. The paintings contain less variety of color and stylistically place more emphasis on outline, giving a rare beauty to the female images.

Buddhist in the case of the Khmer and Cham. By now, these were mature artistic styles, acting independently of Indian models. Local variations produced original results in architecture and sculpture, notably the stupas and sanctuaries of Pagan in Myanmar (Burma), the mountain temples of Angkor and its provincial towns in Cambodia, the distinctive style of bronze manufacture in Sukhotai, and the unusual sculptures of the Champa at Dong Duong. From the 9th to the 13th century, the cities of Angkor and Pagan were the main political and cultural centers of two profoundly different civilizations, the Burmese and the Khmer. Although they differed in their aspirations, the two cultures nevertheless helped each other develop, as exemplified by the Buddhist sanctuaries of Pagan and the Hindu monuments of Angkor. Burmese architecture made exclusive use of brick and stucco. Sanctuary walls were typically lined with plaster, which acted as a surface for the interior wall-paintings, while exterior decoration was confined to the simple molding and projecting pediments that framed the doors. Panels of glazed terracotta, illustrated with didactic scenes, were sometimes placed around the hemispherical, bell-shaped stupas. Classical Burmese sculpture consists of bronze, stone, and stucco images of Buddha,

style from southern India (seventh to eighth century). These styles were preserved by Sinhalese art and transmitted to regions of Southeast Asia.

BURMESE, KHMER, AND CHAMPA ART

The spread of Indian culture was partly a result of commercial contacts with the peoples of Southeast Asia and partly the interaction between the Indian and Southeast Asian courts of the day during the first centuries of the modern era. Among these kingdoms were ancient Funan at the mouth of the Mekong, Sriksetra in Burma, Dvaravati in Thailand, and the more easterly Linyi in Vietnam – all inhabited by people of diverse ethnic stock and language and

Temple of Ananda, Pagan, Burma, late 11th century. This temple is a magnificent example of Pagan architecture.

influenced by different aspects of Indian culture. Subsequently, from about the seventh or eighth century, each of these areas was involved in a process of unification, culminating in the foundation of the Cham and Khmer civilizations, and later, in the 13th century, the Thai civilization. Different religious beliefs determined the artistic orientation of these cultures – Buddhist in the case of the Burmese and Thai, Hindu and

View of the richly decorated Khmer mountain-temple of Bayon, Cambodia.

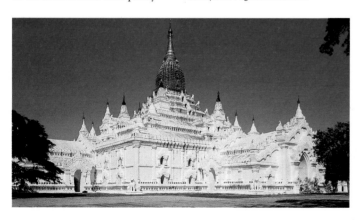

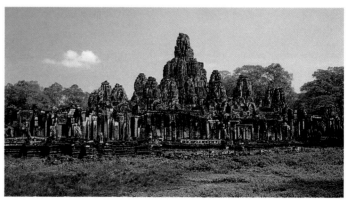

partly derived from Indian art but distinguished by the stylized modeling and the development of a flamelike skull protuberance.

The best examples of classical Khmer art and architecture can be found at the remains of the awe-inspiring ancient city of Angkor. Its sculpture is predominantly Hindu in influence, with rounded statues and shallow reliefs carved on temple walls. The high technical level of Khmer artists is evident in both architecture and sculpture. It is manifested in the skilled use of sandstone blocks in building and in the free-standing statuary, which displays smooth lines and a strong frontality, conveying magnificently the supernatural power of the Hindu divinities. Khmer sculpture is also characterized by the faint smile on the faces of the deities.

To a large extent, Champa art parallels that of its neighboring civilization and is manifested in numerous Hindu temples, particularly at My Son in the north and in the ninth century Buddhist complex of Dong Duong. Rich and imaginative sculpture was also produced, in which diverse influences were blended with great originality.

THE ART OF JAVA

In Java, the earliest examples of classical Indian-influenced art date from the eighth century, such as the simple cubiform temples of the Dieng plateau. Under the rule of the Srivijaya dynasty (c.AD778– 856), the great stupa of Borobudur was built in central Java. This stupa, which remains the largest Buddhist monument in the world, was constructed in the form of a gigantic *mandala*, or diagrammatic aid to meditation.

The Hindu temple complex of Prambanan, near Yogyakarta, dates from slightly later than Borobudur, and its architectural and artistic features show that Buddhism and Hinduism coexisted in Java at that time. Stone sculpture is represented by the sensuous and graceful bas-reliefs, depicting in lively detail either previous lives of the Buddha (*jataka* stories) or tales from Hindu epics. The freestanding stone sculpture from the period has a distinctive monumentality and smoothness of line, while the bronze sculpture, which reflects styles from southern and northeastern India, is particularly graceful. The cultural focus moved to eastern Java in AD929. The finest examples of eastern Javanese temple architecture and sculpture date from the 13th and 14th centuries. The arrival of Islam in the 15th century was to provide another rich new source of inspiration, particularly in the fields of calligraphy and metalwork.

Cover of a terrace, Borobudur, Java, 8th–9th century AD. This monument is rich in splendid didactic sculptures.

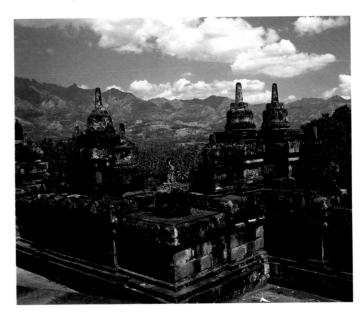

PAGAN AND ANGKOR

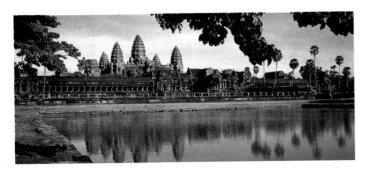

The Buddhist sanctuaries of Pagan represent an original application of the Indian temple to Buddhist architecture. In the classical Burmese version, the temple was built on two levels divided up at various points. A square platform with rising terraces supported the central cubic body. This was covered by a pyramidal structure and surmounted by either a bell-shaped stupa of Burmese derivation or by a miter-shaped roof.

In Khmer art, the sanctuary was a monument of sophisticated symbolism, as can be seen in the classic example of Angkor Wat. The pyramidal structure was intended to reflect the harmony and perfection of Mount Meru, the dwelling place of the gods. The sacred area is reached through an entrance gate, and a long causeway leads across the first platform on which the temple stands. A complicated system of galleries and steps links the adjoining areas to the last platform. In the center of the terrace is the temple with its characteristic towers, square in plan with a tall, curvilinear roof. The temple is decorated in bas-reliefs, the most famous of which is the *Churning of the Milky Ocean.*

View of Angkor Wat, first half of the 12th century. This magnificent Hindu temple was dedicated to Vishnu. In the center, the mountain-temple rises up, surrounded by moats that allude to the sea and galleries that symbolize the mountains. In this microcosm, the sacredness of the Khmer kings was protected by Vishnu.

Buddhist sanctuaries, Pagan. The political and artistic center of Burma, Pagan flourished from the 11th to the i3th century, its variety of architectural forms deriving mainly from Indian influences. One of the most important Pagan civic monuments is the 11th-century library.

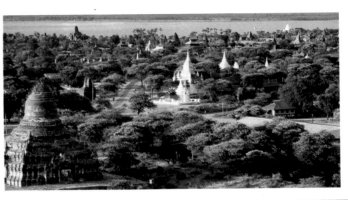

ANCIENT CHINESE ARCHITECTURE

Ancient Chinese monuments, whether great palaces, temples, or small private dwellings, were characterized by the repetition of units. Even in the case of the simplest of houses, the design followed an arrangement of similar-sized rooms. The standard unit was the *jian,* a rectangular room or space enclosed by walls or columns. In the most ancient period, the *jian* measured approximately 9½ x 19 ft (3 x 6 meters), but after the Tang dynasty the dimensions grew progressively bigger.

The system of repeating these areas along a horizontal or longitudinal axis was a characteristic feature of the imposing pavilions (*ting*) of the great palaces and temples, providing large rooms of harmonious proportions. The buildings were almost never isolated but planned in groups based on precise coordinates, with covered passageways to connect one pavilion with the next. The result was a system of linked but separate structures – a blueprint very different from that of Western architecture, in which various functions tended to be united under the same roof.

The sequence of pavilions was generally connected along a longitudinal axis facing south or southeast, interspersed by a succession of courtyards. In the center was the principal building, with the lesser ones

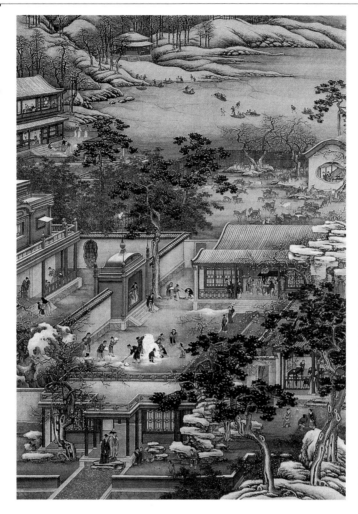

placed to its right and left and sometimes in front or behind it. Elsewhere, there might be a central building at the meeting point of two axes, with the secondary buildings placed around on all sides. In one quite common type of habitation, typical of northern China, the buildings were constructed around the four sides of one

Artists of the court of emperor Qianlong (reigned 1736–95), The Labors of the Twelfth Month, *painted on canvas.*

central square or rectangular courtyard. In more important residences, groups of smaller buildings with courtyards might be assembled around the central construction.

of the purer Chinese prototypes. Narrative painting developed during the Eastern Han dynasty (AD25–221) and the successive period of the Six Dynasties, also known as the Three Kingdoms (AD220–280). Wall-paintings and handscroll paintings became favorite modes of expression. The narrative of the horizontal scrolls was read from right to left, while the walls of temples, tombs, and palaces were adorned with processional scenes of figures drawn with flowing outlines and bright colors. The palette was richer than that previously used – when red, yellow, and black predominated – and was perhaps inspired by lacquer painting.

The Six Dynasties ushered in a period of stark political instability for several centuries, during which China was split between north and south and ruled by various dynasties. From AD386 to 557, the Chinese-assimilated proto-Turkish population of the Tuoba-Wei dominated the north. They played a fundamental role in the diffusion of Buddhist teachings. This was the era of the great cave temples. The oldest site, founded in the fourth century by itinerant monks, was that of Dunhuang in Gansu province, which consisted of hundreds of caves decorated with sculptures and frescoes. In AD440, the Wei conquered Dunhuang, and many important works of art were produced under their patronage. With splendid

THE GOLDEN AGE OF CHINESE ART

Much information about the pictorial art of the Han period comes from the painted decorations on lacquer and pottery, and from sculpted stone figures. Few silk paintings have survived, but some tombs have revealed wall-paintings indicating that Han artists excelled in figure

painting. Landscape was merely the background for the narration of human and mythical events: the notion that it might constitute a subject in its own right did not enter into the cultural considerations of the time. The introduction of Buddhism into China in the first century AD opened up new artistic possibilities and perspectives. The rich iconographic tradition and compositional techniques of Buddhist painting were fused with those

Wall-painting from a royal tomb, Da Horinger, Inner Mongolia, Han period. The depiction of horses, a common theme at this time, indicates the social rank of the dead man. It follows a trend that has a precedent in the tomb of Qin Shihuang (220–210BC).

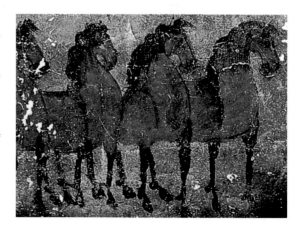

CHINESE SCULPTURE

In China, sculpture was traditionally a relatively popular means of expression, especially in a religious context. During the eastern Han dynasty (AD25–221), stone funerary sculpture – often of considerable dimensions – was produced alongside smaller objects of terracotta, gilded bronze, jade, and other materials.

The spread of Buddhism from the fifth century onward exercised a strong influence on this form of stone statuary. In the grandiose figures of Buddha and Bodhisattvas carved in the rock of the

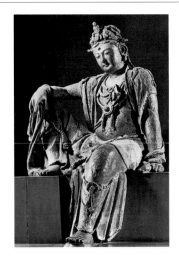

Wooden figure of the Bodhisattva Guanyin, Song dynasty. Museum of Fine Arts, Boston.

frescoes in bright colors portraying traditional Buddhist scenes, the depiction of landscape became increasingly important from about the sixth century onward.

A school of court painting developed alongside the collective tradition of itinerant artists. The artist Gu Kaizhi (AD344–406) worked in the capital of the southern Jin, near present-day Nanjing. Two important paintings (though not in their original form but in later copies) are attributed to him: *Advice of the Governess to the Court Ladies* and *The Nymph of the Lo River*. In these balanced compositions, the elegant, softly outlined figures of

women and dignitaries, colored in ink on silk, are still more prominent than the landscape, which is confined to essentials and indicated with lines of uniform thickness and light shading.

The Sui (AD581–618) reunified China, and the following Tang dynasty (AD618–907) reorganized the empire and gave a fresh impetus to the arts. The desire to create new rules of conduct after a long period of disorder and fragmentation

Avalokitesuara, late Tang period. British Museum, London. This painting on silk from Dunhuang in Gansu dates from the tenth year of the reign of Tianfu. Bamboo paper was just starting to be used at this time.

cave temples of Yungang (Shanxi) under the Wei dynasty, the full, sensual forms found in Indian sculpture were interpreted in a more two-dimensional style. The combination of Buddhist art with the Chinese linear painting tradition resulted in a new form of expression. The stylization and spiritualization of figures became even more pronounced from the end of the fifth century, as seen in the caves of Longmen in Henan and in the surviving bronze images of the time. During the Tang period, Buddhism reached its greatest development, although only a few specimens are known of the great seventh- and eighth-century pieces of bronze, wood, and clay

Small nephrite figure of a chimaera, Han period.

sculpture. This is due largely to the purge of Buddhist art in the ninth century. Surviving pieces of sculpture from the Tang era include the beautiful *mingqi* – tiny glazed or painted figures that had been placed in tombs as part of the funerary furnishings since the Han period. Many splendid examples of wooden religious sculptures were produced during the Song dynasty: one of the more popular subjects of the 12th and 13th centuries was Guanyin, the merciful Bodhisattva, depicted standing or seated in a pose that evokes great serenity and dignity.

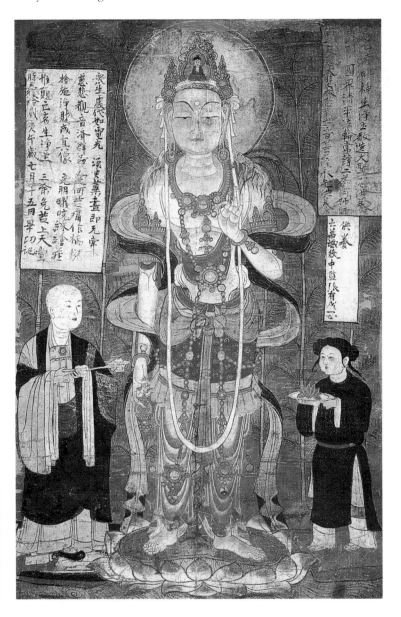

was reflected in the arts, with a codification of standards and techniques. This period saw the birth of landscape painting, due principally to developments in the use of color. Li Sixun (AD653–718) and Li Zhaodao (AD670–730) brought life to a decorative style associated with the court environment. It was characterized by an increased emphasis on the linear element, but it was also enriched by the use of bright colors – clearly the influence of the great wall-paintings of Buddhist temples. The predominant tones were cobalt blue and green (produced from copper), with light touches of gold. Court painting was also the province of Yan Liben (AD600–73), to whom *The Scroll of the Thirteen Emperors* is attributed. His imposing figures represent the image of the sovereign according to Confucian convention. In the eighth century, the

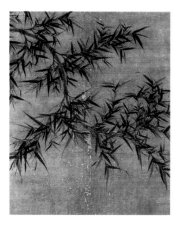

Wen Tong (1018-79), Bamboo, *Song period, c.1070. Chinese artists of the Song period made use of a particular conventional brushstroke to paint plants.*

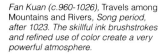

Fan Kuan (c.960-1026), Travels among Mountains and Rivers, *Song period, after 1023. The skillful ink brushstrokes and refined use of color create a very powerful atmosphere.*

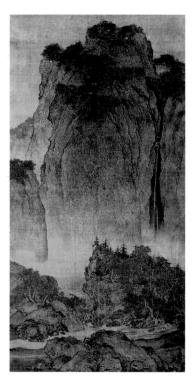

poet and painter Wang Wei (AD699–759) initiated a new style of landscape painting. He introduced the ink-splash technique, using black Indian ink. The style relied less on the importance of the line and more on the gradations of the monochrome ink, representing the infinite variations of landscape. This allusive, poetic style of painting, impressionistic in effect and defined as "poetry without words," was particularly appreciated by intellectuals in later periods. Through suggestion rather than description, it could create a magical atmosphere that expressed the contemplative spirit of the scholar. The work of the artist Wu Daozi (AD689–758), a contemporary of Wang Wei, was highly acclaimed by generations of critics. He produced handscroll paintings and wall-paintings for temples and palaces. His powerful, expressive line and almost calligraphic brushstroke evoked the admiration of his contemporaries, feeding the legend that he was capable of infusing his figures with life. During the period of the Five Dynasties (AD907–60), landscape painting reached a new peak. Jing Hao (c.AD870–940) set the generic standards with his *Bifagi* ("Essay on the Use of the Brush"). This exhorted the painter to pursue absolute

YAN LIBEN: "PORTRAIT OF AN EMPEROR"

Seventh century AD; from The Scroll of the Thirteen Emperors; *20 x 21 in (51.3 x 53.1 cm); Museum of Fine Arts, Boston.*

This work by Yan Liben (AD600–673) depicts the sovereign standing between two markedly smaller dignitaries, who reach only to his shoulders. He rests his forearms on their folded arms. The dominant colors of the robes are pink, red (for the emperor), and black, with touches of white and gold. A thin, pleated tunic reaches the ground and partly covers the emperor's red shoes. Other finely decorated red and pink articles of clothing are partially concealed by the sumptuous black overgarment, which has a red border and is decorated in gold. The long sleeves cover the hands, which, for ritual reasons, are left invisible and protected. Long fringes hang from the complex headdress to mask the sacred face. The officials are bearded like their lord, but their costumes are less elaborate.

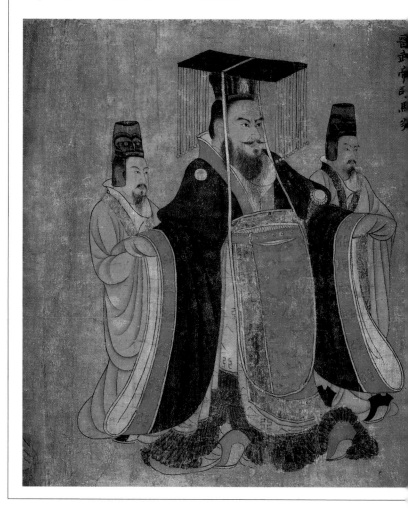

truth, not in the sense of outer appearances but in correspondence with the principles of nature. Through the humble observation of natural forms, the artist could discover their eternal and essential characteristics; by concentrating on these, he would be able to formulate the language to translate it into a powerful, visual experience of the universe.

A tendency toward realism derived from this process of contemplation is evident in the

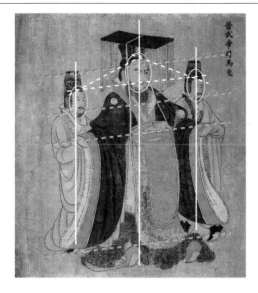

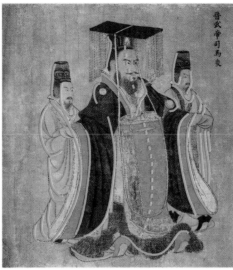

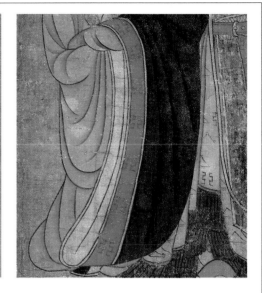

▲ 1. The composition is very simple, almost symmetrically arranged around a vertical central axis. More than one-third of the space is occupied by the emperor. The two dignitaries stand slightly in the background on either side of the sovereign, where they form a sort of frame to the expanse of the central figure; the arrangement emphasizes the prominence of the emperor. This impression is also conveyed by the use of color; the minor figures are painted in the same colors as the main figure, but in lighter tones. The two smaller heads are positioned at the acute angles of a triangle. The planes of alignment of the tips of the sleeves and hands of the principal figure and the chin and hair of the two attendants are thus not horizontal to the base of the painting.

▲ 2. The layout of the painting is characterized by ink outlines and areas of color. The lines around the major figure mainly take the form of crescents and waves and are accentuated by the movement of the sleeves and the right-hand figure. The strokes of the brush on the silk are rapid and confident, building up a composition of curves that wind in and out of one another, dissolving and reforming to construct recognizable forms. By these subtle and delicate means, the painter of the scroll even manages to suggest the heavy weight of the portly protagonist. The few straight lines are gentle but have a powerful, expressive presence. For example, the headdress of the emperor, with its long fringes, serves as an emblem of the royal personage.

▲ 3. The shape and volume of the clothing is determined by the clearly established outlines. The moderation of the line is of great importance, however, and the stroke is not uniform but varied in strength and thickness to suggest texture and shadow. The latter is particularly clearly drawn in the costumes of the minor figures, where strokes of darker pink indicate the depths of the folds; deeper tones of black are used for the folds of the emperor's overgarment. True shadows do not appear, even on the faces. Realistic portrayal is of no interest to the painter, who aims purely to create a composition containing the essential features of its subjects. It is through the omission or refinement of textures lacking symbolic value that the work seems to attain a spiritual quality.

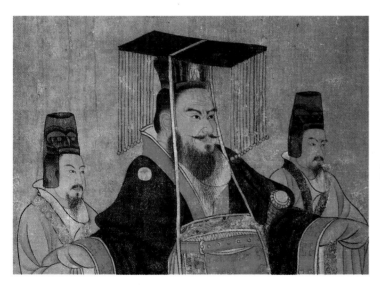

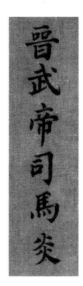

◄ 4. The faces of the dignitaries lack expression, and the features have few personal details. Absorbed in their duties, the men seem devoid of individuality. The face of the central figure is quite different: he is the emperor, lord of his age and the embodiment of his kingdom. The prominent ear, the furrowed brow of a wise man, and the lines around the mouth and eyes all represent the features of a monarch singled out as a characterful and important individual.

◄ 5. The inflection of the marks used to create the ideograms follows the pattern of the rest of the work. From a strictly artistic viewpoint, there is no distinction between the picture outline and the ideogram; calligraphy here is art and as much a painting as the picture itself. The confident hand that created the characters is the same as the one that modulated the outlines of the figures, depicted the facial features, and colored the garments. In this culture, there cannot be beautiful poetry without beautiful painting; in fact, many Chinese artists were also poets. Works of art were individual yet communal and appealed as much to the eye as to the intellect.

work of the painters of the Song dynasty (AD960–1279). This was partly stimulated by neo-Confucianism, which spread with the arrival of the dynasty and nurtured faith in man's ability to understand the world by means of attentive and thorough observation of natural phenomena. This is not a matter of scientific investigation in the Western sense of the term but of a search for the *li* – the principle or essence of every phenomenon. It was believed that it was possible through deep concentration to approach knowledge of single phenomena and, at a higher level, to gain intuition of the universe in its totality. This would reveal a synthetic rather than analytical vision of the world. Similarly, the artist was to paint that which he knew to exist in a particular place, not that which could be perceived from a single viewpoint. A landscape, therefore, should not be seen from one particular angle, as in Western art, but from an abstract viewpoint that would embrace the whole scene. Chinese perspective is mobile: it does not restrict the spectator to one fixed position but shifts around to create a series of different viewpoints, as experienced by a traveler. The great period of realistic painting dates from the accession of the northern Song dynasty (AD960–1127). The search for the absolute truth of nature culminated in the work of Fan Kuan (c.AD960–1026). In his *Travels among Mountains and Rivers,* the mountain scenery of northern China is depicted with such realism that the spectator is made to feel he is actually there. The powerful presence of the mountains is evoked in a simple and logical fashion, with particular emphasis on the vertical elements of the composition. In his *Early Spring* (1072), Guo Xi (c.1020–90) skillfully portrays a mountain landscape dominated by a towering peak, using gentle touches of light and shade to great effect. The carefree spirit of the painters of the early part of the dynasty is characterized by their far-reaching compositions. This was gradually lost to a stiffer style of impersonal, official court painting, which adhered to set formulas and inflexible rules. The painters

of the Academy school, founded by the emperor Hui Zong (reigned 1101–25), embodied this tendency, devoting themselves mainly to nature studies featuring flowers and birds.

Li Tang (1050–1131) represents a transitional stage between these two styles; although he belonged to the Academy school, his style was still strongly individual. His great mastery of the brush influenced two major painters of the southern Song dynasty (1127–1279): Ma Yuan (active c.1180–1224) and Xia Gui (active c.1200–40), both of whom also had links with the court. With these two artists, landscapes lost strength and monumentality and became more delicate and imbued with a sense of sadness that verged on romanticism. Nevertheless, their contribution revived contemporary painting with the introduction of a new type of decentralized perspective. Making freer use of the brush, they employed bold, vigorous strokes to depict the sharp outlines of mountains and trees. The melancholy spirit, typical of paintings of this period, was partly owing to the new political situation that resulted after the loss of the northern regions and the establishment of a new capital at Hangzhou in the south. Painting, now influenced by the soft landscape of southern China, became a means of communicating thoughts and emotions rather than a precise instrument for depicting external reality. It was no longer a matter of studying and describing nature

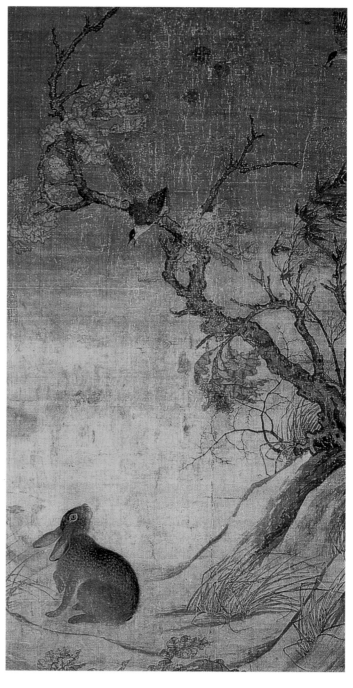

Cui Bo (active c.1060–85), Magpies and Hare, 1061, Song dynasty. Painted in ink on silk, this natural scene appears on a vertical scroll.

Xia Gui (active c.1200-40), detail from Rivers and Mountains, Pure and Distant, Song dynasty. In this horizontal scroll, the landscape loses any monumental aspect and unfolds rather tentatively. Rendered in ink on paper, the scene is delicate and imbued with a slightly melancholic air.

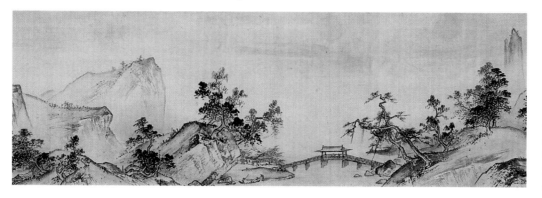

but of borrowing its forms in order to express the sensations and spirituality of the artist. This was the period of the poetic style of painting established by Wang Wei. Su Dongpo (1037–1101), also known as Su Shi, Wen Tong (1018–79), and Mi Fu (1051–1107) were among the finest exponents of this form of impressionistic art. A sense of detachment was

PORCELAIN

Early experiments during the end of the Eastern Han period and the Wei and Jin dynasties eventually led to the production of fine porcelain during the Sui and Tang dynasties. The first workshops were in the north. Kaolin, a special type of clay, was an essential ingredient of the paste used to make porcelain and was fairly common in the northern regions of China. During the Song dynasty, porcelain was also being manufactured in the workshops of Jiangxi in the south. Song porcelain products are generally simple, without the rich decoration typical of Tang ceramics. Their outstanding beauty is manifest in the delicacy of the body and lid, which are generally mono-chrome. The porcelain of the Yuan (1260–1368), Ming (1368–1644), and Qing (1644–1912) periods is more lavishly decorated. The Ming dynasty was the golden age of

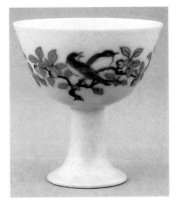

Small porcelain stem cup, Chenghua period (1465–87).

White porcelain Meiping vase with sancaï "three-color" decoration, Ming period. Musée Guimet, Paris.

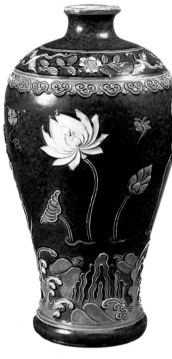

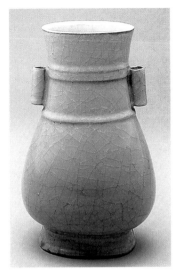

white porcelain with cobalt-blue underglaze decoration. There were further experiments during this period and the ensuing Qing dynasty with various deco-rative techniques using enam-eled glazes. Styles ranged from *doucai* (contrasting colors) to *wucai* (five colors), and two that developed under the Qing dynasty, known as *famille verte* and *famille rose*.

In addition to a notable produc-tion of pieces in earthenware and stoneware, celadonware (Chinese stoneware with a

delicate green glaze) achieved excellent results. Although the technical quality of porcelain was being refined during the Eastern Han era (AD25–220), it is the pieces created during the Song dynasty that are still considered the most remarkable.

Guan ceramic vase with tubular handles, southern Song dynasty (1127–1297).

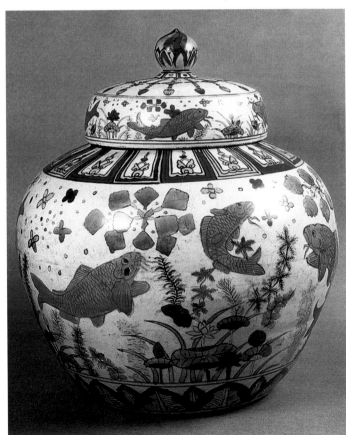

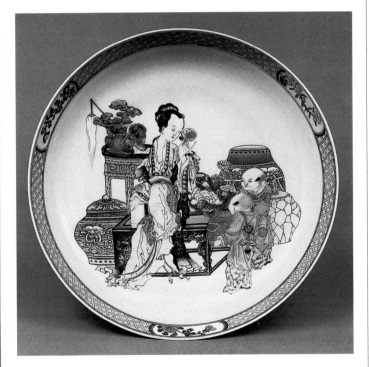

Large porcelain jar with wucai decoration, Jiajing period, mid-16th century. Musée Guimet, Paris. One of a pair, this lidded jar perfectly represents the style of the period.

Porcelain plate with overglaze enamel decoration, Yongzheng (1723–35). British Museum, London. Plates like this one, typical of Qing taste, were extremely popular and were the subject of many imitations in Europe.

expressed in the starkness of the brushstroke, which became almost calligraphic – a simple mark that suggested and evoked more than it described.

THE KORYO ART OF KOREA

The division of the Korean peninsula into three distinct territorial units – Koguryo in the north (37BC–AD668), Paekche in the southwest (18BC–AD660), and Silla in the southeast (57BC–AD935) – led to a differentiation of art forms. The small Buddhist sculptures in bronze or clay from the Koguryo temples were typical of the style of the northern Wei (AD430–534); the plastic art of Paekche showed the influence

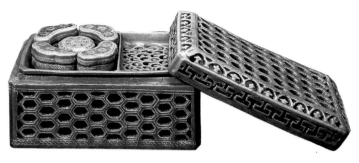

of the Chinese Liang dynasty (AD502–57). The great granite temples, built after the unification of the country under Silla rule (AD668–918), echo the Chinese Tang style, surpassing it in the sculpture of figures. Traces of Indian influence, as seen in the massive legs and the fan-shaped drapery at the bottom of the garments, were perhaps the result of repeated visits to India by Silla Buddhist monks and pilgrims.

Glazed celadon cosmetic box, Koryo period, second half of the 12th century. National Museum, Seoul.

The Great Silla style was characterized by the sculptures of Buddha and Bodhisattvas. These were set in the artificial caves of Sokkuram, south of the Silla capital Kyonju in southeastern Korea. Close contacts with China were fundamental to the development of tomb wall-paintings, as exemplified by the realistic

style of Zol Kuh from the mid-sixth century. Although there are no surviving examples of the paintings from the Great Silla period, it is known that there was an office responsible for the Fine Arts. In the Koryo period (AD918–1392), the capital was moved to Kaesong, north of Seoul, and this led to the transfer of many arts and crafts workshops, which maintained their unique styles and techniques. Painting, too, was strongly encouraged by artists of the imperial house, among them the emperors Hing Jong (1095), In Jong (1123–46), and Kong Min (1352–74). Sculptors of the time favored a more naturalistic approach to figures, which were now produced in a freer style and possessed recognizably human features. Artistic influences

THE PAINTING OF THE THREE KINGDOMS

Painting has played an important role in Korea since antiquity. Tomb paintings, particularly in the Koguryo tombs, include the depiction of the life of the dead person, the animal guardians of the four cardinal points, and celestial figures – all of them subjects that originated in the Chinese tomb decorations of the Han dynasty. In Korea, such decorations lasted long after the Han period and into the seventh century. Among these are the Great Tomb of

Kangso, the tomb of Naeri with its landscape pictures, and Chin'pari with its animal motifs. Buddhist influence soon produced decorative motifs featuring lotus blossoms and flower garlands, which were used to border decorated areas and adorn ceilings. There is evidence from the royal tombs of the Sabi period (AD538–660), situated at Paekche, that each fragment of polished stone was decorated with the animal guardians of the

Wall-painting of a hunting scene from the tomb of Muyong Ch'ong of Koguryo, period of the Three Kingdoms (mid-fifth century).

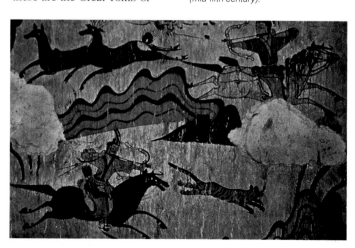

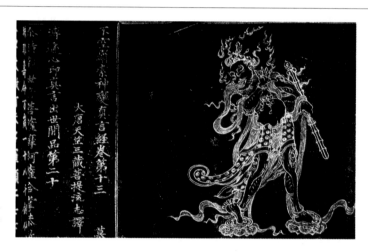

four directions, as seen in the Koguryo tombs. The construction of brick pagodas created a demand for decorated tiles and provided a new stimulus for Korean painting. Artists produced unrivaled masterpieces in this medium, some of which were among the earliest examples of landscape art in eastern Asia.

Documentation of painting from the Great Silla period is all too sparse, although the excellent quality of a fragment of the *Avatamsaka sutra* (AD754–55), painted in gold and silver, testifies to the level of refinement attained by the artists

Sutra of the sermons of Buddha, 1275, Koryo period. Cho Myong-Gi Collection, Seoul.

of the time. During the Koryo period, there were professional painters, such as Yi Nyong (12th century) and amateurs such as the monk Hyeho, who devoted themselves to depicting landscapes both in paint and monochrome ink.

The decoration of ceramics was also an important element of the painting of the Koryo period. Delicate flowers, plants, and birds adorned elegant celadon-wares, which rivaled their Chinese counterparts in grace.

introduced by the Mongol invasion of 1231 resulted in an increased amount of decoration in sculpture, an abundant use of jewelry, and a more relaxed portrayal of the human figure, which was characterized by slanting eyes. At the same time, the rising popularity of Zen Buddhism signaled a marked decline in the creation of effigies and cult objects. Major contributions to the art of the Koryo dynasty came in the field of ceramics with the development of celadonware, a type of porcelain notable both for its form and linear decoration. The influence of China, initially of the Five Dynasties and later of the Song and Yuan dynasties, helped create beautifully balanced and extremely delicate products.

JAPANESE ART

In Japan, in the fourth and third centuries BC, the cultivation of rice and the transition from a nomadic existence to farming laid the foundations for the Yayoi culture, which became renowned for its pottery and metalwork. Technical proficiency in the latter field produced weapons, utensils, and necklaces and achieved particular originality in both the form and decoration of bronze bells, known as *dotaku*. These may have had a ritual function or symbolized fertility. The ornamentation was both geometrical and naturalistic, and the same motifs were used for decoration in red on earthenware crockery. From the third and fourth

centuries AD, the *kofun*, large burial mounds, were the burial sites of a warrior aristocracy; this is indicated by the quantities of weapons and armor found in them. The beginning of the Asuka period (c. AD552–645) brought more awareness of Chinese culture and close diplomatic links with Korea, and it led to the adoption of writing with Chinese characters. The improvement of techniques in woodworking during the Hakuho period (AD645–710) contributed to the development of rural and religious architecture. Shintoism inspired both sacred and domestic architecture and was responsible for the sanctuaries of Ise and Izumo, dedicated to the cult of the founding divinities (*kami*). The arrival and diffu-

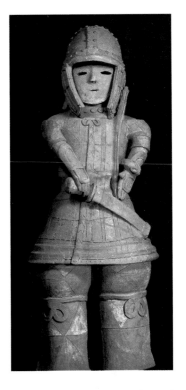

Terracotta warrior, Kofun period, fifth–sixth century. Archeological Museum of Aikava.

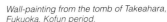

Wall-painting from the tomb of Takeahara, Fukuoka, Kofun period.

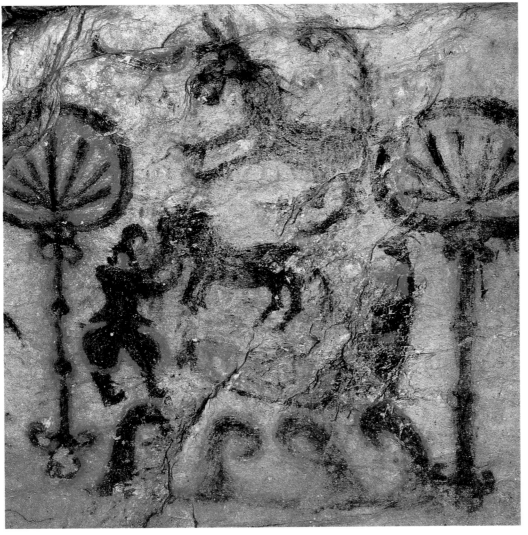

sion of Buddhism in about the sixth century brought a swift transition from a nonanthropomorphic art to the creation of large sculptures. These initially represented Shaka, the historic Buddha; Yakushi, the Buddha of medicine; his assistants Nikko and Gakko; and the Bodhisattva Miroku. They were followed later by Amida, the Buddha of the Western Paradise, and the Bodhisattvas Kannon and Seishi. The strengthening of political power and the unification of the nation, together with the explicit support of the new doctrine by the court, brought about a proliferation of architectural and sculptural works associated with Buddhism. The temples of the sixth, seventh, and eighth centuries observed the canons of Chinese and Korean architecture: a regular plan with pavilions on a north/south axis, with the southern portal (*nan daimon*) as the main entrance; a golden hall (*kondo*) to accommodate the principal

THE BIRTH OF A NATIONAL STYLE OF PAINTING

Prince Shotoku Taishi and – it is presumed – his two sons are the subjects of a painting in ink and color on paper (c. AD684). It is a typical example of a Hakuho work, with one shoulder of each figure positioned farther forward so that it is in alignment with the head.

Although none have survived to the present day, it is known that the wall-paintings depicting the different Paradises of Buddha in the Horyuji temple formed an integral part of the pilgrimage circuit. Plump bodies were highlighted by clear outlines and shading of an Indian and central Asiatic derivation.

Chinese influence, however, is evident in a painting on hemp from Kichijoten (c. AD773), which shows the goddess of beauty and fertility. The round and delicate face, the neat hairstyle, and the flowing garments are typical of an elegant lady of the Tang court. The *Illustrated Sutra of the Past and Present Karma* (c. eighth century) is a blend of painting and calligraphy in which the story (from right to left) of the life of the historical Buddha and his previous existences is interspersed with landscape elements, forming sections for individual episodes and anticipating a practice common to the illustrated hand-scrolls of the Heian period. It was during the

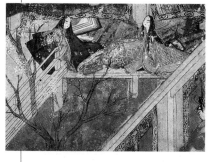

Detail from the Genji monogatari emake, *c.12th century. Tokugawa Reimeikai, Tokyo.*

Descent of Amida, 11th–12th century. In this painting in color on silk, Amida comes down Mount Koya with his court to meet the deceased.

Taizokai Mandala, tenth century. This painting on silk is an important Buddhist work of art.

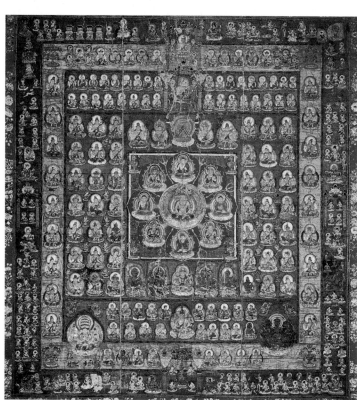

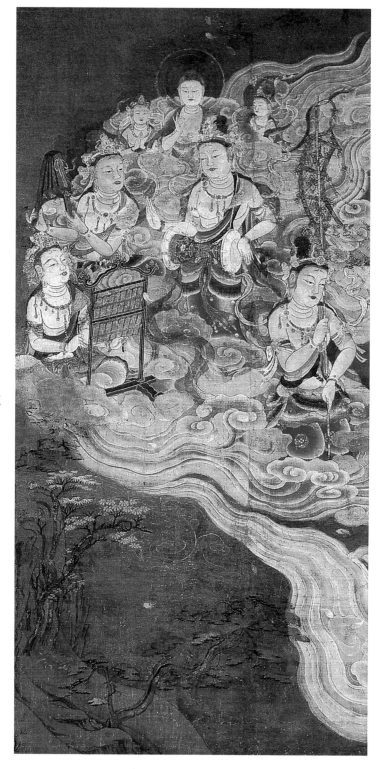

early Heian period (AD794–893) that the Indian inspiration of the iconography of esoteric Buddhism imparted an element of sensuality to the bodies and faces of the deities. Increasingly, the *mandala* became a magical or mystical "diagram," the symbolic image of the universe of Dainichi and a visual aid to meditation. The representation of the nirvana of the historical Buddha (*nehanzo*) followed the canonic tradition, with the body of Sakyamuni lying on a catafalque, surrounded by monks and laity, in a landscape that also reflects the grief for the departure of the Master. This pictorial genre, a modification of a Chinese tradition of sacred painting, employed bright colors with light touches of gold and silver in the background. The late Heian period (AD894–1185), with its fear of the Buddhist "decadence of the Law" (*mappo*), provided rapid impetus for the diffusion of the redeeming cult of Amida. The theme of the Descent of Amida (*Amida raigo*) and his celestial court – to lead the dead to the Western Paradise – became a popular source for limitless pictorial representations.

The birth of a national style (*yamato-e*) at this time represents the establishment of a pictorial genre with secular subjects in typically Japanese surroundings, very much in contrast to the Chinese (*kara-e*) tradition. Perhaps the oldest work in this style is the *Shigisan engi emaki* of the 12th century, although the undisputed masterpiece of the genre is the *Genji monogatari emaki* (the illustrated scroll of the *Tale of Prince Genji*), an unequaled visual accompaniment to one of the greatest works of Japanese literature.

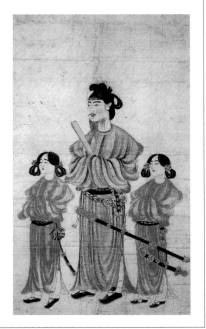

Prince Shotoku Taishi, c. AD684. Imperial Collections, Tokyo. This work in ink and color on paper is considered a masterpiece of Hakuho painting. The two youngsters at the sides of the prince are probably portraits of his sons.

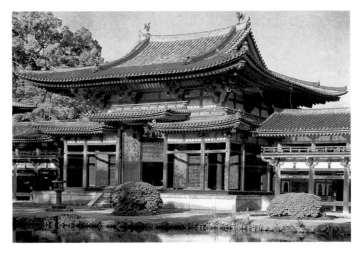

Pavilion of the Phoenix in the Buddhist temple of Byodoin di Uji, Honshu, Heian period, 11th century. The structure of the building and its roofs follows the shape of the mythical bird.

image of the cult; a pagoda (*to*); a refectory; and a reading room (*kodo*).

In keeping with these features, the Horyuji temple (AD607) of Nara remains a valuable testimony to Chinese-influenced Buddhist architecture, since no wooden architecture of this period survives on the mainland. The Shaka Triad in the golden hall, with its stiff frontal pose, the flattening of the garment folds, and the tranquil smiles, shows the iconographical characteristics of the Chinese style of the northern Wei dynasty. Examples of tomb paintings depict processions of men, women, and mythical animals. In about AD700, the wall-paintings of the Horyuji temple celebrated the greatness of Amida (Buddha of Infinite Light) and his celestial court in a style reminiscent of Indian art.

The advent of the Nara period (AD710–84) and the formation of a centralized bureaucratic state, with its "Capital of Peace" at Heijo (present-day Nara), saw the wide diffusion of Buddhist architecture and iconography. The major temples commissioned huge statues of Buddha: the *Buddha of Healing* (c. AD718) in gilded bronze, flanked by two Bodhisattvas, in the Yakushiji; the smooth-surfaced bronze triad, of which only the head of Buddha survives, in the Kofukuji; the *Great Buddha of Supreme Light* in the Todaiji temple, the casting of which was said to have used up all of Japan's copper resources; and the *Triad of Vairocana* (759), in the Toshodaiji temple. During this period the earliest sculptural portraiture developed, exemplified by the dry lacquer (*kanshitsu*) statue of the monk Ganjin.

During the Heian period (AD794–1185), the excessive power of the Buddhist clergy induced the imperial court to move the capital to Heiankyo (present-day Kyoto). Town planning, while on a wider scale, retained the perpendicular grid of broad streets. The spread of esoteric Buddhism (*mikkyo*) and the recognition of Dainichi as the supreme Buddha led to an increased number of sculptural and pictorial subjects. Residential architecture developed the so-called *shindenzukuri* style, which was characteristic of aristocratic homes and featured a harmonious blend of buildings and gardens.

Gilded bronze sculpture of Shaka Triad, Golden Room of the Horyuji temple, Nara, Asuka period, c. AD623.

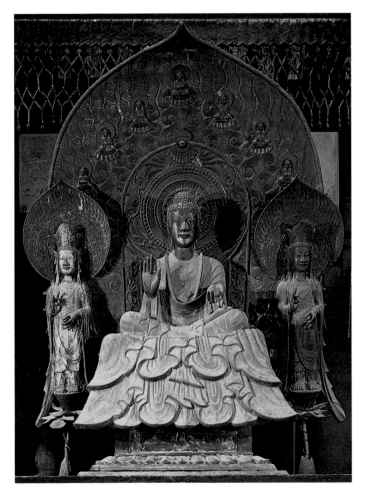

CLASSICAL ART OF SUB-SAHARAN AFRICA

In Africa, particularly in the areas of the Niger and Congo River basins, a number of artistic cultures have been identified between the 12th and 16th centuries, adding to older, existing ones. All expressed themselves in original ways and are particularly known for their classically perfect sculptures.

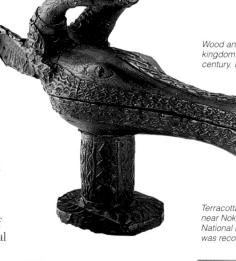

For a long time, Europeans believed the culture of sub-Saharan Africa to be static. It was not considered possible that the various extant styles of sub-Saharan African art could be the result of an evolutionary process based on individual creative talent and the spread of cultural information. The precarious conditions of conservation, the climatic factor, and the perishability of materials prevented the survival of many of the works that could have testified to this stylistic evolution. The majority of works in wood that have been preserved do not date from before the 19th century.

Wood and metal Kola nut container, kingdom of Benin, Nigeria, late 19th century. Institute of Arts, Detroit.

SAO POTTERY

The so-called Sao culture (the name was apparently a derogatory expression used by Islamic invaders to denote the native "pagans") appeared in the vicinity of Lake Chad between 500BC and AD1600. The Sao buried their dead in

Terracotta head from the Rafin Dinya site near Nok village, Nigeria, 500BC–AD200. National Museum, Lagos. This sculpture was recovered in1954, buried under a

thick layer of alluvial deposits. Broken at the base of the neck, it may originally have been part of an impressive, full-sized figure.

THE ANCIENT CIVILIZATIONS OF WEST AFRICA

Historians and archaeologists are now attempting to reconstruct the past of Africa's sub-Saharan regions, piecing together the scant references that constitute the history of African art. Information is sparse: the geographical distribution of finds from the ancient kingdoms lacks continuity, and the map of Africa shows a continent still largely unexplored archaeologically. Research tends to focus on what seems to be the richest region for ancient artifacts, the Niger River basin, which crosses the modern republic of Mali, part of the republic of Niger, and the federal state of Nigeria, ending in the delta that flows into the Atlantic Ocean.

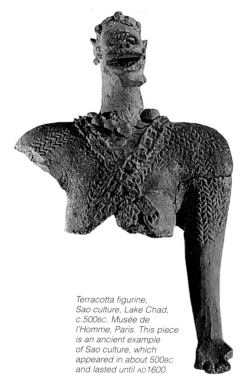

Terracotta figurine, Sao culture, Lake Chad, c.500BC. Musée de l'Homme, Paris. This piece is an ancient example of Sao culture, which appeared in about 500BC and lasted until AD1600.

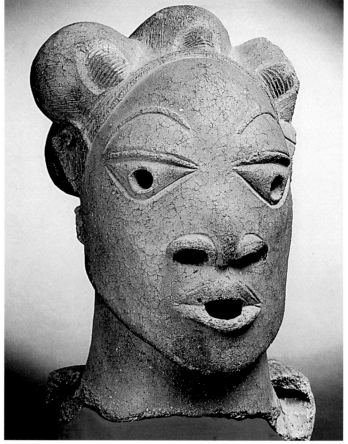

182

huge jars, set vertically in the earth and sealed with an inverted bowl, the base of which protruded above ground level. Various bronze ornaments and much pottery ware, including figures of ancestors and human figures with animal faces, have been discovered in connection with these graves. The human images have been identified as masked people, but were possibly representations of mythical heroes. Sao culture seems to have reached its peak between the 10th and the 16th centuries, a period to which more than 15,000 pottery finds, some still to be fully interpreted, can be dated.

CULTURES OF THE LOWER NIGER BASIN

The most ancient and important tradition of African plastic art outside the Nile Valley originated in the regions that correspond to present-day Nigeria. More information exists on the artistic past of Nigeria than any other part of the African continent. What emerges is an artistic development spanning 2,500 years and dating from at least the middle of the first millennium BC. Although there are enormous gaps in our knowledge of this period, it is still possible to date some of the fundamental phases that help determine the history of Nigerian art. The earliest of these phases is the Nok culture, dating from 500BC to AD200; later there is the style of the Ife kingdom, reaching its peak between AD1200 and 1400; and the style of the Benin kingdom from 1400 to 1900. There is documentation, too, of independent artistic development in the styles of the Igbo-Ukwu (ninth to tenth century) and the Owo (15th century). Examination of common stylistic elements suggests that some of the artistic forms that developed in Nigeria were descended from the Nok culture or, at least,

THE "LOST-WAX" CASTING TECHNIQUE

To begin the so-called lost-wax technique, a wax model is made of the object to be cast, and this is then covered with clay. When it is put in the fire, the clay casing bakes and the melted wax runs out through small channels. Molten metal is then poured into the clay mold through the same channels, filling the space left by the wax. Once the metal has cooled, the clay casing is broken open and the sculpture removed. As the beautifully sculpted bronze head shown below illustrates, this refined technique produces finely detailed works of great craftsmanship – usually associated with much later metalwork. The technical procedures and equipment used to craft metal and clay were probably the independent invention of an already existing alloying and casting technology. Until the early 16th century, Benin sculptors used predominantly "gunmetal" – an alloy of copper, tin, and zinc – suggesting both local and trans-Saharan sources of raw material. From the 16th century onward, brass was used, obtained via trade with Europeans, who at the time were traveling down the West African coast.

Bronze head, kingdom of Benin, Nigeria, 9 in (23 cm) high, early 16th century. Metropolitan Museum of Art, New York.

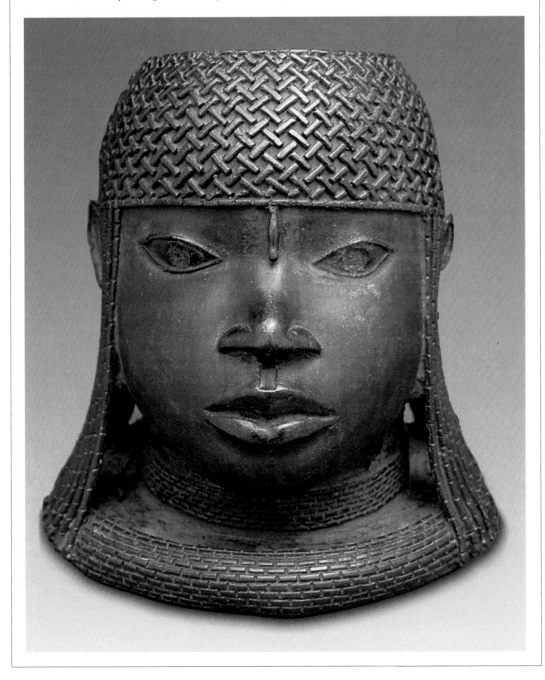

from an artistic tradition of which the Nok is the only known manifestation. No archaeological finds have yet been attributable to the millennium separating the Nok and the Ife cultures. Ife art shows a gradual evolution from the rigid naturalistic style of the classical period to increasingly stylized forms that gave rise to two major currents: the art of Benin, extending until the present, and the various modern styles of Yoruba art.

NOK ART

The Nok culture takes its name from a mining village situated on the high central plain of Nigeria, where the most ancient Nigerian sculptures known to date were excavated in about 1950. These small pottery sculptures, or fragments of other almost life-size sculptures, consist of both human and animal

figures. In the stylized human figures, the head is represented geometrically as a cylinder, cone, or sphere, often decorated with an elaborate hairstyle. The nostrils, pupils, mouth, and ears are for the most part indicated by a groove, while the lines that describe the facial features – particularly those depicting the eyes – are cleanly and precisely carved; the stylized mouth and beard often project from the rest of the face. To produce such large, nearly life-size figures in pottery must have required particular skill, and in common with all sub-Saharan African pottery, open fires instead of kilns were used for firing the items. The Nok culture flourished from 500BC to AD200, and it is within this period that we find the earliest evidence for a tradition of pottery sculpture in West Africa. The stylistic differences found within the Nok region mean that we

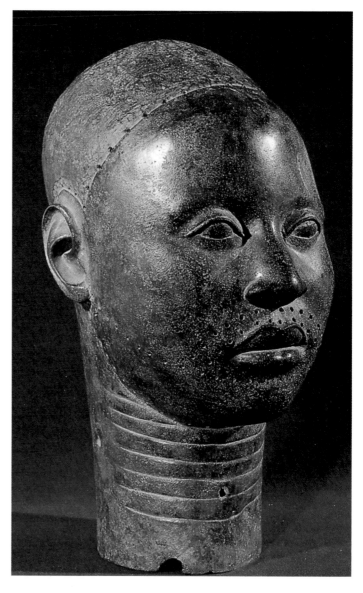

Terracotta head, Nok culture, Nigeria, 14 in (36 cm) high, c.500BC. National Museum, Lagos.

Copper and zinc head of an Óni (king), kingdom of Ife, Nigeria, 12 in (31 cm) high, 12th–15th century. Museum of Ife Antiquities, Ife.

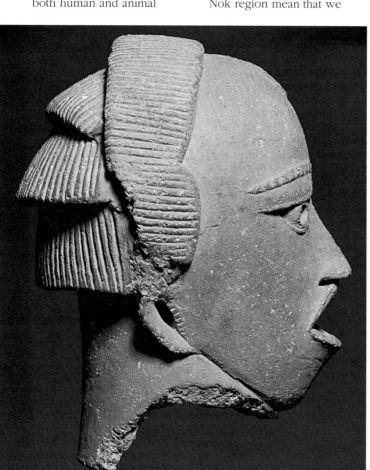

cannot be sure that we are dealing with a single artistic population, and the evidence is not sufficient to conclude that the Nok culture is directly ancestral to other, later Nigerian forms.

IFE ART

Ife art, which flourished between the 12th and 16th centuries, was discovered in 1910 by the German ethnologist Leo Frobenius, at a time when Nok art was still unknown. It baffled Western critics, who resorted to citing

Egyptian or Greek influences to explain this gracefully naturalistic art form that was quite unlike any of the examples so far discovered on the African continent. Subsequent finds at Ife revealed some decidedly African features, such as the accentuation of the size of the head in relation to the rest of the body, and demonstrated how far removed Ife naturalism was from the classic European tradition.
For centuries, Ife was an important city-state of the Yoruba. Its importance was due in part to the creation

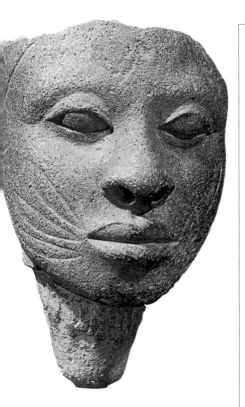

Pottery head of a woman, kingdom of Ife, Nigeria, 5 in (12.5 cm) high, 12th–15th century. National Museum, Lagos.

THE BRONZES OF IGBO-UKWU

Igbo-Ukwu is a small village in southeastern Nigeria, in the region now inhabited by the Igbo people. Excavations here have brought to light a number of bronze objects, the first of which were unearthed accidentally during the course of digging work to install an underground tank. The bronzes found fall broadly into three categories: a repository of ceremonial objects; articles found in a burial chamber of a high-ranking member of society; and items discovered in a well, including a splendidly decorated vase with ceremonial insignia. All of the objects found, made of an alloy of copper, tin, and lead, showed complete mastery of the lost-wax casting technique. A characteristic element of the

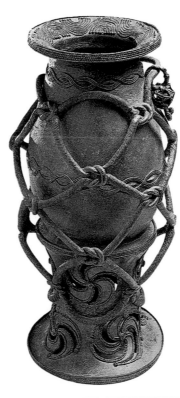

Igbo-Ukwu style (ninth to tenth century) is the detailed and delicate surface decoration of objects, featuring tiny figures of insects and small animals, and the addition of fine wires arranged to emphasize the shape of the piece. The vase illustrated is enveloped in a stylized woven net, possibly inspired by the type of net that would have been used for carrying containers. This is a style unique to the African continent, and nothing is known of its provenance or subsequent development. Although there is no similar style in the same area today, scholars maintain that the descendants of the ancient culture of Igbo-Ukwu are the Igbo people who still live in the region.

Bronze ceremonial vase, Igbo-Ukwu, Nigeria, 12.5 in (32.3 cm) high, ninth to tenth century. National Museum, Lagos.

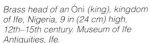

Brass head of an Óni (king), kingdom of Ife, Nigeria, 9 in (24 cm) high, 12th–15th century. Museum of Ife Antiquities, Ife.

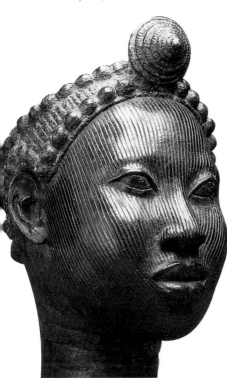

myth of the Yoruba, which tells how the supreme god Olodumare is supposed to have sent 16 minor divinities to create the world and found the various Yoruba kingdoms. One of these lesser deities was Oduduwa, founder and first king (Óni) of Ife. Although it is impossible to date the beginning of Ife artistic development, it was clearly established prior to AD1200 and was producing bronze objects for the kingdom of Benin by the end of the 15th century. It can, therefore, safely be assumed that Ife art reached its apogee between these two dates. The Ife style is visible in one of the nine copper-alloy sculptures found in the village of Tada and on the small island of Jebba along the Niger River; the local Islamic population worshiped these statues in the conviction that they had been brought there

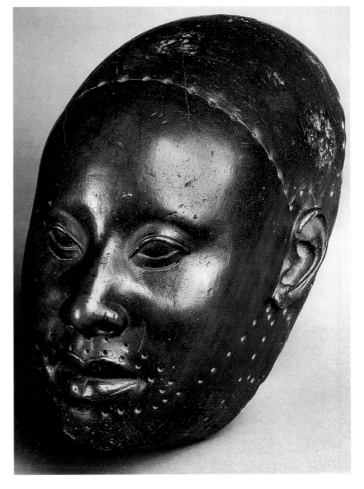

Copper mask of the Óni Obalufon, kingdom of Ife, Nigeria, 13 in (33 cm) high, 12th–15th century, National Commission for Museums and Monuments, Lagos.

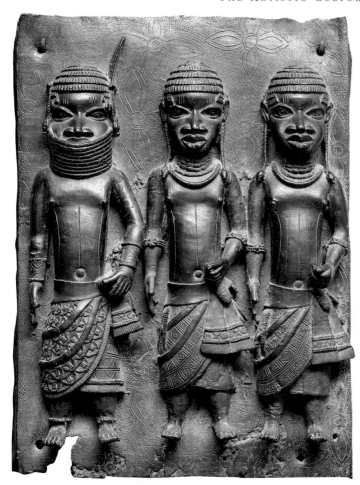

Bronze ornamental plaque, kingdom of Benin, Nigeria, 17 in (45 cm) high, c. mid-17th century. Berggruen Collection, Geneva.

THE KINGDOM OF BENIN

Oral tradition relates that when each king (*Oba*) of Benin died, his head was dispatched to Ife for burial, and a brass head was sent from Ife to be placed on the altar of his ancestors. Toward the end of the 14th century, however, the *Oba* of Benin asked the *Óni* of Ife to

send a foundry worker to teach his people how to produce their own commemorative heads of the sovereign. In reality, the oldest bronze heads of Benin are somewhat different from those of Ife. This is probably explained by the fact that when the technique of casting was introduced, the Benin style was already mature. Benin art continued to evolve until 1897, when British soldiers ransacked and

SEATED FIGURE

One of the most mysterious works of African art, this seated figure matches the Ife style but was found together with the so-called Tsoede bronzes in the village of Tada, on the banks of the Niger. It is distinguished from all other Ife sculptures by its complex asymmetrical position, virtually unique in African sculpture, which generally favors a frontal or symmetrical position. The sculpture is also unusual

in the proportions of the head and other body parts, which resemble that of a real human body. In other figures from Ife, the head measures about one-quarter of the total height and the legs are markedly smaller.

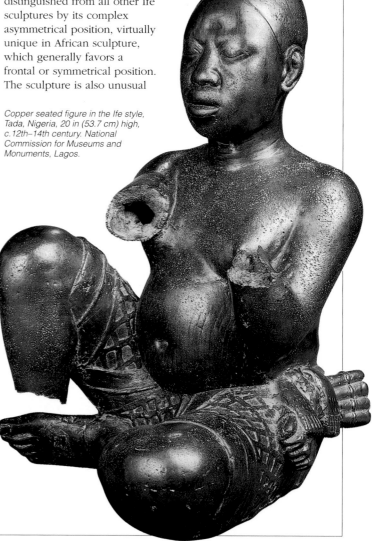

Copper seated figure in the Ife style, Tada, Nigeria, 20 in (53.7 cm) high, c.12th–14th century. National Commission for Museums and Monuments, Lagos.

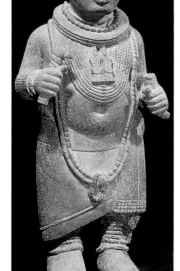

by Tsoede, the mythical hero who founded the Nupe royal dynasty. In 1969, the sculptures were transferred to the National Museum, Lagos. The true origin of the "Tsoede bronzes" remains a mystery. They appear to be derived from at least two different stylistic centers – Ife and Owo, for example. It is feasible, however, that they may come from another important center of production that has not yet been identified. Examination of the alloy (which is mainly copper with the addition of tin) leads to the conclusion that these are works that were made before any contact with any European culture.

Brass statue of an óni (king), kingdom of Ife, Nigeria, 18 in (47 cm) high, 12th–15th century. National Commission for Museums and Monuments, Lagos.

COURT ART

The art of Benin was the art of the royal court. Artists in Benin City were organized into guilds, such as those for brass smiths or wood sculptors. The members lived and worked within particular areas of the city. Their artistic output was tightly controlled by the king (*Oba*), and the objects they produced, whether brass castings for royal shrines or other artifacts for the palace, were solely for the use of the *Oba*, who was seen as a divine figure.

The courtyard verandas of the royal palace of Benin were built of mud-brick and wood and were supported by massive wooden pillars. In the 16th and 17th century, these were decorated with rectangular cast brass plaques commemorating battles and documenting court ceremonies. This kind of documentation is more common in Africa than is usually recognized. On some of these plaques, there is an attempt to imitate Western-type perspective, possibly copied from conventional rectangular book illustrations.

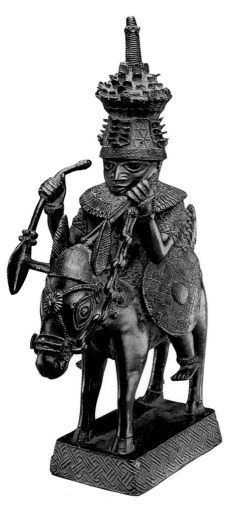

Bronze statue of a warrior on horseback, kingdom of Benin, Nigeria, 18 in (47 cm) high, mid-16th century. Institute of Arts, Detroit.

destroyed the Nigerian city. A treasury of brass and ivory objects was recovered from the palace before it caught fire, and this found its way to England, where the treasures were later dispersed among various museums in the West. Benin art is conventionally subdivided into three stylistic phases. The early period is prior to the changes in Benin art that resulted from European trading in the late 15th and early 16th centuries, and the middle period spans the 16th and 17th centuries. Together, these two periods include the works that Europeans regard as being of greatest aesthetic value. In the late period, which dates from the 18th century to the British conquest, there was an increase in the size of the objects produced and in the standardization of style.

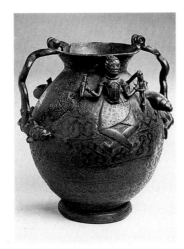

Rounded bronze vase with decorative handles, kingdom of Benin, Nigeria, 9 in (22.5 cm) high, mid-17th century. National Museum, Lagos. The striking decorative figures have been finely created in bas-relief.

THE OWO STYLE

Owo (Nigeria) was another of the many city-states of the Yoruba people. Geographically situated between Benin and Ife, Owo seems to have played a transitional cultural role between these two civilizations. Objects found in Owo, which probably date from the 15th century, display clear affinities with the late art of Ife and that of Benin. Stylistic comparisons suggest that the technique of bronze casting must have traveled from Ife to Benin by way of Owo. The woman's head shown below illustrates how the Owo artists could use terracotta to produce work as fine as the metal objects more usually associated with them.

Bronze statue of a warrior, possibly Owo style, Nigeria, 44 in (115 cm) high, 14th–15th century. National Commission for Museums and Monuments, Lagos.

Terracotta head of a woman, Owo culture, Nigeria, 7 in (17.4 cm) high, 15th century. National Commission for Museums and Monuments, Lagos.

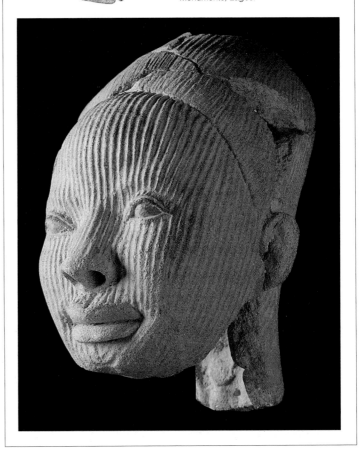

THE IVORIES OF BENIN AND THE KONGO

Ivory was used in Benin for much of the king's ceremonial apparel, including bracelets and even the handles of fly swatters. Heavily decorated elephant tusks, up to 5 feet (1.5 meters) long, were attached to the bronze heads that were kept on the altar of the royal ancestors. Saltcellars, spoons, trumpets, and other objects were commissioned by the Portuguese in coastal Sierra Leone, Benin City, and the kingdom of Kongo. Indeed, the earliest African art objects documented by a European collector were the Kongo trumpets, or hunting horns,

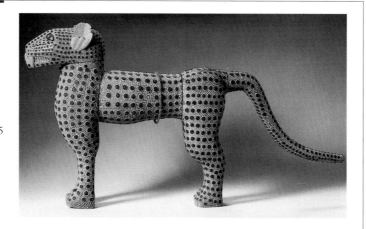

dating from 1560, in the inventory of the household of Cosimo the Great, first grand duke of Tuscany. Closely resembling the horn shown below, these may have been a gift to the

Leopard, kingdom of Benin, Nigeria, ivory with copper inlay, 18 in (47 cm) high, late 19th century. Property of Queen Elizabeth II , British Museum, London. The figure of the leopard is recognized as one of the symbolic representations of the Oba, or king.

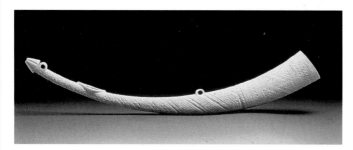

Medici popes or may have been brought into the family by the Grand duchess Eleanor of Toledo.

Ivory hunting horn, kingdom of Kongo, Kongo-Portuguese style, Angola, 24 in (63 cm) high, 14th–17th century. Museo Preistorico ed Etnografico Luigi Pigorini, Rome.

Terracotta figure of a warrior, Djenné style, culture of the inner Niger Delta, Mali, 14 in (38.1 cm) high, 13th–14th century. Institute of Arts, Detroit.

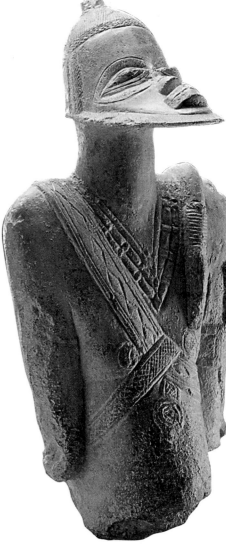

CULTURES OF THE INNER NIGER DELTA

The region of Mali, situated at the confluence of the Niger and Bani Rivers, is known as the inner Niger Delta. It is dominated by a vast alluvial plain crossed by a network of waterways, above which rise strips of land that are spared during flood times. This land

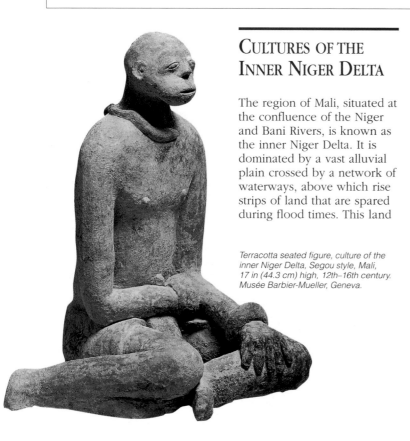

Terracotta seated figure, culture of the inner Niger Delta, Segou style, Mali, 17 in (44.3 cm) high, 12th–16th century. Musée Barbier-Mueller, Geneva.

has been populated for many centuries, and signs of human settlement and ironworking date from as early as the second century BC. Today, traces are emerging of some of the many riverine cultures that made up the ancient empires of Ghana and Mali. Since 1978, many hundreds of sites have been uncovered, and a wealth of pottery sculptures dating from between the 12th and 16th century have been excavated from them. Ranging in height from 11 to 23 inches (30 to 60 centimeters), these items include human or animal figurines molded in clay and decorated with rough engravings. Variations in type are attributed to diverse styles in the centers of production, for example Bankoni/Segou and Djenné. The Djenné style is characterized by markedly

elongated heads, with huge eyes, heavy eyebrows, and a mouth form that juts out powerfully from the rest of the face. Hair, drapes, ornaments, and scars are roughly incised or stamped, producing the effect of a successful blend of modeling and carving.

STONE FIGURES FROM THE VILLAGE OF ESIE

This figure forms part of a group of about 800 soft stone sculptures found in woodland near the village of Esie, Nigeria. They include male and female figures, mostly seated, with tall, elaborate hairstyles and necklaces. The ancestors of Esie's present-day inhabitants are said to have found the sculptures already in situ when they arrived in the area at the end of the 19th century. The origin of the figures is explained by a legend about a group of foreign visitors turned into stone.

Stone figure from the village of Esie, Nigeria, 27 in (70 cm) high, pre-1850. National Museum, Esie.

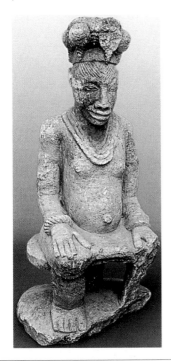

AFRO-PORTUGUESE IVORIES

Among the first African objects to reach Europe were fine ivory carvings imported by Dutch and Portuguese merchants during the Renaissance. They are commonly referred to as Afro-Portuguese ivories because they are thought to have been commissioned by the Portuguese from native African artists. In fact, they are recognizably African, embellished by certain motifs derived from European iconography: hunting scenes, Portuguese heraldic subjects, and Latin inscriptions. It seems that African craftsmen created objects for their earliest Portuguese customers that had originally been made for their own use, modifying the forms and ornamentation to suit the tastes of their clients.

Three styles of Afro-Portuguese ivories have been identified, attributable to three distinct areas of production. The oldest ivories are in the Sapi-Portuguese style, from Sierra Leone between the late 15th century and early 16th century. They were made by artists of the Sapi (Portuguese *Çapes*) population, at the behest of the first Portuguese merchants. Characteristic of the style is the representation of the human head, which resembles that of certain ancient stone sculptures found in Sierra Leone – a vestige of a forgotten local culture. Another typical feature is the gracefulness of the relief decoration, which leaves much of the surface free.

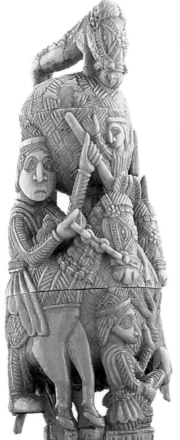

It appears that from the mid-16th century, Afro-Portuguese ivories no longer came from Sierra Leone but from the kingdom of Benin (in present-day Nigeria) and were made there by local artists. This is the so-called Benin-Portuguese style. The ivories in the Kongo-Portuguese style were made by artists of the ancient kingdom of Kongo (in the north of modern Angola). The style is recognizable in only a very few objects, almost exclusively hunting horns.

Ivory saltcellar, kingdom of Benin, Bini-Portuguese style, Nigeria, 7.5 in (19.2 cm) high, first half of the sixth century. Ethnic Museum, Ambres. The skill of the local craftworkers was recognized by the Portuguese.

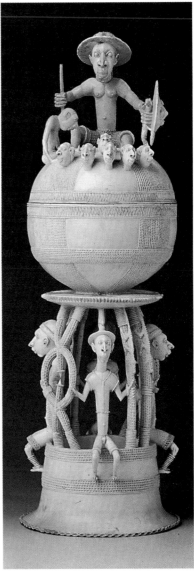

Ivory saltcellar, Sapi-Portuguese style, Sierra Leone, 16 in (43 cm) high, late 15th–early 16th century. Museo Preistorico ed Etnografico Luigi Pigorini, Rome.

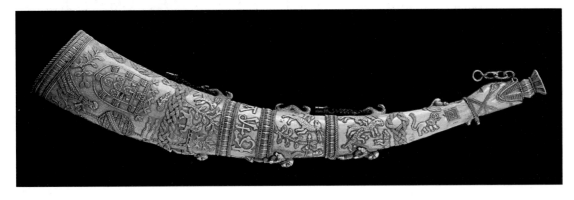

Ivory trumpet or hunting horn, Sapi-Portuguese style, Sierra Leone, 24 in (63.5 cm) high, late 15th–early 16th century. Paul and Ruth Tishman Collection of African Art, Los Angeles.

The Artistic Cultures of Asia & Africa

500BC: Sao culture (c.300BC–AD900) widely established around Lake Chad; in Ceylon, the cities of Anuradhapura and Polonnaruva prosper. **321–185BC:** under the Maurya Dynasty, Indian

Buddhism reaches its zenith. **206BC:** Han Dynasty imposes its rule in China. **142BC:** King Mithridates I of Parthia, of the Arsacid Dynasty, conquers Mesopotamia. **c.AD200–300:** in Japan,

the kofun culture spreads, seen in the ancient tombs and mounds destined for members of the warrior aristocracy. **224–226:** Sassanid Dynasty, under Prince Ardashir, initiates its rule over

Persia. **320–550:** Gupta Dynasty, founded by Chandragupta I, established in northern India. **636:** Muslims conquer Syria. **645–710:** during the Hakuho period, in Japan, Shinto

500BC–AD250   **250–500**   **600–800**   **900–1000**

▼ AFRICA

The development of Nok culture in Nigeria (500BC–AD200) brought a rich production of terracotta sculptures in animal and human forms.

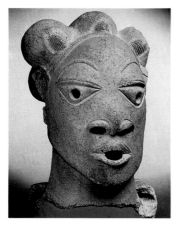

Terracotta head from the Rafin Dinya site near Nok village, Nigeria. National Museum, Lagos.

CHINA

The introduction of Buddhism into China in the first century AD opened up a new iconographic, narrative language, which was developed during the Eastern Han dynasty (AD25–221) and the successive period of the Six Dynasties (220–280).

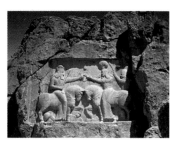

Bas-relief depicting the investiture of Ardashir I (AD224–41), valley of Naqsh-i Rustam, Persia (modern-day Iran). Ardashir, who founded the Sassanid dynasty, was a follower of the Zoroastrian religion.

▼ INDIA

The Gupta period (370–550) constitutes the classic age of Indian art. During this time the typology of the Hindu temple was established, and sculpture was notable for its sensitive, elegant modeling.

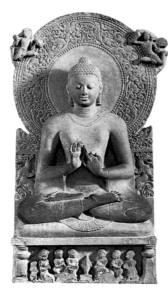

Sandstone statue of preaching Buddha, fifth century. Archaeological Museum, Sarnath, India.

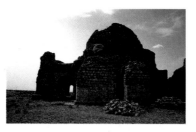

Remains of the small palace of Bahram V (420–40), Sarvestan, Persia (modern-day Iran).

◄ SASSANID PERSIA ▲

Rock reliefs were prolific throughout the Sassanid dynasty (224–651). They were often figurative in subject and associated either with investiture of the sovereign by a divinity or with war exploits. Sassanid art had a profound influence on subsequent Iranian art and, consequently, on the decorative arts of the medieval Mediterranean region.

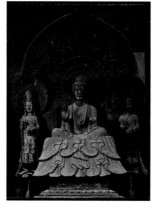

Gilded bronze sculpture of Shaka Triad, Golden Room of the Horyuji temple, Nara, Asuka period, c.623.

▲ JAPAN

Under the Asuka kings (c.552–645), the oldest Buddhist monastery in Japan, the Horyuji at Nara, was built - a rare example of wooden architecture, with obvious allusions to Chinese models. China was also a key influence on sculpture: the Shaka Triad (c.623), for example, reflects the style of the northern Wei.

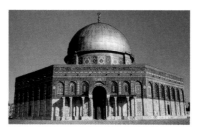

The Dome of the Rock, Jerusalem, completed in 691.

▲ ISLAMIC EMPIRE

The most imposing Islamic monuments, such as the Dome of the Rock, Jerusalem, and the Great Mosque of Damascus, date from the period of the Ummayad caliphate (661–750). Of a similar age are the tempera mural decorations of Qusayr'Amra, in Jordan, a rare example of Islamic painting.

▼ EGYPT

The Fatimid period (969–1171) saw the production of brooches, bottles, and flagons in rock crystal and sought-after transparent quartz. The finished products, prized for their purity, also found their way to the West.

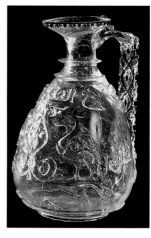

Rock crystal jug with flower and bird decoration and inscription, 992–1011. Museum of Silverware, Palazzo Pitti, Florence.

▼ BURMA

Pagan, capital from 1044 to 1287, was the major center of Burmese Buddhism, a culture influenced by Indian forms. Markedly original were the temples divided into levels, the bell-shaped pagodas, and the production of stylized sculptures of the Buddha in bronze, stone, and stucco.

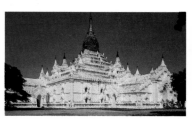

Temple of Ananda, Pagan, Burma, late 11th century.

sanctuaries are built. **732:** Charles Martel's victory at Poitiers stems the Arab advance in the West. **750:** With the defeat of the Umayyads, the Abbasids become the new caliphs of Islam and move the heart of the empire into Mesopotamia. **c.800–900:** an elegant artistic culture develops in the Nigerian villages of Igbo-Ukwu. **930–1250:** during the eastern Java period, Indonesian art attains great splendor. **1040:** Seljuk Turks conquer Khorasan and establish their capital in Isfahan. **c.1267–1276:** China ruled by Kublai Khan, nephew of Genghis Khan, initiating Yuan dynasty. **c.1300:** an original artistic culture for the royal court develops in Benin. **c.1490–1510:** ivories in the Sapi-Portuguese style are produced in Sierra Leone.

1 1 0 0   1 2 0 0   1 3 0 0   1 4 0 0 – 1 5 0 0

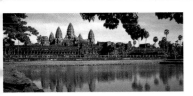

View of Angkor Wat, first half of the 12th century.

▲ CAMBODIA

Among the important shrines of the flourishing Khmer civilization of Angkor (8th to 13th centuries) were the temples of Angkor Wat. The temple reliefs and lifesize statuary exhibit exceptional technical skill.

JAPAN

Dating from the 12th century is the *Genji monogatari emaki*, a masterpiece of Yamato-e, Japan's national style of painting: in contrast to the Chinese tradition, secular subjects were generally adopted.

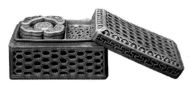

Glazed celadon cosmetic box, Koryo period, second half of the 12th century. National Museum, Seoul.

▲ KOREA

During the Koryo period (918–1392) there was great artistic development around the new capital, Kaesong. Pottery painting and celadon production, with linear forms and decoration, showed great originality. In sculpture, models displayed a new naturalism, while sumptuous decoration and jewelry had a Mongolian influence.

▼ ISLAM

From 800, in Syria, Egypt, Persia, and Spain, the complex technique of metallic luster ceramics took root. Vases and tiles produced between 1200 and 1300 at Kashan, Persia, were in particular demand.

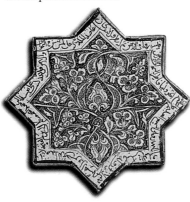

Persian metallic luster tile, with floral decoration and Islamic script. Al-Sabah Collection, Kuwait.

XIA GUI

(active c.1200–40)

Chinese painter, associated with the imperial court. The delicate melancholy of his landscapes reveals him as a master of mood and artistic invention.

▼ KOREA

The Koryo period (918–1392) is notable for the refined quality of its painting.

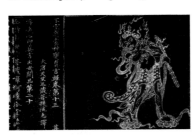

Sutra of the sermons of Buddha, 1275, Koryo period. Cho Myong-Gi Collection, Seoul.

MA YUAN

(active c.1180–1224)

Chinese painter who perfected a dramatic style of painting with a skillful interplay of mass and space.

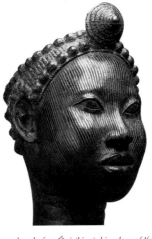

Brass head of an Óni (king), kingdom of Ife, Nigeria, 9 in (24 cm) high, 12th–15th century. Museum of Ife Antiquities, Ife.

▲ AFRICA

The art of the Yoruba city-state of Ife (12th–15th century) reveals original African features, as in its sculpture of human figures, with their markedly disproportionate heads and bodies.

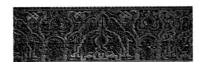

Detail of decoration in wood from the medersa, or school, of Misbahiya, mid-14th century. Fez, Morocco.

▲ ISLAM

Western Islamic art exhibited many original features, exemplified particularly by the Moorish style in Spain. Popular products included textiles and ivory or wood carvings. The fine, nonfigurative decoration typical of Islamic art was applied to mosques and other buildings, household objects, and jewelry. The products of particular workshops were much sought after by collectors at the time.

▼ CHINA

The Ming Dynasty (1368–1644) is renowned for its production of white porcelain with blue underglaze, incorporating many new styles.

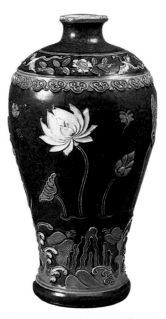

White porcelain Meiping vase with sancaï "three-color" decoration, Ming period. Musée Guimet, Paris.

▼ AFRICA

From 1400 onward, ivory objects, typically African in workmanship and decoration but carrying certain motifs derived from European iconography, were exported to the West. Different styles included the Sapi-Portuguese and the Benin-Portuguese and were applied mainly to hunting horns.

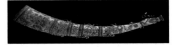

Ivory trumpet or hunting horn, Sapi-Portuguese style, Sierra Leone, 24 in (63.5 cm) high, late 15th–early 16th century. Paul and Ruth Tishman Collection of African Art, Los Angeles.

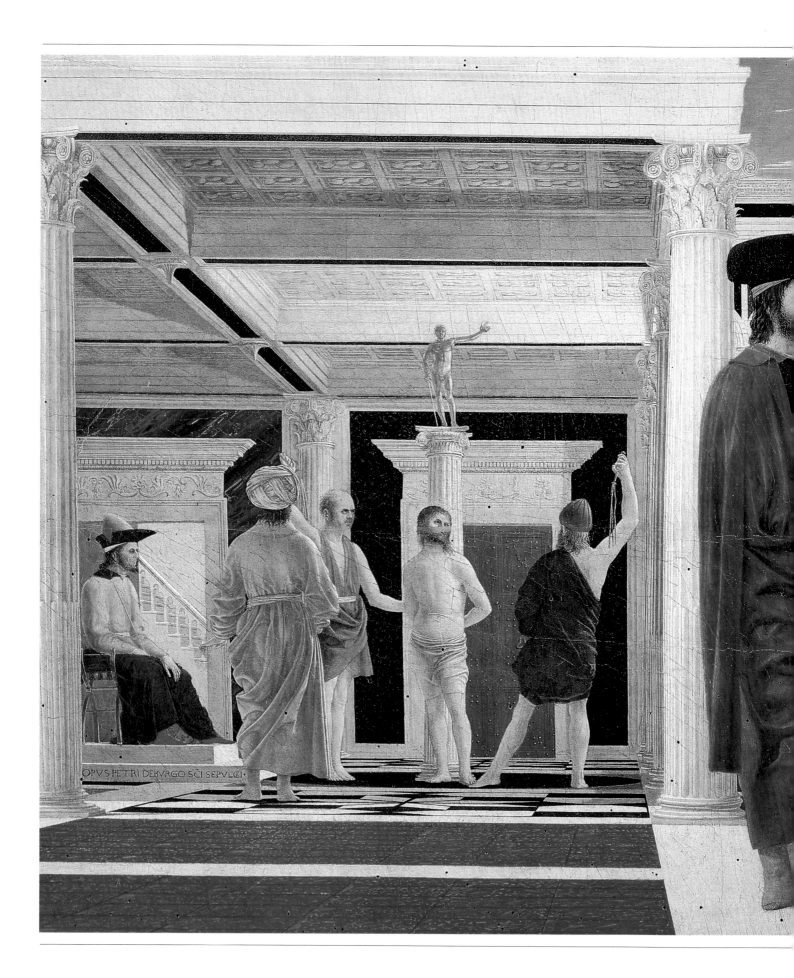

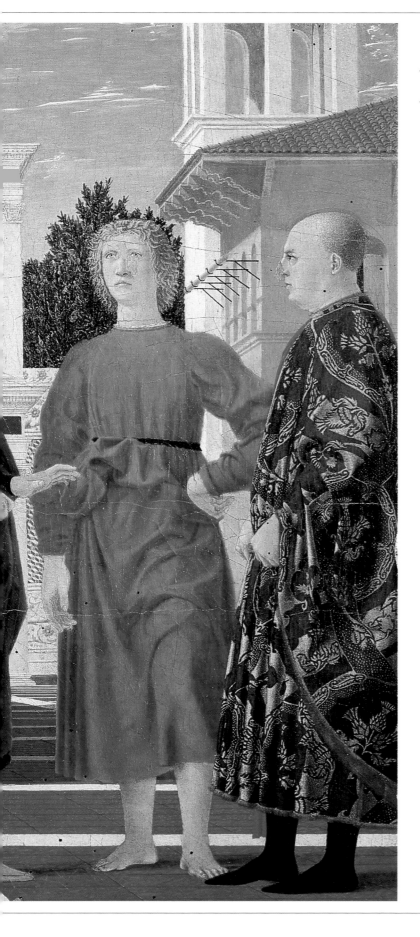

FROM THE GREAT CITIES OF EUROPE TO THE FOUR CORNERS OF THE WORLD

The Triumph of the City
Gothic Art
The Early Renaissance
The High Renaissance

Baroque & Rococo: the City & the Court
The 17th Century: the Age of Spectacle
The Splendors of the 18th Century

Artistic Cultures of Asia & the Americas
The Art of Asia
Pre-Columbian Art

Piero della Francesca, The Flagellation of Christ, 1463–64. Galleria Nazionale delle Marche, Urbino, Italy.

The Triumph of the City

GOTHIC ART

From the middle of the 12th century, a totally new style of architecture emerged in the great cathedrals of northern France. Incorporating improved building techniques and a new perception of symbolic values, this style quickly spread throughout Europe, where, in many countries, it would endure for three centuries or more. This was Gothic art, a prolonged and highly original phase in European culture.

The revolutionary new architectural styles and building techniques first used in the mid-12th century on the construction sites of the cathedrals of northern France quickly spread to England, central Europe, Italy, and Spain. In some countries this "Gothic" architecture was to rule until the beginning of the 16th century. The term "Gothic" was first coined by early Renaissance architects as a means of deriding all architecture created in a medieval style. The word itself referred to the idea of a barbaric past of the Dark Ages and, more specifically, to the "Goths" – a Germanic people who invaded Italy in the fifth century and sacked Rome. However, the term

Durham Cathedral, begun 1093, view of the nave. The structure is bulky and the components are separate, but the ribs on the vaulting compartments run down the piers. For the first time a sense of structural coherence overlaid the solid mass of the supports.

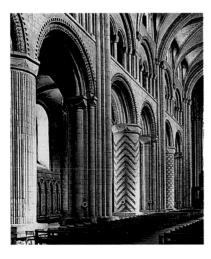

was to lose its derogatory overtones, and, by the Baroque age, great architects such as Borromini and, later, Guarini were quick to appreciate the technical quality and originality of form of these Gothic buildings. In the 19th century, new sensitivities to the picturesque by the English critic John Ruskin, and structural analysis by the French architect and leader of the Gothic Revival in France, Viollet-le-Duc (1814–79), led to a reappraisal of the social and religious qualities of the Middle Ages. Some 20th-century studies of Gothic art have perhaps laid too much emphasis on trends linked to the evolution of style or to geographical location. Others, like those by the art historian Erwin Panofsky and the critic Otto von Simson, have indicated links with scholastic philosophy or with metaphysics of Neo-Platonic origin. Meanwhile, critics such as Georges Duby have upheld the importance of the role of social and religious context.

In architecture, which more than the any other art category personifies Gothic culture, innovation grew out of a progressive mastery of geometry and composition. With new advances in technology, organization, and planning, building methods changed. Construction sites became efficient and economic, and the development of specialized areas, such as carving and

FROM SAINT-DENIS TO CHARTRES

Abbot Suger, a profound mystic, became abbot of Saint-Denis, Paris, in 1122. In 1140, he inaugurated the new basilica, intended as a burial chapel for the Capetian monarchs. This was the first truly Gothic building. Although he completed only the choir aisles and west entrance block, his vision of a ring of stained glass windows expanded the precious shimmer of the altar furniture into an aesthetic of mystic light. The oldest aesthetic dictate, "all that which exists is light," was echoed in the new edifices in the Ile de France, with an extraordinary use of stained-glass windows adorned with figures. The glorification of the portal, which had to be rich and light as a sign of Christ and

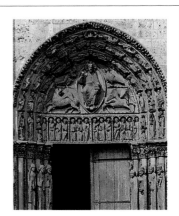

Detail of the Portal Royal, Chartres Cathedral, 1145–70.

a true door to the salvation of man, was a forerunner of the great sculptures that were to appear at the entrances of Notre-Dame in Paris and Chartres Cathedral. It is really in the shadow of these great building sites that theologians like Theodore of Chartres and William of Conches found an obvious counterpart in the logicality of the Gothic structure, with its impression of everything soaring upward. Their speculations on creative energy, *anima mundi* and its other aspect, *ornatus mundi*, is reflected in the elaboration of detail in the varied and wonderful repertory of sculpted decoration.

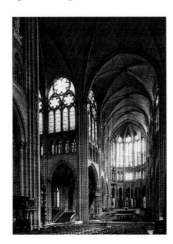

View of the mid-13th-century interior of the basilica of Saint-Denis (1140–1281).

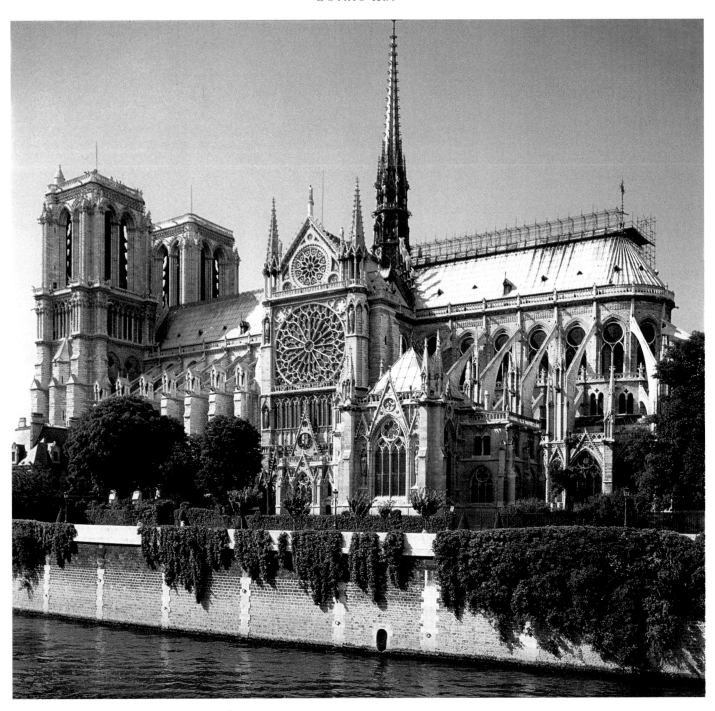

layout, enabled work to be allocated and integrated into orderly sequences. The task of the architect became both more intellectual and more independent, and names like Pierre de Montreuil (c.1200–66), Peter Parler (1333–99), and Ulrich von Esingen, came to be known. The new style, known as *opus francigenum,* spread rapidly as the competition between bishops to build cathedrals grew more intense,

and it was consolidated by the dominance in the 13th century of the French monarchy throughout northern France. Impressed by the economical use of time and materials, the growing monastic orders – Cistercians, Franciscans, and Dominicans – adopted the Gothic style. Building plans began to circulate outside the strict confines applied by the masons and were used by architects and patrons.

Notre-Dame, Paris, 1163–1258. Unlike most cathedrals, Notre-Dame still represents the heart of its city. After eight centuries, it remains a point of reference for French art, from its foundations, built in 1163 on the site of an old temple dedicated to the Roman god Jove, to the 19th-century restoration work by Viollet-le-Duc. The portals retain some of the original sculpture. The transept was added in the 13th century. The interior is dominated by the soaring vaults, the feeling of infinite space, and the austerity of the cylindrical columns in the double aisles.

THE GOTHIC CATHEDRALS

The rebuilding of Chartres Cathedral – the Romanesque structure was destroyed by fire in 1194 – provided a prototype for the new Gothic style. The earliest complete Gothic building was Laon Cathedral (1160), and a different system of encircling bay supports was used at Bourges

(1195). The Chartres plan of single aisles, small triforium, and vaulting bays was simpler. The plan is a longitudinal central body with side aisles, a short transept, and a choir with ambulatory and radial chapels. The main structural elements are the slender pillars topped by pointed arches, which separate the side aisles and rise to form high cross-vaults. The thrust was carried on flying buttresses to allow for large window openings. Set between two towers, the facade is pierced by a large rose window. As Gothic style flourished, the early variations at Noyon (1150) and Notre Dame (1163) were super- seded by developments at Soissons, Rheims, Amiens, and Beauvais.

In the mid-13th century, Gothic art followed the route of monks and pilgrims to Spain, where cathedrals were built at Salamanca, Burgos, and Leon. In England, at Canterbury and Westminster, French design gradually gave way to linear and decorative styles, culminating in the 14th- century perpendicular style. German regions adapted this style early in the 13th century in the Liebfrauenkirche of Trier and the cathedrals of Strasbourg and Cologne.

Sarmental Portal, Burgos Cathedral, Spain, 1221–1567. In Spain, Gothic architecture showed a strongly realistic drive with exceptionally lively reliefs.

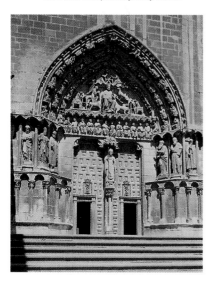

THE SUPREMACY OF DRAWING

Villard d'Honnecourt, a 13th- century architect from Picardy,

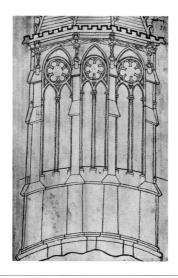

created his compilation treatise "Livre de portraiture" in about 1235 to provide Gothic architects with models and examples in technical drawing. From an ornamental leaf to plans for a nave at Rheims, Villard designed geometric systems and attempted to unveil, through drawing, the rational spirit that he saw as governing creation. This, he believed, should be adapted in the work of the artist, whether it be in the

Villard d'Honnecourt, copy of the Choir of Rheims. Bibliothèque Nationale, Paris.

details of a capital or the span of a bridge. Architectural plans became an important part of Gothic art. Although the drawings for the bell tower of Strasbourg Cathedral were intended to aid building work, their depiction of details of the decorative fretwork and delicately colored statues show the pictorial and luminous effects to which architecture could also aspire.

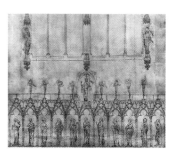

Studio of Nicolas Wurmser, detail of the design for the facade of Strasbourg Cathedral, late 14th century. Musée de l'Oeuvre de Notre-Dame, Paris.

THE PARLER FAMILY

The Parlers were an important German family of masons in the 14th century. Heinrich I (b. c.1300), who trained on the site of Cologne Cathedral, built the Heiligkreuzkirche at Schwäbisch-Gmünd, where he was master mason and responsible for the late Gothic German style. One of his sons, Peter (1333–99), was a leading figure of the late Gothic European style. After his apprenticeship at Schwäbisch- Gmünd with his father, he worked in Strasbourg, Cologne, and Nuremberg, before being summoned to Prague to finish the cathedral started by Matthias of Arras. Peter introduced new ideas that connected the windowed triforium arcade to the main upper windows, and he developed intricate rib patterns for the vaulting. He was then employed by Charles IV in the most important Prague workshops. Peter's son Wenzel worked on Vienna Cathedral, and another family member, Heinrich III, is recorded as having worked on Milan Cathedral in 1392.

Cologne Cathedral, begun in 1248.

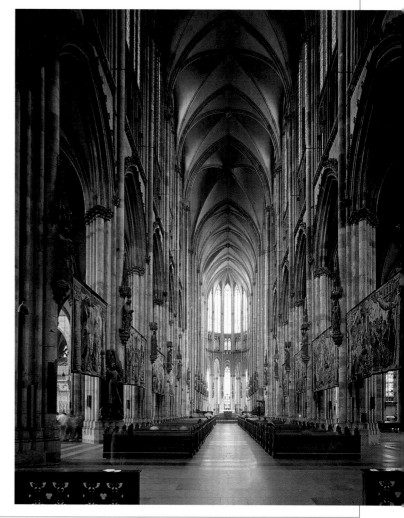

STAINED GLASS

The art of stained glass was an integral part of Gothic culture. At the beginning of the 13th century, Western master masons came together from far and wide to work on the construction site of Chartres Cathedral. This remains one of the few cathedral interiors that retains the original stained glass. Work in glass is an art of many disciplines. As well as its technical evolution, well documented by Theosophus and others, this medium carried rich

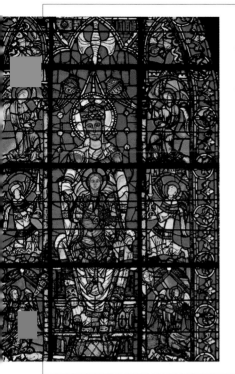

Notre Dame de la Belle Verrière,
detail from a stained-glass window
in Chartres Cathedral,
early 13th century.

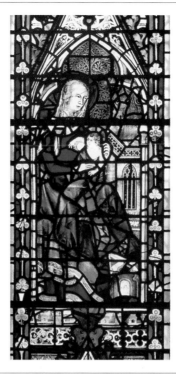

Robert Master, Madonna and Child,
detail from the stained glass in the
west window of York Minster.

symbolism and iconography, much of the meaning and impact of which is lost to us today. Organic forms fit well with the compartmentalized sections. For the "Tree of Jesse," a popular subject first used by Abbot Suger in the Saint-Denis window, curving sections were used to contain within the branches the Kings, the Virgin, and the hierarchy of heaven. Medallions and lozenge shapes were commonly used to divide the events of the great stories of the Bible, the life of Christ, and, most enduring of all, images glorifying the Virgin, the focus of devotion, especially during the 13th century. Most striking of all was the glorious color that streamed into places of worship all across Europe, bringing light and meaning to the promise of eternal enlightenment from heaven.

ARCHITECTURE IN ITALY

From the start of the 12th century, Italian architecture was characterized by many different aspirations, which combined to create an architectural culture of great vitality and a striking geographical diversity. On the one hand, Franco-Burgundian influences began to filter through with the foundation of Cistercian monasteries from Chiaravalle to Fossanova, and they were partially adopted by new orders, in particular the frugal Franciscans and Dominicans. Challenging these ideas was the tenacious Romanesque tradition, which was well able to serve the needs of the new city states. This was the case in the Po Valley of northern Italy, although the church of Sant'Andrea in Vercelli and the top colonnade of the Baptistry of Parma already showed concessions to the new style from the north side of the Alps.
Another important influence

on Italian architecture was offered by the classical heritage, dominated by the early Christian basilicas in Rome, and in the Imperial revivals in Italy, splendidly interpreted by Frederick II of Germany (1194–1250), who was crowned emperor of Rome in 1220. This complex combination of influences was profoundly interlinked with equally multifaceted developments in other Italian art forms, making it difficult to recognize coherent and unambiguous patterns. From a historical point of view, Gothic represented a distinct change, which counteracts the traditional understanding of an uninterrupted transition from the Romanesque to the Renaissance (epitomized by the work of Brunelleschi). By the 13th century, the Franciscan and Dominican orders, together with the Humiliati, a penitential association of the laity specific to the Po Valley, were pushing for simpler constructions and more usable space. As a result, the ceilings of nave and aisles,

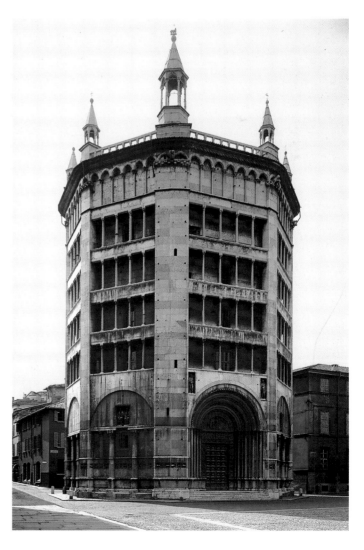

Baptistry of Parma (1196–1216).

THE DOMINICANS

Two Dominican monks, Sisto and Ristoro, are traditionally credited with the planning and construction of the Church of Santa Maria Novella in Florence. The plan of the building, a Latin cross with square chapels jutting out from the east side of the transept, was used for Franciscan models. The dynamic concept differs, from the slender cross vaults to acute pointed arches separating the nave, but with a greater spatial unity. In the second half of the 14th century, Andrea di Bonaiuto painted the wonderful frescoes for the adjacent Spanish Chapel, in which the picture of the Church of the Triumph of the Faith closely resembled Arnolfo di Cambio's design for the cathedral, Santa Maria del Fiore. The spatial integrity of the building is already implicit in Arnolfo's plan of 1294, but the dome of the fresco model is augmented by Brunelleschi's octagonal drum that carries the dome. Another example of Dominican theology is

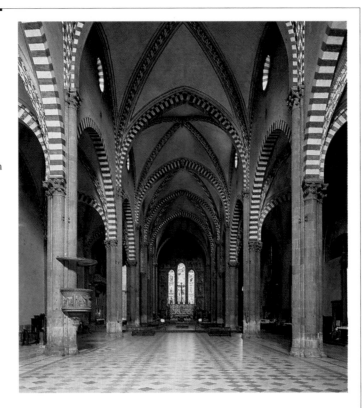

Bonaiuto's fresco cycle showing Thomas Aquinas dominating the allegorical figures of all the liberal arts and the sciences of the theological *cursus*.

Santa Maria Novella, Florence, interior, begun in 1279.

Andrea di Bonaiuto, Triumph of St. Thomas Aquinas, *1365–67, the Spanish dome, Santa Maria Novella, Florence.*

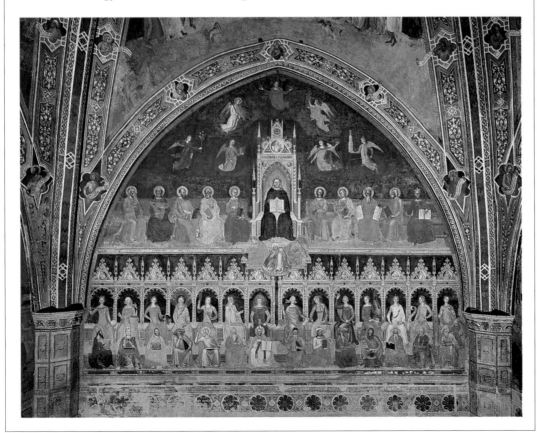

whether vaulted or wooden, were adjusted to reduce the differences in height between the side aisles, while the widely spaced pillars gradually diminished the excessive mix of straight and curved lines by the use of wide-diameter arches, either pointed or completely rounded. The result was a geometric architectonic image that was rationally coherent in design. The surrounding walls became a surface for the multicolored decorations of cycles of legendary scenes, which were either painted on, as in the buildings at Assisi, or sculpted, as in the facade of Siena Cathedral. Seen from this point of view, Giotto's bell tower in Florence represented an extraordinary return to the integrity of surface articulation.

Despite the obvious French influences in the Upper church of Assisi or in San Francesco, Bologna, with its radial chapels around the choir, the Dominicans and Franciscans consciously respected civic needs and erected buildings of strong public character, as is clear in Santa Maria Novella and Santa Croce in Florence. Out of this situation the image of the civic cathedral took shape: from Siena to Orvieto, Lecce, and Bologna. Milan provided an opportunity for later revisions of the French innovations, especially as regards decoration (triforia, rose windows, spires, pinnacles). Other integrations are beautifully exemplified by the crowning of the Baptistry of Pisa and its neighboring cemetery, the Camposanto. That these developments were closely modeled on the art of goldsmiths is evident in the two great facades of Orvieto and Siena, with the microarchitecture of *ciboria* (dome-shaped canopies above the high altar), pulpits, and funerary monuments – works in which artists such as Giovanni

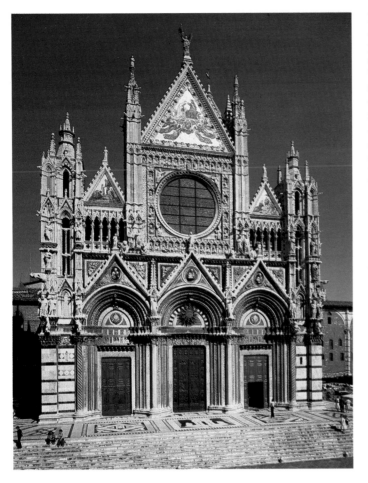

Facade of Siena Cathedral, built and reworked from 1284 to 1382.

Pisano (c.1248– 1314) and Arnolfo di Cambio participated. Also characteristic of the new age was the versatility of great architects who were generally competent artists in a wide range of different fields, including draftsmanship. Such artists include Giotto and Arnolfo di Cambio in Florence, and Giovanni Pisano in Siena. The Italian cities developed rapidly to reach economic independence, and this fostered numerous new civic buildings with a versatile mixture of Gothic pinnacles, colonnaded porticos, and sculptural detail. Clustered around the central square, magnificent town halls, hospitals, and urban palazzos were built, and work continued on the cathedrals. The echo of classical architecture, which retained vestiges of the ancient rules of proportion,

ARNOLFO DI CAMBIO

Florentine sculptor and architect Arnolfo di Cambio (1245–1302) was greatly inspired by the heroic classical style of Nicola Pisano, whom he assisted as a young man. His work also shows an awareness of the French Gothic linear values. Among the many buildings in Florence attributed to him are Santa Croce and the Palazzo Vecchio. He was master mason of the new cathedral of Florence, begun in 1296.

was strongest in Rome. It was also seen at the court of Frederick, which in Castel del Monte interpreted Cistercian Gothic in noble, classical forms. The octagonal cathedral crossings provided a monumental example, which was to extend the geometric styles beyond the confines of the cathedral, to be applied to the fountains of city squares. It is also in the cathedrals of Pisa, Siena, and Ancona that another example of geometric order emerges: the cupola set above the transept and the body of the nave.

TOMBS AND MONUMENTS

The tomb for Cardinal de Braye was created by Arnolfo di Cambio, a pupil of Nicola Pisano and collaborator of his son Giovanni, for the Church of San Domenico in Orvieto in

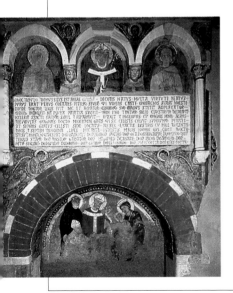

Tomb of Abbot Cotta, Sant'Ambrogio, Milan, 1267.

1282. Even in a reconstructed state, this work is obviously that of a sculptor, marking the rising social standing of artists. It also proves the importance that this microarchitecture – as seen in the tabernacle of the church of San Paolo Fuori le Mura in Rome – was beginning to take on in the development of contemporary architectural language. Simplicity and geometric order were adopted in the plans for Santa Maria del Fiore (1296) and the Palazzo Vecchio (1299). Arnolfo's compositions also initiated the rising interest for funerary monuments as patronage commemoration, set in elaborate architectural relief compositions that supplanted the more conventional insets. Among the most important 13th-century examples are the *arcosolia* (wall tombs) in

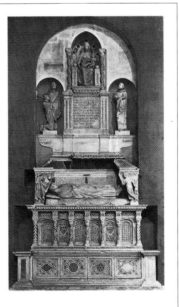

Arnolfo di Cambio, Tomb of Cardinal de Braye, San Domenico, Orvieto, 1282.

Salamanca Cathedral, where architecture, sculpture, and painting join together to express the theme of a celestial Jerusalem.

SCULPTURE

The construction sites of the great cathedrals also became the most important sculptural workshops, dedicated to the decoration of facades, spires, and, above all, portals. The mid-12th-century Portal Royal of Chartres shows how closely and harmoniously the sculpted figures conformed to the disposition of the architecture, without any loss of expression or drama. Saint-Denis and Notre-Dame in Paris became prototypes for composition and iconography, which were complex and carefully worked out. Saints and episodes from the Bible, often of apocalyptic inspiration, were displayed on these great facades in coherent and hierarchical arrangements. Then, in the early 13th century, in the north and south portals at

Chartres, the program of the "heavenly kingdom" was developed as a full integration of homage and celebration, with the deep colonnaded porticos giving a full articulation to the order of Christ's Second Coming. At Rheims and Amiens, the porticos are flattened back into the modulations of the facade, and the figures stand out as personalities that show expressive gestures. The drapery folds take on an independent substance, implying a range of formal nuances and emotions that contrasts with the repetitive components of the architectural settings. By mid-

century, in the transept portals of Notre Dame, this variation becomes graceful and sinuous, seen in the tympanum narratives of St. Stephen and the Virgin. The compositions have become connected to the meanings of the incidents.

Funerary carvings were a characteristic genre of 14th-century France. The face of the *gisant* (recumbent figure on the tomb) was made in the likeness of the deceased, and the *pleurants* (weepers) represented the mourners at the funeral. Begun by Louis IX (St Louis) in the 13th century for his own dynasty, these sculptures often

imitated the tomb of Philip III, made by Pierre de Chelles and Jean d'Arras between 1298 and 1307. Toward the end of the 14th century, the elegant linear style and increasing taste for realism reached its peak with Claus Sluter (c.1340–1405), whose vivid and solemn realism is embodied in his dynamic works of art for the Charterhouse of Champmol. In Italy, the pulpits of Nicola Pisano (active c.1258–1278) for the Baptistry of Pisa and Siena Cathedral already showed the transition from the Roman heritage of *gravitas* toward more integrated forms. In the

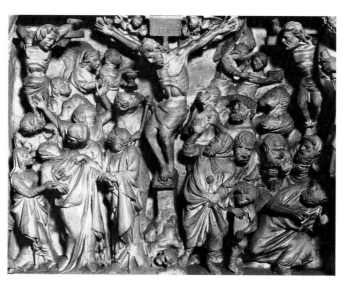

Tino di Camaino and assistants, base of the Easter candelabrum for the tomb of Filippo d'Angió, San Domenico Maggiore, Naples. Filippo d'Angio was prince of Taranto and emperor of the Orient.

THE PULPITS OF NICOLA AND GIOVANNI PISANO

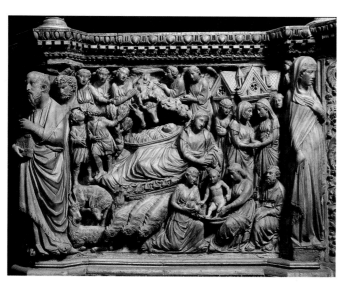

Nicola Pisano, Nativity, pulpit of Siena Cathedral, 1265–68.

Giovanni Pisano, Crucifixion, pulpit of Sant'Andrea, Pistoia, Italy, 1301.

compositional rigor and powerful relief work that are clearly classical in origin. In his work on the pulpits of the cathedrals of Pistoia (1301) and Pisa (1302), his son Giovanni heightened these Gothic tensions. An impetuous, dramatic energy, centered on the major points, such as the Cross of the Passion of Christ, invests the figures with an amazing variety of effects and creates a strong sense of tragic power.

As the mendicant Franciscan and Dominican orders took more and more to preaching, special liturgical sites, such as the pulpit, took on greater significance. Through the works of the great Pisano family in Siena, Pisa, and Pistoia, the pulpit became the element that best illustrates the development of Tuscan sculpture. Nicola trained in the court of Frederick II, as the transference of the Castel del Monte architectural design to his pulpits at Pisa (1260) and Siena (1265) would seem to indicate. His *Childhood* and *Passion of Christ* reveal a

case of his son Giovanni, these betrayed a stay in France that had liberated his expressive talent into rounded and full modeling. This was later displayed in his statues for Siena Cathedral and the pulpits for the cathedrals of Pistoia and Pisa. The Pisa school produced Giovanni di Balduccio, who inspired the sculptors of Lombardy with new ideas, and Tino di Camaino (c.1285–1337), who brought Gothic sculpture to southern Italy. Finally, Giotto's radical style of painting was to influence many fellow sculptors, as shown by Andrea Pisano (c.1290–1349) in the reliefs for the door of the Baptistry in Florence and in those for the bell tower of the cathedral, where he was *capomaestro* from 1340 to 1343.

THE CHARTERHOUSE OF CHAMPMOL

Founded as a family mausoleum by Philip the Bold in 1383, the Charterhouse of Champmol near Dijon was one of the most important religious and artistic centers of the dukedom of Burgundy during the late Gothic era. Today, the site of the destroyed charterhouse is occupied by a psychiatric hospital, but some important

Claus Sluter, Moses' Well, Charterhouse of Champmol, Dijon, France, 1395. The sculpted group is one of the masterpieces of late Gothic naturalism.

works still survive, such as the facade of the church and the *Moses' Well*, which was carved by Claus Sluter during the last ten years of the 14th century. These, together with the duke's tomb and its *pleurants* (weepers), now housed in the Dijon Museum, are among some of the greatest European masterpieces of late Gothic naturalism. The town museum still preserves four panels, painted for the altarpiece of Champmol, showing the *Life of the Virgin* by the Flemish artist Melchior Broederlam from Ypres.

Melchior Broederlam, Flight into Egypt, side panel of an altarpiece, c.1399. Musée des Beaux-Arts, Dijon, France.

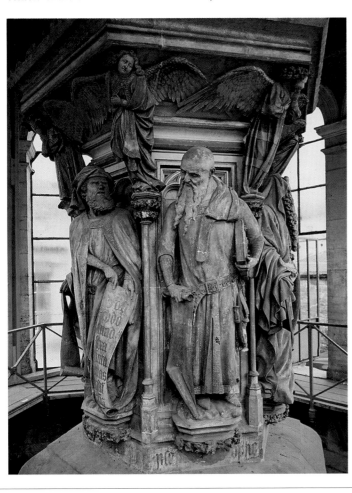

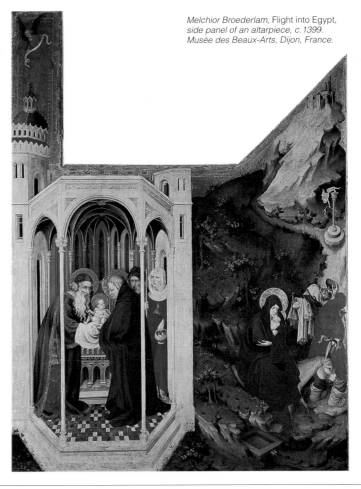

PAINTING

Gothic pictorial art interacted with architecture and displayed a surprising variety of form. With stained-glass windows, artists were able to exploit the opportunity created by vast openings in the wall to fill them with light, color, and narrative. In France, the pictorial culture of the 13th and 14th centuries is represented far more strongly by the stained-glass masters of Chartres, Bourges, and the Sainte-Chapelle than by fresco painters. Gothic painting developed its own rich style, both religious and secular, north of the Alps. A fluid linear quality typified manuscript drawing, while an increasing naturalism replaced the exaggerated Romanesque style. While only vestiges of wall paintings remain, these, along with the illuminations, reveal subject matter mainly from the Old Testament, the Apocalypse, the childhood of Christ, the life of the Virgin, the Passion, and the Last Judgment. Pictorial art in Italy followed a different course, emerging as altarpieces, fresco cycles, and painted crosses. The great altarpieces, which were particularly characteristic of central Italy, became progressively structured in large compositions, yet most have since been broken up

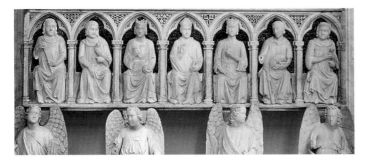

Tino di Camaino and Gagliardo Primario, Tomb of Mary of Hungary, 1325. The front of the tomb is supported by angels and shows the portraits of the sons of Mary and Charles II. Angevin rulers liked to be depicted with their descendants on their tombs.

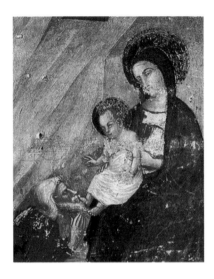

Ferrer Bassá (1285–1348), Madonna and Child, *detail of fresco, San Miguel Chapel, Convent of Pedralbes, Barcelona, 1345–46. Bassá's work shows the influence of Sienese culture. Employed at the Aragon court, he studied at the Papal Palace at Avignon and shared with Lorenzetti a lively naturalism.*

and dispersed into private and museum collections. Furthermore, many of the fresco cycles have suffered irreparable over-painting and erasures throughout the years. In Spain, the principal medium for pictorial culture was the *reredos*, a large compartmentalized screen behind the altar, either painted or sculpted. On the Iberian peninsula, this genre attained a level of experimentation and grandiosity unknown anywhere in Europe, to the point of becoming a major architectural element. At this time, the most readily communicated art form throughout Europe was the miniature. The popularity of illustrated books grew to become an expression of the ideas and tastes of the rich and scholarly. These books typified Gothic art, which increasingly favored naturalistic forms and miniature scenes from everyday life.

The complex profile of Italian painting was dominated by a radical change that took place at the end of the 13th century in Umbria and Tuscany (Assisi, Florence, Siena); this was the arrival of a new artistic language that marked the confluence of various influences. Of these, the most significant were the Romanesque tradition of western Europe, concentrated in the Po Valley; the Byzantine, along the Adriatic and in the south; and the classical, still active, especially in Rome and the surrounding regions. The historical importance of the renewal of the figurative arts – led in painting by Giotto and Cimabue, and in sculpture by the great Pisano brothers and Arnolfo di Cambio – lies therefore not so much in the artists' rejection of the late Byzantine influence as in the richness of their realistic synthesis. The Byzantine culture had produced mosaics and painted fresco cycles of quality, as in the decoration of San Salvatore in Chora. The vibrant

Anonymous, Pope Nicholas Offering the Model of the Sancta Sanctorum, *east wall, Sancta Sanctorum, Rome.*

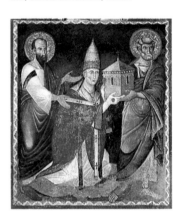

FRANCISCAN ARCHITECTURE

In 1228, the Basilica di San Francesco was begun in Assisi, two years after the saint's death. This long building project revealed the bitter quarrel between those who adhered strictly to St. Francis's ideals of poverty – evident even in the first paintings of him in the Sacro Speco at Subiano – and those who supported the inclusion of the Franciscan phenomenon in the affairs of the Church. Unlike St. Bernard, who had founded the Cistercian Order in the 12th century, St. Francis had not introduced aesthetic ideals into new monastic foundations, but went about restoring small rural oratories. Otherwise, the brothers' work was purely mendicant. The building had the triple function of a burial place, a conventual church, and a papal chapel. The Lower Church, which perhaps represented the first phase, was soon followed by the more ambitious project of the Upper Church, which was rich in

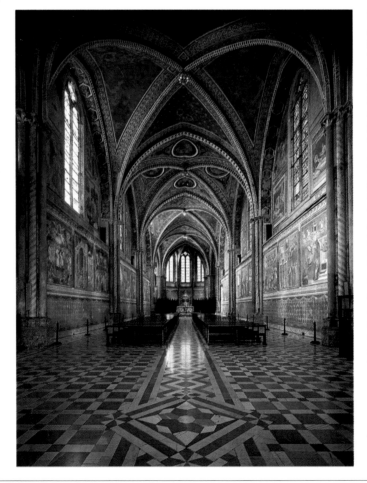

French Gothic elements, such as Angers cathedral and the unified space of episcopal chapels. The building itself stressed the relationship between his preaching mission and Christ's mission, which was also emphasized in Giotto's cycle of frescoes, the *Life of St. Francis*, as well as by Dante in Canto XI of *Paradiso* in his *Divine Comedy*. Franciscan architecture soon gained a hold throughout Roman Catholic Europe. Favoring wide, well-lit spaces, walls were decorated with scenes from the Passion, the Nativity, the Life of the Virgin, saints, and the beatified who encouraged a life of charity. Franciscan convents and churches were prominent in the cities, and it was here that many great artists worked, from Giotto to Piero della Francesca, and from Leonardo to Titian. Vying with the Dominicans, the Franciscans were philosophers and theologians, teaching in the universities and influencing the culture of the courts.

View of the Upper Church toward the apse, Basilica di San Francesco, Assisi.

luminosity and the narrative style revealed in the distinctive and individual altarpieces and fresco cycles testify to a coloristic and compositional freedom far from the concepts of a mystic and divine space usually associated with the Byzantine heritage. Of great significance was the work of Il Cavallini and of Filippo Rusiti (active 1319–30), who represented the classical Roman school of the 13th century, and whose frescoes and mosaics show an important link between their style and the concrete conception of reality created by Giotto in the pictorial cycle of St. Francis of Assisi. With the first defeat of the Swabians in 1266, Charles I came to rule over southern

THE PAINTED CRUCIFIX

The Painted Cross from the Church of San Sepolcro in Pisa (now housed in the Museo Nazionale di San Matteo) is an extraordinary example of how the Crucifixion was

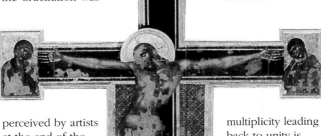

perceived by artists at the end of the 12th century. Christ is shown standing erect and majestic in his luminous incarnation, his eyes wide open. There is no hint

Cimabue, Crucifix, before 1284. Museo dell'Opera di Santa Croce, Florence.

of suffering, but a sense of defeating death in the very instant at which he dies. Around him, the *Story of the Passion* unfolds, crowded with figures and multicolored turreted buildings. The medieval aesthetic of

multiplicity leading back to unity is orchestrated here with a skillful balance of forms and colors. In contrast, a century later, Cimabue painted a *Christ* for Santa Croce, a work badly damaged in the Florence flood of 1966. In this, Christ's suffering eyes are closed and his

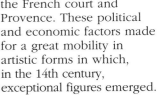

Anonymous, Painted Cross no. 15, from the Church of San Sepolcro. Museo Nazionale di San Matteo, Pisa.

bruised body is twisted, falling away from the rectangular cross in an agonized curve. The story is restricted to the grief of the Virgin and St. John, the simplicity of which serves to give the work more power. A generation later, Cimabue's pupil Giotto would paint his own powerful *Crucifix* in Florence's Santa Maria Novella.

Italy and strengthened the development and culture of Naples, in close relationship with the pontifical court and with the Guelph bankers of

Tuscany (the Guelphs were members of a medieval Italian political party that supported the papacy against the German

emperors). However, he retained the ties with the French court and Provence. These political and economic factors made for a great mobility in artistic forms in which, in the 14th century, exceptional figures emerged.

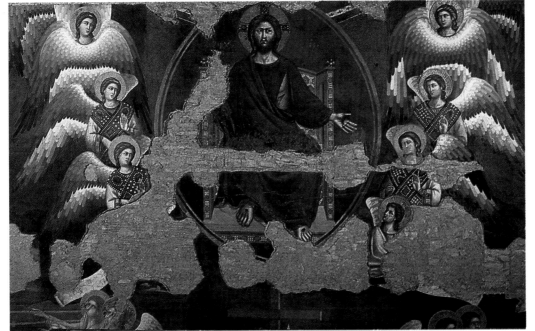

Il Cavallini, detail from The Last Judgment, Santa Cecilia, Trastevere, Rome, c.1293.

PETRARCH AND SIMONE MARTINI

The Italian poet and scholar Francesco Petrarca, known as Petrarch (1304–1374), is seen as the first critic of modern art. A personal friend of Simone Martini, he commissioned a portrait of his beloved Laura from the Sienese master (this is now lost, but it is mentioned in one of his sonnets). A great collector of classical manuscripts, he also commissioned the artist to illuminate the frontispiece of a priceless Virgilian manuscript. While being a great judge of Gothic painting, Petrarch seems to have preferred Martini's elegant works, with their refined patterns of color, such as those in the San Martino Chapel in the Lower Church of Assisi (c.1320). A narrative account in decorative shades, it was an intensely lyrical work, like the poetry of Petrarch's own masterpiece, *Canzoniere*. At this time, classical manuscripts were being recovered, and Petrarch was the first to

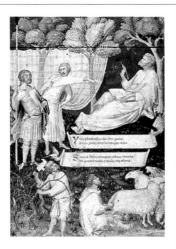

Simone Martini, Apotheosis of Virgil, *frontispiece of the* Commento a Virgilio di Servio, *1340–44. Biblioteca Ambrosiana, Milan.*

propose new standards of realism for paintings and sculptures based on criteria drawn from these classical texts. The great architect and humanist Leon Battista Alberti (1404–72) was the successor to this style, which was later seen as a critical moment in the history of art.

Simone Martini, Death of St. Martin, *Lower Church, Assisi, c.1326.*

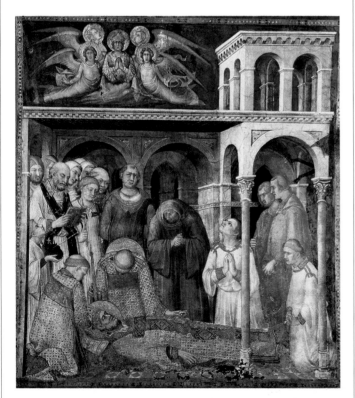

GIOTTO:"LAMENTATION OVER THE DEAD CHRIST"

1304–06; fresco; 78¾ x 72¾ in (200 x 185 cm); Arena Chapel, Padua, Italy.

The Gothic building of the Arena Chapel was erected by an important banking family, the Scrovegnis, and decorated by Giotto with the *Story of Mary* and the *Story of Jesus*, a cycle that is viewed as one of the greatest masterpieces of medieval art. The *Lamentation* is one of numerous separate pictures that run in horizontal bands in three layers around the sides and choir wall of the chapel. The figure of the dead Jesus, naked in Franciscan poverty, is gently laid on the ground, while the holy women tend his body, the disciples weep, and, above, the angels share in the grief of the mourners. The harsh rocky outcrop and leafless

▶ *1. There is much activity in the work, with each saintly mourner depicted with a distinct identity. Christ's mother clasps the dead body to her and appears controlled in her grief. Mary Magdalene holds Christ's feet, gazing at the wounds from the nails. The two contemplative older men to the right are Joseph of Arimathea and Nicodemus; they seem detached from the rest of the group in their mourning. To the left are the companions of Mary, who wail and weep, displaying the anguish and emotion that Mary cannot express. The bare rocky outcrop cuts diagonally across the landscape behind the figures, separating them from the darkened sky beyond.*

tree reinforce the sense that a superhuman tragedy is being played out on a barren Earth. There is a powerful sense of unremitting sorrow.

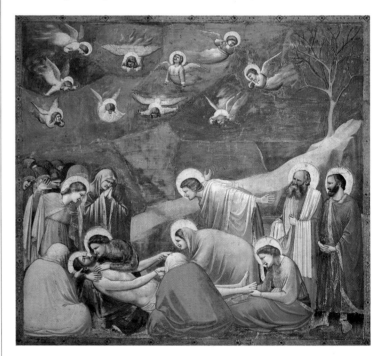

GIOTTO AND THE SIENESE ARTISTS

The convincing three-dimensional style and illusion of space that Giotto created in his painting through the use of receding planes produced a

The great Florentine artist Giotto di Bondone (1267–1337) began work in Cimabue's studio, before working in Rome and Assisi, where he produced some of his greatest masterpieces for the Franciscans. These are chracterized by a powerful sense of pictorial space. By 1300, he was famous and influential as a painter and architect throughout Europe.

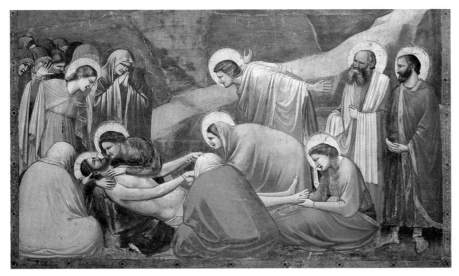

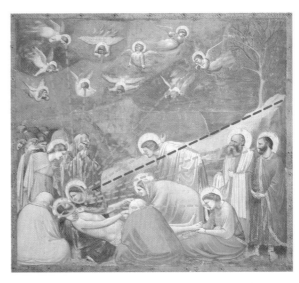

▲ 4. Giotto had an innovative fresco technique that relied on very specific color combinations. A different section of the damp, fresh plaster was worked on every day; these sections, which can be seen in the sky, were known as giornate, from giorno, Italian for "day". The figures of the angels are skillfully painted, showing effectively and precisely their vitality and movement, as well as their grief. The intense blue of the sky throws into relief the soft colors of the mourners' garments.

▼ 2. The harmonious shapes of the cloaks on the figures are striking. Unlike northern European painters, who used the human form as a framework upon which to hang drapery, Giotto firmly defines the bodies beneath the cloth. The impressive forms are not interrupted by bulky folds. The composition is arranged in clear, separate shapes, the figures isolated in their bleak surroundings, each imbued with its own sense of grief and desolation at the death of Christ. The two figures in the foreground, seen from the back, create an illusion of extra space in front of the body of Christ. Above, the contorted bodies of the angels in the sky are painted in short curves as they swoop and somersault.

▶ 3. The focus of the scene lies in the lower left-hand corner, in which mother and son commune. The eyes of all the secondary figures are resting on the image of the dead Christ, their faces painted with precision and power. The spur of rock that descends from the right follows the same direction as their gaze. The lone and leafless tree on the arid hillside stands as a bare, background reminder of the horror and emptiness of death.

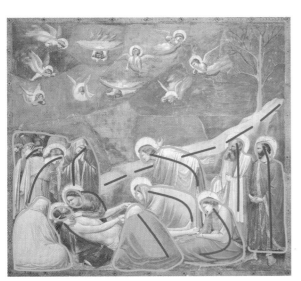

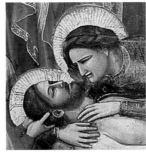

◀ 5. One can see how the pathos of the composition is centered on the two heads of Mary and Christ, creating a very human, tender, scene. The action takes place at eye level, which turns the familiar scene into a real and very moving drama. This contrasts with other religious scenes of the time, which were characterized by a sense of remoteness and a feeling of awe. The halo of Christ is different from those of Mary and the other figures, which distinguishes him from his disciples. The surprising serenity on the face of the Virgin may be due to her inner certainty that Christ will rise again. Giotto seems to have pursued this attitude in the work, which imparts a sense of despair and suffering that is intense but not hopeless.

naturalism in which dramatic themes predominated. The composition and the actions and emotions of the human figure were given full value. His work reveals an intellect open to all the factors of reality, in search of a unifying meaning. The new pictorial realism and its increasingly soft nuances of color owed much to the support of the monastic orders of the Dominicans and Franciscans. Their attachment to city life explains the great wealth of private commissions (in such buildings as Santa Croce in Florence), which enhanced the success of the Giottesque school and that of its leading figures: Stefano, Maso di Banco, and Taddeo Gaddi. The Gothic influences that penetrated the Giottesque tradition had already marked Sienese painting. This is evident in the refined linear and chromatic sensitivity of Duccio di Buoninsegna,

DUCCIO DI BUONINSEGNA

Founder and most celebrated exponent of the Sienese school, Duccio (1260–1318) is famous for his *Maestà*, the beautiful double-sided altarpiece commissioned in 1308 for Siena Cathedral. Breaking away from Byzantine tradition, Duccio's painting displayed an exquisite sensitivity, with superb use of color, elegant modeling, and a lively narrative.

AMBROGIO LORENZETTI: "THE EFFECTS OF GOOD AND BAD GOVERNMENT IN THE COUNTRY"

Circa 1337–39; detail from fresco; 138 x 276 in (350 x 700 cm); Sala dei Nove, Palazzo Pubblico, Siena.

This large fresco was painted by the more "Florentine" in style of the two Lorenzetti brothers, following his commission by the Republic. It is the most important secular fresco cycle of the 13th century in Italy, full of political and literary allegories. Here, we see a detail of the countryside from the right-hand side of the fresco. It shows the "effects of good government" in the country and depicts daily routines, such as farming, fishing, and hunting. The other side of the picture, not shown, represents the city, based on Siena, which in the 12th century had waned in power yet remained one of the major artistic centers in Europe.

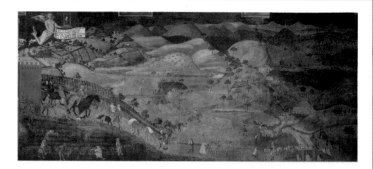

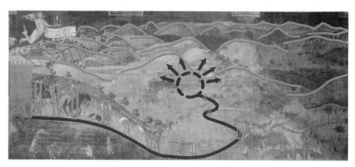

▶ *1. Lorenzetti uses a receding scale to depict subjects farther away on a smaller scale than those in the foreground. This type of recession, which does not use precise vanishing points, involved converging lines that would later be familiar to Brunelleschi and Masaccio. This method was already widely and effectively used in the Florentine paintings of Giottesque masters.*

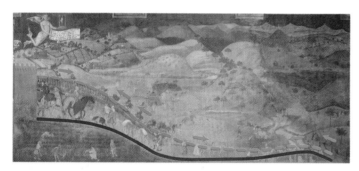

◀ *2. On leaving the city, the road crosses the lower part of the fresco from right to left. We see the merchants' caravan heading toward Siena, about to cross the bridge. Farther on, two merchants advance, along with the peasants leading heavily laden donkeys. The nobility are leaving the city to go hunting. For the cultured medieval citizen, the country was a wild, dangerous place. Now, in the 14th century, it is presented as a thriving rural area.*

▼ *3. This is the first great landscape in Italian art. It portrays the work of farm laborers: plowing, sowing, harvesting, and threshing the grain, and a man waiting outside the mill. The places and activities are painted with warmth in soft pinks, fresh greens, and various shades of ochre. Lorenzetti clearly intended to depict the countryside as a rural and tranquil contrast to town, one that was accessible to the urban patricians.*

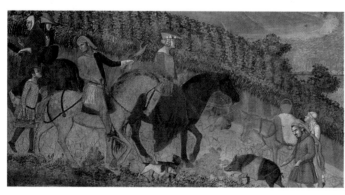

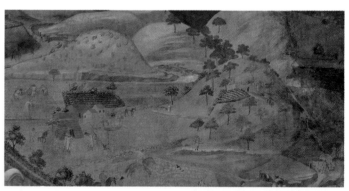

▲ *4. This detail shows a couple out riding. The lady, painted in red, white, and golden yellow, has fair hair curled under her hat, and a low-cut dress. Following her is her young knight, who is talking to a servant on foot; the knight carries a falcon on his gloved wrist, a sign that he is a nobleman. Two dogs complete the group. As they descend, peasants come toward them; one leads a pig, another has a laden donkey, and a third sits at the roadside. The nobles appear serene, and the peasants' work does not appear to be too arduous.*

▶ *5. Good government guarantees security for all the region. This is shown in the allegory by means of Security (Securitas) appearing in the form of an angel. She flies high above the well-cultivated landscape. In her right hand, she holds a scroll which bears the legend: "all ye who are honest walk and sow without fear while this woman rules over the community having taken it from the rule of kings." In case of any doubt, in her other hand she carries a gallows with a hanged king.*

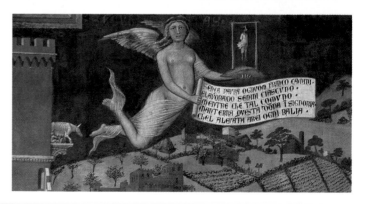

CENNINO CENNINI AND THE GIOTTESQUE ARTISTS

Probably written in the Veneto at the end of the 13th century, Cennini's *Il Libro dell'Arte* is one of the last examples of medieval artistic repositories, a technical manual containing the secrets of the artist's studio and the traditions of the artisan. Moreover, Cennini, who was a pupil of Agnolo Gaddi, confirms in his praise for good fresco technique the greatness of the

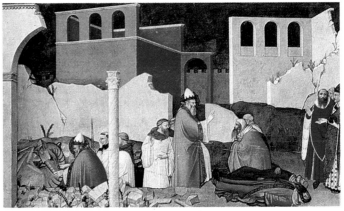

Maso di Banco (active 1341–46), St. Sylvester Restores to Life Two Magicians, *Bardi Chapel, Santa Croce, Florence, c.1340–45.*

Giottesque school. During the 14th century, it had influenced important figures, such as Taddeo Gaddi, who painted the *Life of the Virgin* in the Baroncelli Chapel in Santa Croce, Florence (finished 1336), and Maso di Banco, whose

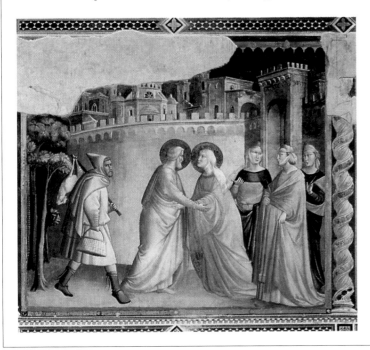

Legend of St. Sylvester (1341–45) is in the Bardi Chapel, also in Santa Croce. These were pupils of Giotto, who developed his artistic precepts in the 13th century. Cennini records the long and hard apprenticeship in the Florentine studios, where artists learned how to paint frescoes with subtle effects of light and shadow, works that would withstand the test of time. Cennini explained how the imaginative use of line and color helped create a more natural realism in painting.

Taddeo Gaddi (c.1295–36), Life of the Virgin, *Baroncelli Chapel, Santa Croce, Florence.*

CIMABUE AND GIOTTO

"The transience of fame on the wave of reflection" – the first great critical debate in the history of Italian art – appears in Dante's *The Divine Comedy*. This has prompted much discussion as to whether the importance of Cimabue, who freed painting from a slavish dependence on Byzantine culture, has been obscured by his pupil Giotto's rise to fame. The move toward greater realism was confirmed by Cimabue's influence on Villani, Ghiberti, and Landino, and was openly credited by Vasari, in his *Lives of the Most Excellent Painters, Sculptors and Architects*. He describes Cimabue as the first to abandon the "stiff Greek style" in drawing and coloring, remarkable for those times. However, Vasari writes that the decisive step was taken by Giotto, who restored the link between art and nature, first by using nature as a model and then by surpassing it. He eventually inspired whole

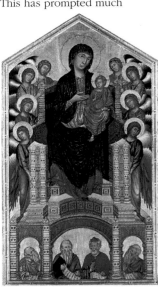

Cimabue, Madonna of the Holy Trinity, *1285–86. Galleria degli Uffizi, Florence.*

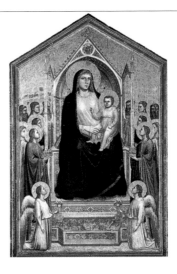

Giotto, Madonna Enthroned, *1310. Galleria degli Uffizi, Florence.*

generations of painters to become involved in the "new modern manner." In about 1400, the Florentine painter and writer Cennino Cennini wrote that "Giotto translated the art of paint from Greek to Latin."

who transformed Sienese painting from the Byzantine tradition to the Gothic. Due to the work of certain of its artists, Siena was launched into a fruitful exchange of ideas with French Gothic art and, in particular, with the exiled papal court at Avignon. Such work included the refined painting of Simone Martini (c.1284–1344), which quickly appealed to the humanistic taste of Petrarch, and the warm expressiveness of Pietro Lorenzetti (c.1280–1348). The long survival of the Giottesque school has been interpreted as a symptom of artistic fatigue and indecision, especially in Florence. In this respect, the Black Death of 1348 is considered by some as a watershed between an age of progressive renewal and a period of pessimistic contraction.

OTHER ITALIAN SCHOOLS

What emerged most clearly in the second half of the 14th century was the vitality of areas outside Tuscany, which had already been affected by Giotto and his followers, and by the

Giovanni da Milano, Pietà, 1365. Galleria dell' Accademia, Florence.

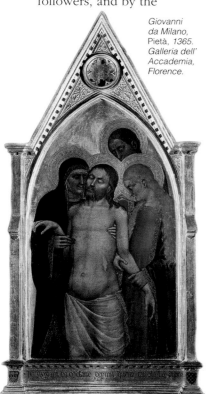

THE "MAESTÀ" PAINTINGS

Siena's devotion to the Virgin Mary is a recurring theme in the art of the city, from the decoration on the facade of the cathedral, begun by Giovanni Pisano (1284 onward) to the *Maestà* ("majesty") masterpieces of Duccio (1309) and Simone Martini (1315). The links with the historical awareness of the city, where religious and civic feelings met, are manifested in the many chronicles describing the triumphal procession that accompanied Duccio's *Maestà*, from his studio to the high altar of the cathedral. Painted for the victory over the Florentines at

Duccio di Buoninsegna, Maestà, 1309. Museo dell'Opera del Duomo, Siena.

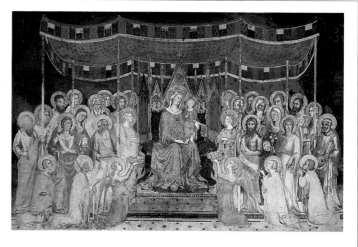

Montaperti, even recorded by Dante in his Divine Comedy, the great altarpiece shows, on one side, the *Story of the New Testament* and, on the other, that of the enthroned Virgin and saints. Simone Martini painted his earliest surviving work, the large *Maestà* fresco

Simone Martini, Maestà, 1315. Palazzo Pubblico, Siena.

for Siena Town Hall, with similar celebratory intentions. He magnified the elegance of line and color with which Duccio had founded a new school of Sienese painting.

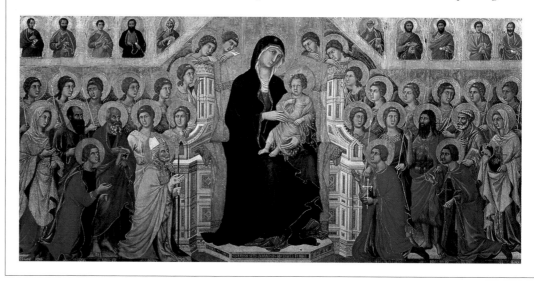

progressive economic and cultural exchanges with Europe north of the Alps. Such was the case with the strongly dramatic 14th-century Bolognese art, or that of Rimini, which was more courtly and emotive. Padua and Verona, touched by the influence of Giotto and by the emergence of strong personalities and active studios, were more inclined to Gothic linearism than to Tuscan plasticity. However, they were subject to Byzantine influences, still

preeminent in the unique case of Venice. Lombardy, which from the end of the 13th century tended toward realistic detail and immediacy of expression, created one of the highest periods of International Gothic. This style was characterized by a refined, exquisite sense of grace and elegance. By 1350, the great innovator Giovanni da Milano (active 1346–69) was working in Florence; his major surviving work is the decoration of the

Rinuccini chapel in Santa Croce. The great exponent of the international Gothic style was Gentile di Fabriano (c.1370–1427) from central Italy. He became master of the typically exquisite style that swept through Europe. The circulation of illuminated books, which had spread artistic innovations in the early Middle Ages, had now been reinforced by the more direct and radical migration of artists themselves. In Italian commercial and religious centers, the ascendancy of Giottesque painting reversed the flow. Filippo Rusuti was invited by the king of France to paint at Poitiers and at Saint-Denis in the first decades of the 14th century; a little after 1320, the great Parisian miniaturist Jean Pucelle arrived in Tuscany, where he was able to acquire a sounder mastery of the use of space to pass on to his French colleagues; and Matteo Giovannetti of Viterbo was involved in the decoration of the Papal See at Avignon, allowing Italian advances in plasticity to penetrate the linear style of Burgundy. Artists,

Altichiero, Crucifixion, *Basilica del Santo, San Giacomo Chapel, Padua, 1374–79. The composition, crowded but balanced, expresses the taste for Gothic detail.*

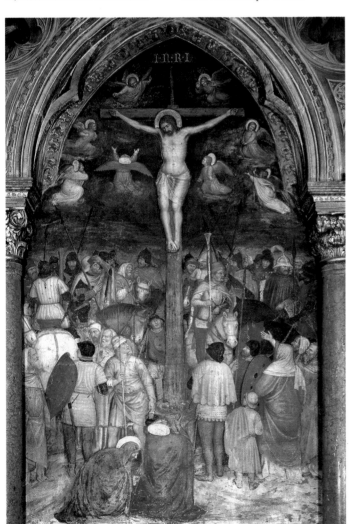

perhaps from Naples, painted frescoes in the castle of Esztergom in Hungary; Charles VI commissioned works from Tommaso da Modena for Prague and Karlstein; more than once, painters from the Venetian school took what they had learned from Giotto and Altichiero (active 1369–84) to Austria, as in the Abbey of San Floriano and the Stefansdom in Vienna. During the 14th century, the number of medieval pilgrim trails increased and led to new destinations comparable with the established holy routes to Santiago, Rome, and Jerusalem.

The construction sites of cathedrals and palaces were also meeting places where architects and builders from all over Europe could

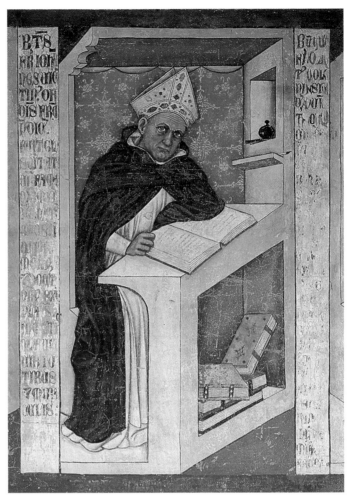

exchange ideas. In order to work in these centers, where architecture, painting, and sculpture interacted to meet the rapidly changing requirements of the buildings and their patrons, artists required a grounding in all artistic forms. Of all the arts, drawing became the unifying factor and, at the same time, an instrument of visual emancipation, by virtue of its capacity to reexplore constantly the ideal forms of real objects. Albums of drawings were compiled, few of which survive today. However, those that do survive testify to the growing need for common

Tommaso da Modena, Albertus Magnus, *Seminary, Dominican capitulary, Treviso, 1352. The fresco shows a doctor of the Church and is part of the* Life of St. Nicholas *cycle.*

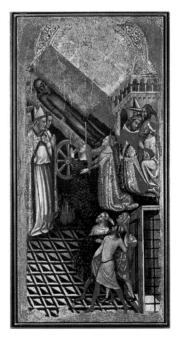

Vitale (degli Equi) da Bologna, Bishop Theophilus Taking the Body of the Saint to Constantinople, *begun 1351. Pinacoteca Nazionale, Bologna. This shows an episode from the* Life of St. Anthony.

principles, as in the *Livre de Portraiture* of Villard d'Honnecourt (13th century), and to the demand for models and studies, as in the *Taccuino* of Giovanni De' Grassi.

Alongside the artist, the figure of the commissioning patron also became more visible. Inscriptions, or *tituli*, placed within paintings recorded their names, often beside those of the artists. A later innovation, however, was the inclusion actually within the painting of the donor's image, almost always shown in an attitude of devotion and sometimes positioned to balance the composition, as in *San Ludovico di Tolosa* by Simone Martini, where the donor, Robert of Anjou, appears in the painting. This was one of the ways in which the artistic convention of portraiture became established.

DIVERGING PATHS

The Pisan artist Francesco Traini was *au courant* with the painting of Avignon. In the second half of the 14th century, the subject of death became a focus for artists. Among the works produced was the *Triumph of Death*, identified by some as by the same Traini. Coastal towns attracted lively exchanges of skills and artistic styles. Of particular interest was the Angevin court of Naples, where Giotto, di Bianco, and Pietro came into contact with the French style that was prominent in the royal palace. The consequences of this are most apparent in the mid-14th century in the activity of Roberto Oderisi (second half of the 14th century), splendidly attested by the decoration of the Incoronata church in Naples. His influence reached as far

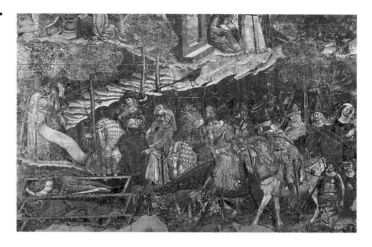

Master of the Triumph of Death, Triumph of Death, left-hand side of the fresco, Camposanto, Pisa, c.1336.

as Palermo, a port much engaged in the importing of every type of art.

In the area around Padua, highly distinctive schools of painting, capable of great expression, joined together and expanded. This was also the case in Bologna, where the university had a continuing relationship with Paris, chiefly by way of manuscripts; this partly

explains why Bolognese miniatures met with such success. Highly sensitive to the linear style from France, Vitale da Bologna (c.1309–60) appeared in about the mid-14th century, the founder of the city's school of painting and a

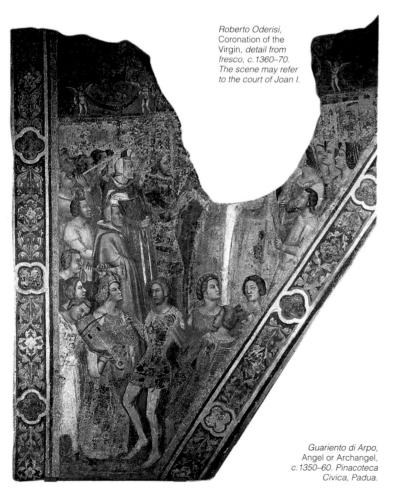

Roberto Oderisi, Coronation of the Virgin, detail from fresco, c.1360–70. The scene may refer to the court of Joan I.

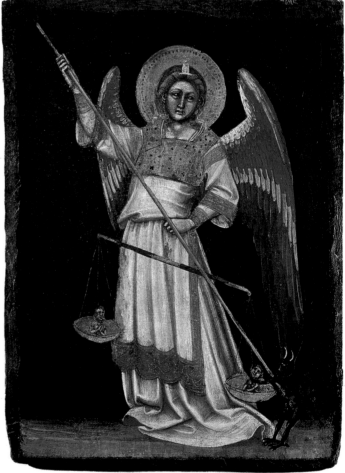

Guariento di Arpo, Angel or Archangel, c.1350–60. Pinacoteca Civica, Padua.

figurative, intensely expressive interpreter of Gothic composition and color.

Two very different artists from Modena found their way out of the Emilia region. One was Tommaso, who was active mainly in Treviso. He had a courtly taste in painting and a sharp eye for costume, which may have earned him the commissions from the court of Prague. The other was Barnaba (active 1367–83), who settled in Genoa to take commissions that still required Byzantine elements – though with a hint of Paduan vitality. The courts of Padua and Verona encouraged the activity of local artists, who, drawing on the impressive landscapes by Giotto, renewed the traditional Byzantine language and achieved results of great formal elegance, as in the *Angelic Hierarchies* by Guariento di Arpo (active

1338–70). Giusto de' Menabuoi (c.1330–90) moved in 1370 to Padua, where his virtuosity in depicting throngs of people in dynamic architectural settings using delicate color was realized. Altichiero was at work here in the same decade, following Giotto's example in creating great narrative cycles, in which dense urban scenes and pictures crammed with crowds of people are set into solid spatial and compositional structures. Lombard painting of the late 13th century reveals a propensity for realism and narrative style, especially in the secular cycle at the castle of Angera. An analogy is to be found in the frescoes of Matris Domini in Bergamo, in those of Sant'Abbondio in Como, and in the lively decorative illustration of the *Liber Pantheon*. The influence of Giotto's stay in

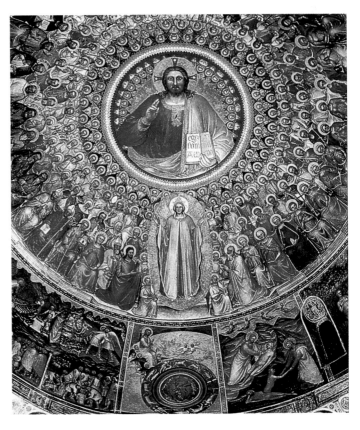

Giusto de' Menabuoi, Pantocrator, *Baptistry Vault, Padua, 1375–78.*

THE CITY

The Effects of Good and Bad Government in the Town and in the Country (1337–39), painted by Ambrogio Lorenzetti for the Sala dei Nove in the Palazzo Pubblico in Siena, shows in a broad, flowing manner that which, more synthetically, is the meaning of the statue from a door in Milan, of *Saint Ambrose Offering the City of Milan to the*

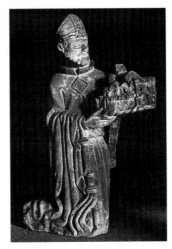

Ambrogio Lorenzetti, The Effects of Good and Bad Government in the Town, *1337–39, Palazzo Pubblico, Siena.*

After Giovanni Balduccio, St. Ambrose Offering the City of Milan to the Virgin, *mid-14th century. Civic Collection of Ancient Art, Milan.*

Virgin. The same urban focus of the two works – one representing the point of communication between the city and the world outside, and the other representing civic responsibility – has a clear symbolic meaning of the relationship between Christian virtue and orderly society. As bishop of Milan in the 14th century, St. Ambrose stood against the emperor and imposed civic moral order.

Milan (1335–36) was first seen in the *Crucifixion* of San Gottardo in Milan, in the *Storie Mariane* in Chiaravalle, and in the abbey of the Humiliati in Viboldone, which was also visited by Giusto de' Menabuoi. In the middle of the century, Giovanni da Milano, who had previously trained in Lombardy, began working in Florence on the frescoes in the Rinuccini Chapel of Santa Croce and on the exquisite *Pietà* (1365). The meeting between Tuscan formal strength and Lombard expressiveness is documented in the hagiographic cycles of the oratories of Mocchirolo, Lentate, and Solare. It was against this background, marked by the presence of Petrarch and by the creation of the extraordinary library of Pavia, that one of the most important schools of illustration came to maturity. Works such as *Guiron le Curtois, Lancelot du Lac,* and the *Messale 757* were produced, as well as

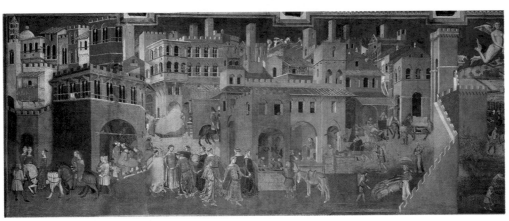

illustrations by Giovannino De' Grassi for Gian Galeazzo Visconti's *Book of Hours.* Lombard sacred painting favored frescoes to painting on panels; altarpieces were generally sculpted in marble or wood or were substituted by objects of gold or silver, following the more refined

Master of the Wilton Diptych, Richard III presented to the Virgin, *c.1400. National Gallery, London.*

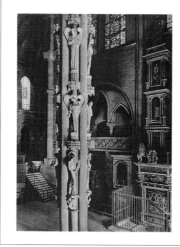

taste of the court. The Lombard influence was soon felt in Piedmont where, from the late 13th to the early 14th century, a strongly expressive Gallic style asserted itself, as in Sant'Antonio in Ranverso. In France, too, thanks to court patrons, first in Paris then in Burgundy, the elements of renewal in figurative culture were to be found mainly in illustrated books. Although the large Parisian frescoes disappeared, as in the Sainte-Chapelle and old Louvre palace, important cycles can still be found in the Haute-Loire and at Toulouse, where the close relationship with the art of illumination can be identified, as can Italian influences. Panel painting (much of which has been lost) centered on Paris, at least until 1380, where the aesthetic ideals formulated at the time of Saint Louis IX were developed. New stimuli came from Italian artists working in Avignon, especially toward the mid-14th century, and from Flemish artists based in Paris, Bourges, and Dijon, who were more closely involved with book illustration. Evidence of this, toward the end of the century, can be seen in the celebrated *Wilton Diptych*, painted in Paris for English patrons.

Few frescoes remain in England, and most painting is preserved in manuscript form – much of it influenced by the earlier Celtic libraries and

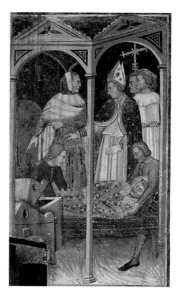

The Master of Lombardy, Translation of the Body of St. Stephen, *c.1380. Oratorio di Lentate sul Seveso, Milan.*

scholaria in the monasteries. In England, Matthew Paris was a monk of St. Albans, a historian and prolific illustrator (active 1217–59). He has left evidence of lively exchanges in court and ecclesiastical circles of both a

---

THE BOHEMIAN COURT OF CHARLES IV

Born in Prague, Charles IV of Luxembourg (1316–78) became the third emperor of the Holy Roman Empire (1355–78). He was one of the most sophisticated and adventurous rulers of his day, founding the spa town of Karlsbad (now Karlovy Vary). As a child, he grew up in the cultured court of his mother's family in Paris and later moved to northern Italy. Praised by Petrarch before his death in 1378, he succeeded in becoming king of Bohemia, Germany, Italy, and Burgundy, as well as becoming Holy Roman Emperor. During his reign, art and architecture flourished: he founded the university, the Karolinum, and built the famous bridge over the Moldau and the castle of Karlstein (started in 1348), a favorite residence of his. Charles IV's greatest master builder in Prague was Peter Parler, who directed the building of the cathedral from 1352. Architecture was by no means the only branch of the arts to flourish under Charles IV. Miniaturists from this period bequeathed exquisite codices, such as the *Velislav Bible,* the *Liber Viaticus* of John of Neumarkt, and the *Evangeliarum* of John of Troppau.

THE HARMONY OF ARCHITECTURE AND SCULPTURE

The capitals of Milan Cathedral and the *Pilasters of the Angels* testify to the great constant of Gothic cathedrals – the close relationship between architecture and sculpture. This is not merely

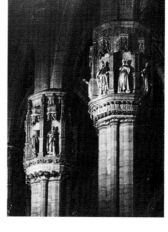

decorative but is of great iconographic meaning. The *Pilasters of the Angels*, inside the portals of the transept of Strasbourg Cathedral, date from 1220 to 1225. The sculptor, who had probably worked on the site at Chartres,

Pilasters of the Angels, *Strasbourg Cathedral, 1220–25.*

Capitals in Milan Cathedral, late 14th century.

placed the angels inside false niches formed by Gothic brackets and pediments made to represent the city. This figurative tradition, widespread on the portals and facades of the cathedrals, was to find a new application in the capitals of Milan Cathedral. Completed at the end of the 14th century to designs by Giovannino De' Grassi, they were criticized by the Frenchman Jean Mignot. However, the church authorities replied that they respected proportions analogous to Vitruvian rationality, and that their decorative merit was strictly related to the iconography. The "Gallery of Saints" was transferred from the portals and facades to the pilasters, where it lined the pathway of the faithful to the altar.

AVIGNON

During the 14th century, the Papal Seat was centered at Avignon. As desired by Benedict XII, the main pontifical residence reflected the image of a castle-convent, characterized by turrets and high walls. The Palazzo Nuovo, commissioned in the middle of the century by Clement VI, conceived the interior as a sumptuous court, with salons, great stairways, and halls.

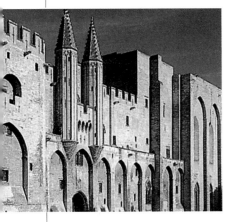

Everywhere, decorations abounded with corbels, portals, and windows designed with great finesse. In these rooms and the adjoining chapels, the full flowering of the Avignon pictorial school could be found, with the refined realism of Matteo Giovannetti meeting the graphic elegance of French artists. Matteo, who painted the frescoes between 1343 and 1347 in the chapels of San Marziale and San Giovanni, reproduced the strong Tuscan architectonic style of the early 14th century in a lively chromatic way. In many rooms, there were courtly scenes in elegant natural surroundings, in which every action and detail carried a moral message that ensured its popularity in ecclesiastical residences.

Papal Palace, Avignon, 1342–52.

Matteo Giovannetti, Ezekiel and Jeremiah, audience chamber, Papal Palace, Avignon, 1342–52.

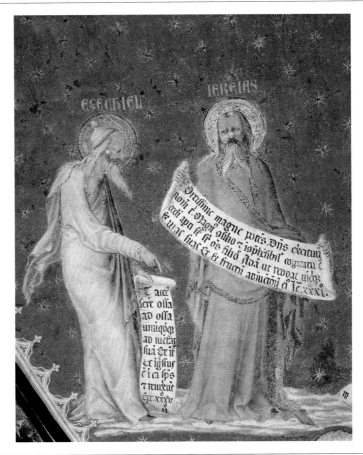

literary and graphic kind. His restless line shows amusing, graceful figures full of activity. Another important example of English manuscript art is the *Douce Apocalypse* painting (late 1260s), which dramatized

Petites Heures of the Duc de Berry, Nativity, c.1410. Bibliothèque Nationale, Paris.

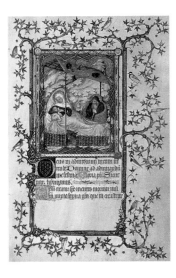

Revelation and pictured exuberant figures. Executed with linear confidence, they also suggest drawing from life and have a sense of volume. A rare example of English panel painting is the Retable at Westminster Abbey (mid-

Giovannino De' Grassi, letterhead of the Offiziolo of Gian Galeazzo Visconti. Biblioteca Nazionale, Florence.

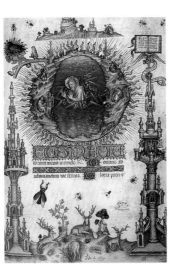

13th century) made at the time French and Italian artists visited the court of Henry III, bringing the sinuous line and delicate detail of the international style. Melchior Broederlam (active 1381–1409), who painted the altarpiece of the Charterhouse of Champmol, was also influenced by book illustration. In this Charterhouse, Claus Sluter brought Burgundian sculpture to new heights of artistic expression: the *Annunciation* of the portal and the *Moses' Well* are remarkable for their strength of composition, finely drawn figures, and deep emotion. Illustration had already begun a process of international renewal, thanks to Jean Pucelle (active c.1319), who incorporated into his delicate yet dynamic linearity a formal solidity and narrative style that were of clear Italian origin. Flemish influence brought an even greater,

distinctly bourgeois, realism. The Duc de Berry and Philip the Bold created two of the most refined courts in Europe, attended by great illustrators such as Hainaut and the Master of Boucicaut, who achieved extraordinary power of expression through freedom of design and intensity of color. In the middle of the 14th century, the imperial court of Charles IV transformed Prague into a great artistic center. In about 1340, Sienese delicacy arrived in Bohemia with the Master of the Altar of Hohenfurt. In 1357, the castle of Karlstein accommodated artists of varying tastes and backgrounds: alongside the Italian tone introduced by Tommaso da Modena, there were elements of a sharper realism in the Kreuzkapelle. Prague, too, would have a great sculptor and architect in Peter Parler, who, with a new realism, would influence the artistic vision of all Europe.

THE EARLY RENAISSANCE

In the 15th century, humanism, a new intellectual movement, broke with medieval scholastic traditions and renewed an appreciation of language, literature, and the wonders of the ancient world. In Italy, artists looked back to the art of Rome, while, in Flemish cities, the sense of "renewal" was expressed in a move toward greater naturalism. The combination of these two interpretations gave birth to modern European art.

Interest in the classical world had never been very strong in the Middle Ages. However, it emerged as the driving force in the development of European culture from the middle of the 15th century, a period of revival known as the Renaissance. The recovery and imitation of ancient texts and classical sculptures led to a marked transformation of intellectual life, which encompassed the study of human relations in literature (hence the term humanism) as well as philosophy, art, and historical biography. Those engaged in the rediscovery of Latin and Greek texts, including the poets Petrarch (1304–74) and Poliziano (1454–94), were also interested in art and artists. The study of classical authors and their works, notably Pliny (AD23–79) and his *Historia Naturalis,* and *De Architectura* (before AD27) by Vitruvius, favored

Lorenzo Ghiberti, Joseph in Egypt, *Porta del Paradiso, Baptistry, Florence, 1425–52.*

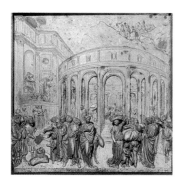

THE COMPETITION OF 1401

In 1401, the *Arte di Calimala*, a merchant guild, commissioned a competition for the design of a pair of bronze doors for the Baptistry in Florence. The subject given was the sacrifice of Isaac by his father Abraham. Seven Florentine sculptors were chosen to compete, including the young Lorenzo Ghiberti (1378–1455), a trained painter and goldsmith, and Filippo Brunelleschi (1377–1446). In both reliefs, the theme is of divine intervention. The boy is on the altar with his father putting the knife to his throat, the angel intervenes, and the ram is visible in the background. The ass drinks water between the two servants. The guild preferred Ghiberti's subtle, beautiful, and more spiritual composition, but Brunelleschi's is the more dramatic and daring work, full of naturalistic observations and tensions.

Filippo Brunelleschi, The Sacrifice of Isaac, *1402. Museo Nazionale del Bargello, Florence.*

Lorenzo Ghiberti, The Sacrifice of Isaac, *1402. Museo Nazionale del Bargello, Florence.*

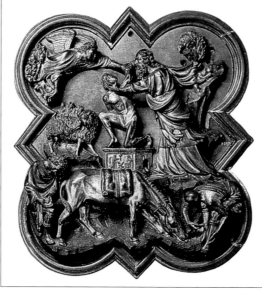

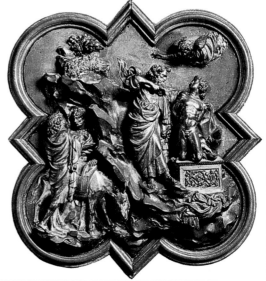

an upsurge in the ideal of "rebirth." This concept of revival also found expression in the figurative arts and in architecture. It ranged from the *Triumphs of Caesar,* created by Andrea Mantegna (1431–1506) for the court of the Gonzagas, who ruled Mantua for 300 years, to the design by Leon Battista Alberti (c.1404–72) for the Tempio Malatestiano, Rimini. The link between humanist studies and the figurative arts was particularly evident in the methods used for the interpretation of art itself; these were initially borrowed from classical rhetoric: *ekfrasis,* an analytical and descriptive narrative system, became the basis on which humanist circles in the Po Valley judged and appreciated the delicate and fantastical art of Pisanello (c.1380–1455) and Gentile da Fabriano (c.1370–1420). Elsewhere, composition, which in the art of rhetoric was the essential element in the construction of a speech, became a principal criterion for artistic theory; this was cited by Leon Battista Alberti in his influential book

Jacopo della Quercia, Tomb of Ilaria del Carretto, *Duomo, Lucca, Italy, 1406–07. The sepulchre, commissioned by the ruler of Lucca in honor of his second wife, was decorated on the sides with classical motifs, cupids, and garlands in imitation of ancient sarcophagi.*

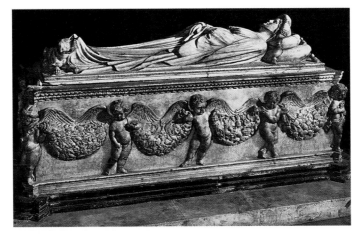

Andrea Mantegna, Trumpeters and Flag Bearers, *detail from the* Triumphs of Caesar, *1480–95. Royal Collection, Hampton Court, England. This work, which was created for the Gonzaga court, conveyed the power of Ancient Rome – a popular theme among the aristocracy.*

JACOPO DELLA QUERCIA

The greatest Sienese sculptor of the 15th century, Jacopo della Quercia (c.1371–1438) was a contradictory man whose work successfully combined Gothic and Renaissance elements. His tomb for Ilaria del Carretto is one of the most serene masterpieces of its time. The reliefs for San Pietro in Bologna show a classical energy and strong realism; they inspired Michelangelo, who saw them in 1494. Among his other masterpieces are the *Fonte Gaia* (1414–19) in Siena and the polyptych of the Trenta family at San Frediano, Lucca.

De Pictura (1435), a work marking the transition from medieval attitudes to the new humanist outlook on the arts. This link with the literary world shows a desire to instill in the figurative arts a sense of social interaction and responsibility.

Change was also seen in architecture, thanks partly to the architectural theory of Antonio Averlino, known as Filarete (c.1400–69), which attempted to explain in scientific terms the component pieces of construction. The literary influences on painting and sculpture changed decisively after the last medieval book of prescriptions, dating from the late 14th century. Writings on art such as those by Leonardo da Vinci (1452–1519) and Albrecht Dürer (1471–1528) now gained greater authority.

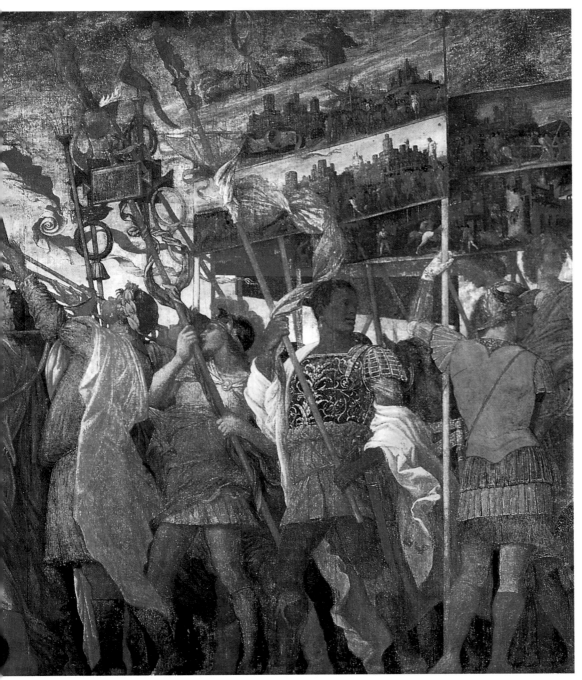

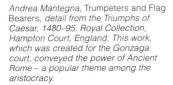

Donatello, St. George, *1417. Museo Nazionale del Bargello, Florence. This statue was specifically designed to fit an external niche in the church of Orsanmichele in Florence.*

NEW IDEAS

The revival of antique texts and sculptures led to a general feeling of artistic rebirth, typified by the pioneering art history book *Lives of the Most Excellent Painters, Sculptors, and Architects* by Giorgio Vasari (1511–74). This was published in its expanded form in 1568. The literary form of biography had been developed by the 15th century, particularly in Tuscany. In works such as Ghiberti's *Commentari* (c.1445) and the anonymous *Life of Filippo Brunelleschi*, the authors combined praise of one or more artists with an emphasis on the primacy of new "modern" ideas over traditional values. The beginnings of the *rinascita*, or "rebirth," especially in painting, are identified with the movement toward realism as instigated by Cimabue (c.1240–c.1302) and Giotto (1267–1337) during the 14th century. According to Vasari, this Golden Age advanced from

THE PATH OF EUROPEAN NATURALISM

In the North, Flemish art was transformed by the dramatic and lively naturalistic style, which had its roots in Florence and traveled north via Burgundy. The Flemish environment, which nurtured van Eyck (died 1441) and the Master of Flémalle, (thought to be Robert Campin, active 1406–44), was a place of learning and of the diffusion of knowledge, as were Burgundy and central southern Germany. They were all receptive to influences and new ideas from elsewhere. Here, Konrad Witz (c.1400–46) achieved his forceful vision of realism through sculptural form and a meticulous attention to detail, while Stephan Lochner (1410–51) used shaded colors and a luminous opalescence, reminiscent of the work of Stefano da Verona (1379–c.1438). The network of ecclesiastical and trading relationships that was active in the 15th century favored a continuous exchange of works and ideas between countries. The work of the great French miniaturist and painter Jean Fouquet (1420–81) spanned and combined elements of Flemish, French, and Italian painting. The works resulting from his stay in Rome in 1447, such as the *Diptych of Melun* (c.1450), echo the Roman style of Filarete, Fra Angelico, and

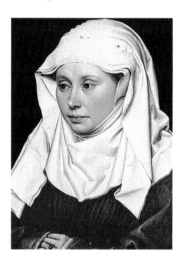

Robert Campin, Portrait of a Lady, c.1420–30. National Gallery, London.

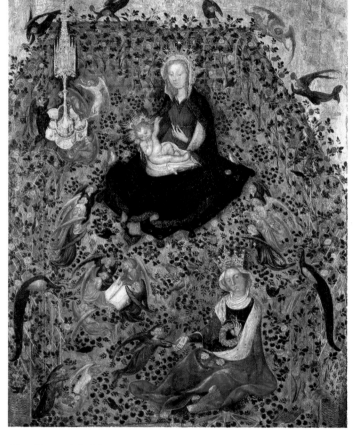

Stefano da Verona, Madonna of the Rose Garden, c.1420. Castelvecchio, Verona.

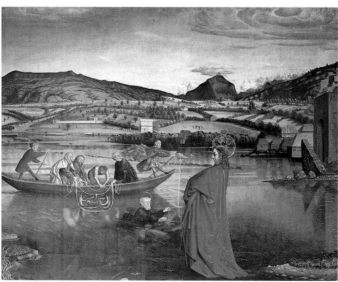

Konrad Witz, The Miraculous Draft of Fishes, *1444. Musée d'Art et d'Histoire, Geneva.*

Masolino, while his miniatures, such as the *Antiquités judaïques*, reveal his imagination at its most expressive. Another artist who was able to blend Flemish influences with those of the Po Valley was the Spaniard Bartolomé Bermejo (c.1440–1500), whose work shows strong links with van Eyck's intense naturalism. This Spanish style, which was resonant with Flemish and Burgundian echoes, reached Naples and influenced the work of Colantonio (active c.1440–70) and members of his workshop. Ludovico Sforza, the Duke of Milan, also arranged for illuminated codices for wedding plans to be sent from the principal Milanese studios to the court of Aragon. It might have been expected that this variety would result in an uneasy juxtaposition of conflicting styles, but the clear and penetrating naturalism of the portraits of Antonello da Messina, as well as those by Colantonio himself, prove this was a successful combination.

THE DOME OF SANTA MARIA DEL FIORE

In his enthusiastic report of Filippo Brunelleschi's dome (1420–36) for Santa Maria del Fiore, Florence, Leon Battista Alberti records the "structure so great, challenging the sky, wide enough to cover with its shadow all the people of Tuscany." Brunelleschi's *Vita* and Ghiberti's *Commentari* give two very different accounts of the competition for its design. The dome needed to be set on an existing octagonal drum constructed during the 14th century according to a plan by Arnolfo di Cambio. Manetti describes Brunelleschi waiting to be called by the wardens of the cathedral and the consuls

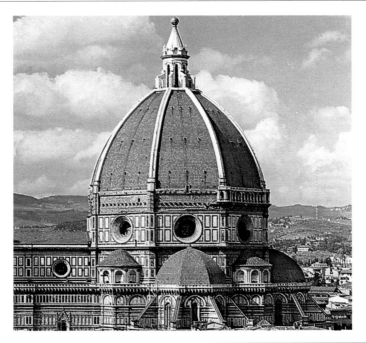

of the Wool Guild, who would soon realize that he was the only architect capable of raising a dome large enough to cover the tribune without the help of scaffolding. Ghiberti claimed that the project was the result of a collaboration, which was then abandoned because he had other work to carry out. Brunelleschi dismissed "centering" and, instead, created a curtain wall and two vaults that allowed the dome to support itself, rising toward the lantern. The discovery of this engineering technique has always been attributed to Brunelleschi, who transformed and modernized this 14th-century building.

Filippo Brunelleschi, dome of Santa Maria del Fiore, Florence.

the art of Masaccio (1401–28) through to works by Perugino (c.1450–1523) toward a newfound natural truth; he wrote in 1550: "we shall see all things infinitely improved, compositions with many more figures, richer in ornamentation; and design that is better grounded and more true to life…the style lighter, the colors more delicate, so that the arts will be close to perfection and to the exact imitation of the truth of nature." The changes from the Gothic

style that occured in architecture are more difficult to recognize. The design of the dome of Santa Maria del Fiore by Brunelleschi followed the classical experiments of Alberti, and it was later praised by Alberti in his first theoretical work on the arts, *De Pictura,* which he dedicated to (among other leading artists) Brunelleschi and which earned him a

Filippo Brunelleschi, central and side aisles in San Lorenzo, Florence, c.1420.

reputation as a supreme innovator. The complex changes of the time also affected the Rome of Popes Eugenius IV and Nicholas V. After the schismatic crisis of Avignon in 1377, they intended to reaffirm the central authority of the See of Saint Peter by emphasizing the Imperial and Christian past of the city and by defining the requirements for the reconstruction of the Vatican basilica in terms that still expressed the Gothic aesthetic. For example, Nicholas V's famous *Testamento* placed great emphasis on light and refinement.

The return to classicism, whether as the standard for harmony and proportion in the design of monuments or in the revival of details from antiquity, became a distinguishing factor in the development of the new architecture. Brunelleschi demonstrated this change in taste and renewed interest in classical style in the designs of his two Florentine basilicas, San Lorenzo and Santo Spirito, where he tackled the problems of Vitruvius' theory of order and attempted to create an

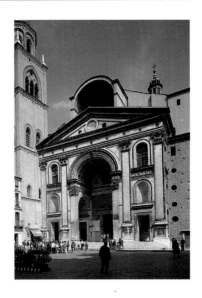

Leon Battista Alberti, facade with triumphal arch of the church of Sant'Andrea, Mantua, Italy, 1470.

ordered, harmonious balance that paralleled the discovery of perspective by painters at the same time. Brunelleschi's meticulous design for the capitals commemorated the most prestigious Roman remains and were probably perfected during a stay in the city. The preference in the Tuscan Romanesque style for the inclusion of marble in the walls also recalls classical models.

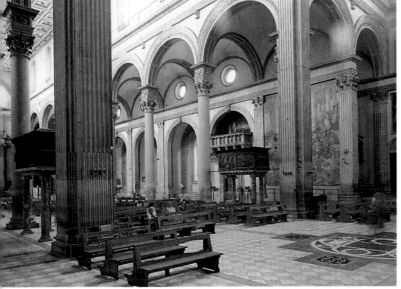

SCIENTIFIC PERSPECTIVE

The new direction taken by the arts in its quest for linear perspective cannot be attributed to the revived interest in antiquity alone. It is significant that the architect Brunelleschi was the first to raise the problem of perceiving depth in rational and mathematical terms. He did so, initially, with his panel for the competition of 1401 for the door of the Florentine baptistry and, later, in his experiments in perspective that are recounted by his biographers. The most striking evidence lies in Brunelleschi's architectural works, in which space is immediately perceived according to his unifying, linear perspectival definition. Similarly, in painting and sculpture – most notably, in the works of Masaccio and Donatello – perspective re-interpreted the realism of Giotto and Arnolfo. Structural orderliness led to a definition of depth, which was characterized by a unifying principle that reconciled real and figurative space. Alberti likened a painting to a window open to the world in which, thanks to "legitimate construction" or perspective, the true representation of the relationship

Domenico Veneziano, altarpiece of the Magnolias, Galleria degli Uffizi, Florence, 1445–47. Domenico was the first Venetian to be influenced by Florentine art and artists such as Fra Angelico and Filippo Lippi.

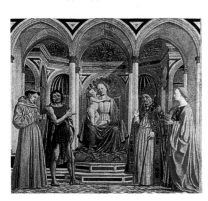

MASACCIO: "THE HOLY TRINITY"

Fresco; 22 x 10 ft (6.67 x 3.17 m); Santa Maria Novella, Florence; c.1426–28.

This work is possibly the last piece created by Masaccio, who died at the age of 27 in 1428. The fresco, a representation of the Trinity, broke new ground in painting. It depicts an altar within the interior of the chapel, which is notable for the vigorous treatment of its architecture and the variety of building materials – chiefly brick, plaster, marble, and stucco – included. Two columns with Ionic capitals support an arch, behind which a barrel-vaulted coffered ceiling, drawn in perspective, recedes toward a second arch, also supported by columns. Against this painted impression of space and depth hangs the crucified Christ. Behind him is

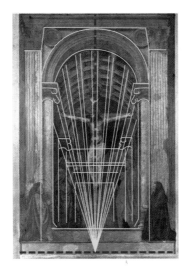

▲ *1. The building depicted in the fresco was inspired by Brunelleschi's architecture. The perspective gives an impression of a concrete space in which the columns and the figures strikingly stand out. The horizon line and the vanishing point have been drawn according to the central perspective system, with the horizon line placed above the altar to accentuate the height of the chapel. A collection of lines, forming acute angles from the point of origin, follows the supporting lines of the capitals. Slight irregularities in the height of the figures and the near-axial position of the Trinity breathe life into the painting, giving the viewer a very real sense of standing inside a chapel before a sacred image.*

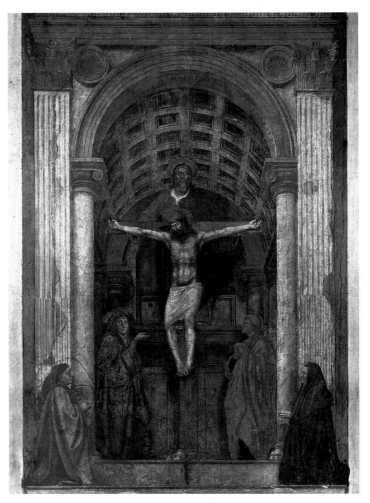

God, bearded and strong, and between their two heads the Holy Spirit is shown as a white dove in flight. Standing on the chapel floor beside the Cross are, on the left, the Virgin and, on the right, St. John. By the entrance step, seen in profile, are the kneeling figures of a man and a woman, the donors of the work, depicted as suppliants. This hierarchical arrangement, with God at the top and the donors at the bottom, conforms to medieval interpretation. Below the altar scene is a skeleton, with an inscription warning of the transience of life (not shown here).

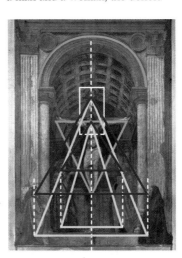

◄ *2. The composition is dominated by the triangle representing the Trinity. The positions of the divine and human figures, and the space allotted to them, is determined by their importance. Four regular triangles, with the vertex pointing upward, link the human figures to the divine, while the Crucifix is contained in a triangle with its vertex pointing downward. Regular quadrilaterals unite the lower pairs of figures and the Trinity. The Divinity is enclosed inside an arc, and the triangle with its vertex pointing downward, in which hangs the figure of Christ, links the divine to the human.*

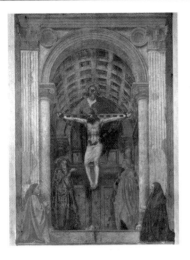

◀ 3. The artist has not distinguished the human figures from the divine by size or matter. However, the donors, Lorenzo Leni and his wife, are outside the sacred space of the chapel, while the foreshortened figures of St. John and the Virgin Mary are positioned inside the sacred area. The Virgin, with her hand and glance turning outward, acts as the channel between the divine and the human. Christ and God the Father are viewed from the front, with God shown full face, to be contemplated by the viewer. The wings of the Holy Spirit are curved, focusing the observer's attention on the head of Christ as it flies from the Father.

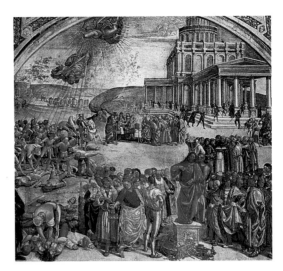

Luca Signorelli, Story of the Antichrist, Chapel of San Brizio, Duomo, Orvieto, 1499–1504. The cycle containing this work marks the apogee of Signorelli's art. Possibly a pupil of Piero della Francesca, he was capable of creating scenes in perspective that were full of vitality and diverse figurative poses.

▶ 4. Masaccio's treatment of color reveals a subtle rhythm. The soft tones accentuate the silence surrounding the mystery of the Trinity, while the divine figures emerge from the dominant tones of gray and red. The donors stand out against the background: on the right, the somber gray of the woman is placed beside the rust-red of St. John, while, on the left, the flame-red of the male figure's robes contrasts with the Virgin's dark gray robes. God's mantle is red on the Virgin's side and gray on St. John's side. Architraves, arches, and the ledge on which God's feet are defined in red, while the verticals in the painting are defined by shades of gray.

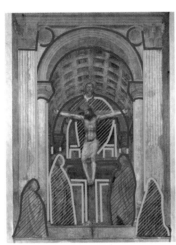

between the elements depicted can be seen. This definition of space, where everything converges toward a single vanishing point – the story line, the arrangement of the figures, and the measured play of light and color – provided the ideal form for Florentine painting in the early 15th century. This new point of departure can be seen in the work of Masaccio, from the polyptych for the Santa Maria del Carmine in Pisa (1426) to the cycle of the Brancacci chapel, Florence (1427), in which the aim to portray the state of mind and moral positions of the main figures is always apparent. The need to depict emotions and inner turmoil continued to grow in importance during the 15th century, reaching its zenith in the work of Leonardo.

FLEMISH ART

An equally strong realistic movement in Flanders and Spain led to a style of painting that analyzed objects in the most minute detail. The goal of the artists of this movement was to achieve as high a level of realism as possible. Employing many and varied techniques of color application for the maximum impact, this pursuit of ideal representations of reality relied on the sheer luminosity of the colors. The portrait painting of Jan van Eyck (c.1390–1441), Hans Memling (c.1440–94), and Rogier van der Weyden (c.1400–64) achieved high levels of expressiveness and insight. Their artistic approach won strong

▼ 5. The donors kneel in contemplation, portrayed as people fully aware of their own humble place in the sacred story. The pyramidal balance of the folds of their mantles are conspicuous against the pale color of the columns on either side. The subtlety with which the age, sex, character, and social status are rendered, together with the strength of their profiles and hands, produces two fully formed, fairly naturalistic characters. Vasari commented of the artist: "It was Masaccio who perceived that the best painters followed nature as closely as possible…" In contrast, the divine figures are less well characterized; individualism has no place in beings of spirit and faith.

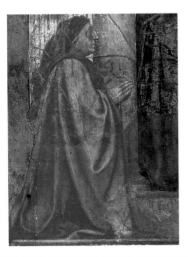

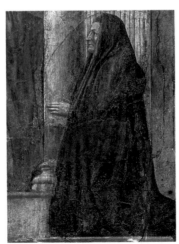

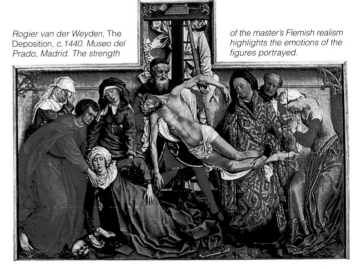

Rogier van der Weyden, The Deposition, c.1440. Museo del Prado, Madrid. The strength of the master's Flemish realism highlights the emotions of the figures portrayed.

support from the *Devotio Moderna*, a religious movement active from the middle of the 14th century onward. The group's spirituality relied on personal immersion in the sacred story.

The impact on iconography can be seen in the narrative composition of sacred works of art and in the heightened realism of the details, a common characteristic of northern European art.

FRA ANGELICO'S FRESCOES IN SAN MARCO, FLORENCE

The frescoes painted in the cells of the monastery of San Marco by Giovanni da Fiesole (1387–1455), better known as Fra Angelico, are evidence of the close rapport between the new pictorial ideas of the 15th century and the contemporary *osservante* ("observance") reforms of the most important religious orders. In fact, the *osservanza* required the renewal of the original Dominican Rule and a grounding in contemporary affairs through preaching. This phenomenon was linked to the spirituality of the Flemish *Devotio Moderna*, which centered around a symbolic union with the life of Christ. Fra Angelico and his fellow monks chose to portray events from the Passion, often accompanied by the figure of a Dominican in meditation. These simple but vivid representations made use of the recent advances in perspective and the depiction of space; every detail is drawn with a harmonious sense of geometry and proportion. The effect of color on light, central to the Dominican aesthetic, gave color the symbolic and natural values of immediate perception.

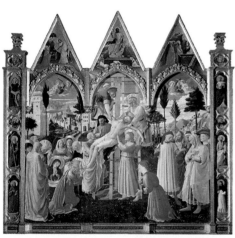

Fra Angelico, Deposition, 1430–34. Museo di San Marco, Florence. This work is known as the Santa Trinita altarpiece, because it was carried out for the church of that name; the three vertexes were painted by Lorenzo Monaco (c.1370–1422 or later).

Fra Angelico, Annunciation, Monastery of San Marco, Florence. 1438–46.

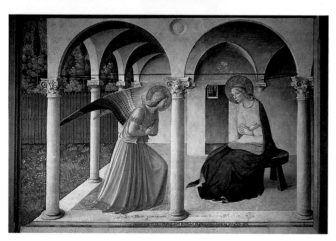

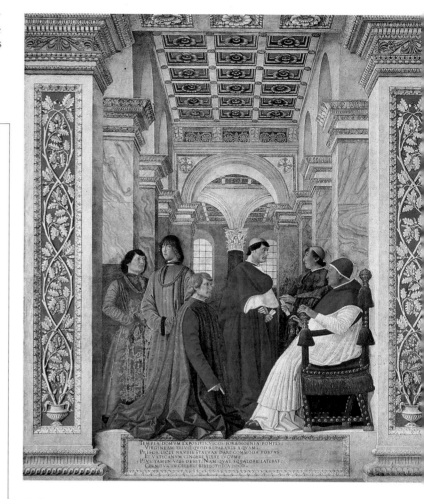

Melozzo da Forlì, Sixtus IV Appointing Platina, 1474–77. Vatican Museums, Vatican City. Melozzo, a pupil of Piero, combined amazing illusionistic effects with the realism he absorbed from Justus of Ghent.

DEVOTION AND HISTORY

To a certain extent, the Italian phenomenon *osservanza* was linked to the *Devotio Moderna*. Observance led the principal monastic orders to revive their original rules during the course of the 15th century in order to establish a more positive relevance to everyday life. Sacred art underwent a renewal in its didactic and devotional purposes. The concepts of spatial and compositional construction needed to be in keeping with the new expectations of art – of its imagery and what was communicated, which were increasingly shaped by a growing need for self-identification. This change in style and its subsequent development in Dominican circles can be seen in the frescoes painted by Fra Angelico in the cells of the monastery of San Marco in Florence, and in Leonardo's *The Last Supper* (c.1495) in the refectory of Santa Maria delle Grazie in Milan. The cult of the Immaculate Conception, popular among the Franciscans, led to the mysterious iconography of *The Virgin of the Rocks* (1508), painted by Leonardo for the Milanese Foundation of San Francesco Grande. Many convent churches in the Po Valley and the Alps acquired very simple and didactic Passion cycles, which were often based on Nordic engravings, particularly those of Albrecht Dürer, which also dealt with the same

THE BRANCACCI CHAPEL

"From Giotto on, Masaccio is the most modern of all the old masters whom we have ever seen," wrote Vasari, who advised Michelangelo to teach everybody but to learn from only Masaccio. His fresco cycle of the life of St. Peter and other scenes in the Brancacci family chapel in the church of Santa Maria del Carmine, Florence, reveal a completely new approach, the success of which lies in its narrative synthesis. This relied on an assured creation of spatial depth to link the episodes through perspective and geometric structure, as can be seen, in *The Expulsion from Paradise*, in which the Archangel points to the world of chastisement. A more complex composition can be seen in the arrangement of the Apostles around Christ and Peter in *The Tribute Money*. Their heads are placed on the same level as those of the main protagonists, but they gradually recede while remaining in proportion. The faces, painted from Roman busts and full of concentration, are turned to Christ and Peter. Vasari wrote: "We see the boldness with which Peter questions Our Lord, and the attentiveness of the Apostles as they stand in various attitudes around Christ, waiting for His decision." In 1428, Masaccio went to Rome and left the Brancacci frescoes unfinished.

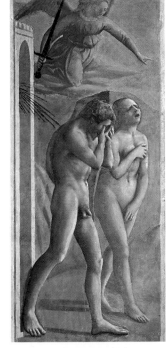

Masaccio, The Expulsion from Paradise, Brancacci Chapel, Santa Maria del Carmine, Florence, 1424–25.

Masaccio, The Tribute Money, Brancacci Chapel, Santa Maria del Carmine, Florence, c.1425.

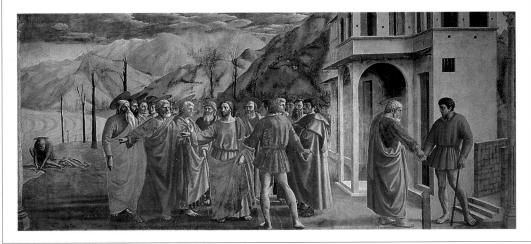

themes. The Augustinian monks, too, were encouraging figurative and architectonic art of the first order, from Santo Spirito in Florence to the Incoronata in Milan, and Santa Maria delle Grazie at Gravedona. Historical events had an impact on art, too. The ending of the pope's exile in Avignon and the return of the papal seat to Rome came about through a complex series of councils. The first ones were held in Constance (1414–18) and Basel (1431–37), followed by meetings in Ferrara and Florence (1437–39), where doctrinal and political problems were discussed, such as the nationalistic demands of Bohemia, the Jewish question in Spain, and the great effort to reunite the Eastern churches around St. Peter's See. From these debates arose the many Eucharistic themes tackled by artists all over Europe. In Ghent in 1432, the *Adoration of the Lamb* for St. Bavo was completed by Jan van Eyck (his brother Hubert died before finishing it); in Siena, Sassetta completed the polyptych (1423–24) for the Wool Guild; and, in Belgium, *The Last Supper* (1468) by Dieric Bouts was created as part of his major work, the Louvain altarpiece, which depicted the Sacraments of St. Peter.

THE TEMPIO MALATESTIANO

Sigismondo Malatesta, Lord of Rimini, decided to build a chapel as a family mausoleum in 1447. His chosen site was the convent church of San Francesco, where the Florentine artist Giotto had painted frescoes in the apse during the 13th century. The complete restoration of the building was planned by Leon Battista Alberti and executed by Matteo di Pasti of Verona. The decoration in relief was carried out by the Sienese painter Agostino di Duccio (1418–c.1481). San Francesco was transformed from a brick church into a secular "temple" (known as the Tempio Malatestiano), with a new external marble shell. The south facade recaptures the Vitruvian order with a copy of the triumphal arch of Augustus, flanked on each side by smaller, blind arches resembling Roman aqueducts. The pagan effect is created by the exquisite reliefs of Sigismondo, his wife Isotta, the Malatesta arms, cherubs, and signs of the Zodiac. The two huge elephants that support the sarcophagus represent the Malatesta heraldic emblem. The Tempio, however, remains unfinished. It is famous for its *Crucifixion*, a marvelous work possibly painted by Giotto in about 1310, as well as the fresco showing the tyrannical Sigismondo kneeling in prayer before the patron saint, a reference to a visit made by Piero della Francesca to the temple in 1451.

Interior of the first chapel on the left, Tempio Malatestiano, Rimini.

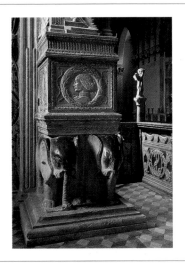

MANTEGNA IN MANTUA

When visiting Mantua in 1494, the great Giovanni de' Medici, the future Pope Leo X, expressed his admiration for the *camera picta* (painted room) and the decorated apartments in the Gonzagas' palace. The frescoes of the so-called *Camera degli Sposi* (1471–74) and the nine canvases depicting the *Triumphs of Caesar* (c.1484–95) were considered to be central to the role played by Mantegna and the Mantuan circle in paving the way for the "modern manner."

When Mantegna was appointed court painter at Mantua in 1460, he entered one of the key centers of humanist culture. His greatest contribution to that culture was the *Camera degli Sposi*, where he painted a series of frescoes to glorify his patrons, the Marquis Ludovico II Gonzaga and his wife. The frescoes depict group portraits of the Gonzaga family, scenes from court life, and images from classical mythology. Motifs from classical

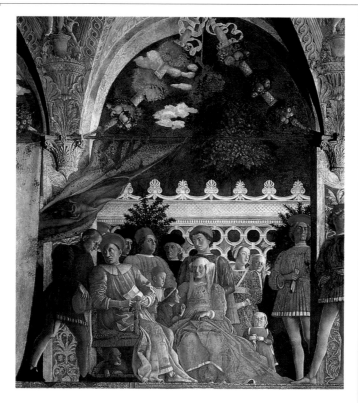

architecture and bust medallions of the Caesars were included – creating a clear visual link between the Gonzagas and the great figures of the Roman Empire.

Andrea Mantegna, Ludovico II with His Wife Barbara of Brandenburg, His Sons, and His Court, *detail from the frescoes in the* Camera degli Sposi, *Castello di San Giorgio, Mantua, 1471–74.*

certainties of medieval life. The *Uomini Illustri*, painted by Masolino (1383–c.1440) in the Palazzo Orsini di Montegiordano in Rome, probably served as a model for other cycles, such as that of Andrea del Castagno (c.1421–57) at the Villa di Legnaia. This included the *Uomini d'arme*, later copied by Bramante (1444–1514) in Milan for Gaspare Visconti. Similar intentions lay behind other iconographical themes, such as those of the Muses, the Arts, or the classical philosophers, which were of interest to the principal courts of the time. Perugino (1450–1523) in the Collegio del Cambio in Perugia, and his assistant Pinturicchio (1454–1513) at the Borgia apartments in the Vatican, gave the Muses and Arts a courtly and detailed rendering, with the aim of connecting classical themes with those of the Christian tradition. The Florentine Academy, led by the humanist philosopher Marsilio Ficino (1433–99), featured philosophers in its paintings. The individual was glorified

EARLY RENAISSANCE THEMES

During the Early Renaissance, artistic themes were generally linked to the rediscovery of the classical world. This was exemplified by such works as Mantegna's *Triumphs of Caesar* and the *Stories of Hercules* by Giovanni Antonio Amadeo (1447–1522), which identified a new view of man, whose destiny was guided by personal virtues and abilities. This idea sought to distance humanity from the previous, secure relationship with God that had been one of the few

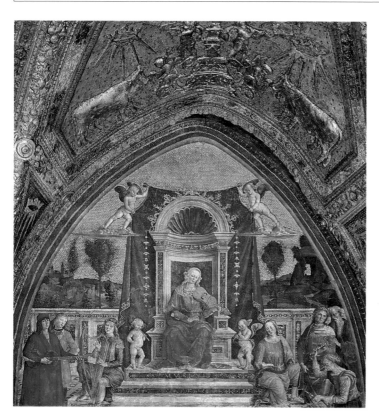

Studio of Pinturicchio, La Musica, Borgia Apartments, *Vatican City, 1492. Christian subjects are placed alongside pagan themes in the frescoes on the walls of Alexander VI's apartment.*

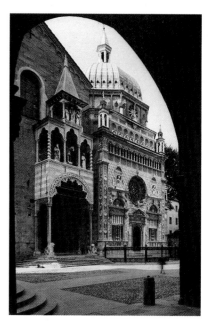

Giovanni Antonio Amadeo, exterior of the Colleoni Chapel, *Bergamo, Italy, 1470–75. Amadeo assimilated Florentine culture, interpreting it through a vivacious style of decoration typical of Lombardy.*

ANDREA MANTEGNA: "OCULUS OF THE CAMERA PICTA"

1473; fresco; Camera degli Sposi, Castello di San Giorgio, Mantua, Italy.

The oculus is in the center of the ribbed vault of the *Camera degli Sposi*, a room 26 feet (8 meters) long, rebuilt to allow Mantegna's sequence of frescoes to unfold. The paintings celebrate and glorify the family of the Marquis of Mantua, Ludovico Gonzaga II (1447–78). The space is transformed into a pavilion, with a series of pilasters appearing to support the dome. The oculus, or painted opening, shows a summer sky. The painted architecture and the

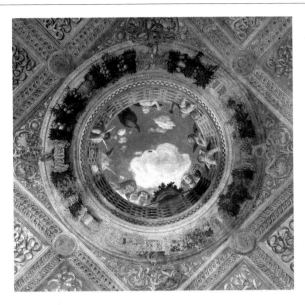

iconography, in which traditions of courtly painting, antiquarian decoration, and experimentation have been combined, make this room an undisputed

Renaissance masterpiece. The oculus is about one-quarter of the size of the room and is surrounded by a foreshortened marble balcony, with a decorative garland below.

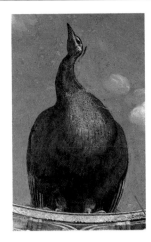

▶ *3. The peacock is notable for its shimmering specks of color that change from blue-green to violet. The artist has portrayed the bird accurately, without any exaggeration. The wheel is an old solar and cosmic symbol. It is clear that the learned Mantegna knew the Christian and magical symbolism of the peacock as a sign of eternity and incorruptibility and the destroyer of serpents (that is, deceivers and traitors), with the power to transform base matter into good. From its high perch, the bird watches over the house of Gonzaga.*

▼ *4. The formal arrangement of the balcony is enlivened by the figures peering over the edge. The winged putti, cherubs rather than angels, are taken from antiquity, while the orange tree (grown by the Mantuan lords) and the obscure figure of the young Moorish slave or Saracen maidservant are symbols of opulence. Another classical reference is the ladies of the court who, caught in the golden light reflected from the marble parapet, resemble the Three Graces.*

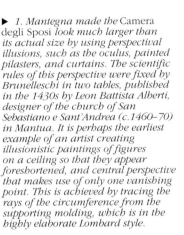

▶ *1. Mantegna made the* Camera degli Sposi *look much larger than its actual size by using perspectival illusions, such as the oculus, painted pilasters, and curtains. The scientific rules of this perspective were fixed by Brunelleschi in two tables, published in the 1430s by Leon Battista Alberti, designer of the church of San Sebastiano e Sant'Andrea (c.1460–70) in Mantua. It is perhaps the earliest example of an artist creating illusionistic paintings of figures on a ceiling so that they appear foreshortened, and central perspective that makes use of only one vanishing point. This is achieved by tracing the rays of the circumference from the supporting molding, which is in the highly elaborate Lombard style.*

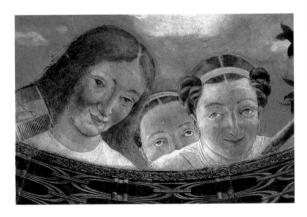

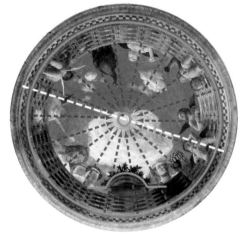

▶ *2. The strict but relatively simple perspectival solution is complex in its realization, since the balcony itself and the figures peering over it must always appear foreshortened at every point on the circle. Seen from below, the precarious position of the tub holding the orange tree catches the eye. It is given symmetry by the groups of figures on either side, in direct relation to the larger cloud and the peacock opposite. The axis of vision from the tub to the bird bears no precise relation to the walls or the diagonals of the dome and expresses, within the limits of the perspective, the painter's freedom of composition, regrouping the figures in an informal and "natural" way.*

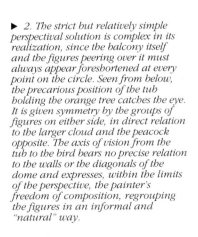

▼ *5. The broad braided garland of leaves and fruit around the oculus was a popular motif. A symbol of Venus, derived from the cornucopia, and signifying the abundance of nature's gifts, it serves as a sign of generosity toward guests. The garland is in an intermediary form between the painting of architecture and the depiction of nature, and it precedes the scenic murals that soon become popular at court. It forms part of the sculptural and iconographic classicism that is an original element of the work by this early Renaissance artist.*

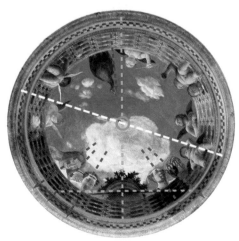

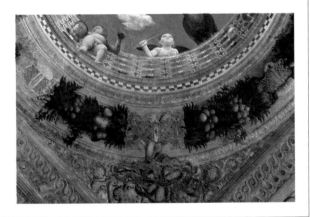

toward the more esoteric and obscure aspects of ancient culture. The growing interest in hieroglyphics, notably in Bologna, Rome, and Venice, was exemplified by the *Hypneromachia Poliphili*, an illustrated romance published by Aldo Manuzio in which the gradual achievement of beauty is interpreted as a mystical journey. Repeated attempts were made to reconcile these tendencies with medieval tradition by emphasizing the continuity between classical culture and Christian truth. Pico della Mirandola (1463–94) was a key figure in this pursuit. The change of focus onto history and the individual favored the development of a new ideal of the city. Ideas were forwarded by leading theorists, such as Filarete, who outlined a

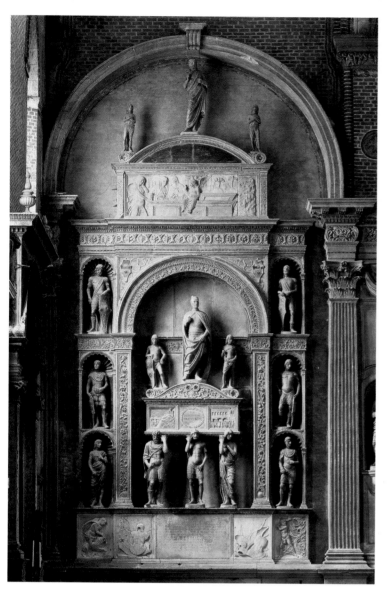

Pietro Lombardo, Tomb of the Doge Pietro Mocenigo, Santi Giovanni e Paolo, Venice, 1476–81. *The sculptor has paid homage to the political and military qualities of the deceased.*

and was depicted as the master of his own destiny. This increased the popularity of individual funerary monuments, boosting the fortunes of Italian sculptors such as Desiderio di Settignano (c.1430–1464), Andrea Bregno (1421–1506), and Pietro Lombardo (1435–1515). This also provided opportunities for new experiments to be made in architecture, as seen in the Portinari Chapel in Milan and the old sacristy in San Lorenzo in Florence, which was carved for the Medici.

URBAN PORTRAITS AND FIGURES

The popularity of portrait painting and the ever greater prominence given to patrons and donors of art (even in the cycles of sacred stories such as those painted by Ghirlandaio (1449–94) in the Santa Trinita in Florence) showed man in a new light – as master of his natural and historical environment, able to take control of his own fate. Neo-Platonic teaching, which Marsilio Ficino (1433–99) held to be the basis of Christianity, was prominent in Florence during the late 15th century and led

MILAN UNDER THE SFORZAS

Between 1464 and 1468, Vincenzo Foppa (c.1427–1515) painted the frescoes for the ancestral chapel built by the Medici banker Pigello Portinari behind the apse of Sant'Eustorgio in Milan. The chapel was a fusion of architecture, sculpture, and Milanese painting, typical of style that flourished during the reign of the duke, Francesco Sforza. It celebrated St. Peter Martyr, standard-bearer of the Dominican order and a model of life for the patrons buried within. Foppa elaborated the humanistic language typical of Lombardy, with its compositional clarity and simplicity, understated realism, straightforward naturalism, and brilliant colors. Bernardino Butinone and Bernardo Zenale, two artists from Treviso, were later commissioned to collaborate on painting *The Stories of St. Ambrose* in the Grifi Chapel in San Pietro in Gessate, a church linked to the reformed Benedictines of Santa Giustina. The story unfolds in continuous sequences, displaying Zenale's mastery of perspective and composition and revealing the influence of the Sforzas. Butinone's nervous and metallic figurations seem closer to the house of Este, which governed Ferrara, Modena, and Reggio. The family was linked with Ludovico il Moro of Milan through his wife, Beatrice d'Este.

Bernardo Zenale, The Judgment, *San Pietro in Gessate, Grifi Chapel, Milan, c.1490.*

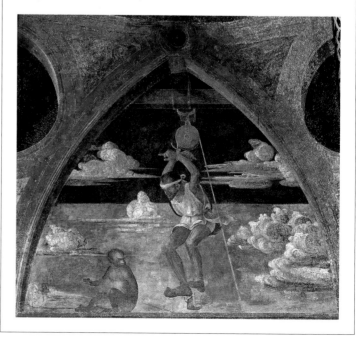

THE 15TH-CENTURY CYCLES IN THE SISTINE CHAPEL

Pope Sixtus IV Della Rovere summoned the best Umbrian and Tuscan painters to Rome in 1428 to decorate in fresco the lower walls of his new chapel: Signorelli (c.1441–1523), Perugino (1445–1523), Ghirlandaio (1452–1525), Cosimo Rosselli (1439–1507), and Botticelli (1445–1510) came to paint stories from the Old and New Testaments. An element of competition emerged between the various pictorial styles, which included Botticelli's ability to render the stories as decorative friezes, copiously borrowing from the Roman repertory of antiquity.

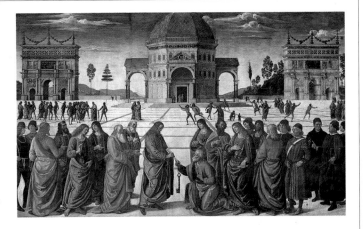

Pietro Vannucci, called Perugino, The Delivery of the Keys, *Sistine Chapel, Vatican City, 1481.*

Sandro Botticelli, Episodes from the Life of Moses, *Sistine Chapel, Vatican City, 1481–82. This work is contemporary with* The Birth of Venus.

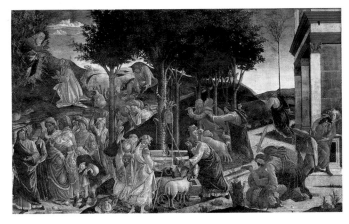

Perugino preferred ordered spaciousness and perspective, while a simpler, narrative style with overcrowded landscapes characterized the work of Rosselli and Luca Signorelli. In this remarkable contest, the compositional and narrative precepts set down in 1435 by Leon Battista Alberti reached maturity. Some of these would soon be glimpsed in the youthful aspirations of Raphael (a pupil of Perugino) and Michelangelo (a former pupil of Ghirlandaio). Nearby is the chapel of Nicholas V, beautifully decorated by Fra Angelico between 1447 and 1449 with the *Lives of Saint Lawrence and Saint Stephen.* These reveal a emphasis on narrative detail that is new to the artist.

in San Pietro in Milan; the Emilian altarpieces by Ercole de' Roberti; and the fresco cycles dedicated to the *Stories of St. Ursula* (1490–95) and *St. George* (1502–07) by Vittore Carpaccio. The Sistine Chapel and its pictorial splendors may be thought of as the ideal celestial city. Theater and festivals aroused interest, too, as seen in Leonardo's efforts in the staging of games for Ludovico il Moro, and in the public demand for a true Vitruvian theater to be created in the palace of Cardinal Riario. This taste for

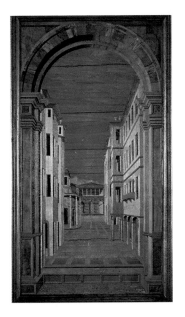

Fra Giovanni da Verona, tarsia, Monteoliveto Maggiore, 1503–05. The stalls in Monteoliveto are inlaid with characteristic subjects such as animals and fantastic views of the city.

scenography entered figurative art at various levels and is evident in the secular Ferrarese cycle painted by Cosmè Tura (c.1430–95), Francesco del Cossa (c.1436–78), and Ercole d'Antonio de' Roberti (1448–96) at the Schifanoia Palace. The sacred cycle of the *Life of the Virgin* and the *Passion of Christ* by Rogier van der Weyden (1400–64)

vision for a new city – Sforzinda – in his *Trattato,* or in the city plans sketched out by Francesco di Giorgio. Biblical themes and classical texts were combined in a new definition of an orderly and functional city, which set out to reflect, in the Aristotelian sense,

harmonious cohabitation. These ideals were often far removed from the reality of city life, but the concepts were rapidly adopted in the figurative arts, where subjects were increasingly placed in urban settings, which were often given the role of protagonist in a

narrative. The repertory was vast: the backgrounds to Mantegna's paintings in the Ovetari Chapel in Padua (1453); Perugino's *Vision of St. Bernard* (1493); Gentile Bellini's large canvases of urban ceremonies; the *Stories of Saint Ambrose* (1489–93) by Zenale and Butinone

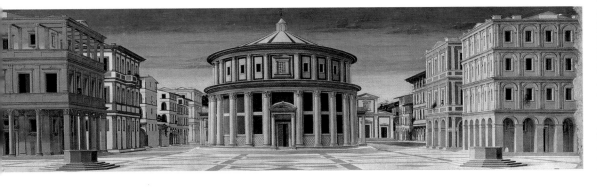

School of Piero della Francesca, Idealized View of the City, *Palazzo Ducale, Urbino, c.1480. An idealized townscape is pictured here, perhaps intended as a theatrical backdrop.*

PIERO DELLA FRANCESCA: FROM BAPTISM TO RESURRECTION

Piero della Francesca portrayed Christ in two memorable works, *The Baptism of Christ* (c.1450) and the *Resurrection of Christ* (between 1459 and 1469). The dignified and classical figure of Christ in *The Baptism* is bleached white, suggesting the ritual purification of the baptism, and is juxtaposed with the whiteness of the tree. The dove, symbol of the Holy Spirit, is carefully placed directly above Christ's head. Three angels look on, separated by the tree from the mortal and physical world, and a neophyte stands behind John the Baptist, preparing for his own baptism. His nakedness is a symbol of humility, contrasting with the grand outfits of the priests behind him. The landscape displays an unprecedented naturalism; the outline of what may be Sansepolcro can be glimpsed, tiny and insignificant, in

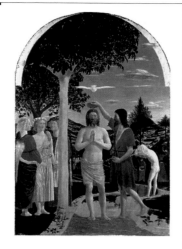

Piero della Francesca, The Baptism of Christ, *c.1450. National Gallery, London.*

the background. In the masterpiece *Resurrection of Christ*, the grave figure of Christ is reminiscent of an ancient hero. He is about to wake the sleeping figures, symbolizing the elevating of the world to a new plane of religious consciousness.

Piero della Francesca, Resurrection of Christ, *late 1450s. Pinacoteca Comunale, Sansepolcro.*

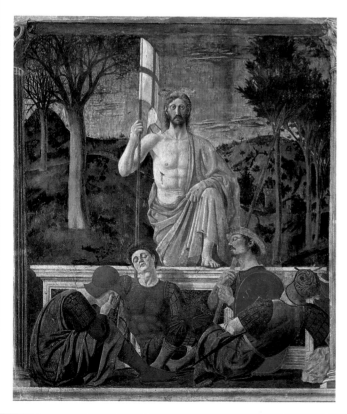

displays a pictorial transposition of rhythms and contexts that enlivened sacred painting. Due to the traditional tastes of art patrons in the Po Valley and the ongoing construction of medieval cathedrals that began in the previous century, Gothic culture retained its vitality, especially in southern Italy. It was evident in the work of Paolo Uccello (1396–1475) and of Andrea del Castagno (1419–57) on the mosaics of St. Mark's in Venice. Through looking at the works of artists such as Giacomo Jaquerio, Pisanello, and Jacopo Bellini it is clear that the artistic climate of the Renaissance was still evolving. The stylistic trends introduced during the mid-15th century by Mantegna, Vincenzo Foppa, and Giovanni Bellini (c.1432–1516), among others, continued stylistic trends started by earlier generations of artists, notably the feeling for atmospheric color and light, which glorified antiquity and illustrated a reverence for and interest in nature. The dramatic intensity of Donatello's sculptures in Padua had considerable influence at this time. A realistic style that harkened back to traditional values was taking shape in Lombardy, involving an effective and invigorating sense of history, while, elsewhere, artists such as Bellini and Giorgione (c.1477–1510) portrayed man in an ideal, naturalistic environment. Signs of a broader, more encompassing trend were appearing in what was to become the modern manner. The presence of Leonardo Da Vinci in the Po Valley encouraged the continuing progress of this style during the last two decades of the century. At the same time, many of the great workshops were

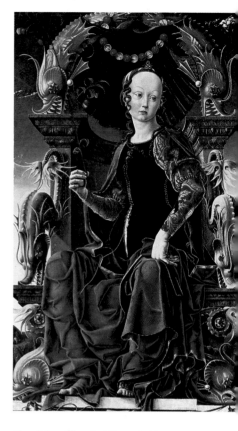

Cosmè Tura, Allegorical Figure, *1460. National Gallery, London. Strange, spiky forms, characteristic of the nervous energy of Tura, fill the picture. He was the first major painter of the Ferrara school.*

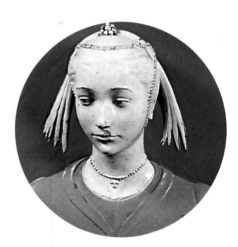

Andrea della Robbia, Tondo with Portrait of a Young Person, *glazed polychrome terracotta. Museo Nazionale del Bargello, Florence. Andrea della Robbia imparted a grace and elegance to his figures.*

establishing interaction with one another, including the Florentine schools of Verrocchio, the della Robbia family of sculptors, and the schools of Fontainebleau.

The second half of the 15th century was also distinguished by the great pictorial experiments of Piero della Francesca (c.1410–92), who worked between his native town of Sansepolcro and the sophisticated Adriatic courts of Urbino and Rimini. His theory of perspective, as set out in his *De Prospectiva Pingendi*, found expression in works bearing great significance, from *The*

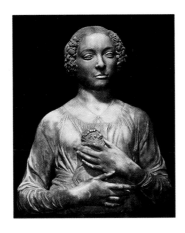

Andrea Verrocchio, Lady with a Nosegay, *1480s. Museo Nazionale del Bargello, Florence. Verrocchio portrays his subject with naturalistic charm, showing the details of the hands and the flowers.*

Legend of the True Cross (c.1452–57), which decorates the chancel of San Francesco in Arezzo, to *The Flagellation of Christ* (c.1463–64) at Urbino. In Piero's work, time and space attained absolute definition: they were harmoniously calculated in every smallest detail, but always with a mystery in the gestures and expressions of the figures.

THE DELLA ROBBIA FAMILY

Luca della Robbia (c.1400–82), his nephew Andrea (1435–1525), and Andrea's son Giovanni (1469–1529) were the key members of this Florentine family of sculptors, particularly renowned for glazed terracottas with splendid white, blue, yellow, green, and brown enamel. Much admired until the 19th century, their work has not enjoyed much critical acclaim since. Luca, whose art can be compared to that of Ghiberti, created works full of expressive vigor, including the *Visitation in San Giovanni Fuorcivitas* in Pistoia and the *tondi* (roundels) showing the Apostles and the Evangelists in the Pazzi chapel in Florence. Giovanni created the *Opere di Misericordia* for the frieze for the Ceppo Hospital in Pistoia.

THE SCHIFANOIA FRESCOES IN FERRARA

During the rule of the Dukes Borso and Ercole d'Este, the Schifanoia fresco cycle of the *Months of the Year* was painted in Borso's palace in Ferrara. It was executed by the leading painters of the 15th century school of Ferrara:

Cosmè Tura, Francesco del Cossa, and Ercole de' Roberti. Based on the 14th-century theme of the *Triumphs* and the older work of the *Months of the Year*, the lavishly illustrated cycle borrows from the astrological texts of the time, using their symbols and icons. There was a previously unknown freedom in the depiction of the allegorical scenes, which makes use of a wide field of reference, from courtly occupations to antiquity, all expressed in brilliant color. The perspective, too, always bold in its foreshortening effects (in the style of Mantegna), is impressive, and the works are lively and imaginative overall.

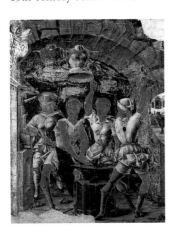

Ercole de' Roberti, The Forge of Vulcan, *from The Month of September, Schifanoia Palace, Ferrara, c.1470.*

DONATELLO IN PADUA AND FLORENCE

Donatello spent a long period in Florence, first as Ghiberti's pupil and later working on the reliefs for the Old Sacristy of San Lorenzo. He was in Padua in 1443 to 1453. Here, he re-assessed his relationship with classicism and reacted against established classical principles, giving free rein to his imagination. In the reliefs for the Paduan high altar (1446–50), the relief technique known as *stiacciato* – a perspectival solution obtained by means of a dense superimposition of planes to achieve depth – places the restless, crowded scenes of the *Miracles of St. Anthony* into wide architectural structures. The popular nature of the subjects reveals an attempt to rework established motifs with a dramatic realism, in which light was used to create depth. His use of foreshortening and the play of light effectively express anguish in the reliefs for the pulpit of San Lorenzo in Florence. Finished by Donatello's assistants after his death in 1446, the scenes from *The Passion of Christ* seem to contradict the certainties that were established in the early Tuscan Renaissance.

Donatello, Showing the Host to the Mule, *from the* Miracles of St. Anthony, *Basilica of St. Anthony, Padua, 1447.*

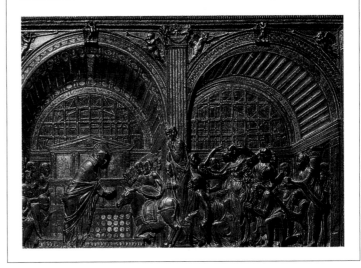

THE SPREAD OF HUMANIST ART

From its inception, the influence of the humanist movement spread across Europe. The church councils set up in the early part of the 15th century served as meeting points, providing opportunities for cultural exchanges and increasing the circulation in Europe of classical manuscripts and new artistic ideas. For example, Masolino worked in Hungary between 1425 and 1427 in the retinue of Cardinal Branda Castiglioni. Through this connection, the ruler, Matthias Corvino (1440–90), commissioned a series of illuminated manuscripts by the most important studios of the Po Valley in the second half of the century. Through these contacts the slow penetration of Italian artistic and architectural ideas into western and northern Europe began. While the Gothic style prevailed, some of these new ideas were adopted, especially the excessively antiquarian style of the sculptors of the Po valley, which was evidently more in keeping with the Gothic ideal than the diversity of perspectival and compositional themes advocated by Leon Battista Alberti. The Late Gothic culture of the Burgundian courts had encouraged a realistic attention to detail. The quest for an ideal luminosity of color was pursued by an assortment of Flemish artists who were capable of combining the sculptural values favored by Claus Sluter (active c.1380) and his followers with a firm

Colantonio, Crucifixion. Thyssen-Bornemisza Collection, Lugano, Italy.

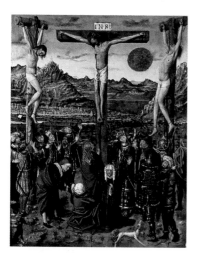

grasp of perspective that accentuated the feeling of depth in their paintings. This marked the birth of a vigorous pictorial tradition that extended from the Low Countries to the Alsace of Martin Schongauer (1453–91). It conquered even the most sophisticated Italian courts, such as those of Florence, Ferrara, and Urbino, with the works of van der Weyden, Justus of Ghent, Hugo van der Goes (c.1435–82), and Pedro Berruguete (c.1450–1504) becoming popular. Before long, the "infinite landscapes" of van Eyck were emulated, with urban features added, in the portraits of Battista Sforza and Federico da Montefeltro painted by Piero della Francesca.

The great age of Flemish painting, which was supported by the thriving merchants of Flanders, marked the rise of the technique of painting with oils on panels. The skill and vibrancy of their work

Martin Schongauer, The Sacred Family. Kunsthistorisches Museum, Vienna.

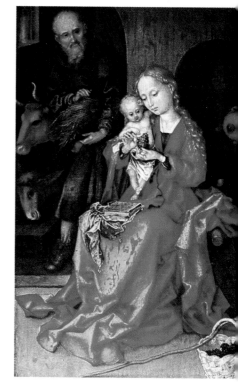

allowed the artists to give the fullest possible expression to Flemish figurative ideals, which originated in the workshops producing illuminated books such as the *Les Très Riches Heures du Duc de Berry,* illustrated by the Limbourg Brothers and Jacquemart de Hesdin in about 1410. The polyptych of the *Adoration of the Lamb,* painted by the brothers Hubert and Jan van Eyck in 1432, was erected in Ghent Cathedral. At about that time, Jan painted the *Arnolfini Marriage* and the *Rolin Madonna,* which displayed a masterly use of color that defined with vibrant precision the smallest and most distant detail in an almost photographic manner. Portrait painters sought to idealize human characteristics, while the ample draperies of the costumes gave a solid presence to the figures, who were often absorbed

in reflection and clearly contained in their own space. This decade also saw the start of the career of Rogier van der Weyden, who had an intense interest in the

THE INFLUENCE OF ROGIER VAN DER WEYDEN

Little is known of the early works of Rogier van der Weyden, and any evaluation of him as an artist is usually based on the few works attributed to him, including the *Last Judgment* (1444–48), commissioned for the Hôtel Dieu of Beaune in Burgundy. It is a large, ambitious work on nine panels, vividly depicting the judgment of anguished souls.

The painting that is generally considered his masterpiece is *The Deposition* (1440). This work is quite unlike that of his teachers Campin and van Eyck; it is far more powerful and emotive, with the grief and the tears on the

faces of the mourners portrayed in meticulous detail. An extremely influential artist, by the mid-15th century van der Weyden had established a busy workshop and enjoyed an international reputation. His

technical skill and self-confidence led to his ability to take on commissions of a monumental scale. He was known and visited by many Italian artists, and ideas and techniques were exchanged between them. References to him are found in the *De Icona* by the Italian humanist theologian Nicholas of Cusa.

Rogier van der Weyden, Last Judgment altarpiece, Hôtel Dieu, Beaune, France, c.1444–48.

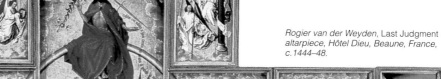
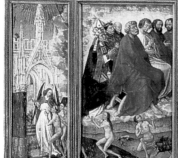
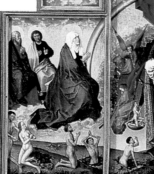
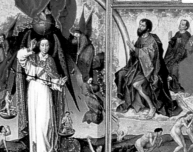
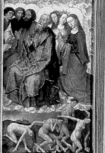
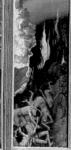

ANTONELLO AND BELLINI: A FEELING FOR NATURE

Little is known about Antonello da Messina's life, but his familiarity with the work of Piero della Francesca and the time he spent in Venice in 1475 are established facts. From an early age, Antonello acquired a clear and disciplined sense of spatial values, as can be seen in his geometric background design. The Venetian scenery heightened his lively sense of color, adding an intense and mystical nature to his later painting of the lagoon at Venice. This search for inner truth made Antonello one of the greatest portraitists of all time. He had contact with Flemish painting, firstly during

his training in the Neapolitan studio of the court painter Colantonio. Among the Venetians encouraged to follow in his footsteps were, most notably, Giorgione (1477–1510) and Giovanni Bellini (c.1430–1516). In creating his work *Transfiguration*, Giovanni abruptly abandoned the sharp, precise style of his brother Gentile and his brother-in-law Andrea Mantegna that he had earlier employed. In his liberal use of color and his mastery of half-light, Giovanni succeeded in expressing his feelings on the mysteries of creation and the natural world.

Giovanni Bellini, Transfiguration, late 1480s. Capodimonte Museum, Naples.

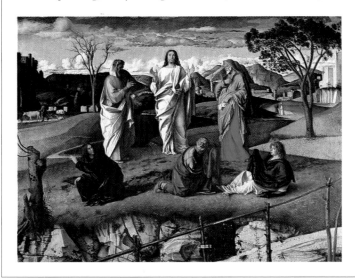

compositional and sculptural themes of wooden sculpture. He dramatically articulated complex forms in his compositions, accentuating his animated figures and their unambiguous gestures and expressions. It is clear that the artist's consuming interest was for the figures as compositional factors, and the *Madonna of San Luca* shows his sensitivity, which allows subtle variations of emotion in his figures to disturb the symmetrical limitations that his predecessors imposed on their work. His journey to

Italy in 1450 involved an exchange of works and ideas with other artists, and the impact of this can be best traced in portraiture. While van der Weyden accepted the influence of Italian painting, the Bruges artist Hans Memling (c.1430–94) exemplified the distinctiveness of Flemish art by developing and expanding the compositional techniques within his own culture. Also in Bruges, Petrus Christus (died c.1475) was influenced by van Eyck, but in a more simplified style and with an intimate, devotional tone,

while Dieric Bouts (died 1475) showed great affinity with van der Weyden – he painted figures set in beautiful, shimmering landscapes. Bouts also experimented with perspective and was highly influential. His major work

was the altarpiece in the church of St. Pierre in Louvain. Painting in the north, then, was also going through a radical transformation, with innovations of techniques and ideas in figurative and landscape painting.

THE GHENT ALTARPIECE

The great Flemish masterpiece, the Ghent Altarpiece, with its principal panel of the *Adoration of the Lamb*, was placed in the cathedral of St. Bavo in Ghent in 1432. It was begun by Hubert van Eyck and completed by his brother Jan after his death in 1426. The outer panels depict the Annunciation and the donors and John the Evangelist and John the Baptist. The central panels depict biblical scenes, groups of angels, processions of the blessed, and Adam and Eve. The theme is the Redemption and the story of mankind, with the lamb as an Eucharistic and apocalyptic symbol. The Gothic city depicted in the background is the Holy City of Jerusalem, under the guise of a typical Flemish urban center. The vibrant and diverse colors, the wholly accurate details and, above all, the analytical naturalism that captures the most distant detail as clearly as the objects in the foreground, are all outstanding. The altarpiece can be seen as heralding the beginning of the Flemish Renaissance in painting, the result of a growing mutual assimilation of ideas. Regional styles were interacting along traditional lines of communication dictated by trade and history, in both directions from the Lower Rhine to Tuscany, from Paris to Rome, and from Seville to Naples and Palermo. Out of all these influences, a single "Renaissance" style was born.

Jan van Eyck, Adam, detail from the Ghent Altarpiece, St. Bavo, Ghent, Belgium, 1432.

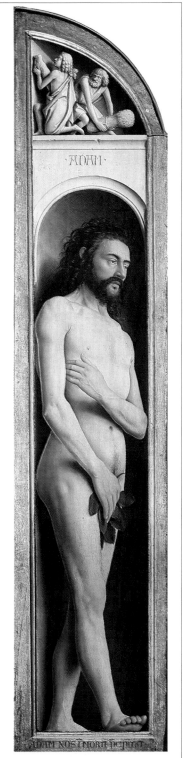
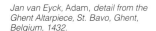

THE HIGH RENAISSANCE

In the 16th century, the Italian Renaissance reached almost unsurpassed heights of cultural and intellectual achievement. The turbulent political climate in Italy was ideal for the spread of the High Renaissance and Mannerism, the latter style already showing tendencies toward the Baroque.

Today's understanding of the Italian Renaissance recognizes the continuity of a number of features from the 15th to the 16th century. This is in contrast to earlier thinking, which maintained that certain major events, such as the discovery of the Americas by Columbus in 1492, marked the beginning of a completely new age that was identifiably "modern." There were turbulent political events that brought about the end of the independent city-states; imperial claims to sovereignty by the French and then Hapsburg rulers; the rise of Protestant reform; stimulating contacts with new cultures; and, simultaneously, a flourishing cultural scene rich in creativity and inventiveness. Such a combination of events is difficult to locate in any other one period. In the Vatican, works by Raphael (1483–1520) and Michelangelo (1475–1564), such as the Stanza della Segnatura (Room of the Signature) and Sistine Chapel, reflected the current climate of change and were received with wonder by their first observers. The Italian architect, painter, and art historian Giorgio Vasari (1511–74) documented the fortunes of the Renaissance in Rome in his *Lives of the Most Excellent Painters, Sculptors, and Architects* (1550). Vasari outlined the progression of the Renaissance following the death of Raphael and the sack of Rome in 1527 (the climax of the imperial-papal struggles when imperial forces invaded and devastated the city), its spread throughout Europe, and its variety and complexity. He also wrote of the concern of the art world to establish an understanding of itself, which is confirmed by the number of treatises written on the subject, many of which helped form the aesthetic ideals of the moment. Vasari's *Lives* also provides an explanation of differences between the art of the 15th century and that of the early 16th, stating that earlier art "lacked that spontaneity which, although based on correct measurement, goes beyond it without conflicting with order and stylistic purity. This spontaneity enables the artist to enhance his work by adding innumerable inventive details." The 15th-century

Piazza del Campidoglio, Rome. The pavement design is by Michelangelo.

artists had "missed the finer points…ignoring the charming and graceful facility that is suggested rather than revealed in living subjects…. Their works also lacked the abundance of beautiful clothes, the imaginative details, charming colors, many kinds of building and various landscapes in depth." According to Vasari, these qualities were introduced with Leonardo da Vinci (1452–1519) and concluded with Michelangelo, when the climax of the modern phase was reached. For Jacob Burckhardt, a 19th-century Swiss historian, Michelangelo was the first contradictory element of the Renaissance. In either case, the artist's long, productive lifespan covered a critical era.

ROME, CAPITAL OF THE RENAISSANCE

As the Italian courts of Milan, Naples, and Florence tussled over which was the most powerful, the Roman popes Julius II (1503–13) and Leo X (1513–21) offered hospitality to a group of artists from these leading principalities. The first significant arrival was that of Donato Bramante (c.1444–1514), following his fruitful stay in Milan at the court of Ludovico il Moro, a rich cultural environment where he had made the acquaintance of such artists as Leonardo da Vinci and Luca

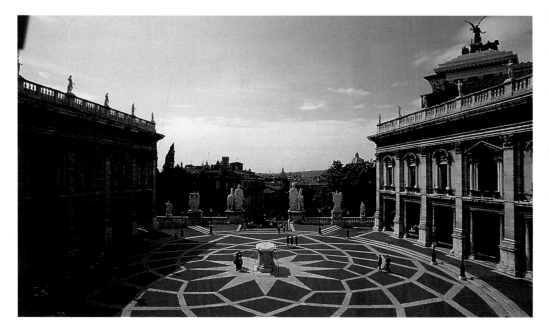

ARCHITECTURAL HERITAGE

The 16th century inherited a wealth of sumptuous architecture from the previous century. For the rich, there were the palazzi, magnificent city residences such as Brunelleschi's Palazzo Pitti in Florence (c.1440) and the Palazzo dei Diamanti in Ferrara (1492) by Biagio Rossetti (c.1447–1516). The country form of the palazzo, the villa with its gardens and orchards, was also introduced during this period. Elsewhere, the severe or incongruous architecture of buildings such as the Maschio Angioino in Naples and the Palazzo Ducale in Urbino was reformed. Churches were designed in a new style, and from Ferrara to Pienza, new urban areas were planned with rationalized form to create the ideal city.

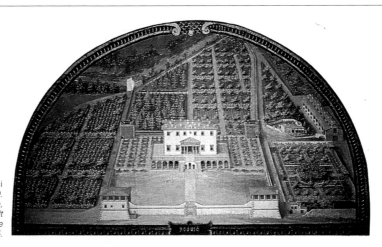

Giusto Utens, View of the Medici Villa at Poggio a Caiano, 1559. Monuments and Fine Arts Service, Florence. The villa was built by Giuliano da Sangallo for the Medici in about 1485.

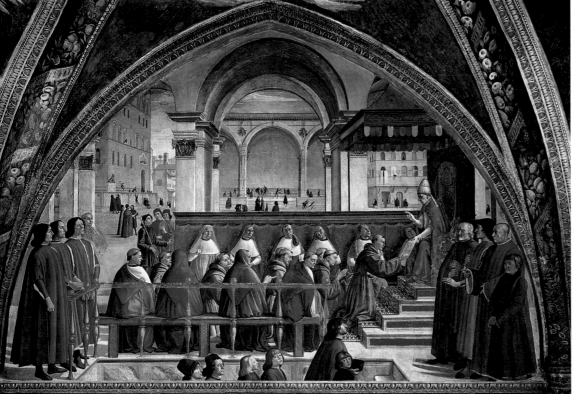

Left: Domenico Ghirlandaio (1449–94), Confirmation of the Rule of St. Francis, 1485. Santa Trinita, Sassetti Chapel, Florence. Portraits of the Medici family are included in this painting of the humanist city.

Below: Benedetto da Maiano (1442–97) and Il Cronaca (1457–1518), Palazzo Strozzi, Florence, 1489–1504. The clean, elegant design of this building, after Brunelleschi, was still being copied as late as the 19th century.

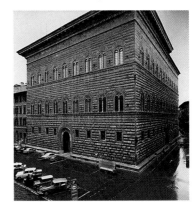

Below: Antonio da Sangallo the Elder (1453/55–1534), Church of San Biagio, Montepulciano, 1518–45. The elderly master translated the rationalism of 15th-century architecture into a Bramante-style church.

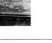

Francesco Laurana (c.1430–1502), Castel Nuovo, with the arch of Alfonso of Aragon, Naples, 1453–58. In the Maschio Angioino, reconstructed for the triumph of Alfonso the Magnanimous, Laurana erected an arch of classical derivation, two stories high and decorated with imposing reliefs.

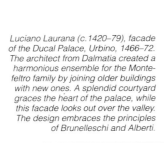

Luciano Laurana (c.1420–79), facade of the Ducal Palace, Urbino, 1466–72. The architect from Dalmatia created a harmonious ensemble for the Montefeltro family by joining older buildings with new ones. A splendid courtyard graces the heart of the palace, while this facade looks out over the valley. The design embraces the principles of Brunelleschi and Alberti.

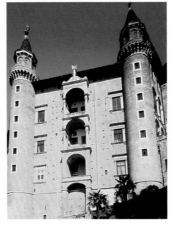

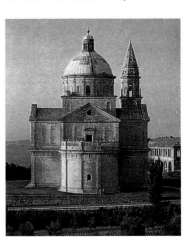

Pacioli (c.1445–1517). In 1504, Julius II gave Bramante the task of organizing the reconstruction of the basilica of St. Peter, which was to be centralized around a large cupola. Bramante had already adopted the design of a round sacred temple (*tempietto*) at San Pietro in Montorio (1502), which is a revival of the early Christian *martyrium* (church built in honor of a martyr). In 1506, the pope laid down the first stone of the new Vatican basilica and, in the same year, the antique sculpture known as *Laocoon* was discovered in a vineyard on the Esquiline hill. This depicted the myth of Laocoon, a Trojan priest who, with his two sons, was crushed to death by snakes. Such discoveries presented exciting new challenges for artists. The young Michelangelo had already grappled successfully with some of these in his sculptures of *Bacchus* (1497) and *David* (1501–04), and in certain ways with his *Pietà* (c.1498–1500), now in St. Peter's. The draw of Rome was such that Florence found it hard to keep its most brilliant artists in the city, even though Leonardo's unfinished *Battle of Anghiari* briefly adorned the Council Chamber of the Republic in the Palazzo Vecchio. Michelangelo was commissioned to paint the *Battle of Cascina* on the opposite wall, but got no further than preparing a full-size cartoon for the project before being summoned to Rome by Julius II in 1505.

MICHELANGELO: "CREATION OF ADAM"

1508–12; vault of the Sistine Chapel, Vatican City.

Michelangelo painted the frescoes for the ceiling of the Sistine Chapel (built by Pope Sixtus IV) between May 1508 and October 1512. They were commissioned by Pope Julius II, who wished to compensate Michelangelo for a previously abandoned project. The *Creation of Adam* is one of nine central panels in the highest part of the vault. Alternately small and large, these panels depict the main stories from the book of Genesis. This large fresco measures 15¼ x 7¼ feet (4.8 by 2.3 meters). It is the fourth in the series but was among the last to be completed. The scene illustrates God

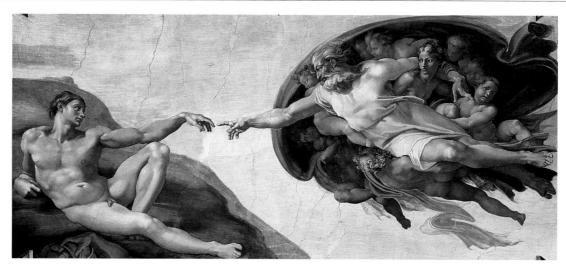

suffusing Adam, his new creation, with the gift of life. He extends his forefinger to touch that of Adam. The "paternal right hand" (papal hymn *Veni Creator Spiritus*) of God transfers immense power to the waking "first man." God's index finger points with authority and definition, while Adam, who is not yet fully alive, can barely lift his hand. The might of God is confirmed in his stern gaze, fixed on Adam, who in contrast looks awe-struck and submissive.

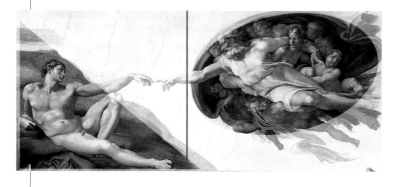

▲ *1. The composition is based on a rectangular layout, which can be roughly divided into two squares. The right-hand side is dedicated to the Creator, and the left to Adam. The name Adam is derived from the Hebrew word for "ground," and the figure rests on a stable, triangular area of barren earth. God, in the other section, is borne aloft by angels and surrounded by dramatic swirls of fine cloth. The empty sky in the center of the picture is important, as it provides the background to the joining of the two hands, the point of communication and the focal point of the painting. It emphasizes the division between the infinite power and divinity of God and the finite world of man, his creation.*

▼ *2. There is a symmetry and a connection between the two figures that is fundamental to the work. This can be shown by long, gently curved lines joining the figures. The main line follows the curve of the arms, passes through the hands, and joins the shoulders. The eyes of God gaze directly into those of Adam, and the bodies and limbs of the two figures are also linked along parallel planes. The viewer's eye is directed from right to left and back again, in a pendulum-like arc, which creates subtle associations and references between the two figures in what is almost an illusion of curved space. The Creation and the Last Judgment are the two situations in which the mystery of contact between humankind and Creator can be contemplated. Here, the artist has approached the enigma of this subject and given it form.*

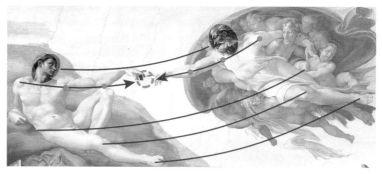

RAPHAEL AND MICHELANGELO

The most active artist of the early years of the 16th century was the passionate Bramante. According to Vasari, it was he who brought Raphael, a pupil of Pietro Perugino (c.1445–1523), to

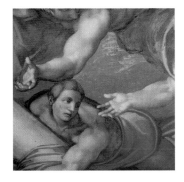

Rome. However, it was to Michelangelo that Julius II gave the commission for his monumental tomb to be placed in the old St. Peter's. Only the *Moses* group and the

Michelangelo, Last Judgment (detail of right-hand lunette), fresco, Sistine Chapel, Vatican City, 1536–41. The fresco depicting the Last Judgment covers the entire end wall of the chapel. The vast composition replaced former works by Perugino.

extraordinary *Slaves* series remain, but even these give the impression of form dramatically escaping from the material, a successful achievement of the ambitious aspirations of the artist. The pope seemed to want to give equal opportunities to the two great rivals, assigning Raphael to the decoration of the three *stanze* ("rooms") in

▼ 3. Michelangelo was clearly intent on adhering strictly to the story in Genesis, to which the nine central panels of the ceiling in the Sistine Chapel are dedicated: "So God created humankind in his image, in the image of God he created them" (Gen. 1:27). Michelangelo's representation of the Creation of Adam perfectly encapsulates these words. The physical forms of the two figures are the same, their strong, well-muscled physiques

precisely depicted – Michelangelo made numerous life studies for this scene – with a careful use of light and shade. The dotted lines showing the center of gravity of the bodies flow in the same direction, as do the lines along the lower edges of the bodies. Positioned in this way, the divine form is convex and the human concave, almost as if the imprint of God is being transferred to man.

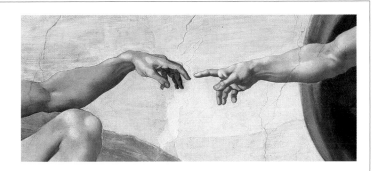

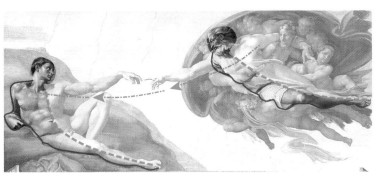

▲ 5. Much has been said about the contact that is about to take place between the two index fingers. There is almost a spark between them, as if a transmission of energy is taking place. The divine breath of life is translated into physical contact, or, more exactly, virtual contact. Between the two fingers lies the love of the Father for his creation and, simultaneously, the unbridgeable gap between the divine and the human. The impression of a current flowing through the arms

is produced by the undulating line connecting the bodies through the arms. The power and life that flow from God's finger recall the words of a papal hymn: "Thou...Finger of the paternal right hand...Pour thy love into our hearts, Strengthen us infirm of body...." Michelangelo's pupil Ascanio Condivi said: "Where God is seen with his arm and hand extended, he is almost giving Adam the rules of what he should or should not do."

► 4. Michelangelo has endowed Adam with a perfect anatomical form, one that epitomizes the glory of the Renaissance figure. The muscular, vigorous body encapsulates both strength and elegance. In accordance with Genesis, Michelangelo has directly modeled the figure of Adam on that of God; his hands and legs mirror those of the Father. Chiaroscuro is very important in this painting, and the quality of the modeling reaches heights of great excellence. This is in spite of the limitations of the medium – shading and, above all, glazing were particularly difficult to achieve in fresco work. Recent restoration of the chapel has revealed that the colors used were strong, varied, and surprisingly bright. Vasari described Michelangelo as the climax of a gradual evolution since Giotto.

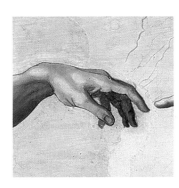

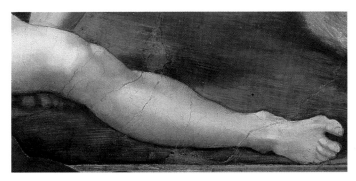

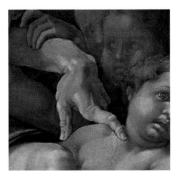

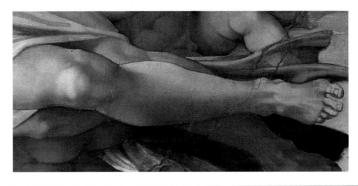

PROPHETS AND SIBYLS IN THE SISTINE CHAPEL

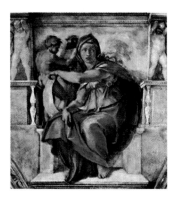

Michelangelo's decoration of the Sistine Chapel between 1508 and 1512 involved a wide variety of images, the sources and interpretation of which are still debated. Scenes from Genesis, the Old Testament prophets and sibyls (female seers), and the ancestors of Christ record the Creation of mankind and the road to salvation initiated by the Jewish people and completed in Christ's Incarnation. There are also clear allusions to the role of the Church and the Papacy at a time of great difficulties for the ruling pope. Michelangelo's composition uses classical architectural elements to frame episodes and support the figures. Particularly imposing and colorful are the sibyls and the prophets. As Vasari wrote: "These figures…are shown in varied attitudes, wearing a variety of vestments and beautiful draperies; they are all executed with marvelous judgment, and invention, and they appear truly inspired to whoever studies their attitudes and expressions." These attributes of Renaissance painting – variety, invention, and expressiveness – led to the creation of powerful characters that would have an impact on all subsequent art.

Michelangelo, Delphic Sibyl, *fresco, Sistine Chapel, Vatican City, 1509–10.*

Michelangelo, detail of lunette of David, *fresco, Sistine Chapel, Vatican City, 1511–12.*

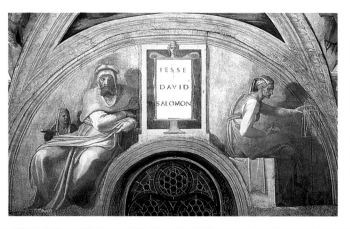

the papal apartments and Michelangelo to the ceiling of the Sistine Chapel. Burckhardt felt that Raphael's paintings in the Stanza della Segnatura were the harmonious manifestation of philosophical truth (as seen in his *School of Athens),* theological truth (*Disputation over the Holy Sacrament),* and poetic truth (*Parnassus*); to his mind, these paintings embraced the course of history from ancient to modern times, using compositional and chromatic values governed by simple, straightforward rules: order, measure, and a delicate, gentle style.
Michelangelo was pursuing other aims in his represent-ation of biblical figures and stories on the ceiling of the Sistine Chapel. He used what Vasari described as "new inventions and novel attitudes," "fresh ways of expression," and "perfect foreshortenings" to express the dramatic story of the effect of freedom on man, as he treads the path of history laid down by God. Michelangelo's complex style of composition and unique method of depicting volume – related to contemporary sculptural experiments in representing the human body – were supported by choices of color and light of surprising clarity and decisive contrast. Vasari claimed that Bramante secretly took Raphael to look at the Sistine Chapel, radically changing the latter's way of painting. When the ceiling was finally revealed in October 1512 – after four and half years of intense creativity – to the amazement of all who witnessed the event, it contained many elements of Florentine Mannerism, as epitomized by the work of artists such as Andrea del Sarto (1486–1530) and Jacopo Pontormo (1494–1556).

THE SCHOOLS OF NORTHERN ITALY

As the 16th century dawned, certain elements of Venetian painting that were rooted in the previous century flourished in works by artists such as

Leonardo da Vinci, Portrait of a Musician, *c.1485. Pinacoteca Ambrosiana, Milan.*

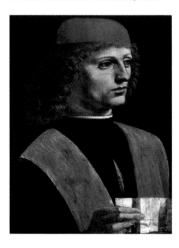

Giovanni Bellini (c.1434–1516). The *sacre conversazioni* ("holy conversation"), the sacred theme of his San Zaccaria Altarpiece (1505), was painted in warm, suffused tones that give a serene naturalism to the figures, landscape, and architecture. The same range of colors appears in the work of Giorgione (c.1477–1510), an artist with such confidence in his composition that he often did without preparatory sketches, creating his paintings by means of color and light. The atmospheric feel of Giorgione's art, seen clearly in *The Tempest,* highlights his links with Leonardo and his school. Titian (c.1488–1576) developed alongside Giorgione, and in 1508 the two artists were engaged to decorate the exterior of the Fondaco dei Tedeschi in Venice. Venice quickly attracted other artists: Albrecht Dürer (1471–1528), the great German artist, returned there in 1505 to further his studies of antiquity and humanism. Despite the turmoil of the political wars in Italy (1494–1530), by the beginning of the 16th century, the Venetian school of painting held great power and influence, its painters enjoying supremacy throughout Italy and Europe. Traditionally a sea-trading capital, Venice became one of the richest states in Europe, its prosperity and artistic influence resting as much on its mainland territories, which included Padua and Bergamo, as on its great sea empire, which encompassed lands from nearby Istria to Cyprus (acquired in 1489).
In the meantime, despite Venet-ian domination, wider artistic styles were emerging and spreading throughout northern Italy. A large group of students and admirers of Leonardo, who had returned to Florence after the fall of the Sforza court, were shaping an early form of the Mannerism that was to dominate central Europe by the mid-16th century.
In the Duchy of Milan, Benedetto Briosco (active

THE MYSTERY OF GIORGIONE

Over the centuries, a number of factors have fueled the mystery that surrounds the Venetian artist Giorgione: his premature death, the continuing debate about his autograph works, the loss of the Fondaco dei Tedeschi frescoes, the alleged rivalry with Titian, and the suggestion,

Giorgione, The Three Philosophers, 1507–10. Kunsthistorisches Museum, Vienna.

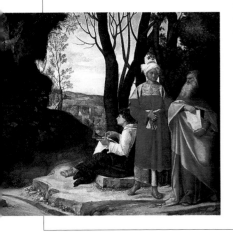

without support, that Giorgione belonged to the Jewish community. As a result, his paintings have proved difficult to understand.

Only a few years separate Giorgione's two most representative works – *The Tempest* and *The Three Philosophers*. Both paintings have been seen to contain biblical references (the theme of Adam and Eve for the first work and the Magi for the second). Mythological and secular meanings have also been detected: *The Tempest* as an erotic allegory, for instance, or references to the three ages of man in *The Three Philosophers*. Radiography has revealed radical alterations during the creation of the works; the young soldier in *The Tempest* was initially a female nude, while one of the philosophers was previously a Moor. This suggests a considerable amount of manipulation of the subject matter and implies that the final outcomes were

Giorgione, The Tempest, c.1505–06. Galleria dell'Accademia, Venice.

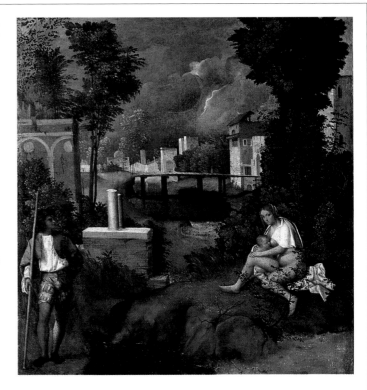

deliberately left ambivalent. The most prevalent feature, however, is the artist's fascination with the moods of nature: his treatment of tones and evocative touches

of light create an unusual atmospheric density. In this regard, Giorgione, of all the Venetians, was the closest in style to Leonardo da Vinci.

THE LAST SUPPERS OF LEONARDO AND DÜRER

Leonardo da Vinci had painted his *Last Supper* by 1498. The series of wood engravings by Albrecht Dürer known as *The Passion* included a *Last Supper* and can be dated from between 1509 and 1511. In little over a decade, the Renaissance had been given its most important

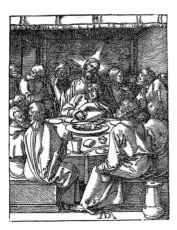

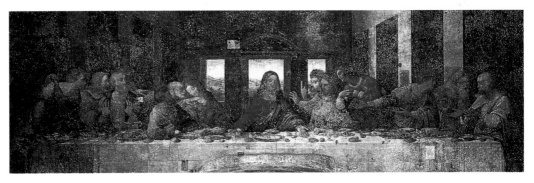

Leonardo da Vinci, Last Supper, Refectory of Santa Maria delle Grazie, Milan, c.1498.

Albert Dürer, Last Supper, *wood engraving, 1509–11. Musei Civici, Padua.*

prototypes for one of the favorite subjects of 16th-century sacred art – the renewed interest in this subject coincided with the debate on the doctrine of the Eucharist stimulated by the Reformation. The iconography of Leonardo's version is rich in new ideas, some taken from the

Dominican culture of the monastery in which the work was painted and some linked to the figurative tradition of Lombardy. The artist's choice to portray the moment following Christ's shocking announcement that "one of you shall betray me" gave him the opportunity to explore the reactions of the apostles. The size of the figures, their position in the foreground, and the unusual perspective mean that the observer is drawn into the emotion of the scene, just as

Dominican friars would have desired. In his engraving, Dürer takes up the drama and movement of Leonardo's painting. He shows John having fallen into the arms of Christ, indicating the close relationship between Jesus and this young apostle. Later, the theme would be developed by Veronese (1528–1588), among others. With little feeling for the spiritual, Veronese transformed the holy meal into a triumphal banquet for the princes of the Church.

1483–1517) was involved in the decoration of the facade of the Certosa at Pavia, giving a courtly appearance to the antique classicism of the Lombard style. However, it was Bramantino (c.1465–1530) who experimented with new and more expressive forms as he explored abstraction in his *Adoration of the Magi* (c.1500). In Bologna, Lorenzo Costa (c.1460–1535) and Francesco Francia (c.1450–1517) collaborated in decorating the walls of the Oratory of Santa Cecilia. Their unified style, rich in references to Perugino and Raphael, combined spiritual meaning with great intimacy. Ideas circulated quickly, partly thanks to the popularity of engravings, one of the most significant areas of Renaissance art. While Dürer introduced his wood-engraving cycles *The Passion* and *The Life of the Virgin* into northern Italy, influencing the direction of 16th-century painting

particularly around the Alpine areas, the Bolognese engraver Marcantonio Raimondi (c.1480–1534) spread the Raphaelesque style through Europe. Copies, engravings, and drawings of great masterpieces such as Leonardo's *Last Supper* became another means of diffusing new forms, and the travels of artists became crucial to the development of art, carrying ideas from one place to another. For example, in the early years of the century, Sebastiano del Piombo (c.1485–1547) visited Rome, bringing the Renaissance of Venice in contact with that of Rome, while Jacopo Sansovino (1486–1570) traveled from Florence to Rome and then on to Venice.

Donato Bramante, Tempietto, San Pietro in Montorio, Rome, 1502.

Mathias Grünewald, Crucifixion, c.1511/12. National Gallery, Washington, D.C..

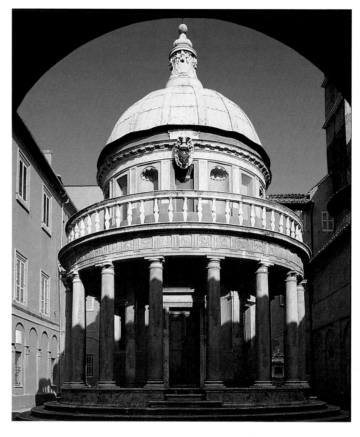

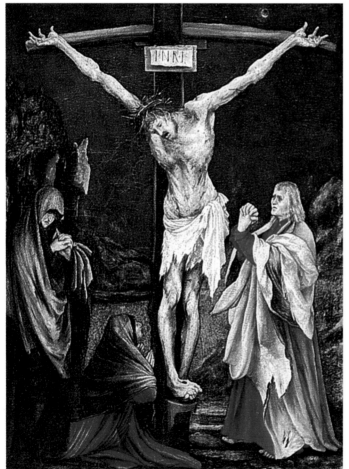

THE ROME OF THE MEDICI

Agostino Chigi's elegant Villa Farnesina (1508–1511) was designed by the Sienese architect and painter Baldassare Peruzzi (1481–1536) in the classical style of ancient Roman villas. The interior was lavishly decorated by some of the finest artists in Rome, including Peruzzi himself, who painted the false perspective views in the Salone delle Prospettive, and Raphael, who painted his famous *Galatea* fresco (1511–12). The classical style also interested Raphael, who even followed extracts from Pliny to create his plan for the Villa Madama, which was never finished.

In 1514, the year Bramante died, Raphael's architectural work was finally recognized. He was summoned to Rome to continue the rebuilding of St. Peter's by Leo X, a Medici pope who favored artistic links between Florence and Rome (Julius II had died in February

1513). Raphael was joined by Giuliano da Sangallo, head of the leading Florentine family of architects, and Fra Giocondo (1433–1515), a Veronese humanist friar. Fra Giocondo was an expert on classical architecture and editor of an important illustrated edition of Vitruvius – the 1st-century Roman architect – which was published in Venice in 1511. Giuliano da Sangallo also had a vast knowledge of Roman antiquity and, in the latter part of his life, resided in Rome.

THE SANGALLO FAMILY

Giuliano Giamberti da Sangallo (c.1443–1516), his brother Antonio the Elder (c.1453–1534), and their nephew Antonio the Younger (1484–1546) were among the most eminent architects of the Florentine Renaissance. Giuliano designed the church of Santa Maria delle Carceri at Prato (1485–92) and the Medici Villa at Poggio a Caiano (from 1480), while his brother created the church and fine palazzi at Montepulciano. Although trained in Florence, their nephew was mainly active in Rome, where he designed the Palazzo Farnese, which was finished by Michelangelo.

However, his best-known buildings were in Tuscany, and in 1516, the year he died, he provided designs for the facade of the Medici church of San Lorenzo in the thriving Tuscan capital, Florence. Andrea del Sarto painted his *Birth of the Virgin* in the atrium of Santissima Annunziata, Florence, in 1514. The painting reflects the architectural ideals

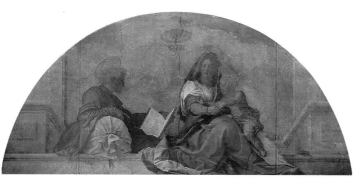

Andrea del Sarto, Madonna del Sacco, fresco, Santissima Annunziata, Florence, 1525. The name is taken from the sack on which St. Joseph is leaning.

of Giuliano da Sangallo and clearly shows the influence of Dürer in the movements and expressions of the figures. In Rome, Raphael's work also showed an increased awareness of movement, color, and light, typified in his *Fire in the Borgo,* in the passionate luminosity of the *Expulsion of Heliodorus,* in the intense color of the *Mass of Bolsena,* and in the wonderful night scene of the *Liberation of St. Peter from Prison.* The wealth of commissions received by Raphael and his natural sociability encouraged the formation of a group of students and collaborators that included Perino del Vaga (c.1500–47), Giulio Romano (c.1499–1546), and Giovanni da Udine. Raphael's architectural tastes centered around the classical style – evident in Palazzo Branconio and Villa Madama – and the master and his followers employed ancient styles of decoration for the loggias of the Vatican. Before long, Raphael had reached heights of power and influence unknown to any previous artist. As the result of a rather mysterious agreement between the pope, Baldassare Castiglione, and the artist himself, he undertook to re-assert the historical image of

THE VATICAN GARDEN HOUSE AND THE DOME OF ST. PETER'S

The architecture of the High Renaissance took a variety of forms. The Raphaelesque and classical culture produced a naturalistic and pictorial type of architecture, sumptuously interpreted by Pirro Ligorio (1510–83) in the gardens of the Vatican. The crucial role played by Michelangelo in architectural works for the papacy led him

to adopt an increasingly individual and subjective understanding of structures and the orders, transforming them into dynamic new forms. Pirro Ligorio, the architect of the Villa d'Este at Tivoli, built the *casino* (garden house) for Pius IV in the Vatican Gardens in accordance with the humanist ideal of man's harmony with nature. The structure is on the slope of a hill and is surrounded by flights of steps, niches, courtyards, and loggias. The whole of the facade is

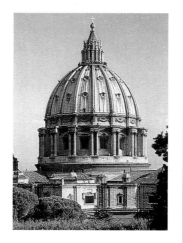

Michelangelo, Dome of St. Peter's, Vatican City, 1546–64.

decorated with classical motifs and mythological scenes, which continue even more abundantly on the interior. At about the same time, Michelangelo was working on a model for the dome of St. Peter's, the final part of his design for the basilica. Rejecting Antonio da Sangallo the Younger's wild Mannerist design, he reinstated some of Bramante's original features, but he kept the Florentine ribbed dome rather than Bramante's hemisphere. When Michelangelo died in 1564, the drum, with its system of buttressing consisting of projecting paired columns alternating with large windows, was under construction. Another of his designs that he never saw completed was the magnificent entrance hall of the Laurentian Library in Florence. This was built from a model produced in 1557.

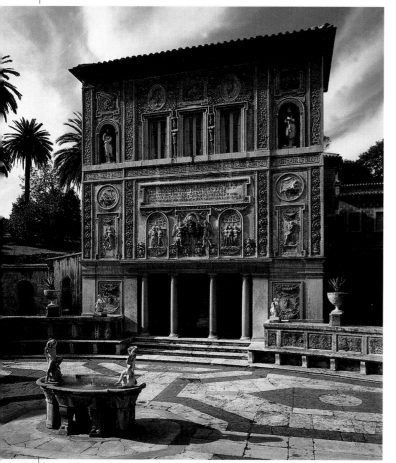

Pirro Ligorio, garden house of Pope Pius IV, facade, Vatican City, 1558–62.

Baldassare Peruzzi, Palazzo Massimo alle Colonne, Rome, 1532–36.

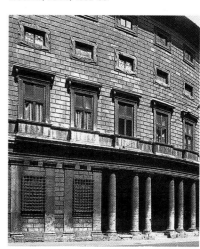

LEONARDO DA VINCI: "VIRGIN OF THE ROCKS"

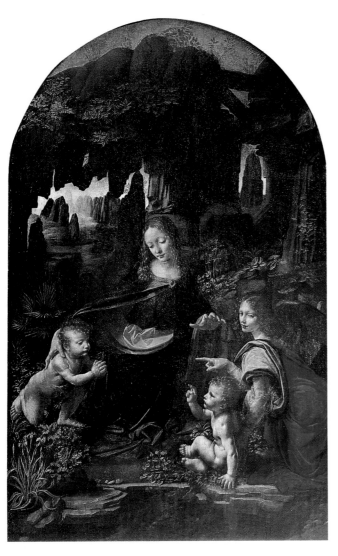

Circa 1483–86; oil on panel (transferred to canvas); 78 x 48 in (198 x 123 cm). Musée du Louvre, Paris.

The Virgin Mary has her right arm around the shoulders of infant St. John the Baptist, who kneels in prayer. Her left hand, slightly open, hovers above the head of the seated Christ child. A kneeling angel points at St. John with his right hand, while his left supports Christ. The figures occupy a large part of the composition; they are placed against a dark background of jagged rocks rising to an arch, through which a misty landscape may be glimpsed.

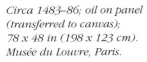

► *1. The painting can be divided into four parts by a vertical axis through the face of the Virgin and a horizontal axis that links the head of John, the hand of Mary, and the face of the angel. Just below this, a parallel line links John's hands with that of the angel. A second vertical axis joins the Virgin's hand with the angel's underneath and the face and body of the Christ child. Farther to the right, a third axis from a rocky pinnacle in the cavern passes through the figure of the angel and highlights the spiral composition in the lower right-hand corner. As the gazes of the Virgin and John converge on Jesus, the lines joining their heads form a regular triangle, although perspective makes the two sides that meet on the Christ child seem longer. A circle drawn around this triangle passes through all four faces, while the lines that meet above Mary's head form a pyramid that contains all the figures.*

▼ *2. The composition has a great spatial dimension to it. The figures rotate around the central axis in the body of Mary; their actions and positions create the effect of a conical shape that encloses them, its apex at the top of Mary's head. The Christ child, at the edge of the cone, puts his hand out toward the observer. A diagonal connects the infant to the area of light in the background, creating an oblique spatial dimension between both upper and lower areas and light and dark. Above the figures, arched rocks echo the shape of the panel and seem to trap the energy created by the interaction below. A deep and mysterious spiritual tension governs the relationships among the figures, the surrounding space, and the colors, created by the variety of planes and volumes hidden in the work.*

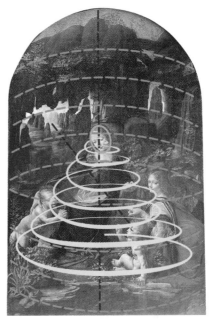

▼ *3. Light filters through the gaps in the rocks in the background, but does not illuminate the figures. Instead, they are captured by a smoky half-light that picks out delicate faces, soft flesh tones, and exquisite curls. The skin of the Virgin is a source of light in itself. Known as sfumato, this technique of blending different areas of color and tone was introduced by Leonardo. The rock formations in the background are defined and then almost reabsorbed by the light, vanishing into an ethereal mist. Leonardo described this as atmospheric or "aerial" perspective. It is based on the optical effects of absorbed and reflected light and involves a careful grading of color according to the density of the atmosphere. The rocks are darkest in the foreground, becoming paler and taking on a bluish tone toward the horizon, where eventually they are obscured in the mist.*

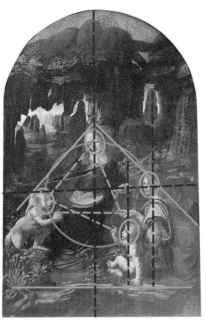

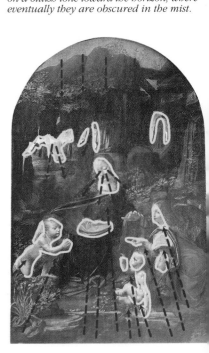

◄ *4. A variety of plant life, depicted in detail, is included in the area between the infants and in the space beyond Mary and the angel, representing the presence of nature. The same attention has been paid to the definition of the physical environment, with naturalistically painted rocks, crags, and caverns. Part of Leonardo's writings was concerned with geology, and he is regarded as one of the founders of this science. Another crucial element of the work is the sense of dampness, an impression given by the plants, the half-light, the recesses, and the quality of the air. Traditional interpretations cite the cave of the Nativity and the cave of the Sepulcher as the inspiration for the rocky background. Whatever the origins of the subject and its wild setting, it is a truly romantic vision.*

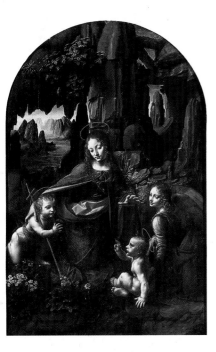

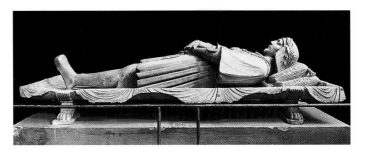

Bambaja, Tomb of Gaston de Foix. Museo del Castello, Milan.

the city of Rome as the capital of the Christian world with an ambitious archaeological and construction project.

In 1512, after returning to Milan for a short time, Leonardo da Vinci also made the essential trip to Rome, by then a mecca for any painter in Italy and northern Europe: Raphael himself had come in 1508 to decorate the Vatican apartments of Julius II. Leonardo's young friend Agostino Busti, also known as Bambaja (1447–1522), was also there, enthusiastically gathering suggestions for future Milanese funerary monuments, but although Leonardo's interest in classicism was important, it was also limited. After a brief stay in Rome, he accepted an invitation from the French king Francis I, calling him to

Amboise, where he remained until his death. Here, he put forward important suggestions for the royal residence of Romorantin that were later abandoned in favor of the chateau of Chambord, where echoes of Leonardo embellish the rooms. Homage to his style is evident in early 16th-century French architecture, which turned away from the defensive structure of castles, preferring instead the elegant construction of court palaces such as those at Gaillon, Chenonceaux, and Blois.

NORTHERN ITALY IN THE AGE OF TITIAN

During the first two decades of the 16th century, Milan and other northern Italian city-states were subject to severe dynastic strife. Having reconquered Milan from the Sforza's in 1515, the French king Francis I ruled the duchy until 1521, when he lost it to his great rival, the Hapsburg emperor Charles V. During this time, the Milanese art scene was dominated by

▲ *5. This second version of the painting is housed in the National Gallery, London, and is also attributed to Leonardo. It contains the same features as the Louvre work, but there are variations: the angel's clothes are different and less striking; the shapes of the heads are not as graceful, particularly that of the Christ child; the texture of the rocks is different; the damp atmosphere has almost disappeared; and the wonderful naturalness of the interaction among the figures has deteriorated into rather affected glances. These variations have raised the question of whether this is a genuine work by Leonardo or a copy by a pupil. It is known that Leonardo left the London version in the chapel of San Francesco Grande in Milan, for which it was painted. There is much uncertainty surrounding Leonardo da Vinci and his works, some of which were damaged or disappeared not long after completion. Others were handed to his followers to be copied. As a result, some of the remaining paintings by Leonardo are occasionally attributed to other artists.*

RAPHAEL'S VATICAN STANZE

Raphael's decoration of the Vatican apartments for Pope Julius II began with the Stanza della Segnatura. In a cycle about the human intellect that asserts the ideals of goodness, truth, and beauty, the artist included his *School of Athens,* with its theme of philosophy, and *Disputation over the Holy Sacrament,* with its theme of theology. The former is a summary of the history of philosophical thought. It centers on the figures of Aristotle and Plato, who are depicted in the center of a large building reminiscent of both classical basilicas and the new St. Peter's. Raphael tried to achieve complete balance in the composition, the variety of figures shown forming a

Raphael, School of Athens, Stanza della Segnatura, Vatican City, 1509–10. The new frescoes for the Vatican apartments replaced older ones by Andrea del Castagno and Piero della Francesca.

Raphael, Expulsion of Heliodorus, Stanza d'Eliodoro, Vatican City, 1512.

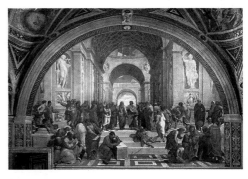

representation of the ideal relationship between the different philosophical beliefs. In the later, and more dramatic, Stanza d'Eliodoro, painted between 1511 and 1514, the

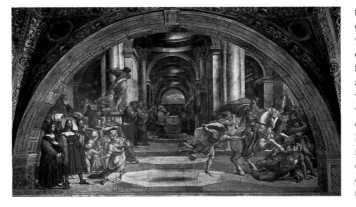

theme is divine intervention on behalf of the Church. In this work, Raphael showed quite different influences. There are, for instance, hints of Michelangelo's Sistine Chapel in the weight and build of the figures, while touches of Venetian art, especially that of Sebastiano del Piombo, are also evident. These more dynamic works depend on a stronger use of light and color, typified by the drama of the *Expulsion of Heliodorus.*

TITIAN AT THE CHURCH OF THE FRARI

In the great Gothic church of Santa Maria Gloriosa dei Frari in Venice, Titian worked on two altarpieces that progressively moved away from the rigid centralized compositions of the Early Renaissance to form a new style. In the *Assumption of the Virgin* (1518), the composition follows the dynamism of the action. To the excitement of the apostles below, angels raise the Virgin toward the open arms of the Lord. It is a picture of motion, light, and color, in which all the movement follows a circular rhythm, immersed in an atmosphere of golden light, moving from the dark tones of the earth to the brilliance of the heavens. In *Madonna of the House of Pesaro*, commissioned in 1519 for a lateral altar in the Frari, Titian adopted a strong diagonal composition in preference to the traditional centralized scheme. He placed the Virgin Mary to one side,

against one of two vast columns that soar up and disappear out of sight. The configuration of the saints and donors conforms to Titian's diagonal-triangular principle, the primary point of the triangle being the Virgin's head, the other points formed by the heads of the two kneeling chiefs of the Pesaro family.

Titian, Madonna of the House of Pesaro, 1519–26. Santa Maria Gloriosa dei Frari, Venice.

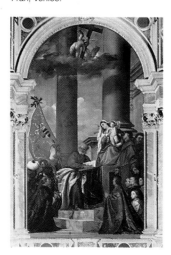

Bramantino and the young Bernardino Luini (c.1480–1532). Bramantino's painting and architecture synthesized classicism into a sense of intimacy and pathos, while Luini combined the example of Leonardo with new ideas picked up from his direct contact with Raphael's work. As a result, Luini is the most

Sebastiano del Piombo, Pietà, c.1520–25. Museo Civico, Viterbo, Italy.

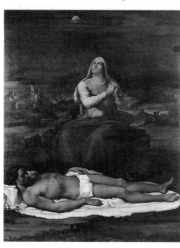

"Roman" of Lombard Renaissance artists, as can be seen from his frescoes at the sanctuary of Saronno.

In Venice, Titian succeeded Giorgione following his early death in 1510, and it is thought that he completed a number of the former's unfinished works. Exploiting color to the full, Titian created powerful compositions, skillfully distributing figures according to color contrasts in the skin and clothes, as seen in *Sacred and Profane Love* (c.1515). One of his first public commissions, the *Assumption of the Virgin* for the church of Santa Maria Gloriosa dei Frari, established his reputation as a colorist. In this, the traditional design of an altarpiece was superseded by a vast and dramatic arrangement of figures rendered in rich colors and bathed in light.

Contact between Venice and Rome was kept alive by Sebastiano del Piombo, one of Michelangelo's most skillful

collaborators. Sebastiano was one of the main exponents of a style that united Venetian colorism with the sculptural character of Roman painting, and was called to Rome by Agostino Chigi to participate in the decoration of the Villa Farnesina.

The work of another Venetian painter, Lorenzo Lotto (c.1480–1556), reveals links between Lombardy and the Marches, where he painted, and northern cultures. As a young man, Lotto had had contact with Raphael and the master's painting of the Stanza della Segnatura. An almost theatrical style illuminated the work of Lotto, as can be seen in the scenes in the Oratory of Suardi and in the altarpiece of the church of San Bernardino. Across northern Italy, there was a move toward a clearer and more emotive representation of Catholicism, creating a bastion of Catholic iconography against the onslaught of Lutheranism. One of the most interesting examples is the site of Sacro Monte at Varallo, where architecture, sculpture, and painting were all combined to re-create the holy places of

Jerusalem in a series of chapels on the hill. Greatly influenced by Franciscan culture, which encouraged total immersion in Catholic ideology, the leading artist was Gaudenzio Ferrari (c.1471–1546), who used a highly theatrical form of representation to depict the episodes from the life of Christ. In both frescoes and sculptures, his crowded scenes had great expressive impact. A similar example can be found in the decoration of Cremona Cathedral, where artists of different extractions worked between 1515 and 1520. As a result, there are a number of different styles, varying from the restrained, late 15th-century compositions of Boccaccio Boccaccino, through important contributions by Altobello Melone and Gerolamo Romanino (c.1484–1560), to the almost barbaric and anti-classical drama of Pordenone (c.1483–1539). Pordedone's work was remarkable for the immediacy of his figures, recalling those of Michelangelo in the Sistine Chapel.

Lorenzo Lotto, Madonna of the Canopy, 1521. San Bernardino, Bergamo, Italy.

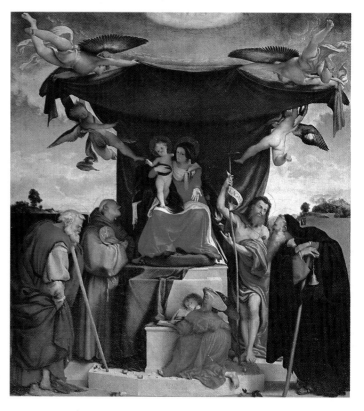

SACRO MONTE AT VARALLO AND THE MORBEGNO ALTARPIECE

The work of Gaudenzio Ferrari is probably the best reflection of the spiritual art favored by the religious culture of the time, especially in the Alpine areas marking the border between Catholicism and Protestantism. The activity of this Piedmontese painter began at the mountain shrine of Sacro Monte at Varallo, which was begun in 1486 by Franciscan monks and continued in the 17th century with the addition of many other chapels. Gaudenzio's decoration of the chapel dedicated to the Crucifixion gives a dramatically visual backdrop to the setting and the statues that animate it. At Morbegno, Gaudenzio painted a wooden altarpiece carved by Giovan Angelo del Maino. The statue of the Virgin

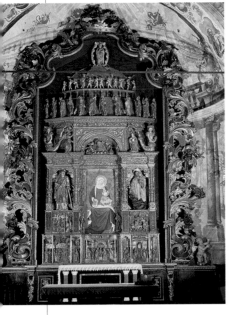

Giovan Angelo del Maino, Gaudenzio Ferrari, and assistants, Assumption Altarpiece, 1516–26. Sanctuary of Morbegno, Italy.

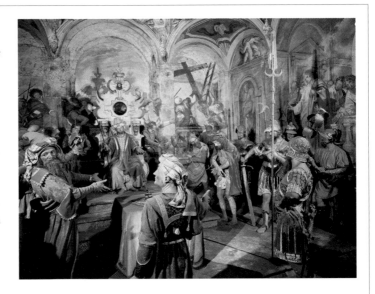

Christ Condemned, *Chapel XXXV of Sacro Monte, Varallo. The statues are by Giovanni d'Errico (c.1560–1644), and the frescoes, painted in about 1611, are by Morazzone (c.1571–1626), a follower of Gaudenzio Ferrari.*

Mary is part of a scheme depicting the episodes of her life. The setting is more restricted than that at Varallo, but the narrative richness and spiritual aura are the same.

In Parma, the originality of Renaissance painting owes much to the merging of Lombard and Venetian styles. The youthful work of Correggio (c.1489–1534) was significant, but after 1518, when he moved to Parma and absorbed other influences (Raphael's *Sistine Madonna*, c.1512–15, was in nearby Piacenza), he developed an ingenious personal style. In the dome of San Giovanni Evangelista in Parma and the abbess' room in the convent of San Paolo (1518), the artist's illusionistic compositions soften the narrative.

Gerolamo Romanino, Love's Yearning, 1531–32. Castello del Buonconsiglio, Trento, Italy.

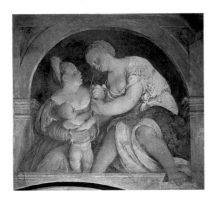

CORREGGIO AND PARMIGIANINO

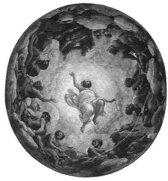

In the early 1520s, two great northern Italian masters, Correggio and Parmigianino (1503–40), made an important contribution to the art of decoration with their frescoes for the church of San Giovanni Evangelista in Parma and the Rocca di San Vitale in Fontanellato, respectively. Both Correggio in his *Vision of St. John the Evangelist* and Parmigianino in his *Myth of Diana and Actaeon* display their innate talent for naturalism. In the San Giovanni dome there are various Roman, and mainly

Raphaelesque, features, but Correggio frees the scene totally of architectural elements, leaving the figures in a vortex of light and clouds. This anticipates the most liberal of Baroque compositions. While still young, Parmigianino,

Correggio, Vision of St. John the Evangelist, fresco in dome, San Giovanni Evangelista, Parma, 1520–23.

Parmigianino, Myth of Diana and Actaeon, ceiling in the Rocca di San Vitale, Fontanellato, c.1522.

from nearby Fontanellato, was influenced by Correggio. However, he was already proving himself more fluent and refined than his elder, preferring more intimate scenes. His trip to Rome in 1524 and contact with Michelangelo eventually led him away from the High Renaissance style toward Mannerism, accentuating the formal aestheticism and delicate balance, while maintaining a highly refined sense of color and composition.

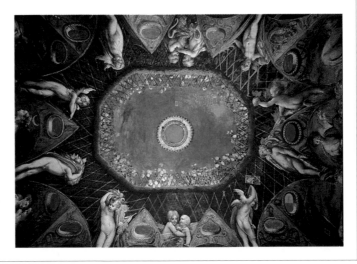

ROSSO FIORENTINO'S "DEPOSITION" AND PONTORMO'S "VISITATION"

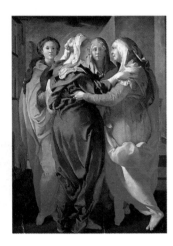

Jacopo Pontormo, Visitation, 1528. Pieve di San Michele, Carmignano, Italy.

Rosso Fiorentino, Deposition, 1521. Pinacoteca, Volterra, Italy.

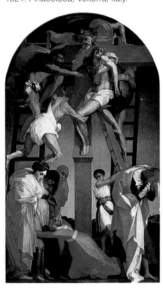

Both students of Andrea del Sarto, Rosso Fiorentino and Jacopo Pontormo were among the most ardent anticlassical interpreters of Renaissance developments, and particularly those of Michelangelo. The *Deposition* by Rosso and the *Visitation* by Pontormo show how the restless Florentine culture could take the striking colors and daring compositional formulas of the Sistine Chapel and apply them to works of extreme formalism. Sometimes their use was highly figurative, as in the expressive moments of the *Deposition,* and at others they were employed in fluent and transparent chromatic fields, as in the *Visitation*. In the metaphysical setting of Rosso's altarpiece, the figures are positioned in sharp planes of light and shade. Pontormo's painting appears to have a double image, the onlookers repeating the features of the protagonists in a frontal view. Florentine painting was reaching a disconcerting crisis with this juxtaposition of reality and illusion, and search for spiritual meaning.

MANNERISM

The diversity of Italian High Renaissance art was remarkable. Artistic trends merged, crossed over, and pulled away from one another, enriching the style of individual artists and exerting a profound influence on the main artistic centers of Rome, Venice, Florence, Bologna, and Milan. An early 16th-century traveler to the Italian peninsula seeking to admire the revival of classical style in the works of Raphael and Michelangelo would have been shocked to see the daring experimentation being carried out by Correggio in Parma and Pontormo and Rosso Fiorentino (c.1495–1540) in Florence. In 1520, Raphael died, and seven years later Rome was sacked. The entire decade was beset with catastrophe, from plagues and famine to sieges and battles. Its effect on the artistic world was the dispersal of artists, particularly those who had learned their skills from Raphael. Polidoro da Caravaggio moved to Naples and then to Sicily; Giulio Romano went to Mantua; Berruguete to Spain; and Rosso Fiorentino and Sebastiano Serlio (1475–1554) to France.

Veronese, Feast in the House of Levi, 1573. Galleria dell'Accademia, Venice. Painted initially as the Last Supper, *this painting was considered an inappropriate treatment of the subject by the Inquisition. The title was therefore changed.*

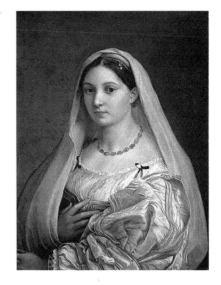

Raphael, Portrait of a Lady or The Veiled Lady, *1516. Palazzo Pitti, Florence.*

As a result, the "modern" style became diluted, reinterpreted by some and refuted by others. This was the start of the period in art labeled Mannerism – from the Italian *maniera,* meaning "style" – the precise definition and boundaries of which remain the subject of debate. The most widely held opinion is that it originated in a crisis of the Renaissance and marked a break with classicism. Indeed, the first signs of an anti-Renaissance direction can be seen in the work of Piero di Cosimo during the late 15th century. Another point of view regards it as regional, evolving from the art produced in Milan and Venice during the 1520s

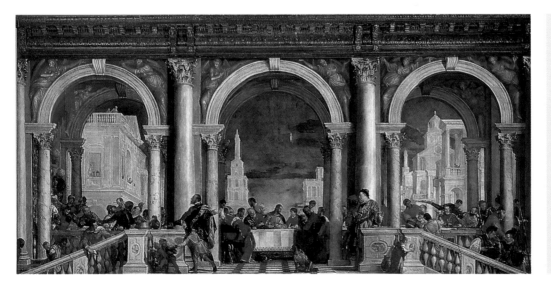

MICHELANGELO'S SLAVES

In 1505, Pope Julius II summoned Michelangelo to Rome to work on his tomb, an ambitious design for a magnificent monument to be placed in the old St. Peter's. Over time, the plans for the project were repeatedly modified, and many of the sculptures for the work were never completed: the artist himself spoke of "the tragedy of the tomb."

Michelangelo's *Slaves,* which were to be placed under a group of *Victories,* were completed in two stages: the first in 1512 to 1513 (presently in the Louvre, Paris) and the second in about 1532 (in the Accademia in Florence). These figures, which emerge from the stone as if they are trying to escape from it, represent Michelangelo's expression of ideal form recovered by

"freeing" the figures from the marble. The unfinished state of these figures has led to many symbolic meanings being given to their dramatic forms. They were subsequently acquired by Duke Cosimo I, who had them installed in a grotto in the Boboli Gardens.

Michelangelo, "Crossed-Leg" Captive, 1530–34. Gallerie dell'Accademia, Florence.

An examination of Michelangelo's work, starting with the *Doni Tondo* (c.1503) and the Sistine Chapel (1508–12) and culminating in the Medici tombs in Florence (1520–34) and the *Last Judgment* (1536–41), reveals how much he had contributed to this development.

There are also different interpretations of the impact on art and architecture of religious upheavals both before and after the Council of Trent (a council of the Catholic Church that met between 1545 and 1563 to address the powers of the

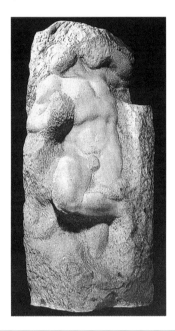

Domenico Beccafumi, Birth of the Virgin, c.1540–43. Pinacoteca Nazionale, Siena.

and 1530s. Unfortunately, most artists' biographies do not record periods of crisis, with the exception of cases such as Pontormo, who Vasari suspected of heresy or madness at the time of his

painting the frescoes in San Lorenzo, Florence(1546–1551), and Michelangelo, who left an extraordinary testimony of his spiritual torment in his poetry. Current interpretations of Mannerism stress the anticlassical feeling that arose in the early 1500s. Following this point of view, the work of artists such as Dosso Dossi (c.1489–1542) in Emilia, Pontormo, Rosso Fiorentino, and Domenico Beccafumi (1485–1551) in Tuscany can be interpreted as experimental, challenging classical rules and often introducing elements of northern European art. However, a continuing debt to the "masters" of the High Renaissance is also evident in their work. For example, while Pontormo clearly borrowed elements of Michelangelo's style, he took them to the limits of license and subjectivity. Soon after, in Venice, Tintoretto, Veronese, and the Spanish artist

El Greco (1541–1614) would in their own styles conclude this fullness of Renaissance harmony.

It seems most likely, as Vasari suggests, that Mannerism was both born out of the Renaissance and was a fundamental part of it – a modern style in which the artist's own interpretation superseded the imitation of nature. Vasari recognized a substantial balance between Mannerism and realism – a "spontaneity which, although based on correct measurement, goes beyond it" – even though he personally preferred the individual approach, provided it was supported by good judgment. Seen in this way, Mannerism is both the main variant within the culture of Renaissance art and a protagonist in the debate between subjectivity and objectivity, between the individual and reality. Humanism – a secular cultural and intellectual movement during the Renaissance that interested itself in the literature, art, and civilization of ancient Greece and Rome – had already addressed this duality. After the brief but intense period when Raphael and Bramante were in Rome, when art seemed to reach the pinnacle of harmony and grace, the two poles of the argument soon revealed themselves as extremes in a very difficult relationship.

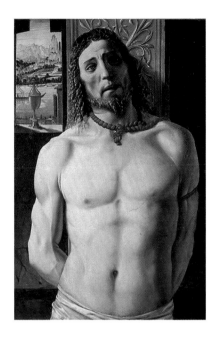

Donato Bramante, Christ at the Column, c.1480. Pinacoteca di Brera, Milan.

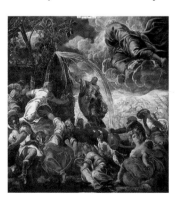

Tintoretto, Moses Striking Water from the Rock, 1575–77. Scuola Grande di San Rocco, Venice. This painting belongs to one of the most famous cycles of late Venetian Mannerism.

TINTORETTO

Jacopo Robusti, known as Tintoretto (1518–94), was the Venetian master of dramatic Mannerism, and there is a great psychological depth to his portraits. Influenced by Titian and the expressionist Roman style of Pordenone, his series for Venice's Scuola Grande di San Marco and Scuola Grande di San Rocco and his pieces for the Doge's Palace were among his most notable works. So, too, were the religious works the *Last Judgment* in the Madonna dell'Orto in Venice and the *Discovery of the Body of St. Mark* in the Brera Gallery, Milan. Tintoretto's large body of work, produced at tremendous speed, deeply influenced the Baroque movement.

ANTI-RENAISSANCE ART

During the development of the figurative art of the Renaissance, certain anticlassical reactions sprang up as early as the turn of the 16th century (the classical Humanism of Donatello and Masaccio was already three-quarters of a century old). One was in the work of the Milanese artist Bramantino, a painter and architect of great formal sensibility. In his *Virgin of the Towers,* he reveals his talent for perspective in the foreshortening of the mysterious figures in the foreground, with a monumental framing of the figures and

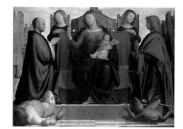

Bramantino, Virgin of the Towers, c.1515. Pinacoteca Ambrosiana, Milan.

architecture behind. A fluid rhythm in the color and composition of the garments unites the figures, with their unusual, curious faces. Giulio Romano arrived at his

pictorial style by a very different route. An assistant of Raphael in the Vatican apartments, he went on to build and decorate the Palazzo Te in Mantua. His interest in the most naturalistic aspects of classicism led him to challenge the rules of the Roman architect Vitruvius, which were at the heart of Renaissance architecture. He experimented with puzzling images, distortion, humor, and a primitive form of vitality, as seen in the Sala dei Giganti in the Palazzo Te. The entire room was

decorated with turbulent figures, their surroundings collapsing about them, in a vision that could not be farther from the harmonious ideals of the Renaissance spirit.

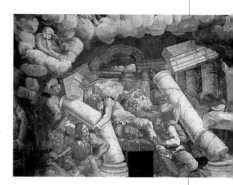

Giulio Romano, The Fall of the Giants, 1532–34. Palazzo Te, Mantua, Italy.

Papacy and the role of bishops). Apart from contact documented between certain artists and Lutheran circles, including Michelangelo himself, the strong individualism of Protestant thought and the intellectualism of certain of its aristocratic followers found favor with the more emotive and sophisticated artistic trends of the time. In response, the Catholic Church encouraged a popular form of art through commissions that concentrated on making the content and meaning of its teachings clear and effective. The confident tone of Gaudenzio Ferrari, as well as the nobler, more imposing style of Titian in the years of the *Madonna of the House of Pesaro,* were used by the Catholic Church to support its cause. Moreover, a new sense of realism emerged in the painting of the Brescian artists Girolamo Savoldo (c.1480–after 1548) and Moretto (1498–1554), which emphasized the devotional aspects of their subjects, strengthening and enobling the emotive content with deep color and dazzling patches of light – glimpses of the future style of Caravaggio. A very different style can be found in the formalism of Parmigianino. His elegant, rarefied figures, from his

Madonna of the Long Neck (1534–40) to the frescoes for the semidome and vault of the high altar of Santa Maria della Steccata in Parma (commissioned 1531), were based not on Renaissance principles of balance, but on Mannerist tensions. A younger contemporary of Correggio, Parmigianino left Parma for Rome in 1524 and was probably familiar with the developing Tuscan Mannerist style. His idealized paintings are full of artifice and refined compositional elements. Raphael's pupil, Giulio Romano, produced similarly provocative results in Mantua. His architecture and decoration of the fantastic Palazzo Te for Federigo Gonzaga – built and decorated at great speed between 1527 and 1534 – deliberately go against rules of style and measurement in an attempt to capture the most vital and basic aspects of nature. This is not a place of tranquil symmetry but the subject of experimentation and ambiguity, where the distinction between architectural space and decoration is challenging and unclear. Such ideas were highly successful in Protestant Flanders and Germany, where convention was periodically challenged by outbursts of interest in diversity and misrepresentation.

THE RENAISSANCE OUTSIDE ITALY

The two main political powers of Europe in the early 16th century were France, under King Francis I, and the Hapsburgs, under Emperor

Charles V. Both recognized the potential of the Italian Renaissance to promote their royal and imperial images in suitable classical forms. With the arrival at the royal court in Fontainebleau of Rosso Fiorentino, Francesco

Albrecht Dürer, Adam and Eve, 1507. Museo del Prado, Madrid.

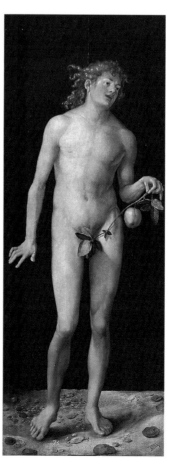

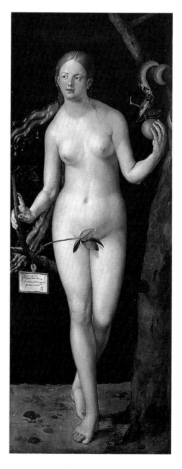

Primaticcio (1504–1570), and Sebastiano Serlio, Mannerism was introduced into France, where it was assimilated by the eclectic, naturalistic tastes of the French world.

Flemish artists were also much in contact with Rome and Italy from the early 16th century. Quentin Massys (c.1466–1530) and Mabuse, also known as Jan Gossaert (c.1478–1532), gradually introduced greater restraint into their painting, initially taking inspiration from Leonardo da Vinci. Tapestries based on Raphael's cartoons were woven in Brussels, thus strengthening the Renaissance feel in the work of artists such as van Orley, in terms of composition and classical taste, while Pieter Bruegel the Elder (c.1525–69) borrowed from Venetian pastoral paintings to create his pictures of Flemish country peasants. There is, however, no hint of Italian classicism in the work of the German artist Hieronymus Bosch (1450–1516). At times realistic and at others fantastic, the mystical nature of his painting was later admired by the Spanish king Philip II. Engraving played an important role in these areas of northern Europe, both as a way of spreading figurative examples and as an independent art form. There were a number of important centers for engraving, such as Antwerp, and the discipline had its own prominent artists, including Lucas van Leyden (c.1494–1533). One of the most significant events in the life of this gifted painter and engraver was his meeting with Albrecht Dürer, the leading figure of Renaissance art in central Europe. Dürer's activities as engraver, painter, and theorist took a decisive turn after a trip to Venice in 1505. His religious works, such as the *Trinity* (1511) in Vienna, became increasingly imposing, with a more mature sense of color. There were important exchanges of ideas on portrait painting, including a new

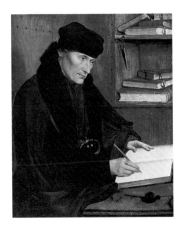

Quentin Massys, Portrait of Erasmus of Rotterdam, *1517. Galleria Nazionale d'Arte Antica, Rome. This portrait of the famous Dutch humanist and Renaissance scholar was painted for Thomas More.*

THE HAPSBURGS AND THE VALOIS

The imperial image of Charles V – king of Spain and Holy Roman emperor from 1519 to 1556 – was the subject of many portraits. At his residences in Augsburg and Brussels, he entertained the greatest painters and sculptors of the time; in turn, they created whole galleries of portrait paintings and sculptures, as well as plaques, medals, and coins. While the image of Charles V was associated with portraiture, by Titian in particular, from his first portrait painted in 1532 to the superb equestrian picture of 1548, that of his son Philip II is linked with a grand architectural project – El Escorial in Madrid. Conceived as a sanctuary,

Titian, Equestrian Portrait of Charles V, *1548. Museo del Prado, Madrid.*

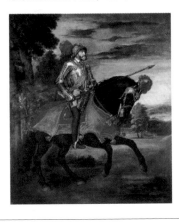

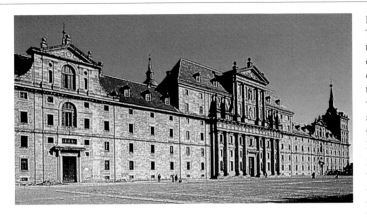

Front view of El Escorial, Madrid, 1563–84.

monastery, residence, and fortress, the building was begun by Juan Bautista de Toledo in 1563 and completed by Juan de Herrera in 1584.

In France, the equivalent showpiece residence of the ruling Valois was at Fontainebleau, where, in 1528, the architect Gilles de Breton transformed the existing medieval castle into an impressive royal residence at the request of the king, Francis I. His design of the palace was influenced by ideas from Italy, based on those of Vitruvius and Alberti. In 1541, the Bolognese architect Sebastiano Serlio, whose writings on Italian Renaissance architecture were published throughout Europe, was appointed *architecte ordinaire*. The most classical section of the palace's regular exterior is the Porte Dorée, with superimposed loggias set between Giant order columns, while the Mannerist style seen in the sequence of windows was echoed inside by Rosso Fiorentino and Primaticcio. Their painting and stuccowork in the Grande Galerie decorated every surface. In 1541, Giacomo da Vignola (1507–73), architect of the Chiesa del Gesù in Rome, worked alongside Primaticcio, and in the 1560s, the Belle Cheminée was completed in a French Renaissance style. The pictorial freedom of Primaticcio, developed by the Fontainebleau school, differed from the experimentalism of Serlio; this led to a new French architectural style, largely through the talent of Philibert de l'Orme (c.1510–70).

Gallery of Francis I, Palace of Fontainebleau.

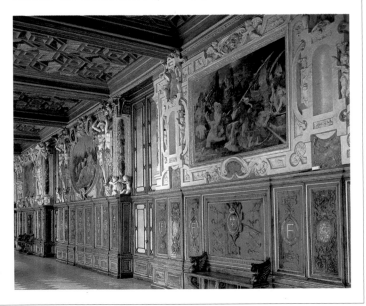

THE WORK OF BOSCH

Hieronymus Bosch was born in 's Hertogenbosch in northern Brabant, Germany, and probably remained there all his life. The rich and imaginative symbolism of his work reveals a knowledge of alchemy, magic, and mystical subjects, linking him to the allegorical culture of the Middle Ages. Popular tales, temptations of saints, biblical episodes, and divine judgments were his chosen subject matter, rarely dealing with more traditional religious themes. Fantastic creatures, monstrous demons, cross-breeds, and strange inventions fill his canvases, their fancifulness matched by an equally refined style. Each detail is rendered with great attention to composition and color, while the entire work emerges out of the careful assembly of every component. Any underlying moralism in Bosch's work is tempered by the friendly and humorous atmosphere of the paintings, into which many people have read all sorts of esoteric meanings.

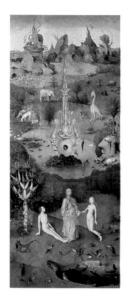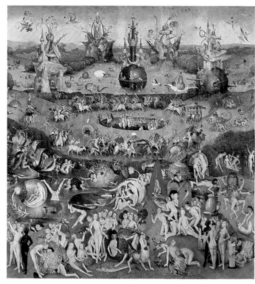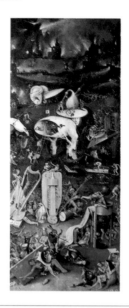

Hieronymus Bosch, Garden of Earthly Delights, *triptych, 1503–04. Museo del Prado, Madrid.*

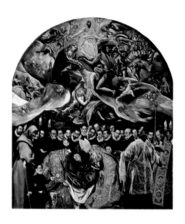

El Greco, The Burial of Count Orgaz, *1586. Museo de San Tomé, Toledo. This extraordinary painting is one of the great masterpieces of late Mannerism.*

perception of realism and psychology. Dürer approached landscape painting with a great scientific curiosity, matched only by that of

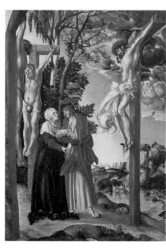

Lucas Cranach the Elder, Crucifixion, *1503. Alte Pinakothek, Munich. In a Mannerist style, the German master places the Crucifixion foreshortened to the right, in a new interpretation of the traditional composition.*

Leonardo da Vinci, later discovering other talented landscape artists among his compatriots, such as Albrecht Altdorfer (c.1480–1538). The extent of the influence of Dürer's engravings in Europe is clear from the number of elements that were borrowed from his series of *The Passion* and *The Life of the Virgin,* which were used again and again in many famous Renaissance works.

Also part of this fertile exchange between North and South were two artists inspired by the Roman Renaissance: Hans Burgkmair and Hans Holbein (c.1498–1543), both from Augsburg, where Charles V had his main residence. Naturally, at Augsburg the emperor was eager to exploit as much classicism as he could to aid his imperial image, and the Italian artist Titian is known to have visited the city, providing further evidence of the mobility of Renaissance art. Elsewhere in Germany, the "expressionist" Mannerism of Lucas Cranach the Elder (1472–1553) and the sculpture of the great Tilman Riemenschneider (c.1460–1531), whose earliest works were characterized by Gothic elements, were being developed. Members of the Nuremberg-based Vischer family were also fine sculptors, their large wooden altarpieces decorated with stories and emotions expressed with great communicative force. These works were part of the sacred art of the Alpine and Pre-Alpine areas, which used sculpture, painting, and small-scale architecture to portray a very solid reflection of human faith – at times incorporating the Italian phenomenon of Sacro Monte – as well as wooden polyptychs.

In Spain, the rule of Charles V, who succeeded his grandfather Ferdinand, had a profound effect on the country's art and architecture, particularly after the court was moved to Madrid. Between 1527 and 1568, the Italian-inspired Palace of Charles V in the Alhambra at Granada was built; it is the only surviving architectural work of Pedro Machuca. The large project of El Escorial for Philip II, designed and constructed in part by Juan Bautista de Toledo (died 1567), who was succeeded by Juan de Herrera (c.1530–97), followed some of the strictest classical designs in Europe. In the first half of the 16th century, Spain was dominated by Flemish-style architecture as well as a Spanish style of ornamentation known as Plateresque decoration. Composed of a mixture of Moorish, Gothic, and Renaissance

EL GRECO

Domenicos Theotokopoulos, known as El Greco (1541–1614), moved to Venice from Greece in about 1567. He worked with Titian and admired the work of Tintoretto, before visiting Rome in about 1570. He then moved to Madrid to work on the palace-monastery of San Lorenzo at El Escorial. He lived in Spain for the rest of his life. The luminosity and inherent spiritualism in his work, the innovative compositions of some of his paintings, and the sumptuous use of color make El Greco one of the great masters of the passage between High Renaissance and Baroque.

FROM SANSOVINO TO PALLADIO

The development of Renaissance architecture in the Veneto region began with Jacopo Sansovino (1486–1570), a Florentine sculptor and architect who fled from Rome to Venice after the sack of Rome in 1527. After the first experiments in the new style of Mauro Codussi (c.1440–1504) in Venice, seen in the church of San Giovanni Crisostomo (1497–1504), Sansovino decisively introduced classicism to Venice by giving the medieval square of St. Mark's the appearance of a Roman forum. The architectural styles of the Procuratie Vecchie, the Loggia of the Campanile, and the Library all have great sculptural force, skillfully contrasting light and shade. Another architect to leave after the sack of Rome was Michele Sanmicheli (1484–1559), who returned to his native Verona. Working under the Venetian Republic, mainly as a military architect, he spread the Roman Renaissance style throughout the Veneto and in Dalmatia, where

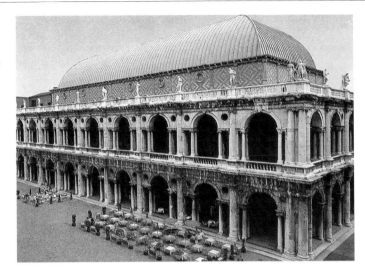

he built fortifications. Meanwhile, farther inland, between the cities of Padua and Vicenza, the talents of the young Palladio (1508–80) were beginning to emerge. His acquaintance with humanists such as Trissino, Barbaro, and Cornaro assured him a classical education, full of universal ideals, and with a solid grounding in the architectural principles of Vitruvius. Palladio managed to go beyond the rhetoric and theory, avoiding too pedantic an approach to the

ancient world. He justified his often anticlassical choices by pointing out the independent validity of contemporary architecture as a part of the continual search for improvement. He won the commission to rebuild the Palazzo della Ragione (now the Basilica) in Vicenza, which became the focal point of the city. With great confidence in his plans, Palladio created a new concept of space where rhythm and design depended on the sculpting of

the framework and the alternation of light and shade. He showed particular skill at adapting his ideas to different types of buildings and environments, as exemplified by the splendid series of villas in the Veneto countryside and in the churches of San Giorgio Maggiore and the Redentore, in the urban setting of Venice.

The Basilica of Vicenza, restructured by Palladio, 1549–1616.

Jacopo Sansovino, (also known as Jacopo Tatti), Madonna with Child, 1503. Loggetta, St. Mark's Square, Venice.

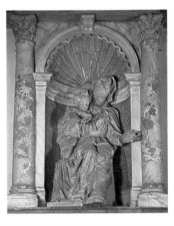

elements, it adorned portals, windows, courtyards, and vaults of castles, churches, and convents from Seville to Toledo – the ancient capital of Spain where El Greco settled in the last quarter of the century – and the university city of Salamanca. As Renaissance elements gradually came to dominate, the decorative style became simpler and more imposing. There were also changes in the painting styles. In the wake of predominantly Flemish influences, evident in the works of Pedro Berruguete in Avila and Toledo, the first signs of Renaissance influence appeared in the work of Yáñez de la Almedina and Fernando de Llanos, who took the Florentine models of Fra Bartolomeo and Andrea del Sarto to Valencia, a major artistic center, in the second decade of the century.

Although both Charles V and Philip II were great admirers of Titian, they never managed to persuade him to take up residence at their courts. One major part of the development of Renaissance sculpture in Spain was the influx of weapons and armor from Lombardy. The great historical scenes on shields and breastplates paid homage to ancient designs and interpreted them with skilled craftsmanship. Similarly, Spanish sculptural decoration was spurred by the Italian tradition of funerary monuments, and the best examples were comparable to the contemporary plastic art of Lombardy and Florence. Leone Leoni (c.1509–90) and his son Pompeo (1533–1608) from Milan became the principal sculptors at the Spanish court. The political and artistic ties between Lombardy and Spain

Giovanni Battista Moroni, Portrait of Count Pietro Secco Suardo, 1563. Uffizi Gallery, Florence. This full-size, unsentimental, and rather analytical representation shows the modern style of portraiture.

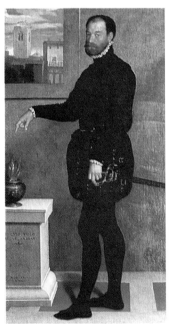

were a determining factor in the development of European art in the course of the 16th century. One example of the dynamism these cultural exchanges provided can be seen in the work of Pellegrino Tibaldi (1527–96), a painter and architect born in the Alpine foothills of Lombardy. Tibaldi trained in Rome, where he came under the influence of Michelangelo, and was called to Milan by Cardinal Carlo Borromeo to give architectural form to the edicts of the Council of Trent; he was then sent as a painter to the Escorial of Philip II. From the Venetian territories, meanwhile, came the fame and example of the great architects Andrea Palladio (1508–80) and Scamozzi (1552–1616), while Giovanni Battista Moroni (c.1525–1578) became renowned for his full-length portraiture.

GOTHIC ART

1115: St. Bernard joins the Cistercian abbey of Clairvaux in northern France. **1140:** Abbot Suger initiates significant architectural innovations in the abbey of Saint-Denis, which anticipate the great age of Gothic art. **1182:** Nicholas of Verdun, sculptor and enameler of the Mosan school, works at Klosterneuburg, near Vienna; St. Francis born in Assisi. **1215:** Domingo de Guzmán (St. Dominic) founds the Order of Preachers. **1220:** Frederick II of Sweden, King of Sicily and Germany, crowned emperor. **1242:** completion of Durham Cathedral, initiating the English Gothic style. **1255:** the Palace of the Popes is built, a rare example of French taste influencing Italian architecture. **1266:** Angevins rule kingdom of Sicily. **1274:** Death of St.

1100   1150   1200   1250

▼ SAINT-DENIS

The ogival-vaulted ambulatory of the choir of the abbey church of Saint-Denis, completed in 1144, constitutes the first example of Gothic architecture.

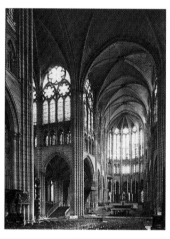

View of the interior of the basilica of Saint-Denis (1140–1281).

▼ CHARTRES CATHEDRAL

In 1145, the facade of Chartres Cathedral was built: the carvings of its three portals, with their complex program of iconography, represent a masterpiece of early Gothic sculpture.

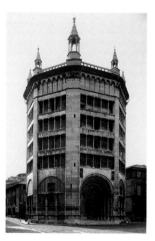

Detail of the Portal Royal, Chartres Cathedral, 1145–70.

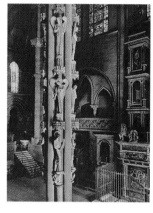

Anonymous, Painted Cross no. 15, from the Church of San Sepolcro. Museo Nazionale di San Matteo, Pisa.

▲ CENTRAL ITALY

Many examples in 12th century of painted crosses depict the crucified Christ, flanked by St. John, the Virgin, and (sometimes) scenes of the Passion.

LINCOLN CATHEDRAL

The vault of the choir of Lincoln Cathedral, built in 1192, exhibits unmistakable features of English Gothic.

Baptistry of Parma (1196–1216).

▲ BAPTISTRY OF PARMA

The baptistry created by Antelami reveals, especially in its upper interior structure, the earliest application of the Gothic in Italy.

▼ STRASBOURG CATHEDRAL

Dating from the 12th to the 14th century, this cathedral demonstrates the link between architecture and sculpture in the Gothic age.

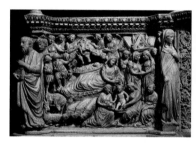

Pilasters of the Angels, Strasbourg Cathedral, 1220–25.

▼ BASILICA DI SAN FRANCESCO, ASSISI

With its blend of local Romanesque and French Gothic forms and its painted decoration by the greatest artists of the 13th and 14th centuries, the basilica di San Francesco in Assisi (1228–53) constitutes an exceptional document of Italian art.

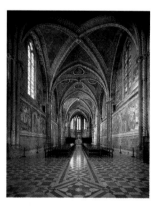

View of the Upper Church toward the apse, Basilica di San Francesco, Assisi.

▼ NICOLA PISANO

(1215/20–1278/84)

A sculptor and architect with his cultural roots in southern Italy, Nicola Pisano set Italian sculpture on a new course, using both classical and Gothic elements. His son Giovanni was also a superb sculptor.

Nicola Pisano, Nativity, pulpit of Siena Cathedral, 1265–68.

▼ CIMABUE

(CENNI DE PEPPO)

(active 1272–1302)

Influenced by the Pisanos, the Florentine painter Cimabue reinterpreted traditionally Byzantine pictorial styles.

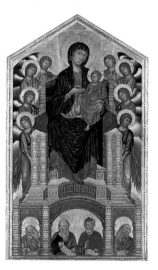

Cimabue, Madonna of the Holy Trinity, 1285–86. Galleria degli Uffizi, Florence.

Thomas Aquinas. **1285:** Arnolfo di Cambio constructs the ciborium for San Paolo fuori le Mura in Rome, influenced by the Parisian rayonnant style. **1306:** Dante Alighieri begins writing the *Divina Commedia*. **1309:** Pope Clement V removes papal seat to Avignon. **1311:** Duccio di Buoninsegna paints his *Maestà* for the high altar of Siena Cathedral. **1326:** Jean Pucelle illuminates a famous Bible, today housed in the Bibliothèque Nationale, Paris. **1350:** the eccentric painter Vitale degli Equi is active in Bologna. **1335:** Giotto paints a (lost) Gloria, surrounded by knights and heroes, in Milan. **1344:** Simone Martini dies at Avignon, having lived there at the papal court for four years. **1348:** devastating plague epidemic in Europe.

1 3 0 0   1 3 5 0   1 4 0 0

◀ GIOTTO
(c.1267-1337)

The revival of naturalism in terms of space and form by this Florentine painter and architect brought about a revolution in Western painting. Giotto's artistic reputation has remained consistent over the centuries, although Vasari's famous claim that he was "born amidst incompetent artists" has long since been considered obsolete.

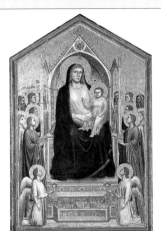

Giotto, Madonna Enthroned, 1310. Galleria degli Uffizi, Florence.

▼ MASTER OF THE TRIUMPH OF DEATH

This eccentric artist has been identified with Traini from Pisa. Only traces remain of the once famous frescoes in the Camposanto, the casualties of World War II bombing.

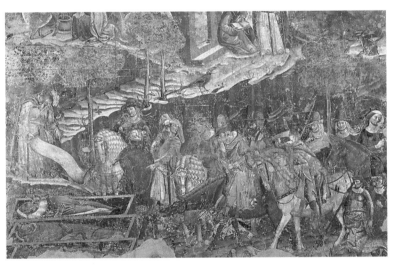

Master of the Triumph of Death, Triumph of Death, left-hand side of the fresco, Camposanto, Pisa, c.1336.

◀ SIMONE MARTINI
(c.1284-1344)

An elegant interpreter of the courtly world, the Sienese painter Simone Martini transfigured reality with pictorial delicacy and grace, providing the foundations for the international development of the Gothic style.

Simone Martini, Apotheosis of Virgil, frontispiece of the Commento a Virgilio by Servio, 1340–44. Biblioteca Ambrosiana, Milan.

▼ GIOVANNI DA MILANO
(GIOVANNI DI JACOPO DI GUIDO)
(active 1346-69)

This Lombard painter revived the moribund Giottoesque tradition in Florence.

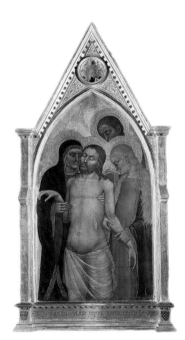

Giovanni da Milano, Pietà, 1365. Galleria dell' Accademia, Florence.

▼ GIUSTO DE' MENABUOI
(c.1330-90)

A Florentine painter active in Lombardy and Veneto, Giusto de'Menabuoi was inspired by the innovations of Giotto. He linked Byzantine and Romanesque styles to formulate an original artistic language.

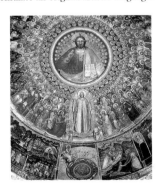

Giusto de' Menabuoi, Pantocrator, Baptistry Vault, Padua, 1375–78.

▼ THE WILTON DIPTYCH

Created by an unknown artist, the profusion of gold and elaborate detail in this celebrated diptych indicate the English taste for linear complexity and lavish color effects.

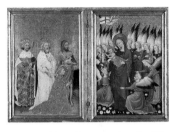

Master of the Wilton Diptych, Richard III Presented to the Virgin, c.1400. National Gallery, London.

▼ FRANCE

A number of miniaturists were active at the court of the Duc de Berry, including the Flemish brothers Paul (or Pol) and Jean de Limbourg.

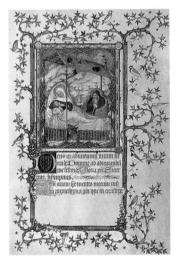

Petites Heures of the Duc de Berry, Nativity, c.1410. Bibliothèque Nationale, Paris.

THE RENAISSANCE

1401: death of Flemish sculptor Claus Sluter. 1404: John the Fearless succeeds his father as Duke of Burgundy, inheriting Flanders from his mother and playing a dominant role at the French court. c.1425: birth of French miniaturist and painter Jean Fouquet, notable for his humanistic sense of form and space. 1428: death of Masaccio, aged only 28. 1442: Alfonso V of Aragon and Sicily conquers kingdom of Naples and lays the foundations for Spanish domination in Europe. 1443: arrival of Donatello in Padua begins the spread of Renaissance forms through northern Italy. 1464: death of Filippo Brunelleschi, Florentine architect and sculptor, fundamental figure of early Renaissance. 1492: Ferdinand of Aragon and Isabella of Castile conquer Granada,

1 4 0 0 – 2 0

▼ JACOPO DELLA QUERCIA
(c.1374-1438)
Following in the tradition of the Pisanos, this Sienese sculptor progressed beyond pure Gothic, leading the way toward a humanist form of sculpture.

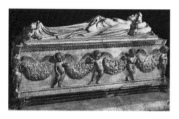

Jacopo della Quercia, Tomb of Ilaria del Carretto, Duomo, Lucca, Italy, 1406–07.

▼ MASACCIO
(TOMMASO DI GIOVANNI)
(1401-28)
The Florentine painter Masaccio revolutionized the course of art within only a few years.

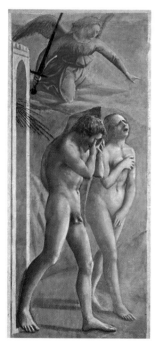

Masaccio, The Expulsion from Paradise, Brancacci Chapel, Santa Maria del Carmine, Florence, 1424–25.

1 4 3 0 – 4 0

▼ FRA ANGELICO
(c.1395-1455)
A major painter of the Florentine Renaissance, Fra Giovanni da Fiesole, earned the popular name Fra Angelico. In the late 1430s his works were fundamentally innovative in composition, color, harmony, and perspective, drawing great inspiration from Masaccio. In *The Annunciation*, volume reminiscent of Masaccio has been chastened into something more slender, but no less spacious, seen in the proportions of the arcaded loggia and the vermilion clad angel.

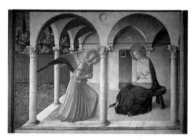

Fra Angelico, Annunciation, Monastery of San Marco, Florence. 1438–46.

▼ ROGIER VAN DER WEYDEN
(c.1400-64)
The leading Flemish painter of his time, Rogier van der Weyden was close to van Eyck and Campin and was extremely influential throughout Renaissance Italy.

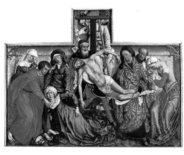

Rogier van der Weyden, The Deposition, c.1440. Museo del Prado, Madrid.

BOTTICELLI
(SANDRO FILIPEPI)
(1445-1510)
Almost all of Botticelli's life was spent in Florence. His studio was always busy and his output was large. At the peak of his career, he was the most popular painter in Florence. However, his style was soon outdated and he died in obscurity.

1 4 5 0 – 6 0

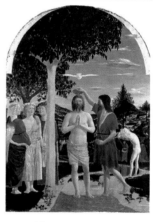

Piero della Francesca, The Baptism of Christ, c.1450. National Gallery, London.

▲ PIERO DELLA FRANCESCA
(c.1415-92)
By means of "divine proportion", this Tuscan painter proclaimed the interrelationship of nature, humanity, and architecture. His combination of Masaccio's modeling, Urbino court geometry, Angelico's enameled tones, and northern naturalism resulted in works of striking modernity.

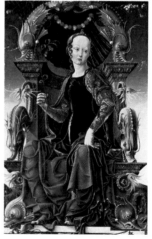

Cosimo Tura, Allegorical Figure, 1460. National Gallery, London.

▲ COSIMO TURA
(c.1430-95)
A painter from Ferrara, Tura was a major representative of the local school. His work is marked by exuberance and fantasy, displaying late Gothic elegance and tension.

1 4 7 0 – 8 0

LEON BATTISTA ALBERTI
(1404-72)
This Italian architect and theorist parted company with the Florentines and formulated the ideal of a new classicism, which still prevailed in the 16th century.

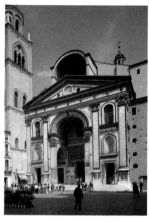

Leon Battista Alberti, facade with triumphal arch of the church of Sant'Andrea, Mantua, Italy, 1470.

▼ BRAMANTE
(DONATO DI PASCUCCIO D'ANTONIO)
(1444-1514)
An architect and painter trained in Urbino, the great Renaissance figure Bramante gave new form to ancient classical models.

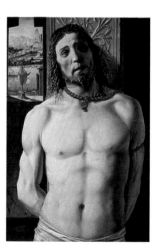

Donato Bramante, Christ at the Column, c.1480. Pinacoteca di Brera, Milan.

last Arab kingdom in Spain. **1494:** Charles VIII, having married Anne, heiress to Brittany, becomes king of Italy. **1517:** Martin Luther launches Protestant religious reform. **1519:**

Charles of Hapsburg, lord of Flanders and king of Spain, elected emperor as Charles V. **1527:** imperial troops invade Italy and ransack Rome. **1545:** opening of Council of Trent, convened to re-

unite Catholicism. **1548:** Turkish architect Sinan builds mosque in Ahmed Pasha, Istanbul. **1550:** first edition of Giorgio Vasari's *Lives of the Most Excellent Architects, Painters, and*

Sculptors published in Florence. **1566:** rebellion in Netherlands against Spanish rule. **1575:** El Greco settles permanently in Spain after prolonged stays in Venice and Rome.

1490 – 1500   1510 – 20   1530 – 40   1550 – 70

HANS HOLBEIN THE YOUNGER
(c.1498-1543)
This German painter and engraver was influenced both by Grünewald and the artists of the Paduan Renaissance.

▼ LEONARDO DA VINCI
(1452-1519)
Painter, sculptor, architect, engineer, and writer, Leonardo examined nature scientifically and is recognized as the most original and complete representative of the Renaissance.

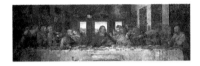

Leonardo da Vinci, Last Supper, Refectory of Santa Maria delle Grazie, Milan, c.1498.

▼ HIERONYMUS BOSCH
(JEROEN ANTHONISZ. VAN AEKEN)
(c.1450-1516)
Bosch was a Flemish painter, whose magical and alchemical allusions – in the context of a style that is still Gothic – gave his works an unmistakably surrealistic dimension.

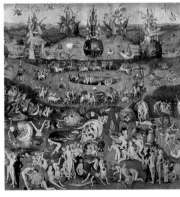

Hieronymus Bosch, detail from Garden of Earthly Delights, triptych, 1503–04. Museo del Prado, Madrid.

PARMIGIANINO
(FRANCESCO MAZZOLA)
(1503-40)
The painter and portraitist Parmigiano produced distinctively elegant and visionary works that were Mannerist in style and represented a reaction against classicism.

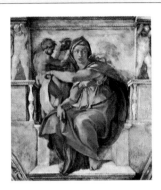

Michelangelo, Delphic Sibyl, fresco, Sistine Chapel, Vatican City, 1509–10.

▲ MICHELANGELO BUONARROTI
(1475-1564)
The great Tuscan sculptor, painter, poet, and architect Michelangelo was indisputably the greatest figure of the High Renaissance. His late works point the way to Mannerism and Baroque.

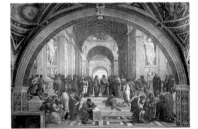

Raphael, School of Athens, Stanza della Segnatura, Vatican City, 1509–10.

▲ RAPHAEL
(RAFFAELLO SANZIO)
(1483-1520)
This painter and architect from Urbino was influenced by the art of ancient Greece and Rome. He developed a coherent, poised, and grandiose style that incarnates the Renaissance ideal of perfection.

▼ GIULIO ROMANO
(GIULIO PIPPI)
(c.1499-1546)
Roman painter and architect, Giulio was a pupil and later chief assistant of Raphael. He was one of the major figures of Mannerist art, and he introduced an exuberantly provocative version of Roman classicism to the court of the Gonzagas.

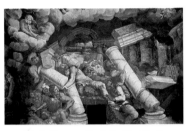

Giulio Romano, The Fall of the Giants, Palazzo Te, Mantua, Italy, 1532–34.

▼ TITIAN
(TIZIANO VECELLIO)
(c.1485-1576)
This Venetian artist was considered to be the greatest painter of the Venetian 16th-century Renaissance. He was unrivaled in his powerfully expressive handling of color.

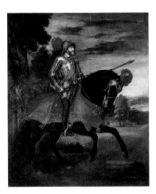

Titian, Equestrian Portrait of Charles V, 1548. Museo del Prado, Madrid.

PIETER BRUEGHEL THE ELDER
(c.1525-69)
A Flemish painter influenced by Bosch, Brueghel revived the tradition of northern social and landscape painting.

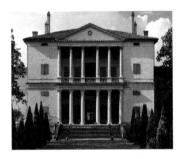

Andrea Palladio, Villa Cornaro, Piombino Dese, near Padua, Italy, 1551–53.

▲ PALLADIO
(ANDREA DELLA GONDOLA)
(c.1508-80)
An architect and theorist from the Veneto, Palladio was trained in the precepts of ancient art, and his work was based on a free reinterpretation of the classical style. This later became known as Palladianism and was extremely popular in Britain. His influence also extended throughout Europe and later to the US.

▼ TINTORETTO
(JACOPO ROBUSTI)
(1518-94)
The Venetian Mannerist painter Tintoretto produced dynamic paintings full of subtle effects of light and shade, which elicited an emotional response.

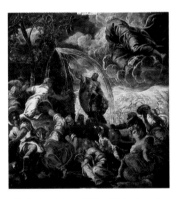

Tintoretto, Moses Striking Water from the Rock, Scuola Grande di San Rocco, Venice, 1575–77.

THE 17TH CENTURY: THE AGE OF SPECTACLE

In the late 16th and early 17th century, a style with its roots in Italy evolved out of Mannerism, expressing new ideas about the world, nature, and human relationships. New concepts of the role of art in relation to civil and ecclesiastical power emerged, as well as a changed attitude toward the private individual's enjoyment of beauty.

During the 17th century, the Catholic Church, by now fully recovered from the schism of the Reformation and more confident of its power following the meetings of the Council of Trent (1545–1563), began to exploit art as a means of disseminating new doctrines. In much the same way, the great European monarchies entrusted artists with the task of creating suitably magnificent and persuasive images of their grandeur.

BAROQUE ARCHITECTURE

The Baroque was a highly theatrical style that relied on illusion, rhetoric, and extravagance for its effects. Over the years, these characteristics have provoked differing reactions: they were rejected during the Neoclassical era, but they have been praised in modern times. The basic elements of the style remained fairly consistent during the course of the 17th century and the first half of the 18th century. Though much altered, they were still utilized in a way that can be termed Late Baroque. The essential characteristics of the Baroque architectural style were the transformation of natural shapes, the alteration of classical proportions, methods of shrinking or expanding

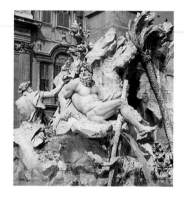

Gianlorenzo Bernini, detail of the Fountain of the Four Rivers, Piazza Navona, Rome, 1648–51. The four rivers – the Danube, Nile, Ganges, and Rio de la Plata – represented the then-known world and hinted at the Church's global influence.

space, and illusionism. These combined to increase the emotional charge of works of art and to create effects of surprise and wonder that were far beyond common experience. Artists strove for an unbroken continuity between internal and external spaces, between painted and architectural space, and between artifice and nature. This sometimes led to the use of natural elements, such as water and light, as well as the combination of techniques and effects from different types of art, making the onlooker play the dual role of spectator and actor.

PIAZZA NAVONA

Built to the express wishes of Pope Innocent X Pamphili, the Piazza Navona in Rome is typical of the Baroque idea of urban space. It transformed the area in front of the Pamphili family palace and the church of Sant'Agnese in Agone into a suitable setting for public entertainment. Indeed, the large open space is contained within the outlines of the ancient Roman racetrack, the Hippodrome of Domitian. The central focus was the Fountain of the Four Rivers (1648–51) by Gianlorenzo Bernini (1598–1680), which probably echoes the temporary structure erected as part of the celebrations of Innocent's election. It exemplifies the synthesis of nature and art, with water gushing from a hollow rock, on which sit personifications of the four continents and the greatest rivers then known. From this base soars the obelisk, symbol of man's aspiration toward the infinite, surmounted by the

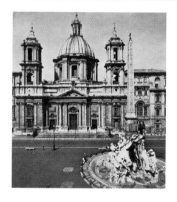

Piazza Navona, Rome. This view shows Bernini's Fountain of the Four Rivers and the facade of Sant'Agnese in Agone.

Piazza Navona, Rome. The Fountain of Neptune can be seen in the foreground.

emblem of the Pamphili family. Two smaller fountains in the piazza, also by Bernini, and the facade of the church of Sant' Agnese (1653–57) by Francesco Borromini (1599–1677) provide a balance to the central fountain. The church's high dome and twin bell towers, along with the vertical axis of Bernini's fountain, contrast with the piazza's horizontal planes.

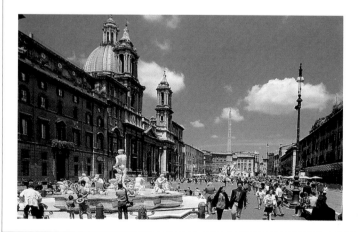

THE URBAN SPACE

The consolidation of great nation states in which power was centralized, the emergence of capital cities as seats of government and symbols of power, and a growth in population and traffic (both pedestrian and wheeled) all contributed to an urgent need to redefine the city. Baroque planning imposed an ordered structure based on a web of wide, straight thoroughfares, which linked a series of focal points, such as gateways, churches, and palaces. To give the townscape a more orderly appearance, continuous streets were created and the facades of important buildings were integrated

Aerial view of St. Peter's, Vatican City. The Vatican buildings, parts of which were altered after Bernini's time, typify Roman Baroque architecture and urban planning.

THE PLACE ROYALE

The Place Royale (now the Place des Vosges) was laid out in 1604 in the then-aristocratic quarter of Paris on land owned by the Crown. Its understated elegance is a product of both its proportions – it is a true square – and the uniformity of the facades that conceal the individual

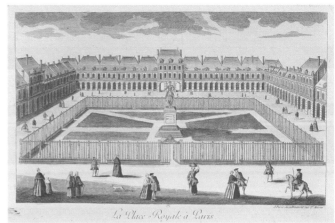

La Place Royale à Paris.

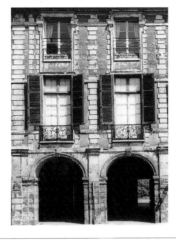

Daumont, Place Royale, Paris *(now the Place des Vosges), 18th-century print.*

Place des Vosges, detail of one of the houses.

houses. Variety is provided by materials: white stone for the architectural framework, red brick for the walls, and gray slate for the roofs. Only the roofs and chimneys demarcate the individual buildings, which have shops at ground level, family residences above, and attics for servants. In the center of the north and south sides, the Pavillon du Roi and the Pavillon de la Reine face each other, providing the square with a central axis; in the middle stands a statue of Louis XIII.

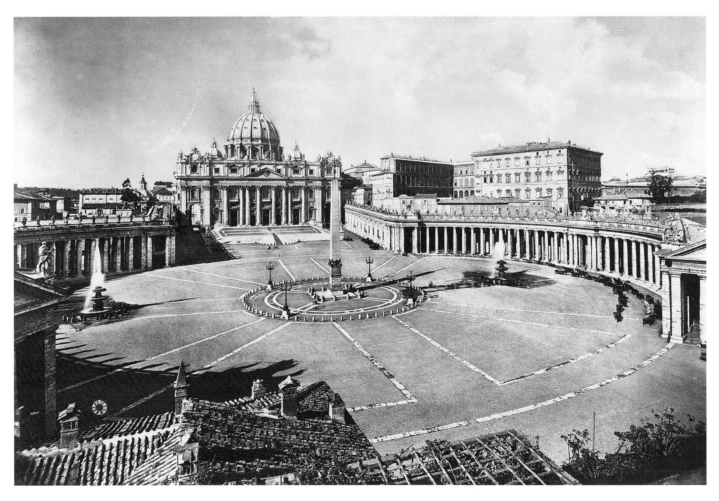

ST. PETER'S SQUARE

Bernini's project for St. Peter's Square was submitted in its definitive form in 1657 and was vigorously supported by Pope Alexander VII Chigi. The colonnaded piazza, linked to the basilica's facade by a small square, is enhanced by the obelisk erected by Domenico Fontana for Sixtus V, as well as by two fountains sited at the focal points of the oval space. Bernini's proposal made the most of the grandeur of the great colonnaded semicircles, which are four columns deep, underlining the symbolic power of the square – they are stretched out toward the city and the world beyond, like the arms of the Church. The variety of visual effects and perspectives balances the relationship between the horizontal space of the piazza and Michelangelo's dome on the basilica itself. A planned third section of colonnade was to have closed the square, but this was never built. Instead, the opening of the great boulevard leading from the church in the 1940s has compromised the sense of enclosure that Bernini sought.

View of St. Peter's Square, Vatican City.

Plan of St. Peter's basilica and piazzas, Vatican City.

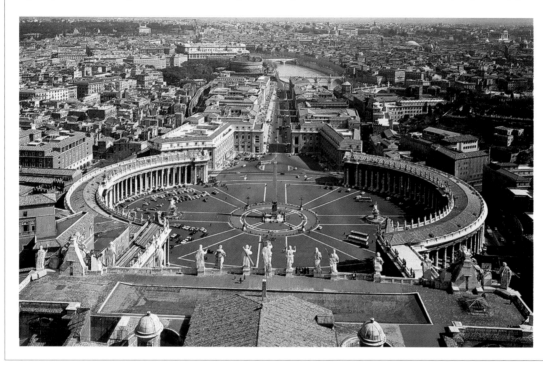

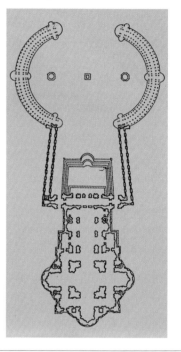

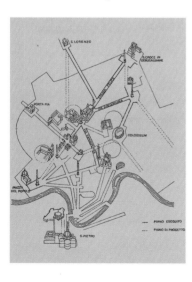

Schematic plan (based on that by the modern scholar Giedion) for the prospective reorganization of Rome under Pope Sixtus V (1585–90). The aim was to create wide, straight thoroughfares, which linked the most important churches. In this drawing, a solid line denotes work actually carried out.

wherever possible to form a harmonious urban fabric. Rome led in this process of urban transformation, and Sixtus V, pope from 1585 to 1590, entrusted the task to the architect Domenico Fontana (1543–1607). The project entailed the construction of straight roads directly linking the seven main basilicas of Rome, several of which were situated in the outskirts of the city. Its practical purpose was to revive depopulated districts outside Rome's historic nucleus and to enliven the holiest of cities. During the course of the century, other building works contributed to the creation of the modern image of Rome: Pope Innocent X (1644–55) commissioned Gianlorenzo Bernini and Francesco Borromini to design the Piazza Navona, and Alexander VII (1655–67) commissioned St. Peter's Square by Bernini, the Piazza di Santa Maria della Pace by Pietro da Cortona (1596–1669), and the Piazza del Popolo by Carlo Rainaldi (1611–91).

As the century progressed, Paris also assumed a more symmetrical appearance. The French capital began to change into a modern city during the reign of Henry IV (1589–1610), who built the Place Royale. This was innovative in its regular geometric shape formed by residential buildings of uniform appearance – such squares were conceived as a setting for a centrally placed statue of the sovereign. Built between 1604 and 1612 in the Marais district of Paris, the Place des Vosges, as it is now called, was the first example of this new urban

BORROMINI

Francesco Castelli, known as Borromini (1599–1677), learned his craft working at Milan Cathedral as a pupil of Francesco Maria Richino (1584–1658), the greatest Milanese exponent of Baroque. From at least 1619 onward, Borromini worked for Maderno and Bernini in Rome, until he received commissions for the convent and church of San Carlo alle Quattro Fontane (1635–41) and the Falconieri and Spada palaces there. The most memorable of his many buildings in Rome include the Chiesa nuova and Oratory for the Congregation of San Filippo Neri and the churches of Sant'Agnese and Sant'Ivo alla Sapienza. Borromini, who eventually took his own life, was one of the most original and inventive exponents of Baroque architecture, which he imbued with soaring upward movement and powerful chiaroscuro effects. He was also one of the finest of a succession of artists, architects, and sculptors, who, from the Middle Ages well into the 18th century, moved from the valleys and foothills of the Lombard Alps into the mainstream of Italian and European art.

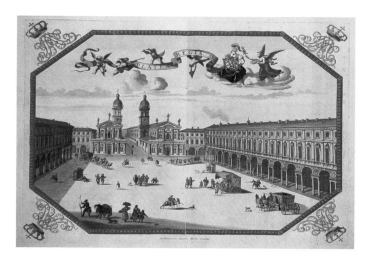

Blaeu, Piazza Reale, Turin, engraving. Library of the Royal Palace, Turin. The great square is notable for the symmetry of the palaces and Juvarra's churches.

countryside. André Le Nôtre (1613–1700) laid out the Tuileries gardens and the Avenue des Champs-Elysées and created the landscape and gardens of the great Palace at Versailles.

The Italian city of Turin, capital of the dukes of Savoy from 1563 onward, underwent similar changes in urban planning; it was transformed by architects such as Ascanio Vitozzi (1539–1615), who created the Piazza Castello and the Via Nuova, and Carlo di Castellamonte (1560–1641), who expanded the city following the grid system used in the original Roman *castrum*. In 1638, he planned the Piazza Reale, now Piazza San Carlo, which was inspired by the Place Royale in Paris, though here closed by two churches with facades by the later Baroque architect Filippo Juvarra (1678–1736).

Pérelle, Place Dauphine, engraving. The square was planned during the reign of Henry IV as part of a plan to rationalize Paris.

feature, and it was followed by the Place Dauphine on the Ile de la Cité. Under the Regent Marie de Médicis (1610–17), the interest of the French Court shifted to the construction of imposing buildings, such as the Palais du Luxembourg. Following the accession of Louis XIII (1617–43), work was resumed on altering and enlarging the Palais du Louvre, but it was only under Louis XIV (1661–1715), when the monarchy felt fully secure, that Paris was transformed into a great capital city. Louis XIV made

his chief minister, Colbert, directly responsible for urban planning, and he oversaw such projects as the creation of the circular Place des Victoires, designed by Jules Hardouin-Mansart (1646–1708), and the polygonal Place Vendôme. The old city walls were demolished and replaced by concentric rings of boulevards, with avenues and streets radiating out toward the surrounding

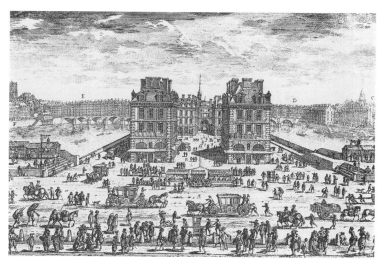

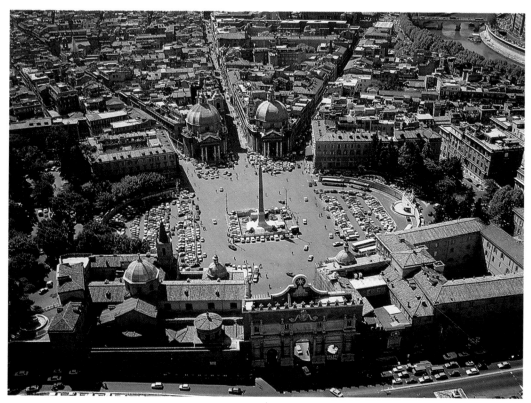

Aerial view of the Piazza del Popolo, Rome. On the far side of the square are the churches of Santa Maria di Montesanto (1662–75) and Santa Maria dei Miracoli (1675–81), by Rainaldi, Bernini, and Carlo Fontana. In the foreground is the Porta del Popolo; the facade facing the square was designed by Bernini (c.1665).

THE MANSARTS

François Mansart (1598–1666) was appointed architect to Louis XIII of France in 1636. He was one of the creators of the *style classique*, which developed from the cultural renaissance in 16th-century France and replaced the Mannerist style with a more purely classical and distinctively French version of the European Baroque. His great-nephew and pupil Jules Hardouin-Mansart became royal architect in 1675 and built the Palace of Versailles around an earlier building by Louis Le Vau, as well as the dome of the Invalides in Paris (1680–1707). His designs for city squares made him an influential town planner in his day. The Mansarts gave their name to the high, steeply pitched "mansard" roof.

THE CHURCH

By the mid-16th century, enthusiasm for the centralized plan as the ideal form for liturgical buildings was waning. After the Council of Trent, Counter-Reformation tendencies within the Catholic Church began to advocate a return to the basilica type. The Gesù (1568–71), the mother-church of the Roman Jesuits

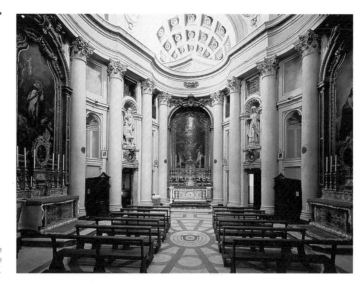

Francesco Borromini, San Carlo alle Quattro Fontane, Rome, view of the interior, 1638–67.

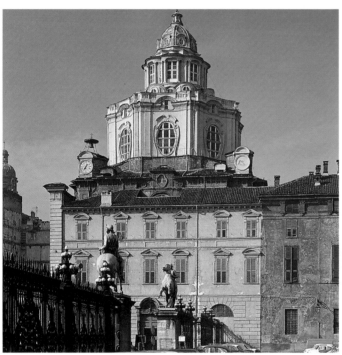

Guarino Guarini, San Lorenzo, Turin, cupola on octagonal base, 1668.

designed by Jacopo Vignola (1507–73), combined both longitudinal and centralized designs, while its monumental dome served both as a visual climax and as an allusion to the symbolic journey of the soul toward God, which begins below in the nave. Elsewhere, Vignola varied the centralized type, providing the church of Sant'Anna dei Palafrenieri (c.1570) with an oval rather than circular ground plan, a device that remained pop-

architect Guarino Guarini (1624–83) rejected the idea of a dome as an enclosing bubble by accentuating certain sections left open to reveal a complicated play of light. Domes also became important features in the urban landscape. In designing the church of Santa Maria della Salute (1631–48) in Venice, Baldassare Longhena (1598–1682) recognized the group of domes of St. Mark's as a model for developing a new emphasis on exterior spaces. At the Roman church of Sant'Ivo alla Sapienza (1642–62), Borromini gave an overall unity to the design by mirroring the ground plan in the outline of the base of the cupola; as the dome rises, it transforms into a perfect circle, while

ular through the 17th century. Baroque church architecture tends to stress either the longitudinal axis, formed by the pathway from the entrance to the altar, or the vertical axis, formed by the altar and the dome, with increasingly daring effects. This was the case at St. Peter's when, in 1607, Carlo Maderno (1556–1629) added a nave and aisles to Michelangelo's centrally planned church. Borromini was later to create dramatic tensions in his interior spaces by drastic variations of scale, while the Turinese engineer and

BAROQUE CHURCH FACADES

In Baroque architecture in general and in ecclesiastical buildings in particular, the facade was extremely important, acting as the element of mediation between internal and external spaces.

In Rome, this idea can be traced back to the late 16th-century church of the Gesù, the facade of which was designed by Giacomo della Porta (1533–1602). It is bipartite, with a strong central axis, emphasized by the double tympanum and portal. During the 17th century, church facades became increasingly important in

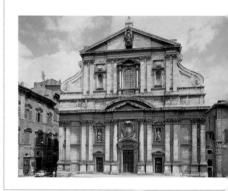

Giacomo della Porta, facade of the Gesù, Rome, 1568–71.

the decorative motifs suggest a continual acceleration of the upward movement of its structure.

Guarino Guarini, San Lorenzo, Turin, interior of dome. Guarini also designed the dome of the Chapel of the Holy Shroud in St. John's Cathedral, Turin.

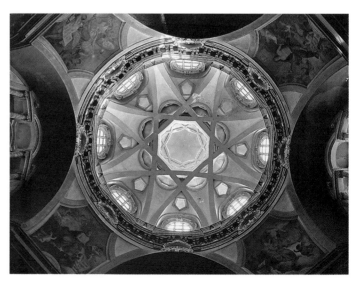

urban areas. Pietro da Cortona's Santa Maria della Pace (1656–57) has an emphatically projecting portico, while the movement in the convex upper section is countered by the flanking walls that curve back to form a fan-shaped space. Bernini reinterpreted Cortona's ideas in Sant'Andrea al Quirinale (1658–61), where the interior and exterior are linked by the exedra, or colonnade, while the convex pronaos, or projecting porch, invites the passerby in. These features are repeated inside the church, marking the boundary between the oval space for the congregation and the main altar. Alternating concave and convex walls were also used by Francesco Borromini for San Carlino alle Quattro Fontane (1667). His facade is like a theater curtain revealing playful, illusionistic scenery and provides a taste of what was to come in the 18th century. The many churches built after the Sack of Rome in 1527 and through the High Baroque period lend harmony to Rome's townscape.

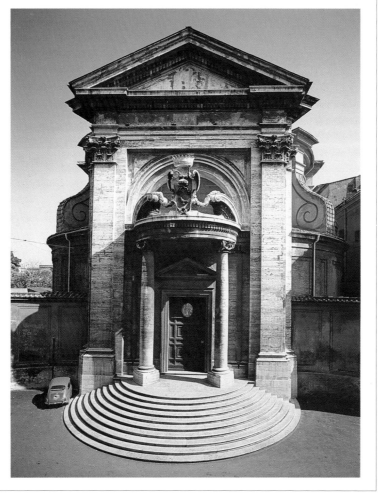

Gianlorenzo Bernini, facade of Sant'Andrea al Quirinale, Rome, 1658–71.

Montecitorio, designed by Bernini for the Pamphili family (1650–55). Its long facade is in five sections, with a projecting central portion and slanting lateral wings; the pilaster bases and window cornices look as if they have been hewn out of rock. The entablature of the portal was originally supported by pairs of telamonic figures (later removed by Carlo Fontana), a motif that was to be widely used in High Baroque architecture in Austria and Central Europe, especially by Johann Bernhard Fischer von Erlach (1656–1723). An even more influential design was Bernini's facade for the

CARLO MADERNO

Carlo Maderno (1556–1629) was a transitional artist who bridged the styles of Mannerism and Baroque in Rome. A nephew and pupil of Domenico Fontana, he designed the facade of Santa Susanna (1595–1603). He was appointed by Pope Paul V as architect of St. Peter's and designed its facade and nave, adopting a basilical plan contrary to Michelangelo's intentions.

THE PALAZZO

The most important aristocratic residence to be built in Rome during the first half of the 17th century was the Palazzo Barberini, designed during the reign of Pope Urban VIII. In 1626, the project was entrusted to Carlo Maderno and was completed after his death by Bernini, assisted by Borromini (1630–32). Its H-plan was inspired by the traditional layout of country villas; the courtyard, flanked by two short projecting wings, introduces the central block, which has an open loggia and entranceway placed on an axis with an oval space that leads out to the garden. Despite being innovative, the design was not imitated for some time in Rome. On the contrary, great emphasis was laid on the facades of city buildings, as occurs at the Palazzo di

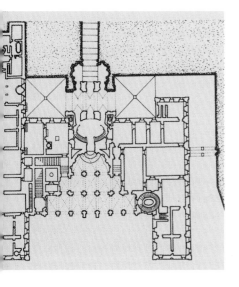

Plan of the Palazzo Barberini, Rome.

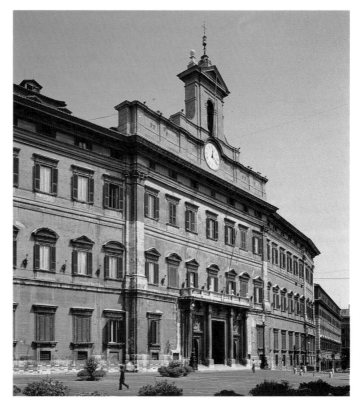

Gianlorenzo Bernini, facade of Palazzo di Montecitorio, Rome, 1650–55.

Palazzo Chigi in the Piazza Santi Apostoli. The central projecting section of the front elevation has pilasters on high bases and is framed by two lateral wings; it is emphasized by a large projecting cornice and balustrade. This design is echoed in Vienna in the Liechtenstein Palace, on which Domenico Martinelli (1650–1718) started work in 1692, and in the city palace of Prince Eugène of Savoy

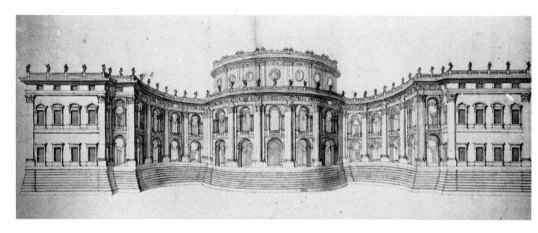

Gianlorenzo Bernini, design for the new facade of the Louvre, first proposal, 1664–65. Musée du Louvre, Paris.

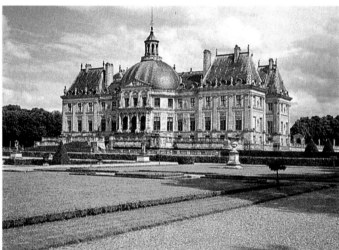

Louis Le Vau, Château Vaux-le-Vicomte, 1657–61. The château, with its garden by Le Nôtre, was built for Nicolas Fouquet, Louis XIV's chief minister.

(1696) and the Schönborn-Batthyány Palace, both by Fischer von Erlach.

The plan of the Barberini palace was exported to France when Bernini was summoned to Paris in 1665 to submit designs for the enlargement of the Louvre.

His first proposal consisted of two grand salons, one above the other, giving their shape to the central oval from which, on the exterior, two concave wings project. This design, derived in spirit from Borromini, was not approved. In his next design, Bernini envisaged a massive block with slightly protruding cornerstones set on a base hewn to resemble a reef emerging from the sea, in complete contrast to the austere lines of the building itself. Work began on this project in 1665, immediately

THE ROYAL PALACE OF VERSAILLES

Versailles is the key expression of 17th-century absolutism and epitomizes the ethos and taste of Louis XIV's reign. It was adopted as a model by other monarchs throughout Continental Europe until the end of the 18th century. Work began at Versailles in 1661, building around the nucleus of a hunting lodge constructed by Louis XIII in 1624. Louis Le Vau was responsible for the project and designed the central section of the new palace, the two wings forming the courtyard, and the garden facade. When the king decided to move the royal court and government to Versailles in 1677, Jules Hardouin-Mansart was

commissioned to enlarge the palace, adding the vast entrance courtyard and two immense wings north and south of the central block. From the outset, the palace was envisaged as the fulcrum of an urban system set in a landscape that appeared to stretch to infinity. André Le Nôtre, in charge of the king's parks and gardens after 1662 and the inventor of the "French garden," drew on the Italian tradition of symmetry for his network of axial pathways. Designed to appear endless, they are punctuated by unexpected pavilions, clipped trees, and open spaces. In this way, Le Nôtre increased the sense of space and scale, emphasized by steps, terraces, large expanses

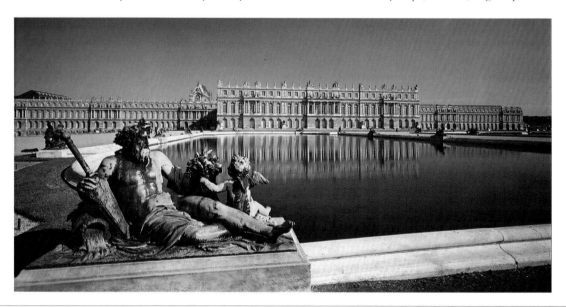

Louis Le Vau, Palace of Versailles, garden facade, 1661–90. Le Vau designed many of the buildings at Versailles, which Louis XIV visualized as a symbol of his reign, almost more of a king's city than Paris itself.

THE MODERN "APPARTEMENT"

In the 17th century, convenience and comfort became increasingly important in French private residences and especially in the *hôtels particuliers*. This led to the introduction of rooms of various sizes for specific uses: the *antichambre*, a waiting room and, at times, dining room; *chambre de parade*, a reception room; *chambre à coucher*, a bedroom; the *cabinet*, a study for work and receiving business visitors; and the *garderobe*, or privy. Grander houses would also have had a salon and sometimes a gallery, An earlier arrangement of interconnecting rooms *en enfilade* was generally abandoned in favor of *appartements doubles*.
In royal residences, the king would often receive state visitors in his bedchamber, which was fittingly decorated with sumptuous stuccowork, gilding, and painting. The royal bed was placed in an alcove, separated from the rest of the room by a low balustrade. Later on, doors were installed behind the alcove, leading to the most private *boudoir*, or dressing room.

after Bernini's return to Rome, but soon came to a stop. A commission formed by Charles Le Brun (1619–90), Louis Le Vau (1612–70), and Claude Perrault (1613–1688) successfully argued for the adoption of classicism as the canonical French artistic style, in preference to copying Italian taste. As a result, a colonnade was added to the eastern facade of the palace in homage to the architecture of classical antiquity.
Unlike the Italian palazzo, the French *hôtel particulier* was connected to the street by a half-open courtyard, or *cour d'honneur*. The living quarters, or *corps de logis*, were set further back. As the century progressed, the *hôtel* generally became a U-shape around the courtyard, cut off from its urban environment as in Jean Androuet Du Cerceau's Hôtel de Sully (1624–29) in the Marais district of Paris. The courtyard of the Hôtel Lambert (1640–44), built by Louis Le Vau on the Ile Saint-Louis for Nicolas Lambert, was surrounded by a continuous Doric entablature, giving a sense of continuity to the space, reinforced by the gently curved concave corners at both "ends" of the facade.

THE CHURCH OF THE INVALIDES

Jules Hardouin-Mansart was commissioned by Louis XIV to build a new chapel (1680–1706) among the existing buildings of the Hôtel des Invalides military hospital and home for war veterans (1670–76). It is constructed on the main axis of Les Invalides, with an oval sanctuary added to a central plan. It is topped by a dome inspired by Michelangelo's cupola of St. Peter's in Rome, although this French version is considerably taller. The windows of the lower drum, separated by pairs of columns, illuminate the interior while also supporting the first masonry ceiling. The windows of the second drum light the space between the first dome and a second one, visible through the wide central aperture of the spheroidal vault

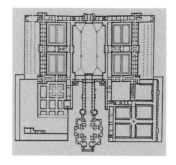

Hôtel des Invalides, Paris, plan of the whole complex, 1670–1706. Created as a home for war veterans, the building needed to express the ideas of grandeur and sovereignty that inspired Louis XIV's military campaigns.

beneath it. A third, lead-covered dome forms the outer shell and is topped by a lantern ending in a pinnacle inspired by the Gothic tradition. Mansart's plans also included two quarter-circle wings, adapted from Bernini's designs for St. Peter's Square, but these were never built. Construction of Les Invalides coincided with almost the entire period of Louis XIV's military campaigns, (1667–1714) through which he sought to dominate Europe.

Jules Hardouin-Mansart, Church of the Invalides, Paris, 1680–1706. The French architect interpreted the themes of the Baroque church with a majestic classicism.

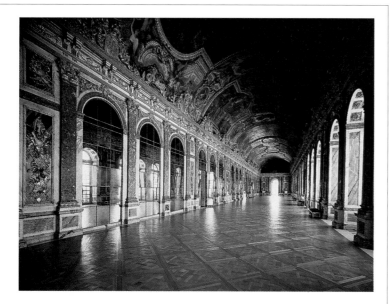

of reflecting water, and spectacular fountains. The palace's interior decoration, under the charge of Charles Le Brun, represents the peak of virtuosity in French Baroque art, especially Hardouin-Mansart's Hall of Mirrors (1678–84).

Jules Hardouin-Mansart and Charles Le Brun, Hall of Mirrors, Palace of Versailles, 1678–84. The immensely long mirrored gallery was intended to rival the Louvre gallery in size and magnificence, which entailed changing Le Vau's earlier plan.

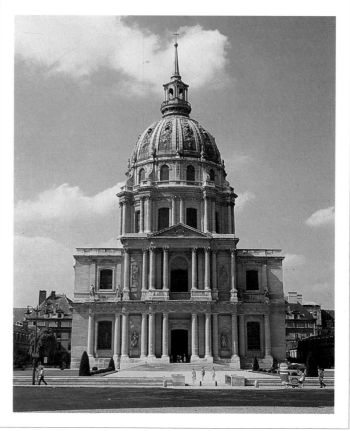

259

PAINTING IN ITALY

The foundations of Baroque painting, laid in Rome during the last decade of the 16th century, were based on two fundamentally different approaches: classicism, espoused by Annibale Carracci (1560–1609), and realism, associated with Michelangelo Merisi da Caravaggio (1571–1610). Throughout the entire 17th century and beyond, the means of expression and stylistic options of European painters revolved around these two poles as they aimed at a fusion of all the arts, whether through grand illusionistic effects or by

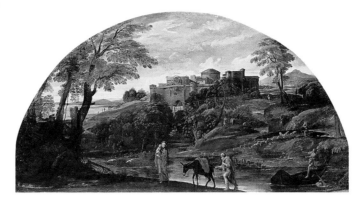

Annibale Carracci, Flight into Egypt, c.1604. Doria Pamphili Gallery, Rome. Carracci's work foreshadows the landscapes of Nicolas Poussin and Claude Lorrain.

capturing the reality of daily life. Annibale Carracci arrived in Rome in 1595. In his decoration of the Palazzo Farnese (1598–1601), he adapted the compositional solutions of Michelangelo's ceiling for the Sistine Chapel and was also influenced by Raphael, especially by his frescoes in the Farnesina. In the Farnese cycle, which depicts the loves of the gods, Carracci reinterpreted Correggio's evocative and sensual style through a more detailed exploration of natural reality. It was a more mature sequel to his earlier

STILL LIFE

One of the most popular genres of 17th-century painting takes its name from the Dutch *still leven*, used to describe paintings of inanimate objects. Still lifes enjoyed great success all over Europe, including Spain, France, Flanders, and Germany. In Italy, the genre was reinvigorated by Caravaggio and his followers, who saw still lifes as an opportunity to express the ideal values of painting. They depicted

rarefied, almost abstract, compositions, which touched on the moralizing theme of *vanitas* – the contemplation of death, the passage of time and the transitory nature of life, and the fading of the senses. This can be seen in the celebrated still lifes of musical instruments by Evaristo Baschenis (1607–77).

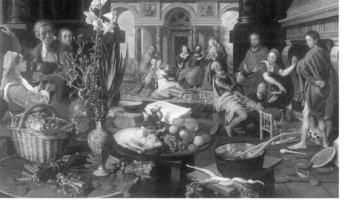

Pieter Aertsen (1508–75), Christ in the House of Martha and Mary, 1553. Boymans Van Beuningen Museum, Rotterdam, the Netherlands.

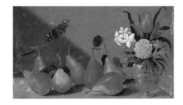

Fede Galizia (c.1578–1630), Still Life. Pinacoteca Ambrosiana, Milan. The particular tranquillity of Lombard realism is revealed in this skillful composition of pears, and flowers.

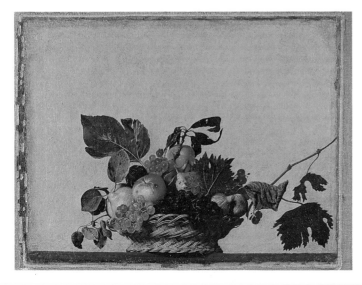

Caravaggio, Basket of Fruit, 1596. Pinacoteca Ambrosiana, Milan. Against a dazzling yellow background, the artist depicts a wicker basket of freshly picked fruit in vibrant colors. The seemingly haphazard arrangement of fresh and drooping leaves symbolizes the fullness of life on the brink of decomposition.

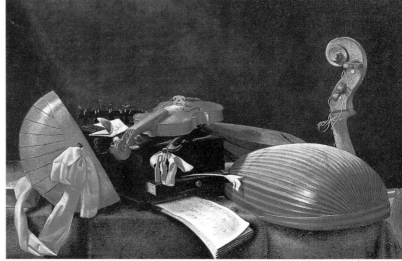

Evaristo Baschenis, Musical Instruments. Accademia Carrara, Bergamo, Italy. The trompe-l'oeil effect of Baschenis' still lifes has tended to overshadow his talent for composition. In this late work, each voluptuously rendered object is like a still life in its own right.

MILANESE PAINTING

In the 17th century, Milanese painting was given a great boost with the commissioning of two series of paintings for Milan Cathedral to celebrate the beatification (1602) and canonization (1610) of Cardinal Charles Borromeo. The most powerful scenes in these cycles were by Giovan Battista Crespi, known as Il Cerano (1567/68–1632). Other notable artists at work in Milan were Giulio Cesare Procaccini (1574–1625), Pier Francesco Mazzucchelli, known as Il

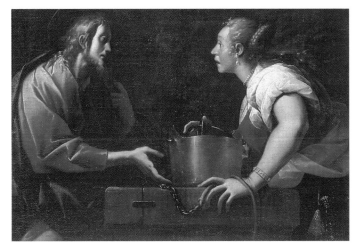

Morazzone (1573–1626), and Antonio d'Enrico, known as Tanzio da Varallo (1580–1635), a fervent adherent of Caravaggism. A terrible outbreak of plague in the city in about 1630 killed many outstanding cultural figures in Lombardy. In the following years, the sensitive, complex painter Francesco Cairo (1607–65) achieved considerable renown.

Il Morazzone, Christ and the Samaritan Woman at the Well, *c.1620–26. Pinacoteca di Brera, Milan. The artistic scene in Milan was dominated by the realist tradition and by the introspective Counter-Reformationist influence of the Borromeo archbishops.*

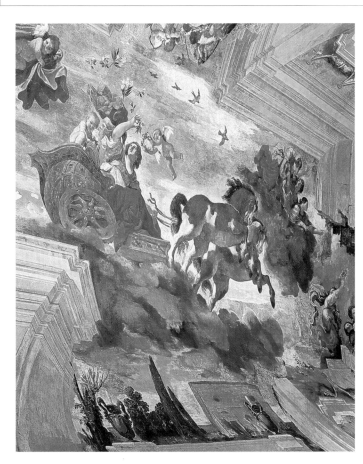

Guercino, Aurora, *detail of ceiling fresco, Casino Ludovisi, Rome, c.1621. The feigned architectural surrounds and framework were designed and painted by Agostino Tassi (c.1566–1644).*

work in the Accademia degli Incamminati in Bologna, which he had executed with his brother Agostino (1557–1602) and his cousin Ludovico (1555–1619). Carracci's art combined the pursuit of ideal beauty with

or Guercino (1591–1666), with his melancholy evocations of antiquity; and Guido Reni, the chief exponent of an elevated style that proved much to the taste of the Academicians and won him many commissions.

The young Caravaggio arrived in Rome in 1593 and began producing the first "anti-Academic" pictures, still lifes, and genre paintings blending moral values with naturalistic glimpses that had an extraordinary visual lucidity. Outraged opposition to what came to be known as

Guido Reni, Atalanta and Hippomenes, *1618–19. Museo del Prado, Madrid. This large painting is constructed with intersecting diagonal lines, interruptions, and readjustments of the rhythm. The Mannerist elements are tempered by Reni's graceful classicism.*

a close observation of natural reality, plus a breadth of vision inspired by classical models both ancient and contemporary. His success drew other artists from northern Italy to Rome: Francesco Albani (1578–1660); Domenico Zampieri, or Domenichino (1581–1641), who brought a lyrical element to classicism; Giovanni Francesco Barbieri,

GUIDO RENI

The Bolognese painter Guido Reni (1575–1642), influenced by Mannerism and the Carracci brothers, was considered a great master in his day, rivalling even Raphael. A thoughtful painter who balanced widely differing influences, he created his own, classicist version of the Caravaggist style in the *Crucifixion of St. Peter* (1604–05). His extensive frescoes in Rome culminated in his *Aurora* (1612–14) for the Casino Rospigliosi, and his reinterpretation of the Renaissance reached its high point with his *Massacre of the Innocents* (1611–12), *Atalanta and Hippomenes,* and the *Labors of Hercules* for the Gonzagas. A disturbing undercurrent in his images of the Magdalene can also be found in his masterly, bravura treatment of *David with the Head of Goliath* (1604–05). This echoes Caravaggio's gruesome treatment of the subject.

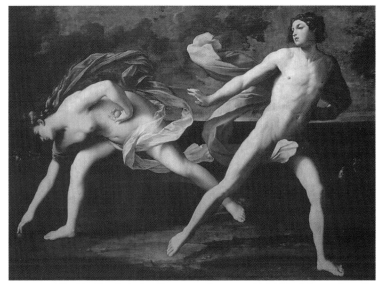

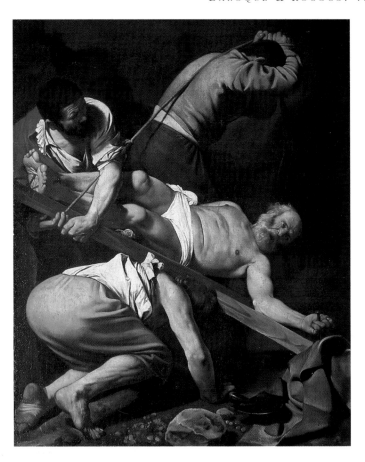

Caravaggio, Crucifixion of St. Peter, Cerasi Chapel, Santa Maria del Popolo, Rome, 1600–01.

CARAVAGGIO

Michelangelo Merisi da Caravaggio (1571–1610) was a pupil of Simone Peterzano before he left Milan for Rome at about the age of 20. There, he worked for Giuseppe Cesari (1568–1640), a powerful, sought-after artist who later turned against him, and was befriended by the cultivated but louche Cardinal Francesco Maria del Monte. He and his dissolute circle influenced Caravaggio as his view of the world and art matured. In his early 20s, he painted a succession of masterpieces for the cardinal – *The Fortune Teller, The Music Party, The Card Players, The Lute Player, St. Catherine, Medusa,* and *The Basket of Fruit* – which had a tremendous influence on European Baroque art. Important commissions for patrons and the chapel of St. Matthew in San Luigi dei Francesi, the French church in Rome, were followed by works in which increasing radical naturalism and revolutionary illuminism led to the *Death of the Virgin* (c.1605). Arrested for murder in 1606, he escaped to Naples, where he painted his *David* and *The Madonna of the Rosary.* In Malta, he completed *The Beheading of St. John the Baptist* and, in Messina, Sicily, *The Raising of Lazarus,* before returning to Naples in 1609. He soon left again for Tuscany, however, where he died of malarial fever at the age of 39.

CARAVAGGIO: "CALLING OF ST. MATTHEW"

Circa 1597; oil on canvas; 126 x 133 in (322 x 340 cm); Contarelli Chapel, San Luigi dei Francesi, Rome.

This is one of a set of three paintings – the other two are the *Inspiration of St. Matthew* (altarpiece) and the *Martyrdom of St. Matthew* (on the right) – that adorn the Contarelli Chapel. This painting, situated on the left-hand wall, shows the unexpected calling of Matthew, a tax collector, by Jesus. The scene takes place in a room with bare plaster walls. Below and to the left of a dusty window, a mature man (Matthew) and three very young men are seated around a table; a fourth, much older man is standing beside Matthew. Caravaggio creates a sense of modernity by using flamboyant, contemporary dress. Toward the right, standing with his back three-quarters turned to us, is St. Peter; behind him stands Jesus, his head turned toward Matthew and his right arm and hand stretched out toward him. The order in which Caravaggio executed the paintings for the Chapel of Cardinal Contarelli is not clear. It is possible that the *Inspiration of St. Matthew* was commissioned as early as 1591. The *Calling of St. Matthew* can be dated from between 1598 and 1599. In the interval between the two works, a great rivalry developed between Caravaggio and Giuseppe Cesari (who was responsible for the ceiling frescoes) over who was to be given the task to decorate the walls. During this time, Caravaggio's work showed a slow progression from a light tonality to a fully mature dramatic style based on strong contrasts of light and shade.

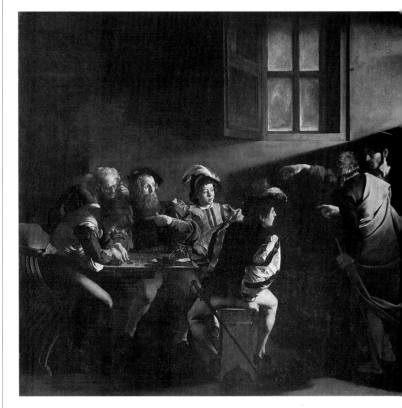

Caravaggismo (Caravaggism) greeted the artist's paintings in San Luigi dei Francesi (1599–1602) and Santa Maria del Popolo (1600–01). In these, scriptural stories are depicted with brutal reality, heightened by strong chiaroscuro and an apparent lack of any divine element. The paintings express an extremely radical and anti-conformist moral stance, which had its roots in the work of Charles and Frederic Borromeo in Milan. The first phase of Caravaggio's career, when he painted in vivid, glossy colors, was followed by work in which light effects became increasingly dramatic and accurately observed. Caravaggio's pictorial sensitivity, based on the study of reality rather than the observation of academic rules, appeared diametrically opposed to the assimilation by the Carracci brothers of classical and Renaissance models. The unrestrained use of light and shade to evoke atmosphere, imagery, and emotions excited the admiration of Caravaggio's contemporaries and became a style in itself, "in the manner of Caravaggio" or "Caravaggesque." Caravaggio's influence, although extensive, is difficult to pinpoint; he

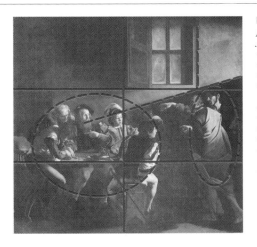

▲ *1. X-rays of this painting reveal many corrections and changes, showing that Caravaggio clearly planned out the composition on the canvas. The edge of the window shutter marks the vertical axis and center line of the picture, while the bottom of the window and table edge create straight lines that divide the painting horizontally in three. The beam of light from high on the right and the cross formed by the frame of the window panes in the top section suggest the divine presence. While the central zone is devoted to the drama played out by the figures, the legs of the men and furniture at the bottom create a crowded, lively interaction of highlights and diagonals.*

▼ *2. The tension and drama in this painting are created by the relationship between light and shade. Here, a beam of bright light from the right passes over the head of Jesus, meets the shutter, and illuminates the figures of the tax collectors on the left. Additional light from the foreground highlights the sleeve of the young man with his back to us, as well as the back and right side of Peter and the hand and face of Jesus. This dramatic interplay of light transforms the canvas into an image of great immediacy.*

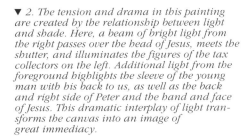

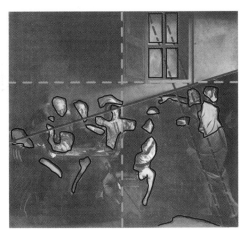

▶ *3. The line created by the succession of heads progresses from its highest point – the head of Jesus – in a curve punctuated by shadows, light, and colors; these correspond to the rhythm of the hands, sleeves, and legs. Veinings of color, as well as of light and shade, run through the doublets, sleeves, legs, and the folds of material. Touches of intense light illuminate the most significant elements in the story: the hands of the old man and the youth counting the coins paid as tax; Matthew's questioning face and hand; and Jesus's neck, ear, cheek, and nose. Christ's hand echoes the function and gesture of that of God in Michelangelo's* Creation of Adam *on the ceiling of the Sistine Chapel.*

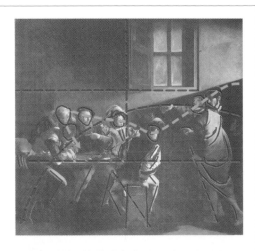

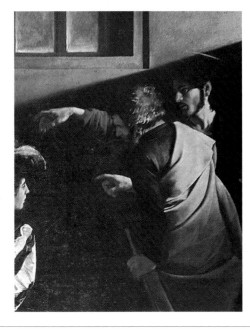

▲ *4. The detailed treatment of the five figures around the tax collector's table holds the viewer's attention: the flashy style of the youths' clothes and the opulent garments of the older men; the hands on the coins; and the various complexions and hair, which differ according to age. The greed of the two figures on the left is conveyed by their failure to participate in – or even notice – the event that unfolds so close to them. Yet all this detail, and the extraordinary skill with which it is depicted, does not detract from the cohesion and vigor of the whole picture – nor from its significance.*

▶ *5. Caravaggio, a notoriously violent and rebellious man, lived at a time when tragic social and religious conflicts, new ideologies, and economic and political upheavals were changing the face of Europe. More uncompromising than almost any other artist, his fervent, radical approach to religion made him hostile to the hierarchy and officialdom of the Roman Catholic Church. Here, the religious message is ambiguous. God's grace falls upon a sinner, Matthew, and the redeeming gesture of Jesus is repeated, in a lower key, by Peter, father of the Roman Church. The viewer may infer from this that he or she, too, may be called by God at any time.*

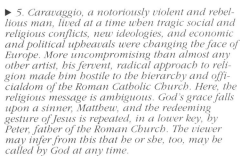

never had his own workshop or pupils in the formal sense. The *Caravaggisti*, those painters who were influenced by his work and attracted by his dark and mesmerizing settings and by his brutal realism, often conveyed no more than a superficial echo of the master's depth and drama. Most of his followers lacked the necessary perception to capture the subtle portrayal of tragedy and human suffering that made Caravaggio's work truly great. In Naples, Battistello Caracciolo (1570–1637) was the most faithful of the *Caravaggisti*, but Jusepe de Ribera (1591–1652), from Valencia in Spain, was more innovative. He aimed for a

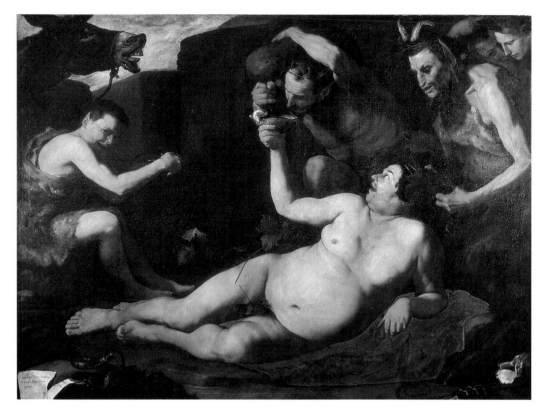

summoned successively to Naples to decorate the sumptuous Cappella San Gennaro in the cathedral. Their classicizing style was embraced by local artists such as Massimo Stanzione (1585–1656) and Bernardo Cavallino (1616–56), reaching its most fervently Baroque and monumental expression in the work of Mattia Preti (1613–99) and Luca Giordano (1634–1705). In Rome, a third variety of the Baroque style was led by Pietro da Cortona (1596–1669), who executed the magnificent ceiling decoration of the gallery in the Palazzo

Jusepe de Ribera, Drunken Silenus, 1626. Capodimonte Museum, Naples. This was painted when Ribera, as painter to the viceroy, was overwhelmed with commissions during the last years of his strictest naturalism. Subsequently, he used brighter, more extravagant colors and a more candid, though sometimes solemn, realism.

depiction of reality that confronted the grotesque and deformed, breaking the rules of decorum in order to show harsh reality even in the poorest settings. Between 1630 and 1640, the painters Domenichino, Reni, and Giovanni Lanfranco (1582–1647) were

Andrea Pozzo, Ascent of St. Ignatius into Paradise, detail of ceiling fresco, Church of Sant'Ignatius Loyola, Rome, 1691–94. The illusionistic perspectives created in this fresco are highly convincing.

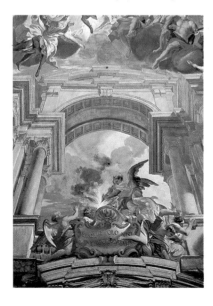

PAINTING IN GENOA

In the 17th century, Genoa was one of the main economic and cultural ports of Europe and welcomed artists such as the Flemish painters Rubens (1577–1640) and van Dyck (1599–1641); the painter and sculptor Pierre Puget (1620–94) from Marseilles; and Cornelis (1592–1667), Lucas de Wael, and many others from Flanders and the Netherlands. Homegrown artists included Luca Cambiaso (1527–85), who ran a successful workshop in the city.

In the wake of important 16th-century artists were portraitist Bernardo Castello (1557–1629), his son the decorative painter Valerio Castello (1624–59), who, with Domenico Piola (1627–1703) and the latter's sons and assistants, left behind a huge body of decorative work in the ecclesiastical buildings and palaces of Baroque Genoa. The fresco painters Giovanni Andrea de Ferrari (c.1598–1669) and, notably, Gregorio de Ferrari moved toward a more pronounced High Baroque interpretation of color and composi-

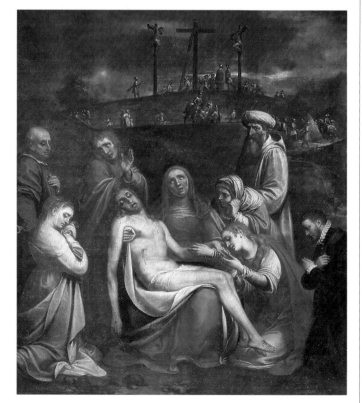

tion. In the work of Bernardo Strozzi (1581–1644), the realistic tradition taken from Caravaggio was melded with the brilliant late Baroque style.

Luca Cambiaso, Pietà, detail, Santa Maria Assunta di Carignano, Genoa, before 1575. Cambiaso's painting shows how Genoese Mannerism was already moving toward 18th-century classicism.

Barberini (1632–39). Here, a dynastic allegory of the Triumph of Divine Providence occupies the central field and appears to be played out in the open sky, so that the spectator feels that the interior of the palace has been invaded by a cast of supernatural characters both sacred and profane. The illusionism of Giovan Battista Gaulli, who painted the ceiling of the church of the Gesù, and of Andrea

Pozzo (1642–1709) in the church of St. Ignatius (1691–94), is a synthesis of many genres of art – such as *bambochades* (peasant scenes), battle scenes, land and seascapes, and official or "display" portraits – which anticipate the 18th century.

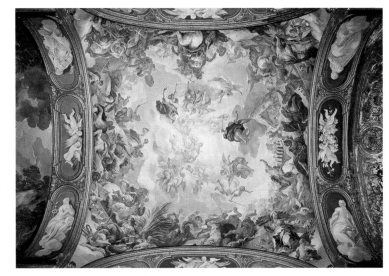

Luca Giordano, Triumph of Judith, ceiling fresco, Treasury Chapel, Certosa of San Martino, Naples, 1704. Luminosity, a Venetian treatment of color, ease of invention, and elegance permeate this example of High Baroque.

A VENETIAN REVIVAL

A renewel in Venetian painting was signaled by the arrival of Domenico Fetti (1589–1623) from Rome, the German Johann Liss (c.1595–1631), and the Genoese Bernardo Strozzi. They had all assimilated the lessons of Caravaggio, Rubens, and the Carracci. In the later 17th century, the dark "tenebrist" style, which involved an emphatic use of chiaroscuro for dramatic effect, gradually gave way to a brighter, more sumptuous style of painting, particularly in the work of Pietro Liberi (1605–87). The arrival of Luca Giordano from Naples and Giovan Battista Langetti (1635–76) from Genoa presaged the more atmospheric work of Tiepolo and his contemporaries.

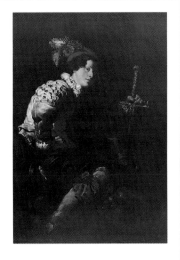

Domenico Fetti, David, 1617–19. Accademia, Venice. An elegant painter of medium-sized and small pictures, Fetti offers his interpretation of a popular Baroque subject.

Bernardo Strozzi, Christ Mourned by the Two Marys, 1615–17. Pinacoteca dell'Accademia Ligustica, Genoa. Strozzi's work contains echoes of Caravaggio, Rubens, and the Sienese Mannerists.

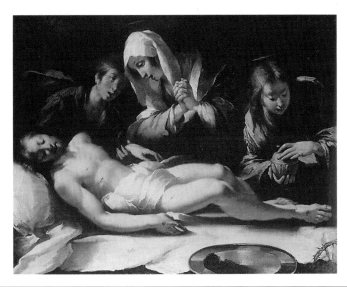

ITALIAN SCULPTURE IN THE 17TH CENTURY

During the late 16th and early 17th centuries, in the Rome of Pope Sixtus V and in Milan during the time of Cardinal Charles Borromeo, sculptors carefully observed principles laid down by the Council of Trent and adhered to the Mannerist tradition. The lessons learned from Michelangelo and the impetus toward strongly animated work led to the emergence of Baroque taste, which found expression in the style of the Lombard sculptor Stefano Maderno (c.1576–1636). The beauty and emotive charge of the recumbent figure of Maderno's *St. Cecilia* (1601) in Santa Cecilia in Trastevere, Rome, appeal to the onlooker with an immediacy that is both realistic and idealized, lifelike and theatrical. This synthesis of types and effects provided the pattern along which sculpture was to develop during the Baroque age. Francesco Mochi (1580–1654) also heralded the emergence of a new artistic language with his *Angel of the Annunciation* and *Annunciate Virgin* (1605–08). The polished smoothness of the marble surfaces and the audacity

of the composition can be seen as the final, refined turning point of Mannerism and suggested new ideas. With his equestrian statue (1612–20) in memory of Ranuccio Farnese, which graces the Piazza Cavalli in the town of Piacenza, Mochi broke free once and for all from the legacy of his teacher, Giambologna, and the Renaissance and late Mannerist models. His ideas were later reworked by Gianlorenzo Bernini and in monumental statuary throughout Europe.
Bernini was born in Naples and was the pupil of his father, the late Mannerist sculptor Pietro Bernini (1592–1629). He studied the work of Giambologna, and

GIANLORENZO BERNINI

The son of a sculptor, Gianlorenzo Bernini (1598–1680) was influenced by ancient Greek and Roman art and by the 16th-century Italian masters. He was awarded the commission for the bronze *baldacchino* (canopy) in St. Peter's in 1624, and he continued to work on the cathedral and the colonnade around the piazza as sculptor and architect until shortly before he died. His architectural commissions include the Palazzo Montecitorio and Palazzo Barberini in Rome, as well as unexecuted projects for the Louvre. His *Ecstasy of St. Theresa* in Santa Maria della Vittoria and the *Blessed Ludovica Albertoni* in San Francesco a Ripa are among Rome's most celebrated sculptures.

of the great 16th-century masters, as well as the sculptures and architecture of antiquity in Rome. Cardinal Scipione Borghese, the nephew of Pope Paul V, became Bernini's patron. He sculpted a series of marble statues for the Cardinal's Roman villa: *Aeneas and Anchises* (1618–19), *The Rape of Proserpine* (1621–22), *David* (1623), and *Apollo and Daphne* (1622–24). These works encompass all the elements of 17th-century sculpture: dynamic poses; twisting bodies; expressive faces and gestures; a smooth and gleaming finish to the marble surfaces; virtuosity and mimetic skill; compositions conceived in the round and effective when viewed from any angle; and an emotional and spatial involvement with the viewer. Bernini's connection with Maffeo Barberini, who became Pope Urban VIII in

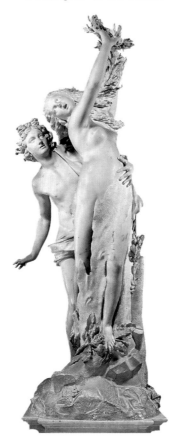

Gianlorenzo Bernini, Apollo and Daphne, marble, 1622–25. Borghese Gallery, Rome. This is considered one of the greatest masterpieces of 17th-century secular sculpture.

1623, lasted for 20 years and afforded Bernini a position of unrivaled prestige and brought him the most sought-after commissions of the day. As early as 1624, the pope entrusted him with the task of creating the bronze *baldacchino* (a structure in the form of a canopy) to be placed under Michelangelo's dome in St. Peter's as the focal point of the entire basilica. This was completed in 1633 with the help of several assistants, including the young Borromini, who arrived from Lombardy after gaining experience as a sculptor at Milan Cathedral. In 1629, following the death of Carlo Maderno, Bernini was appointed architect to St. Peter's. He began to transform the decoration of

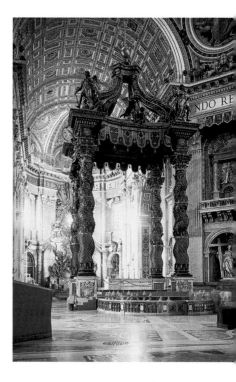

Gianlorenzo Bernini and Francesco Borromini, baldacchino over the high altar of St. Peter's, Vatican City, bronze, wood, and marble, 1624–33.

THE CORNARO CHAPEL

From 1646 to 1652, Gianlorenzo Bernini made a decisive step toward one of his most cherished goals, a new visual and emotional interpretation of the subject of St. Theresa, in his famous marble group, the *Ecstasy of St. Theresa*. This Spanish Carmelite nun was recognized by the Church of the Counter-Reformation as one of its most charismatic saints. In the Cornaro family chapel in

Santa Maria della Vittoria, Rome, Bernini placed her at the center of a theatrical altar, swooning in ecstasy as a young angel pierces her heart with a golden arrow, a symbol of divine love. Like a grandiose high-relief sculpture come to life, the saint appears to be suspended in air, illuminated by light flooding in from on high through a hidden source. Together, the whiteness of the marble and intensity of the light heighten the spiritual charge of the saint's mystical experience and stir the senses, creating an extremely sensual and emotive effect. Portrait statues of the patrons who commissioned this work occupy two balconies of richly colored marble set in recesses on either side of the chapel. They gaze out at the saint, underlining the explicitly theatrical approach of the whole composition.

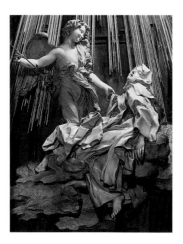

Gianlorenzo Bernini, two details of the Cornaro Chapel, Santa Maria della Vittoria, Rome. In two recesses on either side of the central sculpture are the spectators, members of the aristocratic Cornaro family.

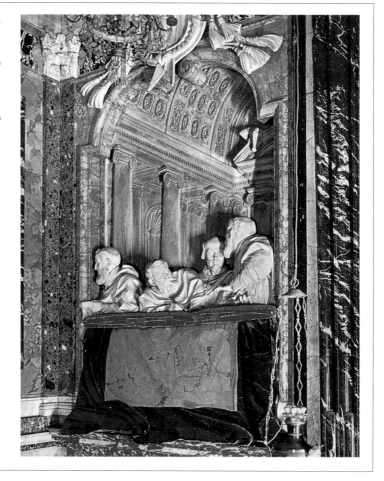

the interior of the basilica, inserting niches containing sculptures in the four piers of the crossing under the dome, and designing the great church's furniture and furnishings, papal tombs, and the polychrome marble cladding of the nave. In addition to his work for the Vatican, Bernini also carried out private commissions, helped by assistants in his highly organized workshop. These included fountains such as the Triton Fountain in the Piazza Barberini and portrait busts of, among others, Cardinal Scipione Borghese (1632) and his mistress Costanza Buonarelli (c.1635). Bernini's ability to exploit the effects of light gave even his court portrait busts – such as that of Louis XIV, sculpted in 1665, and now in the Musée du Louvre, Paris – a vitality that was to inspire 18th-century portrait sculptors.

After the death of his protector and the election of Innocent X Pamphili, Bernini was passed over in favor of Alessandro Algardi (1595–1654). He had trained in the Carracci academy in Bologna and had developed an explicitly classical manner, consolidated during his time at the court of the Duke of Mantua (1622) and in

Gianlorenzo Bernini, Costanza Buonarelli, detail of portrait bust, 1635. Museo Nazionale del Bargello, Florence. This is one of Bernini's most outstanding pieces of portrait sculpture.

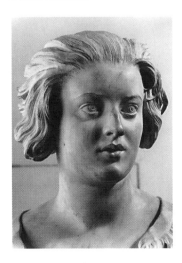

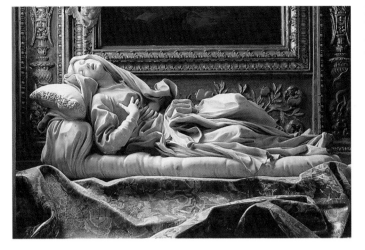

Gianlorenzo Bernini, The Blessed Ludovica Albertoni, Altieri Chapel, San Francesco a Ripa, Rome, 1671–74.

Venice. Algardi settled in Rome in 1625, where, until his promotion to Bernini's post, he worked on the restoration and completion of ancient statues belonging to Cardinal Ludovisi and made contact with fellow Emilian artists working in the city, as well as the French artist Nicolas Poussin (1594–1665). He produced monuments of a subtle, classical dignity for the pope, which were often enlivened by dramatic realism, as is demonstrated by a marble altarpiece for St. Peter's, *Pope Leo I driving Attila from Rome* (1646–53).

His later work, such as the bronze statue of Innocent X (1649–50), made concessions to the Baroque and had a certain affinity with Bernini's style. This is most evident in his portrait sculpture, for example the bust of *Olimpia Pamphili* (c.1645)

During Innocent's papacy, Bernini worked mainly on private commissions, including the Cornaro Chapel in Santa Maria della Vittoria (1644–52). However, his most spectacular fountain, that of the Four Rivers in the Piazza Navona (1648–51), was a papal commission for Innocent X. His works had a profound effect on the appearance and character of Rome and were pivotal for Italian and European Baroque artistic culture. The accession of Alexander VII Chigi in 1655 returned Bernini to St. Peter's in triumph, with the task of designing the piazza in front

THE FOUNTAINS OF ROME

The theatrical open spaces of Baroque Rome were greatly enlivened by fountains, visual pivots for the urban scenery that expressed a connection between nature and artifice. Gianlorenzo Bernini created new concepts and designs for fountains, one of the most famous being the Triton Fountain in the Piazza Barberini (1642–43). He enhanced the pedestal of the fountain by adding exuberant dolphins around the base. Above, the sea god Triton blows a jet of water into the air through a conch shell. Standing in a corner of Piazza Barberini is Bernini's Fountain of the Bees (1644), also commissioned by the Barberini family. Here, the family coat of arms is vividly brought to life in the form of the bees enclosed in the gigantic shell. Soon after, in Piazza Navona, Bernini built his celebrated Fountain of the Four Rivers (1648–51), which was adopted as the site of an annual water festival. The great

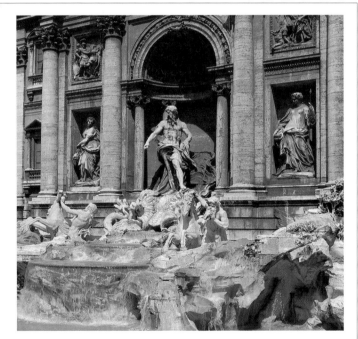

18th-century tradition of urban embellishment derived from these prototypes is exemplified by the Trevi Fountain (1732–63) by Niccolò Salvi (1697–1751), which was carved by Pietro Bracci and Filippo Della Valle. The fountain complements the

Niccolò Salvi, Pietro Bracci, and Filippo Della Valle, Trevi Fountain, Rome.

urban scenery and open space, the rigid classicism of its architectural backdrop being contrasted with the exuberant plasticity of the statuary groups.

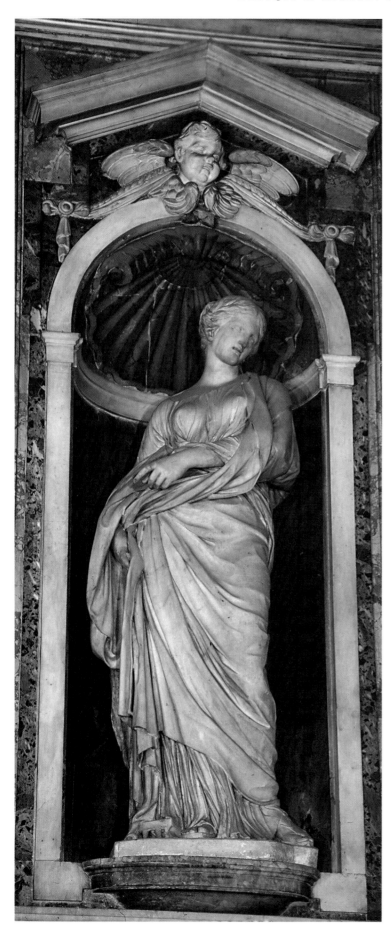

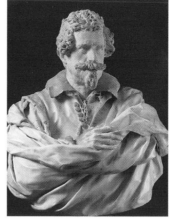

Giuliano Finelli, Michelangelo Buonarroti the Younger. *Casa Buonarroti, Florence.*

François Duquesnoy, St. Susanna, *Santa Maria di Loreto, Rome, 1629–33.*

of the basilica to provide a prelude to the pilgrimage path through the church's interior, the symbolic significance of which Bernini enhanced with works of art. These culminated in the vision, through the *baldacchino* under the dome, of the *Cathedra Petri* (1657–66), a setting for the papal throne that occupied the huge apse at the east end of the basilica. This housed the wooden throne believed to have been used by St. Peter himself, and Bernini's grandiose treatment by which it is elevated – supported by four huge bronze figures of the Doctors of the Church – ensures its potency as a symbol of papal supremacy. Bernini's last commissions included *Angels with the Symbols of the Passion* for the Sant'Angelo bridge, largely sculpted by his pupils to his designs, and *The Blessed Ludovica Albertoni* (1671–74) in the Altieri chapel in San Francesco a Ripa. Shown in her death throes, the subject is framed by two shallow wings leading from the chapel and lit by rays of light. This theatrical display strengthens the emotional impact of the work despite the austere, contemplative

treatment that reflects the deep religiosity of Bernini's last years. Many of his pupils continued to express his artistic language – including Ercole Ferrata (1610–86), Antonio Raggi, (1624–86), Paolo Naldini (1619–91), and Cosimo Fancelli (1620–88) – though after the deaths of Ferrata and Raggi, Roman sculpture and stucco decoration shook off the comparative restraint of the Baroque era and embarked upon the rich ornamentation of full-blown Rococo. The exuberant artistry of Bernini and Cortona and Borromini's flights of imagination were countered by artists who counseled restraint, balance, and measured control; in short, a reaffirmation of classical values. Like Algardi, the Flemish sculptor François Duquesnoy (1597–1643) was in the vanguard of this movement; he left Brussels for Rome, arriving in 1618. A great friend of Poussin, he too was influenced by Titian's *Bacchanal* (1518–23), clearly discernible in his

Giovan Battista Foggini, Vision of St. Andrew Corsini, *Church of the Carmines, Florence, 1685–90.*

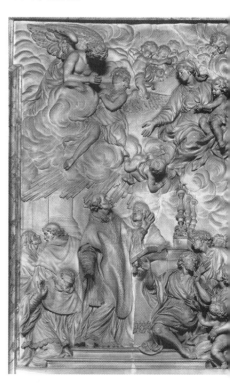

THE BAROQUE ALTAR

With his figure of St. Cecilia (1601), Stefano Maderno introduced a change in the architectural and decorative structure of the altar from traditional Renaissance designs. She is shown lying on her side, encased within an ante-pendium that resembles a sarcophagus. Later, in the Cornaro Chapel (1646–52), Bernini detached the altar from the wall, turning it into a convex stage on which a narrative takes place. His *Cathedra Petri* (1657–66) in the Vatican basilica is a theatrical creation reminiscent of temporary structures for open-air festivities and a clear statement that sculpture had been liberated from architectural structure.

Bernini collaborated with Alessandro Algardi, Domenico Facchetti, and others on the altar of St. Paul's Church in Bologna (1638–43). The result was classical in style but was executed in polychrome marble. Open to the rear, its exedra and columns held a

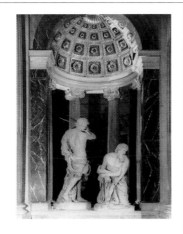

Alessandro Algardi, The Beheading of St. Paul, *Capella Spada, St Paul's Church, Bologna.*

Stefano Maderno, St. Cecilia, *1601, Santa Cecilia, Trastevere, Rome.*

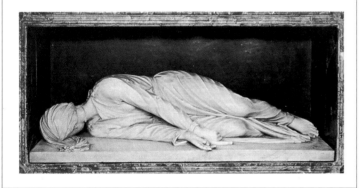

sculptural group, *The Beheading of St. Paul,* in place of the usual painted altar-piece. During the second half of the 17th century, when the influence of Roman decorative art was paramount, a foretaste of the 18th-century's decorative extravagances could be seen in the altar of St. Louis Gonzaga in the church of St. Ignatius, which contained the marble altarpiece (1699) of Pierre Legros. It was also evident in the St. Ignatius chapel (1695–99) in the Gesù in Rome, by Andrea Pozzo.

creations with putti (*Sacred Love and Profane Love*), which were avidly collected. He worked with Bernini on the *baldacchino* in St. Peter's, but his most typical work is the statue of *St. Susanna*, in which the dignity of the figure is matched by its subtle grace. Neapolitan realism also played an important part in

17th-century sculpture, represented by the work of the Tuscan sculptors Pietro Bernini, Giuliano Finelli (1601–57), and Andrea Bolgi (1605–56). Cosimo Fanzago (1591–1678) from Bergamo was the most outstanding of the Neapolitan sculptors and was also a talented architect who brought the Lombard style and Bernini's influence

to southern Italy. His links with Caravaggism led him and other sculptors active in the mid-17th century to adopt a generally realistic and naturalistic approach, though often tinged with a certain austerity and drama, reminiscent of the Spanish painter Francisco Zurbarán's paintings. In Genoa, the French sculptor Pierre Puget (1620–94) blended local traditional style with those of Bernini and Pietro da Cortona, creating scenes in relief carving of great delicacy. Filippo Parodi (1630–1702), a Genoese sculptor, had gained experience in Rome before going to Venice; his sculptural creations show the influence of Bernini, as does the work of Alessandro Vittoria (1525–1608). Venice also gave Flemish sculptor Justus Le Court (1627–73) the opportunity to show his inspiration from Rubens and Bernini in an original and individual group for the high altar of Santa Maria della Salute, the altarpiece for which was sculpted by Orazio Marinali (1643–1720), one of the best exponents of the Venetian style. Marinali was receptive to the new decorative style that was to become popular in the 18th century, and he was in charge of a successful workshop in Vicenza where his brothers Angelo and Francesco also worked. Eventually, Bernini's influence reached northern Italy, inspiring a veritable forest of statues for Milan Cathedral, notably those by Dionigi Bussola (1612–87), whose traditional, popular realism was influenced by the Baroque style. Giuseppe Mazzuoli (1644–1725), a pupil of Bernini, was active in Siena and throughout Tuscany, while Giovan Battista Foggini (1652–1725) was working in Florence in Baroque style, as can be seen in his elaborate altarpiece (1685–90) in Santa Maria del Carmine.

PAPAL TOMBS IN THE AGE OF BERNINI

In 1628, Pope Urban VIII Barberini commissioned his own tomb from Bernini, to be sited within a niche in the apse of St. Peter's. Finished in 1647, this was to become the prototype for Baroque and High Baroque papal and monumental tombs. The sculptor, drawing on the Medici family tombs by Michelangelo in San Lorenzo, Florence, and from Gian Giacomo della Porta's monument to Pope Paul III in St. Peter's, demonstrated his grasp of how to apply pictorial values to sculpture. At the top of the monument is the figure of the pope in bronze, frozen in death on his throne, hand raised in blessing, and with Death personified as writing the epitaph of the pontiff. The lively, almost Rubensesque figures of Charity and Justice are in translucent Carrara marble, their more earthly substantiality bridging the gap between the onlooker and the pope. Bernini changed his approach for the tomb of Alexander VII Chigi (1671–78), eschewing an overtly dramatic approach in order to accentuate its celebratory meaning and its theological and moral significance. Dominating the work, the pope's ascetic marble likeness kneels on high in prayer in order to achieve salvation. A sumptuous pall of red jasper spread out below is slightly raised by a bronze skeleton with an hourglass and surrounded by four figures of the Virtues. The intelligence and pictorial solutions of the two monuments was to be copied in various forms throughout the rest of the 17th century, as well as in the 18th century. This is evident in the work of Antonio Canova, who was also influenced by the strict classicism of Alessandro Algardi's marble monument for Leo XI (1634–43) and its austere pyramidal composition.

Alessandro Algardi, Monument to Pope Leo XI de'Medici, *St. Peter's, Vatican City.*

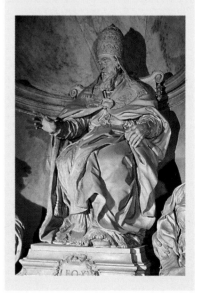

ARTISTIC REVIVALS

There are numerous examples of great masters who were undervalued in their day, and even those appreciated by their contemporaries gained greater stature when reassessed with hindsight. In the second half of the 16th century, a time when art was in a state of turmoil as Mannerism gave way to the Baroque, three outstanding painters with very distinctive styles ventured beyond the tastes of their age to experiment with new techniques, shapes, colors, and lighting effects that would only be fully appreciated much later. Today, they are held in much higher esteem than they were during their lifetimes.

TINTORETTO

Jacopo Robusti, known as Tintoretto (1518–94), spent almost all his life in his native city of Venice. He worked in Titian's workshop for a short time but had no particularly influential teachers. He was inspired by Michelangelo's grand manner and by Jacopo Pontormo's handling of light, and his work shows a typically Venetian sense of space and color. His rapid, sweeping brushstrokes and the speed at which he worked can be seen in the great cycle of sacred paintings in the Scuola Grande di San Rocco (begun 1564), in those in the Doge's Palace, and in his large paintings in the church of the

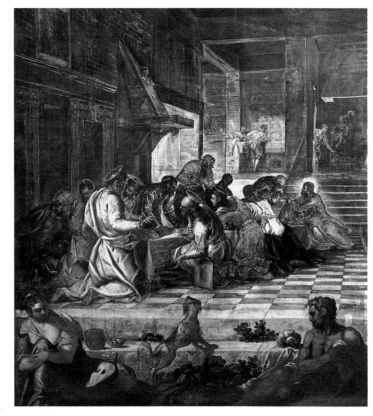

Tintoretto, The Last Supper, Scuola Grande di San Rocco, Venice, 1579–81.

Madonna dell'Orto and the Scuola Grande di San Marco. Each of his versions of *The Last Supper* is unique, while his dazzlingly accomplished battle scenes, his remarkable portraits with their striking immediacy, and the beautiful women in his *Susanna and the Elders* (c.1556) and *Christ and the Woman Taken in Adultery* (1545–48) illustrate his amazing versatility. In order to increase the dramatic impact of

his paintings and to capture the complex poses of his figures, Tintoretto prearranged his compositions using small wax models on a stage and experimented with lamps to achieve striking chiaroscuro contrasts.

VERONESE

Paolo Caliari, known as Veronese (1528–88), was a native of Verona but moved to Venice at the age of 28. Having seen works by Giulio

Romano in Mantua and studied paintings by Parmigianino, he had already developed his own distinctive brand of classicism: balanced and harmonious in composition, but with a lively, often festive, content and an ability to combine anecdotal incidents with a calm sense of dignity. His wall and ceiling frescoes in the Palladian Villa Barbero at Maser, near Treviso, show views of the surrounding countryside and architecture populated by youthful aristocratic and divine figures. The license he took with sacred subjects such as a scene commissioned for the refectory of the convent of Santi Giovanni e Paolo – *Feast in the House of Levi* (1573) – attracted censure from the Inquisition. He was asked to account for the presence of "buffoons, drunkards, dwarfs…and similar vulgarities." This and his other large religious feast scenes painted during the 1560s, his *Allegories of Love* (c.1575) painted for Emperor Rudolph II, and his many historical and mythological paintings provide a fascinating panorama of one of the most dazzling social milieux of the age. In contrast to Tintoretto's religious intensity, Veronese excelled at depicting the theatrical splendor of Venice in its Golden Age.

Paolo Veronese, The Last Supper, 1573. Pinacoteca di Brera, Milan.

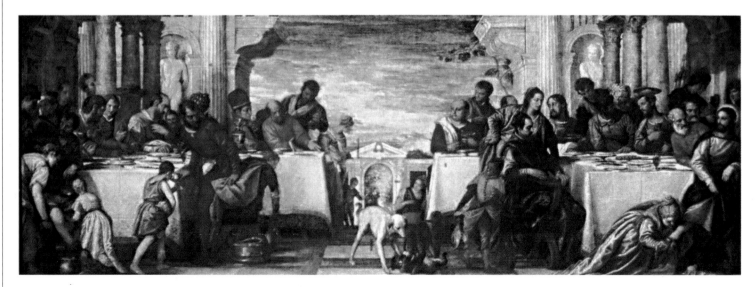

EL GRECO

Domenicos Theotokopoulos, or El Greco (1541–1614), was born on the island of Crete, which was then a Venetian territory and home to a flourishing school of icon painters. He later moved to Venice and is thought to have been a pupil of Titian, although his work shows more of Tintoretto's influence; on a visit to Rome, he saw both Michelangelo's frescoes and Raphael's paintings. He then moved to Spain in about 1575 and lived in Toledo until his death. Like Tintoretto, he tried out his ideas with model figures and a miniature stage before starting to paint. His dramas were those of a mystic religiosity tinged with suffering, which prefigure the Baroque, although his elongated shapes were more Byzantine than Mannerist. His tense scenes shot through with shafts of light are reminiscent of another solitary artist, Lelio Orsi (1511–87), while the energetic handling of his sitters anticipates Velázquez' portraits. Such masterpieces as *The Burial of Count Orgaz* (1586), *The Resurrection* (1605–10), *Adoration of the Shepherds* (1612–14), and *Pentecost* (1600–10) illustrate his rejection of both classic and naturalistic styles. His chilling *Portrait of a Cardinal* was to inspire Francis Bacon and other modern artists.

El Greco, Portrait of a Cardinal, *c.1600. Metropolitan Museum of Art, New York. The subject of this portrait is probably Don Fernando Niño de Guevara,*

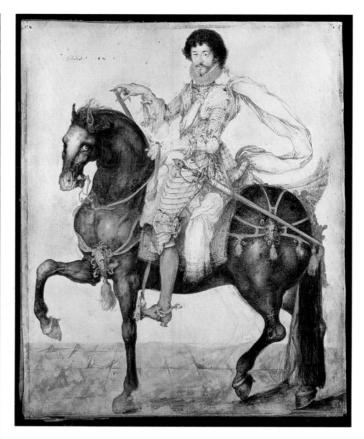

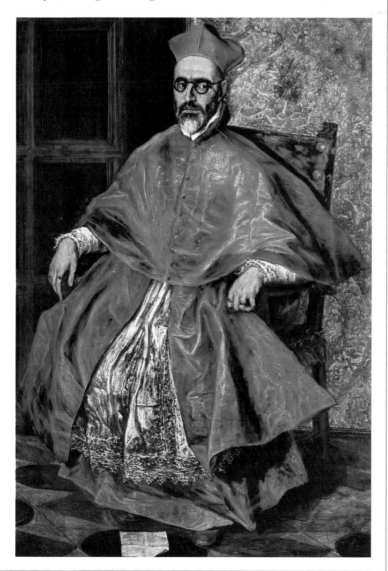

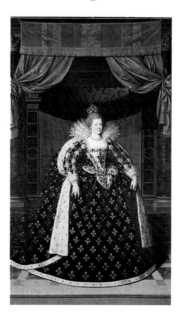

Jacques Bellange, Portrait of Henry II, Duke of Montmorency, on Horseback, *watercolor. Musée Condé, Chantilly, France.*

PAINTING IN FRANCE IN THE 17TH CENTURY

Painters working in Paris and the rest of France followed divergent paths during the early 17th century. Ambroise Dubois (1534–1614) and Martin Fréminet (1567–1619), members of the so-called Second School of Fontainebleau, produced outstanding works in the Mannerist style, while the small but splendid court of the Duke of Lorraine was captivated by the elegant, whimsical paintings of Jacques Bellange (active in Nancy from 1602 to 1616). Many artists rejected Mannerism, however, including Frans Pourbus II the Younger (1569–1622). After nine years in the service of the Duke of Mantua, he became court painter in Paris in 1609 and specialized in portraits and religious pictures such as *The Last Supper* (1618).

Despite Marie de Médicis' commission of Rubens for the sumptuous cycle of historical and allegorical paintings for the gallery of the Palais du Luxembourg (now in the Louvre), there was little change in

Frans Pourbus II the Younger, Portrait of Marie de' Médicis, Queen of France, *c.1610. Musée du Louvre, Paris.*

GEORGES DE LA TOUR: "THE PENITENT MAGDALEN"

Circa 1640–44; oil on canvas; 52½ x 40 in (133.5 x 102 cm); Metropolitan Museum, New York.

The artist painted four different versions of this subject, which lent itself to an exploration of the "nocturne," or night scene – the scene is set in an enclosed, candlelit interior. The style of the work is clearly in the Caravaggist tradition. The theme of the penitent Magdalen, still in her prime and shown contemplating the worldly goods and vanities that she rejects, occurs frequently in 17th-century European Catholic art, from Guido Reni to Artemisia Gentileschi (c.1596–1652). The figure is seated, her legs almost in silhouette, while the upper part of her body is better lit. Her face is turned away, shown almost entirely in profile, and her hands are clasped on a skull resting on her lap. Nearby, a small mirror with an elaborate frame stands on a table; in front, there is a lighted candle. Jewels lie scattered on the table and on the floor.

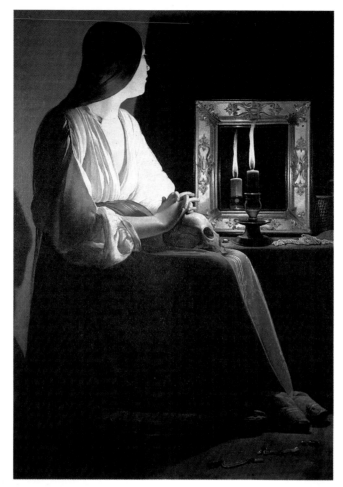

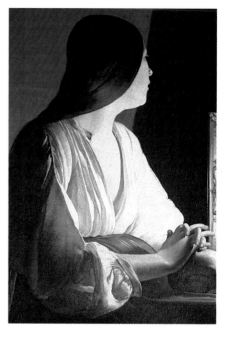

► *3. Without seeing the Magdalen's eyes, it is not clear if she is looking at the flame or its reflection. The candle is burning down, and the flame will soon go out. It is a real flame with light and warmth, whereas the reflection is an illusion in the blackness of the rectangle. Nothing else is reflected as the candle burns away, suggesting the passage of time.*

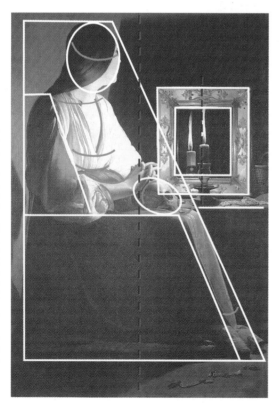

◄ *1. The composition is unusual yet simple, dominated by the still, solid figure of the Magdalen. A series of three irregular trapeziums can be seen in the form of her figure as a whole, a part of her arm in the foreground, and her underskirt. In the upper area of deepest shadow, the mirror is outlined by its elaborate gilded frame, broken only by the shape of the candle and its reflection, which almost bisects it. The rounded forms of the head and skull are echoed in the curves seen in the more strongly lit areas of the figure.*

► *2. The austerity of the compostion helps focus attention on the essentials. The artist draws attention to significant details, emphasizing the curtain and floor against the dark areas to balance the pictorial structure. The major effects are created by the strong contrasts of light and shade, and the whole work is based on this type of dialogue of opposites – not only in pictorial terms. Dazzled by the violent red and yellow light in the obscurity of her room, the Magdalen holds the skull, a symbol of the vanity of worldly wealth, and gazes at the source of illumination. In a typically Baroque image, she contemplates both the true light of the candle and its reflected light in the mirror.*

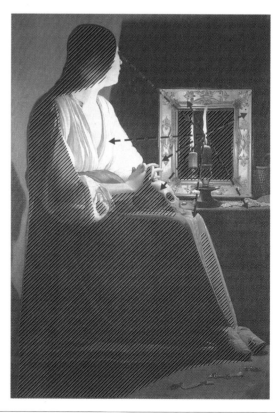

◄ *4. Warm tones suffuse the seated woman's head, shoulders, and face. The ivory hues of her open blouse and skin contrast with the bright red of the undergarment. A skillful and meticulous application of tone on tone conjures up the shadows that fall between the fabric and the skin and in the folds and pleats of the fabric. The variety of shades within an apparent uniformity of colors reveals tremendous virtuosity. The handling of the long, glossy hair, with its smooth and sinuous line, shows the same mastery and intensity and illustrates the quality of the painting.*

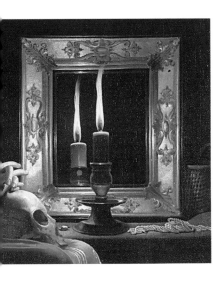

▼ *5. Light barely penetrates the lower part of this scene, in contrast to the more dramatic lighting of the upper half. The dully gleaming jewels are barely discernible on the floor. La Tour's subtlety and delicacy shine through the darkness, typifying an artistic culture that did not hesitate to express itself in a complex and ambiguous manner. His skillful lighting effects reveal a debt to Caravaggio, whose style La Tour may have learned from artists such as Honthorst.*

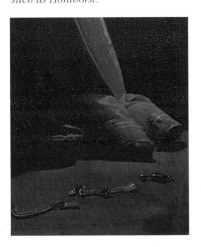

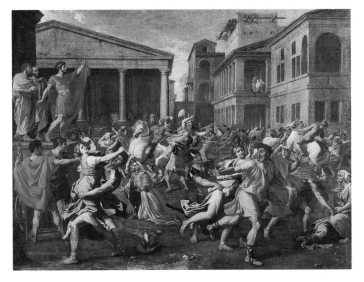

Nicolas Poussin, Rape of the Sabines, *c.1637. Musée du Louvre, Paris.*

prevailing tastes. Young French painters continued to perfect their technique in Italy, and from 1610 onward, many became followers of Caravaggio, including Simon Vouet (1590–1649), Vignon, Regnier, Tournier, and, above all, Valentin de Boulogne (1591–1632). On the whole, Valentin reworked themes introduced by Bartolomeo Manfredi (1580–1620), but his "cabinet" pictures – paintings of a suitable size and subject to adorn the walls of bougeois homes – have a remarkable psychological depth. Vouet's knowledge of 16th-century Venetian painting is reflected in his high coloration and subtle palette in paintings such as *Time Subjugated by Hope, Love, and Beauty* (1612). As France's economic and political strength grew – from 1624 onward Cardinal Richelieu was Louis XIII's chief minister – many artists were encouraged to return to Paris. As chief court painter, Vouet set the fashion for "lyrical" painting, which satisfied the demand for a brilliant and decorative style. A more Caravaggist way of

painting found favor in the south of France and Lorraine, where Georges de La Tour (1593–1652) was active. During the Regency (1643–61), a reaction in favor of greater elegance of drawing and form, inspired by classical models, was further stimulated by the

NICOLAS POUSSIN

The foremost interpreter of 17th-century classicism, Nicolas Poussin (1594–1665) studied first in Rouen and then in Paris, as a pupil of Lallemand. He was familiar with the Fontainebleau Mannerists as well as Raphael and his school. In 1624, Poussin went to Bologna, where he was influenced by the classicism of the Carracci Academy and Guido Reni before moving on to Rome. There, working alongside artists such as Pietro da Cortona and Giovanni Lanfranco, he experimented with the use of color in the style of Titian (*Death of Germanicus*, 1627). During the years 1630 to 1640, he abandoned the Baroque in favor of a rigorously classical style, moving toward a rational clarity and archaeological precision, seen in *Rape of the Sabines*. He was summoned to Paris in 1640 to oversee the decoration of the Grande Galerie of the Louvre, as well as to paint altarpieces and create frontispieces for the royal press. He decided to return to Rome after only two years, and spent the rest of his life there. Later, the Neoclassicists were to draw inspiration from his superb late landscapes, which included *The Funeral of Phocion* (1648). However, during the Romantic era, his reputation waned.

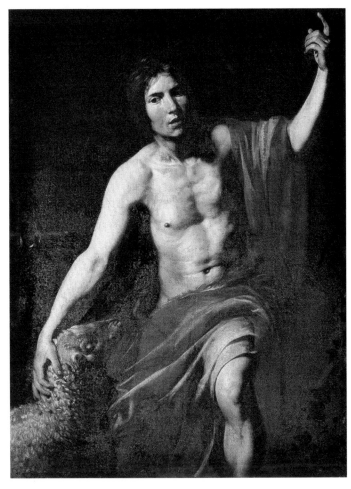

Valentin de Boulogne, St. John the Baptist, *Santa Maria in Via, Camerino, Italy, c.1628–30.*

LA TOUR'S CANDLELIT INTERIORS

Working in Lorraine, Georges de La Tour developed his own, very distinctive interpretation of Caravaggism. He was influenced by the work of the Dutch painters Gerrit Honthorst (1590–1656) and Hendrick Terbrugghen (1588–1629), and it is possible that he spent time in Rome in about 1616. His strict sense of composition and effective handling of indirect light combine to create a reflective atmosphere that is imbued with a sense of inner life. Candlelit scenes are particularly associated with the artist – his first known work, *The Payment of Dues* (c.1615) shows a candlelit interior with figures crowded around a ledger. In *The Flea Catcher*, he portrays a solitary figure, creating a powerful sense of intimacy and demonstrating his trademark mastery of light and shade.

Georges de la Tour, The Flea Catcher, c. 1634. Musée Historique Lorrain, Nancy, France.

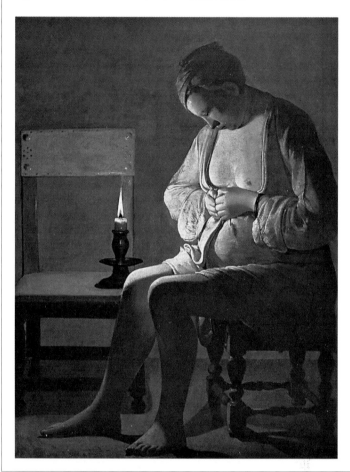

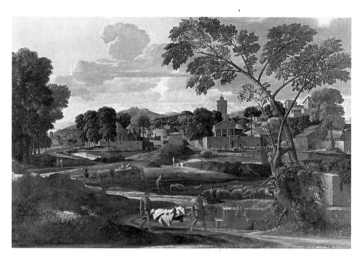

Nicolas Poussin, Funeral of Phocion, 1648. Collection of the Earl of Plymouth, Oakley Park, Shropshire. The classical view of nature and the outlines of the scattered buildings capture the viewer's attention over the sad and subdued historic episode taking place in the foreground.

painting. One of the founder members, Philippe de Champaigne (1602–74), was born in Brussels but worked in Paris from 1621 onward; his historical subjects and portraits combined psychological insight with an almost photographic accuracy. Among the most influential figures of the time was Eustache Le Sueur (1616–55), who painted in a restrained manner inspired by classical antiquity, as is

Claude Lorrain, Landscape with Apollo and Mercury, c.1645. Doria Pamphili Gallery, Rome. Born in Lorraine, the artist spent most of his life in Rome. There, Lorrain combined Bolognese classicism with his Caravaggist interest in light to produce a richly Baroque landscape style.

movement toward classicism in Rome and by the example of Nicolas Poussin, who pursued his career in the papal city from 1624 onward. Poussin's classicism was inspired by Raphael and Titian and was to remain a point of reference for French art, thanks to its formal perfection and refined intellectualism. This was also true of the work of Claude Gellée, known as Claude Lorrain (1600–82), who worked mainly in Rome and was influenced by Flemish painters in the city. Lorrain's idealized style of landscape painting was famous for its formal perfection and timeless quality.

The founding of the Académie Royale de la Peinture in Paris (1648) was a turning point for French

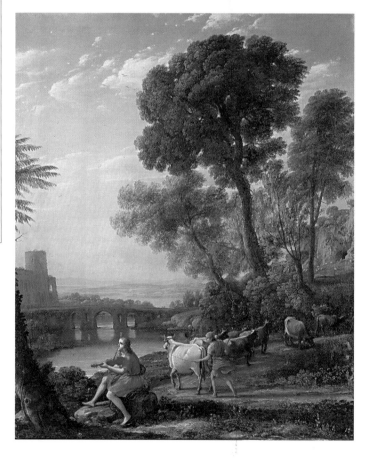

shown in his *Apparition of the Virgin to Saint Martin,* (1654). Charles Le Brun followed Poussin's example and traveled to Italy, staying there for four years. This multitalented artist painted religious subjects and was an extremely skilled decorative painter. From 1656 onward, he supervised the interior decoration of Vaux-le-Vicomte, the château of Louis XIV's chief minister, Colbert, who supported Le Brun's appointment as director of the French

celebrating the king's power. His last works, such as his two *Nativities,* reminiscent of Poussin, were more intimate and emotional.

Another 17th-century French master, Jacques Callot (1592–1635), also came from Lorraine; he worked in Rome and Florence until 1621, when he returned to France. His etchings, with their meticulously defined figures and the originality and scope of his themes and compositions, made a lasting contribution to Baroque art.

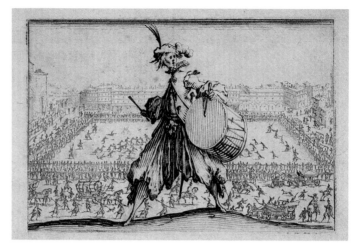

Les Caprices, Les Bohémiens, and *Les Grandes Misères de la Guerre* express his sympathy for all that was strange, sad, and unusual about contemporary life and inspired many later artists, including Goya.

Jacques Callot, The Drummer Boy *or* A Game of Football in the Piazza di Santa Croce, Florence, *1618–19. Galleria degli Uffizi, Florence. This great etcher from Lorraine completed a series depicting popular celebrations for Cosimo II, Grand Duke of Tuscany. His etchings show great originality of composition and his taste for the macabre.*

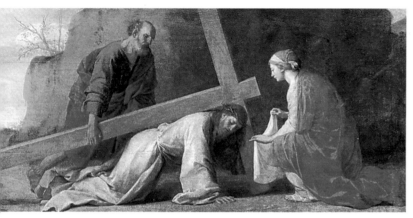

Eustache Le Sueur, Christ Fallen Under the Cross. *Musée du Louvre, Paris. This panel, painted for the church of St. Gervais, Paris, was removed during the French Revolution.*

Academy and its school and, from 1661, of the Gobelins tapestry factory. Le Brun established the grand style of Louis XIV's reign, and in his paintings for Versailles he was able to display his classicism in sumptuous mythological, allegorical, and historical compositions

Charles Le Brun, The Holy Family with the Sleeping Baby Jesus, *1655. Musée du Louvre, Paris. Religious paintings were only one of the strengths of the versatile Le Brun.*

SCENES OF PEASANT LIFE BY THE LE NAIN BROTHERS

Born in Laon, northeastern France, the three Le Nain brothers, Antoine (c.1593–1648), Louis (c.1593–1648), and Mathieu (c.1607–77), were already working in Paris when they were still very young. They established themselves as portraitists as well as painters of the grand manner, producing religious and mythological works. However, their most interesting pictures are

those of peasant life, such as *The Peasants' Meal* (attributed to Louis Le Nain). These are works that transcend genre painting: the everyday reality of the world of humble people is captured with an absolute frankness of observation that discloses the innate humanity of the subjects and their high moral dignity. However, his weaknesses include a certain awkwardness of composition.

Louis Le Nain, The Peasants' Meal, *1642. Musée du Louvre, Paris.*

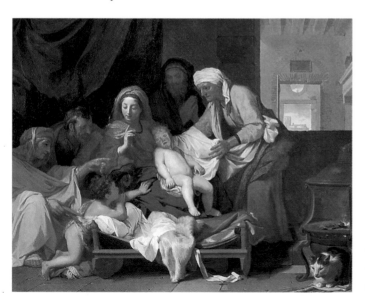

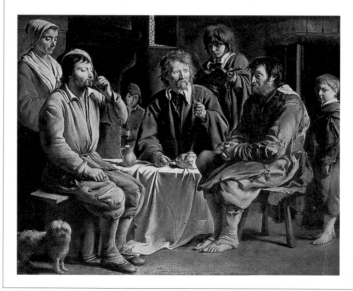

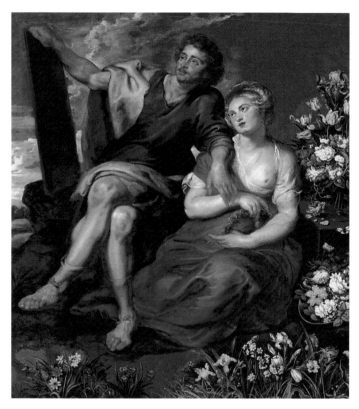

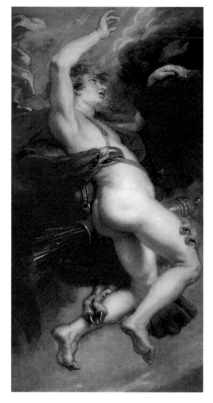

Peter Paul Rubens, Pausias and Glycera or Pastoral Idyll, c.1613. John and Mabel Ringling Museum of Art, Sarasota, Florida. Rubens was always happy to collaborate with other artists: the flowers in this picture were painted by Osias Beert the Elder.

Peter Paul Rubens, Rape of Ganymede, c.1637–38. Museo del Prado, Madrid. The painting's subject is taken from Ovid's Metamorphoses. The figure of the young man is reminiscent of one of the sons in the ancient Roman group statue of Laocoön, and the harsh, bright colors recall Caravaggio's naturalism. Rubens often returned to these sources in his more sensual paintings, translating them into images of dazzling sensuality.

FLEMISH PAINTING IN THE 17TH CENTURY

The name of Peter Paul Rubens dominates Flemish painting of the 17th century. Having trained in Antwerp and learned much from studying other artists' works during his time in Italy (1600–08), Rubens proved himself a master of all genres of painting, including religious, mythological, and allegorical works, portraits, and landscapes. He drew designs for sculptures and tapestries, including *The History of Decius Mus,* (1616–18), for the Genoese nobleman Nicoló Pallavicini, and was also interested in architecture as well as stimulating and coordinating the activities of a wide circle of fellow artists. Many worked alongside him in his studio, collaborating with him on ambitious works commissioned by local and foreign patrons, such as those for the ceiling of the Jesuit church of St. Ignatius in Antwerp (1620–25). Rubens was a rich, cultured artist, with patrician and royal patrons all over Europe. He painted the allegorical cycle of the life of Marie de Médicis for the gallery in the Palais du

Peter Paul Rubens, Triptych of the Descent from the Cross, 1612–1614. Cathedral of Our Lady, Antwerp. The pictorial decoration of this church and of the Church of St. Ignatius, also in Antwerp, marked the apogee of the Baroque in Flanders and a return to a taste for religious imagery after many works of religious art had been destroyed by Protestants in 1566–67 and 1581. The side panels show The Visitation and The Presentation in the Temple.

PETER PAUL RUBENS

By the age of 20, the Flemish painter Peter Paul Rubens (1577–1640) was a member of the Antwerp painters' guild. Between 1600 and 1608, he lived in Italy, studying the example of Veronese, Titian, Tintoretto, the Caracci, and Caravaggio, and on his return to Antwerp was appointed court painter to Archduke Albert and the Infanta Isabella. He also completed important commissions for Marie de Médicis, Regent of France, and for the wealthier churches and members of the bourgeoisie. A polished and thoroughly cultivated man, he served as Ambassador to the Netherlands and to Charles I of England, visited Spain, had many friends among scholars and artists, and had two happy marriages. Van Dyck was one of his many pupils.
Rubens was a very prolific artist with an astonishing ability and great inventiveness. His daring compositions gave his paintings, sketches, and drawings a tremendous vitality.

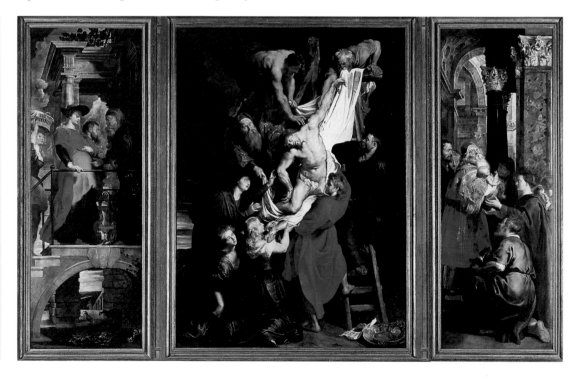

SCULPTURE IN FLANDERS

Many Flemish sculptors were extremely prolific, and some, like François Duquesnoy, met with success abroad. The most gifted and famous member of a family of artists, Duquesnoy worked in Rome from 1618 onward and made his name as a brilliant interpreter of the classical style. Later in the century, the influence of Rubens extended to sculpture, as did that of Roman Baroque. This is evident in the work of Artus Quellinus the Elder (1609–68), a sculptor of note who was active in Amsterdam, where he was commissioned in 1650 to carve sculptures for the new town hall. Lucas Fayd'herbe (1617–97), a pupil of Rubens, was a gifted ivory carver, architect, and sculptor. Among his more famous works are the

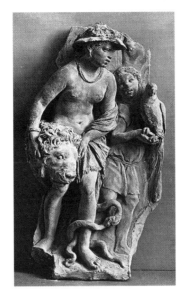

Quellinus the Elder, Africa, 1650. Terracotta model for the Town Hall, Amsterdam.

François Duquesnoy, Sacred Love Conquering Profane Love, 1629. Spada Gallery, Rome.

statues of the Apostles in the church of Saints Michael and Gudula in Brussels, the funerary monument of Bishop Cruesen in Malines Cathedral, and, in the same city, the reliefs in Nôtre-Dame de Hanswyck. The most outstanding of the Walloon sculptors was Jean Delcour (1627–1707), who studied with

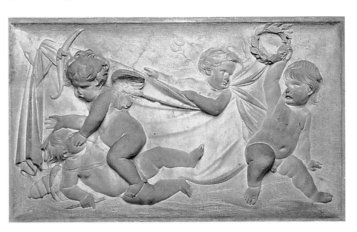

Bernini in Rome before returning to Liège in 1657. Many artists enriched the churches with elaborately decorated altars, choirstalls, screens, confessionals, and pulpits. One of the finest examples is the large wooden pulpit carved by Hendrick Frans Verbruggen for Brussels Cathedral in 1699.

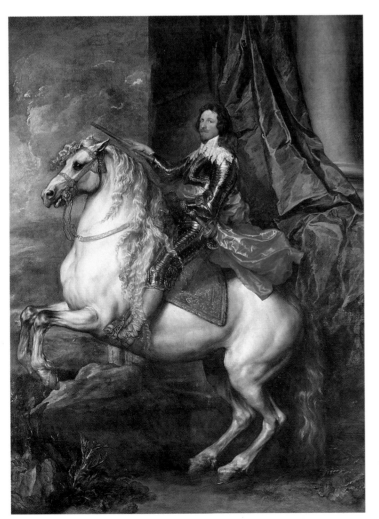

Anthony van Dyck, Portrait of Prince Thomas of Savoy on Horseback, 1634. Sabauda Gallery, Turin. This Flemish artist traveled widely, painting the rich and powerful, from Genoese bankers to the Stuart royal family. His successive posts as court painter to the Archduchess Isabella in Brussels and to Charles I in London did not limit his range of subjects. He painted people with an extraordinary, realistic elegance and with psychological depth.

Luxembourg (1621–35, now in the Musée du Louvre); the painted ceiling in the banquet hall in the Palace of Whitehall, London (1629–34); and a series of paintings inspired by Ovid's Metamorphoses for the Torre della Parada, a royal hunting lodge near Madrid (1636–38).

THE COURT AT BRUSSELS

From 1598 to 1633, Archduke Albert (who died in 1621) and his wife Isabella, the daughter of Philip II of Spain, ruled the Spanish Netherlands from Brussels. The city slowly recovered after the disasters of the sacking of Antwerp and the Protestant iconoclasm, and Flemish life and culture flourished – social improvements began in the city, the University of Louvain was developed, and painters at court included Otto van Veen (one of Rubens' teachers), Rubens himself, Jan Brueghel the Elder (1569–1625), and Anthony van Dyck. While at court, Rubens painted portraits of both the Archduke and

Archduchess, with background landscapes by Brueghel; from 1625 to 1628 he also designed the Eucharist series of Brussels tapestries, some of the sketches for which are in the Fitzwilliam Museum, Cambridge; the printer's device for Christopher Plantin; and a frontispiece for Justus Lipsius' Opera Omnia.

Peter Paul Rubens, design for printers' mark for the Plantin Press, 1627–28. Plantin-Moretus Museum, Antwerp.

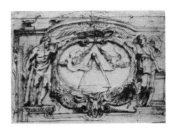

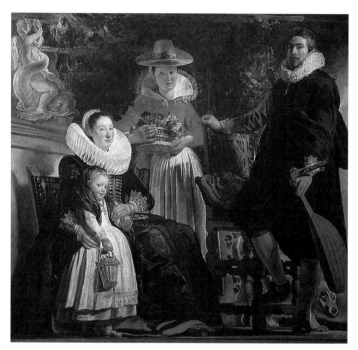

Jacob Jordaens, The Painter's Family in the Garden, *c.1620–22. Museo del Prado, Madrid.*

As a young man, Anthony van Dyck worked with Rubens. After his first visit to London in 1620 to the court of King James I, van Dyck went to Italy (1621–27), staying in Genoa for a considerable time and visiting Venice, Rome, and Palermo. He returned to England in 1632, after which he concentrated mainly on portrait painting, remaining there as court painter to King Charles I for the rest of his life, with the exception of a visit to his homeland in 1634. The work that he produced influenced other artists well into the 18th century. In contrast to van Dyck, Jacob Jordaens (1593–1678) achieved fame throughout Europe without leaving his native Antwerp. Many Flemish artists specialized in the production of cabinet pictures for private collectors, and during the early part of the century in Antwerp this specialization was the virtual monopoly of the Francken family. Their paintings are characterized by a minute attention to detail and a skilful handling of paint, enlivened by elegant Mannerist touches. Genre scenes were given new vigor in the work of Adriaen Brouwer (c.1605–38), who was a pupil of Frans Hals in Haarlem, while Frans Snyders (1579–1657) was an out-standing painter who specialized in the portrayal of animals and landscapes. Both he and his brother-in-law Paul de Vos (c.1596–1678) worked with Rubens. Another prolific artist based

Frans Snyders, The Fruit Seller. *Museo del Prado, Madrid.*

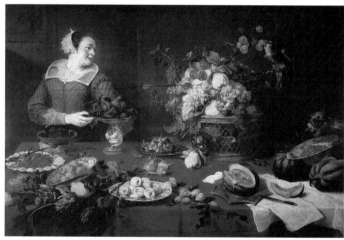

ARCHITECTURE IN FLANDERS

Following Antwerp's conversion from an outpost of Calvinism – the Christian doctrines as interpreted by the French protestant reformer and theologian John Calvin (1509–64) – into a bastion of the Counter-Reformation, two new churches were built: the church of St. Augustine (begun 1615) by Wenzel Coebergher (c.1560–1634) and the Jesuit Church, now St. Charles

Franciscus Aguillon and Pieter Huyssens, St. Ignatius, now St. Charles Borromeo, interior, Antwerp.

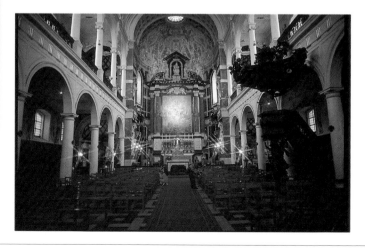

Borromeo (c.1615–25), by the architects Franciscus Aguillon (1567–1617) and Pieter Huyssens (1577–1637), possibly with the help of Rubens. He also provided the drawings for the statues on the facade as well as the entire decoration of the ceiling (destroyed in a fire in 1718) and various paintings. The espousal of an extravagant Baroque style by Flemish architects is evident in the church of St. Michael in Louvain (1650–71), designed by the Jesuit Willem van Hess (1601–90). There, references to Italian churches (notably the Gesù in Rome) and rich decoration are combined with an emphasis on height and verticality which shows the continuing influence of Gothic taste. The houses in the Grande Place, Brussels, most of which were designed by Guillaume de

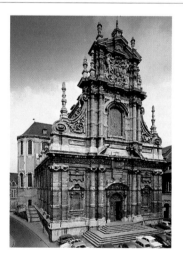

Willem van Hess and Jan Steen, facade of the Jesuit Church (now St. Michael's), Louvain.

Bruyn (1649–1719), have exuberant exterior decoration grafted onto a more traditional and deeply rooted Flemish style.

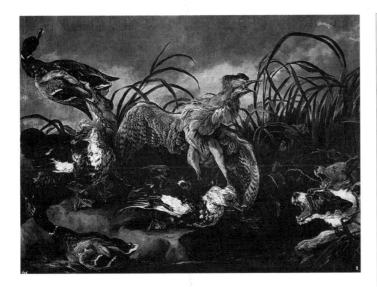

Jan Fyt, Ducks and Waterfowl Surprised by Dogs. *Museo del Prado, Madrid.*

in Antwerp was Jan Fyt (1611–61), who brought new refinements to the handling of paint. Abraham Brueghel (1631–97), the last of the famous dynasty of Flemish painters, moved to Italy in 1659, where he settled first in Rome and then in Naples. During his time in Italy, he produced flower paintings with an ease of execution and attractive composition and color.

DUTCH LANDSCAPE PAINTING

The development of landscape painting in the Netherlands was stimulated by a desire to emulate the Flemish masters. Haarlem was an important center for this new approach, and it was here that Esaias van de Velde (c.1591–1630), who supported a more "realistic" approach to landscape painting, was working. By the 1620s, he had found a like-minded contemporary in Hercules Pietersz Seghers (1589/90– 1633/38), a talented artist whose paintings and etchings depicted views taken directly from nature as well as imaginary landscapes – some incorporating erotic elements of a type that later appealed to Rembrandt. Jacob van Ruisdael (c.1628–82), one of the most outstanding Dutch landscape painters, was much admired by 18th-century and Romantic artists.

Jacob van Ruisdael, A Gleam of Sun. *Musée du Louvre, Paris.*

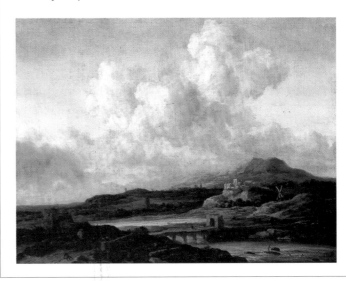

THE NETHERLANDS IN THE 17TH CENTURY

This period saw a great flowering of Dutch art, especially of cabinet and small-scale pictures of all types: portraits, landscapes, marine paintings, domestic interiors, architectural vistas, and still lifes. Official commissions were often for group portraits of civic worthies such as city guilds and military companies in the United Provinces (now The Netherlands). During the 1620s, the established Utrecht master Abraham Bloemaert (1564–1651) was a late convert to Caravaggism, influenced by one of his pupils, Gerrit van Honthorst (1590–1656). Like Dirck van Baburen (1595–1624) and Hendrick Terbrugghen, van Honthorst had spent time in Rome. The evocative, atmospheric candlelight in many of his paintings earned him the name "Gerard of the Night Scenes." But the last flicker of Dutch Caravaggism died away with Terbrugghen's death in 1629; van Honthorst abandoned his earlier style in favor of classicism and went on to work at the English, Danish, and Dutch courts.

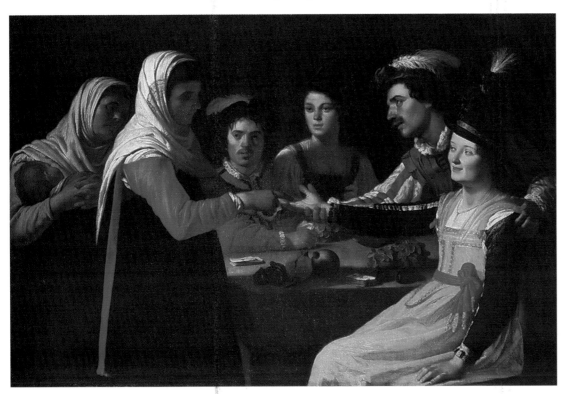

Gerrit van Honthorst, The Fortune Teller, *c.1617. Galleria degli Uffizi, Florence.*

Born in Antwerp, the great portraitist Frans Hals (1581/85 –1666) spent most of his life in Haarlem. He left Mannerist convention behind, restoring truth, vigor, and spontaneity of pose and expression to his subjects, and made the most of his skill at capturing a likeness with swift, sure brushstrokes, as can be seen in his "character" portraits painted during the 1630s. Far in advance of contemporary European artists, Rembrandt van Rijn

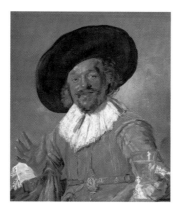

Frans Hals, The Merry Drinker, *detail, c.1630. Rijksmuseum, Amsterdam. Hals' paintings have a tremendous sense of vitality and are full of the pleasures of living in an upwardly mobile, free, and enterprising society.*

REMBRANDT VAN RIJN

Already an established master, Rembrandt van Rijn (1606–69) left his native Leiden for Amsterdam in 1631. He made a good marriage in 1634, which brought him connections and many important commissions, including *The Anatomy Lesson of Dr. Tulp* (1632), *The Night Watch* or *The Militia Company of Captain Frans Banning Cocq and Lieutenant Willem van Ruytenburch* (1642), and a number of group portraits. Completed with a richly colored palette, they demonstrate his genius for composition and the handling of color and light. Thereafter, Rembrandt was less sought after since his manner became more introspective. His *Self Portrait as St Paul* (1661) and *Homer* (1663) date from this period. As his art became less realistic and increasingly cerebral and religious, running counter to deep-seated Dutch cultural conventions, it acquired an austere, mysterious grandeur. This is particularly noticeable in his etchings – some 300 of which survive – including the famous *Christ Healing the Sick* (c.1642–45) and his powerful *Three Crosses* (c.1661).

was not only a painter of exceptional originality but also a superb draftsman and etcher. In about 1625, he set up a workshop in his home town of Leiden and concentrated on examining how light delineates shapes within evocative atmospheres, while also exploring the inner psychology of his subjects. Over the years, his expressive power grew in subtlety and insight, partly as a result of his experience in painting penetrating portraits. Some 80 self-portraits recorded the phases

Rembrandt van Rijn, The Anatomy Lesson of Dr. Tulp, *1632. Mauritshuis, The Hague. This work was painted during Rembrandt's early years in Amsterdam, when the city was Europe's greatest mercantile center.*

REMBRANDT VAN RIJN: "ANATOMY LESSON OF DOCTOR DEYMAN"

1656; oil on canvas, fragment; 39½ x 52 in (100 x 132 cm); Rijksmuseum, Amsterdam.

This is all that remains of a large group portrait after it was damaged by fire in 1723: the upper part and most of both sides are missing, but the lower part with the signature has survived. The work was commissioned by

the Surgeons' Guild some 24 years after Rembrandt painted *The Anatomy Lesson of Dr. Tulp* for the prominent physician Nicolaes Tulp. In that work, he had revolutionized the tradition of group portraiture. Instead of portraying a group of juxtaposed figures, he unified the composition by uniting their interest in the action of the lecturer above the corpse. In 1632, when the first *Lesson* was painted, Rembrandt was 26, well regarded, prosperous, and

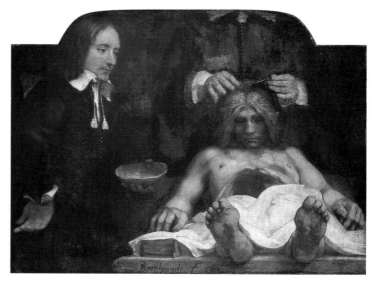

▼ *1. This fragment is only the central part of a large composition (known through a drawing) which showed figures watching the dissection from both sides. The corpse, with raised head and in foreshortened perspective, is contained within a triangle. The hands of the man who is dissecting, above and on either side of the dead man's head, form a smaller triangle; the dead man's chin is its apex, pointing down toward the gaping ventral cavity. The spectator's face, right hand, and what appears to be a small bowl in his left hand form an isosceles triangle. Rembrandt's compositions were often based on diagonal lines and tangential planes. Here, the composition appears as a dihedron, with three-dimensional depth.*

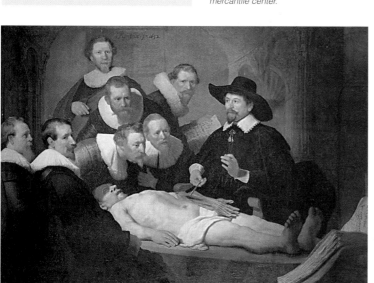

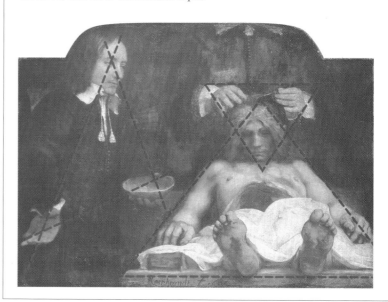

on the brink of an advantageous marriage to Saskia van Uylenburgh. In 1656, after years of spectacular success, he was poor, almost forgotten, and obliged to auction off his belongings because of bankruptcy. In this picture, he concentrates on the essentials: the watching figure of the spectator, the hands of the surgeon, and the body of the unfortunate Joris Fontein undergoing dissection.

▶ *2. Rembrandt's early works bore traces of Caravaggism, but in later works he handled light in a less theatrical way. In this painting, the dissected body is in full light, while deep shadow fills the ventral cavity. A golden light unites the scene, linking the surgeon's hands and the face and hands of the spectator. The light also reveals that the bowl in the spectator's hand is probably the trepanned cranium of the hapless Fontein. By following the diagonal lines that join the picture's salient features, the observer discovers its focal point, the exposed brain under the hair.*

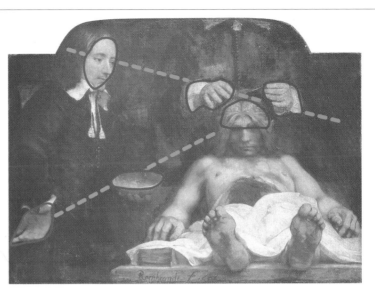

▼ *4. Rembrandt was a well-educated man, living in a culturally rich country that was dominated by a mercantile aristocracy and with a vibrant religious life, both Calvinist and Jewish. Among the treasures he sold later in his life to pay his debts were engravings by Italian masters, including Mantegna. The foreshortened view of the corpse is reminiscent of Mantegna's* Dead Christ *(after 1466, Brera Gallery, Milan), although the cadaver here does not appear as tranquil: the strong arms stretch out toward the foreground, and deep shadows hollow the eye sockets and the cheeks. The brightest and warmest area of color in the fragment illuminates the exposed brain: glowing deep pink and gold. The skin has been pulled back so that it frames the face. The head, supported and inclined forward, seems to have been lifted in an effort to retain the identity and dignity of the man.*

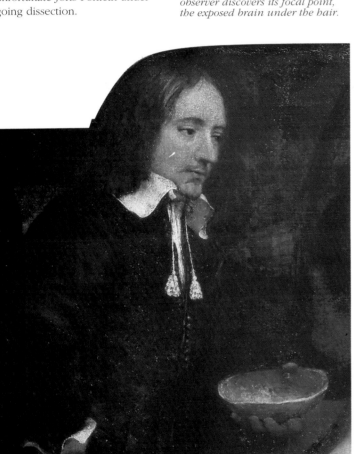

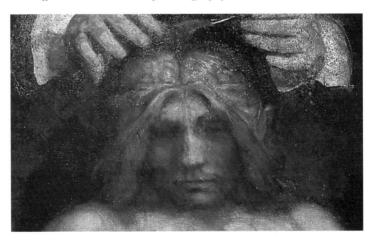

▼ *5. Rembrandt carefully defines the skilled hands of Dr. Deyman, who is performing the autopsy, and shows us exactly how he operates. Subtle touches of color, from red to white, shape the fingers, and his hands are emphasized by the white cuffs. A white thread of paint delineates the blade of the scalpel, which is probing the brain. Rembrandt does not use space as a device for dramatic emphasis; his restrained and masterly use of light can effectively express drama or even intense passion.*

▲ *3. Dr. Calcoen, the surgeon watching the dissection, gazes dispassionately but intently at the hands wielding the scalpel. The cuff of his right sleeve is resting on his hip, and the indistinctly drawn, reddish hand is bloodied and appears somewhat unclear. It is the indifference with which he holds the top of the skull in his other hand that makes it look like an unremarkable small bowl at first glance. He calmly follows the progress of the autopsy. He is a young man, well dressed in the usual austere style of this Protestant city, capable and sure of himself. The portrait is perfect, enhanced by the restraint of its treatment and the rejection of superfluous detail.*

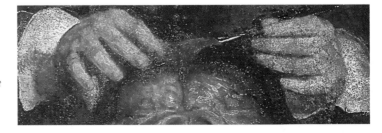

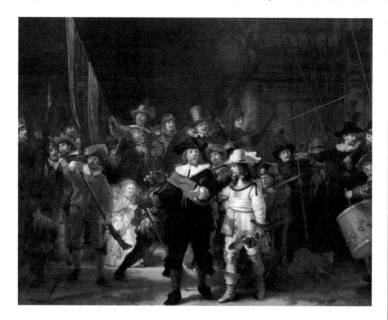

Rembrandt van Rijn, The Night Watch, *also known as* The Militia Company of Captain Frans Banning Cocq and Lieutenant Willem van Ruytenburch, *1642. Rijksmuseum, Amsterdam. This large painting was commissioned by the members of one of the companies of militia men who kept the peace in the free city of Amsterdam. After cleaning, the picture was found to be a far brighter scene than was formerly believed.*

of his life rather like an autobiography, and later they gradually became more introspective. Immediately after moving to Amsterdam in 1631, he became the most sought-after painter of the day for portraits of the city's *haute bourgeoisie.* His *Anatomy Lesson of Dr. Tulp* dates from this period. With his famous *The Night Watch* (also known as *The Militia Company of Captain Frans Banning Cocq and Lieutenant Willem van Ruytenburch*), painted in 1642, Rembrandt created a fresh and unusual

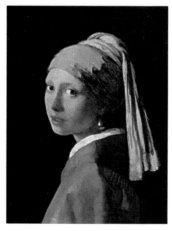

Jan Vermeer, Head of a Girl with a Pearl Earring, *1660–65. Mauritshuis, The Hague. Unusual for Vermeer's works, the sitter is shown isolated and without a context.*

Carel Fabritius, View of Delft, *1652. National Gallery, London. The unusual composition of this painting has a collection of objects and a figure in the left foreground, with a background view of the church surrounded by a low boundary.*

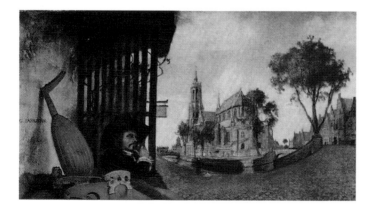

JAN VERMEER: "THE LACEMAKER"
Circa 1669–1670;
9½ x 8 in (24 x 21 cm);
Musée du Louvre, Paris.

This small picture is meant to be viewed from close up. A young girl of Delft is seated at a small, sloping table at work on a piece of lace. She has all she needs within reach, including a book. There is no need for a lamp, since there is enough daylight.
The work is intended primarily as a portrait or perhaps as a cabinet picture to grace the wall of a middle-class house in Delft. It is ideally suited to this purpose, its eloquent calm ensuring that the

owners would never tire of looking at it. The painter must have known that his work would appear to its greatest advantage in such a setting. At an easy distance from Amsterdam, the gateway to the world and the port through which beautiful objects were imported from far and wide, Delft was an important center for the production of pottery, and its inhabitants enjoyed prosperous, untroubled lives. Vermeer depicted mainly women from various walks of life, rarely formally posed but full of dignity and usually occupied in daily activities. Relatively few of his meticulously considered works have survived.

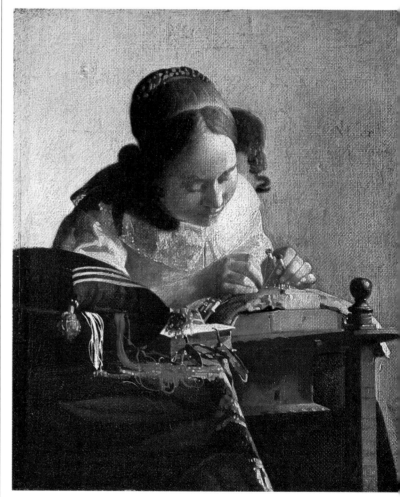

interpretation of the group portrait by dividing the figures into several smaller groups and portraying them moving, instead of in static, poses, emphasized by his

handling of the complex lighting effects.
Rembrandt had many pupils in Leiden and Amsterdam, including Gerrit Dou, Govaert Flinck, Samuel van

282

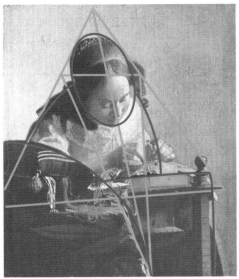

▲ 1. The subject of the painting is lit by a diffuse, soft light and is placed against a pale background of almost plain canvas. The composition can be broken up into different areas of color and shape; the curved, dark mass of the tablecloth, cushion, and sewing equipment is in sharp contrast to the softer, light colors of the girl's dress. The oval of the head is framed by the hair and the neutral background, and the angular, detailed sewing desk crisply reflects the light. The surface of the sewing desk can be seen as the base of of a triangle, the other two sides enclosing the figure as she leans over her sewing. An oblique line running from the lower edge of the tablecloth through the girl's face provides the axis of the picture, dividing the darker left hand side from the right.

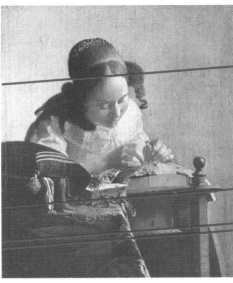

▲ 2. The light falls from the upper right hand side of the picture, roughly following the lines of the top of the sewing desk. The illumination is soft and natural, suggesting that it emanates from an open window just out of view. The girl is bathed in a warm glow, like the light of early morning. The yellow of her blouse, her warm complexion, and the shine of her hair all reflect and enhance the light. These reflective elements, and the fact that the light source is outside of the scene, give the illusion that the girl herself is somehow radiant and is herself the source of light. This radiance gives the figure a more three-dimensional quality than the objects around it.

▼ 3. The girl is concentrating intently, and her gaze is closely linked to her busy hands. The whole composition draws the viewer's eye in to this meticulous industry, the hand and the mind at work; the other details of the painting are merely there to frame this activity. This painting captured the essence of an age of inquiry. In 1664, Thomas Willis had described the appearance and functions of the brain, nervous system, and muscles in his Cerebri Anatome, while Pascal's Pensées, his reflections on thought and conscience, were post-humously published in 1670, at about the time that Vermeer was painting The Lacemaker.

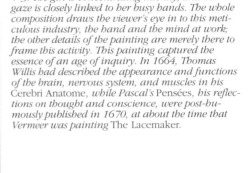

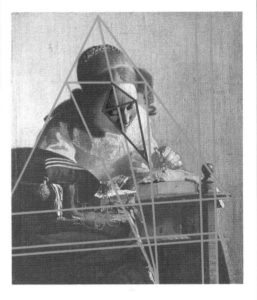

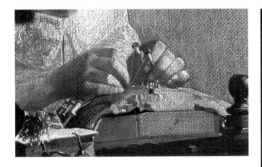

▲ 4. The girl's hands manipulate the thread, which is stretched between the bobbins held in her left hand and the pins marking out the lace design on the little cushion. Other bobbins, not in use at this moment, hang down to one side of the cushion. The work is modest: the girl is young and has undertaken a relatively simple design. Her fingers work deftly and precisely, and Vermeer is masterful in his representation of the proportions and the position of the hands and fingers.

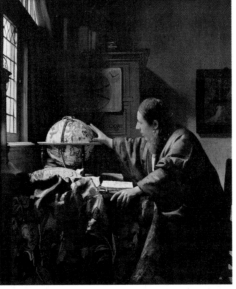

◄ 5. The Astronomer, (1668, Musée du Louvre, Paris) was among Vermeer's late works and again took the theme of dialogue between the mind, eyes, and hands, reinforced by objects – the book, telescope, and celestial sphere. The table carpet is the similar to that in The Lacemaker. This subject is a variation on a theme that had already been used in many genre paintings following the foundation of the Dutch East India Company in 1602. Dutch artists mirrored the subsequent developments in the science and technology of navigation with what were essentially portraits of books, instruments, and rooms, as well as the men who used them. What distinguished Vermeer was his genius for handling the world he created with affectionate detachment, which stems from the conceptual structure of the picture hidden beneath the obvious realism. Vermeer was active at a time when Baruch Spinoza (1632–77), the cerebral Jewish philosopher, was rejecting the personal God of Christians and Jews in favor of a God of rational order and structure, to whom man offered an intimate, silent, intellectual love that constituted true freedom. An equivalent depth of thought seems to be present in Vermeer's meditations, with their inner light, scientific approach, and silent and ordered view of reality.

Hoogstraten, Carel Fabritius, and Nicolaes Maes. In 1650, Fabritius (1622–54) moved to Delft and, inspired by his adopted city, gained a reputation for his vibrant, colorful paintings and his exploration of perspective, demonstrated by his View of Delft (1652). Delft was also home to the painter Emanuel de Witte (c.1617–92), famous for his massive and dramatic church interiors, and Jan Vermeer (1632–75), whose later paintings were generally domestic interiors, peopled by calm figures who are usually occupied in leisure or work activities and which convey feelings of serenity through their purity of color and an exquisite, sensuous light.

STILL LIFE

By 1610, Roelant Savery had introduced flower painting to Utrecht. It proved to be a popular genre, and Ambrosius Bosschaert (1573–1621), an outstanding still-life painter, had considerable success with his flower paintings. The *vanitas* theme, usually involving a penitent and sorrowing figure surrounded by symbols of the transitory nature of earthly life such as a skull, candle, or rose, was a favorite of Leiden artists and also of David Bailly (c.1584–1657). Willem Claesz. Heda (c.1594–c.1682) and Pieter Claesz. (1597/98–1661), who both worked in Haarlem, dealt

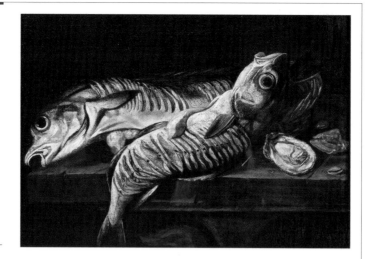

Abraham van Beyeren, Fish. Musée des Beaux-Arts, Dunkirk. This is painted in oils on a wood panel.

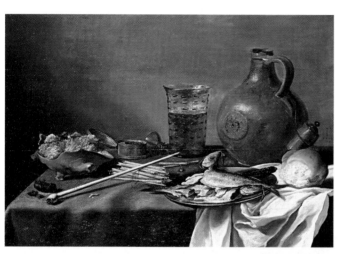

with the fleeting nature of human life, painting in subdued colors; they influenced Jan III van de Velde (c.1620–62). In contrast, the splendid still lifes painted in the second half of the century by Willem Kalf (1619–93) and Abraham van Beyeren (1620/21–90) are full of rich color and light effects, skillfully depicting various materials. The Dutch love of nature and exploration meant that painters were eager to depict a variety of subjects, especially botanical.

Pieter Claesz., Still life with Glass of Beer, 1644. Musée des Beaux-Arts, Nantes.

Pieter Claesz., Still life with Ham. Musée des Beaux-Arts, Dunkirk.

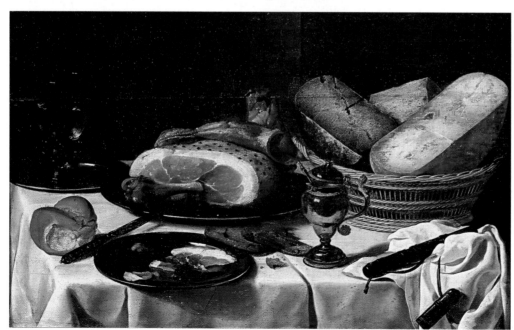

THE 17TH CENTURY IN SPAIN

The 17th century was the golden age of Spanish painting, thanks to a tremendous surge of artistic activity throughout Andalusia and especially in Seville, the economic, cultural, and spiritual center of Spain. Gradually, however, many artists gravitated to Madrid, attracted by the presence of the royal court, although church patronage continued to play a very important role throughout the kingdom. During the first 20 years of the century, the dominant artistic trend was naturalism, further stimulated by the spread of Caravaggism and by works of art that reached Spain from Italy. An accurate depiction of reality and the orchestration of the interplay of light and shade were evident in the early works of the first generation of great 17th-century artists in Seville: Francisco Zurbarán (1598–1664), Diego Velázquez, and Alonso Cano (1601–67). Velázquez' youthful works, such as *Old Woman Cooking Eggs* (1618), already showed a powerful artistic language,

DIEGO VELAZQUEZ

Diego Rodriguez de Silva y Velázquez (1599–1660) trained in Seville under Francisco de Herrera (1585–c.1657) and Francisco Pacheco. In 1622 and 1623, Velázquez visited Madrid, where the Duke of Oliváres admired his work, leading to his appointment as court painter. In 1629, he went to Italy and visited the main centers of artistic activity, traveling from Genoa south to Naples. He was an immensely successful painter, and though influenced by Caravaggio, he tempered his own realism by constant attention to the aesthetic qualities of the composition. His impeccable, balanced, and sober use of color, and his controlled and elegant brushwork, made him a master whose work was immune to the vagaries of fashion and an admirably restrained painter in the great theater of the Baroque world. His painting remains a yardstick against which other artists are measured.

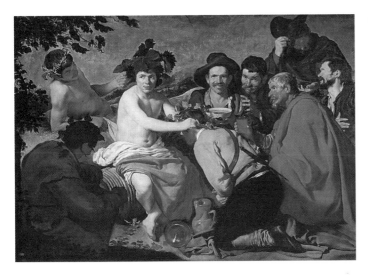

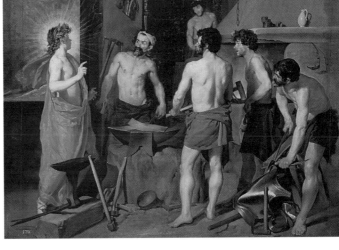

Diego Velázquez, The Topers *or* The Triumph of Bacchus, *c.1624. Museo del Prado, Madrid. In this work, the artist gives a modern interpretation of the Roman myth.*

Diego Velázquez, Las Meniñas, *1656. Museo del Prado, Madrid. In Velázquez' most famous court painting, he depicts the Infanta Margarita Teresa with her maids.*

Diego Velázquez, The Forge of Vulcan, *1630. Museo del Prado, Madrid. In this masterpiece, the artist shows his skill in combining mythology with everyday life.*

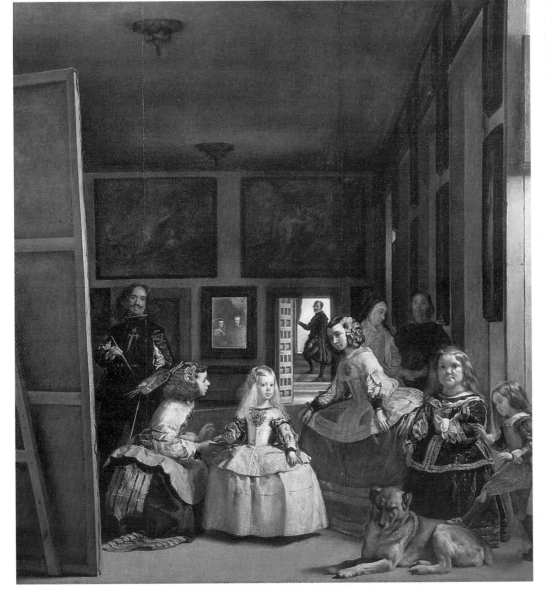

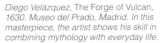

used to convey the everyday life of ordinary people. His treatment of religious subjects shows an equally realistic portrayal of form and chiaroscuro, an interest shared with contemporary Sevillian sculptors. In 1623, Velázquez first came into contact with Philip IV, from whom he was to receive many portrait commissions. He studied Titian's paintings in the royal collection in Madrid and met Rubens (who was in Madrid in from 1628 to 1629), but he reached the height of his powers after his travels in Italy between 1629 and 1631, which made a profound impression upon him. His work is distinguished by a free and agile technique, using touches of vibrant and

Alonso Cano, St. Bernard and the Madonna *or* The Miracle of the Lactation. *Museo del Prado, Madrid.*

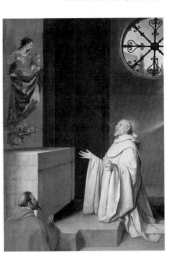

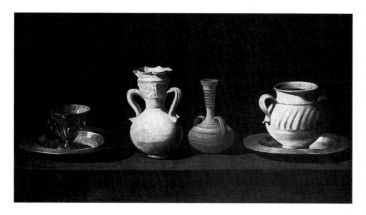

Francisco Zurbarán, Still Life, c.1630. Museo del Prado, Madrid.

FRANCISCO ZURBARAN

Influenced by the School of Seville, Francisco Zurbarán (1598–1664) had already set up his own workshop in Llerena by about the age of 20. There, he completed his admirable series of 21 paintings for the church of St. Madeleine, Seville. He was appointed official painter to the city of Seville and settled there in 1629, moving to Madrid in 1658, where he died. Zurbarán painted religious figures, monks, and saints in meditation and prayer. Many of these are set in shadowy, undefined surroundings, although the figures themselves possess a massive solidity. His masterly use of color was enhanced by an amazingly brilliant intensity of light, which is most evident in his still lifes. These simple scenes, sculpted by light, are idealized but realistic, imbuing everyday objects with a sense of the sacred.

softly shaded color and swift, looser brushwork to achieve a rare interplay between reality and illusion. The painter and sculptor Alonso Cano developed from an early lively naturalism toward the pursuit of a Renaissance-inspired ideal beauty, while Francisco Zurbarán's paintings convey an austere Iberian spirituality. In his figurative paintings, the sculptural figures stand out against dark backgrounds, epitomized in his *Vision of St.*

Francisco Zurbarán, The Lying in State of St. Bonaventure, c.1629. Musée du Louvre, Paris.

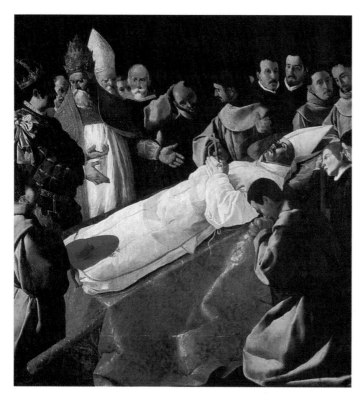

DIEGO VELAZQUEZ: "THE SPINNERS"

1657; oil on canvas; 86½ x 113¾ in (220 x 289 cm). Museo del Prado, Madrid.

Also known as *The Fable of Arachne*, this last great work by the Sevillian master shows the interior of the tapestry factory of Santa Isabela in Madrid. In the background, in a space filled with strong light, several fashionably dressed women seen in profile or with their backs to us examine tapestries hanging on the walls; one has her face turned toward the industrious tapestry workers.

In contrast to the brightly lit background, the foreground is largely in shadow. On the right, a beautiful young woman with her back to us sits at a skein-holder, looking diagonally toward the alcove; beside her is a girl, bending over a basket. Balancing the composition, on the other side of the canvas, is an older woman working with a distaff and spinning wheel who appears to be in conversation with the young girl on her right. Between the two groups, another girl sits in the shadow, stretching out her hand as if to stroke the sleeping cat.

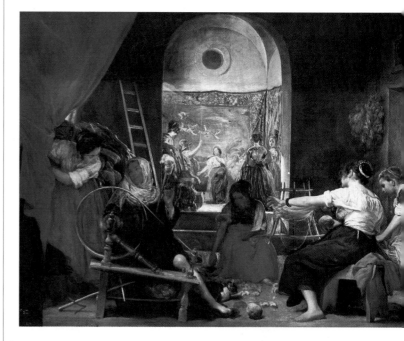

▶ *1. This scene within a scene echoes the Baroque practice of inserting a theatrical or balletic interlude into an opera. Velázquez took inspiration for this work from the myth of Arachne in Ovid's* Metamorphoses. *Portrayed in the form of a tapestry on the far wall is the concluding episode of the myth – the competition between the young weaver and the goddess Athena is being played out in the foreground. In the background, Athena, radiant in her armor, has assumed her divine form; she raises her hand to strike the young Arachne, punishing her arrogance at challenging her weaving ability by turning her into a spider. By implying that the artistry of the weavers can excite the envy of the gods, the painter was entering an important debate of the time as to which was more valuable, the artisan or the artist, skill or creativity.*

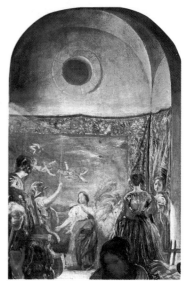

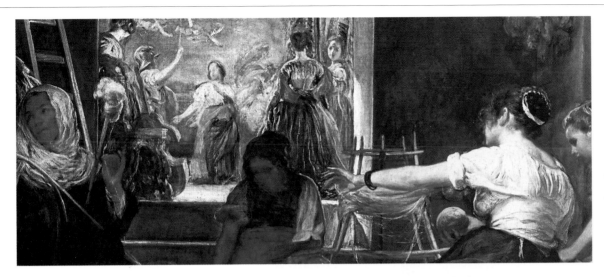

◄ *2. The lighting in the two settings is very different; in the background, clear daylight illuminates the pale blues, grays, and pinks of the tapestry, the composition of which is based on Titian's Rape of Europa (1559–62). Spatial depth is achieved by a gradual blurring of outlines and a lightening of the colors as the scene recedes farther into the background. In the dimly lit foreground, our attention is drawn to the illuminated figure of the young weaver, who, pointing past the shaded figure in the center, redirects our gaze to the drama being played out in the alcove.*

► *3. In the guise of an old woman, as she first appeared to Arachne, Athena sits at the spinning wheel. It is turning so fast that the spokes are not visible. The blurring effect on objects behind the rotating wheel is evident: the rear bracket of the wheel itself, the women's clothes, and especially Athena's hand behind the wheel, at the point near the hub where the spokes are closest together. It is in such details that Velázquez' extraordinary skill in translating what he observed to the canvas is evident. Velázquez demonstrates what Baroque art was all about: revealing the workings of nature and thought, rather than superficial effects.*

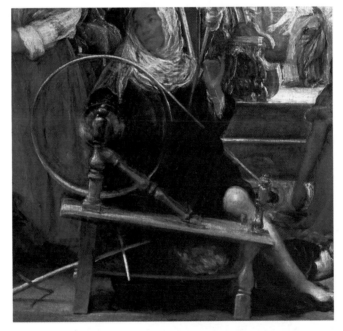

▼ *4. The composition operates on two levels. In the foreground, two groups of paired figures, punctuated and linked by the girl in the center, are sited along diagonal lines. These lead the eye to a spherical shape on the floor, a compositional element that is echoed by the round window above the tapestries in the background. The scenes are separated by a vertical plane of shadow which includes the wall with the arch and the deep stairs up to the alcove. Splitting the painting in this way enabled the artist to combine the humble – a simple scene of weavers at work – with the heroic, blurring the distinction between mythology and everyday life.*

▼ *5. The painter's exceptional talent as a colorist, his creativity in composition, and his superb draftsmanship are all employed to re-create a contemporary scene here in the foreground, which is being played out simultaneously with the mythical narrative. The presence of the dozing cat, the womens' bare feet, and the remnants of wool scattered on the floor combine to present us with an extremely naturalistic scene. In contrast to the more exalted world in the background, the rich reds and browns that the artist has used in this section of the painting lend it a more earthy and practical atmosphere.*

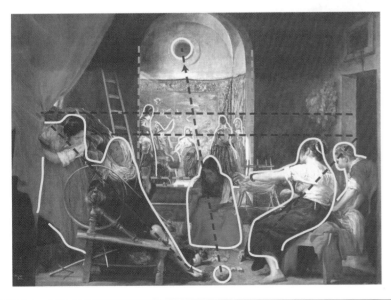

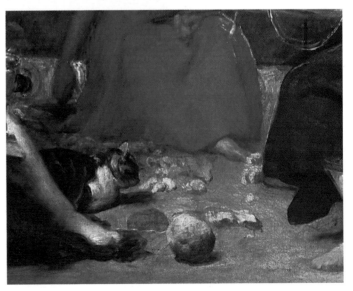

Peter Nolasco (1629), while his still lifes are intense and vibrant. Toward the middle of the century, Bartolomé Estebán Murillo (1618–82) became extremely successful, having learned much from the previous generation of Sevillian painters such as Francisco Ribalta (1565–1628), whose style remained vigorously Caravaggesque, and the melancholy, strange

Bartolomé Estebán Murillo, Young Beggar, c.1645. Musée du Louvre, Paris.

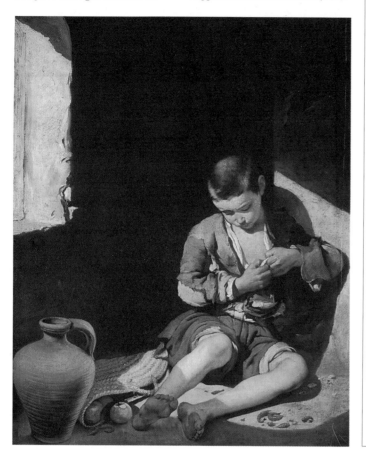

SCULPTURE IN SPAIN

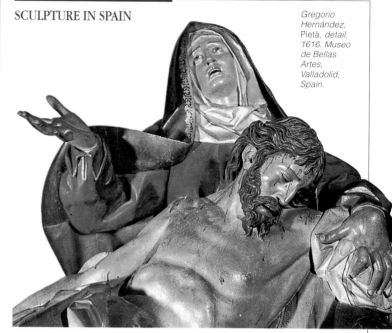

Gregorio Hernández, Pietà, detail, 1616. Museo de Bellas Artes, Valladolid, Spain.

Some of the most outstanding works by 17th-century Spanish sculptors were devotional pieces in polychrome wood. Those of Gregorio Hernández (1576–1636), the greatest sculptor of the Castilian school, are imbued with an intense, passionate expressivity.

The polychrome sculptures of Juan Martínez Montañes (1568–1649), a sculptor active in Seville and a friend of Francisco Pacheco, possessed a powerful naturalism yet strove to convey a spiritual message. Some of his most important commissions, including *Christ of Clemency* (1603–06), are in Seville Cathedral. Montañés was an important influence on his contemporaries Velázquez, Zurbarán, and Alonso Cano. Cano gradually adopted more elegant shapes in his work, aiming at a softer and more idealized approach in both his sculpture and his painting.

ARCHITECTURE IN MADRID

During the 17th century, a huge amount of new building and urban development took place in Madrid, reflecting its new role as the capital city. The most important buildings were for the Royal Court. During the late 16th and early 17th centuries, the Alcázar Palace, in the westernmost part of the city, was enlarged and altered from 1561 onward under the supervision of Juan Bautista de Toledo (the building was destroyed in a fire in 1734). He was succeeded as the leading court architect by Juan Gómez de Mora, who also designed the Plaza Mayor and was involved in the construction of El Escorial, the huge monastery-palace in the foothills of the Sierra de Guadarrama near

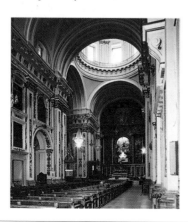

Francisco Bautista, interior of Cathedral of St. Isidore, Madrid, c.1622–60.

Plaza Mayor, Madrid, begun 1590.

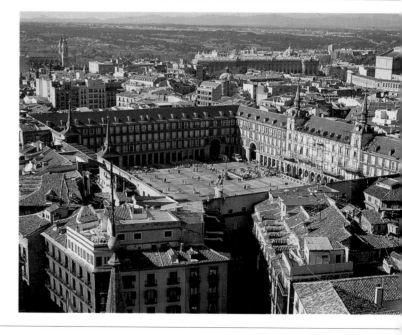

Luís de Morales (1520–86), whose religious paintings, particularly his many Madonnas, enjoyed considerable popularity.

Francisco Rizi, Annunciation. *Museo del Prado, Madrid.*

Murillo's devotional pictures are above all pleasing to the senses, emphasizing the consolatory aspects of religion with a sweetness that sometimes borders on the cloying. His tenderness of vision, which met with

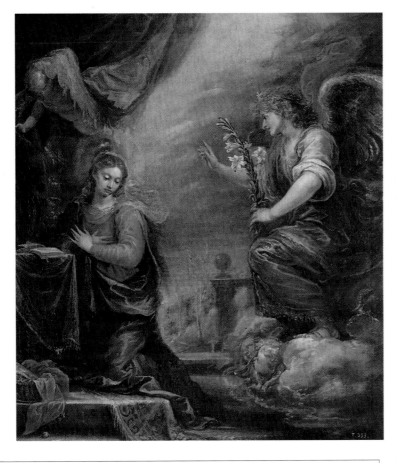

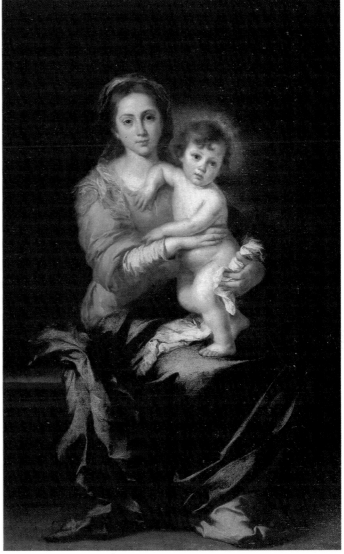

Bartolomé Esteban Murillo, Madonna with the Infant Jesus, *1650–60. Palazzo Pitti, Florence.*

Madrid, built at Philip II's behest. Alonso Carbonel and Giovanni Crescenzi (1577–1660) also worked on El Escorial as well as designing the Palace of the Buen Retiro

El Escorial, south facade, begun 1563.

(1623–29), the sovereign's summer residence in eastern Madrid, which was partially destroyed in 1640. A Jesuit priest, Francisco Bautista (1594–1678), was appointed architect of the new cathedral of St. Isidore.

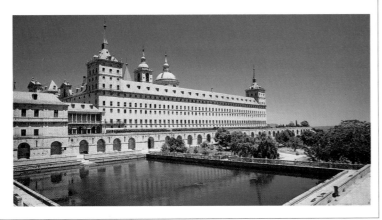

prolonged popularity, can be seen even in his genre scenes. The paintings of Juan Valdés Leal (1622–90), by contrast, were full of energy and drama. It was at this time that Flemish influence, ranging from Rubens to van Dyck, again played a decisive role in Spanish art, and Baroque taste prevailed in the development of large-scale fresco decoration in the grand manner. The greatest exponents of this style were Francisco Rizi (1614–85) and the court painters Juan Careño de Miranda (1614–85) and Claudio Coello (1642–93).

THE HAPSBURGS AND THE 17TH CENTURY

In the 16th century, an irreparable schism developed in Central Europe: the north espoused the Protestant cause while the south, on the whole, remained Roman Catholic. During the Thirty Years' War (1618–48) this split deepened, ending with the Peace of Münster under which the German nation was no longer a political unity – over 300 small states were recognized – and the House of Austria tightened its grip on Bohemia, which lost all political autonomy. The country had come under the control of the Hapsburgs

PRAGUE DURING THE REIGN OF RUDOLPH II

Rudolph II of Hapsburg (King of Bohemia 1575–1611, and emperor 1576–1612) gathered together a prodigious collection of paintings, sculptures, and *objets d'art* in Prague Castle and surrounded himself with artists from all over Europe. Goldsmiths, gemstone cutters such as Ottavio Miseroni, and painters, including

Hans von Aachen (1552–1615), Bartholomaeus Spranger from Antwerp, Joseph Heintz of Basel, and Giuseppe Arcimboldo (1527–93) from Milan, rubbed shoulders with sculptors such as Adriaen de Vries from Holland, a pupil of Giambologna. The result was a tremendous flowering of culture at the court and the production of some of the most outstanding examples of international Mannerism.

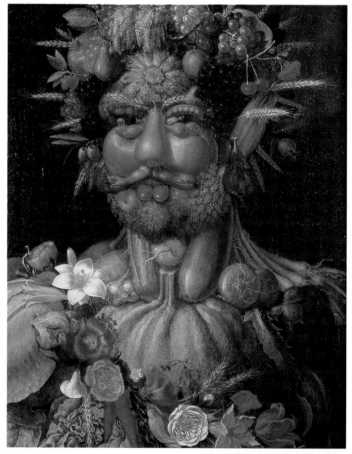

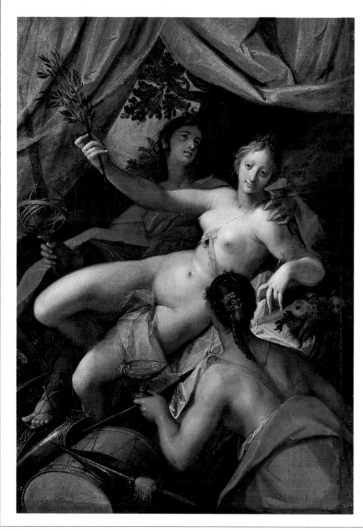

Giuseppe Arcimboldo, Rudolf II as Vertumnus, c.1591. Skokloster Castle, Sweden. This strange Mannerist painter outrageously combines and subverts conventions of both imperial portraiture and still life.

Hans von Aachen, Allegory of Peace, Happiness, and the Arts, 1602. State Hermitage Museum, St. Petersburg. A court painter from 1592 onward, this artist also found favor with Rudolf II's successor, the Emperor Matthias.

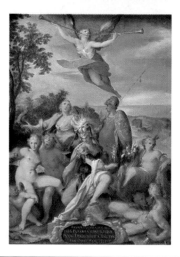

Bartholomaeus Spranger, Allegory of the Reign of Rudolf II or Allegory of the War against the Turks, 1592. Kunsthistorisches Museum, Vienna. As with von Aachen, the influence of Italian Mannerism is obvious.

in 1526, and by the turn of the century the presence of Rudolph II's court in Prague had transformed the city into a lively center of international culture. From 1581 to 1611, Bartholomaeus Spranger (1546–1611), one of the greatest pre-Baroque Mannerist artists, was active in Prague. He is best known for his mythological pictures

such as *Minerva Conquering Ignorance* (c.1591). Although the Thirty Years' War blighted artistic activity in Central Europe until the midcentury, the larger cities, Vienna and Prague, soon recovered their ascendancy, and the southern zones began to flourish. With the Hapsburg dynasty and the Catholic religion established,

many Italian architects were attracted to the empire, particularly during the first phase of building activity. As early as 1621, Count Wallenstein entrusted his magnificent new palace in Prague to Andrea Spezza (died 1628). In the same city, the Jesuit College (Klementinum) and the Leopold Gate (c.1670) were

designed by Carlo Lurago, the Czernin Palace was begun in 1668 by Francesco Caratti, and the church of the Crusader Knights (1679–88) by the French architect Jean-Baptiste Mathey (c.1630–95) was also built. In Munich, Agostino Barelli (1627–99) was responsible for the Church of the Theatines (1663) and for beginning the

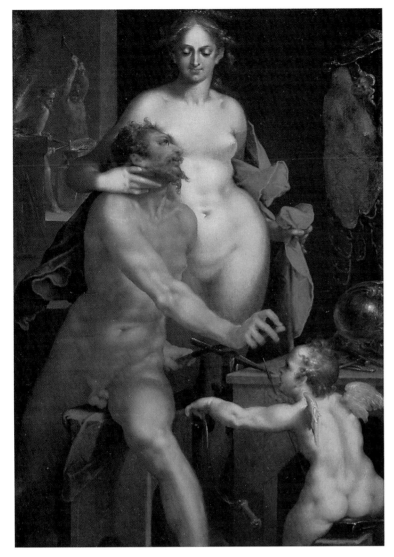

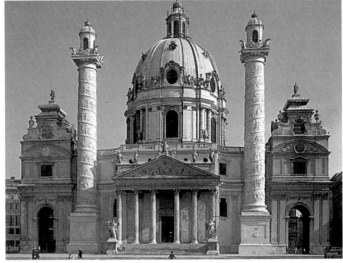

trated urban development in Vienna did not, however, destroy the ancient plan of the city. The new districts effectively encircled the old nucleus. The ring road on the site of the old city walls was lined with palaces and gardens, many designed by Johann Bernhard Fischer von Erlach (1656–1723), the leading Austrian architect, between 1690 and 1700.

Johann Bernhard Fischer von Erlach, Karlskirche, Vienna, 1716. The church was commissioned by Emperor Karl VI in fulfillment of his vow made during the 1713 plague. The life of St. Charles Borromeo, Archbishop of Milan and patron saint of the plague, is illustrated on the columns.

Francesco Caratti, Czernin Palace, Prague, detail of the facade, begun 1668. Appointed architect to Prince Czernin in 1668, Caratti held the post until his death in 1677.

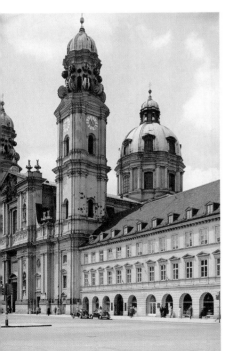

Bartholomaeus Spranger, Venus and Vulcan, c.1610. Kunsthistorisches Museum, Vienna. Spranger worked first in Rome, and then from 1575 in Vienna at the court of Maximilian II. In 1580, he went to Prague, where he became court painter to Rudolph II in 1581.

Agostino Barelli, facade and dome of the Church of the Theatines, Munich, 1663–74. Barelli spent many years working for the religious order founded by St. Gaetano of Thiene.

Nymphenburg Palace (1664), which was completed by Enrico Zuccalli (1642–1724). In Vienna, Carlo Antonio Carlone designed the Jesuit church of the Nine Angelic Choirs (1662) and Filiberto Lucchese the Leopold wing of the Hofburg Palace (1661–68). The great era of Austrian Baroque began only after 1683, the year the Turks were defeated and Hapsburg power assured. The concen-

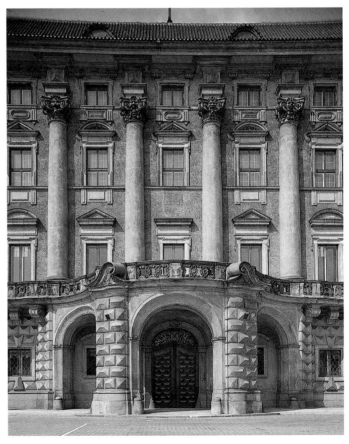

ROYAL PALACES IN VIENNA AND BERLIN

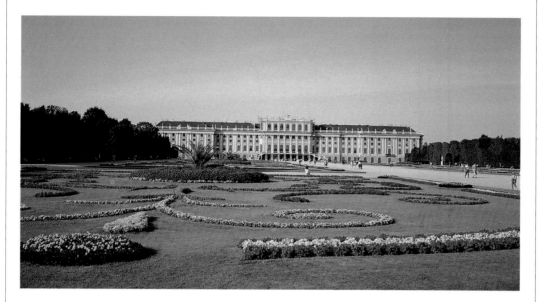

Begun in 1695 from a design by Fischer von Erlach, the construction of the Schönbrunn Palace was not complete until the mid-18th century. This was Vienna's answer to Versailles, an expression of Austria's leading status as a European monarchy. The architect's original plans had been even more ambitious, fusing elements of Roman architecture with massive and imposing French models, such as Bernini's project for the Louvre and Hardouin-Mansart's Palace of Versailles, and also perhaps making reference to ancient architecture in the East. In 1698, another grandiose building project was launched: the Royal Palace in Berlin, designed by the architect and sculptor Andreas Schlüter for the Elector of Brandenburg, who became the first king of Prussia in 1701. The palace was destroyed in 1945.

Johann Bernhard Fischer von Erlach, Schönbrunn Palace, Vienna, begun 1695.

THE 17TH CENTURY IN ENGLAND AND SCANDINAVIA

The English preference for classical architecture was confirmed by the success of Inigo Jones (1573–1652), a versatile architect inspired by the theories and buildings of Andrea Palladio, whose work he first encountered during his visits to Italy (1597–1603 and 1613–14). With the Stuart monarchs James I (1603–25) and Charles I (1625–49) as his patrons, Jones designed the Queen's House at Greenwich (begun 1616), the Banqueting Hall for the Palace of Whitehall (1619–22, decorated by Rubens in 1634 to celebrate the reign of James I), and Covent Garden (c.1630). Christopher Wren (1632–1723), a strict classicist, was the leading architect during the second half of the century and was

The City of London with St. Paul's Cathedral, c.1860. Guildhall Library, London.

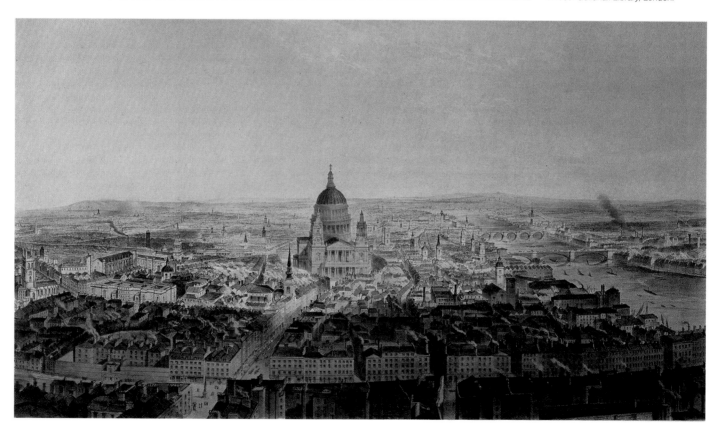

responsible for the many City churches, including St. Paul's Cathedral, which was rebuilt after the Great Fire of London in 1666 (estimated to have destroyed 13,200 houses). English painting started to emerge from isolation from the reign of James I onward with the arrival of foreign artists, among them the Flemish painters Paul van Somer (1577–1621) and Daniel Mytens (1590–1656). Charles I was a great collector and passionate about art: Rubens was invited to London, as were van Dyck, who settled in the capital in 1632, and Orazio Gentileschi,

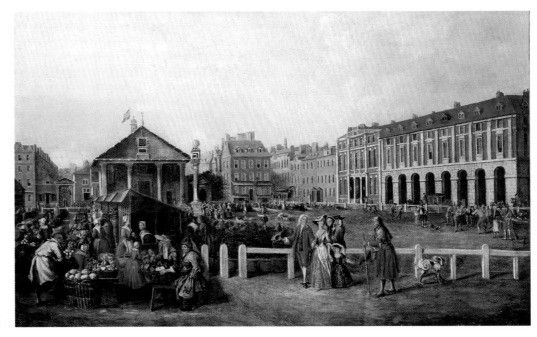

Balthasar Nebot, Covent Garden Piazza, *c.1750. Guildhall Library, London.*

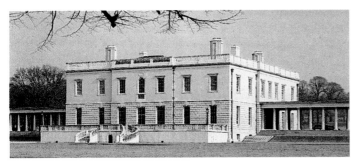

Inigo Jones, Queen's House, Greenwich, London, begun 1616.

a follower of Caravaggio, who arrived from Pisa in 1626. Toward the end of the century, large-scale mural decorations were first made fashionable by Antonio Verrio (c.1639–1707), whose classicism influenced James Thornhill (1675–1734), the artist responsible for the

INIGO JONES

A great admirer of Palladio and Scamozzi, Inigo Jones (1573–1652) was the foremost exponent of late-Renaissance classicism in England, where his work left an indelible mark; it also influenced 18th-century architecture in the US. His most successful projects included country houses (the Queen's House at Greenwich and Wilton House), the Banqueting Hall in Whitehall, and the enlargement of St. Paul's Cathedral. He was famous in his day for his designs for the royal court's masques. An interesting collection of his drawings has survived, including designs for the Palace of Whitehall.

decorative paintings inside the dome of St. Paul's Cathedral and the Painted Hall at Greenwich Hospital. In Scandinavia, there was intense architectural activity in Stockholm after Gustavus Adolphus (reigned 1611–32) made it his capital. Early influences were mainly French and Dutch; one of the most notable figures was Nicodemus Tessin the Elder (1615–81), who designed the majestic Drottningholm Palace (begun 1662). The park was laid out by his son Nicodemus II (1654–1728), who was also the architect of the Royal Palace in Stockholm. The classical style was also used in Denmark in the Rosenborg Palace commissioned by Christian IV, who during his reign (1588–1648) promoted many major building projects.

PAINTING IN SWEDEN

Queen Christina of Sweden (1632–54) was one of the greatest royal collectors of the 17th century, and, before her conversion to Catholicism and subsequent decision to live in Rome, she filled Stockholm Castle with sculptures, paintings, coins, and gold- and silverware. Many of the works had been looted from Prague when the troops of Gustavus Adolphus ransacked the Imperial Palace there during the Thirty Years' War. Among the many artists at her court were portraitists such as the Dutchman David Beck and the French painter Sébastien Bourdon

(1616–71). The German David Klocker Ehrenstrahl (1628–98) was one of the most prolific artists during the following reign of Charles XI. His formative years were spent in Amsterdam, but he had also visited France, Italy, and England. A skilled portraitist and landscape painter, he brought Italian and French Baroque taste to Sweden. In the monumental allegorical works commissioned from him by the Dowager Queen Edvige Eleonora, he introduced the high Baroque style of Pietro da Cortona and Charles Le Brun to a northern audience.

Sébastien Bourdon, Anthony and Cleopatra. *Musée du Louvre, Paris.*

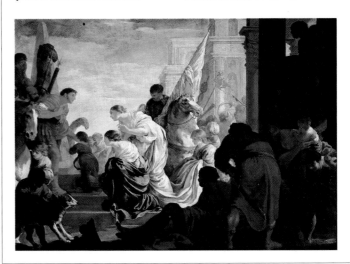

THE SPLENDORS OF THE 18TH CENTURY

The century of the Grand Tour was also the Age of Reason, an era during which artists throughout Europe adopted a cosmopolitan style, molded by the influence of great capital cities such as Vienna, London, and Paris. A taste for all that was exquisite, vivacious, and charming found expression in a stylistic blend of elegance, parody, and tenderness.

Although the term "the Enlightenment" refers specifically to the philosophy of the 18th century, it has often been applied more generally to the culture of the age. Faith in the power of reason and the importance of scientific research was implicit in all intellectual and cultural activities – including the various disciplines of art.

FROM BAROQUE TO ROCOCO

In such a climate, both the production of and interest in art flourished. As the emphasis on Baroque diminished and became fragmented, the role of art ceased to be seen as a tool of influence and persuasion. Increasingly, art was required to fulfill the purely aesthetic function of translating and communicating thought through beauty. For the Venetian Francesco Algarotti (1712–64) and other 18th-century artistic theorists and patrons, the word "beauty" had the precise meaning of graceful and pleasing forms. This was ideally expressed in elegant and beautifully rendered paintings, exemplified by the vivacious and charming allegorical portraits by Jean-Marc Nattier (1685–1766). Within a comparatively short period, the Baroque evolved into High Baroque, also known as Rococo, especially when applied

THE GRAND TOUR

Although traveling for pleasure and instruction was already enjoyed by the privileged classes, the 18th century saw a rise in the popularity of the Grand Tour. This was a tour of the chief cities and sights of Europe to complete a young person's education. The favorite destination was Italy,

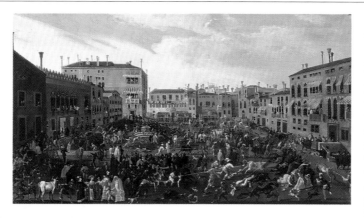

Joseph Heintz, The Feast of the Bulls in Campo San Polo, *1648. Civico Museo Correr, Venice.*

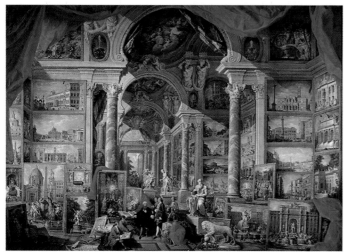

Giovan Paolo Pannini, Gallery, *from* Views of Modern Rome, *1759. Musée du Louvre, Paris.*

Philipp Hackert, Dockers Unloading in the Port of Messina, *detail. Museo Nazionale di San Martino, Naples.*

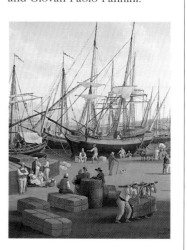

of their travels. They purchased original paintings or less expensive copies and commissioned new works. Venetian townscapes were highly sought after, especially those by Canaletto, as were views of famous cities, Rome and Naples in particular. Heroic scenes and Arcadian landscapes were also very popular, as were views of contemporary festivals and street scenes, such as those by Joseph Heintz (1600–1678), Philipp Hackert (1737–1807), and Giovan Paolo Pannini.

visited for its exceptional artistic treasures and natural beauty. Travelers often set off from northern Europe and journeyed along the Italian peninsula, recording their observations in travel journals and sketching their impressions. The Grand Tour generated a desire among its participants to bring back souvenirs as tangible reminders

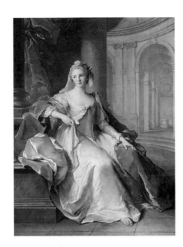

to architecture and the decorative arts. The term "Rococo," derived from the French *rocaille*, was originally applied to a type of decoration with asymmetrical, sinuous, and convoluted lines. Later, the name acquired a deliberately

Jean-Marc Nattier, Portrait of Madame Henriette as a Vestal Virgin, 1749. Detroit Institute of Arts.

Jean-Marc Nattier, Portrait of Madame Maria Zeffirina, c.1751. Galleria degli Uffizi, Florence.

mocking connotation. Strictly speaking, *rocaille* denoted an agglomeration of stones, whether real or artificial, shells, and other materials that mimicked natural objects and structures. Stylistically, it was inspired by shapes and objects found in nature, usually complementary to Arcadian themes and congruent with the tastes of the fashionable and elite circles. Through the contribution of Juste-Aurèle

Meissonnier (1695–1750), an aesthetic theorist and designer, the Rococo style became very fashionable during the Regency of the Duke of Orleans (1715–23). It reached its peak, however, during the reign of Louis XV (1743–74), when it influenced every form of artistic activity and became synonymous with the Pompadour style, named after the king's famous and highly influential mistress Madame de Pompadour.

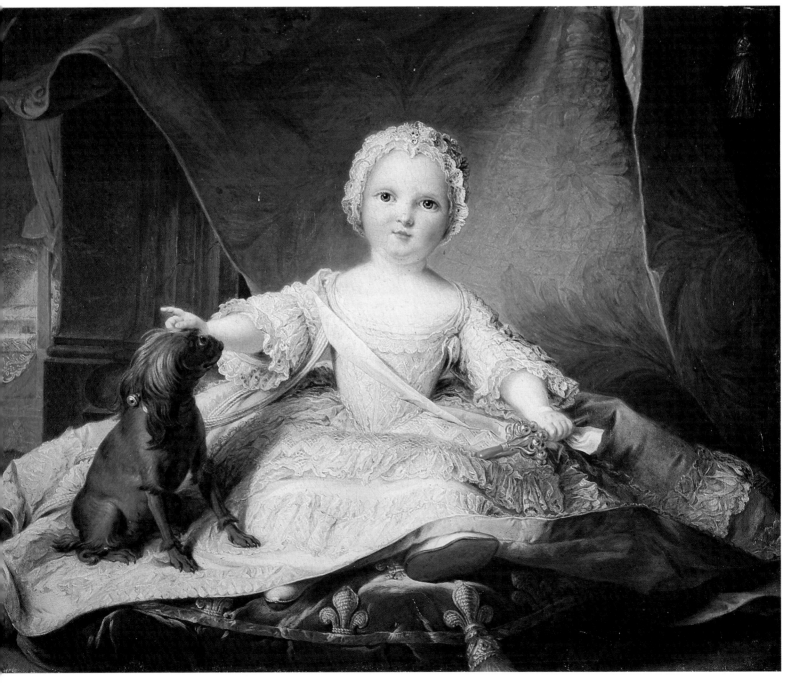

ROCOCO ARCHITECTURE

Although Rococo architecture originated in France, it was far less pronounced there than it was to be later in Germany and Austria. Few buildings were extravagant in appearance, even among those intended to impress, such as the Petit Trianon, which was designed by Ange-Jacques Gabriel (1698–1782) for Louis XV and built in the park at Versailles. There was, however, a more fundamental shift in taste among the autocratic rulers and in the Catholic Church of central Europe. By the 1720s, several architects, including Johann Fischer von Erlach (1656–1723), Lucas von Hildebrandt (1668–1745), and Johann Michael Fischer (1692–1766), were already involved in the construction of palaces and churches in the new style, notably in Austria, Germany, Bohemia, and Poland. These buildings had a new lightness to them, and their structures were enhanced by decorative features with curved, elongated lines. The eye was no longer caught by a single, central focal point but by a rhythmic succession of spaces. Leading examples of this style are Vienna's Karlskirche and the Church of St. John Nepomuk in Prague, with their very impressive and effective combinations of frescoes and sculptural decorations. In Italy, architecture evolved into a High Baroque that came from the legacy of Francesco Borromoni (1599–1667), whose style was influenced by Rome

Johann Michael Fischer, Benedictine Church at Ottobeuren, Bavaria, 1748–67.

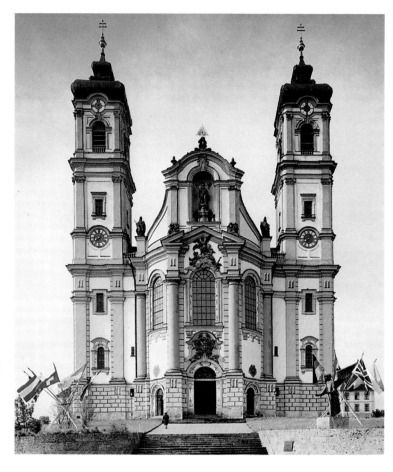

Johann Fischer von Erlach, Karlskirche, Vienna, begun in 1716. This eclectic church combines various stylistic features.

PIRANESI AND ROME

One of the most important precursors of Neoclassical and Romantic architecture, Giovanni Battista Piranesi (1720–78) was more influential as an etcher than an architect. Born in Venice, he trained as an architect and in 1740 moved to Rome, where he designed his only built work, the Church of Santa Maria del Priorato (1764–65). In his printed work, however, Piranesi advocated Rome's position in the classical world. In

Giovanni Battista Piranesi, View of Campo Vaccino, etching from Views of Rome. Gabinetto dei Disegni e delle Stampe, Florence.

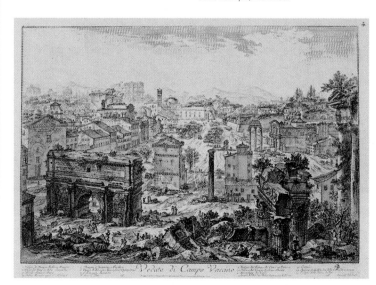

rather than by the French Rococo. The most prominent architect of this stylistic era was a Sicilian, Filippo Juvarra (1678–1736). A pupil of Carlo Fontana (1634–1714) in Rome, Juvarra made his name at a comparatively early age in the service of Victor Amadeus II of Savoy in Turin. His works included the King's Palace of Aranjuez, and his most entrancing building is the Basilica of Superga (1716–31) in Turin. Featuring lively verticality in the form of an elongated dome atop a traditional drum base, the design of the basilica rejected old-style features and extravagant shapes in favor of a freer spatial rhythm, giving a dynamic structure to the building. Juvarra's masterpiece is probably his hunting lodge, the Stupinigi Palace (1729–33), near Turin. Designed to be viewed from the end of a long, straight avenue, the building is enlivened by an airy cupola, and the ample light provided by its many windows. Perhaps the greatest exponent of Late Baroque in Italy was the architect Luigi Vanvitelli (1700–73), who trained under his father and painted accomplished townscapes, which often achieved the effect of theatrical scenes. The combination of courtly elegance and a talent for designing on a monumental scale served him well when building the Palace at Caserta (1752–70) for the King of Naples. Inspired by Versailles, this enormous and imposing building, set in a vast park, combined solemnity with grace and variety. The gardens were embellished with statues, often exuberantly combined with fountains.

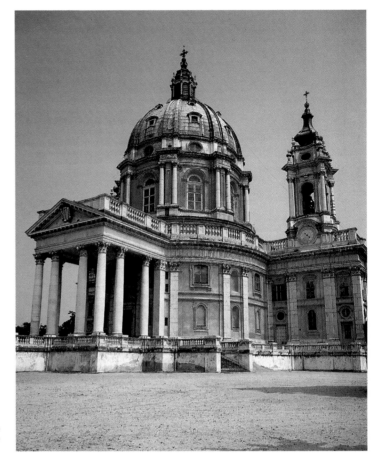

Filippo Juvarra, Basilica of Superga, Turin, 1716–31. It was built for Victor Amadeus II, who was the first member of the Savoy dynasty to become king.

German art historian Johann Winckelmann had identified as the ideal of beauty and perfection. Piranesi supported his thesis in his polemical work *On the Architecture and Magnificence of the Romans* (1761).
It was, however, his *Views of Ancient and Modern Rome* (published from 1745), with its poetic images of Italian ruins and antiquities, that was so effective in molding the Romantic ideal of Rome abroad. His series *Carceri d'invenzione* (c.1745) was a subjective depiction of fantastic and imaginary prisons that evoked a nightmarish, hallucinatory world.

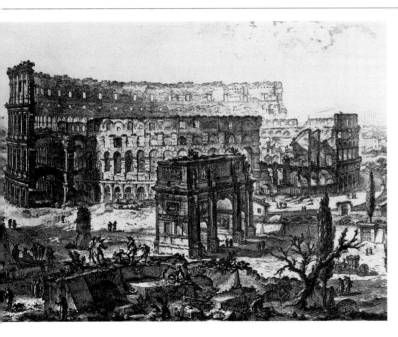

Roman Antiques (1756), he sought to interpret the entire Roman civilization and its ethical and symbolic values. Piranesi maintained that Roman art, with its splendor and loftiness, surpassed Greek art, which the

Giovanni Battista Piranesi, View of the Arch of Constantine and the Colosseum, etching from Views of Rome. Gabinetto Nazionale delle Stampe, Rome.

Giovanni Battista Piranesi, The Well, etching from Carceri d'invenzione. Calcografia dello Stato, Rome.

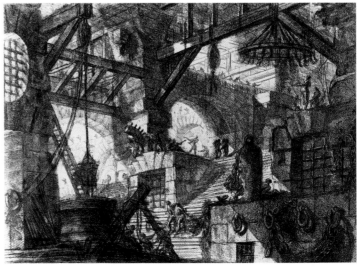

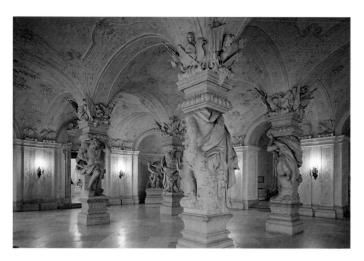

Although architectural works reflected the varying characteristics of different countries, they also expressed, for the first time, a common artistic language. The execution of town plans was more evident in some capital cities than others; for example, Rome continued to develop within the basic structure adopted during the 17th century, while Juvarra began the process of organizing the city of Turin according to a grid plan that still survives. Several new palaces were built in Vienna, sited at intervals around the old center of the city. The most important of these was the Belvedere, built from 1714 by Johann Lukas von Hildebrandt for Prince Eugène of Savoy, not far from where the Karlskirche was built. Meanwhile, the great

Johann Lukas von Hildebrandt, Hall with Atlas-caryatid pillars by Lorenzo Mattiellis, Upper Belvedere, Vienna, 1721–22.

Johann Lukas von Hildebrandt, Upper Belvedere, Vienna, 1720–24.

A New Style in Town Planning

During the 18th century, a new and effective style of town planning emerged. In Europe, this occurred largely because political power remained in the hands of a very few nobles. The form of entire cities could be dictated by autocratic rulers, and a capital city's appearance became a matter of prestige. Monarchs vied with one another to employ the virtuosos of the day, who were usually itinerant artists and architects. This movement among countries and the various royal patrons largely encouraged the development of a greater homogeneity in style.

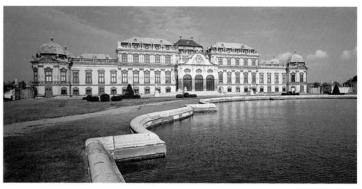

ST. PETERSBURG AND THE HERMITAGE PALACE

Founded by Peter the Great as the new capital of Tsarist Russia, St. Petersburg was constructed according to the plans of Domenico Trezzini (c.1670–1734), who designed the broad, straight thoroughfares or "prospects" along which the first majestic palaces were subsequently built.

A fellow Italian architect, Bartolomeo Rastrelli, followed his father, a sculptor, to Russia, and was responsible for the city's Rococo embellishment under Empress Elizabeth. One of the best examples of his work is the Winter Palace, which was built in the years 1754–62. Facing the historic Fortress of Peter and Paul, the palace epitomizes the style known as "stone Baroque" and, in contrast to the opulence and bright, multicolored decoration admired by Muscovites, the refined elegance of its clean lines and shading of well-matched colors

shows how European artistic influence could coexist with Russia's artistic heritage and cultural tradition.

During her reign, Catherine the Great ordered the construction of a large number of public buildings, later boasting that she had found a wooden city and left one of stone. These

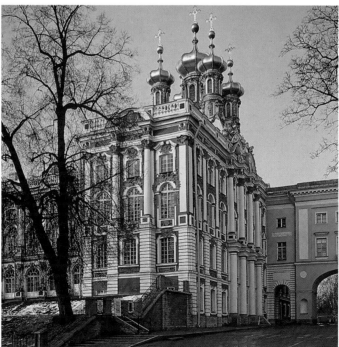

commissions included the Academy of Fine Arts and the Little Hermitage, both designed by Vallin de la Mothe, and a theater by Antonio Rinaldi, who also designed the beautiful Marble Palace. These buildings signaled the waning of the fashion for the playful, lighthearted tone of Late Baroque and heralded the emergence of the Neoclassical style. The Academy of Science by Italian architect Giacomo Quarenghi (1744–1817) displayed the new criteria of severity and restraint. Catherine the Great's personal museum, the Little Hermitage (1764), housed the first great collection of European paintings. When the collection outgrew the building, a second museum, the Great Hermitage (1775–82), designed by Juri Felíten, was built beside it.

Bartolomeo Francesco Rastrelli, Chapel of the Imperial Palace, Tsarskoe Selo, St. Petersburg, 1756.

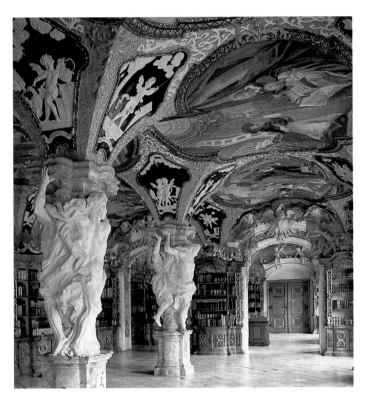

Franz Ignaz Holzinger, Atlas-caryatid pillars in the library of the Benedictine monastery of Metten, Germany.

abbeys in the countryside of Eastern Europe were also built on a scale comparable to that of the edifices in towns. The Abbey of Melk (1702–1714) in Austria was designed by Jakob Prandtauer (1660–1726) on a site above the Danube, so it appeared to rise out of the rock.

At the beginning of the 18th century, Tsar Peter the Great founded the city of St. Petersburg. This drew artists and architects of many nationalities to Russia, including the Italian architect Bartolomeo Rastrelli (c.1700–71), who designed churches and imperial

Jakob Prandtauer, interior of the Church of Saints Peter and Paul, Melk, Austria, 1702–14.

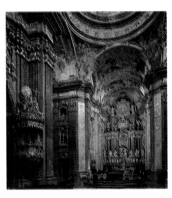

DOMESTIC LIFE

An innovation of High Baroque was the accommodation of inhabitants' comfort into the most grandiose and impressive aristocratic residences. In Continental Europe, the nobility developed a taste for country retreats, where they could escape formal life, while even palaces included

residences such as Tsarskoe Selo (1756), that were noted for their distinctive, hybrid, but brilliantly conceived version of the High Baroque style. In Scandinavia, a style became prevalent during the mid-18th century that combined Austrian and French Rococo. At Amalienborg in Copenhagen (laid out 1750 to 1754), Nils Eigtved (1701–54) built one of the finest urban groups outside France, consisting of four palaces arranged around an octagon and four streets.

domestic quarters. To this end, an increasing proportion of interior space was devoted to the private lifestyle of the upper classes,

in the form of libraries, small sitting rooms, reading rooms, boudoirs, and music rooms. Despite the growing complexity in internal

ILLUSIONISM AND "INQUADRATURA"

The art of illusory architectural perspectives, or *inquadratura*, has been described as painting that deceives the eye. What is merely painted relief appears solid, making it difficult to determine where the fictional sculptural and architectural decoration ends and real space begins. Although this technique predates the 18th century, some of the most stunningly effective ceiling and wall frescoes were achieved during this era. They were typified by convincingly three-dimensional compositions of figures or gracefully arranged garlands and floral wreaths. During this period, fashion in *trompe l'oeil* changed from a taste for architectural compositions to one that was more Rococo in style,

concentrating on pictorial and decorative effects. Robust and "solid" portrayals of perspective gave way to asymmetrical decoration in the form of scroll or spiral motifs, convoluted brackets, and airy cupolas that appeared to be open to the heavens.

The leading exponent of the architectural Baroque style of illusionist painting was Andrea Pozzo (1642–1709), who wrote a textbook on perspective for painters and architects. His work provided the inspiration for an Emilian school of painters and family studios in Lombardy. It was, however, the Venetian Tiepolo who took the technique to new heights, with his renderings of celestial skies.

Ubaldo Gandolfi (1728–81), Hercules Welcomed to Mount Olympus, 1779–80. Malvezzi Palace, Bologna.

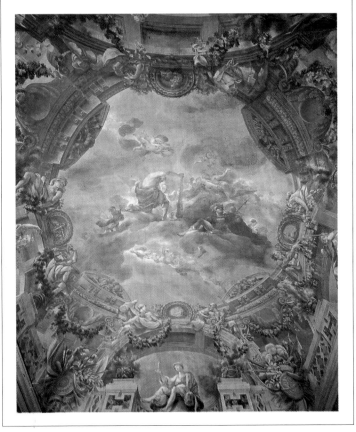

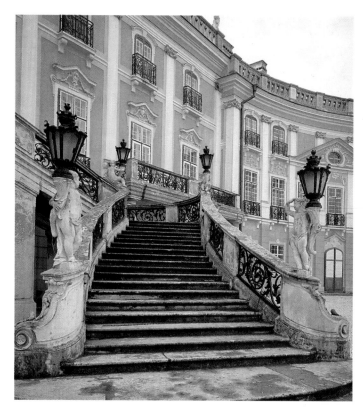

Johann Lukas von Hildebrandt, detail of facade, Upper Belvedere, Vienna.

planning necessitated by the inclusion of the domestic elements and the division of informal and formal realms, 18th- century buildings tended to be presented as a harmonious whole. This was apparent in the use of statuary. Outside, statues were mounted on pilasters and displayed in special niches, while inside, they occupied entrance halls and corridors. These statues perpetuated the Baroque sense of movement, untrammeled and yet disciplined.

ECCLESIASTICAL SCULPTURE

The new aesthetic criteria produced particularly interesting results when applied to ecclesiastical sculpture. The workshop of Milan Cathedral was active in its production of

marble statues, commissioned to complete the sequence of figures that adorned the exterior walls and the roof between the pinnacles. In this lavish display of works, the statues of the Viggiù school are particularly significant, especially those by Elia Buzzi. The stucco

decorations by the great Sicilian sculptor Giacomo Serpotta (1652–1732) differ in style from the typically Rococo archetypes. The fluid linearity of the simple, yet highly imaginative, reliefs, as seen in the Oratorio del Santissimo Rosario in Palermo, echo the sublimity of the classical style. The use of stucco in large-scale statuary was typical of certain artistic groups, as well as a specialty of specific schools. Diego Carlone (1674–1750), an outstanding sculptor of stucco figures, belonged to a dynasty of Lombard painters and sculptors and produced work for various European courts until the middle of the 18th century. The predominance of family workshops among Italian sculptors and artisans, especially in northern Italy, was traditional practice, dating from medieval times. Among those active during this period were Bernardo and Francesco Maria Schiaffino from Genoa and Jacopo and Andrea

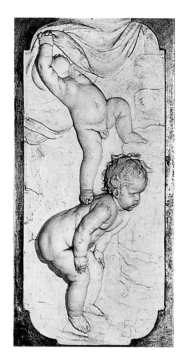

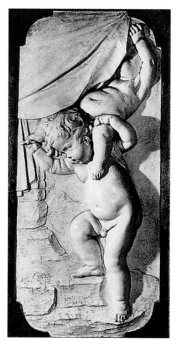

Giacomo Serpotta, plaster putti, Oratorio del Santissimo Rosario in San Domenico, Palermo, 1710–17.

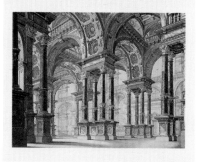

Giuseppe Galli-Bibiena (1695–1757), sketch for a grand hall stage design, pen and ink and watercolor sketch. Accademia di Belle Arti, Bologna.

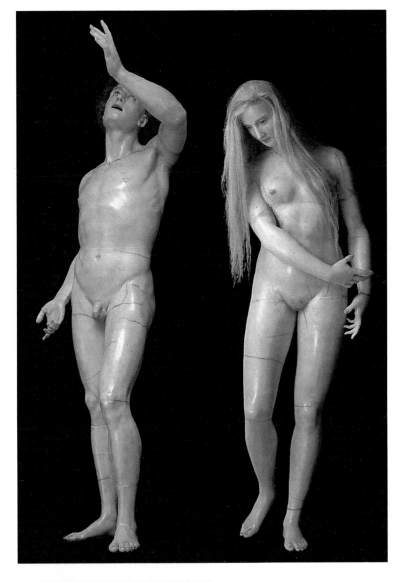

Ercole Lelli (1702–66), Adam and Eve, 1742–51. Museum of the Department of Human Anatomy, Bologna University. These two anatomical wax statues were created specifically for teaching purposes. They were typical of the age of the Encyclopédie, *published in 1751–76.*

Brustolon from Venice. The most industrious and versatile family team was led by Andrea Fantoni (1659–1734) from Bergamo, whose skills in wood carving can be seen in the altar of the Sottocasa chapel, Clusone Cathedral.
In central Europe, Austrian and German sculptors proved to be the most expressive interpreters of

Andrea Fantoni, altarpiece, Church of Santa Maria Maggiore, Bergamo, Italy, c.1705.

NEW STYLES IN GARDEN DESIGN

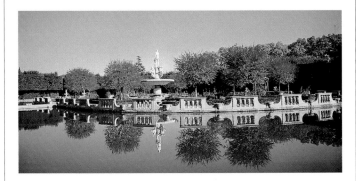

Alfonso Parigi the Younger, Bacino dell'Isolotto (ornamental island in small lake), Boboli Gardens, Florence, 1618.

Keeping apace with the prevailing trend in 18th-century architecture and the decorative arts, garden design adopted a more picturesque style than had been employed in the previous century. Extensive *tapis verts,* or lawns, replaced the rigid, ordered avenues and formal flower beds. As a result, gardens became more romantic and less rigid. The park and palace of Caserta, near Naples, was built and designed by Luigi Vanvitelli, and they epitomized at its best the spirit of the Italian Baroque. They also echo the designs at Marly,

near Versailles, designed for Louis XIV by the more conservative Antoine Coysevox. They have in common an impressive scale, but the plans and styles of the gardens could not be more different. Coysevox kept the ornate *rocaille* motifs to a minimum, preferring a more restrained and linear classical style.

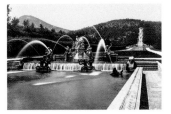

Gaetano Salmone, fountains, Park of Royal Palace of Caserta, 1783.

Luigi Vanvitelli, Great Cascade with Goddess Diana Bathing, Park of Royal Palace of Caserta,1785–89.

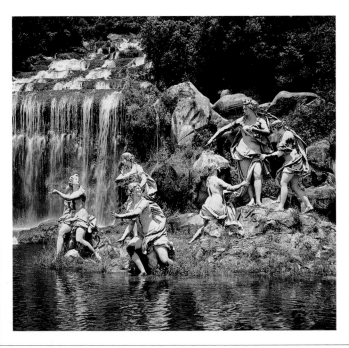

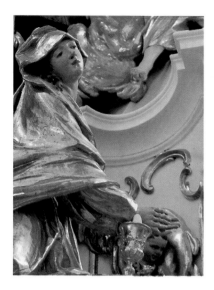

Johann Baptist Straub (1704–84), Religion, high altar, Church of the Augustinian Canons, near Weilheim, Bavaria, 1763–64.

INTERIOR DECORATION

Widely used in sculpture, wood and stucco now took on an important role in interior decoration. The Rococo style was particularly recognizable where decorative themes were inspired by natural forms. Sinuous flowing lines transformed rocks, birds, and flowers into sheer fantasy. These characteristics clearly distinguish the Rococo style from that of the Baroque, in which ornamental motifs tended to be expressed with greater symmetry. The most refined and elaborate examples of Rococo decoration were to be found in the designs of François de Cuvilliès

Detail of the state apartment (reiche Zimmer) of the Residenz in Munich. François de Cuvilliès was responsible for the decoration of these rooms in the residence of the Electors, later Kings, of Bavaria. He collaborated with other famous artists at court.

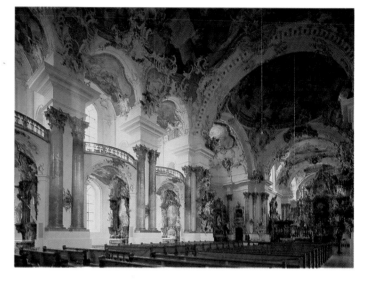

(1695–1768). Flemish by birth but French by education, Cuvilliès went to Munich in 1725, where he was appointed Court Architect to the Elector of Bavaria. He was a talented designer of large, elegant buildings, and his most ambitious work is reflected in his splendid designs for interiors. Both the Amalienburg hunting lodge in the park at Nymphenburg

Johann Michael Fischer, interior of the Church of the Benedictines at Zwiefalten, Württemberg, 1738–65. The decoration is by Johann Michael Feichtmayr (c.1709–72).

Palace and the lodge near Brühl Castle illustrate Cuvilliès' dazzling, lively interiors, in which he fused to perfection architecture, decoration, and furnishings. His extensive use of stucco and lacquer added to their splendor.

the spirit of High Baroque. Johann Michael Fischer (1691–1766) and his lavish decoration for the Benedictine Abbey of Ottobeuren attests to this. The Bohemian school played an important role, as many artists converged on Prague in a surge of activity. Among them was Mattia Bernardo Braun (1684–1738), who had learned his craft in the Austrian Tyrol and specialized in religious figures. Braun adopted the High Baroque style, which was in vogue, and brought to it his own expressive liveliness. A collection of his work in the National Gallery in Prague is proof that the Rococo flamboyant style could, when appropriate, take on a moving, highly dramatic tone. A more restrained style was evident in some of the work of Ferdinand Maximilian Brokof (1688–1731), but for the most part, his wood carvings remained extremely elaborate. In certain respects, Brokof's expressive work, such as the sculptures decorating the Church of St. Gall in Prague, go beyond Baroque rhetoric and illustrate the influence of 18th-century taste.

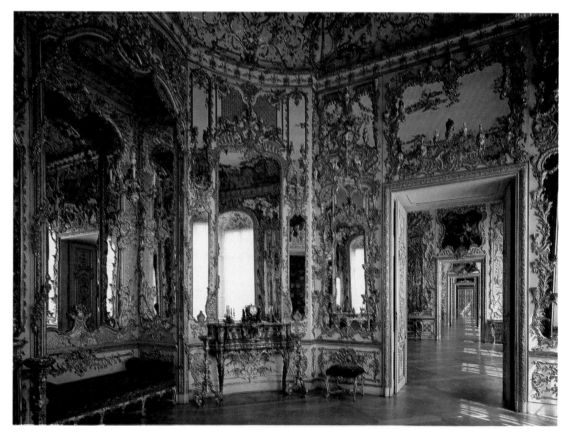

THE ART OF TAPESTRY

Founded in 1667, La Manufacture des Meubles de la Couronne, known as the Gobelins factory, faithfully reproduced impressive scenes by various well-known painters in the form of large tapestries that glorified the reign of Louis XIV. Charles Le Brun's allegorical subjects celebrated the munificence of Louis XIV depicted as Alexander the Great. Another set of tapestries, the *Maisons Royales*, showed the splendor of court life against a backdrop of stately architecture

director of Beauvais and, later, Gobelins, designed *The Loves of the Gods* (1734–37), which were set in highly ornate frames embellished by floral gardens. Charles Coypel designed 28 cartoons illustrating the "chivalrous" deeds of Don Quixote, featuring historical scenes set in medallions and elaborate sculptural *trompe-l'oeil* motifs. Parrocel designed tapestries commemorating the arrival of *The Turkish Ambassador* (1734–37), and Desportes contributed the delightfully fantastic (and inaccurate)

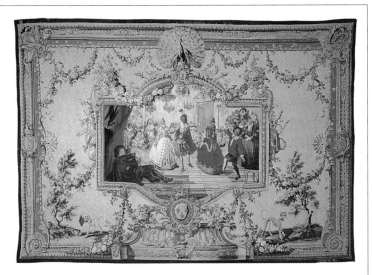

Charles Coypel, The Ball in Barcelona, *one of* The Stories of Don Quixote *set of tapestries, Gobelins, 1732–36. Musée du Louvre, Paris.*

François Boucher, Neptune and Anymone *from* The Loves of the Gods *tapestries, Beauvais, 1757. Petit Palais, Paris.*

exoticisms of *The New Indies*. In his role as head painter at the Spanish court, Francisco Goya (1746–1828) produced an extensive series of tapestry cartoons for El Escorial and for the Prado. The scenes displayed the artist's liveliness and verve, and the works evoke the grandeur and spirit of Rococo in Spain.

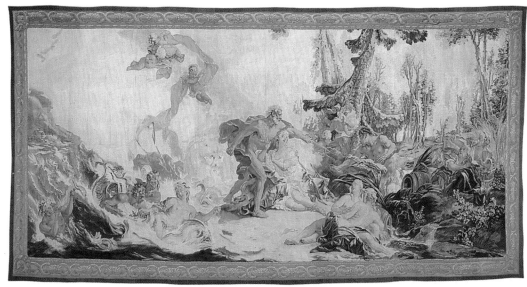

Charles Le Brun, Alexander Besieging Babylon, *from* The History of Alexander, *Gobelins, c.1661–65. Palace of Versailles.*

and magnificent surroundings. When the production of tapestries resumed at the start of the 18th century, three factories, at Aubusson, Gobelins, and Beauvais, assumed a new role and style. Tapestries were no longer employed to cover vast areas of walls and were often woven to fit into a wooden framework. Moreover, the more subtle and varied colors enabled them to compete with paintings as they depicted decorative and fashionable subjects. Well-known painters designed the cartoons or patterns: Boucher, who was

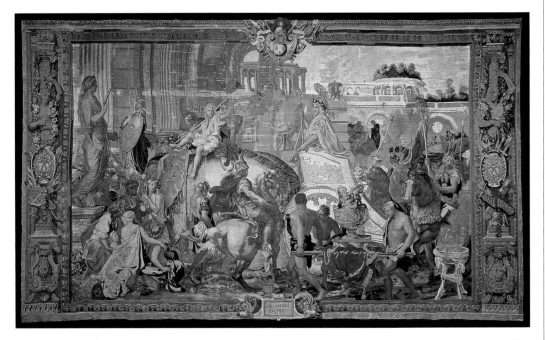

NEW FURNITURE STYLES

FRANCE

Comfort and practicality were given greater consideration in the design and production of furniture during the 18th century; some styles introduced at this time are still recognizable in modern-day furnishings. The repertoire of 18th-century furniture is mainly French in origin and included the *secrétaire,* or writing desk, with hidden drawers; the *bergère* armchair, with a seat cushion and upholstered arms; the *marquise,* or deep-seated armchair for two; the *chaise-longue,* or daybed; the *console,* either a wall bracket or a side table, often with a mirrored back; movable corner cupboards; and the *commode,* a decorative, chest of drawers for the drawing room.

A variety of small tables were produced: tea or tray tables; dressing tables with little drawers, mirrors, and cosmetic pots; and tables specifically designed for gaming, embroidery, or water-color painting. Many other items of indoor and outdoor furniture were often taken from the design books of architects and decorators. The more elaborate pieces were made by cabinet-makers and embellished by gilt-

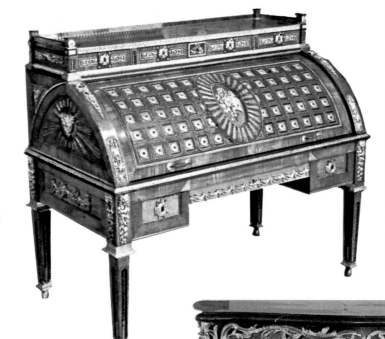

David Roentgen, cylinder-top desk, c.1785. Commissioned by the king as a gift for Catherine II, this desk features straight lines, geometric marquetry, and minimal use of gilt-bronze, all of which denote the Louis XVI style and the first phase of French Neoclassicism.

J. Demoulin, commode, c.1760. The dimensions and the sinuous curves of this item are typical of rocaille taste. The front is lavishly decorated with Oriental, lacquered scenes and the asymmetrical gilt-bronze ornamentation is fantastical.

bronze mountings. Jacques Dubois (1694–1763), François Oeben (1720–1763), Charles Cressent (1685–1768), and Louis Delanois (c.1731–1792) were some of the most gifted craftsmen of the Regency period and the reign of Louis XV. During this time, French furniture in particular was famous for its original designs and craftsmanship. The serpentine outlines, cabriole legs, and curved chair backs were enhanced by lavish wrought-bronze designs, with exquisite marquetry, mother-of-pearl or tortoiseshell inlay, and plaques of painted porcelain.

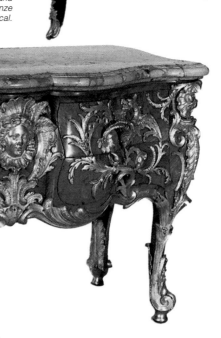

ITALY

Turin and Venice were the main centers of production for fine furniture in Italy. Well-known architects such as Benedetto Alfieri (1699–1767) and Filippo Juvarra worked on furniture designs in Turin, as did the outstanding craftsman Pietro Piffetti (c.1700–77). Famous for his technical skill, elegance, and originality of form, Piffetti preferred the extravagant and unusual in the sculpted and wrought ornamentation of fantastic creatures, a taste he had acquired in Rome. He also favored fine marquetry, tortoiseshell, and ivory inlays. Venetian furniture had a distinctive style: in place of ornamentation made from

Charles Cressent, commode, made c.1730, shortly before the Regency period. This item of drawing room furniture retains the characteristics of the Late Baroque; the dragon handles reflect the fashion for chinoiserie, while the gilt-bronze mounts signal the transition to the Rococo style.

precious woods and bronze, craftsmen in Venice preferred exquisite, delicate carving, very fine gilding, and imitation Chinese lacquer. Less expensive furniture was decorated with stencils (often by typographers like Remondini di Bassano), which were affixed to imitation lacquer and then colored. The art of the Venetians became more highly specialized; furniture was produced from treated softwoods, mainly pine, and painted in delicate shades with Arcadian scenes, landscapes,

Workshop of Maggiolini, chest of drawers. Typical of Giuseppe Maggiolini's work, this piece is characterized by straight lines and decorated surfaces, with Neoclassical motifs depicted in the marquetry.

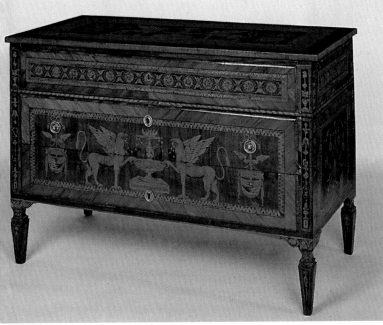

and chinoiserie inspired by the paintings of popular artists, such as Giandomenico Tiepolo (1727–1804). The applied arts in Parma were dominated by the Duke's architect, Ennemond-Alexandre Petitot (1727–1801), who introduced a very refined French style to the Bourbon court. In Milan, Giuseppe Maggiolini (1783–1814), whose work was popular throughout Europe,

Giuseppe Maria Bonzanigo (1745–1825), armchair, 1775. The personal touch of Bonzanigo in this version of Louis XVI-style furniture is evident in the intricate carving of the arms and legs.

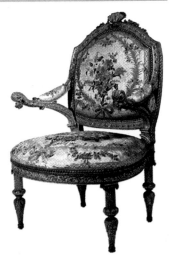

carried out marquetry decoration to his own designs and to those of fine Neoclassical artists such as Andrea Appiani (1754–1817). Florentine taste soon favored all things Neoclassical; craftsmanship was encouraged by the court, evident during the time of Marie-Louise de Bourbon and Elisa Bonaparte, when the architect Giuseppe Cacialli (1770–1828) redesigned and refurbished rooms in the Pitti Palace in a very elegant style. The Genoese aristocracy adopted Rococo refinement to suit their own tastes, with marble tops, beautifully grained olive wood, and marquetry flowers echoing 17th-century still-life paintings.

THE GREAT FRESCO PAINTERS

As sumptuously decorated reception rooms grew in popularity, frescoes assumed a dominant role, gradually covering virtually all the wall spaces, as well as the ceilings. Artists who specialized in painting frescoes formed workshops, making it common practice for each member to concentrate on a particular skill. While the master of a workshop usually specialized in painting figures, one assistant would concentrate on the painting of *trompe l'oeils* or feigned architectural details (*inquadratura*), which often formed the frames of frescoes, while other assistants would specialize in the painting of flowers or still lifes. Some workshops would effectively travel around between spring and autumn, working successively in capital cities throughout Europe. Typical was the well-established team headed by Carlo Innocenzo Carlone (1686–1775), which was in great demand in Italy. The Carlone workshop painted series of frescoes in the cathedrals of Asti and Monza, in palaces in Brescia, Bergamo, and Como, as well as in churches and palaces across Austria, Germany,

Poland, and Switzerland. Most notable were the decorations in Augustus Castle in Brühl, Ludwigsburg Castle, and the Belvedere in Vienna, where the frescoes depict enchanting mythological scenes and allegories celebrating the life of Prince Eugène. Carlone's style was very explicitly Rococo, both in his drawing technique, brimming with vivacity, and in his use of subtle pastel hues, without the strong effects of chiaroscuro. Carlone produced many easel

Carlo Innocenzo Carlone, The Triumph of Reason, detail from the ceiling fresco in the drawing room of Villa Lechi, Montirone, Brescia; Italy, 1745–46.

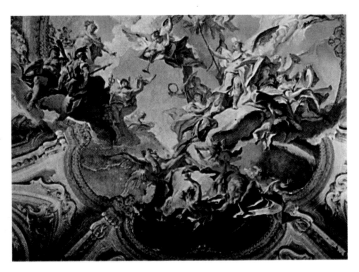

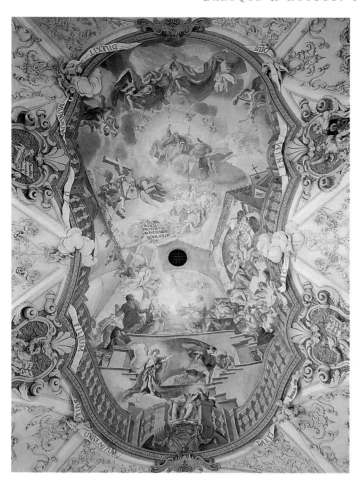

ITALIAN PAINTING

The inclination toward the High Baroque style was first visible in Italy in the early 18th century in the gradual departure from somber colors and adoption of a light, airy palette. The paintings of Luca Giordano (1634–1705) in Naples represent a definite, but not complete, step away from the intense sentimentalism of the Neapolitan school and toward a less explicit and more enjoyable art. In Naples, Giordano decorated the inside of the Treasury dome in the charterhouse of St. Martin. He traveled frequently, for work or simply for artistic curiosity, to see the output of other artists in Florence, Venice, and Spain.

Gregorio de Ferrari (1647–1726) in Genoa introduced a new and radiant fluency

Cosmas Damian Asam, Vision of St. Bernard, *fresco in the Abbey Church, Aldersbach, after 1720.*

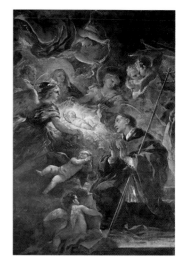

Luca Giordano, San Lorenzo Giustiniani Adoring the Christ Child, Santa Maria Maddalena, Rome, 1704.

in his work, reinterpreting old themes and subjects from the preceding century with a fresh and original touch. This is evident in the series of frescoes executed for the palaces of the Genoese aristocracy, especially in the allegorical paintings for the Palazzo Rosso. In Lombardy,

Gregorio de Ferrari, Summer, fresco, Palazzo Rosso, Genoa, c.1679–88.

paintings, which were executed in a similar style; he had considerable influence on Austrian and German painters, who usually sought inspiration from the Venetian masters, as did Carlone himself. Hence, the artistic atmosphere in Italy shared traits with that of neighboring countries, as illustrated by the work of such artists as Johann Michael Rottmayr (1654–1730), who also worked in Prague; Cosmas Damian Asam (1686–1750), who belonged to a great dynasty of German painters; and Franz Anton Maulpertsch (1724–96). Towering above his contemporaries in artistic stature was Giambattista Tiepolo, who was revered for his expressive ingenuity and the virtuosity of his brushwork.

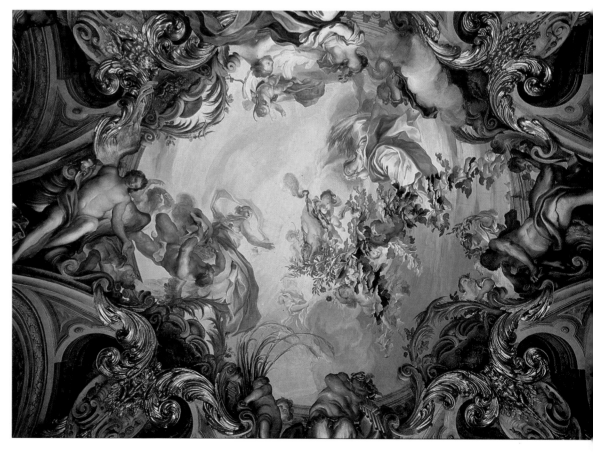

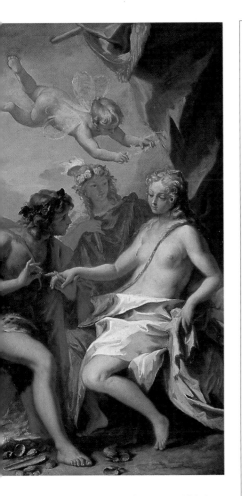

Sebastiano Ricci, Bacchus and Ariadne, *c.1713. Chiswick House, London.*

Stefano Maria Legnani, known as Legnanino (1660–1715), moved away from the academic style of the Roman artists toward the High Baroque, investing his paintings with an expressive sentimentalism that echoed the style of Borromini. Besides numerous altarpieces, Legnanino is known for the luminous frescoes in the Palazzo Carignano in Turin and in the central nave of Monza Cathedral. Another influential painter was Sebastiano Ricci (1659–1734), responsible for the superb ceiling fresco in the Palazzo Colonna, Rome. Like de Ferrari, he used a freer and more varied interpretation of the style of Correggio in order to keep in line with contemporary stylistic trends. Ricci also made use of his

SOCIETY PORTRAITURE

Rosalba Carriera (1675–1757), a hugely successful interpreter of Venetian Rococo, displayed an unequaled ability to capture the delicacy of her era. The exquisite refinement of her portraiture epitomized the ideals of fashionable society, and her spontaneity and grace earned her countless commissions from members of the European elite. Carriera's predilection for pastels was shared by La Tour, Largillière, Nattier, and, later, Mengs and the Swiss painter Liotard, all of whom successfully exploited the "splendor, fragility, and transparency" that breathed new life into portraiture. According to the *Encyclopédie* (the French encyclopedia published under the direction of Diderot), this was unique to the medium. In portrait paintings, sitters no longer adopted solemn and ceremonial poses; instead, they sought to convey a certain cultural distinction, a personal, distinct character, and a fashion-

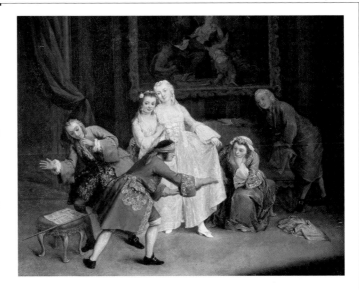

Pietro Longhi, Blindman's Buff, *1744. Collection of Queen Elizabeth II, Windsor Castle.*

able, cosmopolitan elegance. These elements were all rendered through the new medium of pastel coloring, the effects of which, far from being insipid, were robust yet at the same time soft and powdery.

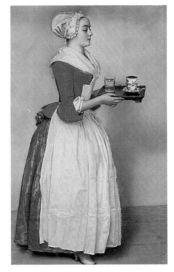

Jean-Étienne Liotard, La Belle Chocolatière, *1744–45. Gemäldegalerie, Dresden.*

Rosalba Carriera, Portrait of a Lady, *c.1720–30. Galleria Sabauda, Turin.*

Pietro Longhi (1702–85) painted some lively and somewhat superficially light-hearted compositions, along the line of the Dutch genre, depicting Venetian domesticity and the often comic activities of high society. His good-humored pictures are known for their luminosity, the use of delicate hues, and the thin and well-blended application of paint. Although reminiscent of Carriera's work, the paintings share certain features with contemporary English pieces.

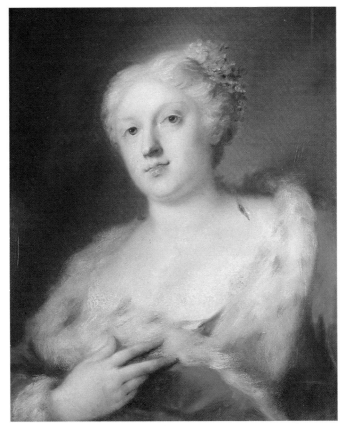

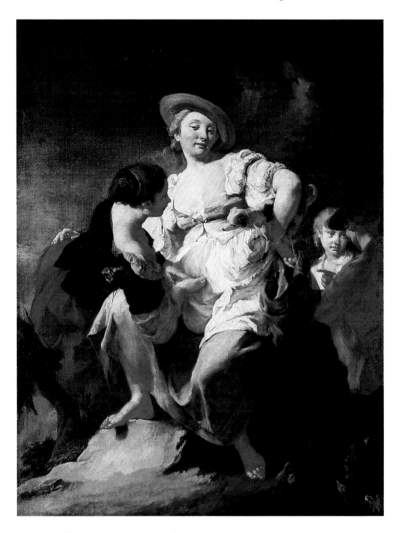

Gian Battista Piazzetta, The Fortune Teller, 1704. Accademia, Venice.

profound knowledge of the techniques used by Venetian colorists during the 16th century, and he was one of the early leading figures in the revival of Venetian decorative painting. His

work was much in demand in many cities, for both easel and fresco paintings. While in London and Paris, Ricci was instrumental in the dissemination of the new style.

The Venetian school, which included only artists working in the city itself, was slower in embracing the Rococo style. However, a few decades later, following the rise of Ricci, Tiepolo, and a group of painters known as *vedutisti*, a new Venetian style came about. It was characterized by unprecedented force of movement and brilliant color schemes.

Other Italian painters tended

Sebastiano Ricci, Punishment of Love, Marucelli Palace, Florence, 1706–07.

THE STRANGE WORLD OF ALESSANDRO MAGNASCO

Despite recent reevaluation and research, Alessandro Magnasco (1667–1749) remains a largely enigmatic figure. Seeking to appeal to a market that was highly cultured and sophisticated, he emp[loyed a very expressive and bold narrative style, using violent,

Alessandro Magnasco, Quakers' Meeting, c.1704. Galleria degli Uffizi, Florence. This was painted at the court of Ferdinand de' Medici, the dynasty's last great artistic patron.

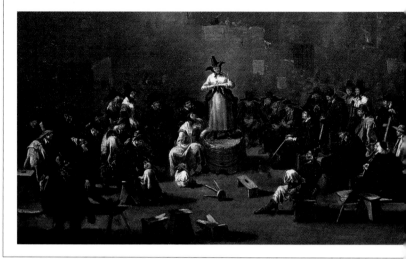

to retain strong chiaroscuro contrasts with distant echoes of Caravaggio. The Bolognese painter Giuseppe Maria Crespi (1665–1747) was an artist of renowned originality, drawing his inspiration from the great Venetians – Correggio and Baroccio in particular, and also the early "Caravaggesque" works of Guercino. His paintings, often derived from genre subjects and mythologies, are invested with an uncanny naturalism, inspiring such newcomers as Gian Battista Piazzata. In their varied

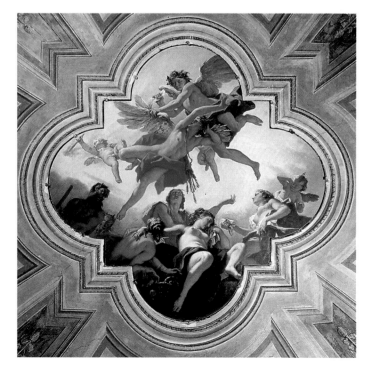

rapid brushstrokes revealing flecks of white paint, to illustrate nonconformist themes that can be linked to the literature of the time. Magnasco was born

Alessandro Magnasco, Refectory of Franciscan Friary, c.1740. Museo Biblioteca e Archivio Civico, Bassano del Grappa, Italy.

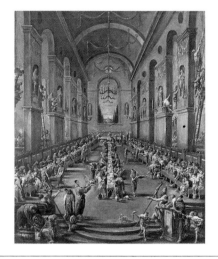

in Genoa but moved to Milan when young. There, he was swayed by the strong moralistic inclinations of the late 17th-century Lombard school and its leanings toward Realism. As a result, he rejected superficial subjects that delighted rather than instructed and, in keeping with the philosophy of Realism, abandoned the "grand manner" of painting. He preferred to paint "minor" subjects, featuring characters castigated by society, such as paupers, gypsies, rogues, and vagabonds. His use of sharp, angular lines is known to have influenced later painters. Some of the most unusual subjects depicted in Magnasco's paintings are the poor and humble figures of the Trappist orders and Capuchin friars; stranger still are his scenes of witchcraft. He completed many versions of paintings of Quaker meetings and of Jewish worshipers in synagogues. These themes reflect the artist's long-standing interest in spiritualism and his participation in lively, albeit clandestine, debates about the

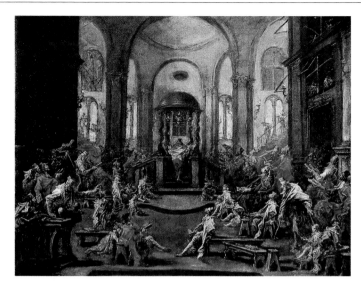

Alessandro Magnasco, Synagogue, c.1730–35. Museum of Art, Cleveland, Ohio.

nature of religion that were popular among freethinkers at the beginning of the Age of Enlightenment.

ART ON THE MOVE

Luxury coaches, invented in Hungary and eventually appearing in western Europe, led to a golden age of coach design and decoration. The decorative arts were lavishly applied to this privileged mode of transportation. Glass and mirrors, carpets, inlaid woods, and gold and silver leaf transformed the bulky, lumbering vehicles into artistic showcases. Rubens painted a state coach for the imperial family, and during the 18th century, the ruling Bourbons commissioned

coaches and sedan chairs that were magnificent examples of decorative art, executed by well-known artists. The carriage museums in Madrid and Lisbon house two of the most interesting collections of their kind. Moreover, there are many paintings that depict the pomp and circumstance that accompanied the arrival of royalty or ambassadors in capital cities, with the long processions of richly decorated, horse-drawn carriages.

Martin van Meytens the Younger (1695–1770), two details from Isabella of Parma's Arrival in Vienna on October 5, 1760. Schönbrunn Castle, Vienna.

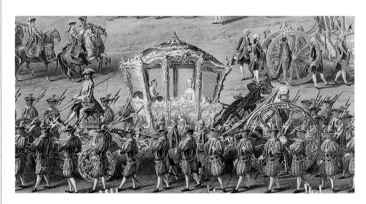

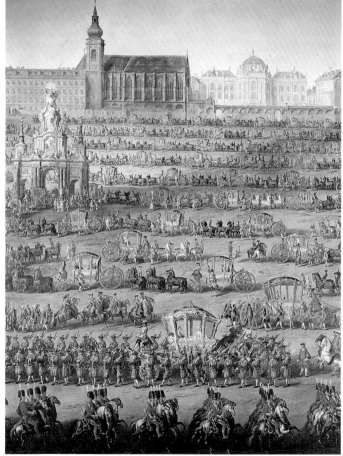

DECORATION IN THE PALACE OF WÜRZBURG

The Prince-Bishop of Würzburg, the regional capital of Lower Franconia in Germany, commissioned the Bohemian architect Balthasar Neumann (1687–1753) in 1719 to build him a palace in the center of the city. Johann Zick was initially engaged in 1749 to paint the *Banquet of the Gods* and the *Goddess Diana at Rest* in the reception room, but he was later replaced by Giambattista Tiepolo, who was hired for the decoration of the banqueting room (1750–52), for which statues and ornamental stucco had already been commissioned. The theme of the decoration, chosen by two of the court's Jesuit priests, was inspired by a series of historic episodes that had taken place in the medieval

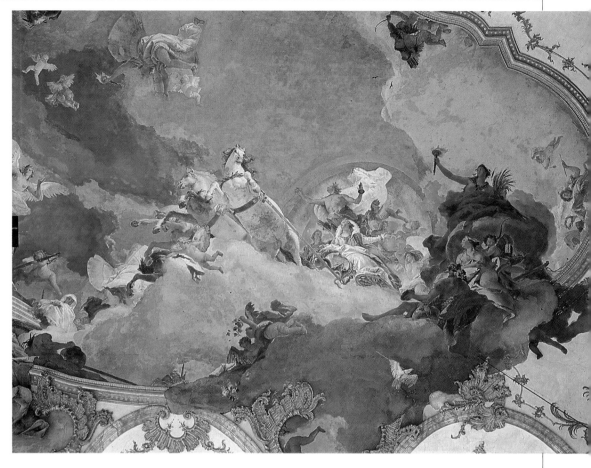

Giambattista Tiepolo, Apollo's Chariot, detail of the ceiling of the imperial drawing room, Würzburg Residenz, Germany.

Balthasar Neumann, view of the grand staircase, Würzburg Residenz, Germany.

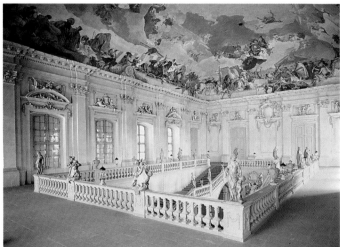

city. One of these, chosen by Tiepolo and his sons Giando-menico and Lorenzo to be portrayed on the walls of the banqueting hall, was the marriage of Frederick Barbarossa to Beatrice of Burgundy, while the ceiling was given over to the great illusionistic scene of Apollo driving the bride to meet the emperor in his chariot.

The free and original interpretation of the historical and celebratory theme, and the sumptuous and intense colorist treatment, were greatly admired. Tiepolo was also commissioned to paint the vast ceiling above the grand staircase, where he summed up the concepts and artistic language that he had first used in 1740 when decorating

the Palazzo Clerici in Milan and in his frescoes for the Palazzo Labia in Venice. The fresco is a mythologically inspired narrative that pays tribute to the Prince-Bishop. He is honored by the gods of Olympus and Fame, personified as a woman holding his portrait aloft, while allegories of the four continents cluster around, all serving as a device to show

greater aerial perspective and depth and the dramatic effects of color and movement. Tiepolo apparently intended Europe to symbolize the unity of the arts, cleverly incorporating portraits of himself, the architect Neumann, and the sculptor Benigno Bossi.

Giambattista Tiepolo, America, detail of the fresco on the ceiling of the grand staircase, Würzburg Residenz, Germany.

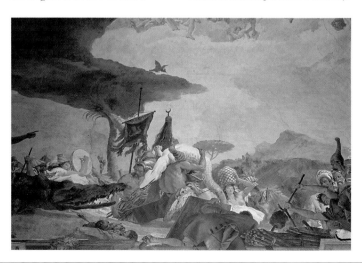

310

interpretations, compositional originality, and choice of iconography, these painters showed how susceptible they were to the new taste in art. Thus, their ingenuity lies in their fresh response and progressive approach to painting. The Genoese painter Alessandro Magnasco (1667–1749) is considered to have been ahead of his time, given his choice of unusual and provocative subjects, his use of quickly applied brushstrokes, and his sharp, angular forms. In Rome, where academicism survived longest, Pompeo Batoni (1708–87) was one of the first to reintroduce the classical style, which heralded the end of Rococo, from the middle of the century onward.

Tiepolo was eager to learn from the great past masters and from those with whom he worked. He had a genius for composition, an appealing theatricality, and an unshakable conviction that the artist should be

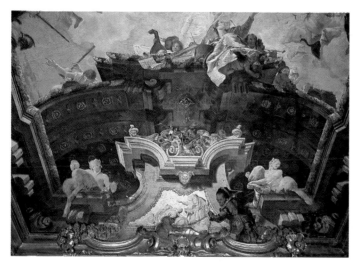

Giambattista Tiepolo, detail of the fresco in the tapestry room, Clerici Palace, Milan, 1740.

Giambattista Tiepolo, The Chariot of the Sun, detail of the fresco in the tapestry room, Clerici Palace, Milan, 1740.

Giambattista Tiepolo, The Moderation of Scipio, fresco, Casati-Dugnani Palace, Milan, 1731.

able to communicate even the most dramatic subjects in a beautiful, grandiose manner.

After his early successes, which led to the commission for the biblical frescoes in the Archbishop's Palace in Udine (1724–25), Tiepolo was always in demand. He employed the assistance of *quadraturisti* or *trompe*

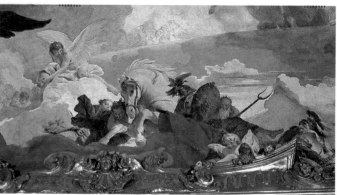

l'oeil specialists when the commission called for architectural perspectives. From the mid-18th century

onward, his sons Lorenzo and Giandomenico worked alongside him. Commissions were plentiful for Tiepolo's easel paintings, often of religious subjects, and for frescoes, mainly in the ceremonial reception rooms of royal and aristocratic palaces. During the period when the Hapsburgs were consolidating their hold on Venice and Lombardy, the nobility in these regions sought to uphold its prestige by building lavish new palaces. Tiepolo went from Milan (where he

painted frescoes in the palaces of Casati-Dugnani and the Clerici) to Venice to execute the *History of Anthony and Cleopatra* in the Palazzo Labia, with architectural perspectives by the virtuoso Bolognese *quadraturista* Gerolamo Mengozzi-Colonna. From there, Tiepolo moved to the Palace of Würzburg, then on to Madrid to paint the *Glory of Spain* fresco on the ceiling in the throne room of the royal palace. Tiepolo's prolific output spans almost the entire course of the century. By the time of his death in Spain in 1770, new trends, such as Neoclassicism together with the first stirrings of Romanticism, had started to push his work out of fashion. It was at about this time that a young admirer of Tiepolo was establishing himself – Francisco Goya.

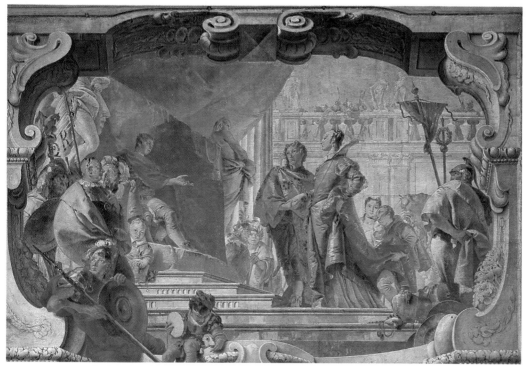

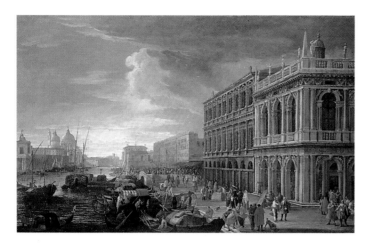

TOWNSCAPES: THE VENETIAN SCHOOL

While large-scale paintings in the "grand manner" were still popular in the 18th century, less spectacular works, much more modest in size and subject, were also sought after for personal enjoyment.

Luca Carlevaris, Venice: View of the Quay with the Mint and Customs House Point, c.1706. Corsini Palace, Galleria Nazionale d'Arte Antica, Rome.

Views (*vedutas*), usually of townscapes, accounted for a large share of this market and were bought as souvenirs of the Grand Tour. The great European cities were gradually adopted as suitable subjects for paintings, usually in the form of panoramic views or close-ups of sites noted for their monuments or beauty. In every large city, workshops specializing in these townscapes proliferated. Venice produced some superb

CANALETTO: "ST. MARK'S SQUARE"

1727–28; oil on canvas; 19½ x 32 in (50 x 82 cm); National Gallery, Washington, DC.

Giovanni Antonio Canal (1697–1768), known as Canaletto, painted this work for the merchant and collector Joseph Smith in 1727–28, along with five similar paintings. This view shows the facades of St. Mark and the Doge's Palace, the loggia of Sansovino with the soaring bell tower on the right, and St. Mark's column, just visible in the background, not far from the water's edge. Much of the government of Venice was located in this area, while the fiscal and economic headquarters were located in the Rialto district. The figures in the paved square can be grouped into social classes by the clothes they wear. The entire square was traditionally the preserve of the aristocracy, to the exclusion of ordinary citizens.

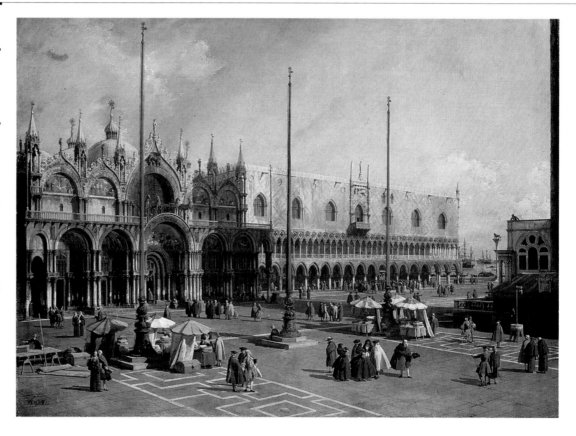

▶ *1. Canaletto based his townscapes on a scrupulous adherence to the rules of perspective. Before painting in color, he undertook a geometric construction of the scene, with a detailed perspective grid. In this case, the construction of the perspective is known technically as "accidental," with the two vanishing points (V.P.) situated outside the picture on the horizon line to restrain the foreshortening and tapering effect so that the buildings were given due importance and value. The artist also used a camera obscura to help with the accuracy of his composition.*

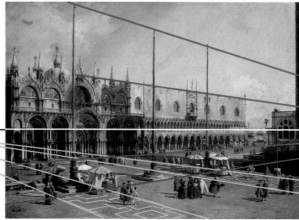

V.P.   Horizon Line

painters of this genre, following earlier examples by Marco Ricci (1676–1729) and Luca Carlevaris (1667–1730), who both attempted to apply what they had learned from the Roman school and the Dutch landscape masters. Venetian townscape painting (*vedutismo*) developed its own style and manner, distinct from the landscape painting of other regions.

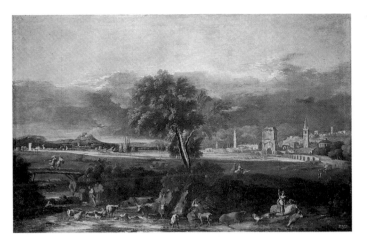

Marco Ricci, Landscape with City on a River, *c.1705. Gemäldegalerie, Dresden.*

The most notable examples were by Canaletto (1697–1768), Bernardo Bellotto (1721–80), and Francesco Guardi (1712–93). Having initially worked as a scene painter with his father, Canaletto then furthered his artistic education in Rome. He returned to Venice in about 1720 and started to produce accurate portrayals of his native city from real life, although he later painted from drawings. His highly original method of

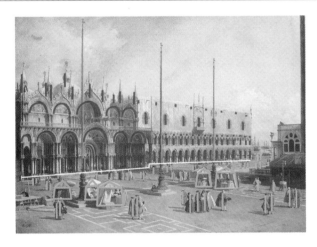

▲ *2. The townscape is affected by the pattern of the buildings that rise to varying heights from the flat land. It is also governed by a closely observed and insistent rhythm: that of the flagpoles, the colonnade, and the gallery, with their arches, groups of columns, and the pinnacles of the buildings. The parading crowd brings the townscape to life. In the main square and in the upper parts of the buildings, the composition is more expansive; in the lower sections, more crowded.*

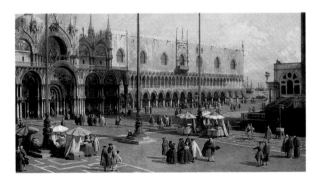

▲ *3. The late afternoon light falls on the rose facade of the palace, the gold of the mosaics, and the ornamental details of the basilica. In juxtaposition with these tones are the contrasting shades of cerulean blue and turquoise of the sky. The shadow cast by the bell tower contributes to the distribution of the chiaroscuro; shadows are never black but interpreted in different shades of brown and always subtly tinged with red.*

▼ *4. Standing on a rostrum under an awning near one of the porticos is a figure preaching to a small crowd. His clothes suggest that he is a monk or friar, possibly a Dominican. The Doge's Palace also housed many government offices, which would have been visited by Venetians as well as visitors from the mainland. In St. Mark's port the gondolas thread their way between the larger vessels.*

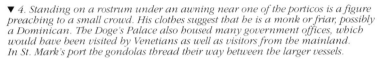

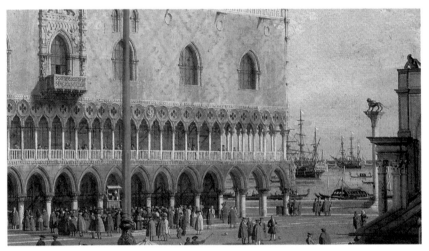

▼ *5. Canaletto coolly analyzes and describes daily life in the famous square. In front of the basilica there are three booths with goods on display and in trunks, shaded by large umbrellas and awnings. Dotted across the square are magistrates in wigs and long robes, aristocrats in all their finery, and members of the bourgeoisie, swathed in dominoes and capes, as required by the laws of Venice. A merchant is dismantling his stall, its covers lying on the ground revealing the trestle table. Canaletto's minute attention to detail and his sharp observation of everyday life in his native city echoes the Dutch genre painters, whose paintings of daily life are unrivaled in their detail.*

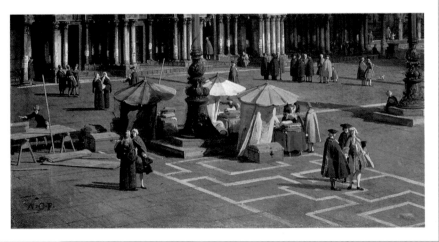

working, the meticulous attention to detail, the descriptive accuracy of his figures, and his breadth and range of perspective make his work all the more appealing. For composition and accuracy, Canaletto used a *camera obscura,* (an apparatus with which images are projected onto a flat surface by a convex lens in an aperture) to help him capture wide-angle views on canvas. Resorting to such technical aids in no way compromised the artist's skill at handling light or the immediacy of his figures, which were brought to life by a few brushstrokes. Canaletto painted a very wide range of views, often repeating a subject but always varying his treatment of it. His style, therefore, is easily identifiable despite the fact that many others worked with similar subjects. The artist's work met with immediate success, the English elite proving to be the most enthusiastic patrons. Canaletto moved to England in 1746 and, for the next ten years, painted numerous landscapes, townscapes, and views of country houses. During this time, a change in his range of color became noticeable. Canaletto's nephew, Bernardo Bellotto, also a painter, emulated his themes

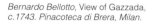

Bernardo Bellotto, View of Gazzada, *c.1743. Pinacoteca di Brera, Milan.*

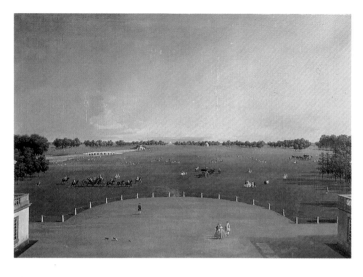

Canaletto, Badminton Park from the House, *1748. Badminton House, Duke of Beaufort's Collection. Many members of the English nobility and royalty were great art collectors at this time.*

Francesco Guardi, St. Mark's Square, *c.1760–65. National Gallery, London. This painting presents a view of Venice looking across St. Mark's Square toward the basilica.*

Guardi, one of a large family of painters, also specialized in townscapes and returned to some of the subjects and settings first painted by Canaletto. He interpreted them in a very different way, working with extremely light and rapid brushstrokes and producing scenes crowded with figures, some just barely sketched. His works stand apart for their dynamism and vitality and, on occasion, they evoked a haunting melancholy. Although best known for his view painting, Guardi later created imaginary scenes, or *capricci,* that sought to convey emotion and atmosphere rather than document real life. Of all

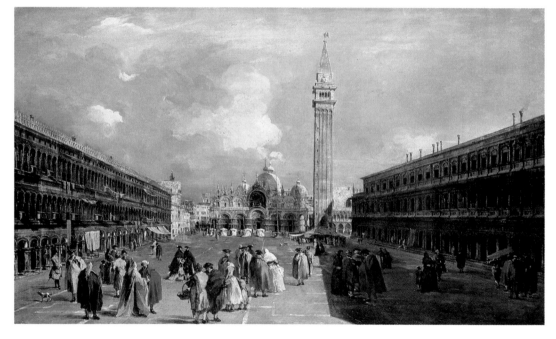

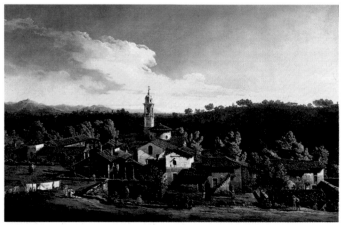

and treatment of perspective but used a colder, darker palette and gave his scenes a more polished, lively quality. After painting many Italian townscapes and landscapes (among them his famous view of Gazzada near Varese), Bellotto left Italy and went to Dresden in 1747, and he also visited various cities in central Europe. He painted some very fine and meticulously accurate views of Warsaw. The Venetian artist Francesco

the townscape painters, Guardi is most closely identified with the spirit of the Rococo. As the style gradually gave way to Neoclassicism, however, Guardi evolved as a painter, and his work went on to inspire many of the more introspective 19th-century artists, who preferred to express their own, personal emotions and artisic outlooks, rather than to be content with strictly descriptive and objective painting.

EUROPEAN PORCELAIN IN THE 18TH CENTURY

European porcelain competed with Rococo sculptures and paintings as the most fashionable items of interior decoration, and they were often smaller, more brilliantly colored versions of the former.

The Meissen factory, named after the German city, was the most influential and active European ceramics factory during the first half of the 18th century. At its peak, over a thirty-year period it produced an unrivaled variety of ornamental wares. With the appointment in 1720 of Johann Gregorius Höroldt, a distinguished painter and color chemist, the Meissen factory began to adopt East Asian decorative motifs and to adapt them to European tastes. Distinct European floral motifs, such as the *Deutsche Blumen,* began to appear, and decorations by distinguished painters were reproduced on porcelain surfaces.

The Meissen factory's first sculptor, Johann Gottlieb Kirchner, specialized in animal figures. He was succeeded by Johann Joachim Kändler, the witty and original creator of statuettes based on street entertainers, peddlers, harlequins, or figures from mythology. His counterpart at the Nymphenburg factory was Franz Anton Bustelli, who was appointed *Modellmeister* in 1754 and remained a dominant figure until his death in 1763. His series of southwest of Paris, attained an outstanding reputation for the distinct color schemes employed in the decoration of wares. Several shades of blue were gradually introduced: *bleu lapis, gros bleu,* and *bleu nouveau,* the latter added in 1763. Also, the famous *rose pompadour,* a brilliant pink, was introduced in 1758. Among the master craftsmen working at Sèvres were the sculptor Etienne Maurice Falconet, who reproduced Boucher's Arcadian world in biscuit porcelain, and Jean-Antoine Houdon, who created exquisite statuettes of lovers or mythological scenes. The factory was saved from closure in 1759 by Louis XV. The growth in popularity of porcelain in European court circles led to the foundation of various centers of production, among them the Capodimonte factory, where Giuseppe Gricci, Francesco Celebrano, and Filippo Tagliolini were among the best sculptors.

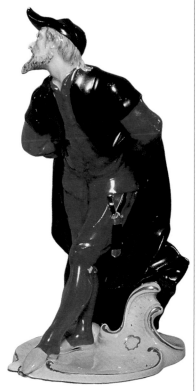

Franz A. Bustelli, Pantaloon, *Nymphenburg, 1760. Victoria and Albert Museum, London.*

Anonymous artist, Keeping Account of Expenditure, *Meissen. Capodimonte Museum, Naples.*

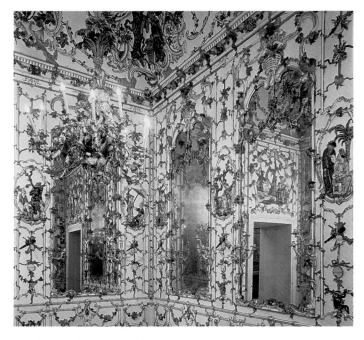

Giuseppe Gricci, Porcelain Room, Capodimonte,1757–59. Capodimonte Museum, Naples.

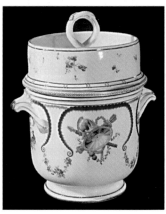

Cooler, 1762, Sèvres. Musée Ile-de-France, Paris.

porcelain figures representing 16 characters from the *Commedia dell'Arte* embody the essence of the south German Rococo. The Sèvres Porcelain Factory, which was transferred in 1756 from Vincennes to Sèvres,

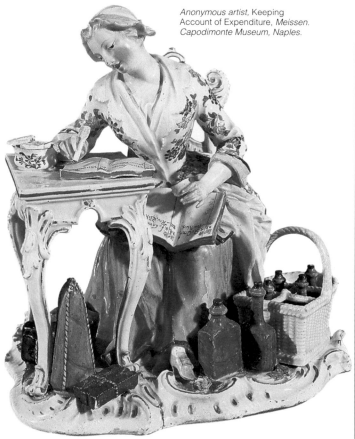

GENRE PAINTING

During the 18th century, there was a tremendous amount of variety in the subject matter of genre painting, which usually represented scenes from everyday life. Such work often depicted the lives of commoners, including beggars, soldiers of fortune, and tradespeople. One of the most popular subjects was the depiction of women engaged in domestic tasks. These paintings were collectively known as *bambocciate,* or scenes of "trivial" subjects. An eye for exaggeration and the grotesque was often a characteristic of this style. Flemish and Dutch artists accounted for the majority of genre painters, and Austrian and German painters followed their lead. Many of these, working in Italy as well as in their native lands, were loosely connected with a group of *bambloccianti* painters who had converged

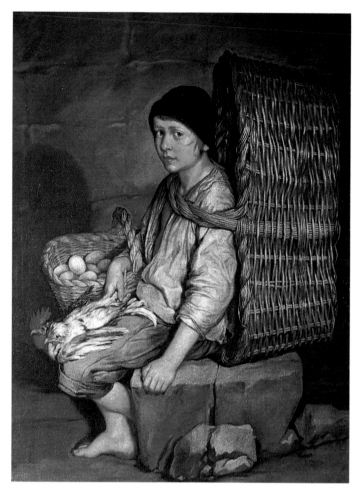

Giacomo Ceruti, Seated Errand Boy with Baskets, *c.1736. Pinacoteca di Brera, Milan. Here, Ceruti reinterprets Lombard realism, a style that had reflected the concern for the humble, as advocated by the Borromeo archbishops. However, true to the style of 18th-century artists, he focused on the picturesque and folkloristic aspects of working-class life.*

on Rome during the previous century. Of the many practitioners of low-life and peasant scenes, certain painters stand out as exceptional; these include the Italian Giacomo Ceruti (c.1698–1767), who was principally active in Brescia. The English artist William Hogarth (1697–1764) dealt with similar subject matter, but his bitter and witty comments and his moral reflections on the society of his day place him in a different, more satirical artistic category.

FRENCH PAINTING

French painting was largely dependent upon and centered around the Court, which provided the artists with commissions, support, and patronage. It adopted a graceful and voluptuous Rococo style that often co-existed with a concern for realism that was gained through a profound knowledge of the Flemish school. French painters were also influenced by the enduring academic tradition of the Bolognese and Roman schools, which they equated with a particular period in the 17th century, and the work of Nicolas Poussin (1596–1665).

The enchanting paintings of Jean-Antoine Watteau (1684–1721) set the agenda for the development of art in 18th-century France. The *commedia dell'arte* and masked performers are a recurring theme in the artist's work, reflecting his early career as a costume designer. The reception of his paintings was so successful that he was soon made a member of the Academy,

HOGARTH'S PROGRESS

William Hogarth's skill and experience as an engraver and illustrator of books influenced his choice and treatment of themes for his paintings, which have a definite theatrical quality. His starkly realistic and bitingly satirical portrayals of London life during the first half of the 18th century were inspired by contemporary theatrical plots.
The artist started work on his first anecdotal pictures in the early 1730s; these were *A Harlot's Progress* (of which only engraved copies survive), followed by *The Rake's Progress* (1733–35). Hogarth used such "modern" subjects as a vehicle for his attempt to draw attention to what he saw as a decline in social values, which was often linked to prostitution and alcoholism. In his famous narrative sequence *Marriage à la Mode* (1743–45), he adopted an exaggerated, mocking narrative voice, bringing his penetrating powers of observation to bear on the aristocracy. The paintings are handled in a free and energetic style and enriched by a dynamic and lively palette.

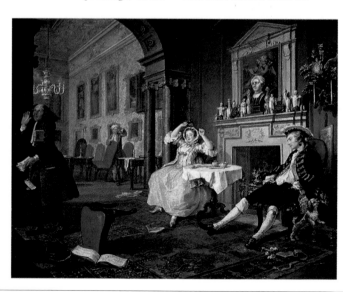

William Hogarth, Shortly After the Marriage *from* Marriage à la Mode, *1744. National Gallery, London.*

JEAN-ANTOINE WATTEAU: "L'INDIFFERENT"

1717; oil on canvas; 10 x 8 in (26 x 19 cm); Musée du Louvre, Paris.

This small painting, also known as *The Nonchalant Young Man*, depicts a young man during the last years of Louis XIV's reign or at the beginning of the Regency period. He is either mid-dance or, as the poet Paul Claudel preferred in his analysis of the picture, about to start dancing. Claudel describes

him as "a messenger of mother-of-pearl, herald of the dawn, half fawn, half bird…a creature of the woods…with one arm outstretched while the other, with a sweeping gesture, unfurls a poetic veil…his whole *raison d'être* contained in the measured advance he is about to make." The contrived gesture and theatrical stance suggest a ballet dancer who has just entered the stage and is silhouetted against a wooded backdrop.

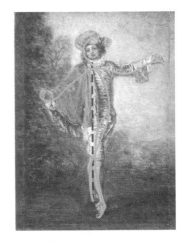

▶ *1. Clad in silk and lace, the figure dominates the picture and is clearly outlined against a fanciful landscape scene. The artist has captured his subtle movements – his body is perfectly poised – and the figure is reminiscent of a china statuette or tableau vivant. This effect of suspended animation is achieved with a undulating, curved line that traces the axes of the body. The curvature of the outstretched leg, the slightly tilted head, and the raised arms and hands all combine to give him a featherlike lightness. The strategic positioning of the figure at the center of the canvas gives the composition a symmetrical stability.*

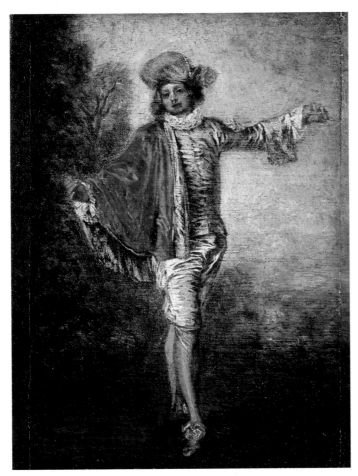

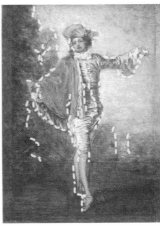

◀ *2. The shape of the figure is delineated by assured and lively drawing, its outline lit by tiny highlights on the small folds of the garments, which help to impart a sense of movement. The suggestion of movement is typical of Rococo paintings, as is the tendency for an artist to imbue figures with a glowing, reflective light. The treatment of the figure is repeated in the surroundings: the uneven ground, the soft, curving outline of the trees, the fluffy clouds, and the evocative, vibrant colors.*

▶ *3. The figure is bathed in light and acquires great sculptural definition through the interplay of light and dark and the rapid, virtuoso brushstrokes that transform simple highlights into radiant, gleaming shades of white, yellow, and orange. Watteau conveys a subtle anxiety, which filters through the grace and lightheartedness of his work. These highlights breathe life into the rippling folds of the iridescent material, evident in the beautiful touches of russet tones.*

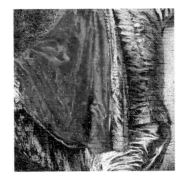

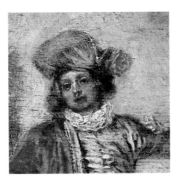

▶ *4. The head stands out against the pale sky, while the hat has been infused with an evanescent quality. Its large, raised brim partially reveals the forehead, and the flesh-pink of the trimming echoes the color of the cheeks. The young man's gaze, both intent and weary, is shown in golden-brown shadow. The outline of his adolescent face, his red, fleshy lips, well-defined eyelids, and fine hair create a sensual and sensitive head. His expression and general languor possibly suggest melancholy.*

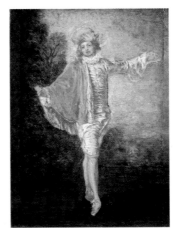

◀ *5. The figure pauses, motionless, in a setting that is both symbolic and ambiguous. To the left of the figure, the light diffuses gradually through the clouds and trees, casting a haziness across this side of the painting. The dancer's face and the front of his leg are lit by a frontal source, reminiscent of theater footlights, that defines the physical features. These intimate details give great depth to a work that at first glance appears to be merely a playful and sensual expression of* joie de vivre.

JEAN-ANTOINE WATTEAU

Abandoning the "grand manner" of Louis XIV's court painters, Jean-Antoine Watteau (1684–1721) preferred to draw his inspiration from the great Dutch and Flemish artists of the 17th century and from the etchings of Jacques Callot (1592–1635). With *Embarkation for Cythera*, one of the most famous and mysterious pictures of the century, Watteau introduced the theme of the *fêtes galantes*, which was to play an important part in *rocaille* art. He viewed the world as a "theater of nature," where members of the fashionable social circles indulged themselves in leisurely pleasure. Watteau's subjects, often inspired by the theater, echo the fanciful characters from the *commedia dell 'arte*; his colors provide a surreal touch to the Arcadian beauty that he strove to capture. He showed anecdotal flair and a good knowledge of the Dutch masters in his genre paintings, which portrayed poverty with an enigmatic and graceful melancholy. His cosmopolitan taste and sensibility contributed to the ambiguous complexity of his work – its wealth of allusions, equivocal meanings, and the often baffling, phantasmagoric quality that reflected the contradictions of the era.

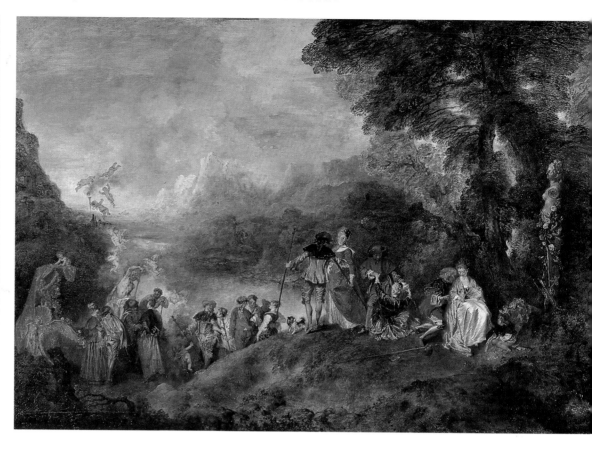

Jean-Antoine Watteau, Pilgrimage to the Island of Cythera *or* Embarkation for Cythera, *1717. Musée du Louvre, Paris.*

SILVER TABLEWARE

In the 18th century, great importance was attached to elegance in table settings, whether for sumptuous banquets or more modest occasions and informal meals. A wide range of flatware in silver or silver-gilt was displayed alongside porcelain serving dishes and tableware; plates of various types were also cast in precious metals, as were coffee and chocolate pots, cups, and soup tureens. The leading production centers were Paris and London, but superb silverware was also produced in Moscow, Lisbon,

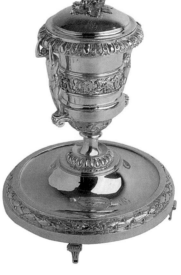

Jean-Simon Pontaneau, French silver-gilt table centerpiece, 1789.

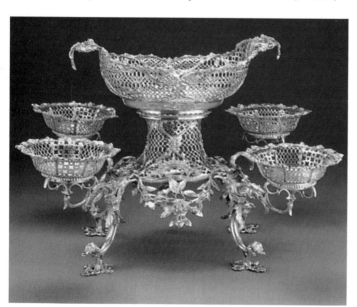

Thomas Pitts, English silver centerpiece with five supporting baskets for fruit, 1763.

Naples, and Madrid. High-quality silver was also now being imported to Europe from North and South America.

and he became a specialist in the *fêtes galantes* genre, which depicted figures in pastoral settings. Despite Watteau's sure touch and the frequently ironic and light-hearted nature of his works, there is an undercurrent of melancholy, a sense of the temporal nature of life and of pleasure in his most significant paintings. The idea of the fleeting moment is often the subtext of his pictures; for example, his work *Embarkation for Cythera* expresses a particularly fragile atmosphere. Of the French school, the work of François Boucher (1703–70) typifies the fullest expression of Rococo. A court portrait painter whose career spanned the Regency and continued into Louis XV's reign, Boucher captured the spirit of Rococo and was responsible for propagating the Pompadour style. Respectful of the Roman

MADAME DE POMPADOUR

The Marquise de Pompadour (1721–64), mistress of King Louis XV, gave her name to a style that prevailed from 1745 for two decades in France. The Pompadour style was full-blown Rococo, expressed with tremendous panache in the architecture and decoration of the enchanting châteaus built at Crécy, Fontainebleau, Champs-en-Brie, and Bellevue. A patron of free thinkers, most notably Voltaire and Rousseau, Mme. de Pompadour lent her support to the publication of the *Encyclopédie* after a decree had been passed to suppress it. She also took a great interest in painting under the tutelage of Boucher, whose spirited work embodied the style of her epoch. The marquise commissioned *The Light of the World* (1750) and other religious subjects from Boucher for the chapels of her country houses and her Paris residences. Boucher produced several portraits of the king's mistress: the first in 1750, her official portrait of 1756, and another in 1759, in which the artist captures both her private and public face. Boucher alludes to her artistic taste and cultural interests by surrounding her with exquisite objects. Similarly, the lively pastel portrait executed by Maurice Quentin de Latour (1704–88) conveys a subtle homage to Mme. de Pompadour's intellectual abilities: beside her, she has the most recent volume of the *Encyclopédie*, the publication of which she personally endorsed, as well as Montesquieu's *L'Esprit des Lois*, Voltaire's *Henriade*, and Guarini's *Le Berger Fidèle*.

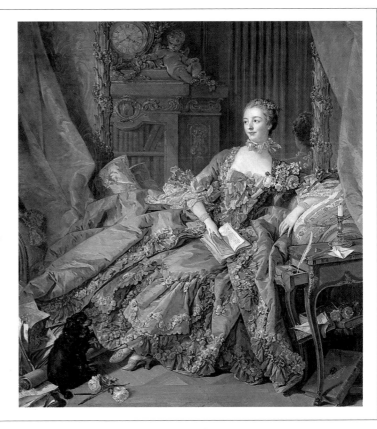

François Boucher, Madame de Pompadour, *1756. Alte Pinakothek, Munich.*

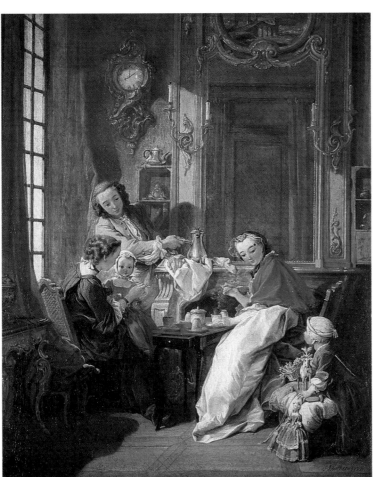

academic tradition, especially after his stay in Rome, Boucher was also influenced by the Venetian school and, in particular, by Sebastiano Ricci. He was a faithful follower of the Baroque masters and was known not only for his portraits but also for his landscapes, designs for porcelain and tapestries, and his stage sets. Boucher represented an aristocratic and worldly approach to painting (he was known for flattering and even seducing his sitters), but the faithfully studied realism that stemmed from Flemish roots was still discernible in his work, as it was in that of his

François Boucher, Family Taking Breakfast, *1739. Musée du Louvre, Paris.*

Jean-Honoré Fragonard, Bolting the Door, *1778. Musée du Louvre, Paris.*

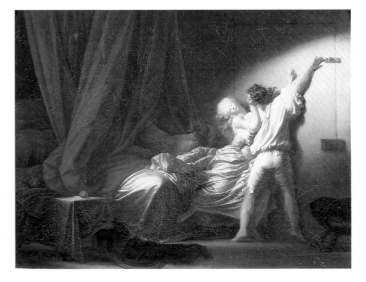

JEAN-BAPTISTE-SIMEON CHARDIN

A keen social observer, Jean-Baptiste-Simeon Chardin (1699–1779) had a genius for portraying the lives of 18th-century Parisian petite bourgeoisie, who passed their days in modest rooms that were becoming increasingly comfortable living spaces to be enjoyed and appreciated. The details of the world of the respectable lower-middle class – their humble household and everyday objects – were rendered in modest canvases in warm, rosy tones with a delightful naturalism. The measured, discerning ethos of the 18th century is perfectly demonstrated in Chardin's work. His paintings such as the *Child with the Spinning-top*, *The Copper Fountain*, *The House of Cards*, *Still Life with Jar of Pickled Onions*, and *The Housekeeper* show the development of the artist's coherent vision, his sensitivity, and his methods of representation. In his final years, he successfully turned his hand to the medium of pastels.

contemporaries. It was clearly evident in the work of Chardin, whose descriptive virtuosity in his portrayals of still lifes and bourgeois domestic scenes made him one of the most admired painters of the mid-18th century. Chardin's pupil, Jean-Honoré Fragonard (1732–1806), in surprising anticipation of the Impressionist movement, captured the immediacy of his subjects via rapid brushwork and a rich impasto.

Jean-Honoré Fragonard, The Progress of Love, 1771–73. Frick Collection, New York. This is one of a series of four scenes depicting the awakening of love in the heart of a young girl, commissioned by Madame du Barry, who succeeded Madame de Pompadour as the king's favorite. The series did not find favor with her, however, and Fragonard failed to secure consistent and highly placed patronage.

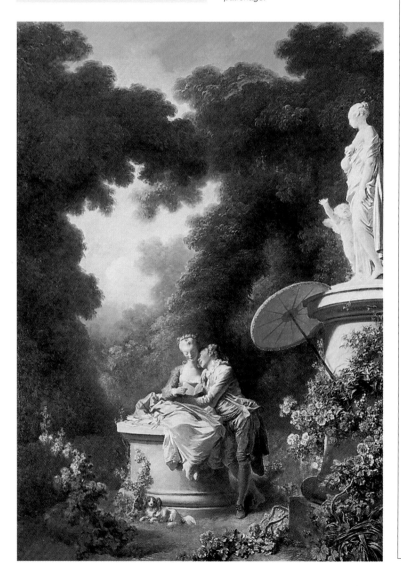

JEAN-HONORE FRAGONARD: "MUSIC"

1769; oil on canvas; 32 x 26 in (81 x 65 cm); Musée du Louvre, Paris.

Painted when the artist was at his most successful, this portrait, also known as *Portrait of Monsieur de la Bretèche*, shows a musician with his instrument, probably a lute. He is shown seated with his back to the viewer but looking over his shoulder. In accordance with prevailing fashion, he is wearing makeup. His curly, tousled hair is half covered by a plumed cap, his robe is partially off one shoulder, and he is wearing a bright yellow shirt with a white collar. Toward the upper right-hand section of the painting a music score is spread open.

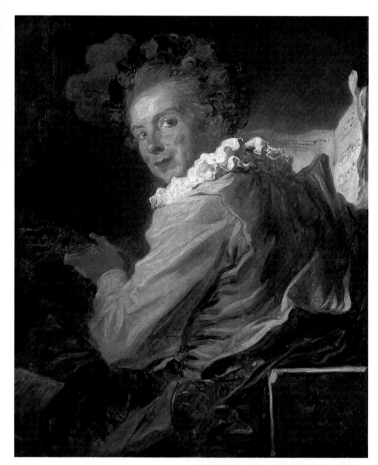

▶ *1. The composition is organized along oblique lines. A diagonal runs from the top right-hand corner, with the subject's torso occupying the lower right-hand triangle and his hand, forearm, head, and shoulders occupy the triangle in the upper left-hand section. The forearm and the head are positioned on two diagonal lines. Oblique lines can be traced from his right shoulder, across his back, and along his left leg. With the forearm, these create an impression of recession from foreground to background, while the diagonal of the head directs the face upward and slightly forward from the back to the front.*

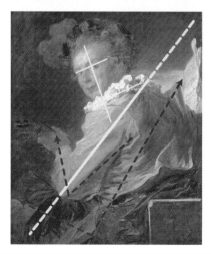

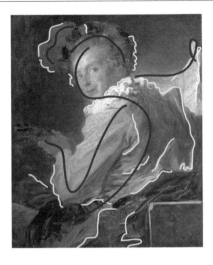

◄ *2. The composition is constructed according to an irregular variation of curved lines and movement, in keeping with the character of Rococo art. A sinuous style of drawing characterizes the whole of the figure, defining it in space by bringing it closer to the picture plane. This treatment is complemented and partially contrasted by the use of energetic contours. The artist has employed brushwork that can either define or blur the outlines. There are no acute angles among the fragmented and varied curves, and the right angle formed by the chair is softened by the use of white. The relative rarity of acute angles in Rococo art distanced it from the Gothic and Renaissance styles, while its realism and naturalism indicated a new artistic approach.*

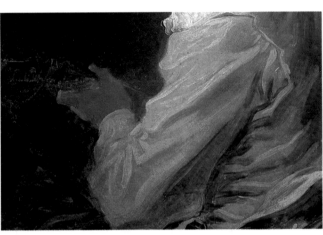

▼ *3. The painting conveys a strong sense of action unexpectedly interrupted and a moment seized, while the lively brushwork expresses a mood of spontaneity on the part of the artist himself. However, closer examination reveals that, in fact, precision governs every line. The alternation of brilliant highlights and dramatic chiaroscuro bring a vitality to a composition that might otherwise have lacked dynamism.*

▲ *4. The vibrant, resplendent color follows the rhythm of the brushwork in a harmonious, almost melodic manner. The rich yellow of the sleeve gives way to warm, colored shadows, where the fabric is enlivened only by a few rapid strokes of white paint. The sketchy white collar is loosely rendered with a Rembrandtesque touch. The edges of the musical score are curled, and the pages appear to be blown by a soft breeze. The reddish hues that characterize this work give the picture a warm and translucent quality.*

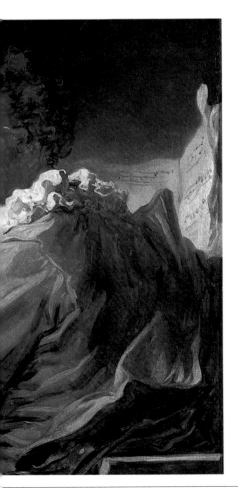

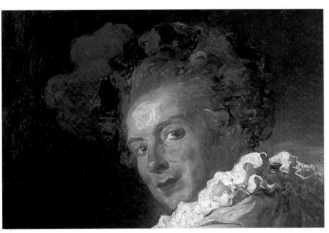

▲ *5. From the initially monochrome foundation of the ground, touches of red, brown, green, and white build a face with expressive lines and gaze. Above the forehead the hair is disheveled and curly, emerging from underneath a brilliantly colored scarlet hat. Shadows shape the slightly sagging cheeks, and the full, well-defined lips are enlivened with red. In the subject's glance, which is penetrating and rather serious, Fragonard seems to anticipate Impressionism in his commitment to canvas of a single fleeting "impression."*

JEAN-HONORÉ FRAGONARD

Influenced by his teachers Boucher and Chardin and their feeling for the *rocaille* figurative culture, Jean-Honoré Fragonard (1732–1806) breathed new life into the Rococo movement with his inspirational ease of style and elegant treatment of his subjects. His invigorating handling of color and his strongly expressed naturalism were reminiscent of the Dutch master Hals and the mature style of Rembrandt. Fragonard's paintings featured beautiful, pastoral settings, erotic scenes, and amorous encounters, and they show a sensuous and tactile application of color. They are among the period's most representative artistic achievements.

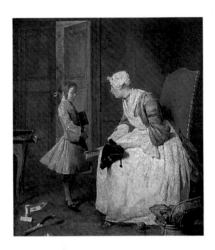

Jean-Baptiste Chardin, The Governess, 1738. National Gallery of Canada, Ottawa. Chardin's paintings of children have a charming delicacy.

THE ENGLISH SCHOOL

Although they were affected by contemporary trends, 18th-century English painters were openly antiacademic. Their work began to show signs of a Romantic sensibility during the second half of the century, especially in their tendency to place figures in the middle of wide stretches of landscapes and impart a greater sense of immediacy. Although the work of Sir Joshua Reynolds (1723–92) shows a certain Rococo flair in his handling of subjects, the strength of his images lies in the subtlety and indeterminate quality of his portraits, the use of natural settings, and the suggestion of

THOMAS GAINSBOROUGH: "MR. AND MRS. ROBERT ANDREWS"

1749–50; oil on canvas; 28 x 48 in (70 x 118 cm); National Gallery, London.

This painting celebrates and commemorates the marriage of the young Robert and Frances Andrews in November 1748. The couple is shown beneath an oak tree on their estate near Sudbury, where Gainsborough was born. The setting enables him to express his gift as a landscape painter, while displaying some of the vast grounds of the house – confirming the couple's social status. During the reign of George II, Britain was already a great world power. The ruling class had grown rich from the products of their lands (in the foreground of this painting, the artist includes sheaves of newly scythed wheat), colonial trade, and financial speculation. The lesser gentry, or squirearchy, was also sharing in this prosperity and felt secure

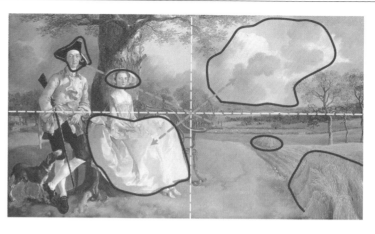

because of its growing influence in Parliament.

This portrait, which remained in the Andrews family until 1960, perfectly documents the style of the young Gainsborough. He was influenced by the work of the great 17th-century Dutch landscape artist Jacob van Ruysdael, while already moving toward a Romantic style. English painters were not disposed to the extra-vagant and frivolous *rocaille* fashions that held sway in Continental Europe. Instead, they assumed a preference for formality and an emphasis on tradition that led to an early espousal of Neoclassicism (incorporating some characteristics of Rococo), which in turn evolved into a form of Romanticism.

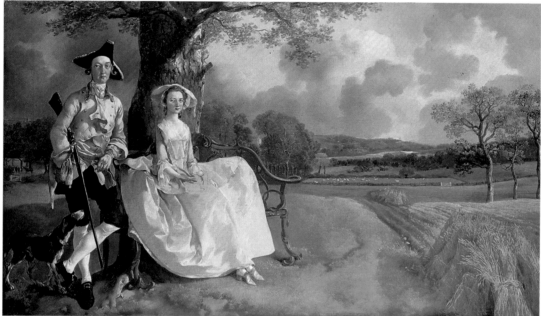

▼ *1. The painting's dimensions conform to the rules of the Golden Section. The canvas can be split into two overlapping squares; their division runs just below the horizon and slightly higher than the upper bodies of the subjects. At first glance, the left-hand square appears to be a double portrait and the right-hand square a landscape. These two sides are fused by the artist's harmonious use of color and the continuity provided by the background. The "positive" element of the great oak tree behind the couple has a symmetrical relationship to the "negative" emptiness centered in the right-hand square.*

▼ *2. The "empty" half of the picture, the landscape, enables the artist to construct a perspective view of the composition without resorting to the use of distortion. The viewer's gaze is led to the couple on the left-hand side, the natural central point of interest in the composition. Linking various important elements, diagonal alignments lead us toward the unusual placing of the focal point in the distance. The painting displays a deep love of nature in all its freedom and beauty that is typical of English sensibility; in this, the work prefigures the Romantic movement.*

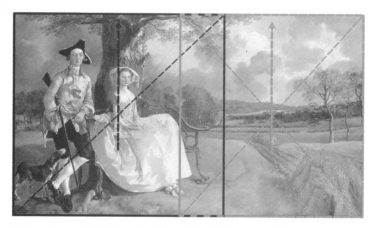

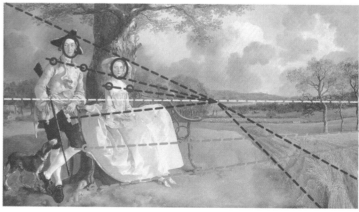

◀ *3. The amount of space devoted to the landscape paradoxically serves to emphasize the two figures. Frances Andrews is the more prominent of the two, the fullness of her pale blue skirt corresponding to the shape of the clouds in the background. The meticulously drawn sheaves of wheat are symbolic references to fertility – highly appropriate in a portrait of a newlywed couple.*

▼ *4. The indications of social status are more evident in the male figure. His magnificent gun – a country gentleman's sporting weapon – indicates prestige and distinction. A whimsical but coherent interweaving of lines combines the shape of the tree roots, the legs, the gun, and the dog. The painter creates a naturalistic portrait full of light. His brushwork is deft, with a delicacy of glazing and a transparency rarely seen in oil colors. He used long brushes and well-diluted color to achieve these effects, most evident in the highlights of the fabrics and the texture of the skin.*

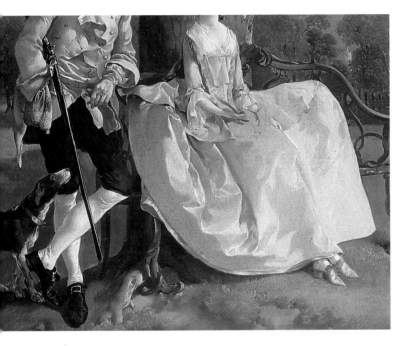

▼ *5. The contrast between the crisp outlines of the tricorne hat, the comfortable cut of the jacket, and the neatly tied stock around his long neck provide examples of English elegance that even the French Court emulated in this era. While the bark of the tree is painted with light brushwork, the woman's hands remain enigmatically unfinished. The subject's represent the English upper class, in their country home, with its distinctions of rank and wealth. They have delicate but clear-cut features, elongated faces, unsmiling mouths, and a composed, slightly superior air.*

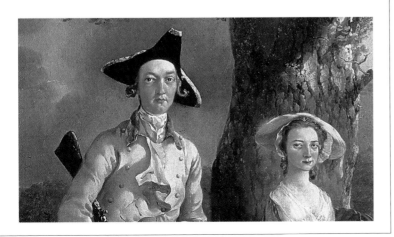

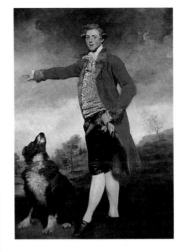

Joshua Reynolds, Portrait of John Campbell, Lord Cawdor, 1778. Cawdor Castle, Scotland.

intimacy. The apparently cold and detached approach to portrait painting that is often displayed in the works of Sir Thomas Gainsborough (1727–88) is offset by his choice of attractive and enchanting settings; his works are painted in a style that heralded the work of 19th-century landscape artists.

Filippo Tagliolini, sculptor, and Giovanni Battista Polidoro, painter; Bench in the Real Passeggio, Reale Fabrica Ferdinandea, Naples, c1790–95. Capodimonte Museum, Naples. This was part of a large set used as table decoration during the dessert course; it illustrates the influence of Rococo in the Neoclassical era.

FROM ROCOCO TO NEOCLASSICISM

The architectural theorist Francesco Milizia documented his views of the Baroque style in 1785 in a savage indictment. He viewed it as already hopelessly old-fashioned. Under his definition of Baroque, much that belonged to High Baroque was mistakenly included. Rococo was already past its peak in central European architecture by the 1780s. In terms of domestic interior decoration and furnishings, best represented in France by the "Louis XV" style, Rococo was going out of favor in Europe by about 1770. In large European cities, Neoclassicism grew in popularity, and where taste was more conservative, there was a return to the academic traditions of the Bolognese and Roman schools. The Louis XVI style in furniture, which became fashionable during the 1770s and 1780s, was characterized by ornately carved wood or stucco decoration. It was tantamount to a variation on the Rococo theme but with a preference for straight

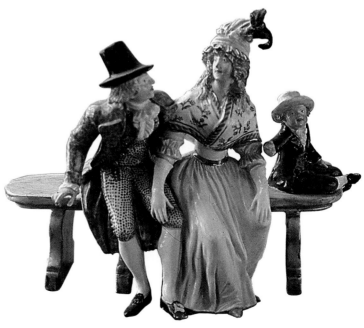

FRANCISCO GOYA: "THE THIRD OF MAY 1808: THE FIRING SQUAD ON MOUNT PIUS"

1814; oil on canvas;
96 x 121 in (266 x 345 cm);
Museo del Prado, Madrid.

This painting, one of Goya's most famous, was particularly influential, later inspiring the war paintings of Manet and Picasso. The canvas shows the execution by firing squad, on a mound near Prince Pius' house, of some partisans who had taken part in the riots of May 1808 against Joseph Bonaparte, whom Napoleon had placed on the throne of Spain. Napoleon's fortunes took a turn for the worse soon after these riots. The dramatic scene takes place at night, in a lonely spot near Madrid's Royal Palace (shown as a large, dark shape on the right in the background). Goya is commemorating the patriots' bravery but keeps an objective, detached view of this very modern method of slaughter. In the foreground on the right, the firing squad is lined up; on the left, in front of the leveled guns, are the martyrs of independence, gathered around a figure in a white shirt and illuminated by the yellow light of the lantern placed on the ground.

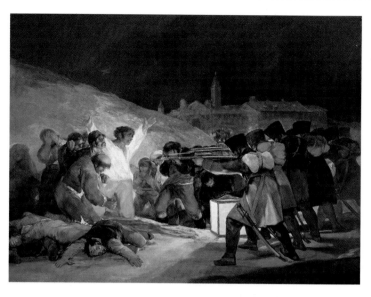

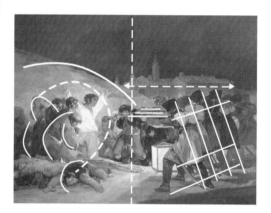

▲ 1. The composition is based on two opposing groups: the one on the right is structured with straight lines that run across the soldiers and their muskets, seen in perspective; the one on the left is arranged along curved lines around the man in the white shirt. In the background, the horizontal lines of the buildings predominate. On the left, the mound and the clothes of the central figure provide reflected light; more light comes from the lantern.

▼ 2. Through the darkness, two bright sources of light project dazzling rays, exposing the expressive details of the faces and stances and the pool of blood that has soaked into the ground. In the semi-darkness stand indistinct figures in dramatic poses, and on the ground lie the motionless figures of the executed men, streaked with red. Lit by harsh rays of light, the rebel group emerges from the darkness.

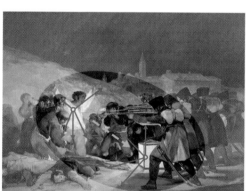

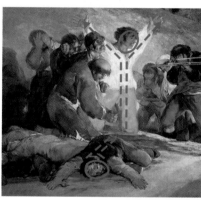

▲ 3. The central figure holds out his arms like a man crucified and screams, showing defiance through his pose and gesture. The bright white and yellow stand out against the subdued color of his surroundings, contributing to an arresting and dramatic image. In the foreground, a body lies with its arms outstretched.

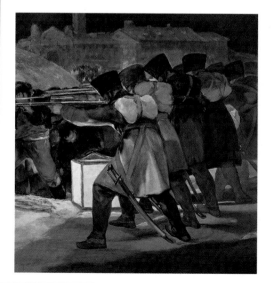

◀ 4. The soldiers line up with a well-drilled military rigidity, carrying out their orders like machines, each with the same tensed stance, their legs apart for greater stability when the recoil comes. They form a chorus of gray and browns, which varies only in the colors of their knapsacks. A pale, cold light, from a source outside the picture toward the right foreground, illuminates their backs and flanks; this is the same light that falls on the bodies lying on the ground to the left. The painter intended that the viewer should notice the firing squad only after studying and empathizing with the condemned man.

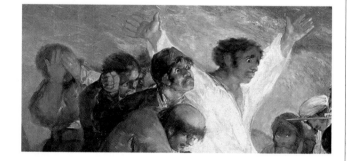

▲ 5. Firm brushstrokes, interspersed with touches of black, portray the faces of the Spaniards on the center right of this detail. Each face has its own identity; they are like masks illustrating despair, the whites of their eyes showing terror, and their expressions contorted with fear and horror. A smoky red is present in the skin color, adding to the vigorous chiaroscuro effect. Goya has invested his composition with a great sense of freedom, and his use of color shows a move toward contemporary art.

lines, a limited range of floral iconography and pattern, a more measured rhythm, and a new, less luxuriant repertoire of decoration. In effect, the gregarious, rich Rococo style gave way to a more austere and serious artistic sensibility. With gradual and various modifications, Rococo gradually progressed toward Neoclassicism with no discernible, abrupt break. As these stylistic changes took place, Francisco Goya exerted great influence on the direction of art. During his career, the artist witnessed the twilight of the age of benevolent despotism. His work was to prove pivotal for contemporary late 18th-century and early 19th-century art.

Francisco Goya, The Great Goat, 1797–98. Lázaro Galdiano Museum, Madrid. This is one of eight paintings commissioned by the Duchess of Osuna for her country house at Alameda. The subject, similar to that of etching No. 60 of Los Caprichos, enabled Goya to combine his flair for fantasy with savage attacks on the Church's abuses and exploitation of superstitions and fears, which were deeply rooted in the popular imagination.

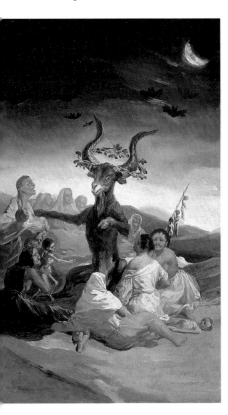

THE IMPORTANCE OF GOYA

Francisco de Goya y Lucientes (1746–1828) was one of the most influential figures in Spanish art. He was also extremely important in the development of modern aesthetic sensibility and was a forerunner of Romanticism, both in the content of his paintings, with their in-depth exploration of reality and references to the dream world, and in his very original technique. His work embodies his personal imaginative visions, defying traditional academicism and conventional subjects. Goya described himself as a pupil of Velázquez, Rembrandt, and nature: from Velázquez, he acquired a feeling for softly shaded color, applied in layers; from Rembrandt, his predilection for dark and mysterious background settings; and from nature, he took an endless variety of forms, some beautiful, some not.

Goya was a keen observer of contemporary society and recorded the sense of unease caused by Spain's moral and political crisis in the closing years of the 18th century. He also portrayed with dexterity the picturesque quality and gaiety of the life of Madrid's *majas*; the religious life of the people (seen in his frescoes for the chapel of San Antonio de la Florida, 1798); and the enthusiasm for progress and technology (*The Air Balloon*, 1818–19). Goya was liberal-minded, a man of the Enlightenment, and his social circle was made up of progressive intellectuals. He turned his attention to the world of the dispossessed – in *The Wounded Mason* and *Winter* (1786–87), for example – and later to the mysterious world of sorcery and witchcraft, which was already popular among writers of the time. He also strongly and graphically denounced injustice and cruelty and the false morality and bigotry

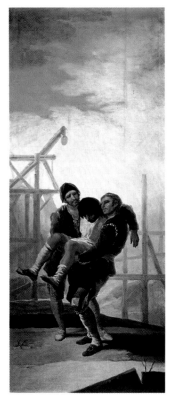

Francisco Goya, The Wounded Mason, (originally The Drunken Mason), 1786–87. Museo del Prado, Madrid.

of religious hypocrites. In his *Los Caprichos* series (1797–99), Goya highlighted the evils of ignorance and superstition, attempting to exorcise them with his mercilessly lucid portrayals.

As chief Court painter, he painted superb portraits of the Spanish nobility and royalty, often influenced by Velázquez; echoes of the famous *Las Meniñas* are evident in *The Family of Charles IV*. Using extraordinarily skillful pictorial effects, he accurately portrayed the Rococo opulence of furnishings and fashions and the aristocratic assurance of his subjects' poses, while subtly recording the pettiness and vanity of a corrupt and complacent ruling class. The French invasion, the subsequent popular uprising, the horrors of war, and the disillusion at the realization that the supposed liberators were merely new oppressors prompted Goya to bear witness to events either in a realistic or an allegorical manner; his series of etchings *The Disasters of War* (1810–20) brings to mind Callot's earlier series. In 1819, he became seriously ill and grew more introspective. He embarked on the strange and brilliant "black paintings" cycle, which combined a very personal vision with his persistent religious themes. His preoccupation with human folly lasted right up until his death in 1828.

Francisco Goya, The Family of Charles IV, 1800. Museo del Prado, Madrid.

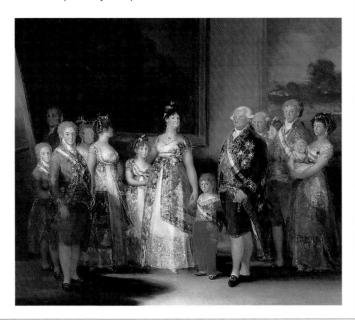

THE 17TH CENTURY: THE AGE OF SPECTACLE

1598: the edict of Nantes puts an end to the religious wars in France; Catholicism is recognized as the state religion, but the Huguenots are granted leave to worship. **1603:** the reign of James I of England, the son of Mary Stuart, begins. **1604:** the Dutch painter van Mander publishes his *Book of Painting*, a collection of biographies of northern artists in the manner of Vasari; in Paris, the Place Royale is laid out, now the Place des Vosges. **1624:** Cardinal Richelieu, now Prime Minister, holds the reins of French politics. **1625:** the Dutchman Pieter van Laer, known as Il Bamboccio, is in Rome; his work will inspire the so-called *bamboccianti*, painters of gypsy and peasant life. **1633:** Galileo appears before the Inquisition for his acceptance of the Copernican system. **1633–1639:** Pietro

1600   1610   1620   1630

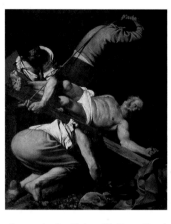

▲ **CARAVAGGIO**
(1571-1610)
The great Italian painter broke radically with the Mannerist tradition, showing religious scenes in an everyday setting. Light and shade are charged with symbolic value in his work. The influence of his style rapidly spread throughout Europe, influencing countless artists, whose work became known as "Caravaggesque." For centuries, his work would remain a point of reference for certain tendencies in realist movements.

Caravaggio, Crucifixion of St. Peter, Cerasi Chapel, Santa Maria del Popolo, Rome, 1600–01.

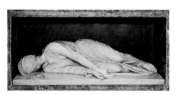

Stefano Maderno, St. Cecilia, 1601, Santa Cecilia, Trastevere, Rome.

▲ **STEFANO MADERNO**
(1576-1636)
A sculptor from the Ticino, Switzerland, Maderno worked in the classical manner, achieving a pathos and simple naturalism that would resurface in certain aspects of the Baroque.

▼ **GUIDO RENI**
(1575-1642)
Using Caravaggio's work as his starting point, Italian painter Guido Reni developed a classical style in pursuit of an aesthetic ideal.

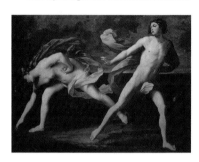

Guido Reni, Atalanta and Hippomenes, 1618–19. Museo del Prado, Madrid.

▼ **JACQUES CALLOT**
(1592-1635)
An engraver from Lorraine, Callot produced original work devoted to the bizarre and picturesque aspects of his day. His work was an inspiration for future geneations of artists.

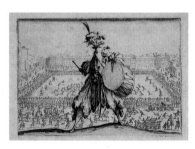

Jacques Callot, The Drummer Boy or A Game of Football in the Piazza di Santa Croce, Florence, 1618–19. Galleria degli Uffizi, Florence.

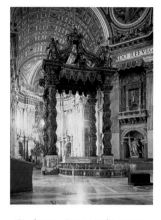

Gianlorenzo Bernini and Francesco Borromini, baldacchino over the high altar of St. Peter's, Vatican City, 1624–33.

▲ **GIANLORENZO BERNINI**
(1598-1680)
A central figure in Roman Baroque, the Italian architect and sculptor Bernini viewed space as a theatrical setting that has the power to astonish and involve the viewer.

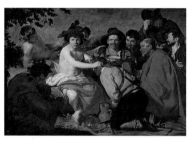

Diego Velázquez, The Topers or The Triumph of Bacchus, c.1624. Museo del Prado, Madrid.

▲ **VELÁZQUEZ**
(1599-1660)
Undisputably one of the greatest and most influential painters of all time, the Spanish master Velázquez developed a fluid, vibrant, and extraordinarily modern style.

FRANCESCO BORROMINI
(1599-1667)
With a masterful technique, this architect from the Ticino, Switzerland, created an original style in which concave and convex elements modulate the space.

▼ **NICOLAS POUSSIN**
(1594-1665)
The French artist Poussin produced rigorous and balanced historical and biblical paintings that made him the greatest interpreter of 17th-century classicism.

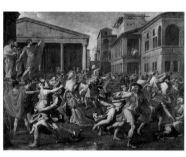

Nicolas Poussin, Rape of the Sabines, c.1637. Musée du Louvre, Paris.

▼ **PETER PAUL RUBENS**
(1577-1640)
The important Flemish painter Rubens anticipated Baroque poetics with his continuous and illusory vision of space, animated by emotional luminous effects.

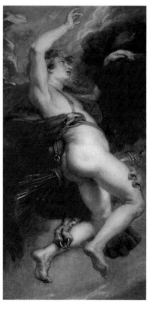

Peter Paul Rubens, Rape of Ganymede, c.1637–38. Museo del Prado, Madrid.

da Cortona paints the fresco of the Triumph of Divine Providence on the ceiling of the Palazzo Barberini in Rome. **1643:** Louis XIV, the Sun King, accedes to the throne of France, under the regency of his mother Anne of Austria. **1644:** the rule of Queen Christina of Sweden begins. **1648:** the Treaty of Westphalia marks the end of the bloody Thirty Years' War; Spain formally recognizes the independence of the United Provinces. **1656:** birth of Fischer von Erlach, the Austrian architect. **1664:** death of Zurbarán, the great interpreter of the Golden Age of Spanish painting. **1665:** Bernini is summoned to Paris to extend the Louvre palace. **1666:** the Great Fire of London. **1682:** the court of Louis XIV moves to the Palace of Versailles. **1683:** the Turks besiege Vienna.

1 6 4 0   1 6 5 0   1 6 6 0   1 6 8 0 – 1 7 0 0

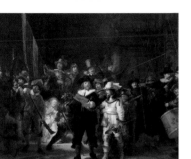

Rembrandt van Rijn, The Night Watch, 1642. Rijksmuseum, Amsterdam.

▲ REMBRANDT VAN RIJN
(1606-69)
The Dutch painter and engraver used strong light effects to give his work – especially his portraits – a strong emotional impact. In a century of fine painters, he is considered one of the greatest.

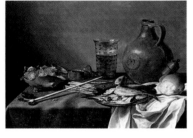

Pieter Claesz., Still life with Glass of Beer, 1644. Musée des Beaux-Arts, Nantes.

▲ PIETER CLAESZ.
(1597/98-1661)
Linked to the Haarlem School, the Dutch painter Pieter Claesz. devoted himself to painting still lifes, a highly popular genre in northern Europe.

CHARLES LE BRUN
(1619-90)
French painter Le Brun's grandiose version of classicism exemplifies the stately, imposing manner of the time of Louis XIV.

▼ BARTOLOMÉ ESTEBAN MURILLO
(1612-82)
Initially close to do Alonso Cano and to Ribera, the Spanish artist Murillo subsequently developed a more delicate style, translated into serene devotional pictures. In the 19th century, a predilection for more sympathetic, graceful figures made him one of the most popular painters of the time.

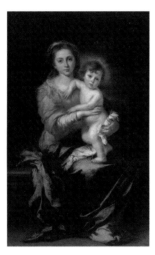

Bartolomé Esteban Murillo, Madonna with the Infant Jesus, 1650–60. Palazzo Pitti, Florence.

▼ LOUIS LE VAU
(1612-70)
Part of the court of Louis XIV, this key French architect was responsible for a series of intensely theatrical and dazzling buildings, including the Palace of Versailles.

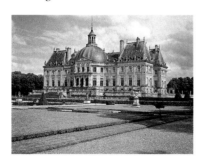

Louis Le Vau, Château Vaux-le-Vicomte, near Paris, 1657–61.

▼ JAN VERMEER
(1632-75)
Originally from Delft, the Dutch artist Vermeer created clear images – often interior scenes – with understated figures and powerful, intimate atmospheres.

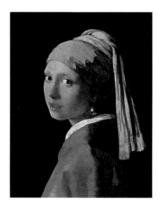

Jan Vermeer, Head of a Girl with a Pearl Earring, 1660–65. Mauritshuis, The Hague.

▼ GUARINO GUARINI
(1624-83)
An Italian architect and engineer, Guarini was also a scientist and author of treatises. He evoked a sense of the infinity of space in his work, rationally placing geometrical elements in multiple combinations.

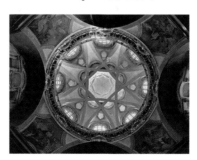

Guarino Guarini, San Lorenzo, Turin, interior of dome.

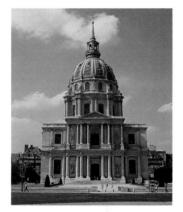

Jules Hardouin-Mansart, Church of the Invalides, Paris, 1680–1706.

▲ JULES HARDOUIN-MANSART
(1646-1708)
French architect. A favorite of the Sun King, he carried out many of his self-celebratory programs in a grandiose, classical style.

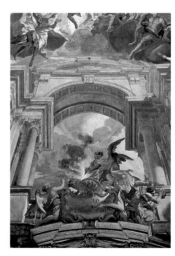

Andrea Pozzo, Entry of St. Ignatius into Paradise, detail of ceiling fresco, Church of Sant'Ignazio di Loyola, Rome, 1691–94.

▲ ANDREA POZZO
(1642-1709)
This Italian painter, stage designer, and mathematician produced paintings – notably ceiling designs – with illusionistic perspectives. A lay brother in the Jesuit order, he often used his art for propaganda purposes.

THE SPLENDORS OF THE 18TH CENTURY

1700: death of Charles II of Hapsburg, King of Spain; his designated successor is Philip V, nephew of Louis XIV. **1703:** Peter the Great, Tsar of Russia, founds the city of St. Petersburg. **1707:** the Union between England and Scotland creates Great Britain. **1708:** the alchemist Böttger discovers how to make porcelain, which spreads with great success throughout Rococo Europe. **1715:** the reign of Louis XV begins in France. **1720:** birth of etcher and architect Piranesi, known for his engravings of ancient Rome. **1722:** building begins of the Belvedere Palace in Vienna, by von Hildebrandt, a great exponent of Austrian late Baroque architecture. **1752:** François de Cuvilliés, refined interpreter of Rococo decoration, moves to Munich as court

1700　　　　1710　　　　1720　　　　1730

▼ JAKOB PRANDTAUER
(1660-1726)
Austrian architect whose monastic buildings incorporate grandiose and delicate forms that integrate with the surrounding natural environment.

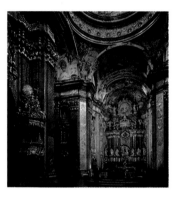

Jakob Prandtauer, interior of the Church of Saints Peter and Paul, Melk, Austria, 1702–14.

▼ ALESSANDRO MAGNASCO
(1667-1749)
Ligurian by birth but Lombard through his education, Magnasco developed an original painting style, in which swarms of darting figures emerge from vast architectonic and landscape backdrops.

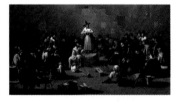

Alessandro Magnasco, Quakers' Meeting, c.1704. Galleria degli Uffizi, Florence.

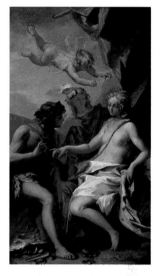

Sebastiano Ricci, Bacchus and Ariadne, c.1713. Chiswick House, London.

▲ SEBASTIANO RICCI
(1659-1734)
A painter from the Veneto region, Ricci was successfully active in many Italian cities. He drew on elements of Correggio's style and used color schemes reminiscent of Veronese, achieving painterly effects that are markedly modern.

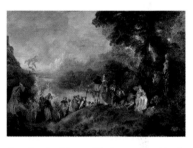

Jean-Antoine Watteau, Pilgrimage to the Island of Cythera or Embarkation for Cythera, 1717. Musée du Louvre, Paris.

▲ JEAN-ANTOINE WATTEAU
(1648-1721)
French painter Watteau was influenced by Rembrandt and Rubens. He blended delicate color and realistic detail to create an exquisite and elusive artistic language.

▼ ROSALBA CARRIERA
(1675-1757)
The delicate pastel portraits of this Italian painter were commissioned throughout Europe. They express a polished, sophisticated image of 18th-century aristocracy.

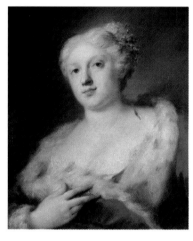

Rosalba Carriera, Portrait of a Lady, c.1720–30. Galleria Sabauda, Turin.

▼ COSMAS DAMIAN ASAM
(1686-1739)
From a family of artists, this German architect and painter remained attached to Baroque illusionism but achieved graceful and delicate Rococo effects.

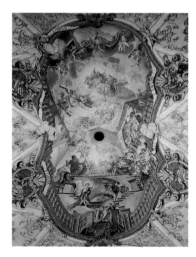

Cosmas Damian Asam, Vision of St. Bernard, fresco in the Abbey Church, Aldersbach, after 1720.

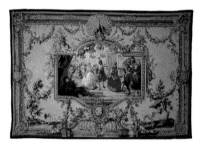

Charles Coypel, The Ball in Barcelona, from The Stories of Don Quixote set of tapestries, Gobelins, 1732–36. Musée du Louvre, Paris.

▲ CHARLES-ANTOINE COYPEL
(1696-1752)
Coypel was a French painter, decorator, and playwright from of a large family of painters connected to Louis XIV. He worked on historical and mythological themes.

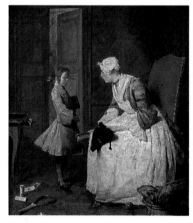

Jean-Baptiste Chardin, The Governess, 1738. National Gallery of Canada, Ottawa.

▲ JEAN-BAPTISTE-SIMEON CHARDIN
(1699-1779)
The work of French painter Chardin was linked with that of the Le Nain brothers and the 17th-century northern artists. He portrays a serene bourgeois world free from any facile sentimentalism.

architect. **1740:** Frederick II is elected King of Prussia, an example of 18th-century Enlightenment despotism. **1746:** birth of Francisco Goya, Spanish painter who straddled the development of art in

the 17th and 18th centuries. **1750:** death of Juste-Aurèle Meissonnier, French architect and engraver and the first theorist and interpreter of the *rocaille* taste. **1754:** building of the Kungliga

Slottet palace in Stockholm. **1756:** birth of Wolfgang Amadeus Mozart in Salzburg. **1762:** Catherine II of Russia, known as Catherine the Great, accedes to the throne. **1769:** Watt patents the first steam

engine. **c.1770:** the Louis XVI style spreads in furnishings. **c.1775:** work on the Hermitage, designed by Felíten, begins in St. Petersburg. **1785:** death of the Venetian painter Pietro Longhi.

1 7 4 0　　1 7 5 0　　1 7 6 0　　1 7 7 0 – 9 0

▼ GIAMBATTISTA TIEPOLO
(1696-1770)
The Italian painter Tiepolo applied a fresh palette, extraordinary illusionism, and compositional richness to allegorical, historical, and mythological themes – a highly successful formula in 18th-century Europe.

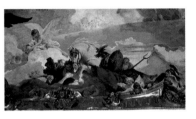

Giambattista Tiepolo, The Chariot of the Sun, detail of the fresco in the tapestry room, Clerici Palace, Milan, 1740.

▼ JOHANN MICHAEL FISCHER
(1692-1766)
German architect Fischer trained in Bohemia and created stunning religious buildings in rich Rococo forms.

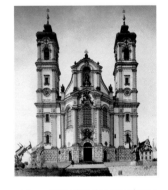

Johann Michael Fischer, Benedictine Church at Ottobeuren, Bavaria, 1748–67.

JEAN-ETIENNE LIOTARD
(1702-89)
The refined technical skill of this painter from Geneva was particularly evident in his miniatures and pastel works. Liotard painted delightful court portraits and elegant genre figurines.

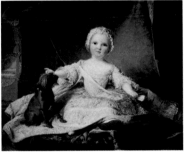

Jean-Marc Nattier, Portrait of Madame Maria Zeffirina, c.1751. Galleria degli Uffizi, Florence.

▲ JEAN-MARC NATTIER
(1685-1766)
Active in Holland and his native land of France, Nattier concentrated on portraits of female sitters, often allegorical in character and with an elegant, graceful style.

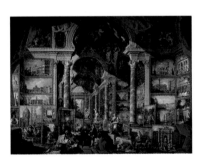

Giovan Paolo Pannini, Gallery, from Views of Modern Rome, 1759. Musée du Louvre, Paris.

▲ GIOVAN PAOLO PANNINI
(1691/92-1765)
Italian painter Pannini was also a respected stage designer. He followed the style of the Bologna-based Bibiena family, owing his fame to the views, both real and imaginary, of the Eternal City.

▼ FRANCESCO GUARDI
(1712-93)
A great interpreter of Venetian views, Guardi distanced himself from the clear precision of Canaletto and portrayed the city with a sensitivity that anticipated the Romantics.

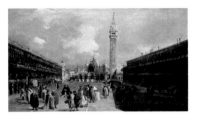

Francesco Guardi, St. Mark's Square, c.1760–65. National Gallery, London.

▼ FRANZ ANTON BUSTELLI
(1723-63)
A Swiss porcelain modeler, Bustelli was active in the porcelain factories at Neudek and the Nymphenburg Palace. He translated into china the graceful forms of the Rococo period, favoring mythological scenes and characters from the commedia dell'arte.

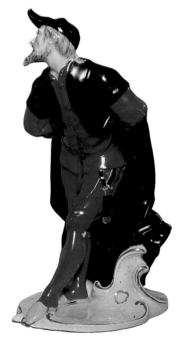

Franz A. Bustelli, Pantaloon, Nymphenburg, 1760. Victoria and Albert Museum, London.

▼ SIR JOSHUA REYNOLDS
(1723-92)
The great English painter and art theorist applied the concept of the "Grand Manner" to portraiture, ennobling his sitters while achieving results of seductive naturalism.

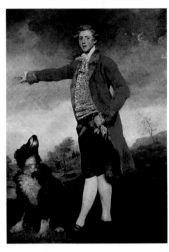

Joshua Reynolds, Portrait of John Campbell, Lord Cawdor, 1778. Cawdor Castle, Scotland.

▼ LUIGI VANVITELLI
(1700-73)
An Italian architect and painter knowledgeable in both the tradition of antiquity as well as the Baroque, Vanvitelli successfully balanced representational and functional demands in his commissions.

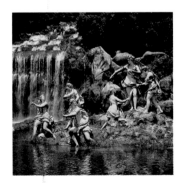

Luigi Vanvitelli, Great Cascade with Goddess Diana Bathing, 1785–89, Park of the Royal Palace of Caserta, Italy.

THE ART OF ASIA

The regional variations of Islamic art had a powerful impact on the Old World, while from India to China, ancient civilizations and new states continued to develop interesting styles of art. The golden age in Japan was renowned for its creative techniques and beautiful objects, which were to have a great influence on European art.

In the 12th century, 500 years after Muhammad's flight from Mecca to Medina, the creed of Islam extended its influence from the western region of the Mediterranean to the archipelagoes of Indonesia. Muslim art, therefore, could no longer be thought of as a regional culture, but instead could justifiably be regarded as universal.

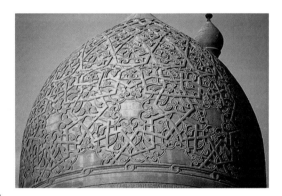

Dome of the Mausoleum of Sultan Kayt Bey, Cairo, 1472–74. This is a splendid example of the so-called "florid" dome, from one of the oldest and most important centers of Islamic art in the Mediterranean.

distant sources, and unify them. From Spain to central Asia and India, fundamental Muslim features were modified by strong regional currents. An important feature of Islamic society was the mobility of its populations. One of the duties of a Muslim was to make a pilgrimage to Mecca, and, as a consequence, the arts were nourished not only by the influences arising from foreign invasion but also by those resulting from internal migration.

ISLAMIC ART

An important characteristic of Muslim history was the frequent invasions by various tribes from the East and, in particular, from central Asia. In the 11th century, semi-nomadic tribes of Turkish origin who had converted to Islam (but nevertheless retained much of their original culture) invaded first Persia and then Anatolia. There were also incursions into Indian territories, but the outcome there was variable, due to the diverse cultures (Hinduism, Buddhism, and Jainism) that were already present. In this way, very different elements – some Chinese, others from central and southwest Asia – were blended with ancient traditions. The Islamic world was always able to assimilate artistic ideas, even from

METALWORK

Metalworking is one of the many decorative arts that has always been highly prized in the Islamic world. The transfor-

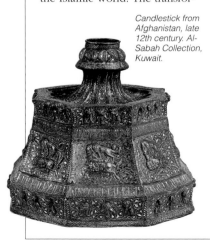

Candlestick from Afghanistan, late 12th century. Al-Sabah Collection, Kuwait.

mation of an inert metal into a glittering and precious object was a valued process. Islamic metal craftsmen, heirs to the tradition set by the Sassanid and Byzantine civilizations, among others, perpetuated and then reinterpreted these skills. The austere life led by the prophet Muhammad inhibited the use of precious materials by artists, and the amount of gold and silver inlaid in the bronze, brass, and copper articles was always extremely small. It was in order to avoid the accusation of violating Koranic precepts that the technique of damascening (ornamenting by etching or inlaying) was developed. The astonishing virtuosity of the artists is evident in articles produced by the cultivated 13th-century Mosul school, the more austere Khorasan school, 14th- and 15th-century Iranian workshops such as the Shiraz, and the Mameluke metalworking shops of Syria and Egypt. The most common objects were large bowls, jugs, pitchers, and goblets, of which fine specimens exist in various museums around the world. In a class apart are the small Veneto-Saracenic metal objects produced in Damascus and Cairo for the Western market. They are distinguished by the Latin and Arabic signatures of the artists and the coats of arms of the Venetian nobility.

THE MAMELUKE ARCHITECTURE OF CAIRO

Of all Muslim cities, Cairo was the most remarkable for its urban architecture. Although few monuments survive as examples of its development in the Fatimid (AD969–1171) and Ayyubid (1171–1250) periods, the Mameluke age (1250–1517) saw an unprecedented surge of activity that is still visible today. Many huge buildings, both secular and religious, attest to the role that architecture, in the form of mosques, *medersas* or Koranic schools, and mausoleums – and sometimes all three under the same roof – played in public life. The glory of the sultans was measured in terms of the great architectural achievements. These massive constructions were built in stone and almost all surmounted by domes, which evolved in form from the primitive ribbed and spiraled Aytimish cupola (1383) to the "florid" cupola, typified by the mausoleum of Sultan Kayt Bey. The outer northern wall of the *medersa* mosque of Sultan Hasan (1356–61) is strikingly modern and is one of the towering masterpieces of Islamic architecture. Such works played a key part in expressing the importance of Cairo in the Near East during the period of Mameluke rule.

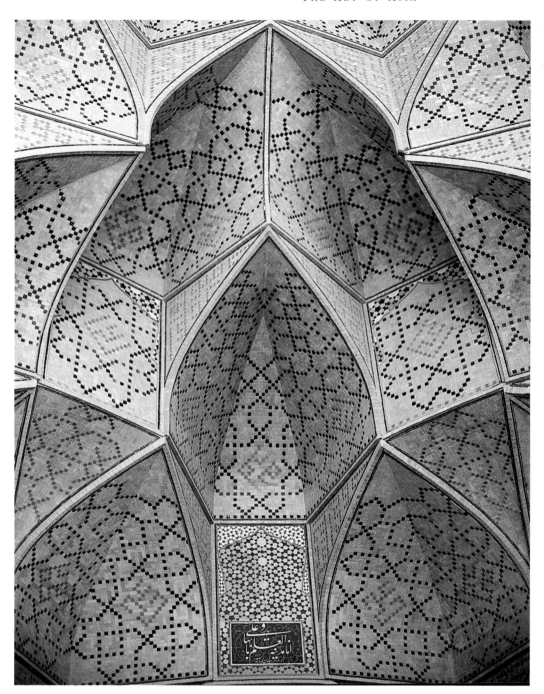

Detail from the Seljuk Friday mosque at Isfahan. The architectural complexity of the muqarnas is highlighted by the geometric pattern of the decoration.

SYRIA AND EGYPT

Syria and Egypt were governed by the Ayyubid (1171–1250) and Mameluke (1250–1517) dynasties between the 12th and early 16th century. The monuments of Damascus, the extraordinary citadels of Aleppo, and the entire urban center of Cairo (including its huge cemeteries) all date from these periods. The architecture was highly original, both in terms of military fortifications (in Syria, these were strongly affected by the architecture of the Christian Crusaders) and of mosques, palaces, baths, and caravanserais (inns where caravans stayed overnight). Black and white stone had already been widely used for portals, while *muqarnas* (honeycombed niches) were employed not only in traditional corners but also in portals and even in the outer balustrades of balconies in minarets.

The decorative arts of Syria and Egypt were equally impressive. Metalwares were often embellished with gold and silver inlays. In the Mameluke age, ornamentation featured inscriptions, applied with long strokes in flowing cursive script, alternating with heraldic motifs. The art of blown and enameled glass – popular in Syria – demonstrated supreme skill and invention. Equally skilled work was produced in textiles, and the fabulous silk materials made in the imperial factories of Damascus, Cairo, and other places in the Near East supplied a growing European market for light silks, damasks, and muslins.

RUGS AND CARPETS

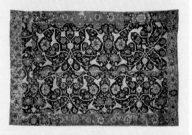

Knotted Persian rug from Herat, late 16th century. Museo Poldi Pezzoli, Milan.

The most famous of all Oriental arts linked with the Islamic tradition is undoubtedly that of knotted rug- and carpet-making. This activity is very ancient, as demonstrated by biblical references, with the oldest surviving antique specimen dating from the fifth century BC. Handmade rugs initially replaced the reed matting and animal hides of nomadic tents and gradually became more elaborate. Woven on looms in Turkey, the Caucasus, Persia, central Asia, and India, there were also workshops in Spain, North Africa, and Egypt. The early carpets were generally knotted in wool, and only a few luxury specimens were made of silk. Craftsmen used natural animal or vegetable dyes right up until the end of the 19th century. The type of knot (Turkish or Persian) involved not only the use of a particular technique but also a special iconography. Turkish rugs and carpets (and likewise those of the Caucasus and central Asia) have predominantly geometrical decorative designs and are often based on the repetition of a specific motif, known as the *gùl*, which can vary in shape and size. Colors – especially in examples of nomadic manufacture – are limited in number. Persian carpets (as in the most famous examples produced by Safavid workshops in the late 16th and 17th centuries) are notable for their floral and naturalistic patterns (including hunting subjects), numerous colors, and a detailed method, which was also imitated in India. These carpets were admired by travelers such as Marco Polo and by Renaissance artists including Ghirlandaio, Holbein, Lotto, Crivelli, Bellini, and Tintoretto.

IZNIK CERAMICS

During the Ottoman era, the ancient Byzantine city of Nicaea in Asia Minor, previously the seat of two church councils in AD325 and AD787, became an important center of ceramic production. The range of wares

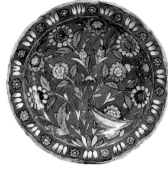

Ceramic plate from Iznik, 16th century. Al-Sabah Collection, Kuwait.

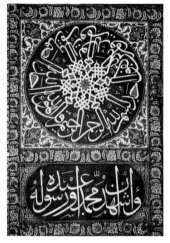

Ceramic tile from the Sokollu Mehmet Pasha mosque, Istanbul, 1571.

included both decorative ceramics and wall tiles. Apart from the abundance of local material – Nicaea enjoyed excellent supplies of clay, water, and wood – there were two other relevant factors: the entrepreneurial approach of Armenian craftsmen and the decision to imitate Chinese blue-and-white porcelain. This was particularly popular at court after the arrival in the early 16th century of many specimens for the exclusive use of the sultan. The imitation of Chinese styles was soon superseded, however, and new colors such as turquoise, sage green, and purple were introduced. However, the finest and most elegant pieces were those decorated with the pigment known as sealing-wax red, or "Armenian bole." Known in the 19th century as Rhodes-style red pottery (since it was thought to have been produced on the island of Rhodes), such wares were already being imitated in Italy in 1600. Enormous quantities of tiles were produced at Iznik on an industrial scale but with exquisitely precise craftsmanship. They were used as ornamentation for the mosques in Istanbul, which were commissioned by the great sultans and designed by the celebrated architect Sinan. The most wonderful example of this decoration, consisting of dozens of different types of tile, can be seen in the mosque of Rustem Pasha (c.1560).

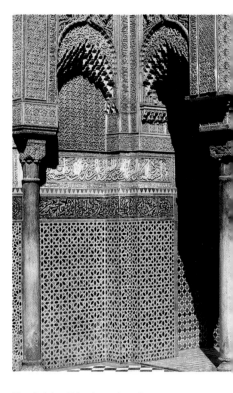

Detail of the al-'Attarin medersa Fez, Morocco, 1325. Fez was founded in 1275 as the capital of the Merinids, who centered religious instruction around the institution of the medersa.

THE TIMURIDS

Incursions from the East continued over the centuries. The Mongols of Genghis Khan (1162–1227) and his descendants invaded China and overran much of the Near East, creating an empire that extended as far as Europe. Although these vanquished peoples were rapidly converted to Islam, particular Chinese traits remained in the general Muslim artistic heritage – the lotus design, for example. Some towns were sacked and burned, never to recover, but the subsequent period of peace, described as the *pax mongolica,* witnessed intense commercial activity. Timur (1336–1405), also known as Tamerlane, set his seal on the history of the Near East at about the end of the 14th and beginning of the 15th century. He conquered vast territories and challenged the might of the growing Ottoman power in Anatolia, where he was finally defeated. The mosques and other buildings of Samarkand, Tamerlane's capital, are clad in splendid multicolored tiles – Persian in taste and style – and bear lofty double domes (a technique already employed by the Ilkhan dynasty). They provide shining examples of the opulence and ostentation of the Timurid court. The heirs of Tamerlane – Ulugh Beg, Shah Rukh, and Baysunghur – were renowned for being generous patrons and promoters of literature. The 15th century saw the production of many precious manuscripts, in particular those in which the arts of writing, illustration, and bookbinding were combined to convey an overall effect of great refinement and originality.

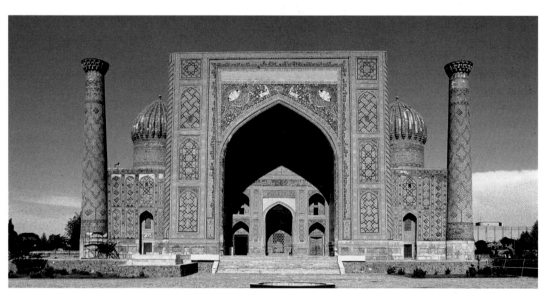

Medersa in Registan Square, Samarkand, Timurid era. This city in east Uzbekistan was Tamerlane's capital in the 14th century.

THE WESTERN MEDITERRANEAN

Western Islamic art and architecture in Morocco and Spain presents a fairly uniform pattern, as seen principally in the productions of the Merinid dynasty – notably the medersas, or theological schools, of al-'Attarin (1323–25) and Bu 'Inaniyya (1348–59) at Fez in Morocco – and those of the Nasrids in Spain, also known as the Moors. The glory of the latter dynasty (wiped out in 1492 by the definitive Christian conquest) is best exemplified by the astonishing architecture of the Alhambra in Granada. This fortified palace is laid out in distinct large areas – the public section with the Court of Myrtles; the Tower of Comares, which contains the Throne Room; and the private section, around the Court of the Lions. The courtyard is crossed by two small channels that divide the area according to the Koranic model of Paradise. Facing it are large rooms, which through the use of stucco and the arabesque display a wholly successful integration of architectural detail and fine decoration, particularly in the *muqarnas* of the domes. This art form had a great impact on European architecture and ornamentation. Initially practiced in Spain by the *mudejar* artists (Muslims working on Christian commission), it was reintroduced in the 19th century as part of the neo-Moorish style.

In the field of the decorative arts, of particular note are the lustre pottery ware of Paterna, Mislata, and Manises, the carpets known as the "carpets of the admirals" that featured heraldic motifs, and the extraordinary textiles with decorated floral and geometrical patterns that were manufactured during the Nasrid period in Granada, Alicante, and Seville. Western art was also influenced by Islam in its workings of wood, ivory, gems, and glass.

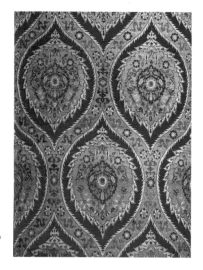

Ottoman silk cloth, 17th century. Museo del Bargello, Florence.

OTTOMAN ART

In the early 14th century, a small local dynasty of central Asian stock under the leadership of Osman ("Othman" in Arabic), gradually took control of the Near East. These were the Osmanli or Ottoman Turks, who first conquered the Balkans and then, in 1453, under Mohammed II (1432–81) defeated the Byzantines and

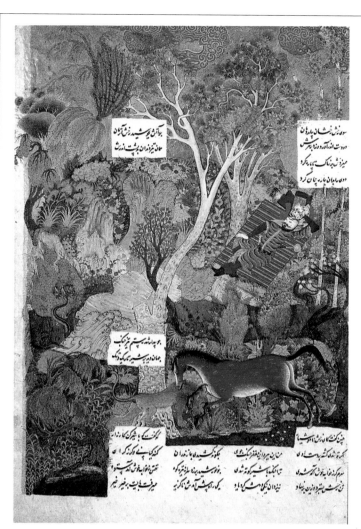

MINIATURES

Few examples of Islamic painting survive, whether on panel, canvas, or in the form of a fresco. Although the Koran does not explicitly prohibit naturalistic representations of humans, animals, and plants, tradition has always excluded such artistic forms in public places. In Muslim art, therefore, painting is represented by the art of the miniature. These works act as the illustrations to particular texts and, as such, constitute an integral part of the book in its entirety.

The style of the miniatures depended on the subject of the book – science, an epic, romance, or history. For example, scientific books were characterized by a very distinctive and traditional style. Texts were often translated from the Greek for subjects such as astronomy (for example the *Forms of the Fixed Stars* of 1009), astrology,

Miniature from the Shah-Nama *("Book of Kings") by Firdausi, probably from Tabriz, c.1500. British Museum, London.*

Miniature by Bihzad illustrating the construction of a palace, Herat, 1494. British Library, London.

medicine, herbals, and animals. The most celebrated literary epics were Persian, written by the poets Firdausi (the famous *Shah-Nama,* or "Book of Kings") and Nizami, and were illustrated from the 14th century onward. Renowned painters included Ahmad Musa and his pupil Shams-al-Din (late 14th century) and Riza-i Abbasi (late 16th century). An entirely separate genre, highly popular in the Ottoman empire, was that dealing with the genealogy of sultans. The Indian schools of miniature painting under Hindu influence, on the other hand, had their own individual styles.

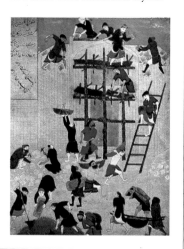

occupied Constantinople. Thanks to a succession of great sultans, in particular Suleiman the Magnificent (1520–66), the Ottoman empire extended its territories, dominating the whole of North Africa, Egypt, Syria, and the holy sites of Mecca and Medina. In the 16th century, it spread westward into Europe as far as Vienna. Although the empire was made up of many different races and had a number of principal cities, it was nevertheless centrally organized, and society was structured in a pyramidal

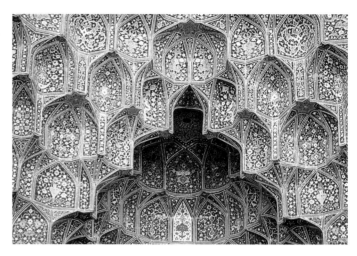

Detail of the honeycomb cells of the muqarnas *from the mosque of Imam, Isfahan.*

PERSIA AND ISLAMIC INDIA

After the turbulent period of Timurid invasions, Persia was ruled by the Safavid dynasty (1502–1722), which ushered in one of the most peaceful and prolific periods the country had ever known. The kingdom achieved a hitherto unequaled

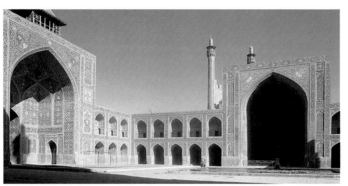

fashion with the sultan at its summit. Ottoman architecture owes most of its splendor to its greatest architect, Sinan Koca Pasha (c. 1489–1580). His designs were influenced by the Byzantine style of the Balkans and were based on a central dome, as at Shehzade (1543–48), Suleimaniyeh (1550–57) in Istanbul, and Selimiyeh (1569–75) at Edirne, with *exedrae* (recesses at the end of rooms), half-domes, and secondary domes. This wholly rational architectural model was easily recognized and exported all over the Ottoman-dominated world, from Yemen to Cairo, from Damascus to Budapest, and from Sofia to Tripoli. The centralized empire encouraged the gathering of court artists, who formed *naqqashkane* – art workshops specializing in making decorative motifs that were then applied to various media: glass, metals, ceramics (the pottery of Isnik is celebrated), and textiles that rivaled the impressive wares of Venice.

View of the mosque of Imam at Isfahan, a great monument of the Safavid era.

measure of prosperity and creativity during the first phase of the reign of Shah Tahmasp (1524–76) and then, more importantly, with Shah Abbas the Great (1571–1629) at the end of the 16th century, when the capital was moved to Isfahan. Artistic splendor is evident in the fabulous architecture of the capital (Royal Square, the Royal Pavilion of Ali Qapu, and the palaces at Chihil Sutun and Hasht Bihisht) and also in the sensual and refined art of miniature painting and carpet-making, which reached its pinnacle here. The Safavid period marks the beginning of more open relations with the West, the fruits of which were later to be developed under the Zand and Qajar dynasties, when there would also be an Achaemenid revival. The Mughal emperors (1526–1858) of central Asia likewise proclaimed themselves descendants of the

BHAG:
"PORTRAIT OF SHAH JAHAN"
From the emperor's album; ink, color, and gold on paper; 15 x 10 in (38.8 x 25.7 cm); Metropolitan Museum, New York.

This miniature is the work of a Muslim or Hindu Indian painter who worked at the court of the emperor Shah Jahan (1628–58), the fifth Moghul sovereign. The miniature portrait, which followed the example of the Persian

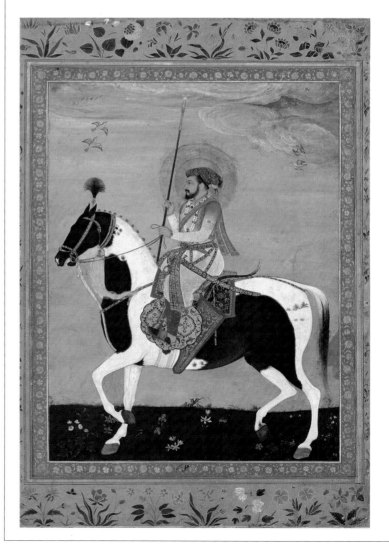

Timurids. In fact, the history of the Islamic penetration of India dates from long before this; there had already been incursions in AD711, 1001, and 1026, while in 1192 the institution of the sultanate had been established in Delhi. At various times and in various places, many local lords declared their independence, but none attained the importance and continuity of the Moghul nobility. The names of Babur, Humayun, Akbar, Jahanghir, and Shah Jahan are associated with stunning archi-

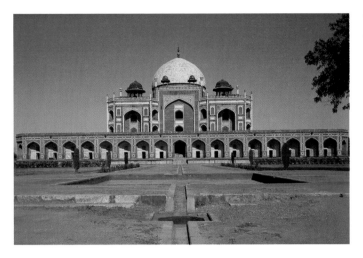

Mausoleum of the Moghul emperor Humayun at New Delhi, built between 1568 and 1580.

tectural achievements. For the Moghuls, gardens were artificial creations of primary importance. Considerable skill and immense resources went into planning formal gardens on the Persian model, such as those laid out in Kashmir, and all the great capitals were worthily embellished. Two notable examples were Fatehpur Sikri (1570–85), an extraordinary city of red

---

tradition, was extremely popular under the Islamic rule of the Moghuls and went through a phase of particular splendor in Shah Jahan's reign. The depiction of the sovereign riding a horse was a traditional subject in Asia, derived from Persian examples dating from the Sassanid era. The painted frame contains a scene occupied entirely by the figure of the emperor on horseback. The inner frame is made up of a red border speckled with delicate gold decoration. The border itself is surrounded by other bands, containing a profusion of decorative motifs found also in other parts of the picture, as on the saddle and the emperor's costume.

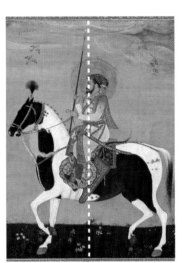

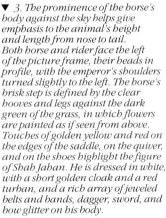

▼ *3. The prominence of the horse's body against the sky helps give emphasis to the animal's height and length from nose to tail. Both horse and rider face the left of the picture frame, their heads in profile, with the emperor's shoulders turned slightly to the left. The horse's brisk step is defined by the clear hooves and legs against the dark green of the grass, in which flowers are painted as if seen from above. Touches of golden yellow and red on the edges of the saddle, on the quiver, and on the shoes highlight the figure of Shah Jahan. He is dressed in white, with a short golden cloak and a red turban, and a rich array of jeweled belts and bands, dagger, sword, and bow glitter on his body.*

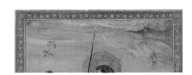

▲ *4. In the upper part of the picture, the depiction of the clouds suggests a storm, either shortly to arrive or passing high over the tranquil meadow. The point of the rider's spear punctuates this area, and the surrounding brushstrokes form rings, wisps, and knots in a mesh of lines and picturesque effects of light and shade. This creates a striking contrast to the flat, uniform style of the lower part of the picture. Another lively and realistic touch, unthinkable in other periods of Indo-Islamic art, is provided by the birds in flight below the clouds. Barely sketched, and in shades that are almost transparent against the turquoise sky, they appear distant and fleeting.*

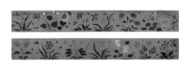

▲ *1. The figures of the horse and rider are drawn with precision and stand out clearly against the background. The lines flow smoothly, conveying the rhythmic movements and steps of the horse, subtly rendering the animal's shape. The chromatic interplay of the brownish black and white is emphasized by a continuous flow of curves and countercurves. The elasticity of the horse's shape, reinforced by its light and rhythmic step, contrasts with the stiff posture of the rider. The emperor sits upright in the saddle and gazes into the distance. The composition consists of fields of color, some of them boldly defined, others minutely decorated. The structure of the image is thus based on the opposition of the static and dynamic, the solid and the delicate.*

▲ *2. The painting, intended to glorify the Grand Moghul, is designed along a central vertical axis, highlighted by the strong oblique line of the spear. The horizon, however, is placed very low. The sky is a light turquoise color that fades upward into yellow; the clouds are simply masses of vapor, without the graphic detail of the Chinese style. These elements convey a feeling of atmospheric space and of a gentle movement of air. Around the emperor's head is a halo of gold, symbolizing his regal spirituality, a device borrowed from Buddhist art. The portrait also has some sense of depth and a rounded quality that is faintly suggestive of a Western art style, a reflection of the cosmopolitan and tolerant nature of the Grand Moghul's court.*

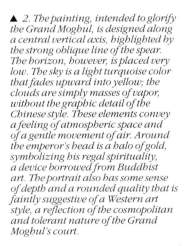

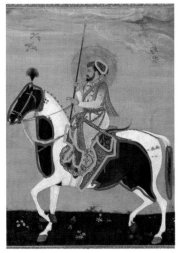

▲ *5. The upper and lower edges of the frame merit special attention. Groups of flowers decorate the golden background in a neat and harmonious arrangement. The two-dimensional treatment of the flowers does not prevent the various species from being identified. Depicted in small clumps or bunches, they show distinct characteristics. The artist uses similar colors in different areas, passing from light blues to pinks and from reds to yellows in a beautiful sequence of shapes and shades. In the variety of flowers represented, the Moghul style of painting emulates the Persian tradition. This can also be seen in the ceramic decoration of buildings. It has been verified that there were Persian artists at the Moghul court.*

sandstone built by Akbar, and the Taj Mahal (c. 1640), the white marble mausoleum erected by Shah Jahan. The magnificence of the Indian royal courts was proverbial and was reflected in all the arts, including miniatures, which were influenced by contemporary Hindu styles.

MEDIEVAL NON-ISLAMIC INDIA

A fragmented political scene, together with the spread of new Hindu movements, helped formulate two fundamental aspects of medieval art in India: first,

the varied nature of artistic trends that assumed very different forms according to each region, and, second, the growing importance of the temple and its religious sculpture. The symbolic

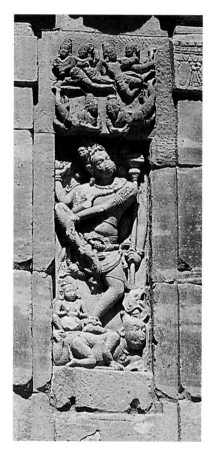

Relief of Dancing Shiva, Virupaksha temple, Pattadakal, Karnataka (formerly Mysore). This example of Western Chalukya art dates from the first half of the eighth century.

MEDIEVAL INDIAN TEMPLES

In the centuries following the Gupta period, the design of the Indian temple became increasingly complex. The most evident change was in the vestibule, which now opened to the east, projecting out of the facade and containing a number of colonnaded, covered rooms. The cubical cell of the sanctuary, on the other hand, increased in height as towers began to be built on top. The shape of the structure was either curved or resembled that of a terraced pyramid; as a

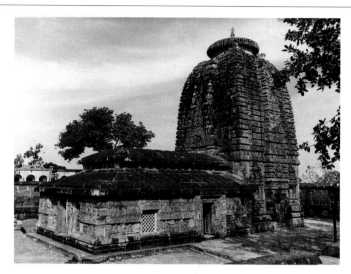

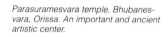
Parasuramesvara temple. Bhubanes-vara, Orissa. An important and ancient artistic center.

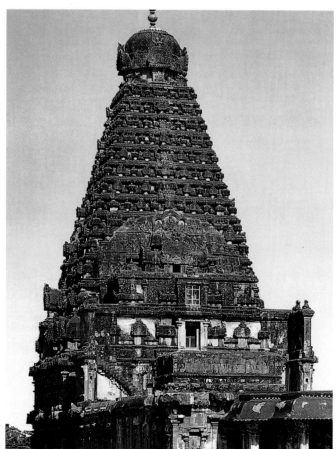

Temple of Brihadisvara at Tanjore, southwest of Madras in the state of Tamil Nadu. Dating from the 12th to the 13th century, this temple exemplifies the artistic climate of the Chola dynasty.

general rule, the former type was associated with northern Indian temples, the latter with those of the south. However, this type of construction was superseded when a pyramid-shaped roof was adopted for the projecting entrance of all Indian temples. Subsequent developments included the terraced platform on which the sanctuary was erected and the grand portal, which allowed access from the east to the terrace steps. The significance of the Indian temple would not have been complete, however, without the sculptural decoration, which covered much of the building with philoso-phical-religious imagery.

decoration of temples and the representation of the divine image became increasingly the focus of acts of ritual devotion and, at a higher level, aids to meditation.

It was in this context that the major monuments of medieval India originated. In the north-east, the most important center was Bhubanesvara, the site where many sanctuaries were built between the 7th and 12th centuries. In central-northern India, the Khajuraho temples were built during the Chandella dynasty (10th–11th century). Their sandstone walls embodied a series of sculptures featuring particu-larly striking erotic images that symbolize the bliss of union with the divine. In the south were the rock temples of Mahabalipuram, built in the Pallava era, with images inspired by mythical subjects, and the early eighth-century Kailasanatha temple at Kanchipuram, one of the dynasty's most astonishing architectural achievements. Also in southern India, the

THE SPREAD OF PĀLA ART

Although Buddhism had vanished from the rest of India, under the Pāla dynasty (8th–12th century) it endured in the northwest of the country, inspiring a school of art that excelled in stone and bronze sculpture. The tradition of pilgrimage to the main religious centers, Nalanda and Bodh Gaya, was also revived, and as a result of the contacts made by the pilgrims, Pāla art was exported to the lands of Southeast Asia, the Himalayan regions, and parts of China.

Although the results of this influence took different forms and covered different periods of time, the most profound impact was in the area of sculpture. Typical Pāla examples were recreated with great innovative flair in Burma and Indonesia and tastefully perpetuated in Tibet, where the Pāla style also extended to painting.

One of the most popular and widely adopted types of Pāla

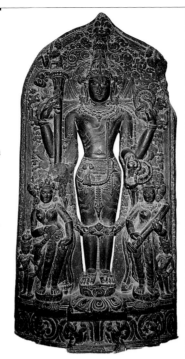

A Pāla stela with figure of Vishnu.

art was the elongated stela, rounded or pointed at the top, on which was carved the image of Buddha surrounded by the eight significant events of his life.

Early Western Chalukya dynasty introduced some original variations in the apsidal shape of the Durga cave temple at Aihole (7th–8th century). While the temple tradition continued as late as the Vijayanagar period (14th–16th century) in the south, symbolizing Hindu resistance to the advance of Islam, bronze sculpture found widespread appeal under the Chōla dynasty (9th–13th century). These small figures were veritable masterpieces in terms of technique and formal beauty. Together with the bronze statuary of the Pāla and Sena dynasties (8th–13th century) in the north, they marked the arrival of a purely secular sculptural tradition.

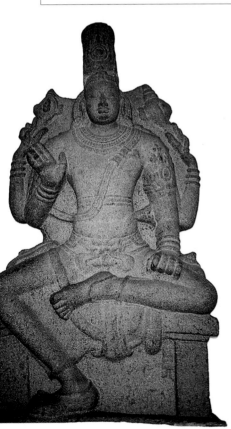

Figure of Vishnu, Pallava art from southeastern India, fifth to ninth century.

SRI LANKAN ART

The island of Ceylon (Sri Lanka) had always been influenced by the art of India. The monumental buildings of the Pollonaruwa period (8th–13th century) were made almost exclusively of brick covered with stucco. Among the many beautiful architectural features that graced the new capital were the bell-shaped stupas, Buddhist hall-temples such as the Lankatilaka, and circular

Detail of the sculptural decoration at the circular temple of Vatadage. This is an excellent example of Pollonaruwa art from northwestern Sri Lanka.

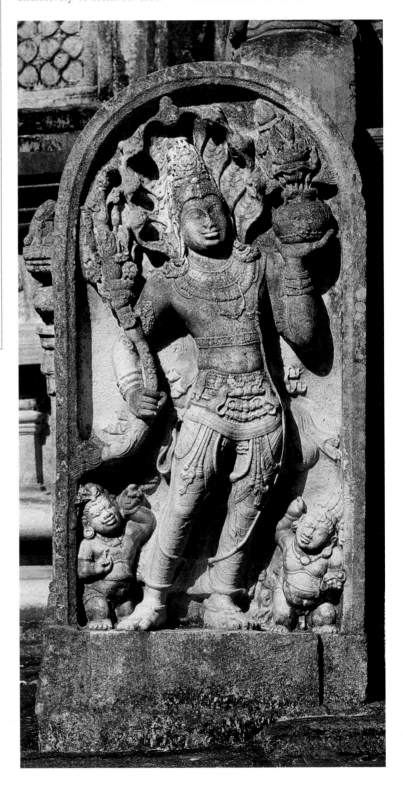

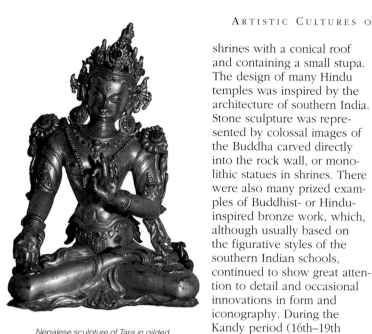

Nepalese sculpture of Tara in gilded bronze, 17th century. Museum of Art, Bombay. Despite the isolation of the Himalayan region, its art was predominantly influenced by Indian art, Buddhism, and Hinduism. Occasionally, the presence of more ancient polytheistic and animistic forms was evident.

shrines with a conical roof and containing a small stupa. The design of many Hindu temples was inspired by the architecture of southern India. Stone sculpture was represented by colossal images of the Buddha carved directly into the rock wall, or monolithic statues in shrines. There were also many prized examples of Buddhist- or Hindu-inspired bronze work, which, although usually based on the figurative styles of the southern Indian schools, continued to show great attention to detail and occasional innovations in form and iconography. During the Kandy period (16th–19th century), considerable progress was made in the decorative arts using ivory, wood, and precious metals. The objects created were often derived from local tradition.

NEPALESE ART

The art of the Himalayan regions was, to a large extent, founded upon contacts with Indian culture, and, as with Indian art, it was of religious inspiration. Distinctive characteristics were present, but it remained the historical and cultural expression of a very fragmented region. Nepalese architecture produced examples of Hindu temples with a number of wooden roofs alongside stupas – similar in type to the ancient forms at Sañchi, with a hemispherical dome topped by a cubical structure, on which the eyes of Buddha were painted. The Gupta style was the principal – though not the sole – source of Nepalese sculpture and was represented by Hindu and Buddhist works in stone and metal.

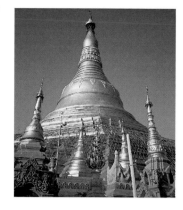

The large bell-shaped stupa of the Shwedagon Pagoda at Rangoon.

THE ART OF BURMA AND THAILAND

After the fall of the Burmese capital of Pagan in 1287, artistic activity in successive dynasties (14th–19th century)

TIBETAN PAINTED SCROLLS

In addition to its architecture and sculpture, the art of Tibet is remarkable for its *thang-kas* – paintings on cotton in tempera colors. The most frequent subjects are the divinities of the Tibetan Buddhist (Lamaist) pantheon, the masters of the Tibetan sects, and the *mandalas*. The latter are circular diagrams representing the cosmos and constituting one of the most sophisticated aids to Buddhist meditation. From the outer square, the devotee passes gradually from one enclosed space to the next, arriving finally at the center of the *mandala*, where the image of a divinity resides, the symbol of the learning thus achieved. The paintings are difficult to date on the grounds of style, not only because their religious nature meant artists always needed to follow strict artistic rules but also because of the widespread custom of faithfully copying old paintings. Producing a copy of an image is very common in Oriental art, and the reproduction is never considered inferior. The most important factor is that the replica should be faithful to the original in all respects.

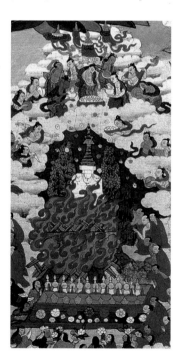

Detail of a Tibetan thang-ka showing Buddha on the funeral pyre, 19th century. Musée Guimet, Paris.

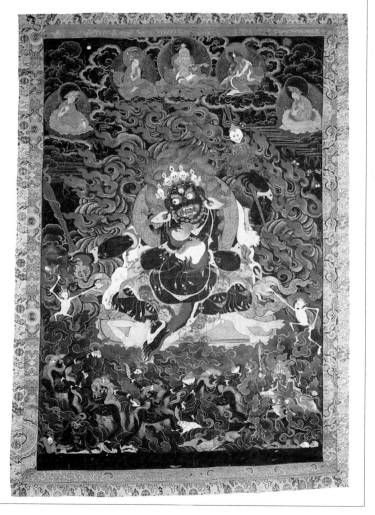

Tibetan thang-ka showing the fierce deity Mahakala, 19th century. British Museum, London.

was associated with attempts to restore Burma's unity. In the ancient 14th-century capitals of Sagaing and Ava and the later capitals of Amarapura (18th century) and Mandalay (19th century), there are still remains of some of the royal monuments, including the palace and tombs in Mandalay. The prevalent form of architecture was the bell-shaped stupa (such as Rangoon's Shwedagon Pagoda), built on an octagonal, denticulated plan and tapering upward from its terraced base. Buddhist sculpture in wood, bronze, and gilded lacquer focused mainly on images of Buddha that were sometimes adorned with royal insignia. The ancient pictorial tradition of Pagan was nevertheless continued in the wall-paintings that can still be seen at Sagaing (17th century) and Amarapura (19th century). The second half of the 13th century saw the rise of the earliest Thai kingdoms, which adopted the names of their capitals, Sukhotai and Chiang Mai. Influenced by the art of

The Naga temple and the "Dated" temple in the Panataran enclosure, eastern Java, 14th century. In the course of the 15th and 16th centuries, Java was converted to Islam, and the grand Indonesian architecture, rich in decoration and sculpture, was no longer built. The two temples pictured were both dedicated to Shiva.

SUKHOTAI AND AYUTTHAYA SCULPTURE

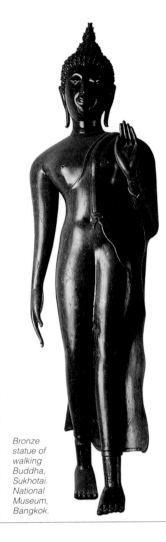

Bronze statue of walking Buddha, Sukhotai. National Museum, Bangkok.

The principal styles of Siamese bronze statuary are found in works from the cities of Sukhotai and Ayuthaya. The former, dating from the 14th century, defined an image of Buddha that was perhaps the most evocative of all representations of the Master as *maha-purusa* (superior essence). Particularly in its statues of the "standing Buddha," a form of iconography fairly common throughout Southeast Asia, the art of Sukhotai overcomes the restrictions imposed by the material and conveys the spirituality of the image in a wonderfully ethereal way. The art of Ayutthaya, in the

so-called U Thong style (13th–15th century), represented the Buddha occasionally in a seated position, touching the ground with his right hand. The iconography, known as *Maravijaya* ("the victory over Mara") refers to the episode of the victory of the Master over Mara, the tempter deity, and the attainment of illumination. The U Thong style was of composite character, with clear references to both Khmer and Sukhotai art, featuring smooth surfaces and fluid contours.

Three statues of the Maravijaya Buddha (the victorious Buddha), Wat Pradu Songtham temple, Thailand.

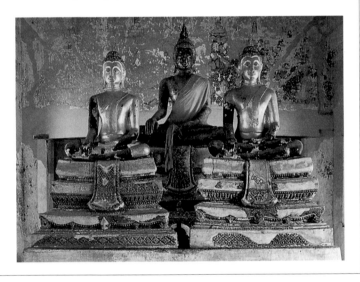

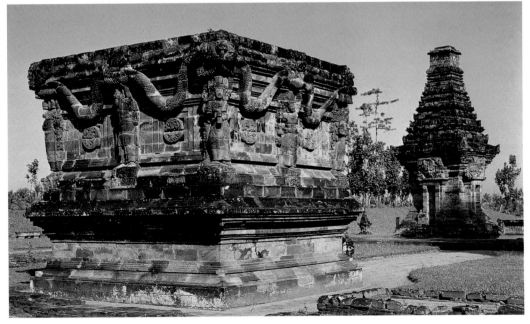

Sri Lanka, the Sukhotai period marked the beginning of their art and the birth of architectural and sculptural styles. It provided important models for the later development of Ayutthaya art between the 14th and 18th centuries. Architecture, in brick and laterite, consisted of bell-shaped stupas with differently styled base-platforms, monasteries, and reliquary towers. The latter, square and denticulate in shape, were built on a stepped base and surmounted by a tall, curved dome. In contrast, however, the art of Chiang Mai was founded on the tradition of the oldest cities of Thailand and was characterized by an individual "northern" style.

YUAN, MING, AND QING CHINA

Zhao Mengfu (1254–1322) was one of the first generation of Yuan painters. Heavily influenced by the ancient masters of Chinese art, he attempted to rediscover the spirit of the past and recreate it in his work. Zhao's austere style, which appears simple and lacking in precision, was in strong contrast to that of the academic painters with their brilliant colors and virtuoso forms of decoration. Following on from Zhao, the "four great masters" of the Yuan period – the landscape artists Huang Gong-wang, Ni Zan, Wu Zhen, and Wang Meng – became very active, mainly in the south. They specialized in

CALLIGRAPHY

Calligraphy has always been one of the most important art forms in China, and the different styles have been classified rigorously since ancient times. Within this medium, the artist traditionally expressed the energies of the natural world by means of gestures: the pen acted as an extension of the human body, providing the instrument through which these forces could be released. The formulation of a single character went beyond its mere graphic meaning, transforming it into a pure, self-sufficient entity. It was the *changli*, or constant principle inherent in all natural beings, that gave the artist the instantaneous ability to create this. Fundamental to the art of calligraphy is the belief that artistic expression is an immediate, apparently spontaneous act, although in reality it entails much thought and inner preparation. This way of thinking was nurtured and influenced by *chan*

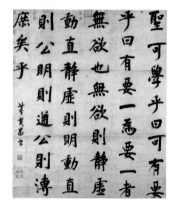

Quotation from an essay by Dong Qichang (1555–1636), ink on paper.

Buddhism (*Zen* in Japanese), with its principle of illumination and by the ancient Taoist theories concerning the intuitive comprehension of the essence of the perceptible world. There is perhaps no other art that expresses so freely the inner feelings of the artist and yet remains contained within such strict rules.

Detail of poetry by Mi Fu (1052–1108), ink on silk.

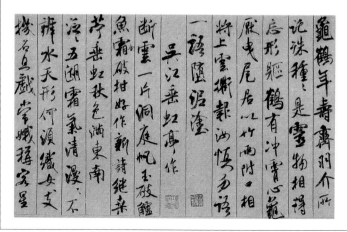

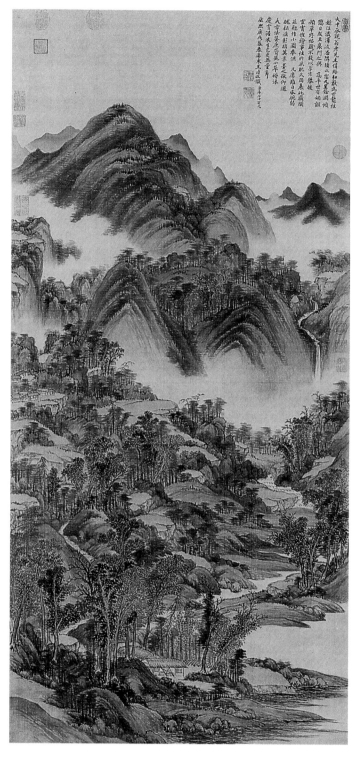

Wang Shimin (1592–1680), Landscape, ink and color on silk.

"literate" painting, and their work combined the talents of the painter, poet, and calligrapher. Huang Gong-wang (1269–1354) used his brush with a light touch to create luminous atmospheres, adding soft, delicate shadows in ink. More eccentric than Huang but still a follower of Taoist doctrines, Ni Zan (1301–74) communicated a sense of mystery and serene detachment from worldly reality in his works. During the Ming period (1368–1644), artists turned their attention to an extremely broad range of

CHINESE LACQUERWARE

Lacquer is a resin extracted from the tree *Rhus verniciflua* and is used as a preservative to cover materials such as wood or bamboo. It can be applied in an almost limitless number of coats, a lengthy process because each coat must dry slowly in a humid atmosphere before another can

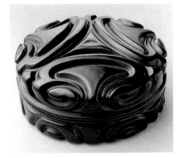

Carved lacquer box, dating from 1272–1368.

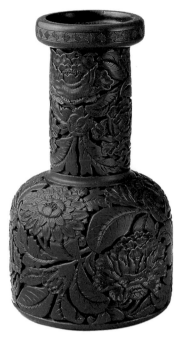

Carved lacquer vase with floral decoration, c.1403–24.

be applied. Used since the Shang era, lacquer was already widely favored during the Han dynasty in the production of beautifully painted objects, such as those found in the tomb of the marchioness of Dai at Mawangdui. Carved lacquerware was produced from the 12th century onward. This form was most highly developed during the Yuan and Ming periods and was to gain special recognition in the 18th century during the reign of the emperor Qianlong (1736–95). As the piece is carved, the varying shades of each layer of lacquer are revealed. Geometrical and floral motifs were most common in this work, but there were also landscapes and scenes of everyday life in gardens and pavilions. As on porcelain objects, the dragon also featured frequently.

DECORATIVE MOTIFS

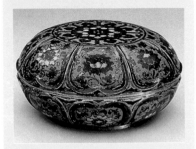

Round cloisonné box with lotus motifs, 1450–56.

The most common subjects in the decoration of porcelain, textiles, lacquer, and *cloisonné* are flowers, fruit, real and mythical birds and animals, and, more rarely, landscape. The designs are found in various combinations that symbolize messages of good fortune or traditional and familiar Chinese proverbs. The decorated surface is often broken up into separate areas of different designs, none of which is necessarily connected to the next. In works of art and on craft objects, the dragon (*long* in Chinese) is often encountered. The appearance of this composite creature, sometimes winged with a snakelike body covered with scales and hooked claws, was a sign of good luck. The emblem of power and dignity in historic times, it later came to represent the country itself. The feminine counterpart of the dragon, also considered to bring good fortune and symbolizing the empress, is the phoenix (*feng* or *fenghuang*) – a fabulous winged creature that embodies all the virtues of the peacock, the crane, and the pheasant. The most common decorative flowers are the lotus, the peony, the chrysanthemum, and the cherry blossom, the "flowers of the four seasons." Each symbolizes a particular virtue and may be used singly or in a group.

Shen Zhou (1427–1509), Strolling with a Walking Stick, c.1485, ink on paper. Like the other panels on these pages, Shen Zhou's work is large in scale: 62½ x 28½ in (59 x 72.2 cm).

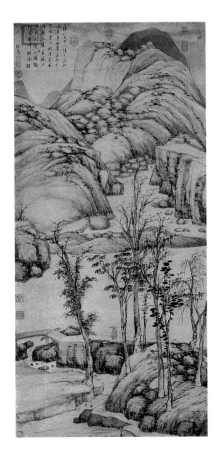

styles and traditions. Dong Qichang (1555–1636), a talented painter and art critic, theoretically subdivided Chinese painting into two distinct categories: the "northern" consisted of artists linked with the academy and court, while freer and more individual "southern," or scholar-painters, originated in the Tang era with Wang Wei, and which was considered by him to be the superior of the two. The two main schools of the Ming period, that of Zhe in Zhejiang and Wu in Jiangsu, subscribed respectively to the northern and southern trends. Tai Jin (1388–1462), a professional painter and chief exponent of the Zhe school, continued the tradition of the Song Academy, drawing particular inspiration from Ma Yuan and Xia Gui. Shen Zhou (1427–1509), founder of the Wu school of Suzhou, and his pupil Wen Zhengming (1470–1559) were, for the most part, the best examples of scholar-painters. Among the more notable scholar-painters of the succeeding Qing dynasty

(1644–1912) was Hong Ren (1610–64), who was renowned for the pure line work of his ethereal landscapes, reminiscent of Ni Zan. The style of Gong Xian (1620–89) was completely different. His scenes, bathed in an aura of mystery, were realized with thick brushstrokes of dark ink, almost tragic in tone. While Zhu Da (Bada Shanren, c.1616–1705)

Ni Zan, Pavilion Among the Pine Trees, ink on silk panel, 1354.

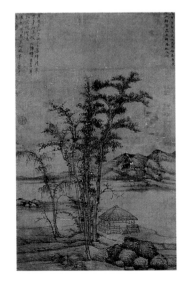

and Shi Tao (c.1641–1710) represented the more eccentric and individualistic aspects of Qing painting, traditional painting was exemplified by the "four Wangs": Wang Shi-min (1592–1680), Wang Jian (1598–1677), Wang Hui (1632–1717), and Wang Yuanqi (1642–1715). They were conservative rather than innovative, paying tribute to the great masters of the past.

KOREAN ART OF THE YI DYNASTIES

Despite the transfer of the capital city to Seoul in 1394, the invention of the Korean alphabet (1443), and the official repudiation of Buddhism in favor of neo-Confucianism, landscape painting in the 15th century was still influenced by the Chinese traditions of the northern Song. However, it was not long before the so-called Li-Kuo manner became modified by the adoption of styles that reflected the characteristics of the Wu school (of southern Song derivation) of Ming China. The representation of animals and bamboos

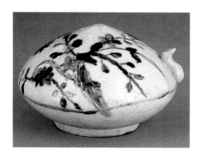

Small water container, blue-and-white porcelain, Choson dynasty, 15th-century. National Museum, Seoul.

was accomplished with vigorous, decisive brush-strokes and a strong color contrast that placed emphasis on height rather than depth. The invasions of the Japanese in 1592 and the Manchus of the Qing Dynasty in 1627 provoked a patriotic reawakening and was the source of a new artistic wave that rejected the Chinese traditions. The realistic painting of Chong Son (1676–1759) was followed by that of the Kim Hong-do genre (1745–c. 1814), which depicted scenes of peasants and craftsmen. Today, these paintings provide a valuable source of information about the customs, clothing, and native landscape of the time.

THE GOLDEN AGE OF JAPANESE ART: KAMAKURA PERIOD

After the prosperity and elegance of the Heran era (AD794–1184), a climate of growing tension and widespread disorder heralded inevitable change. Between 1185 and 1192, the increasing

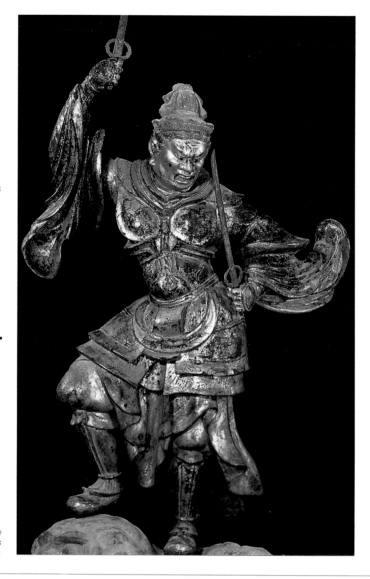

Knijiki-do, Sculpture of Ten, one of the Celestial Kings defending Buddhism. This work has now been restored in Tokyo.

KOREAN PAINTING OF THE YI DYNASTIES

The adoption of Confucianism as official doctrine during the Choson dynasty (1392–1410) had a powerful impact upon Buddhist painting. Although Buddhism continued to be popular for some time, it never again enjoyed royal favor and did not regain the position of artistic predominance it had possessed during the Koryo period. Despite the fact that they were undoubtedly familiar with the paintings of the Chinese court artists still working in the southern Song style, Korean painters of the 16th century developed their own landscape style, concentrating on wide views rather than foreground

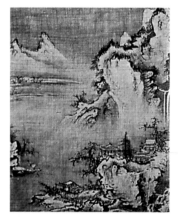

Panels from Landscapes of the Four Seasons, ink and color on silk, 14 x 11¼ in (35.2 x 28.5 cm), Choson dynasty, 15th century. National Museum of Art, Seoul. Attributed to Ahn Kyon, this work shows the influence of the Zhe school and Ming art, though the strong, fragmentary design reveals the native style.

subjects. The broad landscapes, punctuated by minute details, had an impact on Japanese ink painting of the Muromachi period (1338–1573).

The long pictorial tradition of the Zhe school, which had molded many court artists in the early Ming period, was certainly important to artists such as Kang Hui-an (1419–64). The strong, confident ink strokes, the fine treatment of rocks and precipices, and the sharp contrast between the images and the pale background, as used in *Sage Resting on a Rock*, are good examples of what came to be defined as the style of the Korean Zhe school.

The appearance of a new style known as *chingjong sansu* (realistic landscape), pioneered

by Chong Son (1676–1759), marked the transition toward a more overtly nationalistic form of painting. Another genre much to Korean taste was that of Sin Yun-bok (mid-13th century) and of Kim Hong-do (1745–c. 1814), who endeavored to portray the upper and working classes respectively. The work of Kim Tu-ryang (1696–1763) likewise stemmed from direct observation, according to a practice that was probably derived from the *silhak* movement (pragmatic school of thought). One pictorial form succeeded another throughout the 18th and 19th centuries, with such artists as Kim Chong-hui (1786–1857) and Hong Se-sop (1832–84) helping to continue the development of a truly indigenous style.

militarization of the provincial aristocracy and the open conflict among the great families and religious leaders caused the political power to shift from the Kansai region in the Kyoto area to Kamakura in the Kanto region.
Although Kyoto remained the seat of imperial power and the country's cultural and artistic center, the control of the nation was effectively handed over to the new military governor – the *bakufu* – and to the *shogun* (commanders-in-chief), who were to retain power until the 19th century. The Buddhist clergy, showing both political and religious initiative, continued to patronize and inspire the arts. Buddhist architecture and sculpture of the early Kamakura period were devoted to reconstruction and renovation following the destruction caused by natural disasters and civil wars. Though some artists reverted to the plastic art forms of the Nara period (AD710–794), great sculptors such as Kaikei (1185–1220) and Unkei (1148–1223) developed the technique of *yosegizukuri* – using separate blocks of wood to create large sculptures – as is shown in, for example, the Todaiji monastery and the Kofukuji at Nara. They also introduced technical innovations such as *gyokugan*, the

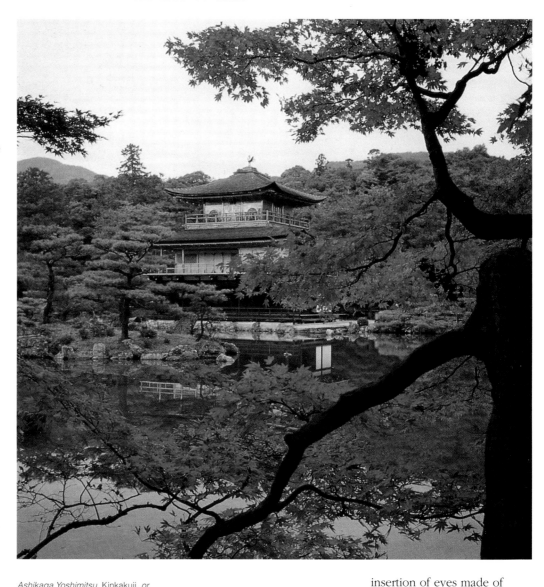

Ashikaga Yoshimitsu, Kinkakuji, or Golden Pavilion, Rokuonji, Kyoto, late 14th century. .

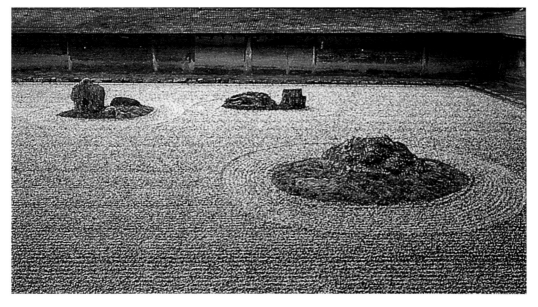

Ryoanji dry garden (kare sansui), Kyoto, 16th century. This famous dry garden is attributed to Soami.

insertion of eyes made of crystal. The sculptures of *chinzo* (religious personalities) and warriors were lauded for being very true to life.
While the iconography of esoteric Buddhism and its various cults continued with the standard forms, such as the symbolically complex *mandalas*, the rise of new religious cults and the Zen sect stimulated a fresh approach to representation. In secular art, the *amato-e* tradition continued, with illustrations of tales (*mono-gatari*), historical accounts (*rekishi monogatari*), and stories of war, uprisings, and diaries (*nikki*). The *History of the Heiji Era* ("*Heiji mono-gatari emaki*"), recounting the 12th-century battles fought at Kyoto for the succession to the

PRINTS OF THE FLOATING WORLD

The peace and prosperity of the Edo (or Tokugawa) period, the development of a wealthy merchant class, and the shifting of political power from Kyoto to Edo all helped create a society based on pleasure, with activities revolving around social centers and the *kabuki* theater. The world of the courtesan inspired the painting of feminine beauty (*bijin ga*), with emphasis on portraits of individual women and on the splendor of the kimono. The innovative approach of the theatrical prints of Katsukawa Shunsho (1726–92) paved the way for the experimental work of Katsukawa Shun'ei (1762–1819), the Utagawa school – directed by

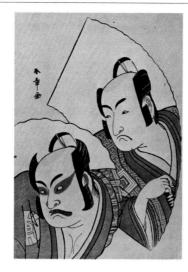

Katsukawa Shunso, Matataro IV, The Actors Ishikawa Mon no Suke II and Bando. *The portraits are positioned between two fan shapes.*

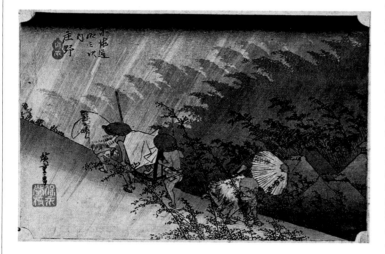

Ando Hiroshige, Sudden Rain Shower at Shono, *one of 53 prints from* Fifty three Stages of the Tokaido Road, *1833–34.*

Toyokuni (1769–1825) – and the original works of Toshusai Sharaku (active 1794–95). Derived from genre painting (*fuzokuga*), the prints of the "floating world" (*ukiyo-e*) took their name from the nature of the subject matter, which focused on leisure activities, sensual delights, the rules of etiquette, and refined taste. Often equated with themes such as glory, fame, and beauty, the floating world did not represent an escape from everyday life but a way of life in itself. The meaning and the characters with which the name *ukiyo-e* were written were

the 17th century, as well as the line engravings of secular subjects, an activity that has evolved to this day. After the initial black-and-white prints (*sumizuri*) of Moronobu (1618-94), the first color, red, was introduced, followed in 1710 by yellow and green. At times the color, particularly black, was mixed with lacquer (*urushi*) or glue to obtain a thicker, shinier medium. The application of several different colors began in about 1764, with different blocks for each color. Suzuki Harunobu (1725–70) perfected this technique in his "brocaded prints" (*nishiki-e*) of beautifully elegant women.

Torii Kiyonaga (1752–85) achieved a delicate balance between the worlds of reality and imagination by gradually elongating the female figure. With his attentive eye, Kitagawa Utamaro (1735–1806) captured the details of life in the Yoshiwara in his portrayals of archetypal feminine beauty. Katsushika Hokusai (1760–1849) embarked on his great landscape series, *Thirty-six Views of Mount Fuji* and One *Hundred Views of Mount Fuji* (1830–32 and c.1834–40), and Ando Hiroshige (1797–1858) depicted the landscapes along the famous highway linking Kyoto and Edo in his *Fifty three Stages of the Tokaido Road* (1833–34).

changed in the 17th century from the Buddhist understanding of *ukiyo* as the "floating world" to that of the more specifically erotic "world of pleasures." The districts catering for such pleasures – Yoshiwara in Edo, Shimabara in Kyoto, and Shinmachi in Osaka – were authorized by the shogunate government and became popular centers of social activity. The introduction of woodengraving in about the eighth century was principally concerned with the printing of Buddhist texts, but later, from the 15th century onward, production also consisted of illustrations for stories and adventures (*otogi zoshi*). These were the precursors of the illustrated stories and novels of

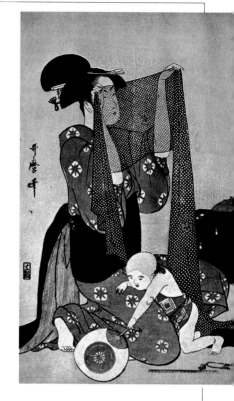

Kitagawa Utamaro, Women Making Clothes (one of three panels). *The influence of Utamaro reached the Western art world.*

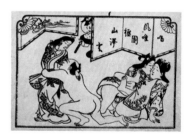

Hishikawa Moronobu, Three Couples. *This artist was the first great master of ukiyo-e.*

Katsushika Hokusai, View on a fine breezy day, *from* Thirty Six Views of Mount Fuji.

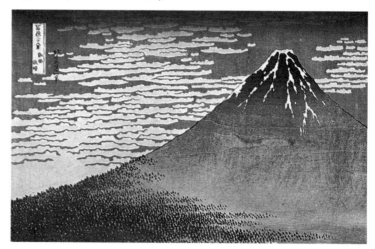

throne, constitutes one of the greatest examples of Kamakura pictorial narrative. The accuracy and faithfulness of the illustrations make it also a particularly important record of contemporary costume.

MUROMACHI PERIOD

Initially, the accession of the shogunate of the Ashikaga family (1334–1573) caused a rift within the imperial family and the division into the so-called southern and northern dynasties (Nanbokucho). Established at Muromachi, the shogunate built temples, towns, and palaces and established official relations with Yuan and Ming China.
The extravagant, ostentatious nature of the arts of this period was in keeping with the wish to display outward signs of prosperity in the home. The shogunate felt a need to exhibit its wealth as a sign of power in its confrontations with the increasingly rich and numerous feudal lords, or *daimyo*.
In the field of architecture, Ashikaga Yoshimitsu attempted to combine the residential (*shinden-zukuri*) and more conventional warrior (*buke-zukuri*) styles in the famous Golden Pavilion, or *Kinkajuki*, of 1397. Ashikaga Yoshimasa (1434–90) repeated

Sesshu Toyo, Landscape, *ink on paper. National Museum, Tokyo. This expressive work has been achieved with the minimum of materials.*

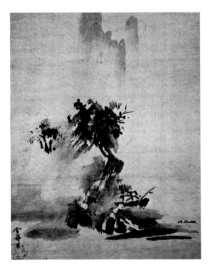

the experiment just as elegantly in the Silver Pavilion, or *Ginkakuji*. Both were originally intended as residences but were subsequently transformed into Buddhist temples. The spread of Zen Buddhism and the associated use of tea as a stimulant during long hours of meditation popularized this drink to such an extent that its consumption came to be accepted as an art form known as the *cha no yu* (tea ceremony). The drinking of tea was carried out in idyllic surroundings, accompanied by objects of worship, flower arrangements (*ikebana*), and delicate paintings in ink. The ceremony took place in simple, austere buildings, such as a pavilion or teahouse situated in a beautifully tended garden. The contemplation of the garden had inspired a new type of architecture, known as *shoin-zukuri* (studio), with wide verandas looking out over enchanting lakes. The Zen garden was a small space in which all the natural elements were gathered together. Water was replaced by sand and gravel to create a dry landscape (*kare sansui*), of which one of the most famous examples is the Ryoanji in Kyoto.
The aesthetic aspect of nature in all its harmony and proportion was the central subject of the priest-painter Sesshu Toyo (1420–1506). With unrivaled mastery of the brush, he applied a Japanese interpretation to the technique of handling space, as proposed by Chinese painting of the time. Three generations of eclectic artists, Noami (1397–1471), Geiami (1431–85), and Soami (died 1525) – painters, poets, garden architects, masters of the tea ceremony, and shogunate councilors – continued the tradition of sketching in ink, focusing on naturalistic subjects. Sesson Shukei (1504–89) applied the same treatment to imaginary landscapes, yet in a far more lyrical style.
The Azuchi-Momoyama period (1574–1614), with its continual

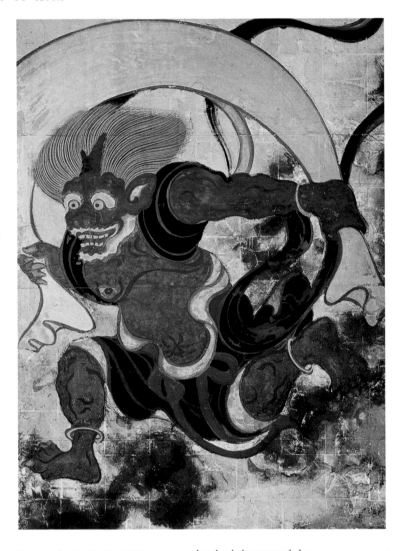

Tawaraya Sotatsu, The God of Wind, *(detail of screen), color on a gold background. Kenninji, Kyoto. In this dynamic work, the artist juxtaposes small and large areas of color.*

struggles over control of the country and led by Oda Nobunaga (1534–82) and Toyotomi Hideyoshi (1536–98), saw the continuation of the Kamakura tradition of building fortified residences – a trend reinforced by the spread of firearms and the arrival of the first Europeans in about 1543. Increasingly, art became a means of demonstrating political power, and the castle, with its complex and effective fortifications, frescoes, and paintings on screens and sliding doors, became testimony to this show of strength. The appointment of Tokugawa Ieyasu to the shogunate in 1603 put an end to the wars

that had devastated the country for decades and ushered in the longest period of peace that Japan had ever experienced, known as the Edo period (1603–1867). The refined simplicity of the Imperial Pavilion of Katsura (begun in 1620) contrasted with the taste for extravagant decoration, evident in the mausoleum of Ieyasu at Nikko (1634–36). In painting, various styles and influences went hand in hand; this was demonstrated by the styles of the Rinpa school of Ogata Korin (1658–1716) and Sakai Hoitsu (1761–1828), the naturalism of Maruyama Okyo (1733–95), the Chinese-inspired *nanga* or "Southern" painting of Ike Taiga (1723–76) and Yosa Buson (1716–83), and the woodblock prints of supple women and famous actors from Edo (modern Tokyo).

PRE-COLUMBIAN ART

During the early years of the colonization of the Americas, Europeans were confronted with flourishing civilizations that revealed a very advanced level of cultural development. The highly impressive artistic works of these native peoples ranged from monumental stone temples to extremely refined and original goldwork.

The American continent had evolved its own cultures and powerful empires prior to the arrival of the Spaniards in 1492. Europeans, represented by the wealthy, dominant monarchies as well as the humble colonists, destroyed, destabilized, and transformed the peoples of the Americas and their cultures. The nomadic tribal cultures of the great plains are not as well documented because of the perishable nature of their goods.

However, many of the material cultures of Mexico, Guatemala, and the Central Andes have survived, leaving spectacular ruins and artifacts.

THE ART OF MESOAMERICA

Mesoamerica, or Middle America, is the term recognized by geographers and archaeologists to describe the vast territory extending from central Mexico to the western regions of Honduras and El Salvador. The highly developed civilizations of these areas share a common heritage, evolved from what is regarded as the "mother culture" of the Americas, the Olmec civilization, which existed between 1700 and 400BC. The development of agriculture in Mesoamerica led to the formation of simple village communities, which, in the course of time, became increasingly complex. Their development culminated in the appearance of the so-called "high culture" of the Olmecs, who occupied a territory along the coastline of the Gulf of Mexico. Artists and craftsmen found aesthetic expression in the creation of works that often served as offerings to their deities, providing a means of placating the gods and exorcising the difficulties of everyday life through worship.

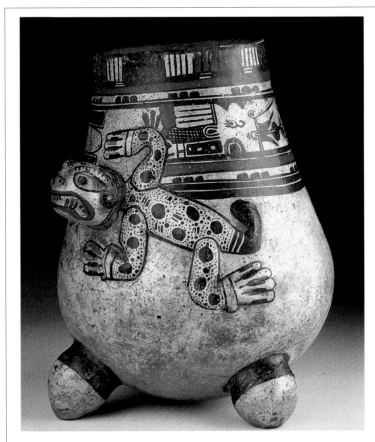

Polychrome tripod vase with a jaguar, Gran Nicoya, c.1000–1350. National Museum, Costa Rica.

THE LAND BETWEEN TWO OCEANS

The long land-bridge that links the two Americas, separating the cultures of Mesoamerica to the north from those of the Andes to the south, exhibits an extremely rich and complex history of archaeology and art. In fact, it may be regarded both as a meeting and dispersal point of diverse traditions. Mesoamerican cultures influenced an area consisting of El Salvador and Honduras in the north to western Nicaragua and Nicoya, Costa Rica, in the south. Painting and sculpture were integrated in pottery, with receptacles being decorated with representations of animals and divinities related to the Mesoamerican pantheon. In sculpture, there were gigantic statues of humans standing over

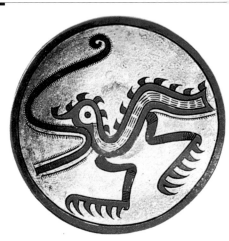

Cup with polychrome decoration, Coclé style, Panama.

animals and tables for grinding maize *(metates),* giving an impression of vigor and realism. The working of jade was also important. Eastern Nicaragua, Costa Rica (except for Nicoya), and Panama, on the other hand, were more closely related to the South American cultural traditions. In ceramics, the *Coclé*

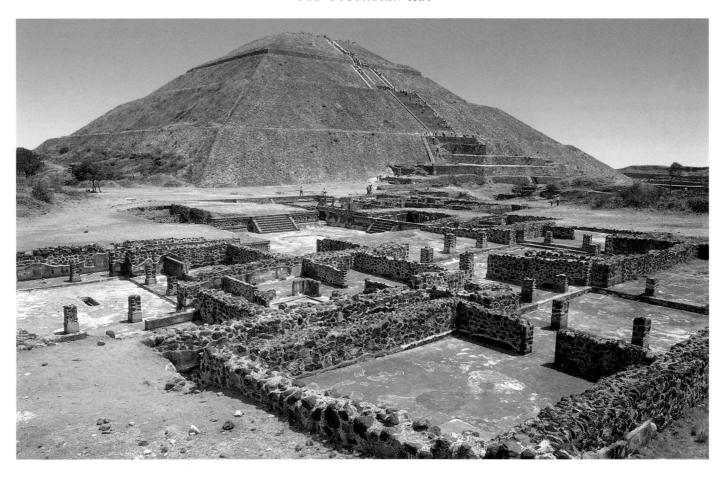

Pyramid of the Sun, Teotihuacán, Mexico.

(Panama) style of pottery is renowned for its exuberant colors, while in Costa Rica, ovoid multicolored vessels, with feline heads and legs in relief, became the most common form of pottery. Goldwork was also highly developed, similar both in technique and form to that of Colombia.

Metate in volcanic stone, first to fifth century AD. National Museum, Costa Rica.

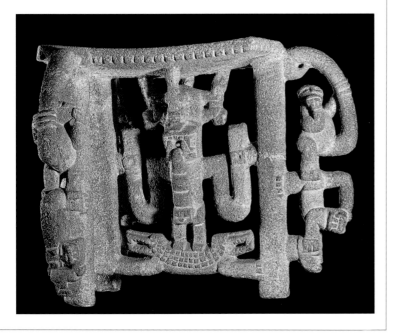

In the valley of Mexico, art objects were still confined to female terracotta figurines associated with fertility rites. The Olmecs, on the other hand, had already mastered certain techniques to produce works that would endure in Mesoamerica for centuries, notably ceremonial platforms, temple pyramids, glyphic writing, stone sculpture, and the ritual calendar. Sculpture often took the form of gigantic monolithic heads realistically portraying eminent persons, until the culture declined in about the fourth century BC. A more mature expression of art is revealed by the highly developed cultures of the Classic Period (AD250–900). This stage of development saw the growth of the great city of Teotihuacán in the valley of Mexico, the largest metropolis on the entire American continent. Buildings, wall-paintings, and ceramics from the city reveal a society characterized by intense religious activity and a serene devotion to the gods. The Zapotec culture of Oaxaca is deservedly considered important, not only for its monumental architecture and its numerous stelae but also for the complex iconography found on terracotta funerary urns. The Totonacs, who settled along the Gulf coast, skillfully fused various cultural

Colossal monolithic head in basalt, Olmec culture, Mexico.

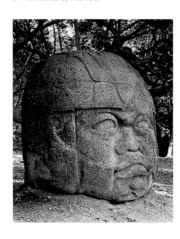

THE PAINTED MURALS OF BONAMPAK

In 1946, painted murals were discovered at Bonampak, in the rainforests of Chiapas in southern Mexico. These are considered to be some of the most important works of their kind in ancient America. The murals cover the whole wall of a small building – a commemorative monument built by a Maya king who reigned in the Classic period from AD776. The paint-

Detail from mural with figures of Maya dignitaries, Bonampak, Chiapas, Mexico.

Detail of Maya mural showing dignitary and figures with zoomorphic masks, Bonampak, Chiapas, Mexico.

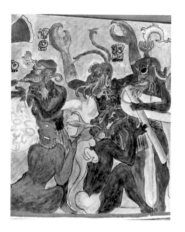

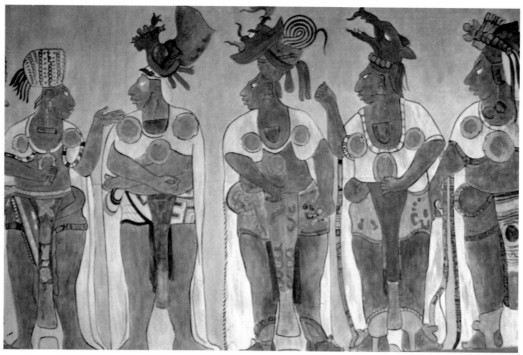

ings are perfectly preserved, thanks to a layer of limestone that had completely covered them for centuries. Although sober in style, certain details were emphasized by the use of a variety of bright colors; for example, the minute portrayal of objects and ornaments that are flaunted by several individuals. The scene depicts a warring expedition that ends with the capture and sacrifice of prisoners and the glorification of the victorious monarch, who performs rituals in honor of the gods.

The paintings of Bonampak not only reveal crucial information about episodes in the life of the Maya ruling classes but also reveal the presence of an artist who succeeded in combining the strict conventions of official art with individual creativity. Such freedom of expression appears particularly in the psychology of the main figures and in the attentive portrayal of some of the protagonists, whose features may be recognized in various scenes of the fresco cycle.

influences to create excellent pieces of stone sculpture and anthropomorphic pottery, with realistic portrayals of high-ranking individuals.

In about AD900, successive invasions by peoples from the north put an end to the finely balanced Classic cultures and initiated the post-Classic period (AD900–1521). This was characterized by more warlike subjects and a religious belief system that was often founded upon the ritual of human sacrifice in order to appease the divinities. The forms of art were designed to be awe-inspiring and to make manifest the tremendous power of the gods. The Toltecs, who disseminated much of this new vision of the world, were the first people in Mexico to work precious metals; but it was the Mixtecs who were responsible for unifying Mesoamerica on the artistic plane. Gifted craftsmen, they excelled in making objects decorated with mosaics and in painting deerskin codices that recounted dynastic histories, in working gold, and in producing polychrome pottery. Later, Aztec art principally took the form of stone sculpture, its powerfully expressive images spare and severe, conveying a strong sense of anguish.

The history of the Maya is to some extent separate from that of Mexico. It was during

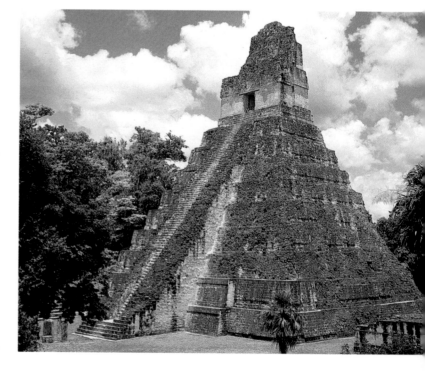

Temple I, Tikal, Guatemala. The steep stepped pyramid, topped by an altar or sanctuary, is typical of Maya temple-pyramids in the rainforests of Guatemala.

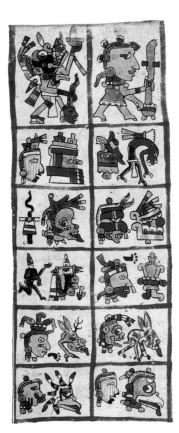

Rare example of an Aztec calendar. Bologna University Library.

the Classic period that Maya artistic production, centered predominantly in the rainforests of Petén, reached its highest levels of achievement. City-states like that of Tikal, which was spread over 6 square miles (16 square kilometers), were to emerge, characterized by tall buildings, especially temple-pyramids built of limestone and faced with lime stucco, and a profusion of sculpture, which was often used to decorate the most important of these structures. In the post-Classic period, architects began to adopt the horizontal plan, exemplified by grandiose, colonnaded buildings. Other noteworthy areas of artistic production included earthenware, stucco sculpture, jadeite working, and wall-painting.

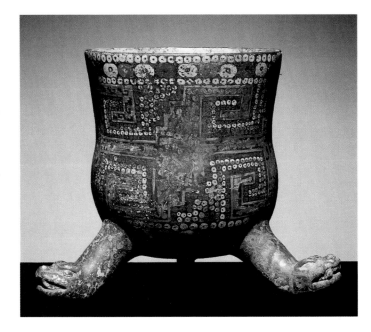

Polychrome ceramic vase with geometric designs and figures and three splayed feet in the shape of snakes, Mixtec culture, late post-Classic period (1300–1521). National Anthropological Museum, Mexico City.

THE PARADISE OF TLALOC

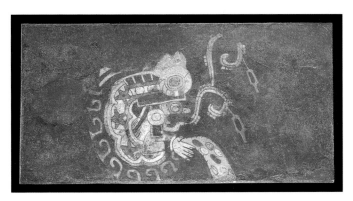

No other pre-Columbian city in Mexico is so rich in pictorial works as Teotihuacán. In one of its greatest monuments, the complex of Teplantitla, there is a fresco known as "the Paradise of Tlaloc," because the unknown artist portrays a place of delight, serenity, and eternal plenty. Designated for all the dead who had honored the gods in life, it is presided over by Tlaloc, the rain god and one of the most important gods in the Teotihuacán pantheon. High up on the wall is the image of Tlaloc, majestic and

The god Tlaloc from a mural painting at Teotihuacán, Classic period (AD250–900).

hieratic, the bearer of gifts. Lower down, however, in an entirely different style, in which the artist gives full play to his creative fantasy, is the representation of a tropical paradise, indicated by the lush vegetation, it is inhabited by tranquil folk who spend their time in games, repose, singing, and contemplation. This is a vision of the blessed life promised to those who, throughout their lifetime, had faithfully honored Tlaloc.

Fragment of mural depicting plant and flower motifs, Teotihuacán. National Anthropological Museum, Mexico City.

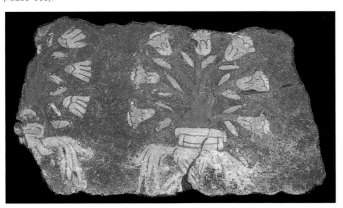

THE ART OF THE CENTRAL ANDES

Present-day Peru and the northwest part of Bolivia constitute the geographical-cultural area known as the Central Andes. Despite the challenge posed by the harsh terrain and inimical climate, or perhaps because of this very fact, cultures flourished that were more highly developed than any others in South America. The extraordinary works of art created by the people of pre-Hispanic Peru are often difficult to date precisely, but it is known that the cultural foundations of the ancient civilizations of the Andes were already firmly established at the settlement of Chavín de Huántar between 1000 and 300BC. This center was renowned for its religious ideology and artistic style. Its magnificent stone temples were designed with steps that opened out onto broad squares. Its sculpture included both bas-relief and carving, and its pottery, dark in color, was strongly figurative. During the third century BC the Chavín culture declined, to be succeeded by other regional cultures, notably the Moche of the northern coast

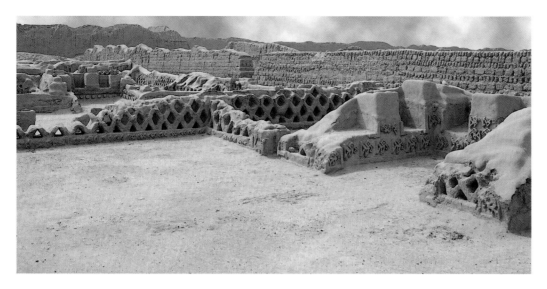

The ruins of Chan Chan, Chimú culture, Moche Valley, Peru, 1000–1450.

and the Nazca on the southern coast. Over a period that lasted until AD600, they both displayed an advanced level of artistic expression. The Moche state built large *huacas* (temple structures with steps) in adobe (sun-dried clay bricks), and decorated them with frescoes. The Moche culture is well known for its ceramic art, which was often found accompanying the deceased to their tomb. The pieces were strongly naturalistic, with a tendency toward molded forms.

The Nazca are known for their ceremonial centers and cities. Bright polychrome colors characterized both pottery and textiles, the latter being of particular refinement and indicative of Nazca artistic sensibility. The cloaks and ponchos were adorned with geometrical or naturalistic motifs and utilized a number of sophisticated techniques, including embroidery, brocading, fine needlepoint, and delicate lacework. Around AD600, the city of Tiahuanaco (Bolivia), situated at about 13,000 feet (4,000 meters) from Lake Titicaca, imposed its rule over a large part of Peruvian and Bolivian territory. Over time, Tiahuacanoid culture initiated a trend toward political and cultural unification. The artistic

style of Tiahuanaco can be clearly seen in its monumental architecture such as stone temples with staircases, imposing ceremonial precincts, and gigantic anthropomorphic monoliths. The Gate of the Sun is famous for the complex religious scene carved in the architrave, portraying the "Staff god," one of the most important deities of the ancient Andean pantheon.

Perhaps because of the over-exploitation of local resources by the state, Tiahuanaco went into decline in about the year AD1000, and other regional cultures found new strength, with their art clearly inspired by earlier local traditions. In this period (AD1000–1476) after the collapse of Tiahuanaco, small warring states fought one another for supremacy. The most dynamic

of these states was that of the Chimú, a confederation of dominions with its capital at Chan Chan in the Moche Valley, the empire of which expanded along the northern coast of Peru. Chimú art styles can be seen in monumental architecture, decorated with geometrical or figurative bas-reliefs. Ceramic art, usually black in color, exhibits a repetition of themes. In contrast to the less developed ceramic style is the splendid metalwork, which reached a very skillful and advanced technical level in the manufacture of *tumi* (ceremonial knives), funeral masks, and *orejeras* (ear ornaments). The Chimú confederation declined with the rise of the Inca civilization. A small tribe from the valley of Cuzco that had always been struggling to survive, the Inca gradually but inexorably subjugated surrounding tribes and then expanded to create an empire that stretched from southern Colombia to central Chile. A territory of this size needed

ELDORADO

For centuries, one of the most enduring American myths has been that of Eldorado. It originated, not by chance, in Colombia. Here, goldwork was very highly developed, both in terms of technical

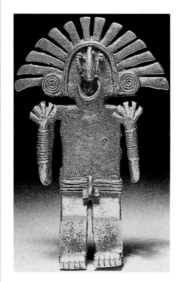

Gold anthropomorphic pendant, Tolima culture, Colombia.

proficiency and artistic originality. Colombia was also the site of many archaeological discoveries that revealed the presence of advanced cultures, such as the ceremonial centers of San Agustín and the underground tombs of Tierradentro. Gold, both in its pure state and as a copper alloy (*tumbaga*), was a prominent ingredient of its art. The metal, extracted from the mines or obtained by leaching from river water, was first used in about the second century BC.

The Quimbaya, Tolima, and Calima cultures, more than any others, excelled in the quantity and quality of their production. The Valdivian culture (2300BC) of Ecuador was the first civilization in the entire American continent to use molded terracotta for artistic purposes. From here

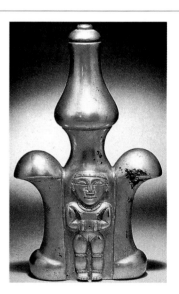

Golden box to hold limestone, Quimbaya culture, Colombia.

on, the skill in the production of earthenware and realistic sculpture was to characterize each successive phase of the culture's development.

THE ICONOGRAPHY OF THE NAZCA CULTURE

Between 400BC and AD550, the culture of the Nazca people flourished in the oases of the coastal desert of southern Peru. They established a powerful centralized state that controlled several coastal valleys, where towns and ceremonial centers were built. The art of this people, often linked to religion, was distinctive mainly for its delicate pottery with polychrome designs. It is possible to trace the development of manufactured earthenware objects based on the diversity of these decorative motifs. At first, these consisted principally of naturalistic patterns: in addition to the emphasis on mythical figures and the presence of trophy heads, great prominence was given to zoomorphic subjects. The Nazca bestiary was extraordinarily varied: it included monkeys, snakes, felines, and, above all, fish and aquatic mammals, which were represented as particularly ferocious. Subsequently, motifs became more conventional and bombastic, with a prevalence of warlike themes. As Nazca culture declined, colors became less varied and motifs were endlessly repeated.

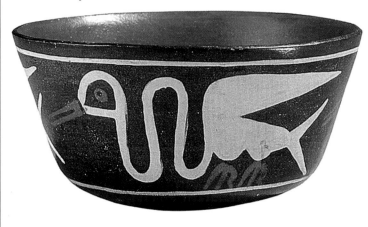

Polychrome cup, Nazca culture, southern coast of Peru.

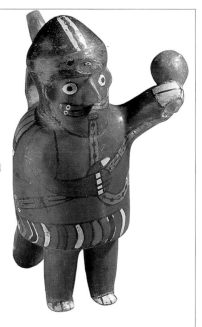

Polychrome earthenware anthropomorphic bottle, Nazca culture, southern coast of Peru.

to be governed by an efficient state organization, and the bureaucratic mechanism established for this purpose took advantage of all the sociopolitical and technical structures already present in Andean society. While the art and architecture of the Inca was less elaborate and more functional, the skill and sophistication of the artists is still impressive. Their metallurgy was especially advanced: they introduced the technique of inlaying shortly before the Spanish invasion and developed a wide range of iconography, especially eagles and condors. The Inca were also renowned for the strength of their masonry – the tight-fitting rectangular stone blocks that characterize their buildings are incorporated into the foundations of modern buildings at Cuzco, the capital of the Inca.

Black ceramic bottle, Chavín culture, northern coast of Peru.

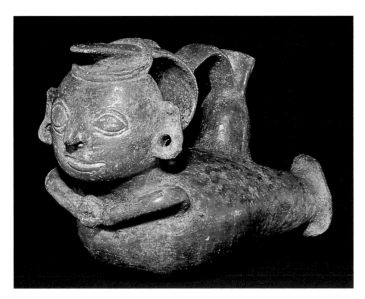

Earthenware anthropomorphic bottle, Vicus culture, southern Peru, AD100–400.

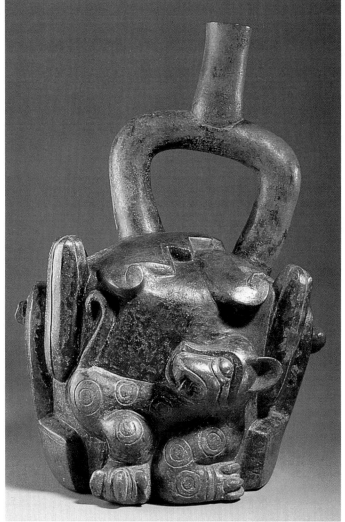

ARTISTIC CULTURES OF ASIA & THE AMERICAS

AD263: Chinese mathematician Liu Hui fixes value of Greek pi at 3.14159. **375:** in India, the Gupta Empire attains its maximum expansion. **550:** in Central America, the Maya civilization reaches its apex of splendor. **622:** Muhammad leaves Mecca for Yathrib (Medina), thus initiating Muslim chronology. **c.750:** technique of paper manufacture spreads from China to India. **980:** birth of Persian philosopher and scientist Avicenna, author of *The Canon of Medicine*, a medical encyclopedia that became known to the West through its Latin translation. **900:** golden period of Japanese culture commences, including the *monogatari* literary genre. **969–973:** foundation of city of Cairo, capital of Islamic caliphate of Fatimids. **c.1000:** movable-type printing invented in China.

AD 250–700 | 700–1000 | 1100 | 1200

▼ PERU

During the period of Nazca culture (440BC–AD550), there was a rich production of polychromatic ceramics with naturalistic motifs.

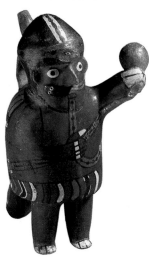

Polychrome, anthropomorphic earthenware bottle, Nazca culture, Southern coast of Peru.

▼ CENTRAL AMERICA

Under the ancient Maya empire (fourth to fifth century), the period of the city-state commenced. The sacred precincts were characterized by tall pyramids.

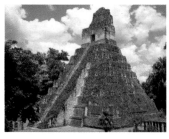

Temple I at Tikal, Guatemala, Maya culture, fourth to fifth centuries.

MEXICO

The artistic civilization of Teotihuacan (first to seventh century), the "place of the gods," was characterized by extraordinary buildings decorated with sculptures and paintings. In the complex of Teplantila, an unknown artist painted the "paradise of Tlaloc," a fresco dedicated to the god of rain.

▼ INDIA

During the time of the Pala dynasty (8th–12th century), there was a profusion of sculpture in stone and bronze. Particularly common were *stelae* in elongated form, carved with episodes from the life of Buddha, with his figure in the center. The same sculptural models were found in Burma and Tibet.

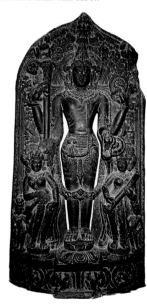

Stele with figure of Vishnu, Pala Dynasty, 8th–12th century.

▼ PERU

Chan Chan became the capital of the Chimú confederation (1000–1476) and was notable for its monumental clay architecture, with geometrical decoration and motifs in relief. There was an extraordinary development of gold-working techniques: production of *tumi* (knives), funerary masks, and *orejeras* (ear ornaments). Pottery, however, was less imaginative and varied, being mostly black.

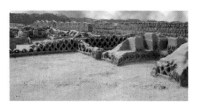

View of ruins of Chan Chan, Moche valley, Peru.

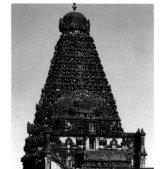

Temple of Brihadiswara at Tanjore, Cola period, 12th–13th century.

▲ INDIA

The bronze sculpture of the Cola Dynasty (9th–13th century) was of high technical quality and of striking formal elegance. The structure of the Indian temple was more complex than that of the Gupta age: taller, with hive-shaped spires, or in the shape of a stepped pyramid. Sculptural reliefs were of great importance and were associated with religious and philosophical programs.

CENTRAL AMERICA

From about the 11th to the 14th century, in an area that included Salvador and northern Honduras and stretched as far as western Nicaragua and Nicoya, there was a rich production of finely painted and modeled pottery. This included receptacles with religious and zoomorphic decoration.

SRI LANKA

Sinhalese art products were influenced by their Indian counterparts. During the Polannaruwa period (8th–12th century), important temples were built, including that of Vatadaga, or Wa Ta Da Ge, circular in plan and decorated with immense stone-carved images.

▼ THAILAND

The city of Ayuthaya, Thai capital from 1350 to 1767, produced sculpture that showed the influence of other Thai schools, notably that of Sukhotai (fluid lines and innovative walking Buddha) and the Khmer-influenced Lopburi (crowned Buddha images). Architectural forms include bell-shaped stupas and Khmer-style reliquary towers with curved roofs.

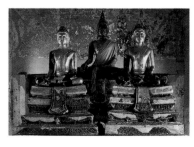

Three statues of Maravijaya Buddha, Wat Pradu Songtham temple, Ayuthaya, Thailand, 13th–15th century.

PERSIA

In about the 13th century, the Mossul School was famed for its finely worked, damascened metal objects.

CHINA

The 13th century saw the continuing production, begun in the previous century, of lacquered wooden and ivory objects, in which the lacquer was applied in a number of superimposed layers and left to dry for a lengthy period. The painter Zhao Mengfu (1254–1322), one of many innovative Yuan artists, captured the rhythms of landscape and everyday life in a naturalistic manner.

1198: death of Arab-Spanish philosopher and scientist Averroè, famous for his comments on Aristotle's writings. **1200:** Incas settle in Cuzco and Aztecs in the valley of Mexico. **1260:** paper money circulates in China. **1365:** Tamerlane proclaims himself heir to Genghis Khan and restores Mongol Empire. **1392:** Choson kingdom established in Korea, destined to last until early 20th century. **1440:** under the rule of Montezuma II, Aztecs extend power throughout central-southern Mexico. **1492:** Christopher Columbus lands on shores of West Indies. **1519:** Spaniard Hernán Cortés conquers Mexico. **1635:** Japanese shogun Togkugawa Iemitsu persecutes Christians and prohibits foreign trade. **1658:** Indian Moghul empire reaches its zenith. **1722:** Afghans conquer Persian Empire.

1 3 0 0   1 4 0 0   1 5 0 0   1 6 0 0 – 1 8 0 0

▼ WESTERN MEDITERRANEAN

Mid-14th century architecture exhibited various homogeneous elements. One masterpiece in the Merinid age (1258-1420) was the al-'Attarin medersa, in the Moroccan capital of Fez. Another is the splendidly decorated Alhambra at Granada, Spain, a rare example of civil architecture from the Nasrid dynasty (1231-1492).

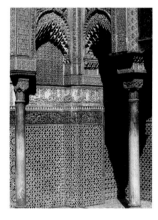

Detail of the al-'Attarin medersa, Fez, Morocco, 1325.

▼ NI ZAN
(1301–74)

Together with Huang Gongwang, Wu Zhen, and Wang Meng, the Chinese painter Ni Zan (a follower of Taoism) formed the group of the "four great landscapists" of the Yuan period : scholar-artists, poets, and calligraphists.

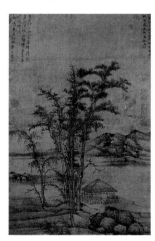

Ni Zan, Pavilion in the Pines, 1354.

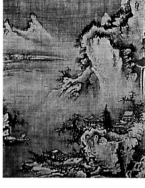

Ahn Kyon (attributed), one of the panels of the Landscape of the Four Seasons, 15th century.

▲ KOREA

During the Choson dynasty (1392-1910) a national style of painting evolved, partly influenced by Chinese art and partly by folk traditions.

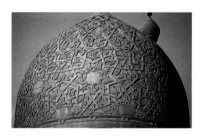

Dome of the mausoleum of the sultan Qaytbay, Cairo, 1472–74.

▲ SYRIA AND EGYPT

The impressive architecture of the Mameluke era (1250-1517) included medersas, mosques, and palaces, topped by florid domes. The *muqarna* was in common usage. Artists and craftsmen produced metal objects damascened in gold and silver, articles in blown glass and enamels, and expensive textiles.

▼ ASIA MINOR

As Iznik pottery developed from the 15th century, typically elegant wares, decorated in red sealing wax, were produced.

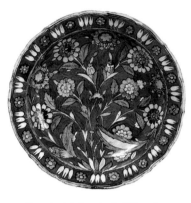

Ceramic plate from Iznik, 16th century. Al-Sabah Collection, Kuwait.

▼ PERSIA

The art of knotted carpets, already thriving in the fifth and fourth centuries BC, continued into the Safavid period (1502-1736). There was an important school of miniatures in the city of Tabriz (1524-76). The work of the prominent artist Sultan Muhammad (active c.1510-45) mingled the Tabriz tradition with the eastern style of Herat.

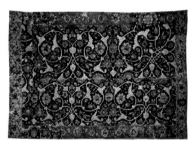

Knotted rug from Herat (northeastern Persia), late 16th century.

NEPAL

Influenced by Indian art, Himalayan sculpture consisted of works in bronze and stone associated with Buddhism and Hinduism. The Newari school of painting was notable for adopting diverse styles. Alongside the stupa, original forms of the Hindu temple were built, covered by multiple wooden roofs.

▼ KATSUSHIKA HOKUSAI
(1760–1849)

This Japanese engraver and painter was a master of the *ukiyo-e*. The French artist Toulouse-Lautrec was influenced by his vigorous, ornamental calligraphy.

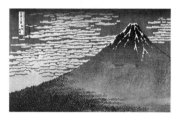

Katsushika Hokusai, View on a Fine Breezy day, from Thirty-six Views of Mount Fuji.

▼ TIBET

Many paintings were produced on vertical scrolls *(thang-ka)*, using tempera on cotton. Subjects were mainly religious and philosophical.

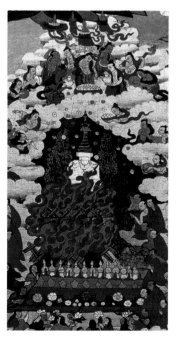

Detail of a Tibetan thang-ka, showing Buddha on a funeral pyre, 19th century.

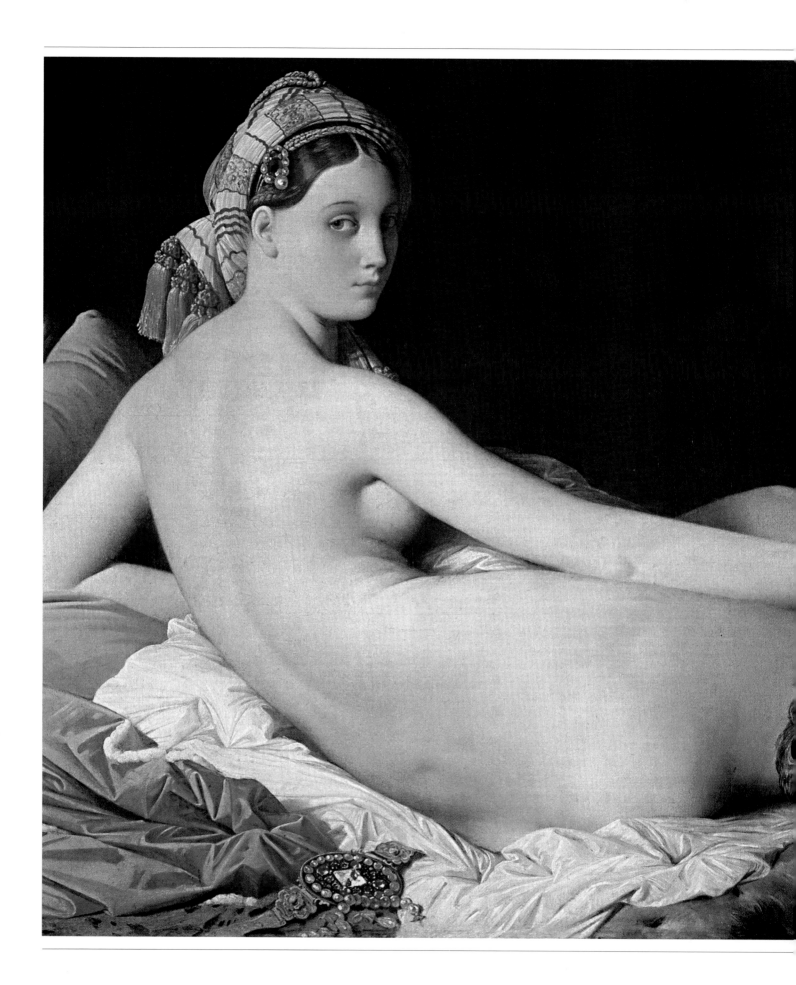

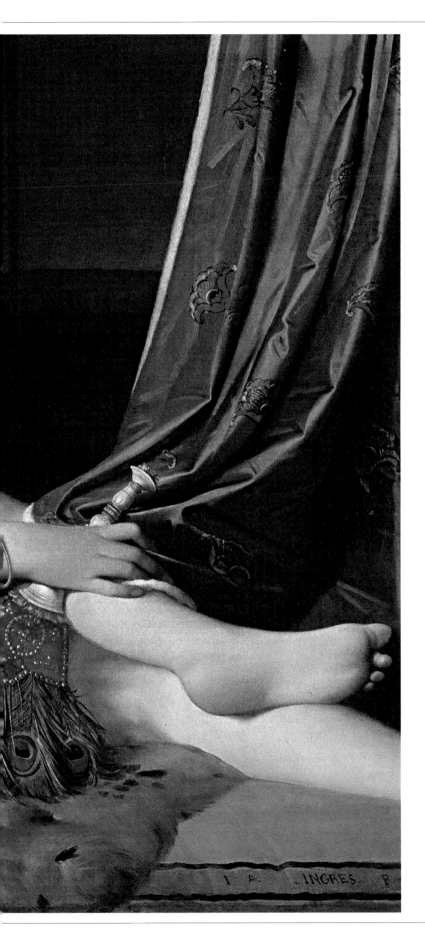

ART, COMMERCE, & INDUSTRY

The 18th & 19th Centuries
Neoclassicism
Romanticism
Orientalism
A Return to the Past

Art Styles in the Industrial 19th Century
Official Art
The Creation of the Metropolis
Art, Technology, & Industry
Furnishings & Fashions
The European Influence

Jean-Auguste-Dominique Ingres, La Grande Odalisque, *1814.*
Musée du Louvre, Paris.

The 18th & 19th Centuries

NEOCLASSICISM

Inspired by the excavations of the Roman cities of Pompeii and Herculaneum, finds from which were popularized by lavish publications detailing the treasures, a renewed interest in the arts of antiquity spread rapidly across Europe and to the New World. This major movement was fully established by the 1770s and manifested itself throughout the decorative and applied arts in a direct imitation of Greek and Roman models.

The term "Neoclassicism" is given to a clearly definable taste in Europe that was based on the pursuit of beauty through the imitation of models drawn from antiquity. The instantly recognizable style of this new movement was clear in all aspects of art. With its sources in the Grand Tour, it emerged between the mid-18th and early 19th century through the ideas of scholars such as German painter Anton Rafael Mengs (1728–79) and archaeologist and art historian Johann Joachim Winckelmann

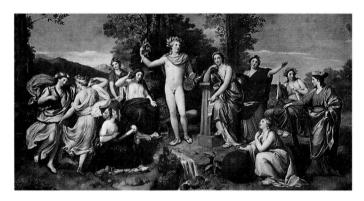

Anton Rafael Mengs, Parnassus, *ceiling painting, Villa Torlonia (formerly Villa Albani), Rome, 1760–61. Perhaps Mengs's best-known work, this painting,* commissioned by Cardinal Albani, depicts the Olympian gods. The Greek pantheon was a favorite subject with Neoclassical artists.

(1717–68). They shared strongly held beliefs based on classical ideals, which were already being revived elsewhere in Europe. Neoclassicism was probably at its most creative during the short, intense period known as the Empire style. Later, some elements of the movement interlinked with those of Romanticism, a relationship that was to destroy the style from within. Neoclassicism was a comprehensive style that embraced painting and architecture, literature and

UNCOVERING THE ART OF ANTIQUITY

Following the discoveries at Herculaneum (1738) and Pompeii (1748), both near Naples, extensive archaeological excavations were carried out in and around Rome during the last quarter of the 18th century. The finds, such as those at the

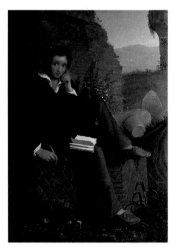

Joseph Severn, Shelley at the Baths of Caracalla, *1845. Keats Shelley Memorial House, Rome. This portrait by Severn (1793–1872) bears witness to the popular taste for backdrops of ancient ruins.*

Lateran (1779–80), attracted a steady flow of visitors to the Eternal City, already an essential stop on the Grand Tour – a standard feature in the education of English gentlemen. The cosmo-

politan community of Rome swelled as enthusiastic observers came to admire the newly discovered masterpieces. According to Winckelmann, the prime theorist of Neoclassicism, sculptures such as the *Apollo Belvedere* and the *Laocoön* epitomized the antique qualities of calm, simplicity, and noble grandeur that were so desirable.

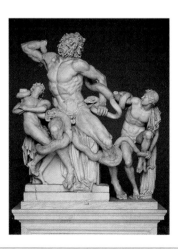

Laocoön, *2nd century BC, Museo Pio-Clementino, Vatican City. This famous marble sculpture was uncovered in 1506 during excavations in the Domus Aurea.*

The Apotheosis of Homer, *from* Antiquités étrusques, grecques et romaines, *vol. III, by Pierre-François Hugues, 1766–67. This work is based on classical Greek vase painting.*

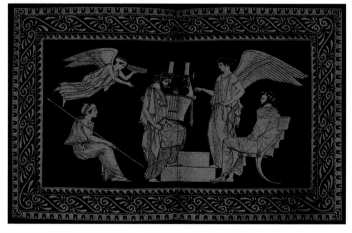

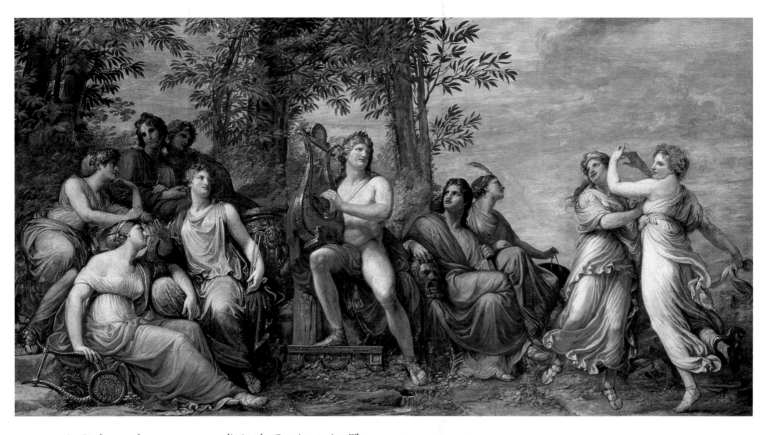

Andrea Appiani (1754–1817), Parnassus, Villa Reale (now the Museum of Modern Art), Milan, 1811. The Villa Reale, built by Leopold Pollak in 1790 for Count Barbiano of Belgiojoso, was given to Napoleon in 1802. This fresco, Appiani's last work, decorates the ceiling of the dining room. With its theme of Apollo and the Muses, it was intended as a tribute to the Bonapartes as patrons of the arts.

music. It also made an impression on the applied arts, where it inspired the design of fabrics, jewelry, furniture, and ceramics. As the movement became more established, the characteristics of the Neoclassical style varied from country to country – as did the name. For example, it became the sober Regency style in England and the grandiose Empire style in France. In Germany, it was expressed in the comfortable, relaxed Biedermeier style; in Scandinavia, it was the light, airy Gustavian style, typified by the use of light-colored wood. In North America, it resulted in the simple Federal style.

ORIGINS OF THE STYLE

As symmetry was gradually introduced into the lavish ornamental motifs of the Rococo style, so the Neoclassicist ideas slowly began to spread. Work from this transitional period retained some delicate grace while displaying some distinctly Grecian traits. The new aesthetic revealed a reaction against the excesses of Rococo ornamentation and the frivolity of the prevailing fashion for curved lines, in favor of what was seen as the noble simplicity of antiquity. This weariness with Rococo style was evident from the 1730s onward in the writings of Voltaire (*Le Temple du goût,* 1730), the architect Jacques-François Blondel (*De la distribution des maisons de plaisance,* 1737), and the abbot Le Blanc (*Letters to the Count de Caylus,* 1737–44). Many Neoclassical ideas were founded in the scientific ideals of the French Encyclopedists, who believed in the enhancement and promotion of public morality through art. French philosopher Denis Diderot sought to make virtue appealing and render vice ridiculous and unattractive, linking the concept of beauty to goodness. He advocated the social responsibility of the creative artist, whose work would be destined for the collective well-being and education of the community.

ARCADIA AT VERSAILLES

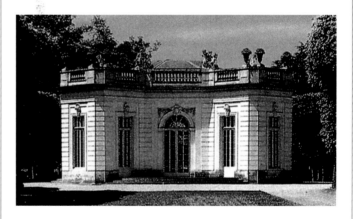

Ange-Jacques Gabriel, the Petit Trianon, Versailles, 1762–68.

In 1762, architect Ange-Jacques Gabriel (1698–1782) started work on his great masterpiece, the Petit Trianon, set in a garden on the estate at Versailles. It was a perfectly balanced building of simple uniformity, with a facade that was symmetrically articulated at right angles to form a closed, independent rectangle.

It demonstrates many typical traits of Neoclassical architecture, not least in its clarity of structure. The building contrasts with the Neo-Gothic architecture found along the winding roads of the English landscape.

INSPIRED INTERIORS

Motifs from the frescoes of Herculaneum were incorporated into interior decoration designs across northern Europe. Divided into small octagonals and squares edged with red, the designs featured nymphs, *putti* (infant boys), dancers, spirits, birds, and small mythological scenes. The decoration stood out against a pale blue background, with delicate grotesques, garlands, capitals, little columns, and perspectives that lead to infinity. Copies of paintings uncovered at Pompeii and Herculaneum soon became very fashionable in England, not least in the form of Wedgwood's exquisite white china figurines. The first "Etruscan" interiors, known then as "Pompeiian," appeared in the villas designed by the Scottish architect Robert Adam (1728–92). The light, graceful rooms were the most intimate and relaxed of the period, their interiors created by artists such as Angelica Kauffmann (who was in England between 1766 and 1781).

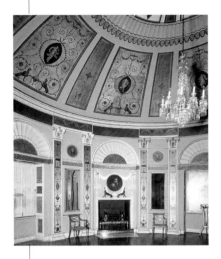

James Wyatt I (c.1748–1813), Cupola Room, Heaton Hall, Manchester, 1772. With this interior, Wyatt brought the delicate refinement of his Neoclassical decoration to a city undergoing industrialization.

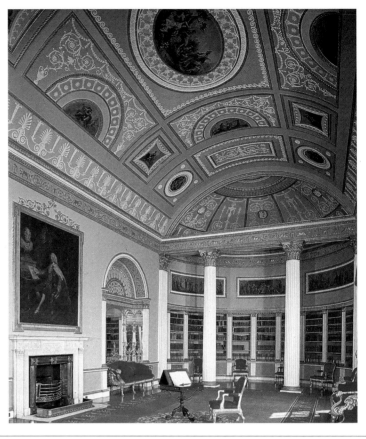

Robert Adam, the library at Kenwood House, Hampstead, London, 1767–69. Here, Adam blended an imitation of the ancient with a taste for comfort and intimacy.

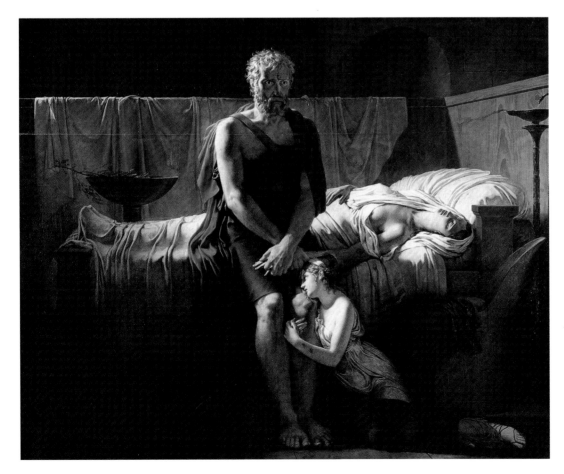

ITALIAN SOURCES

Academic interest in the past was animated by a deep longing for renewal during the 18th century. It was appropriate, therefore, that the new art style evolved in Rome among the ruins of a dead civilization and its treasures, including the stuccowork of the tombs in the Via Latina, the ruins of the imperial palace at Spoleto, in the Albani and Borghese villas, and the setting up of the Pio-Clementino Museum in the Vatican City. These were joined by the excavations at Herculaneum in 1738 and at Pompeii a decade later. Rome was renowned as the

Pierre-Narcisse Guérin (1774–1833), The Return of Marcus Sextus, 1797–99. Musée du Louvre, Paris. The heroic theme, inspired by Roman history, and the artist's skillful effects in the definition of the folds and drapery cannot conceal the first stirrings of the nascent Romantic movement. The horror aroused by the republican wars prompted many Neoclassical artists to turn to harsher, bloodier themes.

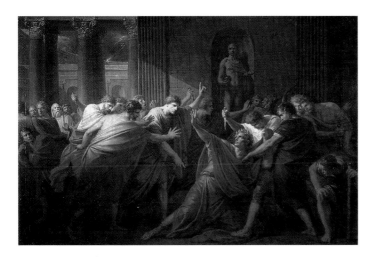

Heinrich Friedrich Füger (1751–1818), The Assassination of Caesar. Historisches Museum der Stadt, Vienna. While in Italy, the Austrian artist Füger met Mengs and absorbed elements of the Neoclassical style from him. Füger gained numerous commissions, including frescoes for some of the ceilings in the palace of King Charles III of Spain at Caserta.

been superseded by new forms such as cherubs and winged cupids, which adorned bedrooms and studies. Meanwhile, the famous tripod with sphinxes from Pompeii had a considerable influence on Empire furnishings. Joseph-Marie Vien (1716–1809), a

JOHANN JOACHIM WINCKELMANN

The influential German Johann Joachim Winckelmann was the key theorist of Neoclassicism. In his widely read volumes *Reflections on the Imitation of Greek Art* (1755) and *History of Ancient Art* (1764), he proposed the study of ancient art by means of a reasoned method. Winckelmann recommended that one should take a fresh look not only at the statues

international capital of artistic excellence, but Naples, too, now became an obligatory stop for cultured Europeans on the Grand Tour. The ruins at Herculaneum aroused a great deal of interest and excitement. King Charles founded the Herculaneum Academy to spread the knowledge of the new discoveries, publishing eight large volumes on the finds

between 1757 and 1792. In *Antiquity and Herculaneum,* all the bronzes and frescoes that had been uncovered were reproduced. Prints and illustrations faithful to the originals facilitated the rapid dissemination of the newly discovered decorative motifs. By the end of the century, the kind of ornament derived from ancient Roman decoration by Raphael and his school had

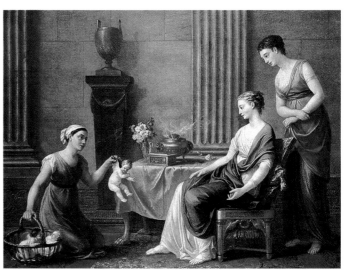

MADAME RECAMIER AND THE GREEK STYLE

The wife of a wealthy banker, Madame Juliette Récamier, "whose beauty and whose grace make one think of Venus," as Jean-Baptiste Bernadotte reportedly said to Joseph Bonaparte, was captured on canvas in

several different guises. In a painting by David, she is pictured reclining barefoot on a sofa; Dejuinne painted her dressed in white as an innocent reader in a room of the Abbaye-aux-Bois; and Chinard portrayed her as a nymph with partly exposed breasts. In François Gérard's portrait, commissioned by Prince Augustus of Prussia, both her dress and the chair on which she poses are inspired by Greek style. The Récamier home, Hôtel Récamier, was lavishly decorated by Charles Percier and Pierre-François-Léonard Fontaine, with clear references to Greek and Egyptian style. Far from leading the life of an idealized classical goddess, Madame Récamier suffered her fair share of hardships, including an unconsummated marriage and unhappy love affairs.

François Gérard, Portrait of Juliette Récamier, *1805. Musee Carnavalet, Paris. During the Napoleonic era, wives, mistresses, and sisters imposed their taste on high society.*

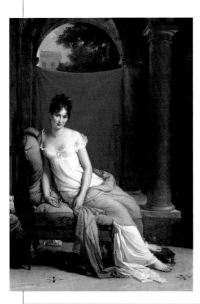

former teacher of Jacques-Louis David, was the first to introduce the so-called "Pompeiian style" in his painting *The Cupid Seller* (1763) by setting a scene with Greek details in a Neoclassical interior. Excavations were also undertaken in Tuscany in the first half of the 18th century, from which collections were established. In his seven-volume *Recueil d'Antiquités* (1752–67), Count de Caylus mistakenly expounded a theory that the Etruscan civilization was older than that of the Greeks. A new interest in Egypt also arose in Rome, inspired by the obelisks and ancient sculptures discovered at Hadrian's Villa in Tivoli. After Napoleon's Egyptian campaign in 1798, a new fashion sprang up – Egyptian Neoclassicism.

Joseph-Marie Vien, The Cupid Seller, *1763. Musée du Château, Fontainebleau. The artist's antiquarian leanings are here used to portray a vision of idle Parisian society in the declining years of Madame de Pompadour's influence.*

and vases of antiquity but also at the whole of the ancient Greek civilization. An enthusiastic and near-fanatical scholar, he perceived an ideal beauty in the cool elegance of Greek art, the perfection of which seemed to him to transcend nature. It epitomized the "noble simplicity and calm grandeur," whereby harmony of line determines form and is more important than color. While Winckelmann recommended the adoption of ancient forms, he disapproved of cold copying, emphasizing the importance of recreating the true Greek spirit. Standing before the *Apollo Belvedere* Winckelmann warned, "At first glance you may see no more than a lump of marble, but if you know how to penetrate the secrets of art you will see a marvel."

ANTON MENGS AND FRANCESCO MILIZIA

Winckelmann's beliefs influenced many artists, including Anton Rafael Mengs who met the great theorist in 1755. His treatise on "Beauty in Painting" was paraphrased by Daniel Webb in his book *Inquiry into the Beauties of Painting* (1760): beauty was the perfect expression of an idea, since art was above nature. The ultimate aim of painting lay, therefore, in selecting

beautiful subjects found in nature, purified of all imperfection. Mengs drew on the works of many past masters: from the ancient Greeks he learned an appreciation of beauty; from Raphael, expression, composition and the treatment of drapery; from Correggio, the skill of chiaroscuro and a sense of beauty; and from Titian, the use of color. His best-known work, the ceiling painting *Parnassus* (1760–61) in the Villa Albini (now Villa Torlonia) in Rome, was significant for breaking with the illusionism of the Baroque style and became the visual manifesto of his theories. According to his fellow theorist Francesco Milizia (1725–98), an artist should choose the most perfect individual elements in nature

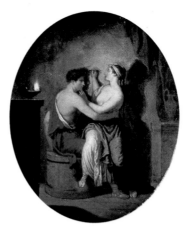

David Allan (1744–96), The Origin of Painting, *1775. National Gallery, Edinburgh. Allan's work illustrates the popular Neoclassical taste for allegory.*

and combine these to form an ideal whole. This would achieve a true representation, based on the artist's own personal vision.

THE FRENCH REVOLUTION

Neoclassicism was not simply an archeological and aesthetic phenomenon but a complete ideology. As well as its governing theoretical methods, which called for continuous application, there were also historical and social implications. In France, in particular, the movement had strong moral associations and was linked to a shift toward a more austere social outlook. The fall of the monarchy had dramatic repercussions throughout Europe. Fueled by a financial crisis and a deep-seated social malaise, which had permeated the nation since the 1770s, the protest finally erupted into the Revolution of 1789. In the same

NEO-PALLADIAN ARCHITECTURE

The most loyal disciples of architect Andrea Palladio (1508–80) were the English architects who regarded the work of the Italian master as a bridge between the extremes of classicism in the 16th century and the Neoclassicism that had emerged. Palladio was a model architect to follow, not only for those in search of Renaissance concepts of form but also because the simplicity and grandeur of his

buildings were strong examples on which to build classical architectural prototypes. Palladian-style architecture spread rapidly and was favored by wealthy patrons as an expression of their rank and power. Known as Neo-Palladianism, the style suffered a setback after the death of Scottish architect Colen Campbell in 1729 but was revived by the traditionalist Sir William Chambers. It later gave way to the innovations of Robert Adam. The style reappeared in the US with the work of Thomas Jefferson.

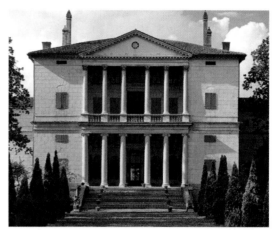

Andrea Palladio, Villa Cornaro. Piombino Dese, Padua, 1551–53. This villa features on its facade a rare example of a loggia and a double layer of columns. This design would be taken up, with many variations, in the plantation houses of the American Deep South.

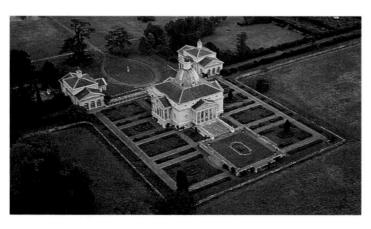

Colen Campbell, Mereworth Castle, Kent, 1722–25. Here, Campbell, author of Vitruvius Britannicus, *applies great elegance to the design of a country house. The large, central structure is derived directly from Palladio's Villa Rotonda (later known as Capra), Vicenza.*

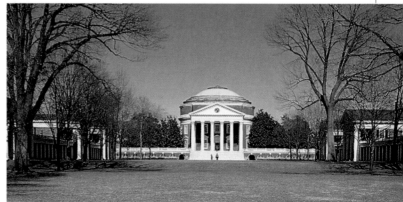

Thomas Jefferson, The Rotunda, *University of Virginia, Charlottesville, 1823–26. The theme of the rotunda is based on the work of Palladio, of which the facade is typical, as well as on the Pantheon in Rome.*

UNATTAINABLE GRANDEUR

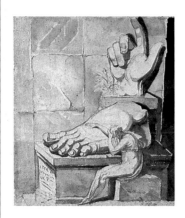

Henry Fuseli, *The Artist Moved by the Grandeur of the Ancient Ruins, 1778–79. Kunsthaus, Zurich.*

When studying works of art from antiquity, artists could only feel disheartened by the awe-inspiring examples of the grandeur to which they aspired. This despair was felt keenly, recalling the dark frustrations of 17th-century irrationalism: the fear of that which was yearned for and yet considered to be unattainable. The artist Giovanni Battista Piranesi, who moved from Venice to Rome, engraved dramatic views of the ancient city, inspiring a new attitude toward antiquity, in which Roman architecture was considered superior to Greek.

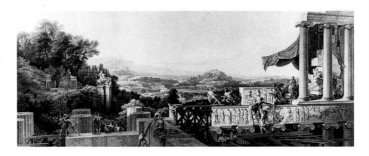

Karl Friedrich Schinkel, *Vision of the Flowering of Greece, engraving by Wilhelm Witthoft, 1846. Staatliche Museen Preussischer Kulturbesitz, Kupferstichkabinett, Berlin.*

Elsewhere, the mark of Romantic sensibility was already appearing: Karl Friedrich Schinkel (1781–1841), a leading German architect of the 19th century, produced idealized visions of imaginary Gothic cathedrals and Greek landscapes. One of his projects left on the drawing board was for a grandiose palace on the Acropolis in Athens designed for Otto of Wittelsbach.

year, the Estates General – the nobility, clergy, and commons – met to establish constitutional controls. Divisions within the Estates General led to the formation of a National Assembly by the Third Estate. During these tumultuous years, the ideological, social, and political foundations of the Neoclassical language were laid down, providing eloquent expression to the passionate political ideals of the Revolution.

A moral Utopia was sought in the aesthetic models of perfection of the ancient world, with the key players in the Revolution exploring history, art, and the nature of antiquity in their search for universal ideal truths. While art did retain its prerevolutionary educational function, its instructive themes upheld an austere, stoical morality that was representative of the new political agenda. This was expressed in the terse oratory of revolutionary leaders Robespierre and Saint-Just.

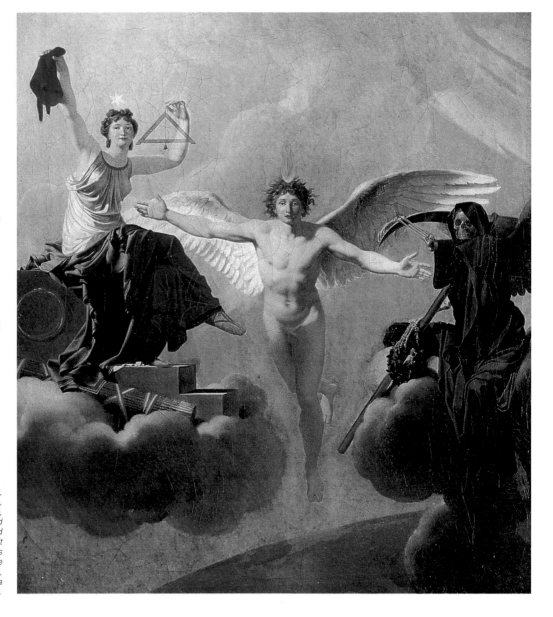

Jean-Baptiste Regnault (1754–1829),
Liberty or Death, *1795. Kunsthalle, Hamburg. An engraver of note, Regnault revealed a love of pure form and outline in this work, which was inspired by classical sculpture. Regnault represents visually one of the phrases used by radical revolutionaries during the period known as the Terror (c.1793–95), his winged youth offering the people a dramatic choice – liberty or death.*

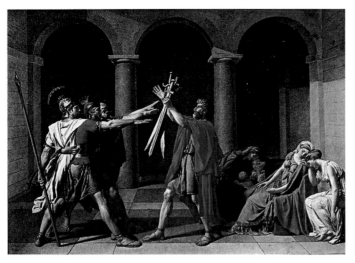

Jacques-Louis David, The Oath of the Horatii, *1784. Musée du Louvre, Paris.*

ART AS PROPAGANDA

The artist most closely associated with Neoclassicism in France was Jacques-Louis David (1748–1825), who expressed more powerfully than any other artist the spirit of the age. He was one of the earliest supporters of the French Revolution: a friend of Robespierre and a deputy of the Convention, he was among those who clamored for the King's death in 1793. His work reveals the moral strictness, sobriety, and austere severity that he learned from classical art under the tutelage of Joseph-Marie Vien, pioneer of Neoclassicism and a director of the French Academy in Rome.

The Oath of the Horatii cannot be regarded wholly as an appeal to republican sentiments, given that it was commissioned for the king by the Count of Angivillier. However, the painting shows a solidarity with the intense illusionism of the antique and celebrates the qualities of courage, temperance, respect for the law, and patriotism. The artist was commissioned in 1790 to paint *The Oath of the Tennis Court*: "To immortalize our ideas," said the purchasers, "we have chosen he who has painted Brutus and his dead son and the Horatii, the French patriot whose genius has pervaded the Revolution." After making some preliminary sketches, the artist did not complete the commission. The fall of Robespierre and the changing political climate led to his imprisonment in 1794. After his release – on the plea of his royalist wife – he produced *Rape of the Sabine Women* (1799). This was seen as an appeal for peace and helped the artist regain his status and position.

These were momentous times in France, with art and culture powerfully reflecting the drama of historical events. For the first time, museums came to be regarded as useful instruments for furthering public education: the Louvre was opened to the public in 1793. Morality was taught and disseminated through public monuments that were dedicated to general ideas or individuals. The cult of the personality evolved from Plutarchian ideals and gradually

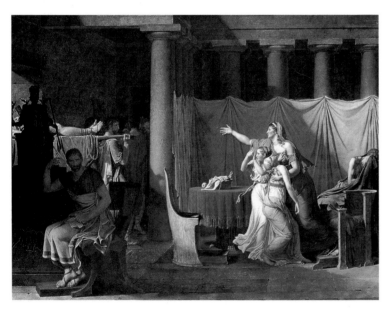

Jacques-Louis David, Brutus Condemning his Son, *1789. Musée du Louvre, Paris. The stoicism of the Roman father contrasts sharply with the gestures of the shrieking, grief-stricken women. This gender characterization was typical of the period.*

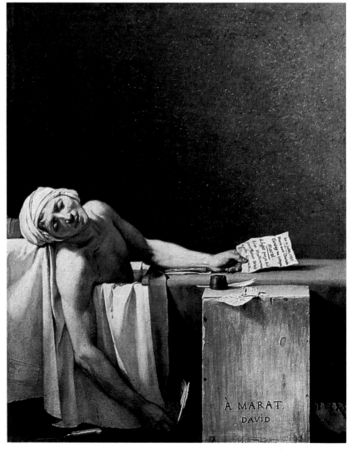

Jacques-Louis David, The Death of Marat, *1793. Musées Royaux des Beaux-Arts, Brussels. David's celebrated painting of the murdered Jacobin recalls works depicting Christian martyrs.*

NAPOLEON, THE SUPREME NEOCLASSICAL HERO

General Napoleon Bonaparte was 28 when he first visited David's studio. David regarded him as a hero: when he was in danger because of his friendship with Robespierre, Napoleon offered him a secret hiding place in his encampment in Italy. Seeking to glorify the emperor's image, David painted him crossing the Alps on May 20, 1800. He is depicted against a mountainous background, advancing not on foot but, unrealistically, on horseback. As fiction and reality merge, he assumes a dramatic, mythical dimension.

Napoleon's exploits were documented on canvas by a variety of European artists. His career from

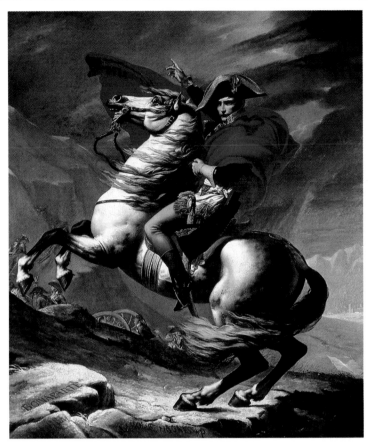

Jacques-Louis David, Napoleon Crossing the Alps, *1801. Musée National du Chateau de Malmaison, Rueil. Here, the hero of the battle of Marengo is shown in an idealized, mythical pose. In reality, he had crossed the Saint Bernard pass clumsily "sliding on his breeches."*

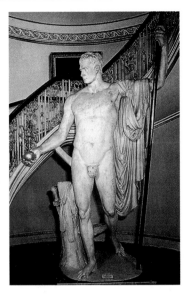

Antonio Canova, Napoleon as Mars the Peacemaker, *1803–08. Apsley House, London. Canova's heroic nude, shown advancing bearing Victory, scepter, and the imperial mantle, was not to the emperor's taste.*

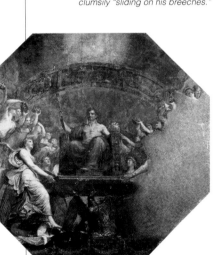

Andrea Appiani, The Apotheosis of Napoleon I, *throne room of the Palazzo Reale, Milan, 1808. In this fresco, the King of Italy, supported by the Eagle and by the Victories, is crowned by the Hours.*

general to emperor and king was depicted in larger-than-life historical imagery: he is seen beaten back from the Alps like Hannibal; victorious in Egypt like Caesar; and restored as emperor like Charlemagne. For about twenty years, Napoleon, who was neither handsome nor athletic, was wholly transformed by artists into the supreme Neoclassical hero. The entire Bonaparte family was made the subject of work by the great Neoclassical sculptor Antonio Canova (1757–1822). Napoleon's sister was portrayed as a Roman goddess in *Pauline Bonaparte Borghese as Venus Victorious* (1804–05), while his mother,

Letizia Ramolino, was the model for a terracotta in the collection at Possagno, Canova's birthplace. The sculptor also created a heroic nude marble statue of Napoleon, endowing him with all the qualities of a Greek god – just as the Romans had portrayed Augustus as divine and the young Marcellus as a "prince of youth." Titled *Napoleon as Mars the Peacemaker*, the statue was later duplicated in bronze (1811).

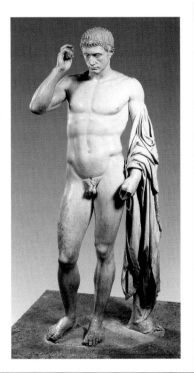

Roman statue of Marcus Claudius Marcellus. Musée du Louvre, Paris. The young nephew and son-in-law of Augustus, who died in 23BC, is portrayed in heroic nude pose as princeps iuventutis, *the heir apparent of his uncle.*

took hold. Napoleon, its greatest embodiment, came to be seen as the one man able to lead France out of the blind alley of the revolution without sacrificing the principles of 1789. David's life-size portrait, *Napoleon in his Study* (1812), was a magnificent example of pure propaganda. Depicted

with the stillness and dignity of a classical statue, the emperor is elevated to heroic status, a model of moral virtue. Also of note for its powers of glorification is *The Empress Josephine in Coronation Robes* (1807–08) by François Gérard (1770–1837), a former pupil of David.

ANDREA APPIANI

Andrea Appiani (1754–1817) was Napoleon's official painter in Italy. Between 1803 and 1817, he praised the Emperor's achievements in a series of panels in the Caryatid room of the Palazzo

Reale in Milan. As the number of subjects multiplied, his pictorial language became increasingly complex. He used powerful chiaroscuro effects in the style of Caravaggio, the austere and metallic colors suggesting moral strength, contrasted with a delicate

they embody feeling but also suggest, in their stylized rigidity, man frozen on the eve of his decline, his submergence into a new order in which he was no longer master of the Earth. During the 19th century, the social change brought about by industrialization rendered the optimism that had characterized the Age of Enlightenment problematic. The lucidity, extreme refinement, and exquisite sense of composition of the best Neoclassical works came to give way to more troubled, tormented expressions – which would develop into Romanticism.

NEOCLASSICAL SCULPTURE

The Italian sculptor Antonio Canova created many works of classical mythological subjects, pursuing an ideal beauty based on reason, according to the aesthetic of the day. He was commissioned to sculpt the monument for Pope Clement XIV (1783–87) in Santi

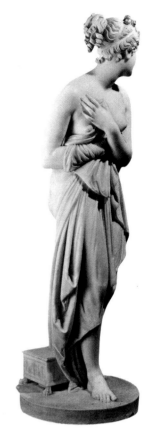

Antonio Canova, The Italic Venus, *1804–12. Galleria Palatina, Florence. The theme of Venus, standing erect or reclining and as a single figure or part of a group, recurs in the work of Canova, who used it to express sensual beauty and divine dignity.*

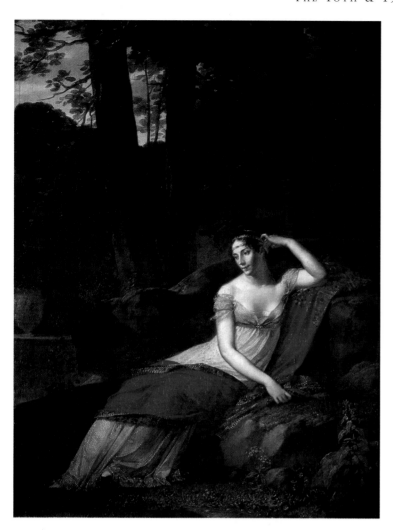

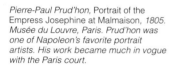
Pierre-Paul Prud'hon, Portrait of the Empress Josephine at Malmaison, *1805. Musée du Louvre, Paris. Prud'hon was one of Napoleon's favorite portrait artists. His work became much in vogue with the Paris court.*

use of pastel that was typical of a certain type of sensuous Neoclassicism. Two tendencies emerged: the minute came to be juxtaposed with the monumental, and the miniature and cameo with the colossal. The works of Pierre-Paul Prud'hon (1758–1823) typified the ongoing influence of the sentimental Enlightenment concept of *sensibilité* on Neoclassical art. Even in the work of David, who shared the enthusiasm of his day for classical models and patriotic ideals with heroes and martyrs, an element of the sensual may be found: in his *Mars Disarmed by Venus and the Graces* (1824), martial virtue

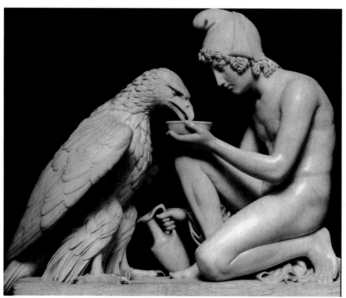

is forsaken in favor of pure sensual pleasure. David's Greek and Roman heroes depict a revolutionary sentiment that is interwoven with dignity and gravity:

Bertel Thorvaldsen, Ganymede with Jupiter as the Eagle, *1817. Thorvaldsen Museum, Copenhagen. The artist portrays the dialogue between the beautiful Trojan youth Ganymede and Zeus, in the guise of an eagle, with a restrained tenderness and delicacy.*

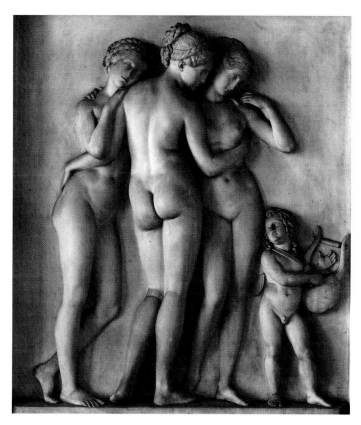

Bertel Thorvaldsen, The Three Graces, Accademia di Brera, Milan. The theme of the Three Graces was a popular subject in Neoclassical art, calling as it did for the portrayal of three female nudes, their arms entwined around one another, each figure depicted in a different pose.

sumptuous drapery. Nevertheless, Canova remained essentially a follower of the Baroque movement and tended to confuse classicism with sentimentality, sometimes veering toward artificiality. His *Three Graces* (1816) and his statue of Pauline Bonaparte Borghese as Venus demanded a visually three-dimensional perspective. This contrasted strongly with Bertel Thorvalsden's (1768–1844) *Three Graces, Hebe* (1816) or *Ganymede with Jupiter as the Eagle* (1817) which are essentially static, and frontal. Denmark's most important Neoclassicist and one of the leaders of the movement, Thorvaldsen spent the majority of his working life in Rome, preferring to work from copies rather than live models. Such was the admiration for his statue of *Jason* (1802–03) that the sculptor was ensured a constant stream of commissions. Thorvaldsen was not a profound observer of character, and his work has been criticized by some modern critics for being rather

Apostoli, Rome. In accordance with Winckelmann's canon of "noble simplicity and calm grandeur," he dispensed with rich ornamentation and the use of superfluous marble for

cold and devoid of feeling. However, Thorvaldsen still deserves to be ranked alongside Canova and John Flaxman as one of the greatest Neoclassical sculptors.

THE DECORATIVE ARTS

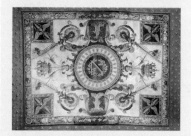

Contemporary copy of the carpet in the throne room at the Tuileries Palace, 1807–09. Musée National du Château de Malmaison, Rueil.

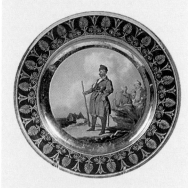

Simeon Chiflar, plate from the Guriev service showing a cossack from the Black Sea, c.1817. Imperial China Factory, St. Petersburg.

Many leading artists made significant contributions to the decorative and applied arts during the Neoclassical period. The Empire style was developed by two French architects, Charles Percier (1764–1838) and Pierre-François-Léonard Fontaine (1762–1853), who produced designs for fabrics, metalwork, furniture, and other crafts. Compatriot Pierre-Paul Prud'hon applied his skills to the design of the cradle for Napoleon's son, the infant King of Rome. In England, Josiah Wedgwood (1730–95) had a considerable influence on the growing demand for china in the Neoclassical style. In 1775, he invented a dense hard stoneware known as jasperware, which he used as a background for applied decoration. John Flaxman created designs for Wedgwood, while the Adam brothers designed for Matthew Bolton, famous for his Sheffield steel plating and his objects in gold and silver plate. Classically inspired wallpaper also became very popular during this period, not in the usual dark colors but with specially created lighter-toned designs and patterns.

NEOCLASSICAL FURNITURE

The elaborate decorations, smooth curves, and gilded ornamentation of Rococo furniture was followed by the straight lines and austere geometric motifs of Neoclassicism. Robert Adam was the first to embrace the new colors and tones, embellishing his furniture with delicate Neoclassical motifs. Georges Jacob (1739–1814) became the emperor's highly acclaimed cabinetmaker; he substituted maple, oak, beech, cherry, and apple wood for the more fashionable mahogany, which was difficult to obtain because of the ban on importing goods from the British colonies. Palmettos, small rose windows, acanthus leaves, and sphinx heads were the most popular bronze decorations. Pompeiian

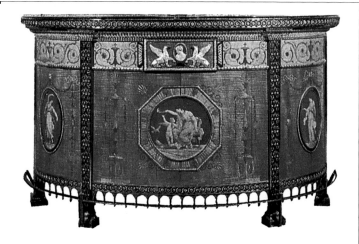

Robert Adam, commode. Adam's furniture is famed for its intricacy of detail and overall balance of design and painted decoration.

tripods were used as bases for tables and small pieces of furniture; chairs were modeled on the curule chair (used by the highest civil officials of

ancient Rome); and beds on the triclinium (dining couch). English and French Neoclassical furniture was adopted throughout Europe. In Russia, for example, Catherine II's Scottish architect Charles Cameron (1745–1812) designed fine pieces in Adam's style.

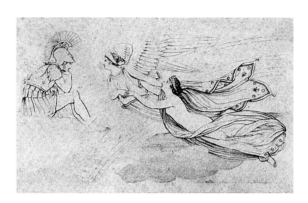

John Flaxman, Venus Wounded by Diomedes Returns to Mount Olympus, 1793. The majority of Flaxman's illustrations of the Greek classics are housed at the Royal Academy of Arts, London, where he was Professor of Sculpture. Shown here is a drawing for the Iliad.

ENGLISH MASTERS

English painting at the end of the 18th and beginning of the 19th century maintained a certain independence regarding the strict canons of Neoclassicism, displaying a characteristic gracefulness and a strong feeling for nature. Sir Joshua Reynolds (1723–92), the first president of the Royal Academy of Arts, painted his *Parody of the School of Athens* in 1751, in which he affirmed that imitation was "a perpetual exercise of the spirit, a continual invention."

This was the age of the great English portraitists: Reynolds, Gainsborough (1727–88), and Sir Thomas Lawrence (1769–1830) combined the fascination with nature, light, and life itself with the luminous elegance of the human face. In the early 1790s, the painter and sculptor John Flaxman (1755–1826) published his engraved illustrations for Homer's *Iliad* and the *Odyssey*, which immediately became famous throughout Europe. Using his knowledge of Greek vase painting, Flaxman dispensed with the illusion of space and reduced volumes to unshaded outlines, giving his figures a sense of unreality and ghostliness that made them resemble imaginary creatures. At this time, England was undergoing the upheavals of the Industrial Revolution, and many new technical advances were reflected in art. In his *Experiment on a Bird in the Air Pump*, of 1768, Joseph Wright (1734–97), painted a young girl weeping over a bird killed in a scientific experiment. One of the most versatile British artists in the 18th century, Derby-based Wright depicted the scientific and technological advances of the time – often painting his work by candlelight.

GERMAN MASTERS

In Germany, the writer and scholar Johann Wolfgang von Goethe (1749– 1832) made a distinction between so-called "noble" nature – that which is viewed from a higher and pure level of perception – and "common" nature, as perceived by the observer. He argued that classical art did

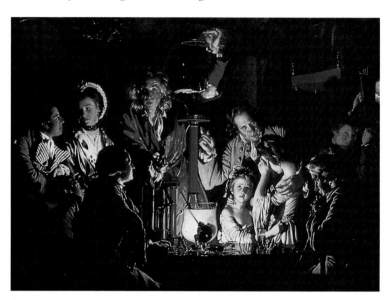

Joseph Wright, An Experiment on a Bird in the Air Pump, 1768. National Gallery, London. As the 18th century progressed, contemporary science, with its instructive language and moral teaching, became a suitable subject for art.

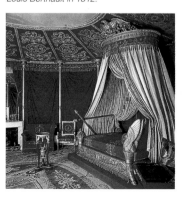

The Lantern Room at Rosendal, private residence of Charles XIV. This palace is recognized as one of the most spectacular examples of the Empire style in Sweden. Its sumptuous furnishings were all made by local artists.

THE MALMAISON STYLE

Josephine Bonaparte acquired the Château de Malmaison on the outskirts of Paris in 1799. After Napoleon was installed as Consul, the Château was enlarged and decorated by Percier and Fontaine. It subsequently became the most sophisticated example of interior decoration, a model of style for the famous visitors who attended the receptions and political meetings held there. Warm mahogany interiors housed stucco panels with Pompeiian-style dancers, extravagant drapery, and ornamental army trophies, while the song of exotic birds imported from the US, Brazil, and Africa filled the air. The French style could also be seen to luxurious effect in the interiors of the Winter Palace at St. Petersburg, those of the Casita at the Escorial in Madrid, and in the private residence at Rosendal of King Charles XIV of Sweden.

Josephine Bonaparte's bedroom at Malmaison, refurbished by Louis Berthault in 1812.

THE NEOCLASSICAL CITY

The Baroque concept of the city had favored the lavish embellishment of individual buildings and features in the urban centers, but it held little regard for the city as a whole. In contrast, the Neoclassical approach was more ambitious and idealistic, with architects envisaging the city as a harmonious, visually balanced environment. At the Adelphi in London, Robert and James Adam created a single complex of buildings, a group of austere houses that were almost devoid of decoration. This project was challenged eight years later by the Adams' great rival William Chambers (1723–96), who embarked on the construction of his great public work, Somerset House, with its massive columns and an imposing archway running parallel to the River Thames. John Nash (1752–1835) undertook the remodeling of Regent Street and Regent's Park in London, combining freedom and formality to produce a brilliant, harmonious marriage between street and garden. In Paris, Percier and Fontaine, Napoleon's chief architects,

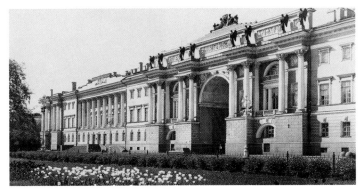

Karl Rossi, The Senate and the Synod buildings, St. Petersburg, 1829–34.

celebrated the emperor's victories with the beautiful Arc du Carrousel (1806–08). In Milan, Giovanni Antonio Antolini (1756–1841) designed the Bonaparte Forum (1801), a vast circular piazza with the Sforza castle at its center, surrounded by mansions with Doric porticoes. In Germany, Karl Friedrich Schinkel transformed the appearance of central Berlin, and Leo von Klenze (1784–1864) reshaped the center of Munich. Warsaw took on Neoclassical features, thanks to Domenico Merlini

John Nash, Cumberland Terrace, Regent's Park, London, 1825–27.

(1730–97), as did Copenhagen, through the work of Christian Frederick Hansen (1756–1845). From the time of Catherine the Great to that of Alexander I, St. Peters-burg rose from a small

wooden town to an impressive stone city. Giacomo Quarenghi (1744–1817), Karl Rossi (1775–1849), Luigi Rusca (1758–1822), Kazakov (1733–1812), Ivan Starov (1745–1808), Zacharov (1761–1811), and Thomas de Thomon (1754–1813) abandoned traditional Russo-Byzantine forms to transform the city into a grand Neoclassical vision. In the US, Washington, DC, was another capital city that was rebuilt to the new specifications. It was laid out by Pierre-Charles L'Enfant (1754–1825) according to a V-plan based loosely on Versailles, with broad avenues converging on the Capitol and the White House.

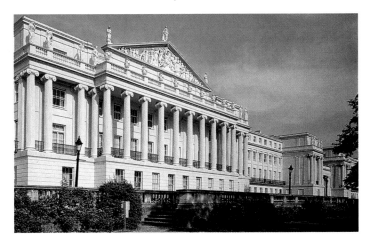

not repudiate nature but was in itself a higher and more faithful form of naturalism – "naturalistic idealism." In 1777, he designed the Altar of Good Fortune, a sphere symbolizing restless desire, standing on the cube of virtue, placed in the idealized landscape of his garden at Weimar.
Heroic Landscape with Rainbow by Joseph Anton Koch (1768–1839), who lived in Rome from 1795, is a mythical vision described by the artist as "a great Greek landscape." In this work, behind the crystalline atmosphere and the sculpted precision with which the shepherds and sheep are drawn, the order set out by the artists of the Renaissance is lost. The viewer's eye does not focus on any one single point

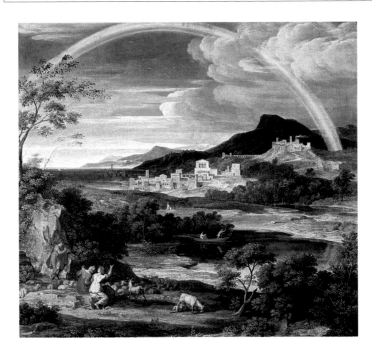

Joseph Anton Koch, Heroic Landscape with Rainbow, 1805. Kunsthalle, Karlsruhe.

ROBERT ADAM

During time spent in France and Italy, the young Robert Adam (1728–92), the best-known member of a family of Scottish architects, became a pupil of the architectural draftsman C.L. Clérisseau and a friend of the etcher Giovanni Battista Piranesi (1720–78). He returned home in 1758 and, with his colleague and rival William Chambers, was made architect to George III. Adam's interiors were exquisitely delicate, drawing from a repertory of classical motifs. His style strongly influenced decorative art. With his brother James (1732–94), he set out their theories in *The Works in Architecture of Robert and James Adam* (1773–78), published in 1822. Together, they planned the ambitious Adelphi project for a residential area along the River Thames.

but wanders all over the painting, absorbing its wide range of emotions.

INGRES: STRADDLING TWO STYLES

The works of Jean-Auguste-Dominique Ingres (1780–1867) represent the apotheosis of the Neoclassical style, while equally hinting at future developments in art. His canvases – particularly his early works – portray all the elements of formal splendor, sober elegance, and an adherence to models of the past (above all the works of Raphael, whom he studied in Italy). In his later paintings, a subtle sensibility, a widespread sensuousness, and an extraordinary psychological insight were expressed, forming a transitional link between 18th-century art and the French painting of the Second Empire.

In his teacher David's work, it was the moral and political subject matter that achieved supremacy, while in that of his own it was the purity of form, developed through the some-times artificial exquisiteness of proportions. These were calculated to emphasize the eroticism and delicate sensuality of his nudes and to give the illusion of a perfect balance. However, Ingres was harshly criticized for this by David: "weak feet, hands…arms and legs a third too short or too long." In an official work such as *Napoleon I Crowned* (1806), the emphasis of the curves and diagonals were in total opposition to Neoclassical composition. For the poet Charles Baudelaire, the work evoked "an impression that is hard to explain, and which, in itself, sums up in indefinable proportions uneasiness, annoyance, anxiety." Ingres' bathers (one of his favorite themes), odalisques, and Oriental women represented an exercise in "academic perfection," marking the birth of a style

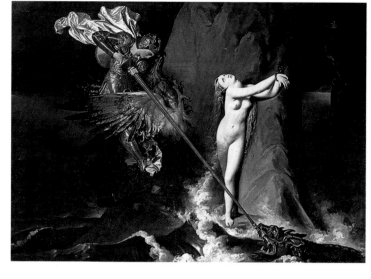

Jean-Auguste-Dominique Ingres, Roger Freeing Angelica, 1819. Musée du Louvre, Paris. The Renaissance tales of Ariosto were transposed by Ingres into a romantic setting in which he could demonstrate his mastery of the nude.

characterized by a languid, soft, expressive eroticism that was very different from that of artists such as Boucher and Fragonard. His later portraits of European nobility best illustrate the great psychological depth of his work.

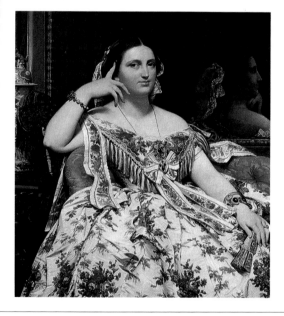

Jean-Auguste Dominique Ingres, Madame Moitessier, 1856. National Gallery, London. The precision and richness of detail in the costume enhance the sensual beauty of the flesh and the graceful curves of the body.

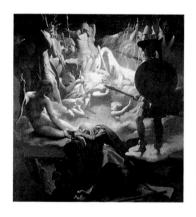

Jean-Auguste-Dominique Ingres, The Dream of Ossian, 1813. Musée Ingres, Montauban, France. James Macpherson published his bogus odes by Ossian in 1762–63, a work full of themes that would be picked up by the Romantics. Half a century later, Ingres used them as his inspiration for this painting.

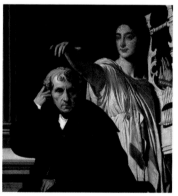

Jean-Auguste-Dominique Ingres, Luigi Cherubini and the Muse of Lyric Poetry, 1842. Musée du Louvre, Paris. A difficult and controversial painting, this portrait of the most famous Parisian composer of the day combines classical iconography with a perceptive portrayal of the subject wearing the dress of the modern intellectual.

NORTH AMERICA

In America, the Neoclassical style enjoyed a particularly long life and a rich variety of expressions. Following the Declaration of Independence in 1776, a distinct style, influenced by European models, evolved and became the pride of a young nation. The Virginia State Capitol (1785–96) was designed by Thomas Jefferson and was inspired by the small Maison Carrée at Nîmes. The model's Corinthian style was replaced by plainer, Ionian ornamentation. The Englishman Benjamin Latrobe (1764–1820), the first fully professional architect to work in the US, decorated his capitals with tobacco leaves and those of the Capitol in Washington with ears of corn. The American painter Benjamin West (1738–1820) ennobled historical events in his work, with paintings such as *Death of General Wolfe* (1770), which broke with Neoclassical conventions by depicting the figures in contemporary dress, and *William Penn's Treaty with the Indians* (1771–72).

By looking at the development

INGRES

Born at Montauban, France, Jean-Auguste-Dominique Ingres first studied in Toulouse before enrolling at David's studio in Paris in 1797. He became the most admired and influential of the French painters, his studio frequented by countless leading figures of society. He was Director of the French Academy in Rome and Professor at the Ecole des Beaux-Arts, just two of many official appointments and honors.

of the Neoclassical style in various countries, it is clear how the premises originally codified by Winckelmann culminated in a sensibility that foreshadowed Romanticism. The reaction to the artificiality of the Rococo movement in favor of a severity of line, color, and form began to reveal a human complexity that had lain hidden beneath the frivolity of earlier 18th-century high art.

A ROMANTIC NEOCLASSICISM?

As Neoclassicism turned to antiquity for its ideal models, so Romanticism yearned for an alternative to everyday reality, aspiring to the truth of the soul and the freedom of irrational impulses. The similarities between these two stylistic trends became more obvious during the decades leading into the 19th century,

AN ARCHITECTURAL UTOPIA

The two most daring and imaginative architects of the Neoclassical era were Etienne-Louis Boullée (1728–99) and Claude-Nicolas Ledoux (1736–1806). Both believed in the simplicity of geometric forms – spheres, cubes, cylinders, and pyramids – which, according to Platonic ideals, "live in nature." Although Boullée's great treatise on architecture was not published until 1953, his prolific teaching meant that he was possibly more influential than Ledoux. He regarded his work as "the architecture of shadows," but his projects became increasingly fantastic and eccentric – and were often unrealized. His design for a library (1783–85) was a Utopian monument to learning, romantic and dreamlike, while that for a monument to Newton (1784) was a 500-foot (150-meter) high sphere – a cosmic globe that was to "sparkle with light and banish all shadows."

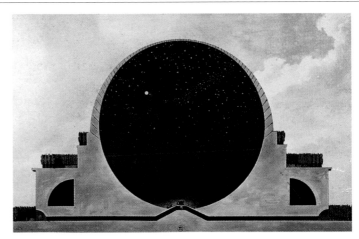

Etienne-Louis Boullée, Cenotaph to Newton, *1784. Boullée's project was never realized, but the design shows how Neoclassical architecture aspired to a monumental grandeur that would have far surpassed that of ancient Rome. Here, the enormous globe – which symbolizes Newton's discoveries – is combined with a Roman mausoleum, surrounded by cypress trees.*

Ledoux took up Boullée's ideas and designed other very imaginative works. Again, many of his projects did not progress beyond the drawing board, such as his plan for the "ideal" cemetery including a giant sphere that would act as a central chapel. From his designs for the "ideal" city, Ledoux planned and partly constructed the industrial center of Chaux at Arc-et-Senans (1774–79); its saltworks remain one of the most celebrated monuments of industrial architecture.

Jean Broc (1771–1850), The Death of Hyacinthus, *1801. Musée des Beaux-Arts, Poitiers, France. The love between Apollo and the Spartan youth Hyacinthus was brought to an abrupt and tragic end by an athletic accident: the god hurled a discus which dealt the boy a fatal blow. Using this myth as his subject matter enabled the artist to portray the pathos of the male nude.*

at which point they more or less coincided – for example, in the work of Ingres. Neoclassicism and Romanticism are two sides of the same coin – both movements reacted to the extravagance of the Rococo style by returning to human values, but whereas Neoclassicism was driven purely by reason, Romanticism was motivated and led by emotion. Antonio Canova's statue in marble of *Cupid and Psyche* (1787–93), although quintessentially Neoclassical in style and structure, marked the boundary between Neoclassicism and Romanticism. This work unconsciously reflects the Romantic concept of humankind's perpetual longing for the unattainable, in that the embrace of the two figures demonstrates the beauty of an unfulfilled union. The longing for a distant and seemingly more appealing age (albeit that of the ancient

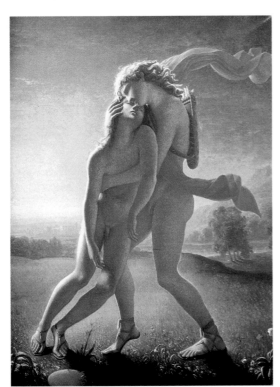

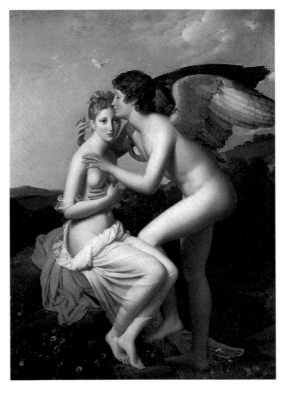

François Gérard, Psyche Receives Cupid's First Kiss, *1798. Musée du Louvre, Paris. This painting still displays a certain Rococo gracefulness in its depiction of the classical myth linking body and soul in love.*

JEAN-AUGUSTE-DOMINIQUE INGRES: "OEDIPUS AND THE SPHINX"

*1808; 73 x 58 in (188 x 149 cm);
Musée du Louvre, Paris.*

Ingres increased the original measurements of this picture before exhibiting it at the Paris Salon, probably in 1825. The subject is the meeting between Oedipus and the sphinx in a desolate place at the gates of Thebes. The painting shows a rocky cave in which the nude figure of the prince confronts the mythical monster. Over his right shoulder, the hero wears a red mantle, which falls against his left thigh. His left foot is placed on a large rock, and two spears lean against his right shoulder, their points resting on the rock. To the left, the sphinx sits in the shadows on a pile of rocks, while below, in the foreground, a foot and some bones are depicted. These are remains of the sphinx's victims – wayfarers she has eaten for failing to find an answer to her riddles. On the lower right of the composition, an animated male figure gestures in the distance.

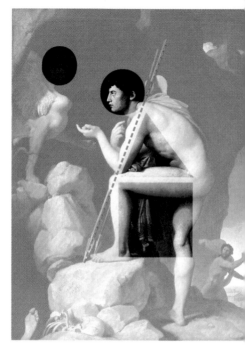

▲ *2. Taking inspiration from the classical world and Neo-Platonic thought, Ingres has structured the human figure using geometric forms of precise symbolic significance. The picture contains a square, a triangle, and a circle. The square represents terrestrial solidity, stability, and balance and is placed in the space created between the bent and straight legs of Oedipus. The triangle, also a stable form but dynamic and linked to the world of the emotions, is positioned between the arm and the torso, seats of the heart and the liver. The circle, enclosing the head, is the shape of harmony, without beginning or end.*

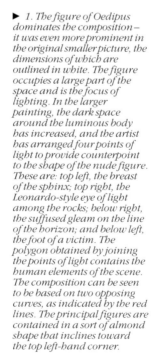

▶ *1. The figure of Oedipus dominates the composition – it was even more prominent in the original smaller picture, the dimensions of which are outlined in white. The figure occupies a large part of the space and is the focus of lighting. In the larger painting, the dark space around the luminous body has increased, and the artist has arranged four points of light to provide counterpoint to the shape of the nude figure. These are: top left, the breast of the sphinx; top right, the Leonardo-style eye of light among the rocks; below right, the suffused gleam on the line of the horizon; and below left, the foot of a victim. The polygon obtained by joining the points of light contains the human elements of the scene. The composition can be seen to be based on two opposing curves, as indicated by the red lines. The principal figures are contained in a sort of almond shape that inclines toward the top left-hand corner.*

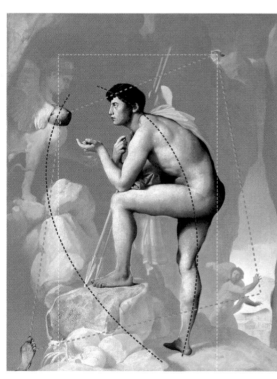

▶ *3. The light that illuminates Oedipus and the rocks in the foreground comes from an undefined source but falls upon the stone and the golden skin of the figure. The nude figure stands out against the dark background, its outline drawn with sharp precision. This is very evident in the right leg, where the full light on the calf fades by fine gradations into the shadow of the foot and upper thigh. In the luminous masses on the left-hand side of the painting, the draftsmanship is also very strong. The breast of the sphinx, defined by the light and the chiaroscuro, has a sumptuous maternal nudity that alludes to the later tragedy that was to befall Oedipus. (After he had solved the sphinx's riddle, the monster killed herself. Oedipus's fate was to marry his own mother, who, when she discovered the truth, hanged herself.)*

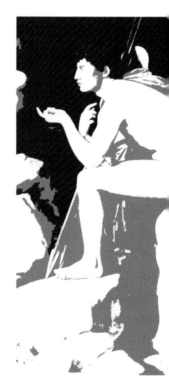

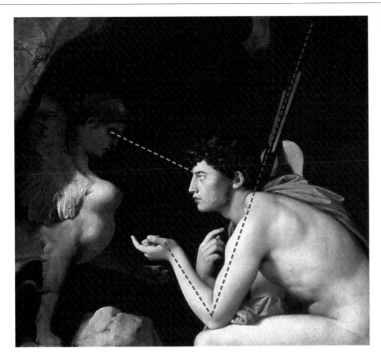

▲ 4. *The stable posture of Oedipus contrasts with the motion of the small figure on the right: the red and orange-red mantles unite the two figures, warming their flesh tones. In both cases, the material is creased or fluttering in the breeze in contrast with the smooth and solid mass of the naked flesh. This detail shows Oedipus meeting the eye of the sphinx, with his forefinger curved toward her breast. The clarity of the scene leaves no room for mystery or ambiguity.*

▼ 5. *The sole of a human foot is illuminated against the darkness in the bottom left of the painting, while a pile of bones and a skull are outlined against the rocks in the foreground. The superb contours and lucidity of form outline a tragic still life. With the sphinx positioned above, space for the dead is contained in the left-hand side of the composition. Space for the living, in the form of the gesturing figure in the distance, is on the right. Oedipus is positioned firmly in the center, his fate undecided.*

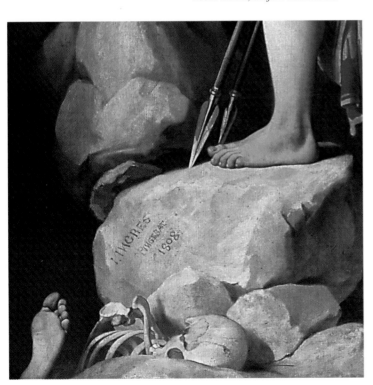

world) is a fundamentally Romantic notion. Thus, a powerful and emotional undercurrent finds its way into the paintings of David, particularly in his depictions of individual pathos, more usually in female subjects. These are typically bestowed with an aura of dignity and nobility or a collective sense of despair and passion. In contrast to the serene

of French Heroes who Died for their Country Gathered in Heaven by Ossian* (1800–02) is a veritable phantasmagoria; *Mlle. Lange as Danae* (1799) shocked its audience with its forthright eroticism; while both *La Pietà* (1787) and *The Funeral of Atala* (1808) displayed unconventional religious feeling. The language of natural forces, both within and

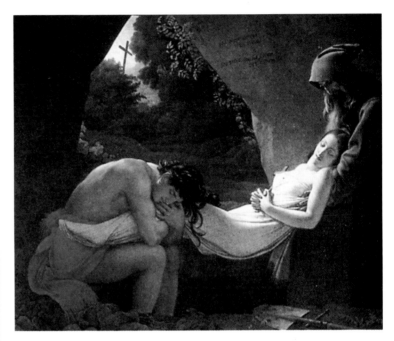

Anne-Louis Girodet-Trioson, The Funeral of Atala, *1808. Musée du Louvre, Paris. Girodet-Trioson, a pupil of David and Gros, exhibited this canvas at the 1808 Salon.*

classicism advocated by Winckelmann, there are blood-curdling scenes, such as Lica being hurled away with brute force by Hercules in Canova's sculpture (1795–1802); similar subjects are also present in the work of Flaxman. Antinaturalism and the more explicit themes of the early Romantic movement emerged against the historical background of the restoration of the monarchy in France. One artist who stands out during this period is Anne-Louis Girodet-Trioson (1767–1824). Of his best-known works, *Endymion Sleeping* (1793), has a dreamlike quality; *Shadows*

around humankind, had by now established itself and would go on to find its most exuberant expression in the Romanticism of Henry Fuseli, William Blake, Caspar David Friedrich, Théodore Géricault, Ingres, and Goya. If it is true that "from the sleep of reason monsters are begotten" (Goya), it is also true that a rationalist Utopia has, at its innermost core, a mysterious and superhuman background inhabited by obscure feelings, arcane voices, and echoes from a fantastical world. Typical examples of these elements are the angelic figures portrayed by the German artist Philipp Otto Runge (1777–1810), the rampant exoticism presented in the work of Delacroix, and the troubled skies painted by Constable and Turner.

ROMANTICISM

Romanticism was not so much a style or manner as a multifaceted movement that represented changing ideas and a new artistic sensibility. Various themes characterized this sensibility, from patriotism and nostalgia to the probing of the depths of the soul. Individualism and the cult of the self combined to create a mood that found its expression in a number of different artistic outlets.

Figurative art played a vital role in the European movement known as Romanticism, which began in music, literature, and the theater, and only later embraced painting and sculpture. It emerged in the late 18th century and continued to evolve throughout the 19th century. The term encompassed various concepts, such as man versus nature, the complexity of the psyche, religion, politics, and history. Unlike the preceding artistic movement, Neoclassicism, which was expressed through an easily recognized style and precise forms, Romanticism had less clearly defined outlines. It was an indication of mood as well as taste, a collective expression of the prevailing European spirit – often accompanied by a degree of extreme emotion.

CONTINUITY AND RENEWAL

During the Neoclassical phase, which partly overlapped with early Romanticism, there were hints of the styles and ideas that would follow. Neoclassical artists had already sought to distance themselves from the gaudiness and fussy over-decoration of the preceding Rococo style. They tackled moral problems, the clash of ideals, and the concept of a harmony that is both external and spiritual (as expounded by Johann Winckelmann, who was one of the key theorists of Neoclassicism). However, the Romantics went further than the Neoclassical artists would ever have contemplated, even though both were searching for the same truths about the human soul. They attempted to explore a deeper, darker level of the human spirit, moving definitively away from the shallowness of the Rococo movement. At the same time, the Romantics recovered some of the more troubled and dramatic themes examined during the Baroque period. During the 19th century there was a distinct change in attitude toward the aesthetic and ethical model of the ancient Greeks, which since the Renaissance had by and large provided the basis for artistic endeavor. For Goethe, this change in attitude became a seminal period of insight in the development of man and his acquisition of spiritual maturity. Later, the writings of Nietzsche would address the disturbing, irrational aspects that lay hidden beneath the polished, sophisticated image of Greek civilization. The notion of antiquity as the essence of natural harmony was challenged

ART AND MADNESS

For the Romantic painters, madness was no longer an abnormal or bizarre subject but a constituent part of humanity. Insanity and disease were portrayed by Franz Xavier Messerschmidt (1736–83), in his "character head" sculptures (1770–83), mostly modeled in lead. Francisco Goya painted himself with Dr. Arrieta, as a tribute to the man who had nursed him through a long illness. He portrayed himself as a sort of Ecce Homo, with the suggestion of a crown of thorns. During the same period, the artist began his grim, visionary "Black Paintings," which show human cruelty while expressing an understanding of the fear that could cause it.

In France, Géricault produced a series of portraits of inmates

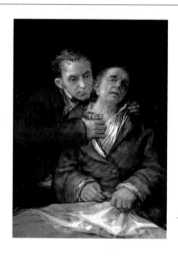

Francisco Goya, Self-Portrait with Dr. Arrieta, *1820. Institute of Art, Minneapolis.*

at the Salpêtrière asylum. With their fixed expressions, they are symbols of a disease that is an integral part of the human condition.

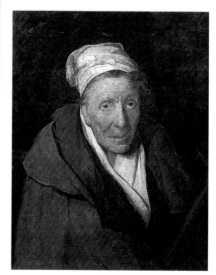

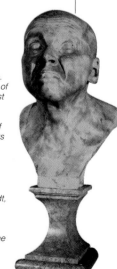

Théodore Géricault, Envious Madwoman, *Musée des Beaux-Arts, Lyons, France. At the request of the psychiatrist Georget, the artist carried out portraits of mental patients from 1820 to 1821.*

Franz Xavier Messerschmidt, Head of a Character, 1774– 83. Österreichische Galerie, Belvedere, Vienna.

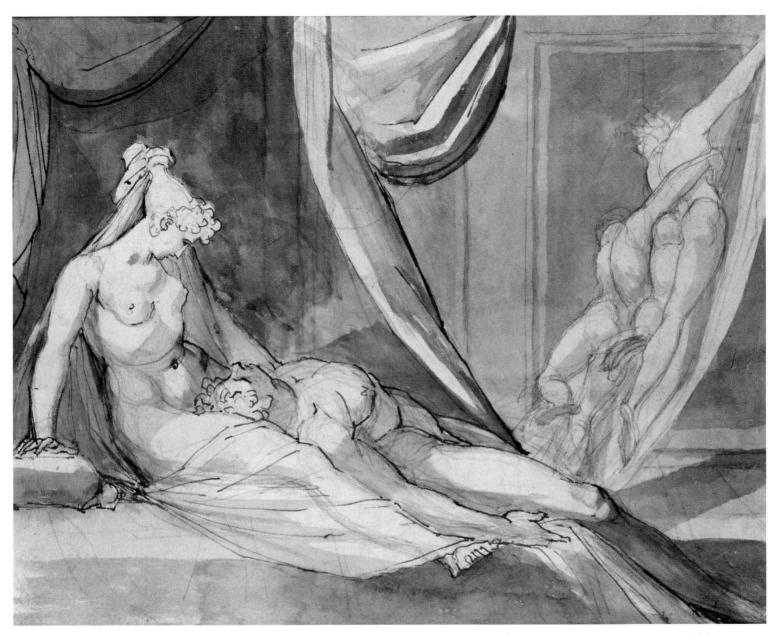

Henry Fuseli, Sleep and Death Bear the Body of Sarpedon *(from the* Iliad, Book XII). *Victoria and Albert Museum, London.*

by Edmund Burke in his *Inquiry into the Origin of our Idea on the Sublime and Beautiful* (1756), which argued against the finite concept of beauty and the classical conception of nature as harmony. Antiquity was interpreted in an nonclassical way by the Danish artist Nicolai Abraham Abildgaard (1743–1809) and, later, by the Swiss-born artist Henry Fuseli (1741–1825), as well as by other visionary painters. The occult, the significance of dreams, notions of infinity, a yearning for distant and exotic lands, anxiety, and the predominance of emotions were among the wide variety of themes that concerned the Romantics.

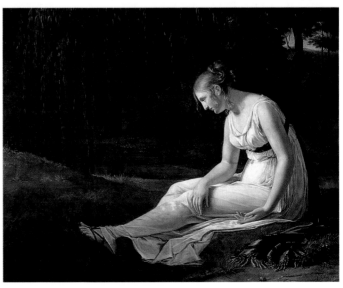

Konstance-Marie Charpentier, Melancholy. *Musée de Picardie, Amiens, France. This painting, exhibited at the Salon of 1801, was inspired by the despairing figure of Camilla in the* Oath of the Horatii (1784) *by David, Charpentier's teacher. The artist powerfully conveys the feeling of isolation and abandonment.*

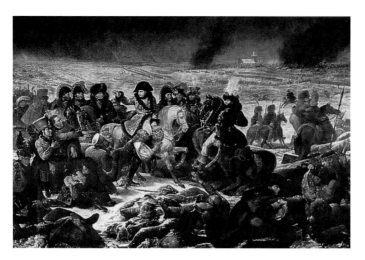

work was tempered by the figure of the Emperor, mounted heroically on a white horse. The canvas is said to have so pleased Napoleon that he made Gros a baron of the empire. Gros' approach was more candid than was traditional for "official" artists and it anticipated the darker style of the Romantics, in which mankind could be shown in its struggle against nature,

Jean-Antoine Gros, Napoleon at the Battle of Eylau, *1808. Musée du Louvre, Paris.*

BEFORE ROMANTICISM

Jean-Antoine Gros (1771–1835) was one of the most avid disciples of French artist Jacques-Louis David (1748–1825). As official war painter of the Napoleonic era and portraitist of illustrious figures of the empire, Gros was commissioned to paint the Emperor on a visit to the camp at the Battle of Eylau (1808). He portrayed the dead in stark reality – lying in the snow, their twisted bodies and frozen expressions showing graphically the horrors of this battle between the French and Russian armies in which about 25,000 men perished. The tragedy of the

Théodore Géricault, The Raft of the Medusa, *1819. Musée du Louvre, Paris.*

John Singleton Copley, Watson and the Shark, *1778. National Gallery of Art, Washington, D.C..*

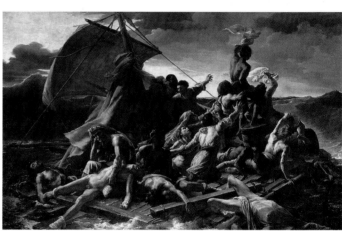

THE MYTHOLOGY OF THE NIGHT

In contrast to the Apollonian clarity that dominated the aesthetic ideal of Neoclassicism, the "Romantic night" became a protagonist in its own right for some artists. It was peopled with spectral apparitions, strange, ambiguous creatures, and fantastic figures like those in the paintings of Henry Fuseli. Night was expressed as the secret moment of human experience, inhabited by the most terrifying psychic forces. The success of the nocturne, which became an elaborate musical form during this period and was favored by Chopin, was partly responsible for the theme being adopted and explored by visual artists. A night setting greatly intensified the emotional significance of an ocean horizon, a Gothic ruin gripped the victim of forces beyond its control. The American painter John Singleton Copley (1738–1815) reconstructed a real-life event in a commissioned work: *Watson and the Shark*. The shark is a very real physical creature, yet at the same time it symbolizes the mighty force of nature with which man can be in conflict or which can even take his life. The men in the boat struggle to save the figure of Watson in the water while also fending off the animal. Théodore Géricault also chose to paint a real event. In his *Raft of the Medusa,* he portrays the makeshift raft on which the surviving passengers and crew were abandoned. The terrible scene Gericault forces us to contemplate shows death and suffering without any nobility or dignity. The victims have a long and drawn-out fate ahead of them. There is no

Caspar David Friedrich, The Sea of Ice, *1824. Hamburger Kunsthalle, Hamburg.*

strong color, only a sickly light and the murky, violent sea. Exhibited grudgingly by the artistic establishment at the Paris Salon in 1819, this radical work proved highly controversial, its grim subject matter challenging traditional artistic rules. *The Raft of the Medusa* became extremely important as a symbol of Romanticism in art, and Géricault's work would prove to be inspirat-ional for artists such as Delacroix.

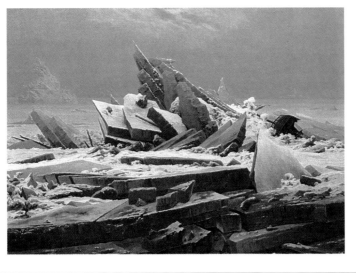

FRIEDRICH AND THE NORTHERN EUROPEANS

In *The Sea of Ice* by Caspar David Friedrich, man is absent, devoured by the awe-inspiring and adverse elements; there are no traces of the shipwrecked crew in the icy landscape. Glimpses of small sections of the boat are visible between the slabs of ice, which form a silent

pyramid rising up to the sky. It is thought that the sea of ice symbolized the "frozen" political climate and the despondent mood surrounding the struggles for German independence from Napoleon's forces. For Friedrich, nature was like a living, organic creature,

by frost, or a forest where trunks and branches became ghostly, distorted patterns. There were clear parallels in the operas of Wagner, which exemplified many of the themes of Romanticism in music. One powerful portrayal of the night was produced by George

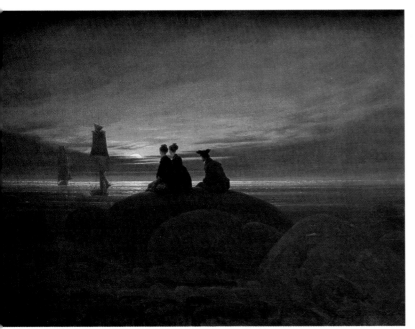

George Stubbs, Lion Attacking a Horse, *1769. Tate Gallery, London.*

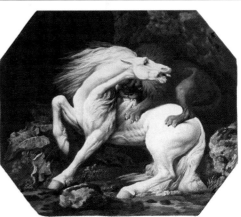

Caspar David Friedrich, Moonrise over the Sea, *1822. Neue Nationalgalerie, Berlin. It is not so much Friedrich's spirit of existentialism as his portrayal of nature as the protagonist of the piece that was to have such a profound influence on landscape painters in Europe.*

Stubbs (1724–1806) in *Lion Attacking a Horse*. The white horse rears in terror as a lion springs onto its back out of the darkness. The contrast between the proud nobility of the domestic animal and the savagery of the wild beast becomes a symbol of the opposing energies that inhabit the human soul and sustain its mystery.

The figures in the canvases of Caspar David Friedrich, such as those in *Moonrise over the Sea,* cast their eyes toward a limitless horizon, lit by a pale, distant moon. Their silent contemplation seems dominated by the night. Although these figures are placed at the very edge of the land and are completely anonymous, the viewer can empathize with them.

THE WAYFARER

The concept of nature that emerged with the Romantic movement gave rise to the figure of the wayfarer, depicted widely in art as well as literature and music. The wayfarer, or wanderer, was a person who had renounced the comfort and security of a home in order to travel through a mysterious and perhaps hostile world, not knowing whether he would ever return. This theme, illustrated predominantly in

Ludwig Adrian Richter, Wayfarer Resting in the Mountains.

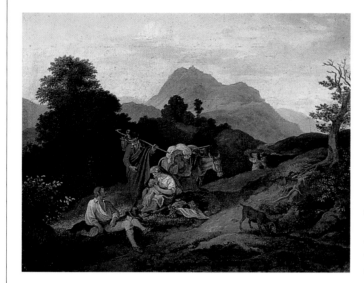

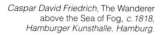
Caspar David Friedrich, The Wanderer above the Sea of Fog, *c.1818, Hamburger Kunsthalle, Hamburg.*

German culture, arises from an anthropological concept whereby man no longer finds himself at the center of events and is unable to control them: indeed, very often the world displays a lack of harmony and order that he cannot comprehend or face up to. Romanticism frequently portrayed nature at its most dramatic: raging tempests, bleak, mountainous landscapes, and forests where one could become forever lost. These landscapes are

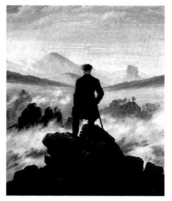

places of extraordinary bleakness and solitude, where man moves aimlessly and wearily, impelled by an irrational quest for the absolute. Wanderers often peopled the canvases of Ludwig Adrian Richter (1803–84) and Caspar David Friedrich, who successfully captured the essence of the wayfarer's long and uncertain journey. *The Wanderer above the Sea of Fog* is one of the most famous paintings of the Romantic movement: it symbolizes solitude, expresses despair, and explores the mystery that engulfs the figure, whose gaze is turned toward the abyss. This canvas represents the experience of human life as the ultimate journey, one that leads toward infinity and death.

Oakwood shows the remains of human endeavor laid open to the forces of the cosmos. This painting may be interpreted as a parable of the divine, suggesting a promise of eternity. The painter often looked to his religious faith for answers to metaphysical questions. It portrays an uncertain, mysterious universe, the workings of which can be glimpsed but are never fully revealed and can never be controlled.

The grand Romantic work of Johan Christian Dahl (1788–1857) was stylistically close to that of both Friedrich and the Norwegian landscape painter Gustav Carus (1789–1869). Carus was also a writer, geologist, physiologist, and naturalist. Both men were friends of Friedrich. The portrayals of the Norwegian landscape by these artists pioneered a new spirit of Norwegian nationalism, and work was produced with a definite Nordic identity. The artists aims were similar to those of the *Sturm und Drang* writers, a proto-Romantic movement that sought to free German arts from French influence.

untameable and unpredictable. The artist's uncommissioned painting *The Cross in the Mountains* (1808) caused a sensation when it was first exhibited as an altarpiece in the castle at Tetschen: the crucified Christ was almost lost in his surroundings, which became the symbol of a cosmic, existentialist grief. During the Neoclassical period, such emotion would have been attained through noble and detailed expression, exemplified by the tomb of Maria Cristina of Austria

Caspar David Friedrich, Abbey in the Oakwood, *1809–10. Staatliche Museen, Berlin.*

by the sculptor Antonio Canova.

For Friedrich, ancient ruins became the symbol of a world of solitude, where

mankind's vain and futile enterprises are lost in a bleak, intensely cold and ghostly landscape. The artist's *Abbey in the*

THE ENGLISH MASTERS

Joseph Mallord William Turner (1775–1851) was one of the greatest of all British painters and a key exponent of Romantic landscape art. His *Snowstorm: Hannibal and his Army Crossing the Alps* is an awesome work, a masterful expression of the power and mystery of nature. It shows Hannibal at the mercy of nature, which has turned against him, rather than as master of his own destiny. This reversed the idea of David's composition, *Napoleon Crossing the St. Bernard Pass* (1800), which portrayed

Napoleon as a new Hannibal. The natural elements completely dominate the composition, and the figures (even that of the elephant) appear tiny and helpless. Turner's work took to extremes the lyrical immersion in nature that had been portrayed earlier by Alexander Cozens (1717–86), and it went beyond the immediacy of the vision of John Constable (1776–1837), culminating in a kind of "mysticism of light." Thomas Gainsborough (1727–88) had already explored the enigmatic magic of color with his fluid, shadowy brush-strokes. According to Sir Joshua Reynolds (1723–92),

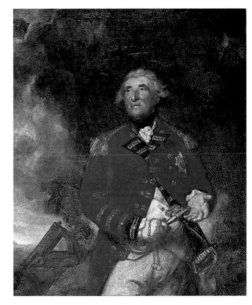

Sir Joshua Reynolds, Lord Heathfield, 1787. National Gallery, London. President of the Royal Academy and a distinguished theorist of painting, Reynolds was the most popular portrait painter among the aristocracy of his time.

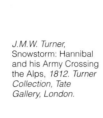

J.M.W. Turner, Snowstorm: Hannibal and his Army Crossing the Alps, 1812. Turner Collection, Tate Gallery, London.

the artist should paint "in the same way in which nature creates her own works." The aristocratic tradition of the portrait was continued by Reynolds, Gainsborough, and Sir Thomas Lawrence (1769–1830), who was court painter in 1792.

ECSTASY AND ESTRANGEMENT

The treatment of time by Romantic artists tended to fall into two categories. Sometimes, it appeared to be compressed by the whirling mass of dramatic events, a portrayal that was particularly common in the works of Delacroix and Géricault. Elsewhere, however, it appears that time has suddenly ceased to exist and cannot be perceived or contemplated. At such moments, man finds himself estranged, and the literal meaning of the word "ecstasy" as "outside one's own mind" is applicable. This definition calls to mind Friedrich's portrayal of the human condition, where nature serves as a vast backdrop against which the irreconcilable solitude of

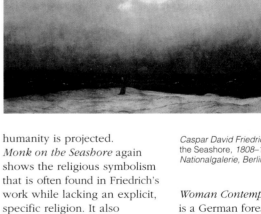

humanity is projected. *Monk on the Seashore* again shows the religious symbolism that is often found in Friedrich's work while lacking an explicit, specific religion. It also conveys the presence of a mystery before which man no longer has any power: he can contemplate it, but to be able to measure himself against this anonymous force, he must come "out of himself." The word "monk" comes from the Greek for "alone," and we share his powerful sense of loneliness with him. The artist's chosen setting for his painting *A Man and a*

Caspar David Friedrich, A Man and a Woman Contemplate the Moon, 1830–35. Neue Nationalgalerie, Berlin.

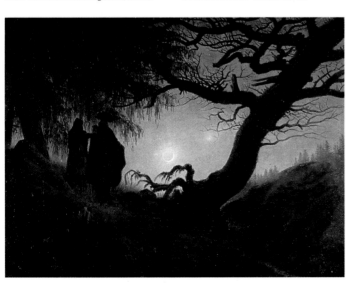

Caspar David Friedrich, Monk on the Seashore, 1808–10. Neue Nationalgalerie, Berlin.

Woman Contemplate the Moon is a German forest, in which there is no visible path for the figures to follow. Among the dark silhouettes of the trees linger two figures who look across the landscape at the moon, which hangs low in the night sky. A symbol of Christ, the moon indicates a hope given to humankind; it is also a sign of the supernatural world in which that hope may be eventually fulfilled.

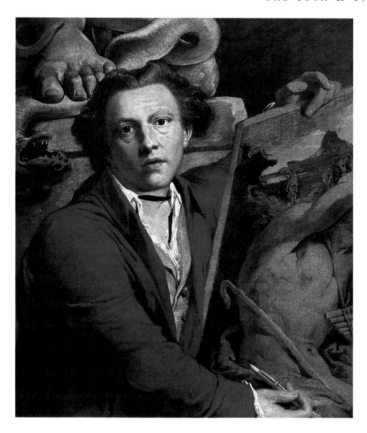

James Barry, Self-Portrait, 1803. National Gallery of Ireland, Dublin.

BLAKE AND THE VISIONARY PAINTERS

The concept of existential loneliness that emerged with Romanticism signaled the end of the Utopian ideals of the Enlightenment. At the same time, the artists' vision broadened in their attempt to paint "that which is not seen." Figures became less heavy and more immaterial, less concrete and defined, in contrast to the precision of Neoclassicism. Figures no longer portrayed only beauty but were molded by the energies of the human soul, sometimes distorted or uneasy, often disorderly and impulsive. Artists were invested with a new responsibility, almost as the re-creators of a lost paradise, imparting a divine message that could be revealed only through the medium of art. William Blake (1757–1827), the visionary and prophetic poet and artist, proclaimed: "The man who raises himself above all is the artist; the prophet is he who is gifted with imagination."
The Swiss-born Henry Fuseli, after settling in England, transformed the graceful, symbolic fauna of Neoclassicism, such as butterflies and horses, into strange, ambiguous monsters of the imagination.
The dream, with all its irrational implications, became the realm of fantasy, terrifying images, and erotic

HENRY FUSELI

Swiss-born artist Johann Heinrich Füssli (1741–1825), widely known as Henry Fuseli, was pushed by his father toward a career in the Church. However, he developed an aversion to religious dogma, preferring to read Milton, Dante, Homer, Shakespeare, and the medieval German heroic epic the *Nibelungenlied*. He lived in Italy from 1770 until 1777 and moved to London in 1780, where he settled and became a member of the Royal Academy of Arts. One of his most illustrious pupils was William Blake. He was buried with full honors in St. Paul's Cathedral.

THE APOCALYPTIC FORCES OF NATURE

Nature, to the Romantics, ceased to be a mere backdrop to human affairs and became a living organism that was both extreme and multidimensional. It no longer bore the intentionally reassuring characteristics of Arcadia, expressing itself through hurricanes, raging fires, and earthquakes.
The Last Days of Pompeii by the Russian artist Karl Pavlovitch Brüllov (1799–1852) shows in lurid colors the horror of that fateful day. The outstretched arms, the heads bent back to look at the threatening sky, and other gestures show the sense of terror among the figures. These expressions conform to the classical vocabulary introduced in the *Stanze*, the series of rooms in the Vatican that Raphael decorated for Julius II and Leo X. Elsewhere, the same theme of horror and cataclysm was developed in a decidedly anticlassical sense. John Martin (1789–1854) was one of the more visionary English painters of the 18th century. His unusual effects of light and the contrasts between a dramatically apocalyptic landscape and tiny figures create an almost supernatural effect. He drew on biblical and Oriental themes, for example the canvas of *Sadak Looking for the Waters of Oblivion* (1812), taken from Persian legend, and *The Fall of Baylon* (1819), which is painted in the same grandiose manner. Martin was famous throughout Europe and appealed particularly to French writers such as Huysmans, Sainte-Beuve, Victor Hugo, and Théophile Gautier. Henry Fuseli, in his painting *Satan Calling to Beelzebub over a Sea of Fire*, advanced even farther toward the abyss: the main figure is both majestic and sinister, while the figure rising from the depths with its indistinct features seems to bring to life the monstrous forms of the human soul.

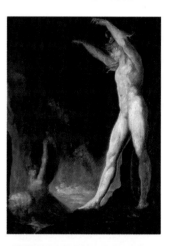

Henry Fuseli, Satan Calling to Beelzebub over a Sea of Fire, 1802. Kunsthaus, Zurich.

Karl Pavlovitch Bryullov, The Last Days of Pompeii, 1830–33. Russian State Museum, St. Petersburg.

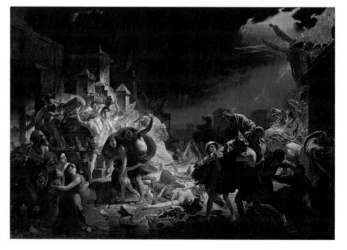

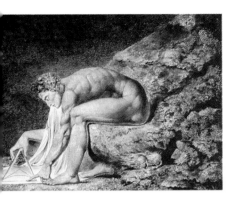

temptations. His
contemporary, the Irish
historical painter James Barry
(1741–1806) was, according
to Blake, misunderstood and
unappreciated by the art
world. Affirming his strong
belief in his own greatness,
Barry portrayed himself in
Self-Portrait, wearing the
garments of the Greek
painter Timantes.
For William Blake, "the
world of the imagination is
the world of eternity," where
truth and illusion, experience
and fantasy, the real world
and the supernatural, have
no dividing line. To Blake,
if "the doors of perception
were cleansed, everything
would appear to man as it
is, infinite." Blake, along with
exploring the spiritualism of
biblical subjects, also sought
a common, unifying
cosmology to all mythology
– classical, Nordic, Semitic,
and Oriental. In reviving
the form of the medieval
miniature, Blake devised a
new technique to blend the
meaning of the text with
the style in which it is
presented, synthesizing
narrative and decoration.
His figures retained a
classical beauty and purity of
line that approached those
of the Danish-born German
painter and draftsman Jakob

*Philipp Otto Runge, Morning, 1808.
Hamburger Kunsthalle, Hamburg. This
painting operates on several levels,
from the principal image in the frame
to the surrounding figures that are
full of allegorical meaning.*

SLEEP AND REASON

Fuseli's *The Nightmare* is an
enigmatic image that transcends
reason, while Goya's *The Sleep
of Reason Produces Monsters* is
an allegory of the irrational fears
that lie behind rational thought.
Both illustrate sleep and dream-
states and explore how illusion
and fantasy are inextricably
bound up with reason.

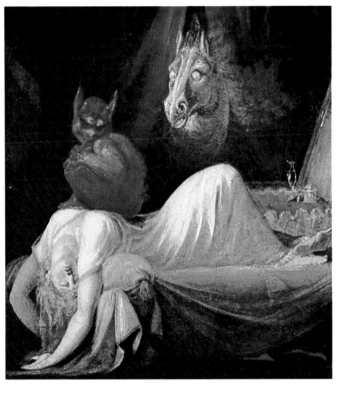

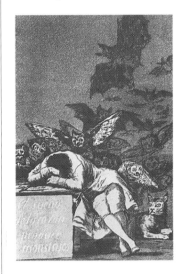

*Francisco Goya, The Sleep of Reason
Produces Monsters, Capricho No. 43,
etching and aquatint, 1797–98.
Private Collection.*

*Henry Fuseli, The Nightmare,
1790–91. Goethemuseum, Frankfurt.
This is one of several versions of
Fuseli's original 1781 painting.*

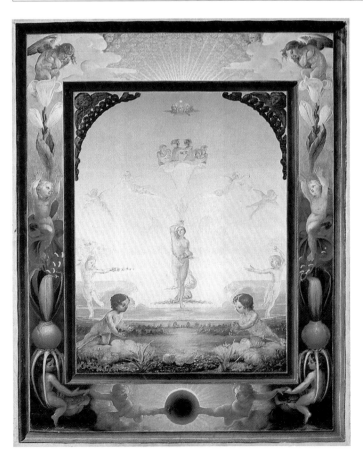

Carstens (1754–98).
The German artist Philipp
Otto Runge (1777–1810)
took refuge in the myth of
childhood, which he idealized
as a beautiful, happy time
in which love remained pure
and innocent. He often used
the stability of the family in
his work as a mirror of the
entire range of human
relationships. In his series
Die Tageszeiten ("The Times
of the Day") begun in about
1796, Runge aimed to extend
such harmony to the whole
universe. This ambitious
project depicts nature with
allegorical personages that
allude to human destiny
and have some religious
and political significance.
A chapel was to have housed
the work, which, combined
with music and poetry,
prefigured Wagner's dream
of *Gesamtkunstwerk* – a total
expression of words, music,
and theater.

GOYA

The two chief aspects of Romanticism are combined in the work of Goya: the exploration of the frontiers of a deeper life and the integration of historical fact. In *The Colossus*, Goya portrays the giant as bestial and strangely still. He stands against the dark and misty skies, hovering above a land populated by fleeing people. The painting represents the looming catastrophe of war and the abandonment of humanity to the destructive force of instinct. Other key Goya works include *Saturn Devouring His Own Son* (1821–23), an allegory of Spain destroying her own people, and a "reportage" of 65 etchings, *The Disasters of War*, executed between 1810 and 1820. In these, the artist illustrates the massacres, rapes, violence, assassinations, profanities, and crimes committed by both the French and Spanish armies during the Napoleonic occupation. An obscure, curious, and irrational element was apparent in Goya's work. In his series of etchings *Los Caprichos* (published in 1799), there is none of the gaiety often dominant in similarly titled works by Tiepolo, Fragonard, or

FRANCISCO GOYA

Francisco de Goya y Lucientes (1746–1828) was the son of a poor goldsmith in Saragossa. In 1763, he moved to Madrid and, after a period of travel, he returned in 1776 to become a successful artist. He became Principal Painter to King Charles IV in 1799. In 1811, Joseph Bonaparte granted him the Royal Order of Spain. After the fall of the Napoleonic Empire, Goya once again worked for the Spanish court. With the restoration of Ferdinand VII's absolutist regime, the artist left Madrid for Paris and in 1825 settled in voluntary exile in Bordeaux, where he died after a final burst of activity. His work has since greatly influenced and inspired artists, particularly the 19th-century French painters.

POLITICAL PAINTING

Artists have illustrated the exploits of monarchs and generals since antiquity. Among the most celebrated examples are the high reliefs of the Arch of Constantine and Trajan's Column; the lost fresco cycle of Charlemagne's palace at Aachen, depicting the Emperor's victories in Spain; and Andrea Mantegna's historic portraits of the family of the marquesses of Mantua in the *camera picta* of the castle of San Giorgio (1471–74). Entire Italian dynasties were portrayed in vast cycles: Alessandro Farnese (who became Pope Paul III in 1534) employed Francesco Salviati and Taddeo Zuccari, while Giorgio Vasari began the apotheosis of the House of Medici in the Palazzo Vecchio in Florence in 1556. Later, Peter Paul Rubens executed a series of paintings to glorify Henry IV and Marie de' Médicis for the Luxembourg Palace in Paris (1625). As for the Spanish, Giambattista Tiepolo was summoned to Madrid by the monarch Charles III and paid to exalt the sovereign, the dynasty, and its victories. His *Glory of Spain* (1765) on the ceiling of the throne room of the Royal Palace celebrated the whole royal family.
The Napoleonic occupation of

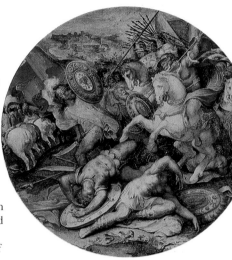

Taddeo Zuccari, Pietro Farnese Defeats the Enemies of the Church, *1562–63. Palazzo Farnese, Sala dei Fasti Farnesiani, Caprarola, Italy.*

Peter Paul Rubens, Apotheosis of Henry IV and Proclamation of the Regency of Marie de' Médicis, *c.1625. Musée du Louvre, Paris.*

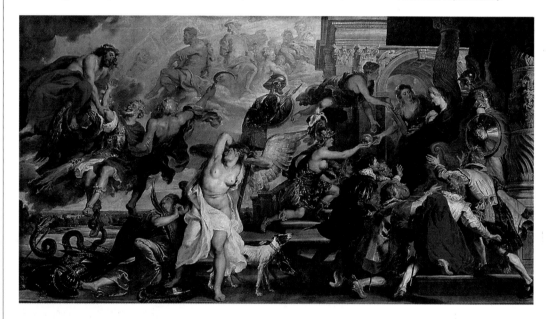

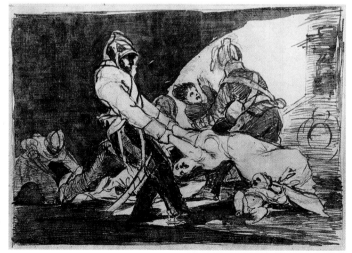

Spain ended in 1814, but even before the restoration of Ferdinand VII, Goya began works commemorating events that took place during the Spanish uprising. His *Third of May 1808* (1814) marked a turning point in artistic representation of war, as the tragedy of human conflict had never before been portrayed with such pitiless honesty. This approach had nothing to do with the heroism and chivalry of conventional historical painting;

Francisco Goya, Not Even These, *c.1810. Museo del Prado, Madrid.*

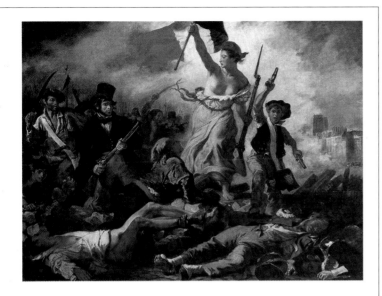

Eugène Delacroix, Liberty Leading the People (July 28, 1830), *1830. Musée du Louvre, Paris.*

instead, it deals with the death of liberty, with the artist acting as spokesperson for the people. The power of his expression of horror, outrage, and violence

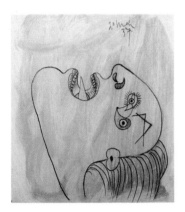

Pablo Picasso, study of a woman's head for Guernica, *May 20, 1937. Centro de Arte Reine Sofia, Madrid.*

Arnulf Rainer, Hiroshima Cycle, *1982. Städtische Galerie im Lenbachhaus. Munich.*

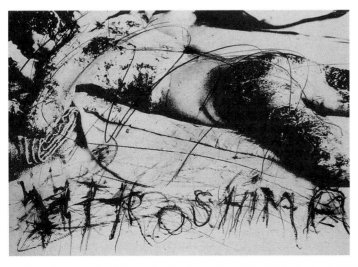

would not find its equivalent until the 20th century with Picasso's *Guernica* (1937) and with portrayals of previously unimagined devastation, such as *Hiroshima Cycle* by Arnulf Rainer.
In one of the most famous – and controversial – political paintings of the 19th century, *Liberty Leading the People (July 28, 1830)*, Delacroix celebrates the Parisian uprisings of 1830. The heroine, who holds aloft the French flag, personifies a new collective hero in art: the people.

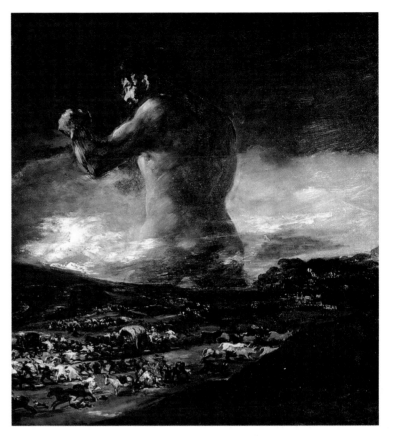

Francisco Goya, The Colossus, *c.1808–12. Museo del Prado, Madrid.*

Guardi. The artist also questioned the excesses of his imagination in *Capricho No. 43*, a self-portrait. His head lies against a solid base, a metaphor for order within the world, while he is in the middle of a nightmare. He entitled the piece "The sleep of reason produces monsters," adding, "imagination abandoned by reason generates monstrosity; together they form the mother of the arts and the origin of marvels." This phrase sums up the aesthetic ideal of Romanticism, for which art does not "redeem" sickness, irrationality, or death but actually emanates from the same source.
Goya's work was extremely advanced for its time, demonstrating an astonishing technical skill in both etching and painting. His works are characterized by problems and conflicts, unknown in 18th-century iconography, and a sparse, bleak treatment of landscape. Goya's portraits often reveal the extraordinary inner complexities of the human soul – they can illustrate at once arrogance, authority, and a sense of emptiness. Even when he was painting official canvases such as the celebrated group portrait *The Family of Charles IV* (1800–01), the human frailty of the subjects was made apparent.
Goya's technique for painting nudes was to have a decisive influence on late Romantic and even Impressionist painting. His *The Maja Nude* (1800) is probably one of the most famous nudes in the history of art. He was also master of fresco painting, as is clear from the terrifying "black paintings" (1820–22) from the "House of the Deaf Man," his country home, which were transferred to canvas in 1873. Unique for his time, Goya prefigured many of the themes of modern art in a wide-ranging body of work that displayed an unrivaled intensity of expression.

THE SOLDIER: HERO OR ANTI-HERO?

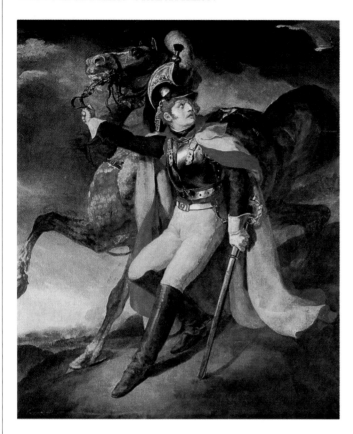

Among the most memorable portraits of the soldier during the early 19th century were those of Napoleon, notably by Jacques-Louis David. His idealized Napoleon did not represent the individual so much as the archetype of heroism. A significantly less heroic portrayal of the soldier was Géricault's *Wounded Cuirassier*, painted at the time of Napoleon suffered a defeat in the "Battle of the Nations" at Leipzig (October 16-19, 1813) and exhibited at the Salon in

Théodore Géricault, The Wounded Cuirassier, *1814. Musée du Louvre, Paris.*

1814, the year of the Emperor's abdication. The image of a terrified horse being restrained by a soldier, who looks back to where the battle rages, is tinged with sadness and disillusionment, suggesting that an epoch has drawn to a close. The painting, with its flat slabs of color, renders its subject unappealing and marks an end to the portrayal of the soldier as a superman and hero.

EUGENE DELACROIX

The most important painter of the Romantic movement in France, Eugène Delacroix (1798–1863) began his career in Baron Guérin's workship. There, he met Théodore Géricault, who would prove to be a key influence. Among the other painters he admired was Constable. Influential in terms of subject matter were his travels in 1832 to Morocco, Algeria, and Spain. After years of battles with the Salon, he was given official approval at the Universal Exhibition of 1855.

THE FRENCH MASTERS

Eugène Delacroix used literary, exotic, historical, and also contemporary events as subjects for his paintings. When he showed the *Massacre at Chios* at the Paris Salon in 1824, it caused a sensation. Suddenly, art no longer neede to refer to antiquity but could presume

to document the age in which the artist was living. Delacroix sought "that expressive force, that energy, that audacity" that he could not find in the canons of David's ideal of eternal

beauty. This "force" later emerged in Géricault's compact, solid forms based on the contrast between light and shade. The atmospheric luminosity of Delacroix's landscapes and the brilliant,

EUGENE DELACROIX: "THE ABDUCTION OF REBECCA"

1846; oil on canvas; 32 x 40 in (82 x 100 cm); Metropolitan Museum of Art, New York.

This work, which illustrates a popular fictional dramatic scene, is signed and dated at bottom left. It belongs to the artist's fully mature period; a second version is housed in the Louvre. The subject is based on the romantic novel *Ivanhoe*, written by Sir Walter Scott in 1820. It recounts a tale of the wars between the Normans and Saxons at the time of Richard I (1189–99), known as Richard the Lionheart. In the foreground, Rebecca, a rich young Jewish woman, is lying

across the haunch of a horse, held between two men in flamboyant costumes; one holds her by the waist, the other by the legs. Below right, in the middle ground, a knight in armor, with his cloak billowing in the wind, spurs on his mount to reach the victim. In the upper background, amid trails of smoke, stands a castle in flames.

▶ *1. The animated composition follows a rigorously studied plan, its balance established by two main right-angled axes. The vertical axis falls from the edge of the tower to the right hands of the horseman and the girl, then to the left leg of the abductor seen from behind. The horizontal axis is lower down, passing through the feet of the standing abductor and the rear hooves of the horse. Above this axis, the movement of the composition is arranged in a series of intersecting lines and contours.*

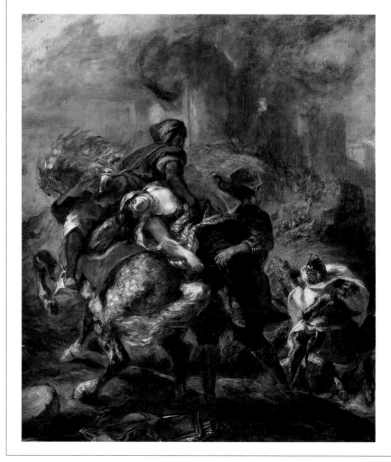

fierce light of Morocco brightened his palette with stronger colors. It released him from the academic technique of chiaroscuro and enhanced the freedom of his brushwork.

The same vital energy was echoed in the vibrant, tense postures captured by the animal sculptor and painter Antoine-Louis Barye (1796–1875). This artist brought an extraordinary

vigor to his violent portrayals of fights between tigers, crocodiles, and other wild beasts. These paintings contrasted strongly with the monumental stillness and sublime calm of Neoclassical

art, which was based on precise aesthetic principles. With the advent of Romanticism, sculpture became an almost contra-dictory medium as regards the ideal theories of the new

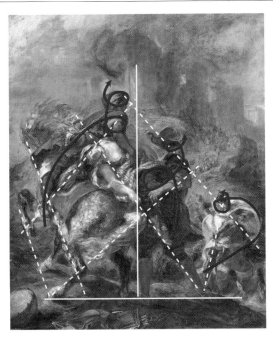

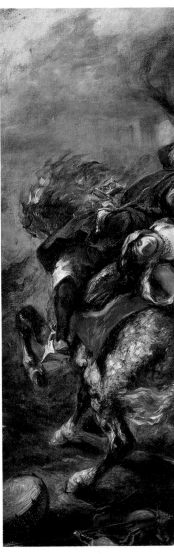

▼ 2. The painting is full of energy and drama. This shines through, not only from the compositional plan, but also from the dominant line from which the form is composed. The use of curved lines accentuates the sense of continuous, dramatic movement, resiliently bounding and rebounding from one form to another. The dynamic tension of these curves binds together each element of the composition, creating a single dramatic whole.

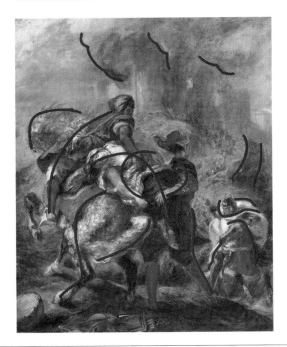

▼ 4. The vigor of the brushwork is key to the painting's powerful effect. The artist's movements are immediate and energetic, evident in the flowing brushstrokes. Light also plays an important role in the strong emotive content of the picture. In the atmosphere darkened by the smoke of the fire, the light floods on to the two "good" figures, the woman and the knight rushing to her assistance. The light makes them the two focal points of the scene, although more space is given to the abductors and the horse. Particularly successful is the dramatic way in which the artist captures every posture, gesture, and movement of both the humans and the animals.

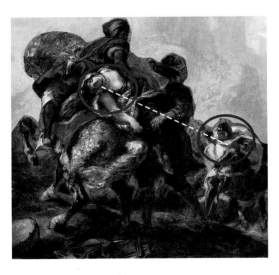

▼ 5. The castle ramparts emerge from the darkened background of smoke like an apparition. The smoke spirals up in great plumes, painted with energetic brushstrokes. Although the smoke is contained in the upper third of the picture, the light it reflects invades the scene in the foreground. The orange in the clouds and the red and yellow streaks in the flames serve as indications of movement in the scene.

▲ 3. A closer look at the juxtaposition of colors reveals the careful prelim-inary research and planning that characterizes Delacroix's work. The pure colors are laid on the canvas in adjacent tones that anticipate the experiments of the Impressionists. The contrast is made up of complem-entary warm and cold tones; for example, the red cloth and the green saddle, the blue area of the sky among the orange clouds and the brown of the horse's mane. The background has cold touches of green alternating with warm burnt ochre. The basis of the painting is the rhythmical cadence of blue-greens and brown-reds, and flashes of white tinged with flesh tones or silver.

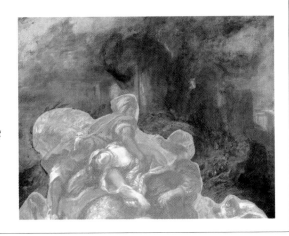

ROMANTIC DEATH

The subject of death, which had been portrayed by the Neoclassicists as a moment of universal nobility for humanity in general, became for the Romantics an artistic device for the expression of individual tragedy.

The same themes that had been illustrated by David or Canova were now burdened with a dark sense of tragedy. Dead or dying figures became symbols of disintegration and decay, particularly, as seen in the despairing figures painted by Géricault and Delacroix. The

Girodet-Trioson (1767-1824), the sleeping figure of Endymion, with his young, almost childlike body, is bathed in such an intense light that it seems it could almost consume him – a reminder of the closeness of the state of sleep to that of death. His interpretation, a reminder of the fleeting mortality of both individuals and society, contrasts with the earlier Neoclassical idealization of the past through myth.

The American historical painter Benjamin West (1738–1820) returned many times to the theme of death and was

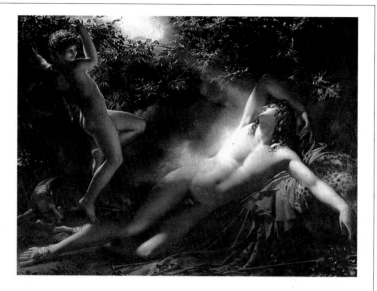

successful in portraying contemporary scenes of war and destruction with the pathos and heroism of a classical tragedy, while still investing his work with an immediacy and contemporary relevance. His apocalyptic *Death on a Pale Horse* was important in the

Benjamin West, Death on a Pale Horse, *1796. Institute of Arts, Detroit.*

Anne-Louis Girodet Trioson, The Sleep of Endymion, *1793. Musée du Louvre, Paris.*

Romantic movement, and it was hailed as prefiguring Delacroix. West settled in London in 1763 and became the most successful historical painter of his day, enjoying a profitable association with George III. He succeeded Reynolds as President of the Royal Academy in 1792.

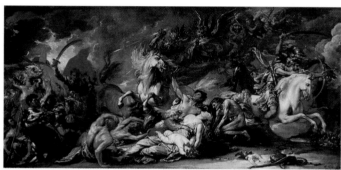

past became almost an organic and changing state of decay rather than the static moment captured in Neo-classical painting.

The Death of Sardanapalus, which illustrates a mythical antiquity with precision and detail, is similar in mood to that evoked by Gustave Flaubert's novel *Salammbô* (1862), set in ancient Carthage. Delacroix expresses the relentless certainty of dissolution and decay; his use of sumptuous decoration is a veneer that conceals the inevitable progress toward death. The painting was harshly criticized for its rejection of French classicism in both subject matter and style, not least its bold and dynamic treatment of color.

Sleep, too, can be seen as a state in close proximity to death. In *The Sleep of Endymion* by Anne-Louis

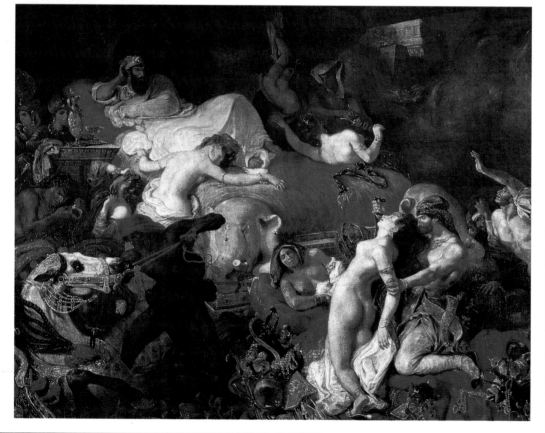

Eugène Delacroix, The Death of Sardan-apalus, *1827. Musée du Louvre, Paris.*

THE PEOPLE

The heroism of the people who fought for their country and their faith and who maintained a link with tradition was often used as subject matter to express grand Romantic political and moral ideals. Delacroix's *Greek Woman among the Ruins of Missolonghi* glorifies the inhabitants of the Greek city, which they destroyed rather than surrender to the Turks. The Italian painter Francesco

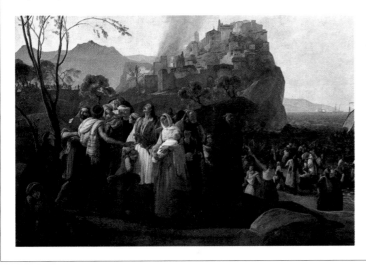

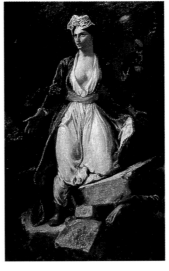

Eugène Delacroix, Greek Woman among the Ruins of Missolonghi, *1826. Musée des Beaux-Arts, Bordeaux.*

Francesco Hayez, The Refugees of Parga, *1831. Pinacoteca Tosio Martinengo, Brescia, Italy.*

Hayez, who in 1841 was proclaimed a "national painter" by the Italian patriot Giuseppe Mazzini, portrayed the people in the role of a Greek chorus in his *Refugees of Parga*. His Romantic subjects never quite lost their sharp academic outline. The idea of nationhood developed during the 19th century, when "the people" became a single entity, treated as a coherent individual. The idealization of the masses would sometimes lead to stereotypical generalizations of nations or cultural groups, often bordering on the ridiculous. Romantic artists often showed the people engaged in struggles, battles, and other emotionally intense scenes; this theme was also much in evidence in the narrative prose, poetry, and opera of the time.

aesthetic; hence, it was poorly represented as an art form at this time. *Carnage* (1834) by Auguste Préault (1809–79) appears as a menacing and visionary attack on violence, while Romantic individualism found expression in the celebrated medallions of Pierre-Jean David d'Angers (1788–1856). He represented the characteristics of his famous sitters (including Delacroix, Friedrich, Victor Hugo, Byron, Paganini, and Rossini) almost to the point of caricature.

THE ITALIAN MASTERS

In comparison with other cultures, the development of Romanticism was slow in Italy, in literature as well as in painting. Its principal characteristic was the attribution of historical significance to individual events, particularly those associated with the unification of Italy. Francesco Hayez (1791–1882) did not possess the dramatic impetus, nor perhaps the expressive truth, of French painters; for him, the pictorial fury with which Delacroix translated the immediacy of events was entirely foreign. He was, however, the most important figure in the transition from Italian Neoclassicism to Romanticism. Images became more refined in Italian painting as draftsmanship was combined with a notable solidity. The artist's illustrations often assumed the character of a symbolic romance or, in their lyrical and sentimental handling of melodramatic events, shared an affinity with current musical performances in Italy. Hayez favored a theatrical style, using backdrops, wings, costumes, and a balanced arrangement of the characters. The scenery was dictated by a desire for documentary accuracy, and he developed a symbolic sense of gesture in his style, which is perfectly exemplified by *Melancholy*.

Francesco Hayez, Melancholy, *1842. Pinacoteca di Brera, Milan.*

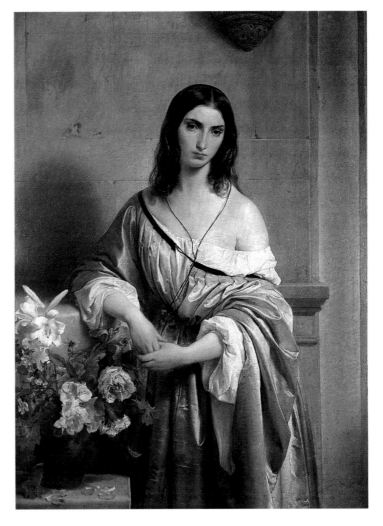

ORIENTALISM

Following the British expansion in India during the first half of the 18th century, Napoleon's Egyptian Campaign in 1798, and the French conquest of Algeria in 1830, an idle curiosity about these distant lands grew into a specific interest that influenced European taste in general. An element of the exotic permeated trends in literature, music, and the visual arts throughout the 19th century.

In the early 18th century, the influence of the Orient in art was of a purely decorative nature. Viewed through Western eyes, the Orient evoked by Western artists was a fanciful and distinctly Europeanized place, exemplified by the works of Giambattista Tiepolo, François Boucher, Nicolas Lancret, and Charles-Joseph Natoire. The increasing interest in the East was echoed in the realm of music, for example in the compositions of Rameau and Mozart, particularly Rameau's *Les Indes galantes* (1735), and Mozart's *Die Entführung aus dem Serail* (1782).

By 1770, the vogue for chinoiserie – the imitation of Chinese style, primarily in decoration and furniture –

Jean Etienne Liotard, Woman with a Tambourine, c.1735–40. Musée d'Art et d'Histoire, Geneva.

THE EGYPTIAN STYLE

Following Napoleon's campaign of 1798, the Egyptian style became fashionable throughout Europe. It was favored for the furnishings of grand town houses and was also adapted to less ostentatious dwellings. Decorated furniture, fabrics, goldwork, jewelry, and porcelain all featured such details as sphinxes and caryatids. The French ceramics manufacturer Sèvres produced dinner services with sumptuous designs of hawks, sphinxes, and hieroglyphs. Many villas and palaces displayed the popular taste for the Egyptian style: Napoleon's residence at Elba, the Villa di San Martino, where he was exiled between 1814 and 1815, was a triumph of the interior decorator's art, complete with an Egyptian room and gardens

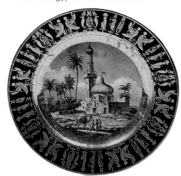

The Temple of Hermopolis, *"Champollion" Sèvres vase, Museo degli Argenti, Florence.*

Jacques Swebach (1769–1823), Mosque at Rosetta, *Sèvres plate from the Egyptian dinner service.*

embellished with pillars and obelisks. Tombs shaped like small pyramids and obelisks begin to fill cemeteries, such as Montparnasse and Père Lachaise in Paris and Kensal Green in London. These were

derided by the English architect and propagandist of the Gothic Revival Augustus Welby Northmore Pugin (1812–52) in his *Apology for the Revival of Christian Architecture in England* (1843).

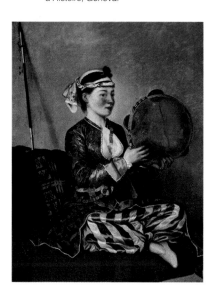

that had been popular in the Rococo period was beginning to fade. However, there remained a number of notable enthusiasts of the Chinese style, particularly in the field of architecture. For example, in 1799 Venanzio Marvuglia (1729–1814) created a "Chinese Palace" at Villa La Favorita in Sicily as a refuge for King Ferdinand IV. Soon after, at the beginning of the 19th century, Oriental style was extravagantly revived by John Nash (1752–1835) in his reconstruction of the Royal Pavilion in the English seaside resort of Brighton.

PRE-ORIENTALISM

Although Orientalism did not become a well-defined style until the 19th century, its roots can be traced to a general love of exotica in the 18th century. Artistic treatment of Eastern subjects took the form of charming, picturesque recordings of artists' travels through Eastern countries, with scenes clearly refined to suit the tastes of a European audience. Of particular note is the work of the Swiss pastel painter and engraver Jean Etienne Liotard (1702–89), who painted

women dressed in Turkish costume, paying careful attention to detail and displaying an unprecedented degree of sensitivity to the subject. After spending four years in Constantinople from 1738, Liotard even chose to retain the Turkish dress and beard that he had adopted while abroad. Another 18th-century artist to venture East was Luigi Mayer (c.1755–1803), who traveled through the Ottoman Empire between 1776 and 1794, sketching and painting panoramic landscapes, ancient monuments, and the Nile and its surroundings.

THE EGYPTIAN INFLUENCE

During the late 18th century, the East was not only a rich source of inspiration for decorative themes and motifs but also yielded great scientific discoveries. In order to meet the need to give a sound methodological basis to these new studies, in 1793 a special school was set up in the Bibliothèque Nationale in Paris for the teaching of Arabic, Turkish, and Persian. Egyptology, followed later by Assyriology, soon became the fashionable hobby of

Karl Friedrich Schinkel, The Queen of the Night, *1815. Hochschulbibliothek, Berlin. This picture, a scenery design for Mozart's* The Magic Flute, *is inspired by iconography of the Virgin Mary.*

PUBLIC DISPLAY

With the advent of the 19th century, grand monuments to conquests of exotic lands appeared increasingly in the public squares and avenues of Europe. To commemorate his Egyptian campaign, Napoleon ordered the erection of a fountain adorned with exotic decorations, and he gave Parisian streets Egyptian names, including rue Damiette and rue du Caire. Subsequently, the fashion for Egyptian ornamentation was widely embraced – disseminated through D.-V. Denon's illustrated *Voyage dans la Haute et dans la Basse Egypte* (1802) and the Institut d'Egypte's magisterial *Description de l'Egypte* (1809–28) – and became particularly successful in the US.

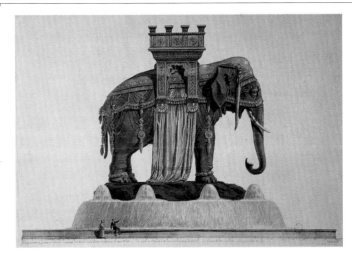

Jean-Antoine Alavoine, fountain sketch for Place de la Bastille, c.1814.

In England, to commemorate Nelson's victory in the Battle of the Nile in 1798, several Egyptian-style buildings and interiors were created. Egyptian features were freely mixed with other styles, such as Neo-Gothic and Neoclassical.

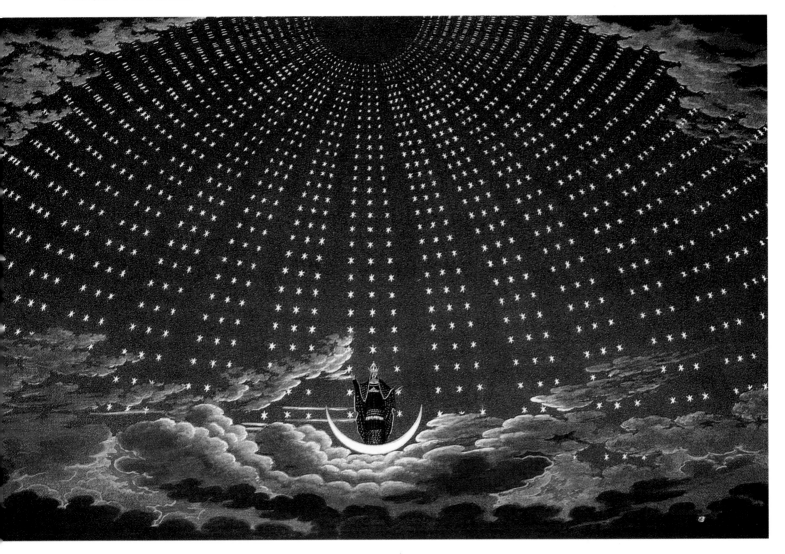

INTERIOR DESIGN

Between 1750 and 1753, Giambattista Tiepolo painted a series of frescoes at the residence of the Prince Archbishop of Würzburg. These included personifications of the four continents on the ceiling of the staircase in the Kaisersaal. Painted with triumphant, whimsical verve, the theme was widely imitated in simpler forms in private houses. Exotic countries and voyages to faraway lands provided the subject matter for spectacular *papiers panoramiques* – brilliantly colored wallpapers that adorned drawing and dining room walls. The sources of such images of distant imaginary worlds were often found in literature, such as Jean-Jacques Rousseau's story *La Belle Sauvage*, Montesquieu's *Lettres persanes*, and the writings of Voltaire, Diderot, and Bougainville.

Jean-Gabriel Charvet, The Savages of the Pacific Ocean, *wallpaper design, 1804. Musée des Ursulines, Maçon.*

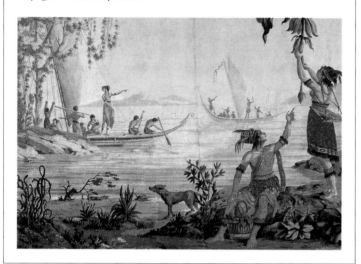

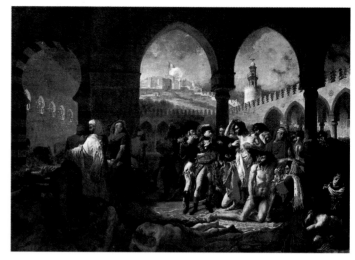

Antoine-Jean Gros, March 11, 1799, Bonaparte Visits the Plague Victims of Jaffa, *1804. Musée du Louvre, Paris.*

Thebes and other Egyptian articles, housed them at the Vatican. Here, in 1836, Gregory XVI opened the Egyptian Museum, its walls painted like those of the palaces on the banks of the Nile, and its ceilings adorned with golden stars sparkling against a cobalt blue sky.

Anne-Louis Girodet-Trioson, The Revolt of October 21, 1798 in Cairo. *Musée du Château, Versailles.*

THE ROMANTIC ORIENT

Major historical events in the East contributed greatly to its increased topicality in the West: Egypt gained independence from the Ottoman sultans in 1805; the Greek War of Independence against the Turks took place between 1821 and 1830, during which Lord Byron died at Missolonghi (1824); and the French conquered Algeria in 1830.

the educated classes. Much admired were the works by Baron Antoine-Jean Gros (1771–1835) and Anne-Louis Girodet-Trioson (1767–1824) that documented Napoleon's Egyptian campaign; these were elevated to the rank of "great" paintings and accorded the status of official art. For the first time, the East was explored, reorganized, reassembled, and finally reborn in the monumental *Description de l'Egypte*. This study was published in 24 volumes (1809–28) by the Institut d'Egypte, founded by Napoleon for the purpose of studying Egyptian civilization. In Rome, at the Palazzo Braschi, an Egyptian Room was established to display all the gifts brought by Napoleon to Pope Pius VI. His successor, Pius VII, acquired the collection of Andrea Gaddi, and, along with statues from

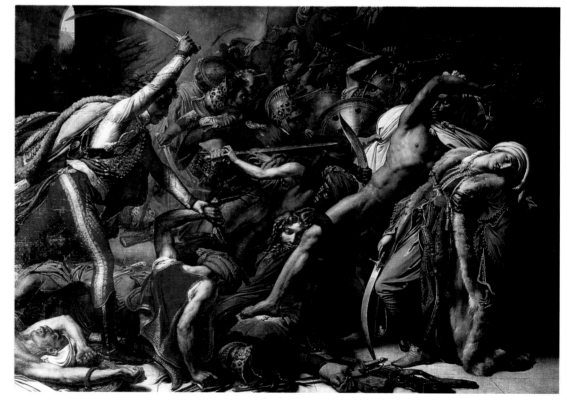

THE CHINESE INFLUENCE

Rococo asymmetry lent itself to the incorporation of chinoiserie, which reached the height of its popularity in the 18th century. European craftsmen drew freely on the decorative motifs found on goods imported from China. The first major application of the Chinese style for an interior design was in Louis Le Vau's Trianon de porcelaine at Versailles, built in 1670 and later destroyed. The style was adopted in court residences across Europe. Schönbrunn Palace (1695–1711), the summer residence of the Habsburgs just outside Vienna, had a Chinese room as well as gardens – laid out in about 1705 by Jean-Nicolas Jadot de Ville-Issey – that included pagodas and tea houses. The second quarter of the 18th century saw a revolution in garden design, as irregular Chinese models replaced formal designs. In England, the Chinese example was combined with a romantic eclecticism to produce the Anglo-Chinese garden. In 1757, the English architect Sir William Chambers published his *Designs of Chinese Buildings...* and, in 1772, his *Dissertation on Oriental Gardening*, condemned by Horace Walpole as disgraceful. Despite its detractors, the Chinese theme was taken up in garden and palace design throughout Europe. Most memorable are the pavilion at Sans Souci in Potsdam (1754–57) and Catherine the Great's Chinese palace at

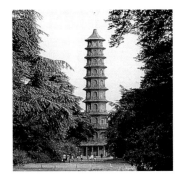

Sir William Chambers, pagoda at Kew Gardens, London, 1757–62.

Oranienbaum in Germany (1762–68); the Chinese palace in the grounds of Villa La Favorita in Sicily; the Chinese pavilions in the gardens at Cibalka in Prague (1818–24); and at the Wilanov Palace in Poland (c.1805). During the 19th century, chinoiserie was superseded by other exotic tastes, such as Turkish, Egyptian, Gothic, and Greek.

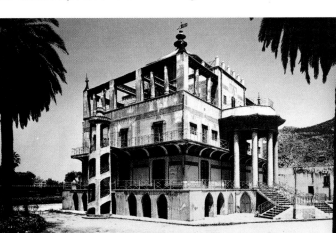

Venanzio Marvuglia, Chinese palace in the grounds of Villa La Favorita, Palermo, Sicily, 1799–1802.

The Orient, as it was perceived by Europeans, included such countries as Greece and Algeria; although technically outside the geographical area of the Orient, they were nevertheless categorized with Egypt as exotic, Eastern lands.

A single trip to the East was sufficient to provide many painters, Eugène Delacroix (1798–1863), Alexandre-Gabriel Decamps (1803–60), and Théodore Chassériau (1819–56) among them, with a new and inexhaustible aesthetic vocabulary. Others undertook lengthy tours, familiarizing themselves with different aspects of the culture of the indigenous populations, which they faithfully reproduced in small-scale genre scenes. The Scotsman David Roberts (1796–1864) and the Frenchmen Eugène Flandin (1809–76) and Eugène Fromentin (1820–76) illustrated their travels in paintings and diaries. Emile-Jean-Horace Vernet (1789–1863) brought to his paintings his experience of traveling in Algeria, Morocco, Egypt, Syria, Palestine, and the Crimea. Primarily a military painter, Vernet is best known for his imposing battle scenes, but he also painted animal subjects inspired by his travels. The Spanish artist Mariano Fortuny y Carbo (1838–74), who visited Morocco twice, was another notable producer of battle paintings. The English painter

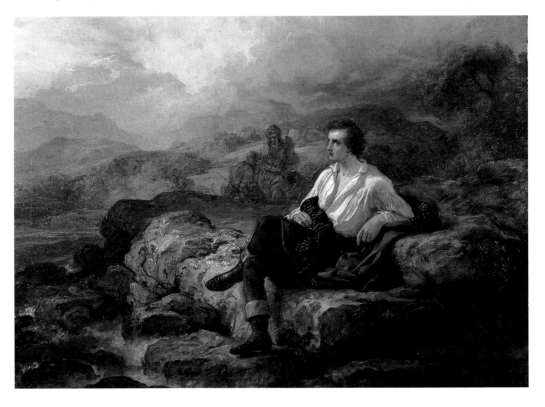

Giacomo Trecourt (1812–82), Byron in Greece, 1859–60. Pinacoteca Malaspina, Musei Civici, Pavia, Italy.

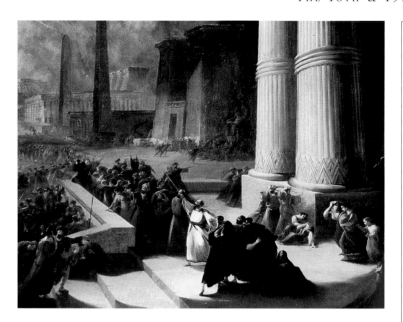

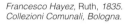

With Ingres' late work, *Turkish Bath*, the role of the pure, chaste, Neoclassical nude as an expression of moral dignity gave way to that of the Romantic nude as an expression of wantonness and hedonism. *Turkish Bath* positively exudes steamy air, heavy scents, and the languid laziness of the women's bodies. Following Ingres' sensuous vision, any feminine form shown in an Oriental setting,

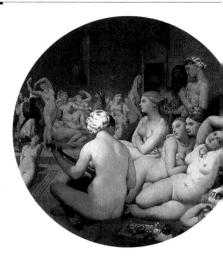

Francesco Hayez, Ruth, *1835. Collezioni Comunali, Bologna.*

Jean-Auguste-Dominique Ingres, Turkish Bath, *1859–63. Musée du Louvre, Paris.*

John Frederick Lewis (1805–76) recorded his ten-year sojourn in Egypt on canvases notable for their meticulous precision and attention to detail.

For many of the Romantic artists, the "journey to the Orient" was essentially a voyage to a place beyond reality: a haven for the soul and a refuge from everyday life. These exotic lands served as a kind of multicolored, alluring mask of the more mysterious side of the human psyche. Many artists who succumbed to this allure never actually set foot in the East, including Ingres (1780–1867), John Martin (1789–1854), and Francesco Hayez (1791–1882). In some cases, literary sources proved as inspirational as first-hand experience. Lord Byron's series of Oriental poems, Victor Hugo's *Les Orientales*, the *Itinéraire de Paris à Jérusalem* by Chateaubriand, and works by Heinrich Heine, Dumas Père, Alphonse de Lamartine and Théophile Gautier were among the sources widely enjoyed.

For the Romantics, the exotic was often explicitly linked with the erotic, founded on the myth that the Levant (modern-day Lebanon, Syria, and Israel) enjoyed a laxity of morals quite unthinkable in Europe. Eroticism became an

John Martin, The Seventh Plague of Egypt *(detail), 1823–24. Museum of Fine Arts, Boston. The biblical world provided rich subject matter for the Orientalists.*

area free from moral conventions; bodily sensations were no longer idealized but seen in all their carnal and sensual reality. The link between eroticism and the female nude was developed further in the second half of the 19th century, when the so-called *pompiers* (the humorous name given to artists seen as having little talent) in France and the Victorian painters in England created images more overtly erotic than had ever been seen before in the history of painting.

THE END OF THE DREAM

With the development of steamships and the railroads, the opening of the Suez Canal in 1869, and the increasingly widespread use of photography, the East became more accessible and familiar. Likewise, the influence of Western customs and costumes spread to the East, even leading some local ladies in Turkey to discard their traditional garments in favor of crinolines from the House of Worth in Paris. Gradually, the Orient was

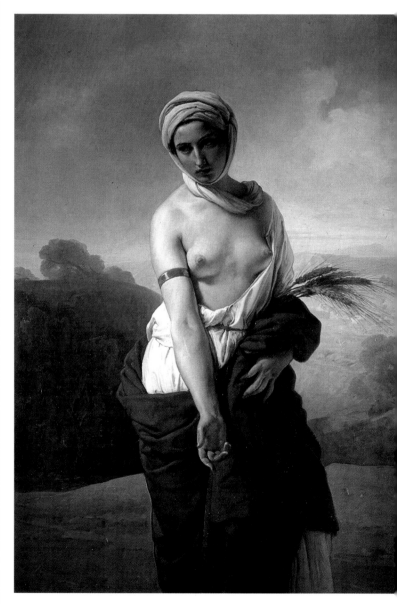

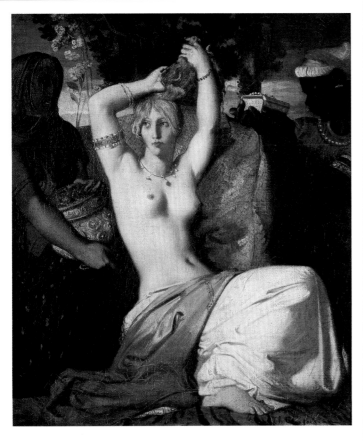

whether mythological, biblical, or real-life, was portrayed as an icon. *La Toilette d'Esther* by Théodore Chassériau, a pupil of Ingres', and *Ruth* by Hayez are just two examples of biblical subjects imbued with a powerful atmosphere of desire and melancholy. Such

Théodore Chassériau, La Toilette d'Esther, 1841. Musée du Louvre, Paris.

sentiments had been conveyed with a sense of modesty by Delacroix (1798–1863) in *The Women of Algiers*, a rich and exotic work inspired by his trip to Morocco in 1832.

Eugène Delacroix, The Women of Algiers, 1834. Musée du Louvre, Paris.

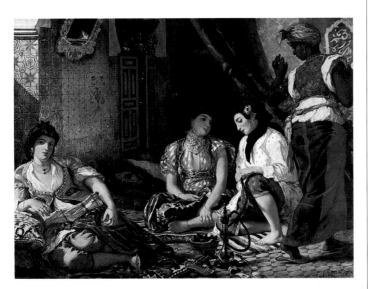

stripped of its mythological aura. In 1826 in Istanbul, Mahmud II suppressed the janissaries, and Western reforms were introduced to the capital by various organizations, including those devoted to law, education, and the economy.

Some artists now began to represent a harsher vision of the Orient – blind beggars, cripples, filthy streets, and peeling plaster – that was at variance with earlier, idealized images. The French poet Gérard de Nerval told Théophile Gautier that he regretted having formed his own idea of Egypt in his imagination. The real Egypt having been "bitterly impressed on my memory," he had lost an imaginary, wonderful place in which de Nerval could take refuge with his dreams.

Large numbers of Europeans now beat a path to exotic locations. Merchant adventurers, missionaries, and, above all, soldiers, brought back objects from the Old World. These became a source of inspiration for the production and wide availability of a range of goods: furniture, clothing, trinkets, and even games displayed the Oriental stamp, while interior and garden design were both strongly influenced by the styles of the East.

At the end of the century, the mythical Orient enjoyed a final season of splendor, corresponding with the demise of the odalisque. Artists from vastly differing schools were united by the liveliness of treatment that they brought to Oriental themes: they included the French sculptor and painter Jean-Léon Gérôme (1824–1904), Gustave Boulanger (1824–88), Georges Clairin (1843–1919), Mariano Fortuny y Carbó, and Hans Makart (1840–84). In 1873, Jules-Antoine Castagnary wrote: "Orientalism is dead," yet twenty years later, the Société des Peintres Orientalistes was founded, with Gérôme as honorary president.

Giuseppe Castiglione, Collection of Good Luck Symbols, ink and color on silk, 1723. National Palace Museum, Taipei, Japan.

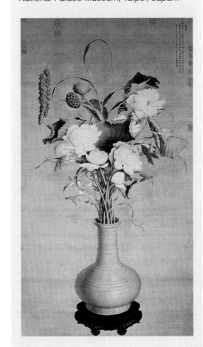

A RETURN TO THE PAST

During a hundred-year period that began in the late 18th century, artists returned, once again, to an exploration of the styles of earlier times. This was not a revival of classical or Renaissance art but of the medieval art that had been practiced until the advent of 15th-century Florentine art. It represented a certain reluctance to search for new, modern forms.

The 19th century was to see a profusion of revived styles, the predominant one being the Neo-Gothic. It originated in England during the 18th century in a quest for the picturesque, and it manifested itself in various ways in different countries. The *troubadour* style appeared in France between 1780 and 1820, inspired by the myths of chivalry. More specific types of revivalism were the Neo-Romanesque and 15th-century Florentine styles.

REVIVING MEDIEVAL STYLES

The development of these revivals in Europe may be understood partly as an expression of nationalistic feeling, for it represented a nostalgic return to long-forgotten or neglected forms of art. In Germany and England, the Gothic tradition constituted a continuation rather than a revival, with artists showing a greater understanding of the historical weight of the style and reworking it from a romantic point of view. In contrast to the Neoclassicism that had had such a profound effect on art, the Neo-Rococo style was reintroduced by the Goncourt brothers (who wrote *The Art of the 18th Century*, 1859–65) and practiced by painters such as Tassaert and Roqueplan. The French Renaissance architectural style of the Loire châteaux was readopted, as was the Henry II furniture style. In 1850, Léon de Laborde (1807–69), an aristocratic historian, politician, explorer, Louvre curator, and amateur photographer, proclaimed his nationalistic vision of the French Renaissance in his *Renaissance of the Arts at the French Court.*

William Burges (1827–81), Neo-Gothic bookcase with biblical scenes, 1859–62. Victoria and Albert Museum, London. The revival of the Gothic style in England accompanied a renewed interest in national culture and religion.

MEDIEVAL COMPASSION

For some 19th-century artists, the return to the medieval aroused positive emotions of brotherhood, innocence, and Christian charity. Heinrich Anton Dähling (1773–1850) was inspired by Heinrich von Kleist's *Das Kätchen von Heilbronn*, while Ferdinand Theodor Hildebrandt (1804–74) concentrated on the paternal sentiments of a knight.

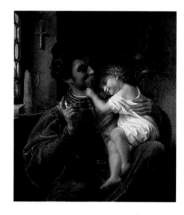

Heinrich Anton Dähling, Kätchen von Heilbronn and Count Wetter von Strahl, 1825. Niedersächsisches Landesmuseum, Hanover.

Ferdinand Theodor Hildebrandt, Warrior with his Son, 1832. Preussischer Kulturbesitz, Nationalgalerie, Staatliche Museen, Berlin.

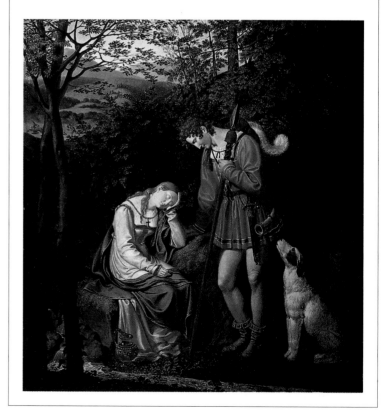

NORTH AND SOUTH

During this period, many great contemporary artists found an irreconcilable problem in the duality of classicism and medievalism, pagan mythology and Christian iconography, North and South, and German and Mediterranean culture. They felt that this caused them to oscillate between two mutually incompatible outlooks. The young Goethe, for example, was seduced by the impetus of the medieval revival, but, as an adult, under the influence of Winckelmann, he came to embrace the very reverse properties – simplicity, measure, and balance. The Nazarenes endeavored to establish harmony between the two opposites, the ideal incarnated by Raphael and the spirit of German tradition. In Overbeck's *Italy and Germany*, the women representing the two extremes sit happily together.

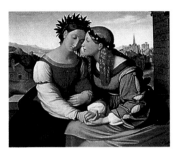

Johann Friedrich Overbeck, Italy and Germany, *c.1815. Bayerische Staatsgemäldegalerie, Munich.*

It was a time of rationalism and enlightenment; in England, antiquity, the Christian Middle Ages, the Renaissance, and the Industrial Revolution, all came to be regarded as golden ages of the past that could be looked back upon as Utopian examples. Rushing to the rescue of art – a victim of the degeneration and corruption of its time – were artistic brotherhoods such as the French Primitives, the German Nazarenes, the Italian Purists, and the English Pre-Raphaelites, who all harked back to former traditions in order to give true meaning to their work.

THE NEO-GOTHIC

The Neo-Gothic or Gothic Revival took various forms in different parts of Europe. In England, one of its earliest manifestations was in the landscape garden. Here, from the first half of the 18th century, without any pretense of faithful imitation, Greek temples, Chinese pagodas, Gothic buildings, and artificial ruins were placed side by side. In 1799, Ercole Silva, the Milanese author of *The Art of the English Garden*, wrote that ruins such as these "recall past times and arouse a feeling of compassion mingled with melancholy." The ruin became a relic that could evoke a lost past. An element of the picturesque contributed to the birth of the Gothic Revival, in that art no longer adopted the classical principles of beauty but was rather aiming to produce thoughts and feelings through powers of suggestion. In reaction to the Palladian formality of Inigo Jones (1573–1652) and the Baroque classicism of Sir Christopher Wren (1632–1723), whose St. Paul's Cathedral in London was completed in 1711, the

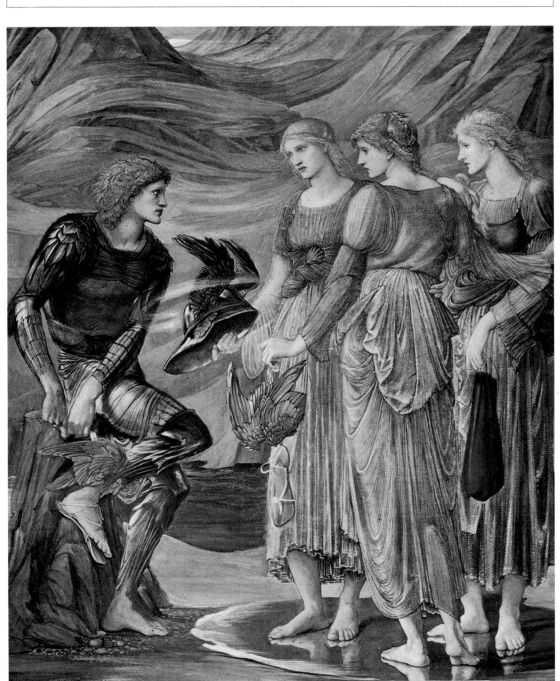

Edward Burne-Jones, The Arming of Perseus, *1877. Southampton Art Gallery, England. The* Cycle of Perseus, *inspired by William Morris'* The Earthly Paradise, *depicts imaginative tales of the hero on a mysterious planet.*

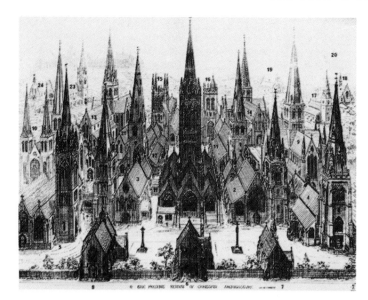

A.W.N. Pugin, frontispiece to Apology for the Revival of Christian Architecture, 1841.

Revival. The medieval revival was hailed by younger generations and received the official sanction of philosophers and poets. In 1772, the young Johann Wolfgang von Goethe (1749–1832), a law student at Strasbourg, wrote an essay on German art and dedicated it to the memory of Erwin von Steinbach, one of the builders of Strasbourg Cathedral. Goethe viewed Gothic architecture as embodying the noblest human aspirations and quest for eternity. Friedrich

Schlegel, an admirer of Greek civilization, turned to late Christian medieval art around 1790 and was converted to Catholicism. Novalis, in his essay "Die Christenheit oder Europa" ("Christianity or Europe", written in 1799 but published posthumously in 1826, 27 years after his death), perceived in medieval Christianity a lost Europe united by faith and love. In Munich, Georg Joseph Ritter von Hauberrisser (1841–1922) built the resplendent Rathaus (1867–74); the castles of Ludwig of Bavaria revived the Gothic culture of myths and legends, through which the

man of letters Horace Walpole (1717–97) laid out the garden of his country villa just outside London at Strawberry Hill, Twickenham, in a mixed style of Rococo and Gothic. Walpole, author of *The Castle of Otranto* (1764), made liberal use of architectural structures that lacked any historical authenticity, and in so doing created a setting that would fire the imagination and conjure up the atmosphere of distant times. Between 1796 and 1813, James Wyatt (1748–1813) built the residence of Fonthill Abbey for the eccentric William Beckford. This constituted an extraordinary Gothic spectacle of immense proportions, which ended up falling apart during a single night in 1825.

Johann (Anton Alban) Ramboux (1790–1866), The Construction of Cologne Cathedral, engraving, 1844. Stadtmuseum, Cologne. Containing works of art, souvenirs of Frederick I, and the Dreikönigen-schrein (the reliquary of the Magi given to Otto I), the cathedral of Cologne represents a historic symbol of the German Empire.

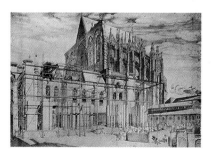

Reaction against such wild fantasies in stone, typical of many of the earlier buildings, came from architects such as Augustus Welby Northmore Pugin (1812–52) and Sir George Gilbert Scott (1811–78), who brought scrupulous precision to their work in the Gothic Revival style.
The Neo-Gothic style was also widely used in smaller, more mundane buildings. A variety of country houses were built in this style, their plans taking into consideration any irregularities in the terrain. Perfectly adapted to their surroundings, such homes, with their lavish use of many materials and meticulous interior decoration, suited the needs of the new middle-class owners. From 1840, the classical design of the compact, regularly proportioned house was almost wholly superseded.
In Germany, the revival of figurative Gothic culture seemed to be affected by anti-French sentiments. The restoration of Marienburg Castle, the old seat of the Order of Teutonic Knights; of Cologne Cathedral, absolute symbol of High Gothic in its full splendor; and of the monuments on the Rhine appeared to signify a return to native roots. Similarly, the celebrations of the tercentenary of the death of Albrecht Dürer in 1828 set the triumphant seal on the Gothic

THE GERMAN UTOPIA

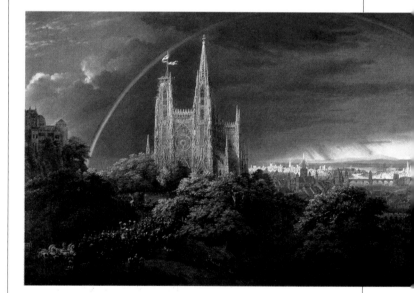

Karl Friedrich Schinkel, Medieval City, 1815. Preussischer Kulturbesitz, Nationalgalerie, Staatliche Museen, Berlin.

During a journey to Italy between 1803 and 1805, the architect and painter Karl Friedrich Schinkel (1781–1841) became fascinated by the Venetian Gothic and Moorish styles, the monuments of Sicily, and Milan Cathedral. In his oil paintings, enormous Gothic cathedrals are dramatically silhouetted, the backlighting emphasizing the effect of delicate filigree work. Gothic, for the German architect, was a romantic aspiration and an unrealizable ideal. His cathedrals were products of a poetic imagination, divine yearnings that had no counterparts in

reality. In his own architecture, Schinkel was reluctant to face seemingly insurmountable practical difficulties, convinced that the building technique of the medieval masters had been wholly lost. Instead, he introduced models from Greek antiquity into the architecture of his day. This constituted a sort of Byzantine Romanesque style and became an expression of a wish to return to the pre-industrial times.

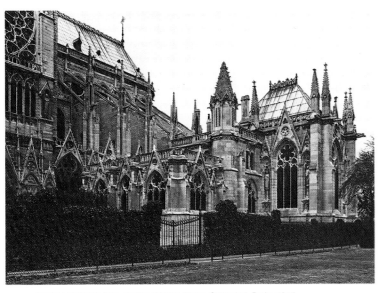

Eugène Viollet-le-Duc, vestry of Notre-Dame Cathedral, Paris, 1847.

with its glorious medieval past. The architects who built in the medieval manner were also those who were restoring the churches damaged over time and in revolutions. The notion of repairing cathedrals and abbeys was associated with a form of national identity that went hand in hand with Catholicism. Henri Labrouste (1801–75) and Eugène Viollet-le-Duc (1814–79) stimulated theoretical study of the Gothic by confronting the challenge of combining the Gothic Revival with new building techniques and materials. For Viollet-le-Duc, the cathedral became an organic unity, which he once described as a paneled struc-

ture supported by a skeleton of ribs. For his successors it became a structure of glass supported by a skeleton of metal. Thus, in the various 19th-century revivals, romantic nostalgia for the past mixed with enthusiasm for the present. Gothic boldness would eventually be converted into new forms that made no reference whatsoever to medieval times.

THE NAZARENES

In 1809, the young German painters Franz Pforr (1788–1812) and Johann Friedrich Overbeck (1789–1869) founded the Brotherhood of

eccentric Ludwig escaped the contemporary world. In Vienna, new Gothic buildings included the Votivkirche (1855) of Heinrich von Ferstel (1828–83) and the Rathaus (1872) of Friedrich von Schmidt (1825–91).

In Italy, the return to the medieval reflected the rise of nationalism and the move toward Italian unification. Work was resumed on Milan Cathedral and the facade of Santa Maria del Fiore in Florence. Pietro Selvatico (1803–80), theoretician, militant critic, architect, and a passionate defender of Primitive art, was commissioned in 1862 to study a project for a "complete restoration" of the Gothic palace of Piacenza. This was a typical example of an attempt by a former great city to reaffirm its own urban identity through the presence of Neo-Gothic architecture. It became the ensign of a city's independence, and as such the monumental cemetery of Pisa, the cathedral of Orvieto, and the Gothic monuments of Venice were all depicted in historical paintings and in the works of foreign artists.

In France, the Neo-Gothic style took on the guise of a sentimental and political movement, in which the monarchy identified itself

INGRES AND THE NAZARENES

Certain similarities can be found between the puritanical spirit of Pforr and the style of Ingres, which was defined by David and his school during a particular period of the artist's activity as "Gothic" and "dry and clipped." In Pforr's *The Entrance of Rudolf of Hapsburg into Basle in 1273*, the minute detail of faces and costumes of the animated crowd filling the narrow streets

Jean-Auguste-Dominique Ingres, Entry into Paris of the Dauphin, the Future Charles V, 1821, Wadsworth Atheneum, Hartford, CT.

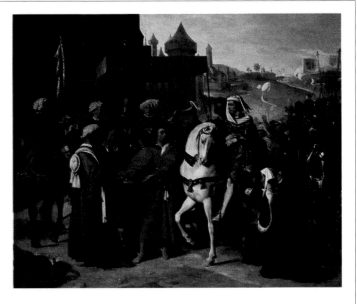

Franz Pforr, Entrance of Rudolph of Habsburg into Basle in 1273, 1808–10. Städelsches Kunstinstitut, Frankfurt.

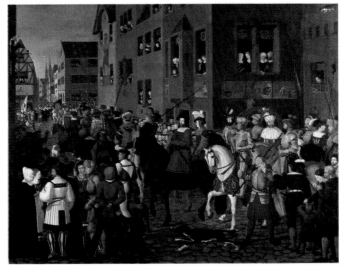

seems to be an informed interpretation of a scene from medieval life; in fact, the painting displays anachronisms that spring from the wish to revive a lost age.

In his *Entry into Paris of the Dauphin, the Future Charles V*, Ingres discarded the excessively primitive nature of Gothic painting, as revived by Pforr, with its absence of atmosphere, depth, and pathos, preferring soft brushwork to the dry technique of the Nazarenes.

St. Luke in Vienna. They settled in Rome a year later, where they lived and worked with new recruits in the convent of Sant'Isidoro del Pincio. Because of their flowing hair and monklike appearance, they were called the Nazarenes. Within the confines of the Brotherhood, their daily life was based on fraternity and ascetic poverty. As artists, the members set out to revive the art of painting by following an ideal of simplicity and sincerity, in conflict with the academic principles of their time. Their reworking of ancient sacred art was based on a sobriety of

Philipp Veit, The Empyrean and the Spheres of the Planets, *fresco, 1818–24. Sala Dante, Villa Massimo, Rome.*

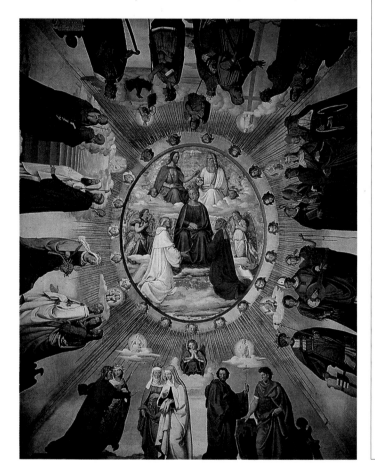

THE ITALIAN PURISTS

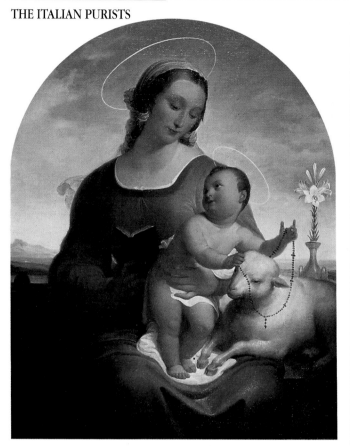

In Italy, Purists, in common with the Nazarenes, shared a reaction against academic dogma. Although they were not preoccupied with religious and philosophical matters, they rejected chiaroscuro, plasticity of form, and courtly mannerisms. The objectives of the movement, as written in 1843

Tommaso Minardi, The Virgin of the Rosary, *1840. Galleria Nazionale d'Arte Moderna, Rome.*

by Antonio Bianchini and signed by Tommaso Minardi (1787–1871) and the sculptor Pietro Tenerani (1789–1869), were to rediscover the art of Cimabue, Fra Angelico, and the early works of Raphael.

THE FRENCH PRIMITIVES

Two students of David, Pierre-Henri Révoil (1776–1842), an author of medieval romances, and Fleury-François Richard (1777–1852), heralded what was to become the *troubadour* style by reviving the subjects and style of the medieval age in their paintings. A vision of chivalry was the subject of Révoil's *The Tourney*, exhibited at the Salon of 1812. His research into the costumes and architecture was conducted with the scrupulous love and care becoming to the illumination of a medieval codex, and he achieved a superb vision of the period. By contrast, Paul Delaroche (1797–1856) interpreted historical, religious, and literary subjects with factual accuracy and a particularly theatrical tone. Another medievalist, Hippolyte-Jean Flandrin (1809–64), imitated the style and iconography of the Italian artists, drawing upon the Byzantine and Giotto-inspired repertories for his frescoes in the church of Saint-Germain-des-Prés in Paris (1846).

Pierre-Henri Révoil, The Tourney, *1812. Musée des Beaux-Arts, Lyons.*

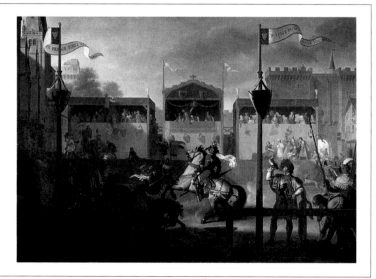

color and line that had many sources of inspiration, including Fra Angelico, the early works of Raphael, and older northern masters from Van Eyck to Dürer. For the Nazarenes, art was a divine mission, which was elevated to the level of true faith. The celestial origin of sacred art was celebrated by Philipp Veit

from the canons of official portraiture.

The original spirit, derived from the masters of the 15th century that had brought the Nazarenes together, lasted only for a short time. The fresco cycles that decorated the home of the German consul Bartholdy (1816–17) and the Villa Massimo already

showed affinities with the style of the Renaissance of the early 16th century. Pforr died before the age of 25 and Cornelius was summoned, with Heinrich von Olivier (1785–1841) and Julius Schnorr von Carolsfeld (1794–1872), to Munich by Ludwig. The king encouraged a popular, educational style of painting and commissioned them to adorn the city's public buildings with patriotic, humanistic frescoes.

The art of the Nazarenes assumed an official role with Cornelius' paintings – which formed part of the Glyptothek (1819–30), the museum of ancient art designed in a Greek style by Leo von Klenze. Thanks, too, to Carolsfeld's cycle of the *Nibelungen* (1827) for the Königsbau (the royal residence in Munich open to visitors), an artistic interpretation of national mythology assumed an educational function.

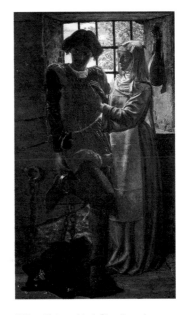

William Holman Hunt, Claudio and Isabella, *1850. Tate Gallery, London.*

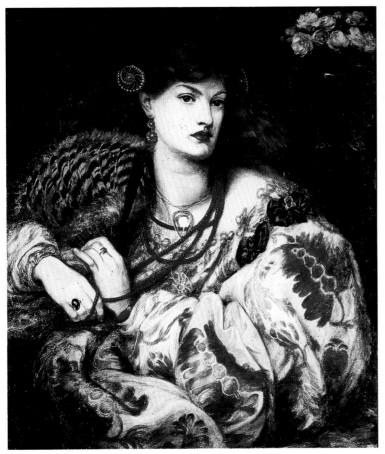

Dante Gabriel Rossetti, Monna Vanna, *1866. Tate Gallery, London.*

(1793–1877) in his frescoes in the Villa Massimo of Rome (1819), where he represented the three great Italian poets – Dante, Ariosto, and Tasso – alongside the saints and fathers of the church. Between 1826 and 1839, Peter von Cornelius (1783–1867) gave artists sacred status in the loggias of the Munich Pinakothek (1826–30) and the Stadel Institute of Frankfurt with his *Triumph of Religion in the Arts* (1829). In portraits, there was a mood of contemplation. In the intimate portrayal of friends, pictures reveal subtle nuances of character in a style far removed

John Everett Millais, Lorenzo and Isabella, *1848–49. Walker Art Gallery, Liverpool, England.*

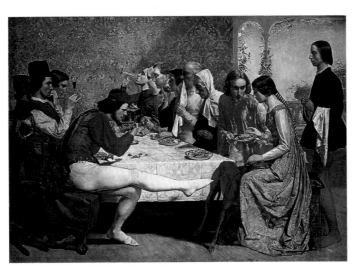

THE PRE-RAPHAELITES

Between 1825 and 1860, life in England underwent profound changes as a result of the Industrial Revolution. In a country soon to be transformed by coal and steel production and its peripheral side effects of poverty and

pollution, the luminous, sharply focused paintings of the Pre-Raphaelites provided a form of escape. The Pre-Raphaelite Brotherhood was formed in 1848 by William Holman Hunt (1827–1910), Dante Gabriel Rossetti (1828–82), and John Everett Millais (1829–96). They were later joined by others, including Ford Madox Brown (1821–93) and Edward Coley Burne-Jones (1833–98). They initially signed their works with the initials PRB, causing much controversy and scandal.

The champion of the movement, however, was writer and critic John Ruskin (1819–1900), who, in addition to promoting the Gothic style, helped reinforce the group's sense of moral commitment and social awareness. He envisaged art as a means of saving the human race and fulfilling the most important human aspirations. In contrast to the pretense and artifice of academic painting, Pre-Raphaelite art looked afresh at techniques used by artists before the time of Raphael. Studying nature in detail to rediscover its inner meaning, the Brotherhood sought to communicate with the forgotten sources of spirituality. However, the early purity of spirit was later lost.

THE 18TH & 19TH CENTURIES

1761–65: Scottish poet James Macpherson publishes the poems of Ossian, which are immensely successful in Romantic Europe. 1764: German archaeologist Winckelmann completes *History of Ancient Art,* signaling the dawn of modern art history, dealing with the history of art as a language, instead of the individual in the manner of Vasari. 1765: Maria Theresa of Austria appoints her son Joseph II as co-ruler and institutes a comprehensive policy of reforms. 1773: a papal bull suppresses the Society of Jesus. 1776: America declares independence. 1781: the first edition of *Critique of Pure Reason is* published, an important work by German philosopher Immanuel Kant. 1787: Spanish architect Juan de Villanueva commences building of the Museo del

1760–70   1780   1790   1800

▼ ANTON RAFAEL MENGS
(1728-79)

This German painter and theorist of Neo-classicism studied ancient art and the work of Raphael in Rome. He was famous in his day for his explicit reinterpretations of past masterpieces.

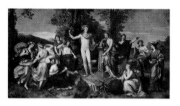

Anton Rafael Mengs, Parnassus, ceiling painting, Villa Torlonia (formerly Villa Albani), Rome, 1760–61.

▼ FRANZ XAVIER MESSERSCHMIDT
(1736-83)

Messerschmidt was a German sculptor who departed from the Austro-Bavarian Baroque tradition. His busts were later used in the study of human pathology.

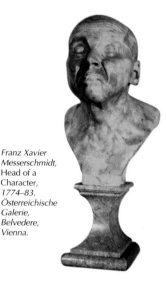

Franz Xavier Messerschmidt, Head of a Character, 1774–83. Österreichische Galerie, Belvedere, Vienna.

▼ JACQUES-LOUIS DAVID
(1748-1825)

French painter Jacques-Louis David was probably the greatest exponent of Neoclassicism. For him, antiquity not only provided the model for his sober painting, but also served as a moral example.

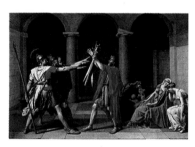

Jacques-Louis David, The Oath of the Horatii, 1784. Musée du Louvre, Paris.

▼ SIR JOSHUA REYNOLDS
(1723-92)

An English painter, theorist, and the first President of the Royal Academy, this great portraitist of society figures was frequently inspired by models of classicism. His ideas about art and the role of the artist, expressed in his *Discourses,* had a profound effect on the history of English painting.

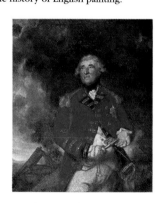

Sir Joshua Reynolds, Lord Heathfield, 1787. National Gallery, London.

J.M.W. TURNER
(1775-1851)

An original and gifted artist and colorist, the English Romantic Turner is considered one of the greatest landscapists of all time.

▼ FRANCISCO DE GOYA
(1746-1828)

The great Spanish painter and etcher distanced himself from the traditional Rococo vein, bringing a fresh approach to painting in which he expressed his individual anxieties and those of contemporary society.

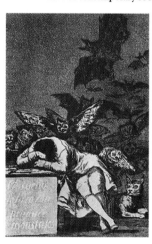

Francisco Goya, The Sleep of Reason Produces Monsters, Capricho No. 43, etching and aquatint, 1797–98. Private Collection.

▼ VENANZIO MARVUGLIA
(1729-1814)

This Italian architect Marvuglia freely combined classical and foreign styles.

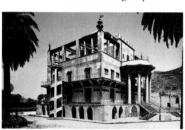

Venanzio Marvuglia, Chinese palace in the grounds of Villa La Favorita, Palermo, Sicily, 1799–1802.

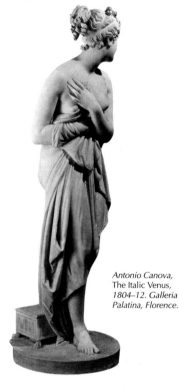

Antonio Canova, The Italic Venus, 1804–12. Galleria Palatina, Florence.

▲ ANTONIO CANOVA
(1757-1822)

A Venetian sculptor, painter, and draftsman, Canova translated Winckelmann's ideals of "quiet grandeur and noble simplicity" into exquisite marble statues.

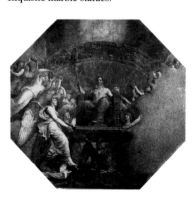

Andrea Appiani, The Apotheosis of Napoleon I, throne room of the Palazzo Reale, Milan, 1808.

▲ ANDREA APPIANI
(1754-1817)

The Lombard painter Appiani was an exponent of Italian Neoclassicism.

Prado, in a sober Neoclassical style. **1789:** outbreak of French Revolution. **1795–1815:** German composer Ludwig van Beethoven composes his most famous works. **1800–01:** Goya paints *The*

Family of Charles IV, an unflattering portrait of the Spanish royal family. **1804:** Napoleon crowned emperor at Notre-Dame, Paris. **1814–19:** the principles of royal succession and

legitimacy are the basis of a new vision of Europe, as sanctioned by the Congress of Vienna. **1816:** during a visit to Rome, Géricault studies Michelangelo's art. **1825:** Death of Swiss painter Henry

Fuseli, celebrated for his visionary works. **1830:** Eugène Delacroix, leader of the French Romantic school, paints *Liberty Leading the People.* **1848:** foundation of Pre-Raphaelite Brotherhood in London.

1 8 1 0   1 8 2 0   1 8 3 0   1 8 4 0

KARL FRIEDRICH SCHINKEL
(1781-1841)
In his early projects, this German architect combined a range of styles, including Gothic.

▼ THOMAS JEFFERSON
(1743-1826)
Loyal to the principles of Palladio and antiquity, this American statesman and architect applied classical canons to the architectural culture of the US.

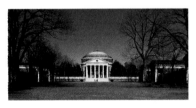

Thomas Jefferson, The Rotunda, University of Virginia, Charlottesville, 1823–26.

▼ JEAN-LOUIS-THEODORE GERICAULT
(1791-1824)
This French painter, engraver, and sculptor admired the work of Michelangelo. Romantic by disposition, he produced paintings of dramatic vigor and vitality.

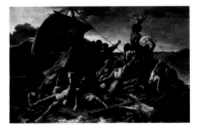

Théodore Géricault, The Raft of the Medusa, 1819. Musée du Louvre, Paris.

JEAN-ANTOINE GROS
(1771-1835)
A favorite of Napoleon, this French painter's dramatic vision of history surpassed the classicist compositions of his master, David.

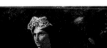

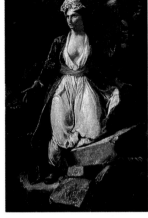

Eugène Delacroix, Greek Woman among the Ruins of Missolonghi, 1826. Musée des Beaux-Arts, Bordeaux.

▲ EUGENE DELACROIX
(1798-1863)
Influenced by the work of Rubens, this French painter broke with the academic style, adopting a free and spontaneous approach to painting.

▼ JOHN NASH
(1752-1835)
Accomplished in a range of styles, the English architect John Nash is best known for his development of Regent's Park and Regent Street in London. He translated the ideas of the Picturesque movement into architecture.

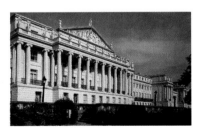

John Nash, Cumberland Terrace, Regent's Park, London, 1825–27.

▼ CASPAR DAVID FRIEDRICH
(1774-1840)
The greatest exponent of German Romantic painting, Friedrich produced work that was permeated with a sense of mystery and desolation in face of the immensity of nature.

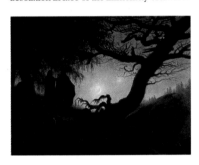

Caspar David Friedrich, A Man and a Woman Contemplate the Moon, 1830–35. Neue Nationalgalerie, Berlin.

▼ FRANCESCO HAYEZ
(1791-1882)
The Italian Romantic painter Hayez brought a melodramatic effect to his historical themes, involving the spectator emotionally.

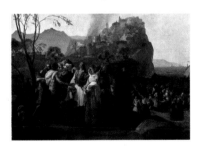

Francesco Hayez, The Refugees of Parga, 1831. Pinacoteca Tosio Martinengo, Brescia, Italy.

A.W.N. PUGIN
(1812-52)
This English architect was the chief theorist and propagandist of the Gothic Revival.

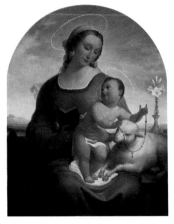

Tommaso Minardi, The Virgin of the Rosary, 1840. Galleria Nazionale d'Arte Moderna, Rome.

▲ TOMMASO MINARDI
(1787-1871)
Adhering to the conservative position of Purism, the Italian painter Minardi revived the style and themes of the work of the Italian "primitives."

▼ EUGENE-EMMANUEL VIOLLET-LE-DUC
(1814-79)
This French engineer, architect, and theorist on restoration of medieval monuments recommended the Gothic as the model for a national style.

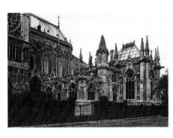

Eugène Viollet-le-Duc, vestry of Notre-Dame Cathedral, Paris, 1847.

OFFICIAL ART

Official art is the name given to a style of painting that flourished in Europe in the second half of the 19th century under the auspices of the established middle classes, the new ruling powers, and the official academies of painting and sculpture that prospered from the 17th to the 19th century.

The style and subject matter that dominated European painting in the second half of the 19th century arose from a complex mix of historical and sociological factors. State patronage, church influence, and the growth of the middle classes all encouraged the painting of pictures with historical, mythological, and allegorical subject matter. Exhibitions to show this work were organized by the academies or salons, and, as the mouthpieces of such institutions, the artists involved enjoyed a privileged position in society. The exhibitions were held in buildings such as palaces and museums, and the works

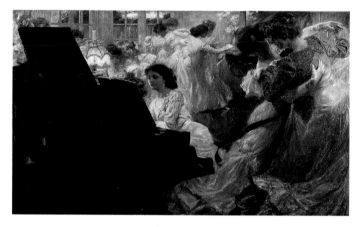

ranged in subject from the universal to the municipal. Many private exhibitions were also held in bourgeois homes as a declaration of the owner's wealth.

Joseph Marius Avy (1871–1939), Le Bal blanc, 1903. Musée du Petit Palais, Paris. Dancing became a popular diversion – as well as a status symbol – for the rising class of the bourgeoisie.

PUBLIC ART

Following a period of estrangement marked by Romanticism, the marriage of artists and institutions was renewed in Rome in the early 19th century by the Nazarenes, a group of German artists who revived the art of monumental frescoes. Their works, didactic and nationalistic in tone, paved the way for the creation of official forms of painting, sculpture, and architecture. Ludwig I in Munich, the Bourbons in Paris, and Frederick William III in Berlin encouraged such art as confirmation

CONTEMPORARY LIFE

Paintings of scenes from everyday life became a popular genre in England in the middle of the 19th century. *The Derby Day* by William Powell Frith (1819–1909) is a realistic portrayal for which

William Powell Frith, The Derby Day, 1856–58. Tate Gallery, London.

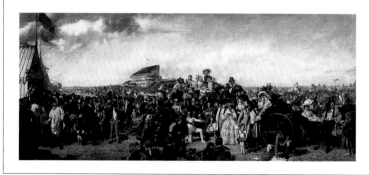

the painter employed professional studio models and followed the strict academic rules then in vogue. His crowd contained popular stereotypes, such as prostitutes, fashionable ladies, criminals, and dandies. Such was the painting's success that barriers were erected around it when it was exhibited to restrain the general public. Social

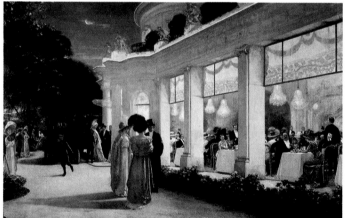

realism in art continued to grow in popularity until the turn of the century. *An Evening at the Pré-Catalan* by Henri Gervex (1852–1929) was almost a tribute to modernity, featuring a car,

Henri Gervex, An Evening at the Pré-Catalan, 1909. Séligmann Collection, Paris.

electric lights, and the Brazilian aviator Santos-Dumont to represent modern aviation.

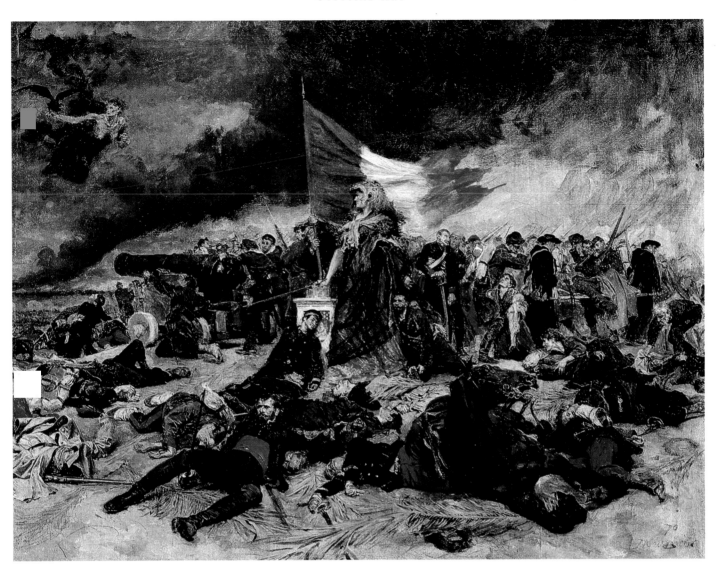

Jean-Louis-Ernest Meissonier, Siege of Paris, 1870. *Musée d'Orsay, Paris.*

of their own sovereignty. Between 1830 and 1908, the new regimes in Europe saw art as a means of celebrating national achievements. After the French were defeated at Sedan in 1870, Classicism in France was promoted as a form of nationalistic ideology linked to anti-Prussian feeling. Ernest Meissonier (1815–91) celebrated the campaign triumphs of Napoleon I and III in detailed canvases, while the frescoes of Puvis de Chavannes (1824–98) redefined symbolic art, presenting an enigmatic, sparse view of history with little color or line work. In England, in 1836, work

began on the project of decorating the new Houses of Parliament in Westminster, London, a building intended to encapsulate a national style. It involved artists such as Richard Redgrave (1804–88), William Dyce (1806–64), and John Tenniel (1820–1914). Elsewhere, a high moral tone was taken by Ford Madox Brown (1821–93), whose frescoes for Manchester Town Hall (1878–93) illustrated episodes of the city's history. The second half of the century saw an "art for art's sake" philosophy emerge. Adherents to this included Thomas Armstrong (1832–1911) and Randolph Caldecott (1846–86), who worked on the decoration of Bank Hall in Derbyshire (1872–73).

THE COURT PORTRAITIST

The German artist Franz Xavier Winterhalter (1806–73) displayed an extraordinary technical proficiency and opulent sense of style, exemplified by his portrait of Elizabeth of Wittelsbach,

empress of Austria. The success of his portraits of royalty and the nobility lies in a carefully contrived simplicity of mood, with just the right combination of splendor, arrogance, and charm. His subjects were as attractive and seductive as the clothes they wore to proclaim their status.

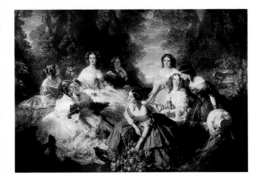

Franz Xavier Winterhalter, Portrait of the Empress Eugénie Surrounded by Maids of Honor, 1855. *Musée National du Palais de Compiègne.*

THE MUSEUM

Museums became the temples of public art, where past and present met to perpetuate tradition and where the total experience of an individual work of art derived from a fusion of its setting, decorative value, and subject matter. Following the restoration of the Bourbons, museum doors in Paris were opened to artists: Louis XVIII handed over the rooms of the Senate to the Ecole moderne de la France, which became the Royal Gallery of the Luxembourg Palace, henceforth reserved for modern painting. Under Charles X, new rooms in the Musée du Louvre were decorated with frescoes devoted to France, the sovereign-protectors of the arts, and the arts themselves. *The Apotheosis of Homer* (1827) by Ingres was both a glorification of the arts and a homage to the artistic policy of the Restoration. Louis Philippe commissioned a team of artists, including Eugène Delacroix (1798–1863), François Gérard, Horace Vernet, and Ary Scheffer (1795–1858), to execute a series of battle paintings for the Historical Gallery of Versailles, opened in 1836.

New museums were opened in many other European cities. In London, the Royal Academy of Arts was transferred to Burlington House in 1869 and separated from the National Gallery. In Madrid, the Prado Museum (1819) was extended in 1870 to accommodate all of the religious paintings from the Trinity Museum. Artists working at the Kunsthistorisches Museum in Vienna between the years 1872 to 1891 included Viktor Tigner, Hans Makart, Michael Munkacsy, Franz Masch, and the brothers Ernst and Gustav Klimt. In Amsterdam, in 1885, the Rijksmuseum was established in a grandiose building designed and built by Petrus Josephus Hubertus Cuypers (1827–1921).

Infallibility (1870) increased the power of the ecclesiastical authorities, who used art as a tool of propaganda. The increased wealth of the bourgeoisie led to a new and much larger source of interest and income for the art world. Formerly, patronage had been the preserve of the royal court and the nobility; the patrons of later 19th-century art, however, were often from the middle class rather than the aristocracy. Now, it was not only the palaces of Versailles and the Tuileries that could boast art fit for a king; the less exalted residences of the wealthy middle class were also decorated with fine paintings. The wonderful buildings constructed by Haussmann in Paris reflected a social hierarchy arranged vertically, where bourgeois families lived on the higher, more expensive floors.

In England, the prosperity of the middle class derived from Britain's growing commercial and industrial power. After the Parliamentary Reform Act of 1832, the patronage of the arts by the middle classes mirrored their growth in power and influence.

Jean Béraud, Mary Magdalene Before Jesus, 1891. Walker Collection, Paris. Here, a biblical event takes place within a bourgeois context, the traditional Christ figure surrounded by modern figures.

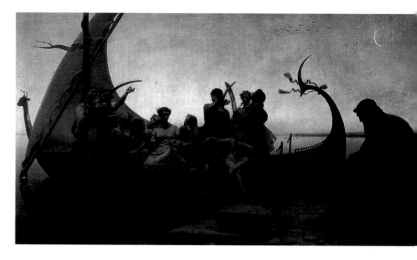

Charles Gleyre (1806–74), Evening, or Lost Illusions, 1843, Musée du Louvre, Paris. The traditional subject matter of myth and legend found its way into the homes of art collectors. This work is a relatively informal and intimate portrayal.

THE SALONS AND THE ACADEMIES

Huge crowds regularly flocked to the exhibitions at the Paris Salon and London's Royal Academy of Arts. The public showed extraordinary interest in the paintings on display, some of which were protected by barriers and guarded by the police. The fear was not of malicious attacks on the works themselves but of over-enthusiastic crowds getting too close. Artists whose work was selected for exhibition enjoyed immediate success,

THE SALON OF 1863

The paintings exhibited at the Paris Salons represented only a small fraction of those submitted to the exacting jury, which took care to make sure that academic standards rather than creative genius remained the prime criterion. To pacify the many protesters, Napoleon III created an alternative salon in 1863 to enable the public itself to judge the merit of the works on exhibit. Most of the people who visited the Salon des Refusés that year went in a spirit of hostility. At the Salon of 1863,

Eugène-Emmanuel Amaury-Duval (1806–85), The Birth of Venus, 1863. Musée des Beaux-Arts, Lille, France.

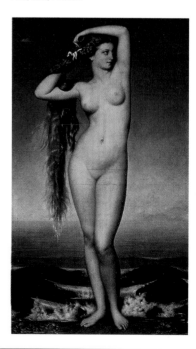

CHURCHES AND PALACES

Supported by the restored monarchy, the Church in France embarked on a new moral crusade. The mystic leanings of Napoleon III's consort, the Empress Eugénie, had led to religious buildings being filled with votive paintings and to the restoration of many churches damaged during the years of the revolution. The new dogmas of the Immaculate Conception (1854) and Papal

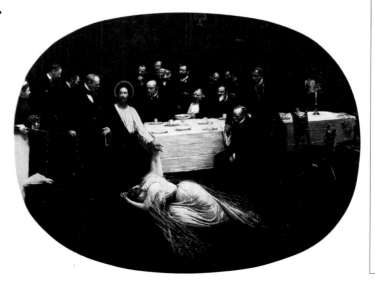

and the value of their paintings was greatly increased. As a result, a recognizably "academic style" developed as artists sought to create works of art that appealed to the exhibition selectors. Horace Vernet (1789–1863), Jean Léon Gérôme (1824–1904), and Alexandre Cabanel (1823–89) were among those artists who enjoyed such high esteem in the second half of the century. Another of their number, Adolphe William

Bouguereau (1825–1905), once boasted at the height of his fame, "Every minute of mine costs a hundred francs."
Run according to a strict hierarchy, the French Academy of Painting and Sculpture had been dissolved in 1793 by David and the Abbé Grégoire because,

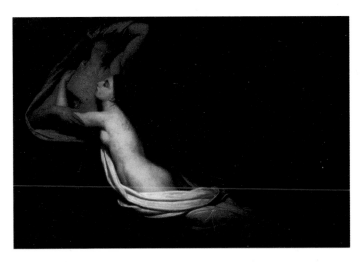

Ary Scheffer, The Shadows of Francesca da Rimini and Paolo Malatesta, *1835. Wallace Collection, London. This Romantic subject was popular in paintings and also found fortune in musical compositions.*

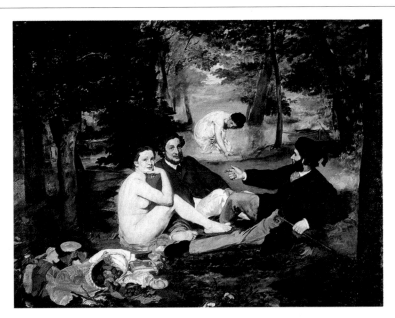

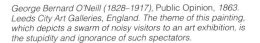

George Bernard O'Neill (1828–1917), Public Opinion, *1863. Leeds City Art Galleries, England. The theme of this painting, which depicts a swarm of noisy visitors to an art exhibition, is the stupidity and ignorance of such spectators.*

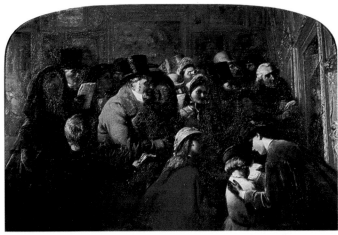

Edouard Manet, Déjeuner sur l'Herbe, *1863. Musée d'Orsay, Paris.*

the emperor himself purchased a nude by Cabanel, regarded as perfectly decent and wholly unsensual because of the mythological subject matter. However, *Déjeuner sur l'Herbe* by Edouard Manet (1832–83) was judged by the jury to be vulgar and was turned down. Gérôme (and to a lesser extent Cabanel) proved to be the most bitter adversary of the Impressionists and of the work of Manet in particular. He strongly opposed an exhibition of Impressionist paintings donated from the Caillebotte collection that was due to be held at the Musée du Louvre.

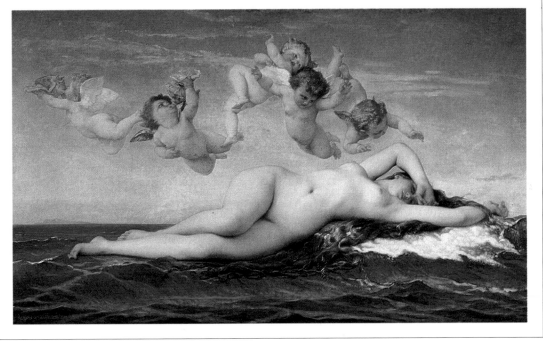

Alexandre Cabanel, The Birth of Venus, *1862. Musée d'Orsay, Paris. This work earned the artist entry into the Académie des Beaux-Arts.*

ART DEPICTS SCIENCE

Doctors and men of science were the embodiment of the 19th-century's belief in progress, and their influence permeated the art world. Luigi Sabatelli (1772–1850) exalted science and Florentine scientists in his sculpture *Galileo's Pulpit*, which was commissioned by Leopold II in 1841 for the Congress of Italian Scientists. The naturalist Anton Dohrn of Stettin founded the Marine Institute of Naples between 1872 and 1874, and Hans von Marées (1837–87) was commissioned to create a fresco for the library of this scientific institute. In France, the eminent scientist Dr. Jules-Emile Péan was painted by Henri Gervex in 1887.

Henri Gervex, Doctor Péan Demonstrating at the Saint-Louis Hospital his Discovery of the Hemostatic Clamp, *1887. Musée de l'Assistance Publique, Paris.*

Hans von Marées, The Pergola, *fresco, 1873. Geological and Marine Institute, Naples.*

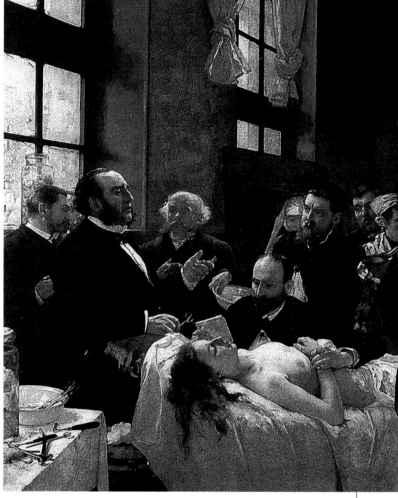

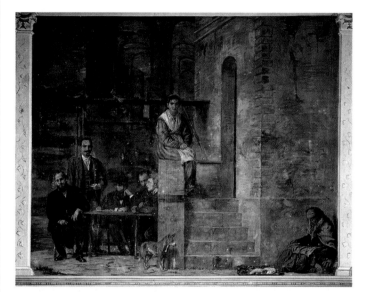

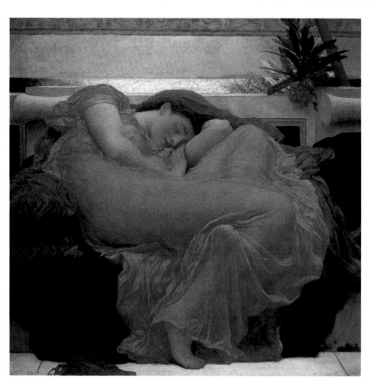

as stated in the Salon guide for that year, "the main characteristic of genius is independence." William Blake and Jakob Carstens, among others, also dismissed the institutions as too didactic. However, in the mid-19th century, they were a necessary testing ground for painters of "serious" art and won the endorsement of painters such as Frederic, Lord Leighton (1830–96), who praised the Royal Academy of Arts in London. Overall, the academies became more and more influential, placing greater emphasis on formal, didactic works than on the more spontaneous approach that had previously been so important in artistic training.

Frederic, Lord Leighton, Flaming June, *c.1895. Fundación Luis A. Ferré, Museo de Arte, Ponce, Puerto Rico.*

ACADEMIC APPROVAL

The French state was eager to patronize artists and issued invitations to them to preside at official openings and other public occasions in Paris. The status of "official artist" was hugely prestigious; artists were indulged by the Salon and by clients, and some were even decorated with the Legion of Honor. At the beginning of the 19th century, many of London's artists lived modestly in the poorer parts of the city, but soon those endorsed by the institutions took advantage of their growing status and moved to more salubrious areas of London.
Luxurious and exotic

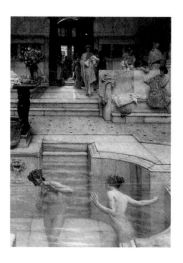

Sir Lawrence Alma-Tadema, A Favourite Custom, *1909. Tate Gallery, London.*

mansions were fashionable among the wealthier artists, most notably Lord Leighton's in Holland Park, which followed a design by George Aitchison (1825–1910). Its outstanding feature was an exotic Arab vestibule. Designed by Walter Crane (1845–1915) and Randolph Caldecott, this Moorish-style room was richly decorated with Persian tiles and a mosaic fountain. Sir Lawrence Alma-Tadema (1836–1912) had two studios in his home: one with Pompeiian decorations for himself and the other, featuring German paneling, for the use of his wife, also a painter. In France, the painter Ernest Meissonier (1815–91) commissioned for himself a luxurious Neo-Renaissance palace in the Place Malherbes, Paris. If one of the strongest motivations of Romanticism was a yearning to be some-where else, to return to the past through mythology and exoticism, then the painting of the so-called *pompiers* and the artists of the Victorian age favored precisely the opposite: antique, Oriental, historical, and allegorical themes were all used metaphorically. The reality of the present was of more interest to them than the remote past. While Romanticism strained to

THE "POMPIERS"

The French academic painters of the second half of the 19th century were described as *pompiers* – an ambiguous term that either signified the notion of ostentation and pomposity or referred generally to the nude figures of David, which were often depicted with plumed helmets (jokingly compared to the headgear of French firemen, or *pompiers*). The *pompiers* took great pleasure in detail. Their delight in anatomical precision eliminated any possibility of uncertainty as well as any hint of sentiment or drama. The portrayals of Venus in works by Cabanel and Bouguereau, for example, have no individual character: the female figures are invariably beautifully formed, soft and shapely, sensual yet maternal, all at the same time. They presented the ideal of woman as an embodiment of pleasure, elevated to aesthetic and (by reason of the allegorical theme) moral heights. These works reflect the decadent tastes of the Second Empire, with its penchant for prostitution, sensuality, and luxurious living.

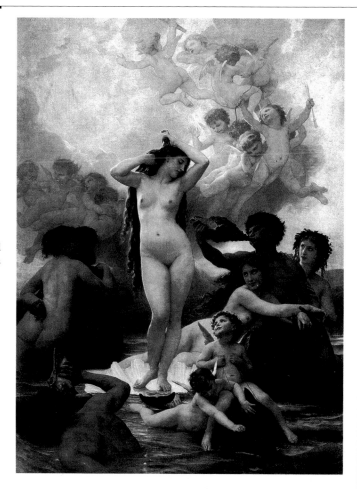

Above: William-Adolphe Bouguereau, The Birth of Venus, *1879. Musée d'Orsay, Paris. This painting contains echoes of the work of Ingres.*

Jean-André Rixens (1864–1924), The Death of Cleopatra, *1874. Musée des Augustins, Toulouse. Rixens depicts a subject popular in painting since the 17th century.*

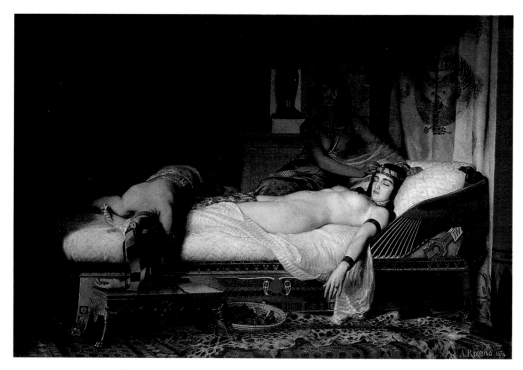

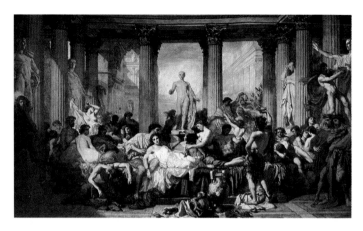

Thomas Couture, Romans of the Decadence, *1846–47. Musée d'Orsay, Paris. The corruption and hedonism of the imperial society is depicted with a moralistic tone.*

grasp whatever was distant, unknowable, or elusive, academic painting was more direct and made the subject matter much more accessible to the observer.

This new attitude also led to a fresh definition of technique and style: the painting surface was smooth, almost polished, and every effort was made to achieve

the greatest possible accuracy and precision. The pursuit of historical accuracy was sometimes taken to excessive lengths, since even the most minute of details had to be verified. Such paintings required months of laborious study: Meissonier struggled with *The Battle of Friedland* for 15 years, and Mariano Fortuny y Carbó (1838–74) spent his entire life planning *The Battle of Tetuan.* When Lord Leighton exhibited his *Venus Disrobing for the Bath* in

1867, the allegorical content and the pure, brilliant style of the painting silenced any criticism, mocking the forces of moral repression and indirectly celebrating the sensual world. Refinement of technique came to be understood as the very criterion of the work's morality. To the prospective buyer it implied honesty and hard work, and pristine surfaces were associated with integrity and professional conscientiousness, which, in the eyes of

the bourgeoisie, guaranteed quality. Praise was given for the amount of time spent on an accurate rendering of an outline or for evenly balancing the brushstrokes. This was especially the case with some very large-scale works, such as *Romans of the Decadence* by Thomas Couture (1815–79). These

Mariano Fortuny y Carbó, The Sons of the Painter in the Japanese Room of his House, *1874. Museo del Prado, Madrid. Here, Japanese culture, having lost its novelty value, is used simply as a decorative device.*

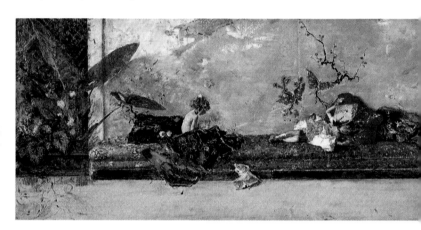

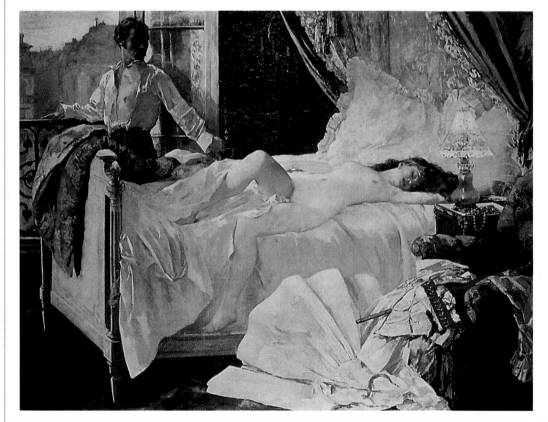

Henri Gervex, Rolla, *1878. Musée des Beaux-Arts, Bordeaux.*

THE GERVEX SCANDAL

Even an "official" painter of the caliber of Henri Gervex (1852–1929), commissioned to create frescoes for the Hôtel de Ville and the foyer of the Paris Opéra Comique, was refused permission to exhibit a work at the 1878 Salon on the grounds of unacceptable subject matter. Its subject taken from a poem by Alfred de Musset, the painting depicted Maria, a young prostitute, lying on a bed, and Rolla, a desperate *bon viveur* about to commit suicide. On the advice of Edgar Degas (1834–1917), Gervex had added a pile of clothes tossed to the ground in the right-hand corner, a detail that was enough to get the canvas condemned for its moral laxity. When the work was later exhibited at a dealer's in the Chaussée-d'Antin, it created a considerable stir.

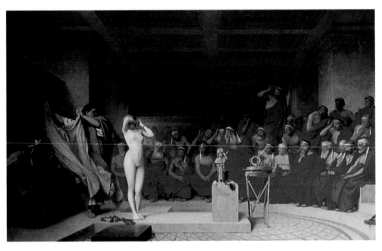

Jean-Léon Gérôme, Phryne in the Areopagus, 1861. Kunsthalle, Hamburg. The representation of the myth of beauty persuading justice appealed greatly to French tastes.

immense canvases were much in vogue until the 1880s, when the artists themselves discreetly began to buy works produced by the Impressionists.
A further sign of the gradual breakdown of the academic tradition was to be found in the arguments that took place between the writer and influential art critic John Ruskin and the American painter James Abbott McNeill Whistler (1834–1903). Whistler's atmospheric and impressionistic painting *Nocturne in Black and Gold:*

Cesare Maccari, Cicero Denouncing Catiline. Palazzo Madama, Rome. The newly born Italian nation looked to republican Rome for its model of national unity.

The Falling Rocket (1875) was judged by Ruskin to be like "flinging a pot of paint in the public's face." Whistler sued for libel and won his case in 1878 (he was awarded only a farthing in damages and no costs, leaving him bankrupt). In contrast with such innovative and controversial work, the highly finished painting of the *pompier* artists started to appear dated.
Meissonier died in 1891 and Paul Baudry in 1886, without having completed the cycle of *Joan of Arc* intended for the Paris Panthéon. The works of Jean-Leon Gérôme (1824–1904) enjoyed continued success at salon and academy exhibitions throughout the latter half of the 19th century. In the less fashionable areas outside of the main cities, *pompier* art continued to attract an enthusiastic following.

INSPIRED BY ANTIQUITY

At the beginning of the 19th century, Lord Elgin, British ambassador to Turkey, brought back to England a large collection of sculptures (the Elgin Marbles) from the Parthenon. Later, in 1846, Sir Charles Newton organized an expedition to Asia Minor to examine the mausoleum of Halicarnassus. This interest in antique sculpture and admiration for classical ruins were the inspiration for many of the works of the English painter and sculptor George Frederick Watts (1817–1904) and Lord Leighton. The paintings of ancient Rome by the Dutch-born, naturalized English artist Sir Lawrence Alma-Tadema were also the product of exhaustive studies of classical art. During his visits to Naples, Pompeii, and Herculaneum, he assembled a large photographic archive of Roman monuments, sculptures, frescoes, and sketches.
In *The Flautist's Rehearsal* of 1861, Gustave Boulanger (1824–88) recorded what was in effect a festival, staged in the courtyard of Napoleon's palace, which was suitably decorated with Pompeii-style frescoes by Gérôme. Present was the artist and writer Théophile Gautier, who encouraged members of the state-run Comédie Française to perform classical Greek and Roman dramatic works.

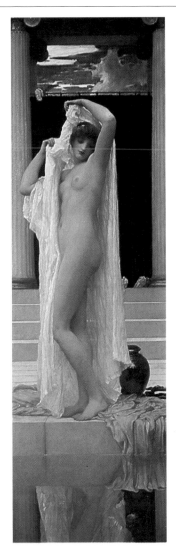

Frederic, Lord Leighton, The Bath of Psyche, c.1889–90. Tate Gallery, London.

Sir Lawrence Alma-Tadema, Phidias and the frieze of the Parthenon, 1868. Museum and Art Gallery of Birmingham, England.

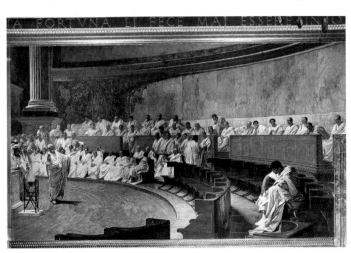

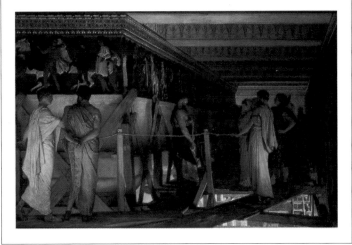

THE CREATION OF THE METROPOLIS

In the 19th century, the capital city was planned and constructed – or reconstructed – as an all-encompassing urban organism, with structured districts surrounding an aesthetic and functional center. The metropolis was provided with infrastructures and services, with buildings and areas allocated for specific uses.

The equivocal beauty of the industrialized 19th-century metropolis is hauntingly evoked by Charles Baudelaire in the lines of his poem "*Les Sept Vieillards*" ("The Seven Old Men") from his famous collection *Les Fleurs du Mal* (1857): "Swarming city, city full of dreams, where in broad daylight a ghost clutches the passerby! Mysteries everywhere flow like sap along the narrow canals of the great giant." Here, behind the vivid imagery we catch a glimpse of the contrasts inherent to the modern city:

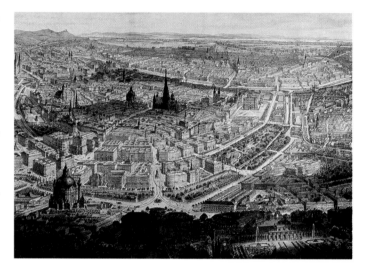

G. Veith, View of Vienna, *1873. This engraving shows an example of town planning from the end of the 1850s. The previously unoccupied ring of fortified walls is transformed into an area of green space and public services alongside the ancient city center.*

this is a place that inspires the loftiest of dreams, yet its practical infrastructure includes the basest of elements, such as sewage and drainage.

For the 19th-century middle-class city dweller, the real masterpieces of the age were the palaces of power for government and business; the terminals for land and

CASTLES AND THE GOTHIC REVIVAL

The castle, that most evocative and mysterious setting of the medieval world, fascinated·novelists from the late 18th century onward, and Horace Walpole, man of letters and collector of art and armor, was one of its greatest enthusiasts. Sir Walter Scott described how Walpole's villa at Strawberry Hill, London, was gradually transformed into a feudal castle by the addition of towers, turrets, galleries, corridors, friezes, fretworked ceilings, castellated walls, and pierced windows; inside, the walls were decorated with bossed shields, armor, bucklers, and jousting lances, typical accoutrements of chivalry. Gothic castles provided the setting for such novels as Walpole's *The Castle of Otranto* (1764) and Sir Walter Scott's *Ivanhoe* (1819) and *Castle Dangerous* (1831). Throughout 19th-century Britain, numerous castles were built in the image of those in the stories of Scott and Walpole: Harlaxton Manor in Grantham, Lincolnshire, by Anthony Salvin (1831–37); Cardiff Castle by William Burges (1865); and Scarisbrick Hall in Lancashire (1837–45) by A.W.N. Pugin. In Continental Europe, Stolzenfels was built on the

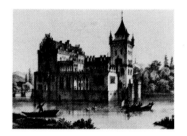

Georg Pezolt, Castle Anif, Salzburg, 1838–48. Freed from the chains of classical models, the castle-villa is one of the first examples of picturesque experiment inspired by the Middle Ages.

Rhine, designed by Karl Friedrich Schinkel (1836); Anif in Salzburg (1838–48) by Georg Pezolt; the medieval-revival Borgo in Turin by Valentino (1882); the Château de Pierrefonds (1858–67), on the outskirts of Paris, by Eugène-Emmanuel Viollet-le-Duc; and Château de Challain-la-Potherie (Maine-et-Loire, 1847–54) by René Hodé.

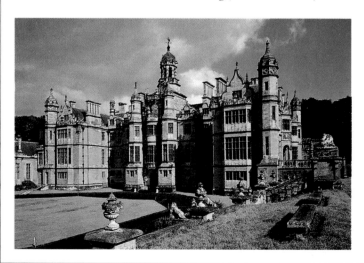

Anthony Salvin, Harlaxton Manor, Grantham, Lincolnshire, 1831–37. In addition to Gothic Revival, English architecture derived inspiration from the late Renaissance style of Elizabeth I and James I.

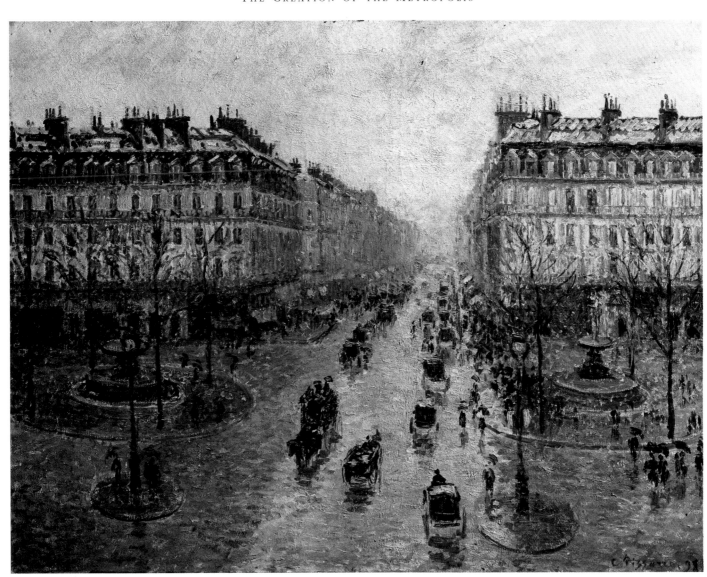

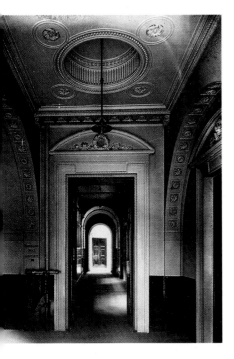

John Soane, Bank of England (detail of waiting room), London, 1788–1805. The tasteful, elegant style of Soane's interiors was achieved by his original reworking of more purist forms of classical ornamentation.

sea travel; the commercial premises; the huge buildings for education, healthcare, and entertainment; the public parks; the convenient bridges, and, towards the outskirts, the cemeteries.

The 19th-century city sprang from a series of remarkable transformations caused by industrial and technological developments. Cities became true metropolises as new citizens flocked in from other areas. All the needs of a community experiencing an explosive growth in numbers had to be provided: new streets, water supply, drainage and sewage systems, public and private buildings, and a transportation system that was able to carry large numbers of workers to and from their workplace. Improved public hygiene, a higher standard of living, and significant advances in medicine all contributed to a lower mortality rate at this time of high population growth.

TOWN PLANNING

The mapping out of land development and the application of the new discipline of urban planning were factors in controlling the expansion of large urban

Camille Pissarro, Avenue de l'Opéra in Paris, 1898. Pushkin Museum, Moscow. Bustling Paris life at the end of the century was a recurring subject in Impressionist painting. The fashionable middle classes flocked to the popular Avenue de l'Opéra, which was opened following Haussmann's transformation of the city in the second half of the century.

areas. Regulatory systems transformed the appearance of some of the most important European capital cities, not the least being Paris.

In *Notre-Dame de Paris* (*The Hunchback of Notre-Dame*, 1831), Victor Hugo wrote: "I am not without hope that Paris, viewed from a montgolfier balloon, shall one day greet the observer with such sumptuous lines, such opulence of detail, such diversity of aspects and with that certain something of

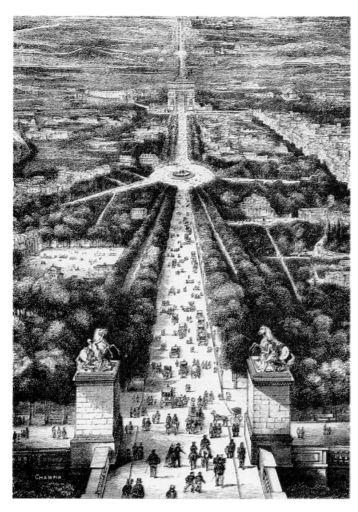

An engraving by Champin of the Champs-Elysées in the middle of the 19th century. Pushkin Museum, Moscow.

establishments, and to improve the state of buildings and movement of traffic along new roads. The changes to the street plan were carried out in three stages. The first phase, from 1854 to 1858, consisted of essential work, of which half to two-thirds of the overall cost was subsidized by the state. This included extension of the Rue de Rivoli, the Boulevard Sebastopol/Saint-Michel, the axis running from Châtelet to

including the Château d'Eau, the Étoile de l'Arc de Triomphe, and the Place du Trocadéro. The third phase saw the completion of a network of streets running through areas such as Les Halles, the Opéra, the Rue Lafayette and Rue de Rennes, Boulevard Saint-Germain, Parc Montsouris, and Parc des Buttes-Chaumont. The purpose of these measures was to integrate parts of the old city into the new layout. This objective entailed the demolition of certain buildings and the absorption of those parts of the city that

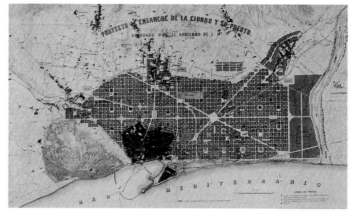

Ildefonso Cerdá, plan for enlarging the city of Barcelona, 1859.

greatness in simplicity, of the unexpected in beauty found in a chessboard." Baron Georges-Eugène Haussmann, Prefect of the Department of the Seine from 1853 to 1870, promoted and prepared his plan for Paris, outlining the picture of a modern city where wide, straight thoroughfares would physically and aesthetically

link its most imposing buildings and monuments. Long boulevards were to cross at star-shaped traffic circles (*ronds-points*) to create rectilinear visual axes and attractive vistas. Haussmann's aim was to give the city a comprehensively modern image, to make the most of its heritage of great monumental

the Hôtel de Ville, and the Avenue de l'Impératrice to the Bois de Boulogne. The second phase, from 1858 to 1868 and beyond, consisted of the construction of streets radiating outward from important road junctions,

were compatible with the new layout.

The result of these changes was a triangular block, formed by the subdivision of the urban fabric along the new radial thoroughfares. The problem of developing these central avenues had to be tackled first; the facades of the buildings had to fit in with the overall character of the neighborhood and with the general appearance of existing buildings. Town halls, schools, museums, theaters, hospitals, and other public places were inserted into the urban setting and linked and integrated by well-planned routes.

In England, a population explosion accompanied the Industrial Revolution, and the consequent phenomenal

BARON HAUSSMANN

The Parisian-born Baron Georges-Eugène Haussmann was largely responsible for the transformation of his hometown into an exemplary modern city. At the behest of Napoleon III, who wanted a capital as grandiose as his ambitions, Haussmann was the first town planner to rip out the historic center of a great city, replacing it with wide streets and avenues. He expelled the working-class inhabitants from the center of Paris and created a series of entirely new districts. His Paris of the Third Empire would become a model for major cities all over Europe and America.

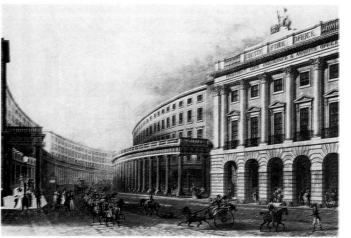

John Nash, Regent Street, London, 1814–20. The regularity of planes and the uniformity of style in this London street constitute a fine example of early 19th-century town planning.

HOTELS, SPAS, AND CASINOS

As the habits and lifestyles of city dwellers changed during the 19th century, certain places outside the main cities became very popular as venues for social and leisure activities. Visiting vacation and seaside resorts, taking the waters at spas, and gambling at casinos were among the new pastimes adopted by the prosperous middle classes. Countless "grand hotels," cafés, spas, and casinos were built during this era. The spa towns of Evian, Aix-les-Bains, Vichy, and Vittel in France; Montecatini, Fiuggi, San Pellegrino, and Salsomaggiore in Italy; Baden Baden and Wiesbaden in Germany; Bath in England; and Karlsbad in Bohemia developed around the buildings provided specifically for visitors.

Spas and seaside resorts offered numerous other attractions:

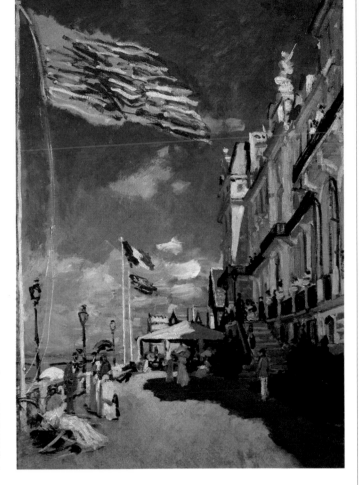

Claude Monet, The Hôtel des Roches Noires at Trouville, *1870. Musée d'Orsay, Paris. Trouville, a famous seaside resort on the Normandy coast, was one of the most popular vacation locations for Parisian society of the Belle Epoque.*

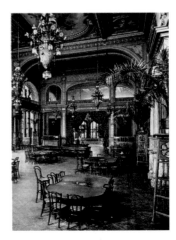

Mariánské Lázně, colonnade of Marienbad, Bohemia, 1884–89. The covered promenade, often constructed of iron and glass, was one of the most fashionable meeting places in late-19th-century spa cities.

casinos, theaters, and dance and concert halls, which in the case of Charles Garnier's Monte Carlo Casino (1878–79) were all accommodated in one building. The architecture of these resorts was modeled on the Neoclassical style, with a predominance of colonnades, pediments, and entablatures. Later, the style became more eclectic, often with Oriental touches. At the end of the century, the widespread use of iron and glass took over, heralding the Art Nouveau style. The success of the coastal resorts – such as Cannes, Nice, the Venice Lido, and Beaulieu-sur-Mer on the Mediterranean, Biarritz and Saint-Malo on the Atlantic, and Deauville,

Henri Beyaert, interior view of the first kursaal, Ostend, 1852. Favorably situated on the North Sea coast, Ostend became one of the most exclusive spas in Europe. The first kursaal (casino), an indoor recreational complex containing rooms for dining, refreshment, and gambling, constructed of wood and stucco with a cast-iron frame, could be disassembled. At the disposal of the War Department, which prohibited the erection of permanent structures on the coastal strip, it was demolished in 1865.

Dieppe, Calais, and Brighton on the Channel - was not only owing to the draw of attractive surroundings and a healthy environment but also to the range of amenities and the level of comfort guaranteed by the large hotels. These grand establishments offered the height of luxury: elevators, central heating, room service, reading rooms, spacious reception areas, music rooms, and gambling or games rooms, as well as gardens and promenades outside.

growth of London meant that civil engineers and legislators needed to cope with a fast-changing city. Between 1840 and 1914, the population of London doubled, while that of Greater London tripled; in the years 1820 to 1914 the radius from the heart of London's built-up area extended out from 2 to 6 miles (5 to 15 kilometers). Growth of the outer suburbs was stimulated by the further extension of the railroads and was additionally encouraged by the opening of the first underground subway system in 1863. The city grew through the construction of housing projects, groupings of houses designed in a similar style, planned on a mass scale, and covering very large areas at a phenomenal rate. These projects, however, were often built by speculative builders (this was the case at least until 1888 when the London County Council was established), especially in the working-class districts where the over-crowded and insanitary conditions appalled educated people and writers such as Charles Dickens. This started the debate on the question of London's suburban development, which eventually led Ebenezer Howard to write his *Garden Cities of Tomorrow* at the end of the century, setting out an original proposition for coping with urban expansion. This was the new town – a self-contained satellite town that benefited from both urban and rural amenities. His ideas were first put into practice in the early 20th century by architects and town planners such as Raymond Unwin and Barry Parker, who laid out the first garden city, Letchworth in Hertfordshire, in 1902.

One of the most important examples of 19th-century town planning was Barcelona, the design for which was drawn up by Ildefonso Cerdá in 1859. The expansion of the city was to take the form of a rectangular grid about 22 blocks wide, incorporating the oldest, central district of the city, the Barrio Gotico, and crossed by two large, diagonal arterial roads. The plans for *ensanche* ("the widening") or expansion are illustrated in Cerdá's *Teoria general de l'urbanización* published in 1867.

The problem of integrating the older urban fabric with the modern city was solved by the Ring system in Vienna, Cologne, Leipzig, Copenhagen, and other northern European cities. This interesting solution meant that the new road system could be accommodated without destroying the original town plan. In Vienna, the medieval fortifications of the city wall enabled Christian Friedrich Forster (1797–1863) to create a belt around which he built the new city. The Ringstrasse, or circular highway, was bordered by parkland along parts of the sloping banks of the fortifications, while new public buildings, including a theater, a library, museums, galleries, and markets, were erected along the outer edge. In 1817, Karl Friedrich Schinkel (1781–1841) drew up a town-planning program for the center of Berlin that laid down the criteria for the construction of public buildings (some of which he designed himself). It also contained plans for the improvement of road and waterway links, including changes to the Spree canal and its banks. Leon von Klenze (1784–1864) and Friedrich von Gärtner (1792–1847) were involved in the expansion of Munich, building the Ludwigstrasse as well as the

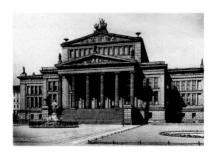

Karl Friedrich Schinkel, Schauspielhaus, Berlin, 1818–21. This building represents a rationalist reworking by Schinkel of a classical Greek construction.

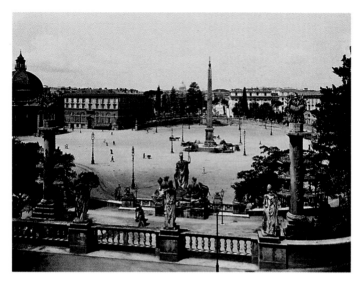

Giuseppe Valadier, reorganization of the Piazza del Popolo, Rome, 1813–20. The piazza solves the problem of linking the city proper with the system of ramps on the east side leading up to the Pincio.

Odeonsplatz, Briennerstrasse, and Königsplatz.

Plans for redefining the image of Italian cities ranged from Neoclassically inspired town plans by Giovanni Antonio Antolini (1756–1841), Luigi Cagnola (1762–1833), and Luigi Canonica (1762–1844) to the work of Giuseppe Poggi (1811–1901), who aimed to turn Florence into a modern metropolis. Enrico Alvino (1809–72) provided a new layout for parts of Naples, and Giuseppe Valadier (1762–1839) reorganized the Piazza del Popolo in Rome.

NEW DOCTRINES

With these changes to city layouts and the growth of many European capitals, it became necessary to reassess the provision for and siting of certain public buildings. Thought had to be given to new buildings in which to house government assemblies and administrative and financial institutions as well as educational establishments, cultural centers, and hospitals. If Balzac was correct in stating, as he did in *La Fausse Maîtresse,* that "architecture is the expression of custom," then the town plans and

architectural styles of the 19th-century city expressed the need for display on the part of an increasingly prosperous middle class. The stylistic complexity of 19th-century architecture, in which classical forms were entwined with references to archaeology and reminders of past styles (such

as Gothic), also exploited new materials and technology. The result was a vast and varied inventory that could be used in the complex planning involved in redefining city spaces and new buildings in response to the needs of a modern society.

Jean-Nicolas-Louis Durand (1760–1834) was among the first to realize the importance of reformulating a planning praxis that needed to include a classification of the type and history of buildings built in the past. In his *Précis des leçons d'architecture* (1802–05), he identified specific types of public buildings (town halls, stock exchanges, law courts, libraries, museums, markets, abattoirs, theaters, hospitals, prisons, and others) and private buildings (including townhouses and rented accommodations) with designs that took the form of "horizontal schemes" (plans) and "vertical schemes" (elevations).

GREAT EXHIBITIONS

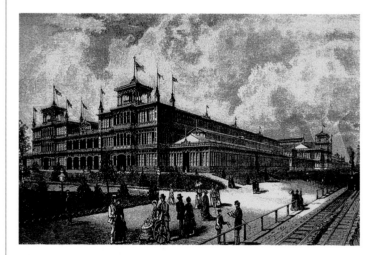

The great exhibitions, organized by various cities from the mid-19th century onward, were open to a wide, international public. As the decades progressed, truly universal-themed exhibitions proliferated alongside those of a more local character. The exhibitions played a significant role in the rapid expansion of industrialization and the

The Machinery Building at the Philadelphia International Exhibition, 1876.

stimulation of international trade – the lifeblood of modern Western civilization. In addition to their symbolic value as temporary unifiers of different geographical areas and cultural spheres, the exhibitions often provided opportunities for architectural experimentation.

THE CRYSTAL PALACE

Erected in Hyde Park in 1851 to house the first international exhibition, the Crystal Palace was the brainchild of Joseph Paxton (1803–65). He was a landscape gardener at Chatsworth in Derbyshire, England, and based the design for the great glass palace on the construction methods that he had developed for his greenhouses. Standard panes of glass set in wooden frames were inserted into a skeleton of iron girders, and guttering was designed to collect internal and external moisture, which then flowed away down hollow cast-iron columns.

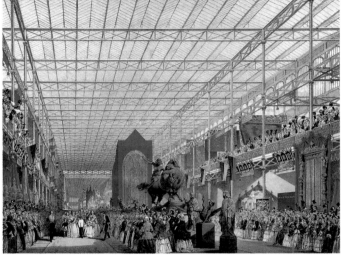

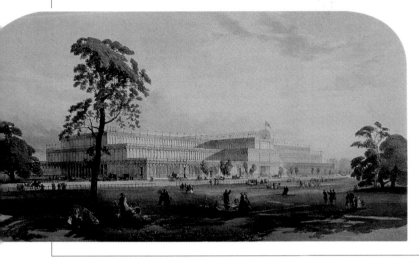

Joseph Paxton, Crystal Palace, 1851.

The five-aisled Crystal Palace had a floor space of 1,848 feet (563 meters) by 407 feet (124 meters) and was built entirely of mass-produced, factory-made sections that were assembled on

An interior view of the Crystal Palace at its original opening. This was destroyed by a fire in 1936.

site. Taking less than six months to complete, it was considered the first, and most significant, example of prefabrication to be used in architectural construction.

For example, the first "universal" event, the Great Exhibition of the Works of Industry of All Nations held in London in 1851, was to prove significant for the development of modern architectural techniques. Crystal Palace, built for the exhibition and the first structure of its kind, found international favor, inspiring a succession of exhibition buildings around the world: New York in 1853; Munich in 1854; Paris in 1855, 1867, 1878, and 1889; Vienna in 1873; Philadelphia in 1876; Sydney in 1879; Melbourne in 1880; Antwerp in 1885; and Brussels in 1888. Not only were these events showcases for industry, technology, and mass production, but they also bore witness to the burgeoning world of decorative arts and the practical application of new aesthetic criteria – later known as the applied arts.

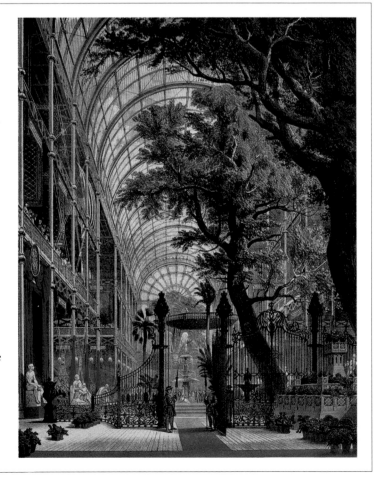

The Coalbrookdale Gates at the Great Exhibition in London, 1851.

Although Durand's lessons helped a succession of 19th-century architects make a choice when it came to changing the face of the city, Eugène-Emmanuel Viollet-le-Duc (1814–79), in his *Dictionnaire raisonné de l'architecture française,* showed how stylistic vagaries

VIOLLET-LE-DUC

Eugène-Emmanuel Viollet-le-Duc (1814–79) was given his first important commission at the age of 24: the restoration of the church of Sainte Madeleine at Vézelay, France. He went on to restore Sainte Chapelle, the Parisian burial place of Capetian kings, and then the cathedral of Notre-Dame. Later, he worked on buildings in Narbonne, Saint-Denis, Chartres, and Carcassonne. Viollet-le-Duc had two guiding principles: firstly, to be true to the original building during restoration (this proved to have disastrous consequences when practiced by less discerning disciples); secondly, based on his observations of Gothic architecture, to ensure that a building displayed the technical virtuosity of the design. This latter principle was put into practice extensively during the 19th century.

HONORE DAUMIER: "THE THIRD-CLASS CARRIAGE"

1863–65; oil on canvas;
26 x 36 in (65 x 90 cm);
Metropolitan Museum of
Art, New York.

This lively multi-portrait shows the interior of a congested third-class railroad carriage – of a type typical of French rolling stock of that era. The carriage has doors to gain access to the very narrow passageways between two facing bench seats, which are placed back to back, until all the space had been occupied. This organization of space allows the painter to produce a multiple portrait. Nineteenth-century artists usually chose the exterior features of the engine and carriages or the railroad station itself as their subjects; however, Daumier, a renowned caricaturist, was more interested in the people. Above their heads, the space remains unbroken.

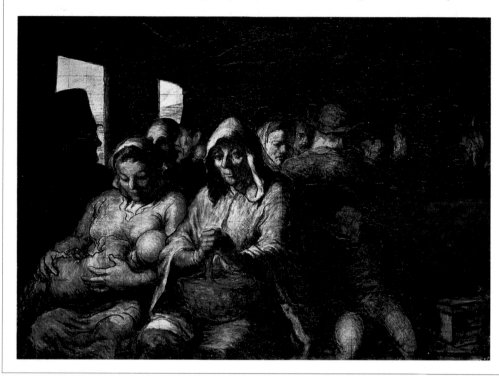

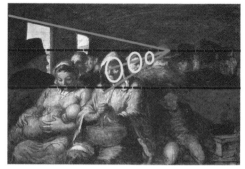

▲ *1. The subject of a busy train carriage fascinated the artist, who painted several versions of this painting. Here, he chooses a rectangular composition, which allows for an all-encompassing wide-angle view. The backrest of the seat in the foreground cuts the composition in two, underlining the rows of heads and faces in the upper half of the canvas. Not an example of accurate perspective with a central vanishing point, the painting also has a second line – that running above the highest heads. Various oblique lines originate from a point fixed on this line, defining homogenous elements in the composition. These lines organize the section of the picture that is most filled with light.*

RAILROAD STATIONS

Théophile Gautier described railroad stations as the "palaces" of modern industry, in which the railroad – the god of the 19th-century – was worshiped. For Marcel Proust, they were special places that contained the very essence of the city.

These cathedrals of contemporary society became the meeting places of different nationalities, the focal point of a vast radiating network of steel stretching out to the ends of the earth. The station – the modern showcase of progress and technology – started to exert its fascination during the second half of the century, as railroads were extended throughout Europe and the US. Architecturally, the great railroad stations combined

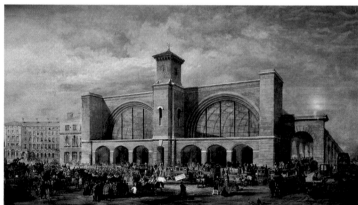

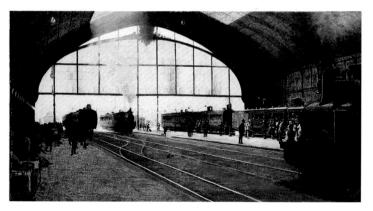

Lewis Cubitt, King's Cross Station, 1851–52. This painting shows the arrival of Queen Victoria at the famous London railroad station.

Angelo Morbelli, The Central Station of Milan, 1889. Civica Galleria d'Arte Moderna, Milan.

references to the past and experimentation with new forms. Typically, they featured the spectacular technological innovation of a vast canopy high above the platforms. The gigantic iron and glass structures of such stations as St. Pancras (1866–68) and King's Cross (1851–52) in London, Grand Central (1869–71) in New York, and Saint-Lazare (1887) in Paris were remarkable for their virtuosity and up-to-date construction.

Each of these great city terminals

▼ *2. A particular rhythm of shapes underlies the composition. Ovals, whole or cut in half, are distributed in horizontal rows, fixing both the rhythm and the successive planes of depth. The distribution of the ovals – the women's knees and the heads and faces of the passengers – becomes denser toward the background. In contrast, the straight lines of the carriage walls, doors, and ceiling are barely defined.*

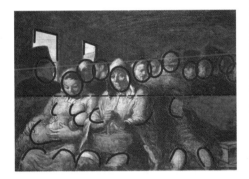

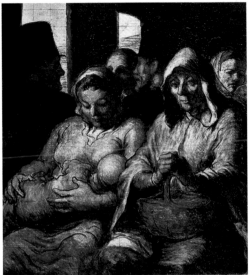

◀ *4. The style of the painting is characterized by visible brushmarks and a strong sense of immediacy. Daumier has painted with a speed that records and preserves the freshness of a first sketch – exactly as in caricature. Some faces, and especially those in the foreground, have the vigorous and conspicuous outlines of a pen-and-ink sketch. Daumier, also a fine engraver, reveals exactly what he wants to say about the two women through their features. With thick-set, robust bodies and holding their suckling baby and basket with equal intensity, they look noticeably alike.*

▼ *5. The light in the picture is neither bright nor diffuse. The figures are chiefly lit by the natural light from the windows on the left, although backlighting also brings the faces into profile against the shade. Both types of light cast well-defined shadows, with clear sculptural relief. But despite being accentuated, the contrast of light and shade does not create a dramatic feeling: what Daumier wishes to convey is reality, with neither softening nor emphasis.*

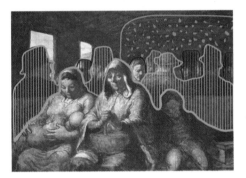

◀ *3. In order to give the picture depth, the painter exploits the succession of portraits, which, arranged in horizontal rows, become smaller the farther they are from the foreground. This is reminiscent of the way in which artists represented space before the scientific concept of perspective was understood, and the layering effect recalls that seen in toy theaters. Here, we see the travelers, most of them strangers to one another, crowded in their seats and forced into an awkward proximity. To emphasize the sense of congestion, the artist chooses the viewpoint of an onlooker occupying the bench that faces the two women and small boy. If depicted from a higher viewpoint, the figures would have appeared to be more comfortably distributed.*

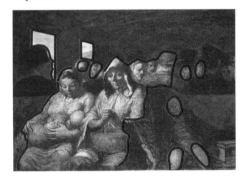

was emblematic of the metropolis it served and was linked to a far-flung network that kept to precisely the same time, marked by the large station clocks. Railroad timetables led to the introduction of standard time, vital if the transportation system were to function.

Franz Schwechten, Anhalter Bahnhof, Berlin, 1872–80.

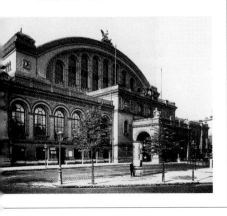

could be rationally explained by changing construction methods. After visiting Italy, many Englishmen, such as George Gilbert Scott (1811–78), Edmund Street (1824–81), William Burges (1827–81), and, notably, the critic John Ruskin (1819–1900), returned home to write about what they had seen. Their ideas had a considerable influence on contemporary architects and planners because they stressed that the essential principles of architectural practice include memory and, by extension, obedience to the styles of the past. In *The Seven Lamps of Architecture* (1849), Ruskin advocated a revival of the Gothic style, which he considered to be the supreme reflection of Nature. He explored this concept further in *The Stones of Venice*, published between 1851 and 1853, in praise of Venetian Gothic.

George Meikle Kemp, Walter Scott Memorial, Edinburgh, 1838–44. Kemp's monument, the winning entry in a competition held in 1838, was conceived as a great tabernacle in the Gothic style.

PUBLIC BUILDINGS

The commemorative or symbolic aspects of official buildings and administrative headquarters were often enhanced by the architect's choice of style. This is evident in London's Neo-Gothic Houses of Parliament designed by Sir Charles Barry (1795–1860) and A.W.N. Pugin (1812–52). Vienna's city hall (1872–84), designed by Friedrich von Schmidt, is another example of Neo-Gothic, as is the Hôtel-Dieu in Paris, by Emile Gilbert and Arthur-Nicholas Diet, and the Préfecture de Police on the Ile de la Cité (1862–66). A more spectacular use of new structural technology was evident in buildings destined

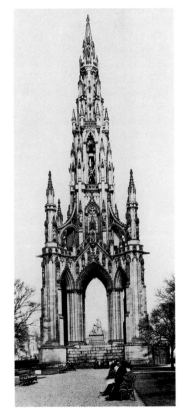

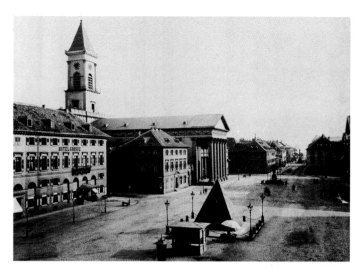

Friedrich Weinbrenner, pyramidal monument, Karlsruhe, 1823. As Inspector of Buildings from 1800, Weinbrenner initiated the Neoclassical revival in Karlsruhe. He designed the Karl-Friedrichstrasse and the Kaiserstrasse (1802–05), the Schlossplatz (1806), the Town Hall (1821), the Palace of the States General (1822), and the Mint (1826).

for educational and cultural use. Fine examples include Berlin's Bauakademie, designed by Karl Friedrich Schinkel between 1831 and 1836; the Ecole des Beaux-Arts in Paris by Félix Duban and Ernest-George Coquart (1871); the Bibliothèque Sainte-Geneviève (1843–50); and the Bibliothèque Nationale in Paris (1854–75), designed by Pierre-François-Henri Labrouste (1801–75). Joseph Duc's design for the Palais de Justice in Paris (1857–68), with its mixture of Italian inspiration and Far Eastern ornamentation, shows how various stylistic influences could be combined. A wealth of Neo-Baroque details,

including colonnades, tympani, and cornices, underlines the complex structure of Joseph Poelaert's Palais de Justice in Brussels (1866–83), making an impressive monumental whole. At a time when industry and commerce were expanding, the designs for stock and commodity exchanges were particularly varied. A typical example was London's Coal Exchange (1844–49) by James Bunstone Bunning, whose circular building had galleries and walkways surrounding the trading floor, surmounted by a wide, glazed dome.

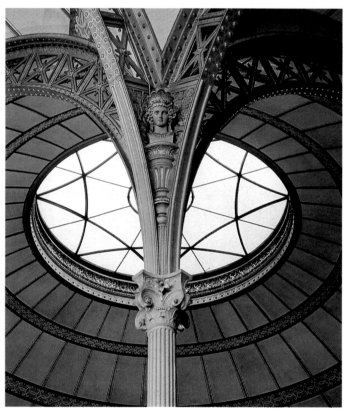

Pierre-François-Henri Labrouste, reading room of the Bibliothèque Nationale, Paris, 1858–68. The characteristic ribbed vault roofing, supported by slender cast-iron columns, represents an early synthesis of engineering and architecture and demonstrates the aesthetic possibilities of iron structures.

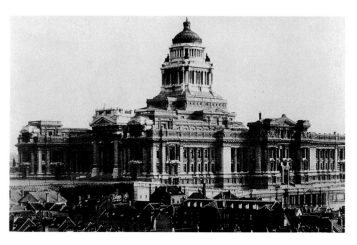

Joseph Poelaert, Palais de Justice, Brussels, 1866–83. This late example of the Neoclassical style is a gigantic building which dominates the center of Brussels. In this respect, it bears comparison with the religious buildings of the ancient East.

THEATERS AND MUSEUMS

Traditionally, certain types of building had been provided to accommodate cultural and recreational activities. Notably, these included theaters (for operas, concerts, ballets, and plays) and stadiums for spectator sports. The stadiums often housed sports events such as horse racing, cricket matches, and tennis tournaments, which people attended primarily in order to socialize. There were also large cafés in city centers and parks, hotels that catered to the increasingly popular habit of taking seaside vacations and health cures at spas, and casinos for gambling.

The theater's shape reached what was virtually its definitive layout by the end of the 19th century. By this time, the elements particular to this architectural form – the seating area, foyer, sloping aisles, galleries, and a division of the internal space between stage, proscenium, and the ceiling over the auditorium – were all in place. Jean-Louis-Charles Garnier's Paris Opéra (1861–75), Karl Friedrich Schinkel's Schauspielhaus (1818–21) in Berlin, the San

CAMILLO BOITO

After spending his formative years in Padua and Venice; Camillo Boito (1836–1914) taught architecture at the Accademia di Brera in Milan from 1860 until 1908. An impressive lecturer, a cultivated scholar, and a relentless traveler, he amassed photographs of works of art from all over the world and wrote countless articles on architecture. Despite his involvement in the demolition of Belle-Epoque Milan and its subsequent reconstruction, his restoration work showed respect for a building's history. However, his architectural work, including the Porta Ticinese in Milan and the Pinacoteca Civica in Padua, was uninspiring. He eschewed the prevailing eclecticism and developed his own version of the "veracious" style, resembling Italian Romanesque-Gothic. Luca Beltrami (1854–1933) was one of his pupils.

NEW MUSEUMS

The 19th century saw profound changes in the organization and role of the museum. Although there are precedents in earlier periods, it was after 1800 that scientific systems of classification took over from personal taste as the rationale for the formation and arrangement of collections. The Great Exhibition, held at Crystal Palace in 1851, symbolizes the urge to classify objects into a strict taxonomic framework. Elaborate catalogues and advanced techniques of display

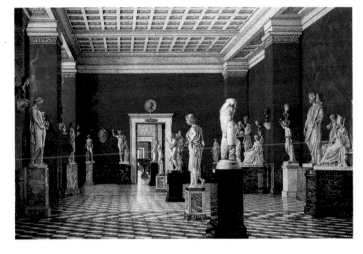

Interior view of the State Hermitage Museum, St. Petersburg, 1852.

Smaller museums with specific functions, intended to act as a celebration of local history or great figures, also appeared in the 19th century. The Thorvaldsen Museum in Copenhagen results from the desire of the sculptor Bertel Thorvaldsen (1768–1844) to establish a monument to his own genius. In 1837, he gave his collection to the city: the museum which bears his name, designed by Gottlieb Bindesbøll, was opened in 1848.

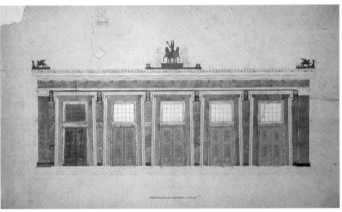

should be "sumptuous" or "systematic". Like the Louvre, the Hermitage in St Petersburg, rebuilt by Leo von Klenze in the 1840s and opened by Nicholas I in 1852, compromised between clarity and spectacle in its displays. The move towards a scientific curatorship influenced the founding of the Altes Museum in Berlin, designed by Karl Friedrich Schinkel.

Camillo Boito, Pinacoteca Civica, Padua, 1879.

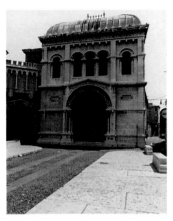

reflected these priorities. Profits from the Exhibition were used to found the South Kensington Museum – renamed the Victoria and Albert Museum in 1899 – which applied these principles to the fine arts and decorative arts as well as scientific collections. Similar museums were founded in Europe and the US, notably in Vienna and New York (the Metropolitan Museum, 1870).

M.G.B. Bindesbøll, Thorvaldsen Museum, Copenhagen, 1839–48.

Karl Friedrich Schinkel, Altes Museum, Berlin, 1823–30.

The development of art history as a discipline also had implications for museum organization. The conversion of the Louvre in Paris from a royal palace to a museum, which opened in 1793, instigated a debate as to whether displays

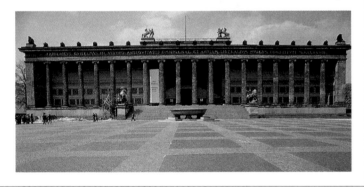

Carlo theater in Naples (1810) by Antonio Niccolini, and the Carlo Felice theater (1825–28) in Genoa by Carlo Barabino, as well as many other theaters and opera houses, have these component parts in common, although arranged differently and with varying interiors, suitable for plays, opera, music, or ballet.
The importance that nationalist governments attached to museums and their close ties with metropolitan and urban life

encouraged their proliferation. Museums assumed the role of guardians of record and power in a full range of cultural spheres. Exhibition space, planned within the wider context of the city, was to become an essential theme for architectural developments during the 20th century. In 1793, the Louvre opened in Paris; a few years later, the museum now known as the Kaiser Friedrich Museum was inaugurated (1797) in Berlin, and, in 1809, a museum

housing the Accademia di Belle Antidi Brera, was opened to the public in Milan. Further testimony to the close interest taken by governments is clear in the number of specialized establishments that were erected all over Europe: the Glyptothek in Munich (1815–34), designed by Leo von Klenze; Karl Friedrich Schinkel's Altes Museum in Berlin (1823–1830); the Victoria and Albert Museum in London (1856–1909), designed by Aston Webb, F. Fowke, and

L.C. Scott; Robert Smirke's British Museum (1823–47), also in London; and the Österreichisches Museum für Künst und Industrie in Vienna (1868–73), designed by F. von Ferstel. Natural history museums also sprang up in the capital cities, including the Naturhistorisches Museum in Vienna (1871–91), the work of Gottfried Semper and K. Hasenauer, and London's Natural History Museum (1871–81), designed by Alfred Waterhouse.

JAILS AND HOSPITALS

The architecture applied to prisons and hospitals during this era illustrates how specific functional needs were linked to stylistic and symbolic expressions of a new political and social climate.

Penal institutions in large cities experimented with ever more effective solutions. The "panopticon," first devised by Jeremy Bentham in 1787, allowed prisoners to be kept under very close surveillance and consisted of a central control area from which wings, housing the cells, radiated outward. The whole construction was punctuated by courtyards and enclosed by a high brick perimeter wall. This architectural plan was used in the House of Correction in Bury St. Edmunds, England (1803–05), and La Petite Roquette in Paris (1826–36) by Louis Hippolyte Lebas. In some cases, adding a Neo-Gothic style gave the prison an imposing and austere appearance, as in Bunning's Holloway Prison (1849–51) in London, making it seem like a castle or an impenetrable fortress.

The effects of medical procedures and hospital organization on the mortality rate were researched between 1760 and 1790 by Howard, Tenon, and Hunczovsky in England, France, and Austria, respectively. Their statistics proved that it was vital to build hospitals divided into separate wards rather than the traditional multifunctional buildings for the sick. The guiding principles for the construction of hospitals (endorsed by the Académie des Sciences in 1786 and analyzed by Jean-Nicolas-Louis Durand in his *Précis des leçons d'architecture* of 1809) were exemplified in the rebuilding of the Hôtel-Dieu (1772–1788), one of the largest hospitals in Paris, designed by Bernard Poyet. The hospital interiors

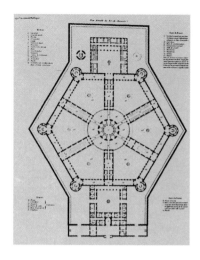

Louis Hippolyte Lebas, La Petite Roquette, Paris, 1826–36. Conceived as a correctional institute for juveniles, this building is constructed on the radiating plan inspired by Jeremy Bentham's "panopticon."

Martin Pierre Gauthier, Hôpital Lariboisière, Paris, 1846–54. Originally named the Louis-Philippe, the hospital's layout of pavilions met the most modern hygiene requirements.

CEMETERIES

In the wake of Napoleonic decrees that forbade individual burial within the confines of inhabited areas, cemeteries required specific consideration as far as town planning was concerned. In his *Historical Dictionary of Architecture,* Quatremère de Quincy singled out the Camposanto at Pisa as a model. He contributed to the diffusion of axial symmetry design in cemetery layout. Tombs and chapels, on the other hand, received a freer treatment, inspired by classical and medieval repertories.

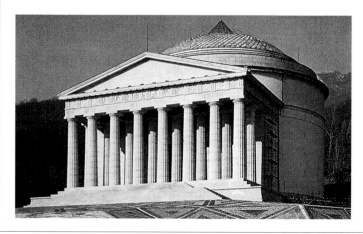

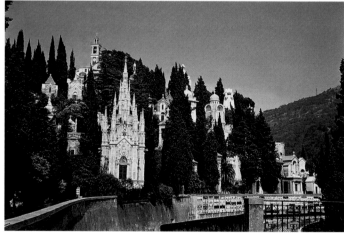

G. B. Rezasco, Staglieno Cemetery, Genoa, Italy, 1844–61.

Temple of Antonio Canova, 1819–20. Possagno, Italy. This famous funeral monument is based on the Pantheon.

were to be subdivided, with the spaces organized according to the various pathologies. Large areas were devoted to bedded wards for in-patients, sited so as to ensure the best sanitary conditions possible, and set in green open spaces. Enclosed walkways linked the various hospital facilities. During the 19th century, many hospitals adopted this layout, including the Lariboisière in Paris, designed by Martin Pierre Gauthier (1846–54); the Royal Herbert Military Hospital at Woolwich, London (1860–64); and St. Thomas' Hospital, also in London (1865–71).

In the late 18th century, new laws requiring burial in designated sites outside the populated areas meant that by the second half of the 19th century, cemeteries of an alternative layout and style to the traditional compact enclosure emerged. Plots allotted to family tombs were designed as funerary monuments, chapels, and buildings in miniature, using the expressive potential of sculpture, and a new symbolic language, to portray the distinctive characteristics of the departed.

ARCHITECTURE AND TECHNOLOGY

"Geometric forms intersected one another...the markets had a square, uniform appearance, like some huge modern machine...an enormous steam engine, a cauldron big enough to satisfy the hunger of a nation, a gigantic stomach, bolted, rivetted, made of wood, glass, and iron...with the power of a mechanical engine driven by the heat of combustion and the dizzying rush...of the wheels." With these words, from *Le ventre de Paris,* Emile Zola describes one of the great transformations of the 19th century: the development of new materials and construction

BUILDING BRIDGES

Structural engineering was one of the disciplines to reap the greatest benefit from the new technology and materials introduced during the 19th century. The Coalbrookdale Bridge in Shropshire, England, built over the River Severn in 1777 to a design by Abraham Darby and John Wilkinson, had a span of nearly 100 feet (30 meters) and was constructed entirely of cast iron. It was the first in a long line of bridge-building feats that clearly illustrated the virtuosity of contemporary structural engineering. In 1801, the American James Finlay patented a design for the suspended level floor. This construction method was later

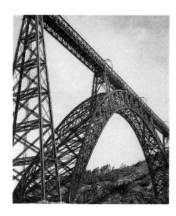

Gustave Eiffel, Garabit railroad viaduct over the River Truyère, France, 1880–84.

G. Rothlisberger, Paderno Bridge, Paderno d'Adda, 1887–89. This strong iron construction inspired by the arch bridges of Gustave Eiffel consists of a straight truss, supported by a parabolic arch with a span of 495 feet (150 meters).

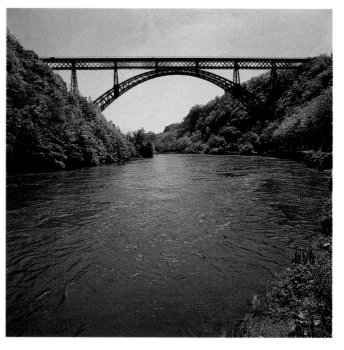

developed by using wrought iron "chains," a process patented in 1817 by Samuel Brown and Thomas Telford. The chain suspension technique was employed to build many bridges in the British Isles: Thomas Telford's Menai bridge in Wales, 1819–26; the Union Bridge over the Tweed at Berwick, by Samuel Brown,

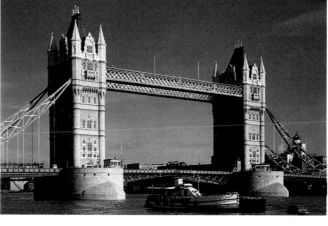

John Wolfe Barry and Horace Jones, Tower Bridge, London, 1886–94. The central structure can be raised to allow ships to pass up and down the Thames.

1820; and Clifton Bridge near Bristol by Isidore Kingdom Brunel, 1829. Further advances in suspension bridge construction were made when J. White and E. Hazard bridged Schuylkill Falls in Pennsylvania (1816), and when the Seguin brothers constructed their bridge at Tain-Touron (1825) over the Rhône. In both cases, drawn metal cables were used instead of chains.

During the second half of the century, designers concentrated their efforts on building structures that used less iron and, increasingly, switched to steel for tensile strength. The famous French engineer, Gustave Eiffel, built the first viaducts over the River Douro at Oporto, Portugal (1876–77), and the Truyère at Garabit, France (1880–84), with a parabolic vertical section supported by hollow columns. Toward the end of the century, moving bridges were introduced with London's Tower Bridge, designed by Horace Jones and John Wolfe Barry. Built between 1886 and 1894, its two large towers, with an upper and lower iron structure running between them, were linked by abutment towers and land ties, and by the chains to the shore spans. The lower level, divided into twin bascules, carried traffic when lowered but could be raised in drawbridge fashion to allow ships to pass.

techniques. Some applications and architectural forms seemed more suited to the use of these new materials than others. There was great interest in the potential use of prefabricated sections, which resulted from industrial production, as the large number of documented experiments shows. The construction techniques first used by John Wilkinson (1728–1808) in his iron bridge at Coalbrookdale, England, were developed by

construction techniques first employed in Joseph Paxton's Crystal Palace. Architects made the most of the ductility of metal structures and of advances in plate-glass manufacturing for large glazed surfaces. At the Exposition Universelle in Paris in 1889, the evolution of this construction technology was clear for all to see with the opening of two great building achievements: the Machinery Hall and the Eiffel Tower. The Machinery

Hall was an imposing steel structure, 1,170 feet (420 meters) long, with a 315-foot (115-meter) roof span. Visitors could be raised to the level of the exhibits, which included heavy industrial machinery and the most advanced technology of the day, on two movable bridges.

The Eiffel Tower, designed by the engineer Gustave Eiffel (1832–1923), soon became an unmistakable emblem of the city and of the technical

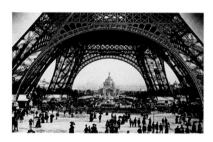

The base of the Eiffel Tower at the Exposition Universelle, Paris, 1889.

Jean-Baptiste Rondelet in his *Traité de l'art de bâtir* (1802), and in the later *Entretiens sur l'architecture* (1863–72) by Eugène-Emanuel Viollet-le-Duc. The production of wrought iron and, later, of steel girders was first carried out on an industrial scale in England between the late 18th and early 19th century. This meant that designers, engineers, and architects could try out new techniques and shapes that exploited the structural versatility of the new materials. Vast exhibition halls were made of iron and glass, using the greenhouse-style

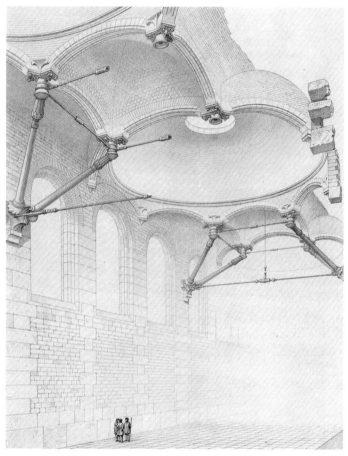

Eugène-Emmanuel Viollet-le-Duc, masonry design from Entretiens sur l'architecture, *1864.*

The Machinery Hall, Paris, from L'exposition de Paris illustrée, *1878.*

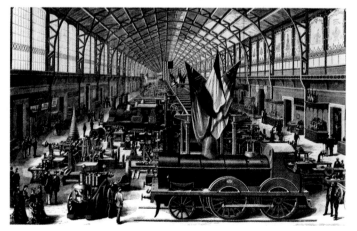

possibilities of modern structural engineering. It could be seen soaring skyward from every district in Paris, its distinctive tapering shape designed to minimize wind resistance and giving, as Gustave Eiffel himself described it, "an impression of strength and beauty."

"URBAN FURNITURE"

Public spaces proliferated and became larger in the 19th-century metropolis. Paris was famous for its boulevards, *passages* (arcades), and cafés with wide terraces. Gustave Flaubert recreates the picture in *L'Education sentimentale.* His preoccupied hero, Frédéric Moreau, wandering through Paris at dusk, notices that the shopkeepers are starting to take down their awnings. As municipal watering carts sprinkle a fine rain over the dusty pavements, an unexpected, cool freshness mingles with the aromas from the cafés. Through their open doors he glimpses, among the silver and gilt, flowers reflected in high mirrors. The crowds walk slowly by and men chat on the pavements. The *ville lumière,* as Camille Mauclaire described it, is the "city of light", where life is lived to the full and where the city is always more than a mere backdrop. In such an environment the various spaces of the metropolis can be enjoyed not only for their impressive appearance but also as places in which people pass their time and live their lives: hence, they must be furnished. Double rows of trees along avenues and around squares, flowerbeds and gardens, bandstands, gazebos, park benches, fountains, railings and gates, protective fencing for young trees, watering systems, and lighting – all these make up what we might describe as "urban furniture". They help to define a city's image and ensure that its open spaces can function primarily as places for recreation and so-cializing. Jean-Charles Adolphe Alphand's work for the city of Paris showed meticulous care in choosing and cultivating the plants and trees that filled the flowerbeds in the streets and parks of the city, calculating their size at maturity and the effect of the color of their foliage.

DEPARTMENT STORES

Department stores introduced a new approach to retail space by displaying and selling every imaginable type of product under one roof. The first department stores were multi-story buildings with vast entrance halls, built using the iron girder construction method. The rest of the building was constructed around these wide, open spaces, which were naturally lit through huge skylights high above. Long, winding staircases led up towards the higher floors, as in Louis Auguste Boileau's Bon

C. R. Franck, Au Moine Saint-Martin, advertisement for the department stores of that name, c.1875. Musée des Arts Décoratifs, Paris.

Jules and Paul Sédille, Printemps department store, Paris, 1882. The cast-iron structure on reinforced concrete foundations is based on a historically derived decorative style.

Marché (1872–74) and Jules and Paul Sédille's Printemps department stores (1882–89), in Paris. The fascination of these places was vividly described by Anatole France in *Le Petit Pierre* (1918). To his hero, as to others, these shops seem immense and full of treasures. He wonders

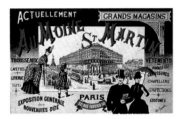

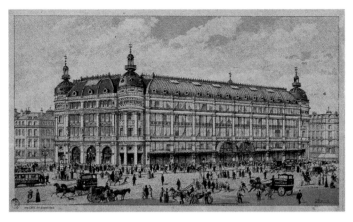

whether they have given him a taste for sumptuous artifacts that has become so strong it has never quite left him. The sight and quantity of materials, embroideries, carpets, feathers, and flowers on sale throw him into a kind of ecstasy, and he is lost in admiration at the affable gentlemen and the gracious young ladies who smilingly proffer these marvels to their indecisive clientèle.

MARKETS AND ARCADES

The 19th century brought the large commercial building into the modern metropolis. As a result of growth in industrial production, space devoted to the sale and distribution of goods in cities expanded rapidly. Various architectural solutions were adopted to meet the new requirements, including large covered markets, where great quantities of goods could be sold under one roof, and arcades made up of roofed pedestrian streets lined with shops.
The purposes for which covered markets were built dictated the shape of the interior. This was not unlike the nave of a church,

often widened by transepts, with stalls arranged around the sides and covered by glazed roofs. Such a layout was seen in Victor Baltard's great development of the Halles Centrales in Paris (1851–66), and Friedrich Hitzig's covered market in Berlin (1865–68), lit by gaslight and complete with storage space. The shopping arcade meant that articles for sale could be

Giuseppe Mengoni, Galleria Vittorio Emanuele II, Milan, 1865–77. This is a typically eclectic work based on the Parisian passages, or shopping arcades.

Friedrich Hitzig, covered market, Berlin, 1865–68. This perspective drawing captures Hitzig's grand vision. Plansammlung der Technischen Universität, Berlin.

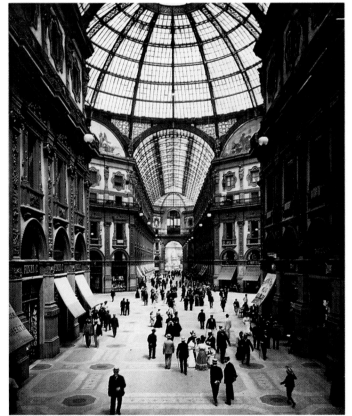

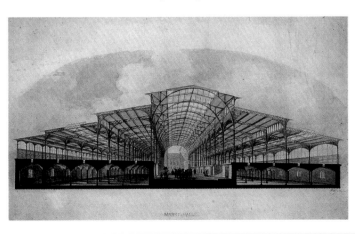

temptingly displayed in the windows, illuminated by natural light from the glass roof, or by gaslight. Among the most attractive were the Galerie d'Orléans in Paris (1829) by Fontaine and Percier; the Burlington Arcade in London (1818–19), designed by Samuel Ware; the Galleria Vittorio Emmanuele II (1865–77) in Milan; and the Cleveland Arcade in Ohio (1889–90).

PARKS AND GARDENS

The complex layout of the 19th-century park was linked to the development of the garden, which, from the late 18th century onward, had undergone a transformation. Parks were no longer the preserve of aristocratic or royal landowners, but were open to the public at large. They varied in size, layout, and character, depending on their metropolitan settings. The relationship between green spaces and built-up areas was sometimes achieved by having a parkland area where the city walls once

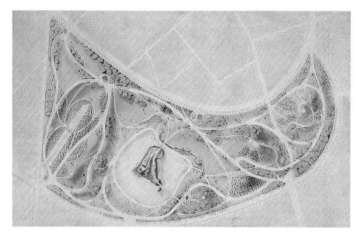

Adolphe Alphand, design for Parc des Buttes-Chaumont, c.1890, Paris. As a colleague of Haussmann, Alphand designed the green-belt system for Paris.

stood. The Stadtpark in Vienna was one example of this, and the 19th-century transformation of Lucca's 16th- and 17th-

century bastions and curtain walls into a promenade, by Marie-Louise de Bourbon, another. Tree-lined avenues or walks – such as the Boulevard Saint-Antoine in Paris or the Real Passeggio di Chiaia in Naples – and the public park, with its clearly defined boundaries and necessary amenities, also introduced greenery into city centers. In *L'art de composer et de décorer les jardins* by Pierre Boitard, designer and scholar of the art of garden planning, three categories of garden were identified: the walk or promenade, the pleasure garden, and the public park. In Britain, pleasure gardens

BOTANICAL GARDENS AND ZOOS

Although the conception of the garden as a setting for the observation of nature and its laws was long established, it was in the 19th century that this idea was applied widely. Gardens were to be used to collate and disseminate knowledge of the natural world: plants were catalogued and rocks, minerals, and animals were put on show. Zoological gardens, where animals were kept, studied, and exhibited to the public, were often sited next to botanical gardens, creating an experience that combined both pleasure and instruction. Collections of tropical plants and palms were contained in hothouses, where

Regent's Park Zoological Gardens, London, 1835. The 19th-century public garden provided both education and recreation for those who visited. The concept of the zoo, with its excellent prototype in London, reflects the positive, comparative thinking of the time.

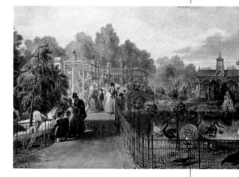

it was possible to recreate the microclimates suitable for the maintenance of exotic species. These buildings were characterized by large areas of plate

glass, with traditional wooden structures progressively replaced with iron constructions. The popularity of botanical gardens and zoos spread rapidly throughout Europe, along with institutions for teaching and research into agriculture and the natural sciences. In 1840, Queen Victoria gave the botanic gardens at Kew to the nation, while the Jardin des Plantes in Paris provided plants and flowers for municipal use. The Leopold park and zoo in Brussels opened in 1851, and in Naples, the fashion was for English-style landscaped gardens alternated with areas of botanic garden.

Richard Turner and Decimus Burton, Palm House, Kew Gardens, London, 1844–48. This articulated structure, with its huge, vaulted central pavilion, is one of the most famous metal greenhouses of the early Victorian age.

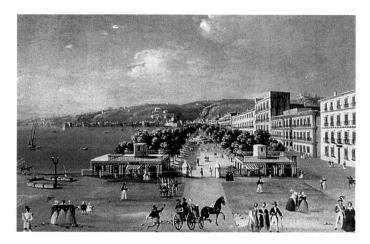

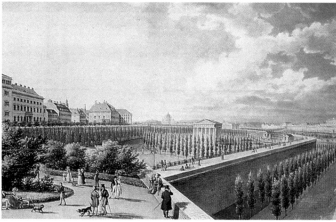

G. Scoppa, Il Real Passaggio di Chiaia, *early 19th century gouache. Often offering a range of special facilities, the promenade by the sea – such as this one in Naples – was a typical 19th-century setting for a vacation.*

P.D. Raulino, la passeggiata sui bastioni, *1824, drawing, Museen der Stadt, Vienna. At the end of this tree-lined avenue in Vienna is a house converted from the old city ramparts.*

were very popular, places where people met and where various recreational activities – entertainment, concerts, and games – could be enjoyed by the aristocracy and the middle classes. Vauxhall Gardens, in London, was one of the most famous of the city's 60 public gardens, which were recorded by Warmick Wroth in *The London Pleasure Gardens*, a

detailed guide published in 1896. The French equivalent of the pleasure garden was the *jardin spectaculaire,* such as the Parc Monceau or the Jardin de Tivoli. In the garden of Château Rouge, the promenades and carefully planned spaces were arranged to make the most of the beautiful site and show the trees and plants to their best advantage.

The progression toward public parks and gardens in the city came about gradually. London squares, built around an enclosed garden and reserved

for the private use of their residents, had already marked a significant step toward the introduction of the modern public garden. The aim of reintroducing nature into the urban landscape lay at the heart of John Nash's 1812 design for Regent's Park, in which a road formed the boundary of an enormous green open space, allowing carriages to take a circular

route around the park. Over the following years, the park was completed, with the addition of large expanses of water, a zoo, a botanical garden, and a number of long, intersecting walks. Such gardens also underwent a gradual change in Germany and France. The Englischer Garten, in what were then the outskirts of Munich, was set in a wooded area with plenty of shrubs and plants and contained a pagoda, an amphitheater, and a temple. Proof of how highly the Volksgarten (the people's garden) was valued is clear from the 1818 plan for the reorganization of the Berlin zoo, or Tiergarten, by P.J. Lenné. Parks were being turned into places where the wonders of nature could be appreciated and where natural science and beauty could be observed at close quarters. This function mirrored that of the great botanical gardens of Europe, which were founded for just such a purpose. The role of these institutions was underlined by their buildings, commissioned to facilitate the study and cultivation of plants. Richard Turner and Decimus Burton's Palm House at Kew Gardens, the Jardin d'Hiver on the Champs Elysées, and the park surrounding the rebuilt Crystal Palace at Sydenham all contributed to the perception and acceptance of the public park as part of the wider green spaces, considered indispensable amenities of a great metropolis.

PLEASURE GARDENS

From the late 18th century onward, a number of pleasure gardens attracted people to the outskirts of London, not only for the enjoyment of nature, the countrified scenery, and the flora and fauna, but also for the many amusements provided: plays, dancing, concerts, acrobatics, and juggling displays. London's Vauxhall Gardens, the oldest and most famous pleasure gardens, could be reached at first only by taking a boat across the River Thames. Once there, visitors could stroll among particularly sweet-smelling plants and orchards of fruit trees, and take the waters at the medicinal springs. Charles Dickens described the pleasures of the experience in "Vauxhall Gardens by Day" from *Sketches by Boz*: "We loved to wander among these

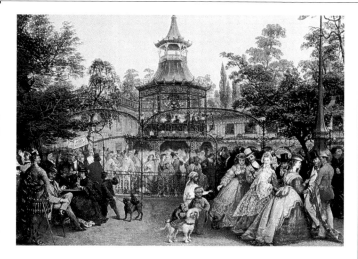

Cremorne Gardens, London, 1864. Follies, or small garden pavilions, were an essential ingredient of the 19th-century pleasure garden.

illuminated groves…The temples and saloons and cosmoramas and fountains glittered and sparkled before our eyes; the beauty of the lady singers and the elegant deportment of the gentlemen captivated our hearts; a few hundred thousand of addi-

tional lamps dazzled our senses; a bowl or two of punch bewildered our brains; and we were happy."

ART, TECHNOLOGY, AND INDUSTRY

As the 19th century progressed, so did methods for reproducing images using various photographic techniques and new printing systems. A vast number of copies of any publication could now be made available, so the dissemination of ideas, styles, and tastes widened and quickened.

The Industrial Revolution, which had started in England and spread to Germany and much of the rest of Europe during the 19th century, brought new developments in the manufacture of everyday, utilitarian objects and in the field of artistic endeavor. The changing face of society also exerted an influence, with the rise of a dynamic and entrepreneurial middle class set to replace the vanished patronage of the church and aristocracy. Rapid advances in technology and new machine tools were essential to the manufacture of consumer goods and mass-produced objects. Henry Cole (1808–82), one of the organizers of the Great Exhibition of 1851, was among the first to appreciate the necessity of forging close links between art and industry. He was instrumental in ensuring that the exhibits, which came from all over Europe, the East, and the US, included manufactured products that were fine examples of art and design. The innovations in industry also led to the development of photography. For the first time, visible reality could be captured and reproduced, so that a moment in time could be frozen forever.

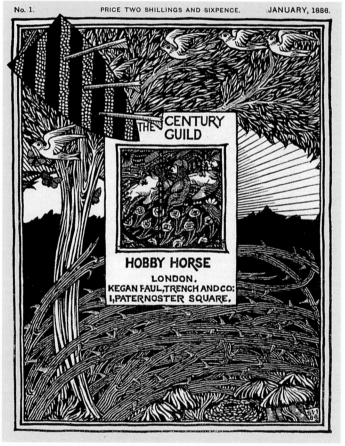

Arthur H. Mackmurdo, title page to Hobby Horse, 1886. This is the journal of the Century Guild, the movement founded by Mackmurdo in 1884.

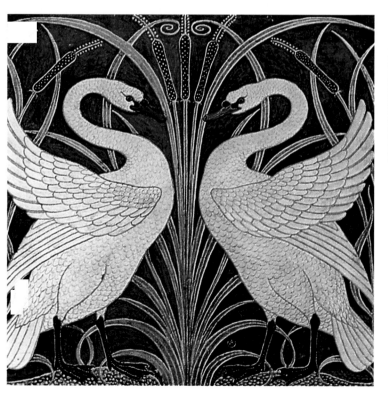

Walter Crane, Swans and Irises, 1877, polychrome tile. Flowers and animals were the most common decorative elements of this period.

THE ARTS AND CRAFTS MOVEMENT AND THE ORIGINS OF DESIGN

The English writer, artist, and social reformer William Morris (1834–96) believed that it was the duty of the new industrial society to develop a fresh, far-reaching aesthetic sense and to be mindful of the value of cultivating the decorative arts. Writing in *The Arts and Crafts of Today*, published in 1889, Morris maintained that if art were not applied to everyday objects, not only would products have no meaning but also there would be a gradual deterioration of the human race if life became purely material and spiritually empty. The effects of the aesthetic measures advocated by Morris would lead to the reevaluation of the decorative arts as an inescapable part of a person's environment. It would also lead to an awareness of design in the manufacture of household goods for a vast number of consumers. With Morris at its head, the Arts and Crafts Movement was at the

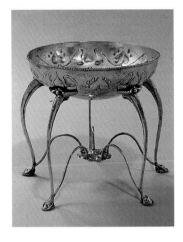

Charles Robert Ashbee, Silver Bowl, Guild of Handicraft, 1893. Victoria and Albert Museum, London. Here, decoration and industrial design are harmoniously combined.

vanguard of stressing the importance of aesthetic awareness in the machine age. Morris's cultural aims were also espoused by the other members of the group. The English architect and designer Charles Robert Ashbee (1863–1942), who founded the Guild and School of Handicrafts in London in 1888, maintained

that constructive and decorative arts were the true backbone of every artistic culture. Meanwhile, the designer and illustrator Walter Crane (1845–1915), author of the didactic collection *Lines and Outlines* (1875), asserted that crafts were the true origins and bases of all the arts. Arthur Mackmurdo (1851–1942), a Scottish architect and designer based in England, initiated the Century Guild and, in 1884, founded the movement's journal *Hobby*

WILLIAM MORRIS AND THE DECORATIVE ARTS

In his numerous writings on the relationship between art and the new society, William Morris stated his case as a supporter of the expansion of the applied arts by exploiting some of the new techniques originally introduced for industrial production. Morris maintained that it was important to dispense with the arbitrary distinctions between "fine arts" and "useful arts,"

William Morris, wallpaper with flowing pattern in shades of yellow, blue, and green, 1882–83.

which had been accepted in the Romantic period, and to recapture the link between visual expression and the use of suitable materials and skills that had been present in the Gothic and Renaissance eras. In 1861 Morris founded Morris, Marshall, Faulkner & Co., which specialized in decorative work. Among the partners in the company were the Pre-Raphaelites Edward Burne-Jones, Ford Madox Brown, Dante Gabriel Rossetti, and the

William Morris, green dining room interior, commissioned by the Victoria and Albert Museum, London.

architect Philip Webb. Morris is best known for the chintzes and wallpapers that he designed between 1872 and 1896. They were instantly recognizable for their inter-twined floral motifs, vine shoots, and leaves arranged in diagonal and scrolled patterns. According to the scholar Peter Floud, composition of the elements in Morris's designs can be classified into four distinct phases: free arrangement of various types of flowers (1872–76); symmetrical repetition along vertical axes (1876–83); motifs arranged along continuous diagonals (1883–90);

and the alternation of scrolled naturalistic detail on dark backgrounds (1890–96). The exhibitions, organized from 1888 onward by the Arts and Crafts Exhibition Society, promoted a design philosophy that reinterpreted the world of useful everyday objects (furniture, materials, rugs, and other household furnishings). In 1890, Morris founded the Kelmscott Press at Hammersmith, extending his ideas to typography by adapting historical models for his typefaces (Golden, Troy, and Chaucer) and for his decorative initials and borders.

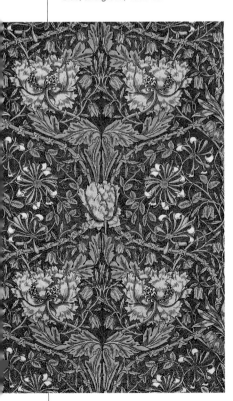

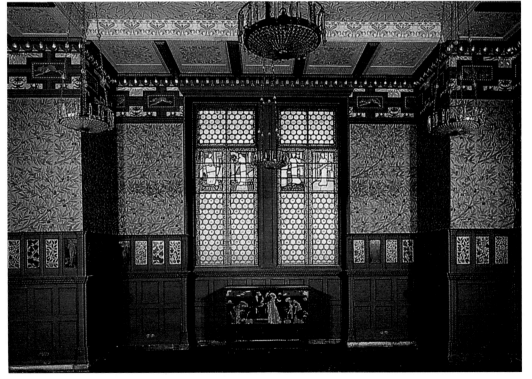

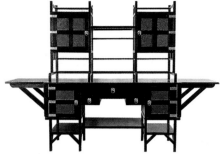

Edward W. Godwin, dresser, 1875. Victoria and Albert Museum, London.

Gottlieb August Pohle, drawing for an adjustable writing desk, 1806. Österreichisches Museum für angewandte Kunst, Vienna.

which the international exhibitions did much to promote. It was at this juncture that the earliest signs of functional aestheticism could be detected in industrial production. This was to prove highly influential during the 20th century, especially in Austria and Germany through the ideas expounded by the *Werkbund* and Bauhaus movements. The processing techniques of traditional and new materials were updated in order to achieve a simplification of objects intended for everyday use.

ART AND PRINTING TECHNIQUES

During the 19th century, changes in printing technology had a great influence on publications linked with the arts, including engraving, etching, lithography and chromolithography, reproductions of works of art, and illustrated guides to ornamentation and costume. A variety of materials reflected these advances: books, magazines, periodicals, catalogs, and advertising posters, all of them primarily intended for mass consumption.

The process of lithography had been invented by Aloys Senefelder in 1798, when he succeeded in transferring onto paper an image that he had drawn in greasy ink on a special kind of limestone. Francisco Goya (1746–1828) was attracted by the immediacy of the effect produced by lithography and was among the first artists to make use of it. In 1819, in Madrid, he created his first lithograph of an old woman spinning, entitled *La vieja hilandera,*

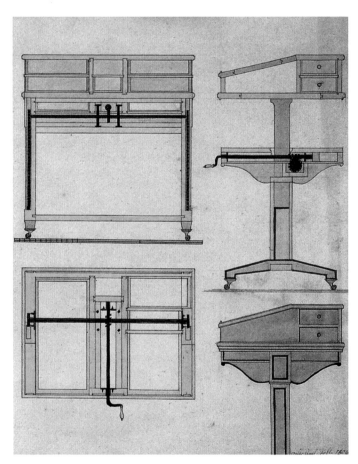

Horse. In his conception of design, particularly graphic printing, Mackmurdo anticipated the style of the Art Nouveau movement.

The expansion of new and faster forms of transportation (notably, the advent of the railroads and faster, powered sea travel) led to a boom in international trade, which industrialized production was able to satisfy, and

The evolution of the forms of such objects was linked to the perfection of mechanical processes, which also took into account the cost of the finished article.

In 1892, the designer Lewis Day (1845–1910) wrote that whether people liked it or not, machinery and steam and electrical power might well have some part to play in the decorative arts of the future.

CHRISTINE'S BOOK

The Danish writer Hans Christian Andersen (1805–75) rose from penury to achieve international fame for his fairy tales, among them the classics *The Ugly Duckling* and *The Little Match Girl*. More privately, he compiled a unique picture book with his friend Adolph Drewsen as a birthday gift for the latter's niece, Christine. The book consisted of a complex collection of over 1,000 illustrations – including clippings from newspapers, reviews, and posters, as well as pages of "popular prints" – stuck into an album. Creative projects of this sort became very popular in the mid-19th century: the pictures, often colored in by hand by the authors, form collages depicting scenes and short stories, accompanied by hand-written phrases and fragments that tell amazing tales. Luxuriant tropical plants, butterflies, parrots, beetles, domestic animals, faraway places, and domestic scenes fill the pages of a second book by Andersen, *Grandfather's Picture Book* (1868). In it, numerous wonderful stories are recounted, some very long. Anderson often chose to include his own drawings: in a new album produced for Christmas, he failed to find enough cut-out pictures to fit his story, so he drew the illustrations himself. He also added the reminder that if the book were to be damaged it did not matter, because it was only intended to be looked at and enjoyed.

Lithograph from Plan géometrique de la ville de Paris, *1876, colored and used in* Christine's Book.

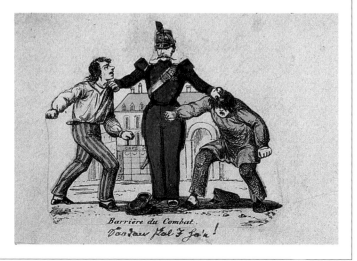

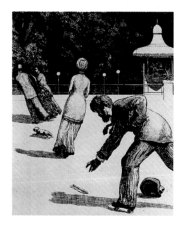

Max Klinger, Action, *from the series*
A Glove, *aquatint, 1881.*

followed, during his years in Bordeaux (1824–28), by some large lithographs of bullfighting scenes – *Los toros de Burdeos*. Many 19th-century artists followed in Goya's footsteps and experimented with the expressive possibilities of the new medium of lithography. Among them were Théodore Géricault with his *Chevaux dans leurs écuries* (1819) and his 13 English lithographs (1821); Eugène Delacroix with his *Hamlet* collection (1834–43); Edouard Manet with his famous *Les Courses* (1864) and *Rendez-*

vous de chats (1868); and Auguste Renoir with *Mlle. Dieterle* (1892). From 1885 onwards, Toulouse-Lautrec produced over 300 lithographs; Pierre Bonnard created lithographs for book illustrations, as well as his famous *Femme au Parapluie* (1896); and Edouard Vuillard produced a collection of lithographs entitled *Paysages et intérieurs* (1899). Other artists to work in this medium included Paul Cézanne, Camille Pissarro, Edgar Degas, and Paul Gauguin.
The new lithographic technique did not prevent

continued interest and improvement in older graphic techniques, such as etching, which had been practiced by artists since the early 16th century. In 1765, designer and book illustrator Jean Baptiste Le Prince invented the aquatint – repeated etchings over a porous ground that produce a wide range of tonal effects.
Artists exploited and promoted significant advances in these graphic techniques, and this led to the development of a branch of publishing specializing in illustrated books of

POSTERS

Printed notices to inform the public of political events, legal matters, judicial sentences, plays, concerts, and entertainments had been a feature of city life for centuries. During the 19th century, a great many technological innovations combined to create a success story: the advertising poster. The introduction of new printing procedures, such as lithography (1798), and the improved forms of presses used in the 1830s were particularly important.
Following the earliest chromolithographic experiments in black and white, the French artist Jules Chéret (1836–1932) perfected the use and effectiveness of the process, printing large numbers of polychrome posters from 1866 onward. Chéret's pictures were often

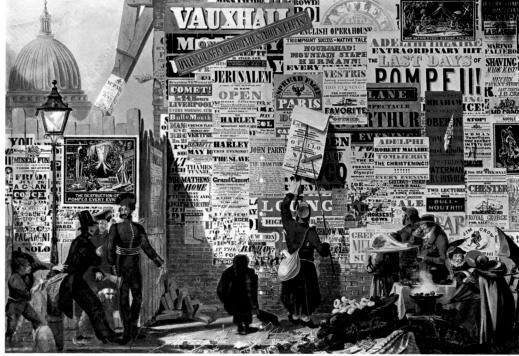

John Parry, A Bill-poster's Fantasy, *1855. Victoria and Albert Museum, London.*

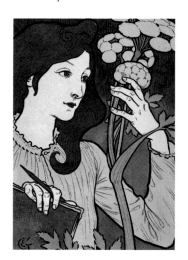

Eugène Grasset, Salon des Cent, *poster, 1894. Bibliothèque des Arts Décoratifs, Paris.*

constructed around a central nucleus, with the internal dynamism of the composition emphasized by effective combinations of colors.
Large publicity posters had a very strong pictorial attraction and minimal but bold lettering. Among the artists who experimented with this new method

of graphic reproduction was Eugène Grasset (1841–1917), whose designs had fluid outlines that resembled his stained glass. Meanwhile, Henri de Toulouse-Lautrec (1864–1901) concentrated his efforts, especially from 1891 onward, on finding a new language for the poster. In his most famous posters (the *Moulin Rouge, Divan Japonais,* and *Aristide Bruant* of 1893), the attention of the observer is captured by the boldness of the picture, the clear outlines of the figures, the warmth and brightness of the flat-toned colors, and the

contrast between black and paler colors or white.
Alphonse Mucha (1860–1939) another celebrated and prolific poster artist, created his first poster design in 1892.
In contrast with Toulouse-Lautrec, he was able to achieve an unusual harmony between his linear drawings and decorative patterns. His female figures, often taken from posed photographs, are surrounded by frames and borders of intertwined Hispano-Moorish motifs and by materials reminiscent of Japanese woodcuts.

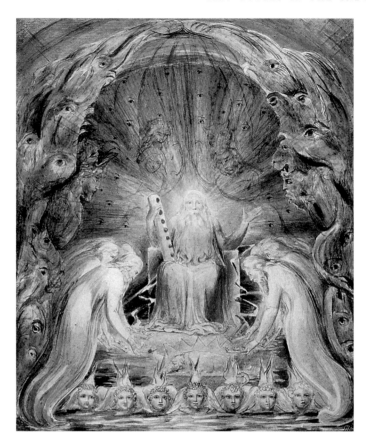

William Blake, The Twenty-four Elders
Place Their Crown Before the Throne of
God, 1805. Tate Gallery, London.
The prints of Blake's illustrations were
to influence and inspire the work
of many "visionary" 19th-century painters.

Pompeo Batoni, Sacro Cuore di Gesù,
1763–67. Chiesa del Gesù, Rome.
This painting by the artist from Lucca
became very popular throughout the
Catholic world through oleographs.
Numerous copies would be produced
until the mid-20th century, as were
various other religious pictures.

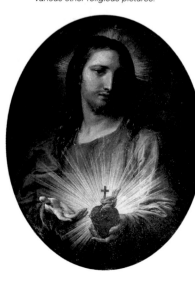

techniques and the simplified insertion of illustrations into books meant that there was a huge increase in the number of illustrated books, children's titles, and themed collections of prints devoted to particular subjects. New developments revived the ancient craft of silkscreen printing, in which silk or another suitable fabric was "painted" with the design to be stenciled and stretched on a rigid frame; successive stencils each marked out areas of different colors. In its updated form, this technique was widely used in industry and by artists.

exceptional quality. They often took the form of special editions of highly prized literary works, republished with the creative contributions of artists whose aim was to translate the writer's expressiveness into rich and immediate images. Examples include William Blake's illustrations for Dante's *Divine Comedy* (1824–27); Aubrey Beardsley's illustrations for Oscar Wilde's *Salome* (1894); Max Klinger's illustrations for Brahms's works, in which the musical score is introduced into the field of iconographic representation; and the series of illustrations by Odilon Redon, produced in three versions, for Gustave Flaubert's *La Tentation de Saint Antoine* (1874). Gustave Doré (1832–83), the most outstanding of the great 19th-century illustrators, brought to life the imaginary world evoked by the great European literary masterpieces, such as Cervantes's *Don Quixote* (1862) and Perrault's fairy tales (1862). The many advances in printing

CHROMO-LITHOGRAPHY

The introduction of colors in the lithographic process, known as chromolithography, came about in 1837. This meant that color printing could now be applied to large surfaces. Once this new process had been perfected, a new type of advertising picture, the poster, was launched with resounding

Ramón Casas, Anís del Mono, chromo-
lithograph, 1898. Department of
Drawings and Engravings, Barcelona.
An advertisement for a popular
Spanish liqueur.

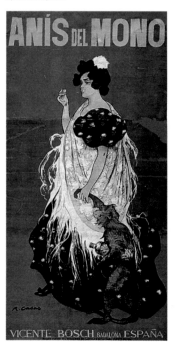

success. The newly discovered means of image reproduction – lithography, chromolithography and, subsequently, photography – can most certainly be considered the forerunners of modern advertising methods. The poster, one of the 19th century's most widely and frequently used publicity tools, was fully able to satisfy the need for mass communication. It invited the observer's perceptual and emotional involvement, which was often intensified by the repeated use of the same message all over towns or cities.

In the 17th and 18th centuries, developments in printing and engraving technology had meant that the Western world's figurative culture could be disseminated throughout Europe. In the 19th century, color reproductions of paintings, townscapes and cityscapes, and photographs of particularly attractive subjects proved very popular. Another popular Victorian product was the oleograph, produced by coating a lithographed print with a pigmented oily varnish. When dry, it was processed with an embossing roller in order to imitate the visual effect of an oil painting's canvas.

THE GRAPHIC ARTS

Printing and publishing underwent tremendous changes during the 19th century. Advances in typographical technology and distribution systems, as well as a general reduction in costs, meant that nearly all printed matter was now within the reach of the general public. Nicolas-Louis Robert made a significant contribution to this progress when he introduced the first machine for the "mechanical" production of paper in 1798. Another invention developed commercially at the beginning of the 19th century was stereotyping. A mold was made by pouring plaster of Paris over a page of

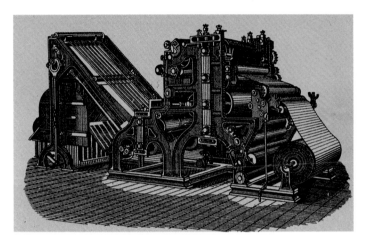

Rotary printing, cutting, and stacking machine, engraving, 1866, United States. The introduction of automation was instrumental in reducing costs.

type and allowing it to set; molten metal could then be poured over the face of the mold in a casting box. Further development of this technique led to *papier mâché* being substituted for plaster to form the matrix, or "mat." The most revolutionary innovation, however, came in the form of Friedrich Koenig's

steam-powered printing machine of 1811 and its successors. On the old hand-operated press, the maximum production was 300 copies an hour, but with the new equipment this could easily be increased to 1,000. Printing became even faster in 1828 with the introduction of the sophisticated four-cylinder press, developed by Augustus Applegath and Edward Cowper, which could print 4,000 copies an hour. Printing presses were not alone in benefiting from new technology. Even bookbinding was increasingly mechanized, and in the 1830s the first books with separate cloth-covered cases blocked in gold appeared. The sewn book could now be trimmed using another newly introduced device, the guillotine. The ensuing increase in printed matter prompted Friedrich Gottlob Keller to invent a machine for grinding wood pulp for making paper. This was to the great economic advantage of publishers of newspapers, catalogs, and other publications with large print runs.

Despite the continual modernization of mechanical processes and raw materials for printing – vital for the growth of publishing and the spread of information in Europe and the US – one problem remained unsolved in the mid-19th century. This was the most crucial phase of the printing procedure: composing text. The first truly reliable composing machines were built in 1866 (Robert Hattersley's machine) and in 1869 (Charles Kastenbein's system). Although these machines brought type together, the time-consuming work of adjusting the line length still had to be done by hand. Only when Ottmar Mergenthaler's Linotype machines came into use (they were first installed at the *New York Tribune* in 1886), followed by Tolbert Lanston's Monotype machines, did the composition of text and line justification finally become automatic processes.

PANORAMAS

In 1787, the Irish artist Robert Barker took out a patent under the name of *Nature à coup d'oeil* for a method of pictorial representation that simulated the appearance of town views and landscapes in an uninterrupted circular form. The patent's description stated that the spectator could turn around in a circle and the reproduction – in the form of a drawing or painting – would create the appearance of a panorama similar to reality. Barker created a number of landscapes and cityscapes using this technique, as if viewed from real places, such as the Calton Hill Observatory on the high ground overlooking Edinburgh or the

roof of Albion Mills in London. Robert Barker's creations were followed by numerous panoramas of places and views transferred onto cloth or paper, among them the *Panorama of Rome* by Adam Breysig (1800), *Vienna* by L. Jansche and Karl Postl (1806), and Karl Friedrich Schinkel's *Palermo* of 1808. The spectator was able to scan the panorama and recognize the highest buildings "at a glance," viewing the skyline and the districts of the city by rotating the angle of vision through 360 degrees. Rural scenes and city panoramas were sometimes accompanied by a commentary describing country life or historical events. There were also scientific panoramas, one being the semicircular drawing

of the Alps by Hans Conrad Escher von der Linth (1803). To make it easier for artists to produce wide canvases that ensured an absolutely faithful reproduction of the scene, "optical cameras" were introduced toward the middle of the century. These were followed by the first cameras for producing daguerreotypes and, a few years later, by photographic prints.

In order to show panoramas as a public spectacle, specially built structures were erected, such as the Rotonde des Panoramas on the Champs-Elysées (1841), the Rotunda in Vienna's Prater (1882), or those in Munich (1880) and Berlin (Rotunda of Sedan, 1883; Kolonial Panorama, 1884).

Ramsay R. Reinagle, Panorama of Berlin, *1814, and* Panorama of Florence, *1812, engravings from an illustrated pamphlet. British Library, London.*

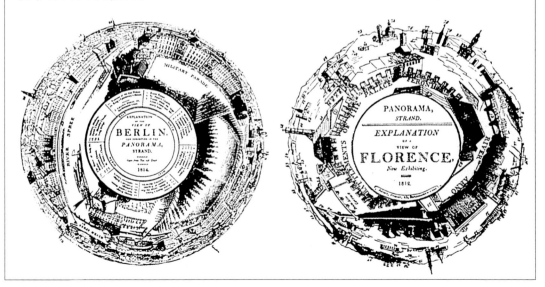

ILLUSTRATED MAGAZINES

The creation of a modern publishing industry moved a step nearer with the introduction of printed illustrations.

The leading daily newspapers had provided pictures for their readers since 1840, when the daguerreotype process came into use. In the early days, periodicals like the *Illustrated London News* or *Illustration*

CATALOGS

Although in a simplified form and often without any illustrations, manufacturers' catalogs were already in use by the 19th century for listing products and mass-produced goods. However, during the course of the century they were to become hugely popular as vehicles for advertising and for providing information. The availability of new graphic technology and picture reproduction was exploited, with technical specifications and pictures of the various products now displayed in black and white or color. Manufacturers soon began to provide these

useful new publication at the great exhibitions, alongside exhibits of their products and activities. Visitors could use them to find out details about any item that took their interest, including specifications and prices.

Both the development of industrial production and the potential for selling to a mass market were greatly helped by the existence of manufacturers' catalogs. They proved to be an indispensable method for reaching customers far and wide and providing an increasingly demanding clientele with a wider choice.

Lithograph from the Catalog of the Paris Exposition of 1862.

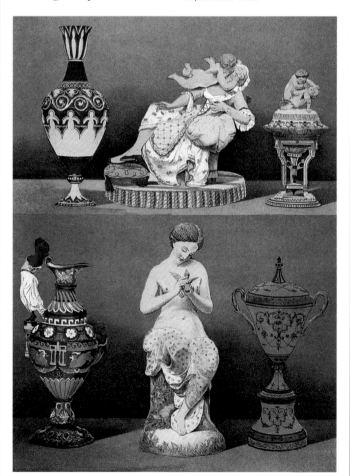

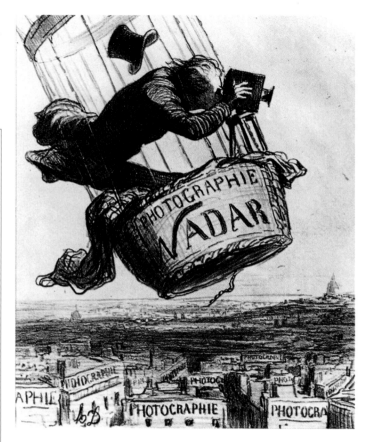

made use of the services of teams of sketchers, who were sent with journalists to create illustrations for news stories. Among the most successful caricatures and cartoons were those by Honoré Daumier, Gustave Doré, and Gavarni for *La Caricature* (1830–34) and *Le Charivari* (1832–1926), satirical reviews that were imitated all over Europe. Daumier's prolific output of drawings, satirizing contemporary fashions and the political and social scene, were outstandingly effective.

The task of faithfully reproducing such drawings and using engraving techniques to prepare the wooden blocks for printing was entrusted to a team of engravers on the permanent staff of the newspapers' headquarters. Toward the end of the century, with the advent of collodion (a colorless mixture of pyroxylin in ether and alcohol), glass plates were used in cameras, so the engraving could be carried out directly from the original with a great saving in time. In 1850, Hippolyte

Honoré Daumier, Nadar élevant la photographie à la hauteur de l'art, *lithograph from* Souvenirs d'Artistes, *appearing in* Le Boulevard, *May 25, 1863.*

Fizeau first experimented with etching a plate with a daguerreotype for printing. Better results, however, were obtained with the so-called "flat-bed" processes, which were used in the following years by Rose-Joseph Lemercier and Alphonse Poitevin to reproduce photographs with typographical inks. The Woodburytype was patented by Walter Bentley Woodbury in 1864 for reproduction by the photoglyptic method, and although the resulting images were exceptionally clear and faithful to the originals, inking was a manual process that proved far too laborious and time-consuming for newspapers and periodicals. Quality printing on such surfaces as newsprint could be achieved only by using relief plates; Firmin Gillot, Charles Nègre, and Edouard Baldus all came to this conclusion between 1853 and 1856.

Among the photomechanical printing processes, screen printing of images proved particularly important. This was first introduced in 1870 by William Leggo and was followed in 1878 by the introduction of similigravure, a halftone printing technique developed by Charles Guillaume Petit. The first example of reproduction of photographs in newspapers dates

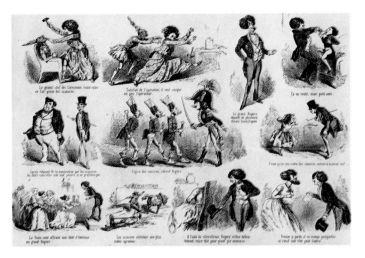

from when Georg Meisenbach put to use the process he had developed and patented under the name of autotype. Further advances in the halftone printing of photographs had to wait until improved forms of

Gustave Doré, Hosannah! Voici les Osanores!, *lithograph, 1849. The great French draftsman and engraver was more celebrated for his classic book illustrations (such as those for the works of Rabelais, Perrault, Balzac, Cervantes, Dante, and Arioso) than for his humorous prints of social criticism.*

screen were introduced. After 1880 a large number of illustrated periodicals were published, especially in the UK, Germany, France, and the US. The various titles were aimed at a vast readership, and publications that aimed mainly to inform and educate were soon joined by specialized periodicals exploiting the communicative power of photographic images.
The introduction of the postage stamp gave rise to a great deal of research into graphic techniques, including gravure and letterpress. The first stamps were issued in England in 1840, starting with the penny black and two-pence blue series, designed by H. Corbould and printed by C. & F. Heath. Both showed Queen Victoria's head.

Penny Black and Two-pence Blue, *1840. These postage stamps were introduced in England following Rowland Hill's reform of the postal service.*

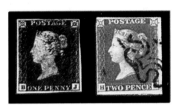

OWEN JONES AND THE GRAMMAR OF ORNAMENT

Detailed studies of ornament and the decorative arts were carried out by the Welsh architect Owen Jones (1809–74), author of many works on the collection and classification of ornamental motifs. His publications were inventories,

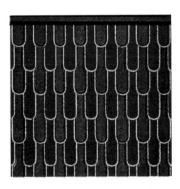

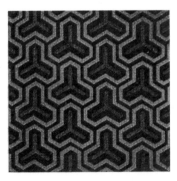

illustrated by plates, which provided descriptions of all the subjects covered. They led to the spread of knowledge and use of stylistic elements belonging to past civilizations and other cultures. His *Plans, Details, and Sections of the Alhambra* (1842–45), *Designs for Mosaic and Tessellated Pavements* (1842), *Illuminated Book*

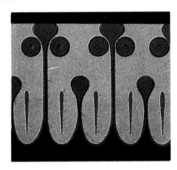

Owen Jones, Egyptian and Chinese motifs, *from plates LI and LIX of* The Grammar of Ornament, *1856.*

of the Middle Ages (1844), and analyses of Italian ornamentation in *The Polychromatic Ornament of Italy* (1846) reveal a meticulously documented syntax of ornament.
Two of Jones's publications were particularly famous: the *Grammar of Ornament* (1856), an encyclopedic work in which the author expounded his own theories on harmony in composition and underlined the importance of studying patterns from antiquity and nature, and *Examples of Chinese Ornament* (1867), which featured 100 color plates showing the decorated surfaces of vases, bowls, and plates. According to Jones, certain general geometric laws can be

traced in the natural world, such as in the structure of a tree or a flower or in the arrangement of leaves transformed into arabesques; these theories were to prove particularly attractive to ensuing generations of artists and architects.
Owen Jones's books also show his particular interest in the psychology of perception: his principles of composition and his studies of line and the arrangement of geometric forms anticipate the early 20th-century Gestalt psychology experiments. An opportunity to try out some of his perceptual theories arose when he was asked to take charge of the interior decoration of Crystal Palace in 1850. Jones implemented Michel Eugène Chevreul's chromatic theories, expounded in his book *De la loi du contraste simultané des couleurs* (1839), by using three primary colors and white to achieve the required effect of infinite space. When viewed from a distance, the yellow of the columns, the blue of the framework and girders, and the red of the background to the exhibit stands tended to blend together, creating a neutral tonality and an indeterminate vibrancy.

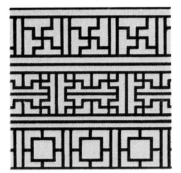

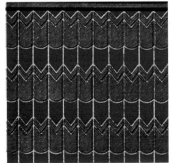

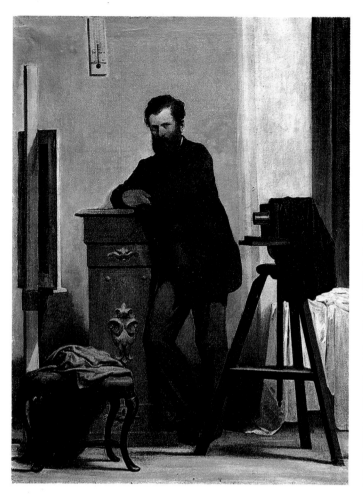

THE ALINARI BROTHERS

The Alinari brothers' company, founded in 1852 in Florence by Leopoldo, Romualdo, and Giuseppe Alinari, was one of the first to devote itself to photography and publishing. The brothers specialized in photographing works of art and architecture, as well as portraiture and landscape photography. The company built up an amazing collection from their numerous photographic assignments, charting the events that took place in the second half of the 19th century. Their illustrated catalogs, published from 1865 onward, contained a wide selection of pictures from an archive consisting of thousands of plates and photographs.

The photographic studio of the Alinari brothers. Archivio Alinari, Florence.

PIONEERS OF PHOTOGRAPHY

The first experiments with the chemical effect produced by light on certain substances were undertaken by Johann Heinrich Schulze and Carl Wilhelm Scheele in the 18th century. Not long after, in 1802, Thomas Wedgwood, son of porcelain manufacturer Josiah, began to experiment with producing images by a photographic process. He managed to obtain silhouette images of leaves and other objects on paper and leather that had been impregnated with silver nitrate and silver chloride. However, it was primarily through the pioneering work of three men – Joseph Nicéphore Niepce (1765– 1833) and Louis Jacques Mandé Daguerre (1789–1851) in France and William Henry Fox Talbot (1800–1877) in England – that photography was born.

Alessandro Guardassoni, Self-portrait with Camera, c.1860. Instituto Gualandi, Bologna.

The world's earliest surviving photograph – now in the Gernsheim Collection, Texas – was produced by the French inventor Niepce. In 1826, he succeeded in making a negative photographic image of the view from his workroom on a sheet of pewter covered with bitumen of Judea.

At the same time, the French artist and inventor Daguerre was carrying out experiments in the reproduction of images by a photochemical process. In 1829, he formed a partnership with Niepce, then he continued their research after Niepce's death in 1833. In 1839 he sold the rights for the daguerreotype and the heliograph (the name given to Niepce's process) to the French government; his work was first presented at a meeting of the French Academy of Sciences in Paris in the same year. Described in detail in a booklet published in 1839, the process involved a silver-plated sheet of copper made sensitive

William Henry Fox Talbot and some colleagues outside his photographic printing establishment, Reading, England, c.1845. Talbot set up this photographic printing works to mass-produce photographs for the publication of The Pencil of Nature.

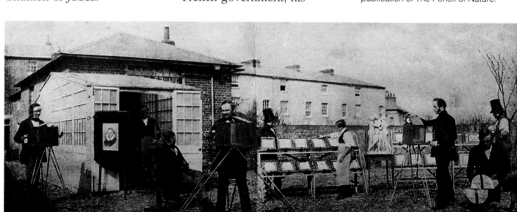

NADAR

Gaspard-Félix Tournachon (1820–1910), better known as Nadar – the pseudonym affectionately given to him by his friends after his nickname *tourne adard* (bitter sting) – is recognized as a photographic pioneer. His eccentric personality was first revealed in the caricatures that he drew for reviews and periodicals from the 1850s onward; each conveyed his highly individual standpoint – ironic, keenly observant, and hypercritical. Nadar was particularly drawn to social events and the literary and artistic climate of 19th-century Paris. He first became involved in photography when planning a series of lithographic caricature portraits of 270 famous people of the time. In order to complete this project, evocatively called the *Panthéon,* he recruited various collaborators, completed many drawings, and took numerous photographs. The operation was repeated for his second edition of the *Panthéon,* in which a few

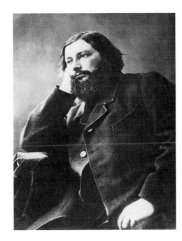

Nadar, photographic portrait of Gustave Courbet, 1861. Archives photographiques, Paris.

changes were made. Nadar's main interest, however, seems to have been in investigating the possibilities of photography as a medium, and he persuaded Gustave Le Gray, the doyen of photography of his day, to give lessons to him and his brother, who was a painter.

In 1854, Nadar opened his own studio at 113 Rue Saint Lazare in

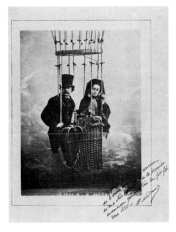

Nadar and his wife Ernestine in a balloon, photographed by their son Paul, c.1865. Nadar took many pictures from the air.

Paris, where he mastered the wet collodion process and specialized in portraits. Until the advent of electric light, he exploited the limited daylight in his studio and achieved original results; his subjects were lit from one side, leaving parts of their faces and body in shadow. This technique sculpted the expressions of the faces in tones

that ranged from white to black, while the absence of a painted backdrop accentuated their faces. Nadar's many portraits of the famous personalities who came to his studio, including Balzac, Delacroix, and Rossini, are documented by the notes and letters that passed between the photographer and his subjects. In 1860, when he had already gained a high reputation in his field, Nadar moved to the Rue des Capucines, to a building that had been used as a photographic studio by Le Gray and the Bisson Brothers. On the front of the building was a huge illuminated facsimile of Nadar's signature. Helped occasionally by his son Paul, he undertook novel projects, such as aerial photography from balloons flying over Paris. He even went so far as to build a prototype steam-powered helicopter (1863). During the same period, he experimented with photographs taken by artificial light; this led to his shooting of the catacombs and the network of sewers under Paris using electric light.

---

to light by exposure to iodine vapor, which produced a light-sensitive layer of silver iodide on the surface of the plate. After being placed in the camera for exposure, the plate was then exposed to mercury vapor to produce an image. At first, the image was fixed in a salt solution, but the method was later improved by the use of hyposulphate (hypo), the discovery of astronomer Sir John Herschel (1792–1871). Unaware of the experiments being carried out by the French inventors, the British scientist Talbot was also working on a technique to record accurate images. On his honeymoon in 1833, he made use of a camera lucida – a sketching aid that enabled the user to produce an accurate drawing of a scene on paper. His frustration at the poor results led to his experimentation with photography, and he discovered a process of exposing sensitized paper in the camera and then

developing it to form a negative image. This could then be contact-printed onto another sheet of sensitized paper to produce a positive print. The process, called "calotype," differed from the daguerreotype in that the resultant negative image could be used to make multiple positive prints, whereas each daguerreotype was a unique image.

Talbot published details of his photographic process early in 1839, six months before the French government released details of the daguerreotype.

THE WORLD THROUGH THE CAMERA

Portraiture was one of the earliest beneficiaries of Daguerre's photographic technique. At first, the exposure times required were too long,

but various improvements were soon introduced that were to reduce exposure times drastically, although the subjects still needed to strike lengthy poses. The contrast and strength of the image greatly improved, and people were intrigued and fascinated by the immediacy and vitality of these daguerreotypes. During the 1840s, photographers like Claudet, Vaillant, and Derussy took thousands of portrait photographs. These included the 400 taken by Scottish landscape painter David Octavius Hill for a project in 1843; he invited fellow Scotsman Robert Adamson to help him complete the task. Photography also proved to be an ideal method of recording historical sites and views of faraway countries, despite the unwieldly equipment, which was difficult to set up outside a studio. Joseph-Philibert Girault de Prangey and Jules

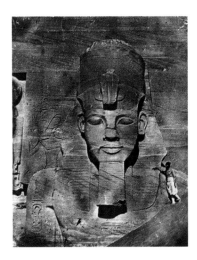

Maxime du Camp, the colossus of Ramesses II at the Temple of Abu Simbel, 1849–51, calotype. Gernsheim Collection, Austin, Texas. From the 1840s, photography was increasingly used for the documentation of archaeological sites.

Itier took about 1,000 photographs during the 1840s while traveling in China and Egypt, and in 1845, Frederick Langenheim captured pictures of Niagara Falls on five plates.

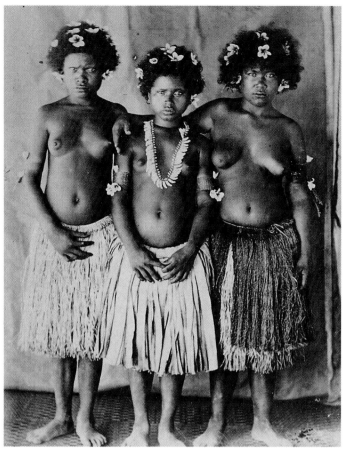

Lamberto Loria, Three Young Women of Matu, *1891–98. Museo Preistorico ed Etnografico Luigi Pigorini, Rome. In the field of scientific photography, photographing different races was considered important for anthropological study.*

later in the 19th century, for example, that photomechanical methods of reproducing photographs made the mass distribution of copies feasible. In 1850, Louis Blanquart-Evrard invented the albumen process for printing photographs on paper; this proved very popular, and he opened a photographic printing works in 1851. In the same year, Frederick Scott Archer published his discovery of a process in which collo-

of the *Société Héliographique.* Portrait and reportage photographs were joined by the novelty *cartes de visite* – photographs pasted onto small rectangles of cardboard. Several poses were recorded on each negative, using special cameras to capture the multiple exposures. Soon,

Carlton E. Watkins, view of Yosemite Valley, California, 1861. Yosemite National Park Museum, California. Photography was an important tool for the study of geographical features.

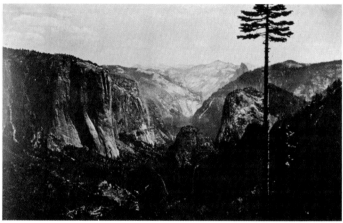

In the same decade, Talbot used his calotype process to take pictures for the illustration of printed matter, publishing in 1844 the first of six parts that were to form *The*

Pencil of Nature – 24 plates with text and photographs by Talbot himself.
Early photographic processes could now provide the various branches of science – from the natural sciences to the observation of the universe – with an effective investigative tool, even though the technical potential of the photographic medium had not yet been fully explored. It was not until

dion acted as a binding agent to keep light-sensitive chemicals on the surface of a glass plate and produce glass negatives. Subsequently, improved collodion and, later, gelatin emulsions were developed and produced on an industrial scale. In 1854, the *Société Française de Photographie* was founded to promote the work of artists and photographers, following the demise

these *cartes de visite* were produced in the millions by virtually every photographic studio in the world. Photography was soon being used for an increasingly diverse range of enterprises. It reached the world of industry via the great international exhibitions, and so much interest was shown in the documentation of exhibits in lavishly illustrated catalogs that people began to appreciate its potential importance in the sphere of advertising. Meanwhile, in the US, photography was used to promote national unity, with Charles Weed, Carleton E. Watkins, and Eadweard Muybridge all undertaking separate expeditions to record the scenery of the Yosemite Valley in California. Exploration of Central America was recorded in 47

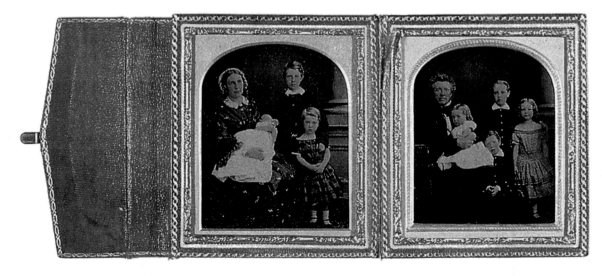

Two photographs of family groups in a portfolio, 1850. Family portraits were now substitutes for miniatures. Photographs could be incorporated easily into jewelry such as necklaces, bracelets, or brooches.

SCIENTIFIC PHOTOGRAPHY

The different forms of scientific photography were to exert a considerable influence on 20th-century art. The naturalistic abstraction of Paul Klee, for example, refers explicitly to the world revealed by the microscope, while the dynamic quality of the images captured by chronophotography were to lead to many of the Futurist and Cubist experiments at the start of the 20th century.

In 1853, Auguste Bertsch and Towler Kingsley took photomicrographs of insects and crystals with a solar microscope. Photomicrography involves taking photographs of very small objects by attaching a camera to the eyepiece of the microscope. (The reverse method – making small photographs of objects by optical reduction – is known as microphotography; Dagron, 1870.)

In the field of astronomy, telescopes and other traditional optical equipment used for

Auguste Bertsch, photomicrograph of a louse, 1853. Société Française de Photographie, Paris.

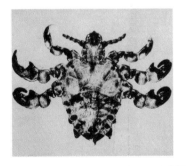

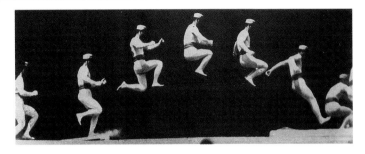

observations were equipped with cameras that made it possible to carry out detailed studies of the Moon's surface (Warren de La Rue, 1852, and Lewis Rutherford, 1865) and the recording of events of particular scientific interest, such as solar eclipses (Porro and Quinet, March 14, 1858).

In 1856, photographs were first taken during gas and hot-air balloon flights for geophysical surveys of territory and mapping, as well as photo-reconnaissance for military purposes. Two years later, Nadar and the Tissandier brothers took the first aerial photographs of Paris. In 1861, Aimé Laussedat experimented with a photogram-metric technique of recording and measuring, which was used by E. Deville to survey the entire surface of the Rocky Mountains. In astronomical photography, definition and precision were achieved by using special plates and improved chemical processing, as demonstrated in a photograph of a comet taken by Pierre-Jules-César Janssen in 1881, and in the *Atlas Photographique de la Lune* (1896–1909) by M. Loewy and P. Puiseux. Photography also proved

Etienne-Jules Marey, Long and High Jump, 1886. Bibliothèque Nationale, Paris.

Lewis Rutherford, The Moon, 1865. Musée des Techniques, CNAM, Paris.

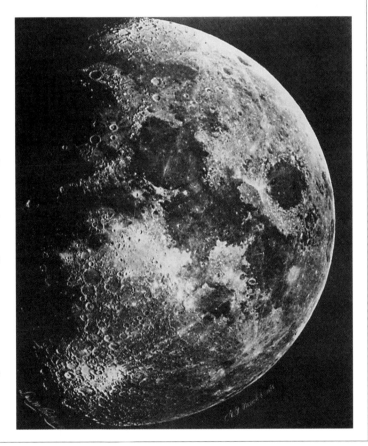

invaluable in medicine. Etienne-Jules Marey (1830–1903) first carried out studies on the physiology of movement, based on the analysis of a sequence of photographs. These were taken using a "photographic gun," which could achieve exposure speeds of one 720th of a second. He also invented chronophotography, used to visualize the structure of movement on a single image. It was Marey's work that inspired Marcel Duchamp to produce his *Nude Descending a Staircase* studies in 1911–12.

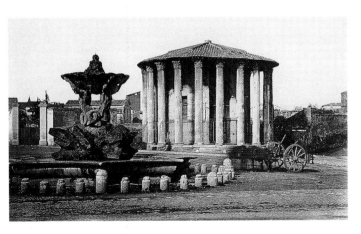

views of important Mexican historical monuments by Désiré Chanay, *Cités et Ruines Améri-caines*, and in 1856 Moulin's photographs provided an original photographic record of little-known episodes in the colonization of Africa. However, photography's greatest potential was not fully realized until cameras were

Robert Macpherson, Rome, a Fountain, and the Temple of Vesta, albumen print, c.1858. Gernsheim Collection, Austin, Texas.

mass-produced in a form that could be used by anyone. In 1888, George Eastman intro-duced the first Kodak camera; he launched the first commer-cially available celluloid roll film the following year. However, the cost of film and equipment remained expen-sive, and it was not until he developed the Brownie box camera in the early 1900s that photography could be enjoyed equally by professional and amateur.

Art Styles in the Industrial 19th Century
FURNISHINGS & FASHIONS

The introduction of new technology made possible the mass-production of furnishings and clothing that had the appearance of traditional, handmade articles but were less expensive and were aimed at a wider market. Taste veered toward extravagant shapes, conspicuous ornamentation, and excess.

The historical, social, and political revolutions that swept through Europe from 1790 to 1840 triggered great changes in both the design and industrial manufacturing processes of furniture, pottery, porcelain, textiles, glass, and other objects. Tastes changed as Napoleonic influence led to the spread of the Empire style, with its roots in the revival of interest in Greek, Roman, and, later, Egyptian art. The most influential exponents of the Empire style were the French architect-designer team of Pierre-François-Léonard Fontaine (1762–1853) and Charles Percier (1764–1838), and the furniture makers Jacob-Desmalter & Cie, founded in 1803.

Small wooden table. Palazzo dei Normanni, Palermo, Italy. One of a pair of tables, this is carved and gilded, with the top in fossil sequoia, bordered in amethyst.

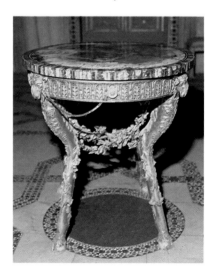

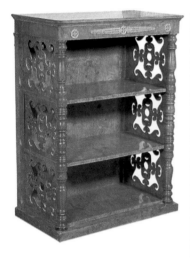

Jacob-Desmalter, ash bookcase, 1839. The French firm of Jacob-Desmalter & Cie consisted of Georges Jacob (1739–1814) and his son François-Honoré (1770–1841).

FURNITURE

In France, fashionable 19th-century ornament for interior decoration and furniture included symmetrically arranged gilt-bronze classical motifs: capitals, palmettes, sphinxes, dolphins, swans, and miniaturized mythical characters and creatures. Also popular were emblems of Napoleonic imperial splendor: eagles, bees, arms (spears, arrows, swords), and, of course, the letter "N," adorned with the victor's laurel wreath. The color and graining of mahogany contrasted admirably with gilt decoration, so furniture makers often used the combination to excessive effect. New items of furniture

MICHAEL THONET'S BENTWOOD FURNITURE

German furniture maker and designer Michael Thonet (1796–1871) pioneered the mass-production of standardized furniture with his process for making bentwood, patented in 1841. This involved placing lengths of beechwood in metal frames and then steaming or boiling them in water and glue until they were soft enough to bend into long, curved rods; they were then left to dry. Since far fewer parts were required than in traditional furniture making, manufacturing was now greatly simplified and far cheaper. Thonet's chair, armchair, and other designs were remarkable for their durability, lightness, and simplicity (the seats and backs of chairs were merely hoops covered with cane). Significantly, given the previously prevailing taste for rich decoration, his pieces were without ornamentation. Models no. 4 (1850) and no. 14 (1859) are the most celebrated Thonet chairs, now

considered hugely important prototypes in the history of the furniture industry. Their lightness and stability made them extremely popular, and over 50 million no. 4's were produced. No. 14 consisted of only six parts, all easily assembled with just ten screws and with caning for the seat.

Michael Thonet, Chair no. 14, 1859.

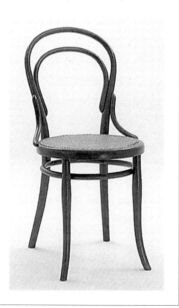

were created: cheval glasses or swing mirrors in varying sizes began to appear, as did ladies' dressing tables and various types of paper-filing and storing devices known as *serre-papiers*.
After the final defeat of Napoleon in 1815, the Bourbon Restoration style ushered in a variety of new

ornamental motifs. Light-colored woods such as ash and cherry were fashionable (they were used in Continental Europe during the British blockade of imports during the war years, 1793–1815), as were curving lines and marquetry or inlays of darker woods or reflective materials. During the

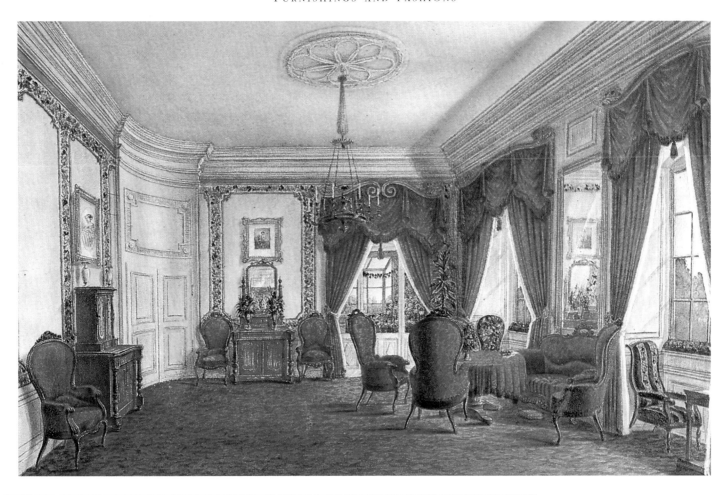

THE BIEDERMEIER STYLE

Characterized by a simple, restrained classicism (the German word *bieder* means plain or conventional), the Biedermeier style spread through Germany, Austria, and northern European countries from 1815. The predilection for furniture with simplified forms and modest dimensions, more suited to bourgeois apartments

than palaces, and the pursuit of comfort and functionalism reflected a new approach to interior design. One of the characteristics of Biedermeier furniture is its light color: ash, maple, cherry, citrus,

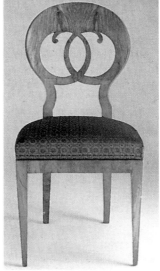

Viennese chair with entwined scroll, c.1820. Private collection, Milan.

Tea room at the Sanssouci Palace, *watercolor, c.1830, Potsdam, Germany.*

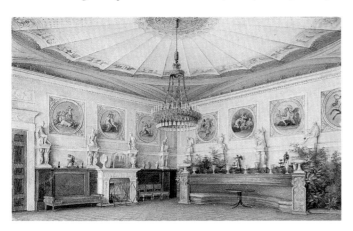

beech, and yew (the last typical in Viennese interiors) were frequently employed. Gilt finishes were applied sparingly or replaced by painted or black and gold inlaid details.

Wilhelm Dünckel, Drawing room at Mannheim Castle, watercolor, 1860. The Neo-Rococo furniture in the room dates from about 1850–60. The overall color scheme is crimson.

postwar years, the bourgeois Biedermeier style developed in Austria and northern Europe. This smaller, more homely furniture in simple, geometric shapes and light woods was typified by *Sekretäre* (bureaus) and *Nähtische* (occasional or sewing tables). Chairs and well-upholstered sofas were designed with greater attention to the user's ease and comfort, including proper back support. It was in this context of "cleaner," more functional lines that the revolutionary bentwood innovations of Michael Thonet met with such success from 1841 onward. An interest in historical styles had already been re-awakened in the previous century, and it increased considerably in the 19th century. Borrowings from the past were combined with current styles in very original ways. The Gothic style, which found such favor in architecture, became the height of fashion in France under Charles X and Louis-Philippe. The "cathedral style," with its attendant spires, pinnacles, and intricate fretwork or piercing, was especially prized. But these Neo-Gothic fancies were not the only point of reference from the past: French furniture designers also reinterpreted Renaissance, Baroque, Louis XV, and Louis XVI styles. During the reign of Louis-Philippe and the Second Empire, which lasted from 1848 until Napoleon III's abdication in 1870, interior decoration underwent a transformation. Walls were covered with tapestries, with double and sometimes triple layers of hangings; chairs and sofas were draped or upholstered with button-backing or quilting; and a distaste for empty spaces drove the wealthy to cram their houses with furniture, furnishings, plants (especially palms and other exotic species), pictures, and *bibelots* (knickknacks). The introduction of coil springs, which replaced

unyielding, tightly packed horsehair, led to many new types of upholstered furniture, including armchairs such as the low, opulent *crapaud* and the Voltaire, the smoking chair, and the pouffe. Among the more intriguing novelties were upholstered seats for the center of a room in which the occupants half-faced each other: the serpentine *confidant* for two and the *indiscret* for three.

THE VICTORIAN AGE

The long reign of Queen Victoria (1837–1901) was to prove a time of great change. For a while, the Regency style remained in favor, the linear Neoclassicism of furniture enlivened by ebony and metal inlay. However, toward the middle of the century and more conspicuously after the Great Exhibition of 1851 and subsequent expositions, there was a far greater stylistic variety and mixture. During the Victorian era, interpretations of a number of artistic influences gave rise to new, sometimes eccentric shapes. The British designers A.W.N. Pugin (1812–52) and William Burges (1827–81) were the

virtuosi of the Gothic Revival Style, while others preferred to rework Baroque and Rococo taste, sometimes combining an eclectic range of shape and ornament with varying degrees of success. A cross-fertilization between Europe and distant cultures – especially China and Japan – was stimulated by the great trade exhibitions held around the world, when countries learned more about one another's technology, vernacular style, and preferences in ornamentation. Unlikely combinations of materials and processes (of which papier-mâché was just one example) were adopted with enthusiasm, and this fresh approach was applied to wood (often used very simply), marble, textiles, and painted panels. Iron, both cast and wrought, was used for garden seats and tables and for indoor furniture, such

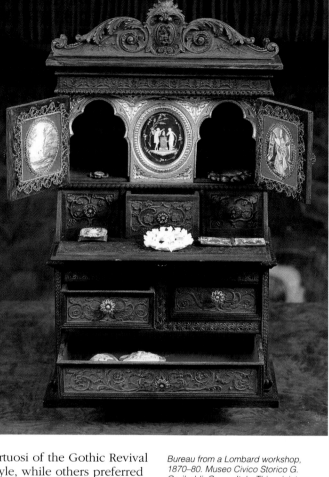

Bureau from a Lombard workshop, 1870–80. Museo Civico Storico G. Garibaldi, Como, Italy. This miniature piece of furniture, made from wood, gilded metal, enamel, and incised coral, is about 12 inches (30 centimeters) high. It is either a workshop model or, more likely, a toy. It is stocked with a number of other miniature objects.

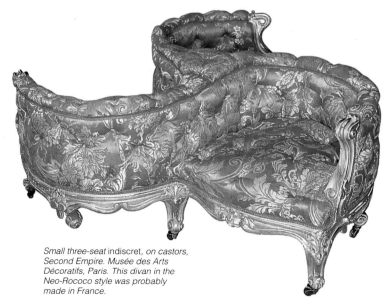

Small three-seat indiscret, *on castors, Second Empire. Musée des Arts Décoratifs, Paris. This divan in the Neo-Rococo style was probably made in France.*

PAPIER MACHE

The technique of molding paper pulp, long practiced in the Far East, was first patented in England in 1772 and used for making small tables, chair backs, firescreens, decorative bed headboards, wardrobe panels, small boxes, and containers. The pulp, made from a mixture of paper, glue, chalk, and sometimes sand, was pressed into the required shape, dried, and then painted or japanned with a dark background color. This was then decorated with multicolored designs, inlays of mother-of-pearl or ivory, or gilding with metal dust. In the early 19th century, papier-mâché products became extremely popular. Jennens & Bettridge of Birmingham, a leading British furniture manufacturer between 1816 and 1864, specialized in inlaid decoration.

as bedframes. Cane and bamboo also became very fashionable.

As more imports made their way to Europe, the appeal of the Orient spread, particularly all things Japanese. Japan took part in the 1862 exhibition in London, and, in the same year, a shop called *La Porte chinoise* opened in Paris, its success ensured by the established, widespread taste for chinoiserie. In 1867, the influential British designer and architect Owen Jones (1809–74) published his *Grammar of Chinese Ornament,* and Far Eastern influence grew further. It manifested itself in delicate pieces of furniture with highly polished surfaces and in a vogue for black lacquer, used in the work of Edward William Godwin (1833–86). Asian influences could also be seen in the highly stylized interiors of James Abbott McNeill Whistler, as well as in the innovative treatment of objects and space by William Morris (1834–96) and other members of the Arts and Crafts Movement.

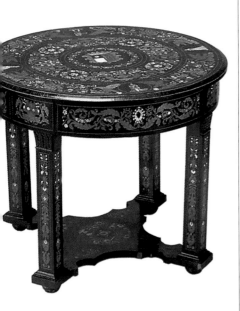

Table inlaid with various woods, mother-of-pearl, and ivory, late 19th century. Fratelli Falcini, Florence. Furniture made from papier-mâché could be decorated to achieve effects similar to this.

NEUSCHWANSTEIN

Ludwig II of Bavaria chose the site of a ruined medieval tower for Neuschwanstein Castle, set on a high rocky outcrop amid the forests of the Bavarian Alps. He commissioned ideas for both the exterior and the interior decoration from Christian Jank, the court stage designer. The decor was to be inspired by the world of Richard Wagner's operas. The walls of the major rooms were painted with frescoes of Germanic legends, and especially the story of Lohengrin, the early medieval chivalric hero with whom the mad Ludwig II identified closely. The Hall of Song emulated a hall of the same name in the Gothic castle of Wartburg, on which Wagner based a stage set for his opera *Tannhäuser,* the Grotto of Venus was built to re-create the Venusberg scene; and paintings in the studio that led to it, as well as the throne room, were reminiscent of the Hall of the Grail in the opera *Parsifal.* All expressed Ludwig's obsession with the world of Wagner, and emphasized the fairy-tale setting.

Neuschwanstein Castle, near Füssen, Bavaria, 1869–86.

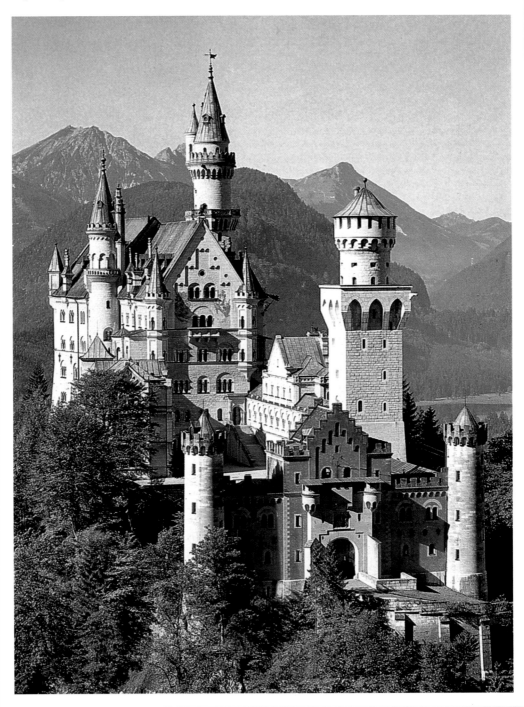

CERAMICS

Neoclassical designs were adopted by many porcelain manufacturers in countries that had fallen under the sway of the Napoleonic Empire, not least because their factories had passed from private to state ownership and were controlled by Napoleon's civil servants. The former Royal Porcelain Factory in Sèvres was famous for its Empire-style ornamentation, picked out in gold on the luminous white biscuit background. Despite the wars with the French, Britain embraced the Neoclassical style with enthusiasm; in Staffordshire, black basalt ware produced by the Wedgwood pottery was embellished with light-colored decoration, inspired by ancient Greece and Rome. As the 19th century progressed, industrial output supplanted the older craft methods of production,

benefiting from the discovery of new processes and of raw materials. Many advances were of crucial importance, including the 1794 invention of a bone-china production process by the English potter Josiah Spode (1754–1827) that could be used on an industrial scale. In 1813, Charles Mason patented ironstone china, and in 1843, Copeland & Garrett of Stoke-on-Trent pioneered the production of parian ware. This pure white porcelain with a slightly granular surface was an excellent modeling medium for busts, figures, decorative dishes, and vases. In the early 1860s, the *pâte-sur-pâte* technique of decorating porcelain in relief was developed at the Sèvres factory; very fine detail was applied in white clay to darker-colored wares, creating relief ornamentation of exceptional quality.
The growth in output of the English porcelain factories, largely due to these

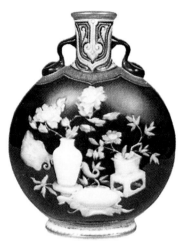

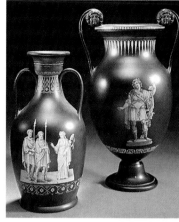

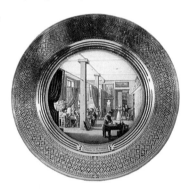

Minton ware flask in pâte-sur-pâte *porcelain with Chinese-style decoration in relief with superimposed layers, c.1870.*

Two black basalt vases with antique-style full-figure decoration, early 19th century. These vases were produced by the famous Wedgwood factory in Staffordshire, England.

Charles Develly, hand-painted porcelain plate, gilt and enamel decoration, 1825. Musée National de Céramique, Sèvres, France.

advances, both satisfied and stimulated a widening export market throughout Europe, the US, and many parts of the British Empire. This was not a one-way traffic, however: from the 18th

BONE CHINA

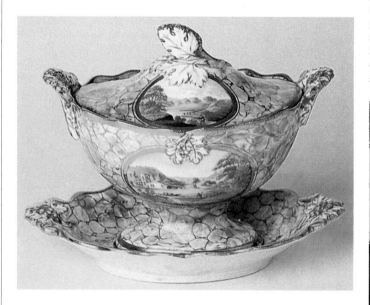

The most influential experiments in the creation of porcelain objects were made at the end of the 18th century by the Staffordshire potter Josiah Spode. He developed a

Small bone-china soup tureen with landscape decoration, c.1815–20. Ridgway factory, Staffordshire, England.

Bone-china sugar bowl, perhaps by John Cutts, 1815–20. Wedgwood Museum, Stoke-on-Trent, England.

porcelain that could be fired at higher temperatures than previously. By adding bone ash to the traditional soft-paste formula, Spode created the characteristic high translucence and white color of bone china.

During the 19th century, several English factories specializing in porcelain, such as Robert Chamberlain and John Rose at Coalport, introduced objects made with this technique.

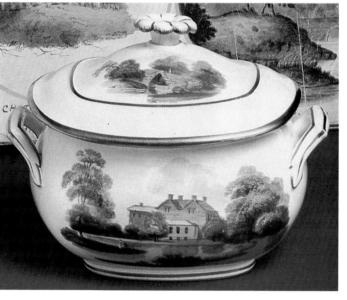

THE PEACOCK ROOM

The American artist James Abbott McNeill Whistler began his working life etching for the US Geodetic Coastal Survey, but left after a short time to move to Europe. There, he was to have a meteoric – and controversial – career. From 1876 to 1877, Whistler undertook the decoration of the dining room in Frederick Leyland's house in Prince's Gate, London. This later came to be known as the Peacock Room, and is now re-assembled in the Freer Gallery, Washington, D.C.. Although certain architectural details of the room had already been created by another designer, the Peacock Room is a good example of Whistler's work, and especially of a style that eliminates the distinctions between a painting and its frame, and between painting and the decorative arts. The room was planned around his painting *La Princesse du Pays de la Porcelaine* (1863–64), which was inspired by Japanese art. Asymmetrical yet harmonious, the scheme contrasted greenish-blue leather paneling with the dark brown-black and gilt of elaborate wooden shelving, originally installed for Leyland's collection of blue and white china. The shelving framed two large wall panels showing peacocks in full, opulent detail, and elsewhere in the room the decoration was based on the birds' breast and tail feathers. The leather-paneled walls were enlivened by a fan-shaped motif with gilt detailing. Writing on interior decoration in 1888, Whistler expressed a hope that he might find the opportunity to display his flamboyant taste and skills in his native US.

James Abbot McNeill Whistler, detail of the Peacock Room, 1876–77. The interior was designed for the dining room of Frederick Richard Leyland's London home.

James Abbot McNeill Whistler, the Peacock Room, detail. The room is now reassembled in the Freer Gallery of Art. Smithsonian Institution, Washington, D.C..

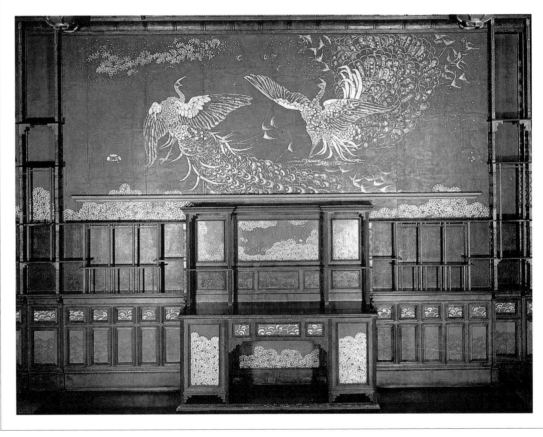

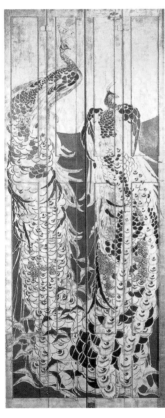

century, Chinese and Japanese ceramics had been imported throughout Europe in large quantities. This led to the adoption of many Oriental designs and shapes, as well as a new use of color and decorative techniques such as cloisonné. In cloisonné, cells made of metal wire are soldered to a metal base to form a design. Molten enamel in various colors is poured into the compartments, leaving the metal tracery visible. The work of the French artist Joseph-Théodore Deck (1823–91), and cloisonné wares produced by the English Minton factory, were of a particularly high quality. After Napoleon's defeat, classical motifs were often combined with extravagant and exotic shapes. There was a return to the Rococo style in the factories at Sèvres and Meissen, where the eclectic designs of Jacob Petit were especially rich. Decoration grew florid and elaborate, in part due to the introduction of chromolithography and transfer designs for pottery; these allowed painted inserts of various scenes, landscapes, still lifes, and even copies of paintings by great masters to be used as ornament.

Among the many porcelain products marketed during the second half of the 19th century were fairings. These were small groups of china figures, souvenirs sold in vast numbers, decorated with a variety of scenes and complete with captions.

There was also a demand for china souvenirs bearing the names and motifs, or arms, of towns and cities; for plates, tiny baskets, and all sorts of little containers; and for many other novelties. China was also used for toys: dolls had china heads, feet, and hands, although biscuit porcelain eventually was used because it was more lifelike. The dolls ranged from babies to fashionable Parisiennes, with beautiful clothes and accessories.

GLASSWARE

The influence of the Far East was not confined to porcelain. It could also be seen in 19th-century glassware, in which the revival of past styles was combined with the many technical innovations so typical of the century. A wide range of ornaments and tableware in cut lead glass was made in England, Scotland, and Ireland, as well as pieces of cameo glass. This was achieved by casing, or covering, a piece of glass with a layer of a different color and then partly removing the surface layer by hand or later, more cheaply, using acid. The

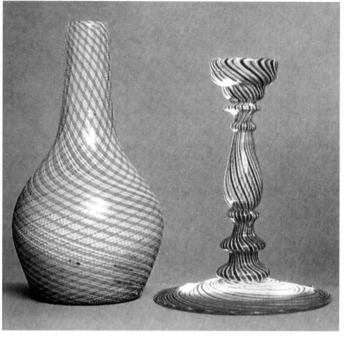

Glass bottle and semifiligree red glass candlestick, both in aquamarine and latticinio, c.1845. Pietro Bigaglia, Murano, Venice.

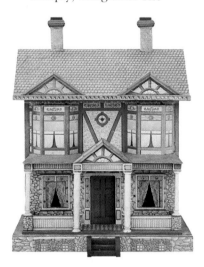

Doll's house by the Bliss Manufacturing Company, color lithograph on cardboard, 1890–1910. This would have been one of the cheaper wooden craft models.

Glass paperweights, 1850–60. The most valuable examples of paperweights were made in France by the Saint-Louis, Baccarat, and Clichy factories.

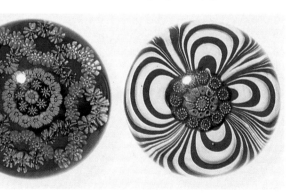

result was a design that stood out boldly against the background. Another technique, cameo incrustation, set molded porcelain reliefs inside a piece of clear crystal, such as a paperweight; these were also known as sulfides. Experiments with color at the New England Glass Company in the US produced the distinctive Peachblow and Amberina, while elsewhere in the US Burmese was introduced, a pale green-yellow shading to pink. In 1810, a white glass treated with metallic oxides resulted in opaline, a slightly milky glass, while

lithyalin, an opaque glass colored to simulate such semiprecious stones as agate and jasper, was patented in Bohemia by Friedrich Egermann in 1829.
The ancient Roman art of mosaic glass, rediscovered by craftsmen in Murano, Venice, in the 19th century, was given a new lease on life in the form of *millefiori* paperweights, launched at the 1845 Vienna Exhibition by Pietro Bigaglia. These small, solid crystal spheres were also made in France by master craftsmen at the Saint-Louis, Baccarat, and Clichy glassworks. The technique of embedding slices of colored glass canes in clear glass, usually arranged as flowers, proved hugely popular.

FASHION

The industrial, technological, and commercial expansion of the 19th century also brought about great changes in clothing and its manufacture. During the early part of the century, flourishing plantations in the southern US allowed imports of cotton into Europe to soar, forcing down prices of the

raw material from traditional suppliers such as India. Machinery was constantly being updated and improved in the cotton mills, which enabled them to produce material for clothing, in addition to other textiles. New textiles were patented, and, with the introduction of the sewing machine, the clothing industry was truly transformed. Factories were established specifically for the manufacture of clothing, large stores were opened in big cities, and fashion magazines such as *Ladies Magazine*, *La Mode illustrée*, *Le Journal des modistes*, *Il Corriere delle Dame*, and *Wiener-Moden-Zeitung* were published in England, France, the US, Italy, Austria, and elsewhere to keep women abreast of what the fashionable were wearing.
During the Napoleonic era, female attire and accessories

Giovanni Boldini, Portrait of Madame Charles Max, 1896. Musée d'Orsay, Paris. This is an expressive image of a late 19th-century Parisian socialite.

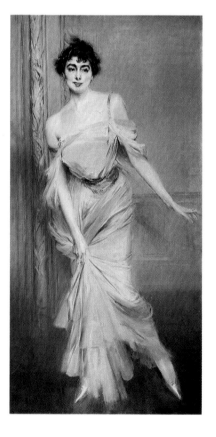

THE ART OF FLOWERS

During the course of the 19th century, artists, designers, and photographers turned their attention to flowers. Flowers appeared in the fabrics and wallpapers of William Morris, on the plates of Christopher Dresser (1834–1904) – where they were dissected and drawn as in a botanical illustration – and in every type of decoration and ornament.

Flower photography was used in experiments with industrial production. Images that were almost pictorial "still lifes" produced by the camera, such as the 300 collodion plates shown by Adolphe Braun at the Paris Exposition Universelle in 1855, made it possible to create a repertory of pictures that could be put to industrial use – applied to fabrics, for example. Flowers, a symbolic theme in the early 20th century, conveyed a sense of harmony to the artist, as Whistler wrote: "The artist should not merely, and blindly, copy every blade of grass but should aim to see instead how the elongated curve of a narrow leaf, balanced by a slender, straight, stem, combine grace and dignity, how strength increases sweetness, obtaining elegance as the final result."

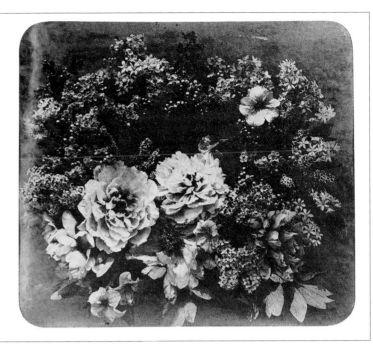

Adolphe Braun, Bunch of Flowers, photograph, 1856. Musée d'Orsay, Paris.

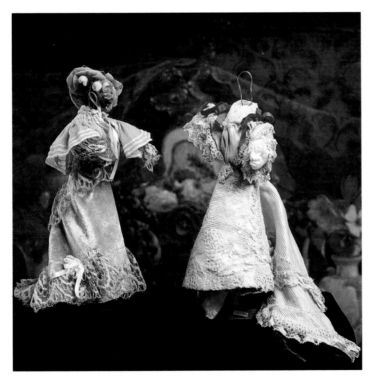

Models of fashionable gowns from the 1880s. Museo Civico Storico G. Garibaldi, Como, Italy. These models are 13 inches (33 centimeters) high and were probably factory samples used for customer selection.

had become progressively simpler and less cluttered. Waists were "out," comfort and freedom were "in," fabrics were light and soft and clung to the figure, and colors were pale. Although

Louis Hippolyte Leroy, one of the creators of the new fashion, survived until the end of the Empire, a few changes had already begun to appear in the early years of the 19th century. Heavier fabrics, more elaborate finishes, long sleeves, more modest necklines, and, most important, wider skirts were introduced. Skirts were full, thanks to starched petticoats and hoops, and at their height, such crinolines measured some 22 feet (seven meters) across. These widest of dresses were held up by a metallic under-structure, to guarantee flexibility and ease of movement despite their volume. In 1855, Millet successfully patented a metal frame known as the crinoline cage, perfected by Auguste Person the following year. The wide skirts contrasted with a narrow waist, which was created with the help of whalebone or steel corsets. During the 1870s, skirts became flatter in front but billowed out at the back in the *pouf*, the *demi-crinoline*, and, later, the *tounure*. These dresses made the most of the new fabrics, including Jacquard silks, satin, ribbons, piping, and lace. In the middle of the 19th century, female fashion was set by women dressmakers who looked to the splendor of Versailles for inspiration; their ideas, shown as fashion plates in magazines, were copied by bourgeois women. There was also a great interest in the theater and in the costumes of actresses, singers, and ballerinas. One of the great figures in 19th-century fashion was Charles Frederick Worth, the first *haute couturier*, who opened his Paris studio in 1857, heralding the modern fashion house. However, the corsets, petticoats, and bulky gowns fashionable women were required to wear were constricting and unhealthy. In 1883, the English Rational Dress Association called for more comfortable, practical dress that followed the figure, with long sleeves and calf-length skirts worn over pantalets, as suggested by the American Amelia Bloomer around 1850.

"LA DERNIERE MODE"

Among the many fashion magazines published in the late 19th century, *La Dernière Mode* is outstanding for its originality. Although published for only six months, from July to December 1874, this exceptional Parisian review offered its readership paper patterns, advice from a range of experts, information on the latest fashions (including those from London), tips on interior decoration, theater and book reviews, exotic and unusual menus for dinner parties, and a social calendar. The articles – of extraordinarily high quality – were all the work of one man, the famous French poet and writer Stéphane Mallarmé, despite being signed by imaginary authors with unusual names.

Art Styles in the Industrial 19th Century
THE EUROPEAN INFLUENCE

*The artistic styles that evolved in 18th- and 19th-century Europe were widely
imitated and adapted in the colonies and the new independent states.
Though the colonial architecture varied according to its locality, a
particularly original style developed in America, one that was
destined to flourish and make an impact internationally.*

In the earliest periods of the exploration and settlement of the New World, the colonists adopted certain elements of European culture that were later to become salient features in American art and architecture. In Massachusetts, the first English colonists built country villages and small towns modeled on the rural communities of southeast England, with the church or meetinghouse as the social and spiritual heart. The earliest colonists, who were for the most part busi-nessmen, traders, and farmers, reached the American continent during the 17th century. The number of colonists rose substantially throughout the 18th century, and they founded an increasing number of colonial villages and towns. Their clapboard houses were two or three stories high, with steeply pitched roofs. Spacious living areas on the ground floor were arranged around

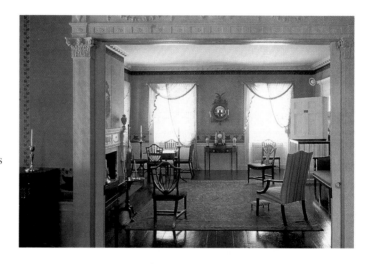

Samuel McIntire (1757–1811), drawing room, Gardner-White-Pingree House, Salem, Massachusetts, 1804. A typical interior in the English taste.

CHANGES IN THEATER DESIGN

In the 19th century, theater design elaborated on the conventions that had been established during the Baroque era. New features to the basic layout included a horseshoe plan and a different arrangement of the stage, stalls, and galleries. The theater was more than a performance space for opera, plays, and other forms of dramatic representation. It was also a focal point for fashionable society and reflected the most current styles and tastes. Through their varying dramatic interpretations, theater produc-tions mirrored cultural trends and captured social moods and changes. The advent of German romantic opera, following in the wake of a theme chiefly found in the first half of the century, reveals the term "romantic" to be descriptive of the quest for an

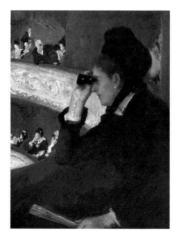

Mary Cassatt (1845–1926), At the Opéra, 1880. Museum of Fine Arts, Boston. This painting illustrates the theater's main social function in the cities of America and Europe – to see and be seen.

all encompassing cultural vision. The famous *Festspielhaus* (1876), founded by the composer Richard Wagner (1813–83) in Bayreuth, Germany, introduced a series of innovations on both a narrative and a decorative level – two aspects that were inher-ently interlinked. Galleries and balconies were eliminated in favor of large, fan-shaped stalls, once it was realized that the audience was most comfort-able when it had a lateral view of the stage. The orchestra was hidden between the stalls and the stage, and the part of the theater occupied by the audi-ence was left in darkness for the duration of the performance. With the invention of electric lighting, actors and singers could now be illuminated in a manner that gave a sense of depth, created shadows, and high-lighted the backdrop.

In the 19th and 20th centuries, theaters were built throughout America and Australia based on the European models. The dramatic trend of Realism once more brought about a revision in the way performances were presented. The attention paid to the accuracy of every detail, historical reconstruction, costume, sets, backdrops, and lighting meant that in the future no single aspect of theatrical production would be judged to be peripheral again.

Cross section of the Opéra de Paris (1860–74). Renaissance features enhance the Neo-Baroque flavor of this building by Charles Garnier (1825–98). The vast, magnificent interior and the use of opulent materials reflect the offi-cially sanctioned style of Napoleon III's Second Republic.

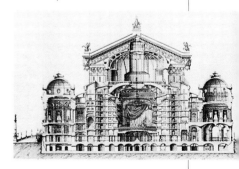

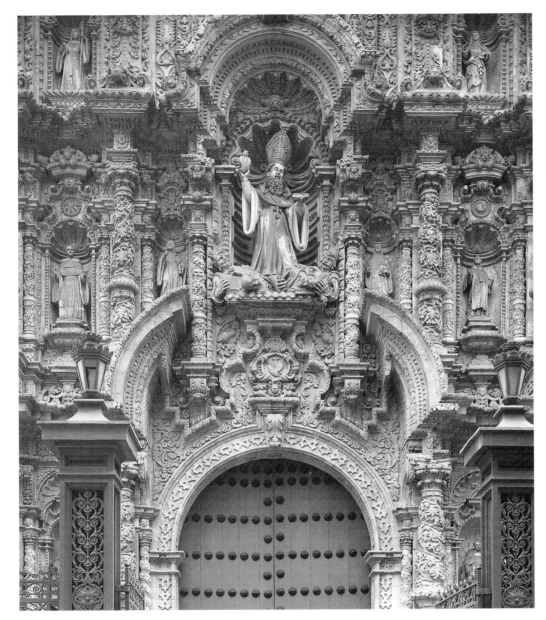

Diego de Aguirre, façade of the Church
of St. Augustine, Lima, Peru, 1721.

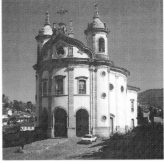

Francisco Araujo, façade of Our
Lady of the Rosary, Ouro Preto,
Brazil, 18th century.

types included fortifications,
churches, and houses, which
had thick stone walls broken
by small openings and long
balconies supported by
wooden structures. The
building methods employed
and the recurrent stylistic
elements, such as expansive
white surfaces and decora-
tively painted supporting
beams, were widely used until
the 19th century. They also
had many features associated
with the traditions of the Native
Americans of the Southwest.

ARCHITECTURE IN AMERICA

During the 18th century, the
French colonization of the
Mississippi and the Great
Lakes had a particular architectural impact on these
regions. The buildings, often
pavilion-style structures, typically featured a wide balcony
surmounted by a sloping,
hipped roof. In New Orleans,
an entire quarter was built
on this model. The French
colonial style, as displayed
in residential and communal
buildings, differed from other
forms of architecture exported
from Europe in that it took
into account the environ-
mental and climatic factors
of North America, especially
the oppressive humidity of
the Mississippi basin.
Examples include the building
system known as *briquette
entre poteaux*. This method
entailed the use of wood,

Juan Correa, screen depicting the
liberal arts, 17th century. Franz Maier
Foundation, Mexico City.

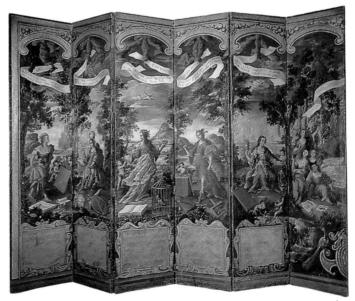

a large central fireplace, which
also served to heat the rooms
on the upper floors.
Spanish colonists established a
number of settlements in the
central regions of America in
the mid-16th century during the
reign of Philip II, including San
Antonio, Santa Fe, and the
coastal zones of California and
Florida. Architectural and
ornamental structures were
clearly modeled on the
Spanish Baroque. Building

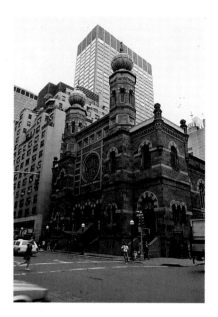

Central Synagogue, Manhattan, New York, 1872. American cities are studded with buildings that appear almost foreign to their modern urban surroundings, having survived constant changes and additions. Synagogues are among the best-preserved and interesting monuments from the 19th century; they exhibit a variety of styles from Moorish to Neo-Romanesque.

PATCHWORK

Patchwork is the art of stitching together various small pieces of cloth that differ in color, fiber, and decoration. The technique originated in China but became very popular in 19th-century North America. It is used for making cushions and quilts in an infinite variety of imaginative designs. Interesting and attractive effects can be obtained by dividing the surfaces into symmetrical patterns and by contrasting or matching colors, shapes, and textures. In this colorful example, an interesting combination of geometrical patterns has been used to create the quilt's overall effect.

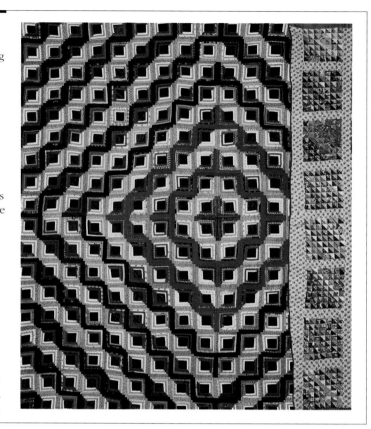

Detail of a quilt with a contrasting border, 1863. American Museum, Bath, England. Patchwork products were among the finest and most elegant articles of domestic handicraft in America.

THE AMERICAN WRITING DESK

In his novel *America*, Franz Kafka (1883–1924) gave a detailed description of the "American desk," a piece of furniture with a special mechanism for regulating the arrangement of compartments, which was very popular in America. The hero, Karl, finds one in his room while he is staying with his uncle in New York: "In his room stood an American writing desk of superior construction, such as his father had coveted for years and tried to pick up cheaply at all kinds of auction sales without ever succeeding, his resources being much too small. This desk, of course, was beyond all comparison with the so-called American writing desk that turned up at auction sales in Europe. For example, it had a hundred compartments of different sizes, in which the President of the Union himself could have found a fitting place for each of his state documents; there was also a regulator at one side, and by turning the handle you could produce the most complicated combination and permutations of the compartments to please yourself and suit your requirements. Thin panels sank slowly and formed the bottom of a new series or the top of existing drawers promoted from below; even after one turn of the handle the disposition of the whole was quite changed and the transformation took place slowly or at a delirious speed."

walls made of stone and stucco, and very large windows, which transformed the living area into a veranda during the day.

The German colonial style, which dates from the landing of William Penn in 1680 and continued into the next century, was quite different. The use of stone in the many villages in Pennsylvania and western Maryland drew on European medieval architecture, while in some regions of New Jersey and in New York there are fine examples of buildings based on traditional Dutch styles. These incorporated construction elements such as multiple-hipped roofs of varying inclination, dormer windows, and stable-type doors. Though the various strands of colonial styles differed noticeably, certain factors bound them all together; these included the variable climactic conditions, the availability of local materials, and the skill of the local craftsmen. On these factors rested the durability of their architecture.

LATIN AMERICAN ARCHITECTURE

The early 19th century saw the independence of the Spanish and Portuguese colonies in Latin America – Mexico in 1821, Brazil in 1822, and Peru in 1823. This brought about new political orders and debates about national identity but had no immediate impact on architectural production. As the century progressed, however, the introduction of the Neoclassical style through the academies began to replace overtly Iberian influences and transform the physical appearance of the Latin American colonial cities. Changes in thinking brought about by the Enlightenment, the growing cultural influence of France, and the desire to break away from retrospective Hispanic culture all had an effect taking various forms in different areas of the continent.

The architecture was often the work of immigrant European

Presidential Palace, Buenos Aires, 1894. Like many contemporary palaces in Latin America, this imposing monument is reminiscent of the European Renaissance style of architecture.

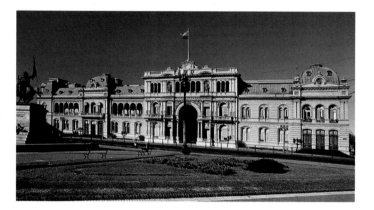

THE CIRCUS

The development of the circus as a form of entertainment, featuring acts by performing animals, acrobats, jugglers, dancers, and clowns, is generally attributed to the Englishman Philip Astley (1742–1814). Of particular importance was the show staged in London in 1768, where the audience was entertained within a circular, covered structure. Performances continued to take place in fixed, indoor places until 1830, when the development of large tents that could be easily dismantled made the circus more mobile. The first circus tents were quite small – 64 to 96 feet (20 to 30 meters) in diameter, with only one central pole. The cover was

A lion tamer from the Barnum Circus. The subduing of such an exotic beast, which was a familiar sight to visitors of the newly established zoos, was an exciting spectacle for adults and children alike.

tied down around the perimeter with guy ropes and pegs, similar to an army tent. With the invention of the two-pole tent by the American Gilbert Spaulding (1811–80), the circus grew in size. Now over 3,000 people could be seated, and with the further development of the system with four-pole and eight-pole tents, capacity increased to 15,000 spectators. The supports were originally wooden, but these were replaced by iron poles and then by light but strong steel supports in sections. Performances could include simultaneous acts by pyramids of acrobats on horseback and trapeze artists flying through the air, introduced for the first time by the gymnast Léotard in 1859. A popular feature of the circus in the second half of the 19th century was the parade of wagons and animals when the troupe arrived in town. The example of the European circus

was spread around the world by companies such as Ringling Brothers and Barnum & Bailey, and the Franconi family. In America, the presence of the railroads and special cars meant that large circuses could travel across the continent with ease.

A company of Mexican acrobats, early 20th century. The skill of troupes in forming human towers and pyramids still fascinates audiences today.

Henri de Toulouse-Lautrec, At the Cirque Fernando, the Ring Master, 1888. Oil on canvas. Chicago Art Institute. Here, the energy and excitement of the horseback rider is successfully captured on canvas.

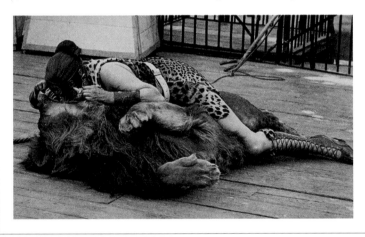

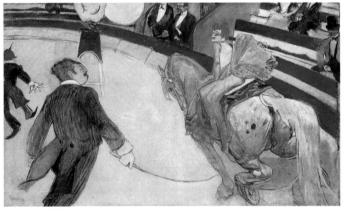

architects. The English architect John Johnson worked on the country house of Saõ Cristavaõ as early as 1812. Frenchmen A.J.V. Grandjean de Montigny (1776–1850) and C.F. Brunet-Debaines (1799–1855) built in Brazil and Chile respectively. In Argentina, there was a strong German influence, evident in the work of Ernesto Bunge. Theaters were important architectural projects, ranging from the sober Teatro Santa Isabel, Recife (1840–46) to the plaster-gilded Teatro Amazonas, Manaos. Europeans continued to under-

take important projects into the 20th century, as seen in the work of the Italian Adamo Boari (1863–1928) in Mexico. However, the predominance of Neoclassical styles and foreign architects was soon challenged in the form of a more self-conscious neocolonialism, initiated by José Mariano Carniero da Cuña and Ricardo Severo in Brazil. Rooted in nationalist ideologies, its intention was to challenge the dominance of European culture. By the end of the 19th century, new materials began to have an impact. In the south, iron

market structures were built by Miguel Aldunate, including the Santiago Market (1868–72) and the Meat Market in Buenos Aires (1889). In Mexico City, the particular trade relations with Europe maintained by Latin America are evident in the anonymously designed iron structure of the Del Chopo Museum. Materials local to individual Latin American countries began to take on significance, as illustrated by the use of traditional tiles by Alejandro Manriques in the Bavarian Beer Factory, Bogotá (1888).

ARCHITECTURE IN THE SUDAN AND INDIA

Occupied by the Egyptians from 1820 and then ruled by the Mahdi from 1881, the Sudan was conquered and colonized by the British in 1898, and its capital, Khartoum, was rebuilt by Lord Kitchener to an octagonal plan in the classical style. Its public buildings were embellished with prefabricated Ionic columns, pilasters, and continuous arcades, even on the facades.

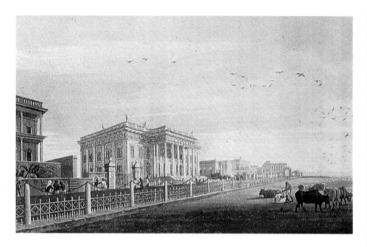

James Baillie Fraser, Esplanade Row from Chouringhee Road in Calcutta, 1815. *Illustration. The Neoclassical style so popular in Britain was echoed in all the cities of the Empire.*

Situated mostly in the city's official area alongside the Blue Nile, it was composed of tree-lined streets and squares, an area with churches and botanical gardens, and a crowded market district. The houses were not built in the local tradition, and instead of being constructed around an inner courtyard in a way that was adapted to the climate, they opened directly onto the street in a northern European manner. It was a triumph of town planning, a veritable "oasis in the desert." In India, there are numerous examples of colonial British architecture in Bombay, in the area around Esplanade Row in Calcutta, and in the designs of Sir Edwin Lutyens (1869–1944) for New Delhi. Oriental

Station and administrative buildings of the Bombay Railway Company, designed by F.W. Stevens (1847–1900), in a 19th-century painting.

elements such as Moghul domes are blended with Western Renaissance planning. Nowhere demonstrates the varied range of British colonial architecture better than Bombay. Its buildings include the Ionic Mint (1829) by Hawkins, the railway station by F.W. Stevens, the Telegraph Office (Renaissance), the great hall of the University (Flamboyant French), the Secretariat (Venetian Gothic, 1874), and Cowper's Town Hall (Doric outside and Corinthian inside).

AMERICAN CLASSICISM

One of the most influential figures in American architecture was the third president, Thomas Jefferson (1743–1826). Scholarly in his approach, Jefferson sought to develop an architecture that expressed the republican ideals of the new nation. By adopting a Palladian style for the designs of his own house Monticello (1769–70), near Charlottesville, Virginia, he rejected the

THE STATUE OF LIBERTY

The construction of a statue of Liberty in New York was originally the idea of a French historian, Edouard de Laboulaye, who had an avid interest in American politics and institutions. He proposed that money should be raised by public subscription so that France could send a monument to America to commemorate the close links between the two countries during and after the American Revolution. Consequently, a Franco-American committee was set up to raise the money and to oversee the construction work. The French sculptor Frédéric-Auguste Bartholdi (1834–1904) designed the colossal statue, which was to stand at the entrance to New York Harbor. He decided to place the statue on the 12-acre Bedloe Island, where the enormous female figure, right hand raised and bearing a torch, would serve as a lighthouse. He enlisted the help of the engineer Gustave Eiffel (1832–1923), who created a steel framework on which the copper figure was modeled. The statue was transported across the Atlantic in 214 cases and reached New York in June 1886. Meanwhile, Richard Morris Hunt (1827–95) made the pedestal on which the statue was to stand. The completed monument was officially inaugurated on October 28, 1886 by President Grover Cleveland. It has since come to symbolize not only the US itself, but also democratic freedom throughout the world.

Statue of Liberty, *1884, Print.*
Bibliothèque Nationale, Paris.

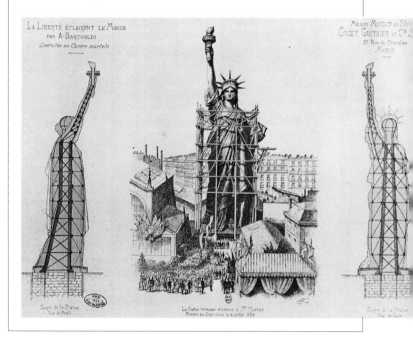

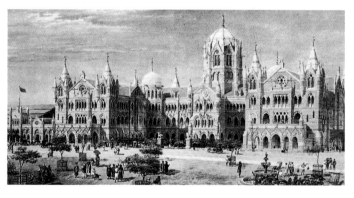

English colonial style of the Virginia tidewater. After the Revolutionary War (1775–83), he found in Roman architecture the style and principles that he had been seeking. He discovered ancient Roman architecture in France, where he was a foreign minister between 1784 and 1789, in both the ruins of Provence and through his links with the Neoclassicist academic circles.

His design for the State Capitol in Richmond, Virginia (1785) was one of the first instances of the front of a classical temple being applied to monumental buildings, and it provided a vocabulary for an architecture of democracy worldwide.

The beginning of the 19th century saw the ascendancy of two parallel architectural trends: the so-called Adam, or

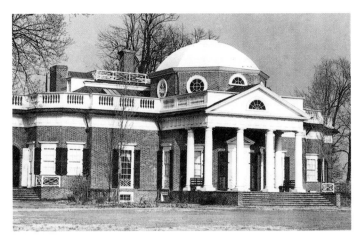

Thomas Jefferson, Monticello, Charlottesville, Virginia, 1772–79..

Federal, style and the Greek Revival style. The former derives its name from the period between 1789 and about 1830 when the United States Federal government was formed. Though it was rooted mostly in British Neoclassicism, a French influence can be discerned, which reflected the pro-French sentiment following the Revolution. It attracted architects such as Charles Bulfinch (1763–1844), Samuel McIntire (1757–1811), and William Thornton (1759–1828). The Greek Revival style reached the peak of its popularity in about 1820 following important archeological discoveries in Europe (the excavations of the Parthenon in Athens began in 1804) and the fashion for all aspects of ancient Greek art and architecture. Bulfinch's design for the third house of Harrison Gray Otis in Boston (1806) exemplifies the Federal style house in its harmonies, composition, and layout, wherein a series of rooms of various shapes – circular, oval, and polygonal – enclose rectangular areas of different sizes.

The first building in the US inspired by Greek architecture was the Bank of Pennsylvania built in 1801. Its architect, Benjamin Henry Latrobe (1764–1820), was the main exponent of the Greek Revival Two of his pupils, Robert Mills (1785–1855) and William Strickland (1788–1854), designed many public and private buildings, which were also based on the orders and canons of Greek art and architecture. These include the Second Bank of the United States in Philadelphia (1824) and the Treasury Building in Washington, D.C. (1842). According to practical, functional needs, these types of building did not necessarily adhere rigorously to the strict rules of symmetry and proportion laid down by the classical orders. However, they were frequently impressive in size and style. A very different historicist impulse emerged in about 1825 in the guise of the Gothic Revival. It was initially inspired by late 18th-century English Gothic architecture. In the late 19th century, interest in it was reawakened by the writings of the English art

SHAKER FURNITURE

Gradually, the various countries and states on the American continent began to crystallize their own cultural identities independently from Europe. Many had chosen America as a refuge from European persecution and as such often had quite different expectations about what America had to offer. Between the 17th and the 19th century, there was a rise in the number of social communities established, who were generally groups of people united by a lifestyle dictated by a particular religious philosophy. The community of Shakers derived its name from the religious society of Quakers, in particular a group that had arrived in America in 1774. They became known as Shaking Quakers because of the dance they performed as part of their religious rituals. They followed a strict lifestyle designed to bring them closer to a more natural way of living: they did away with private property, considered men and women to be equal, and did not recognize racial differences. Their belief in communal life meant greater importance was given to the everyday needs and welfare of the whole community rather than to the wishes of single individuals.

Around the middle of the 19th century, there were many Shaker communities in Kentucky, Indiana, and Ohio. Their arts and crafts products became highly respected, leaving an enduring mark on American culture. Shakers

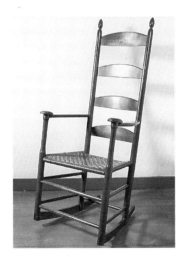

Shaker rocking chair, c.1840. American Museum, Bath, England. There is a minimal amount of ornamentation in this highly functional design.

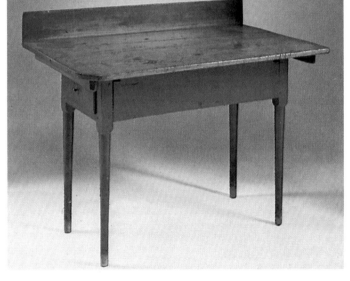

Work table in birch and pine, with drawer and edged work surface, c.1850–60, from the Hancock Shaker community in Massachusetts. This table combines practical simplicity with elegance.

believed that all members of the community should use their skills to make useful and functional objects, in order to satisfy their daily requirements and pursue their way of life without being troubled by the demands of industrial civilization outside. The essential and practical objects they produced, especially their furniture, were renowned for their precise style and high level of craftmanship.

In the second half of the 19th century, the Arts and Crafts Movement in England, with its emphasis on the tradition of simple handcrafted objects, owed much to the Shaker philosophy for its inspiration.

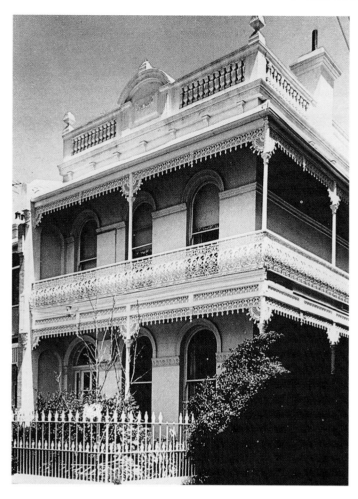

Colonial house, Paddington, Sydney. The style of this building, with its distinct Neoclassical features, reveals a great attention to exterior decoration. A range of ornate elements and details embellish its facade.

critic and social reformer John Ruskin (1819–1900), particularly *Stones of Venice* (1851–53). The work of Alexander Jackson Davis and Richard Upjohn bears this influence. Examples of early English and French architecture were adopted as models, as were Italian Renaissance villas and *palazzi* at a later period. This resulted in the radical eclecticism of the late 19th century. Perhaps its greatest exponent was Richard Morris Hunt (1827–95), whose "Breakers" mansion, built for the Vanderbilt family in Newport (1892–95), was an extravagant Italian Renaissance palace. His other mansions, built for the wealthy of Rhode Island and New York, illustrate his ability to master a whole range of historical styles.

WASHINGTON AND NEW YORK

In 1785, legislation was passed that brought about Land Ordinance. The regulation of the sale of land suitable for both agriculture and construction had become more and more essential with

the growth of large cities. This survey was based on a system of coordinates, in which the land was divided into sections according to longitude and latitude. As a result, the development of all large cities in the US and even the boundaries between the different states was determined by the grid plan.

The plan for the city of Washington, D.C. was drawn up by Pierre L'Enfant in 1791, and that for New York was completed in 1811. Such blueprints had to take into account the rapid increase in the number of buildings within their respective metropolitan areas and the need to establish an urban road network that would provide adequate communications between public buildings and service areas. L'Enfant's designs for Washington stipulated a series of radial thoroughfares that were to be superimposed on the existing rectangular grid. New avenues and streets were designed to cross the city, linking opposite parts of the metropolis by way of wide thoroughfares. The plan for New York, drawn up by a special committee, was

PRESSED GLASS

The US played a very important role in the development of industrial glass production. Even to this day, glassmaking in Europe remains predominantly one of handcrafting, in which individual glasses are hand-blown. In contrast, the technique of pressing glass was introduced to the US in the 1820s. Glass was widely employed in the manufacture of art objects, as exemplified by the wares of factories such as Deming Jarves in Boston and the Flint Glass Manufacturing Company of Pittsburgh. The surfaces of these glass vases, bottles, jugs, and other containers featured raised decoration in the form of abstract geometrical patterns or figures and portraits of famous people,

An assortment of "sandwich" glass jars.

Bottle in blown and pressed glass, c. 1896. Produced by the Democratic Party to commemorate the presidential election attempt by William Jennings Bryan.

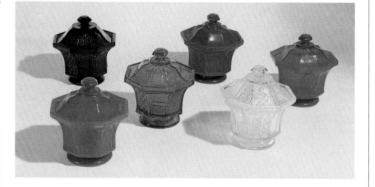

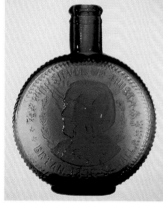

often accompanied by writing and ornamental motifs. In the initial phases, the pressed surfaces were achieved by a so-called "sandwich" method, but from 1828 onward a more efficient casting procedure made it possible to make forms in one piece, representing a considerable saving of time and money.

The technique was further improved during the early 20th century, when the first automatic pressing machines were invented. Particular modeling procedures and a variety of ways of treating glass encouraged experiments with various effects, ranging from opaque to transparent, and unusual color combinations.

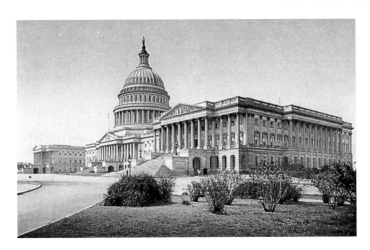

William Thornton and Charles Bulfinch, The Capitol in Washington, D.C., 1827. The Neoclassical style adopted in the Federal capital was used for government buildings in many state capitals.

broadly based on the traditional grid system, with the avenues and streets being numbered over an area of approximately 60 square miles (100 square kilometers). This took into account the potential development of the city over the ensuing decades. The question of urban expansion was closely

analyzed so that eventual growth could be carefully controlled in accordance with the original plan.

CHICAGO: CRADLE OF AMERICAN ARCHITECTURE

Founded in the early 19th century on the site of an American military post on the shore of Lake Michigan, the city of Chicago testifies, perhaps more than any other city on the continent, to the rapid growth of the 19th-century American city. Chicago was particularly notable for its use of wood in building. George Washington Snow (1797–1878) had introduced a technique called the "balloon frame," already in use on the East Coast, in which wooden boards were joined with nails in standardized, commercially available lengths of lumber. The modular wooden framework was then covered and erected singularly or joined with others. It was flexible enough a method to provide a solution for a number of construction problems. The first building in which the balloon-frame principle was used was Chicago's St. Mary's church, in which building costs were cut by more than 40 percent.

Unfortunately, because wood was so cheap and widely used in Chicago, the Great Fire of 1871 destroyed almost one-third of the city's buildings. The history of Chicago was dramatically affected by this event. Work carried out during the following years involved many architects and engineers, who were faced with several problems specific to the city; they needed to reconstruct buildings quickly and in harmony with the existing surroundings, while also guaranteeing that the structures would be safe and reliable in the future. The important consequence of these demands was the development of the fireproof steel

BROOKLYN BRIDGE

One of New York City's most prominent and famous landmarks, Brooklyn Bridge was an archetype of modern American bridge construction. It stands 128 feet (40 meters) high, has a span of 1,595 feet (486 meters), and links the southern part of Manhattan Island to the borough (previously the city) of Brooklyn.

The firm of John Augustus Roebling (1806–69), a German-

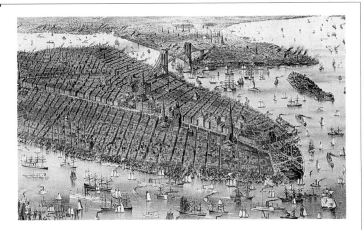

Currier and Ives, New York and Brooklyn, 1875. Museum of the City of New York. This commemorative print was produced to celebrate the opening of the new bridge.

Brooklyn Bridge during its construction. Photograph by John Augustus and Washington Roebling. Museum of the City of New York.

born American engineer, drew up the plans for the bridge in 1867, and the work was completed by his son, Washington Roebling, for its grand opening in 1883. The most striking innovation was the use of twisted metal cables, a technique Roebling had employed in 1842 for an aqueduct over the Allegheny River in Pittsburgh.

Roebling, one of the country's most important bridge builders, was also responsible for the Niagara Railway Bridge (1851–55) and the great bridge over the Ohio River at Wheeling, West Virginia (1856–57), which played an important part in the subsequent development of the suspension bridge.

TIFFANY GLASS

Glassmaker, jeweler, painter, designer, and decorator, Louis Comfort Tiffany (1848–1933) is associated with one of the most original forms of craftsmanship of the late 19th century. Having already undertaken such prestigious commissions as decorating the Red and Blue rooms in the White House (1882–83), Tiffany began to specialize in glassware. Through his experimentation with special laboratory techniques using chemical baths and steam, he produced glittering glass surfaces in iridescent colours, with opaque and burnished nuances.

The Tiffany Glass Company was founded in 1885 and became renowned for the production of naturalistic objects in the colourful and elegant Favrile (patented in 1894), the handmade glass that was the designer's trademark. The subtle effect of transparency and the delicate play of colours could be reproduced on virtually any decorative household object, including the classic Tiffany lampshade. Imaginatively shaped vases,

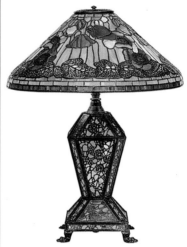

Louis Comfort Tiffany, lamp "Aux Pavots," with bronze and glazed metal frame. Produced post–1900 by Tiffany Studios in New York. Tiffany lamps are still produced today.

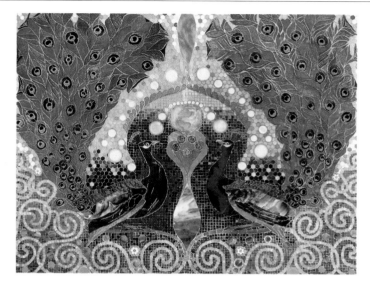

Louis Comfort Tiffany, Peacock Mosaic, 1890–91. The peacock, perhaps because of its decorative potential, was a favorite motif of the Art Nouveau. This panel was made for the house of Henry Osborne Havemeyer in New York.

bowls, and cups were decorated with flower motifs or abstract, flowing lines, and the colour of the glass, whether clear, pearly, opaque, or combined with metals, seemed to vary according to the light. In the 1890s, Tiffany branched out into Europe, taking part in the exhibitions of the Société Nationale des Beaux-Arts in Paris and then in the Exposition Universelle of 1900.

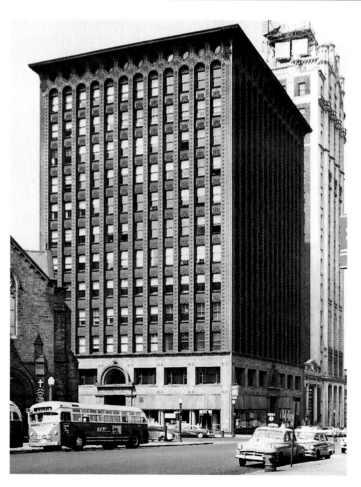

Dankmar Adler and Louis Sullivan, Guaranty Building, 1895. Buffalo City, New York.

frame. Between 1870 and 1880, William Le Baron Jenney (1832–1907), who had been educated at the Ecole des Arts et Manufactures in Paris, developed an unprecedented style of construction that made the most profitable use of available land in the city center by building vertically rather than horizontally. The result of his research was the prototype of the modern skyscraper and indeed the modern office building. Jenney not only explored the technical problems, one of which would be resolved by adopting steel as a building material, but also considered the unique visual perspective of the high-rise block. He paid attention, for example, to the shapes and textures of the facades. In 1879, his firm put up the first of the two Leiter Buildings (today on 208 West Monroe Street), with a composite supporting frame-

work of brick pillars on the outside and steel columns on the inside. This system of construction was further perfected in the Home Insurance Building (1885). Daniel Hudson Burnham (1846–1912), one of the finest architects and engineers commissioned with American urban rebuilding, worked initially with Jenney and then collaborated with John Wellborn Root (1850–91). Their technique employed, at least during its first phase, already well-established materials and techniques, but they later went on to explore unprecedented ways of designing and handling the large external areas of commercial buildings. This form of architecture was applied to offices, government and business buildings, and department stores. Chicago's 16-storey Monadnock Building (1889–92), designed by Burnham and Root, is unusual in having no ornamental features and in its use of bow windows at the top. William Holabird (1854–1923) and

THE SKYSCRAPER

After the devastating fire of 1871 destroyed a vast area of Chicago, the most urgent priority in rebuilding the city was to experiment with materials other than wood – it was vital that they should offer greater resistance to fire. William Le Baron Jenney used iron and steel to construct load-bearing frameworks for his new buildings. This innovation, which made it possible to build multistory blocks, could not have been considered without the introduction of the elevators in 1857. The first steam elevators, invented by Elisha Graves Otis, were replaced in 1870 by C.W. Baldwin's hydraulically operated system and then by an electrical system in 1887. These early blocks still employed historical styles: Jenney built the two Leiter Buildings (1879 and 1890) and the Home Insurance Building (1885) for the Chicago Loop, using metal frames and glass surfaces alternated with pilaster strips with classical capitals. The Tacoma Building (1887–88) by Holabird and Roche and the Reliance Building (1890–95) by Burnham and Root are similar examples.

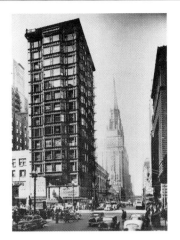

Daniel Hudson Burnham and John Wellborn Root, Reliance Building, Chicago, 1890–95.

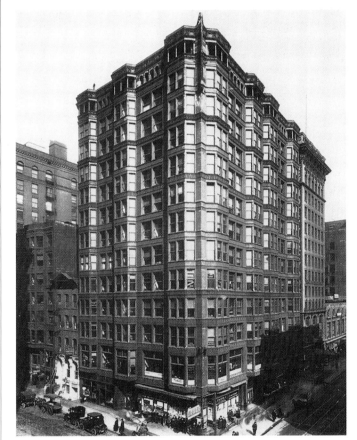

William Holabird and Martin Roche, Tacoma Building, Chicago, 1887–89.

Louis Sullivan (1856–1924) was the first truly modern architect. He produced high-rise buildings with forms that directly expressed their function. He devised a new plan for the skyscraper based on three essential components: a spacious ground-floor entrance lobby, a top floor that would act as a service area for the whole building, and multiple stories in between the two. This revolutionary concept was realized in such projects as the Wainwright Building in St. Louis (1891), the Guaranty Building in Buffalo, which he built with Dankmar Adler (1895), and the Schlesinger & Mayer Building (1899–1904) in Chicago. These were all remarkable constructions considering the problems posed by the limited availability of materials.

that Richardson had applied to Chicago's Marshall Field Wholesale Store (1885–87). For this building, he envisaged a stone facade broken by round arches. For the Chicago Auditorium (1887–89), a huge project consisting of a modern theater, a large hotel, and 11 floors of offices, Sullivan used different materials and original decorative touches in rustic stone for the first three stories and a smooth dressing of sandstone higher up. The auditorium was a truly fine example of Sullivan's architectonic artistic skills. His work here and in other cities (New York, Buffalo, and St. Louis) had a strong influence on later architects, not least for his concern in the harmonization of structural and decorative features in the overall design of a building. In 1893, Chicago's World's Columbian Exhibition proved a setback for architecture in the city. Sullivan's ideas for exhibition buildings were rejected in favor of the more conventional grandiose Roman Renaissance style. It was not until the emergence of the brilliant young architect Frank Lloyd Wright (1869–1959) a generation later that Chicago recovered.

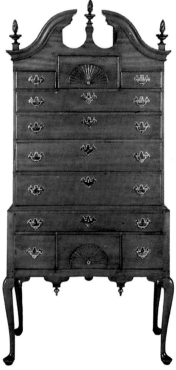

Martin Roche (1855–1927), pupils of Jenney, used a different approach for the face of their Tacoma Building (1889) – as the edifice rises, the decorative features of the string courses (horizontal, projecting bands, often carved or decorated) gradually disappear, returning again higher up before being rounded off at the top by a small arcade of arches and columns. Louis Sullivan (1856–1924) and his partner Dankmar Adler (1844–1900) were two of the leading architects involved in the design of tall commercial buildings. Over 12 years, they put up a number of buildings in which considerations of style and technique were successfully combined and new forms of decoration were used. Sullivan and Adler were influenced by the classicism of H.H. Richardson (1838–86), and they adopted the version of the Neo-Romanesque style

18th-century cabinet. Private Collection, Philadelphia. This particular model was widely copied.

ART STYLES IN THE INDUSTRIAL 19TH CENTURY

1804: an imperial decree by Napoleon insists upon burial of the dead in places outside built-up areas; this results in a new cemetery architecture. **1812:** architects Percier and Fontaine encourage the spread of the Empire style with the reissue of their compendium of ornament *Récueil des décorations intérieures*. **1816–26:** Caffè Pedrocchi in Padua, built by Giuseppe Japelli, exemplifies the eclectic tendencies of contemporary architecture. **1820:** technique of lithography, introduced at end of 18th century, becomes widespread; death of the English architect Latrobe, the greatest exponent of Greek Revival in the US. **1837:** Queen Victoria accedes to the British throne and a new era of national prosperity begins. **1848:** violent popular uprisings

1810　　1820–30　　1840　　1850

▼ JOSIAH WEDGWOOD
(1730-95)
Wedgwood was instrumental in the transformation of a craft form into an example of modern industrial art.

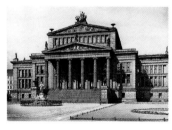

Two black basalt vases with antique-style full-figure decoration, early 19th century. These were produced by the famous Wedgwood factory in Staffordshire, England.

▼ KARL FRIEDRICH SCHINKEL
(1781-1841)
Schinkel, a German architect and pupil of Friedrich Gilly, progressed from the Doric to the Neo-Gothic style.

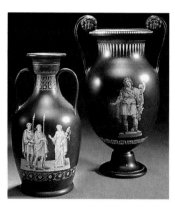

Karl Friedrich Schinkel, Schauspielhaus, Berlin, 1818–21.

JOHN RUSKIN
(1819-1900)
The English art critic and writer John Ruskin was a key champion of the Gothic Revival and the Pre-Raphaelites. His ideas greatly influenced contemporary architects.

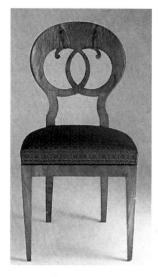

Viennese chair with entwined scroll, c.1820. Private Collection, Milan.

▲ GERMANY AND AUSTRIA
The conservative Biedermeier style in Germany and Austria appealed greatly to the middle classes between about 1815 and 1850. It was characterized by a sober realism in art and a solid functionalism in architecture.

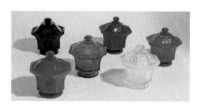

An assortment of "sandwich" glass jars.

▲ UNITED STATES
Between 1820 and 1825, the technique of pressed glass was widely employed by American industry in the decoration of vases, bottles, jugs, and glass containers.

▼ ENGLAND
The 1840 issue of the first postage stamps, which were designed by H. Corbould and engraved by F. and C. Heart, constitutes one of the great innovations in the field of graphic technique during the 19th century.

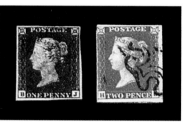

Penny Black and Two-pence Blue, England, 1840.

DANKMAR ADLER
(1844-1900)
A German-born architect working in the US, he was a major figure of the Chicago School. Together with his colleague Louis Sullivan, he made great strides in the integration of architecture and engineering.

ELISABETH VIGÉE LEBRUN
(1755-1842)
This French painter is best remembered for her portraits of female sitters, such as Marie Antoinette, Madame de Staël, and Lady Hamilton.

▼ THOMAS COUTURE
(1815-79)
The historical "costume" works of French artist Thomas Couture represented one aspect of "Official" painting during the time of Napoleon III.

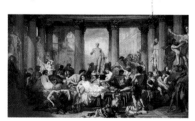

Thomas Couture, Romans of the Decadence, 1846–47. Musée d'Orsay, Paris.

▼ ENGLAND
The expansive glass and steel structure of London's King's Cross symbolized the technological progress of industrial society.

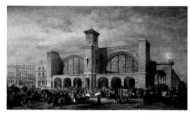

Lewis Cubitt, King's Cross Station, 1851–52.

HENRI GERVEX
(1852-1929)
The French painter Henri Gervex was a typical representative of Official art.

▼ PIERRE-FRANCOIS-HENRI LABROUSTE
(1801-75)
This French architect and engineer created antiacademic, functional forms that combined the late Gothic tradition south of the Alps with the use of innovative materials.

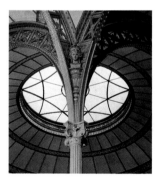

Pierre-François-Henri Labrouste, reading room of the Bibliothèque Nationale, Paris, 1858–68.

in Europe. **1851:** Joseph Paxton builds the celebrated Crystal Palace for London's Great Exhibition. **1852:** Louis-Napoleon crowns himself Emperor Napoleon III of France. **1854:**

Haussmann begins the architectural modernization of Paris. **1859:** town plan of Barcelona is drawn up by Cerdá. **1861:** Unification of Italy. **1862:** Garnier builds the Paris Opéra, an expression of the

architectural exuberance of the Second Empire. **1865–68:** architect Mengoni designs Galleria Vittorio Emanuele II in Milan, a model for other Italian cities. **1872:** South Kensington Museum opens

in London, later named the Victoria and Albert Museum. **1883:** Brooklyn Bridge, designed by the engineer Roebling, opens in New York. **1890:** van Gogh kills himself after a long depression.

1860　　1870　　1880　　1890

▼ Félix Nadar (Gaspar Félix Tournachon) (1820-1910)

A key French photographer and caricaturist, Nadar combined art and photography in his studies of the artistic life of Paris.

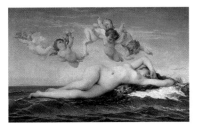

Nadar, photographic portrait of Gustave Courbet, 1861. Archives photographiques, Paris.

▼ Alexandre Cabanel (1808-79)

French painter Cabanel introduced a note of sensuality into mid-19th century academic Parisian culture.

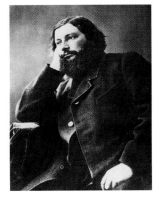

Alexandre Cabanel, The Birth of Venus, 1862. Musée d'Orsay, Paris.

UNITED STATES

In 1865, the Massachusetts Institute of Technology was founded. It conducted research that was to prove important for the technological links between science and the arts.

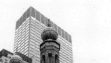

Central Synagogue, Manhattan, New York, 1872.

▲ UNITED STATES

The eclectic tradition of European architecture quickly spread to the other side of the Atlantic.

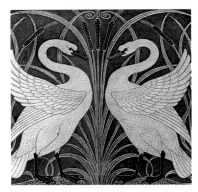

Walter Crane, Swans and Irises, 1877, polychrome tile.

▲ Walter Crane (1845-1915)

Together with William Morris, the English designer and illustrator Walter Crane was central to the Arts and Crafts Movement.

HOLLAND

From 1877 onward, the Rijksmuseum of Amsterdam was housed in a specifically built building designed by Petrus Josephus Hubertus Cuypers (1827-1921), an architect of eclectic taste but with a preference for the Gothic style.

▼ Max Klinger (1857-1920)

The German engraver, painter, and sculptor Max Klinger was influenced by the symbolism of Böcklin. His works had a dreamlike dimension that preempted Surrealism.

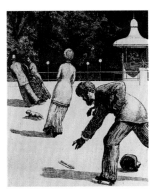

Max Klinger, Action, from the series A Glove, aquatint, 1881.

UNITED STATES

The Statue of Liberty, designed by Frédéric-Auguste Bartholdi and constructed in collaboration with the engineer Eiffel, was unveiled in New York in October 1886.

▼ ENGLAND

Tower Bridge, a raisable bridge across the Thames, exemplifies the great developments in 19th-century structural engineering.

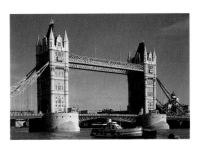

John Wolfe Barry and Horace Jones, Tower Bridge, London, 1886–94.

▼ UNITED STATES

The new face of Chicago epitomized contemporary American architecture.

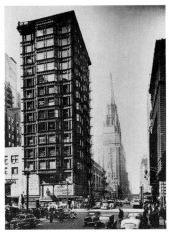

Daniel Hudson Burnham and John Wellborn Root, Reliance Building, Chicago, 1890–95.

▼ Giovanni Boldini (1842-1931)

Society portraitist Boldini imbued his sitters with grace and elegance.

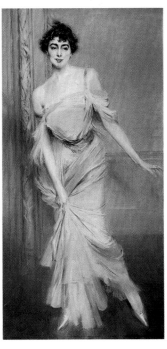

Giovanni Boldini, Portrait of Madame Charles Max, 1896. Musée d'Orsay, Paris.

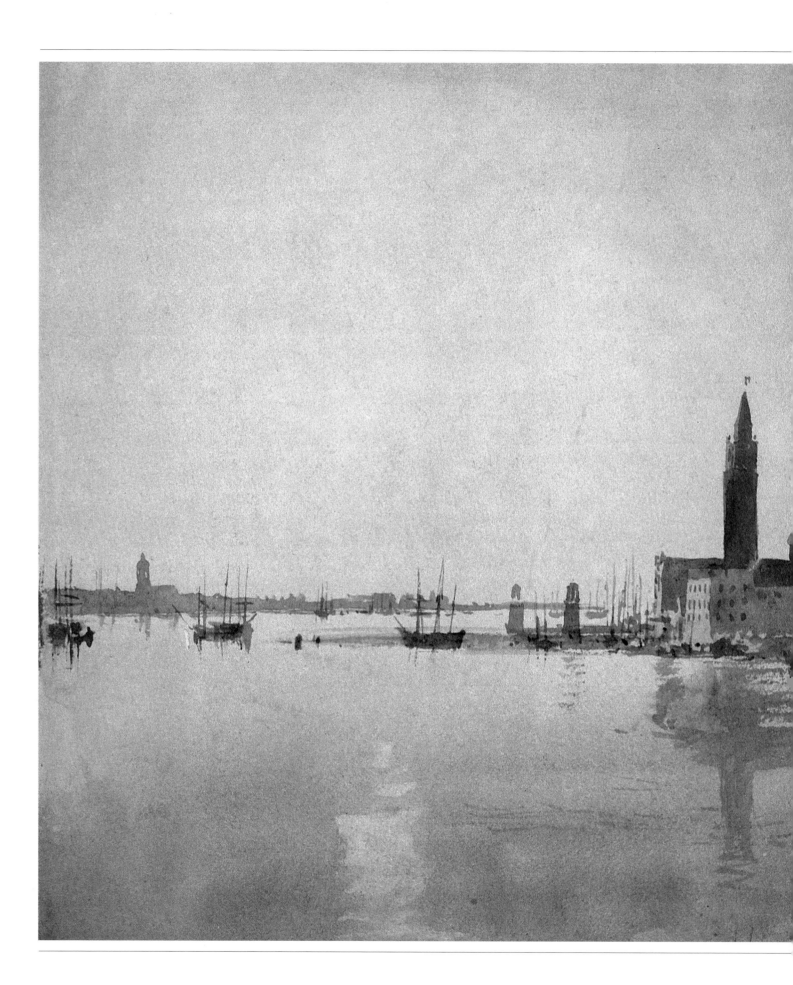

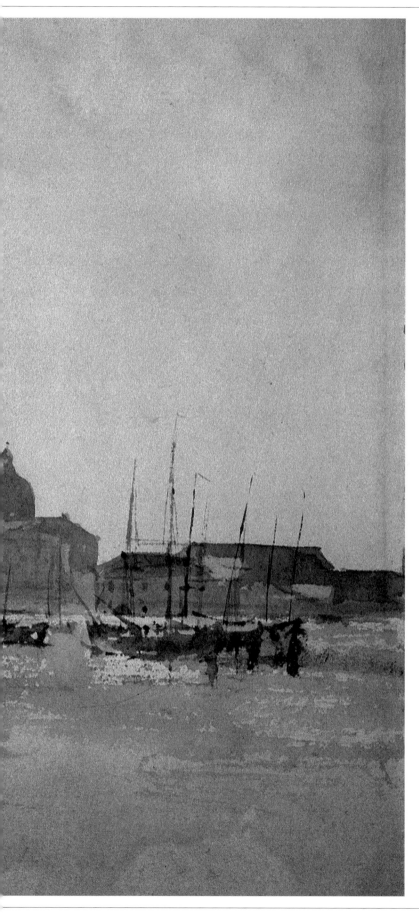

A CRISIS OF TRADITION & THE BIRTH OF CONTEMPORARY ART

Developments in the 19th Century
The Birth of Realism
The Impressionists

New Trends in the 19th & 20th Centuries
Post-Impressionism
The Modern Style

The Art of Africa & Oceania
Artistic Cultures of sub-Saharan Africa
Artistic Cultures of the Pacific

J.M.W. Turner, Venice, San Giorgio from the Dogana, c.1842.
Tate Gallery, London.

THE BIRTH OF REALISM

As the Romantic movement waned, exponents of the visual arts sought to depict the world in a more literal way. Focus shifted away from idealism to a more realistic rendering of nature, social relationships, and the characteristics of the individual, society, and the nation at large. This new realism assumed various forms in the different countries where it took root.

Realism was a historical movement that had a profound influence on the literature and figurative arts of Europe. The most systematic and coherent form evolved in France during the revolutions of 1830 and 1848. It reached its peak during the Second Empire (1852–70) and began to wane in the 1870s. In many different forms, and in varying measures of intensity, Realism spread throughout Europe, from the Russia of Alexander II to the Britain of Queen Victoria; from the Germany of William I to the Italy of the Risorgimento and the Hapsburg empire; and from Scandinavia to countries beyond Europe.

The year 1855 was significant in the establishment of Realism in Europe. It was the year in which Gustave Courbet (1819–77) exhibited his work in Paris in the Pavillon du Réalisme, a building that he himself paid for. He exhibited about forty paintings, including *A Burial at Ornans* and *The Painter's Studio*, which had been refused by the jury of the Exposition Universelle, who instead hailed the work of more traditional masters such as Ingres. In the same year as Courbet's provocative debut, the painters of the Barbizon School showed their art for the first time in a public exhibition. In 1855, the Italian Realist painters, who later became known as the Macchiaioli, met up regularly in the Caffè Michelangelo in Florence. In the field of criticism, the novelist and critic Edmond Duranty published a magazine, *Le Réalisme*, which

THE BARBIZON SCHOOL

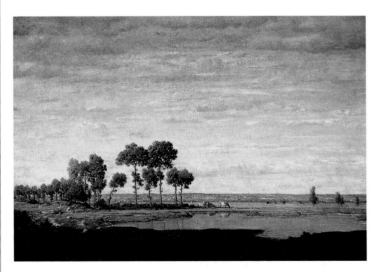

Théodore Rousseau, Spring, 1852. Musée du Louvre, Paris.

Between 1830 and 1850, the village of Barbizon – lying on the outskirts of the Forest of Fontaine-bleau, just outside Paris – became a meeting point for a group of artists that would take its name. The major representatives of the Barbizon School were Narcisse Díaz de la Peña (1807–76), Constant Troyon (1810–65), Jules Dupré (1811–89), Théodore Rousseau (1812–67), and Charles-François Daubigny (1817–78). They did not confine themselves to their immediate surroundings but roamed through the French provinces, from the Auvergne to the Jura and from the Vendée to Normandy. The school constituted a link between Romanticism and Realism, paving the way for the Impressionists. Abandoning the traditional 18th-century approach to landscape painting, the Barbizon artists reverted to a simpler form taken from drawings and oil studies sketched directly from nature. They took a particular interest in the changes in nature from day to day and season to season, recording them with free and subtle brushstrokes. Although they anticipated the Impressionists in painting directly from nature, they still executed their finished works in the studio. The Barbizon artists were united in their opposition to academic conventions and in their shared interest in landscape art, but each had his own personal interpretation and style. In Rousseau's early works there lingered an element of romanticism that manifested

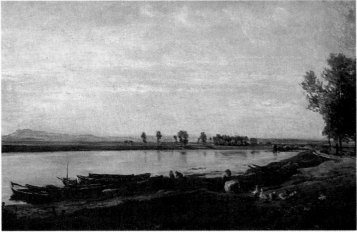

Charles-François Daubigny, View of the Banks of the Seine at Bezon. Musée du Louvre, Paris.

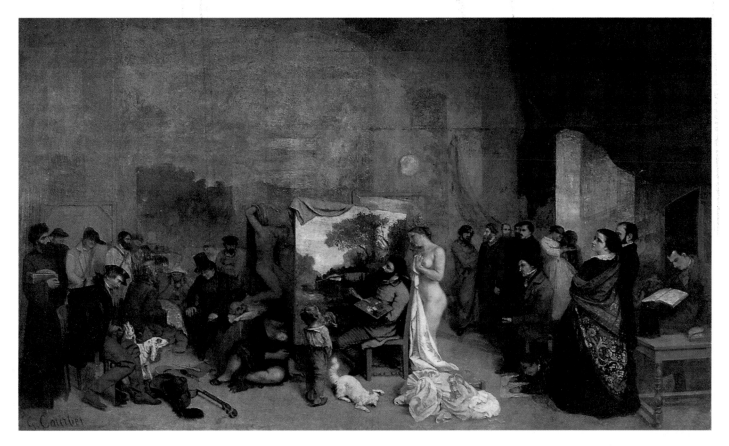

Gustave Courbet, The Painter's Studio, *1854–55. Musée d'Orsay, Paris. Despite the picture representing, in the words of the artist, "a real-life allegory," the harsh realism in the treatment of the subject and figures was judged unseemly, and the work was refused by the Salon of 1855. Delacroix, on the other hand, thought it worthy of praise.*

itself in a sense of mystery, transcendence, and mystical contemplation. He immersed himself in nature and the solitude of the countryside in order to find himself. For this artist, nature became a refuge and a place of nostalgia. It compensated for the frustrations of the social and political hopes of the July Revolution of 1830 and the revolution of February 1848 (Rousseau left Paris forever in 1849), as well as for his refusals by the Salons of 1835 and 1837 and the disillusion engendered by the growth of industrial society. Whereas Rousseau tended to favor a more solid and static pictorial structure, contrasting the horizontal elements of the ground with the verticals of the trees, Daubigny showed sensitivity to natural movement and variations in light. There is nothing theatrical about his work; he painted innumerable landscape views along the Oise River from the confines of his studio boat. During the 1860s, his painting became freer, embracing the vivacity of his sketches at a time when the bold innovations of the Barbizon School were beginning to be cramped by its own formulas.

became the principal organ of the movement between 1856 and 1857. In *Le Réalisme*, published by Champfleury in 1857, the same year that Flaubert's *Madame Bovary* appeared, no single definition of reality was proposed and no attempt was made to represent a fixed world, as in the daguerrotypes of the period. Instead, the world was seen as fluctuating and mobile and composed of complex elements and contradictions, qualities that were central to the Realist mode of expression.

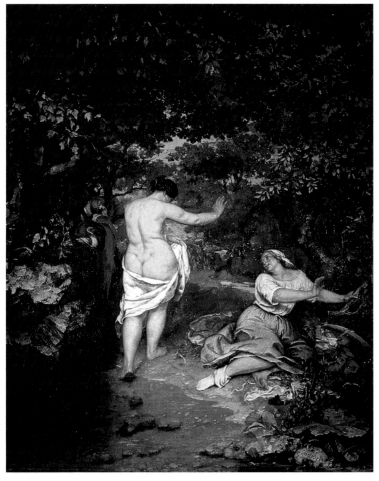

Gustave Courbet, The Bathers, *1853. Musée Fabre, Montpellier, France. Here, the classical theme of female beauty, as interpreted by Rubens and the 16th-century Venetian painters, is given a more realistic touch. The curvaceous shape of the woman, only partially covered by her drape, caused a scandal at the Salon of 1855.*

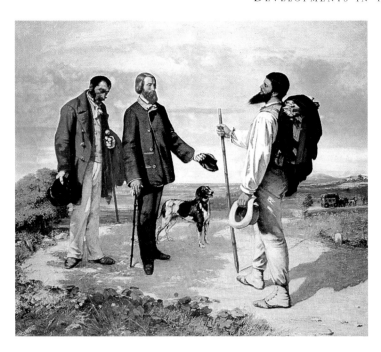

ORIGINS

Courbet wanted to create art from life and worked on "concrete" representations devoid of traditional moral values and prejudices. This was the fundamental characteristic of Realism, no matter how complex and varied the themes and modes of expression. The subjects represented were drawn directly from life because, in Courbet's own words, "an abstract, invisible object that does not exist is outside the province of

Gustave Courbet, The Meeting or "Bonjour Monsieur Courbet," 1854. Musée Fabre, Montpellier, France. The artist depicts himself meeting the art collector, and purchaser of the painting, Alfred Bruyas.

painting." New themes came to replace the paintings of allegorical and mythological subjects that featured in the moralistic ideals of academic art, which were supported in France by Napoleon III, who was proclaimed emperor in 1852. A much broader range of experiences was now envisaged. Subjects included workers, the poor, and the homeless, while the traditional idea of beauty was replaced by one of somber plainness. Even though one could speak of realism in the landscapes of the Flemish school of Ruysdael and Paulus Potter in the 17th century, and certain social issues were present in the realistic art of Caravaggio or Ribera, these subjects took on a wholly

PORTRAITURE

Discarding academic forms and classical models, the new genre of portraiture focused on the contemporary middle class. The vivid and unsparing image of Ingres' imposing *Monsieur Bertin the Elder* exemplified the power of the emergent social class. This "Buddha of the bourgeoisie" paved the way for a body of middle-class portraiture that had different connotations from country to country.
In Spain, Federico de Madrazo y Küntz (1815–94) proved himself a master of the techniques and styles of portrait painting and became a teacher and guide for later generations. In Germany, Anselm Feuerbach (1829–80),

an artist who tried his hand at both historical and allegorical compositions, excelled in paintings of contemplative women, such as his portraits of Nanna Risi and Lucia Brunacci. Franz von Lenbach (1836–1904) was a celebrated society portrait artist noted for his acute observation and terse style. The Italian artist Giovanni Boldini (1842–1931), for a short while a disciple of the Macchiaioli, discovered English portrait painting in London and made a name for himself in that genre among Parisian society after 1871.
In the US, Thomas Eakins (1844–1916) brought a sharp, precise sense of realism to his portraiture and group scenes. The most famous painter of the genre, John Singer Sargent (1856–1925), who celebrated the world of the Belle Epoque, brought the virtuosity of his silken brushwork to both the delicate flesh tones of his female sitters and the rustling materials in which they were dressed. Finally, in Russia, Ilya Repin (1844–1930) painted the celebrities of his time with realism and

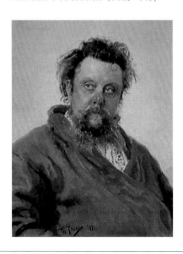

Ilya Repin, Modest Mussorgsky, 1881. Tretiakov Gallery, Moscow.

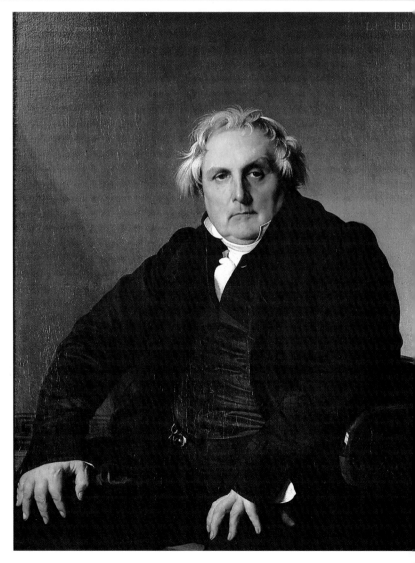

Jean-Auguste-Dominique Ingres (1780–1867), Monsieur Bertin the Elder, 1832. Musée du Louvre, Paris.

new meaning in the century of the Industrial Revolution. There was a "democratization of art," stimulated by the progressive uprising of 1848 and by new subversive incentives. In January 1848, Karl Marx and Friedrich Engels published in London their "Manifesto of the Communist Party", which called for an international working-class revolution. The new attitude was a result of the political and social disillusionment with the Second Empire, the advances of science, the rise of new critical approaches to history, and the development of humanitarian concerns. In the realm of painting, chosen subjects were drawn from daily life, not merely as an opportunity for protest but also as a

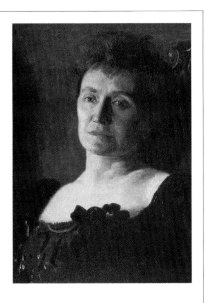

Thomas Eakins, Edith Mahon, *1904. Smith College Museum of Art, Northampton, Massachusetts.*

a sharp eye for detail, as can be seen in his sprightly *Modest Mussorgsky* and in *Tolstoy at Work* (1887). Meanwhile, photography had made a great impact on the portraiture business, with photographers creating sumptuous backdrops for their clients, placing them in false gondolas or under grand canopies. However, photography remained the humbler medium of portraiture, and those wishing to pass their own image down through the generations still preferred the skills of a painter.

document of contemporary habits and customs. More interest was shown in people and their problems, and artists sought to make more direct and immediate contact with reality in contrast to the conventions of academic tradition. The roots of Realism were borne out of the crisis within the Romantic movement. Although it rejected many of the principles of Romanticism – the exotic and historical subjects, the lofty ideals, and the supremacy of the imagination – other elements of the Realist cause reflected the true Romantic spirit: the expressive truth of the plain and ugly; the reverence for natural beauty in its imperfect, unfinished state; the attention to individual, regional, and ethnic peculiarities; and the elevation of the artist to a heroic level. But the Realist painters did not seek to transform what they saw into Picturesque or Sublime works; they appreciated these scenes for their very ordinariness. Delacroix's motto of "belonging to one's own time" was adopted by Realist painters in a narrower, more specific context. But it was English painting from the early 19th century, with its feeling for nature, that the earliest signs of Realism began to appear.

THE ENGLISH LANDSCAPE ARTISTS

John Constable (1776–1837), and Richard Parkes Bonington (1802–28) both exhibited with great success at the so-called "English Salon" of 1824. Together with Joseph Mallord William Turner (1775–1851), they were largely responsible for introducing a new approach to landscape painting that was to have a major influence on European art. They brought to landscape painting a respect for the actual location, a belief that the commonplace was worth painting and that changing atmospheric effects (light and weather) were an essential part of the landscape.

THE SELF-PORTRAIT

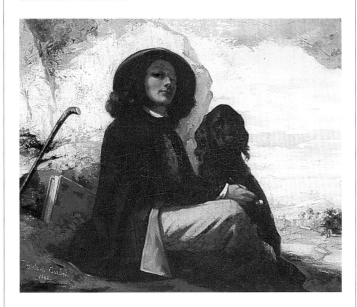

Gustave Courbet, Courbet with a Black Dog, *1844. Petit Palais, Paris.*

During this period, artists became heroic figures of their times and chose to represent themselves and their friends and colleagues in an imaginative range of poses. Gustave Courbet compared himself to Rembrandt in the depiction of his own likeness. His self-portraits range from the sharp, egocentric youth absorbed in self-praise to the final expression of his agony through the image of a trout in its death throes. More than a sensitive still life, this work is a tragic self-portrait of an artist who had suffered repeated disappointment: first, in the fall of the Paris Commune; second, in his imprisonment; and, finally, in his eventual exile to Switzerland.

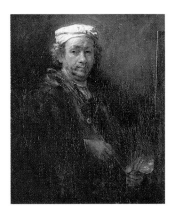

Rembrandt, Self-Portrait at the Easel, *1660. Musée du Louvre, Paris.*

Gustave Courbet, The Trout, *1872. Kunsthaus, Zurich.*

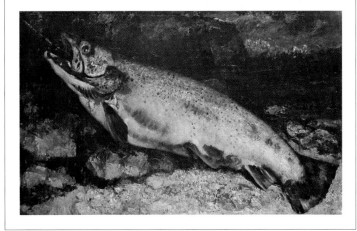

461

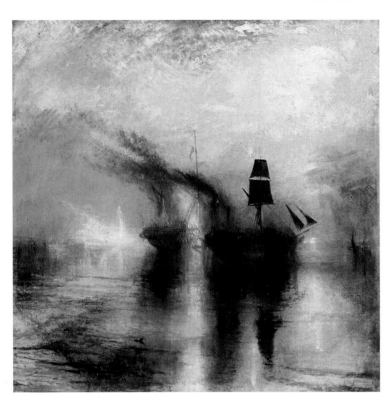

J.M.W. Turner, Peace – Burial at Sea, 1841. Tate Gallery, London.

TURNER

In his visionary paintings, J.M.W. Turner expressed the majesty of the "sublime"; he transcended empirical facts in favor of a fluid world, where the fusion of the four elements generated primordial energies. The present was dissolved in the past, visual experience in memory, and the particular became universal, vanishing in a timeless representation. *The Burning of the Houses of Lords and Commons, October 16, 1834,* of which there are two versions, becomes an apocalyptic vision; the painting of Admiral Nelson's old ship, *The*

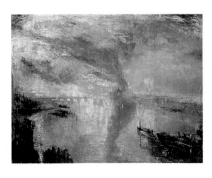

J.M.W. Turner, The Burning of the Houses of Lords and Commons, October 16, 1834. Cleveland Museum of Art, Ohio.

Fighting "Témeraire" tugged to her last Berth to be broken up, 1838, is a sad symbol of human destiny. The artist lashed himself to a mast of the ship *Ariel* in order to sample the stresses of snow, smoke, wind, and water at first hand. He later transformed the experience into a ghostly interpretation, which appears to be at the center of a vortex of cosmic energy, in his painting *Snow Storm: a Steamboat off a Harbours Mouth* (1842). Turner did not confine himself to a romantic vision of nature. Following his first trip to Italy in 1819, he experimented with a new form of naturalism in his landscape painting, which was based on the direct observation of truth, without resorting to any idealized or stylized form. This came to fruition in subsequent years, with a number of sketches in oils in which the artist worked on the themes of sky and sea. Some of Turner's lively experiments in oils anticipate the works of Constable, and the light that suffuses his mature works looks forward to the art of the Impressionists.

J.M.W TURNER: "RAIN, STEAM, AND SPEED – THE GREAT WESTERN RAILWAY"

1844; oil on canvas; 38½ x 48 in (98 x 122 cm); National Gallery, London.

This painting is part of the Turner bequest, which was made in 1856, a few years after the artist's death. It consists of over one thousand drawings, watercolors, and oil paintings, the majority of which are housed in the Tate Gallery, London. One of Turner's most famous works, *Rain, Steam, and Speed – The Great Western Railway* shows a train, bathed in a haze of morning light, traveling into the foreground over a bridge. Just in front of, and below, the

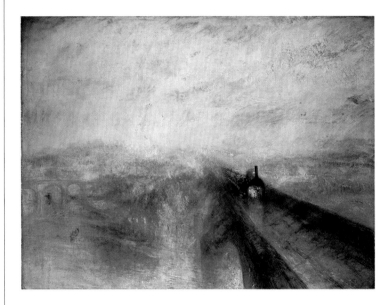

▼ *1. The composition is divided by two right-angled axes into almost equal parts, both horizontally (above and below, sky and earth) and vertically (left and right). Top and bottom are suffused with golden light, while left and right share similar features of depth. In the lower right quarter, dark tones prevail, whereas in the lower left quarter, there are fewer dark and heavy colors, and the space is dominated by a blend of lighter tints. In both these quarters, lines clearly in perspective lead the observer's eye into the distance and specifically to the light in the center, which is the focal point at which everything disintegrates. The perspective, left to the observer's intuition, relies on the shape of the bridges and the train to suggest an infinite expanse.*

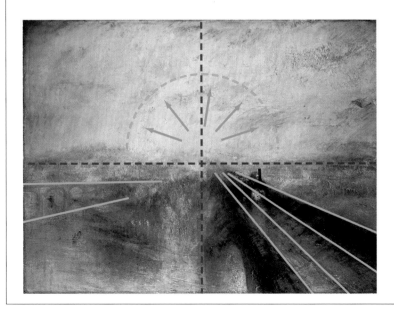

locomotive is a broad arch in which luminous yellows suggest the reverberation of the water. On the left, in the distance, are four arches of another bridge, which are delicately reflected in the gold and blue surface of the river. Between the two bridges is a boat, and near the center, on the bank of the Thames, are the light-colored shapes of figures dancing.

▶ *3. Although the form of the train is distinguishable, there is a sense of its being lost in the surrounding light and atmosphere. Similarly, the bridge, painted in various shades of brown and maroon, is shot through with flashes and streams of light. The end of the train is at some invisible point, enshrouded in sheets of rain. The veil of steam obscures the shape of the second arch.*

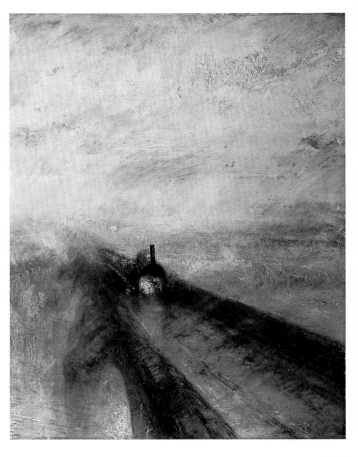

▼ *4. On the left-hand side of the picture, the arches of a second bridge rise out of the water. The delicate color and tender brushwork create a calm, tranquil effect. The leisurely flow of the water is rendered in soft, warm gold and hazy gray-blues. The small boat on its surface is completely detached from the eddies of light and steam given off by the train. There is no break from left to right in the handling of the landscape, but the left side is bathed in a slow, gentle sweep of rain and light, while the right side is pervaded by the sense of speed, not only of the train itself but also of the air that it stirs into violent movement.*

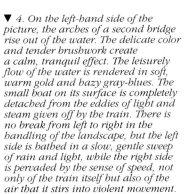

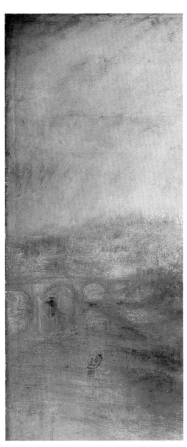

▲ *2. The most striking feature of the painting is the light – a dense light of atmospheric vibrations, dominated by warm, golden yellow tones that culminate in the absolute splendor of white. Only in the lower sectors do darker colors converge to define and surround specific subjects. The relationship between dark and light that separates and links the lower and upper parts of the picture corresponds to Goethe's color theories, in which a color is simultaneously associated with light and shadow. Here, yellow mingles with brown in the large bridge, and brown is present in the yellow reflection of the river, as seen in the area of the lower central part of the picture. Water enabled Turner to find correspondences between sky and earth and to discover infinite possibilities of echo and reflection between soft blue and golden yellow.*

▶ *5. The luminous effects of the painting are achieved by combining oil colors with watercolor techniques. This enabled Turner to obtain effects of brilliant color, such as the glowing yellows, and to combine them with transparent washes, as shown in the water. This technique helped to create the "melting" backgrounds, such as that of the sky, with its range of soft and deep blues, restful yellows, and gleaming whites. Above all, this method eliminated the need for painting in fields of color: in every part of the picture, color changes imperceptibly from one tone to another, so that it is impossible to tell where one color begins or ends. The style continues and develops the processes of disintegration and reconstitution of color and light exemplified in 18th-century Venetian and French paintings; it also anticipates Impressionism. In this and other paintings by Turner, we can see the sensitivities of the artist freeing him from the constraints of the artistic conventions of the time.*

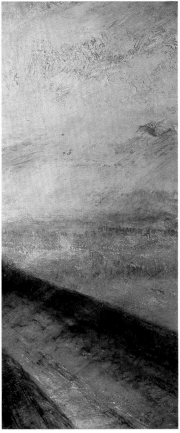

BEFORE AND AFTER TURNER

With Albrecht Altdorfer (c.1480–1538), nature became one of the principal vehicles of expression for the artist attempting to convey the vastness of the universe. In his *Battle of Alexander at Issos*, the most original feature is the great depth of the scene. The sun lights up the clouds, symbolizing the divine and solar qualities of Alexander, victorious over the enemy. These symbolic qualities of alternating sunshine and shade would reach a climax in the work of Turner. His paintings are comparable to Claude Lorrain's mythological compositions; in the paintings of both artists, luminosity spreads from a central point of the canvas. The traditional view of history as an ordered progress, which was upheld by academic history painting, was challenged by Turner's extension of the form to include representations of

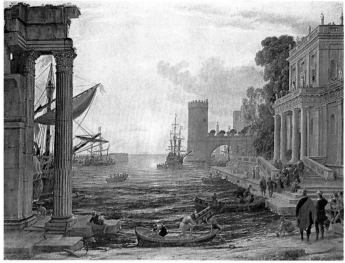

nature as chaotic and apocalyptic. His extraordinary view of nature was a pivotal point in 19th-century painting, enabling later artists to present nature and rural life as subjects in their own right. As such, Turner was a strong influence for the European realists. Nonfigurative art of the late-19th and 20th centuries often revived Turner's handling of light and color. The play of light on natural forms was integral to the paintings of the Impressionists and the Post-Impressionists. The abstract paintings of Paul Klee (1879–1940) reveal a vision of nature set out in the arrangement of luminous shapes. Mattia Morena (b.1920) carries the violence of natural events to extremes, with spurts and blotches of color.

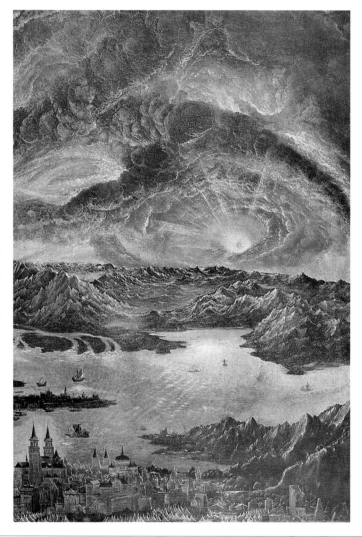

Albrecht Altdorfer, The Battle of Alexander at Issos, *(detail), 1529. Alte Pinakothek, Munich.*

Mattia Moreni, Natura viva, *1956. Civico Museo d'Arte Contemporanea, Milan.*

Claude Lorrain, Sea Port with the Embarkation of the Queen of Sheba, *1648. National Gallery, London.*

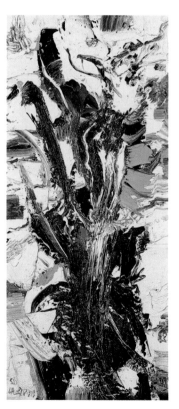

CONSTABLE

Like Turner, John Constable was primarily a landscape artist, but while the former was a tireless traveler, Constable was essentially a painter of English scenes. His subjects are the places that he knew and loved: the country landscapes of Suffolk, Dedham, Salisbury, the River Stour, and Hampstead. Throughout his life, he enjoyed a quiet, open-air existence, firm in the conviction that nature was the clearest revelation of God's presence. Sheaves of hay, hedges, trees, and streams were the impetus for divine contemplation and worship. The poet Wordsworth – so akin to Constable in many ways – expressed in the preface to his *Lyrical Ballads* (1802) why rural scenes were preferable to those of parkland: "in that situation our elementary feelings exist in a state of greater simplicity and consequently may be more accurately contemplated and more forcefully communicated." This idyllic fusion of man with his surroundings, where "the passions of man are incorporated with the beautiful and permanent forms of nature," is the Garden of

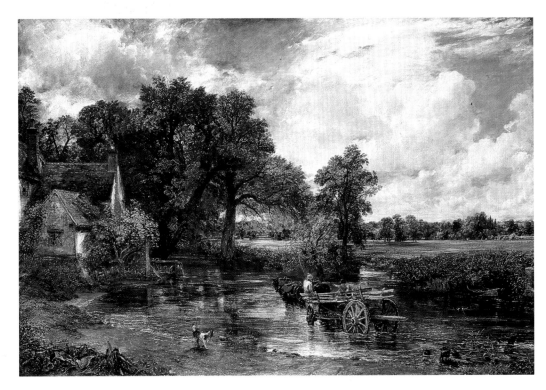

COROT

Camille Corot (1796–1875) was unrivaled in capturing on canvas the atmosphere of nature – trees, paths, and water were all enveloped by some untouchable and indefinable spirit. In due course, the results of his work would be absorbed into the works of the Impressionists. His immaterial light uses the relationship of colors to heighten the sculptural value of his paintings. His "unfinished" sketches were presented in exhibitions as true, valid, complete works of art. It was Baudelaire who defended Corot's landscapes at the Salon of 1845, defining the difference between a "finished" picture, painted with careful attention to detail, and a "complete" work, which might have been only roughly sketched. Corot visited Italy as a student from 1825 to 1828, documenting in small sketches and paintings his first-hand

Eden – a metaphor of purity and truth contrasting with the industrial reality of the city. In Constable's small oil studies (as opposed to the large canvases intended for Academy exhibitions), Constable shunned the conventional compositional elements – framing devices and central motifs – and concentrated instead on capturing the changing effects of light and atmosphere. His studies of clouds between 1821 and 1822 had precedents in the work of Alexander Cozens (1717–86), who, in his depiction of clouds and other natural phenomena, discerned something mysterious and beyond rational thinking. Constable went further: in his studies there is no trace of beginning and end. His depictions of clouds and rivers seem to spill over the edges of the sheet. They move rapidly and unexpectedly in every

direction, within a space that seems totally free and infinite. Constable used chiaroscuro to dramatic effect, transforming his tranquil rural scenes with the shadows created by the clouds. His rapid painting technique conveys immediacy, using touches of pure white spread with the flat brush. His vibrant brushstrokes fill the canvas with light and vitality.

REALISM IN FRANCE

English painting had an impact on 19th-century French art, initially in the romantic landscapes of Delacroix (1798–1863), who saw Constable's paintings at the Salon of 1824, and in the works of the Barbizon School. There are several strands linking Constable to Delacroix and the Impressionists, and equally to Courbet and Géricault, whose trip to England in 1820 became a source of inspiration for realistic paintings, such as *The Lime Kiln* (c.1822).

Camille Corot, Souvenir of Morte-fontaine, *1864. Musée du Louvre, Paris. This painting has echoes of the classical style of Lorrain, but the suspended enchantment of the contemplative scene also takes it toward values that would be part of Symbolism.*

John Constable, The Hay Wain, *1821. National Gallery, London. Considered one of Constable's masterpieces, this work depicts a gentle rural scene – a favorite of English painters.*

IL PICCIO

Giovanni Carnevali, known as Il Piccio (1804–73), broke with the classical tradition of landscape art in his views of the Alpine foothills, in which he showed nature in its tragic grandeur, purity, and radiance. Il Piccio interpreted the tradition of Correggio, Bernardo Luini, and the 16th-century Venetian school freely, filtering it into his paintings through

thick brushwork in imposing atmospheres and plays on light. He began by making sketches, the styles of which anticipated modern landscape painting, and then finished them in the studio. During his lifetime, Il Piccio was a famous portrait painter, as attested by his portraits of the Accademia Carrara in Bergamo.

Il Piccio, Landscape with Tall Trees, *1844–46. Galleria d'Arte Moderna, Milan.*

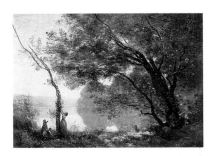

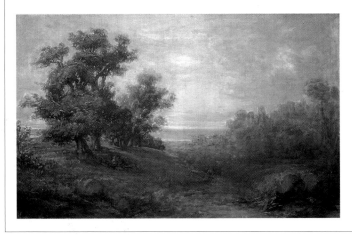

JEAN-BAPTISTE-CAMILLE COROT: "THE WOMAN IN BLUE"

1874; oil on canvas;
31½ x 20 in (80 x 50.5 cm);
Musée du Louvre, Paris.

This is one of the last paintings by Corot, who died at the age of 79 in 1875. It is a full-length portrait of a young woman at a dressing table, her elbow resting on a piece of clothing, hand on chin. In her other hand she is holding a folded fan. She wears an elaborate blue dress in the style of the age, sleeveless, with a low neckline, and tight-fitting at the bust. The woman is seen almost in profile: the lower part of the body is a three-quarter view from the back, while her face is turned slightly toward the observer. Two landscape pictures in the background and a rather basic treatment of the rest of the room complete the scene. This work is not the most famous of Corot's paintings, nor at the time the most appreciated; he was an artist who usually concentrated on contemplative landscapes. It is, however, representative of the work that Corot produced, above all, for himself: *in situ* landscape sketches and portraits, particularly of women. Although tense and severe, the picture still captures some intimate grace.

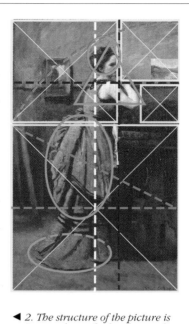

▶ *1. The proportions of the painting are classical, the base and height conforming to the Golden Section – the name given to the proportion used in ancient and Renaissance art and architecture in which the third term equals the sum of the first and second. A network of geometric lines and curves was drawn over pictures and plans of buildings to find balance and harmony in their design. Here, the structure of the Golden Rectangle uses a series of four squares that proceed from the bottom in a counterclockwise direction to divide up the compositional space. The vertical center line and the perpendicular lines, extending the sides of the third square to the left and to the bottom, form other rectangular areas. The forms of the figure are contained within three ellipses and an equilateral triangle.*

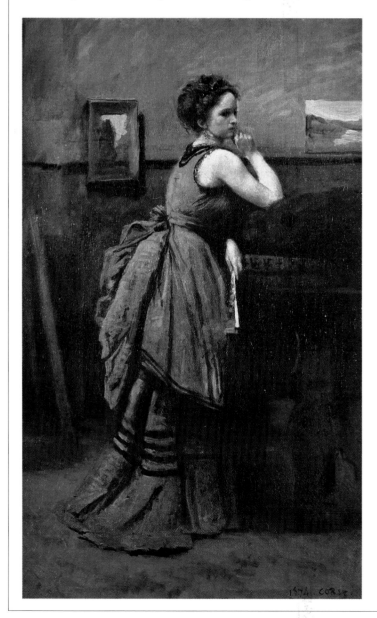

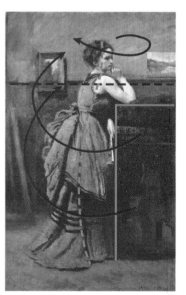

◀ *2. The structure of the picture is quite complex, calculated according to Renaissance rules, and very unusual for this period. It is like a secret design that the painter has woven into the work in order to give it an enigmatic balance, an effect that was probably lost on his contemporaries. Corot constructs the interior as if it were a landscape. High up in the painting, air and light flow around the figure and envelop her. The table that she leans against confers a sense of stability and becomes the central structure around which the space is organized. The light comes from the foreground and the left, embracing much of the figure and giving it substance. The interplay of dark colors and softly luminous flesh tints help accentuate the slight twisting of the body.*

▶ *3. In Corot's precise and solid composition, the line and color of the brushwork exhibit a freedom that echoes the experiments of the Impressionists, already working at that time. The brushstrokes are not fused but left visible and seem to have been directed by an inner impulse that helps give them expressive value. The painting as a whole appears, therefore, to be driven by a vital force that rises up through the figure, touching the bust and the head, and spreads outward to illuminate the upper part of the background. "The real is a part of art: feeling completes it," wrote the painter, who claimed that he interpreted with his heart "to the same extent as with my eyes."*

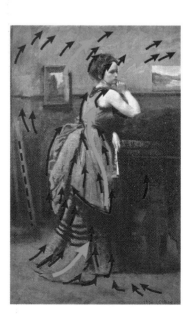

▼ *4. The lines are not sharp but are clearly perceptible and firm in character. The surroundings and the background, except for the easel on the left, are defined with straight, right-angled lines, while the lines of the woman's figure are soft, flowing curves. These vary in length, as with the blacks that outline the dress and decorate the skirt and drapery. The subtle use of color helps create a sense of naturalism about the figure.*

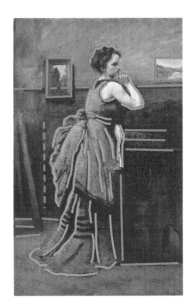

▼ *5. In a method already practiced by Vermeer, Corot creates echoes in the face of the painted landscapes on the wall behind the figure. Vertically, the face is made up of lines that radiate from the closed fan, with patches of light forming and supporting the larger features. Neither the foliage of the trees in the landscapes nor the woman's hair are given precise graphic definition. In contrast, the shadows of the woman's eye sockets are very dark, mirroring the broad shadows of the trees in the pictures.*

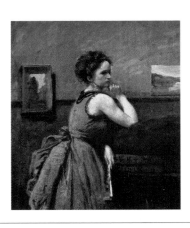

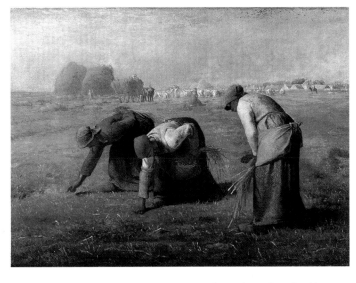

Jean-François Millet, The Gleaners, 1857. Musée d'Orsay, Paris.

observation of the countryside around Rome, which he subsequently composed in the studio. The artist had a natural gift for selecting and simplifying natural detail, which placed him in the French tradition of Claude Lorrain. His Breton women seem like mythical figures, and his later landscapes become ideal, timeless places inhabited by nymphs, shepherds, and gods. At the same time, nature in this guise was also understood by the artist in terms of measurable proportions, which anticipated the "geometrical" landscapes of Paul Cézanne.

MILLET

Jean-François Millet (1814–75) was the first artist to choose the theme of rural life as the subject for his paintings. He depicted peasants in large scenes, positioning them in isolated groups in the foreground. They are austere figures with great dramatic presence, even though their facial features are hidden. Millet's peasants do not have the crudeness of those in Courbet's works: the attitudes of the somber figures, softened by the evening light, are self-absorbed, tinged with melancholy, and somehow timeless. Their shapes are

simple and rendered with broad strokes and harmoniously blended colors. These peasants do not belong to a given region but take on a wider significance, becoming representative of humankind's dependence on the land. This realism, with all its social and humanitarian implications, was that of a deeply romantic and religious individual whose interest in art went back to childhood. Millet's early days

were spent in a village in Normandy, in an enclosed, somber environment, supervised by a pious priest who based his lessons on the Bible and Virgil's *Eclogues*. His future path became clear in 1849, when he met the painters of the Barbizon School following an apprenticeship in the Paris studio of Paul Delaroche. There, he had made a start with paintings of mythological subjects in a Romantic vein. Millet never emulated the heroic, revolutionary style of Courbet but instead retained a traditional element in his compositions, investing his ordinary subjects with poise and nobility. From his time in Barbizon, he painted works from memory, transcending any specific reference to reality.

DAUMIER

Honoré Daumier (1808–79) began as a designer and lithographer with the satirical weekly *La Silhouette*. He then contributed to the *Magazine de la Caricature*, edited by

RUSTIC LIFE

Millet's *The Sower* became the symbol of man at work. The direct and close bond with nature was reflected in the mood and tone – the weary rhythm of everyday toil in a dull, oppressive light. Meanwhile, Jules Breton (1827–1906) lived in a provincial rural community where the pattern of daily life was tied in with the observances of the Church.

Jules Breton, The Blessing of the Wheat, Artois, 1857. Musée d'Orsay, Paris.

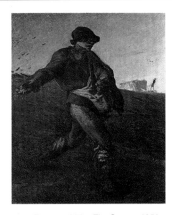

Jean-François Millet, The Sower, 1850. Museum of Fine Arts, Boston.

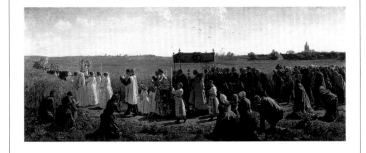

middle class, and the professional ranks of judges, lawyers, and doctors. He conveyed a sense of human suffering through his images of Christ, Don Quixote's adventures, and the actors of the commedia dell'arte.

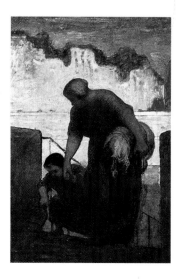

Honoré Daumier, The Washerwoman, 1863. Musée d'Orsay, Paris.

Aubert, and the weekly *La Caricature* of Charles Philippon, who also founded *Charivari*, in which Daumier published a series of biting caricatures of political and social celebrities. The artist drew on the Parisian working class for inspiration in his own "Human Comedy" in an inspired blend of the real and the visionary. He made almost 4,000 lithographs (including 100 in the celebrated "Robert Macaire" series) and turned to painting in his later years. He successfully combined the popular language of the lithograph (which owed much to English prints of caricatures and contemporary life) and the refinement of late Romantic painting, which was self-taught. Daumier documented workers' conditions, women's struggle for emancipation, the emergent

COURBET

The catalog compiled by Gustave Courbet for the exhibition at the Pavillon du Réalisme in 1855 contained the famous "Manifesto of Realism", outlining the artistic theories of the man who would be known as the master of 19th-century European Realism. Courbet's defiant and unconventional approach was far removed from the nostalgia for a lost tradition, dreamed of by the Pre-Raphaelites, or the historical painting of the *pompiers* (the derogatory term given to French academic painters). Courbet's art was concrete, almost tangible, even in the handling of the paint, which was laid on with a spatula rather than a brush, in what he described as "a wholly physical language." In *A Burial at Ornans* (1849–50), familiar provincial folk are depicted life-size, raising regional painting to the level of historical art. The subject is contemporary life, the actual moment of a burial in a stark, gloomy landscape

Gustave Courbet, Lady with a Parrot, 1866. Metropolitan Museum of Art, New York.

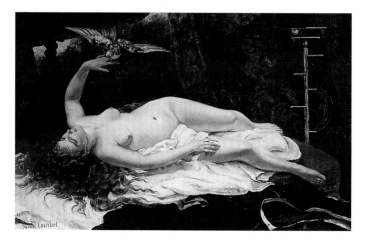

GUSTAVE COURBET: "A BURIAL AT ORNANS"

1849–50; oil on canvas; 124 x 263 in (315 x 668 cm); Musée d'Orsay, Paris.

The painting shows the last part of a Catholic funeral ceremony – the lowering of the coffin into a grave at the cemetery of Ornans in the Franche-Comté, where Courbet was born in 1819.

With such large dimensions, the painter was able to portray more than fifty life-size figures. In the center foreground is part of the empty hole; on the left are the priest, the pallbearers, and the coffin; behind the grave are officials; on the right are female mourners – separated from the men according to Catholic custom – and, in the foreground, a dog.

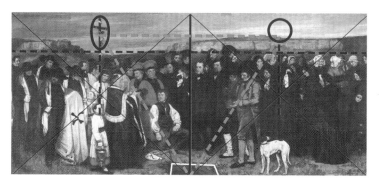

▲ *1. Courbet's finely composed painting is made up of two identical rectangles, which are very close to squares. In the left half, we see the officiating priest, dressed in black robes and reading the words of the liturgy. There are also two altar boys, a clergyman carrying the processional cross, and four pallbearers in black, with the bands for lowering the coffin over their shoulders. Between them, the coffin is covered by a white drape with black crossed bones, over which is placed a red mat. Behind the grave, there is a man bent on one knee, two men in gowns and red toques, and a group of men. The women stand to the right. Above the figures, beyond the ideal line of the horizon, extends the broad landscape of green hills and rocks. If vertical lines were drawn through the center of the composition and through the two separate rectangles, it would be possible to trace the base of an imaginary triangle, its apex in the grave.*

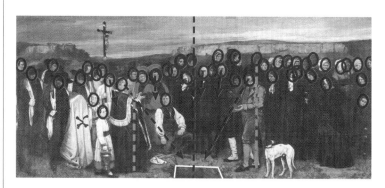

▲ *2. The different sizes of the people and their varying distances from the foreground place them in a succession from left to right, constituting a rhythm along the whole length of the picture. This rhythm varies according to the arrangement of the figures and whether they are facing the grave, looking at, or talking to, their neighbors, or turned in another direction. Only four of the people are looking out of the painting toward the observer. The imposing figures of the priest and the fashionably dressed man beside the dog constitute, through position and color, key reference points in horizontal space, dividing it into three parts that are almost equal. The expressive faces show that this is not a random gathering but a reunion of acquaintances, all of the participants with their own individual presence.*

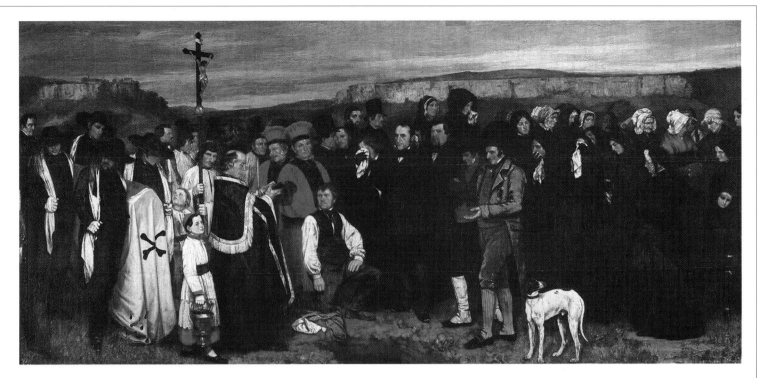

▶ 3. The source of the light in the painting is not specific. The folds of drapery covering the coffin suggest that it is illuminated from the left, while the shadows on the dog indicate a light source the right. There is even a feeling that light emanates from somewhere in front of the scene, which has the effect of giving the spectator a sense of involvement. The color is extremely rich and of uniform tones that are dense and earthy. The color also plays a part in defining the rhythm: in the group on the left, whites and blacks alternate with bright reds; in the central group, there are somber areas of black and red with touches of white; from the center toward the right is a black mass with touches of various colors. The earth in the foreground and the hills and sky in the background frame the long line of people and reinforce the solemnity of the scene.

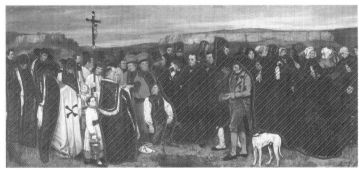

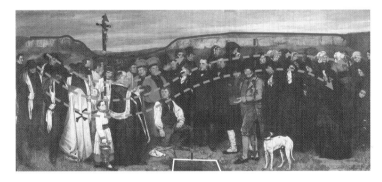

▲ 4. The scenery occupies barely a third of the picture's surface; it is painted in wide areas of color with scanty detail. Nevertheless, the landscape has a powerful presence, like the group of people it contains. The composition consists of a series of planes, from front to back, which help to organize the space and give it volume. The group in the foreground on the left is the nearest to us, while the group on the right is the most distant. Contrary to what may have appeared at first sight, the figures are not arranged in straight procession, but in a kind of S-shape of curves and counter-curves, revolving around two imaginary axes: the cross and the well-dressed man in the foreground. The movement of the group of figures echoes the shape of the undulating hills in the background.

▼ 5. Courbet addressed his subject with extreme deliberation. "I maintain," he asserted, "that painting is essentially a concrete art and should, in fact, consist only in the representation of real and concrete things." As a rule, the paintings submitted for exhibition by the Salon had to be of a size proportionate to the importance and category of the subject. Courbet chose the size approved for a historical or mythological theme for this ordinary funeral in a local setting; he saw it as an event as important as the burial of a king. This is evident in the detail with which he portrays the people of Ornans and the splendid array of whites, reds, and blacks. The varied colors of the clothes worn by the figure with the dog indicate a gentleman of property, while the elegant black hats and red toques distinguish members of groups noted for their honesty, devotion, and generosity.

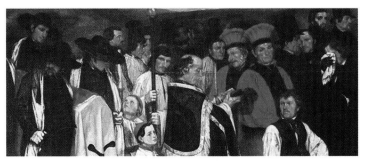

that exudes the smell of the soil. It is a secular, anti-heroic painting, unlike those of Jean-Pierre-Alexandre Antigna (1817–78), in which the people are seen to struggle in a theatrical and melodramatic manner against a hostile fate. This canvas was the forerunner of other monumental pictures inspired by the rural events and customs of Courbet's native Franche-Comté. In *The Stone-breakers* (1849, destroyed during World War II), he renounced traditional methods of figural painting, both in his choice of subjects and the way he represented them. Unlike Millet's figures in *The Gleaners*, the protagonists in Courbet's painting are not invested with dignity and monumentality (for which reason Millet's painting was more warmly received by critics and the public than Courbet's). *The Painter's Studio – A Real Allegory Summing Up Seven Years of my Artistic and Moral Life* (1854–55) was the centerpiece of Courbet's exhibition in the Pavillon du Realisme. In it, he presents himself as the artist-hero, seated in the middle of his studio, paintbrush poised

LABOR

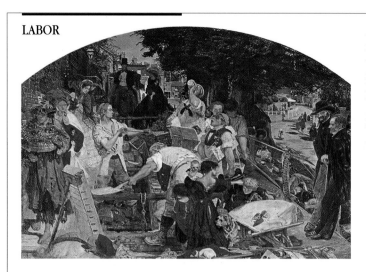

The objective of Realism entailed both the representation of the characteristics and customs of contemporary life and a commitment to exposing social issues that needed to be redressed. The latter aspect can be seen in the sculptures of Constantin Meunier

(1831–1905), who gave a new sense of monumentality and authority to the figures in his *Monument of Labor*, Place de Trooz, Brussels. In *Victims of Labor,* Vincenzo Vela (1820–91) showed the heroism of everyday life in his depiction of a mine disaster. *Work* by Ford

Madox Brown (1821–93), is a meticulously executed portrayal of a London suburb showing people from various walks of life. The theme of work would be the subject of great attention in Soviet Realism, which celebrated factory workers, rural workers, and soldiers.

Ford Madox Brown, Work, 1852–63. Manchester City Art Gallery, England.

Vincenzo Vela, The Victims of Labor, bronze relief, 1882–83. Galleria Nazionale d'Arte Moderna, Rome.

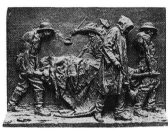

over a canvas of a landscape. Assembled around him are all the significant influences of his life. In a letter to Champfleury, Courbet wrote that the people on his right are "friends, fellow workers and art lovers … those who live on life" and on his left is " the world of the commonplace … the exploiters, the exploited, those who live on death." The

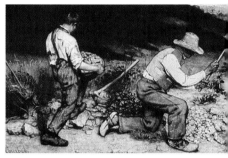

Gustave Courbet, The Stone-breakers, 1849. Formerly in the Gemäldegalerie, Dresden.

portraits on the right are identifiable – among them are Champfleury and Baudelaire – but we are left to speculate on the identity and meaning of the characters on the left. Courbet is best known for his figure paintings, but he was also a prolific painter of landscapes. For him, nature was a direct sensation; it had substance and physical consistency and was modeled by light, which is no accidental element but a palpable structure of reality itself.

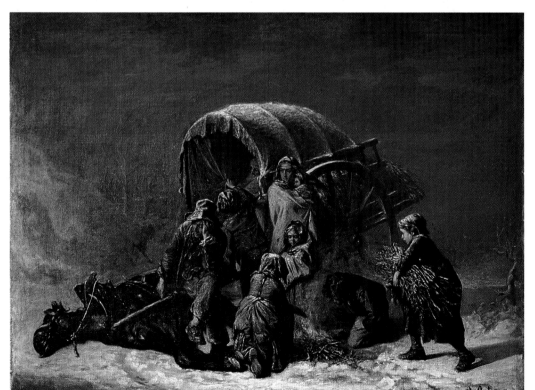

Jean-Pierre-Alexandre Antigna, The Forced Halt, 1855. Musée des Augustins, Toulouse, France.

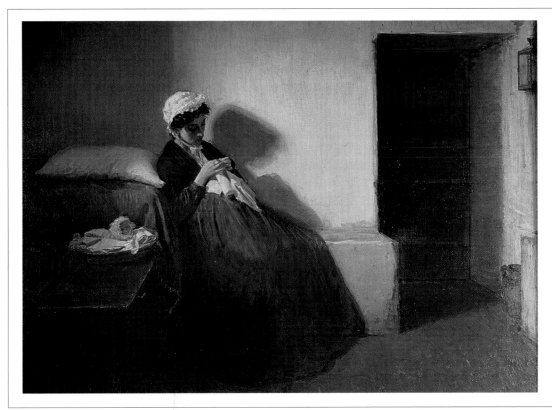

WORKING LIFE IN NAPLES

Gioacchino Toma (1836–91) depicted the interiors of contemporary bourgeois homes with a restrained intimacy, while his concern for social problems can be seen in his representations of the sufferings of the Neapolitan people. *Luisa Sanfelice in Prison* was inspired by the pioneering efforts of the first democratic women in Italy. This subject is shown calmly awaiting her execution during the Bourbon repression of 1799. From about the same time are two works, *La ruota dell'Anunciata* and *Il viatico dell'orfana*, which confirm the artist's concern for the life of the Neapolitan working classes. Having lost its status as the capital of Sicily, Naples was in industrial and social decline.

Gioacchino Toma, Luisa Sanfelice in Prison, *1877. Museo di Capodimonte, Rome.*

REALISM IN ITALY

The persistence of academic tradition in Italy delayed the establishment of a Realist movement. Realism eventually manifested itself in various regional schools and the many ruling cities that existed during the period of political fragmentation. Despite this diversity, a unifying trend did emerge. It was articulated on a national level during the 1870s in the work of the Macchiaioli movement, with its emphasis on reality and truth. During the second half of the century, a number of independent artists' colonies sprang up all over the country, from Resina to Naples, and from Rivara in Piedmont to Pergentina in Tuscany.

The Dutchman Anton Sminck van Pitloo (1791–1837), who held the chair of landscape art at the Naples Institute of Fine Arts, persuaded the Southern painters to free themselves from the shackles of conventional scenic art in favor of open-air painting and to capture their first impressions in studies and sketches. The lesson was learned by the so-called Posillipo School, of which Giacinto Gigante (1806–76) was the chief representative. Working with oils and watercolors, the Naples-born artist soon broke away from van Pitloo and painted his spontaneous and original views of Posillipo and its surroundings in the Gulf of Naples (he published his collection of lithographs, *Vedute di Napoli e dintorni*, in 1830). These met with great success at the courts of the Bourbons and the Tsars; Gigante assembled an *Album di vedute dell'Isola* for the Tsars in 1846.

The Vasto-born Filippo Palizzi (1818–99) worked initially with the Posillipo School and then introduced his descriptive and analytical Realist manner to Naples. In his mostly small-format canvases, the artist brought a sentimental, anecdotal quality to his close-up studies of domestic animals.

Giacinto Gigante, Sunset at Caserta, *1857. Museo Nazionale di San Martino, Naples.*

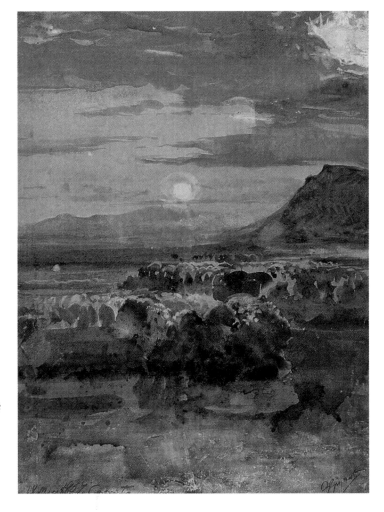

He showed the influence of both Flemish naturalism and Baroque still life, whereas his brother Giuseppe Palizzi (1812–88) found inspiration for his subjects and style in the French painting of Corot and Courbet, whose works he had admired during his visit to Paris. In 1867, Giuseppe Palizzi was joined in Paris by Giuseppe de Nittis (1846–84) from the so-called Resina School, which was established shortly after 1860 on the western slopes of Mount Vesuvius for the painting of subjects from real life. The school enjoyed the support of Adriano Cecioni (1836–86), theorist and apostle of the Macchiaioli movement. It shared the same principles of registering impressions directly from nature and using large patches (*macchie*) of color rather than chiaroscuro. The Resina School was shortlived and dispersed after about five years.

The Neapolitan Domenico Morelli (1823–1901), a friend of Filippo Palizzi, renounced the traditional local style in favor of large-scale compositions, following the international aesthetic-literary trend. Michele Cammarano (1835–1920), from the Palizzi School, alternated

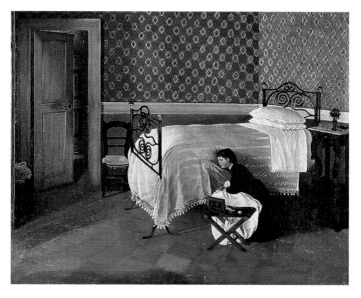

Adriano Cecioni, Interior with Figure, c.1867–70. Galleria Nazionale d'Arte Moderna, Rome.

subjects of a domestic type with patriotic themes and images of contemporary life. The Roman Antonio Mancini (1852–1930) was taught by Morelli at the Naples Institute of Fine Arts. Splashes of light and brilliant, sparkling colors, applied with a soft, fringed brush, characterized his everyday scenes of Neapolitan street urchins, acrobats, and priests. These images reached beyond the comfortable picturesque and attained a level of enlightened dignity. Under Hapsburg domination, Lombardy pursued its own identity. The Milanese brothers Domenico Induno (1815–78) and Gerolamo Induno (1825–90) participated enthusiastically in the patriotic activities of the Risorgimento – the five decades of struggle for liberation from foreign rule, culminating in the unification of Italy in 1870 – and provide detailed documentation of local events in their works. Theirs was a confined world of dressmakers, soldiers, and laborers, concerned only with their daily work and their dreams. To them, history was a chronicle of simple

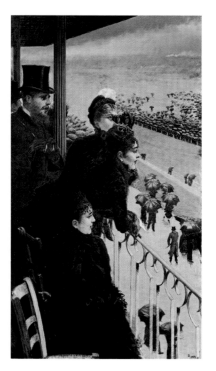

Giuseppe de Nittis, panel from the triptych Races at Auteuil, 1881. Galleria Nazionale d'Arte Moderna, Rome.

people and small events in their lives, reality a matter of feelings that needed no melodramatic emphasis.

The Brescian Angelo Inganni (1807–80), who worked in the studio of Francesco Hayez, renounced large canvases and big historical events in favor of small pictures that reveal him as an observer of everyday occurrences in the streets, lanes, and elegant districts of Milan. Mosè Bianchi (1840–1904) of Monza who painted views of Milan and the provinces, portrayed the local middle class with satirical grace. Emilio Gola (1851–1923) used bright colors for his canal scenes of Milan and Brianza and portrayed the elegance of his aristocratic female figures with a modern touch. In Piedmont, landscape painting found ample scope in the romantic works of the artist and politician Massimo d'Azeglio (1798–1866) and its finest exponent in Antonio Fontanesi (1818–82). Born in Reggio Emilia, but Piedmontese from 1848 once he had decided to take part in the first war of independence, Fontanesi did not belong to any specific regional school but assimilated a broader European culture in the course of his continuous travels. In Paris, the artist made contact with the French landscape artists and befriended Corot;

in London, he studied the works of Turner and Constable; in 1867, he attended the studio of Cristiano Banti, which was associated with the Macchiaioli school, in Florence; and he taught at the Imperial Academy in Tokyo. He died in Turin, where he had taught for some years at the Albertina Academy. One summer in Rivara, a group of Piedmontese and Ligurian painters came together, including Carlo Pittara (1836–90), Alfredo d'Andrade (1839–1915), and Vittorio Avondo (1836–1910), with the purpose of painting from natural scenes. The Rivara School, founded in 1862, reached its peak between 1865 and 1870, spreading the gospel of realistic landscape painting throughout northern Italy. In the Veneto, Giacomo Favretto (1849–87) painted small pictures of popular Venetian scenes with a rich and lively sense of color. Guglielmo Ciardi (1842–1917), from Treviso, trained at the Venetian Academy. He was stimulated by his contact with the Tuscan Macchiaioli movement to paint in a more sensitive and robust manner, as is evident in his views of the Lagoon and sunny landscapes. The Venetian Federico Zandomeneghi (1841–1917) likewise came under the Macchiaioli influence in Florence, painting popular scenes before leaving for Paris, where he remained, absorbing the spirit of Impressionism until his death.

THE MACCHIAIOLI

The Macchiaioli movement attracted artists from all over Italy, who had common social interests and political opinions. Many of them had been personally involved in the Risorgimento. Differing in personality and style, the principal exponents of the movement (which saw its most active years during the short period between 1854

THREE MACCHIAIOLI PAINTERS

NINO COSTA

Although he was a member of the Macchiaioli, Nino Costa (1826–1903) felt closer in spirit to Corot, with whom he became friendly in Paris in 1862. His scenes, which were quite classical in structure, were nevertheless free from the constraints of academic tradition, with juxtaposed *macchie* of color that anticipated the landscapes of Giovanni Fattori. It is possible that Costa was influenced by the Nazarenes (based in Rome from 1810) and shared their purist approach to art.

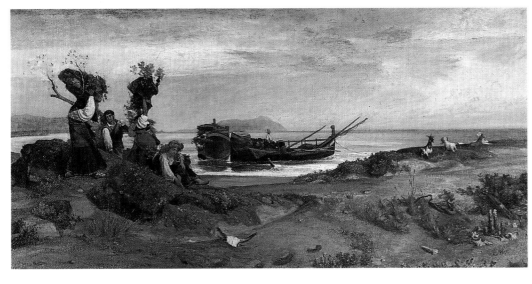

Nino Costa, Women Loading Wood at Anzio, *1852. Galleria Nazionale d'Arte Moderna, Rome.*

SILVESTRO LEGA

Originally from the area of Romagna, Lega eventually settled in Florence. He joined the Macchiaioli group with reservations and went to live at the house of a wealthy family in the quiet countryside of Pergentina. Here, he painted in the open air, together with the Macchiaioli members Borrani, Abbati, Sernesi, and Signorini,

Silvestro Lega, The Pergola, *1868. Pinacoteca di Brera, Milan.*

who had been members of the Pergentina School since 1865. In his pictures of orchards and gardens around Florence and his views of the country between the Africo and the Arno rivers, Lega brought a more gentle, poetic touch to his handling of *macchie.* The restrained use of this technique provided an outlet for his classicist inclinations, his aristocratic temperament, and the purist training he

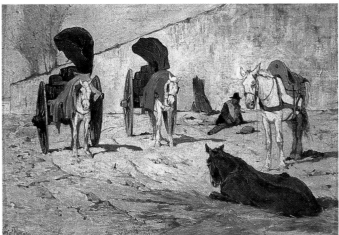

Giovanni Fattori, Roman Carts Resting, *1873. Galleria d'Arte Moderna, Florence.*

had received from Mussini. In his composition *The Pergola*, the artist conceals the underlying geometry – suggested by the brick paving and the trellis – with the dappled light that filters through the foliage.

GIOVANNI FATTORI

One of the most outstanding personalities of the Macchiaioli was Giovanni Fattori. His artistic development was slow. He was greatly influenced by Nino Costa, who advised him to abandon the romanticism of historical subjects and look instead to the truth of nature. He used the *macchie* to telling effect in a vivid series of small paintings, bringing to them simple, Impressionistic touches. He also painted sober military scenes that showed lines of weary marching soldiers, their features

masked with dust, or patroling sentries in a deserted landscape evaporating in the heat of the sun – reality dissolving in a poetic vision.

Fattori's restless nature led him to explore beyond the bounds of events, as interpreted by other Macchiaioli painters. A great portraitist and an excellent engraver (as evidenced by his own etchings), he combined rough, vigorous drawing with a feeling for color that was sometimes brilliant, sometimes a subdued pearly gray of diffused light. His later works developed a more tragic tone, the result of an inner struggle, the lack of recognition, and disillusion with his country.

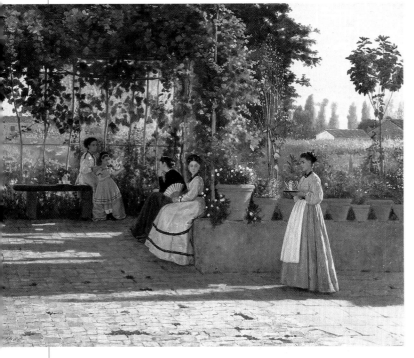

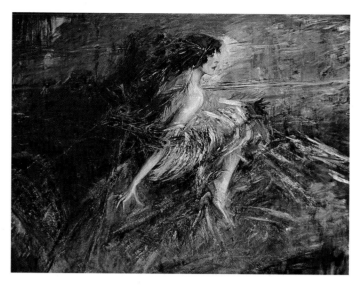

Giovanni Boldini, *Marchesa Luisa Casati*, 1914. Galleria Nazionale d'Arte Moderna, Rome. Boldini was one of the most prestigious portrait painters of the Parisian set.

Signorini (1835–1901), Giovanni Fattori (1825–1908), and Adriano Cecioni; the Roman Nino Costa (1826–1903); the Neapolitan Giuseppe Abbati (1836–68); the Venetian Federico Zandomeneghi; Silvestro Lega (1826–95) from Romagna; and Giovanni Boldini (1842–1931) from Ferrara.

The need to raise 19th-century Italian art from a provincial level to a broader international plane was the concern of two particular members of the movement: Telemaco Signorini, who developed the group's basic theories, and Diego Martelli (1839–96), critic and art patron, who wrote works on Impressionism, the relationship between Romanticism and Realism, and on the artists

Daumier, Manet, and Giuseppe de Nittis. The Macchiaioli met at the Caffè Michelangelo in Florence, where they discussed how to represent nature without any literary interpretations and how to develop an art based not on the interplay of geometry and perspective but on color variation and modulation. The *macchie* of color, which already characterized the work of the Neapolitan School, now had a more precise and unique purpose. Based on strong contrasts of light and shadow, achieved by juxtaposing different color tones, it gave a new type of definition and clarity to outlines, which was far removed from the conventional forms of drawing and shaping according to academic tradition.

THE HAGUE SCHOOL

The artists of the Hague School shared certain ideas with the French Barbizon painters. The key figure was Jozef Israëls (1824–1911) – sometimes called "the Dutch Millet" – who was concerned more with painting nature than people. Rather than reflecting the novelties of Paris, where he lived between 1845 and 1848, his paintings evoke the melodies of the violin and the heavy shadows of the Jewish quarters of Amsterdam or recall his years in Groningen where he studied to become a rabbi. Jacob Maris (1837–99) was noted for his atmospheric scenes of the countryside – canals and windmills seen in the rain, under and 1860) included the Tuscans Raffaello Sernesi (1838–66), Odoardo Borrani (1834–1905), Telemaco

stormy skies and scudding clouds while his brother Matthias (1839–1917) was more interested in the urban landscape, as his more spiritual nature responded to the influence of the English Pre-Raphaelites. Anton Maure (1838–88) was an original addition to the Hague School, influenced by Millet and very attached to the artistic heritage of Dutch culture. His seascapes and rural scenes feature delicate silver-gray tones and were the first models for the young van Gogh.

Jozef Israëls, When One Grows Old, c.1878. Gemeentemuseum, The Hague.

Jacob Maris, Dutch Landscape, 1890–91. Neue Pinakothek, Munich.

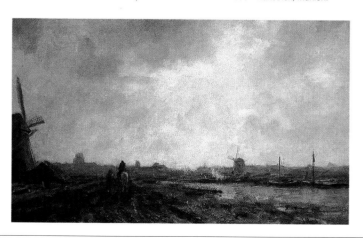

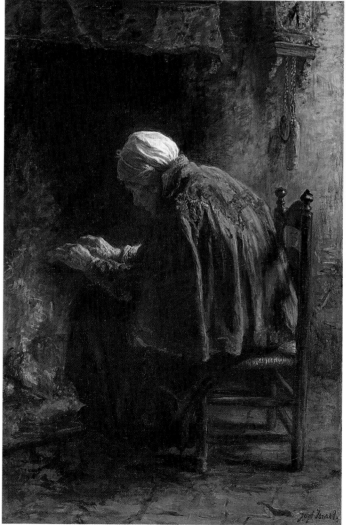

THE ART OF MENZEL

The German painter Adolf von Menzel (1815–1905) paid brief visits to Paris in 1855, 1867, and 1868, during which time he encountered the painting of Courbet. At the outbreak of the Franco-Prussian war, he affirmed his patriotism by supporting and painting William I of Prussia, the future emperor, who defeated Napoleon III and laid the foundations for a unified German nation. Menzel's canvases mirrored contemporary life in middle-class Berlin, with its crowds, street scenes, everyday happenings, and official functions. Later in his career he turned to subjects that derived from the harsher side of industrial society. Sometimes these works were laced with caustic humor or gentle malice. His technique was essentially detailed and descriptive, although occasionally it was more full-bodied, revealing the influence of French colorist brushwork.

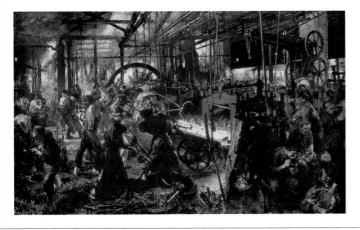

Adolf von Menzel, The Iron Rolling Mill (Modern Cyclops), *1872–75. Nationalgalerie, Berlin.*

REALISM IN THE REST OF EUROPE

The themes of Belgian Realism were partly derived from the nation's industrial revolution, which followed hot on the heels of the English model. On the one hand, this style showed the influence of French artists – Courbet's *The Stone-breakers* was exhibited in Brussels in 1851. On the other, it revived the 15th-century Flemish tradition. This second aspect emerges in the subtle landscapes and tranquil domestic interiors of Henri de Braekeleer (1840–88), whose world hinges on the silent poetry of inanimate objects. Alfred Stevens (1823–1906) also showed a feeling for the structure of objects and a shrewd awareness of everyday life, handling with virtuosity the areas of gray and backgrounds learned from Corot. His brother Joseph (1819–92) remained true to Flemish painting, specializing in animal portraiture, particularly dogs. Belgian landscape painting was centered on Tervuren, on the fringes of the forest of Soignes. Here, a group of artists headed by Baron Hippolyte Boulenger (1837–74) pledged allegiance to the Barbizon School and pursued their definition of light in bold experiments in color that verged on Impressionism and heralded the early 20th-century Belgian landscape painting of Franz Courtens (1854–1943).

In Germany, the Realist movement recalled the work of Dürer and Holbein in its search for objective truth, sometimes in a crude and harsh manner. During the second half of the 19th century, the simple realism of the Biedermeier style of art and design determined and reflected the taste of many middle-class homes. It found gloomier expression in themes inspired by the industrial landscape and new social conditions. There was fresh stimulus, too, from

SOCIAL PAINTING IN BELGIUM

Charles de Groux (1825–70) initially explored historical subjects in his paintings, but from 1848 he moved on to themes concerning social deprivation in urban and rural life. He depicted ordinary people afflicted by poverty in squalid, bleak surroundings. His paintings were marked by deep shadows and were stripped of color. There was nothing here of Daumier's ironic tone but a vein of religious mysticism that conferred a note of languishing sadness to the simplified, yet strong, decisive style modeled on Courbet. Influenced by de Groux, Constantin Meunier (1831–1905) diluted color to the point of austerity in order to document the black depths of the coal mines with their atmosphere of fumes and smoke. He also dealt with themes of this type in his series of sculptures dedicated to the lives of workers.

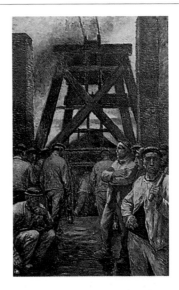

Constantin Meunier, panel of triptych The Mine, *1890–1900. Musées Royaux des Beaux-Arts, Brussels.*

Charles de Groux, Saying Grace, *1861. Musées Royaux des Beaux-Arts, Brussels.*

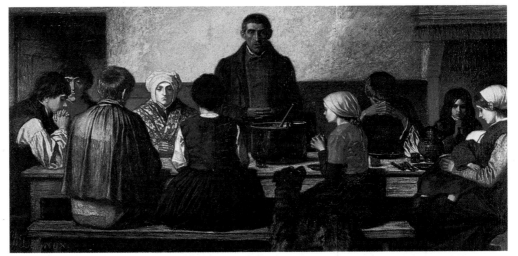

English and French painting: in 1854, Courbet exhibited in Frankfurt am Main to great acclaim; in 1869, Ludwig II of Bavaria invested him with the Cross of the Order of St. Michael.

Wilhelm Leibl (1844–1900) was influenced by Courbet, whom he met in Munich in 1869 and then followed to Paris. Leibl applied colors densely, modulating his light to achieve striking chiaroscuro effects. He subsequently added a somewhat cold, analytical touch to his work, which eventually prevailed. His rigorous technique, incisive brushstrokes, and measured calligraphy are a legacy of the German tradition. Hans Thoma (1839–1924), active in Paris in 1868, also came under the influence of Courbet and the Barbizon School. His early landscapes – usually scenes of his native Black Forest – were romantic,

with touches of the medieval manner typical of the Düsseldorf School. Later, he perfected a delicately luminous style with symbolic overtones. His experiments with light were sufficiently innovative to affect the art of Max Liebermann (1847–1935), who, during his period of realism, painted scenes of orphanages and asylums, peasants and poor people, before moving toward Impressionism in about 1890 and devoting himself to portraiture.

In Austria, too, artists took inspiration from France, paying particular attention to the romantic naturalism of the Barbizon School and Corot. Anton Romako (1832–89), apart from being an accomplished portrait painter, treated historical subjects in a some-

Hans Thoma, The Rhine at Laufenburg, *1870. Gemäldegalerie, Berlin.*

THE OPEN-AIR PAINTING OF JONGKIND AND BOUDIN

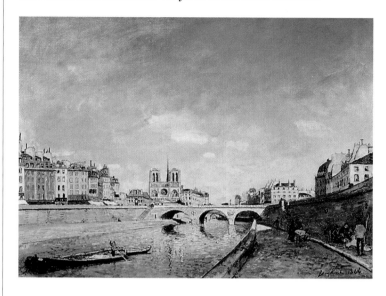

Johan Jongkind, The Seine and Notre-Dame de Paris, *1864. Musée d'Orsay, Paris.*

The touch of Romanticism that lingered on in the painting of the Barbizon School was resolutely abandoned in the work of the

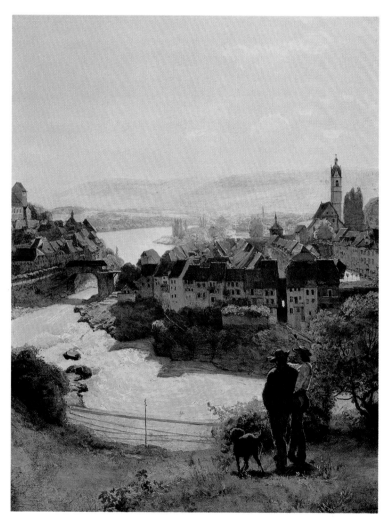

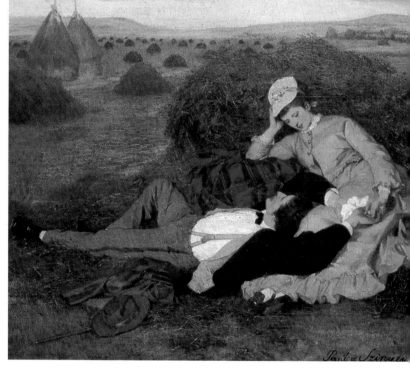

what Impressionist manner, setting events in a dramatic existential context.

An expert in melodramatic chiaroscuro, Mihály von Munkácsy (1844–1900) showed the dark, mystical aspect of the Hungarian soul. Settling in

Pál Szinyei Merse, Lovers, 1873. *National Museum, Budapest.*

Prague in 1872, he remained a romantic Realist, turning his back on Impressionism. On the other hand, Pál Szinyei Merse (1845–1920) painted *en plein*

Dutchman Johan Barthold Jongkind (1819–91), anticipating the arrival of Impressionism. He followed in the path of the Dutch Hague School, drawing and painting in the open air in the Côte-Saint-André in the Dauphiné, which he made his home. His main subjects were air and water

Eugène Boudin, The Beach at Trouville, 1864. Musée d'Orsay, Paris.

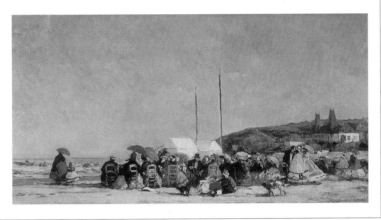

– the fleeting effects of reflected light, vibrating and dissolving in mirages, and the transparency of the water in gray seas under heavy skies. Similarly, the French artist Eugène Boudin (1824–98), whom Corot called the "master of the sea," painted the beaches and harbors of Trouville and Honfleur with freedom and immediacy of perception.

air, a method that he had learned during his trip to Paris in 1852. Typical of his work is *Lovers* (1873), with its delicate, sensitive brushstrokes.

Realism in Romania was modeled on the work of the French Barbizon School where Grigorescu (1838–1907) spent some time. An unhappy passion for Millet's daughter led the artist to return home. Grigorescu's realism took the form of systematic observation of the people and landscapes of his native land, his interest in peasant life going beyond a simple curiosity about local folklore.

Polish Realism, like that of Slovakia and Russia, had a strongly nationalistic flavor, which was concerned with social as well as political questions. The peasants of Henryk Rodakowski (1823–94) are reminiscent of those of Courbet, while Jan Matejko

(1838–93) contained his Romantic impulses in historical reconstructions of costumes and places, which in his *Battle of Grünwald* (1875–78) took the form of a large-scale nationalistic painting.

In northern Europe, there were isolated talents such as Wilhelm Eckersberg (1783–1853). He revived Danish painting in 1820 by founding an open-air school, where artists were encouraged to capture the transitory effects of light outside as opposed to the still artificial light of the studio. Stimulated by the teaching of Eckersberg, Christen Købke (1810–48) brought a profound sense of realism and truth to his precise observations of life in the Danish provinces north of Copenhagen. Mist and cloud envelop his motionless, melancholy figures in a mystical evocation of atmosphere.

THE RUSSIAN ITINERANTS

Realism in Russia was tinged with the mysticism of mankind's divine and eternal suffering. In St. Petersburg and Moscow, a nationalistic form of painting emerged that was only margin-

Ilya Repin, They Did Not Expect Him, 1884. Tretiakov Gallery, Moscow.

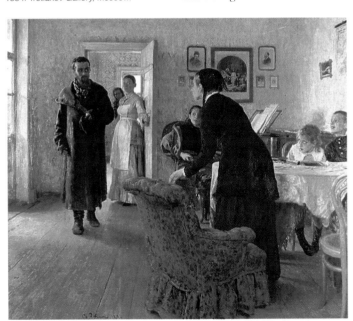

ally influenced by the French example (even though artists, such as Perov and Repin, visited Paris). In his essay the *Aesthetic Relationship between Art and Reality* (1865), Chernyshevski chose to regard the real as superior to the make-believe, and declared that the purpose of art was to educate and emancipate. The new generation of artists

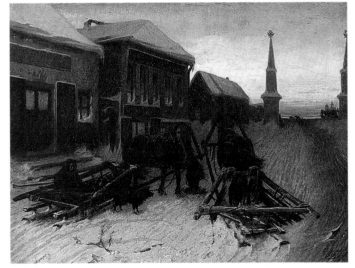

Vasili Perov, The Last Tavern by the City Gates, 1868. Tretiakov Gallery, Moscow.

reacted against the official institutions; in 1863, they established an avant-garde group called the Society of Wandering (Traveling) Exhibitions, which took its name from the exhibitions organized periodically in various parts of Russia. There was a revival of religious and historical painting: in the art of Vasili Surikov (1848–1916), scenes of the past

contained contemporary elements alluding to social and political issues.

The same feature is found in the portraits of Vasili Perov (1834–82), who had become familiar with the work of Courbet and Meissonier in Paris, and in the Russian landscape scenes of Isaak Levitan (1860–1900). Meanwhile, Ilya Repin (1844–1930) revealed a freshness in his representations of people in crowds and in groups.

A NEW APPROACH TO THE RELIGIOUS SUBJECT

During the period of Realism, religious painting became much less dogmatic and no longer specifically illustrated events of the Church. The church calendar and the act of worship were used in a contextual sense, rather than as subjects in their own right. In his painting of the Angelus (a Roman Catholic prayer recited three times a day at morning, noon, and sunset), Millet aimed to convey a general idea of poverty and suffering that reflected the lives of the French farmers and peasants of the early 19th century. Religious painting assumed a regional character in the *Angelus* (1859) of Alphonse Legros (1837–1911), which was praised by Charles Baudelaire at the Salon of 1859 for its genuine portrayal of faith and goodness in country folk. A laical attitude is also expressed in *Three Women in Church*, by Wilhelm Leibl, where the artist dwells attentively, almost obsessively, on ordinary details, from aprons to headdresses. The portraits of the worshipers are drawn with an unwavering objectivity, with the faces of these women expressing the age-old ways of country life.

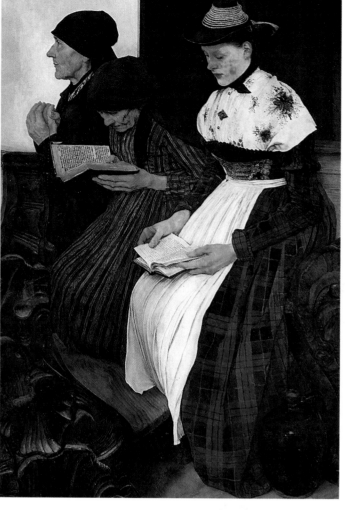

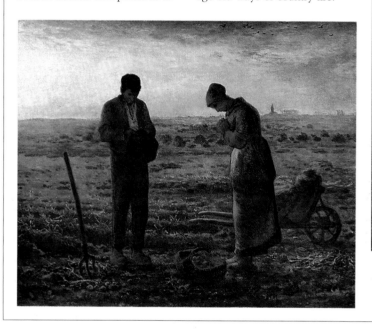

Jean-François Millet, The Angelus, 1857–59. Musée d'Orsay, Paris.

Wilhelm Leibl, Three Women in Church, 1878–82. Kunsthalle, Hamburg.

Carl Fredrik Hill, Landscape on the Seine, 1877. Nationalmuseum, Stockholm.

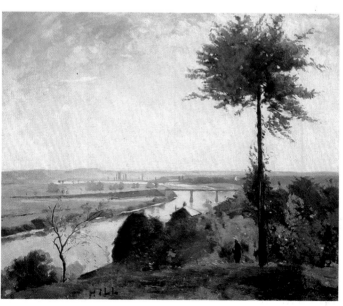

In Sweden, Ernst Josephson (1851–1906) painted portraits characterized by honesty and a touch of irony. He used bold brushwork to imbue the portraits with vitality. With the onset of madness in 1889, however, his figures took on fantastical proportions. The genuine vein of Carl Fredrik Hill (1849–1911), inspired by Corot, was tinged with sentimentality, his landscapes rendered in intense color ranges. On a journey to Paris in 1876, he, too, succumbed to madness.

REALISM IN THE UNITED STATES

The realism that developed in the US was quite distinct from that seen in Europe. While many American artists embraced the concrete and the tangible in their paintings, they also created a strong sense of idealism. Thus the naturalistic renderings of virgin forests and undefiled landscapes of the artists of Hudson River School were sometimes obscured by mysticism. George Caleb Bingham (1811–79) embraced realist concepts inasmuch as he

SATIRICAL MAGAZINES

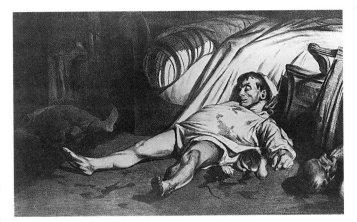

Honoré Daumier, Rue Transnonain, le 15 avril 1834, *lithograph, 1834. British Museum, London.*

As printing techniques were developed in the 19th century, satirical journals became very popular. In England, Charles Keene (1823–91) produced work for *Punch*, while in Germany, Adolf Oberländer (1845–1923) created cartoons for *Fliegende Blätter*. The Russian-born Emmanuel Poiré (1859–1909), better known as Caran d'Ache (from the Russian *karandash*, meaning pencil), worked for numerous French publications. He founded the magazine *Psst!* (1898–99) with Jean-Louis Forain (1852–1931), whose style was more fierce than his own. Forain's work also featured in the *Journal amusant, Courrier Français* and, later, *Figaro* (1914–20). Théophile-Alexandre Steinlen

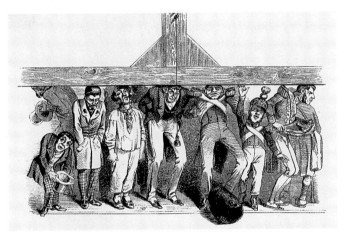

Jean Gérard known as Grandville (1803–47), Human Leveling: the Dream of the Mediocre.

(1859–1923) depicted subjects ranging from Parisian suburbs to feline habits, in magazines such as *Le Mirliton* and *Gil Blas illustré*. The Realists made many brilliant etchings, including

those by Alphonse Legros and James Tissot (1836–1902), who produced faithful representations of contemporary life. The Belgian Félicien Rops (1833–98) began as an illustrator and editor of the *Uylenspiegel*, the political-satirical magazine that he founded. In 1875 Rops founded the International Society of Engravers. His work, ranging from the grotesque to the profane and licentious, had a influence on James Ensor.

of the North Atlantic was celebrated by Winslow Homer (1836–1910) in his famous marine paintings, executed during the 1890s at Prout's Neck in Maine. Homer, who had exhibited among the works representing American art at the Paris Exposition of 1867, expressed his attitude to his art in the words, "When I have selected the thing carefully, I paint it exactly as it appears." Homer's contemporary Thomas Eakins embodied the scientific interest of his generation; he constructed elaborate models and prepared detailed sketches to ensure the accuracy of his pictures. This disciplined naturalism was at odds with the immediacy sought by such artists as those of the Barbizon School. Still-life painting flourished in the US. The works of Martin Johnson Heade (1819–1904), who painted the flora and fauna of his native land, and Joseph Decker (1853–1924) are representative of the preoccupation with visual realism, which climaxed in the *trompe l'oeil* works of William Michael Harnett (1848–92).

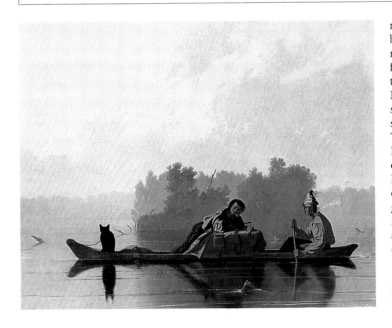

George Caleb Bingham, Fur Traders Descending the Missouri, *1845. Metropolitan Museum of Art, New York.*

represented the commonplace, but his work also displays a romantic influence. He was fascinated by the traders and travelers who navigated the Missouri in their flatboats: strong, purposeful figures in silent, light-filled settings. The Swiss-born artist Frank Buchser (1828–90) recorded the exploits of the North American Indians and the confrontations of Union and Confederate generals in the Civil War. Meanwhile, the sometimes spectacular heroism and courage of the fishermen

HUDSON RIVER SCHOOL

The pride of Americans in their homeland and their desire to celebrate the original features of that virgin territory gained new impetus between 1825 and 1875 in the work of the Hudson River School. It was by no means a local movement, and scenes of the Hudson River landscape were interspersed with those of rivers, mountains, and valleys from all over the country. Thomas Cole (1801–48), who left England for America in 1818, had a poetic and religious feeling for nature. His painting owed more to the imagination than to reality, and his infinite expanses of luminous sky and lofty mountains are reflections of human emotions. Frederick E. Church (1826–1900), a pupil of Cole, traveled beyond his native land, painting not only the Niagara Falls but also little-known sites in South America. Church's emphasis on light created a balance between the solid and the transient, between substance and atmosphere, transforming the subject into apocalyptic, romantic visions. Also important was George Inness (1825–94), whose youthful works show the influence of the Barbizon School in the skillful rendering of light.

THE IMPRESSIONISTS

In the feverish cultural climate of Paris in the 1860s, a group of about 30 artists began to experiment with a new form of expression. They were to go down in history as the Impressionists, their work marking the frontier between modern art and that of their own time. Today, Impressionist paintings are among the most admired and sought-after in the world.

Impressionism did not arise from any specific theory or manifesto. It was more the result of certain artists sharing the same ideas at a particular moment in French history, when the climate helped spread and establish a new style of painting. The movement, with its distinctive artistic style, evolved in quite a complex way. The first signs of its development appeared in the early 1860s, but a collective consciousness was not evident until the period between 1867 and 1869. The motivating force behind Impressionism was the desire of a small number of artists to approach painting in a way completely opposed to that practiced in the official, sacrosanct surroundings of the Parisian institution, the Salon. The artists, who were of widely differing personalities and from a variety of schools, found themselves embarking separately, and quite instinctively, on a new style. The subject matter, techniques, and artistic language of their work were all features that were to set Impressionism quite clearly apart from the traditional world of academic art.

A SHORT-LIVED MOVEMENT

In the late 1860s, three artists – Monet, Renoir, and Pissarro – formed the habit of going to sit on the banks of the Seine

THE FEMALE FIGURE IN IMPRESSIONISM

Almost all Monet's models were female. They were not erotic figures, but forms that captured certain myths – scenes of lost childhood, for example, or of an idyllic garden where women wore sweeping dresses and held parasols that cast shadows over the lush grass. They bring touches of life to the canvas and seem to embrace and regenerate the very essence of being. There is nothing more feminine – and less sensual – than his *Woman with a Parasol* (1875).

Very different from such gentle portrayals was Manet's *Olympia*, a work that caused a great scandal. Shown at the Salon in 1865, it continued the long tradition of the reclining nude, and the composition was based

Edgar Degas, Little Dancer Aged Fourteen Years, 1880. Tate Gallery, London.

Edouard Manet, Olympia, 1863. Musée d'Orsay, Paris.

directly on Titian's *Venus of Urbino*. However, the work was condemned as an outrage to public morality for its brazen portrayal of a courtesan and its glorification of the flesh, said to be almost unreal in its whiteness. Later revived and reinterpreted by Cézanne (1869 and 1873), Picasso (1901), Dubuffet (1950), and Pop artist Larry Rivers (1970), *Olympia* remains

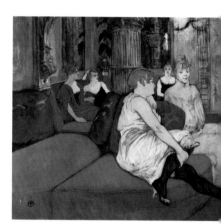

Henri de Toulouse-Lautrec, In the Salon at the Rue des Moulins, 1894. Musée Toulouse-Lautrec, Albi, France.

one of the most celebrated paintings of the period. After Manet's experience, Toulouse-Lautrec was more cautious in showing his risqué works. He presented a collection with great discretion at the Galerie Manzi-Joyant in 1896, because "it could be thought that I want to create a scandal." The theme of the loneliness of women in their most private and intimate moments is explored by

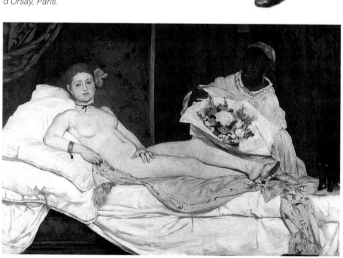

and Oise to paint the country-side. Of paramount interest to them was the reflection of light on the river; it seemed to be constantly moving and giving life to the water. The many colors revealed in the reflections gave them the idea of painting light by applying bands of opposing colors, without using dark tones for the shadows. With this in mind, they brightened up their palettes and divided up the different shades, unaware that they were applying the theory of complementary colors. No particular date marks the birth of the Impressionist movement, although the year 1869 was certainly significant. It was then that Monet and Renoir both painted at La Grenouillère, the open-air café and bathing resort near Bougival. Each completed works that are now viewed as landmarks of early Impressionism. However, it was not until 1874, after a long and arduous quest to master this new means of

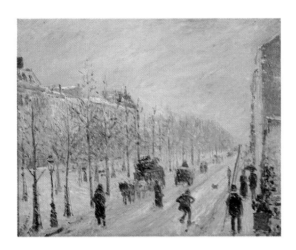

Camille Pissarro, The Outer Boulevards: Snow, *1879. Musée Marmottan, Paris. During this period, Cézanne visited Pissarro in Pontoise. The contact between the two made Pissarro more aware of the sculptural value of composition.*

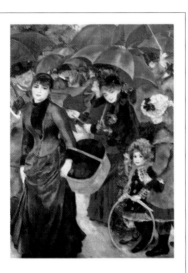

Pierre-Auguste Renoir, The Umbrellas, *1879. National Gallery, London.*

Degas, both in his painting and sculpture. Renoir, on the other hand, glorified the female form, highlighting the ripeness of its curves by bathing women in a soft light full of colors.

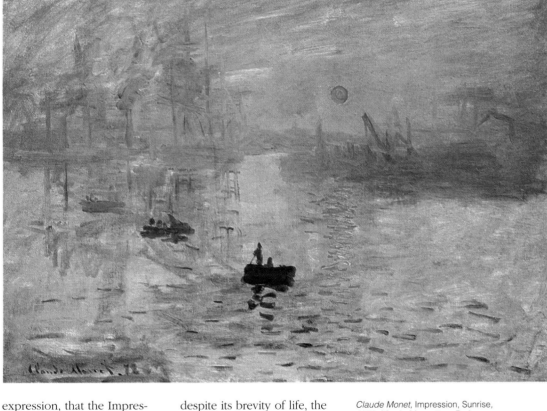

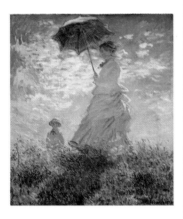

Claude Monet, Woman with a Parasol, *1875. National Gallery of Art, Washington, DC.*

expression, that the Impressionists exhibited their work in public for the first time. By 1880, just six years after that first show, the group had already broken up. It is possible that the process of setting down an "impression" of a scene in a spontaneous, clear, and objective way required a naïve and enthusiastic approach that was, by its very nature, quickly lost. What is clear is that Impressionism occupies an remarkably short period of time in the history of art. Yet despite its brevity of life, the achievements of its artists in these few years are of incalculable importance.

Claude Monet, Impression, Sunrise, *1872. Musée Marmottan, Paris.*

THE PIONEERS OF IMPRESSIONISM

Among the leading Impressionists was Camille Pissarro (1830–1903). Born on the island of St. Thomas in the West Indies to a Creole mother and a Jewish father of Spanish

CAMILLE PISSARRO

The Creole of the Impressionists, Pissarro started drawing as a child in Venezuela. In France, he pursued an active, artistic life, preferring Rouen, Dieppe, and other towns to the capital that so inspired the other artists. His career followed a course of continuous artistic experimentation, which placed him closest to Seurat among the Impressionists. He produced mainly *plein air* paintings of rural landscapes and urban views.

CLAUDE MONET: "GARE SAINT-LAZARE"

1877; oil on canvas;
23½ x 39¼ in (60 x 100 cm);
Musée d'Orsay, Paris.

Monet painted Gare Saint-Lazare many times, displaying seven variations of the subject at the Impressionist exhibition of 1877. This famous railroad station held a particular appeal for the Impressionists and was a constant source of inspiration for their paintings. It was a place of movement and bustle, with its rapid interweaving of figures and forms. In practical terms, it provided a vital link between the capital and the countryside locations frequented by the artists. For Monet in particular, the sources of interest were many: the metallic structures of the buildings and trains, the transparency of the glass roof, and the turbulent effects of the smoke and steam. The central theme of this painting is not the play of light on the architecture and other elements but the way the smoke and steam interact with these strong, yet ethereal, structures.

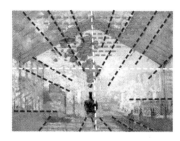

▲ *1. It does not take long to realize that this painting is unusual for an Impressionist work. The view is frontal, there is a vertical axis in the middle of the picture, and at about mid-height to this the imaginary line that links the ends of the roof pitches makes a horizontal axis. These axes are almost perfectly symmetrical. The smoke and the engine are the two main elements on which the composition is founded. At the bottom, on either side of the locomotive, clouds of steam indicate that the train is moving slowly. Bands of lines converge behind the train, emphasizing that the locomotive is coming toward the viewer.*

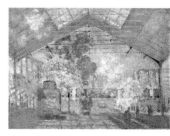

▲ *2. In the background, beyond the station building and its angular roof, the space is a whirl of colors. The yellow, the white and pink tones, the soft greens, and the grays flecked with blue and red form an amalgam of lighter tones of the spectrum. The large buildings do not stand out from the vaporous atmosphere but are hazily perceived in a ferment of colors. Their mass is systematically dematerialized by Monet's typical commalike brushstrokes of bright color. Alternatively, the eye of the viewer could also follow the opposite course, distinguishing the impression of the edifice from the cloud of smoke obscuring the sky.*

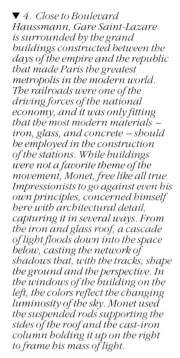

▼ *4. Close to Boulevard Haussmann, Gare Saint-Lazare is surrounded by the grand buildings constructed between the days of the empire and the republic that made Paris the greatest metropolis in the modern world. The railroads were one of the driving forces of the national economy, and it was only fitting that the most modern materials – iron, glass, and concrete – should be employed in the construction of the stations. While buildings were not a favorite theme of the movement, Monet, free like all true Impressionists to go against even his own principles, concerned himself here with architectural detail, capturing it in several ways. From the iron and glass roof, a cascade of light floods down into the space below, casting the network of shadows that, with the tracks, shape the ground and the perspective. In the windows of the building on the left, the colors reflect the changing luminosity of the sky. Monet used the suspended rods supporting the sides of the roof and the cast-iron column holding it up on the right to frame his mass of light.*

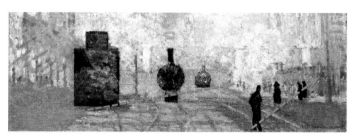

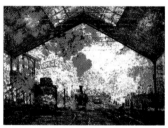

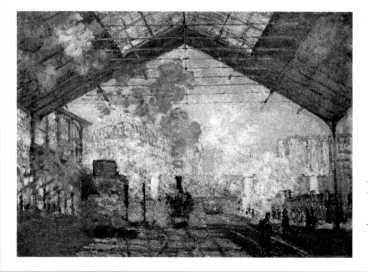

▲ *3. Scanning the picture across its middle from the left side, we see the station building, a train carriage, an engine, and, in the distance, a train billowing steam. The carriage is not moving, and its solid mass is more sharply defined on the right-hand side by the luminous background. In the middle ground, we see a moving engine. Its black metallic mass is enlivened and strengthened by blue reflections. To the right of the engine, some soldiers or railroad workers walk between the tracks, while on the platform the colorfully dressed passengers await the arrival of the incoming locomotive. No emphasis has been given to the human figures, and they have less presence in the painting than the station building, seen foreshortened on the left in the foreground.*

▼ *5. In the background, and in particular to the right, the space seems to be free of any structure. Flowing shapes and volumes formed by iridescent clouds, smoke, and vapor make up the substance of the painting. The encounter between the new architecture and an Impressionist painting is lost in the vague distance.*

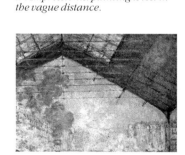

origin, he always painted his exotic canvases in strong and lively colors. He never attempted to portray the lightness of air and water but remained attached to the solidity of his subject matter. His preoccupations with the

rules of composition led him to depict three-dimensional space with minute, separate dots, a technique that would form the heart of pointillism and divisionism. Uncompromising, tenacious, and an anarchist, he was the oldest

of the Impressionists and therefore had some authority in the eyes of the other artists – Cézanne said of him: "He is a man to consult; he is a bit like God."
A participant in all the Impressionist exhibitions,

Pissarro promoted and defended the movement from the beginning, claiming: "The Impressionists are in the right, supporting a solid art based on sensations, and it is an honest viewpoint."
Widely considered to be the

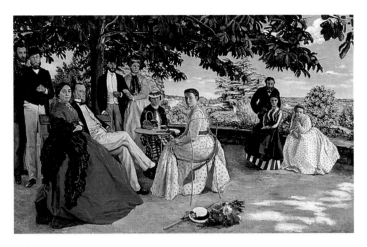

Frédéric Bazille, Family Reunion, *1867–68. Musée d'Orsay, Paris.*

most consistent of the Impressionist group, Alfred Sisley (1839–99) was born in Paris of English parents. He devoted himself almost exclusively to landscapes, mostly painting the countryside to the west of Paris, where he lived. His work was dominated by images of the River Seine, the floodwaters at Port-Marly, rows of poplars, reflections on the snow, and the delicate mist that hung over the fields. The sky was an important element in his work, and he employed various techniques to create a sky that "would not be simply a background." His canvases were not highly esteemed during his lifetime and were less respected than those of the other Impressionists. Little by little his paintings lost their vitality, becoming less interesting and more simplistic.

Claude Monet (1840–1926), the painter most faithful to his

visual sensations, was described by Cézanne as "Only an eye but my God, what an eye!" It was Monet who encouraged the other members of the group to paint out of doors. His canvas exhibited at the first Impressionist show in 1874 was called *Impression, Sunrise*, which prompted

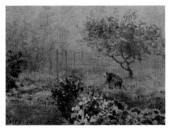

Alfred Sisley, Foggy Morning, *1874. Musée du Louvre, Paris.*

the journalist Louis Leroy to label the whole group the "Impressionists." In Monet's works, form is lost in the quest to depict light. The artist took this to such extremes that he went beyond merely transcribing what he saw: with vague shapes for subjects and colors broken up into thousands of gradations, his paintings verged on the abstract. Together with Monet and Pissarro, Pierre-Auguste Renoir (1841–1919) was one of the first to spread the doctrine of

Impressionism at the end of the 1860s. He filled his canvases with a steady, diffused light, bringing figures and landscapes together under one rhythmic and constant source of illumination. In 1881, he visited Rome, where he found "the wisdom of Raphael," who "like me, looks for the impossible." Impressionism, the "impossible" undertaking

WIND AND SMOKE

Capturing the most intangible elements on canvas constituted the greatest challenge for the Impressionists. For them, everything could be represented – snow, mist, fog, heat, even the

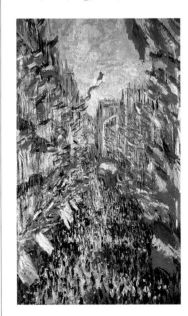

Claude Monet, Rue Montorgueil, *1878. Musée d'Orsay, Paris.*

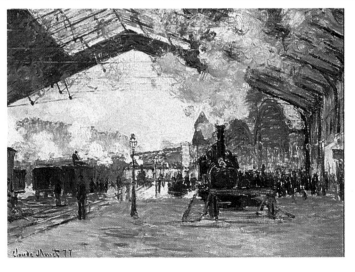

Claude Monet, Gare Saint-Lazare, *1877. Art Institute of Chicago.*

way the wind made shapes in the flags of *Rue Montorgueil* (1878). "Why not a scene of Negroes fighting in a tunnel?", Monet asked his critics, who maintained that fog was not a suitable subject for painting. Gare Saint-Lazare, where the trains from the northern suburbs arrived – "so full of smoke as to make it barely possible to see" – provided particularly challenging material for him; he opted for an approach completely opposed

to the bright, sunlit scenes of the most typical *plein air* art. Mistaking him for a famous painter of the Salon, the superintendent of the Western Railway gave Monet a grand welcome. He stopped all the trains, had all platforms cleared, and filled the locomotives with coal so that they could emit plenty of the artist's precious smoke.

EDOUARD MANET

After several failed attempts to get into the navy, Manet took up painting and studied under Thomas Couture, a famous academic painter of the day. He visited Brazil, Belgium, Holland, Italy, Austria, and Germany and was influenced by the Old Masters, particularly those of the golden ages of Spanish and Venetian painting. His work began to cause controversy in 1863, yet he became the most recognized figure in the Impressionist group, bringing to them his idea of "pure painting."

that seemed to challenge the very shape of nature, found in Renoir's work a unique, structural solidity in his depiction of young women. These figures became increasingly more imposing but were graceful and softly lit:

"I believe I have been able to achieve the grandeur of Antiquity," he declared. Friend of Renoir, Monet, and Sisley, Frédéric Bazille (1841–70) was never a fully committed Impressionist. "I wish to give each subject its own weight and volume and not paint only outward appearances," he said. Tragically, Bazille's career was cut short when he was killed in action during the Franco-Prussian war.

Armand Guillaumin (1841–1927) displayed works at all the Impressionist exhibitions except those of 1876 and 1879. His palette became increasingly brilliant and unnatural. The vivid colors were arranged in sharp contrasts, similar to those found

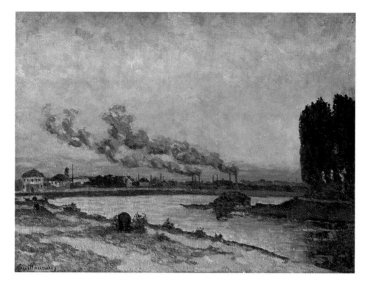

in the work of Paul Gauguin. Berthe Morisot (1841–95), the daughter of wealthy parents and a descendant of the

Armand Guillaumin, Sunset at Ivry, 1873. The artist painted many landscapes, in vivid, contrasting colors en plein air around Paris and along the River Seine.

THE JAPANESE INFLUENCE

The fashion for *japonaiserie* started in France. In 1881, despite the policy of closure that Japan had followed since 1639 (the year in which the governor of Tokugawa completely shut off the country from all Western contact), there appeared in Paris four volumes by Breton on Japanese culture, entitled *Le Japon, ou moeurs, usages et coutumes des habitants de cet empire.* In 1856, Félix Bracquemond had discovered a number of prints by Hokusai (1760–1849) that had been used to wrap up china. Very soon,

enthusiasm for Japanese art spread and began to influence many of the Impressionists. Degas, Manet, Renoir, Pissarro, de Nittis, Gauguin, and Toulouse-Lautrec painted on linen fans in the Japanese style; their wives were portrayed in kimonos and oriental costumes; and Monet designed a Japanese bridge for his garden at Giverny. In 1862, a shop called *La Porte Chinoise* ("The Chinese Door") opened under the arches in the Rue de Rivoli. Whistler shopped there for his blue-and-white china and Japanese costumes, and Manet, Fantin-Latour, Baudelaire, and the Goncourt brothers also visited the

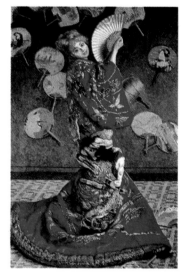

Claude Monet, La Japonaise, 1875–76. Museum of Fine Arts, Boston.

proprietors, M. and Mme. Desoye. Japanese influence on Impressionist art was neither a question of style nor merely the result of curiosity in new and exotic subjects. It was a genuine discovery that helped confirm and shape new artistic ideas. Subjects were viewed from different, unconventional angles, and perspective from a single viewpoint – as practiced in Western art since the Renaissance – was now abandoned. Figures were now depicted at the edge

of, or even leaving, the canvas. In 1890, Pissarro wrote: "The Japanese exhibition is admirable…. I, Monet, and Rodin were very enthusiastic. I'm happy with my effects of snow and floods. These artists have shown that we are right in the way we see nature."

Monet was clearly inspired by Japanese prints for his *La Japonaise* (1875–76). The pose of his wife Camille, with her head tilted and her back curving, the shape of the kimono fastened behind and swirling out at the hem in a great sweep, and the strong colors contrasting with the silk embroidery covering the

Edouard Manet, The Woman with the Fans, 1873. Musée d'Orsay, Paris.

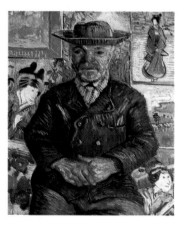

Vincent van Gogh, Portrait of Père Tanguy, 1887. Niarchos Collection, Athens.

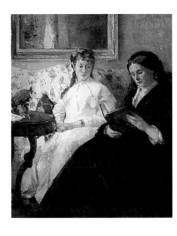

Berthe Morisot, Portrait of the Artist's Mother and Sister, *1869–70. National Gallery of Art, Washington, DC.*

their shows and, in 1868, met Edouard Manet, who became her teacher and close friend. She later married his brother Eugène. The two artists influenced each other greatly, and it was Morisot who persuaded Manet to experiment with the "rainbow palette" of the Impressionists. In her own work, she never used the group's trademark short, broken brushstrokes but retained her own delicate, feathery technique. Morisot's women – reading, cooking, and tending to children – are solid forms with great presence, not figures swept away by the passing moment. Edouard Manet (1832–83) was in many ways separate from the Impressionists. The son of a Paris magistrate, he was a

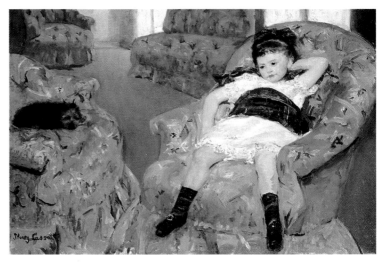

Mary Cassatt, The Blue Room, *1878. National Gallery of Art, Washington, DC. Cassatt, whose favorite themes were women and children, came in contact with Impressionism after meeting Degas in 1887.*

painter Fragonard, exhibited regularly at the official Salon before opting enthusiastically to join the Impressionists. She took part in all but one of

a Japanese screen behind him and oriental prints on the wall. He arranged the writing desk and the objects around the writer in parallel bands with no perspective, following the technique of polychromatic wood-printing.
Also deeply inspired by the composition of Japanese art was Whistler, who produced his *Nocturne in Blue and Gold: Old Battersea Bridge* (1872–75) after seeing Hiroshige's *Edo Bridge,* from his series *One Hundred Views of Edo* (1857).

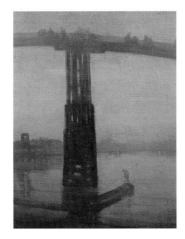

Edouard Manet, Portrait of Emile Zola, *c.1868. Musée d'Orsay, Paris.*

center of the garment all pay homage to the East. But Camille's innocence is a foil for Shok, an aristocratic warrior embroidered on her kimono. He is portrayed by Monet as a grotesque dwarf with a broken sword, warding off the devil. There is a sharp link between the model with her open fan and the background covered with other fans, which accords with the rules of *ukiyo-e* ("pictures of the floating world") in its connection between figure and flat space. Meanwhile, Manet painted Zola seated with

James Abbot McNeill Whistler, Nocturne in Blue and Gold: Old Battersea Bridge, *1872–75. Tate Gallery, London.*

HILAIRE GERMAIN EDGAR DEGAS

The son of a wealthy family of landowners, Degas initially studied law. In 1855, however, he entered the Ecole des Beaux-Arts. Between 1854 and 1859, he traveled in Italy and found himself enthralled by the early Renaissance painters. He began by painting mythological and historical subjects and a number of large-scale portraits, before his encounter with Manet and the other artists in the Café Guerbois. He later joined the Impressionists, though he always remained an artist who preferred painting indoors in neatly defined surroundings than *en plein air.* Degas turned to sculpting in his old age when his eyesight had seriously deteriorated. His famous bronze figures were cast from the wax models that were left in his studio after his death.

fashionable, urbane gentleman painter and friend of the poets Mallarmé and Baudelaire. He sought the approval of the most influential critics and recognition from the official Salon and found their constant rejection very upsetting. In terms of influence, Manet owed his masterly handling of pigment, known as *peinture claire,* to Courbet and Velázquez. Later, Japanese art had a deep impact on his work, and his subjects,

often finished in the studio, became more unreal and flattened. The color was spread directly over the white canvas, with none of the half-tones of the academic painter. His first one-man exhibition, held in 1863 at the Galerie Marinet, was an important event for the Impressionists, who in the same year exhibited at the Salon des Refusés. In the 1870s Manet, influenced by Morisot, had more contact with the group. Leaving his studio to paint outdoors, his work became lighter and more spontaneous, capturing with immediacy the farewells at a port in *Departure of the Folkestone Boat* (1868–71) and catching the sparkle of the water in *The Seine at Argenteuil* (1874). Although a regular participant in their exhibitions, Edgar Degas (1834–1917) never considered himself a true Impressionist, claiming, "There is nothing less spontaneous than my art." The son of a wealthy banker and a Creole woman, he found early inspiration in the work of the Renaissance masters. He preferred painting in his studio to out of doors and favored artificial light over sunlight – he found it highlighted the movements of his famous ballerinas.
Mary Cassatt (1844–1926), from an American banking family with French ancestors, shared with her friend Degas a special love for drawing. She exhibited with the

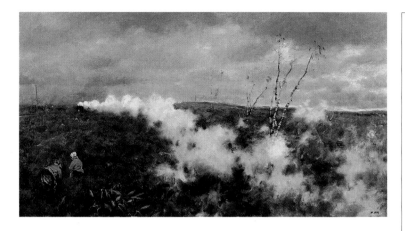

Giuseppe de Nittis, Passing Train, *1869. Museo Civile, Barletta. An Italian painter, de Nittis settled in Paris in 1867 and exhibited with the Impressionists in 1874.*

Impressionists for the first time in 1879. Her linear style and talent for combining separate elements led her to the creation of the colored lithographs and engravings that are among her most successful works. Giuseppe de Nittis (1846–84), a friend of Degas, Manet, Caillebotte, and Toulouse-Lautrec, participated in the first Impressionist exhibition of 1874 with five paintings. His scenes depicting the elegant society of Parisian life and his impressions of London were a great success. In 1878 he was awarded the Legion of Honor. Paul Cézanne (1839–1906) exhibited with the Impressionists in 1874 and 1877 but, like Degas, never identified himself with the group or wholly embraced their ideas. With the exception of Pissarro, with whom he shared a long and productive friendship, they did not completely understand him. When Cézanne started painting, his art was romantic, heroic, and erotic. Initially, he used thick, dark paint, but after meeting some of the group, his palette became lighter. Rather than catching fleeting impressions and the transient effects of light, he preferred to contemplate his subject in order to produce more structured, balanced, and geometric compositions. He gave up his brush for a palette knife, which was better

suited to reproducing the mass and volume of his subjects, and forgot about painting atmospheres. Toward the end of his life, he returned to his home town, Aix-en-Provence, to paint nature "in the sphere, the cone, and the cylinder." He concentrated on landscapes, particularly views of Mont Sainte-Victoire, and claimed: "One must learn to paint from these simple forms; one will then be able to do whatever one wishes." Also difficult to classify as true Impressionists are the French artist and collector Gustave Caillebotte (1848–94), who painted contemporary life in a classical style, and Henri de Toulouse-Lautrec (1864–1901), whose subjects reveal a genuine sense of tragedy.

LIGHT AND SHADOW

Monet intended his unfinished *Déjeuner sur l'herbe* as a sort of painting manifesto of his own ideas. He had hoped to submit it to the 1866 Salon but missed the deadline and abandoned the project in the same year. The first attempts to depict light shining and filtering through foliage and flooding onto the objects below can be seen. The figures are fragmentary, and the light falls from the foliage and spreads shadows onto the white of the tablecloth. The *plein air* painters believed that the color of shade was influenced by the surrounding colors and therefore must shine with a thousand

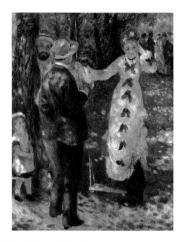

tones and not be strengthened by the use of blacks. This conviction is at the center of such masterpieces as Renoir's *La Balançoire* (1876), in which the variation of light among the trees rustling in the breeze of a summer's afternoon determined the relationship of light and shade. The reflections infuse life and movement into the surface of subjects. The shadows of the trees fall in patches on the clothes, faces, tree trunks, and the pathway of colored spots, and the effect was considered by some critics to be too "daring."

Pierre-Auguste Renoir, La Balançoire, *1876. Musée d'Orsay, Paris.*

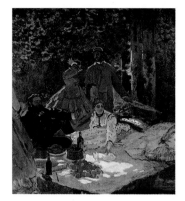

Claude Monet, Déjeuner sur l'herbe, *(detail), 1865–66. Musée d'Orsay, Paris.*

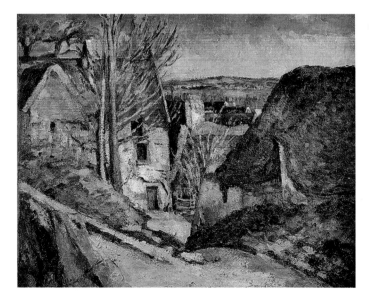

Paul Cézanne, The House of the Hanged Man, *1873. Musée d'Orsay, Paris. Exhibited in 1874 at the first Impressionist show, this was the first picture sold by the painter to a collector, the landowner Armand Doria.*

VARIOUS KINDS OF IMPRESSIONISM

The key protagonists of Impressionism did not work according to any program or plan, nor did they have any preconceived ideas. In fact, they felt liberated and free: Renoir boasted that he did not know from one day to the next what he was going to paint, while Monet claimed he painted just like a bird sings. Although the Impressionists remained a harmonious group, all the artists connected with the movement spent a significant amount of time working independently, resolving any problems they came up against each according to his

PAUL CEZANNE

In 1861, at the age of 22, Cézanne made his first trip to Paris. He then spent a year in Aix-en-Provence as an apprentice in the family bank before returning to Paris, where he met Pissarro. He became involved in Parisian artistic life and from 1874 took part, although on the fringe, in the Impressionists' struggle for recognition. By the end of the century, he was already thought of as a master "apart." In 1907, a year after his death, the retrospective exhibition in Paris confirmed him as one of the greatest artists of all time. In the 20th century, he became a model for figurative and nonfigurative painters concerned with the depiction of volume.

or her own instincts. Even the writer Zola, a friend of Cézanne and great supporter of Manet and Impressionism, could not quite grasp what it was that unified the group. In his articles in *L'Evénement* he tried in vain to find the right definition. There was certainly much discussion about their work among the Parisian painters at the Café Taranne and Café Guerbois, but this almost always proved sterile. "Don't ask me whether a painting should be objective or subjective. I couldn't care less," Renoir would say, uninterested in confronting the stylistic problems that obsessed Cézanne or Seurat.

PUBLIC DISAPPROVAL

At first, Impressionist paintings were not favorably received. To the conservative Parisian public, they appeared unfinished, like mere impromptu sketches. Traditionalists were not about to forgive the artists for what they saw as the destruction of traditional, aesthetic ideals and the introduction of the coarse vulgarity of everyday life into art, without any qualms about the value of their subject matter. In their large canvases, painted *en plein air*, the Impressionists depicted picturesque and sentimental subjects in their paintings. It was therefore difficult for the spectator to find any real

"message" in the images. Initially, the Impressionists were disliked by art critics – Leroy used the term "Impressionist" with derision rather than admiration – and were unpopular with the conservative regime of

Napoleon III. Having been rejected by the Salon, they exhibited in the Salon des Refusés at the adjacent Palais de l'Industrie in 1863, which had been founded by the emperor himself. Attention was focused on the then

scandalous, but today highly admired, *Déjeuner sur l'herbe* by Manet, the work that inspired Monet to start painting his large, unfinished work of the same name in 1865. In 1873, the Impressionists were again forced to exhibit at the

MONET AND WATER

The appearance of water in Monet's work varies according to the location, the light, and the weather. For example, in *The Terrace at Sainte-Adresse* (1867) and *The Seine at Argenteuil* (1875), there are rippling waves, while in Monet's first attempts at *La Grenouillère* (1869), the water is bright with the reflections of boats and trees. At this riverside spot, Monet and Renoir abandoned traditional, solid, compact forms in favor of fragmented brushstrokes and vibrant colors.

In *La Grenouillère*, depth is suggested by the diminishing figures and the sharp diagonals of the boats, the restaurant, and the walkways. Monet was taking on the difficult task of combining the perspective of the buildings with the flat surface of the water. Sisley solved the problem in *Flood at Port-Marly* (1876) by making space almost undetectable, merging sky, earth, and water into a single mass. In his *Waterlilies* series, Monet went further still: the water loses

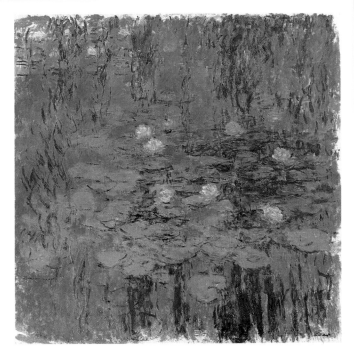

Claude Monet, Waterlilies, 1916–19, *Musée d'Orsay, Paris.*

its identity and can no longer be recognized, appearing thick and saturated with plant life. The absence of shore and horizon also helps give these compositions the illusion of a solid whole.

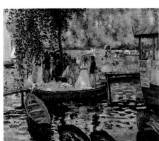

Pierre-Auguste Renoir, La Grenouillère, *1869. National Museum, Stockholm.*

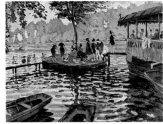

Claude Monet, La Grenouillère, *1869. Metropolitan Museum of Art, New York.*

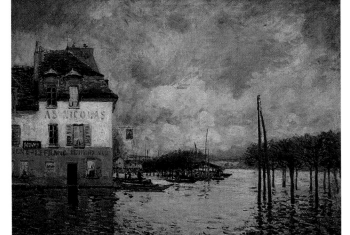

Alfred Sisley, Flood at Port-Marly, *1876. Musée d'Orsay, Paris.*

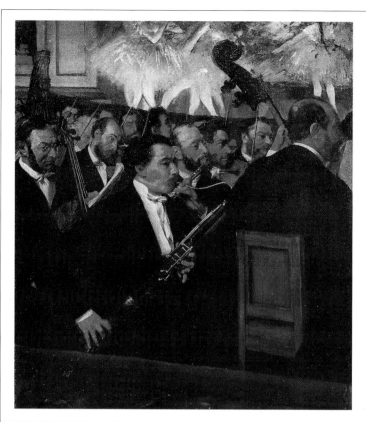

THE THEATER

Degas was a regular attender of the café-concerts at Montmartre and the Champs-Elysées. At the Ambassadeurs, a café frequented by Toulouse-Lautrec, he made a number of pastel drawings. In *The Café-Concert at the Ambassadeurs* (1875–77), the spectators (ourselves included) and the orchestra are seated in shadow against the sparkling lights in the background where the entertainment is taking place. This arrangement, which could be regarded as voyeuristic, is repeated in his *Orchestra of the Opéra* (1868–69). Here, our gaze is directed upward over the heads of the musicians, toward the blurred, barely visible images of the performers on stage. Flickers of light illuminate the legs and tutus of the anonymous

Edgar Degas, Orchestra of the Opéra, *1868–69. Musée d'Orsay, Paris.*

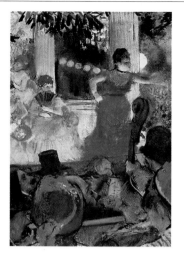

Edgar Degas, The Café-Concert at the Ambassadeurs, *1875–77. Musée des Beaux-Arts, Lyons.*

ballerinas. In contrast, the images in the foreground are sharp and obviously painted with meticulous care. Degas has included the composer Emmanuel Chabrier among the musicians.

Salon des Refusés, hanging their works beside mediocre paintings, because the official Salon remained stubbornly hostile to anything new.

In 1874, the Impressionists organized their own exhibition, featuring a total of 165 works by 39 artists. They called themselves the *Société anonyme des artistes peintres, sculpteurs, graveurs*. Although the show was a financial failure, it was important as the group's first official event. It was held in the Paris studio of the photographer Nadar in Boulevard des Capucines and reunited the artists for the first time since they had dispersed in different directions at the outbreak of the Franco-Prussian War (1870–71). During this war, Monet, who was a fierce opponent of the regime of Napoleon III and was unwilling to sacrifice his life for the emperor, traveled to London. Here he was joined by Sisley and Pissarro, whose home in Louveciennes had been overrun by enemy troops. Influenced by the work of Turner and Constable, Monet and, to a lesser degree,

Pissarro made changes to their style. Their brushstrokes became more transparent and insubstantial and the paintings more atmospheric. Pissarro attributed this to the "*plein air*, the light, and the ephemeral effects of the English landscape painters." In Monet's paintings of the River Thames and London parks, there is lightness of touch that suggests the same north European atmosphere. "I have studied the effects of mist, snow, and of spring," said Pissarro, who had adopted a freer style, with light, rapid brushstrokes. "Without fog, London would not be a beautiful city. It is the fog that gives it its magnificence," wrote Monet, when he stayed in London. He was to return to the city in 1899 and in the winters of the next two years.

Edouard Manet, Boating, *1874. Metropolitan Museum of Art, New York. Manet did not participate in the first Impressionist exhibition in 1874. This picture was exhibited at the 1879 Salon, which the artist regarded as a grander and more fitting showcase for his work.*

FINAL RECOGNITION

It was during his time in London that Monet met with the first great collector of Impressionist art, the French art dealer Paul Durand-Ruel, who had sought refuge in England and taken his collection with him. In his London gallery, he exhibited paintings by Monet and Pissarro. On his return to Paris the following year, he

visited Manet's studio, where he purchased 25 canvases. In 1876, Durand-Ruel organized the second Impressionist exhibition in Rue le Péletier, Paris, in the vain hope of a better financial success than that of 1874.

In the following year, 1877, the Impressionists organized a third exhibition, again in Rue le Péletier. It was a historical moment because, for the first time, they named this show of

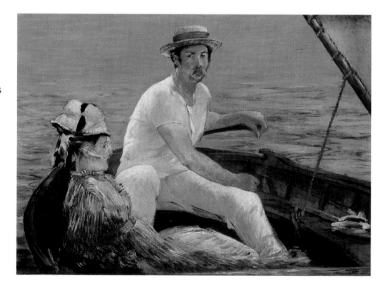

PIERRE-AUGUSTE RENOIR: "LA LOGE"

1874; oil on canvas: 2¾ x 2 ft (80 x 63 cm) ; Courtauld Institute Galleries, London.

This painting, completed by Renoir when he was 33, was shown at the first Impressionist exhibition in 1874. The romantic, fashionable subject of the work was in favor at the time and so was one of only four paintings shown that escaped criticism. In the foreground is a young woman in a black-and-white striped dress, wearing evening gloves, with pink roses in her hair and at her breast. In one hand, resting on the red velvet ledge of the theater box, she holds her opera glasses, while in the other she holds a folded black fan. Her male companion, seated behind her in order to give her prominence, scans the audience through his raised opera glasses. A model, Ninì Lopez, and the artist's brother, Edmond, posed as the society couple.

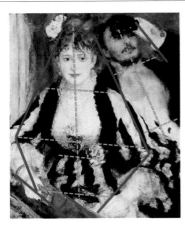

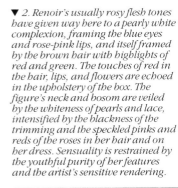

▲ *1. The composition has been carefully arranged to give maximum prominence to the figure of the woman. She is framed by oblique lines in a more or less regular pentagon. To the viewer, the right-hand side (the model's left) appears slightly advanced, defined by the angle of the figure's arm from neck to elbow. The perspective is, in fact, correct, and by following the stretch of limb from the hand to the elbow, one sees that this is indeed farther away than the figure's right hand on the edge of the box. Parallel to the line running from the woman's head to her left elbow is another forming the axis of the man's chest.*

▼ *2. Renoir's usually rosy flesh tones have given way here to a pearly white complexion, framing the blue eyes and rose-pink lips, and itself framed by the brown hair with highlights of red and green. The touches of red in the hair, lips, and flowers are echoed in the upholstery of the box. The figure's neck and bosom are veiled by the whiteness of pearls and lace, intensified by the blackness of the trimming and the speckled pinks and reds of the roses in her hair and on her dress. Sensuality is restrained by the youthful purity of her features and the artist's sensitive rendering.*

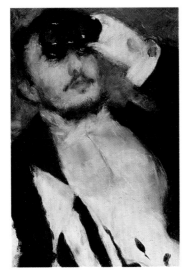

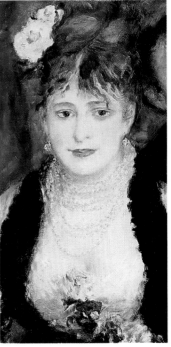

▼ *3. The neck and bosom are a white and flesh-pink color, and her clothing is in striking black and white stripes. A dark but soft-looking black fabric edges the garment and contains touches of blue, green, and some lighter tones. The white in the various textures of her clothing and gloves is accentuated by the light in the painting.*

▲ *4. The woman is given pride of place in the foreground and monopolizes all the light, color, and decoration. Typical of Renoir's female subjects, she is a source of light and enchantment. In contrast, the gentleman is in shadow in the background and wears somber colors. The white of his shirt, scarf, and vest forms a long, downward slope that does not catch the light, and his torso is touched with unreal strokes of black and gray tinted with blue. The shape of his tail coat and even the lapels are hidden in the darkness. His snow-white cuff extends from his sleeve and his kid-gloved hand grips the black binoculars, the lenses of which show the glint of reflected light. The upper part of his face is hidden, but his moustache, beard, hair, nose, and mouth are all carefully depicted.*

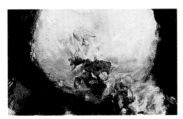

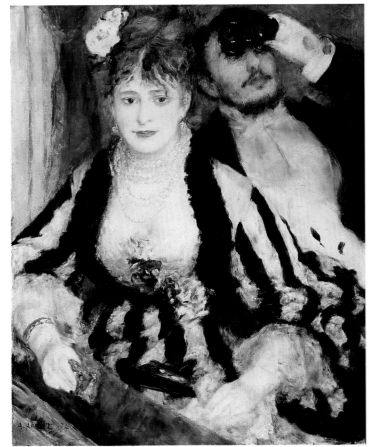

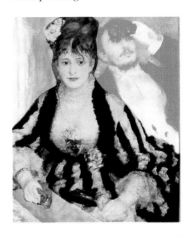

▲ *5. Renoir's expressive skill and freedom with his brush are clearly identifiable in various details of the painting: the two pairs of opera glasses; the black, closed fan; the lace and necklaces around the woman's neck; and the pink flowers, particularly those fastened at her décolletage. Here, the artist shows complete indifference to realistic rendition, however, and we cannot tell if the flowers are fresh and tied in a bunch with ribbons or if they are artificial. They serve to define Renoir's particular quality of Impressionism, which succeeds in giving us the "impression" of a couple in a theater box, perhaps a minute or two before the curtain goes up.*

their finest work "*Exposition des Impressionistes*." It was supported by the first issue of their art publication *L'Impressioniste*, which ran for only a few months. It was the last time that all the members were to exhibit together. Such solidarity weakened at the subsequent shows of 1879, 1880, 1881, 1882, and 1886, with the defection of Cézanne, followed by Monet, Renoir, and Sisley. New names appeared, however, including Zandomeneghi, Gauguin, Redon, Signac, and Seurat. Just as Impressionism was reaching the end of its short life, the artists began to receive public recognition, starting with Monet, who exhibited with the sculptor Rodin in 1889. The success of these two artists increased as the years went by. Durand-Ruel took Impressionism to the US, showing a few paintings in New York in 1886. Dr. Gachet, an art collector and engravings enthusiast, built a studio for the production of etchings, and it was here that Pissarro and Cézanne produced their first graphics. Some of the greatest artists

THE BOULEVARDS

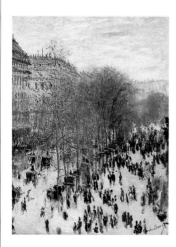

Claude Monet, Boulevard des Capucines, *1873. Nelson-Atkins Museum of Art, Kansas City.*

Toward the middle of the 19th century, Paris underwent a massive rebuilding program to turn into a quintessentially modern city. In the heart of the city, whole districts were demolished to make way for wide, tree-lined boulevards. In literature, Balzac and, later, Baudelaire evoked the daily activities of the ostentatious Parisian life of these great avenues. In art, Monet, Renoir, Sisley, Caillebotte, and Manet produced luminous and airy paintings to document the innovations of the town-planner Baron Haussmann. At the Impressionist exhibition of 1877, the critic Jacques is said to have commented: "So, four Impressionists have given themselves

the mission of reproducing Paris: M. Caillebotte has chosen the street; M. Renoir the ball; M. Degas the theater and the café-concert; Mlle. Berthe Morisot the boudoir. Besides this, of course, there are some excursions to the country, but still rendered by Parisian brushes."

Claude Monet, Carnival at the Boulevard des Capucines, *1873. Pushkin Museum, Moscow.*

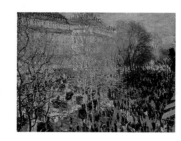

were also the most enthusiastic collectors, such as Degas and Gauguin. The painter and collector Gustave Caillebotte, who exhibited at five of the eight Impressionist exhibitions, bequeathed 65 paintings to the French nation, almost half of which were disdainfully rejected by the Ecole des Beaux-Arts.

INNOVATORS OF PAINTING

The Impressionist painters confronted nature in a very different way from their predecessors. Their new language not only changed traditional conventions, it overturned

the very way of seeing the world and challenged the human relationship with reality. The artists did not record nature as static and unchanging but sought to reflect its constant movement and natural pulse. In a rejection of the age-old principles of academic painting – stillness, symmetry, order, and cleanliness – they cast aside the distinction between foreground and background; the frontal illumination needed for chiaroscuro; the sharpness of outline; the balance of mass and color; and the solidity of form. In Pissarro's words, "The Impressionists have abandoned the three principles of illusion: line, perspective, and the artificial light of academic painting." This apparent lack of respect angered the public and critics alike. Instead of depicting subjects substantively and definitively, the Impressionists adopted a looser style that was lively and immediate and in a continual process of change. In their paintings, executed *en plein air*, these artists captured

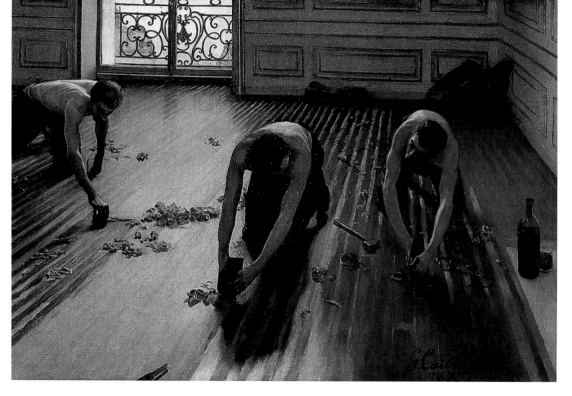

Gustave Caillebotte, The Floor Planers, *1875. Musée d'Orsay, Paris. Although the Impressionists were accused of producing works that were not true to life, this work, shown at the 1876 exhibition, was criticized for its crude realism.*

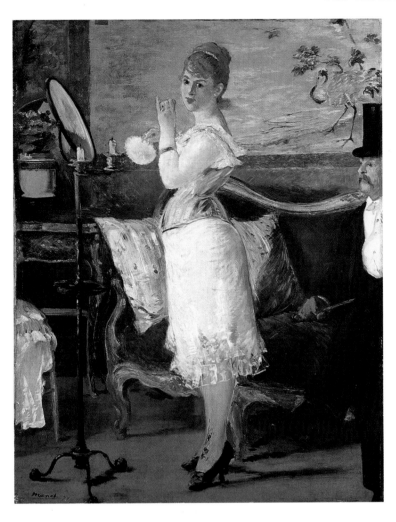

Edouard Manet, Nana, 1877. Kunsthalle, Hamburg. Fifteen years after painting Olympia, Manet returned to the theme of the courtesan. The woman posing was a young actress named Henriette Hauser. The focal point of her petticoats detracts the gaze from the unusual arrangement of furniture in the room and from the presence of the man on the right.

Claude Monet, The Terrace at Sainte-Adresse, 1867. Metropolitan Museum of Art, New York. Confined within an unusual network of straight lines, the many subjects on the terrace and in the sea and sky at this coastal resort near Le Havre are depicted in a dazzling display of blues, reds, yellows, whites, greens, and oranges.

the sighing of the breeze, the constantly changing sky, and the fleeting effects of light reflected on water.

Under the strong influence of the Impressionists, the classical painting of landscapes became more ethereal and misty. Unreal shadows and contrived dark tones were now eliminated, and the paint lost the compact density characteristic of Courbet, who said that painting "is an art of sight and should therefore concern itself with things seen."

The English artist John Constable (1776–1837) had already sought to evoke the "chiaroscuro of nature in the dew, in the breeze, in the flowering, in the freshness, that no painter has yet succeeded in putting on canvas," using rapid brushstrokes and splashes of pure

THE CAFES

The somber mood of Degas' *L'Absinthe* (1876) is emphasized by his use of cold blue and gray shades. Two café regulars are portrayed staring vacantly over their glasses, and the woman's contains the familiar green drink of absinthe. Despite the appearance of spontaneity, in reality Degas' paintings were carefully composed. "No art was ever less spontaneous than mine," he remarked. *L'Absinthe* is not a slice of life captured as it unfolds but an evocation of surroundings and atmosphere. The man and woman pictured are two of the artist's friends, the engraver Marcellin Desboutin, a drinking companion from the Café Guerbois, and the actress Ellen Andrée.

In Manet's *Bar at the Folies-Bergère* (1881–82), we see the audience reflected in the mirror behind the barmaid, with her customer clearly "missing" from the foreground. Thanks to this device, we are given a panoramic vision of the interior. What we see is not the result of realistic observation but the artist's deliberate use of false perspectives. He was nonetheless accused by the critics of incompetence.

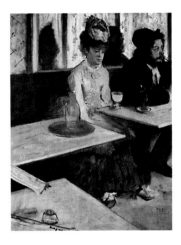

Edgar Degas, L'Absinthe, 1876. Musée d'Orsay, Paris.

Edouard Manet, Bar at the Folies-Bergère 1881–82. Courtauld Institute Galleries, London.

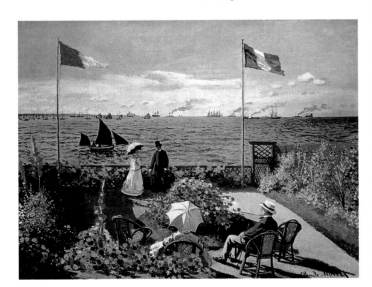

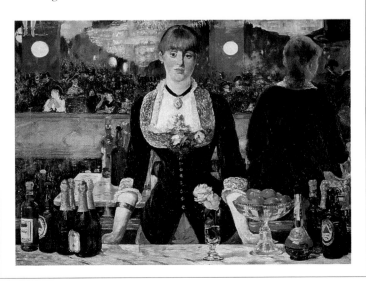

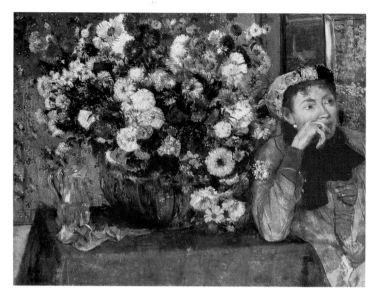

white paint applied with a palette knife. In Impressionism, it is light, broken into all its composite colors, that floods canvases with freshness and captures the constantly

Edgar Degas, A Woman with Chrysanthemums, *1865. Metropolitan Museum of Art, New York. The flowers, the focus of the composition, provide the ideal opportunity for the use of comma-shaped brushstrokes. The cropping of the figure at the edge of the canvas recalls a snapshot image.*

changing atmosphere. The browns and ochres (earth colors) were replaced with the primary colors (red, yellow, and blue), which were blended with complementary colors (green, purple, and orange). Imitating the lively brushstrokes of Delacroix (1798–1863), who had already used pure color and not mixed his paint, the Impressionists broke colors into a thousand fragments, not only dissolving the outline of form but flaking the paint itself in order to reflect back every "impression." The surface, varying in thickness and no longer depicted in uniform colors, came alive, nourished by the quantity and variety of comma-shaped brushstrokes. Many other marks were added to enliven the whole canvas and make it appear in continuous motion, using reflections

optics, which, since the beginning of the 19th century, had developed and been published in various journals. These included theories about the composition of color and the structure of light. In 1839, the chemist Eugène Chevreul published a work on the principles of color harmonies and contrasts and their use in art. These theories were applied directly to the canvases of the Impressionists.

A NEW VIEW OF NATURE

With the advent of Impressionism, the representation of historical subjects lost its supremacy. For these artists, nature was their true mistress: they immersed themselves in it and its visual experience.

ARCHITECTURE

Architecture in itself was not a subject that greatly excited the Impressionists; for them, it was static material. The contents of a city, on the other hand, were a different matter. While individual buildings constituted permanent masses, an avenue or the corner of a square contained life and movement

in the form of the figures as they bustled past. Architecture was of interest only when buildings seemed to "move" in the shimmering light. Gothic buildings, such as Rouen Cathedral, made particularly good subjects, as demonstrated in Monet's landmark series. Bridges over water and constructions built of glass were also favored for their interaction with changing light.

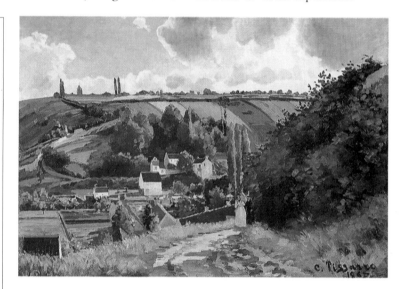

of light and the contrast of complementary colors. The skies of the Impressionists opened up, and the light became millions of particles – opaque, vibrant, and refracting. It went far beyond the delicate, spontaneous brushwork of such artists as Jongkind and Boudin, who had already practiced the art of painting *en plein air.* Impressionism was very much a product of its time, and the movement coincided with the discussion of ideas prompted by discoveries in the field of

Camille Pissarro, The Côte du Jallais near Pontoise, *1867. Metropolitan Museum of Art, New York. This work was well received at the 1868 Salon despite the thick paint, which was applied with a spatula to achieve contrast.*

Monet's beautiful garden at Giverny constituted a world of its own, one that he painted many times before his death in 1926, depicting the leafy branches, delicate little bridges, and waterlilies. With their thousand gradations of color and skillful shading and toning, the Impressionists painted that which by definition could not

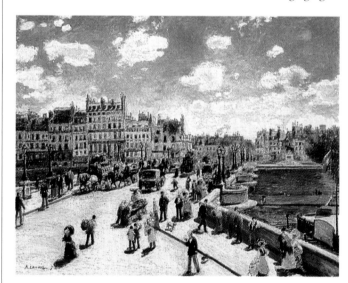

Pierre-Auguste Renoir, Le Pont Neuf, *1872. National Gallery, London.*

PASSING TIME AND CHANGING WEATHER

Monet's famous *Rouen Cathedral* series is the most famous example in Impressionism of the study of passing time and the effects on color of changing weather. The artist painted 30 canvases in total, working at first from a shop directly opposite the cathedral, then later from an apartment nearby. In these pictures, the role of the physical subject as the focus of the work is redundant. Instead, the building serves as the agent through which the artist depicts the infinite changes in the atmosphere. The cathedral becomes literally "swallowed up" (to use Debussy's words) by the colors of the day. The blues, grays, and nuances of brown are carefully arranged according to a harmony (the term explicitly used by Monet) created from the matching of colors and brushstrokes, sometimes thick, sometimes ragged. The very term "harmony" points to the lack of realism in the artist's intentions: these are Monet's reproductions of sensory and psychological impressions, which portray the subject in perpetual metamorphosis. In 1895, 20 of the canvases were exhibited by Durand-Ruel, selling for an astonishing 15,000 francs each.

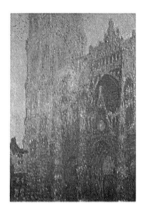 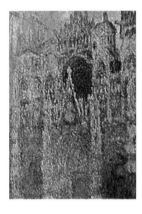 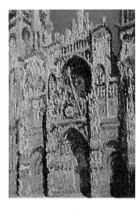 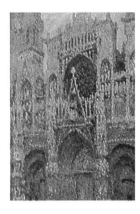 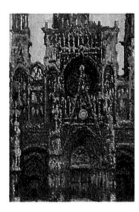

Claude Monet, Rouen Cathedral, Morning – Harmony in Blue, *1892–94. Musée d'Orsay, Paris.*

Claude Monet, Rouen Cathedral, Morning – Harmony in White, *1892–94. Musée d'Orsay, Paris.*

Claude Monet, Rouen Cathedral, Bright Sunshine – Harmony in Blue and Gold, *1892–94. Musée d'Orsay, Paris.*

Claude Monet, Rouen Cathedral, Gray Day – Harmony in Gray, *1892–94. Musée d'Orsay, Paris.*

Claude Monet, Rouen Cathedral – Harmony in Brown, *1892–94. Musée d'Orsay, Paris.*

be painted for the simple reason that it was not physically visible: for example, the qualities of air such as its dampness or its crispness. Even tangible elements no longer existed, except in terms of the aura that defined them at a particular moment in time. For example, in Monet's famous series of 30 canvases of Rouen Cathedral, painted at different times of the day, it is not the cathedral that provides the focal interest but the intensity of light and its effects on the stone. The Impressionists felt that art should be appreciated with all the senses, and they concentrated on the presence of deep sensations rather than the cold reality of a scene. Consequently, psychological perceptions became more important than the "real" subject matter, and the content came to be replaced by visual

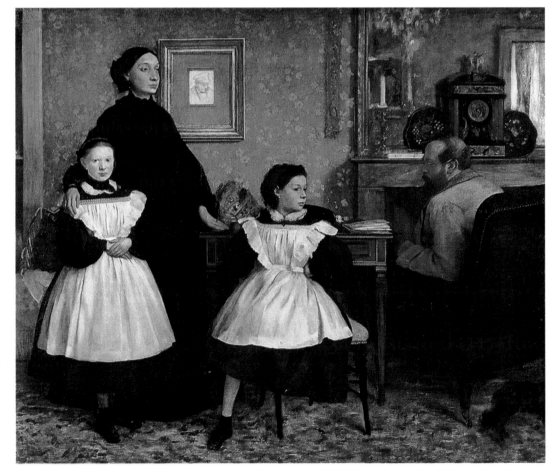

Edgar Degas, The Bellelli Family, *1858–59. Musée d'Orsay, Paris. Standing out against the vibrant background of the floor and walls, the figures recall portraits by Holbein or van Dyck.*

PERCEPTION, LIGHT, AND COLOR

What we perceive is more important to our minds than what is real. For example, the colors of Impressionism are not true to real life. In the works of Degas and Caillebotte, we find an illusory glimpse of social realism in the graceful, melancholy figures of the adolescent ballerinas and in the remoteness of the women working in laundries. For Toulouse-Lautrec, these deep reflections on life produced tragic pictures that evoked feelings of emptiness: the grimace of Yvette Guilbert; the misery of the sins of the flesh shrouded in ambiguous, artificial light; the green, purple, and yellow seediness of the small-town evening; the theater and the cabaret.

Delacroix's color lit up his paintings. It was dynamic, excessive, and exuberant, pouring life over objects and figures and giving them movement. With Impressionism, colors were no longer the means of representation but became instead the focus of representation.

The landscapes of Sisley became watery: water on canvas, for the supreme illusion or supreme realism.

Monet, whose father had been a wholesaler at Le Havre, saw water not merely as a childhood memory but as life itself, as light: "I would like to always be near or on the sea and, when I die, to be buried in a buoy."

Previously unknown forms of light flooded the canvases of the Impressionists with an infinite series of colors. Monet claimed: "The seed of my painting was found in Africa." He was stunned by the light in Algeria, where he spent two years doing military service with the Chasseurs d'Afrique: "One cannot imagine how much I've learned," he wrote. There were other forms of light, too, in Paris, at Argenteuil, Anvers-sur-Oise, Pontoise, London, and many other places. Each had differences in density, purity, and translucence according not only to the place, but to the passing hours, which alter the relationships between colors and the

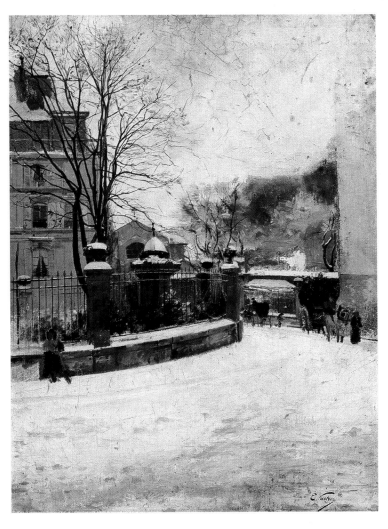

"impressions" of all that the senses could perceive. The colors, reflections, and chiaroscuro that characterize Monet's cathedral series are not there to be seen; they have never existed in reality but are psychological reactions. Whoever looks at these pictures, however, considers the blues, grays, and golds as very true and real in terms of the overall impression they create. Each painter re-created reality according to his or her own perception. This meant that not only did painting no longer have a message to communicate, but also the traditional means of sending that message were lost.

It is in the boldness of these intentions, and in the invention of a pictorial code that could put them into practice, that the extraordinary modernity of Impressionism lies.

In Monet's series of paintings

Edouard Castres, Paris Streets in the Snow, 1872. Oskar Reinhart Collection, Winterthur, Switzerland. This painter from Geneva (1838–1902) interpreted the variations in light found in winter landscapes.

of the River Thames and haystacks, in the geometric sequences of poplars, and in the various façades of Rouen Cathedral, any substance seems to be dispersed by a thousand vibrations. White clouds in the sky, piles of snow along the Seine, ice, mist, and fog are all aspects of nature shown in the very act of dissolving – mirroring a fragile, constantly changing world. Representation lost the natural vestiges that, at the end of the Romantic movement, kept it anchored to reality. In its place came Monet's sunrise, no longer the sun rising, but something quite different – an "impression" of the sun rising.

Federico Zandomeneghi, Along the Seine, 1873. Galleria d'Arte Moderna, Palazzo Pitti, Florence. The tophat of the man with his back to us and the smokestacks in the background are realistic features, adding color and atmosphere to this composition that blends water and land into one.

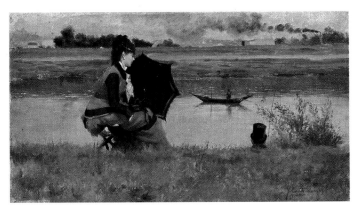

DANCE

The Impressionists flourished during the first 20 years of the *Belle Époque*, when Paris was the undisputed capital of pleasure and entertainment. There was dancing everywhere and at all times, throughout the day and night, in cafés, hotels, public dance halls, and open squares. Grand balls were given by the wealthy, dances were organized for the workers and countryfolk, and there was dancing in the cabarets, circuses, opera, and, of course, the ballet. For the Impressionists, dancing was a natural theme; they captured with ease the slow and fast paces, the grace and the strength of the moves, the sudden stop, the flight, the turn, the way the skirts swept around as the dancers spun. Degas and Renoir were among the most enthusiastic painters of this aspect of Parisian life. Renoir frequented Sunday afternoon-dances at the Moulin de la Galette, while Degas indulged his fascination for life backstage at the Opéra.

Edgar Degas, L'Etoile, 1878. Musée d'Orsay, Paris. Degas interpreted this subject in many different ways. Here, the ballerina shines on her own before the other artists, seen hazily in the background.

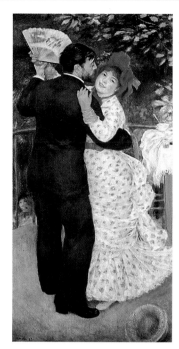

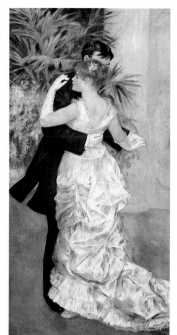

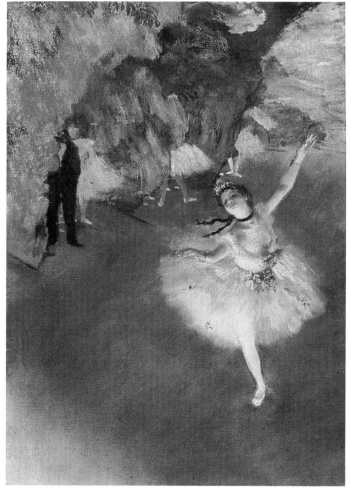

Pierre-Auguste Renoir, Dance in the Country, 1882–83. Musée d'Orsay, Paris. The couple, Paul Lhote and Aline Charigot, blend elegantly into their surroundings with their relaxed pose.

Pierre-Auguste Renoir, Dance in the Town, 1882–83. Musée d'Orsay, Paris. Suzanne Valadon, in a dress with a long train, and Eugène Lestringuez dance against the background of palm trees.

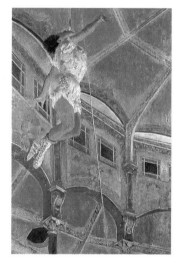

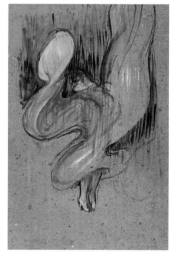

Edgar Degas, Miss La La at the Cirque Fernando, 1879. Musée d'Orsay, Paris. Here, the artist undertook the difficult task of rendering the impression of a circus performer captured in midflight during her act in the air.

Henri de Toulouse-Lautrec, Study for Loïe Fuller, 1893. Musée Toulouse-Lautrec, Albi. Here, the body of the dancer disappears, as Edmond de Goncourt puts it, into a hurricane of material, in a whirlwind of petticoats, in a spiral of light.

very appearance of objects. For the Impressionists, painting became a frenetic activity as the speed of execution required an ever more difficult pace to sustain. Monet did not work for more than a quarter of an hour at a time on any one canvas, because a painting was "the registering of an unrepeatable emotion in an instant of time that will not return." He continually changed canvases according to the hour and the light, choosing the appropriate one from those in his large box. For him, the brisk walk of a man seen in the distance became, from the simple movement registered by the mind, a mere flicker of light on his canvas. For Renoir, the most classical Impressionist and the artist most interested in human subjects, painting was not about representing nature, but feeling it, perceiving it, and seeing it. He favored light-hearted scenes from everyday life and social events. Unconcerned with realism, he gave his paintings a feeling of movement and a sense of rotation, created by the light itself. From this point of view, he could be regarded as the father of movies; he was, indeed, to become father of one of the most celebrated movie directors, Jean Renoir. In Renoir's paintings, there is nothing like the "life" that we find in the works of Delacroix or David, or in Géricault's *Raft of the Medusa*, where the shipwrecked are fixed forever on the canvas. Instead, an indefinable magic draws the images out of the light – images, it seems, that could vanish from one moment to the next.

In *The Dance at the Moulin de la Galette* (1876), the people depicted are not portraits (although some faces belong to Renoir's friends and were painted as a compliment to them), but swirling apparitions created out of light, color, and atmosphere. Renoir, like Monet, was fascinated by the strange effects of light filtering through foliage. His models, placed at tables and under

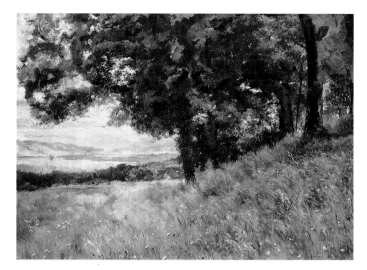

Louis Eysen, Summer Landscape, *1875–77. Städelsches Kunstinstitut, Frankfurt. Eysen (1843–99), born in England and active in Germany, was also a talented wood engraver. In this hilly landscape, the frenzied activity of nature is expressed by the thick carpet of flowers, reminiscent of Monet or Renoir.*

trees and sprinkled with mottled light, were little more than vehicles for the expression of the momentary effects of light and shadow.

For the Impressionists, life as a presence and a reality had been replaced by a mere impression of life, a bewitching, luminous spell that veers toward something vague and indistinct. Life and human identity vanish

into thin air in an iridescent shattering of colors. In the works of Georges Seurat (1859–91), the idea of an impression made of light and color would be carried to extremes. Using contemporary scientific color theories, he applied small dots of unmixed color side by side on the canvas in a technique that became known as divisionism. His masterpiece *Sunday Afternoon on the Island of La Grande Jatte* (1884), shown at the final Impressionist exhibition in 1886, is a visual statement of his ideals.

In Manet's rich use of color we can still detect a sense of

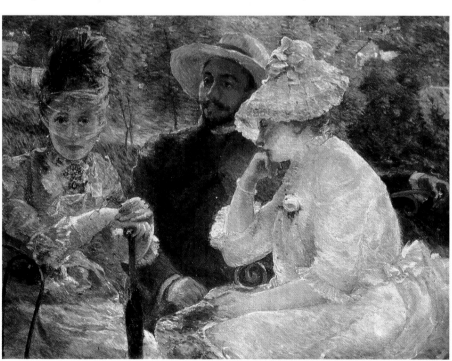

Marie Bracquemond, On the Terrace at Sèvres, *1880. Petit Palais, Geneva. One of the most popular female Impressionists, Marie Bracquemond was married to the engraver Félix and was a close friend of Degas. The most striking feature of this picture is the isolation of each of the figures. Only the man is looking at a member of the group, but his gaze is distant. The dazzling color gives movement to the branches of the trees and heightens the material of the dresses, which are bathed in light.*

PHOTOGRAPHY AND PAINTING

In 1839, the painter Louis Jacques Mandé Daguerre (1787–1851) was developing the daguerreo-type, the first practical photo-graphic process, which William Henry Fox Talbot would perfect later that year. Photography as an art form was slow to assert itself. Baudelaire called it the "refuge of all failed painters," but it was often the painters themselves who made use of it, albeit at times in secret. Delacroix, Corot, and Courbet all took advantage of the new process. Photography established a new approach to reality: in long sittings, it could register gestures, reactions, and expressions that

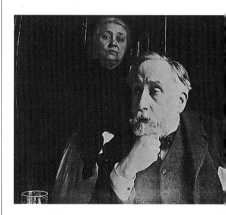

Edgar Degas, Degas and his maid, Zoé Closier, *1890. Bibliothèque Nationale, Paris.*

looked seemingly spontaneous but were in fact cleverly stage-managed by the photographer. New psychological and spatial relationships developed, which Degas took up and examined in detail. He collected *cartes de visite*, photographs the same size as a visiting card, which were mounted in series on cardboard and featured particular subjects (ballerinas, reigning monarchs, actors). The models simulating certain gestures or movements made up a real "theater of vision." The famous André Adolphe Eugène Disdéri (1819–90) earned huge amounts from a celebrated series in which the sitters' poses were in

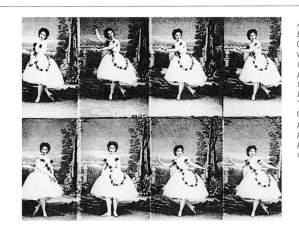

André-Adolphe-Eugène Disdéri, Carte de visite with ballerina. *In about 1860, the photographer made this series that would become known as* The Legs of the Opéra. *The photographic process had a profound influence on tastes in art.*

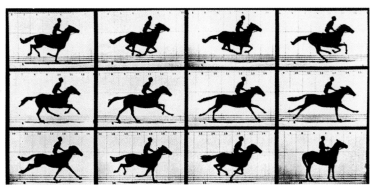

Eadweard Muybridge, The Horse in Motion, *1878. This English photographer, based in the US from 1852, carried out the first important research into the movement of men and animals between 1872 and 1885. The shots are considered important forerunners of cinematographic processes.*

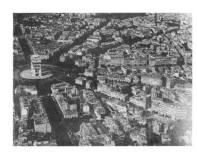

Nadar, View of Paris. *An aerial shot taken during a flight in a hot-air balloon.*

sequence to make them appear more natural. Several scientific questions were resolved by the achievements of photography, particularly with regard to motion. The great Eadweard Muybridge's photographic series of the movements of a galloping horse exposed all the errors previously made by sculptors and painters in their depictions of horses in motion.

Félix Nadar (1820–1910), in whose studio in the Boulevard des Capucines the first Impressionist exhibition was held in 1874, was the subject of a contemporary cartoon with the caption: "Nadar raises photography to the level of art." The most renowned personalities of the day flocked to his studio to be photographed, and in 1863 the intrepid photographer astounded Paris by going up in a hot-air balloon to take the first-ever aerial photographs. This earned him a mention, under the name Ardan, in Jules Verne's novel *De la terre à la lune* ("From the Earth to the Moon", 1865). According to the poet Paul Valéry, Degas was "enamored of photography at a time when other artists despised it or did not dare admit that it could be of use to them." He made prints to explore the effects of light and seek new perspectives. Because he was so

Pierre-Auguste Renoir, The Dance at the Moulin de la Galette, *1876. Musée d'Orsay, Paris. In the New York (Whitney Collection) version, the movements of the figures and the lights and colors as the artist recorded them* en plein air *are even more striking.*

busy during the day, he took photographs in the evening; he wanted to capture the magic of moonlight or artificial light. "Daylight is too easy," he said. An extraordinary type of photograph emerged from Degas' camera, in which light and shade absorb descriptive detail and create spaces around the opaque forms of the female figures. Mallarmé and Renoir were persuaded by Degas to pose for 15 torturous minutes under the heat of nine lamps for a photograph that Degas wanted to give to Valéry: "This photograph has been given to me by Degas, whose camera and reflection can be seen in the mirror," wrote Valéry.

VIEWPOINTS

To achieve the luminous canvas of *Le Pont Neuf* (1872), Renoir sketched the passersby from a window. His brother Edmond had been sent down to hinder their progress so that the artist would have the time to set them down on canvas. There was still something too stiff about these figures seen from above; their movements were depicted through the intellect, not through the eye. In later paintings, Renoir defined them as simple daubs of color. In *Boulevard Seen from Above* (1880), Caillebotte did not look for movement. With meticulous precision, he worked out the arrangement of space in a classical manner. In the view from

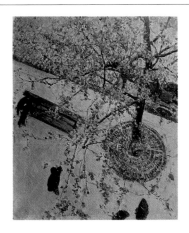

Gustave Caillebotte, Boulevard Seen from Above, *1880. Private Collection, London. Asymmetry, oblique lines, and an aerial view brought freshness to the artist's perception.*

below of *Miss La La at the Cirque Fernando* (1879), Degas defined space psychologically. It is not the audience but we who lift our heads, holding our breath to watch Miss La La balancing in space. Our perception is sharpened by the asymmetry of the figure, which, with all its weight, hovers in the air, occupying only one upper corner of the large surface of the painting. In Renoir's *The Dance at the Moulin de la Galette* (1876), the people dance in and out of the tables in a café in Montmartre. The fluctuating light and the seduction of the composition were to come alive again in the film *A Day in the Country* (1936–46) by Renoir's son Jean, in which he paid homage to Impressionist painting.

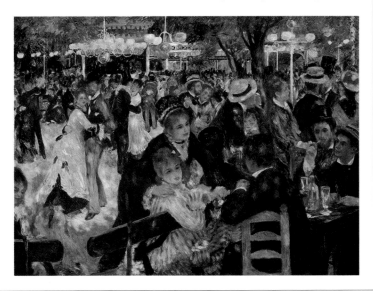

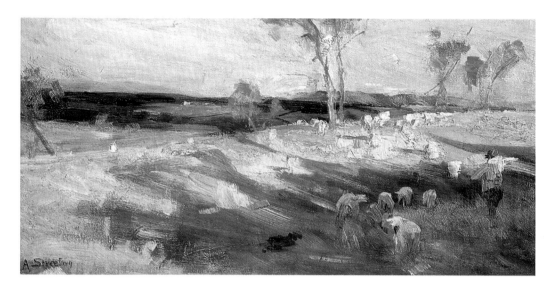

structured composition and an awareness and use of the devices of pictorial representation. Along with Degas, he stands just outside the classification of true Impressionism. The girls in the works of Renoir and Monet are quite different from Degas's young girls. It seems that the instant we see them, they pulsate with that

Arthur Streeton, Impression of a Golden Summer, *c.1888. Ledger Collection, Benalla Art Gallery, Melbourne. The Australian artist Streeton (1867–1943) uses thick brushstrokes to depict the colors of the sunset at Eaglemont, near Melbourne.*

changing, fleeting rhythm of life. The expression of this sense of impermanence – perhaps the very core of

Impressionism – is based on the impressions engendered by the changeability of light. Renoir's two young women dancing, one the subject of *Dance in the Country*, the other of *Dance in the Town*, look as if they could whirl out of the canvas at any moment, smiling as they go. In both paintings, it is the light that

changes and carries life with it. By doing so, it reveals the melancholy hidden deep within the paintings, which, on the surface, are so full of joy and exuberance.

In the paintings of Pissarro and Sisley, everything is presented in a blaze of full, strong sunlight or under the blinding white. However, our eye seems to witnesses constant changes in the atmosphere, which moves in an uneven rhythm across the canvas. While the classical landscape painter captured scenes from nature that will endure forever, untouched by the centuries and the subjectivity of knowledge, both Pissarro and Sisley created landscapes that last only the time of a fleeting glance, before they change again and move onto another moment. In Monet's waterlily paintings, his subject is pure, beautiful plantlife that grows, takes shape and dies, changing color and substance minute

FLEETING EXPRESSIONS

In Degas' work, harmony and beauty are systematically sacrificed to expression. A

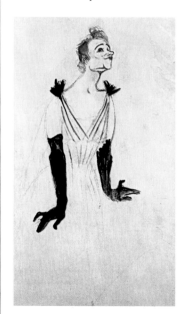

Henri de Toulouse-Lautrec, Yvette Guilbert, *1894. Musée Toulouse-Lautrec, Albi, France.*

woman yawning or bent over her iron, or a young girl lacing up her ballet shoe, re-creates an everyday attitude that, rather than telling us about the person, conceals her behind a mysterious veil. The figures are not disclosed to us; instead, they remain silent and aloof, beyond our reach.

In Degas' *Singer with a Black Glove* (1878), the gloved arm becomes the visual center of the composition, creating a sense of instability in the figure depicted. The grimaces of Yvette Guilbert and the gestures of her hands say far more than a conventional portrait could about this unusual woman, who entertained at the café-concerts and who, "with her white dress, black gloves, and haunted face, could truly appear like a fragile figure evaporating from a bottle of ether" (Edmond de Goncourt).

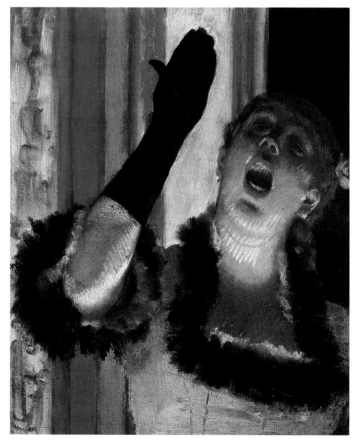

Edgar Degas, Singer with a Black Glove, *c.1878. Fogg Art Museum, Cambridge, Massachusetts.*

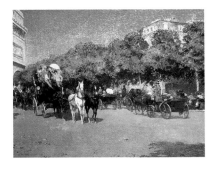

Childe Hassam, Grand Prix Day, *1887. Museum of Fine Arts, Boston.*

by minute, and we see organic material appearing and disappearing. The Impressionists felt that there was a subjective link between the painter, his canvas and the observer, they are inextricably linked and there is a perpetual movement occuring within the works.

THE INFLUENCE OF IMPRESSIONISM

The Impressionist movement brought about a change in the understanding of color. Once the colors of the rainbow had been broken up, there was no turning back. From there were to come new techniques, such as divisionism, as well as the revolutionary idea that color could be the central subject of a painting over and above any other element. In 1895, Kandinsky, having seen Monet's series of haystacks, offered the following definition: "The painting takes on a magical strength and splendor and, at the same time, unconsciously, the subject, the crucial part of the picture, is put in doubt." Color, hereafter, assumed different forms and roles, and the consequences for modern art, regarding theory and technique, were to be enormous.

The influence of Impressionism spread from Paris around the world. Artists everywhere

William Bruce, Landscape with Poppies, *1887. Art Gallery of Ontario, Toronto.*

FRAMING

With Impressionism, the definition of the visual field of a painting was thrown open to experimentation. The relationship between the point of observation and the subject matter of a picture became much less straightforward. In Degas' depiction of the horse races in *At the Races, Gentlemen Jockeys* (1877–80), the differing planes on which the various protagonists are situated separate each of their roles in the picture. Each person is depicted from a different angle, and a large part of the canvas remains empty, almost as if it were a moment of real life. This can also be said of Caillebotte's *Paris, a Rainy Day* (1877), in which the artist chooses a very particular angle from which to paint. He succeeds in presenting with equal importance the figures on the right, the general bustle of the passersby in the middle ground, and the rain-drenched streets and the buildings that intersect and frame the square.

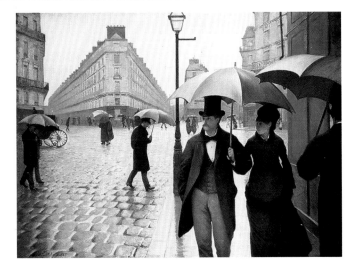

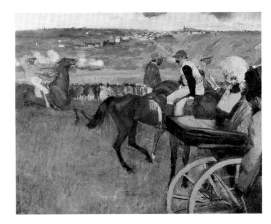

Gustave Caillebotte, Paris, a Rainy Day, *1877. Art Institute of Chicago.*

Edgar Degas, At the Races, Gentlemen Jockeys, *1877–80. Musée d'Orsay, Paris.*

were rejecting academic tradition in favor of this new radiant painting style inspired by the Paris-based group. The Italian painter Federico Zandomeneghi (1841–1917) was just one of many to be inspired by the Impressionists.

He came to Paris in 1874, and, thanks to the influence of the art historian Diego Martelli, he exhibited with the group in 1879, 1880, 1881, and 1886. Shy and reticent, he found it difficult to sell his pictures and was forced

to make a living from his fashion drawings.

Monet's home at Giverny was among the favorite haunts of American artists in France. John Singer Sargent (1856–1925), an American who trained in Paris, recorded his visit in 1887 in a painting. His brief, intense Impressionist period, which lasted from 1884 to 1889, enriched his art, making his drawing freer and less formal and enhancing his portraits. After seeing works by Monet and Pissarro in Paris, Childe Hassam (1859–1935) captured the New York streets on canvas, with light brushstrokes that successfully evoked the atmosphere of the city. In 1898, a group of American painters (of which Hassam was a member) called The Ten, led by J. H. Twachtman and J. Alden Weir, formally introduced the principles of Impressionism into the US.

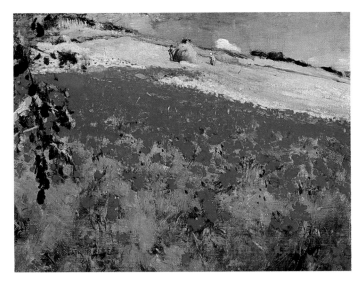

ARTISTS, WRITERS, AND MUSICIANS

During the Impressionist period, there was a great deal of debate between the protagonists of the various arts. They exchanged ideas and discussed politics and cultural issues. Painters, writers, and musicians frequented the same venues and often socialized together.

Manet was at the center of a group that met regularly at the Café Guerbois in the Batignolles district of Paris. He included portraits of other members of the group in his paintings. In *Music in the Tuileries Gardens*, he painted several of the cultural figures of France's Second Empire: the novelist Champfleury; Jacques Offenbach, the "Mozart of the Champs d'Elysées," as Rossini called him and composer of *La Belle Hélène* (1864) and *La Vie Parisienne* (1866); and Baudelaire, who accompanied the artist on his walks through the Tuileries Gardens. In the following year, Baudelaire published *L'Heroïsme de la vie moderne*, in which the new ideal of heroism was no longer something transcendental

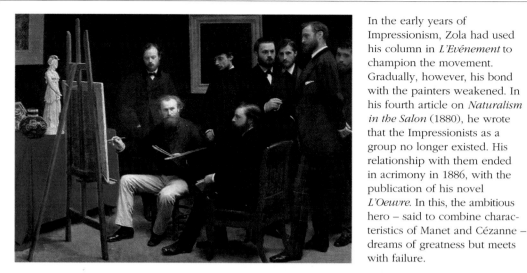

Henri Fantin-Latour, Studio in the Batignolles Quarter, 1870. Musée d'Orsay, Paris. The group of artist-friends resembles a jury examining the painter at work. Each one seems to be giving great thought to the work of the others.

open our eyes to see the heroism of our time all around us." The painter and the writer, both portrayed by Fantin-Latour in *Homage to Delacroix* (1864), met in 1859, and their friendship lasted until Baudelaire's death in 1867. The friendship between Manet and Mallarmé was also enduring,

In the early years of Impressionism, Zola had used his column in *L'Evénement* to champion the movement. Gradually, however, his bond with the painters weakened. In his fourth article on *Naturalism in the Salon* (1880), he wrote that the Impressionists as a group no longer existed. His relationship with them ended in acrimony in 1886, with the publication of his novel *L'Oeuvre*. In this, the ambitious hero – said to combine characteristics of Manet and Cézanne – dreams of greatness but meets with failure.

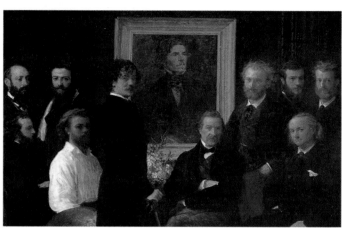

Henri Fantin-Latour, Homage to Delacroix, 1864. Musée d'Orsay, Paris. The group of friends, painters, and writers stands tightly together for the picture. The world of artists, although regarded as one full of envy and differing opinions, appears very close.

various disciplines often crossed: for example, Degas illustrated the novel *La Fille Elisa* by the Goncourt brothers; Manet designed the lithographs for *Cats Meeting* to illustrate the book of anecdotes about cats by Champfleury; and Guy de Maupassant sometimes accompanied Monet on his painting trips. Emile Zola, a childhood friend of Cézanne, appeared with Manet, Renoir, and Bazille in *Studio in the Batignolles Quarter* (1870) by Fantin-Latour. The picture paid homage to Emile Zola as the first supporter of Manet's art: reviewing the 1886 Salon in the pages of *L'Evénement*, the writer advised the readers that it would be a "good investment" to buy Manet's paintings.

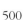

Edgar Degas, Diego Martelli, 1879. Scottish National Gallery of Modern Art, Edinburgh.

Edouard Manet, Music in the Tuileries Gardens, 1862. National Gallery, London. The faces of some of the artist's friends in the picture were painted in the studio from photographs, a method that would become common practice.

but was to be found in the actions of everyday behavior: "All the newspapers provide proof that all we need to do is

lasting from 1873, the year the poet arrived in Paris, until Manet's death in 1883. Mallarmé, who had defended the artist in several articles, mourned his death: "I have seen my dear Manet almost daily for ten years, and now cannot believe he has gone," he wrote to Verlaine. The paths of the artists of

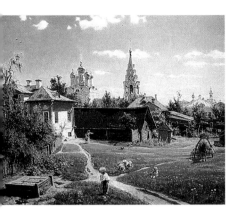

Vasili Dimitrevic Polenov, A Moscow Courtyard, *1878. Tretyakov Gallery, Moscow.*

The Australians William Blair Bruce (1859–1906) and Arthur Streeton (1867–1943) were dedicated *plein air* painters. Meanwhile, artists in Japan shared a kinship with the Impressionists, since they had been influenced by Japanese art. The Danish painter Peder Severin Krøyer (1851–1909) was influential in introducing Impressionism to Denmark. Paul Gauguin, who had married a Danish girl, helped spread the Impressionist theories, showing his own collection in 1889 – including works by Manet, Degas, Cézanne, Guillaumin, Pissarro, Sisley, and Angrand.

Living in Paris between 1873 and 1878, Max Liebermann (1847–1935) came into contact with the Impressionists. He is the only German painter who could be classified as an Impressionist. The Russian Vasili Dimitrevic Polenov (1844–1927) became his country's forerunner for *plein air* painting, while Isaak Levitan (1861–1900), who taught landscape painting at the Moscow School of Art, achieved a romantic lyricism using the Impressionists' "rainbow palette." From Spain came Ramón Casas y Carbó (1866–1923), who showed an affinity with Toulouse-Lautrec, and Joaquin Sorolla y Bastida (1863–1923).

Isaak Levitan, Golden Autumn, *1895, Tretyakov Gallery, Moscow.*

A NEW VIEW OF HISTORY

On June 19, 1867, the Emperor of Mexico, Maximilian of Hapsburg, was shot by a firing squad, together with his generals Miramón and Mejía. As the news spread to France, public indignation turned against Napoleon III, who had imposed the reign of Maximilian and then withdrew the military forces that should have sustained it. Manet worked on the subject for over a year, basing his composition on photographs, documents, and eyewitness accounts. He created four oils and lithographs, which in their structure strongly recall Goya's *The Third of May 1808* (1814), seen by Manet two years earlier when he visited the San Fernando Academy in Madrid. In Manet's final work, romantic sentiments have faded, the warm, soft colors replaced by black and cold greens. There is no sentimentality, only the action itself captured at the very moment the three men were shot. There is none of the romantic rush that characterized Goya's *Struggle against the Mamelukes* (1814), with its excited rhythm of time and action. In Manet's work, time is arrested at that instant. The space is clear and clean, and the emperor is positioned at the center of the trio, like Christ on the cross. However, behind the wall, there is the briefest hint of life beyond this time and place.

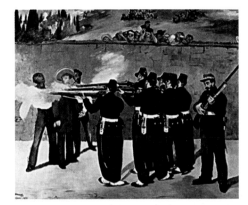

Edouard Manet, The Execution of Emperor Maximilian, *1868. Städtische Kunsthalle, Mannheim.*

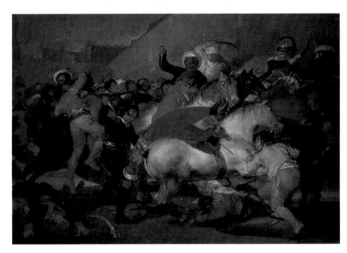

Francisco Goya, Struggle against the Mamelukes, 1814. Museo del *Prado, Madrid. This belongs to the same series as* The Third of May 1808.

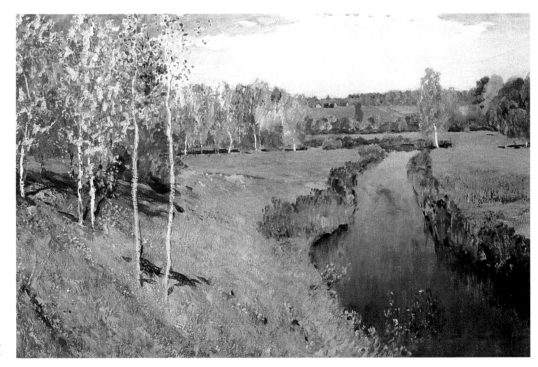

DEVELOPMENTS IN THE 19TH CENTURY

1830: after the July Revolution, Louis Philippe of Orléans becomes king of France; Barbizon School established in the forest of Fontainebleau, near Paris. **1837:** birth of the Dutch painter and engraver Jacob Maris, exponent of the Realist branch of the Hague School. **1839:** French photographer Daguerre invents daguerreotype process. **1845:** coinciding with the Paris Salon, Charles Baudelaire writes his first essay of aesthetic criticism. **1848:** manifesto of the Communist Party, by Karl Marx and Friedrich Engels, is published in London. **1854:** Giuseppe Palizzi returns from Paris, bringing to Naples the most up-to-date information on the works of French painters. **1851:** Courbet exhibits *A Burial at Ornans* at the Pavillon du Réalisme; The Caffè Michelangelo in

1830   1840   1850   1860

▼ HONORE DAUMIER
(1808-79)
Political satire and social denunciation were constant themes in the work of Honoré Daumier, the French draftsman, painter, and sculptor.

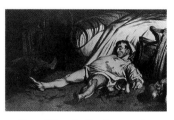

Honoré Daumier, Rue Transnonain, le 15 avril 1834, *lithograph, 1834. British Museum, London.*

▼ JOSEPH MALLORD WILLIAM TURNER
(1775-1851)
Trained at the Royal Academy, the great English painter Turner was an acute observer of natural phenomena, transfigured into lyrical visions full of light.

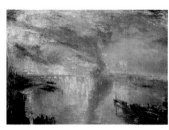

J.M.W. Turner, The Burning of the Houses of Lords and Commons, 16th of October, 1834. *Art Museum, Cleveland, Ohio.*

JOHN CONSTABLE
(1776-1837)
The works of English painter Constable were a romantic response to the natural beauty of his surroundings. In the 1830s, his work became more expressive, aiming less at the careful naturalistic depiction of a scene and more at the immediate recording of light and atmosphere.

▼ IL PICCIO
(GIOVANNI CARNEVALI)
(1804-73)
The Lombard painter Il Piccio was influenced by French art and was a free interpreter of the great Italian tradition. His landscapes are largely concerned with atmosphere and light.

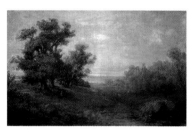

Il Piccio, Landscape with Tall Trees, 1844–46. *Galleria d'Arte Moderna, Milan.*

THEODORE ROUSSEAU
(1812-67)
French painter Rousseau was a member of the Barbizon School, which constituted a link between Romanticism and Realism. He immersed himself in the solitude of the countryside as a refuge from the dissolution caused by the growth of an industrial society.

▼ GEORGE CALEB BINGHAM
(1811-79)
Associated with the current of Realism prevalent in the US, Bingham represented the commonplace while displaying a romantic influence and a sense of idealism.

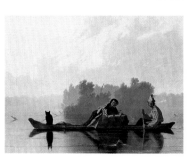

George Caleb Bingham, Fur Traders Descending the Missouri, 1845. *Metropolitan Museum of Art, New York.*

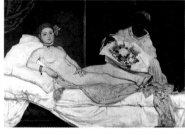

Gustave Courbet, A Burial at Ornans, 1849–50. *Musée d'Orsay, Paris.*

▲ GUSTAVE COURBET
(1819-77)
The paintings of French artist Courbet made a radical break with the prevailing style of academic art, depicting contemporary life with dramatic realism.

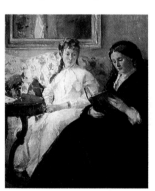

Jean-François Millet, The Sower, 1850. *Museum of Fine Arts, Boston.*

▲ JEAN-FRANCOIS MILLET
(1814-75)
More closely associated with Romanticism than with the new Realism, the French painter Millet produced work that promoted a positive, idealized vision of a hard-working peasantry.

▼ EDOUARD MANET
(1832-83)
Using an extraordinarily innovative style, the French artist Manet chose subjects that reflected the heroic aspect of modern life, as envisaged by Baudelaire. Unpopular in academic circles, his faith in contemporary experience was a major inspiration to early Impressionism.

Edouard Manet, Olympia, 1863. *Musée d'Orsay, Paris.*

▼ BERTHE MORISOT
(1841-95)
A French painter and pupil of Corot, Berthe Morisot developed a style that owed much to Manet in its free brushwork. Her strokes were delicate and feathery rather than in the short and broken style of the Impressionists.

Berthe Morisot, Portrait of the Artist's Mother and Sister, 1869–70. *National Gallery of Art, Washington, DC.*

Florence is headquarters for the group of artists later known as Macchiaioli. **1863:** *Le Déjeuner sur l'herbe* by Edouard Manet, exhibited at the Salon des Refusés, creates a huge scandal. **1867:**

Diego Martelli and Telemaco Signorini found the *Gazettino delle arti e del disegno*, the first Italian art magazine to deal with the latest developments in Europe. **1871:** King Wilhelm I of Prussia

becomes emperor of Germany; the brief revolution of the Paris Commune is suppressed by the army. **1874:** the first exhibition of the Impressionist group is held in Paris. **1879:** discovery of the

caves of Altamira in Spain, revealing wonders of Paleolithic art. **1886:** the art dealer Durand-Ruel presents some of the works of the Impressionists in New York with resounding success.

1 8 7 0   1 8 8 0   1 8 9 0

▼ PARIS
In 1874, the first exhibition of the group of Impressionists was held in the studio of the photographer Nadar in Paris.

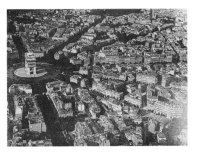

Nadar, View of Paris. *This photograph was taken from a hot-air balloon.*

▼ PAUL CEZANNE
(1839-1906)
Influenced by Pissarro, this key French painter distanced himself from the Impressionists in his use of solidly geometrical forms, a style that was to lead to Cubism.

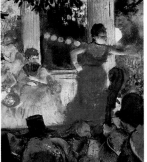
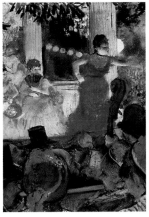

▲ EDGAR DEGAS
(1834-1917)
An admiration for Ingres and the Italian "primitives" persuaded this French painter and sculptor to adhere to the principles of traditional design: his links with Impressionism were mainly thematic.

Edgar Degas, A Café-concert at Les Ambassadeurs, *1875–77. Musée des Beaux-Arts, Lyons.*

▼ VINCENZO VELA
(1820-91)
The Swiss-born sculptor Vincenzo Vela was influenced by Lorenzo Bartolini. He treated social themes with great realism.

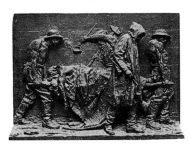

Vincenzo Vela, Victims of Labor, *bronze, 1882–83. Galleria Nazionale d'Arte Moderna, Rome.*

▼ PIERRE-AUGUSTE RENOIR
(1841-1919)
After a formal training, the French painter Renoir turned to open-air painting, depicting with astonishing immediacy figures that vibrated with life and movement. A visit to Italy led him to discover Raphael, after which his figures became more solid, without losing any of their joyful vitality.

▼ HENRI DE TOULOUSE-LAUTREC
(1864-1901)
With his distinctively elegant style that anticipated Art Nouveau, the French artist Toulouse-Lautrec became the ironic, ruthless chronicler of Parisian night life.

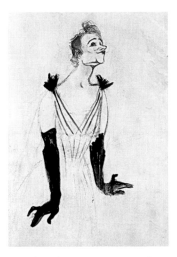

Henri de Toulouse-Lautrec, Yvette Guilbert, *1894. Musée Toulouse-Lautrec, Albi, France.*

▼ CLAUDE MONET
(1840-1926)

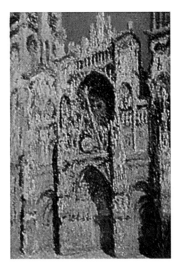

Claude Monet, Rouen Cathedral, Bright Sunshine – Harmony in Blue and Gold, *1892–94. Musée d'Orsay, Paris.*

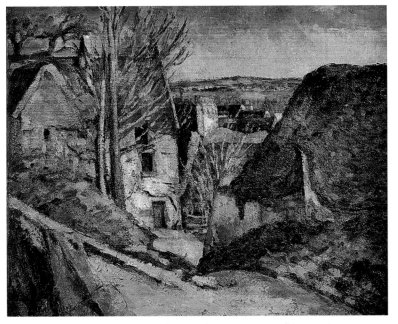

Paul Cézanne, The House of the Hanged Man, *1873. Musée d'Orsay, Paris.*

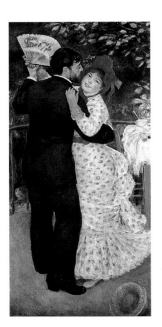

Pierre-Auguste Renoir, Dance in the Country, *1883. Musée d'Orsay, Paris.*

New Trends in the 19th & 20th Centuries
POST-IMPRESSIONISM

*Following the relatively brief flowering of Impressionism, European art –
with Cézanne at the forefront – witnessed the rapid blossoming of diverse
new trends and the formation of new groups of artists, both nationally
and internationally. Among these artists there were some innovative
figures with their own powerful and unique styles.*

During the 1880s, Impressionism seemed to be running out of ideas. Dissent was growing between the various artists, who were now pursuing their own personal artistic experiments. At the same time, there was an emerging trend that sought to distance art from its previously close relationship with nature and give it a more markedly intellectual character.

By historical coincidence, the culmination of a number of significant events in 1886 signaled the final transition to a different artistic climate: the Impressionists staged their eighth and last exhibition; Vincent van Gogh arrived in Paris; Georges Seurat presented a painting that would be the visual manifesto of the new artistic style of Pointillism; and *Le Figaro* published the Symbolist manifesto of Jean Moréas. Furthermore, the publication of Emile Zola's *L'Oeuvre*, which recorded the critical devaluation of Impressionism, put an end to the author's 30-year-old friendship with Cézanne, who could be recognized in the character of the protagonist Claude Lantier, an unsuccessful painter who fails to realize his dreams through a lack of creative flair. The intellectual stimulation and readiness to explore entirely new formal solutions soon created a complex cultural exchange. Thus, it would be hard to separate trends and label individual artists at a time of such interest in, and sensitivity to, new ideas.

CEZANNE'S GREAT THEMES

The desire to investigate what lies at the heart of reality and to understand its essence rather than merely its ever-changing manifestations made Cézanne return in an almost obsessive fashion to certain subjects throughout his productive life. Following his stated aim to organize nature according to geometric forms, he repeatedly painted Mont Sainte-Victoire, the mountain seen from the window of his house in Aix-en-Provence, until he had fully caught its shape and relationship with the surrounding space and the background of sky. In depicting the bay of Marseilles, he subjected even the expanse of open water to the process of structural analysis and solidification.

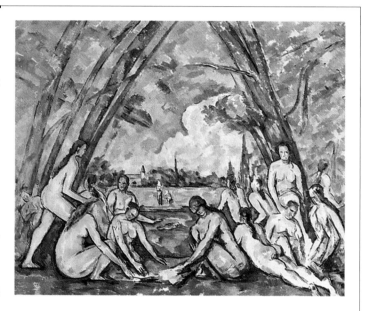

Paul Cézanne, The Large Bathers, *1898–1905. Philadelphia Museum of Art. An arc unites the two groups, linking various planes to the background in a structure of extraordinary power.*

The other subject that fascinated Cézanne was the human figure. He liked to portray statuesque figures based on geometrical shapes, such as his impassive card players and series of firm-bodied, yet completely unsensual, bathers. He dedicated much time to the latter, spending seven years working on the ambitious painting *The Large Bathers*, which represents his personal interpretation of classicism. In this architectural composition, with its tight rhythm and triangular compositional format, human and natural forms are given equal dignity and weight by the use of a limited color range in shades of blue and ochre.

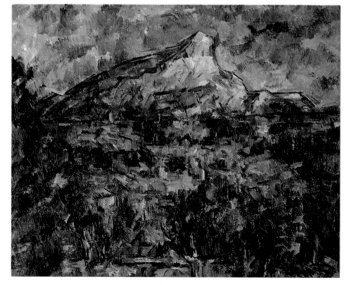

Paul Cézanne, Mont Sainte-Victoire, *1906. Pushkin Museum, Moscow.*

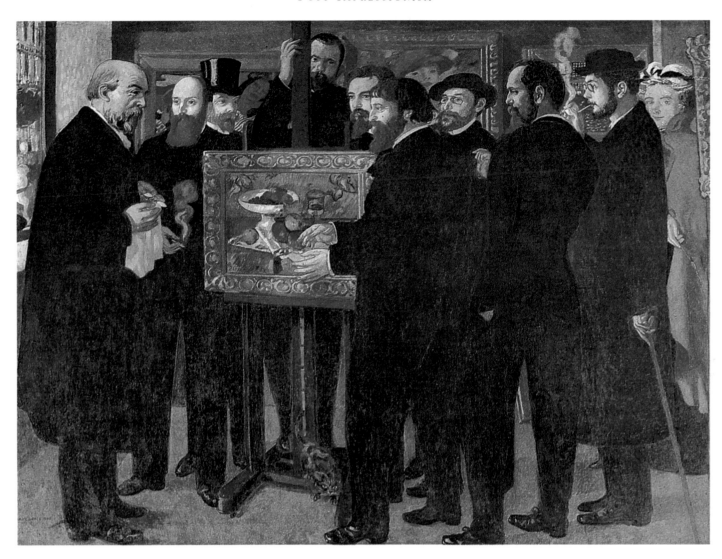

BEYOND IMPRESSIONISM

Cézanne (1839–1906), having distanced himself from the Impressionist movement in 1877, left Paris and returned to Aix-en-Provence. There, he continued to perfect his most important research into "solidifying Impressionism" through the reconstruction of form – this involved analyzing, simplifying, and stripping it of any extraneous visual attributes and creating a harmonious compositional synthesis that was balanced yet rigorous in color and dimension. His intention was to remove objects – landscapes and figures – from the transitory state of the visual experience and restore their solidity, thereby infusing them with a new classical spirit. In order to, in his words, "re-create Poussin from nature," he set out to depict his subject matter "through cylinders, spheres, and cones, all placed in perspective." This approach developed into a trend that would later find expression in the work of of the 20th-century Cubists, but already it was inspiring younger artists in Paris and in Brittany who were experimenting with a totally new type of painting that concentrated on the plastic organization of forms. An exhibition of one hundred canvases by Cézanne, held in Ambroise Vollard's gallery in 1895, together with the enthusiasm shown toward him by other artists (for example, the artist Maurice Denis named one of his works *Homage to Cézanne*), illustrated the profound change in the art scene that took place in the course of just a decade. On show were works by the great master demonstrating his new theories, from the series *The Card Players* to the many versions of landscapes of *Mont Sainte-Victoire* and *The Large Bathers*, in which form was reduced to its most basic elements, carefully studied and tenaciously repeated, and the colors are a sober, harmonious blend of blues, mauves, and grays.

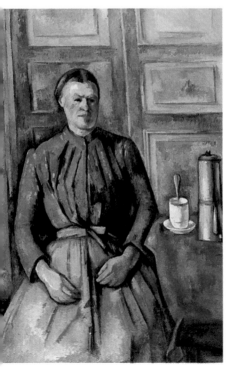

Paul Cézanne, Woman with Coffee Pot, *1893. Musée d'Orsay, Paris.*

Maurice Denis (1870–1943), Homage to Cézanne, *1900. Musée National d'Art Moderne, Paris. The painting shows a group of artists, including Redon, Vuillard, Bonnard, and Denis himself, gathered around a still life by Cézanne.*

PAUL CEZANNE: "THE BATHERS"

1900–05; oil on canvas;
51 x 77 in (130 x 195 cm);
National Gallery, London.

Cézanne worked extensively on the theme of bathers toward the end of his life (1895–1906), producing several versions of this painting. The largest, and perhaps best known, owing to the perfect geometry of its composition, is in the Philadelphia Museum of Art. The version pictured here is perhaps the most synthetist in the treatment of the figures.

The work can be seen as part of the tradition of groups of people in natural scenery that has many examples in arcadian and pastoral art, from Giorgione, Raphael, and Giulio Romano, through Claude Lorrain and Poussin, to Manet and Renoir. Cézanne had great respect for classical tradition, and his aim was to re-create its balance within the new dimension of Impressionist art. In his painting, considerations of composition are essential and permanent, freed from traditional lines of perspective, and there is a assured sense of space.

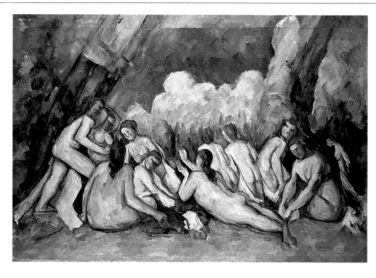

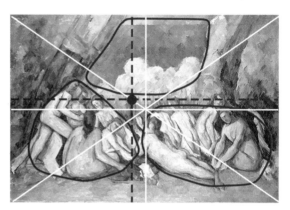

◀ *1. The painting is divided by two perpendicular axes into a lower area of figures and an upper area of landscape. The right and left sides both contain bathers. The composition centers on a hypothetical focal point where the vertical axis crosses the horizon line at the base of the clouds. The eye is naturally drawn to the area between the center of the canvas and the center of the pictorial sections: this is the pivotal point between the two groups of bathers and the area of sky.*

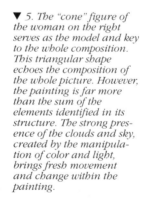

▶ *2. Oblique lines make up the composition and bring dynamism to the perpendicular axes. Arranged in bands, one line follows the tree trunk and the inclined figure on the left of the picture; the other follows the figures that are facing downward in the foreground, from the right-hand side through the center, until it meets the other band. Lesser lines also follow these two bands. Color and light are fused in the same way, creating an overall effect of dense, compact organization around the central atmospheric void.*

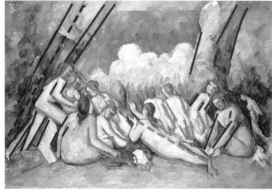

▲ *4. It is easy to see the picture as a composition of geometric shapes: from the left there is a rectangle, an oval, a cone, and an ovoid. The two women sitting at either side are recognizable as cone or pyramid-like figures. For Cézanne, these basic geometric shapes represented what he saw as the bases of many natural forms.*

▼ *5. The "cone" figure of the woman on the right serves as the model and key to the whole composition. This triangular shape echoes the composition of the whole picture. However, the painting is far more than the sum of the elements identified in its structure. The strong presence of the clouds and sky, created by the manipulation of color and light, brings fresh movement and change within the painting.*

▶ *3. Curved lines contribute to the successful combination of figures and landscape. Like the oblique lines, they add to the rhythm of the composition, defining the bathers' bodies and the colored shapes in the vegetation and sky. Using new methods to expand on the experiments of the Impressionists, Cézanne opts for color rather than line in his construction of form and space. Here, the greens and blues of the sky and vegetation are echoed on the bathers' bodies, as are the yellows and pinks, also found in the clouds.*

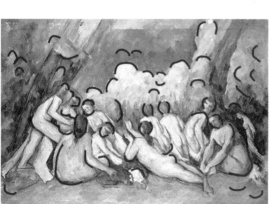

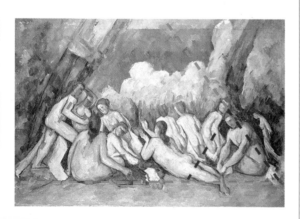

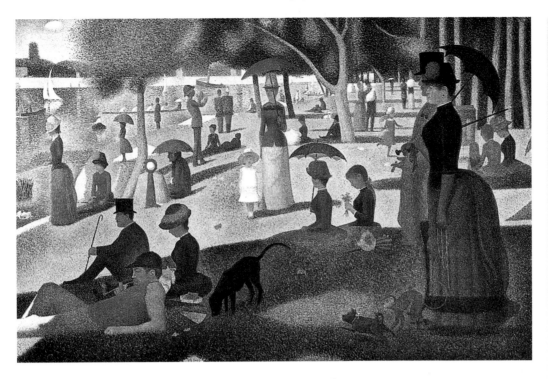

As the innovative and experimental artists of Impressionism and Post-Impressionism flourished, certain strongholds of tradition in the arts remained intact. One such area was that of folk costume and decorative design, a reappraisal of which had its roots in the French Revolution, when the educated classes developed a new interest in traditional dress. Paintings of village folk and scenes from traditional rural life were soon in great demand. One of the most famous of these was the series of pictures commissioned by Murat, King of Naples, which was used to decorate the royal palace. Ethnographic studies promoted great interest in the designs used to decorate everyday objects. These included the ornamental motifs that were traditionally carved into furniture; patterns embroidered onto linen, curtains, and clothing; fabric prints; shaped molds for bread and butter; jewelry designs; motifs used in lace-making and knitting; and decorative designs on plates, candles, and religious objects. The motifs and patterns took the form of flowers, fruit, fret designs, and stylized human and animal forms. City dwellers, trying to cope with the immense changes caused by industrialization (and offered little by the new art styles), found comfort in the visual heritage of their rural ancestors. The trend was reinforced by the municipal authorities, who held events featuring traditional village games, folk dances, and races.

NEO-IMPRESSIONISM

Cézanne's rigorous research into form and structure yielded crucial results for the future of art and laid the foundations for the Cubist revolution. However, he was not the only artist to offer an alternative solution to the empirical experience of Impressionism. Georges

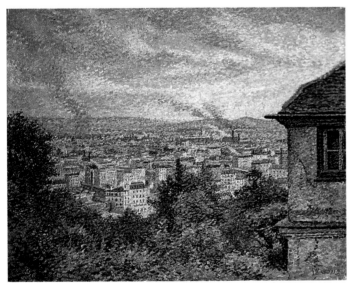

Maximilien Luce (1858–1941), View of Montmartre, *1887. Petit Palais, Geneva. The artifice of the scientific techniques of Pointillism does not detract from the sincerity of the painting's inspiration.*

Seurat (1859–91) attempted to replace the emotional subjectivity of the visual process with a scientific objectivity based on the laws of optics. Between 1880 and 1885, he was already working on the composition of color and form through the analysis of light and breakdown of color into its constituent elements. He adopted the scientific theories of Hermann Helmholtz and Edward Rood, which developed the discoveries of Eugène Chevreul, already well known to the Impressionists, and

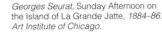

Georges Seurat, Sunday Afternoon on the Island of La Grande Jatte, *1884–86. Art Institute of Chicago.*

experimented with a new scientific painting technique. Instead of mixing the color on the palette, the required shade was achieved on the canvas through the dense application of dots of pure color. When perceived from a distance, the juxtaposed colors were fused into a solid image.

Sunday Afternoon on the Island of La Grande Jatte was shown in 1886 and soon became the "manifesto" of the new technique of Pointillism. In this painting, Seurat offers

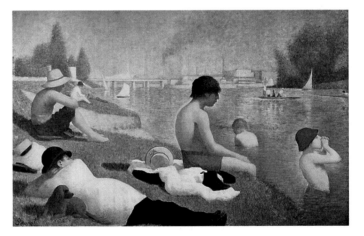

Georges Seurat, Bathers at Asnières, *1883–84. National Gallery, London.*

a critical reworking of a popular Impressionist subject, capturing and crystallizing the scene in a strictly intellectual vision, where all form is reduced to geometric volume and is ordered according to harmonious

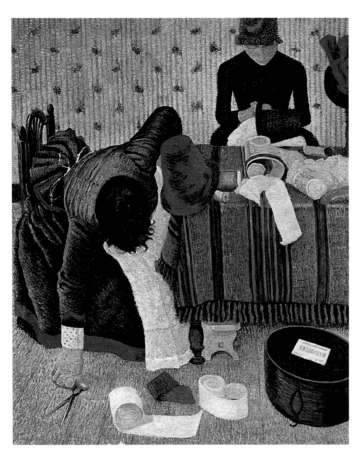

Signac (1863–1935) and the Impressionist artist Camille Pissarro (1830–1903) and his son Lucien. There was also the group of "young chemists," as Gauguin chose to call them, which included Charles Angrand (1854–1926), Henri-Edmond Cross (1856–1910), and Albert Dubois-Pillet (1846–90), as well as the Belgian artist Theo van Rysselberghe (1862–1926). Also affiliated to the movement – which would soon become a fashionable trend – were *pompier* painters such as Jean and Henry Martin, who immersed their traditional subject matter in halos of radiant light.

With the premature death of Seurat in 1891, Paul Signac continued the elaboration of Pointillist theory, arriving at the conclusion that behind the scientific explanation of the technique there was a spiritual aspect, a development that paved the way to Symbolist-style interpretations.

VAN GOGH

The Dutch-born painter Vincent van Gogh (1853–90) was the son of a Protestant pastor, and was himself a lay preacher for a time in the Belgian coal mines. He moved to Paris in 1886, and throughout the year he frequented and painted in Père Tanguy's shop. He exhibited his works at the Café du Tambourin with

Paul Signac, The Milliner, 1885. E. Bührle Collection, Zurich. The theme of millinery, a profession that was very much in demand in the late 19th century, attracted many other artists, including Seurat, Degas, and Toulouse-Lautrec.

relations expressed in light and color.

Seurat's experiments were supported by the critic Félix Fénéon, who vouched for the scientific and methodological foundations of this artistic process and also coined the term "Neo-Impressionism" to describe it. Other enthusiasts for the new style were Paul

THE SOCIETE DES ARTISTES INDEPENDANTS

In opposition to the wishes of admission panels of the official Salons, the Société des Artistes Indépendants was formed in Paris in 1884; under the motto "No jury no prizes," it allowed everybody to submit their work to public exhibition and public scrutiny. Owing particularly to the initiatives of Georges Seurat, Paul Signac, and Odilon Redon, the group soon launched the work of the Neo-Impressionists

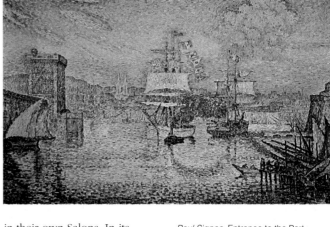

in their own Salons. In its desire to embrace the most diverse and innovative artistic experiences of the Post-Impressionist generation, the society invited the unknown primitive artist Henri Rousseau to exhibit in 1886. In the following year, the group presented work by the Norwegian artist Edvard

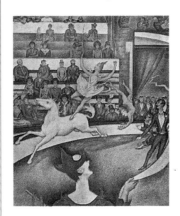

Georges Seurat, The Circus, 1890. Musée d'Orsay, Paris.

Paul Signac, Entrance to the Port of Marseilles, 1911. Musée National d'Art Moderne, Paris.

Munch. Later, in 1911, the society introduced Cubist painting to the general public. Interest resided not only in the ideas and talents of the young artists but also in the lessons of the great artists of the past. Homage was paid to van Gogh in 1891, and the first Seurat retrospective was held in 1892.

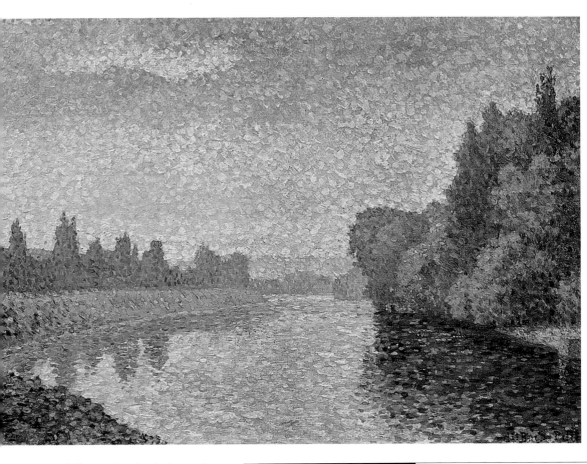

Albert Dubois-Pillet, The Marne at Dawn, 1880. Musée d'Orsay, Paris. In this painting, the variations in light that so captivated the Impressionists are here reinterpreted according to the theories of Seurat and Signac.

soon abandoned his former style (dark, dense colors in large, accentuated brushstrokes) and stark subject matter (figures reflecting the reality of poverty, such as those in *Potato Eaters*, 1885). He turned instead to a lighter style of painting with bright colors and more accessible, cheerful subject matter based on familiar characters and scenes. Although he was attracted and impressed by the technical innovations of the Neo-Impressionists, he was also disappointed by their attitude – some of the painters "disgusted him as people" – and felt that the emphasis on technical solutions, based on visual objectivity, too often led to the neglect or even abandonment of content. Van Gogh's main preoccupation

fellow artists Louis Anquetin (1861–1932), Emile Bernard (1868–1941), and Henri de Toulouse-Lautrec (1864–1901). Van Gogh was also interested in Neo-Impressionism and its theories on the perception of color, and he used its ideas as a basis for his own original technique of fragmented brushstrokes. This can be seen in *Interior of a Restaurant* (1887). In Paris, van Gogh

Emile Bernard, Buckwheat Harvest, 1888. Private Collection. Bernard painted with Gauguin at Pont-Aven, enclosing areas of color with dark outlines.

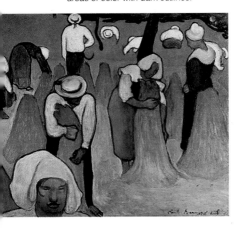

THE THEORY OF NEO-IMPRESSIONISM

Paul Signac expounded the scientific theory of the Pointillist painters in his essay "D'Eugène Delacroix au Néo-Impressionisme," which gave an interpretation of the expressive and emotive values of artistic composition. He stressed the value of using only pure colors and of mixing them only when adjacent on the color wheel: "These colors, in shades between one another and made lighter with the addition of white, will help give the range of tints of the solar spectrum and all their hues…" Signac's advice to Neo-Impressionists on composition was based on that of Delacroix, who never started work on a canvas before establishing a layout: "He will manipulate the lines (direction and angles), the chiaroscuro (tones) and colors (shades) to fit the mood he wants to predominate. The dominant line will be horiz-

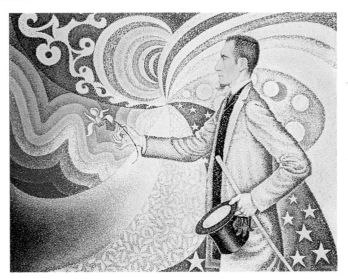

Paul Signac, Portrait of Félix Fénéon, 1890. Museum of Modern Art, New York.

ontal for calmness, ascending for joy, and descending for sadness; all other intermediate lines will represent the many remaining feelings. To add to this interplay of lines, there is an equally expressive and diverse play of colors: warm

shades and light tones go with ascending lines, while cold shades and dark tones go with descending lines; a balance of warm and cool shades and pale and intense tones accompanies horizontal lines. By subjecting color and line to the emotion he wishes to portray, the artist will be doing the job of a poet, a creator."

was a search for the substance and hidden meaning of objects. He pursued this end by means of an expressive and psychological choice of color – "I have tried to express the terrible passions of man with red and with green"– and by the use of undulating rhythms in disjointed brushstrokes that formed the outlines of lacerated and distorted shapes. In 1888, van Gogh moved to Arles in southern France, where he enjoyed a happy period of creativity in the region's beautiful natural surroundings. Some of his greatest works were produced during this period, including

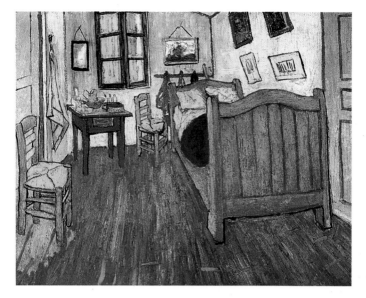

Vincent van Gogh, The Artist's Room at Arles, 1888. Van Gogh Museum, Amsterdam.

the series of 12 paintings entitled *Sunflowers* (symbols of divine sunlight) and the views of his bedroom and the humble objects that furnish it, such as *Vincent's Chair*. Van Gogh dreamed of founding a studio in the south of France, a kind of communal utopia where artists could play an active role in society, and tried unsuccessfully to involve his friend Gauguin in the project when he visited Arles. The period of disillusionment that followed, which led to van

VINCENT VAN GOGH: "STARRY NIGHT"

1889; oil on canvas; 29 x 36 in (73 x 92 cm); Museum of Modern Art, New York.

This picture was painted during during Van Gogh's stay at the asylum in Saint-Rémy. It is dated June 1889, a month after his arrival, and 13 months before his suicide. The artist wrote to his brother, Theo: "My wretched illness is making me work with mute fury, very slowly, but from morning to night without interruption…I believe this will help me get better." The painting depicts a village landscape, with hills in the background, at night. It does

not portray a calm, still night but one where the elements of nature and the human world quiver with tormented emotion, the village reaching up to the sky, with its coils and tangles of movement.
The simple composition centers on the relationship between the vertical lines of the cypresses and steeple and the powerful oblique strokes which, with an accelerating rhythm from left to right, impart a strong dynamic thrust to the line of the horizon. The real expressive impact of the of the composition lies in the color – clear and sharp with unexpected bright yellows that accentuate the coldness of the blues.

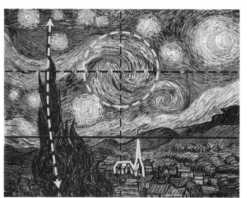

▼ *2. The whole of the area of the sky has been obsessively filled with curved lines of color. Series of short, thick, successive strokes of color set the surface in motion. The darker lines are generally continuous. Their changing directions draw the eye into swirls of dark and light, which create an aura of anxiety and compulsion. The poetic twinkling of the stars, defined by the lighter colors, develops into a frenzied, incessant throbbing.*

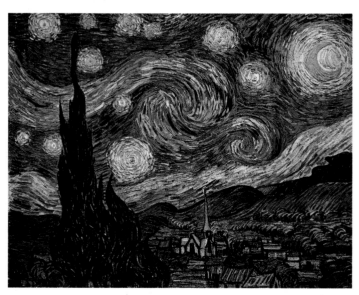

▲ *1. The composition of the painting is straightforward. The night sky occupies approximately two-thirds of the picture, while the other third is dedicated to the landscape. In the foreground and middle ground, the movement proceeds from left to right. The ground and sky are connected by a clump of cypresses that rises from the bottom of the painting on the left-hand side. In the middle of the sky, there is a large, circular whirl of color. Because of its size and prominence, this vortex becomes the central feature of the composition. The landscape that lies beneath the vortex appears to be flattened. The pointed church steeple rises out of the group of buildings, standing out against the hills and extending into the area of sky, like a second line connecting the human world with that above. The band of lines and colors that make up the whirling vortex comes from the extreme left of the picture and goes toward the right, guiding the viewers eye in the same direction.*

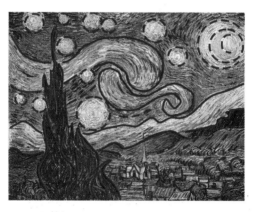

▶ *5. The narrow band of earth lies beneath a dramatic sky and has a well-defined outline. Wide, generally short strokes, in a combination of straight lines and curves, are lit up with flashes of red and yellow. The cypresses in deep and dark green with subtle red lines dominate the landscape: "A cypress tree is beautiful because it has lines and proportions like an Egyptian obelisk," wrote the artist. The base of the band of light along the bottom of the sky is defined by the hills. The impact of van Gogh's style lies chiefly in its pictorial language – his boldness in the application of color, his imbuement of the surface with movement, and his creation of a composition with dynamic contrasts.*

VINCENT VAN GOGH

The son of a Dutch Protestant pastor, Vincent van Gogh (1853–90) had early intentions of a religious career. Plagued by mental illness, he was the "great mad artist" of his century. Like Caravaggio, van Gogh was idolized by those who admired art with a violent emotional impact. With frenetic brushwork and a vivid sense of color and movement, van Gogh was a dramatist of pure art as well as a desperate poet of human suffering. Working within the context of Impressionism, he remained virtually outside the art world of his time. For the variety and richness of his pictorial content and the boldness and originality of his style, van Gogh is one of the leading figures in 19th-century art.

Gogh dramatically cutting off his own ear, marked the start of a deep crisis that resulted in his admission to an asylum in Saint Rémy. The depiction of the fragility and desperation of the human condition (*The Prisoners' Round*, 1890) was translated into a new style of painting that consisted of ever more tormented and violent brushstrokes and increasingly bold and angry colors. This style culminated in the Expressionist-type contortions of the paintings created by van Gogh in his final years (*Starry Night*, 1889, and *Crows in the Wheatfields*, 1890).

THE SELF-PORTRAITS OF VAN GOGH AND GAUGUIN

One of Van Gogh's dreams was to create a commune, a brotherhood built around the practice of art and life with other artists, that would encourage collaboration and reciprocal stimulation and establish the foundations for pictorial research. After moving to Arles in 1888, van Gogh wanted to start up a "Studio of the South," hoping to join forces with his friends Emile Bernard and, especially, Paul Gauguin, whom he would have liked to undertake the role of director. The initiative failed dismally (though it was later revived by Gauguin under the name "Studio of the Tropics"), but the series of self-portraits that followed were akin to a custom popular among Japanese artists – the group of friends dedicated to each other, bearing witness to their commonly held ideals of work and fraternity. While van Gogh likened his portrait to a Buddhist monk, Gauguin depicted himself as the young Jean Valjean, the hero of Victor Hugo's *Les Misérables*, "disguised as a badly dressed and audacious rogue…but all the same with a certain nobility and innate kindness."

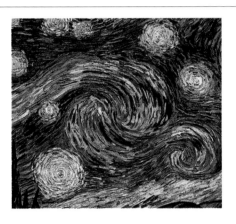

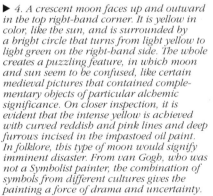

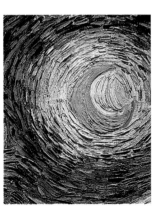

◄ 3. *The central vortex is the most developed feature. Its base rests against another vortex with a well-defined center and a cometlike tail trailing in its wake. Below, a band of bright sky rises, against which the hills are outlined. The shape of the vortex is reminiscent of the Taoist circle, made up of two teardrop shapes, the positive and bright "yang" and the negative and dark feminine "yin," which influence destiny. It is likely that van Gogh learned about Taoism when collecting Japanese prints in Paris.*

► 4. *A crescent moon faces up and outward in the top right-hand corner. It is yellow in color, like the sun, and is surrounded by a bright circle that turns from light yellow to light green on the right-hand side. The whole creates a puzzling feature, in which moon and sun seem to be confused, like certain medieval pictures that contained complementary objects of particular alchemic significance. On closer inspection, it is evident that the intense yellow is achieved with curved reddish and pink lines and deep furrows incised in the impastoed oil paint. In folklore, this type of moon would signify imminent disaster. From van Gogh, who was not a Symbolist painter, the combination of symbols from different cultures gives the painting a force of drama and uncertainty.*

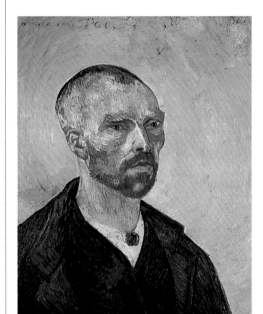

Vincent van Gogh, Self-portrait with Shaven Head, 1888. Fogg Art Museum, Cambridge, Massachusetts.

Paul Gauguin, Self-portrait, 1888. Van Gogh Museum, Amsterdam.

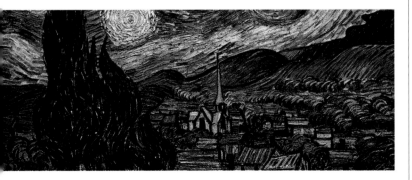

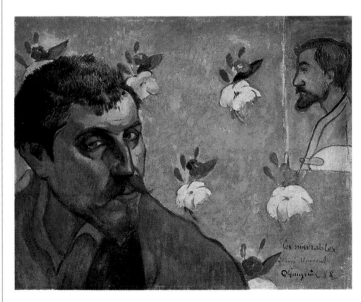

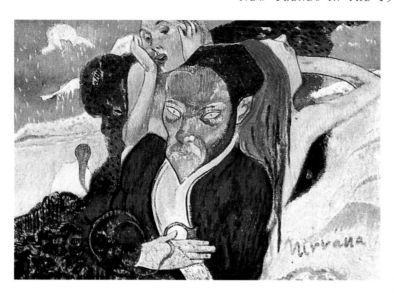

Paul Gauguin, Nirvana, 1889. Wadsworth Atheneum, Hartford, Connecticut. The sitter is Gauguin's fellow artist, Jacob Isaac Meyer de Haan. The two figures in the background appear in the lithograph At the Black Rocks.

PAUL GAUGUIN

If van Gogh typified the artist passionate about his own anguish in an unappreciative society that alienated him to the point of self-destruction, then Paul Gauguin was the daring, nonconformist painter – less complicated, but equally as compelling. Driven by a "terrible longing for things unknown," he fled a bourgeois existence for lands unscathed by Western ideas of progress, conventions, and rules. There, he could express himself with absolute freedom, discovering the spirituality of civilizations that were to him mysterious – "the only ones left that could provoke real emotions." Gauguin came to painting at a late age and was intro-

PAUL GAUGUIN

Paul Gauguin (1848–1903), a friend of Pissarro, devoted himself to art in 1883. His distaste for modern industrial life distanced him from Paris, so he moved to Brittany in 1886, before joining van Gogh in Arles in 1888.
He made his first visit to Tahiti in 1891 and returned there in 1895 after a retrospective exhibition in Paris. He later settled in the Marquesas Islands, where he died in poverty. Inspired by aspects of Japanese and other non-Western art and with a deep concern for the future of contemporary art, he sought to develop a new "synthetist" style that made a complete break with tradition.

duced by Pissarro into the Impressionist circle (he took part in the group's exhibitions of 1879 and 1886). While in Brittany, a region that conserved its popular traditions, he was stimulated by the experiments of Bernard and Anquetin. They sought to replace the fragmented color and fleeting nature of Impressionism with a style that used large areas of flat, uniform color, surrounded and defined by thick, dark outlines – similar to the effect achieved by stained glass. Instead of glorifying color and light, Gauguin aimed for a "silent harmony" of dense hues, vibrant with music, as a background to simplified shapes with foreshortened strokes and completed by large, decorative arabesque lines.

After Brittany, Gauguin visited Tahiti, where, enraptured by the charm of the landscape and the Polynesian people, he rediscovered the emotive and magical value of color and became fascinated by indigenous mythology. His increasing awareness of spiritual concerns in every field of art was reflected in his paintings, which contained new and complex symbols

PAUL GAUGUIN: "TA MATETE"
1892; oil on canvas;
29 x 37 in (73 x 93 cm);
Kunstmuseum, Basel, Switzerland.

This work, the title of which means "the market," was painted during Gauguin's first trip to Tahiti. In the middle of the painting are five island women sitting on a long bench in solemn poses; two pairs of women are locked in conversation, while the woman in the middle of the group is staring forward. A large green and orange strip, perhaps the goods on sale, frames the painting at the bottom. In the background there are some blue-violet tree trunks on areas of green, with the profiles of two men carrying fish in the top right-

▶ *1. The composition of the painting is based on a series of "layers," which, like a stage set, appear one behind the other across the canvas. The sky amounts to just a small, yellow strip broken by branches and leaves, while the band of sea below it is slightly narrower and deeper. The pinkish yellow beach stretches out and winds through the other layers, bringing them closer to the foremost. In this way, the scene has a sense of being viewed from above, even if the backdrop of trees and the figures are two-dimensional. The vertical lines of tree trunks and figures are perpendicular to the horizontals in the background, giving static balance to the composition.*

hand corner. Behind the men lies an area of pinkish sand, which reaches the blue of the sea and, in turn, is bordered by the yellow sky above.

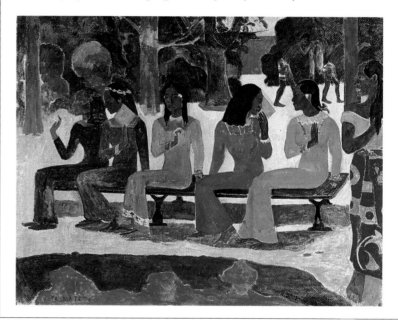

derived from Indian art (for example *Nirvana*, which shows the Dutch Buddhist painter Meyer de Haan); Japanese prints (a current fashion in the West); and Pre-Columbian art, which he knew well through his Peruvian family tradition. Despite these varied influences, the works never lost their spontaneity and decorative gaiety.
Between 1888 and 1900, the artist created a series of stylized pictures in which his dependence on memory, sensation, and the imagination overshadowed the importance

of nature. Looked upon by young artists as their charismatic master, Gauguin advised, "Don't paint from nature too much. Art is an abstraction: extract it from nature and dream of the creation that will result." Gauguin's last great work – *Where do we come from? What are we? Where are we going?* (1897) – appears to be a final and painful meditation on the destiny of humanity, summarizing life's passage from childhood to old age. It pays tribute to Symbolism, which championed the role of

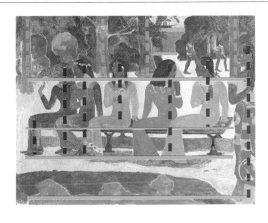

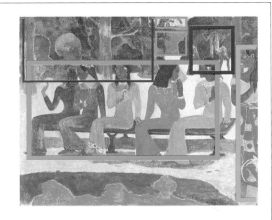

▶ 3. Like a series of decorated glass slides, the layers of the painting create a composition of two-dimensional planes. The first contains the standing woman, the second the figures of the seated women, the third the tree trunks, the fourth the male figures, and the last ones show the distant sea and sky. The depth of the picture is not achieved primarily by perspective or color effects but by the shadows under the bench and the reduction in size of the figures along the different planes, which render the idea of distance. The "primitive" nature of Gauguin's painting, conceived as a cathartic exercise to defy academic convention and look afresh at perspective, was common in much contemporary art.

▼ 2. The seated women and the vertical tree trunks behind are arranged regularly across the canvas in a regular fashion. This regularity is a dominant feature in the painting and arises from the structure, form, and gestures of the women. The figurative style of the seated figures is borrowed from Egyptian art: the faces and legs are in profile and the bodies face forward. The angles the women create are repeated across the picture, while their straight arms and hands provide subtle variations and echoes. Touches of asymmetry give fluidity to the work: the precise arrangement of the heads and faces (two facing the left, one facing forward, and two facing each other); the placement of the central figure on the left-hand side; and the increase in height of the women from left to right. The figure in the foreground is sharply interrupted by the frame, reminiscent of the "photographic cuts" of the Impressionists.

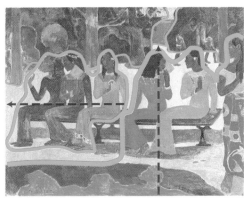

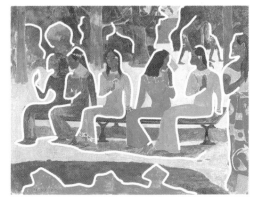

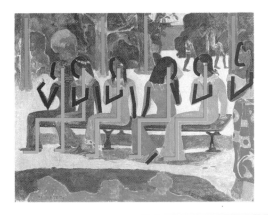

▲ 4. The chromatic composition alternates warm shades of yellow, orange, and red, and cold shades of blue, dark green, and violet, and divides the surface into sections. Strong orange hues (reinforced by greens and yellows) create the sense of foreground at the bottom of the picture. Orange is accentuated in the standing figure, particularly by the red and yellow in her wrap, which create the appearance of a bright orange. The women in red and yellow on the bench reinforce this. Beneath them, the violet shadow establishes the first feeling of depth in the canvas. The farthest "layers" of the painting are in mostly cold colors, creating a sense of distance. The dark colors worn by the three women on the left and the blue shadow under the bench all give an impression of space receding to the left of the picture.

▲ 5. Gauguin applied thin layers of paint to the rough canvas to achieve a tapestry-like effect. By mixing pure pigments, he brought an antique feel to the painting. Two-dimensional planes and three-dimensional illusions govern the composition. The portrait of a foreign place with an unfamiliar way of life has an alienating effect. The link with Egyptian art shows that the scene is not from a "primitive" world but simply a place with an unfamiliar kind of beauty and existence. Compared with the searing inner tensions of van Gogh, Gauguin's choice of subject appears evasive; the disease of civilization is avoided rather than confronted, and the inhabitants of this distant location are idealized as the holders of primal, natural truths.

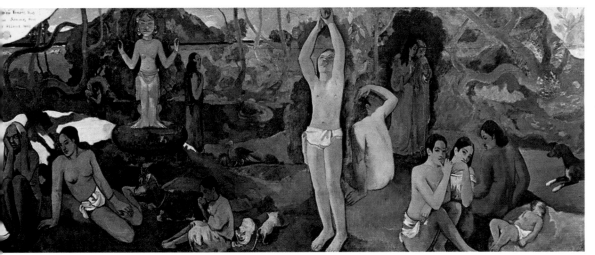

Paul Gauguin, Where do we come from? What are we? Where are we going?, 1897. Museum of Fine Arts, Boston. This powerful painting expresses the eternal questionings of humans; its ambiguities leave it up to the viewer to find the answers.

the imagination in creativity, and allows Gauguin to condense his figurative experiences by combining earlier motifs and characters in a large and highly decorative composition. The harmonious but somber colors enhance the mysterious, ambiguous imagery, creating a powerfully resonant image.

513

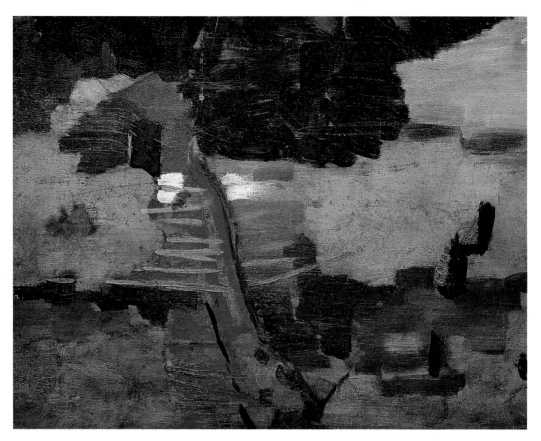

THE PONT-AVEN SCHOOL AND THE NABIS

Maurice Denis's statement that "what Manet was for his generation in 1870, Gauguin was for his in 1890" generally referred to the manner in which Gauguin encouraged young artists to choose their models and styles freely and to draw on figurative sources inspired by all cultures, not just those of the West. Between 1886 and 1888, in the town of Pont-Aven in Brittany, Gauguin gathered a circle of painters around him, including Emile Bernard and Louis Anquetin. Their experiments led to the adoption of a style known as *cloisonnisme*, which was characterized by dark lines enclosing areas of

Paul Sérusier (1863–1927), The Talisman, *1888. Musée d'Orsay, Paris.*

THE NABIS AND ILLUSTRATION

The Nabis felt that the decorative arts were of equal value to painting and devoted much of their time to the graphic arts, illustration, and stage and poster design. Some of the group illustrated books written by literary friends: Maurice Denis illustrated *Le Voyage d'Urien* (1893) by André Gide; Félix Vallotton did *La Maîtresse* (1896) by Jules Renard; and Pierre Bonnard did *Parallèlement* (1900) by Paul Verlaine. Others collaborated on theatrical stage sets, such as Paul Sérusier on *Les Sept Princesses* (1892) by

Félix Vallotton, illustration for La Revue Blanche, *1898.*

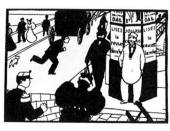

Maurice Maeterlinck and, with Maurice Denis, on *Ubu roi* (1896) by Alfred Jarry. Denis also helped devise designs for the Théâtre de l'Oeuvre in 1893, while Lacombe worked on the Théâtre Rosse.

From 1893, *La revue blanche*, a literary magazine founded by the Natanson brothers, became a prestigious medium for caricatures and sketches and assumed an important promotional role for the "modern" figurative arts. It helped spread the theories of Neo-Impressionism, publishing Gauguin's illustrated account of Tahiti in 1897 and Signac's essay in 1898.

A prolific contributor to the magazine, Toulouse-Lautrec also designed posters for it with Bonnard. Several exhibitions by the Nabis were held at the headquarters of *La revue blanche*. In 1903, its closure was in part responsible for the dispersal of the group.

Pierre Bonnard, poster for
La revue blanche, *1894.*
Bibliothèque Nationale, Paris.

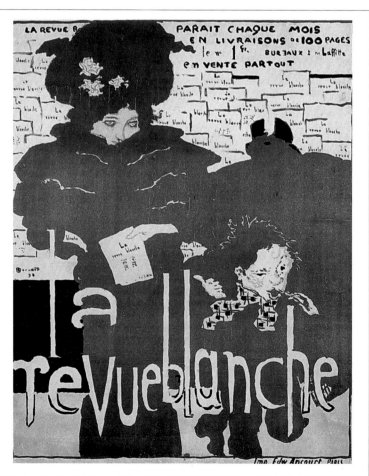

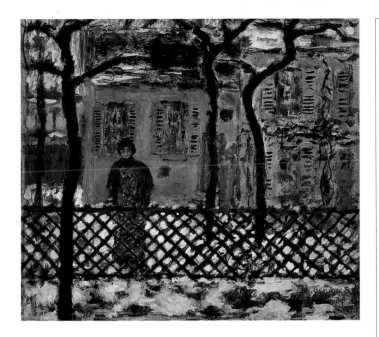

Pierre Bonnard, Behind the Fence, *1895. The State Hermitage Museum, St. Petersburg. Bonnard's sense of light and color is reminiscent of a tapestry, while his sinuous rhythms echo Japanese art.*

intense, pure, and flat color. The effect was highly decorative and marked the emergence of a new attitude toward nature (in contrast to Impressionism), in which inspiration came from memory rather than real life and confined itself to the "essence" of an object, rather than its appearance. Under the guidance of Gauguin in Pont-Aven, Paul Sérusier (1863–1927) painted a landscape in 1888 that summarized this new artistic freedom; it was later named *The Talisman* because of its significance in the develop-ment of Symbolism. Once back in Paris, at the Académie Julian, Sérusier urged his fellow students to seek out the basic roots of art. Among them were Pierre Bonnard (1867–1947), Maurice Denis (1870–1943), Henri-Gabriel Ibels (1867–1936), Paul Ranson (1864–1909), and, later, Edouard Vuillard

Paul Ranson, Nabi Landscape, *1890. Private Collection. The synthesis, the arabesque, the distortion, the wavy articulation, and the interplay of color and outline are all characteristic of the Nabis' works.*

(1868–1940) and Félix Vallotton (1865– 1925). The young painters formed a group in 1892, taking the name of Nabis, "prophets" in Hebrew. Within the group, each artist had his own particular role: for example, Denis was the "*Nabi aux belles icones,*" while Bonnard was the "*Nabi très japonard.*" The group members would all meet periodically in Paul Ranson's studio, which became their "temple." Here, the group experimented with the spiritual, supernatural world of magic through ritual practices. It was Maurice Denis, theorist of the Symbolist movement, who made the famous rallying

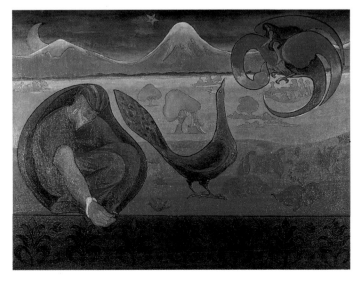

cry to the avant-garde: "Remember that a picture, before being a battle horse, a nude woman, or any interpretation you want, is essentially a flat surface

JAMES ENSOR'S SOCIAL CRITICISM

The existential unease found in the work of van Gogh was an inherent part of the artistic experience of the Flemish painter James Ensor (1860–1949), who, like van Gogh, denounced the hypocritical, banal, and sometimes violent lifestyle of contemporary society. Moved by popular cries for social emancipation and an improvement in conditions for the poor and underprivileged, he translated his concerns into the characters of his work. For example, he produced a series of etchings in 1887 that were devoted to the strike of the Ostend fishermen. Ensor first attracted public attention in 1888 with his painting *Entrance of Christ into Brussels*, a bizarre and grotesque parade of masks, skeletons, and fools that symbolized the empty and false propriety of the ruling classes. The graphic aspect, the sharp outlines, and the visionary effect all combine to create contorted, haunted faces, which, together with the harsh colors, are a prelude to the strong emotional language of Expressionism.

James Ensor, Entrance of Christ into Brussels, *1888. Musée Royal des Beaux-Arts, Antwerp.*

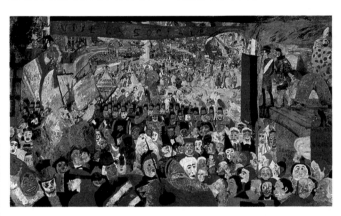

covered in colors assembled in a certain order." While some Nabis portrayed scenes from Parisian life, others painted imaginary and mythological subjects. Nonetheless, the whole group was united in its contempt for naturalism. They translated feeling and emotion into decorative compositions, "synthetist" shapes reminiscent of inlay work, and rhythmic color harmonies modeled after stained-glass windows, medieval enamelwork, and Japanese prints. With their emotional use of color and line they contributed to the breakdown of distinctions between fine and decorative arts at the threshold of the new century. They also heralded the beginnings of Modernism.

GUSTAVE MOREAU: "SALOME DANCING BEFORE HEROD"

1876; oil on canvas; Musée Gustave Moreau, Paris.

Known as the "painter of Salomés," Moreau interpreted this subject many times, producing numerous versions after 1870. Some, like this one, were left unfinished or, in the artist's words "in the process of execution"; in fact, part of his method was to start a painting, then continue it later, often after a long interval. Moreau's Salomé, a symbol of lasciviousness "amid the heavy odor of perfumes," was the inspiration for *A Rebours* (1884), a decadent novel by the important art critic and writer Joris Karl Huysmans, and for the poet José-Maria de Heredía, who described these paintings as having "a magic air in which the smell of poison lingers." In his *Salomé* paintings, Moreau embodied in his work the essence of a particular artistic and literary culture.

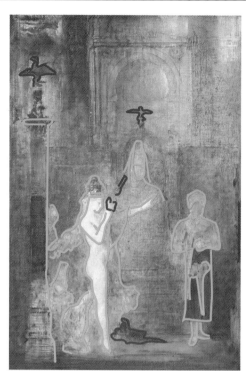

▶ *1. The work is accessible but contains many ambiguities, such the apparition-like figures. Huysmans describes the scene as follows: "A throne like the high altar of a cathedral standing beneath a vaulted ceiling…In the center of the tabernacle set on the altar…the Tetrarch Herod was seated, with a tiara on his head…immobile, statuesque figure, frozen like some Hindu god in a hieratic pose…Salomé slowly glides forward on the point of her toes, her left arm stretched out in a commanding gesture, her right arm bent back…while a woman squatting on the floor strums the strings of a guitar." This figure is only partly visible at the front left-hand side. In front of the left column, "the ferocious Herodias" can just be seen. "The eunuch who stands saber in hand at the foot of the throne" is on the right. The painting has none of the decorative excess associated with decadent art.*

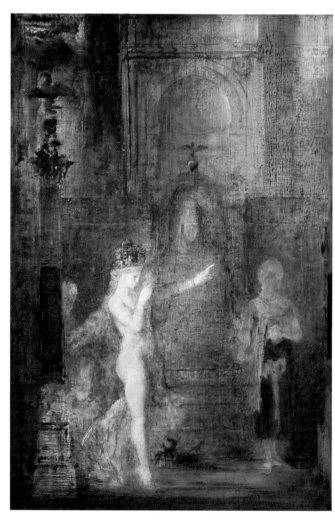

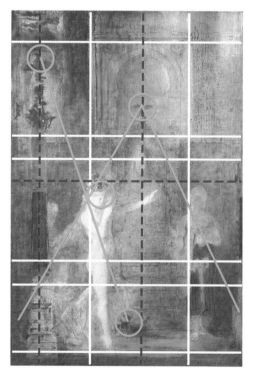

◀ *2. While the figures are not clearly defined, the structure of the composition can be identified more easily. A grid of perpendicular axes lies off center, with a principal vertical axis cutting the throne in half. It appears to be more central because of the left-hand axis running down the middle of the column. Lesser vertical lines connect the left and right sides of the recess behind the throne with, respectively, the figure of Salomé and the figure of the eunuch. The main horizontal axis unites the heads of Herodias, Salomé, and the eunuch, while other horizontal lines above and at the level of Herod's head form a square. This square is repeated vertically in the ethereal but monumental structure in the background.*

SYMBOLISM

The roots of Symbolism can be traced back at least as far as the Romantic trends of the early 19th century. The movement shared strong affinities with similar contemporary developments in poetry, philosophy, and music, creating a synthesis and union of the arts. Its official debut came in 1886, when Jean Moréas launched the manifesto of Symbolist poetry, which included the figurative arts, in *Le Figaro*. However, in reaction to the objective recording of nature that was so characteristic of Impressionism, certain painters had already shown a need to express a "reality" beyond the evidence gained from visual perception – notably the spiritual aspects, allusions, and ambiguities inherent in mere sight.

If it is true that the reality we see – according to Platonic philosophy – is but a poor copy of the world of "ideal forms," then it is the task of the artist, in his or her role as perceiver with an "inner eye,"

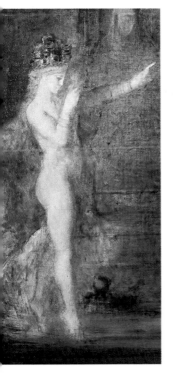

◀ *3. The light seems to enter the interior from above. The heavy dark atmosphere is speckled with dusty red and gold. Colors are evident in the princess's crown and in the milky and alabaster white tones of her skin. The curved but slender nude figure is an ethereal form saturated in light. She appears to be suspended in space. While provocative, Salomé retains a virginal appearance, emphasized by the perfect figure and blonde, fleecy hair. The body is not decorated, but, notably, it bears theatrical conventions such as the crown, a tiptoeing gait, and fine veils. Influenced by the original scenario of the work, the setting has no historic accuracy. The imprecise outlines of the figures and the diffuse light renders the figures insubstantial; they seem almost to be mere suggestions of figures.*

▶ *4. This work gives an insight into Moreau's bold painting technique. He does not apply a preparatory background color to tone down the cold light of the white canvas, which is significant given the darkness of the colors. However, these are illuminated by gold light, and some areas of white show through. The picture is constructed in layers of transparent brown that, applied more or less evenly, outline the shapes, define the planes, and create the atmosphere.*

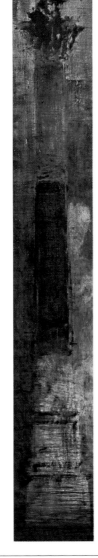

◀ *5. The picture is clearly Symbolist, both in its subject matter and in its formal and chromatic structures. Certain parts seem to disintegrate. Perhaps the animal on the column is a chimera, a symbol of desire that seduces but does not gratify. The tetrarch's throne bears perhaps an eagle, a symbol of alluring military power. Salomé holds a lotus flower, a sign of oblivion and used in Celtic rites to symbolize an evil woman. The hint of flowers at Salomé's feet (withered roses are found more visibly in other versions of the painting) are symbols of love in decay.*

Fleurs du Mal (1857) the most popular source of inspiration for many Symbolist painters in the 1880s and 1890s. They were joined by scientists, such as Eduard von Hartmann and Jean Martin Charcot, who were interested in the imagination and recognized that dreams were a means of expressing as image the fantasies and desires of the subconscious. Symbolism was an international movement that spread throughout Europe, although the forms it took varied considerably. The unifying element was not so much the style – the break with realism did not bring about a uniform end to objective representation and choice of new artistic language – as a refusal to choose contemporary subjects drawn from current affairs and social realism. Instead, artists desired to give substance to content derived from poetry, mythology, and psychological research.

An anticipation of this choice of themes can be seen in the experience of the English Pre-Raphaelites who gathered around Dante Gabriel Rossetti (1828–82) in the 1870s. Once

Gustave Moreau, The Song of Songs, *1893. Ohara Museum of Art, Kurashiki, Japan. In a sensual, mystical atmosphere, the almost scientific naturalism of the detail is engulfed by the wild fantasy of the overall conception.*

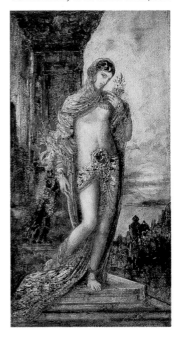

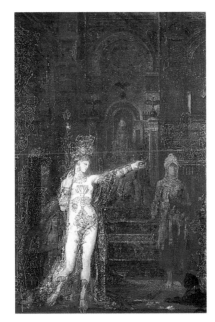

Gustave Moreau, The Apparition, *1876. Musée du Louvre, Paris. This lurid theme appears often in Moreau's work. His use of mysterious, exotic surroundings and intense light and color were to have a great influence upon decadent art.*

again, it was French artists who played the leading role in this debate about aesthetics, which was pursued with intensity by magazines such as *La Revue Wagnérienne* and *Le Mercure de France,* as well as in the philosophical and literary writings of Henri Bergson and Huysmans. In his novel *A Rebours,* published in 1884 and considered by many to be the "bible" of aesthetic decadence, Huysmans describes the work of three painters – Gustave Moreau, Rodolphe Bresdin, and Odilon Redon – as being among the most sophisticated creations. His leading character, Des Esseintes, surrounds himself with their work in order to escape from the vulgarity of everyday existence. Amid a climate of Impressionist realism, Gustave Moreau (1826–98) exhibited *Oedipus and the Sphinx* in 1864, a painting rich in mysterious and fantastic allusions. This work heralded a form of Symbolism drawing on classical and biblical mythology, on medieval legends, and on the fables of *La Fontaine.* This new style

to decipher the hidden meanings and translate them into sensitive forms that can be understood by everybody – that is, as stated by Gustave Kahn, to "objectivize the subjective" as opposed to the tendency, pursued up until this time, of "subjectivizing the objective." The Symbolist poets were the first to explore the relationships between sounds, smells, and colors and to allude to the mysterious affinities between the visible and the invisible. Not by chance was Charles Baudelaire's anthology *Les*

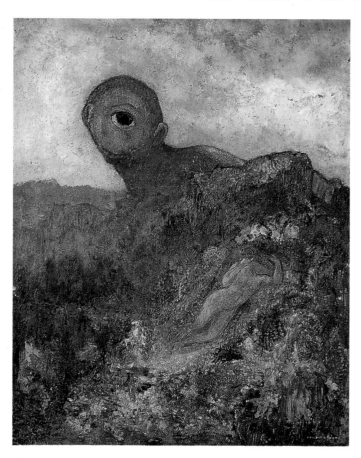

Odilon Redon, The Cyclops, 1898–1900. Kröller Muller Rijksmusum, Otterlo, the Netherlands.

dealt with exotic themes and investigated the subject of death in compositions that were deliberately formal in language, rich in color, and filled with esoteric details and references. Odilon Redon (1840–1916) received much acclaim with the publication of his first lithographic album in 1879, appropriately titled *Dans le rêve* (In the Dream) He followed this with illustrations to Gustave Flaubert's *La Tentation de Saint Antoine* and a number of other successful collaborations with poets and writers. In his series of black-and-white drawings, charcoal sketches, and lithographs completed before 1895, Redon depicted bewildering and contorted images that are both real and unreal, human and monstrous. They are typical of the ambiguity of his visionary art.The influence of French Symbolism throughout the rest of Europe varied in importance from country to country. Research into the unity of the arts was conducted with special enthusiasm by Jan Toorop (1858– 1928) and Johan Thorn Prikker (1868–1932) in Holland, Fernand Khnopff (1858–1921) and Félicien Rops (1833–98) in Belgium, Michail Vrubel (1856–1910) in Russia, Gaetano Previati (1852-1920) and Giovanni Segantini (1858-1899) in Italy, and Edvard Munch (1863-1944) in Norway. Spiritualism was particularly fashionable in Germany, where its artistic treatment drew on the aestheticism of the late Romantic tradition. The *Secession* exhibitions provided an excellent opportunity to advertise the Symbolist aesthetic. An original interpretation of decadent culture, inspired by *fin-de-siècle* literary references, was offered by Arnold Böcklin (1827–1901), an artist who worked in various European cities. Like many German romantics of the second half of the 19th

MOREAU'S SALOME

"Of all artists there was one that threw him into long periods of ecstasy and from whom he acquired both masterpieces: Gustave Moreau. Des Esseintes lingered entire nights in contemplation over the painting representing Salomé…In this work by Gustave Moreau, conceived quite differently from the details in the Bible, Des Esseintes finally found the extraordinary, superhuman Salomé of whom he had dreamed…an overpowering fascination emanated from that canvas. And yet perhaps the watercolor entitled *The Apparition* was more disquieting."
This was how Huysmans recorded Moreau's Salomé in his novel *A Rebours* (1884). The subject was extremely popular in the figurative arts, literature, and music toward the end of the century. This concurred with the misogynous attitude of the Symbolists; in the interpretation given in Heinrich Heine's text, we can see the prototype of the unbalanced, destructive female who seduces Herod to obtain the head of John the Baptist. Moreau had used this subject many times in his works, among which was the famous canvas exhibited at the Salon in 1876; it depicts a dancer whose whole body is tattooed in bold, swirling designs, an effect that adds to the sensuality of the figure.
In contrast to Salomé is the delicate female figure, reclining comfortably on the grass in the painting *The Unicorns*. The unicorns are symbols of chastity and purity, and the work suggests a feeling of serenity and comfort within the mythological subject matter.

Gustave Moreau, The Unicorns, c.1885. Musée Gustave Moreau, Paris.

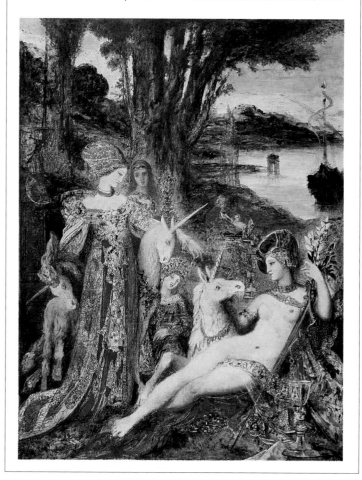

PUVIS DE CHAVANNES

Pierre Puvis de Chavannes (1824–98) was almost contemporary with Gustave Moreau, and the two artists are often associated with one another because of their different interpretations of the same concept of Symbolism. During a stay in Italy, Puvis

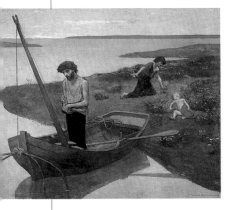

Pierre Puvis de Chavannes, The Poor Fisherman, 1881. Musée du Louvre, Paris.

was inspired to adopt classical models for a large series of allegorical works that celebrated personal and civic virtues. These were hung in various important buildings throughout France (from the Sorbonne and the Panthéon to the museums of Poitiers and Marseilles). His misty, poetic art sought mainly to achieve a linear rhythm applicable to the composition as a whole rather than to the single image. Puvis adopted traditional figurative values and kept his work clear and simple, with delicate, anti-naturalistic colors, in order to obtain an effect of unity. He expressed the fears of the contemporary human condition symbolically, through the nostalgic evocation of an unchanging, archaic world of pure beauty and harmony.

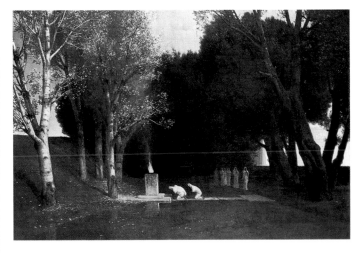

Arnold Böcklin, The Sacred Wood, 1882. Kunstmuseum, Basel, Switzerland.

century, he traveled to Italy, attracted by the myths of classical art. Böcklin was fascinated by mysterious and visionary themes, which he expressed in formal academic terms. His technically flawless methods of composition and representation gave the viewer the feeling that he was fathoming an impenetrable landscape that was both enigmatic and real. The sirens, centaurs, and heroes that Böcklin drew from classical mythology are presented as real, flesh-and-blood men and women, as romantically suggestive as the landscape that surround them. Yet there is also an uneasy feeling about these scenes, which are apparently literary and mythological and

THE ROSICRUCIANS

The growing interest in spiritual matters in the last two decades of the 19th century led to the formation of many societies and groups, first in Paris and then in Brussels. The esoteric Rosicrucian Society was particularly involved in ritual magic and the occult. Its founder, Joseph Péladan, was known for his novel *Le Vice Suprême*

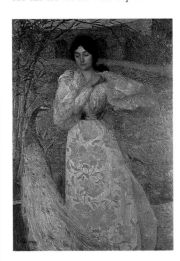

(1884). One branch of the society was devoted to promoting the arts and organizing art exhibitions, concerts, and plays. Between 1892 and 1897, their salons hosted some of the leading European Symbolist painters, who subscribed to the Rosicrucians' aesthetic ideals, including Sèon, Osbert, Previati, Schwabe, Khnopff, and Delville. The rules laid down by Péladan (he referred to himself as "magus"), stated that the shows would be "a demonstration of Art against Arts, of Beauty against Ugliness, of Dreams against Reality, of the Past against the Present." Conventional subjects inspired by reality or nature, such as portraits and landscapes, were banned; instead, the most popular themes were allegories, dreamlike visions, and anything

Jean Edmond Aman (1860–1936), The Peacock Girl, 1895. Musée des Arts Décoratifs, Paris. The painters from the Rosicrucian circle favored allegorical and mystical subjects.

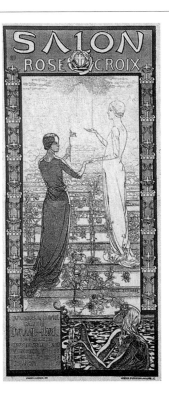

Carlos Schwabe (1866–1926), poster for the first Rosicrucian Salon, 1893. Several of the Rosicrucian artists organized exhibitions, to which various Symbolist painters contributed.

that expressed a mystical conception of art. Péladan's closest disciple was the Belgian writer, theosophist, and artist Jean Delville (1867–1953), who founded the Salon d'art idéaliste in Brussels in 1896 and, in 1900, wrote "La Mission de l'art," an appeal for the spiritual regeneration of art and its followers. Delville was attracted to satanic iconography and also to Wagnerian subjects (*Tristan and Isolde*, 1887). He completed a large allegorical decoration for the Sorbonne entitled *The School of Plato (1898)*, which is now exhibited in the Musée d'Orsay in Paris.

The artist Fernand Khnopff (1858–1921) was present at the first Rosicrucian Salon in 1892. The aristocratic spiritualism of his art was highly admired by Péladan. In his exploration of hidden meanings, Khnopff packed his compositions with mysterious symbols and figurative combinations in a pictorial style noted for its slickness and polish.

yet are imbued with psychological undertones. The artist stated: "A painting must say something and make the spectator think, like a poem, leaving him with an impression, like a piece of music." Max Klinger (1857–1920), who first met Böcklin in 1887 while in Berlin and again later in Florence, could enchant and mystify the spectator with his magical effects and lofty themes. As was pointed out in 1920 by de Chirico, the originality of his work lay in the allusive symbolism that he created by modifying scenes from contemporary life with visions from antiquity. He used images of a timeless world to elaborate upon themes of grotesque realism in order to achieve "a highly impressive dream reality" and "a suggestive and romantic interpretation of modernity." Myth and reality, past and present, the sacred and the erotic, and the ordinary and the extraordinary were all to be found together on his large canvases. His paintings were often of exaggerated complexity, radiating a sinister aura. Klinger was especially interested in graphic techniques and the analogy between art and music, classifying each etching in his series as an opus. His principal aim was to bring about a synthesis of the arts as a means of expressing a broader notion of life. Among a number of works dedicated to this were the painting *Christ of Olympus* (1896) and the sculpture *Beethoven* (1902).

Max Klinger, Judgement of Paris, 1885. Kunsthistorisches Museum, Vienna.

ART AND THE PUBLIC

Given the hostility and resistance – from both critics and public – that met the Impressionists in Paris in the early 1870s, it is easy to imagine the general bewilderment in the more parochial towns and villages at the unconventional styles and subject matter of the Post-Impressionists. Painters such as van Gogh and Gauguin were not popular, and with the onset of the revolutionary avant-garde trends of the early 20th century, the gap between modern art and the general public widened. Very traditional artists still catered for this audience, but public taste was largely satisfied by the low-cost prints being produced by the new lithographic and photo-mechanical techniques. National and patriotic paintings such as those by the Imagerie d'Epinal were popular, as were oleographic prints of religious paintings by the likes of Raphael and Murillo. Art could thus be shared in a context that was readily understood and appreciated. The Church, however, chose to separate itself from the progress of modern art in the late 1800s, continuing to expound its beliefs in traditional terms.

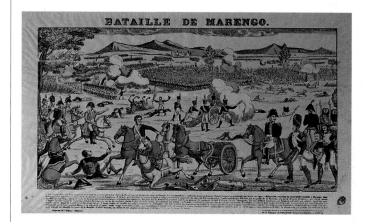

Late 19th-century engraving of the Battle of Marengo.

EXOTICISM AND ROUSSEAU

The myth of Exoticism captivated the minds of many avant-garde artists and writers as the 19th century drew to a close. It represented an escape from the declining spiritual values of bourgeois society and an urge to travel to distant lands uncontaminated by progress in order to pursue a more natural, "savage" lifestyle. Following in the wake of Gauguin's move to Tahiti, Kandinsky traveled around north Africa, Nolde sailed to New Guinea, Pechstein explored China, and Klee and Macke spent time in Tunisia.

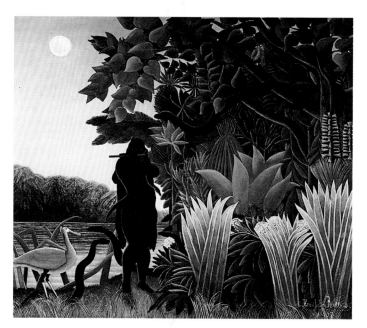

The French painter Henri Rousseau (1844–1910) pursued this same ideal in his quest to capture a spirit of innocence. While still very much rooted in French city life, and for many years a conventional man, he nevertheless projected images of an exotic world of magic and freshness. Known as "Le Douanier" because he worked for the Paris customs service until 1893, he was an untrained painter. However,

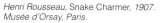
Henri Rousseau, Snake Charmer, 1907. Musée d'Orsay, Paris.

amid much criticism and controversy, the exclusive intellectual elite of late 19th-century Paris at the end of the century claimed to understand the "hedonistic mystifications" of symbolism in his work. Rousseau worked within a climate that borrowed elements from African sculpture and contrasted them with

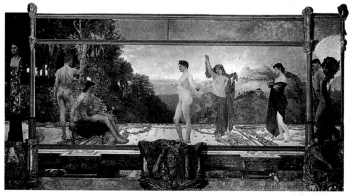

TOULOUSE-LAUTREC AND PARISIAN NIGHT LIFE

A vivid account of the frenetic city life of contemporary Paris is found in the work of Henri de Toulouse-Lautrec (1864–1901), who immersed himself fully in its atmosphere and depicted it with a sharp eye and wry humor. His limited output of paintings and almost all of his abundant series of drawings are devoted to the cabaret and brothel scenes of Montmartre, an area that became famous in the last decades of the 19th century as the home of many painters' studios and art galleries. A draftsman of exceptional talent, Lautrec had an incisive, lively style that could capture effectively the dynamics of gesture. He was attracted above all to the bright artifice of Parisian night life and to the

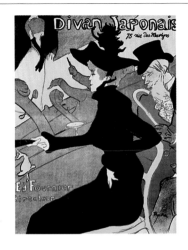

Henri de Toulouse-Lautrec, Divan Japonais, 1892. Bibliothèque Nationale, Paris.

challenge of portraying both the splendor and misery of that underworld. His name was associated with the Moulin Rouge, the night club run by C. Zilder. It was advertised in a series of lithographic posters by Toulouse-Lautrec, a medium to which the artist dedicated himself with passion. La Goulue, Les Ambassadeurs, and Le Divan Japonais, created in the early 1890s, are notable for their original synthesis of form, their thin, elastic lines, and their strong layers of color. Among the many other artists seduced by the feverish air of Monmartre was the young Picasso, who arrived in Paris in the early 1900s. He portrayed the area in paintings such as At the Moulin Rouge (1901).

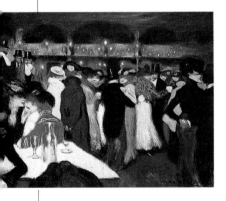

Henri de Toulouse-Lautrec, Moulin de la Galette, 1900. Solomon R. Guggenheim Museum, New York.

Fauvists. He was adored by literary figures, such as Alfred Jarry, whom he had painted in 1894, and Apollinaire, to whom he dedicated The Muse Inspiring the Poet in 1907, as well as by other painters such as Robert Delaunay, whose mother commissioned The Snake Charmer in 1907. He was also a composer of songs, which he performed at the banquet given by Picasso in his honor in 1908.

SOCIAL ART AND THE BIRTH OF DIVISIONISM IN ITALY

At the beginning of the 1880s, there was a general interest among artists throughout Europe in art inspired by social issues – Repin in Russia, Meunier in Belgium, and von Menzel in Germany. Such concerns had been evident in art since the 1840s, for example in the work of Courbet, Millet, and Daumier; a revival now sprang from the diffusion of anarchic and socialist ideas and the belief in the emancipation of the working classes. An equally important factor was the growing dissatisfaction with mannered, realistic subject matter; artists now felt the need to depict more profound material in their paintings and to express more progressive ideas. In northern Italy, which had become industrialized over a comparatively short period of

time, the climate was right for the development of these concerns. At the first Triennial Exhibition in Milan in 1891, works that revealed the fulfillment of these aims included the Oratore dello Sciopero by Emilio Longoni, a provocative denunciation of unemployment, and the Parlatorio del Pio Albergo Trivulzio, with which Angelo Morbelli began a series of dramatic representations of the neglect of the elderly. At the same time, the Milan exhibition marked the first official appearance of a new technique, which had been arrived at independently by each of the artists involved, but was now given more weight by virtue of the works being grouped in a common collection that came under the label of divisionism. Some critics saw a clear link with the scientific theories of Neo-Impressionism, launched by Seurat in 1886 and defined by Signac more than a decade later, while others believed it to be an original but parallel trend, derived from the widespread urge to create a new language of color and light. Divisionism used a technique of placing touches of pure color on the canvas – not in small dots, as in France, but in threadlike, "combed and streaked" brushstrokes. Italian divisionism was not derived from the application of any discoveries in the field

Angelo Morbelli (1853–1919), Feast Day at the Trivulzio Hospice in Milan, 1892. Musée d'Orsay, Paris.

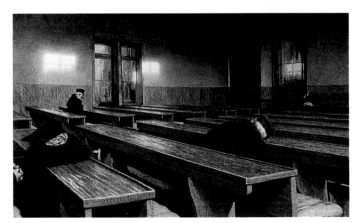

Greek classicism, achieving a style that was unpretentious, shunning facile mannerism and the pretentious intellectualism of "art for art's sake." Rousseau made a name for himself as a primitive artist through the Salons des Artistes Indépendants, to which he was invited in 1886, and gained widespread recognition from 1904 to 1905, when he embarked on his "jungle" scenes, such as Explorers Attacked by a Lion and The Hungry Lion, the latter shown at the Salon d'Automne in 1905 in the room of the

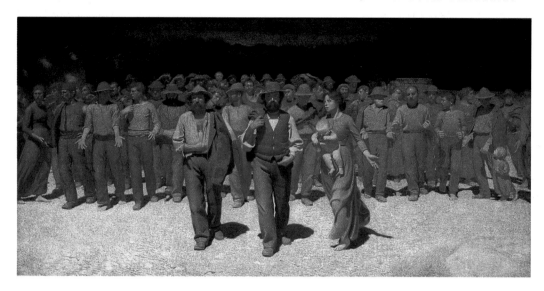

Giuseppe Pellizza da Volpedo, The Fourth Estate, 1898–1901. Galleria d'Arte Moderna, Milan.

of optics (which the artists knew superficially and with which they experimented only in a haphazard fashion), but from the naturalism and effects achieved by Antonio Fontanesi (1818–82) and the artists of the *scapigliatura* movement. With the exception of the work by Previati on the scientific principles of divisionism (published in 1906), the new technique lacked any real body of theory or collective consciousness that might have stimulated the organization of group exhibitions. The most striking example of the use of divisionism to express social concerns was *Il Quarto Stato* (*The Fourth Estate*) by Giuseppe Pellizza da Volpedo (1868–1907). This depicted the confidence and unity of the working classes toward a future of liberation and dignity, inspired by the principle that "it is no longer the time for Art for Art's sake but for Art for Humanity." The technique of dividing light to give form, rendering it insubstantial and ethereal, was also used in symbolic paintings inspired by literature or derived from the artists' dreams and imagination. This was the case with the work of

Gaetano Previati (1852–1920) and Giovanni Segantini (1858–99). Previati was invited to the first Rosicrucian Salon in 1892 by virtue of his adherence to the more mystical currents of international decadence. Here, he presented *Maternità*, an antinaturalist "idéiste" painting, the streaky and vibrating texture of which gave the effect of symbolic abstraction. Segantini's brilliance lay in his ability to escape completely from the usual confines of art and to renew contact with nature and the universal spirit in order to explore the primeval source of his inspiration. Although Milan was the hub of the divisionist movement, producing most of the activity, Genoa and Rome also experienced a climate of lively experimentation, ultimately forming a basis, through the work of Giacomo Balla, for the beginnings of Futurism, which was to develop during the early 20th century.

GIOVANNI SEGANTINI

Of all the Italian divisionist painters, the one who adhered most convincingly to the then widespread practice in Europe of expressing "ideas" in painting was Giovanni Segantini. His art evolved from a realism based on color gradations in the 1880s

Giovanni Segantini, The Two Mothers, 1889. Galleria d'Arte Moderna, Milan.

(*At the Plow*, 1886) to experiments in fragmented light in his most characteristic Alpine landscapes (*Midday on the Alps*, 1891), and to Symbolist compositions celebrating the mystical–pantheistic aspects of nature. Segantini left Milan, where his familiarity with international artistic experiences had been nurtured by the art critic and dealer Vittore Grubicy, and chose instead the serene beauty

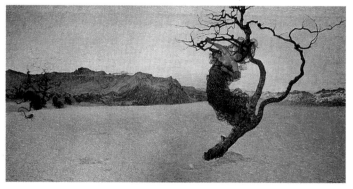

Giovanni Segantini, The Evil Mothers, 1894. Kunsthistorisches Museum, Vienna.

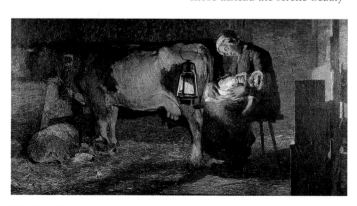

of the mountains, first in Grisons and then the Engadine. Even in these Alpine retreats he kept abreast with critical debate over modern art and was invited to the main European exhibitions, being given a one-man show by the Secessionists in Vienna in 1898.
While some of his works were allegorical (*Love at the Fountains of Life*, 1896) and others inspired by literary subjects (*The Evil Mothers*, 1896–97), Segantini often depicted nature as a symbol of maternity and infantile refuge and, introspectively, as the abode of the mind and the spirit. Yet the image remained sufficiently clear to prevent losing "the living, tangible meaning of natural reality."

THE SCAPIGLIATURA MOVEMENT

While France, in the aftermath of Impressionism, was witnessing a great period of artistic experimentation, Italy was undergoing its own innovations, not least in the development of the *scapigliatura* movement. Almost wholly confined to the Lombardy area during the 1870s, this movement originated initially in literature and then filtered through to the figurative arts. It consisted of a

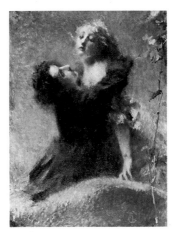

Tranquillo Cremona, Ivy, *1878. Galleria d'Arte Moderna, Turin.*

small group of painters and sculptors united by an anti-bourgeois and antiacademic cause and by their opposition to the theory of the synthesis of the arts, as outlined by the novelist Giuseppe Rovani. The characteristics of the technique adopted by the movement's principal painters,

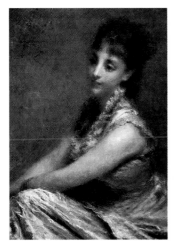

Daniele Ranzoni, Portrait of the Countess Arrivabene, *1880. Galleria d'Arte Moderna, Milan.*

Tranquillo Cremona (1837–78) and Daniele Ranzoni (1843–89), were a taste for dissolving forms and hazy effects in gradations of color, a masterly use of light, airy brushstrokes (in complete contrast to traditional chiaroscuro design), and subject matter taken from the fashionable circles of contemporary life. Cremona achieved a vibrant shimmering effect, particularly in his watercolors and some of his portraits, in which form seems to be ambiguously suspended between the stroke and the image. The result, if somewhat mannered, was not without interest. Ranzoni revealed a great lightness of touch in his exuberant brushwork, but he also endeavored to avoid superficiality and to give plastic consistency to his landscapes and, in particular, to his portraits.

Together with these two artists, the sculptor Giuseppe Grandi (1843–94) experimented with new effects of illumination for his lively pieces of sculpture, creating an uneven surface of creases and folds in irregular projections so that light falling onto the work was broken and split into various colors. In *Monument to the Five Days of Milan,* (started in 1880), Grandi took up the traditional style of commemorative sculpture for the first time in Italy, assembling figures, symbols, and architectural elements in an imposing, exciting, and powerfully luminous composition. His success in overcoming the traditional limits imposed by sculpture were to influence the work of Medardo Rosso during the early 1880s.

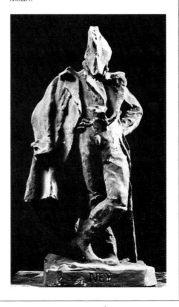

Giuseppe Grandi, Marshal Ney, *1874–75. Galleria d'Arte Moderna, Milan.*

on Velázquez–style effects of light, which appealed greatly to European tastes at the time. Other key artists included Mary Cassatt, a friend of Degas and the Impressionists, who created delicate interpretations of the mother–child relationship, and James Whistler (1834–1903), a nonconformist in both painting style and character. He was the principal exponent in England of the "art for art's sake" movement and produced "symphonic" portraits and landscapes using careful variations in tone.

William Merritt Chase learned his skills in Munich and then returned to New York to teach art between 1890 and 1900. He reflected the local preference for commonplace subjects in urban surroundings and painted in dark, rather unappealing shades. Chase's artistic experiences stimulated the formation of the Ash-can School of painting: a group of progressive American realist painters from illustration backgrounds, among whom were Robert Henri, John Sloan, William Glackens, and Everett Shinn. Without being deliberately controversial or condemning, they portrayed scenes of everyday life with detached, cold objectivity, highlighting social imbalance in the newly industrialized society. This paved the way for the realism of the 1930s and 1940s.

AMERICAN INNOVATORS

The visual arts scene in the United States throughout the 19th century generally looked to developments in Europe, differing in the extent of its attachment to a more markedly realist style. The most popular subject matter was the Wild West, an area that was ripe for exploration

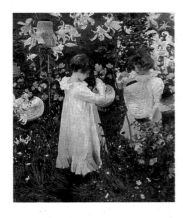

John Singer Sargent, Carnation, Lily, Lily, Rose, *1885–86. Tate Gallery, London.*

and colonization, providing a rich source of original images and material. Scenes from daily life, as well as portraiture, were most convincingly represented, however, by artists whose formative years and artistic endeavors had taken place largely in Europe. The masterly technique of John Singer Sargent centered

LES VINGT

Les Vingt (Les XX) was the name given in the 1880s to an adventurous circle of artists formed in Brussels around the magazine *L'Art moderne*. Their aim was to use art, through a blend of modernism and aesthetics, as a means of modifying and improving the industrial process. The group, founded by Octave Maus and E. Picard, included artists such as James Ensor, Fernand Khnopff, Alfred William Finch (founder of the Finnish divisionist group Septem), and Theo van Rysselberghe. They adopted the style of Post-Impressionism

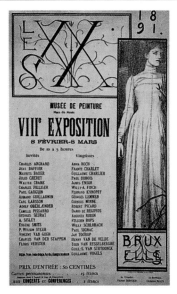

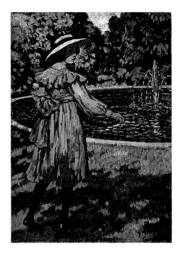

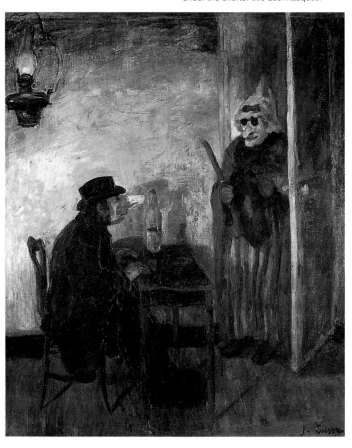

Fernand Khnopff, poster for the Brussels exhibition of Les Vingt, 1890. Khnopff's compositions tended to feature dreamlike, surrealistic images in which the figures are surrounded by a halolike aura.

James Ensor, Les Masques Scandalisées. *Musée Royal des Beaux-Arts, Brussels. This painting was first exhibited in 1881 at the inaugural exhibition of Les Vingt under the shorter title* Les Masques.

and incorporated Symbolist elements into their work. Shows were organized periodically to popularize modern lines of thought and to assert the importance of art in the field of environmental planning. The first exhibition in 1884 included works by Rodin, Liebermann, Whistler, and, subsequently, Redon, Seurat, Gauguin, van Gogh, and Cézanne

Theo van Rysselberghe, Portrait of the Artist's Daughter. *Private Collection. This painting is in a Pointillist style, influenced by the works of Seurat but lacking their symbolic content*

SCULPTURE AT THE TURN OF THE CENTURY

In 1846 Baudelaire published an essay entitled "Why Sculpture is Boring." His sentiments were later to be echoed by the critics, who condemned the current proliferation of ancient sculpture in an academic, late-Romantic style. In particular, they criticized the monumental work destined for urban or funerary use, characterized by a uniformity and pompous solemnity that had become prevalent during recent decades.

However, the establishment of Symbolist ideology in the last two decades of the 19th century challenged this negative judgment. The liberal ideals of the social reform movements had already changed the artist's view of three-dimensional art. This now countered what had become a mannered and often tedious genre with a direct appreciation of the real, preserving references to the great models of the past but dispensing with elaboration and idealization. This new approach was seen in particular in the work of three sculptors: the Belgian Constantin Meunier (1831–1905), who created figures of working people, and Vincenzo Vela (1845-1929) and Achille D'Orsi (1845-1929) in

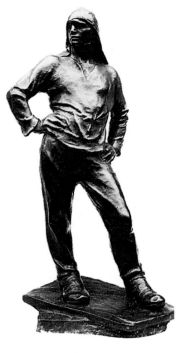

Constantin Meunier, The Stevedore, 1885. Petit Palais, Paris.

Italy. Although the plastic arts in general were generally insufficiently expressive for the Impressionists and Post-Impressionists, they, too, contributed significantly to the rescue of sculpture from solemn rhetoric and superficial realism. Degas demonstrated sculpture's potential for conveying dynamic movement in his scenes of horses and ballerinas that were modeled in colored wax. Renoir came later to sculpture and translated the round, pleasing figures from his paintings into three-dimensional space. Bonnard, who was particularly interested in the tactile values of sculpture and the relation of the surface of the body to the surrounding light, enjoyed a similar success in this medium.

GAUGUIN THE SCULPTOR

Gauguin developed an early interest in sculpture, showing a marble bust of his son Emile at the Impressionist exhibition of 1879, and some wooden sculptures with lightly colored details in 1881. Through the etcher Félix Bracquemond, Gauguin met Ernest Chaplet, a noted ceramicist with an Oriental style. Working with glazed stoneware, Gauguin made about fifty original heads and figures in Breton costume between 1886 and 1887. The anthropomorphic decoration is reminiscent of Inca pottery, which he knew from his childhood in Peru, although an updated technique is used to conform with the spontaneous and concise Impressionist style of modeling. After spending time among the Maori people, Gauguin's sculptural techniques changed. He started to incorporate into his work formal as well as iconographic references to Tiki statues and ritualistic Tahitian idols. His favorite piece, *Oviri* (*The Savage*), was made in Paris and marked a break with Western sculptural traditions and the start of his expressive Primitive phase, seen in the carved wooden bas-reliefs with which he decorated his house in the Marquesas Islands.

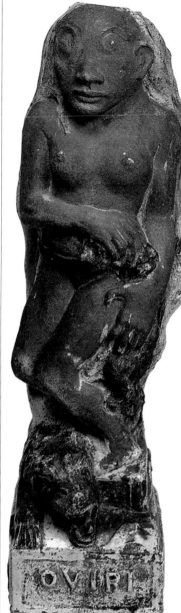

Paul Gauguin, Oviri (The Savage), *1894. Musée d'Orsay, Paris.*

Paul Gauguin, The Swans, *1890. Private Collection.*

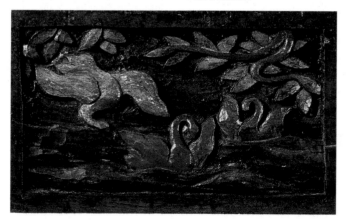

RODIN

Auguste Rodin, who was born in Paris in 1840 and died in Meudon in 1917, was similar in age to many of the Impressionists. He was attracted and inspired by

Auguste Rodin, The Kiss, *1901–04. Tate Gallery, London.*

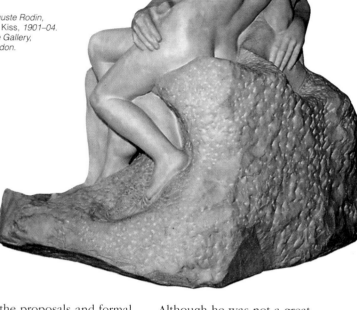

all the proposals and formal suggestions that came from their movement, but also by the newly emerging "idéiste" art – painting from the imagination. A highly gifted artist, who developed great skill as a sculptor, Rodin began his career under the sculptor Carrier Belleuse, working on the decoration of the Commercial Exchange in Brussels. His liberation from academism came through his study of Michelangelo on a trip to Italy in 1875. He was impressed by the epic nature of nude muscular figures and by the technique of "incompleteness." The creation of *The Gates of Hell* in 1880 revealed Rodin's search for a new, vital, and impassioned monumentality with a Dionysian rhythm, in which the core of the sculpture seems to explode into the surrounding space and the figures appear to dissolve in the luminosity of the whole.

Rodin was mainly interested in the subject of movement.

Although he was not a great theorist, it is clear from his thoughts on sculpture, collected by his students and his secretary, the poet Rainer Maria Rilke, that he believed in the need to overcome "closed form" and to "transfer inner feelings to muscular movements; give movement to express life." "The expression of life," he said, "can never be halted or frozen if it is to conserve the infinite flexibility of reality." The statues and groups that he created, both the famous monumental examples and smaller works such as the sensitive nude ballerina figures (*Iris, Messenger of the Gods*, 1890–91), are rarely calm and restful, even when action is not crucial. Rodin was accused by many artists and critics – including Matisse, who visited him in 1906 and sought his advice in the medium – of neglecting the whole, of not achieving a compositional or sculptural synthesis, but rather of proceeding with an assembly

THE GREAT WORKS OF RODIN

Rodin's first sculptural assignment was the ornamental doors (*The Gates of Hell*) for the Musée des Arts Décoratifs, commissioned by the Ministry of Fine Arts in 1880. The narrative scenes, taken from Dante's *Divine Comedy* and from Ovid's *Metamorphoses*, consisted of more than 186 figures in high and low relief, their dramatic passion reflected in the pained faces and exaggerated movements. The doors were never completed and were broken up into smaller sections; Bourdelle then reassembled them according to Rodin's elaborate plan, producing four examples to be found today in museums in Paris, Zurich, Philadelphia, and Tokyo. Various motifs were taken by Rodin and enlarged in later elaborations – *The Three Shadows* (1880), *The Kiss* (1886), and *The Thinker* (1888) – the last being an enigmatic and symbolic meditation on human destiny.

From 1884 to 1886 Rodin worked on the *Burghers of Calais* group, erected later

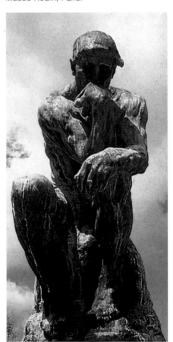

Auguste Rodin, The Thinker, *1880. Musée Rodin, Paris.*

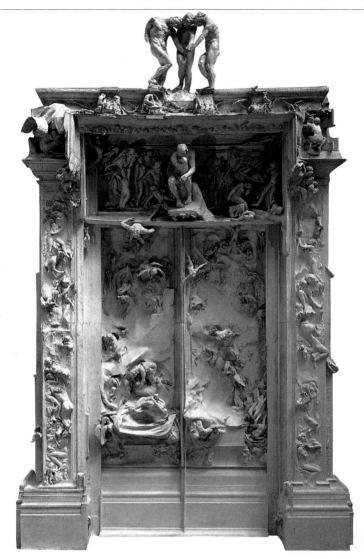

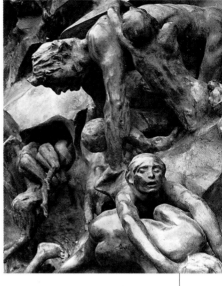

Auguste Rodin, detail of Ugolino and his Sons *from* The Gates of Hell. *Stanford University Museum of Art, California.*

befell the monument to Balzac, commissioned in 1883 by the Société des Gens de Lettres and rejected by them following a discussion over its excessively free technique and its originality, deemed too superficial and inadequate in its portrayal of the subject. Cast in bronze after Rodin's death, it was placed in the Boulevard Raspail in 1939.

Auguste Rodin, The Gates of Hell, *plaster model, 1917. Musée Rodin, Paris.*

in 1895. This was a realistic depiction of the six French citizens who during the Hundred Years' War offered to give their lives to King Edward III if he were to raise the siege on their, by then, destitute city. When Rodin was commissioned in 1885 to sculpt the funerary monument of Victor Hugo, destined for the Panthéon, he planned a group featuring the poet naked and pensive, accompanied by gesticulating Muses. This interpretation, not being sufficiently conventional, was rejected, and the work was not finished (albeit in an altered form) until 1909, when it was placed in the gardens of the Palais Royal. A similar fate

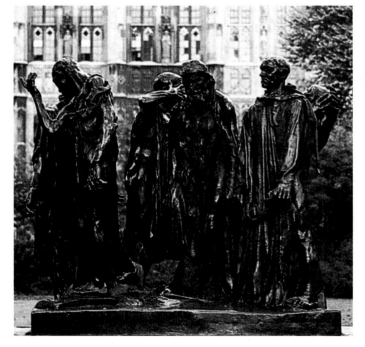

Auguste Rodin, The Burghers of Calais, *1884–86. Westminster Gardens, London.*

of separate details, albeit each realized with the inspiration of genius. However, he continued with his research into the many-faceted and ever-changing profiles of an object, pursuing the organic vitality that seemed to animate the sculpture from within.

A great modeler rather than a sculptor, Rodin found it very difficult to work in stone, so the job of translating his extraordinary inventions into marble was left to the skillful collaborators whom he had gathered around him: Emile-Antoine Bourdelle (1861–1929), who worked as an assistant in his studio from 1893 to 1908, and Charles Despiau (1874–1946). Together with Aristide Maillol (1861–1944), they continued the debate into this new form of sculpture, by now free from academic mannerism and devoted to recapturing essential formal values derived from the relationships between mass and light and filled and empty space, as well as from the rhythmic articul-

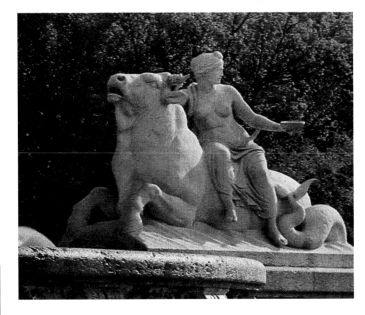

MAILLOL THE SCULPTOR

Aristide Maillol was an artist with a large and varied range of interests. During his highly productive life he worked in many media, concentrating first on painting within the Nabis group, then on tapestry and, later, wood-engraving, including fine, limited edition woodcuts, which he produced for a version of Virgil's *Eclogues*

Aristide Maillol, Torso for the Blanqui Monument, 1905–6. Tate Gallery, London.

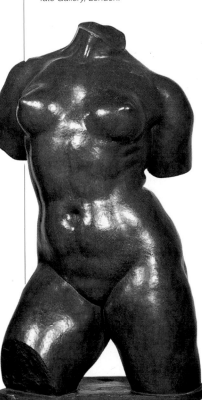

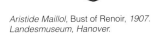

Aristide Maillol, Bust of Renoir, 1907. Landesmuseum, Hanover.

(1913). During the 1890s he began to sculpt in wood and to make terracotta statuettes, which Vollard later arranged to be cast in bronze. Maillol's sculpture was, in style, the exact opposite of Rodin's. Where Rodin's style was emotional, passionate, and highly expressive, Maillol's style was calm and meditative, with smooth, flowing lines. A trip to Greece in 1906 had helped define Maillol's idyllic classical style, although the influence of the sculpture of his friend Renoir, with its round and smooth female shapes, made a significant contribution, as did the sculpture of *The Bathers* by Henri Matisse.

ation of planes and lines. For Maillol this renewal process ranged from a return to the classical ideal forward to the neo-Hellenic plastic arts (he lived in Greece for a year and was inspired by the ancient statues). In contrast, Bourdelle, boosted by his Christian faith, reverted to medieval-inspired sculpture of simplified, robust, and heroic figures.

HILDEBRAND AND CENTRAL EUROPEAN SCULPTURE

The importance of Rodin's work in the field of sculpture, seen in both his own artistic output and in that of his closest followers, was complemented by the impact of the German Adolf von Hildebrand (1847–1921), whose contribution was of a theoretical nature. Attracted to sculpture during a stay in Italy, where he formed friendships with the painter Hans von Marées and the art critic Konrad Fiedler (both, like him, believers in the myth of *Deutsche-Römer*), Hildebrand is not primarily remembered for the quality of his art works, which have even been described as mediocre. His most successful undertaking was the

Wittelsbach Fountain in Munich (1894), with its numerous pools, waterfalls, and groups of figures arranged with great balance and symmetry. However, his literary work, *The Problem of Form in Figurative Art* (1893), was to prove widely influential. Of the two forms of vision distinguished by Hildebrand, the distant view, or, in other words, the complete, synthetic vision, was the more important. In sculpture this meant that the three-dimensional plastic form must be conceived in equally proportioned levels of relief. Out of this came a method – in complete contrast to the impetuous modeling of Rodin – whereby the sculpture was formed around a framework, a technique that involved starting from the outer surface of a block of marble and carving successive levels inward until the entire image was achieved.

This debate on the aesthetic problems of sculpture soon spread interest in Hildebrand's theories throughout Germany, and it was reflected in the work of, among others,

MINNE'S "FOUNTAIN OF THE KNEELERS"

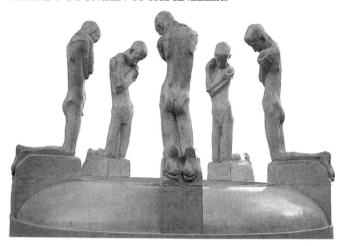

Georges Minne, Fountain of the Kneelers, 1898. Musée des Beaux-Arts, Ghent, Belgium.

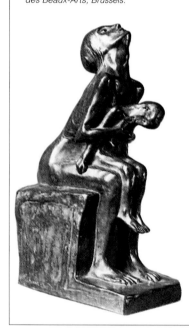

Georges Minne, Mother Weeping for Her Dead Son, 1886, Musée Royal des Beaux-Arts, Brussels.

Influenced by the somber sculpture of Claus Sluter, Georges Minne (1866–1941) interpreted the "idéiste" art of his age in the medieval sculptural style of Flanders. He led his life according to Franciscan rules and interpreted the human condition in melancholy and mournful terms. Minne masterfully expressed his feelings in a large marble fountain, *Fountain of the Kneelers* (1898), surrounded by five nude figures kneeling with their arms crossed on their chests. Elongated and slender, their somewhat severe, formal posture, sculpted in an abstract stylized manner, conveys strong spiritual tension.

"BEETHOVEN" BY KLINGER AND BOURDELLE

The genius of Beethoven has never ceased to inspire artists. Max Klinger's famous theatrical bust of the great German composer was undertaken in 1886, using precious materials (polychrome marble, bronze, ivory, and semiprecious stones for the features), with clear references to the Zeus of Phidias. This was a composite structure in a classical style, yet distinguished by its obvious Symbolist abstraction. Completed in 1901, the sculpture was exhibited at the Vienna Secession exhibition in an area dedicated wholly to Beethoven, an idea originated by Joseph Hoffmann according to the principle of *Gesamtkunstwerk*. In this context, Klinger's work assumed significance because he claimed to have found the unifying element of painting, sculpture, and architecture in the many colors of the varied materials. Moreover, as Hoffmann said, the sculpture confirmed "the connection between plastic arts and space" in a concrete way. For its presentation, Beethoven's Ninth Symphony was specially adapted by Gustav Mahler and performed at the event. Emile-Antoine Bourdelle began a series of portraits of Beethoven in 1888, which, from then until 1929, resulted in more than sixty sculptures.

This obsessive interest can be explained by the artist's identification with the composer and his feelings of spiritual affinity. Equally important was the widespread desire for "total art," which recognized the parallels between the techniques of creating with mass or sound. The last of Bourdelle's Beethoven series was *La Masque Tragique* (1901), a work that anticipated the formal solutions of 20th-century avant-garde sculpture.

Max Klinger, Beethoven, 1901. Museum der Bildenden Kunst, Leipzig, Germany.

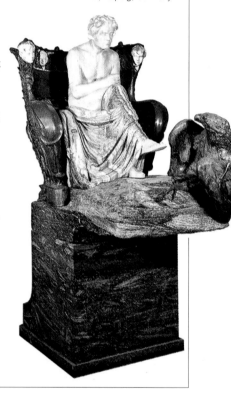

Wilhelm Lembruch, Georg Kilbe, Gerhard Marcks, Max Klinger, Ernst Barlach, and Käthe Kollwitz. In a climate dominated by Symbolist abstraction, these artists honored classicism, explored the revival of the northern Gothic tradition, touched on Expressionist themes that were fashionable at the turn of the century, and proclaimed their support of the Secessionists. Meanwhile, in Belgium, Georges Minne's interpretation of the formal

Gothic style resulted in his slim figurines, such as *The Little Relic Carrier* (1897), with their delicate rhythm and expressivity that are reminiscent of Rodin. Monumental and classical sculpture was ill-suited to take on assymetrical and overly stylized work, and, although some works of great skill and quality was achieved in the field of funerary art, in general Art Nouveau sculptors generally tended to focus on interior furnishings and architectural decoration.

ROSSO

A major contributor to the plastic arts at the end of the 19th century was Medardo Rosso (1858–1928), an Italian artist defined by the Futurist Boccioni as "the only great modern sculptor who has tried to open up sculpture into a wider field and to render in this medium the atmospheric links and the surrounding influences that bind it to the subject." Rosso started in the early 1880s as a member of

the Milanese *scapigliatura* movement, which believed that objectivity and subjectivity were both handicaps to artistic vision, and whose characteristic fusion of figure and atmosphere was revealed in Rosso's earliest compositions, inspired by urban, working-class types (*The Concierge*, 1883, and *Under the Lamppost*, 1883). While visiting Paris, where he was finally to settle in 1889, Rosso became a significant figure in discussions concerning the relationship between Impressionism and sculpture,

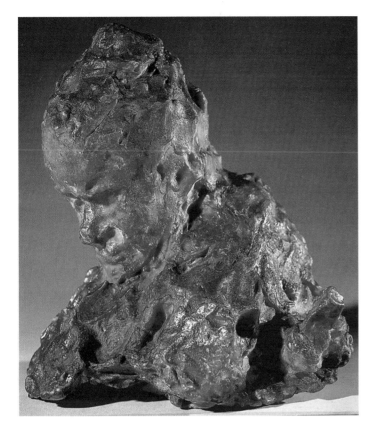

Medardo Rosso, The Concierge, *1883. Private Collection, Biella, Italy.*

a debate that involved him, Rodin, and E. Claris, who acted as spokesman, in the research initiated by *La nouvelle revue*. Described by Apollinaire as "the greatest sculptor alive," Rosso was highly appreciated by Rodin, who seemed to be influenced by certain of the Italian's figures (such as *The Bookmaker*, 1894, and *Man Reading*, 1894–95) – for example, in the diagonal,

Medardo Rosso, The Bookmaker, *1894. Museo Medardo Rosso, Barzio, Italy.*

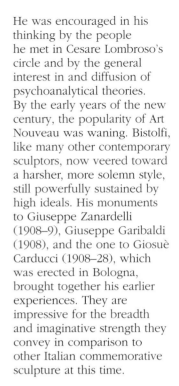

unbalanced line of his *Balzac*. Rosso attempted to "forget the material" and to capture "the intimate essence of reality" through the skillful illumination of his wax models, which he placed under a particular type of light source to give a diffuse, transitory impression. With *Ecce Puer* in 1906, the artist seemed to be aiming not so much for the expression of a fleeting visual experience as for the representation of a moral aspiration or an ideal – an interpretative approach in the Symbolist mold.

BISTOLFI

Leonardo Bistolfi (1859–1933), another Italian working along similar lines to Rosso, came to the attention of international critics as a result of the originality and quality of his sculptural ideas. He refused to adapt modern iconography or significant "ideas" to stylistic formulas of previous traditions, no matter how they were reworked or updated, and instead proposed a new artistic language within the syntax of Art Nouveau, known in Italy as *Stile Liberty*. A fine exponent of modern sculpture, Bistolfi was able to create articulate plastic forms endowing them with expression and vitality and modeling them with a delicate, quivering sensitivity that makes an indelible impression on the mind of the observer. He was an animated artist who showed a great inner tension and who was constantly probing the depths of his own imagination in his search for spiritual values.

Bistolfi spent his formative years in Turin, where he moved in avant-garde circles, which promoted the magazine *L'arte decorativa,* and organized in 1902 the International Decorative Arts Exhibition (for which he designed the poster). Between 1890 and 1900, he created a series of commemorative funerary monuments – *Sphinx*, (1890), *Pain Comforted by the Memory,* (1898), *The Funeral of a Virgin,* (1899), and *The Dream,* (1900) – which earned him the title of "poet of death." In these works, Bistolfi captured the fluid, changing processes of nature and the continual regenerative cycle of death and birth in delicate yet decisive images with little descriptive detail. He was also fascinated by the inscrutable inner logic of dreams, the passage between the conscious and subconscious, and the mysteries of the mind.

Leonardo Bistolfi, The Song of Love from the Bronze Strophes, 1908. Monument to Garibaldi, San Remo, Italy.

He was encouraged in his thinking by the people he met in Cesare Lombroso's circle and by the general interest in and diffusion of psychoanalytical theories. By the early years of the new century, the popularity of Art Nouveau was waning. Bistolfi, like many other contemporary sculptors, now veered toward a harsher, more solemn style, still powerfully sustained by high ideals. His monuments to Giuseppe Zanardelli (1908–9), Giuseppe Garibaldi (1908), and the one to Giosuè Carducci (1908–28), which was erected in Bologna, brought together his earlier experiences. They are impressive for the breadth and imaginative strength they convey in comparison to other Italian commemorative sculpture at this time.

Leonardo Bistolfi (1859–1933), The Dream, 1900. Cimitero Monumentale, Tomba Cairati, Milan.

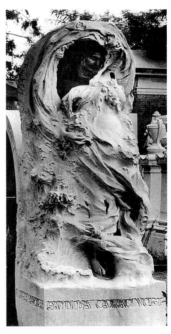

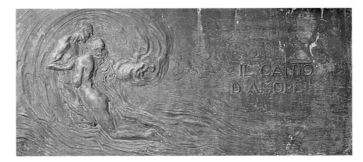

New Trends in the 19th & 20th Centuries

THE MODERN STYLE

Characterized by decorative, curvilinear designs, an innovative new style spread rapidly throughout Europe at the end of the 19th century. Following exotic trends while remaining faithful to regional traditions, this modern style could be seen in art, design, and architecture. It produced particularly fine results in the decorative arts, graphic work, and illustration.

From the end of the 19th century until World War I, the general desire for something new and modern produced innovation in the arts across Europe. Sharing certain formal elements and theoretical bases, the "modern style" was known by different names in each country: *Sezessionstil* in Austria, *Jugendstil* in Germany, Art Nouveau in France, the Liberty style in England, *Modernisme* in Spain, and *Stile Liberty* in Italy. A combination of faith in the improvements that industrial society would bring and a rejection of stylistic eclecticism proved to be the impetus for the creation of a new artistic language that took its inspiration directly from nature. Rich in references to animals and plants and characterized by sinuous asymmetrical lines, the work was lively, highly decorative, and exciting.

THE NEW STYLE

The new artistic language was based on an emphasis on "line-force," which, according to the Belgian painter and architect Henri van de Velde, held the energy of the person that produced it. Part of its appeal was the desire to fulfill a fundamental theoretical principle of Modernism: the application of the same aesthetic criteria to all aspects of industrial production. From construction to cabinet-making, from ceramics to fashion, and from graphic design to wrought-iron work, the functional was combined with the decorative so that useful items could also be beautiful.

The middle classes of modern society, rapidly gaining in economic status, now looked for artistic quality in the industrial products that they purchased. In the field of painting, they favored organic and naturalistic themes, which were expressed through a new relationship between line and surface. Linear and curvilinear arabesques and cool, transparent colors made up compositions based on undulating rhythms in asymmetrical patterns. The thickness of "whiplash" and "dynamographic" lines was dependent on how much energy they were intended to hold.

Characterized as Art Nouveau, this clearly distinguishable style influenced the many artistic movements emerging from Post-Impressionist art, such as the Nabis and the Symbolists, in the last decade of the century. In central Europe, among the members of the Secession, its influence resulted in works full of emotional expression, not just basic descriptive graphics. Henri van de Velde, English artist Walter Crane, the Germans Otto Eckmann and Hermann Obrist, and, above all, Gustav Klimt and

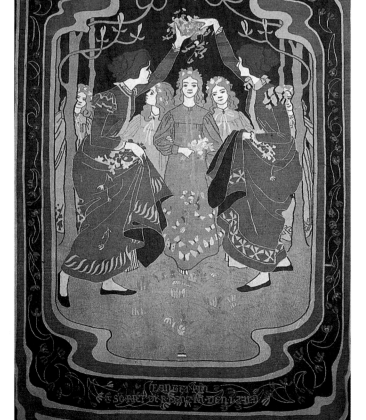

Otto Eckmann, The Coming of Spring, *tapestry, 1896–97.*

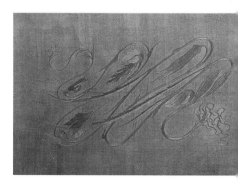

Hermann Obrist, Whiplash, *wool and silk, 1895. Stadtmuseum, Munich.*

VAN DE VELDE AND THE "SPEAKING LINE"

Of all the Modernist architects, Henri van de Velde was the one who best translated and put into practice the theories of *Einfühlung* to give meaning to his work. He based his designs on the principle that every part must satisfy an aspect of the mind: one element would induce tranquility, another excitement, another surprise, and another relaxation.

In a series of essays written between 1902 and 1903, van de Velde discussed the concept of the "speaking line," which he claimed to be a feature distinguishing every historical period and every civilization. He maintained that the slightest of movements, the subtlest change in rhythm, and the smallest variation in the timing or distance of emphasis were all responses to specific moods or states of mind. He defined the modern line as the malleable and elastic product flowing from a primitive current of energy. This was such a tangible and impatient force that it would not allow anything to get in between its points of departure and its final objective.

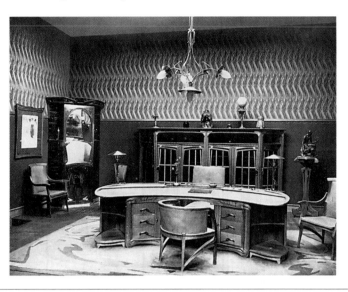

Interior of the Paris shop La Maison Moderne, designed for Julius Meier Graefe, 1898.

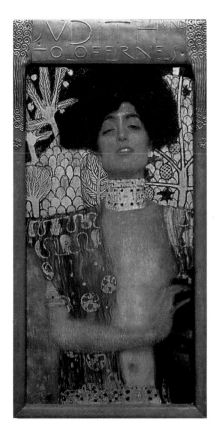

Gustav Klimt, Judith I, *1901. Österreichische Galerie, Vienna.*

Gustav Klimt, Danaë, *1907–08. Private Collection, Vienna. The image of the maiden loved by Jove is elliptical in construction and composed of a mosaic of colors and interlaced arabesques. Reminiscent of Byzantine artificiality, they remove any sense of depth and produce an effect of symbolic abstraction.*

HENRI VAN DE VELDE

The work of Henri van de Velde (1863–1957), Belgian painter, architect, theorist, and designer of furniture and *objets d'art*, bore the same marks of dynamism and abstraction found in compatriot Victor Horta's final works. He was the chief continental advocate of the ideas of William Morris, sharing the search for a clear style with rational structures and similar concerns for the role of the artist in society. Van de Velde strongly supported the need to match art with industry, but his emphasis on the aesthetic value of this marriage meant that he did not believe in mass production. His contributions to the decorative arts – from door handles to complete interior plans for houses – featured mainly ribbonlike, sinuous lines bordering voids. The technique was dominated by a nervous charge that produced a synthetic and dynamic interpretation of the "whiplash" effect.

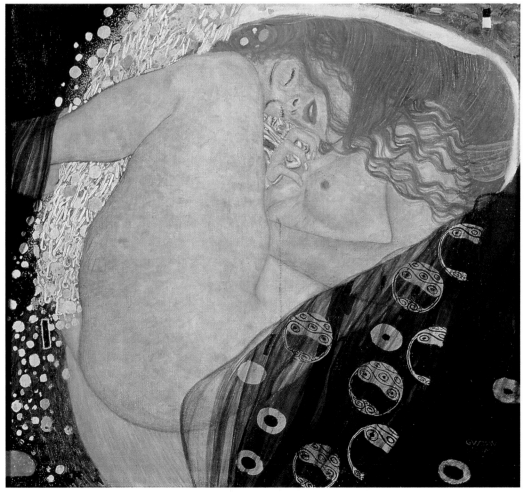

Edvard Munch showed how decoration in art could have both sociological and existential meanings.

Noted architects, painters, and sculptors, who had united in breakaway Secession groups, applied themselves to the

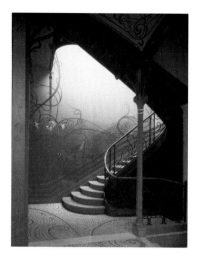

Victor Horta, staircase of the Tassel House, Brussels, 1893.

design of household objects and furniture in the pursuit of a "global art." This would produce an overall harmony, in which there was "a reciprocal assimilation of an interior affinity" among all forms. Horta and van de Velde in Belgium, Guimard in France, Mackintosh in Scotland, Gaudí in Spain, Wagner, Olbrich, and Hoffmann in Austria, and Basile in Italy all used new techniques and materials in a modern, international language. The style was recognizable everywhere, even when it paid respect to local indigenous features, which ranged from Gothic to Rococo, from Celtic art to Moorish art.

KLIMT

Gustav Klimt (1862–1918) was a refined and enigmatic portraitist, a sensitive painter of landscapes, and a skilled draftsman of sensual and delicate female nudes. In his paintings and mural cycles, he combined the intrinsic and the abstract, illusion and decoration, and maintained a harmony between the subject and the ornamentation. In this way, he incorporated the sublimity that was characteristic of the artistic experience at the end of the 19th century.

The son of a goldsmith, he acquired a good reputation in the traditional Viennese art world with his large allegorical paintings in the Burgtheater and Kunsthistorisches

THE VIENNESE SECESSION

"GLOBAL ART"
The Secession in Vienna evolved in 1897 through the initiatives of the writer Ludwig Hevesi; a group of artists that included Gustav Klimt (the first president), Carl Moll, Koloman Moser, and Maximilian Lenz; and the architects Josef Maria Olbrich, Josef Hoffmann, and, later, Otto Wagner. Their intention was to constitute an alternative to the narrow-minded cultural politics of the Viennese Künstlerhaus, which had little contact with the general public. The program stated their aim to "raise the flagging art of Austria to contemporary international standards". For this purpose, they concentrated on frequent, good-quality art

Koloman Moser, poster for the 13th Secession Exhibition in Vienna, 1909.

THE SECESSION MOVEMENT

In the last decade of the 19th century, there was general resentment among artists in certain central European countries about the powers of the art academies and their monopoly of exhibitions. This drove young painters, sculptors, and architects to break from the official organizations and to start up alternative groups, known as Secessions. Their objectives, apart from establishing a style that was Symbolist in orientation, were to free themselves from

historical revivalism, to achieve a fulfillment of the concept of "global art," and to make all modern works of art known internationally in order to encourage cultural exchange. The first groups to be founded were the Munich Secession (1892) and the Berlin Secession (1893). In 1897, the most famous of all, the Viennese Secession, was established. Other artistic societies that came together to oppose ruling institutions included the Roman Secession, whose exhibitions of an anti-academic nature were also a reaction to the radical avant-

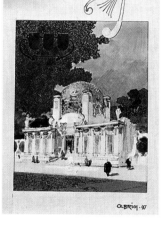

Joseph Maria Olbrich, study for the Secession Palace, 1897. Historisches Museum, Vienna.

garde aesthetic nature of Futurism. It is hard to overestimate the influence of the Secessionists on European art in the early 20th century. Although essentially homogeneous in practice, the Secessionists stimulated the growth of the workshop as a center of creativity, expanding the range of materials and expressive techniques.

Franz von Stuck, poster for the Seventh International Secession Exhibition in Munich, 1897.

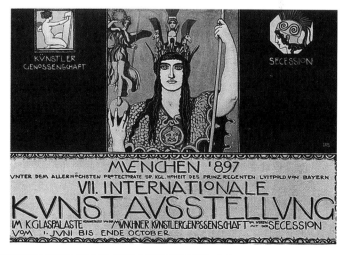

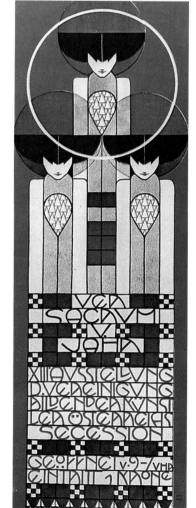

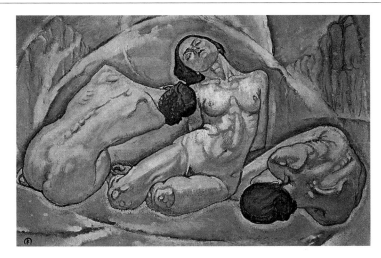

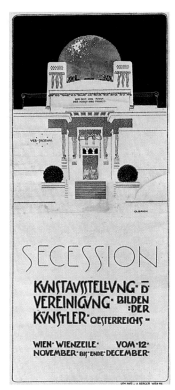

exhibitions – there were 23 shows in the first seven years – with strong didactic support, such as guided tours and free catalogs. The vehicle for communicating their activities and ideas was *Ver Sacrum*, a magazine that featured graphic and literary contributions of a particularly high standard between 1898 and 1903.

The group's desire to create "global art," involving painting, sculpture, architecture, and decoration, brought about the organization of theme-based exhibitions. One work of art would become the center of the show, and the others assumed the role of subsidiary accompaniment. This was the case for Arthur Strasser's *Group of Mark Antony* in 1889 and Max Klinger's *Beethoven* in 1902. Other important events included shows

Gustav Klimt, poster for the Secession Exhibition, Vienna, 1898.

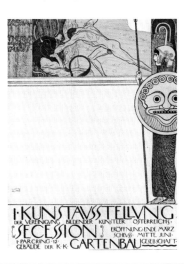

dedicated to the Glasgow School and to Ashbee's Guild of Handicraft Artists in 1900, the large Klimt exhibition in 1903, the Munich Secession show in 1907, and one dedicated to modern Russian art in 1908–9. The success of the first was enough to finance the building of a special gallery, which was designed by the architect Joseph Olbrich as a pavilion and small temple. The frieze at its entrance bears the words "Der Zeit ihre Kunst, der Kunst ihre Freiheit" ("Let the times have their art, and art its freedom").

ARCHITECTURE

The architecture of the Viennese Secession followed along similar lines to the work of Charles Rennie Mackintosh and his Scottish followers. It was directed toward a control of opulence and organic decoration in favor of more rigid systems, with cubic blocks for form and geometric shapes for adornment. The work of the master Otto Wagner (1841–1918) was supported by that of fellow students Joseph Maria Olbrich (1867–1908) and Joseph Hoffmann (1870–1956). Between them, they renovated a large part of Vienna, especially private houses (for example, those on the Wienzeile), in which they endeavored to display modernity in contrast to the historic tastes of previous decades. Instead of Renaissance or Baroque decor, Wagner

Joseph Maria Olbrich, Secession Pavilion, Vienna, 1898.

produced a perfectly smooth facade adorned with majolica tiles brightly painted with flowers. The design covered the whole surface, with every house and every floor receiving the same kind of decoration.

Olbrich, on the other hand, applied the mark of his rather original style to the "artists' village" on the Mathildenhöhe in

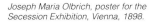

Darmstadt, a project realized entirely by him and commissioned by the Grand Duke Ernst Ludwig for the artist colony's 1899 exhibition. He also introduced a new architectural formula for the construction of exhibition halls in the Viennese Secession building of 1898: a square module, topped by a golden bronze dome incised with a laurel leaf decoration standing between four small towers. This structure was given the uncomplimentary name of the "Golden Cabbage House" by the critics of the time.

By about 1900, Hoffmann's architectural plans also revealed a tendency to take formal elements to a geometric extreme, a characteristic that he developed after the foundation of the Wiener Werkstätte, when he widened the scope of his activity to encompass all branches of craftsmanship. One such area was modern furniture, which he created in elegant and stylized designs, concentrating on functional rather than ornamental form.

Constructed in a simple fashion, the pieces were given proportion through a measured use of the square. Hoffmann said, "I am particularly interested in the square as such, and in the use of black and white as dominant colors, because these clear elements have never appeared in earlier styles."

Joseph Maria Olbrich, poster for the Secession Exhibition, Vienna, 1898.

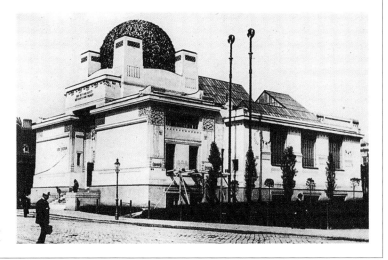

Museum. However, at the dawn of the new century, his designs for the ceiling of the Great Hall of Vienna University disappointed the commissioning authority. Instead of exalting positively the values of science and reason as purveyors of truth, his concept was a comment on the decadence of contemporary society. The portrayal was judged to be too crude, merciless, and erotic. It was his subject matter – nude, elderly, and obese men and women, all

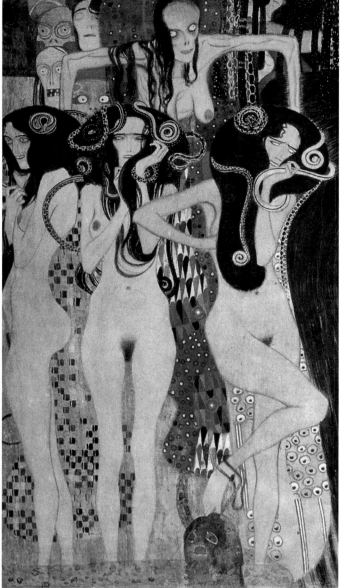

A SWEET ART

In the first quarter of the 20th century, the influence of the new modern art styles reached even the smallest areas of artistic enterprise, including that of pastry-making. During the Second Empire and then in the belle époque, pastry-making reached a particularly high level of artistry – the *Sachertorte*, a miraculous confection invented in Vienna and exclusive to the hotel of the same name, is still enjoyed today. The Modern style, and later Art Deco, had a particular influence on the decoration of pastries, determining its overall style, range of colors, and ornamental details. The art of pastry-making lives on in many European countries, and the finished products are as visually pleasing and appetizing as those that delighted gourmets a century ago. To many devotees, the perfectly made tart, cake, or pastry is considered more delicate and ephemeral than any piece of pottery, its aesthetic appearance at least as important as its taste.

of the *Jugendstil*. He constructed images with mosaic patterns of arabesque colors and designs, which, with their lack of depth, recalled Byzantine arts, while also containing a heavy element of Symbolist abstraction. Two important mural cycles exemplify this technique and represent the perfect synthesis of the sensitive use of space: the first, the *Beethoven Frieze* for the Secession exhibition of 1902, was planned by Hoffmann as an expression of the synthesis of all the arts. The second was the mosaic for the dining room in the Palais Stoclet in Brussels (1905–6), where the abstract figure barely emerges out of the profusion of decoration created with a variety of sparkling precious materials. From this moment onward until the end of World War I, Klimt continued to develop his style by placing great emphasis on abstraction and stylization. He was to become the leading artist of an alternative version to avant-garde abstract art, which had emerged from the same central European culture in the same period.

Gustav Klimt, Beethoven Frieze, *detail, 1902. The frieze was situated in an inconspicuous part of the Viennese Secession Palace.*

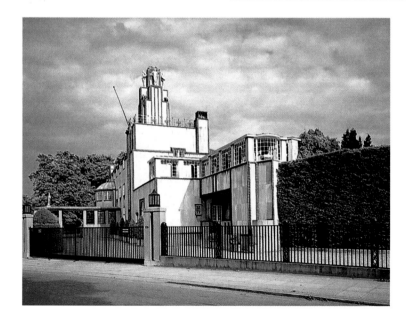

drawn by an invisible force – that upset the authorities rather than his use of the Modern Style. The layout was asymmetrical, the technique was strongly two-dimensional, and the outlines were clear and sumptuously curvilinear – a style that Klimt initiated with other Viennese artists as members of the Secession from 1897.

Between 1900 and 1903, Klimt's style developed the characteristics that would make him the chief exponent

Josef Hoffmann, Palais Stoclet, Brussels, *1905–11. This famous building has a white exterior on which unmolded, colored apertures are arranged.*

GUSTAV KLIMT

Gustav Klimt (1862–1918) took courses at the School of Decorative Arts in Vienna and began work as a painter and decorator of public buildings, together with his brother and other artists. The style they followed was an international form of Symbolism. In 1897, he was the leading figure in the foundation of the Viennese Secession, and after a few years he had become the best representative of the Modern style. In his last years, he showed an appreciation of the avant-garde tendencies of the Expressionists. His extraordinary talent ensured the success of work that contained various expressive materials in one composition, recalling Gothic and Byzantine traditions while also anticipating the multimedia art of the 20th century.

GUSTAV KLIMT: "THE KISS"

1908; oil on canvas; 71 x 71 in (180 x 180 cm); Österreichische Galerie, Vienna.

This work, one of various versions of *The Kiss*, belongs to the period that has been defined as Klimt's "golden" phase, distinguished by intense decorative lyricism and formal stylization. The painting shows two figures on a flower-covered bank in golden surroundings. Their bodies are fused under luxurious clothes, which are adorned with a rich array of colored shapes and designs. The female figure is kneeling, her body in profile, with her head resting on her shoulder and supported by the man's hand. Her face is turned toward the viewer and her eyes are closed. The man is standing and embracing the woman, his embrace forming a union of the two bodies. His head leans forward, resting on the side of the woman's head, and his arm cradles her head and neck. His right hand also rests lightly on her face.

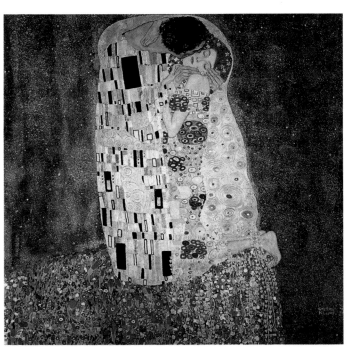

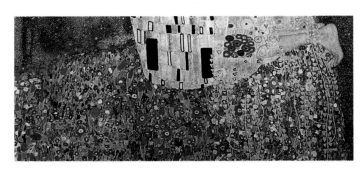

▲ *3. The decoration of Klimt's painting is exuberant, and he achieves a particular golden splendor in the area containing the figures, wrapped in their rich, sumptuous clothing. The dominant color of bright gold is continued in the carpet of flowers, most strikingly in the leaves of the vines on the right. The field of flowers is a life-force that occupies the space in front of the figures and borrows from the colors in their fabrics. Where it meets the background, its borders form a blurred horizon.*

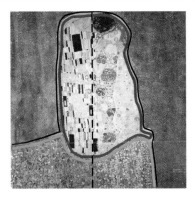

▲ *1. There is an exquisite elegance and sense of order to the composition, created by distinct blocks of color and a pervasion of yellow and golden hues. The two bodies form a rising, elongated mass of color, which stands out against the golden backdrop. The loving relationship between the two figures is expressed through the suggested fusion of their bodies and through the almost identical fabric that swathes them, isolating them from the rest of the world like a layer of skin. If the mass of the figures were cut along a vertical axis, the two sides would be dissimilar and completely asymmetrical. It is the right-hand side that holds most of the elements of the bodies – faces, hands, legs, and feet.*

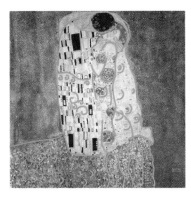

▲ *4. A very sure, precise line defines the different chromatic masses of the composition. It slides around in curves forming the borders of the large masses of color. Elsewhere, a rhythmic series of curved lines carves out minute details of the decoration, both in the clothing and the flowers. Spirals, twisting plant shapes, circles, and ovals are dotted all over the surface of the fabric, the overall effect of which remains subtle, smooth, and serene. In certain parts, it almost seems to create a veil, perhaps symbolizing faded energy and rarefied substance. At the time of painting, advances in scientific analysis under the microscope were revealing similar shapes in nature.*

▼ *2. Space is defined in two dimensions, as in the Byzantine mosaics that Klimt studied in Ravenna. There is no perspective and therefore no sense of depth. The dusty brown in the gold background does not add a sense of depth but helps enrich the sensual atmosphere. The two-dimensional space is made up of many-colored masses, which rarely have natural borders to identify them as particular forms. However, within each of the chromatic masses, the decoration – be it flowers, embroidery, gems, or metals – gives motion to the indicated planes and fills them with light and color. Klimt was clearly inspired by Oriental motifs (he was an enthusiastic collector of Chinese and Japanese objets d'art) and by the work of the French Symbolist painter Gustave Moreau.*

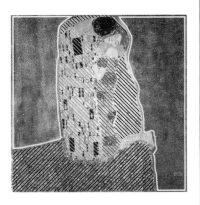

▼ *5. Although the majority of the painting is strikingly, non-naturalistic, in keeping with Klimt's characteristic style, the features of the two figures are depicted more realistically. The flesh of the woman's face, shoulder, and left arm, and the man's fingers, all have a certain sense of plasticity. There is a subtle contrast between the mother-of-pearl pallor of the woman and the amber skin-tone of the man. Klimt uses shadows to depict the man's cheek and eye, which can just be seen. He decorates the heads with stylized flowers and delicately paints the hair. In this isolation and highlighting of parts of the body there is an affinity with religious icons. In these, only certain parts of the saints' bodies were recognizably painted, the rest being decorative, with gold, enamel, and gems.*

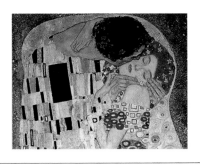

EDVARD MUNCH: "THE SCREAM"

1893; tempera on panel; 33 x 26 in (83.5 x 66 cm); Kommunes Kunstsmalinger, Oslo.

Munch made several versions of this work, including a number of lithographs. It is probably his most famous painting and is part of his exploration of the theme of desperation – he wrote: "I painted the clouds like real blood. The colors are shrieking." The painting depicts the span of a bridge, opening out diagonally from left to right across the lower two-thirds of the composition. In the foreground, a figure dressed in dark colors stands in the middle of the scene. Two male figures can be seen at the top of the bridge, where the diagonal line meets the left edge of the picture. To the right of the bridge, there is a dark hilly landscape surrounding a clear lake or inlet of sea. Above the horizon, the sky is made up of wavy ribbons of bright colors. The bridge is painted in a band of straight lines that begin in the bottom left-hand corner and cover the base of the picture. The rest of the painting is filled with colors regulated by curving lines.

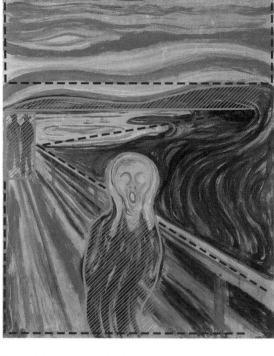

▶ *1. The basic features of the composition are simple. Under the band of sky, the hills are defined by two parallel lines. The lower one runs along the bank on the far side of the water. At the end of this line on the right another line traces the border of the water and the nearest bank, arriving at roughly the middle point of the vertical rectangle containing the two figures. The body of the figure in the foreground is depicted with curving lines that stand out against the straight lines of the bridge. The head, light in tone, stands out against the dark landscape. The perspective, which breaks up on the right-hand side, makes use of straight lines and angles along with curved lines.*

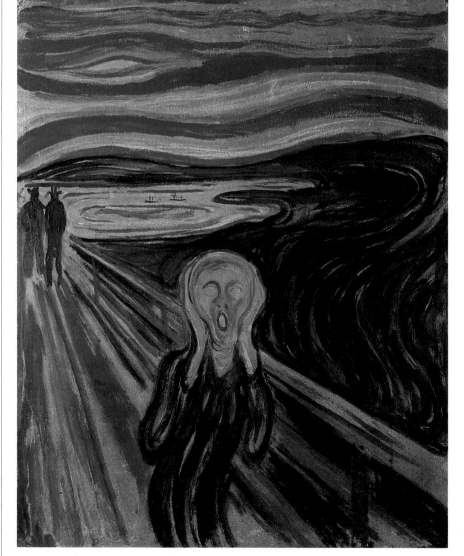

▼ *2. If the picture is observed from the foreground, the eye is pulled toward the straight lines and the corner from which they originate. On the right-hand side, on the other hand, the area moves in bands of curves in which space disappears. The different treatment of the two sides creates a feeling of unease. The crude and violent colors are positioned according to a plan: on the left, in the area of straight lines, yellows and reds predominate; on the right, in the area of curves, blues, greens, and blacks prevail. The brushwork of the figures, forms, and paths is passionately expressive. Realism is denied by the use of wild colors. There is no harmony between the dark and light colors, only violent contrast. The undulating bands of warm colors in the sky only add to the tension.*

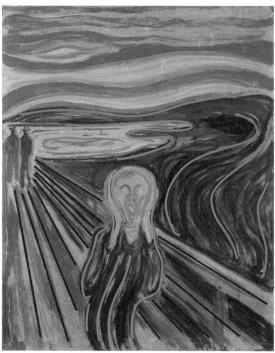

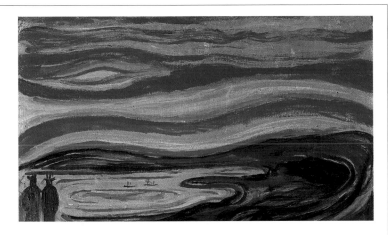

▲ 3. In the top part of the painting, an area of "painting for painting's sake" stands out. The very part that seemed to block in the dramatic turmoil of the lower half with fiery light appears to be something very different when considered in isolation. The harmonious bands of yellow and red with intermittent strips of white, gray, and light blue follow a gentle horizontal rhythm. The blue band is equally undulating and elaborate and moves horizontally from right to left, for the most part above the water. The lake or sea reflects the yellow of the sky, containing twists of lilac and light blue.

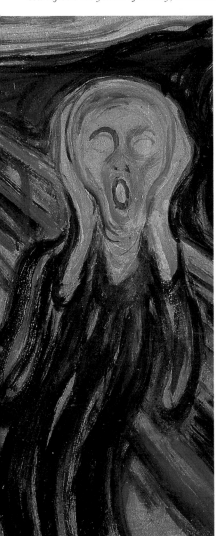

◀ 4. The figure in the foreground appears in the form of ectoplasm – the ghostly substance spiritualists say emanates from a medium during a trance. Psychic beings are said to float in the air and have no particular sexual identity, just like the figure in the painting. With the arms bent upward, the head stripped bare of skin, with light holes for the eyes and open mouth and dark holes for the nostrils, this is the image of deep anxiety. The movement of the figure comes from its base, its hands around the screaming mouth, and the horror expressed in its wide-open eyes.

▲ 5. The reading of a work of art should never be too conditioned by the emotions expressed within it. What is important is that the artist uses the medium to create the intended image of the world. This is what Munch does here, with a juxtaposition of straight and curved lines, warm, light colors, and cold, dark ones. In the area of gloomy colors, the movement of the curved lines mimics that of a sea storm. An enormous surge rises up and breaks, like a "scream" of nature.

MUNCH

If Klimt translated "the precarious survival of form at the end of substance" (Argan) in the rhythmic elegance of his decorative art and equally expressed the reaction of a society in crisis, then the Norwegian Edvard Munch interpreted problems of a similarly existential kind. Using a language that is markedly expressive, his pessimism is full of references to the work of Schopenhauer, the negative philosophy of Nietzsche, and the aesthetics of Wagner. Along with his compatriot Henrik Ibsen (for whom he designed theater posters and stage sets), Munch hated conventional morality, bourgeois prejudices, and hypocrisy. Within the Art Nouveau style and its "dynamographic" lines, he found the ideal language to interpret the principles of *Einfühlung* – the communication of important messages on the big issues of life, love, and death.

With contrasting monochrome areas of color, bordered by thick, continuous, dynamic outlines that go in waves and vortices, the artist sought to express the themes of loneliness, the difficult relationship of love and passion between man and woman, and the insufficient

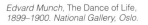

Edvard Munch, The Dance of Life, 1899–1900. National Gallery, Oslo.

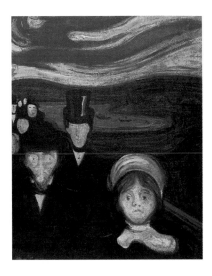

Edvard Munch, Angst, 1894. Munch Museum, Oslo. In the background, the mirrorlike sea (actually a fjord) appears again, as in The Scream. Here, too, the diagonal of the bridge across the landscape is prominent in the foreground.

EDVARD MUNCH

Edvard Munch (1863–1944) studied at the School of Art and Handicraft in Oslo and was heavily influenced by French art, making his first trip to Paris in 1885. At the 1892 show in Berlin, the harshness of his style caused a stir. His most famous works, anticipated the Berlin Secession and Expressionism and created in various versions, were produced between 1892 and 1908. His later work is less appreciated, although it lacks none of the intensity, high quality, and diligence of his earlier art. *Studies of the Artist's Diseased Retina* (1930–34) led to the powerful *Self-portrait at 2:15 in the Morning* (1941–44), an unsparing image of a composed but sleepless old man.

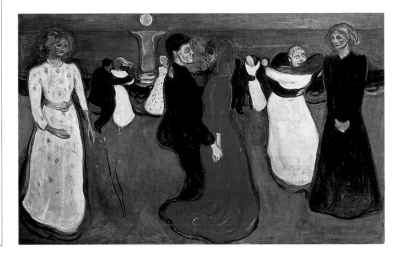

THE MUNICH SECESSION

In 1892, Franz von Stuck (1863–1928), a German painter of traditional leaning, established the first of the Secessions, together with Wilhelm Trübner and Fritz von Uhde (1848–1911). The group was made up of artists who eschewed the avant-garde ideas that occupied the artistic community in favor of naturalism, particularly in the field of the decorative arts. The movement soon became associated with the magazine *Jugend* ("Youth"), which played a crucial role in making the Art Nouveau style part of German culture. In fact, the German form of the Modern style then took the name of the magazine. The artists of the Munich *Jugendstil* (Obrist, Eckmann, and Endell) derived their inspiration for their new decorative vocabulary from the plant and animal world. From the natural world, as Endell said, "you can take the nonrepresentational shapes from which art is created; shapes that awaken our souls with the force of music."

One interesting exponent of the *Jugendstil* was Hermann Obrist (1863–1927), a naturalist, botanist, and sculptor, who set up a workshop in Florence in 1892 and then in Munich two years later. From these centers he organized the production of "organic embroidery," so called because of the spontaneity and rhythm that characterized the work. His wall panel of 1895, which was embroidered with cyclamens in gold silk on a background of turquoise wool, has in time become a symbol of the Art Nouveau style. Its name *Whiplash* derives from the impression it gives of a sudden and rapid force, as portrayed in twisting lines that seem to take off and wind around and around on the two-dimensional surface of the embroidery.

August Endell, Elvira Studio, Munich, 1897–98.

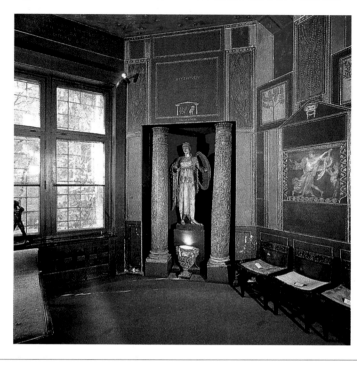

Franz von Stuck, Athene, 1897. Music room, Villa Stuck, Munich.

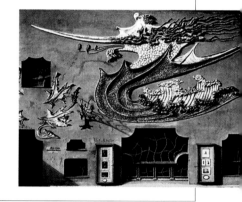

MUNCH AND EXPRESSIONISM

Like Klimt, Munch was also interested in the medium of large mural decoration, and in 1910 he completed a complex cycle on the theme of the Sun in the University of Oslo. He had already finished his ambitious series of works, the *Frieze of Life*, which he described as "a poem of life, love and death." He took over ten years to complete it, aiming to "help people see clearly" and to understand the internal psychological growth of an individual. The project was shown at the Berlin Secession in 1902 and had a profound effect on the development of German art at the beginning of the century, especially on the birth of the Expressionist movement. His woodcuts had a particular influence, prompting a widespread revival of the technique. Munch's first personal show was held in 1896 at La Maison de l'Art Nouveau, the Paris shop designed by Henri van de Velde and opened the previous year. In the gallery, the owner Siegfried Bing displayed paintings, Japanese art, and modern *objets d'art* in the new decorative styles, including glass and ceramic pieces, books, and furniture.

Edvard Munch, The Sun, c.1912–13. Munch Museum, Oslo.

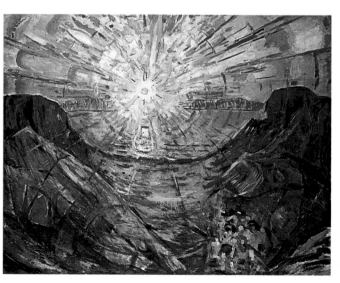

weight given to moral actions in a closed, conformist society. Works like *The Sick Child* (1885–86), *The Scream* (1893), and *Angst* (1894) originated from a view of life that was dominated by death and disease, anxiety and neuroses, and attraction to and rejection by women.

ART NOUVEAU IN FRANCE

In Paris, the floral exuberance of works by Belgian architect Victor Horta was interpreted in unique fashion by Hector Guimard (1867–1942). In his design of the entrances to the Métro stations in about 1900, he gave an urban dimension to the floral genre of decoration that had until then only been used for interiors. Using iron and enameled steel, he sculpted signs, railings, and lampposts in organic forms,

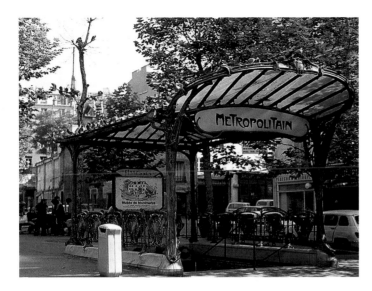

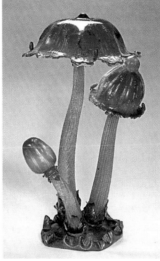

Emile Gallé, mushroom lampstand, 1900.
Musée de l'Ecole, Nancy.

and translucent backgrounds. He painted, carved, and created reliefs of dragonflies, spiders, flowers, and delicate landscapes on his soft-blue-colored glass known as *clair de lune* and on cameo glass. These magical images were often accompanied by lines of poetry by his Symbolist friends, "solidifying the verses of Baudelaire and Verlaine," as van de Velde said. The success of his experiments encouraged other artisans to breathe new life into the art

Hector Guimard, Métro station of the Place de l'Etoile, Paris, 1899. This structure has since been demolished.

with lamps shaped like succulent orchids. Otto Wagner and Joseph Olbrich must have had such ideas in mind when they were commissioned to design the underground in Vienna. The abundance of floral and vegetal decoration is not as visually overwhelming in this

case but is nonetheless characterized by a lightness and freshness.
The main concern of French Art Nouveau, however, was for the *objet d'art*, innovated at the Ecole de Nancy and created with great refinement and a skill that is hard to find elsewhere. The traditional glass production of this French town was dramatically changed by the designer Emile Gallé (1846–1904), who

utilized his knowledge of Oriental glasswork after taking over his father's glassworks in 1874. He also incorporated his interest in plants and insects in a unique style of decoration that made use of some original techniques. In his search for special effects of light and mistiness, Gallé experimented with the addition of pieces of metal, enamel, and pigments in order to obtain changing

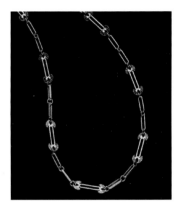

René Lalique, gold necklace, 1900. Private Collection, Parma.

of glasswork, including the brothers August and Antonin Daum, who perfected opaque *pâte-de-verre* for boxes, vases, and small figures, and René Lalique (1860–1945), who was the first to set up large-scale production of precious perfume bottles. Lalique is more famous for his jewelry. Using semiprecious stones, glass, enamel, mother-of-pearl, and even horn (not for its intrinsic value but for its color), his beautiful jewels represented natural subjects such as dragonflies, scarabs, snakes, orchids, and mistletoe. His range of soft colors typified the Art Nouveau palette.

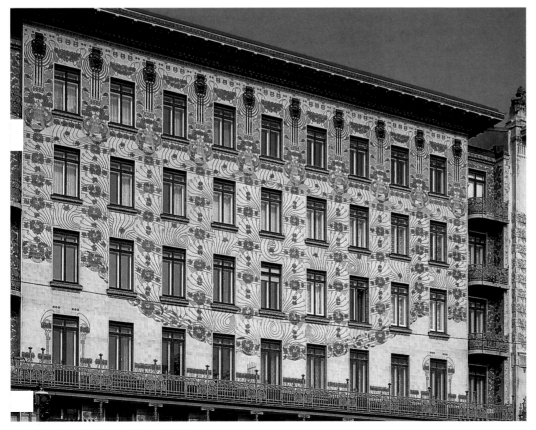

Majolica House, Vienna, 1898–1900. The architect was Otto Wagner, while the design for the majolica on the facade was by Gustav Klimt, who, as decorator, was responsible for the art work.

EIFFEL AND HORTA

In 1889, the engineer Gustav Eiffel (1832–1923) designed a tower for the World Exhibition in Paris. Structured entirely in iron, left visible to show the expressive possibilities of the new material, the Eiffel Tower was to symbolize the modern era. Three years later, in the same vein as the French tower, with its light, slender, vertical outlines somewhat reminiscent of the Gothic style, Victor Horta (1861–1947) adorned the Hôtel Tassel in Brussels with a series of small columns in iron, leaving them blatantly exposed. Instead of the classic style of modeling, they rose up twisting and winding like stalks, opening out into fronds and buds. The plant detail is also present, in a more developed way, in the floor mosaics, the friezes, and the decorative elements in bronze or iron on the banister rail and wall surfaces. The work of this brilliant architect met with such acclaim

that, in a few years, the face of the Belgian capital was changed. This transformation affected the features of private houses, such as gently curving facades softened by large windows and glass doorways (such as that of the Hôtel Solvay, 1894–1900); commercial buildings, such as the Innovation store; and civic buildings. Horta's Maison du Peuple, commissioned in 1895 by the Fédération Bruxelloise du Parti Ouvrier, unites the functionalism and originality of the building with a daring constructional design, which involves a visible framework of steel filled with large panes of glass. Lacking the more elaborate serpentine decoration of his luxurious private houses, the structure is notable for the agile rhythm of the network of its horizontal and vertical elements and the undulating motion of its concave and convex curves.

Victor Horta, Hôtel Solvay, Brussels, 1894–1900.

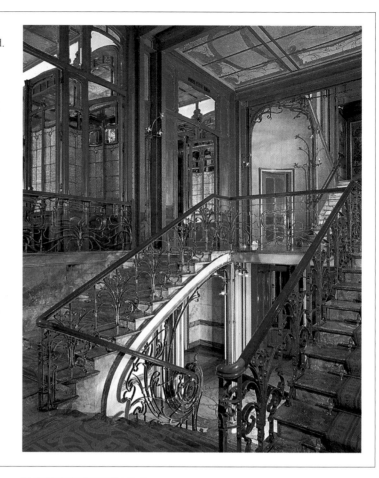

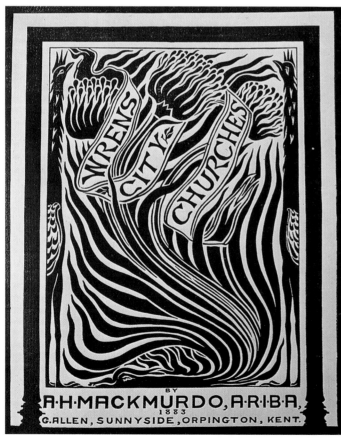

Arthur Mackmurdo, frontispiece for Wren's City Churches, 1883. Victoria and Albert Museum, London.

THE LIBERTY STYLE

Just as the term "Art Nouveau" is linked to a store of the same name opened in Paris in 1895 by Siegfried Bing, the "Liberty" store in England came to be associated with its own particular style of art. Opened in London in 1875 by Arthur Lazenby Liberty, initially for the sale of Oriental fabrics, the shop's merchandise soon came to be characterized by a distinct style based on naturalistic patterns, exploring and developing the ideas of William Morris.

In 1882, Arthur Mackmurdo (1851–1943), Art Nouveau pioneer and designer of stylized, slender furniture, founded the cooperative organization, the Century Guild. Inspired by the ideas of Morris and John Ruskin, the group produced furniture, carpets, wallpaper, and metalwork, aiming to promote and establish decorative art in the same way as William Morris' own company had set out to do. Mackmurdo also turned his talents to graphic design and typography. At the time, there were numerous publications that adopted Art Nouveau graphics, exploiting the expressive power of the flat lines without shadows and the clear, contrasting areas of color. In his title page for *Wren's City Churches*, published in 1883, Mackmurdo presented an original mixture of typography and ornamentation, employing the same undulating motif of meandering lines growing one out of the other that had adorned the back of his famous chair of 1881. In 1884, he started his own periodical at the Century Guild, the highly original and influential *Hobby Horse*, which aimed to embrace all the arts, including literature and music.

BEARDSLEY AND MACKINTOSH

The young English illustrator Aubrey Beardsley (1872–98) came to the critics' attention with his 300 drawings for a version of Malory's *Morte d'Arthur*, which was published by William Morris' Kelmscott Press. He also developed his own unique stylistic mark, based on very artificial figures, immersed in ornamental detail that was secondary but distinct in its superficial elegance and fine line work. A prolific illustrator who worked only in black and white, he skillfully translated the aesthetic spirit of the hedonistic *fin de siècle* culture into his illustrations for Oscar Wilde's *Salomé*, published in 1894. Rich in hidden metaphors and perverse erotic details, the drawings are a sophisticated expression of a cerebral art form. With these and other works published in *The Studio* from 1893 and in *The Yellow*

SALOME: WILDE AND BEARDSLEY

Both Oscar Wilde (1854–1900) and Aubrey Beardsley were part of a group of London dandies who reveled in scandalizing the conventional world with their eccentric and affected behavior. They were also connected by the publication in 1894 of *Salomé*, in which Wilde's poetic text was illustrated with exceptional decorative show by Beardsley. The story of the Jewish princess – "pale...like a white rose reflected in a silver mirror" – described by Wilde with decadent passion, was interpreted by Beardsley with a modern, daring spirit. He uses iconographic motifs and ideas from Japanese art (he dresses her in a kimono), models from the Paris fashion world, and the peacock-feather decorations in Whistler's *Peacock Room*, thereby adhering to the modern tastes and literary predilections of *fin de siècle* intellectuals. From this combination of interests come images that are both puzzling and ambiguous, due to the blend of crudeness and grace, formal elegance and moral perversity, eroticism, and delicate drawing. The character of Salomé – that of a wicked and perverse female – appears in many of Beardsley's women, representing the misogyny of a decadent culture affirmed by a dichotomy between beauty and morality, with beauty always given the advantage. In December 1897, the composer Richard Strauss staged his opera *Salomé* in Dresden. Based on Wilde's play, it was a masterpiece of musical decadence.

Aubrey Beardsley, illustrations for Oscar Wilde's Salomé, *1894: left,* The Climax; *right,* The Dancer's Reward.

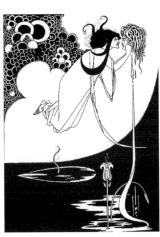

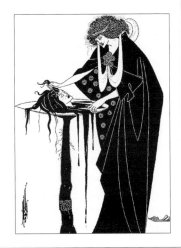

THE ECOLE DE NANCY

The Nancy School was officially founded in 1901 in preparation for participation at the Turin Exhibition a year later. However, the school had been formed over a decade earlier by a group of artists – Emile Gallé, Louis Majorelle, Victor Prouve, Antonin Daum, and Eugène Vallin – who wanted to promote the setting up of modern art industries in the provinces by providing teaching and professional training. Depictions of the animal and plant worlds filled their artistic vocabulary; as Gallé explained: "Our roots lie at the threshold of the forest, in the moss that surrounds the pond." Organic ornamentation predominated in their glass and ceramic pieces and, in particular, in the furniture – original structures crafted in soft, malleable wood in the shapes of insects with long

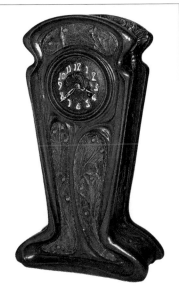

Louis Majorelle, Clock, 1900. Musée de l'Ecole, Nancy.

legs or the winding shoots of young plants. Details in copper or bronze, applied or inlaid on fine wood or mother-of-pearl, added to the appeal.

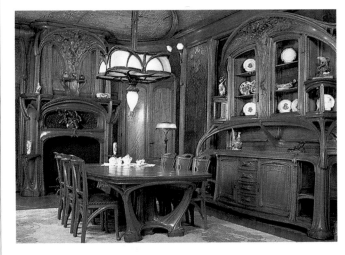

Eugène Vallin, dining room, Nancy, 1903–04.

Emile Gallé, table, Nancy, 1904.

Book from 1894, Beardsley exerted a great influence over graphic art in Europe and, especially, in the US. In the field of furniture, contrasting with the exuberant and precious ornamentation of the French style, and in particular with that of the Ecole de Nancy where echoes of Rococo were still present, a more rational and controlled use of line was adopted in Britain. Greater attention was

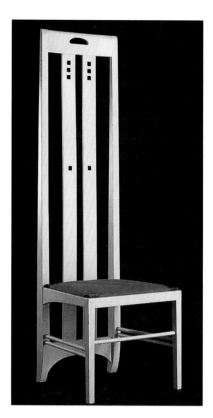

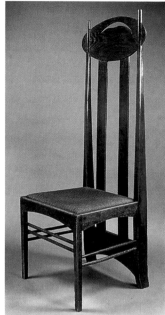

Two chairs by Charles Rennie Mackintosh; left, 1900, from the Hunterian Art Gallery, Glasgow University; above, 1897, from the antiquarian market, Glasgow.

THE CATALAN MODERN STYLE

As the Modern style developed across Europe, the form that it took in each country depended on particular local trends and tastes. In the architectural examples of the Spanish Modern Style, also known as Modernisme, and especially in the extraordinarily inventive work of Antoni Gaudí, a taste for flamboyant Gothic and Moorish styles is evident, as well as a preference for tiles, mosaics, and the use of colors inspired by the Mediterranean tradition. The influence of medieval Catalan architecture was obvious in Gaudí's work – Modernisme art was significant in Catalan nationalism and was linked to the aspirations of the Renaixenca group, which aimed for for political and cultural autonomy. Gaudí regularly encountered members of this group in Barcelona at the house of his friend and patron Eusebi Güell. As a result of knowing Güell, a wealthy industrialist who was eager to

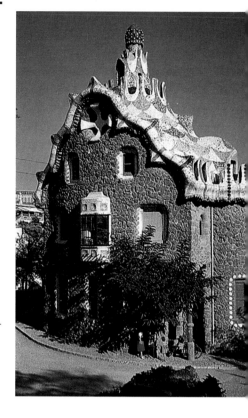

Antoni Gaudí, building in the Güell Park, Barcelona, 1900–14.

paid to practicality, anticipating furniture design in the 20th century.

In Scotland, the designer Charles Rennie Mackintosh (1868–1928) formed The Glasgow Four with Herbert MacNair and the sisters Margaret and Frances Macdonald. The distinguishing points of their style were the preference for straight lines and geometrical shapes, rather than curved lines and organic shapes, and a symmetry of composition based on aligned and parallel elements. In 1897, Mackintosh started on a large architectural project – the design of the Glasgow School of Art. It is an austere, compact building, with a "disturbed symmetry" resulting from the presence of some asymmetrical elements. The features of his rigorously simple architecture, as seen in the Glasgow School of Art and in some privately commissioned houses, are also to be found in his production of furniture, which helped spread the style internationally. He abandoned the use of color and precious decorative detail, adopting instead the exclusive,

sharp black-and-white design of varnished wood and a grid design with checkered bars (which he claimed was of Japanese derivation), seen in his famous high-backed chair.

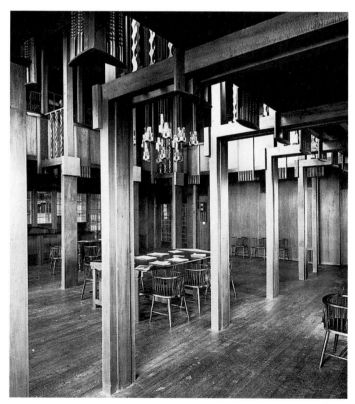

help with all Gaudí's experiments and ambitious plans, the architect was commissioned to design the entrance to the Güell Estate (1884–87), the Güell Palace (1886–87) and the Güell Park (1900) under commission. The park covered 50 acres (20 hectares) and was initially designed as a residential garden suburb, equipped with all the services necessary for a community to function. In his use of styles from the past, Gaudí remained faithful to the principle that to be original required the artist to revisit his or her origins. He mixed these with literary references, whimsical elements, and mystical vision, while also basing his design on the natural movements of the earth. The rocky landscape is broken up into hills and valleys with avenues and seats, sweeping and sloping walkways, and winding colonnades.

Charles Rennie Mackintosh, Glasgow School of Art library, 1897–99. The design for this austere building is based on regular, rectilinear rhythms.

THE ART NOUVEAU POSTER

Typical features of Art Nouveau style, such as the flatness of the colors, the lively chromatic contrasts, and the flora-fauna motifs, proved to be well suited to the new lithographic techniques. The poster enjoyed great success as a principal product of Art Nouveau style: by the turn of the century, there were specialized poster galleries and a host of collectors.

In central European countries, the Secession groups produced a number of dedicated artists in the field of graphic design: Sattler was responsible for the beautiful poster for *Pan*, Heine designed the cover for the magazine *Simplicissimus*, and Zumbusch created the cover for *Jugend*. Also successful were E.P. Glass, F. Heubner, C. Moss, E. Praetorius, M. Schwarzer, and W. Zietara in Germany, and, in Brussels, van Rysselberghe, with his famous poster for the

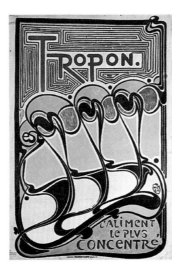

Henri van der Velde, poster for a Tropon food product, 1898.

Jules Chéret, poster for a skating rink.

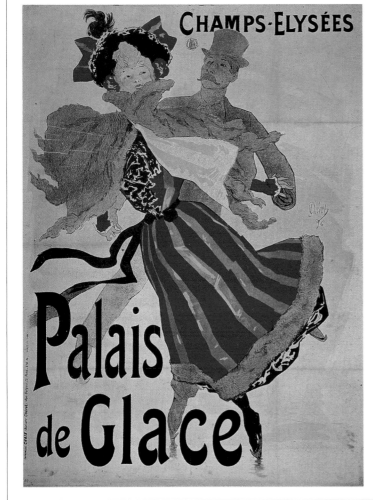

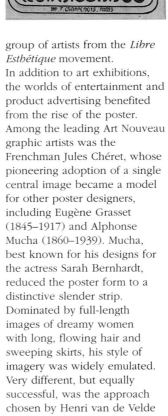

Alphonse Mucha, poster for Sarah Bernhardt, 1896.

Alphonse Mucha, poster for Sarah Bernhardt, 1897. Západoceske Museum, Pilsen.

group of artists from the *Libre Esthétique* movement.

In addition to art exhibitions, the worlds of entertainment and product advertising benefited from the rise of the poster. Among the leading Art Nouveau graphic artists was the Frenchman Jules Chéret, whose pioneering adoption of a single central image became a model for other poster designers, including Eugène Grasset (1845–1917) and Alphonse Mucha (1860–1939). Mucha, best known for his designs for the actress Sarah Bernhardt, reduced the poster form to a distinctive slender strip. Dominated by full-length images of dreamy women with long, flowing hair and sweeping skirts, his style of imagery was widely emulated. Very different, but equally successful, was the approach chosen by Henri van de Velde

for his advertisement for *Tropon*, a canned food product. He made no allowances for the commercial requirements of illustration, instead catching the viewer's attention with a striking design in which the brand name was placed in the middle of a completely abstract composition.

The art of advertising-poster design also underwent interesting developments in Italy. The first exhibition of art for publicity was held in Milan in 1906, paying tribute to the contribution artistic advertising could make to the aesthetic value of the city environment.

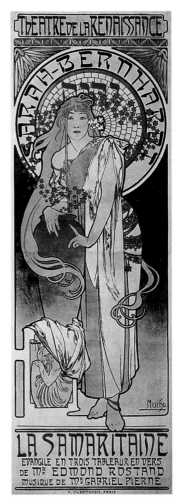

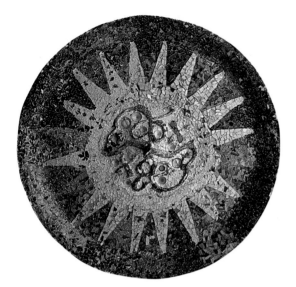

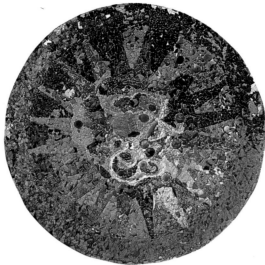

Antoni Gaudí, decorative detail in Güell Park, Barcelona.

Gaudi's design for Casa Milá in Barcelona (1906–10) also looks as if it were the product of ancient movements in the Earth's crust. It has a large rocky facade, "exposed" to the elements and opening into niches, and is sculpted in undulating lines that recall the motion of the sea. Some years before (1905–7), the architect had restored Casa Batlló in the center of Barcelona, covering the entire former structure with a mosaic in colored glass tiles. The disks are arranged at different angles in the walls so that they reflect light in different ways. Gaudí also oversaw the ornamental details of the exterior, which featured wrought-iron work balconies and colored ceramic tiles on the borders of the windows and the roof. Considering the smallest detail of each of his buildings, he also created the interior furnishings, paying special

Antoni Gaudí, Casa Milá, Barcelona, 1906–10,

LA SAGRADA FAMILIA

"The straight line is the line of man and the curved line is the line of God," stated Gaudí, who at the beginning of the 20th century became the apostle of a new mystical and visionary religious architecture. It was regulated by geometric structures, including parabolic curves, ellipses, and

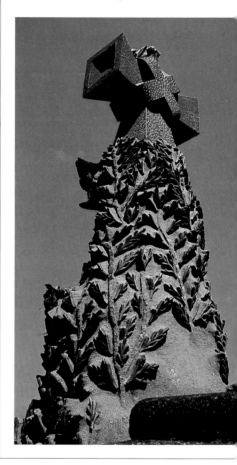

attention to the materials and colors.

Gaudí's *pièce de résistance*, however, was the church of the Sagrada Família, also in Barcelona. Its construction spanned the best part of his productive life and drew not only on his intellectual interest in capturing both the traditional and the modern, but also on an religious commitment that became more mystical as time passed. Begun in 1882, the church is still unfinished today. It remains, however, the most extreme example of the Art Nouveau interpretation of Gothic art.

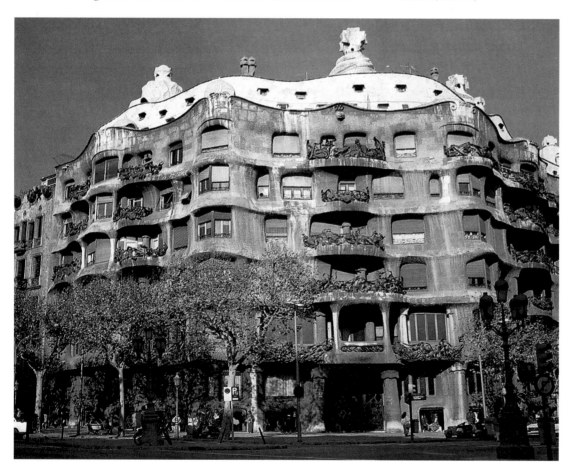

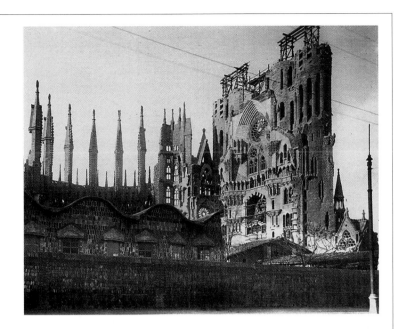

Antoni Gaudí, La Sagrada Familía, Barcelona, begun 1882.

Antoni Gaudí, detail of the cypress-shaped pinnacle decoration, La Sagrada Familía.

hyperbolas. The church of the Sagrada Familía was begun in 1882, following the original Neo-Gothic design by the architect Villar; by 1893, only the apsidal area had been completed. Gaudí's contribution to the project was a complex symbolic plan. Adopting an exuberant and imaginative style, his intervention changed the existing structure and decoration in a way that blended in without appearing artificial. He introduced a

continuous narrative into the decoration, employing popular characters, academic references, and religious symbols in a way that is both realistic and allusive. The features seem to grow naturally out of the architecture, altering and modeling the geometric structure of the front and the towers and transforming the vertical supports into a forest of tree shapes. Work on the Sagrada Familía proceeded with much difficulty, especially since Gaudí felt a need for the church to be incomplete and imperfect. When he died in 1926, only the first of the four Nativity towers was finished. In 1976, the Passion facade was completed, featuring Cubist-Expressionist elements.

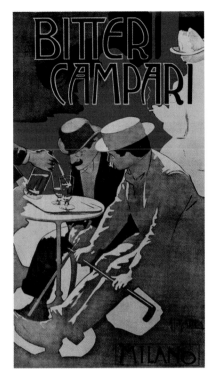

Adolfo Hohenstein, poster for Campari, c.1901. It was printed in the graphics workshop of Ricordi, the music publishers of Verdi and Puccini, of which Hohenstein was artistic director.

production but did not always follow the true Modernist line that the style should cover all forms of design in pursuit of a stylistic unity.

The organizers of the Turin exhibition, held in the Valentino park, included the critic Enrico Thovez, the sculptor Leonardo Bistolfi, the engineer Angelo Reycend, and the painter Lorenzo Delleani. They were attempting to link the Italian experience with that of the rest of the world. The designer of the park's pavilions was the architect Raimondo D'Aronco, whose designs were a combination of the latest innovations in iron and glass construction with the stylistic proposals of Wagner and Olbrich. The pavilions also had decorative features of Islamic and Byzantine origin.

The work displayed at the

Caramba (Luigi Sapelli), designs for La Tavolozza, Théâtre de Monte Carlo, 1902. Here, the great costume and stage designer from La Scala, Milan, ironically based his designs on the Liberty style.

ITALIAN MODERNISM

In Italy, participation in the new wave of Art Nouveau styles came quite late in the day and was limited to a small group of artists working in the areas of decorative art, including designers, furniture makers, and ceramicists. These artist were generally brought together by the magazine *Emporium* and by membership of the Italian society of arts and crafts, Aemilia Ars. In 1902, they took part in a large exhibition of decorative and modern art held in Turin. In

doing so, they established the Italian Art Nouveau movement, named *Stile Liberty* after the fashionable London store. Through *Emporium*, which had been founded in 1895 along the same lines as the English magazine *The Studio*, graphics, typographics, posters, fashion sketches, and cartoons played a vital role as the first evidence of the new style. The Aemilia Ars was founded in Bologna in 1898 as the Italian equivalent of the Arts and Crafts Movement and the Wiener Werkstätte. It advocated a new aesthetic approach to industrial

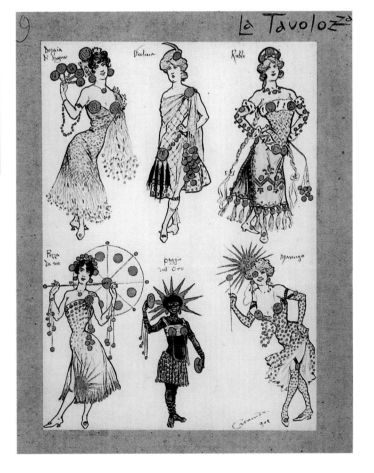

TIFFANY AND ART NOUVEAU

The name of Louis Comfort Tiffany has become synonymous with Art Nouveau style in the US. The designer was inspired by the shapes and colors of French Art Nouveau, although the simple forms of his glass-ware items were more stylized and abstract than French glass products of the same period, which featured more natural, organic shapes. Tiffany's trade-mark design classic, the leaded-glass lamp, encapsulated his particular vision of modern style. First created in the 1880s, following the invention of the electric light bulb, it was produced by the company in colored glass on a bronze stand.

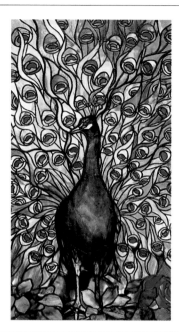

The shade was made of a lead framework filled with glass pieces in flower and animal shapes – a scaled-down adaptation of Tiffany's stained-glass windows. The designer's links with the symbolic heart of the Art Nouveau movement – Siegfried Bing's shop in Paris – were first forged as early as the 1870s, when Bing supplied him with Oriental *objets*. In 1895, Bing asked Tiffany to contribute ten stained-glass windows for the shop: Edouard Vuillard, Pierre Bonnard, Paul Sérusier, and Henri Toulouse-Lautrec were among the artists to contribute designs.

Louis Comfort Tiffany, window detail with a typical motif of peacock feathers.

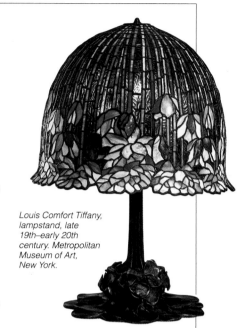

Louis Comfort Tiffany, lampstand, late 19th–early 20th century. Metropolitan Museum of Art, New York.

INDUSTRY, EXHIBITIONS, AND MAGAZINES

The breakdown of the borders between fine art and the decorative arts was one of many factors that contributed to a new relationship between art and industry. The result was an improvement in the visual appeal of all products, including everyday household objects. The aim was to create a new society through the work of craftsman-ship, one in which individuals surrounded by beautiful objects

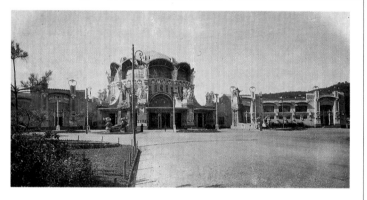

would be better able to reach a higher moral plane. The raising of standards also benefited the less well-off, because the introduction of mass production led to lower prices.

The trade and decorative arts exhibitions of the time were important vehicles for spreading aesthetic ideas and Art Nouveau tastes around Europe and the US. Particularly significant were the World Exhibitions in Paris in 1889 and 1900, and the 1902 Exhibition of Modern and Decorative Arts in Turin. Equally crucial for the promotion of change was the foundation of associations of artists and craftsmen: Morris' Arts and Crafts Society, the

Raimondo D'Aronco, central pavilion of the Turin Exhibition, 1902. Galleria d'Arte Moderna, Udine.

Century Guild, and the Art Workers Guild of Mackmurdo and Crane in England; the Glasgow School in Scotland; the Ecole de Nancy in France; the Wiener Werkstätte in Austria; and the Talaskino and Abrantsevo groups in Russia. Art magazines were another valuable medium for sharing ideas and were in themselves fine examples of graphic art. *Jugend* and *Pan*, *L'Art Nouveau* and *The Studio*, *Emporium* and *Ioventut*, and *L'Arte Decorativa e Industriale* and *Mir Isskuttva* all printed images of works by Art Nouveau artists with critiques of their techniques and style.

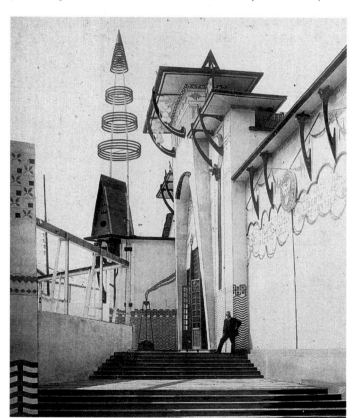

Raimondo D'Aronco, facade of the Galleria degli Ambienti, 1902. Galleria d'Arte Moderna, Udine.

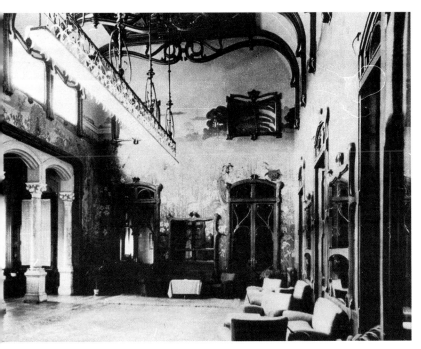

Ernesto Basile, drawing room of the Villa Igea, Palermo, 1898–1903.

SULLIVAN

Gaining rapidly in popularity at the end of the 19th century, Art Nouveau crossed the ocean to find success in the US. The urgent necessity to reconstruct Chicago after the fire of 1871, combined with the talents of architect Louis Henry Sullivan (1856–1924), provided the ideal circumstances for the development of a modern architectural style. New technology and construction in steel gave him the means to build his first famous sky-scrapers, in which the frame of the building, a cellular structure, featured in the external appearance. Sullivan also created a new form of decoration: inspired by Art Nouveau decoration in Europe, he sculpted iron into Gothic spirals and naturalistic forms

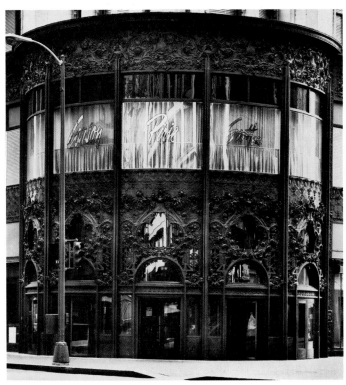

Louis Henry Sullivan, Carson, Pirie, Scott & Co. department store (entrance), Chicago.

Turin exhibition by the up-and-coming Italian artists and craftsmen included furniture designed by the exotic Carlo Bugatti, the refined Eugenio Quarti, and the extravagant Carlo Zen; wrought-iron work by Alessandro Mazzucotelli; painted ceramics by Galileo Chini; decorated glass by Vittorio Zecchin and Giovanni Beltrami; embroidery by Maria Rigotti; and lacework by Jesurum. The quality and aesthetic appeal of the art showcased received international recognition. Immediately following the exhibition in Turin, to which Peter Behrens, Josef Olbrich, and Victor Horta also contributed architectural and furniture designs, there was an explosion of *Stile Liberty* architecture throughout Italy. Although it was initially applied to functional and public buildings such as hotels, cemeteries, and stations, the style soon spread to the private houses of the rich entrepreneurial classes. Many architects employed the style, but the leading names of the day were Pietro Fenoglio (Casa Fenoglio La Fleur, Turin, 1902), Giuseppe

Sommaruga (Palazzo Castiglioni, Milan, 1900, which was decorated with provocative statues by Ernesto Bazzarro and iron work by Mazzucotelli), and Ernesto Basile. The latter produced a number of fine and mature interpretations of Secession stylistic formulas, as can be seen in some of the famous Palermo villas (Villino Florio, 1899–1902, and Villa Igea, 1898–1903) as well as in his furniture designs. These were realized and produced by the firm Golia Ducrot.

with entwined branches and leaves. The ornamentation accentuated the vertical support elements, the doors, and the outline of the lower floors of what were otherwise sober and rational buildings. The Guaranty Building, Buffalo (1895) and the Carson, Pirie, Scott & Co. Store, Chicago (1899–1904) are both buildings in which "the form," according to Sullivan's slogan, "follows function," but without rigidity.

Louis Henry Sullivan, Carson, Pirie, Scott & Co. department store (detail of entrance), Chicago.

NEW TRENDS IN THE 19TH & 20TH CENTURIES

1875: during a trip to Italy, Auguste Rodin discovers the work of Michelangelo; Liberty's store opens in London. **1876:** Third Republic established in France. **1878:** Dostoevsky

publishes *The Brothers Karamazov.* **1882:** Workers' Party founded in Milan; Richard Wagner completes his composition of *Parsifal*; Vincent van Gogh moves to Arles, in Provence;

French composer Eric Satie gains recognition with his *Trois Gymnopédies.* **1884:** publication of *A Rebours*, a novel of cultural decadence, by Huysmans. **1885:** Emile Zola's novel

Germinal, dealing with harsh working conditions in the coal mines, is published. **1886:** last art show by the Impressionists is held in Paris; Seurat's *Sunday Afternoon on the Island of La*

1 8 7 5   1 8 8 0   1 8 8 5   1 8 9 0

▼ GUSTAVE MOREAU
(1826-98)
Trained in the academic tradition, Moreau painted works that reflected the aesthetics and decadence of the age.

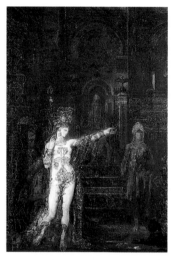

Gustave Moreau, The Apparition, 1876. Musée du Louvre, Paris.

▼ TRANQUILLO CREMONA
(1837-78)
Cremona was a representative of the Scapigliatura movement, influenced by the work of Il Piccio. His painting had a hazy, impalpable quality.

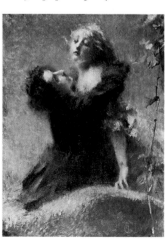

Tranquillo Cremona, Ivy, 1878. Galleria d'Arte Moderna, Turin.

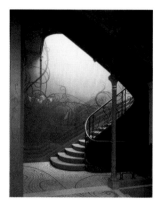

Auguste Rodin, The Thinker, 1880. Musée Rodin, Paris.

▲ FRANÇOIS-AUGUSTE-RENÉ RODIN
(1840-1917)
The great French sculptor brought Romantic sensibility to the tradition of Michelangelo, creating works of vibrant power and strong emotional impact.

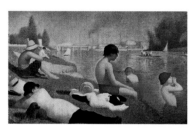

Georges Seurat, Bathers at Asnières, 1883–84. National Gallery, London.

▲ GEORGES SEURAT
(1859-91)
During his short career, the French artist Seurat challenged the tenets of Impressionism, applying scientific theories to the breakdown of colors.

▼ PAUL GAUGUIN
(1848-1903)
Influenced by Japanese art and primitivism, Gauguin produced work that synthesized these styles. His work was later dominated by his fascination for the Polynesian world.

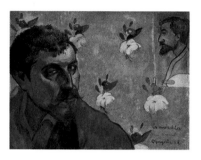

Paul Gauguin, Self-portrait, 1888. Van Gogh Museum, Amsterdam.

▼ GIOVANNI SEGANTINI
(1858-99)
This Italian painter used the Divisionist technique to present a vision of a luminous, spiritualized nature, with overtones of contemporary Symbolism.

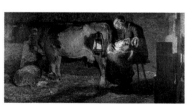

Giovanni Segantini, The Two Mothers, 1889. Galleria d'Arte Moderna, Milan.

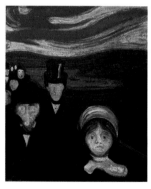

Victor Horta, staircase of the Tassel House, Brussels, 1893.

▲ VICTOR HORTA
(1861-1947)
Using dynamic, undulating lines that were both structurally functional and decorative, the Belgian architect Victor Horta conveyed the essence of Art Nouveau.

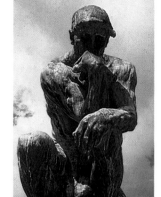

Edvard Munch, Angst, 1894. Munch Museum, Oslo.

▲ EDVARD MUNCH
(1863-1944)
Norwegian painter Munch's tragic vision of human destiny was comunicated by means of strong lines and vivid colors, anticipating the Expressionists. Existential themes such as life and death, melancholy, and absolute despair were recurrent in the art of the 1890s.

Grande Jatte, a visual manifesto of Neo-Impressionsim, is exhibited; Symbolist Manifesto, by the poet Jean Moréas, appears in *Le Figaro*. **1889:** Medardo Rosso moves permanently to Paris.

1891: first Brera Triennial Exhibition, including works of Italian Divisionists, held in Milan. **1892:** Gauguin's first journey to Tahiti. **1893:** Norwegian artist Munch paints his most famous

work, *The Scream*. **1895:** first Biennial of International Art in Vienna. **1897:** Scottish architect Mackintosh draws up detailed plans for the Glasgow School of Art. **c.1900:** Guimard builds stations

and entrance halls of Paris Métro in Art Nouveau style. **1902:** Italian Liberty movement affirmed at Turin Exhibition of Decorative Art. **1905:** Japan wins war against Russia.

1 8 9 5   1 9 0 0   1 9 0 5

▶ ALPHONSE MUCHA
(1860-1939)
Czech painter, commercial artist, and stage designer Alphonse Mucha was influenced by Parisian Art Nouveau; he transformed the female figure into charming arabesques.

▼ PIERRE BONNARD
(1867-1947)
A representative of the Nabis group, the French painter Bonnard revealed his passion for Japanese art in his composition, color, and subject matter.

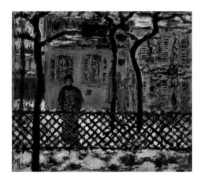

Pierre Bonnard, Behind the Fence, 1895. The State Hermitage Museum, St. Petersburg.

▼ AUGUST ENDELL
(1871-1925)
A German architect and designer, Endell was a leading exponent of the Munich Jugendstil. His forms were inspired by nature.

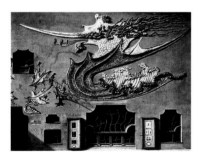

August Endell, Elvira Studio, Munich, 1897–98.

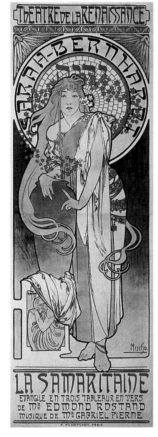

Alphonse Mucha, poster for Sarah Bernhardt, 1897. Západoceske Museum, Plzen, Czech Republic.

▼ JOSEPH MARIA OLBRICH
(1867-1908)
Austrian architect and designer associated with the Viennese Secession, Olbrich had a preference for basic forms and lavish decoration.

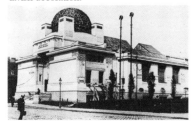

Joseph Maria Olbrich, Secession Pavilion, Vienna, 1898.

▼ LOUIS COMFORT TIFFANY
(1848-1933)

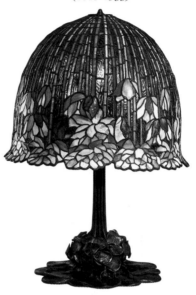

Louis Comfort Tiffany, lamp, late 19th–early 20th century. Metropolitan Museum of Art, New York.

▼ GUSTAV KLIMT
(1862-1918)
Austrian painter and graphic artist Klimt was the leading figure of the Viennese Secessionist movement.

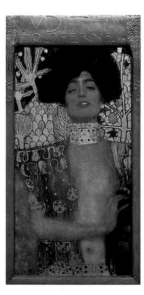

Gustav Klimt, Judith I, 1901. Österreichische Galerie, Vienna.

▼ HENRI ROUSSEAU
(1844-1910)
Known as Le Douanier, this self-taught French painter created a colorful, pristine world of magic and innocence. He is renowned for his jungle scenes.

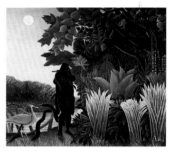

Henri Rousseau, Snake Charmer, 1907. Musée d'Orsay, Paris.

▼ ANTONI GAUDÍ
(1852-1928)
The greatest exponent of Catalan Modernism, Gaudí fused the national Gothic style with effects of fantasy to create extraordinary buildings that verged on the Baroque.

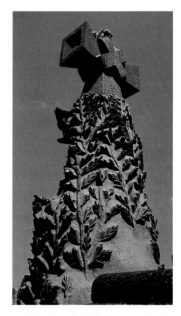

Antoni Gaudí, detail of cypress-shaped pinnacle decoration, La Sagrada Familia, Barcelona.

ARTISTIC CULTURES OF SUB-SAHARAN AFRICA

*Many of the creative traditions of sub-Saharan Africa have a
very long history within certain geographical areas, and particular
forms appear to have remained consistent over several centuries.
In the 19th and 20th centuries, these artifacts have had
a significant influence on European art.*

The artistic heritage of sub-Saharan Africa is extremely diverse. This chapter, however, focuses on its most distinctive manifestation, sculpture. The works featured here originate from a relatively small part of the entire African continent, which has been divided here into four sectors: Western Sudan, the Guinea Forest, the Equatorial Forest, and the Congo Basin.

THE SCULPTURE OF SUB-SAHARAN AFRICA

African artifacts are created first and foremost in order to serve particular social functions. They can therefore only be understood in relation to their original context – in political or religious ritual activities, for example. The motifs are often based on symbolic or cultural ideas rather than natural forms, and their meanings are not necessarily accessible to all members of a given society. The African artist and his patrons do not always come from the same ethnic group, and often the patron's demands and specifications play an important part in the creative process. The aesthetic quality of a particular object is never its sole purpose, but its ability to affect the emotions of those who manipulate and view it constitutes an important aspect of its potency or effectiveness within the controlled context of its use.

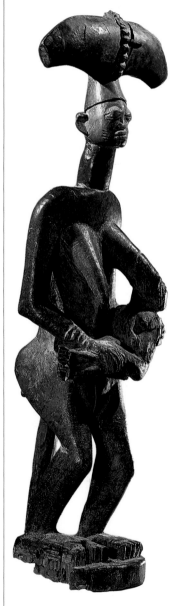

Yoruba mother and child figure, Nigeria, wood, height 28 in (71.5 cm). Metropolitan Museum of Art, New York.

MOTHER AND CHILD FIGURES

The representation of motherhood in plastic art is a familiar subject in the majority of African cultures. It celebrates the fertility of women and revives beliefs in the mythical mother who gave life to humankind – a crucial element within society in that it ensures the continuity of the species. The composition of figures generally consists of a seated or kneeling female with a baby at her breast or on her back. The representation of maternity by most African peoples is characterized by idealism rather than realism. The mother figure usually has an expressive face that conveys a sense of tranquil dignity but seldom shows obvious emotion. Some mother figures from the Congolese area are clearly derived from the Christian iconography of the Madonna and Child, yet these specimens, too, in their formal attitude and cultural significance are typical examples of African sculpture. Recent studies have linked these images to the development of *mpemba* – a new propitiatory *nkisi* cult associated with the magical treatment of gynecological ailments. This activity was very widespread in the Loango and Cabinda areas during the second half of the 19th century.

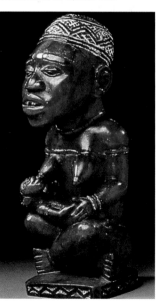

Kongo (Yombe) mother and child figure, Zaire, wood, height 9¼ in (23.7 cm). Museo Preistorico ed Etnografico Luigi Pigorini, Rome.

Dan mother figure, Ivory Coast, wood and pigments, height 25 in (64 cm). Private collection.

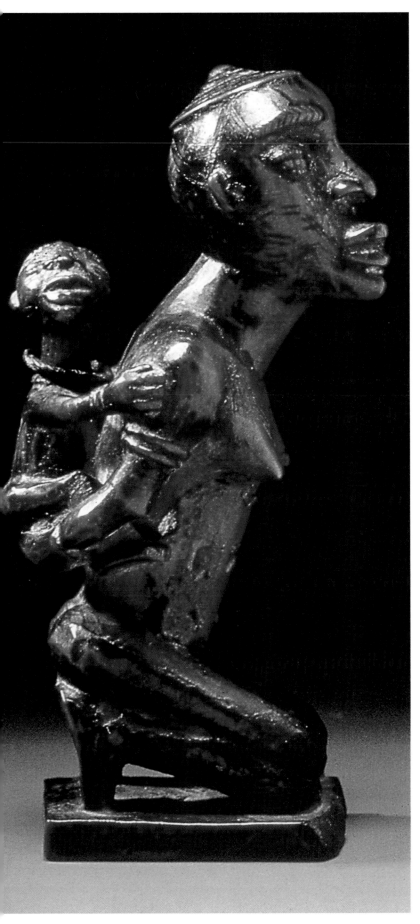

Kongo mpemba *mother figure, Zaire, wood, height 6¼ in (16.2 cm). Museo Preistorico ed Etnografico Luigi Pigorini, Rome.*

"BEAUTIFUL, CORRECT, AND APPROPRIATE"

The aesthetic test of a sculpted object within many African communities is the extent to which it is "beautiful, correct, and appropriate." Efficacy is largely determined by the measure to which it conforms to a model and its overall cultural significance. The model is understood as an ideal formal structure as well as the visual image of an ethical concept. An artifact from a traditional culture of sub-Saharan Africa holds a different cultural significance depending on the social and political organization of the group and on the role of the artist. In unstratified, mobile societies such as the Lobi of northwestern Burkina Faso, for example, there are no professional carvers and no separate role or identity for a person who carves. Anyone who feels the need for another figure for one of the household shrines will carve it himself. Consequently, it is hard to identify any such thing as a Lobi carving style. Furthermore, there is no clear symbolism or iconography that a person refers to in order to create a figure intended for a shrine of a specific type; therefore, only the person who carves it is able to tell the purpose for which the figure will be used. Aesthetic evaluations of carved forms are matters of individual concern among the Lobi. Similarly, the necessary skills and sensibilities required for the making of any kind of artifact are thought to be possessed by every adult member of the community. In contrast, in societies with centralized political institutions, artists have a monopoly on the work for the monarch and court. The need of the ruling class to assert and make legitimate its authority through a series of power symbols led to the creation of a courtly,

ceremonial type of art in ivory, bronze, stone, and wood. Complementary to this style is the popular art, which, by contrast, is associated with magical and religious practices. In a centralized state, the individuality of the artist may be restricted by the need to express the static nature of the monarchy. However, it is wrong to assume that traditional African art cannot express individual creativity. Many examples of creative flair exist and can be attributed to the work of a particular workshop or artist.

Dogon mother figure, Mali, wood, height 26¾ in (68 cm). Private Collection.

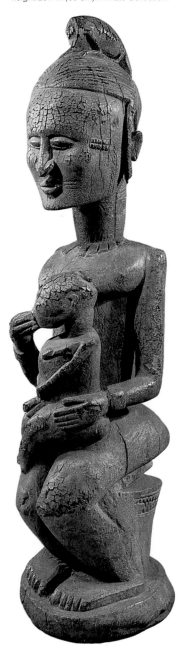

TOMB FIGURES

In the Lower Congo region, groups of commemorative figures in wood or, more rarely, stone were used to indicate the burial places of sovereigns or important individuals. These figures, the oldest of which date from the 17th to the 18th century, may have been simple memorial monuments or may have performed the function of guardians, offering protection against the evils of black magic. Generally, tomb figures depict people seated with crossed legs and bearing symbols of authority, such as a conical or truncated headdress adorned with leopard claws, effigies, or the insignia of the sovereign. Figures of women with children were sometimes placed on the tombs of high-ranking females. These probably represented the sovereign's wives or women of royal blood.

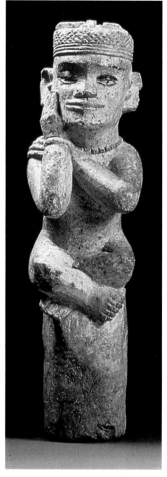

Kongo ntadi *statue, Zaire, steatite and wood, height 13¾ in (35 cm). Museo Preistorico ed Etnografico Luigi Pigorini, Rome.*

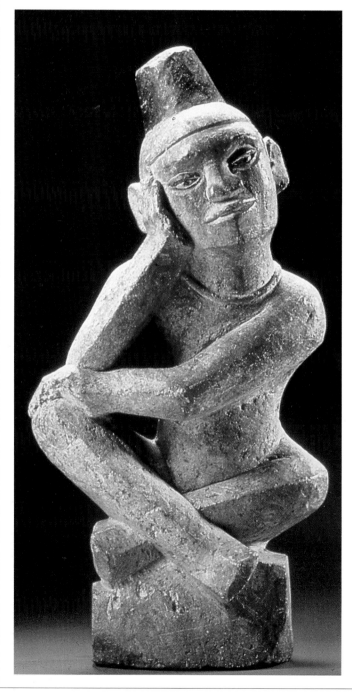

Certain common characteristics in these tomb figures, such as the use of colored pigments on the eyes and mouth, the vaguely Oriental features, and particularly the frequent lack of symmetry (a rarity in African sculptural tradition) were once thought to have been stylistic influences from Asia. However, they are now widely recognized as typical characteristics of the art objects produced in the coastal Kongo. The gestures and postures, as well as the decorative motifs, have been interpreted as expressions of the supernatural.

Kongo ntadi *statue, Zaire, steatite and pigments, height 15 in (38 cm). Museo Preistorico ed Etnografico Luigi Pigorini, Rome.*

MASKS AND STATUES

Although African cultures express themselves artistically in a very wide range of materials and forms, carved wooden statues and masks have attracted most attention from Western scholars and connoisseurs.
The statues usually represent human ancestors, reflecting the importance in African culture of family relationships within lineage-based societies – extended equally to the world of the dead. Ancestors are perceived as a vital force for

Baule seated female figure, Ivory Coast, wood and glass beads, height 14½ in (37 cm). Private Collection.

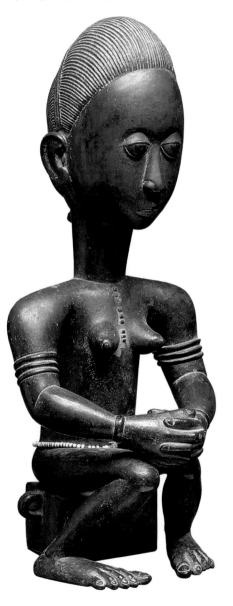

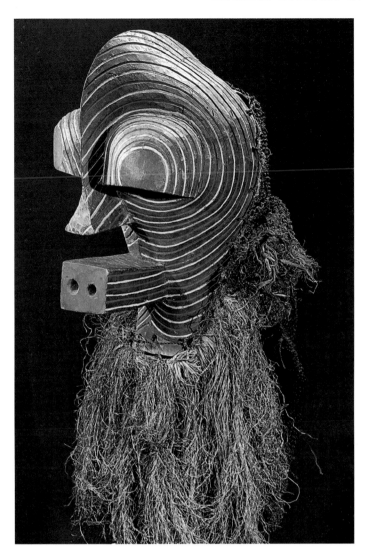

Songye kifwebe *mask, Zaire, wood and plant fibers, height 22 in (55.6 cm). Musée Royal de l'Afrique, Tervuren.*

of ritual acts. It reaffirms the social principles and enduring beliefs of everyday life and thus ensures the collective well-being of the community. In terms of form, masks exhibit a wide range of styles, varying in material, shape, and decoration and also in the manner in which they are worn or carried. As a rule, they are made of carved wood but carry additional decoration in materials of different kinds, some of which may help increase their power. The most common type of mask is designed to be worn over the face; others are helmetlike, veritable pieces of sculpture that are carried on the head. Whatever the form, their value in society remains unchanged, given the role that they play in the most important occasions of collective life.

The mask bears witness to the passing of tribal wisdom to the young in the initiation rites of puberty and provides moral rules by serving as a reminder of the traditional customs of the group. In funeral rituals, it represents the means of dispelling, summoning, and countering the negative forces released by death. In agricultural ceremonies, in order to mark the period of social and cosmic regeneration, the mask celebrates mythical times by recalling tribal heroes. Within secret societies that have political and judicial functions, it serves as an instrument of power and social control.

the entire group and a link between the land of the living and the realm of the spirits. In this sense they are the guarantee of the harmony of the village. In accordance with the values of African art, which are neither descriptive nor imitative, a statue does not depict a particular ancestor. Instead, it reproduces an ideal image that extols the concept of the life-force while also conforming to a number of rules: intentional disproportion of the body parts, with an emphasis on the head and trunk (seats of the life-force) and sexual organs (symbols of fertility); a static pose hinting at the possibility of imminent movement – conveyed by the angles of elbows and knees – and symbolizing the power of the life-force; and the absence of any suggestion of emotion or expression, which gives the figure a detached attitude. These constants are more than a sterile academic exercise. Combined with other formal characteristics of African statuary – harmony, symmetry, luminosity, verticality, and a frontal viewpoint – they boost the value of the figures by highlighting their social and religious significance.

Like statues, masks are a typical form of African plastic art. As an expression of the moral and religious code within a group's culture, the mask is an important attribute

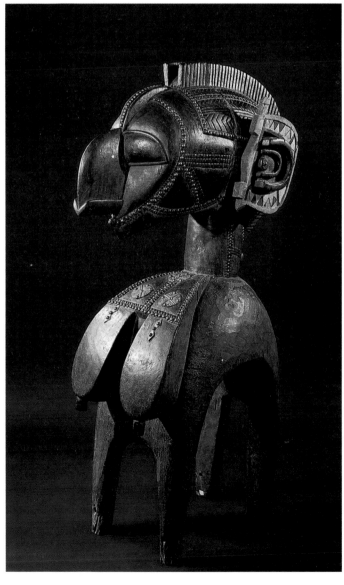

Baga nimba *shoulder mask, Guinea, wood and brass, height 55 in (140 cm). Musée d'Histoire Naturelle, Toulouse.*

SCULPTURAL STYLES OF WESTERN SUDAN

Not all African cultures have developed the figurative plastic arts to the same extent. The richest areas are concentrated in the Atlantic regions of the continent, from Senegambia down to Angola. Traditional styles across this area may vary a great deal, with some being based on geometric designs and others on naturalistic concepts. The geographical area defined as Western Sudan refers to the stretch of savanna in West Africa to the south of the Sahara and to the north of the great forests. It is characterized by a variety of stylistic tendencies, although there is a general preference for abstract forms that rely more on a juxtaposition than on an even succession of parts; this feature is especially evident in the art of the Dogon. Masks, generally in animal shapes, testify to the close, primeval

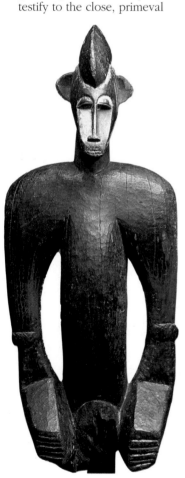

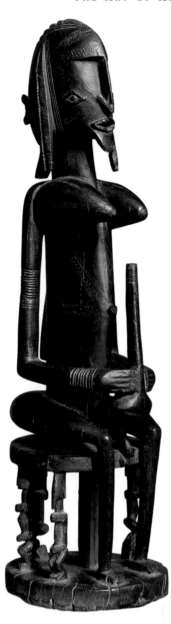

Dogon hermaphrodite, Mali, wood, height 27 in (69 cm). Private Collection.

relationship between humans and animals. From the point of view of structure, the mask is regarded as an individual work, each one endowed with its own meaning, which is directly associated with the mythical-religious universe. Statues represent the life-force of ancestors or the mythical pairing of Heaven and Earth. Geometrical stylization and the skillful balancing of empty and solid areas heighten the solemnity of the ancestral

Senufo male figure, Ivory Coast, wood, height 24¾ in (63 cm). Private Collection.

EQUESTRIAN SCULPTURE

Since ancient times, equestrian subjects have occurred repeatedly in the artistic traditions of many West African cultures. Horses and their riders are associated with the exercise of political, military, or spiritual power. The rider, by reason of his raised position and the potential speed of the horse's movement, becomes the emblem of strength and authority. In this sense, although his standing may vary in different societies, ages, or cultural regions, the equestrian figure in Africa is the symbol of status and alludes to the authority of the ancestors or chiefs. Owned exclusively by the monarch and court, horses, generally mounted by a warrior, were a central subject in the iconography of the Sudanese empires ever since their establishment. This harks back to the mythical horsemen who rode in from the North and who, according to local tradition, were the founders of new states. Terracotta equestrian sculptures have been found principally in the area of the Niger river bend

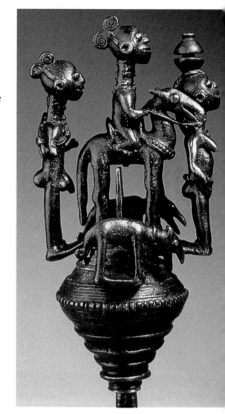

Beafada sono insignia of authority, Guinea-Bissau, copper alloy, height 25¾ in (65.5 cm). Museo Preistorico ed Etnografico Luigi Pigorini, Rome.

Senufo horse and rider. Senufo equestrian figures primarily represent the spirits of the forest, considered to be very powerful.

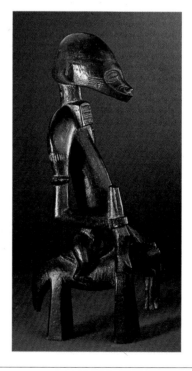

and may be dated from the 13th to the 15th century, when the Mali and Songhai empires were at their peak. The figures celebrate heroic leadership, and their static pose suggests the idea of the stability and permanence of power. The equestrian theme in the area surrounding the Niger river bend has continued in the contemporary art of the Dogon, which shows obvious links with the styles from the past. In Dogon mythology, both horse and rider shared in the creation of the world. Small wooden or iron equestrian figures are assembled in shrines in memory of the mythical character called Nommo, who transformed himself into a horse to haul the arch of creation onto the earth. Beside or above the animal there is always a human figure – the rider-deity Amma, the supreme god who is the universal principle. In Dogon art, therefore, the equestrian theme refers to the "original journey." In terms of form, this idea is conveyed by the relaxed position of the rider and the treatment of his legs, which are purely decorative and firmly attached to the saddle. These elements combine to suggest the mystical nature of the journey and the impossibility of the rider being unseated. The horses and riders represented in Dogon art do not follow any rules of naturalism. Structurally, they are formed from two separate sculptural parts, thus contravening the almost general rule of African art that links the human figure and its horse in an ideally unified whole.

This mystical union is nevertheless emphasized in the art of the Senufo, where the horizontal structure of the horse and the vertical structure of the rider constitute a sculptural unit. Their spiritual oneness and the exchange of strength, which passes without interruption from rider to animal and vice versa, is formally expressed by the columnlike structure, in which the vertical lines of the human figure are followed through to the legs of the horse.

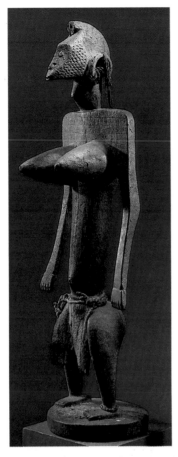

Bamana female statue, Mali, wood, height 29 in (74 cm). Private Collection.

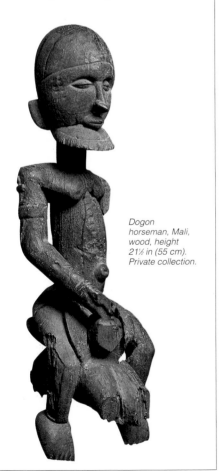

Dogon horseman, Mali, wood, height 21½ in (55 cm). Private collection.

images, which constitute the favorite iconographic subject for a large range of cult objects. The output of the Bamana carvers also includes masks and statues, but it is less varied in style and form than the works of the Dogon. Figurative sculpture is marked by a stiff, powerful style, which contrasts with the flowing lines of the masks and headdresses. The Bamana *tyi warra* (headdresses worn in agricultural rituals) usually combine the attributes of a number of wild animals that can scratch or wound, including the antelope, aardvark, and lion. The headdresses symbolize Tyi warra, a mythical being who taught man to cultivate the land. They are worn to encourage the men as they "wound" and break up the hard soil.

To some extent, the art of the Senufo is similar both to that of the Sudan and of Guinea.

Huge, flat, helmetlike animal masks are very typical, as are smaller human-type masks surmounted by a sculpture in the shape of a bird. Both types of mask are made either of wood or metal, and both are used in the rituals of the *Poro* society. Senufo statues usually show figures standing erect, with a complex hairstyle, an elongated head, a heart-shaped face, and slightly curving shoulders. Their monumental style, which is evident equally in smaller works, is underlined by geometrical reliefs on the chin, breasts, and belly.

SCULPTURAL STYLES OF THE GUINEA FOREST

The number and variety of artistic styles belonging to the groups in the Guinea forest reflects the complex pattern of its different peoples. In their artistic production, the forest people tend to renounce abstract forms in favor of a

more naturalistic approach: edges are more rounded, and the geometric styles of the savanna are replaced by curved lines and closer attention to anatomical proportions. The Baga, Nalu, and Mende populations, which inhabit the western part of the area, sculpt mainly very large animal masks. These are used in female initiation rites or in the secret society ceremonies that dominate the social life of these groups.

The most important works come from the central-eastern part of the area and are made by the Baule. In addition to masks and statues, this group produces everyday objects, such as looms, spoons, and stools, of exceptional quality. The Baule carve large, colorful animal masks that represent mythological animals symbolizing masculinity and small, carefully made masks

Baule double mask, Ivory Coast, wood and pigments, height 11 in (28 cm). Private collection.

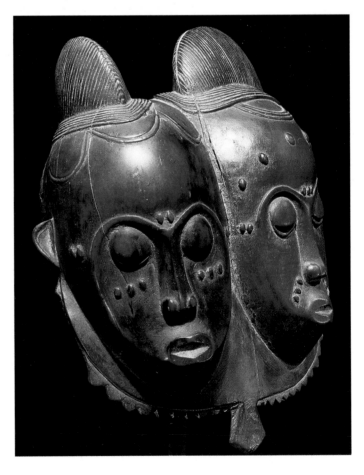

YORUBA EQUESTRIAN SCULPTURE

Equestrian subjects have been used in Nigerian art ever since the time of the ancient Igbo-Ukwu and Benin cultures. Here, as in the old Sudanese empires, horse-riding was regarded as a sign of prestige and authority – the central part of a complex ceremony whereby the ruling class asserted its social distance from the rank and file – as was its exclusive possession of rare and precious objects.

The same equestrian theme can be found today in the Yoruba tradition and is used to convey the notion of distinction and power. The rider is usually represented in a stiff upright position, with reins gathered in the left hand, while the right hand grasps a symbol of authority. The comparative realism of some of these sculptures may indicate, at least among earlier examples, that they were the detailed portraits of illustrious persons or famous warriors. Although Yoruba sculptures show the horse as an attribute of the rider, who is always the principal figure of the pair, a clear ideological link exists between the horseman and his steed: he embodies symbolically the strength of the animal. The subject of horsemanship in African art is not necessarily associated with mythical events or important political and religious persons but is used for objects that demonstrate the status and wealth of the owner. The possession of articles carved with equestrian scenes could confer not only social status on the owner but also increased authority, as a result of associating with the animal's mystical nature and enjoying the power derived from the convergence of human and animal forces. In African cultures, the figure of the horseman has always been seen as a link with prestigious external cultures, the values of which are, in complex ways, assimilated and transformed by local cultures into their own artistic expressions.

Yoruba pillar in the form of a horse and warrior rider, attributed to Olowe of Ise (died 1938), Nigeria, painted wood, height 79½ in (202 cm). Private Collection.

Yoruba divination cup. The horse and rider is the main decorative theme in the production of prophecy cups; the equestrian theme symbolizes the status and economic power of the owner.

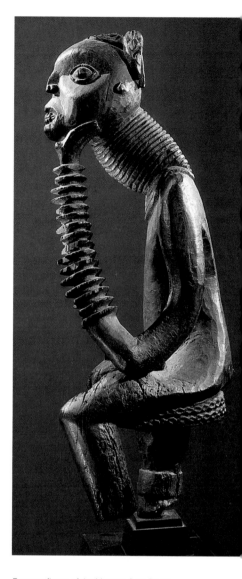

Bangwa figure of the Master of the Rings, Cameroon, wood, height 32¾ in (83 cm). Private Collection.

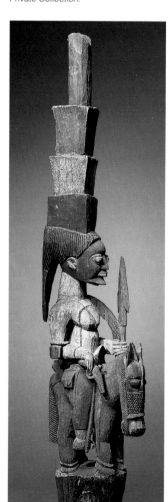

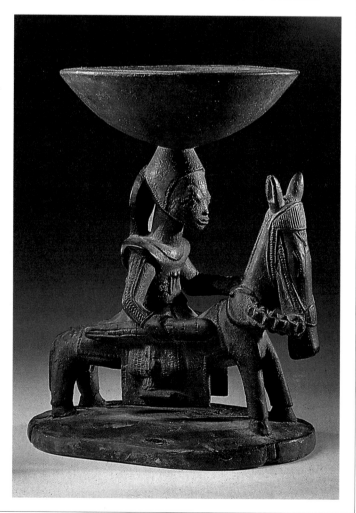

with human features that are used in funeral ceremonies. Statues generally represent ancestors or spirits from the hereafter, which are depicted either standing or seated on a stool. Baule sculpture is noted for its skillful coordination of proportion, its generous and harmonious shapes, and its strict formality. This is evident even in the refined handling of the reliefs and in the elaborate hairstyles and decorative body marks of the figures. The Yoruba of Nigeria, who inherited the ancient sculptural tradition of Ife, have produced an art, still alive today, that draws inspiration from the large pantheon and expresses the centralized social and political structure. Masks, associated with secret societies, vary from the hemispherical polychrome type that are carved out of softwood in a highly expressive style, to heavy forms with a stylized skull, often Janus-faced, used for communicating with the hereafter. The shape of the eyes and mouth are consistent features in masks and statues and, despite subtle local variations, immediately indicate the Yoruba style.

The artistic ways of the Igbo, the Ibibio, and the Ekoi – all ethnic offshoots of the Guinea area – differ somewhat in that they already anticipate the Bantu styles. Characteristic are the heads covered with antelope hide and complex hairstyles. Sometimes Janus-faced, they are used by the Ekoi as dance headdresses in propitiation rites.

The cultures of the Cameroon highlands share common features, notably in the very distinctive artistic products of the Bamun, the Tikar, and the Bamileke groups. Particularly famous are the wooden masks with swollen cheeks, large round eyes, and protruding foreheads, which come in a variety of styles, with either animal or human features; the latter also show variants in the type of hairstyle, some of which reproduce the ceremonial head coverings worn only by chiefs. Typical, too, are the statues and the thrones with female figures, entirely covered with glass beads that serve to embellish and to make the work a status symbol. The Bamun also produce elegant metalwork, including bronze pipes decorated with animal figures, which are given by the monarch as a sign of honor.

Yoruba gelede *mask, Nigeria, wood and pigments. Institute of Arts, Detroit.*

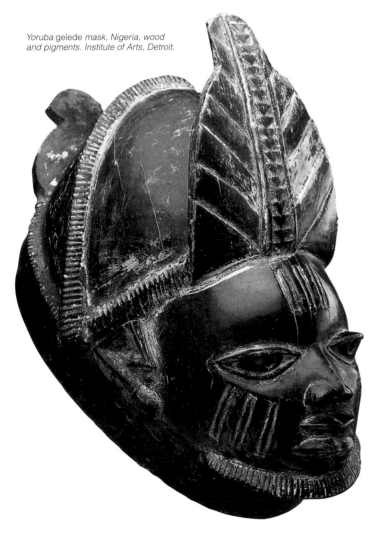

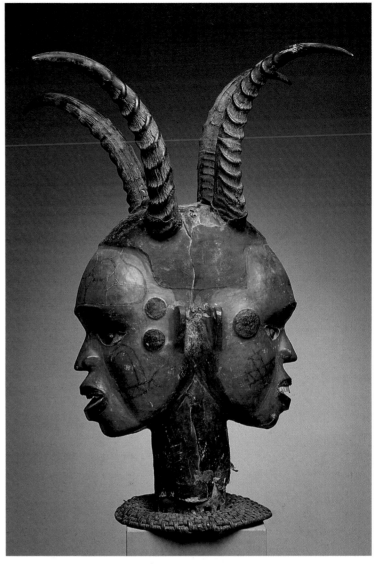

Top of dance head-dress with two faces, Boki art, Nigeria, wood, horn, leather, pigments, and plant fibers, height 21¼ in (54 cm). Private Collection.

ART STYLES OF THE EQUATORIAL FOREST

The Fang people of Gabon and the neighboring groups of the Kota and Kwele between them produce the finest sculpture of the whole equatorial forest zone.

The central theme of Fang iconography is the image of the ancestor, which bears a heart-shaped face and "coffee-bean" eyes. The image is placed on top of a box that contains the bones of a dead person in the belief that it will capture and preserve the life-force. The rigid forms, the dark, glossy patina, and the grave expression of the face constitute formal elements typical of this production. The reliquary figures created by the Kota perform a similar function. These are made of wood and decorated with sheets or strips of copper and brass in an abstract style that presents natural forms in an overall geometrical context. The typical shape of the face, symmetrically divided by the line of the nose and balanced by the arches of the eyebrows, is also found in the female masks of the Fang, as well as in those of the neighboring Kwele group.

SCULPTURAL STYLES OF THE CONGO BASIN

The area of the Congo river basin is noted for its broad range of racial groups and a correspondingly wide variety of sculptural styles. The Kongo people themselves are renowned for their fine carving, both in stone and wood. The stone sculptures of seated figures with crossed legs are deservedly famous; they are placed as guards over the tombs of chiefs and other notable people. Of even greater artistic quality are the wooden representations of ancestors, power figures, "fetishes," and rounded mother figures, all of which are carved with great attention to anatomical detail, though often in an asymmetrical pose. Masters of the art of engraving, the Chokwe have produced sophisticated figures of sovereigns with elaborate headgear – an element that, as in the masks, is a symbol of power. The Chokwe also make other types of ritual mask, characterized by slit eyes set in large, deep orbital cavities, a wide mouth, and a long, slender nose. The Kuba are famous for their aristocratic art associated with the divine monarchy. Their art includes portrait sculptures of sovereigns, idealized and raised to the rank of divinities, and a series of prestigious objects, such as bowls, cups, and boxes, in which the art of geometrical decoration reaches a strikingly high artistic level. The artistic production of the Songye is substantially different from other styles in the Congo basin in that the figurative style shows an almost abstract tendency reminiscent of Cubist art. The Luba have developed a sophisticated artistic tradition that embraces at least ten different influential styles. Statues are rounded, surfaces smooth, and proportions harmonious, while special features are the prominent forehead, the coffee-bean eyes, raised scars on the belly, and crosslike headgear over the back of the neck. The range of sculpted art also consists of everyday and prestigious objects such as headrests and stools with female figures, the most celebrated of which are those in the Luba-shankadi style, with typically flowing hair. A review of the most significant modern expressive forms of the African cultures of this region illustrates the regard in which they are held – and why increasingly numerous and varied studies have been made.

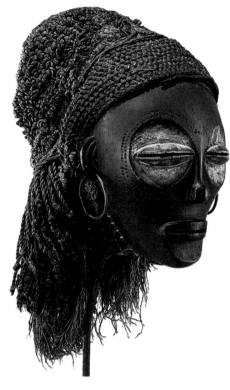

Chokwe mask, Angola, wood, metal, and plant fibers, height 10½ in (27 cm). National Museum of African Art, Washington, DC.

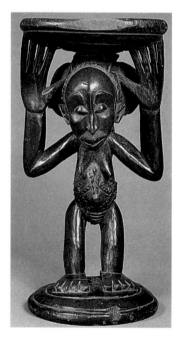

Master of Buli, stool with female figure, late 19th century, Luba-Hemba art, Zaire, wood, height 23¾ in (61 cm). Metropolitan Museum of Art, New York.

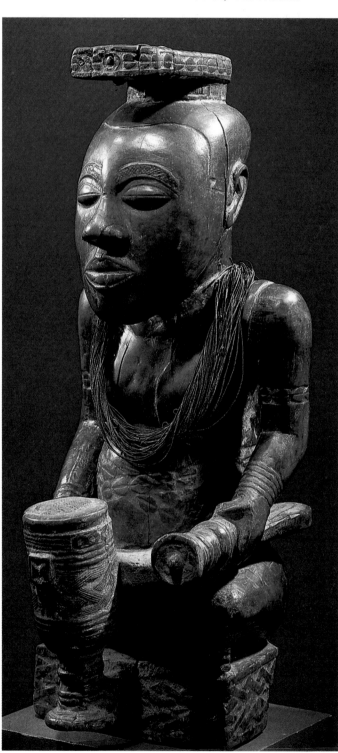

Kuba effigy of King Bushongo Kot A-Ntshey, Zaire, wood and plant fibers, height 20 in (51.1 cm). Musée Royal de l'Afrique Centrale, Tervuren.

MAGICAL SCULPTURES

A range of ritual objects from the Congo basin – in particular from the Kongo area – are commonly known as *minkisi* (sing. *nkisi*) and historically labeled "fetishes." They may consist of a collection of natural objects or may be sculpted from natural materials, such as wood, shell, or animal horn, into human or animal forms. The quality of the *nkisi* is not determined by the type of material – this merely conducts the spirit forces – but by the "magical substances" that it contains. The power of the object can be directed to a variety of purposes, including curing diseases and ensuring success in hunting and trading. The making of a *nkisi* is an operation shared by the sculptor and the *nganga* (initiated ritual expert), who attach certain substances that help harness the power of the object and metaphorically define the uses to which it can be put. The

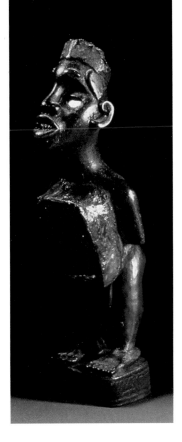

Kongo (Yombe) reliquary nkisi, *Zaire, wood, resin, and mirror, height 12¼ in (31.4 cm). Museo Preistorico ed Etnografico Luigi Pigorini, Rome.*

iron pieces. They often have a menacing expression and an arm raised in a threatening gesture. *Minkondi*, used for mystical attack and defense, were activated by having nails driven into them to arouse their "anger." The *nganga* could then direct this "anger" against, for example, the author of his client's grievance by singing an invocation. The directed "anger" was "engaged" by the client's words and by his act of licking the *bilongo* (magical charge) of the *nkondi*. The third form of *nkisi* is the *mpemba*, which consists solely of carvings of mother and child figures for use in the treatment of gynecological ailments. The characteristics that identify the different categories of *minkisi* – mirror, nails, raised or weapon-brandishing arm – may also be found together in a single sculpture.

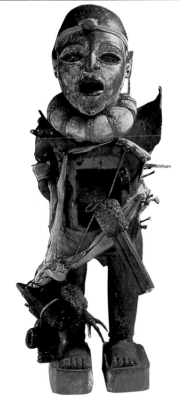

Kongo (Yombe) nkondi, *Zaire, wood and other materials, height 46 in (116.8 cm). Institute of Art, Detroit.*

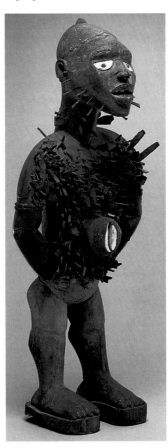

Kongo nkondi, *Zaire, wood, iron, and shell, height 20¾ in (53 cm). Museo Preistorico ed Etnografico, Luigi Pigorini, Rome.*

magic essences can either be inserted into cavities in the object – generally in the abdomen or head – or attached to the outside in projecting containers that are glued on with resin or clay. Traditional *minkisi* figures can be subdivided into three main categories. The first type are reliquary objects, characterized by the presence of a mirror to symbolize light and the clear-sightedness of the *nganga* who is interpreting the event. The second kind are nail *minkisi*, or *minkondi* (sing. *nkondi*), and are imbedded with nails or sharp

Kongo (Vili), nkondi, *Republic of Congo, wood, iron, plant fibers, other, height 44 in (112 cm). Museo Preistorico ed Etnografico Luigi Pigorini, Rome.*

Kongo (Yombe) reliquary nkisi, *Zaire, wood and plant fibers, height 11 in (28.2 cm). Museo Preistorico ed Etnografico Luigi Pigorini, Rome.*

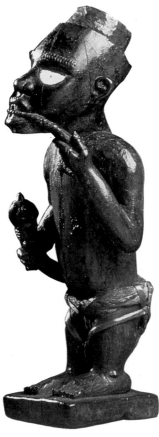

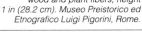

ARTISTIC CULTURES OF THE PACIFIC

Among the most recent discoveries in the panorama of world art are the treasures of Oceania. Dating from several centuries ago, they display a variety of styles and wealth of forms that reflect the size of the area and the scattered archipelagos of the Pacific. As the 20th century progressed, these works aroused increasing interest.

Oceania is a vast area encompassing the Pacific Ocean and its thousands of islands. Its population has evolved gradually over thousands of years, with the Polynesians reaching the last islands only in about the 13th century. The colonists have very different cultures and languages, dating from different periods in history, making it impossible to speak of the art of Oceania as a

Painted tree bark, Australia. Museo Preistorico ed Etnografico Luigi Pigorini, Rome.

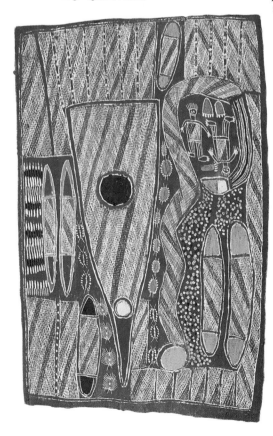

single artistic phenomenon. Nevertheless, major geographical and cultural areas can be distinguished, within which the various art forms and styles share many common features.

AUSTRALIA

The Aboriginal people of Australia grouped themselves into small nomadic groups of hunter-gatherers, who, though they used only a few simple tools, had a very complex social structure and a rich vein of myths and religious beliefs. Art and religion were closely linked in these Australian cultures and were constant features of their daily lives – sacred and everyday objects alike were decorated with engravings and paintings, while myths served as a code of reference from which both the individual and society as a whole drew inspiration. These traditional themes found expression in Aboriginal art, music, and dance. The decoration of sacred objects, even when it appeared to be highly stylized, had a complicated symbolic meaning

that varied from one group to the next. For example, concentric circles represented living creatures or their internal organs, while a series of dots might stand for the footprints left by dancers. Rock paintings showed scenes of daily life inspired by popular myths, as well as sacred subjects that were to be viewed only by those who were initiated. The great rock paintings of Kimberley, in northwest Australia, are highly symbolic. According to the Aboriginals, these paintings contained the essence of water and life. The mouths of the mythological creatures, which they believed to be the source of rain, were repainted annually to ensure continued rainfall and prolong life on Earth. Paintings on tree bark were also very common – especially those of Arnhem Land – and typically depicted legendary creatures, tribal forebears, and themes from mythology.
At the heart of Aboriginal art lay the deep link that existed between myths and society, between humans and the earth. However, the arrival of the European colonists in the 18th and 19th centuries almost shattered this link. Despite this damage, Aboriginal art is now flourishing and today enjoys huge popularity in the international art world.

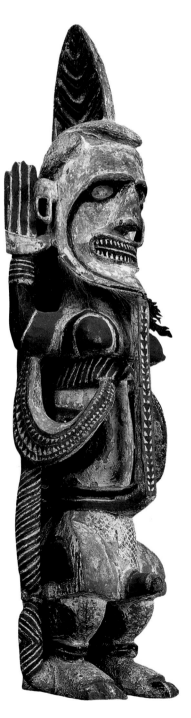

Colored wood Uli statue, New Ireland, Melanesia. Berggruen Collection, Geneva.

MELANESIA

The term Melanesia applies to the group of islands and archipelagoes that extend to the northeast of Australia. They are inhabited by a population that lives on subsistence farming and still retains much of its traditional culture. Although no single art form dominates Melanesia, a large number of local styles and a wide variety of materials and techniques are used.

Individual groups and villages have their own cultural identity, their own spirits, and their own ancestral beliefs, and each has developed a recognizable style and form of artistic expression. Yet several common features can be identified: for example, throughout Melanesia, even the most ordinary objects are decorated with extraordinary delicacy, no matter what technique is applied – carving, engraving, weaving, painting, or "feathering."

The decorative themes and motifs employed all have extremely complex symbolic and allegorical meanings. For this reason, Melanesian art has been the subject of wide study and interpretation by art scholars, and yet, in many cases, the true meaning of the decoration remains a mystery. The principal themes are mythical ancestors, depicted in both human and animal form, and supernatural beings, such as the spirits of the waters and the forests.

New Guinea is the most important center of Melanesian art. It is the largest island in the southern hemisphere and hosts more than 700 different languages. Within this vast mosaic of races, three major areas exhibiting different styles of art have been distinguished. Among the most important of these are the areas around the Sepik river and the Massim (eastern New Guinea). In the Massim, artists are professional figures who enjoy high social prestige; the region is noted

SEPIK ART

The great basin of the Sepik, the principal river of northern New Guinea, is home to people with many different languages and cultures. The extraordinary forms of art that have been developed here make this one of the richest and most important areas of native artistic production. In spite of the cultural and linguistic differences, the homogeneous

Wooden mask, Sepik basin, New Guinea. Museo Preistorico ed Etnografico Luigi Pigorini, Rome.

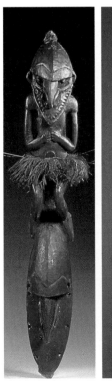
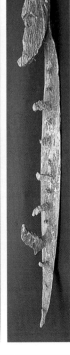

Spirit of war and the hunt, New Guinea. Museo Preistorico ed Etnografico Luigi Pigorini, Rome.

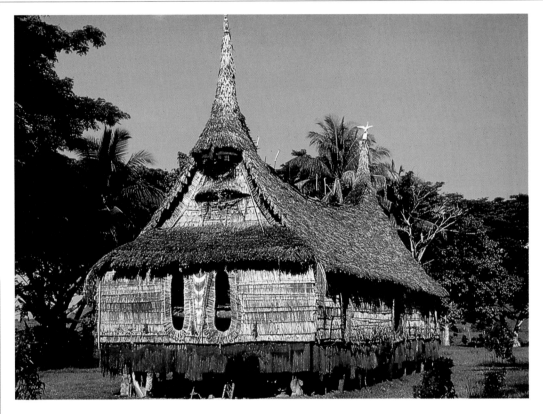

body of styles renders Sepik art immediately recognizable. The dominant elements, especially in the sculpture and painting, are representations of humans and animals (mainly crocodiles, snakes, and birds), which are depicted in a variety of ways, ranging from realistic to extremely stylized. These images appear on numerous objects, such as amulets, masks, drums, shields, orators' stools, and the

prows of canoes. They can also be found on the painted façades and carved posts of the great ceremonial houses. The human and animal figures are generally associated with the spirits (both of forests and rivers and of ancestors) and totemic antecedents. Most of these works are guarded inside the ceremonial "houses of men," which are the focal point of the group's social and religious life. Sometimes these houses are shaped in an idealized representation of the crocodile, the creature regarded as the

Papuan ceremonial house, Sepik basin, New Guinea.

mythical Creator. Although strongly connected with religion, Sepik art does not appear to be a manifestation or representation of a myth or ritual; its deep significance, which is not always a conscious one, lies in the expression of ideas that are fundamental to native culture. These include the place of human beings in the universe, the roles of males and females, and the display of power.

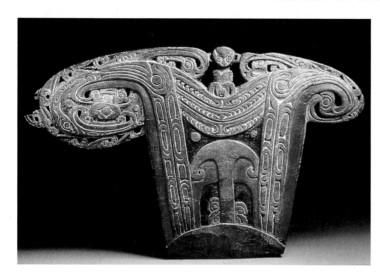

Canoe ornament, New Guinea.

for its impressive ceremonial canoes, on the prows of which are panels with elaborately carved or painted symbolic decoration. The individual parts are highly ornamental and are laden with mythological and ritual meaning. Melanesian culture, despite its contacts – sometimes destructive – with the Western world, is still thriving and is capable of expressing itself through many original art forms, even though these now differ considerably from the traditional art of earlier generations.

POLYNESIA AND MICRONESIA

Contact between visiting Europeans and the peoples of Polynesia had a devastating effect on native cultures. As a result, Polynesian art became virtually extinct long before the end of the 19th century, and so today examples of this work can be seen and studied only in the display cases of the world's museums.

Despite its distant scattering of islands and archipelagoes, Polynesia is inhabited by people who speak similar dialects and whose cultures had many common features. One of the characteristics of the native society was its strict hierarchical structure, and Polynesian art to a large extent reflected these divisions of ranks, both in its ritual and its decorative aspects. Social hierarchy was conveyed through a wide variety of insignia of rank displayed by members of the classes concerned. Among these objects of rank were ceremonial clubs (particularly those of the Marquesas Islands) and scepters, cloaks and feathered headdresses from the Hawaiian Islands, earrings made from whales' teeth, and breast ornaments. The materials most frequently used were wood, bone or ivory, shells, plant fibers, and feathers. The decoration of these objects featured both highly stylized human figures and geometric motifs.

Ceremonial mace, Marquesas Islands, Polynesia. Museo Preistorico ed Etnografico Luigi Pigorini, Rome.

MAORI ART

The Maori are a group of peoples of Polynesian language and culture who live on the islands of New Zealand, the most southerly part of Polynesia. Situated to the southeast of Australia, these islands have fostered the development of complex societies by means of their varied and abundant natural resources. The islands of New Zealand are the most recently populated of the Polynesian archipelago, between the 10th and 14th centuries AD. Because of their geographical situation, they have very different

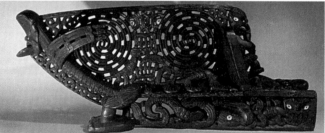

climatic conditions. Hence, although Maori art exhibits similar themes to Polynesian art, it has evolved an individual and independent style that is easily recognizable. The creative talent of Maori artists is most evident in their use of elaborate decoration and

Wooden canoe prow, New Zealand.

adornment, culminating in the so-called "Maori curvilinear style." Wooden statues are very common, but fully rounded figures are rare in comparison with the perforated friezes that adorn ceremonial houses and canoe prows. Human-style figures usually represent ancestors, but a very typical conventional figure is the *manaía* – a stylized human form with the head of a bird, which is depicted both on large wooden friezes and ceremonial objects. Like other forms of Polynesian art, Maori art was largely destroyed with the collapse of traditional culture during the second half of the 19th century.

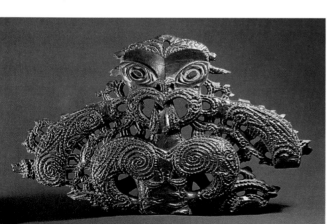

Part of a wooden door jamb in the form of a manaía, *New Zealand.*

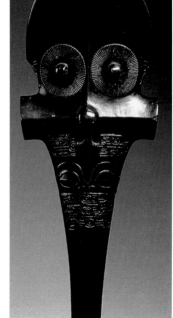

CONTEMPORARY ABORIGINAL ART

The art of the Australian Aborigines was inextricably linked with their social organization and mythology. Contact with the Europeans meant that much of this culture was destroyed, and the few remaining Aboriginal groups were forced to adopt lifestyles that were entirely foreign to them. In some cases, traditional culture was partially retained, resulting in a form of artistic expression that reinterpreted traditional Aboriginal motifs through the medium of new industrial techniques and materials. The earliest forms of this new art dated from the 1930s, but it developed most significantly during the mid-1970s throughout the regions of central Australia.

The distinctive painting style originated among a group that was driven from its native territory in the early 1970s. It then spread to other groups, each of which had an individual style that reflected their differing social and political situations and their different settlement procedures. Mythological themes

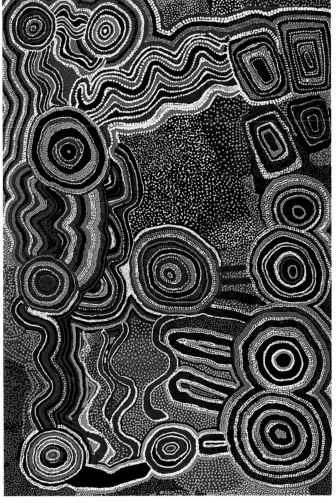

Alan Winderoo Tjakamarra, Dreaming of the Water in the Artist's Land, 1989. Acrylic on canvas.

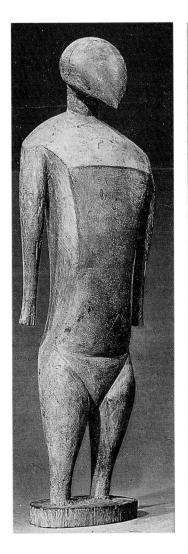

Wooden statuette, Caroline Islands, Micronesia.

Very few examples remain of the wooden sculptures, especially those from Hawaii representing divine beings, because many of them were destroyed by missionaries in the course of their evangelical work. However, still extant are the immense megalithic heads of a ceremonial nature, notably the famous carved stone heads of Easter Island (AD400–1680), and similar examples from Tahiti, Hawaii, and the Austral Islands. The art of tattooing may also be considered a form of artistic expression. It was frequently very rich and elaborate, particularly in the Marquesas Islands and New Zealand. High-ranking individuals often had their entire bodies tattooed in a

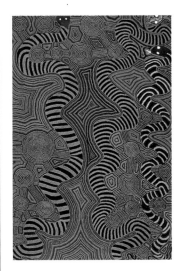

Fred Ward Tjungurrayi, The Journeys of the Three Ancestral Snakes from Jupiter Well to Karrilwarra, 1990. Acrylic on canvas.

are represented by symbolic motifs – concentric circles, curved and wavy lines – painted in a decorative pattern of dots. Contemporary artists, who often have no formal training, now use acrylic colors on canvas rather than the traditional vegetable dyes – and, again contrary to the usual practice in traditional art, they paint exclusively for the Western market. Although their

work is destined for a very different outside world, these artists remain part of the community and reaffirm their role as guardians of the earth (often represented in the pictures). Their role is vital in reestablishing broken links and in expressing the longing for the sacred places that have been lost. Yet their paintings also address issues that have affected their people from the past until the present day.

mass of abstract curved motifs. The art of Micronesia was far less complex in form than that of Polynesia and was expressed mainly in the craft production of attractive artifacts for everyday use.

Notable exceptions, however, were the wooden statues produced by craftsmen in the Caroline Islands. Carved in human form, these sculptures rank among the finest examples of their kind

to be found anywhere in the world. In these highly stylized pieces, the conceptualization of form has been elevated to a high level of abstraction that is remarkably "modern" in feel.

THE ART OF AFRICA & OCEANIA

1804: Usman dan Fodio creates the empire of Sokoto, consisting of Nigeria and Niger. **1814:** Protestant missionary work commences in New Guinea. **1816–28:** authoritarian King Shaka establishes Zulu state and society in Natal. **1824–36:** England sets up five new colonies in Australia, including Port Philip, modern Melbourne (1835), and Adelaide (1836). **1828:** Dutch take control of western New Guinea. **1840:** New Zealand Association, founded by Wakefield, claims New Zealand archipelago in the name of the British crown. **1842:** French military occupation of Marquesas Islands. **1852:** Tekut empire founded in Nigeria by emperor Hadj Omare. **1854:** while France tightens hold on Senegal, Britain grants independence to Orange Free State. **1858:** English explorer John Speke discovers

SUDANESE SAVANNAH · GUINEA FOREST · EQUATORIAL FOREST · CONGO BASIN

▼ SENUFO
Erect, geometric figures are typical of Senufo sculpture.

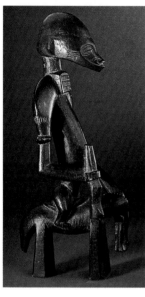

Senufo horse and rider.

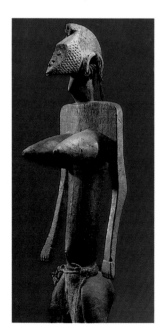

Bamana female statue, Mali. Private Collection.

▼ BAULE
Baule artifacts include polychrome zoomorphic masks and anthropomorphic masks for funerary use. Sculpture is characterized by harmony of form and well-defined decorative details.

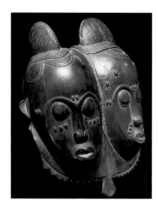

Baule double mask, Ivory Coast. Private Collection.

▼ YORUBA
Heirs to the Ife tradition, the Yoruba still produce art today. Masks are created in different shapes, with unmistakable stylistic detail of eyes and mouth. The theme of the horseman is recurrent in statuary.

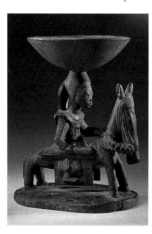

Yoruba divination cup.

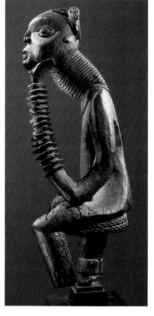

Bangwa figure of the Master of the Rings, northwest grasslands, Cameroon. Private Collection.

▲ CAMEROON GRASSLANDS
The art of the Cameroon grasslands was unified by the use of a common iconography across the many Fons, or kingdoms. The human male figure typically displayed some or all of the regalia of Fonship: stool, prestige cap, calabash, bracelets, and necklaces.

FANG
The dark, shiny statuary is associated with the cult of ancestors, depicting figures with a typically heart-shaped face and eyes like coffee beans.

KOTA
Stylized reliquary figures are made of wood covered with foil or strips of copper and brass. The symmetrical form of the faces is reminiscent of Fang and Kwele female masks.

KWELE
This culture of the Gabon region of western Africa produces a great amount of sculpture, especially masks.

▼ CHOKWE
Talented in woodcarving, the Chokwe represented their sovereigns with sophisticated hairstyles.

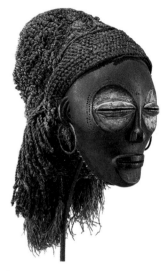

Chokwe mask, Angola. National Museum of African Art, Washington, D.C..

▼ KONGO
Traditional artifacts of the Kongo are *nkisi*, containers for magic substances used in ritual ceremonies. The three principal categories are the reliquary *nkisi*, the *nkondi*, and the *mpemba*.

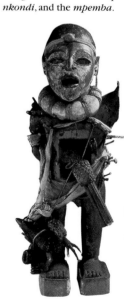

Kongo (Yombe) nkondi, Zaire. Institute of Art, Detroit.

Lake Victoria. **1867**: David Livingstone begins expeditions to the Congo basin. **1884**: two protectorates established in New Guinea: Papua (British) in the south, Kaiser Wilhems Land (German) in the north. **1893**: New Zealand becomes the first nation to grant women the right to vote. **c.1900**: Australian railroads cover almost 9,315 miles (15,000 km). **1908**: Belgium annexes King Leopold II's Congo Free State. **c.1914**: Ethiopia and Libya remain the only free states on the continent of Africa. **1931**: Australia and New Zealand attain full sovereignty within British Commonwealth. **1941**: Atlantic Charter, signed by Churchill and Roosevelt, sanctions the right of popular self-determination. **1960**: process of decolonization makes rapid strides in Africa.

| AUSTRALIA | MELANESIA | POLYNESIA | MICRONESIA |

▼ KIMBERLEY AND ARNHEM LAND

Dating from an age long before colonization, the rock paintings of Kimberley and cork paintings of Arnhem Land have strong religious connotations.

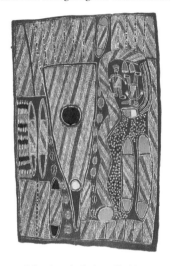

Painted tree bark, Australia. Museo Preistorico ed Etnografico Luigi Pigorini, Rome.

▼ ABORIGINAL ART

Contemporary Aboriginal art, although designed for the Western market, retains symbolic motifs associated with ancient tradition.

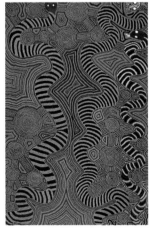

Fred Ward Tjungurrayi, The Journeys of the Three Ancestral Snakes from Jupiter Well to Karrilwarra, 1990.

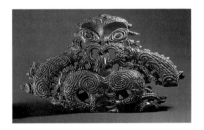

Wooden mask, Sepik basin, New Guinea. Museo Preistorico ed Etnografico Luigi Pigorini, Rome.

▲ SEPIK

Anthropomorphic and zoomorphic figures are common to the different styles of painting and sculpture that characterize the rich art production of the Sepik region. Ceremonial houses protect a variety of objects ranging from drums to shields.

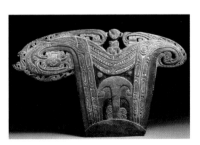

Canoe ornament, New Guinea.

▲ MASSIM

Typical artifacts of the Massim are large ceremonial canoes, their prows decorated with carved tablets and painted with symbolic motifs.

▼ MAORI

Polynesian in language and culture, the Maori have created a curvilinear style applicable to sculptural decoration. The *manaía* is a stylized human figure with the head of a bird, carved on friezes and ceremonial objects.

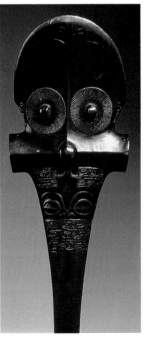

Part of a wooden door jamb, Maori culture. New Zealand.

▼ MARQUESAS ISLANDS

The islands are noted for the production of ceremonial clubs, with geometric or anthropomorphic ornamentation. The art of tattooing is also of remarkable quality.

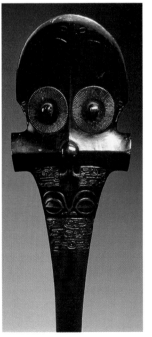

Ceremonial mace, Marquesas Islands, Polynesia. Museo Preistorico ed Etnografico Luigi Pigorini, Rome.

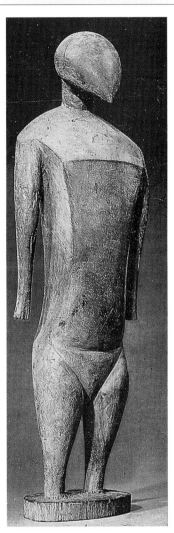

Wooden statuette, Caroline Islands, Micronesia.

▲ CAROLINE ISLANDS

The anthropomorphic wooden statuary of the Caroline Islands is pure, almost abstract, in form.

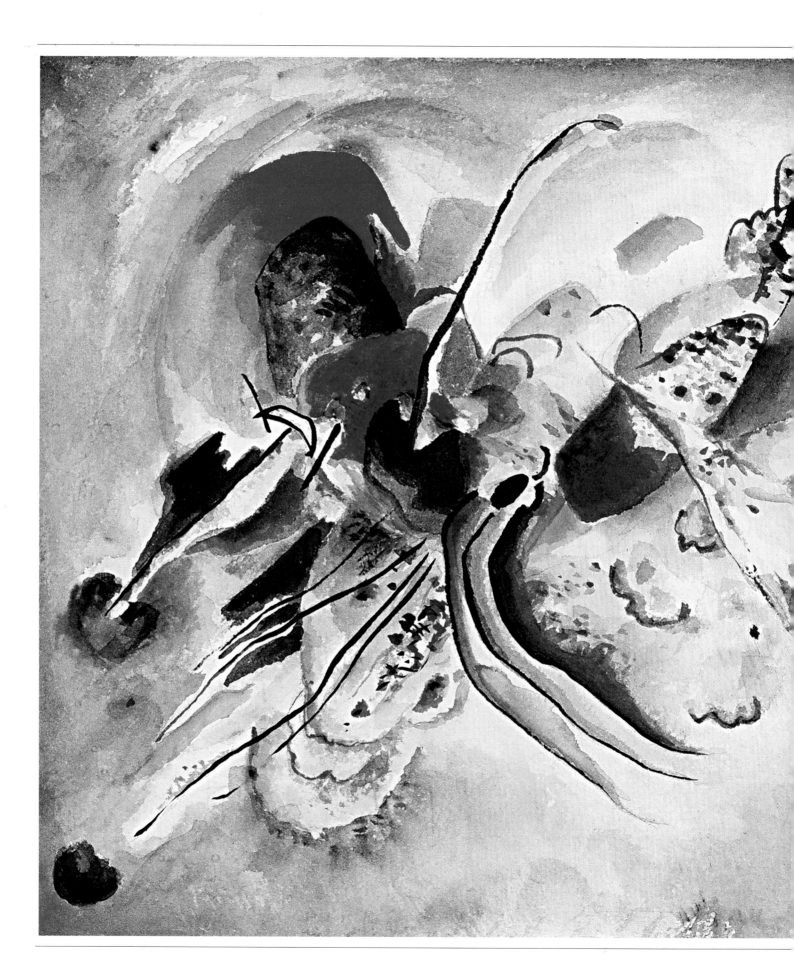

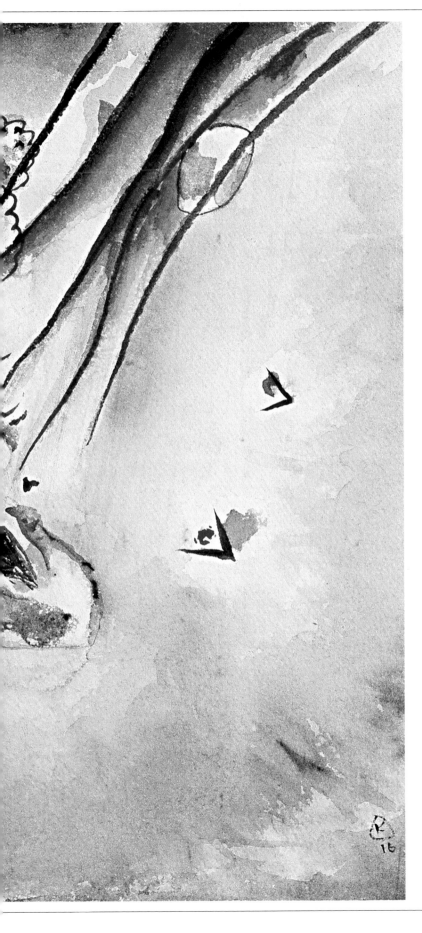

ART OF THE 20TH CENTURY

A Revolution in the Arts
Expressionism & Fauvism
The Great Avant-garde Movements
The New Architecture
Art & Politics

Postwar Developments & Contemporary Art
Art in the Postwar Period
The New Avant-garde & Postmodernism
Architecture in the Second Half of the 20th Century
Toward a New Century

Wassiliy Kandinsky, Painting with Two Red Spots, *c. 1916.*

EXPRESSIONISM & FAUVISM

Certain trends that had developed under Post-Impressionism and Symbolism found expression in experimental art groups from the beginning of the 20th century. Often shortlived, these trends produced new definitions of artists and their work as well as the role of art in society. The main centers for these new ideas included Paris, Berlin, and Dresden.

The first two decades of the 20th century were marked by a rapid series of artistic innovations, which often appeared to contrast with each other but which were all connected by a desire to break with the past. This common aim led to the naming of certain groups of artists as "avant-garde," a term with military connotations that conjured up the image of an advance force expressing an artistic perception that only later would become part of the wider culture.

THE FIRST AVANT-GARDES

The intense artistic experimentation that took place duing the period 1905 to 1916 gave rise to several trends and movements: Die Brücke, the Fauves, Cubism, Der Blaue Reiter, Futurism,

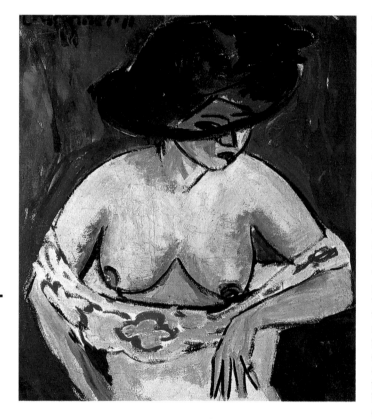

Ernst Kirchner, Half-length Nude with Hat, *1911. Wallraf-Richartz Museum, Cologne. The influence of tribal art is evident in this painting.*

HENRI MATISSE

Matisse (1869–1954) began painting in the 1890s and experimented with Impressionism and Post-Impressionism, influenced by Gauguin, Cézanne, and van Gogh. By 1904, he had adopted the Pointillist style of Signac, and from this he developed the bold colors and broad brushstrokes typical of the Fauves. Throughout his life, color was a key element of his work, which he defined as "the art of arranging in a decorative manner the various elements at the painter's disposal for the expression of his feelings."

Orphism, Suprematism, Constructivism, Vorticism, and Dadaism. These groups investigated new ideas of pictorial language – particularly the use of abstraction – and explored the expressive possibilities of materials and techniques not previously used in art. Part of their motivation was to urge people to abandon their conventional way of seeing things and adopt a fresh look at the ever-changing world. The messages voiced by these groups sometimes baffled society, broadening the gap between traditional culture and avant-garde art. This prompted them to define themselves with clear values and objectives, which were often broadcast using posters and pamphlets. As a unit, the groups could identify and develop alternative ways of exhibiting their art, such as private galleries, cabarets, theaters, and political organs.

Raoul Dufy, Old Houses on the Docks at Honfleur, *1906. Private Collection, Paris.*

EXPRESSIONISM

Many of the first avant-garde movements can be loosely united under the term Expressionism in that they rejected Impressionist art for its superficial relationship with the world.

With positivist culture in crisis, a new concept of time and history based on vitalism and evolution exposed Europe to a less certain vision. New scientific lines of thought, such as Einstein's theory of relativity, combined with social unrest to create a growing lack of consensus, while international disputes were soon to explode into major conflict. Such political tension had a marked effect on the artistic climate. The critic Hermann Bahr wrote of this period: "Never has there been a time so disturbed by desperation, by the horrors of death…. Never has man been smaller. Never has he been more troubled. Never has joy

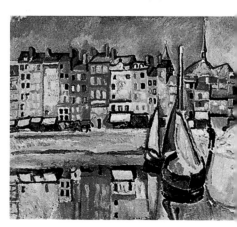

MATISSE'S GOLDEN AGE

Three Matisse paintings stand out for the success with which they depict the artist's vision of an ideal existence – a harmonious relationship between the human figure and the landscape. Each of the three beautifully balanced compositions represents a contemplation of a Golden Age that Matisse found in the light and color of the Mediterranean countryside.

During his stay with Signac in Saint-Tropez in 1904, Matisse started work on *Luxe, Calme et Volupté*, a Pointillist work that he completed in Paris. This modern pastoral image was presented at the Salon des

Henri Matisse, Joie de Vivre, 1905–06, Barnes Foundation, Merion, Pennsylvania.

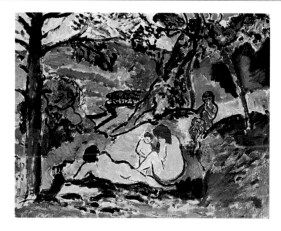

Henri Matisse, Pastorale, *1906. Musée d'Art Moderne de la Ville, Paris.*

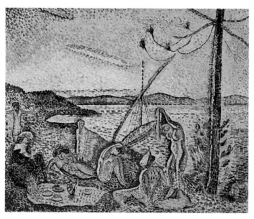

Henri Matisse, Luxe, Calme et Volupté, *1904. Musée d'Orsay, Paris.*

Indépendants in 1905. The title comes from Baudelaire's *L'Invitation au Voyage*, but the subject also refers to André Gide in its invitation to live life intensely according to instinct but led by the intellect.

In *Pastorale*, the group of women sharing a picnic at the sea's edge was transferred to a pleasing countryside scene, with modern shepherds, nymphs, and musicians. The Pointillist dabs of intense color are extended to broader strokes with sinuous outlines. *Joie de Vivre* took up the theme again with a wilder rhythm of colors and arabesques. A reworking of Cézanne's *Bathers*, it combines Gauguin's decorative style with hints of Islamic art.

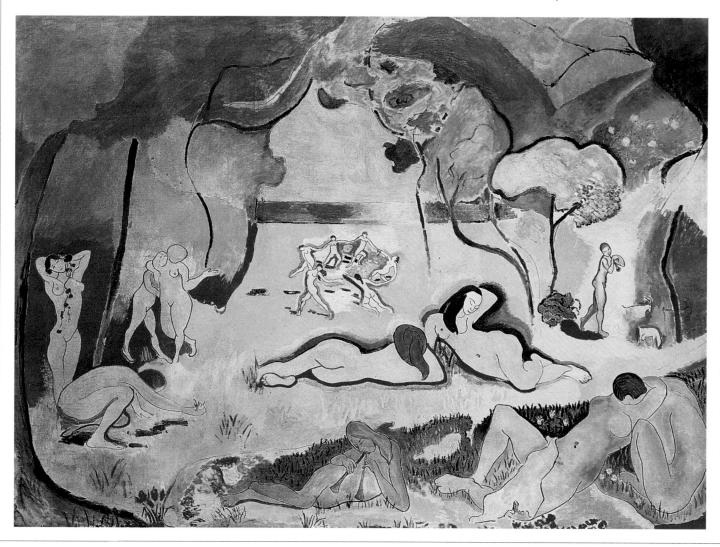

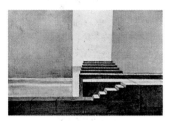
been more absent and freedom more dead. Here is the cry of desperation; man cries out for his soul, a lone cry of anguish rises out of our time. Art also cries out in the dark, calling for help, appealing to the spirit: this is Expressionism." He added: "What the Expressionist is looking for has no model in the past: a new art is beginning. Whoever sees an Expressionist painting…cannot fail to recognize it: what is in front of him is truly without equal. There is only one thing, after all, that all these groups have in common. What unites them is the fact that they have turned their backs on, or rather that they are against, Impressionism." Bahr's account explains the evolution of art in Germany and some countries in the Austro-Hungarian Empire. Artistic developments in France during the same peiod were more concerned with exploring formal values to express a new outlook on the world than with

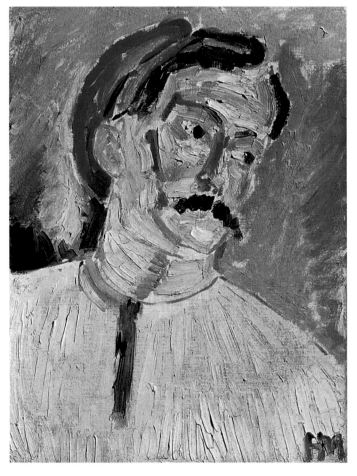

Henri Matisse, Portrait of André Derain, *1905. Tate Gallery, London.*

denouncing the world's problems with a violent Expressionist will as they affect one's physical and spiritual nature.

Following on from the Neo-Impressionism of Seurat and Signac and the Synthetism of Gauguin and Denis, the artists known as the Fauves wanted to reform art by revising its formal elements. They abandoned a realistic use of color and applied pigment with the aim of creating harmonic unity. Matisse stated: "If the methods are so worn out (as in 19th-century painting) that their expressive force is exhausted, then one must go back to the basics…. Our paintings are therefore a form of purification…they speak with immediacy…with elementary material that searches the depths of the human soul. This is the departure point for Fauvism: the courage to rediscover purity in the medium."

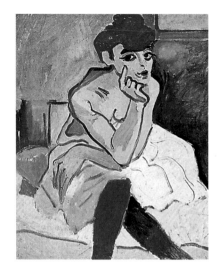

André Derain, Dancer at the "Rat Mort," *1906. Statens Museum for Art, Copenhagen.*

THE FAUVES

The name "Fauves," meaning wild beasts, was a derisive label given by Louis Vauxcelles, art critic of the review *Gil Blas*, at the Salon d'Automne exhibition of 1905. Exhibitors at the show included Derain, Matisse, Vlaminck, Rouault, and Marquet, whose paintings consisted of bright arbitrary colors and distorted lines and looked at the time like the work of savages.

The Fauves had no common program but were loosely joined by a shared rebellion against the academic system, a series of liberation and experiment. Freeing line and color from the bonds of realistic description, the Fauve artists looked back to the juxtapositions used by the Pointillists. They were also influenced by the emotionalism of van Gogh and the decorative values advocated by Gauguin, whose works had been shown and celebrated in Paris at large exhibitions held in 1901 and 1903 respectively. They chose to depict mainly people and landscapes, the subjects they

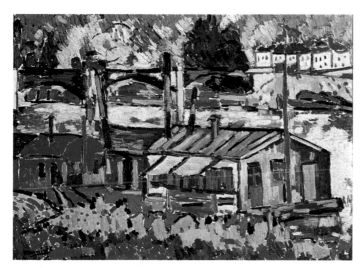

Maurice de Vlaminck, The Bridge at Chatou, *1906. Musée d'Annonciade, Saint-Tropez.*

Kees van Dongen, Woman on a Balcony, 1907. Musée d'Annonciade, Saint-Tropez.

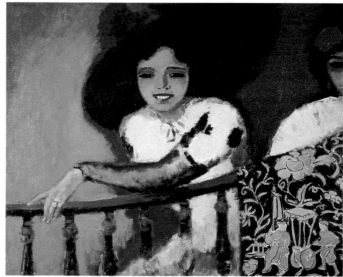

distorted forms were used to create emotive effects, while new harmonies were produced from an interpretation of reality through color and its use in new combinations.

The key figure of the Fauvist movement was Henri Matisse. He met Marquet in 1892 while at the Ecole des Beaux-Arts in Paris and in 1898, when they were both pupils of Gustave Moreau, they decided to work together. They were subsequently joined by Vlaminck and Derain, named the "Chatou Couple" after the Paris suburb where found in the world surrounding them: historical and mythological themes were abandoned entirely. The Fauves also dispensed with the need for perspective or the realities of a scene in their lively compositions.

The vivid colors on their canvases were painted with rapid brushwork and outlined with thick edges, which left ample room for arabesques and ornamentation. Arbitrary chromatic juxtapositions and

GEORGES ROUAULT AND THE FAUVES

Born in 1871, Rouault developed an original artistic style that was fraught with drama and emotion. An apprenticeship in stained-glass window-making deter-mined his later style, which was characterized by intense, thick

Georges Rouault, Head of Christ (Passion), *1938. Hanna Fund, Cleveland Museum of Art, Ohio.*

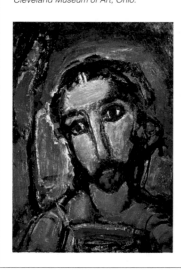

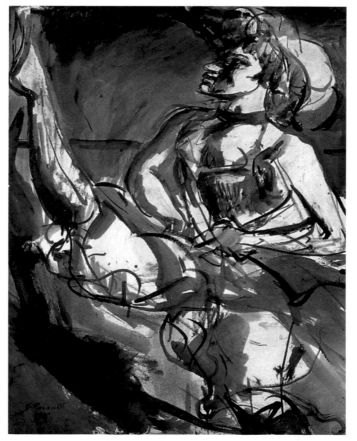

Georges Rouault, Le Chahut, 1905. Musée d'Art Moderne de la Ville de Paris.

color enclosed in black outlines. From 1892 he studied under Gustave Moreau at the Ecole des Beaux-Arts, and this brought him into contact with Matisse and Marquet. Roualt exhibited at the Fauve show of 1905, but, although he rejected Moreau's aestheticism and mysticism, he also remained aloof from the Fauves' primarily formal concerns. His main concern was the content of a painting, and his works from this time are generally in one color, a methylene blue, and bear no resemblance to the bright, varied colors associated with other Fauve artists. After undergoing a psychological crisis in 1898, he had developed a loathing of vice and cruelty and hoped for spiritual renewal through a revitalized Catholic faith. He then portrayed dramatic scenes of religious iconography and tragic human figures, such as prostitutes and social outcasts.

MODIGLIANI'S PARIS DEBUT

Born in Leghorn, Italy, Amedeo Modigliani (1884–1920) arrived in Paris in 1906, when Fauvism was flourishing and Cubism was taking root. The artistic climate was a stimulating contrast to the artist's cultural background,

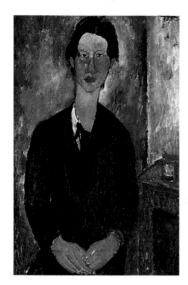

Amedeo Modigliani, Portrait of Chaïm Soutine, 1917. National Gallery of Art, Washington, D.C..

which included 14th-century Sienese painting and Tuscan Mannerism. Working at first as a sculptor, Modigliani joined the lively community at

Montparnasse, where Soutine, Chagall, Brancusi, and Zadkine were based. These were some of the artists who were at the center of that intense concentration of artistic activity that became known as the Ecole de Paris. Modigliani developed a very personal and distinctive style, which combined formal elegance with expressive immediacy. His use of line, with its sinuous, curving rhythms, recalls Botticelli and the Sienese painters, while his succinct and incisive style came from Brancusi and African tribal art. Modigliani was also influenced by the work of Cézanne, which became his

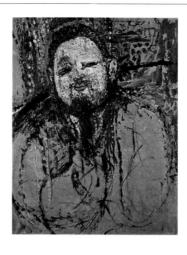

Amedeo Modigliani, Portrait of Diego Rivera, 1916. Museu de Arte, São Paolo, Brazil.

main inspiration for the large series of portraits that he produced after 1914, when the outbreak of war ended his supply of material for sculpture. After working to resolve the problem of the relationship between solid form and background, he attempted to give integrity and depth to inner feelings and moods; his figures show an anguish and resignation that inspires compassion. His poetic figures are slender, with thin necks, blue eyes, and dreamy expressions, while his nudes are erotic, created with sensitive and elegant lines that are more modeled than drawn.

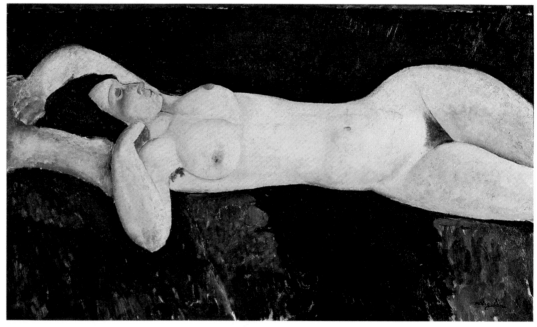

Amedeo Modigliani, Nude with Closed Eyes, 1917. Museum of Modern Art, New York.

MAURICE DE VLAMINCK

In his artistic temperament, his love of excessive behavior, and his anarchic tendencies, Maurice de Vlaminck (1876–1958) was a Fauve in the most radical sense. He applied himself to art with great passion and little academic preparation. An admirer of van Gogh, as a young artist he did not have enough patience to work with a brush and so squeezed paint straight onto the canvas. Under the influence of Cézanne, his slashing brushstrokes and strident colors became more considered and refined over time. His dramatic force is still evident in his landscapes of 1920 to 1930, which, despite their range of softer colors, no longer suggest violence so much as fatalism.

they had painted together; the "Le Havre Three" of Braque (1882–1963), Dufy (1877–1953), and Friesz (1879–1949); as well as the Dutch-born, Paris-based artist Kees van Dongen. While the refined and intellectual Matisse set out to achieve simplicity, balance, and harmony in rich, joyful colors, the instinctive,

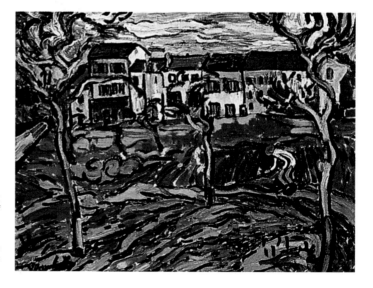

Maurice de Vlaminck, Houses at Chatou, 1903. Art Institute of Chicago. Derain and Vlaminck, the so-called Chatou Couple, both painted beside the Seine. Of the two artists, Vlaminck was more direct and powerful in his use of color.

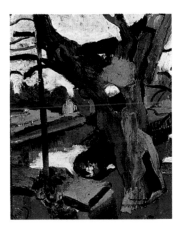

André Derain, The Old Tree, 1904–05. Musée National d'Art Moderne, Paris. The tree was a recurring theme in art during the early 20th century, from Cézanne to Matisse and Soutine.

passionate Vlaminck attacked his canvases boldly and recklessly, expressing his overwhelming vitality in fiery, hot shades. Derain defined his optimistic view of life in paintings of dazzling and sensual luminosity. He was initially influenced by Vlaminck and "discovered" Gauguin along with Matisse during a stay in Collioure in 1905. Braque joined the movement in 1906 at an early stage of his productive life. He translated his perception of reality into original formal constructs that were based on relations between shades of ochre and orange and a balance of geometric rhythms. At the Salon d'Automne of 1906, the Fauves exhibited their work together again. The show included works by Friesz and van Dongen, who depicted the bright social frivolity of Paris, and Rouault, whose work followed a similar direction to that of the Fauves, although he kept himself at a distance. By 1908, the group had dissolved as new influences and ideas emerged. Matisse pursued a poetic direction that was more personal in nature, while Braque focused on the Cubist experiments of Picasso. Derain studied the sculptural composition of Cézanne, to whom the Salon d'Automne dedicated its first large retrospective show.

DIE BRÜCKE

At the same time as the Fauves were establishing themselves in Paris, a parallel group, Die Brücke ("The Bridge"), was forming in Dresden. While the Fauve artists had not produced any manifestos, and their solidarity was founded on recognition of their stylistic affinities, Die Brücke defined itself as a movement; its intention was to break with the past and create a new art that was relevant to modern life. Ernst Kirchner formulated a manifesto, which he transcribed onto a woodcut: "With faith in evolution, in a new generation of creators and connoisseurs, we call together all youth…. We want to create for ourselves freedom to move and to live opposite the well-established older forces. Everyone belongs with us who renders with immediacy and authenticity everything that compels him to be creative." These were not so much aesthetic as existential statements: an appeal to the viewing public as well as artists for a new approach to art. The name "Die Brücke" probably came from the prologue of Nietzsche's "Thus Spoke Zarathustra," where man is described as a bridge "between beast and Superman," but the name

Ernst Kirchner, Five Women in the Street, 1913. Wallraf-Richartz Museum, Cologne.

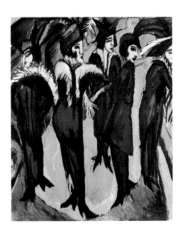

also indicates their desire for a link with other forward-thinking artists. Die Brücke was founded in 1905 by four architecture students – Erich Heckel, Ernst Kirchner, Karl Schmidt-Rottluff, and Fritz

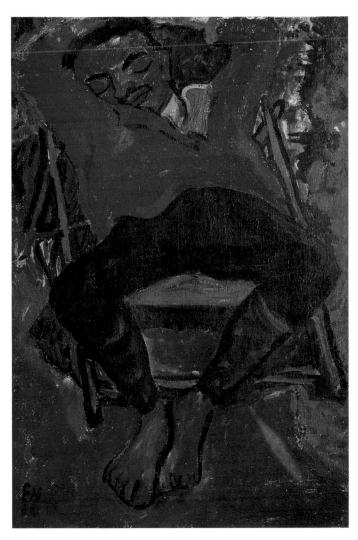

Erich Heckel, Pechstein Asleep, 1910. Staatsgalerie Moderner Kunst, Munich. In this portrait of the drowsy painter, the rules of perspective are subverted in the irrational relationship of the feet in the foreground and the withdrawn head. The disproportionate elements assume an expressive function.

Bleyl – who had halted their studies to dedicate themselves to painting, despite having little or no formal art training. The following year, they were joined by the Swiss artist Cuno Amiet; the German Expressionist and graphic artist Max Pechstein (1881–1955), who later formed a link with the Fauves while in Paris; and Emil Nolde (1867–1956), who was invited to join the group because its members admired his mainly religious paintings, which were judged as "storms of color." In 1910, when

ERNST LUDWIG KIRCHNER

Before turning to art, Kirchner (1880–1938) studied architecture at the Dresden Technical School. A founder of the Die Brücke group, he exhibited a striking use of color and harsh distortion of form. He moved to Berlin in 1911 and exhibited with Der Blaue Reiter group in Munich in 1912. In 1913, he wrote an account of Die Brücke's history and aims, which led to quarrels within the group, causing it to disband. After serving in World War I, Kirchner suffered a nervous breakdown and moved to Switzerland in 1917. He is considered to be one of the masters of Expressionism, contributing a bright, often sunny, range of colors as well as a decisively graphic flair.

AMEDEO MODIGLIANI: "NUDE RECLINING WITH OPEN ARMS"

*1917; oil on canvas;
24 x 36 in (60 x 92 cm).
Mattioli Collection, Milan.*

When he was at the height of his artistic maturity, between 1917 and 1918, Modigliani painted a series of female nudes, of which this is one of the best examples. The painting was exhibited by Berthe Weill in her Paris gallery on the occasion of Modigliani's first one-man exhibition. However, the painting was deemed to be too indecent for public viewing and had to be removed from display.

The canvas is dominated by the reclining figure of a woman. The subject is cut off abruptly above the knees at the lower right corner of the canvas, at the wrist on one side, and at the elbow on the other. The woman's, painted in a warm shade of gold, is lying on a red divan with scattered cushions. A blue-green cushion is tucked under her head and body, giving emphasis to the colors and forms around it. Of the clearly defined features on her long face, the thickly made-up eyes attract the most attention. Her open arms stretch upward and fall away loosely behind her.

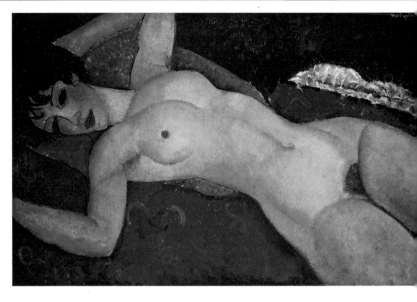

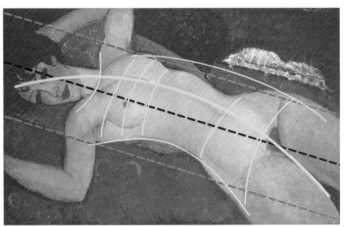

▶ 1. The painting is divided diagonally into three parts. The central and most important section is occupied by the nude figure, which is positioned in a gentle curve. The composition is devoid of straight lines, and there are no hard or rigid elements in the design of the body, the features of the face, or the background. The axes of the body are made up of a series of curves, which are drawn with great structural precision. The divan and those details of the body that would require straight lines in their depiction (and which would therefore disrupt the formal stylization of the nude) are not depicted.

▶ 2. The lines used by the artist follow Art Nouveau and classical Tuscan (especially Sienese) design. They describe, construct, mark, and establish forms and articulate space and chiaroscuro. The vigorous line breaks and joins up again through a combination of curves and arabesque ornaments. Thick outlines stand between light, shade, and semidarkness. The intensely expressive linework establishes depth and the pictorial spaces across the canvas: the figure, the areas around the woman's body, the foreground, and the background. Inflection of line stylizes the form, winding around to create the outlines, elongating, bending, and stretching them to conjure up an idealized form that glorifies reality.

activities transferred to Berlin, Otto Müller (1874–1930) also became a member.

In his *Chronik der Brücke* (1913), Kirchner wrote that much of the inspiration for a change in art came from the city of Dresden itself, with examples of German masters such as Cranach and Dürer, as well as the Oceanic sculpture preserved in the city's Ethnographic Museum. No less important for these young artists was van Gogh, to whom a retrospective show was devoted in Dresden in 1905.

The emotional fervor of Ensor and Munch, communicated in their unusual, violent works with striking and unnatural colors, were also a fundamental influence on the Expressionists. These influences can be found in the paintings of Kirchner, Nolde, and Heckel, which are often crudely and hastily sketched to maintain their expressive impact. Their subjects included busy urban life, particularly its seamy side, and its antidote the countryside.

Unlike the Fauves' optimistic vision of the world, which was influenced by the intuitionism of French philosopher Henri Bergson, the members of Die Brücke expressed dissatisfaction, so their work is more subjective

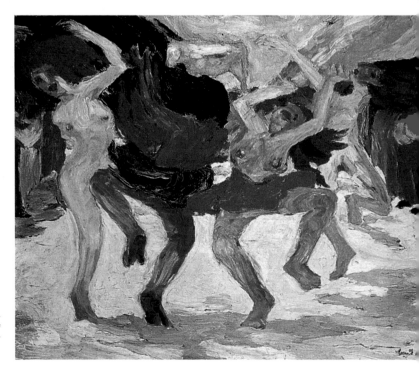

Emil Nolde, Dance around the Golden Calf, 1910. Staatsgalerie Moderner Kunst, Munich. The wildness of the dance is translated freely into color rhythms.

▶ 3. Temperate, placid colors are found in the ochre and red grounds, the dull blue, and the dark blacks occasionally flecked with white. The figure stands out clearly on the dark background. The skin colors are full of light and are almost isolated by borders. Hints of shadows in the red foreground look more like variations in light on the upholstery than true shadow. The soft color of the body is achieved with warm shades of pink and gold, which define the delicate curves. The various dark shades of color in the background make the brighter colors stand out as areas of light. There is nothing coarse or crude about the obvious sensuality of the picture.

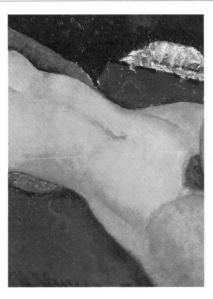

▶ 4. Light is sculpted rather than treated in an atmospheric sense. The grounds are structured, using precise brushstrokes. The body emerges out of a space that is two-dimensional in appearance – the surroundings have no well-defined features and simply provide a background to the nude figure. An ambiguity between the voluminous structure of the body and the background is achieved by lines, thick edging, and dark shading, which rest between the body and the space where it is positioned. The passage from volume to void creates very little sense of depth.

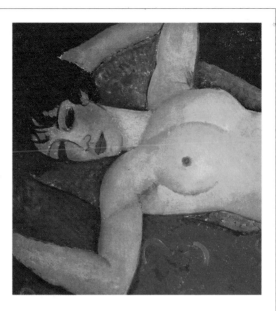

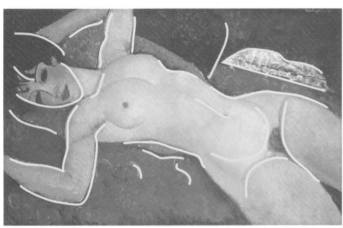

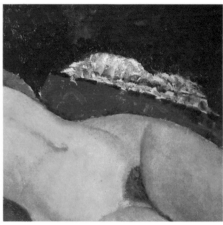

◀ 5. The brushwork is freer than in the artist's earlier paintings. Vibrant strokes accentuate the colors with hints of arabesques and small decorative marks. The dense color is applied in varying thicknesses and tones. The motion is confident and well structured. Elements in the surroundings look almost sketched. The brushwork in the nude figure is constructive: it molds and blends, creating light and shade in gradual transitions of color by amalgamating the basic shades. This treatment of color highlights the luminosity and clarity of the nude figure.

with a psychological charge and a Nietzschean sense of the struggle of the individual against oppressive reality. As well as painting, Die Brücke artists were especially interested in xylography (the art of engraving wood). The appeal of the woodcut was strong for many reasons: its precise marks, which created stark contrasts between black and white; the expressive simplification of form that it encouraged; the sometimes distorted and uncontrolled lines produced by the gouge; and the potential for reproduction and distribution. After the group's first exhibition, of which nothing remains, others followed, held in a suburb of Dresden from 1906 to 1910, and in Berlin from 1911. Various

Emil Nolde, The Ruler, 1914. Galerie Rudolf Hoffmann, Hamburg. Nolde traveled via Russia and Japan to New Guinea in 1913, where his encounter with native and primitive art stirred deep emotions that led to the appearance of new elements in his painting. Here, the human figure is violently deformed in broad sweeps of color.

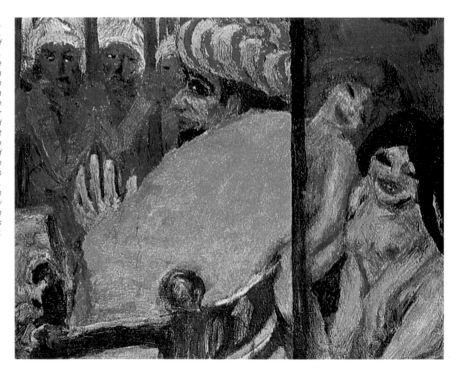

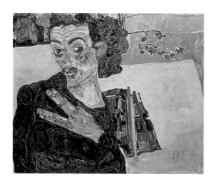

Egon Schiele, Self-Portrait, 1911. Historisches Museum der Stadt, Vienna.

members of the group settled in Berlin in search of an atmosphere that was more open to cultural exchange. Their work was shown at Der Sturm Gallery, owned by Herwarth Walden, who is credited with introducing the term "Expressionism." Walden played host to the protagonists and various trends of Expressionism, from Der Blaue Reiter to the Fauves as well as the Belgians Ensor and Wouters. Expressionism also found fertile ground in the artistic climate of Vienna. Austrian Expressionism was rooted in the work of Gustav Klimt and the Norwegian Edvard Munch, whose powerful images relied on extreme graphic tension in the emotive lines and distorted forms. Such work was a source of inspiration for Egon Schiele (1890–1918) and Oskar Kokoschka (1886–1980). From Klimt, his teacher, Schiele took precious and elegant

EGON SCHIELE

Trained at The Vienna Academy of Fine Arts, Schiele (1890–1918) was influenced by Klimt. He quickly showed a great talent for drawing and developed a particular feel for Expressionism, making him one of its most popular exponents. Schiele's art was both elegant and dramatic, loaded with sensuality and a sense of disquiet, which he achieved through dislocations of line, color, and space. He was also influenced by Freudian psychology, which he sought to apply to his work. He died in the influenza epidemic of 1918.

THE ART OF KOKOSCHKA

Oskar Kokoschka studied at the School of Applied Arts in Vienna. At first, his output was as much literary as artistic, culminating in a series of Expressionist plays. As a member of the Wiener Werkstätte from 1908, he exhibited illustrations for "The Dreaming Boys," his poem dedicated to Klimt. Another exhibit, a painted clay bust entitled *Warrior*, was bought by the architect Adolf Loos, whose relationship with Kokoschka proved to be fundamental. It was Loos who persuaded the artist to abandon the Wiener Werkstätte and his

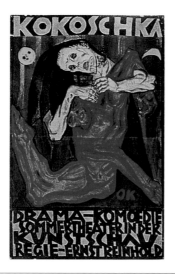

Oskar Kokoschka, poster for Murderer, Hope of Women, *1909. Museum of Modern Art, New York.*

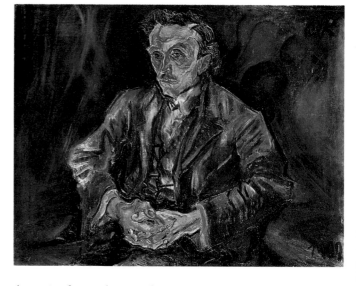

Oskar Kokoschka, Portrait of Adolf Loos. Neue Nationalgalerie, Berlin.

decorative fans and postcards for more radical cultural circles and develop his own Expressionist style. The next year, Kokoschka presented *Murderer, Hope of Women* at the Kunstschau, dedicated to Loos. The sketches he prepared for this work were wild and impetuous, and the provocative poster used the religious motif of the pietà to represent the struggle between the sexes. In about 1909, Kokoschka painted a series of portraits of Viennese intellectuals and

worked as an illustrator for Herwarth Walden's *Der Sturm* magazine in Berlin. The portraits featured scratchy and tortuous linework and a probing analytical treatment of his sitters, which shows them at their most defenseless. This has led to many comparisons with the psychoalanalytical work of Sigmund Freud, who was also working in Vienna at this time.

linework, which he subjected to lacerations and distortions, suggesting the inner contradictions of a reality that appears to be straightforward and serene but is really dominated by death and destruction. His exceptionally skillful drawings were mainly dedicated to erotic themes, expressed explicitly in a bitter and aggressive style. Meanwhile, Kokoschka created a series of portraits noted for their psychological depth, as well as some graphic work that features a nervous, all-expressive line.

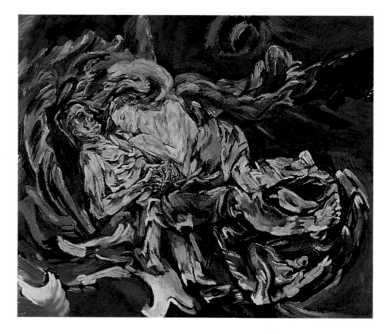

Oskar Kokoschka, The Tempest, 1914. Kunstmuseum, Basel, Switzerland.

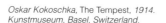

ABSTRACTION AND KANDINSKY

The exhibitions organized by the New Artists' Association of Munich in 1909 and 1910 provided an opportunity to compare the various avant-garde trends in Europe. The association's Russian-born president Wassily Kandinsky (1866–1944) set out the group's aesthetic principles, which later became the basis of the major Expressionist group Der Blaue Reiter. Instead of Die Brücke's form of Expressionism, where emotions were released onto the canvas in aggressive colors and deformed shapes, he declared that the object of art was to reveal the spiritual side of reality by using natural instinct.

The artist should divorce himself from the opinion of the masses and the material concerns of society and focus inward to explore his own character and follow an "inner necessity." Claiming that "objects damage pictures," Kandinsky created his first abstract painting. He justified his choice with the observation that "the more frightening the world becomes (as indeed it is today), the more art becomes abstract" Kandinsky's move toward abstraction was rooted in Symbolism. It was this influence that gave rise to his concern with hidden meanings beyond the appearance of reality and with achieving in painting music's ability to stir the soul without reference to the objects of the physical world. Another influence was Jugendstil, a German style linked to Art Nouveau, which tended toward abstraction in its linework, using arabesques and other decoration. For these artists, the concept of representation or imitation of reality took second place to formal invention, which was allowed to flow freely without regard for rules of symmetry or three-dimensionality.

The exclusion of naturalistic references through linear stylization coincided with the publication of "Abstraction and Empathy" by Wilhelm Worringer (1908). This essay looked at the long-standing tendency in art to evoke reality by using symbolic forms, colors, and lines that exerted a psychological influence on the viewer.

Wassily Kandinsky, Improvisation XX, *1911. State Tretyakov Gallery, Moscow.*

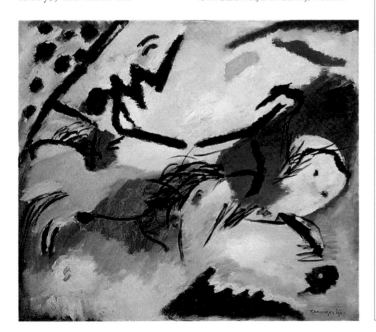

ARNOLD SCHÖENBERG: COMPOSER AND PAINTER

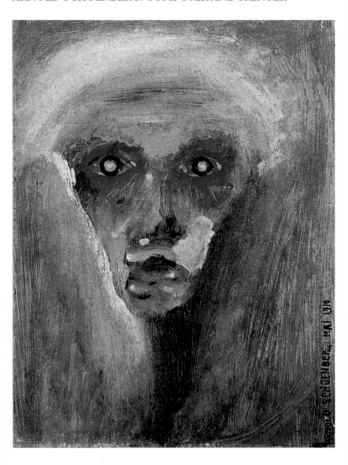

Arnold Schöenberg, The Red Stare, *1910. Städtische Galerie im Lenbachhaus, Munich. The painting is a synthesis of sound and color which Schöenberg claimed to derive from the vibrations of the soul.*

In 1912, Kandinsky dedicated a critique to his friend Arnold Schöenberg (1874–1951), composer and creator of twelve-tone music and a painter of some significant artistic work as an exhibitor with Der Blaue Reiter. Schöenberg wrote an article for the group's *Almanak,* and he participated in their first show, held in Munich in 1911. As well as traditional landscapes and portraits, he also painted what he termed "visions," in which he expressed deep feelings that could not be put in a musical form. Schöenberg and Kandinsky both experienced synaesthesia – an overlapping of the senses whereby colors are "heard" or sounds "tasted." Together, they researched the relationship between the harmony of colors and the harmony of sounds. Schöenberg gave the name *Colors* to one of his *Five Orchestral Pieces* in 1909, and later he laid down his theories of sound-color and "the melody of chromatic tones" in *Treatise of Harmony.* In his excitement following a concert given by Schöenberg in 1911, Kandinsky painted *Impression III (Concert),* a composition dominated by bright yellow, a color that, according to the symbolism adopted by the painter, "resounds like a high-pitched trumpet, played louder and louder." A reading of the letters exchanged between the two friends reveals how they were both absorbed by "the search for dissonance in art and in painting just as much as in music." Kandinsky predicted: "Dissonance in painting and music today will be nothing but consonance tomorrow."

Worringer recognized the ability of an abstract language to communicate meanings that could not be captured in other ways. As well as making a lucid contribution to the theory of abstraction, he produced some of the most direct and pleasing examples of "lyrical" abstraction. Further inspiration for Kandinsky came from a variety of cultural sources: Goethe's *Theory of Colour*, naive and primitive art from Russia; the cult of theosophy; and the expression of synaesthetic experience, for which he studied Schöenberg's work. The Czech artist Frantisek

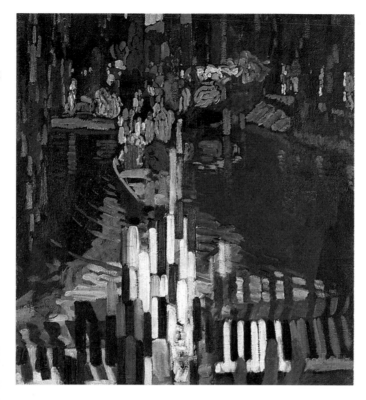

Frantisek Kupka, Piano Keys – Lake, 1909. Narodni Galerie, Prague.

FRANTISEK KUPKA

Before moving to Paris in 1895, Kupka (1871–1957) studied at the Academies of Prague and Vienna. His work was concerned principally with the composition of colored circles and lines and experimented with the translation of music into a visual representation of rhythm and harmony. Particularly noted for the abstract works that he produced from 1911, Kupka is regarded as an important representative of Czech art in the 20th century.

Kupka and the Lithuanian Mikaloius Kostantinas Ciurlionis (1875–1911) are sometimes cited as precursors of abstraction. They both had Symbolist tendencies and experimented with the

translation of music into colors and forms. Ciurlion is created a composition of chromatic waves entitled *The Stars Sonata, Allegro*, while Kupka abandoned representation in his *Piano Keys – Lake*.

DER BLAUE REITER

After setting up the New Artists' Association of Munich in 1909, Kandinsky cofounded Der Blaue Reiter (The Blue Rider) with the German Expressionist painter Franz Marc (1880–1916) in 1911. Kandinsky later explained, "we both loved blue, Marc liked horses, I riders. So the name came by itself." Blue was the color attributed to the spirit by Neo-Platonic philosophy, and it had already assumed Symbolist and "idéiste" connotations. The rider was a regular motif in Kandinsky's work, symbolizing the artist's aspirations. The group continued to pursue the concerns of the New Artists' Association: to lead a renewal of art based on the spiritual, abandoning any

Mikaloius Ciurlionis, The Stars Sonata, Allegro, 1908. Ciurlionis Museum, Kaunas, Lithuania.

THE NEW ARTISTS' ASSOCIATION

Alexei von Jawlensky, Alfred Kubin, and Gabriele Münter, along with other artists who no longer wanted to work within the Munich Secession movement, founded the New

Artists' Association of Munich in 1909. Led by Wassily Kandinsky as president, the group met to discuss the need to make art less bound by realism and more inspired by emotions, and to express this "inner world" directly with "necessary" forms rather than in the hackneyed "secondary" forms of existing artistic styles.

The association held its first two shows in 1909 and 1910, including work by many French Fauves and Cubists, which provoked strong criticism. Such hostility, together with the rejection from the group's exhibition of Kandinsky's *Composition V*, which marked his turn toward abstraction, caused the group to break up.

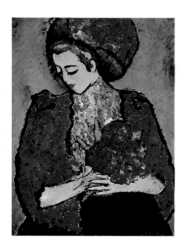

Alexei von Jawlensky (1864–1941), Girl with Peonies, 1909. Städtisches Museum, Wuppertal, Germany.

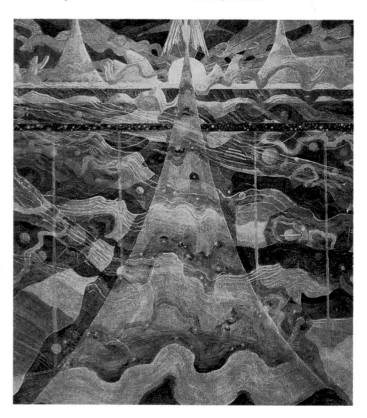

THE WRITINGS OF KANDINSKY

Kandinsky published theoretical treatises through which his considerations on aesthetics became systemic and coherent. The first of these, "On the Spiritual in Art," published in 1911, was reprinted three times in German in the course of a year in response to the interest generated in the idea of abstraction and the artist's investigation into "inner necessities." The text is rich in references to Romantic and Symbolist culture and to theosophy, the theory of relativity, and the field of music. (Kandinsky later published *Sounds,* a collection of 38 poems accompanied by 55 engravings). Its main themes were a "spiritual awakening" through art, the search for harmonies, and the principle of "inner necessity," according to which the artist reaches the soul, not just the eyes, and touches the chords of our innermost being.

In his quest, Kandinsky analyzed color according to its psychological values: "Color is the key. The eye is the hammer. The soul is the piano with its many chords. The artist is the hand that, by touching this or that key, sets the soul vibrating automatically."

Kandinsky's *Point and Line to Plane* (1926), written for the Bauhaus series of books, made an important contribution to the theory of psychology of form, which Kandinsky had studied since 1914. He aimed to establish a grammar of painting through an analysis of all forms, working down to the most simple, geometric, and neat shapes, of which the circle was the most perfect.

Wassily Kandinsky, cover for the first issue of On the Spiritual in Art, *1911–12. Piper & Co., Munich.*

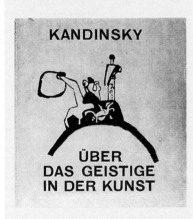

KANDINSKY

ÜBER DAS GEISTIGE IN DER KUNST

concern with representing material reality to create works born out of "inner necessity." As Marc said, they sought to create "symbols that belong on the altars of a spiritual religion." The group's first show was

DER BLAUE REITER "ALMANAK"

In 1912, Der Blaue Reiter issued its *Almanak,* a small volume containing texts, musical scores, and pictures. The book covered a wide range of cultures, from Alaskan Native Americans to Mexicans and Chinese, and the most varied of styles, from folklore to avant-garde. All these works were deemed to be united by a "spiritual awakening": "the reader will find works in our volumes that in this respect show an inner relationship although they may appear unrelated on the surface." For the first time, drawings made by children attracted interest, and, in a controversial text, August Macke wrote, "Are not children, who express themselves directly from their innermost feelings, more creative than followers of Greek ideals?" As far as

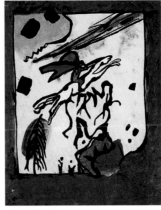

Wassily Kandinsky, cover design for Der Blaue Reiter Almanak, 1911. Städtische Galerie im Lenbachhaus, Munich.

Franz Marc, Yellow Cow, 1911. Solomon R. Guggenheim Museum, New York.

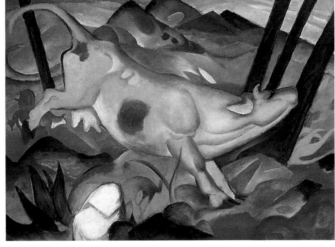

modern art was concerned, the artists of Der Blaue Reiter confirmed their total refusal of the principle of imitation in art and paid tribute to van Gogh, Cézanne, Gauguin, and Rousseau for creating work according to inner feeling rather than outer reality.

organized at the Tannhäuser Gallery in 1911. Works by artists (43 in total) from a wide variety of backgrounds were shown in order to "prove in the variety of forms represented how the inner aspirations of artists are realized in many different ways." As well as the group's founders, exhibitors included Campendonck, Macke, Münter, Schöenberg, Burljuk, Delaunay, and Rousseau. An even greater proportion of international work was included in the 1912 exhibition, which was held at the Goltz Gallery and was restricted to graphic work. Among the exhibitors were the Cubists Picasso and Braque; Die Brücke painters Kirchner and Nolde; Russian abstract artists Malevich and Goncharova; as well as Arp, Kubin, and Klee.

The next year, the group was invited to take part in the first German Salon d'Automne in Berlin. The work included there made it clear that the artists would no longer acknowledge social issues, preferring to cuts themselves off from the outside world. Plans for another exhibition were curtailed by the outbreak of war in 1914, and the group disbanded.

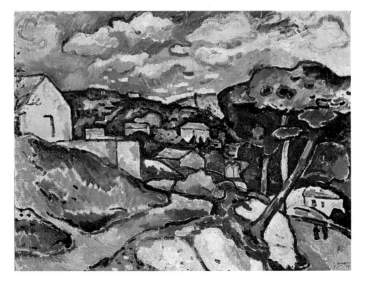

Georges Braque, Estaque, 1906. Musée de l'Annonciade, Saint-Tropez.

THE GREAT AVANT-GARDE MOVEMENTS

The advent of Cubism marked a period of radical revolution in the arts, with a rapid spread of artistic innovations and a great diversification of styles and techniques. Russian, Spanish, and American artists influenced one another, while all felt the powerful draw of Paris, the undisputed focus of artistic life.

Cubism may well have been the most influential movement in the history of art since the Renaissance. Its artists overturned the rules of perspective that had governed painting for at least four centuries, establishing new formal and conceptual ways of working that no artist of the future would be able to disregard.

This important and wide-ranging revolution did not come entirely unannounced, since certain experiments had

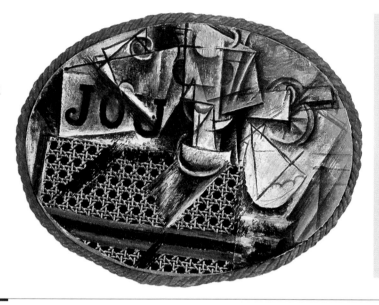

Pablo Picasso, Still Life with Chair Caning, *1912. Musée Picasso, Paris.*

PABLO PICASSO

One of the few painters to become a legend in his own lifetime, Picasso (1881–1973) dominated the art scene during most of the first half of the 20th century. He directed his formidable energies toward various artistic activities, sometimes changing his creative language but always achieving great expressivity. His most famous pictures, and even his swift sketches, reveal his extraordinary versatility and technical brilliance. The co-creator (with Braque) of Cubism and a tireless questioner of tradition, Picasso had a profound influence on Western art and aesthetics. He was the driving force behind the early avant-garde movements, which he later reinterpreted and revitalized.

PICASSO'S BLUE AND ROSE PERIODS

Having first started to paint in the stimulating artistic climate of Barcelona, where he frequented

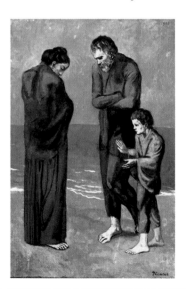

Pablo Picasso, Tragedy, *1903 (Barcelona). National Gallery of Art, Washington, D.C.*

anarchist and avant-garde circles, Picasso spent the first years of the 20th century as a struggling artist alternating between Barcelona and Paris. In 1904, he finally took up permanent lodgings at the Bateau Lavoir in Paris, where Renoir and van Dongen had studios.

During this early Blue Period (1901–04), Picasso used a limited palette of cold blue tones to symbolize his need for introspection. Drawing his subjects from social outcasts, he rejected hedonism and concentrated on themes of poverty and despair. The humanity depicted in his paintings is without hope – lonely, defeated creatures who have lost their vital spark. His subjects have a melancholy, wistful look, with bowed heads and folded arms.

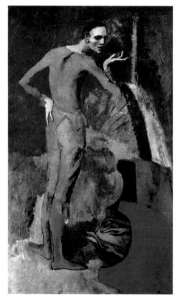

Pablo Picasso, The Actor, *late 1904 (Paris). Metropolitan Museum of Art, New York.*

The works from the subsequent Rose Period (1904–07) reflected a more optimistic and determined attitude to life. Using delicate shades of pink and darker tones of ochre and terracotta, Picasso adopted new subjects for his paintings, which now portrayed harlequins, actors, acrobats, and circus performers. He was fascinated by the performers and their fanciful costumes, generally depicting them in real-life situations away from the limelight. During these years he also created his first sculptures and began to explore plastic form in his paintings.

Blue and pink were important colors in late 16th-century Spanish art and held a variety of connotations. Picasso was influenced by the great Spanish painters Velázquez and Goya, whose works are a constant point of reference in his art.

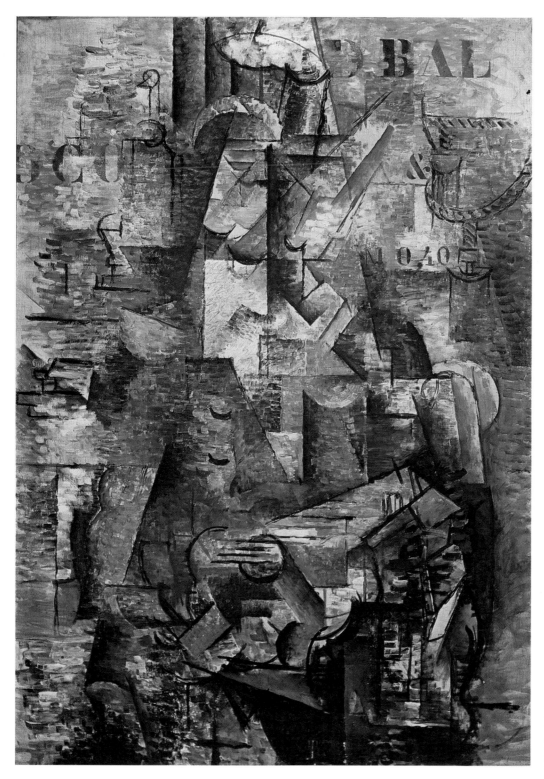

Georges Braque, *Le Portugais*, *1911–12.*
Kunstmuseum, Basel.

Fauves (especially Vlaminck, Derain, and Matisse) had promoted knowledge of synthetic and expressive African sculpture, paving the way for an antinaturalistic and non-imitative use of color.

CUBISM

When *Les Demoiselles d'Avignon* by Pablo Picasso was first seen in 1907, it certainly represented a radical break with the canons of traditional portrayal. No longer governed by the laws of a single, central perspective, artists were able to depict the subject from various simultaneous viewpoints. A purely intellectualized vision – a combination of angular solids and geometric planes – could now be conveyed within a two-dimensional canvas, thus dismissing spatial illusionism. Picasso was introduced to Georges Braque by a mutual friend, the poet Guillaume Apollinaire. The two artists shared a common desire for a new language and worked together for more than seven years. Picasso and Braque sought a way of expressing a more complete and multi-faceted reality (by painting what is *known* about space and shapes, not only what is *seen*). Such is the similarity of their paintings that it is sometimes difficult to identify each artist's work. However, Braque seems to have stayed more in touch with formal values, founded on

already prepared the ground and provided encouragement. In fact, Michel Puy in 1911 acknowledged Cubism as the culmination of the task of simplification undertaken by Cézanne and continued by

Matisse and Derain. Certainly, the lessons learned from Cézanne were fundamental to all avant-garde artistic statements. He had undertaken the challenge to solidify space, to treat objects as geometrical shapes, to portray near and distant elements at the same time and on the same plane,

to sacrifice richness of color for the expression of volumes, and to structure the picture in accordance with mental and rational constructs. Pointillism had also contributed to the adoption of simplified and geometric chromatic plans for the construction of paintings. Similarly, the work of the

GEORGES BRAQUE

A part of the avant-garde movement in Paris from 1900 onward, Braque (1882–1963) followed his own restrained version of Fauvism. Cézanne's influence led him to develop Cubism, and he was regarded as the movement's most "painterly" adherent. Progressing from Analytical to Synthetic Cubism, Braque was among the first to insert letters and numbers into his works and to recognize the scope of collage and *papier collé*. He was a fine graphic artist, but he never gave up his exploration of spatial values in painting and experiments with color.

PABLO PICASSO "LES DEMOISELLES D'AVIGNON"

1907; oil on canvas; 96 x 92 in (244 x 233 cm); Museum of Modern Art, New York.

One of the 20th-century's most famous pictures and widely considered to be one of the first examples of Cubism, *Les Demoiselles d'Avignon* remained in Picasso's studio for some thirty years. He would show the work only to those whose opinion he valued. The title is said to refer to the girls of the brothel in Carrer Avinyó, Barcelona. Five female nudes are depicted; four standing and one seated.

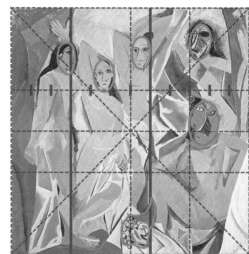

▶ *1. The almost square canvas is divided into three vertical rectangles, which increase in size from left to right. The first is dominated by warm reds, the second by pink and white, and the third by intense blues and reds. Dividing these rectangles into 12 strips, the first rectangle has three strips; the second, four; and the third, five. The rectangles correspond to three phases in the creation of the work. All but the two central figures were changed after Picasso saw African sculptures exhibited at the Ethnographic Museum in Paris.*

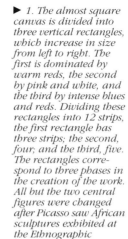

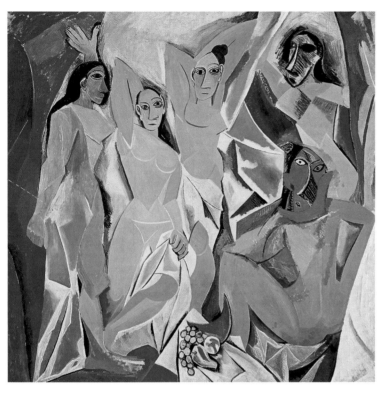

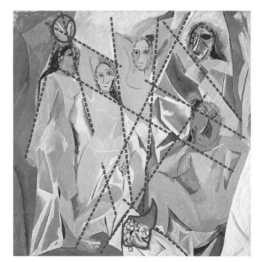

◀ *2. The strongest lines in the composition are oblique and often intersect. This gives a very dynamic appearance, despite the three vertical rectangles and the four upright nudes. Some oblique lines run from the top of the canvas to the still life in the lower foreground. This is a reversed perspective, analagous to Courbet's* Burial at Ornans, *in which the sight lines are directed toward a focal point. The hand in the top left corner is a second point of interest toward which many of the lines flow.*

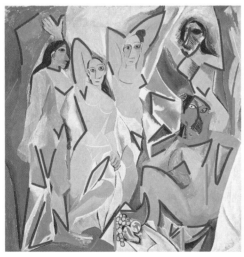

◀ *3. Broken lines dominate the picture, generating acute and obtuse angles where they meet. There are few horizontal or vertical lines, keeping any static element to a minimum. The oblique lines, especially when joined to form angles, give movement to the shapes. The work seems to guide the eye outside its confines so that we, as viewers, must keep returning our focus to the picture. It is in Picasso's treatment of the seated nude that we can detect the beginnings of Cubism. Here, several simultaneous views of the figure are combined in one image.*

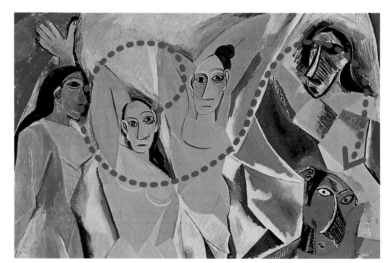

harmonious and rhythmic composition, while Picasso, true to his Spanish blood, was more aggressive, passionate, and dramatic. Recurring themes in the works of both painters include angular human figures – treated like wooden sculpture and possessing an almost sacred solemnity – and landscapes in which small houses were reduced to geometric cube shapes. It was in Louis Vauxcelles's description of this detail in *Gil Blas* in November 1908 that the term "cubism" was coined. Portraits were often of the painters' dealer and collector friends, such as Kahnweiler, Vollard, and Uhde, while the still lifes show fragments, silhouettes, and profiles of objects that appear

At the bottom of the painting, in the foreground, some fruit is arranged as a still life. The dominant colours for the figures are pinks, from flesh colour to bright pink, and, for the background, white and various shades of blue. The women are not portrayed by means of a traditional painterly language, in relation to which they appear variously deformed and in disharmony.

▼ *4. The detail and precision of the still life in the foreground reveal much about Picasso's working methods and his tireless search for new formal structures. Its prominence – in fact its very presence – in a picture that clearly deals with a quite separate subject reflects the influence of Spanish 16th-century painting. The fruit and the table on which it is placed are painted in a way that makes them project out of the canvas towards the viewer. The colors of the background and simplified drawing of the fruit are a tribute to Fauvism. If the viewer imagines the picture without the still life, its shapes lose their dynamism and become agitated and fragmented, like satellites deprived of the planet around which they circle.*

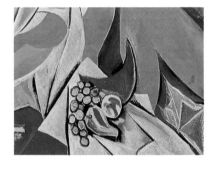

◄ *5. The Cubist portrayal of figures is not to be found solely in the perception and painting of their forms, seen from different angles and through elements of knowledge other than sight itself. The detachment of the part from the whole, the arm shown out of scale compared with the torso, and the emergence of a hand from the top of a girl's head on the left are all Cubist traits. Typical of Picasso's unsentimental style, the protruding hand might be a reference to Goya's painting* The Third of May *(1808), in which the hand of the man about to be executed expresses horror and pleads for help. Unlike traditional paintings, the women's faces are distorted. The girl on the left wears a mask that is less Africanized and less disturbing than the other two pictured. Old and new images are used here, blending traditional and exotic suggestions as a part of the aesthetic revolution in art.*

to interlock tightly as if within a web. Musical instruments were often represented, chosen partly for their formal values – piano keys relate well to spatial rhythm, and the

shape of the mandolin echoes the curves of the female body – and partly in the ever-present hope of achieving a synthesis of painting and music.

Within two years, the process of dismantling form started by Picasso and Braque took fragmentation and obscurity to such extreme lengths that it led to cryptic and indecipherable works. This phase is known as Analytical Cubism, when pyramidal structures of geometrical solids tend to dematerialize through the effect of light shining through them, making them crystalline and forming designs that have been mistaken as abstract. In fact, Cubists sought to penetrate reality to its very depths, investigating its most hidden aspects in order to provide as much information about it as possible. According to Jean Metzinger (1883–1957) and Albert Gleizes (1881–1953) in *Du Cubisme* (published in 1912), the Cubists wanted to circle around the object and, under the control of the intellect, give a concrete representation of several successive aspects of it. Although Picasso and Braque were acknowledged as the two most significant exponents of Cubism in its analytical phase and subsequent stages, neither of them took part in the movement's first official viewing held in April 1911 at the Salon des Indépendants. Works by participating artists –

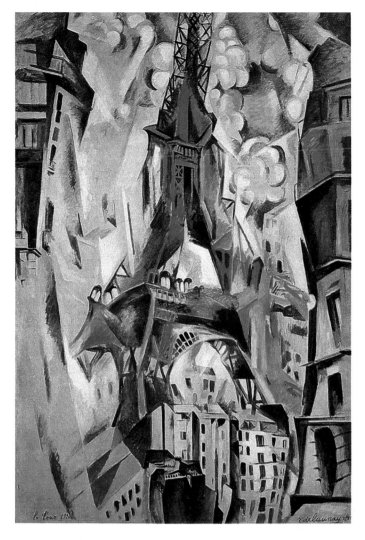

Robert Delaunay, La Tour Eiffel, *1911. Solomon R. Guggenheim Museum, New York.*

Metzinger, Gleizes, Henri Le Fauconnier (1881–1946), Fernand Léger, and Robert Delaunay (1885–1941) – showed very different artistic experiences but were now grouped under one name,

which acquired its own resonance and historic significance. The five painters of the Salon were soon joined

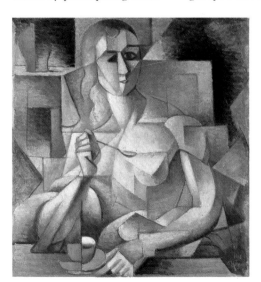

Jean Metzinger, Teatime, 1911. Philadelphia Museum of Art. Metzinger was initially influenced by the ideas of Neo-Impressionism and Fauvism but became a member of the Cubist school after meeting Picasso and Braque in 1910.

FERNAND LEGER

One of the more diverse avant-garde painters, Léger (1881–1955) was, at various times, associated with the Fauvists, Cubists, Orphists, and Futurists. He brought a love of bold imagery and intentionally crude colors to each avant-garde movement, together with the reduction of volumes into regular and usually curvilinear and tubular forms. His paintings also embodied the Purist cult of the machine and used flat fields of color of an abstract quality. Constantly renewing his artistic language and scope, he also tried his hand at mural painting, sculpture, stage design, ceramics, and movies (he collaborated with Man Ray on the film *Ballet Mécanique* in 1924).

THE SECTION D'OR GROUP

The refusal of the Salon des Indépendants to exhibit Marcel Duchamp's *Nude Descending a Staircase* led to the launch of a breakaway group, the Section d'Or (Golden Section), with a large exhibition of 300 works in October 1912 at the Galerie de la Boëtie. Members of the group – Picabia, Gleizes, Metzinger, Gris, Archipenko, Villon and Kupka – had taken up Cubist ideas about the treatment of form and were now moving toward other avant-garde experiments. The works of Picabia and Duchamp revealed new uses of color, themes based on movement, and an avid interest in the mathematical system of proportion (similar to the Golden Section), the study of which had inspired the group's name.

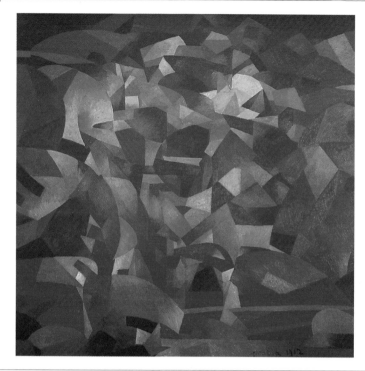

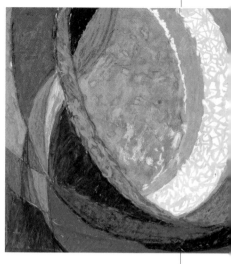

Frantisek Kupka (1871–1957), Etude pour Amorpha, chromatique chaude, 1911–12. Mladek Collection, Washington, D.C.

Francis Picabia, Dances at the Well II, 1912. Museum of Modern Art, New York.

THE CONTRIBUTION OF GUILLAUME APOLLINAIRE

The poet Guillaume Apollinaire (1880–1918) was a frequent contributor to the influential *La revue blanche* from 1902 onward. He had originally confined his critical interest in painting to the works of Seurat, Cézanne, and the Fauves but later became closely involved with the activities of avant-garde artists, acting as their interpreter and theoretician. He wrote a treatise entitled *The Cubist Painters – Aesthetic Meditations* (published in 1913), as well as

reviews and prefaces for the one-man shows of Picasso and Braque and for exhibitions by the so-called Orphists. An enthusiastic apologist for any new artistic development, he wrote the manifesto "L'Antitradition futuriste" for Marinetti in 1913. In 1917, he coined the term "surrealism" when describing his play *Les Mamelles de Tirésias*

Pablo Picasso, Project for a Monument to Apollinaire, (1928). Museum of Modern Art, New York.

Marie Laurencin (1885–1956), Apollinaire and His Friends, 1909. Musée National d'Art Moderne, Paris.

and also contributed to *391*, Picabia's Dadaist review. When Apollinaire died, Picasso designed a wire sculpture

based on one of Apollinaire's poems, "signifying nothing, like poetry and fame."

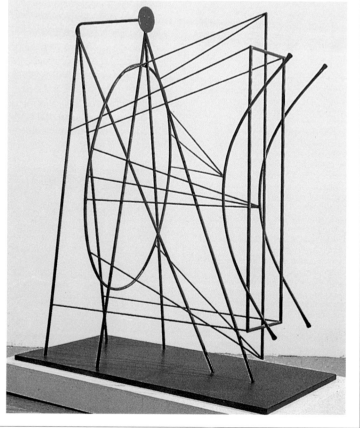

by Roger de la Fresnaye, Marcoussis, and the so-called "Puteaux group," consisting the three brothers Marcel Duchamp (1887–1968), Jacques Villon (1875–1963), and the sculptor Raymond Duchamp-Villon (1876–1918). Later on, the Spanish painter Juan Gris (1887–1927) was associated with the group, albeit loosely. Also in 1911, contacts were made with the Blaue Reiter at Delaunay's exhibition in Munich and with the Cubo-Futurists Malevich and Burliuk. In the same year, Gris' *Homage to Picasso* acknowledged Picasso as the father of a new, historic artistic era, and the Cubist exhibition in Brussels, which was organized by Guillaume Apollinaire, marked the close of the movement's first phase. Other Cubist developments followed, such as so-called Synthetic Cubism and the distinctive Orphic Cubism. In these, the object, which had initially been analyzed and broken into parts (losing any recognizable features) was reconstituted, depicted according to its essential structure and expressed in terms of its most significant components. Cubists now sought to avoid the danger of abstraction and mystification. Instead, they favored a subtle linguistic game of metaphors

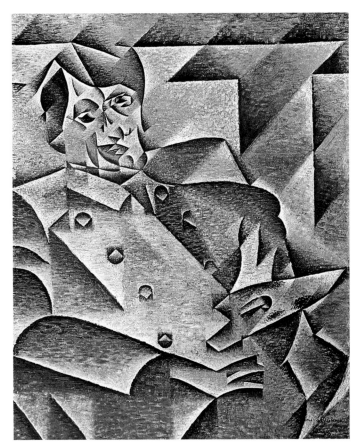

Juan Gris, Homage to Picasso, *1912. Art Institute of Chicago.*

Marcel Duchamp, Nude Descending a Staircase no.2, *1911. Philadelphia Museum of Art.*

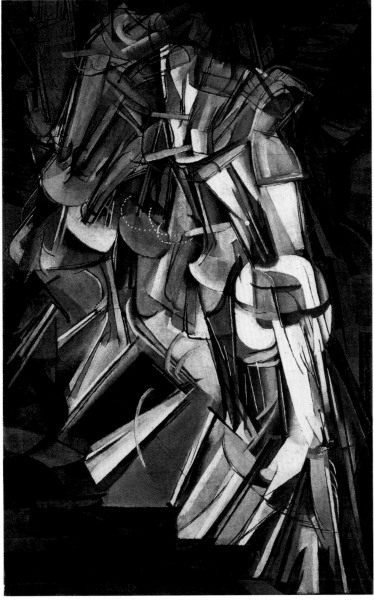

and cross-references between reality and illusionism. Works now featured letters, numbers, and "pieces of reality," such as cloth, newspaper cuttings, stamps, and other *objets trouvés.* The use of these items by Cubists launched the technique of collage and *papier collé,* which was later adopted enthusiastically by Dadaists and Surrealists. Impelled by the need to achieve order and clarity and increasingly repelled by the drab and uniform colors of the majority of Cubist paintings, Juan Gris and, subsequently, Fernand Léger adopted a rigorous structure and more luminous and brilliant colors. The Cubism of these artists is a simple, essential, and schematic language of geometric shapes enriched by flat areas of clear, pure color.

FUTURISM

In contrast with other early 20th-century avant-garde movements, the distinctive feature of Futurism was its intention to become involved in all aspects of modern life. Its aim was to effect a systematic change in society and, true to the movement's name, lead it toward new departures into the "future." Futurism was a direction rather than a style. Its encouragement of eccentric behavior often prompted impetuous and sometimes violent attempts to stage imaginative situations in the hope of provoking reactions. The movement tried to liberate its adherents from the shackles of 19th-century bourgeois conventionality and urged them to cross the boundaries of traditional artistic genres in order to claim a far more complete freedom of expression. Through a barrage of manifestos that dealt not only with

FUTURIST SCULPTURE

Umberto Boccioni published his "Technical Manifesto of Futurist Sculpture" in 1912, despite having completed only two sculptural works at the time. He had developed his new theories after coming into contact with Duchamp-Villon, Archipenko, Brancusi, and Picasso while in Paris. Boccioni's ambition was to make sculpture capable of expressing the dynamic structures of modern society. To this end, he aimed to capture the totality of reality, including psychological and emotional dimensions and all its varied facets in their continual condition of change. The resultant work would be "sculpture of environment," in which he could "fling open the figure and let it incorporate within itself whatever may surround it." The Cubists had already tried a fresh approach to reality, interrupting the continuity of line and breaking up the rhythm of forms according to analytical and geometric conceptions. However, they did not alter the static perception of reality. Futurists aimed to convey all the changes that an object undergoes during movement. After demonstrating the sculptural motion of an everyday object in his famous "bottles" series (*Development of a Bottle in Space*, 1912), Boccioni tackled the theme of movement in the human body, constructing aerodynamic, compressed compositions with a succession of concave and convex shapes. By stretching and distorting his figures, he created "syntheses" of "internal plastic infinity" and "external plastic infinity," as seen in his *Unique Forms of Continuity in Space* (1913). The most conclusive work of Boccioni's sculptural experimentation was his inspired composition *Horse + rider + buildings* (1913–14). The materials chosen for this work, including wood, tin, copper, and cardboard, represented the need to progress from traditional sculpture made in a single material to the use of a multiplicity of colors and materials. Picasso's assemblage of various materials for his sculptures in 1911 and 1912 had already started to change the course of plastic art in Europe. *The Horse* (1914) by Duchamp-Villon showed a remarkable affinity with Boccioni's work, which was also discernible in Lipchitz's solid three-dimensional structures and in Constructivist works.

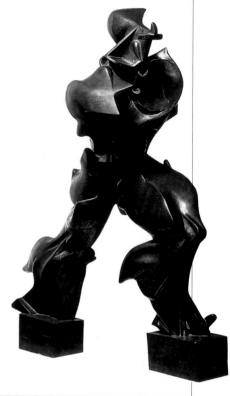

Umberto Boccioni, Unique Forms of Continuity in Space, *1913. Museum of Modern Art, New York.*

UMBERTO BOCCIONI

Initially influenced by Balla's Divisionist theories and interested in the relationship between visual art and psychology, Boccioni (1882–1916) later focused on the effects of industrialization and a need for change in the arts. A knowledgeable and cultured artist, he was associated with early avant-garde movements and was a founding member of the Futurist group. Boccioni was a naturally gifted sculptor and painter, concerned with subtle variations of form, based on rigorous aesthetic considerations. The beauty of his colors and his harmonious development of volume won him many admirers.

Futurism, which started out as a literary movement, had its first manifesto (signed by Filippo Tommaso Marinetti) published in *Le Figaro* in 1909. It soon attracted a group of young Italian artists – Umberto Boccioni, Giacomo Balla (1871–1958), Carlo Carrà (1881–1966), Luigi Russolo (1885–1947), and Gino Severini (1883–1966) – who collaborated in writing the "Technical Manifesto of Futurist Painting" and the "Manifesto of the Futurist Painters," both of which were published in 1910.

Despite being the sole Italian avant-garde movement, Futurism first came to light in Paris, where the cosmopolitan atmosphere was ready to receive and promote it. Its development coincided with that of Cubism, and the similarities and differences in the philosophies of the two movements have often been discussed. Without doubt they shared a common cause in making a definitive break with the traditional, objective methods of representation. However, the static quality of

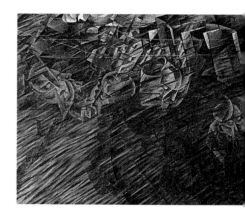

Umberto Boccioni, States of Mind: Those Who Go, *1911. Galleria d'Arte Moderna, Milan. Boccioni painted various versions of his* States of Mind *triptych (*The Farewells; Those Who Go; Those Who Stay*) between 1911 and 1912. The Milan triptych precedes that in the Museum of Modern Art in New York, which was completed after Boccioni's trip to Paris and reveals, if indirectly, his contact with Cubism. A version in the form of a wood-engraving has the same expressive force as the more famous work in oil on canvas.*

various aspects of art, such as painting, sculpture, music, architecture, and design, but with society in general, the Futurists proclaimed the cult of modernity and the advent of a new form of artistic expression and put an end to the art of the past. The entire classical tradition, especially that of Italy, was a prime target for attack, while the worlds of technology, mechanization, and speed were embraced as expressions of beauty and subjects worthy of the artist's interest.

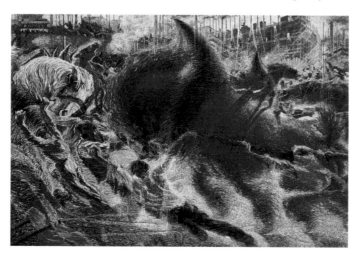

Umberto Boccioni, The City Rises, *1910–11. Museum of Modern Art, New York. Many studies were made for this large canvas, which is a manifesto of Futurism. In fact, it took Boccioni from the summer of 1910 until April of 1911 to complete the work. It was then shown at the Exhibition of Free Art held in Milan.*

Cubism is evident when compared with the dynamism of the Futurists, as are the monochrome or subdued colors of the former in contrast to the vibrant use of color by the latter. The Cubists' rational form of experimentation and intellectual approach to the artistic process also contrast with the Futurists' vociferous and emotive exhortations for the mutual involvement of art and life, with expressions of total art and provocative demonstrations in public. Cubists held an interest in the objective value of form, while Futurists relied on images and the strength of perception and memory in their particularly dynamic paintings.

The Futurists believed that physical objects had a kind of personality and vitality of their own, revealed by "force-lines" – Boccioni referred to this as "physical transcendentalism." These characteristic lines helped inform the psychology and emotions of the observer and influenced surrounding objects "not by reflections of light, but by a real concurrence of lines and real conflicts of planes" (catalog for the Bernheim-Jeune exhibition, 1911). In this way, the painting could interact with the observer who, for the first time, would

Giacomo Balla, Dynamism of a Dog on a Leash, 1912. Albright-Knox Art Gallery, Buffalo, New York.

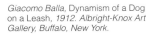

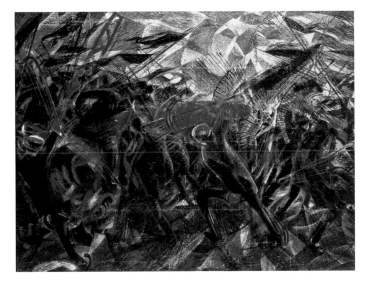

Carlo Carrà, The Funeral of the Anarchist Galli, 1911. Museum of Modern Art, New York.

be looking "at the center of the picture" rather than simply viewing the picture from the front. This method of looking at objects that was based on their inherent movement – and thereby capturing the vital moment of a phenomenon within its process of continual change – was partly influenced by a fascination with new technology and mechanization. Of equal importance, however, was the visual potential of the newfound but flourishing art of cinematography.

Futurists felt strongly that pictorial sensations should be shouted, not murmured. This belief was reflected in their use of very flamboyant, dynamic colors, based on the model of Neo-Impressionist theories of the fragmentation of light. A favorite subject among Futurist artists was the feverish life of the metropolis: the crowds of people, the vibrant nocturnal life of the stations and dockyards, and the violent scenes of mass movement and emotion that tended to erupt suddenly. Some Futurists, such as Balla, chose themes with social connotations, following the anarchic Symbolist tradition of northern Italy and the humanitarian populism of Giovanni Cena.

The first period of Futurism was an analytical phase, involving the analysis of dynamics, the fragmentation of objects into complementary shades of color, and the juxtaposition of winding, serpentine lines and perpendicular straight lines. Milan was the center of Futurist activity, which was led by Boccioni and supported by Carrà and Russolo. These three artists visited Paris together in 1911 as guests of Severini, who had settled there in 1906. During their stay, they formulated a new artistic language, which culminated in works dealing with the "expansion of objects in space" and "states of mind" paintings. A second period, when the Futurists adopted a Cubistic idiom, was known as the synthetic phase and lasted from 1913 to 1916.

At this time, Boccioni took up sculpture, developing his idea of "sculpture of the environment" which heralded the "spatial" sculpture of Moore, Archipenko, and the Constructivists. In Rome, Balla and Fortunato Depero (1892–1960) created "plastic complexes," constructions of dynamic, basic silhouettes in harsh, solid colors.

The outbreak of World War I prompted many Futurist artists to enlist as volunteers. This willingness to serve was influenced by the movement's doctrine, which maintained that war was the world's most effective form of cleansing. Both Boccioni and the architect Antonio Sant'Elia, who had designed an imaginary Futurist city, were "cleansed," and the movement was brought to a sudden end.

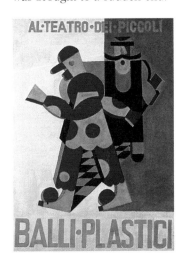

Fortunato Depero (1892–1960), Plastic Dances. Mattioli Collection, Milan,

During the 1920s, some Futurists attempted to revive the movement and align it with other European avant-garde movements under the label of "Mechanical Art." Its manifesto, published in 1922, showed much in common with Purism and Constructivism. Futurism also became associated with "aeropainting," a technique developed in 1929 by Balla, Benedetta, Dottori, Fillia, and other artists. This painting style served as an expression of a desire for the freedom of the imagination and of fantasy.

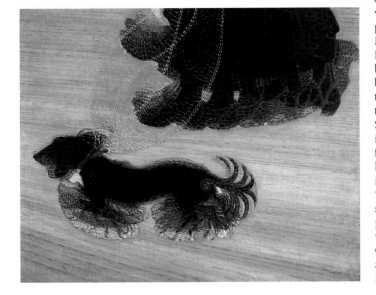

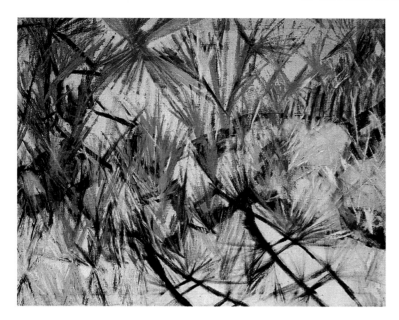

Mikhail Larionov, Rayonist Landscape, *1912. Russian Museum, St. Petersburg.*

EARLY RUSSIAN AVANT-GARDE MOVEMENTS

During the first two decades of the 20th century, Cubism and Futurism were adopted and developed by Russian artists who, except for those living outside Russia, had not previously been involved in the European avant-garde movements. From 1905 until the outbreak of World War I and, subsequently, from the time of the October Revolution until the mid-1920s, three important initiatives were launched in succession: Rayonism, Suprematism,

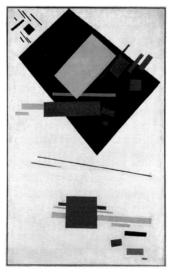

Kasimir Malevich, Suprematism, *1915. Stedelijk Museum, Amsterdam.*

and Constructivism. Founded on intellectual discipline and geometry, these modes entailed original theoretical and pictorial developments along the lines of Abstractionism. Although aware of its legacy in painting and literature, young Russian artists felt burdened by the cultural tradition of realism and rejected it in favor of the new developments in France. They were mesmerized by the collections of Post-Impressionist works by Cézanne, Matisse, and Picasso, which were brought to Russia by wealthy merchants such as Shchukin and Morozov, who allowed public viewings.

Russian artists also admired Italian Futurism, avidly reading translations of the manifestos and attending Marinetti's lectures, held in Moscow from 1910 onward.

The Golden Fleece exhibitions of 1908 and 1909 included works by Natalia Goncharova and Mikhail Larionov (1882–1964) that recalled national tradition in robust primitivist scenes. In 1912, however, work presented at the so-called "Donkey's Tail" exhibition showed that these two artists had already started to embark upon a modernization of Russian painting. Although independent and critical of Western culture, these painters set great store by the Cubo-Futurists' experiments in the use of color, dynamism of line, and the liberation of art from naturalistic representation.

In his "Manifesto of Rayonism" (published in April 1912 and revised in 1913 for the Target exhibition in Moscow), Larionov defined his new artistic theories as "a synthesis of Cubism, Futurism, and Orphism." Rayonism is said to have drawn its inspiration and name from the scientific discoveries of radioactivity and ultraviolet rays, which revealed the sum of rays derived from an object and the dynamic and simultaneous transmission of light. The movement was promoted in Western Europe throughout 1913 and 1914 and was taken up zealously in Rome during 1917, but it failed to survive the upheavals of war. Its main protagonist, Larionov, moved to France to concentrate on stage designs for the Ballets Russes.

Natalia Goncharova, Lady with Hat, *1913. Musée National d'Art Moderne, Paris.*

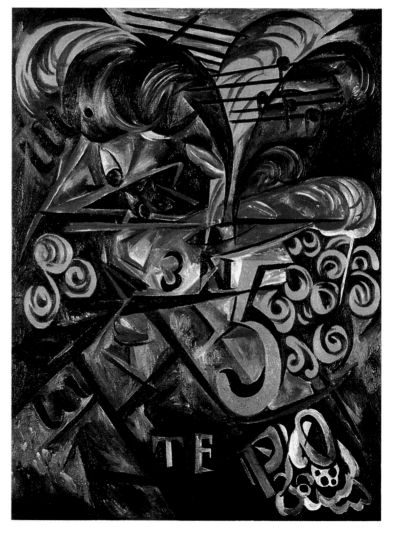

THE STAGE DESIGNERS OF THE BALLETS RUSSES

Russian art had previously been considered barbarous and primitive by a sophisticated western European public, but its national folklore aroused great interest when works were shown at the Paris Exposition of 1900. Seizing every opportunity to promote Russian art, Serge Diaghilev (1872–1929) organized the exhibition *Two Centuries of Painting and Sculpture* in 1906 and brought the music of Rimsky-Korsakov, Mussorgsky, and Borodin to Paris in 1907. Diaghilev staged *Boris Godunov*

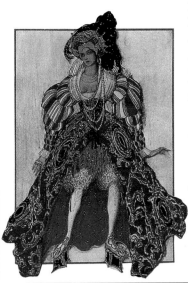

Léon Bakst, The Wife of Potiphar, *costume sketch for* La Légende de Joseph *by Richard Strauss based on the story by Hofmannsthal, 1914. This is taken from the program of the Ballets Russes at the Theatre Royal, Drury Lane, London. Typical traits of Bakst, who worked in a climate of French Symbolism, are his rich color range and his ability to express the precise nature of a character through a costume sketch.*

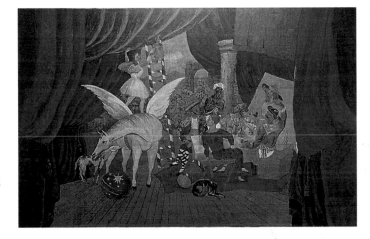

Pablo Picasso, drop curtain for Parade, *1917. Musée National d'Art Moderne, Paris.*

in 1908, with sets and costumes by Golovine, Yuon, and Alexander Benois, and he launched the Ballets Russes in the following year. Together with choreographer Fokine and stage designer Léon Bakst (1866–1924), he revolutionized the concept of dance (which for him was the finest art, being a synthesis of all the others), and introduced a new approach to ballet production. Bakst's settings

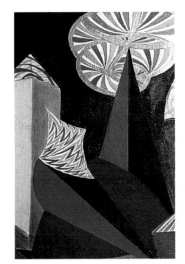

Giacomo Balla, sketch for Stravinsky's Fireworks, *1915. Museo Teatrale, Milan. Balla was a founder of the Futurist movement (this sketch bears his characteristic signature of this period, "FuturBalla") and was one of the first to move toward abstract art through his innovative use of light and motion.*

used intense, vibrant colors and exotic, elaborate costumes, while his stage designs for *L'après-midi d'un faune* and *Daphnis et Chloé* were legendary. The Ballets Russes moved to Monte Carlo in 1912, having become an independent company. Gradually, it moved away from the Russian national tradition, leaving room for various avant-garde artists to contribute ideas. Diaghilev chose his stage designers for their talent and ability to enhance music and movement. Many other artists worked for the ballet company, including Goncharova, Larionov, and Picasso, who in 1917 designed Cubist scenery for *Parade*, written by Cocteau, with music by Satie and choreography by Massine. Derain, Matisse, Ernst, Miró, Utrillo, Gabo, and Pevsner collaborated on an original stage design in transparent plastic for *La Chatte* in 1927, while de Chirico and Rouault designed sets in the company's last year of existence.

The works shown by Kasimir Malevich (1878–1935) at "0.10. The Last Futurist Exhibition," held in St. Petersburg in 1915, represented an important move toward nonrepresentational art. He had sought to "liberate art from the dead weight of objectivity" in 1913 by painting a single black square on a white ground, the sole content of which was "the sensitivity of nonobjectivity."

The aim of this new movement, which Malevich named Suprematism, was to express the absolute supremacy of sensitivity in the creative arts. The goals of his manifesto, produced in collaboration with the poet Maiakovsky, were to liberate painting from the shackles of naturalistic or

symbolic references; to divest it of any practical purpose; and to ensure that it existed only as pure aesthetic sensibility. This involved the composition of elementary geometric shapes, usually squares, which were initially painted black but were later produced in several colors. The quest for purity and immateriality of form reached its logical conclusion in 1918 with a white square on a white ground.

Vladimir Tatlin (1885–1953) exhibited at the St. Petersburg shows held in 1915 and was a pupil of Larionov. His work evolved from the Neo-Primitive style toward more abstract compositions. His stormy friendship with Malevich ended when theoretical disagreements

arose between them in 1917. Malevich continued to reject any connection between the "pure plastic sensibility" of art and the problems of practical

life, whereas the Constructivists, led by Tatlin, held that art had to abandon individual aesthetic stances if it was to help emancipate modern society.

El Lissitzky, Proun 19D, c.1922. Museum of Modern Art, New York. Lissitzky often used his art for political ends as socialist propaganda. Influenced by the ideas of Malevich, he developed the concept of PROUN ("Proekt Utverzdenija Novogo" or "Projects to Promote New Art"). He used the abbreviation, sometimes with a number and/or letter, for the titles of his subsequent works.

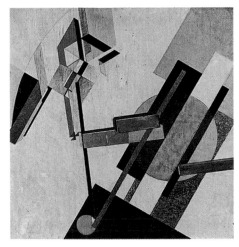

ROBERT DELAUNAY AND ORPHISM

Coined by Guillaume Apollinaire in an article for *Der Sturm* in February 1913, the term "Orphism" was applied to various individual artists. Derived from Orpheus – the name of the mythical poet and musician who could move inanimate objects by his music – it was used to describe a variant of Cubism specifically concerned with color, its dynamism, and its irrational and mystical-spiritual

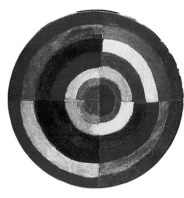

Robert Delaunay, Premier disque simultané, 1912. Burton-Tremaine Collection, Meridien.

implications. Certain painters, including Léger, Picabia, Duchamp, Kandinsky, and the Italian Futurists, had refused to accept the rules of orthodox Analytical Cubism and were described by Apollinaire, somewhat arbitrarily, as "Orphic." He did, however, recognize Robert Delaunay and his wife Sonia Delaunay (née Terk, 1885–1979) as the most significant exponents of this new artistic language, which depicted the object exclusively in terms of planes and color rhythms.

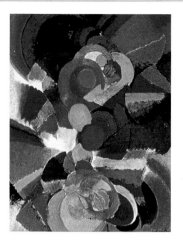

Stanton MacDonald Wright, Abstraction on Spectrum, 1914. Des Moines Art Center, Iowa.

By 1912, after his earlier Cubist and Neo-Impressionist style (typified by *Saint Séverin*, 1909–10, and *La Tour Eiffel*, 1909–11), with its fragmentation, curvilinear distortions, refracted planes, and circles of light, Delaunay moved on to his *Windows* series. He described this as being composed solely of pure color and of color contrasts that developed in time yet were perceived as simultaneous. His *Premier disque simultané* shows a wheel (symbolizing contemporary civilization as well as cosmic energy) of colors in juxtaposition, following a scheme of complementary colors. He pursued an effect of dynamism that had resonances of Futurist theories – it was no coincidence that in April 1913 Boccioni accused the Orphists of plagiarism. Morgan Russell and Stanton MacDonald Wright, two American painters living in Paris, based their theories of Synchronism (which sought new expressive potential in color through "simultaneity") on Delaunay's work.

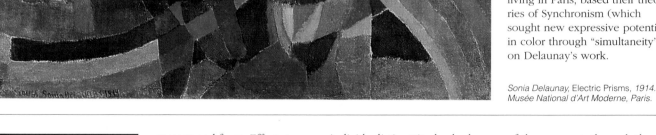

Sonia Delaunay, Electric Prisms, 1914. Musée National d'Art Moderne, Paris.

DADAISM

The upheavals that took place in the art world prior to the outbreak of World War I shared a determination to give the aesthetic message new

content and form. Efforts to achieve this exploited hitherto unexplored methods and techniques. The rupture with tradition and the past was sometimes violent and provocative, and excessively intellectualized and

individualistic attitudes had undermined the message that artists sought to convey to the spectator. However, the value of aesthetic endeavor had never been questioned. No one had refuted the need for art that could be an expression

of the moment, through the rational analysis of structure or the interpretation of rhythms and shades of color.
In spite of earnest experimentation and an eagerness among artists to expound theories, a reaction of radical

denial soon set in. This took the form of a rejection of all artistic creation and culture and of all coherent and rational communication, as if the outbreak of such a dreadful war, the impoverishment of moral values, and the decay of humankind that it revealed made any attempt at communication futile and untimely. The term "Dada," first used in Zurich in 1916, came to stand for a movement inspired by the profane, nihilistic attitudes of artists who rejected the concept of the "creation of a work of art." Instead, banal, everyday objects, bereft of any intrinsic aesthetic value, were adopted for their allusive, symbolic, and conceptual resonances. Works were often dependent upon the artist's choice of a title that exploited double meanings and humorous ambiguities. Dadaists were not interested in formal plastic qualities, preferring to concentrate on a controversial and

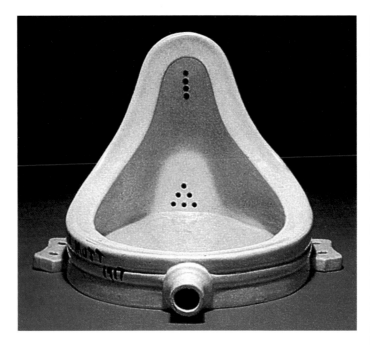

Marcel Duchamp, Fountain. *Galleria Schwarz, Milan. Replica (1964) of the lost original (1917). Dadaists rejected anything conventional. Here, Duchamp gives an all too familiar object the status of a work of art, proving that the value of the subject merely depends on the whim of the artist.*

provocative action that displaced and decontextualized an object, endowing it with multiple meanings. These were the aims of Marcel Duchamp, who proved to be the most interesting and intellectual of all the exponents of Dadaism. Although his early works anticipated and inspired American Dadaism, Duchamp was never recognized as one of the movement's founders. Some of his earliest "ready-made" works such as the *Bottle-Rack* (1914) were bereft of any intervention on the part of the artist, while others were "assisted"; for example, his *Bicycle Wheel* (1913) was fixed to a stool, or *Mona Lisa* (1919), which was adorned with a little goatee beard, a moustache, and a provocative, cryptic caption. His notorious *Fountain* was shown in New York in 1917. While Duchamp was laying the foundations of Conceptual art in Europe and the US, a group of war exiles who had taken refuge in Zürich launched Dadaism in the Cabaret Voltaire, a club opened by a versatile German, Hugo Ball. The movement's manifesto

DADAISM IN THE US

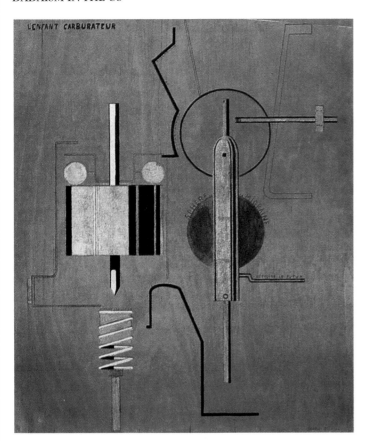

Francis Picabia, L'enfant carburateur, *1919. Solomon R. Guggenheim Museum, New York.*

Marcel Duchamp and Francis Picabia were instrumental in the success of Dadaism in the US. They took part in the 1913 Armory Show in New York (Duchamp exhibited his *Nude Descending a Staircase*), which provided the first important opportunity for a comparison and exchange of ideas between European and North American avant-garde artists. Duchamp and Picabia were fascinated by the level of industrialization and mechanization in the US. Duchamp interpreted these themes in his ready-made works, while Picabia translated them onto canvas in his "mecanomorphic" pictures. On their return visit to the US from 1915 to 1918, they contributed to the *291* review (which Picabia later emulated in Barcelona under the title *391*) and participated in exhibitions at the *291* gallery, which was founded by the photographer and dealer Alfred

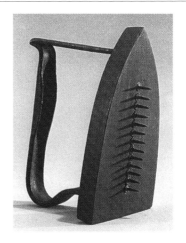

Man Ray, Gift, *1921. Private Collection, Chicago.*

Stieglitz. Here, they were joined by the ingenious Man Ray, a great experimenter with new artistic materials and the ironic and caustic creator of paradoxical objects, which were unmistakably of Dadaist inspiration. Together with Duchamp and Katherine Dreier, Man Ray founded the *Société Anonyme,* the first permanent exhibition devoted to avant-garde art.

MAN RAY: "RAYOGRAPH"

1922; image developed on photographic paper.

With the "rayograph," Man Ray (1890–1976) was able to obtain direct prints on sensitized paper, similar to that used for photographic prints, without using a camera, photosensitive film, or any of the equipment usually needed for printing a negative onto paper as a positive. After placing an odd assortment of objects (or "subjects") on paper that had been treated with silver nitrate, Man Ray used a light to project their outlines onto the paper. In this rayograph, a number of rolled-up and tangled films can be seen, together with the silhouette of a penknife. A photographer, sculptor, draftsman, and painter, Man Ray first came into contact with European avant-garde artists at the Armory Show held in New York in 1913. By the 1920s, other Dadaist artists, including Marcel Duchamp, were working with photography and experimental movies. Other important contemporary artists to explore the use of photographic methods were László Moholy-Nagy (1895–1946), who experimented with new materials and techniques in accordance with the methodology of the Bauhaus, and the painter Hans Richter (1888–1976).

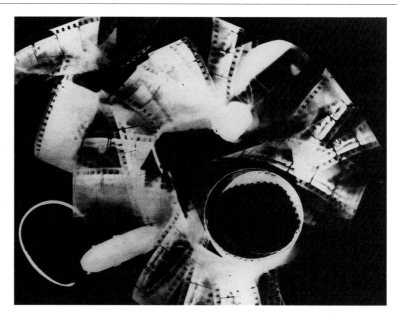

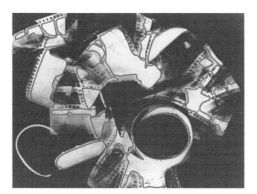

▼ *2. Although Man Ray used neither color nor familiar art materials such as paint, his works were nevertheless produced by a method equivalent to the process of painting rather than photography, and thus in definition approach the character of still-life painting. Whereas painters begin with an idea, select objects, and then create a painting, photographers select an image and capture it. Copies can be made from the negative and may differ through the use of various techniques. Man Ray created just one original photographic impression, selecting and arranging a subject on paper to achieve a desired effect. His composition is a spiral, stemming from the spiral created by the unwinding roll of film.*

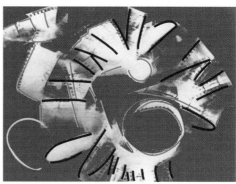

▲ *1. The photosensitive paper has produced a negative image. Originally white, it has darkened in the parts exposed to the light. Those parts that are still white have been shielded from the light by the objects placed on the paper. The black sections have been exposed to direct light, and the gray parts, where objects vary in transparency, have been exposed to filtered light. The finished rayograph shows white and gray shapes on a black background. This was a process of partial abstraction (inasmuch as the finished rayograph bears little resemblance to the original appearance of the objects) and, at the same time, transformation of the original image (inasmuch as the original image is reversed in terms of light and shadow).*

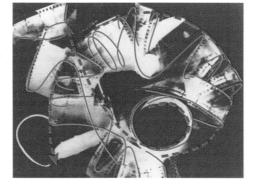

▲ *3. The image is dynamic and encourages the eye to follow the swirls of the snailshell shape formed by the roll of film, which unwinds across the composition. The curves express a smooth, flowing movement. It appears to be a movie film, since the frames are set sideways along the length of the roll. The subject is therefore representing itself: the dynamic medium of the movies, or "photography in movement," becomes movement in the film photographed. These equivocal interpretations of the technical identity of an object and an identity chosen by the artist were a fundamental part of Dadaist poetics. In this case, Man Ray has made deliberate and particular use of the technical process to create ambivalence in his work.*

(published in 1918 by Tristan Tzara) promoted ideology above artistic content and stated that Dadaism should have no meaning whatsoever. Among the founding members were Hans Arp, Marcel Janco, and Richard Huelsenbeck, who were joined in 1918 by Francis Picabia (1879–1953), founder of the Spanish Dadaist movement. When Huelsenbeck returned to Berlin in 1917 and joined forces with George Grosz, Otto Dix (1891–1969), Raoul Hausmann (1886–1971), and John Heartfield (1891–1968), Dadaism also spread through Germany. There, it became recognizably controversial since most of the Dadaists belonged to the League of Spartacus, a radical socialist group that became the German Communist Party in 1919. It found expression in collages and photomontages that violently denounced certain aspects of society. The collaboration between Jean Arp and Max Ernst (1891–1976) in Cologne produced some of Dadaism's most interesting figurative works, including "frottages," created by shading over the texture of an object in order to reproduce its surface image in the form of a rubbing.

JEAN ARP

After training in Weimar and Paris, Jean Arp (1887–1966) moved to Switzerland. He was associated with the Blaue Reiter, early abstract painters, Dadaists, and the De Stijl group, and was a founding member of the Abstraction-Création association of artists. He is best known for his sculptures of the 1930s: large, organic, mainly nonfigurative forms and monumental works often in "anonymous" materials such as cement.

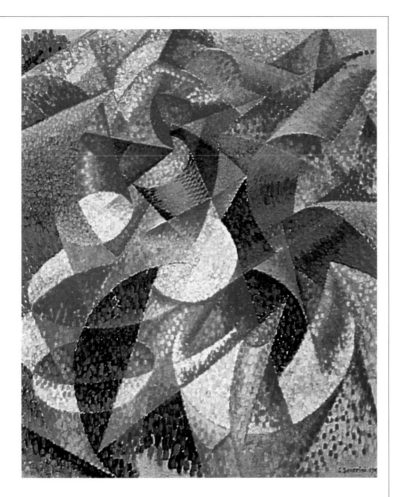

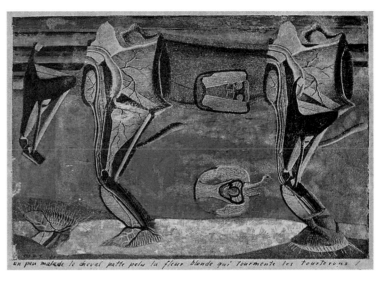

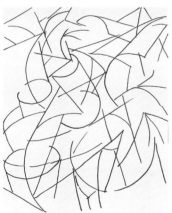

Max Ernst, He's Not Very Well, the Hairy-Hoofed Horse, *1920. Civica Galleria d'Arte Moderna, Turin. Here, Ernst brings the alienating technique of de Chirico to a collage, mixing up and distorting its constituent parts.*

Raoul Hausmann, Tatlin at Home, *1920. Moderna Museet, Stockholm. This Austrian painter made theoretical and artistic use of the new technique of photomontage.*

◀▲ *4. An analagous work can be found in* Sea=Dancer *(1914, Guggenheim Foundation, Venice) by Gino Severini (1883–1966). This Futurist painting is one of a group known as the* Plastic Analogies, *synaesthetic figurative inventions undoubtedly inspired by Marinetti's "literary analogies," and the abstract patterns of music and dance.* Sea=Dancer *brings together the abstract equivalents of two different realities. As Severini explained: "the sea with its dance on the spot, its zigzag movements and scintillating contrasts of silver and emerald, in my plastic sensibility evokes the far-off vision of a dancer covered with sparkling paillettes in her surroundings of light, noises, and sounds."*

GEORGE GROSZ

In 1925, George Grosz (1893–1959) and Otto Dix founded Neue Sachlichkeit (New Objectivity). A popular 20th-century German artist, Grosz experimented with avant-garde techniques. He evolved an elegant and incisive style of portraying anonymous figures that represented the moral decadence of the rich middle-classes at the time of the Weimar Republic in Germany. His collections of drawings have earned him international renown.

Meanwhile, Kurt Schwitters (1887–1948), a lone Dadaist in Hanover, recycled an enormous variety of discarded items for his *Merz* pictures – taken from *kommerz* meaning commerce – which denounced the commercialization of avant-garde art.

During the years immediately after the war, Paris was the focal point of Dadaism. In the movement's last phase,

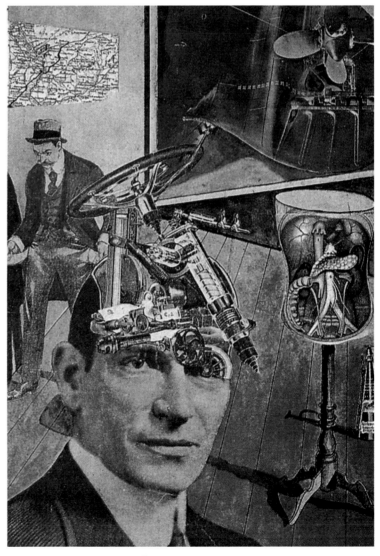

COLLAGE, READY-MADES, AND PHOTOMONTAGE

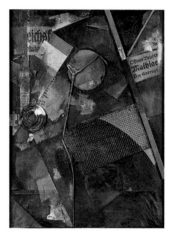

The introduction of new materials into works of art was initiated by the Cubists. Every-day objects were combined with *trompe l'oeil* paintings of objects in their collages and *papiers collés*, used chromatically or metaphorically to give the painting greater reality and spatial autonomy. For his Futurist works *Fusion of a Head and a Window* and *Head + House + Light,* Boccioni used hair, part of a window, and even an iron railing. In answer to Giovanni Papini's criticisms in 1914, he stated that it was

Pablo Picasso, Guitar, Newspaper, Glass, and Bottle, *1913. Tate Gallery, London.*

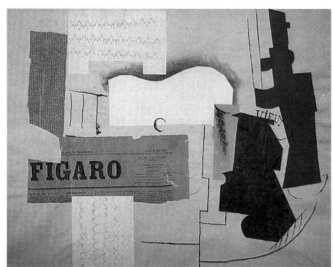

vital to replace imitation with reality in order to increase expressive potential. The Dadaists experimented endlessly with heterogenous materials, either as an expression of admiration for modern technology or as a rejection of industrialized society. Ready-mades were banal objects elevated to works of art through their selection by the artist. Schwitters' *assemblages* were made with discarded items, while Heartfield and Grosz used old photographs and newspapers for their photomontages.

Kurt Schwitters (1887–1948), Merz 25, *1920. Kunstsammlung Nordrhein-Westfalen, Düsseldorf.*

John Heartfield (1891–1968), cover for the magazine Der Dada, *no.3, 1919.*

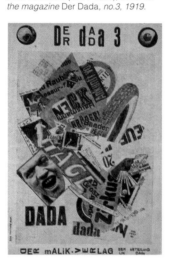

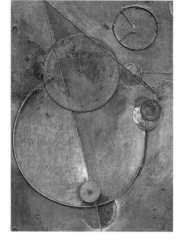

Kurt Schwitters, Revolving, *1919. Museum of Modern Art, New York. In anticipation of Trash Art, Schwitters used bits of rubbish in his collages.*

confrontation grew between Tzara, who remained committed to his nihilistic stance, and André Breton, who took Dadaism as a starting point to develop a new modern movement, which would find expression in Surrealism.

NEO-PLASTICISM

The abstractions of Piet Mondrian (1872–1944) and other Dutch artists of the De Stijl group probably mark the end of the first phase of 20th-century avant-gardism. These artists formed a transitional movement that prepared the ground for the artistic currents of the interwar years: Constructivism, Purism, and late Expressionism. Mondrian coined the name Neo-Plasticism for a new style that his contemporaries and later critics described as an exercise in absolute rationalist rigor, even cerebralism. More recent opinion has stressed the presence of a mystical and irrational content underlying the paintings of the Dutch artists and their theoretical works. In particular, the formal expression characteristic of Symbolism and Cubism in Mondrian's early paintings betrays deep religious and philosophical concerns. It reflects the artist's contact with such thinkers as Schoenmaekers, who explored the relationship between forms and cosmic forces and was familiar with the Romantic

tradition in German culture. Founding his theories on an understanding of the world as one single force governed by mathematical principles of order and harmony, Mondrian believed the role of art was to put the individual in contact with the "universal vibration," to translate inner beauty into free rhythm. He recognized abstraction as the means of expressing the spiritual evolution of humankind. Mondrian, Theo van Doesburg (1883–1931), and a group of painters, sculptors, architects, designers, and poets who had gradually come together – Kok, Richter, Rietveld, Vantongerloo, and Oud –

PURISM

Mechanization inspired many artistic and literary movements of the 20th century, sometimes in admiration and sometimes in firm opposition. The rational, objective, and disciplined aspects of machinery were recognized either as aesthetic precedents or as a threat to all that was beautiful in society. Pure functionality fascinated artists but at the same time puzzled them. Two French artists provided a response to this problematic relationship with the machine age. Under the label of Purism, they expressed their belief in the need for artistic rigor, precision, and impersonality. Both Amédée Ozenfant (1886–1966) and Charles-Édouard Jeanneret (1887–1965), later known as Le Corbusier, wanted a more rational interpretation of Cubism, beyond its literary or symbolic baggage and dynamic or decorative stimuli. Purist theory aimed to restore painting to a primitive purity in which representation would be lucid, self-evident, and geometrical. This ideal of efficiency and essentiality in art could be modeled on the aesthetics of machines and industrial technology, which the two painters recommended as a potential repertory of plastic forms.

modeled their review, *De Stijl,* on the Berlin publication *Der Sturm,* using it as a mouthpiece for the group. Between 1917 and 1918, Mondrian published his long essay *Neo-Plasticism in Painting* which, together with two prefaces by van Doesburg (dated 1917 and 1919) and three manifestos (published in 1918, 1920, and 1921) formed the theoretical basis of Neo-Plasticism. Although Mondrian was the inventor of the movement's stylistic language, it was van Doesburg who tirelessly promoted the movement through contact with avant-garde artists in Europe, from Severini to Lissitzky. Close links had been formed with the Dadaists through another magazine he had launched, *Mecano* (The Hague and Paris, 1922), and with the

Constructivists, with whom he had collaborated on the review *G* (Berlin, 1923–26). He also worked with Arp (on the decoration of the Café L'Aubette in Strasbourg from 1926 to 1928) and alongside members of the Bauhaus. The fundamental aims of the movement (many of which were shared with other avant-garde movements) included the adoption of a universal artistic language; the abolition of individuality on the part of the artists concerned; the identification of art with life (not in terms of the Dada understanding of artistic involvement in life but rather through a conception of life as a pure, internalized activity); and a concentration on all forms of plastic art, from the pure experience of painting to architecture and furniture

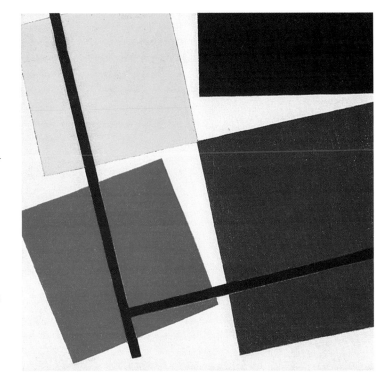

Theo van Doesburg, Simultaneous Counter Composition, *1929–30. Museum of Modern Art, New York.*

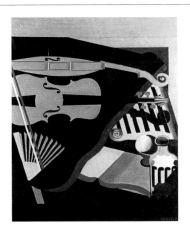

pipes. Clearly delineated against a simple perspective plane, these works adhered to a "general grammar of sensibility" that simplified forms, standardized compositional relationships, and swept away accident and emotivity in favor of a synthesis of lines and chromatic fields. In October 1920, in order to disseminate their purist and rational doctrine, the two artists

in conjunction with the poet Paul Dermée launched a review, *L'Esprit Nouveau,* which was published on a regular basis until 1925. This magazine was probably more effective in making an original contribution to the avant-garde movements in Europe than the rather repetitive and frozen paintings that were being produced by Ozenfant and Le Corbusier.

Amédée Ozenfant, Still Life with Violins, *1919. Musée National d'Art Moderne, Paris.*

Le Corbusier, Pale Still Life with Lantern, *1922. Le Corbusier Foundation, Paris.*

Their main aim was to provide examples of universal values such as order, austerity, and clarity. Other European movements of the time, which were also providing a positive response to the brutality, chaos, and irrationality of war, had much in common with these views. In their manifesto "Après le Cubisme" (published in 1918), Ozenfant and Le Corbusier stated that the greatest joy of the human spirit was the perception of order and the greatest human satisfaction was to be found in helping to bring about, or being part of, this order. Their paintings were almost exclusively still lifes of domestic objects such as jugs, glasses, and

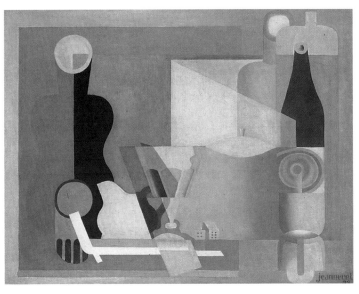

design. The latter was exemplified by Gerrit Rietvald's famous *Red Blue* chair (1918) and the inclusion of influential interior design in the De Stijl exhibition held in Paris in 1923. The Neo-Plasticists were accused of excessive intellectualism in art, of having substituted for emotion the use of pure tones and geometric designs, and of reducing painting to a simple play of colors and ornamental forms. Mondrian's reply was that he had set out to create a free rhythm, like that of jazz, by simple means such as perpendicular lines and primary colors, and sought to impose order on the disorder of the objective world, eliminating any subjective references suggested by curved lines and the emotional use of color. The introduction by van Doesburg of the diagonal line, a dynamic element which, according to Mondrian, destroyed the equilibrium of the composition, caused the two painters to sever contact. By 1924, Neo-Plasticism had run its course.

PIET MONDRIAN

Mondrian's progression toward Neo-Plasticism started during a prolonged stay in Paris from 1911 to 1914, which coincided with the advent of Cubism, a form of art that he credited with having "broken limited form" and liberated the rhythm imprisoned within it. At this time, Mondrian was influenced by the Theosophical Society of Blavatsky and the philosopher Schoenmaekers. He also studied Fiedler's "purovisibilist" theories and principles of harmony and clarity. He was gradually drawn

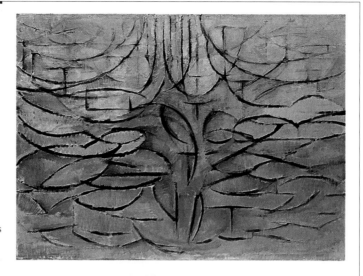

Piet Mondrian, Apple Tree in Blossom, *1912. Gemeentemuseum, The Hague.*

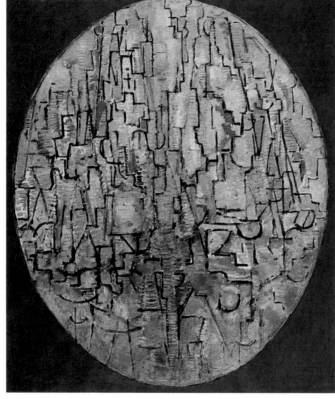

Piet Mondrian, Oval Composition, *1913. Stedelijk Museum, Amsterdam.*

toward an objective stance, divesting his work of any naturalistic reference, reducing his art to stylization, eliminating all individualistic touches and excluding curvilinear and diagonal elements. Mondrian constantly reinterpreted the theme of the tree, a symbol of the link between the real (the earth into which the roots grow) and the spiritual (space, toward which the branches stretch). Between 1914 and 1918 he experimented with ovals (favored by the Cubists), lozenges, and rectangles – while working toward what would be his typical structures, articulated by assymetry; then checks; and finally, in his *Compositions,* by primary colors.

value. To this end, Gropius advocated very high teaching standards for the school. Among the subjects covered were the theory of color and vision and the psychology of form. Pupils were trained in various crafts and were encouraged to experiment with the latest developments. They were also required to master a wide range of technical disciplines. Members of various avant-garde movements were invited to teach at the Bauhaus. These included the painters Johannes Itten and Lyonel Feininger; ceramics expert Gerhard

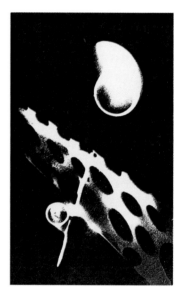

László Moholy-Nagy, picture obtained without the use of a camera, as part of the optical experiments of the Bauhaus, 1923.

László Moholy-Nagy, cover of Gropius Bauhaus Bauten Dessau, *Munich, Albert Langen, 1930. Bauhaus Archives, Berlin. Exiled to the US, Moholy-Nagy formed the New Bauhaus in Chicago.*

THE BAUHAUS

The Bauhaus school was founded in Weimar in 1919 by Walter Gropius (1883–1969), an architect who felt that it was his duty to be involved in the community. Eager to share his conviction that there was no need for a conflict of interests to arise between art and technology, Gropius wanted members of

the Bauhaus school to undertake constructive action that would create a new visual environment for the benefit of society.
Following in the footsteps of William Morris, Henry van de Velde, and the Deutscher Werkbund, the Bauhaus aimed to achieve a synthesis of art, craftsmanship, and industry that would satisfy society's needs, creating mass-market products of high aesthetic

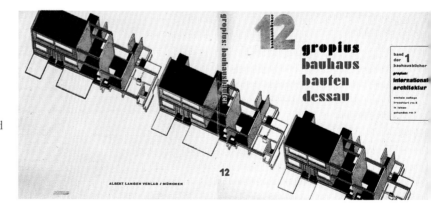

Marcks; stage designer and sculptor Oskar Schlemmer; tapestry designer Georg Muche; and László Moholy-Nagy, a fervent supporter of "applied art," who specialized in metalwork and the artistic use of photography. The impressive caliber of these lecturers made the desired high standards of quality, beauty, and originality more achievable. Moreover, it allowed for concrete expression of the creative potential and imaginative strength of some outstanding contemporary artists. Each artist was entrusted with the task of passing on his or her own personal aesthetic vision, teaching in a clear and lucid manner, in order to build up the school's collective experience of skill and experimentation. The most significant and fundamental contributions to the Bauhaus were made by Paul Klee and Wassily Kandinsky (1866–1944), whose outstanding lectures on theory were published, respectively, in *Pedagogical Sketchbook* (1925) and *Point and Line to Plane* (1926). In these works, the question of space and the sensual and emotional value of colors and forms were explored in a scholarly manner, yet without sacrificing poetic communication or the spiritual and emotional appeal necessary to interpret new meanings in the world of natural forms.

Accused of being a "hotbed of Bolshevism," the Bauhaus closed its doors in the spring of 1925. It reopened in Dessau, occupying a building that was designed by Gropius, and later moved to Berlin. The architect Ludwig Mies van der Rohe (1886–1969) took over as director in 1928, but five years later the school was closed down by Hitler's National Socialist government. Paradoxically, the school's enforced closure enhanced the international influence of the Bauhaus, since many of its masters and pupils left Germany and spread its ideas farther afield, especially in the US, where Moholy-Nagy founded the New Bauhaus in Chicago in 1937. The methodical approach taught by the Bauhaus had a unique influence on subsequent generations. Its example set a powerful precedent for every aspect of aesthetic research conducted according to rational principles.

PAUL KLEE

Paul Klee (1879–1940) had a multifaceted artistic personality, reflecting a broad spectrum of interests and aptitudes that ranged from romantic sensibility to theoretical lucidity. He was in temporary allegiance to various avant-garde movements without adhering to any one tendency. The constant, central theme of Klee's long and varied career as a painter was the analysis of artistic language. His interest lay in discovering a truly expressive medium that would draw (from past and contemporary experiences) those aspects that could most readily be communicated and that could express cosmic totality. Klee's parents and wife were all musicians, and he spent several years pursuing a musical career. His devotion to painting sprang from a visit to Italy early in the century, where Leonardo da Vinci's works made a lasting impression on him. He settled in Munich and made contact with the Blaue Reiter artists, sharing their interest in children's drawing and in non-European cultures that provided stimuli and suggestions for a new, primordial vocabulary of images and signs. For Klee, what children or primitive peoples saw, or the forms that derived from what they saw, were very important insights. Through Delaunay's theories (Klee had translated and published his essay "De la lumière" in *Der Sturm* in 1913) he had discovered the imaginative power, rhythm, and dynamism of contrasting colors. Klee accompanied Macke on a visit to Tunisia in Easter 1914. Overwhelmed by the color of the Mediterranean countryside, he wrote, "color and I are both one: I am a painter." His starting point was always the natural world ("the object of painting is the world, even if it is not this visible world"), which prompted Klee to organize the two-dimensional space of his pictures in free geometric shapes and in areas of brilliant color, which actually refer to reality through mere hints of poetic association. Following the turmoil of World War I, Klee created a new

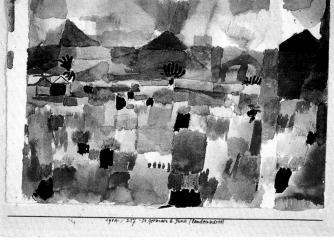

Paul Klee, Saint Germain Near Tunis, *1914. Musée National d'Art Moderne, Paris.*

iconography that combined elements of a figurative language (including the sun, stars, arrows, and birds) with geometric forms in a "pictographic" writing that unified content and image, poetry and painting. It was during this period that Klee was invited to the Bauhaus in Weimar, where he taught from 1920 to 1929. The artist encouraged his students to transform the unreal into the real, the irrational into the rational, and to portray that which exists only in the emotions in graphic terms. These were also the years in which Klee painted his series of "magic

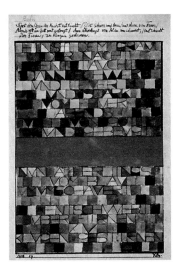

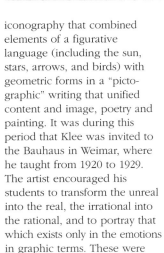

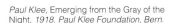

Paul Klee, Emerging from the Gray of the Night, *1918. Paul Klee Foundation, Bern.*

squares." These works were confined exclusively to the expression of color relationships and harmonic rhythms, echoing Schoenberg's polyphonies of the same period. They are based on mathematical schemas, in which the series of numbers found in the division of the canvas produce the same total in a horizontal or a vertical direction, mimicking the "magic square" from which they took their name.

Klee was a versatile and profilic artist, his complete output estimated at almost 8,000 works. In both his art and his teaching, he had an important influence on the art of the 20th century.

WASSILY KANDINSKY: "PAINTING WITH THE BLACK ARCH"

1912; oil on canvas; 46½ x 78 in (118 x 198 cm); Musée National d'Art Moderne, Paris.

Kandinsky's complex international artistic and theoretical formation led him to produce his first purely abstract works in about 1910. His earlier law studies, which had developed his ability to argue and distinguish, provided him with a sound theoretical foundation. He worked in watercolor with particular skill and had a strong, expressive drive. *Painting with the Black Arch* presents forms that cannot be related to objective reality. It consists of three large patches of modulated color, worked upon and interconnected by frequently

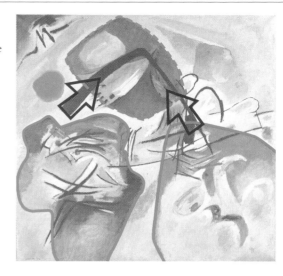

intersecting black linear features. All this stands out against a very pale, partly white background. Presenting his own view of the work, Kandinsky proudly wrote: "it was the first to place painting on the level of purely pictorial expressive means and to eliminate objective elements from the image." He was concerned with extracting the essential qualities of artistic materials, rather than creating an abstraction from natural appearances. A forerunner of expressive abstraction, he was nevertheless a master of composition. His unique organization of picture space – abandoning geometrical perspective and representation in favor of the expressive qualities of color and form – has informed many subsequent generations of artists.

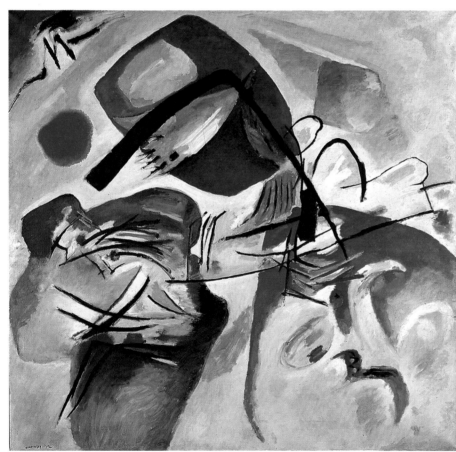

▼ *1. At first sight, the composition appears simple: the two areas of primary color (red and blue) at the bottom are partly aligned, linked by a black arch superimposed on a secondary color of purplish red in the upper half of the canvas. The two primary colors blue and red merge to form purple, a secondary color. The key compositional elements of the painting seem to be enclosed within a circle. The addition of an equilateral triangle, with one side parallel with the bottom edge of the canvas shows how the three corners are, in different and harmonious measure, pervaded by the three main colors. Each of the four surfaces between the curves of the circle and the corners of the canvas is treated very differently.*

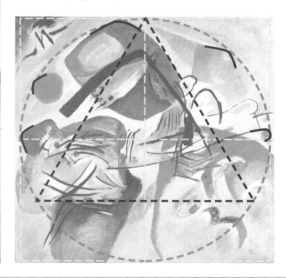

RUSSIAN AVANT-GARDE MOVEMENTS

After the Bolshevik revolution and World War I, a new artistic trend emerged in Europe. Unlike Dadaism's nihilistic stance, the aesthetic individualism of Suprematism, or Mondrian's abstract mysticism, which rejected all political and social value for art, this new movement stressed the need for artists to become actively involved in reshaping society. It declared that the combined forces of art, craftsmanship, and industry could help build a better world. In post-Tsarist Russia, the first Commissar of Education, Anatoly Lunacharsky, was broadly sympathetic toward modern artistic movements and permitted avant-garde artists to play a role in cultural activity and teaching. Considered useful to society, art was expected to concentrate on architecture, the design of manifestos and household objects, and printing. Known as Constructivism, this movement sought to put these revolutionary aims and ideals into practice. It rejected any creativity that did not have a purpose and categorized it as a specific, purely aesthetic activity. From 1915 to 1916, Tatlin (1885–1953) and

◀ *2. For Kandinsky, form was the external expression of inner content. He attributed opposing features to the colors blue and red. Blue, which is centripetal, recedes and is deep and cold; if light, it can be reminiscent of the sky, or, if darker, of the night and the sea. It develops "the element of tranquility," inviting humankind toward the infinite. Red, in contrast, is centrifugal, highly dynamic, and stands out; it recalls fire and blood and is direct. In the center, above them, purplish red achieves a balancing effect: the blue and the red join together and give rise to a different expression, which is suspended between sky and life.*

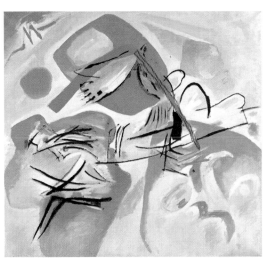

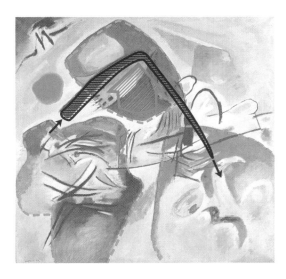

▲ *4. The arch dominates almost all the other, minor black forms, which seem to refer to it and draw on its strength in order to exist. The mass of linear strokes below the arch appear to condense into an image of a knight on horseback. The painting was created in 1912, the same year in which Kandinsky cofounded the artistic move-ment, Der Blaue Reiter ("The Blue Rider"). The image of the horse jutting out of the blue toward the red area, and the heads of the man and horse already projecting beyond the purple and the red, can be interpreted as metaphors of the picture content and what is occurring within it.*

▲ *3. The black arch forms the dynamic link between the two opposing colors and illustrates the route that form takes through color to achieve synthesis. For Kandinsky, black represented the total silencing of color and light, so the arch can be regarded as the annihilation of contrast. Any analysis of 20th-century art requires participation in the artist's mental process. The black arch starts from a hollow above the blue area, which formally generates it, and hits, rather like an arrow or a boomerang, the heart of the red area. It is in the purplish red area that the force of the arch, moving upward and outward, deflects itself in order to descend toward the red area and dissolve.*

▶ *5. For Kandinsky, a painting was a "world" made up of many small parts, each with its own reason to exist within the aesthetic whole. In this work, each area of color holds the universe of color and form: for example, the blue area contains shades of yellow, red, and green, and dots, corners, curves, and right angles. In The Bare Canvas, the artist wrote: "Each line says, here I am! Listen to my secret! A line is full of marvel. A tiny dot, several tiny dots, which become smaller and smaller in one place, larger and larger in another...lots of small tensions which incessantly repeat together: listen to me! but here is the greatest marvel of all: summing up all these voices...within just one painting – the entire canvas has become a single 'Here I am!'"*

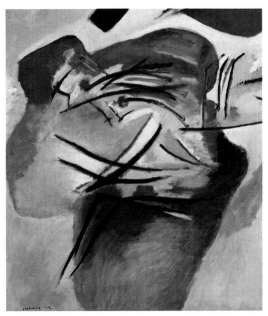

Up with technology! Down with tradition! Up with Constructivist technical progress!" The art produced by Moscow artists who had emigrated, many of them before World War I, was much more in tune with international movements. Artists such as Larionov, Sonia Delaunay, Goncharova, Chagall, and Soutine settled in Paris, where they found the artistic climate more congenial than in their native country.

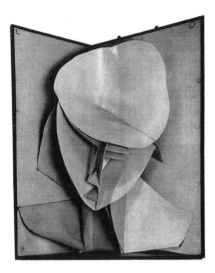

Naum Gabo, Head of a Woman, celluloid and metal, 1917–20. Museum of Modern Art, New York. Sculptors of the avant-garde movements proposed the adoption of new materials in place of traditional ones, such as stone and bronze, in order to make a break with traditional art and to examine new means of expression. One of Gabo's early works, this piece was produced in a Cubist style with folded surfaces and sharp edges.

Rodchenko (1891–1956) made utensils and household objects in iron, glass, and other industrial materials. They were joined by two brothers, Antoine Pevsner (1886–1962) and Naum Gabo (1890–1977), and the Mayakovsky group, organized by Lev (the Left Front), whose manifesto was published in 1923.

After the first flush of shared enthusiasm among the artists, differences soon emerged over methods and results. Following the subsequent schism in the Constructivist group, Pevsner and Gabo espoused the virtues of realism, which, as expounded in their "Realistic Manifesto" of 1920, supported the absolute value of art and

its independence from the structure of society, be it capitalist or communist. Immediately, Rodchenko and his wife Varvara Stepanova delivered their riposte in the "Program of the Productivist Group," airing extreme utilitarian and "functional" views and ending with the exhortation: "Down with art!

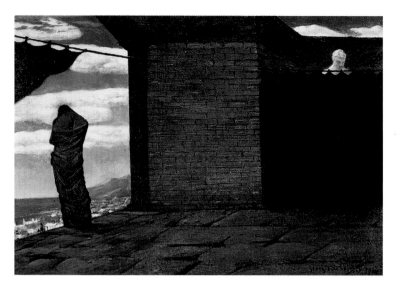

Giorgio de Chirico, Enigma of the Oracle, 1910. Museum of Modern Art, New York.

METAPHYSICAL PAINTING AND VALORI PLASTICI

Giorgio de Chirico (1888–1978) was unimpressed by the avant-garde movements of the years immediately prior to World War I. After leaving his native Greece in 1906, following the death of his father, he studied in Germany. He later moved to Italy, and in 1911, to Paris, where he met Apollinaire. De Chirico was contemptuous of many of the avant-garde painters who he met in France and dismissed the Futurists' contribution to art as worthless.

While in Germany, he was influenced by the work of the Symbolists, and his first mature paintings had a strange, dreamlike quality about them. An admiration for the tradition of the Tuscan school of primitive artists and classic figurative painting was evident in the works of de Chirico and his contemporary Carlo Carrà, with whom he launched a new movement. In the first issue of the group's review *Valori Plastici* (published in 1918), de Chirico called the style Metaphysical Painting. Between 1914 and 1918, the work of de Chirico slowly gained critical recognition in Italy. The artist's work was shown in Paris in 1912 and 1913, and reproductions of his paintings appeared in the American arts magazine *291*, while the originals were shown at the Dada gallery in Zurich. Prior to 1914, the only person to share de Chirico's artistic theories was his brother, Alberto Savinio (1891–1952). He was primarily a writer and musician, who also promoted the work of the poet and Dadaist Tristan Tzara in Italy. Savinio's play, *La chanson de la mi-mort,* which was published by Apollinaire in *Soirées de Paris* in 1913, inspired de Chirico to use mannequins in his painting – disquieting creatures who peopled such

works as *The Philosopher and the Poet* (1914) and *The Seer* (1915). Savinio's "Hermaphrodito" (published by *La Voce* in 1918), a surreal and ambiguous piece, is the literary equivalent of de Chirico's pictorial idiom. In 1917, the two brothers met Carrà, who had already been described as a Metaphysical painter by the art critics Papini and Soffici, and who also seemed to be in search of a link between modern and classical painting. At that time, Carrà sought to escape from Futurism through a new construction of form, hoping

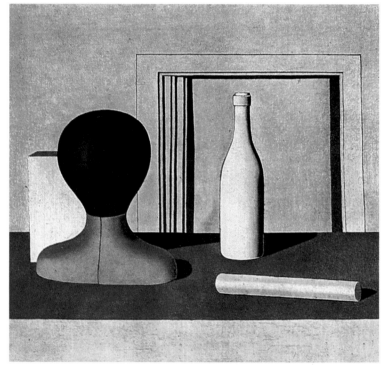

to emulate the Tuscan primitive painters. Sensing that he was on the brink of finding his own, definitive style, his aim was to construct and see shapes anew, and to be "the Giotto of the 20th century". After Boccioni's death in 1916 and Severini's departure for Paris, Carrà was one of the leading artists in Italy, and his

paintings were among the most representative of the quest to recover formal values in art. His earliest Metaphysical paintings were shown at the end of 1917 at the Chini Gallery in Milan. Although sharing the same rarefied immobility as de Chirico's work, Carrà's paintings are less sinister and have a certain mellow, picturesque quality. Carrà explained the theory that underpinned his paintings in *Metaphysical Painting* (published in 1919). The main protagonists of

Giorgio Morandi, Metaphysical Still Life, 1918. Pinacoteca di Brera, Milan.

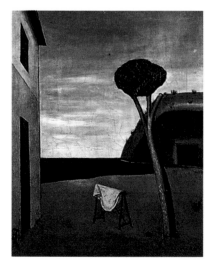

Carlo Carrà, Pine by the Sea, 1921. Casella Collection, Rome. This work marks Carrà's break with the avant-garde. In the climate of a "return to order" of the Valori Plastici, and looking back to Giotto and Masaccio, he moves toward a style that is timeless and uncontroversial, yet bold and poignant.

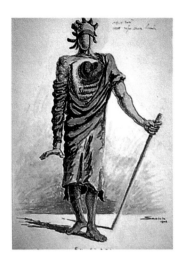

Alberto Savinio, Oedipus Revealed, *sketch for* Oedipus Rex *by Cocteau and Stravinsky, Teatro alla Scala, Milan, 1947–48. Savinio was also the stage designer and chorus master of the production.*

Metaphysical painting were de Chirico and Carrà, but Filippo de Pisis (1896–1956) and Giorgio Morandi were also briefly and peripherally involved. The influence of the style on de Pisis was slight, while Morandi continued to incorporate Metaphysical elements into his work during his long career. He used estrangement and isolation as a means of concentrating and meditating on the plastic and chromatic aspects of reality, rejecting any literary allusion, any sense of mystery, or nostalgia for classical antiquity. After World War I, and with order in Europe apparently restored, the Metaphysical "School" (a misnomer, considering its few, often argumentative members) had run its course. Its successor arose from parallel artistic developments in other parts of Europe where the early 20th-century "renaissance" was taking place, and it made far more general use of formal models in the classical tradition, encapsulating ethical as well as aesthetic values. Derain, Matisse, and Picasso, among others, were subjecting art to close scrutiny and rational evaluation in order to create their own, new and vibrant, classicism.

La Ronda, a literary magazine, and V*alori Plastici,* edited by Mario Broglio and concentrating on the figurative arts, both served as catalysts for idealistic cultural movements in Italy. Published from 1918 to 1921, *Valori Plastici* welcomed theoretical articles and illustrations from contributors who condemned avant-garde experimentalism. Among them were the sculptor Arturo Martini (1889–1947) and the art critic and painter Ardengo Soffici. The review favored a return to classical values and stressed the importance of art as a profession; the European avant-garde movements were criticized for abandoning these principles. Known as the Valori Plastici group, supporters of the review were invited to take part in the exhibition held at Berlin's Nationalgalerie in 1921. Among those who took this opportunity of meeting like-minded German artists from the Magischer Realismus ("Magic Realism") and the Neue Sachlichkeit ("New Objectivity") groups were Carrà, de Chirico, Morandi, and Martini.

GIORGIO MORANDI

Giorgio Morandi (1890–1964) first came to public notice in *Valori Plastici.* A reserved artist, he preferred to work in isolation in his studio in Bologna, exploring and developing his own line of thought in search of poetic purity. Having studied the work of Cézanne, whom he revered highly, Morandi became interested in Futurism. Between 1917 and 1919, he was briefly associated with the Metaphysical School, sharing their admiration of the early 15th-century Italian masters. Certain Metaphysical features are evident in his work from this

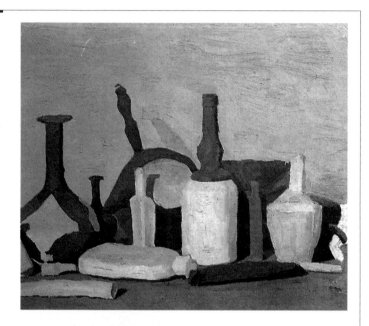

Giorgio Morandi, Still Life with Violet Objects, *1937. Private Collection, Florence.*

period – the formalization of objects and the use of light to make an abstraction of their shapes – which give his pictures the suggestion of a mysterious reality beyond the visible representation. Between 1920 and the late 1930s, Morandi concentrated almost exclusively on still lifes – making bottles, carafes, and fruit bowls the typical iconography of his work. Using subtle, atmospheric combinations of color and a limited tonal range, he imbued his pictures with an intimate serenity. After World War II, he gained international recognition and is widely regarded as one of great still-life artists of the 20th century.

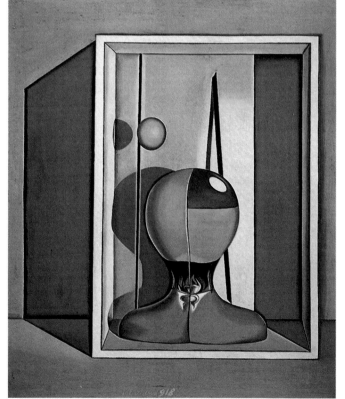

Giorgio Morandi, Still Life, *1918. The State Hermitage Museum, St. Petersburg.*

THE METAPHYSICAL ART OF DE CHIRICO

The typical motifs in de Chirico's work – towers, arcades, statues, and trains – were drawn from nostalgic recollections of his childhood in Greece and later travels in Italy. His love of myth and classical culture made his work very distinctive, executed in an incisive and prominent formal artistic language. De Chirico studied in Munich and admired Böcklin and Klinger's masterly ability to situate mythological scenes in the present, in a rarefied and frozen atmosphere. This meant that when the young artist went to Paris in 1911, he was dismissive of any fragmentation and shattering of form and of the cult of

Alberto Savinio, The Awakening of Carpophage, *1930. Private Collection, Rome.*

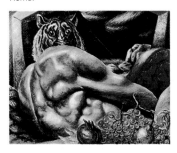

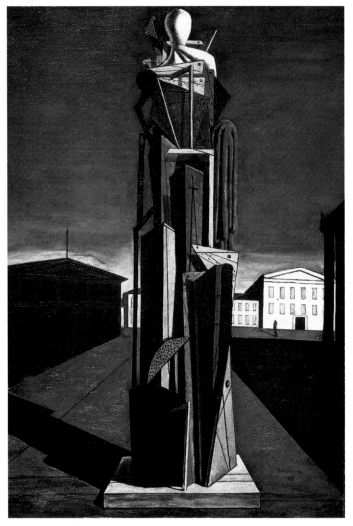

speed and modern technology. His own work was utterly different, portraying scenes with a timeless, motionless atmosphere – deserted squares surrounded by shadowy colonnades, empty and inhospitable buildings, or distant cemeteries. He described his art as "Metaphysical" because it referred to a world beyond the real world. He realized this theory by stripping his subjects of all their usual associations and placing them in new and unusual settings. His paintings had no relation to nature or history, so they did not reveal recognizable details or clues as to their meaning; hence the sense of mystery and disquiet in his works. His strange atmospheres were evoked by the use of dark shadows, anonymous mannequins, the bizarre and alienating juxtaposition of objects, and the enigmatic titles that he chose for the works. This poetic conception of art, "austere and cerebral, ascetic and lyrical," as de Chirico himself described it, was suffused with the philosophy of Nietzsche, who had maintained that art had no logical significance.

Giorgio de Chirico, The Great Metaphysician, *1917. Museum of Modern Art, New York.*

REALISMS

When the Purist artists Ozenfant and Le Corbusier appealed for a "return to order" in art they wished to impose precision on artistic form, constructing works of art with their own calculated equilibrium and intellectual balance, while not ruling out abstract interpretations. Elsewhere in Europe, other artists were also starting to advocate a return to clear and lasting images of real substance. Two discernible trends, which developed simultaneously, pursued this "return to order": one was a geometric style, the other an objective style inspired by naturalism. Evident across Europe was a desire to return to forms that

were immediately recognizable. This change of direction sometimes saw artists explicitly rediscovering their historical roots and national traditions. First seen in the years following World War I, this

trend continued throughout the 1930s, when it was susceptible to exploitation serving the purposes of nationalistic and dictatorial regimes. During the 1920s, two main currents within

avant-garde art often intersected. One strand was the verism of German New Objectivity and Magic Realism,

Otto Dix, The Great City, *triptych, 1927–28. Staatsgalerie, Stuttgart.*

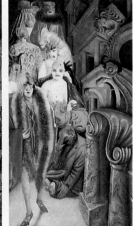

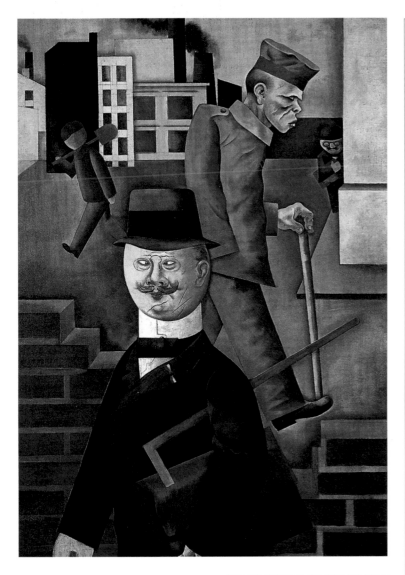

George Grosz, Gray Day, *1921. Nationalgalerie, Berlin.*

MARC CHAGALL

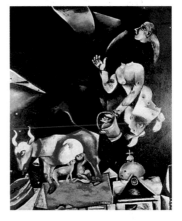

Marc Chagall, To Russia, to Donkeys, and to the Others, *1911–12. Musée National d'Art Moderne, Paris.*

During his long and prolific career, Marc Chagall (1887–1985) drew inspiration from many of the avant-garde experiments, but he did not align himself with any one movement. He was born in a Russian village where Jewish orthodoxy was strictly observed; he later became a pupil of Bakst in St. Petersburg. His interest in Cubism, Futurism, and the color experiments of the Orphists is discernible in his *Self-portrait with Seven Fingers* (1912–13). With the help of Apollinaire, he exhibited at the Der Sturm gallery in Berlin but then returned to Russia in order to support the Revolution. He became involved with the Vitebsk Academy, where he invited members of the Suprematist and Constructivist groups to teach, but the fantasy element in his work was incomprehensible to the Russian authorities and, in 1923, he returned to Paris. His fanciful paintings led André Breton to hail him as one of the precursors of Surrealism in his study *Genèse et Perspectives du Surréalisme* (1941).

Drawn from Russian popular tradition and Jewish ritual, Chagall's iconography makes frequent reference to folklore and his mythical native village where man and beast coexisted peacefully, as well as to the themes of circus and flight. The style of these lyrical compositions, with their vibrant and varied colors, hovers between symbolism, descriptivism, and fable. The racial persecution carried out under Hitler's rule prompted Chagall to deal with more dramatic themes. His *Crucifixion* series, with its dense, dark shades, is highly expressive.

Marc Chagall, Paris through the Window, *1913. Solomon R. Guggenheim Museum, New York.*

and the Italian Novecento group. The works produced by these groups assumed a cold and analytical quality and usually evoked a motionless atmosphere. The second strand was a new form of expressionism that characterized the paintings produced by the "School of Paris" (including Modigliani, Chagall, and Soutine) and which was also apparent in certain works by the German painter Otto Dix and artists of the "Roman School." These works featured strong emotional impulses and violent social tensions, expressed through exaggeration, distortion, and bright colors.

GERMANY

The troubled political and social climate in Germany during the years of the Weimar Republic (1919–33) provoked much critical reevaluation of contemporary art, which, as far as the realms of literature, movies, theater, and the figurative arts were concerned, was still largely expressionist. A progression toward a more rigorous and lucid analysis of reality led to the foundation of the Bauhaus school and of the Frankfurt Institute for Social Research. The move also prompted the director of the Kunsthalle in Mannheim, Gustav Hartlaub, to organize a large exhibition in 1925 under the banner of "New Objectivity". Among the artists

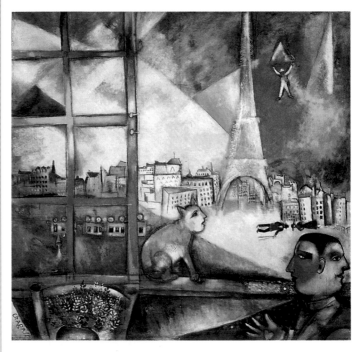

A gifted sculptor, Martini (1889–1947) was influenced by the sculpture of the past as well as by contemporary ideas. His understanding of the meaning and value of the innovative experiments of the avant-garde is revealed in his essay "La scultura, lingua morta" (1945). When young, he was influenced by the work of Adolf Hildebrand and the painter Gino Rossi. His natural talent for modeling in clay and stucco endowed his work with movement and light. His passion for ceramics was demonstrated by his polychrome terracotta works and majolica ware, which inspired Lucio Fontana. His life-size sculptures and monuments, in some cases associated with the Fascist era, reveal his masterly and eclectic control of volume and form and his ability to sculpt any material, including bronze, with an austere inventiveness and expressivity.

who took part were Otto Dix, George Grosz, and Max Beckmann (1884–1950), who had been influenced by Dadaism and had already made themselves unpopular in certain quarters through their denunciation of social in-equalities and corruption. This stance was typified by such works as a set of fifty engravings titled *War* (1923–24) by Dix, and Grosz' collections of satirical drawings, *The Face of the Ruling Class* (1921) and *Ecce Homo* (1927). Other painters, such as Christian Schad, Georg Schrimpf, Georg Scholz, Alexander Kanoldt, and Carlo Mense, also sought to move beyond Expressionism – which they labeled as sentimental and collaborationist. Their aim was art as an objective statement in which rigorous, analytical, and uncompromising draftsman-ship would discipline a measured use of color. Among the favorite subjects of these artists were mercilessly violent erotic scenes, true-to-life portraits, and squalid cityscapes depicting urban alienation. Their subject matter conveyed clear moral judgments and more or less explicit denunciations that, in the changing political climate of the early 1930s, were tolerated less and less.

THE NOVECENTO GROUP

"Magic Realism" was a phrase coined by Franz Roh in a book on Post-Expressionism published in Munich in 1925. What Roh attempted to describe was a tendency that moved toward less ideological art, introducing a suffusion of poetic undertones in an attempt to remove crudeness and harshness. The same phrase was also used by an Italian writer, Massimo Bontempelli, to describe art that rejected reality and cultivated imagination for its own sake, nourished by a sense of the magical discernible in everyday life and objects. This definition provides a key with which to interpret the enchanted atmosphere that permeates the paintings of Antonio Donghi (1897–1963), Cagnaccio di San Pietro, and Riccardo Francalancia.

During the 1920s, there was a tremendous amount of artistic

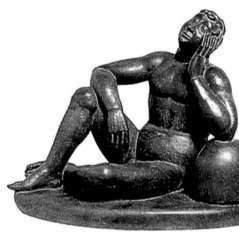

Arturo Martini, The Sleeper, *1921. Private Collection, Monza, Italy. Martini was representative of the avant-garde approach, although never belonging to any particular group. He was asked to write the manifesto of the second Futurist movement in 1920, in which he stressed the need to develop "a wider and more synthetic plastic vision."*

cross-fertilization between Italy and Germany, initiated by the exhibitions of Metaphysical and Valori Plastici paintings in Berlin and Munich. The growing trends all promoted a return to naturalistic portrayal, albeit of a changed and subtly ambiguous character, attempt-ing to convey meanings that went beyond temporal and spatial boundaries. In Italy, the tendency was to harken back to classical or primitive traditions, which were treasured as glories of Italian cultural heritage. Anselmo Bucci (1887–1955) and a group of like-minded artists in Milan formed the Novecento group in 1923. They were determined to promote a new, specifically Italian version of modern artistic styles that were relevant to their own time but mindful of the great masters and schools of painting of bygone ages. In the event, Novecento came to stand for the reactionary style of the late 1920s and 1930s rather than for the achievements of this small group. The term "Novecento" was more commonly used to

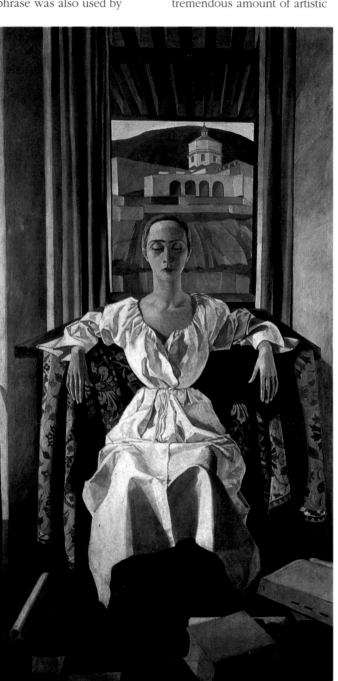

Felice Casorati, Portrait of Silvana Cenni, *1922. Private Collection, Turin, Italy. Typical of Casorati's work at this time, this solemn portrait is set against a meticulously structured background with an artificial perspective.*

THE ROMAN SCHOOL

Several of the artists in Rome who did not take part in the Novecento exhibition of 1929 decided to form an association. Among the members were Scipione (Gino Bonichi, 1904–33), Mario Mafai (1902–65), and his wife Antonietta Raphaël (c.1895–1975), who had worked in Paris with Russian Jewish emigrés such as Soutine and Chagall. The Roman School opposed the weighty classicism of the Novecento and introduced a new style of romantic expressionism. Their works were often hallucinatory and visionary, sometimes surreal, with warm brown and reddish tones and an iconography that drew on Rome's appearance of

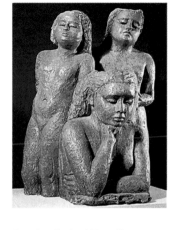

Antonietta Raphaël, Three Sisters, *1936. Galleria d'Arte Moderna, Rome.*

sumptuous decadence. The original trio were later joined by other artists who were opposed to the archaism favored by the authorities: Fausto Pirandello, Marino Mazzacurati, Pericle Fazzini. The writers Libero de Libero and Leonardo Sinisgalli helped found the magazine *Fronte* in 1931, through which the group spread its theories. This project was short-lived and, combined with the early death of Scipione and the frequent absences of Mafai and Raphaël, helped to bring about the demise of the "Roman School" by the early 1930s.

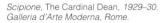
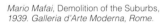

Scipione, The Cardinal Dean, *1929–30. Galleria d'Arte Moderna, Rome.*

Mario Mafai, Demolition of the Suburbs, *1939. Galleria d'Arte Moderna, Rome.*

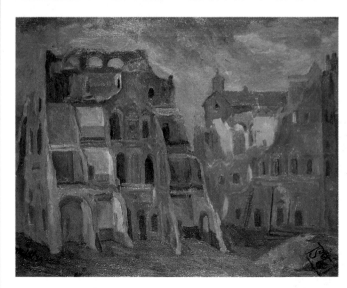

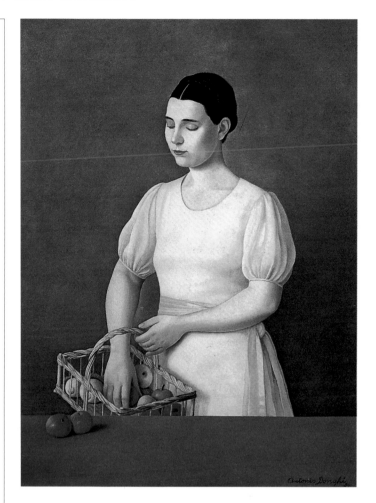

Antonio Donghi, Margherita, *1936. Civico Museo d'Arte Contemporanea, Milan. The light falling on the woman and her static, absorbed state make this apparently everyday portrait somewhat unreal and akin to the style of Magic Realism.*

describe a tendency toward a simplification of form, combined with classical references. Paintings associated with this movement have a monumental quality and are easily understood; they consist of a readily accessible and reassuringly familiar iconography drawn from everyday life and have clear, harmonious forms.

The broad span of styles and number of artists exhibiting at the second Novecento exhibition in November 1929 had grown and diversified, ranging from Futurism to Metaphysical painting and including Carrà, Morandi, Casorati, and Osvaldo Licini (1894–1958), among others. Some of the participating artists were willing to accommodate the propagandist requirements of Mussolini's Fascist government and responded by producing pictures that reflected the regime's ideology, rejecting individualism or any deeply personal themes.

FELICE CASORATI

After studying painting at the academies of Padua, Naples, and Verona, Casorati (1886–1963) exhibited work at the Venice Biennale in 1907. He was a knowledgeable admirer of late 19th-century painting, especially French and German works, but no influence of these paintings or the current avant-garde movements can be seen in his work. A figurative painter, Casorati preferred to elaborate a style of his own, and, like Carrà, diversified into architecture and stage design. His work had a classical flavor to it and a very deliberate use of line and color. He sought to explore spatial values and to convey emotion with mastery and rigor. Described as a "painter of solitude," he earned an international reputation that continues to grow in stature.

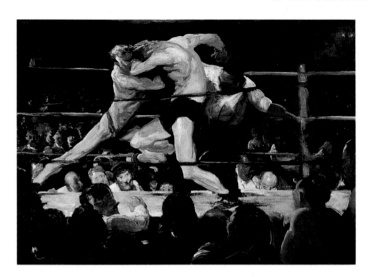

of the European avant-garde movements – which Hopper had encountered while visiting Europe between 1906 and 1910 – incorporating trends from them into their own view of the sociological conditions of their homeland. From the early 1930s onward, they explored the signs and symbols of contemporary reality, expressed in American scenes and architecture, frequently portraying states of loneliness and alienation with almost photographic precision. Bellows' vivid painting of an illegal boxing match, *Stag at Sharkey's,* has been referred to as a landmark of realism. The cold, disenchanted hyper-realism in Hopper's paintings conveys a stance of psychological detachment from the reality depicted. It contrasts starkly with the figurative style and warmth of emotional engagement that characterize the work of artists, such as José Orozco (1883–1949), Diego

Rivera (1886–1957), and David Alfaro Siqueiros (1898–1974). Rivera and Siqueiros looked to the Mayan and Aztec civilizations for a means of strong and immediate communication with their fellow countrymen. They recognized the potential of large murals painted in public places. Monumental and heroic in scale and explicit in nature, they were an effective means of disseminating social and political ideology.

Edward Hopper, Windows by Night, *1928. Museum of Modern Art, New York.*

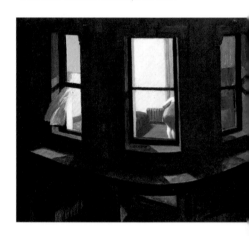

TRENDS IN THE US

The annual exhibitions of the Novecento group in Pittsburgh may have encouraged the trend toward more realistic painting in the US. However, this move had already begun early on in the century, evidenced by the works of The Eight and the Ash-can School. After the end of World War I, two trends emerged in

response to the industrial era: one was preoccupied with formal problems and involved a mechanical iconography; the other was more concerned with content and the theme of social protest. Both movements, however, aimed to revive a "native" style and to lay claim to a specifically American cultural autonomy. George Bellows (1882–1925) and, more specifically, Edward Hopper (1882–1967) adapted the ideas

THE MEXICAN MURALISTS

In his "Call to the Artists of America," published in the Spanish review *Vida Americana* in 1921, David Alfaro Siqueiros urged artists to renew contact with the original art of their land and to depict scenes of everyday life of the indigenous, local people. Together with Diego Rivera, whom he had

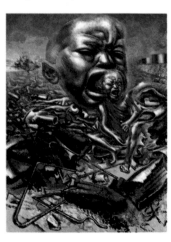

David Alfaro Siqueiros, Echo of a Scream, *1937. Museum of Modern Art, New York.*

met in Paris in 1919, Siqueiros worked on an initiative supported by the Mexican government that sought to combat illiteracy and educate the populace through art, using readily accessible and recognizable images to convey information. The best means of creating art for the people was to paint murals on public buildings ("the streets will be our museums") – easel paintings were better suited to a cultural elite. Stylistically, the murals were realistic interpretations with symbolic allusions, strong in narrative content and full of references, both to contemporary artistic media (such as the movies) and the Pre-Columbian artistic tradition. The artists' admiration for Italian frescoes, which they had studied during a visit to Italy in

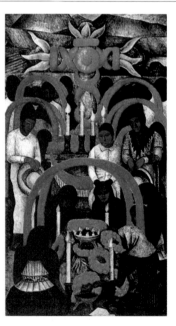

1920, was clearly reflected in their work.
From 1923 to 1928, Rivera worked on a series of vast frescoes for the Ministry of Public Instruction, illustrating

Diego Rivera, The Day of the Dead Man, *1923–24. Public Education Office, Mexico City.*

Mexican life. This touched on work and hardship and the contrasting lives of rich and poor people, as well as celebration and fiestas. The message was articulated in such a way that it could be understood on several levels, and it appealed to a cross-section of society. Following the assassination of General Obregón and subsequent changes in Mexico's political structure, the critical messages conveyed by these murals were no longer tolerated by the government, and the three great muralists – Rivera, Siqueiros, and José Orozco – were forced to leave their homeland. During the period of Roosevelt's New Deal in the US (1933–40), these artists were commissioned to paint large murals on buildings in New York and California.

WOMEN OF THE AVANT-GARDE

In 1980, an exhibition was held in Milan that was devoted to female painters and sculptors of the avant-garde movements. It demonstrated the contribution of women as talented explorers of new artistic expressions and as tireless patrons of the arts in environments that, although intellectually progressive, were often dominated by misogynistic attitudes. Sometimes (as in Marinetti's Futurism), open and provocative contempt for women was expressed. Many female artists were well known, partly through their association with more famous male artists – Gabriele Münter, Suzanne Duchamp, Sonia Delaunay, Sophie Täuber Arp, and Benedetta Marinetti included – and others were famed primarily for their fashionable or eccentric lifestyles, such as the gifted portraitist Tamara de Lempicka. Nevertheless, women gained recognition as artists in

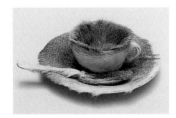

Meret Oppenheim, Fur-lined Teacup, Saucer and Spoon, 1936. Museum of Modern Art, New York.

their own right and were valued for their original work in the movements of Constructivism, Cubo-Futurism, Dadaism, and Surrealism.

Women painters also contributed to the theoretical aspects of avant-garde trends. The manifestos of Valentine de Saint Point, Olga Rozanova, and Vera Pestel helped spread avant-garde ideas to the US. The Surrealist work *Fur-lined Teacup, Saucer and Spoon*, by Meret Oppenheim (1913–85), became one of the most widely known examples of modern art in the US.

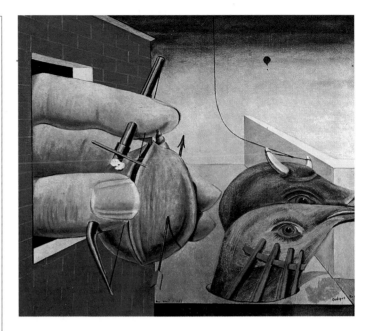

Max Ernst, Oedipus Rex, 1922. Private Collection, Paris.

SURREALIST PAINTING

Although the Metaphysical movement had declined by the 1920s, the advent of Surrealism rekindled interest in this type of painting. The Metaphysical School has been described as the precursor of Surrealism. However, the rational control that governed Metaphysical invention is absent from Surrealism, which sought to convey its message to the subconscious, exploiting involuntary psychic connections of ideas for self-expression. The immediate predecessor to Surrealism in art was, in fact, Dada. Developing from this movement, Surrealism absorbed certain Dadaist principles: in particular, its concepts of complete freedom and of the total interdependence of art and life. However, Surrealism put a positive and constructive emphasis on these motivations, in contrast with Dadaism's nihilistic attitude. Surrealism became politically involved with Marxism, and, in 1930, the name of its official mouthpiece was changed from *La révolution surréaliste* to *Le surréalisme au service de la révolution*. The movement's

official date of birth was in 1924, when André Breton's literary manifesto appeared, in which he explained the theory of "automatism" – acts of spontaneous creation, on which the Surrealist theories were based. Two years later, Breton wrote another article devoted mainly to Surrealist painting.

When the German Max Ernst (1891–1976), the Frenchman André Masson, and the Spaniard Joan Miró met at Kahnweiler's gallery in Paris in 1923, a certain common direction was agreed upon, although it is difficult to identify a specific Surrealist style, since

JOAN MIRÓ

After spending his formative years in Barcelona, Miró (1893–1983) first visited Paris in 1919. Here, he came into contact with the Fauvists, Picasso, and Tzara and absorbed the atmosphere of 20th-century cosmopolitan artistic life. Miró was associated with the Surrealists, signing their first manifesto in 1924. He was the first to give his paintings non-figurative meanings, developing a kind of lyrical abstraction that showed an affinity with Kandinsky. During the 1940s and 1950s, he devoted his energies to ceramics and sculpture, carrying out some important commissions in the US and Paris. His lively use of color and the playful nature of his work earned him a very wide and appreciative following.

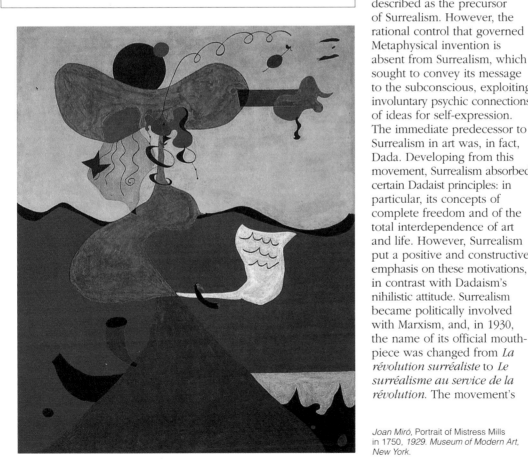

Joan Miró, Portrait of Mistress Mills in 1750, 1929. Museum of Modern Art, New York.

SALVADOR DALÍ: "ILLUMINATED PLEASURES"

1929; oil and collage on wood;
9½ x 13½ in (24 x 34.5 cm);
Museum of Modern Art, New York.

One of Dalí's so-called "hand-painted dream photographs," this painting involves a disturbing combination of images. Below center, a distressed woman with bloody hands is supported by a man; they are both emerging from an upsurging wave. To the left, a bloody arm bearing a knife rises from below. The rest of the canvas is filled with images that are linked by tentative references and arranged spatially in a desert landscape, as they might appear in a dream. Defining his work as "paranoid-critical," Dalí allowed himself to be swept up into a dreamlike dimension, enabling images from the deepest layers of his subconscious to float to the surface. The artist stated: "It does not matter whether others understand my painting, nor does it matter whether I understand them."

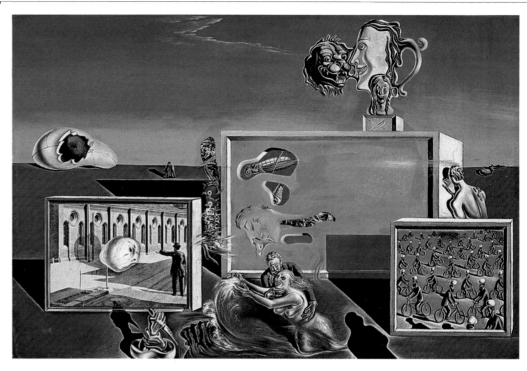

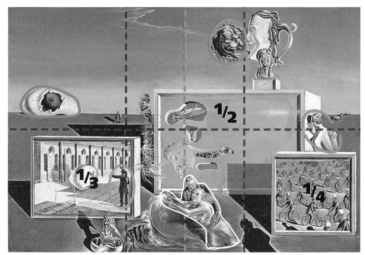

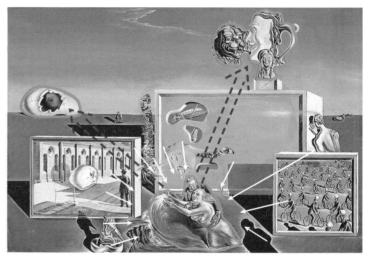

▲ *1. The relationship between the height and the width of the painting is approximately two to three. No compositional structures of particular significance can be detected, other than the placement of the two central figures on the vertical median axis. When the surface is divided into six squares, the animal's head in the upper part of the painting (between the second and the third squares) is balanced by the man with a hat, who falls on the line dividing the fourth and the fifth squares. The deformed, split egg in the first square, and the nude looking inside the box between the third and the sixth are also arranged with a certain degree of balance. When the surface is divided into quarters, no compositional rhythms can be seen.*

▶ *2. The artist paints the figures in a deep void, achieved both by a succession of planes and by perspective, the focal point of which is beyond the right-hand side of the painting, on the horizon line. The resulting distortion of the figures and the perspective is confirmed by the oblique, almost parallel lines that slope from the top of the painting toward the left. These lines are provided by the shadows, generated by a distant light from the lower right foreground. The effect of alienation and of life sequestered is absolute and generates a particular sense of discomfort through the tension created by the rigid arrangement of the three boxes and the apparently casual placing of the other figures.*

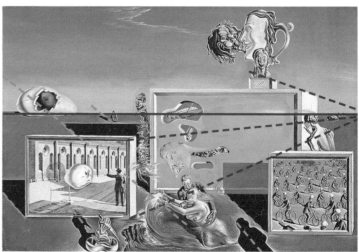

▼ 3. Dominating the composition are three boxes. The presence of contents of some sort is suggested by the small nude figure on the right, who is apparently peering into the large box through a hole in the side. Objects can be glimpsed through misshapen holes in the blue exterior, which seems to become fluid and gush out of the screen to form the wave enveloping the couple. It is possible that Dalí uses the boxes to separate the central couple from the deeper levels of the picture. The box "screens" are also used as a tool to introduce other images to the painting– the artist was fascinated by the idea of multiple imagery. On, or within, the right-hand box, cyclists pedal between diagonally placed dunes.

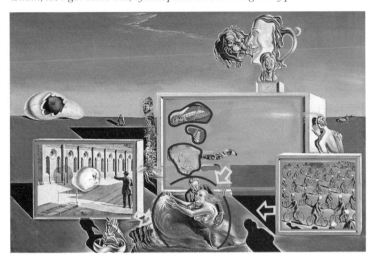

◄ 4. The allusions and references linking the various figurative elements of the painting cannot be defined with any degree of certainty. The impression is that whereas some compositional compartments or "cells" weigh the couple down, two "cells" in particular are the objects of their yearning. Above a fourth box, which resembles a pedestal, is a cup in the form of a woman's head, seen from the front, which generates another, shown in profile. The handles of both cups are visible, and the two women are laughing. The larger of the two is linked to the sneering head of a beast, which looks like a lion from Chinese art. The composite image of the two heads has an ectoplastic quality. The other "cell," placed to the left of the painting, in the direction of the arms of the woman in the central couple, is that of the misshapen and split egg, inside which is a yolk that resembles an apple.

▼ 5. Two elements are inserted as in a collage: the totem at the center left between the two boxes and the architectural photograph on the left, in all likelihood the side of Santa Maria delle Grazie in Milan, the work of Guininforte Solari (1463). Up against the drawing of the building is another ovoid bowl. There are also minor figurative elements dotted about: in the lower foreground a human shadow stretches out, and small figures are apparent near the horizon line.

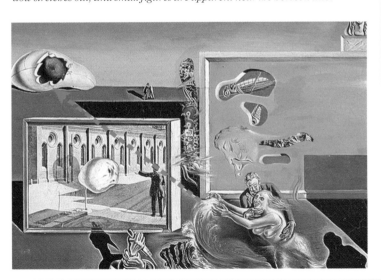

each artist developed his own interpretation of Surrealism. The influence of Freud's psychoanalytical theories is discernible in all Surrealist painters' work. His theories identified the psychological processes of the unconscious, stressed the significance of dreams, and gave meaning to apparently incongruous thought-associations and seemingly illogical free associative ideas. Max Ernst's famous definition of beauty echoes this Freudian influence: "As beautiful as the chance encounter of a sewing machine with an umbrella on a dissection table", suggesting that by matching incompatible realities, new and intriguing aesthetic meanings would be revealed.

Ernst was a highly imaginative painter, endowing dreams and tricks of the mind with a convincing and coherent figurative appearance. His *Elephant Célèbes* (1921) and *Oedipus Rex* (1922) are considered Surrealist masterpieces even though they were painted before the movement was founded. From 1929 onward, the eccentric artist Salvador Dalí (1904–89) employed a visionary and hallucinatory technique in his paranoiac and psychopathological paintings, seeking to call reality into question and to be rid of any rational foundation.

The Belgian artist René Magritte (1898–1967) was

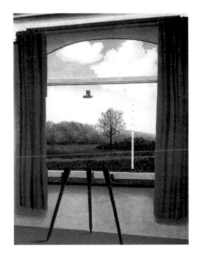

René Magritte, The Human Condition I, *1933. Private Collection.*

the extraordinary creator of paintings with strong conceptual tensions, which emphasized contradictions and double meanings, confounding the observer's expectations and challenging perceptions. Surrealism occupied center stage in the panorama of interwar European culture, partly due to the high quality of Surrealist paintings, and partly because of its ability to encompass artistic, social, and political issues. Although Paris remained the hub of their activity, talented Surrealist artists such as Arshile Gorky, Roberto Matta, and Wifredo Lam were also based in the US.

Salvador Dalí, The Persistence of Memory, *1931. Museum of Modern Art, New York.*

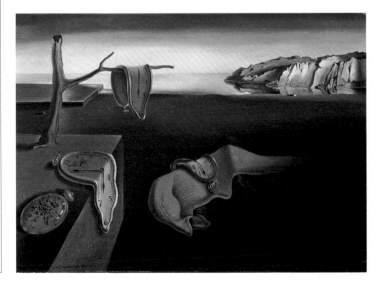

THE NEW ARCHITECTURE

*After World War I, architects in Europe and the US were full of new ideas.
They now thought of buildings not only as prototypes for the future of
architecture but also as an integral part of their surroundings, whether
rural, suburban, or urban. Simplicity masking organized complexity
was the new order of the day.*

By the time the "Exposition Internationale des Arts Décoratifs et Industriels Modernes" opened in Paris in 1925, the interwar Modern Movement had already begun to gather momentum, and the forms and methods of town planning and architecture were undergoing a fundamental transformation. The exhibition marked the success of a specific style that was closely associated with the production of useful objects for the home, interior decoration, and building construction. The entrances and pavilions of the exhibition itself (with the exception of Le Corbusier's ascetic and uncompromisingly modern pavilion, *Esprit nouveau*) demonstrated how the trend toward decorative linearity, later known as "Art Deco," could not only co-exist but also blend happily with more purist shapes or forms typical of the so-called "retro eclecticism." The new style was also compatible with the far more austere and rationalist designs of modern architecture.

ART DECO

Although it is not possible to identify a specific Art Deco style of architecture, during the 1920s and 1930s European and American architects produced designs that relied heavily on the characteristics and nuances of Art Deco. They used the style to enhance the spare, Viennese

MANHATTAN'S ART DECO SKYSCRAPERS

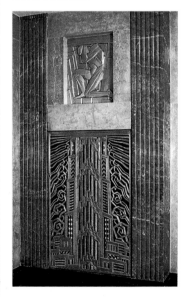

John Sloan and M.T. Robertson, detail of interior decoration, Chanin Building, New York, 1929.

The flowering of the Art Deco style in the US was remarkable for the way that it retained a high quality of detailing in spite of its widespread application. In Manhattan alone, some 150 Art Deco skyscrapers were built within the space of ten years. The style assumed its own recognizable American form, drawing on older, indigenous sources for inspiration and absorbing the ideas of the Chicago School, which had been responsible for developing the modern office building after the Great Fire of 1871. The flamboyance of the new style also created an element of symbolic liberation from

European cultural colonialism, and an opportunity to show how the New World had forged ahead technologically.

Following a visit to the 1925 Paris Exhibition, some members of the Architectural League of New York signed a declaration in favor of encouraging the development of a new architectural style. Its specific aim was to meet American requirements while continuing to apply any useful technical and stylistic lessons to be learned from Europe. The Chrysler Building, designed by William van Alen and built between 1928 and 1930, is among the finest examples of Art Deco in the US. Like the earlier Eiffel Tower in Paris (1889), its slender silhouette soars up above the city surroundings;

Leonard Schultze and J. Weaver, Waldorf Astoria Hotel, New York, 1930–31.

from its high, compact "base," it gradually tapers into a pointed tower with six gleaming semi-circles on each side, surmounted by a steel spire and eye-catching ornamentation. This modern and technically state-of-the-art structure was a fitting headquarters for the highly successful automobile manufacturer, Chrysler.

The architects of the Chanin Building of 1929, John Sloan and M.T. Robertson, were influenced by French designs and introduced extensive decorative detail to door and window frames, iron grilles, and the structure's brick exterior. Ornamentation was also exploited in the design by Leonard Schultze and J. Weaver of the Waldorf Astoria – a modern interpretation of a temple with a centralized plan and domed roof.

William van Alen, Chrysler Building, New York, 1928–30.

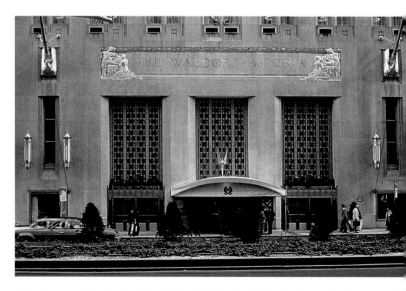

Secession-inspired style of the turn of the century, which had tended to produce a stiff and schematic version of the sinuous, organic principles of Art Nouveau design. Soft curves became angular, and the free, fluid forms of earlier designs were organized into a strict symmetrical style, with the exuberant *fin de siècle* ornament now confined within geometric patterns. Buildings with severe, basic shapes and light, bright exteriors were embellished with cement or

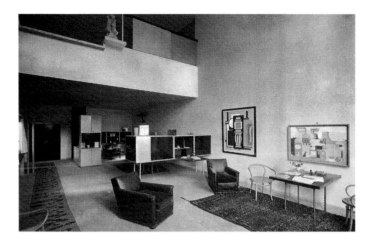

Charles Edouard Jeanneret (Le Corbusier) and Pierre Jeanneret, the interior of the Esprit nouveau *pavilion at the Paris International Exhibition of Decorative and Industrial Arts, 1925.*

sandstone friezes, fascias, and figurative inserts, and their surfaces arranged in ordered and rhythmical patterns. The Art Deco style was widely applied to buildings between the wars. It was used in residential districts, commercial buildings, and places of leisure and entertainment (such as theaters, which were being

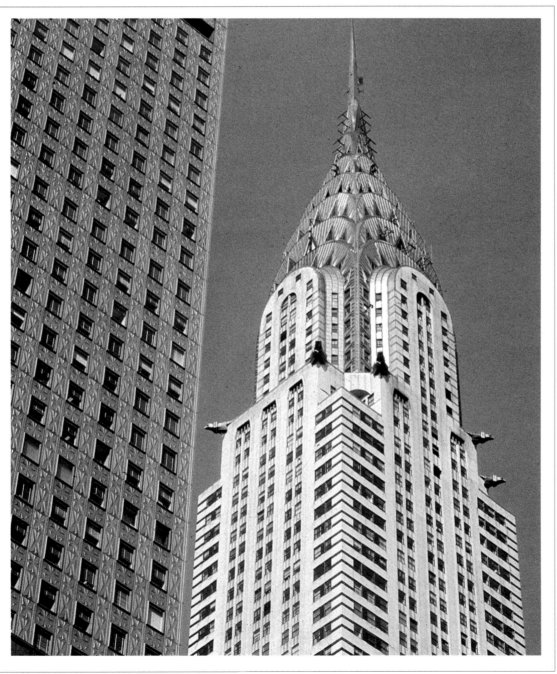

built at a great rate during this period), as well as exhibition halls and department stores. The style soon spread overseas to French colonial cities (Casablanca being a prime example) and to the US, where it met with great success and left its mark on the soaring skyscrapers of Manhattan – and consequently on the New York skyline. It was also used to striking effect in seaside resorts, such as Miami Beach. The new architecture spread rapidly in the wake of increased travel, news coverage, and communications. Capital cities and old urban centers were no longer alone in striving for the newest effects. Minor centers also began to flourish, with new settlements springing up that were instantly elevated to city status.

NEW TRENDS OF THE INTERWAR YEARS

From the turn of the century until World War I, architecture was affected only marginally by the avant-garde movements of Cubism and Expressionism, which were the principal engines of change and innovation in painting and sculpture. Raymond Duchamp-Villon's *La maison cubiste* (Cubist House) project of 1912 and Rudolf Steiner's experimental building at Dornach – a material expression of anthroposophy, the spiritualist doctrine founded by Steiner – were just two

THE ANTIDECORATIVE THEORIES OF ADOLF LOOS

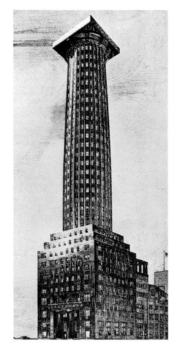

Adolf Loos, project for the Chicago Tribune Building, 1923.

The architect Adolf Loos (1870–1933) worked mainly in Vienna after gaining early experience in the US, where he was influenced by the functionalist Chicago School. In 1908, he wrote a highly contentious article entitled *Ornament und Verbrechen* (Ornament and Crime), an indictment of ornament that attacked the Secession designers, then in vogue in Vienna, and their extravagant use of decoration for furniture

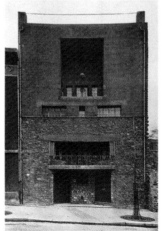

Adolf Loos, Tristan Tzara House, Paris, 1926.

and buildings. Loos had already written a series of articles for the *Neue Freie Presse* and his periodical *The Other,* in which he promoted the ideas that governed his own work, contrasting them with current "stylistic exercises." He maintained that designers and all their artistic scribblings were utterly superfluous. What were needed were new shapes and lines, which should be determined by the requirements of everyday life, comfort, and practicality. In support of his protorationalist beliefs, the highly polemic Loos went as far as to open a Free School of Architecture in 1906. This proved to be a less successful vehicle for his views than his actual commissions (the Villa Karma near Montreux, Switzerland, and the Steiner and Schue houses in Vienna).

examples of the trend. With so much rebuilding to repair war damage required in Europe, attention was once more focused on architecture. This was to be the turning point toward a stylistic renewal, leading to a demand for a break with tradition and the abandonment of historic, national styles in favor of a new, modern, and thoroughly cosmopolitan style. The condition for such a revolution was the belief that

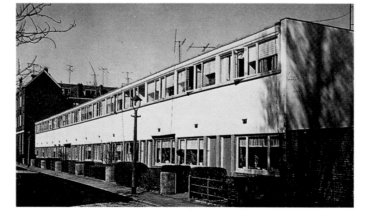

Jacobus Oud, residential unit, Kiefhoek, Rotterdam, 1925–27.

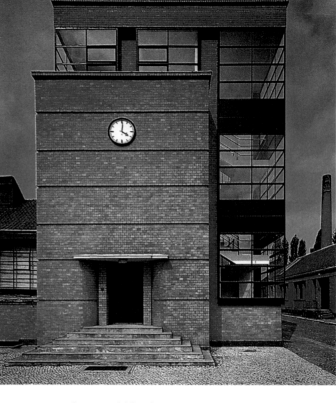

Walter Gropius and Adolf Meyer, Fagus Factory, Alfeld an der Leine, 1911.

systematic analysis could lead to a rational solution to all the problems of postwar society and that cities could be made to function more efficiently and meet the needs of their inhabitants. Moreover, art had to be seen as capable of improving mankind's lot, of contributing to social progress and the democratic education of society. These beliefs were central to the philosophy of Walter Gropius (1883–1969), Ludwig Mies van der Rohe (1886–1969), and Le Corbusier (1887–1965). Each of these architects had his own methods of town planning and organization, and all three saw the relationship between man and his habitat as a unitary problem, in which ethics took precedence over aesthetics. These views were most readily adopted and implemented by countries where progressive opinion had triumphed over reactionary tendencies – social-democratic Germany, the Netherlands, and Soviet Russia. Given that architecture was deemed capable of serving a social need, the most outstanding talents were employed in the public sector. The new, all-encompassing attitude to design was summed up in the famous slogan "from the spoon to the city." This described the architects' determination to surround people with high-quality functional and rational objects and structures, produced at a modest cost through the use of new technology. These mass-produced goods would make life freer, more ordered, and less arduous, solving practical problems and thus giving the city dweller time and space to nourish his mind and spirit. Among all the plans and projects put forward (some of which were decidedly Utopian), the theory was most successfully translated into reality through town planning, in response to the urgent demand for new housing. The prevailing shortage had been caused partly by the war but mainly by the vast increase in the number of people coming to seek work in the industrialized cities. Among the many workers' housing projects were those planned in Moscow and elsewhere in Russia by the German architect Ernst May and, shortly afterward, by Hannes Meyer and Mart Stam, who both taught at the Bauhaus. The Dutch architect Jacobus Oud (1890–1963) created working-class housing in Rotterdam, and Karl Ehn (1884–1957) designed large, innovative residential units constructed around courtyards; his fortresslike Karl-Marx-Hof in Vienna (1926–27) is a prime example. The more progressive architects of the day all formulated new ideas for housing, devising apartment buildings, individual family homes, and terraced houses. In all these cases the brief was the same: space was scarce, so buildings had to extend upward rather than outward; the designs had to be simple, functional, and geometrical, and serve a practical purpose; and technology had to be exploited as much as possible, with the use of mass-produced, prefabricated sections. In addition, the minimum tolerable living space had to be identified; this had to be enough to ensure that each inhabitant would have sufficient air, light, and warmth for a healthy life. The adoption of a rational, modern type of architecture, with its few distinguishing features and little or no regional or historical references, meant that a certain uniformity of style was discernible in the work of European and North American architects. They learned of their contemporaries' ideas and designs through architectural publications, exhibitions, competitions, and conventions, which were held at frequent intervals during the interwar years. In

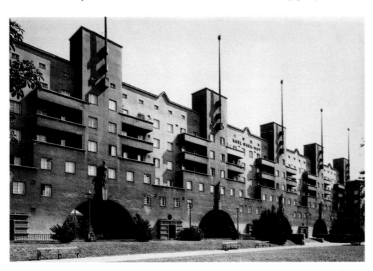

Karl Ehn, Karl-Marx-Hof, Vienna, 1926–27.

THE FIVE POINTS OF LE CORBUSIER

Charles Edouard Jeanneret became famous as an architect under the pseudonym Le Corbusier, which he adopted in 1920. This followed a brief spell as a painter, during which time he and the artist Amédée Ozenfant founded Purism, a movement that encompassed all the arts and was rather like Cubism without its distortions. He had already acquired considerable firsthand architectural experience and was influenced by Josef Hoffmann and Adolf Loos while in Austria. He had also come into contact with Mies van der Rohe and Walter Gropius during his visits to Behrens's studio in Berlin. In 1921, he set up his own studio in Paris, where he was based until shortly before his death in 1965. His projects for "machines for living in" expressed his concept of city architecture as a huge collective organization. They consisted of high-rise residential buildings surrounded by open spaces. These were equipped

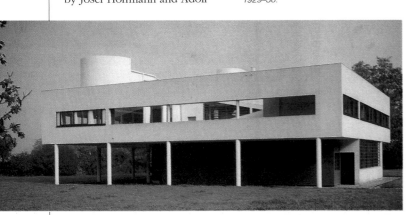

Le Corbusier, Villa Savoye, Poissy, 1929–30.

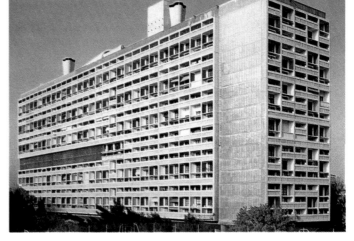

Le Corbusier, Unité d'Habitation, Marseilles, 1947–52.

with their own infrastructures and services to ensure that the individual would not be isolated and would have the opportunity for "self-development." In 1926, Le Corbusier formulated the five points of his architectural aesthetic: the *pilotis* system (free-standing concrete columns that enabled a building's mass to be elevated off the ground); free plan; the roof garden; the ribbon window; and the free-façade composition. The introduction of reinforced concrete had finally freed the architect's hand, and a more flexible layout was possible. Once the building was elevated on supports and no longer in contact with the damp soil, air could circulate under the lowest floor, where there was room for a garden. Alternatively, this could be sited on the top of the unit in the form of a roof garden.

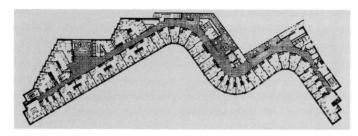

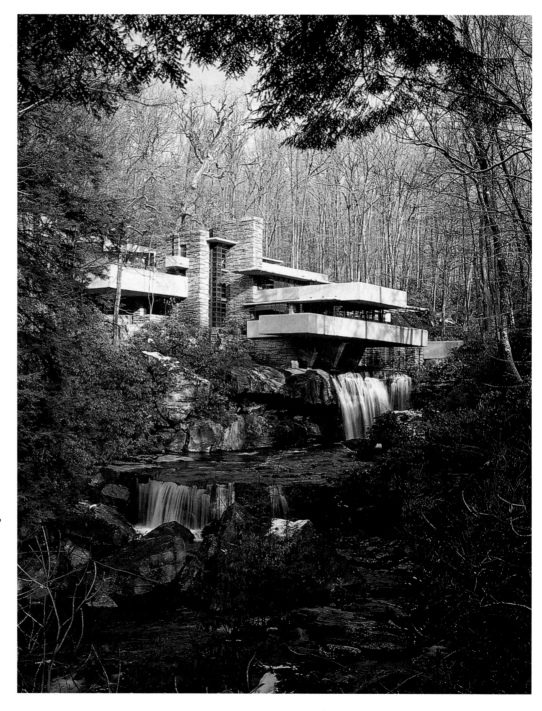

Alvar Aalto, plan of the Baker House dormitory, Massachusetts Institute of Technology, Cambridge, 1947–48.

Frank Lloyd Wright, Kaufmann House, Bear Run, Pennsylvania, 1936–39.

1922, for example, Walter Gropius, Bruno Taut, Hannes Meyer, Hans Scharoun, and Adolf Loos all competed with one another for the commission to design the new head office of the *Chicago Tribune*. Five years later, an opportunity arose to put the new theories into practice when a competition was held for the League of Nations headquarters in Geneva; although Le Corbusier's design was ruled out, his purist credo was subsequently to prove immensely influential. In the same year, Mies van der Rohe, on behalf of the *Deutsche Werkbund* (an association of architects, craftsmen, teachers, and industrialists), submitted a project for an experimental, rationalist housing development in Stuttgart. The resulting project, on which he invited fellow architects Adolf Schneck, Jacobus Oud, Walter Gropius, Bruno Taut, Peter Behrens, and Hans Poelzig to collaborate, made use of the most up-to-date building standardization technology. In 1931, Gropius, Erich Mendelsohn, Poelzig, and Le Corbusier all failed to win the commission to build the Palace of the Soviets in Moscow, a project that was awarded to B.M. Iofan, a modern architect of the "academic" persuasion.

ORGANIC ARCHITECTURE

The contemporaneous style known as "organic architecture" (as it was originally described by Louis Sullivan, the most important architect of the Chicago School) developed primarily as a response to rationalism and was soon enthusiastically adopted in the US. Both trends, however, were architectural phenomena that drew their inspiration from avant-garde artistic experiments that had taken place during the first two decades of the century: Cubism, Abstraction, and Neo-Plasticism. All of these movements played their part in fostering a taste for "clean" lines and a sparing use of ornament to create an architectural style that, while disjointed and asymmetrical, nonetheless achieved a dynamic balance. Mass tended to be treated as compact blocks, allowing for space to be organized in new and unconventional ways. The division of internal space depended on the individual architect's interpretation of how it would best fulfill its particular function and the needs of the occupants. The treatment of the exterior was nonhierarchical, so there was no single, dominant elevation.

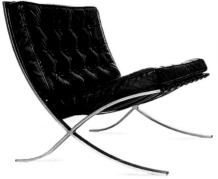

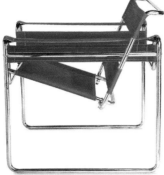

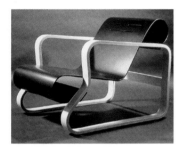

Three chairs, from top left clockwise: Barcelona by Ludwig Mies van der Rohe, 1929; B3 by Marcel Breuer, 1925; and Paimio by Alvar Aalto, 1932. From the late 19th century, architects and designers worked on the creation of mass-produced furniture, often achieving highly original results in terms of line, comfort, and use of materials. Simplicity in manufacture and assembly of components were both important considerations.

The numerous and disparate practitioners of modern architecture, however, shared the wish of those at the forefront of the arts world to sever all links with historic styles, to exploit technology, and to emphasize structural elements rather than hide them under decorative coverings.

In contrast to the rationalists' strictly geometric approach, organic architecture treated space as an organism that should be modified in accordance with its purpose and its environment. It should not impose its own order, nor establish an *a priori* design methodology, but instead develop freely with a variety and richness of form and materials, blending together nature and artifice in a harmonious synthesis.

The American architect Frank Lloyd Wright (1869–1959) was a champion of this design philosophy. He maintained it throughout his long professional life in a wide variety of commissions across the globe. Wright's unique interpretation of "abstraction" and "spatial continuity" was illustrated by preference for free planes and curvilinear rhythms, his adoption of elastic structures and flexible floor plans, and his exploitation of the play of light by using transparent and pierced components. Wright was always aware of the symbiosis between the individual and the architectural space (many of his designs were for family homes, notably his Prairie Houses), and between the individual and nature, respecting the principle that "architecture must exclude anything that clashes with nature and man's character." Wright's philosophy had a profound influence on Euro-pean architecture, particularly in Germany, the Netherlands, and Scandinavia.

THE ITALIAN MOVEMENT FOR RATIONAL ARCHITECTURE

In Italy, the Modern Movement was promoted by the Gruppo 7 – a group of seven young architects from Lombardy (Luigi Figini, Guido Frette, Sebastiano Larco, Adalberto Libera, Gino Pollini, Enrico Rava, and Giuseppe Terragni) – who argued the case for Rational architecture against the monumentalism beloved of the Fascist regime. In a series of articles published in *La Rassegna italiana* from December 1926 onward, the group declared its mission to free architecture from the Futurist avant-garde (reflecting their antipathy for its vehement and individualistic approach) and also from a cultural climate in which Italian architecture did not reflect the spirit of the times. They were also against personal style and original creativity, seeking to establish basic types of architecture based on the criteria of logic, order, clarity, and complete adherence to functionalism. At the same time, they wanted to avoid a total break with the enduring values of classical architecture and the European tradition.

Adalberto Libera was the driving force behind the MIAR (*Movimento Italiano per l'Architettura Razionale*), which in 1928 expanded from the initial Gruppo 7 to include other leading Italian architects, including Giuseppe Pagano (1896–1945). The MIAR held two exhibitions in Rome in 1928 and 1931. Exhibits included interior decoration plans and designs for industrial buildings, models of garages, gas plants, the so-called "electrical houses," and an apartment building built by Giuseppe Terragni for the Società Novocomum in Como in 1927–28.

INTERNATIONAL CONGRESSES AND MODERN ARCHITECTURE

In 1928, architects and town planners founded official channels for the dissemination their new methods – the CIAM (*Congrès Internationaux d'Architecture Moderne*). These congresses were intended to provide a forum for discussion of work in progress all over Europe. The first was held at La Sarraz in Switzerland, where the agenda, drawn up by Le Corbusier, covered several fundamental topics: modern technology and its results, cost control, standardization, education and training in architecture, and the relationship between architecture and the state. The fourth congress, in 1933, was held on board a ship cruising from Marseilles to Athens and focused on the topic of the "Functional City." The delegates' deliberations formed the basis of "The Athens Charter," published in 1942, which explained what the functionalists considered to be the fundamental needs of the individual in relation to town planning: to live, to work, to move around, and to further one's cultural education.

Le Corbusier, study for a city of three million inhabitants from Une ville contemporaine, *1922.*

Le Corbusier, "Plan Obus" for Algiers, 1930.

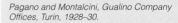

Pagano and Montalcini, Gualino Company Offices, Turin, 1928–30.

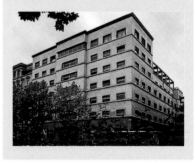

ART & POLITICS

*Soon after the end of World War I, a new and hitherto unknown
quantity became part of the political equation: the ordinary people. Those
in power, especially dictators, used art as propaganda to influence the
masses, and even independent artists often chose to direct their
work and its message at the general public.*

During the interwar years, the state gradually took control of art in many European countries. This was not only the case in nations with totalitarian regimes, for even some democratic governments assumed a "protective" and watchful attitude toward the artist. This led to a blandness of style and a revival of themes and styles that were widely accepted and easily understood. Where work had to have an official seal of approval, artists tended to look toward Classicism or 19th-century Realism for suitable exemplars.

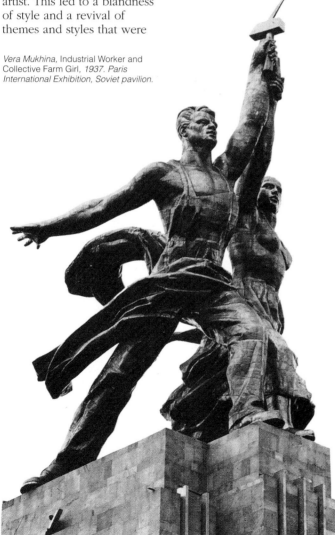

Vera Mukhina, Industrial Worker and Collective Farm Girl, *1937. Paris International Exhibition, Soviet pavilion.*

PAINTING AS INVOLVEMENT: GUERNICA

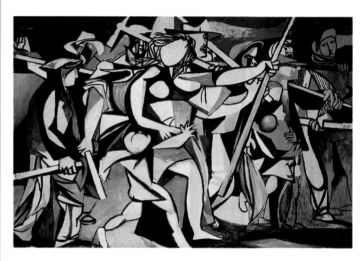

Renato Guttuso, The Occupation of the Land, *1947. National Museum of Fine Arts, Budapest. The work, inspired by the spirit of democracy, has echoes of Picasso.*

One of the most celebrated examples of an artist's direct concern with contemporary events was Picasso's *Guernica,* which came to be considered not so much a record of a historic event but a historic event in itself. It was painted to express the artist's overwhelming emotional reaction to the destruction of the town of Guernica by the first use of indiscriminate aerial bombardment by the Nazis. When the huge canvas went on show in Paris in 1937, it met with an extremely strong response, partly because it recorded such a recent event and partly because of its style. Picasso had expressed his reaction in a language that bridged Cubism and Surrealism, fragmenting and displacing form without making it unintelligible. He had adopted an emblematic iconography: the bull, the horse, the bird, the lamp, and the broken sword all endowed the heroic theme of the story with a universal dimension,

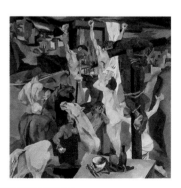

Renato Guttuso, Crucifixion, *1941. Galleria d'Arte Moderna, Rome. The tragedy of war is treated as a religious theme, owing much to Picasso and Expressionism.*

THE ART OF POLITICAL PROPAGANDA

It is not surprising that the totalitarian regimes of Soviet Russia and Nazi Germany, despite their conflicting ideologies, should have favored the same conventionality in art. Above all else, they shared the aim that a particular political message should be successfully conveyed to as wide an audience as possible. It was a prerequisite that this message should be both accessible and persuasive. Inevitably, art became banal, a rhetorical exercise in glorifying the political system. At the 1937 International Exhibition of Art and Technology in Paris, the monumental Nazi and Soviet pavilions vied spectacularly with each other. Their towers reached heights of 187 feet (57 meters) and 108 feet (33 meters) respectively, the former surmounted by the classically inspired Nazi bronze eagle and the latter by Vera Mukhina's imposing steel statue of two figures, *Industrial Worker and Collective Farm Girl*. The German pavilion housed a selection of "pure Aryan art," while the Russians concentrated on examples of "Socialist Realism." These exhibits shared a disquieting affinity, identified and examined by André Breton and Diego Rivera in their 1938 manifesto "Toward an Independent Revolutionary Art."

symbolizing the horrors of war. This example of Picasso's conviction that painters were entrusted with a historic mission to help mold a democratic civil conscience was emulated by other artists. One such artist was Renato Guttuso, who entered his *Crucifixion* in the 1942 Bergamo exhibition as a "symbol of all those who suffer outrage, prison, and torture for their ideas."

Pablo Picasso, Massacre in Korea, *1951. Musée Picasso, Paris. In this canvas, the artist reworked Goya's painting,* The Third of May 1808.

Pablo Picasso, Guernica, *1937. Reina Sofía Museum, Madrid.*

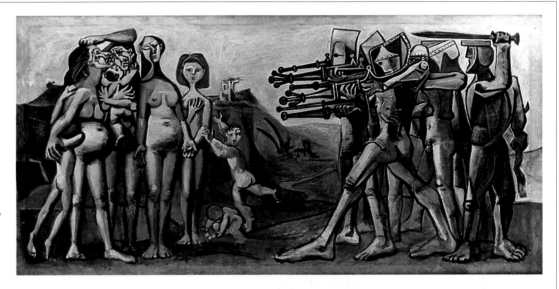

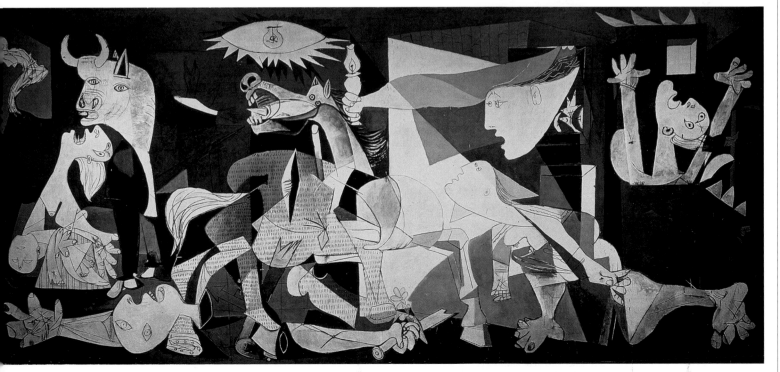

DEGENERATE ART

In 1937, Joseph Goebbels, Propaganda Minister for the Nazi party, entrusted the task of organizing an exhibition in Munich to Adolf Ziegler – a second-rate artist specializing in paintings of Aryan nudes, much admired by Hitler. The exhibition was to concentrate on works from 1910 onward that were condemned as "German art of the decadent period." This large official exhibition of "Degenerate Art" had been preceded in 1933 by several "exhibitions of shame" on themes such as "Cultural Bolshevism" in Mannheim, "Art as the Cause of Moral Decay" in Stuttgart, and "Reflections of Artistic Decadence" in Dresden. Exhibited on the orders of the Führer, they symbolized each museum's "chamber of artistic horrors."

Among the paintings labeled as "degenerate" were those by artists of the Die Brücke, Der Blaue Reiter, and Bauhaus

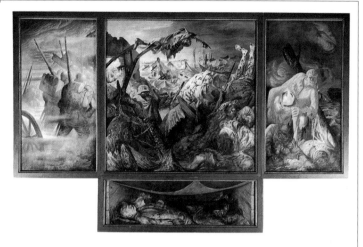

Otto Dix, Triptych of War, *with predella, 1929–32. Staatliche Kunstsammlungen, Dresden.*

groups, and those of Kokoschka (who proceeded to paint a self-portrait of "a degenerate artist"), Dix, Grosz, Beckmann, Barlach, and El Lissitzky. The exhibits were divided into categories, each containing examples of a variety of alleged perversions and physical and mental abnormalities, such as prostitution, insanity, impotence, Judaism, and cretinism.

In 1938, a decree was passed authorizing the seizure of

16,000 works by "degenerate" German artists and by Matisse, Gauguin, van Gogh, Munch, and other great European painters. These paintings were then expropriated by Nazi leader Goering, sold to foreign museums and collections, or burned publicly as a warning to the people.

Petrograd, 1928). All were exponents of the "Socialist Realism" style, which was given official state recognition in 1932 in a Moscow exhibition celebrating the 15th anniversary of the Russian Revolution (previously, the label "Heroic Realism" had frequently been used). While Socialist Realism was being promoted in the USSR, ousting abstraction and sweeping away the vestiges of Constructivism (despite the latter's contribution to revolutionary ideology), in Germany cultural repression was growing increasingly tyrannical. The Bauhaus was shut down in April 1933, not long after Hitler came to power, and museum curators found guilty of having added Abstract and Expressionist works to their collections were dismissed from their posts. Such work was classified as "degenerate art" for its elitist and cosmopolitan nature.

Ben Shahn, Portrait of Sacco and Vanzetti, *1931–32. Museum of Modern Art, New York.*

Recalling in style the 1920s plaster and terracotta busts of revolutionary heroes, Mukhina's pair of rigid figures – heroic workers complete with hammer and sickle – represent the most durable example of Soviet propaganda imagery. The aim was to create "art that was revolutionary in form and socialist in content," using the formal, conservative idiom of 19th-century Russian academicism to depict the USSR's progressive new society and its foundations in the solidarity of the workers. Hence the recurrent themes – rural life depicted as a rustic idyll, manual labor as unquestionably fulfilling, and the glorification of the Red Army – were depicted in the paintings of such artists as Alexander Michailovich Gerasimov (*Lenin on the Podium,* 1929; *Celebration at the Collective Farm,* 1937; *Portrait of Stalin,* 1935); M.B. Grekov (*Takanka,* 1925); and Alexander Alexandrovich Dejneka (*Defense of*

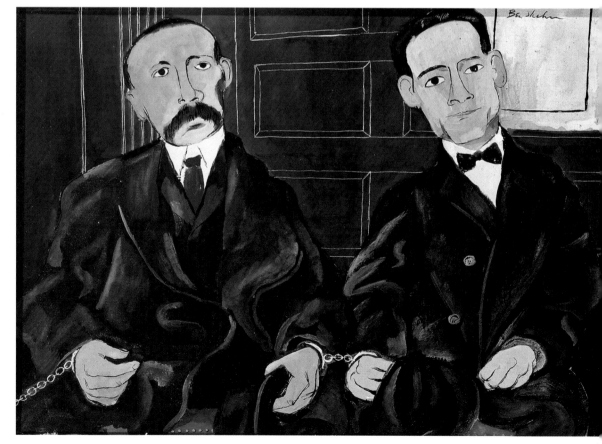

Only paintings reflecting Germanic tradition were deemed acceptable, as well as some examples of the Classical and Romantic revival – the only artistic genres considered by the authorities to be suitable for the promotion of nationalistic ideological integration. Although by no means as liberal as the democratic countries that allowed artists such as Ben Shahn free expression during this era, Italy was nonetheless free of the extreme sectarianism that characterized the cultural agenda of its fascist ally Germany. This was despite Mussolini's vow as early as 1926 "to create a new art, an art of our times, a Fascist art," for his vision was promoted with none of the extremism, violence, or repression displayed in Germany. In fact, throughout the 1930s, Italian art remained fairly eclectic; the Futurists' experimental successors, the young abstract artists associated with the Milione gallery in Milan and the Corrente Expressionist painters, were by and large tolerated. In terms of propaganda and political pressure, the regime chose to use more subtle propaganda to achieve its desired consensus, enlisting the support of artists by organizing a succession of exhibitions, competitions, prizes, and public commissions. Proof of a climate in which two very

"NOVECENTO ITALIANO"

The *Novecento Italiano* movement had its foundations in a group founded by seven painters in Milan: Gian Emilio Malerba, Anselmo Bucci, Leonardo Dudreville, Achille Funi, Ubaldo Oppi, Pietro Marussig, and Mario Sironi. Lino Pesaro, the owner of an art gallery, and Margherita Sarfatti, an influential critic, had recognized a profound awareness of cultural heritage in their work, and in 1922 suggested they should form a mutually beneficial association. Despite its lack of a specific, clearly enunciated stylistic program, the group leaned toward a revival of 19th-century Lombard naturalism that was neither impressionistic nor descriptive, but characterized by a clear, harsh style and Neoclassical iconography. This was in contrast to the Futurist avant-garde and the idealistic *Valori Plastici*. After their debut at the Pesaro Gallery in Milan in 1923 and

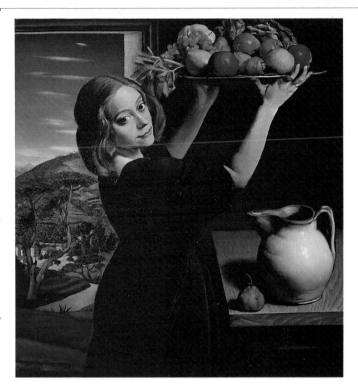

Achille Funi, The Earth, *1921. Private Collection, Bergamo.*

Pietro Marussig, Women in a Café, *1924. Civico Museo d' Arte Contemporanea, Milan.*

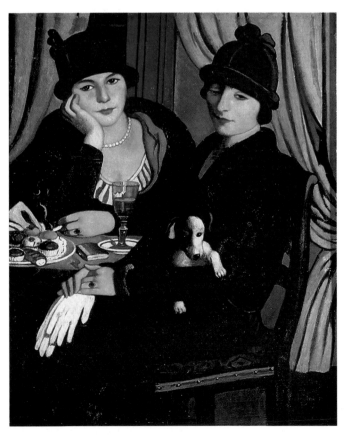

their acceptance the following year at the Venice Biennale (where the exhibition was called "Six Novecento Painters," indicating Oppi's defection), Margherita Sarfatti launched a more ambitious project. She expanded the group to include "all the best artists of the new generation," albeit only those who conformed to certain ostensibly high-minded, politically acceptable principles. The first exhibition of the Novecento Italiano opened at the Permanente in Milan in 1926, and 110 artists participated. From diverse backgrounds, they included Carrà, Casorati, Campigli, Guidi, and Soffici. On the strength of this successful initiative, which demonstrated that contemporary Italian art could no longer be described as "provincial" in character, the Novecento looked abroad and found a capable organizer in Mario Tozzi for their exhibitions in France, Berlin, Buenos Aires, Amsterdam, and Pittsburgh. The group was increasingly associated with the propaganda of the Fascist Sindicati delle Belle Arti and with reactionary work; it disbanded in 1943.

"CORRENTE"

Between January 1938 and May 1940, despite suppression by Mussolini, the journal *Corrente di Vita Giovanile* ("Youthful Trends") was published in Milan. Founded by Ernesto Treccani (b. 1920), this literary, arts, and political periodical welcomed articles expressing advanced views from dissident intellectuals. An offshoot developed in the form of an association of painters and sculptors drawn together by their belief in the artist's right to freedom of choice, unfettered by political agendas.

They refused to take part in the adulation of the nationalist cause (which they identified with the Novecento's Classicism) while also rejecting abstract elitism. Committed instead to a critical approach to contemporary social reality, the Corrente group expressed their views with force

Giuseppe Migneco, Lizard Hunters, *1942. Private Collection, Milan.*

Aligi Sassu, Venetian Horses at Famagusta, *1940. Private Collection, Milan. This painting was exhibited at the Bergamo Prize competition.*

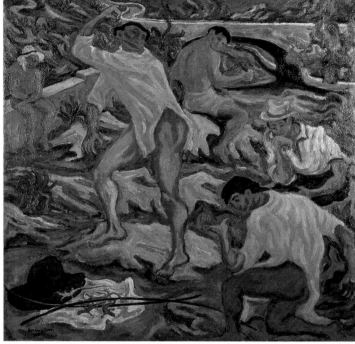

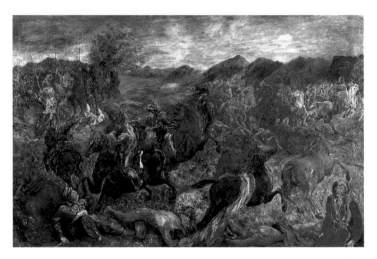

and candor. Expressionist influence was discernible in their work, with its bold, almost crude qualities, distorted lines, tortured shapes, bright colors, and thickly applied impasto.

Corrente's first exhibition was held in Milan in March 1939. It included the work of many young artists, including Birolli, Cantatore, Tomea, Badodi, Cassinari, Megneco, Mucchi, and Cherchi, as well as Sassu, Guttuso, and Vedova – artists who were making a name for themselves in official circles, having participated (successfully in Guttuso's case) in the Bergamo competition. A second exhibition

different political-artistic trends coexisted is provided by the contemporaneous introduction of two competitions on the eve of World War II. The first, the Cremona Prize, was launched by the Fascist extremist Roberto Farinacci to encourage heroic, celebratory painting. Energetic in style, the entries were unashamedly nationalist. The second was the Bergamo Prize, introduced in 1939 and inspired by a more subtle and intelligent approach. Although this, too, sought to check poetic and formal freedom of expression to a certain extent, it also invited cultivated, individualistic entries in order to show that Italian art had not been left behind by international artistic trends. Whereas the Cremona

Mario Sironi, Justice between Law and Force, *1936. Palazzo di Giustizia, Milan.*

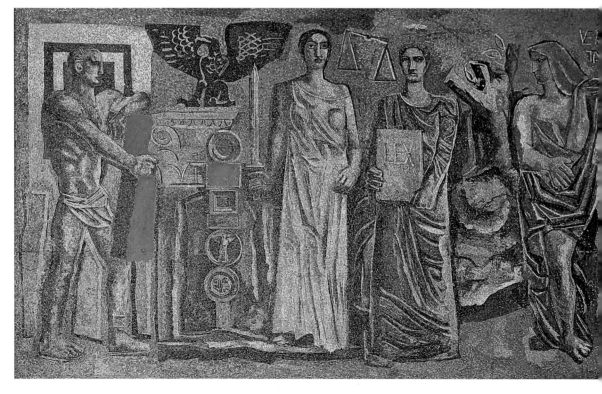

was held in December of the same year. In 1943, the group produced the *Manifesto dei Pittori e Scultori* ("Painters' and Sculptors' Manifesto"), the contents of which were to have considerable influence in the early postwar years, leading to the creation of the *Fronte Nuovo delle Arti* ("New Arts Front").

Emilio Vedova, San Moisè, 1937–38. Private Collection.

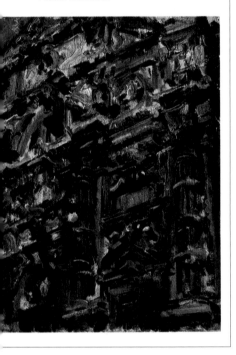

Prize stipulated the subject (e.g. "Listening to Mussolini's Speech on the Radio"), which could be expressed only in a rhetorical style with trite and populist realism, the Bergamo Prize allowed its competitors relative freedom of subject. This enabled them to experiment not only with technique, color, and interpretation, but also to make a sociological or existential comment on the difficulties of life.

THE ART OF POLITICAL ENGAGEMENT

The 1937 Paris exhibition, with its displays of Nazi and Soviet artistic propaganda, also provided a showcase for a work by Pablo Picasso, who had been invited to exhibit mural paintings with allegorical themes. The heavy bombing by the Nazis of the Basque town of Guernica in April of that year had inspired Picasso to produce an ideological painting expressing solidarity with the Spanish Republicans. *Guernica* became emblematic of progressive, sociopolitically inspired art – direct and vivid in language, avant-garde in spirit, and the antithesis of the prevailing conservative styles of political art.

The previous year, when an exhibition entitled *Le réalisme et la peinture* ("Realism and Painting") was held in Paris, an intellectual debate developed about the events unfolding in Spain and the role of modern art. The question was whether a type of art that dealt exclusively with humans, their relationships and problems, and which expressed these themes in terms divorced from both academicism and experimentalism should be freely available to all.

Mural paintings were a particularly suitable medium for this sociopolitical art. Instantly accessible and produced on a large scale, the works were often inspired by familiar stories. They proved popular in Italy, where many were commissioned for the inauguration of the Fifth Triennale at the Palace of Art in Milan in 1933. Their popularity spread to the US, where artists deprived of work through the Depression were employed to decorate airports, schools, and stations with scenes of everyday life. Many contained a strong undercurrent of social protest and were executed with the same stark realism as their European counterparts. Another popular and effective vehicle for political propaganda was movies, the new art form that required substantial financial backing. The regimes of Soviet Russia, Germany, and Italy all called on talented film-makers to put forward their message. *The Triumph of Will* (1936), by Leni Riefenstahl, was just one notable example.

BRANCUSI

Among the artists who worked within the dictates of 20th-century art and those who fought against them in different ways, there were others who seemed to work outside history. One such artist was the Paris-based Romanian sculptor Constantin Brancusi (1876–1957), who refused an offer to join the great Rodin's studio as a student in favor of creating sculptures characterized by a total purity of form. He eliminated from his work everything that was not essential, believing that "what is real is not the external form but the essence of things."

He began with his famous stone work *The Kiss* (1908), in which the entwined lovers' bodies are locked in a shape that recalls Egyptian Middle Kingdom statues of the pharaohs. Several versions were made. Among the works

Constantin Brancusi, Mademoiselle Pogany III, 1931. Louise and Walter Arensberg Collection, Museum of Art, Philadelphia.

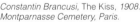

Constantin Brancusi, The Kiss, 1908. Montparnasse Cemetery, Paris.

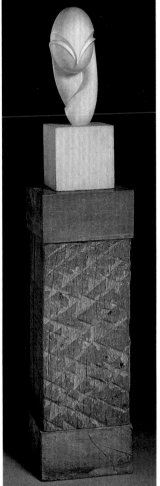

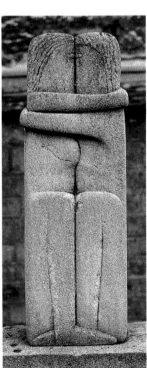

that followed were 17 versions of the bronze statue of *Mademoiselle Pogany*, executed in other materials between 1913 and 1933; six wood versions of the *Cockerel* (1924–49); seven versions of the bronze of *The Newborn* (1915–20); and 22 bronze versions of *Bird in Space* (1919–40). All testify to his attempt to condense and simplify his subject.

In 1938, Brancusi created, among other sculptures, a 98-foot (30-meter) cast-iron version of his famous *Endless Column* for the park at Targu-Jiu in Romania. Ever more distant from the contemporary art scene and current events, he went to India when World War II broke out. Here, at the request of the Maharajah of Indore, he worked on a project for a temple of meditation.

A REVOLUTION IN THE ARTS

1905: Expressionist group Die Brücke is formed in Dresden. **1907:** Picasso completes *Les Demoiselles d'Avignon*, initiating the great period of Cubist art; Pope Pius X condemns Catholic modernism. **1913:** the poet Apollinaire coins phrase "Orphic Cubism" with reference to work of painters Delaunay, Léger, and Kupka. **1914:** Duchamp exhibits the *Bicycle Wheel*, the first of his famous "ready-mades"; World War I breaks out following assassination of Crown Prince Franz Ferdinand of Austria. **1918:** the loss of over ten million lives in the war is commemorated by poets such as Wilfred Owen and painters such as Paul Nash. **1920:** Swiss-born Paul Klee gives lessons at the Weimar Bauhaus. **1923:** art critic Margherita Sarfatti encourages

1905　　　　1910　　　　1915　　　　1920

▼ HENRI MATISSE
(1869-1954)
Considered one of the greatest artists of the 20th century, Henri Matisse was a leading figure of the Fauvist group.

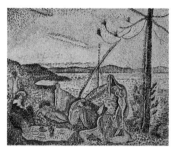

Henri Matisse, Luxe, Calme et Volupté, 1904. Musée d'Orsay, Paris.

▼ OSKAR KOKOSCHKA
(1886-1980)
A painter trained in the time of the Viennese Secession, Kokoschka used the rapid, urgent brushwork of the Austrian Expressionist style.

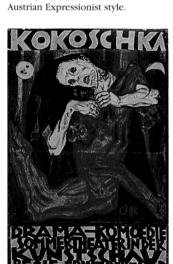

Oskar Kokoschka, poster for Murderer, Hope of Women, 1909. Museum of Modern Art, New York.

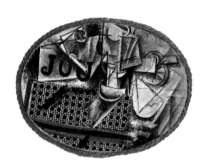

Umberto Boccioni, The City Rises, 1910–11. Museum of Modern Art, New York.

▲ UMBERTO BOCCIONI
(1882-1916)
Boccioni, the Italian painter, sculptor, and theorist of Futurism, used bright colors and bold interpenetration of planes in his work to convey the dynamism of modern life.

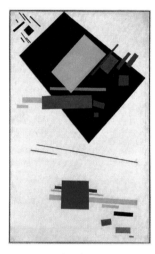

Pablo Picasso, Still Life with Chair Caning, 1912. Musée Picasso, Paris.

▲ PABLO PICASSO
(1881-1973)
Spanish painter, sculptor, and ceramicist Picasso founded Cubism, in which the object and its surrounding space are reduced to facets and planes, showing multiple viewpoints.

▼ KASIMIR MALEVICH
(1878-1935)
The search for essence and pure form led Malevich, Russian painter and founder of Suprematism, to an ultimate level of abstraction.

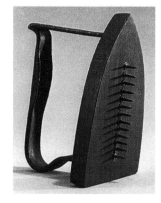

Kasimir Malevich, Suprematism, 1915. Stedelijk Museum, Amsterdam.

▼ AMEDEO MODIGLIANI
(1884-1920)
This Italian painter and sculptor was influenced by African art and Cézanne. He created figures synthetically defined by an elegant line, inherited from Sienese painting.

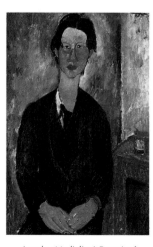

Amedeo Modigliani, Portrait of Chaïm Soutine, 1917. National Gallery of Art, Washington, DC.

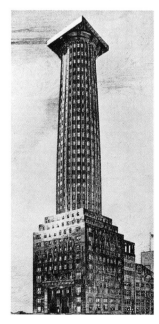

Man Ray, Gift, 1921. Private Collection, Chicago.

▲ MAN RAY
(1890-1977)
A versatile representative of Dada and Surrealism, Man Ray was a tireless experimenter. He was particularly interested in photography and its processes.

Adolf Loos, plan for the Chicago Tribune skyscraper, 1923.

▲ ADOLF LOOS
(1870-1933)

the Novecento group to exhibit at Pesaro Gallery, Milan. **1924:** André Breton publishes *Manifesto of Surrealism.* **1925:** Austrian Alban Berg composes the opera *Wozzeck*; Fascist regime seizes power in Italy. **1929:** crash of New York stock market, causing grave economic crisis in the US. **1930:** Il Milione Gallery, focal point of Italian abstraction, opens in Milan. **1932:** first exhibition of cinematography held in Venice. **1933:** in Germany, Hitler becomes chancellor of the Reich. **1935:** Italian troops invade Abyssinia. **1936:** civil war erupts in Spain. **1937:** Picasso's *Guernica* is exhibited in the Spanish pavilion of Paris Exposition Internationale. **1939:** outbreak of World War II. **1950:** Roberto Longhi founds magazine *Paragone.*

1 9 2 5   1 9 3 0   1 9 3 5   1 9 4 0 – 5 0

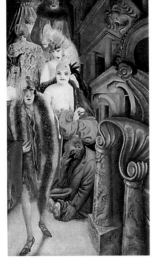

Otto Dix, detail of The Great City, triptych, 1927–28. Staatsgalerie, Stuttgart.

▲ OTTO DIX
(1891-1969)
Dix was a German painter who looked to the northern Renaissance for the development of his Expressionistic style. This was to lead to the disturbing realism of "New Objectivity."

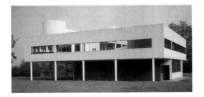

Le Corbusier, Villa Savoye, Poissy, 1929–30.

▲ LE CORBUSIER
(CHARLES-EDOUARD JEANNERET)
(1887-1965)
French architect, painter, sculptor, and town planner, Le Corbusier's designs were marked by rationality and the free use of open space. His revolutionary work provided the departure point for an entire generation of architects.

▼ NEW YORK
The fashion for Art Deco continued throughout the 1930s, becoming applicable even to New York skyscrapers.

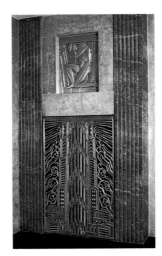

John Sloan and M.T. Robertson, detail of interior decoration, Chanin Building, New York, 1929.

▼ RENE MAGRITTE
(1898-1967)
This Belgian painter's unusual juxtapositions and ambiguous treatment of everyday objects exemplify the essence of Surrealism.

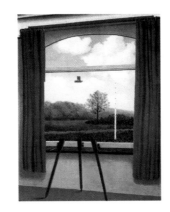

René Magritte, The Human Condition I, 1933. Private Collection.

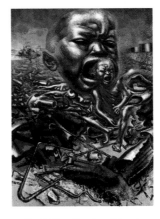

David Alfaro Siqueiros, Echo of a Scream, 1937. Museum of Modern Art, New York.

▲ DAVID ALFARO SIQUEIROS
(1896-1974)
This Mexican painter was inspired by the pre-Hispanic traditions of Latin America. Together with Rivera and Orozco, he portrayed popular epic themes in his murals.

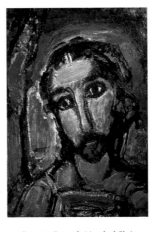

Georges Rouault, Head of Christ (Passion), 1938. Hanna Fund, Cleveland Museum of Art, Ohio.

▲ GEORGES ROUAULT
(1871-1958)
French painter Roualt's strong outlines and glowing tones characterize some of the most dramatic religious images of the century.

▼ ALIGI SASSU
(b. 1912)
The Italian painter Sassu was associated with the "Corrente" movement (1938-40). Influenced by great 19th-century art, he developed an expressionistic style, which he handled coherently in the postwar years.

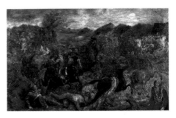

Aligi Sassu, Venetian Horses at Famagusta, 1940. Private Collection, Milan.

▼ PABLO PICASSO
(1881-1973)
Picasso employed a stark, powerful new style to confront the problems associated with the horrors of war and the eternal theme of violence.

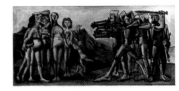

Pablo Picasso, Massacre in Korea, 1951. Musée Picasso, Paris.

ART IN THE POSTWAR PERIOD

While it tore Europe apart, World War II ironically accelerated the globalization of culture and increased the number of artistic centers worldwide. Although figurative art was still being produced, it was in the field of nonrepresentational art that more revolutionary experiments were taking place and in which the avant-garde styles and ideas in the first quarter of the century were developed.

Until the outbreak of World War II, the art scene had been basically dominated by European artists. Even when artistic influences from outside Europe stimulated the emergence of new styles, guidance came primarily from artists within Europe. This was exemplified by the interest van Gogh and Gauguin showed in Japanese art and the attention Picasso paid to African art.

The avant-garde movements of the early 20th century were born in Europe, and it was from Europe – the instigator of world conflict – that the impetus for postwar changes in America would come. In the early 1940s, artists such as the Surrealists André Masson, Joan Miró, Yves Tanguy, and Max Ernst sailed to New York to escape the war. Their ideas soon spread there, thanks to

the promotional work of Peggy Guggenheim, who founded the Art of this Century Gallery in 1942, where she first exhibited the work of Jackson Pollock. However, the rise of art to prominence in New York, especially in the commercial market, did not overshadow the flourishing European art scene, which continued to exert considerable influence and be of great importance.

THE MID-1900S

After the war, artists began to question their role in a society that had experienced such appalling suffering. The roads they took were varied and often contrasting. On the one hand, the widespread feeling of existential malaise fostered the Expressionist figurative painting of the English artists

COBRA

Founded in Paris in 1948, the CoBrA group took its name from the native cities of its founding members: Copenhagen, Brussels, and Amsterdam. Danish artist Asger Jorn (1914–73), Belgian artists Pierre Alechinsky (b. 1927) and Corneille (b. 1922), and Dutch artist Karel Appel (b. 1921) developed a style that could be traced back to German Expressionism in its violent brushwork and distorted forms,

Karel Appel, La Hollandaise, 1969. Galerie Ariel, Paris.

Pierre Alechinsky, Loin d'Ixelles, 1965. Private Collection, New York.

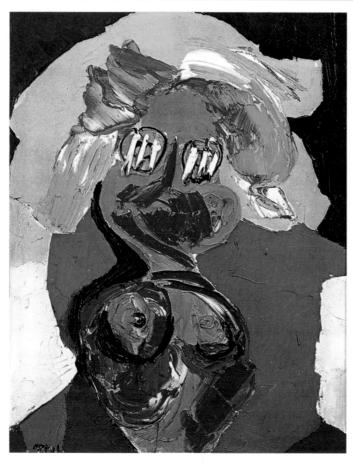

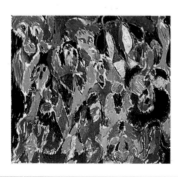

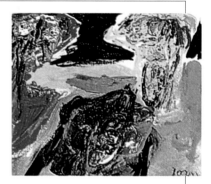

Asger Jorn, Green Ballet, 1960. Guggenheim Museum, New York.

but which proved less somber in its choice of subjects and chromatic range. Although form seemed at times to give way to abstraction, it never stopped being the essential element of their work. It testified to the group's desire to react against the widespread contemporary interest in abstract art. Between 1948 and 1951, they had three exhibitions and printed eight issues of the magazine *Cobra*. However, they soon went their separate ways, and the group dissolved.

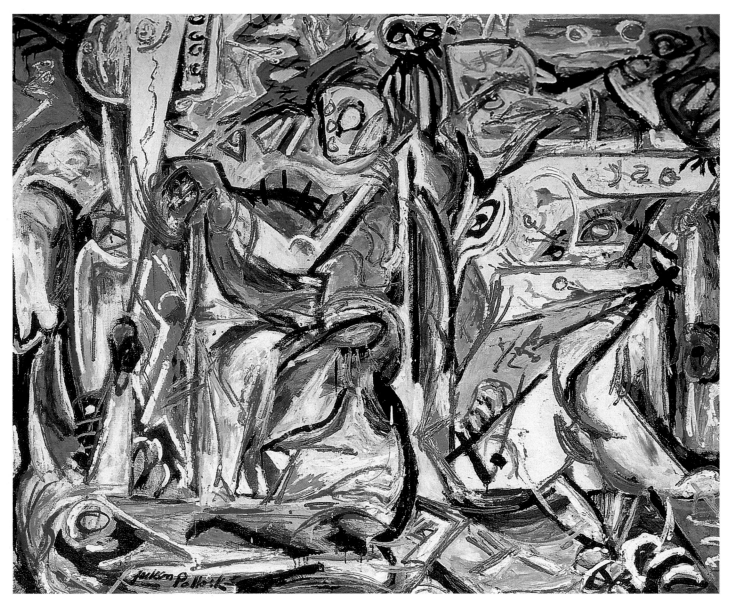

Jackson Pollock, Circumcision, *1946. Peggy Guggenheim Foundation, Venice. Within a structure redolent of Picasso, disturbing figures of a totemic type stand out.*

Francis Bacon (1909–1992) and Graham Sutherland (1903–80), and that of the Danish, Belgian, and Dutch artists of the CoBrA group. The malaise was evident, too, in Spain in the ironic Surrealism of the Catalan painters of the Dau al Set, who aimed to shatter the traditional values preached by Franco's dictatorship. On the other hand, both America and Europe saw a growth in the various manifestations of Art Informel, (art without form), spurred

"DAU AL SET"

The Spanish Dau al Set (which means "the seventh side of the dice" in Catalan) was a courageous attempt to react against the intellectual stagnation of postwar Spain. The group was born in 1948 out of the friendships between the poet Joan Brossa, the philosopher Arnaldo Puig, and the painters Joan Ponç (b. 1927), Modest Cuixart (b. 1925), Antoni Tàpies (b. 1923), and Joan Tharrats (b. 1918). It took its inspiration from the Dada movement, which had become known in Spain thanks to the promotional efforts of Francis Picabia

Antoni Tàpies, Newsprint Cross, *1946–47. Collage and watercolor on paper. Private Collection, Barcelona.*

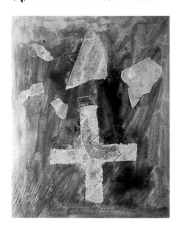

(1879–1953), who had founded the magazine *391* in Barcelona in 1917.

Another source of inspiration was Surrealism, to which Joan Miró (1893–1983) was still making a lively contribution. The Dau al Set adopted its provocative style, creating imaginary compositions that were often tinged with demonic elements. Soon after, Tàpies opted for a calmer type of painting that focused on an examination of the material quality of the paint used. After 1952, when the collective activity of the Dau al Set ceased, he freely embraced the ideas of Art Informel.

FRANCIS BACON: "STUDY FOR A POPE II"

1961; oil on canvas, 59 x 47 in (150 x 118 cm); Modern Religious Art Collection, Vatican Museums, Rome.

In this painting, Bacon reworks one of the most famous portraits by Velázquez, the *Portrait of Pope Innocent X*, painted in 1650 and now found in the Doria-Pamphili collection in Rome. Bacon often reinterpreted works by past masters, and this subject is one that Bacon treated over 40 times. This version is one of a series of six that he painted in 1961. In both artists' paintings, the subject, who is in his 70s, is shown seated on a large chair, wearing a camauro (a crimson velvet cap trimmed with ermine) and a rochet (linen vestment), which in the original is finely ruffled and has lacework, and a short satin mantelletta (sleeveless cape).

However, Bacon's re-creation of the painting is not based on a detailed analysis of the work. When he painted his first portrait of Velázquez's Pope, he had never seen the original, despite his efforts to get hold of a reproduction. Therefore, the subsequent works were all based on his work rather than the portrait by the Spanish master. This, in itself, is an indication of the artist's desire to distance himself from the original and any of its subtle nuances.

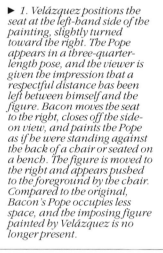
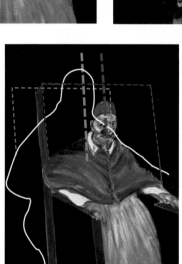
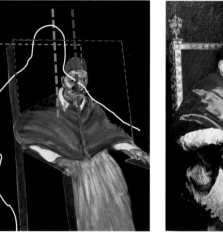
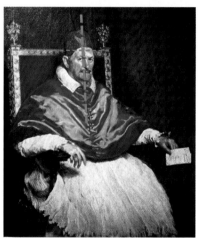

▶ *1. Velázquez positions the seat at the left-hand side of the painting, slightly turned toward the right. The Pope appears in a three-quarter-length pose, and the viewer is given the impression that a respectful distance has been left between himself and the figure. Bacon moves the seat to the right, closes off the side-on view, and paints the Pope as if he were standing against the back of a chair or seated on a bench. The figure is moved to the right and appears pushed to the foreground by the chair. Compared to the original, Bacon's Pope occupies less space, and the imposing figure painted by Velázquez is no longer present.*

on by an urge for the negation of form which, in spite of the avant-garde movements, remained in evidence. Italian artists, in particular, were torn between adopting a Realist language, which seemed more in tune with their political and social needs, and pursuing an interest in Art Informel and the techniques of geometrical Abstraction. The outcome was a composite array of proposals and the production of manifestos promoting the various trends, which in content echoed the style and exhortational tone of the early 20th-century avant-garde.

NEO-REALISM IN ITALY

After the war, Italy searched for an explanation of the recent events that had devastated the country and seeking a stimulus for widespread recovery. It was in this context that "Oltre Guernica" ("Beyond Guernica") was drawn up in Milan as the manifesto of Realism in 1946. The following year the *Fronte Nuovo delle Arti* (New Arts Front) was founded in Venice, a movement that drew its inspiration from Picasso's *Guernica* (1937) and its testimony to social commitment. The strong desire for social

participation provided a common focus for its members, whose styles and tastes varied greatly. While Renato Guttuso (1912–87) and Armando Pizzinato (b. 1910) displayed more inclination toward Realism, artists such as Renato Birolli (1905–59), Ennio Morlotti (b. 1910), Giuseppe Santomaso (b. 1907–90), and Emilio Vedova (b. 1919) were involved in developing abstraction. The heterogeneous nature of the group became clear in 1948 when the Communist Party, with which the artists were linked, was excluded from the government. Indeed, the

▶ *2. The grand chair of the Pope, red and ornate, becomes a black box outlined in yellow and dark green in Bacon's work. The background of the original is a damask red, full of light and enriched with a little yellow that highlights the Pope's satin mantelletta, which is a bright red with a spot of blue. In Bacon's work, the black chair is on a background of the same shade, but the whole composition is toned down: less volume, color, and importance is given to the subject. Velázquez's proud Pope has become a crushed man in Bacon's painting.*

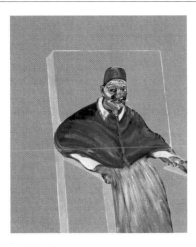

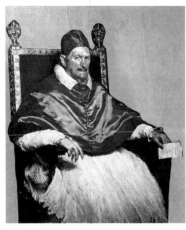

▼ *5. The left hand of Innocent X in Velázquez's portrait emerges from the lace handcuff, which Bacon excludes and rests on the arm of the chair in his painting. Between his index finger and thumb, the Pope is holding out a letter. Could it be an order to his favorites, Bernini and Borromini, or a decree? Bacon's Pope has no dispatch in his hand and does not manifest an air of wisdom and authority. Innocent X is no longer the great Baroque Pope, the powerful nepotist, but a man supported by his chair, disfigured by his anguish. He has become an icon of the violence of the 20th century. It is a painting of extreme pessimism, and Bacon's treatment of this previously proud figure leaves the viewer with a strong sense of unease.*

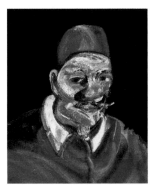

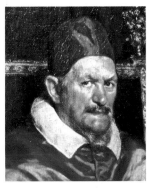

▼ *4. Bacon described his art as "an attempt to remake the violence of reality itself." He portrayed this by disfiguring parts of the image, passing a rag over the fresh paint, or degrading the subject by distorting its physical and psychological appearance. This humiliation is particularly obvious in the hands of the Pope. Their shape is no longer clear, and the streaked colour, which gives movement to the limbs, changes them into hooves with long claws that cling desperately to the arms of the chair. The contrast with the portrayal of the hands in the original is striking. John Rothenstein Rothenstein stated that Bacon's paintings communicated directly and acted immediately on the nervous system.*

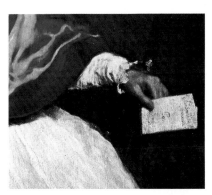

▲ *3. The faces of the figures indicate that Velázquez depicted his Pope as a lively old man, robust and full of color, with thin but firm lips. At that particular period in Rome, it was rumored that the Pope had become involved with his sister-in-law. As a result, there is a sense of a suspicious nature and an ability to control the situation. This is reflected in his look and demeanor, in the different positions of his hands, and in the general dominance of the figure over the chair. On the other hand, the face in Bacon's painting is distorted. The head is no longer held high, and the face is covered in touches of red and blue to give it a swollen effect. Gray and white encrusted areas surround the eyes. The Pope no longer looks imperiously at the observer and avoids eye contact with the world.*

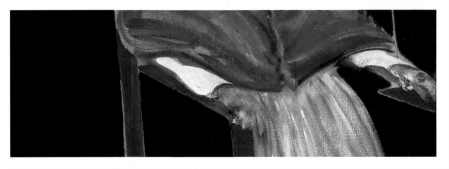

Communist party soon made it clear that they had no time for abstract art, which showed no apparent political commitment and was, therefore, of little value for its propaganda purposes. Through the 1950s, although artists such as Guttuso and Pizzinato stressed the didactic element of the popular style that they had developed, Birolli, Morlotti, Santomaso, and Vedova refused to tolerate any artistic limitations. In 1952 they joined the *Gruppo degli Otto* (Group of Eight) supported by the critic Lionello Venturi, giving free rein to their abstract inclinations.

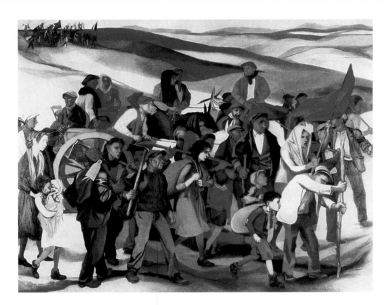

Renato Guttuso, L'occupazione delle terre incolte di Sicilia, 1949–50. Gemälde Galerie, Dresden.

Armando Pizzinato, Bracciante ucciso, 1949. Private Collection.

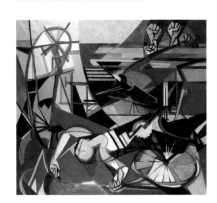

NEO-REALIST CINEMA

During the 1940s, Italian movie-making followed in the footsteps of the art world and turned its attention to the horrors of the war, particularly to the material and psychological havoc it had wreaked. In strong opposition to the propagandist and escapist cinema of the Fascist era, directors such as Luchino Visconti (1906–76), Roberto Rossellini (1906–77),

and Vittorio de Sica (1901–74) sought to represent the miserable way of life of the masses (*La terra trema,* 1948), the atmosphere of the rounding up of partisans during the German occupation (*Rome, Open City,* 1945), and the existential misery to which the weakest, particularly children, were subjected (*Shoeshine,* 1946).

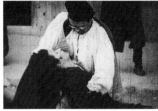

Rome, Open City, *1945. Movie directed by Roberto Rossellini.*

The cinematographic style was basic and rough, bordering on documentary crudeness. The casts were made up mostly of ordinary people rather than actors, and local dialects as well as Italian were used in the dialogue. In *La terra trema,* for example, the inhabitants of Acitrezza in Sicily spoke in their local dialect.

The precarious conditions in which the directors had to work meant they needed to put the stylistic needs of their vision in second place. Rossellini had to shoot *Rome, Open City* with out-of-date film and on makeshift sets.

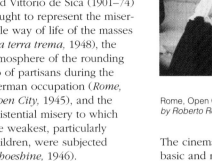

La terra trema, *1948. Movie directed by Luchino Visconti.*

in the US as well, in great part due to Piet Mondrian (1872–1944), who spent the last years of his life in New York.

Within the field of Abstract Expressionism in the 1940s and 1950s, artists such as Barnett Newman (1905–70) and Ad Reinhardt (1913–67) displayed an interest in an even more radical form of Abstraction. Their art was drawn out into a balanced construction of uniform areas of color – "color fields" – that were later to influence the minimalist work of the 1970s. Thus, they bridged the gap between art, which was predominantly instinctive, and the often extreme intellectualization that characterized geometric abstraction.

FORMA 1

The group Forma 1 was founded in Rome in 1947. Its intention was to make a stand against Realism, which was now seen as anachronistic, and to invite comparison with other European artistic tendencies. The group's manifesto was published in the only issue of the magazine of the same name, published in the same year. The members – Carla Accardi (b. 1924), Pietro

NEO-ABSTRACTION

At the end of the 1940s, a conflict developed between Realism and Abstraction between a figurative form of art derived from 19th-century models and a nonrepresentational form, inspired particularly by the De Stijl movement. In Italy, the opposing sides regarded each other with mistrust, the Neo-Realists believing that only they were capable of expressing the urgent need for social change and of communicating in a language that the wider public understood. The Abstract artists, though they did not intend to isolate themselves, wanted to choose their own

direction and not to be used for any political ends. Equally, they sought to keep up to date with the international art scene and distance themselves from

the traditionalism of the figurative style. This reawakening of an interest in Abstraction was not confined to Europe. The movement developed

Carla Accardi, Scomposizione, *1947. Civico Museo d'Arte Contemporanea, Milan. The work marks the pictorial debut of Carla Accardi as part of Forma 1, far removed from her subsequent sign painting.*

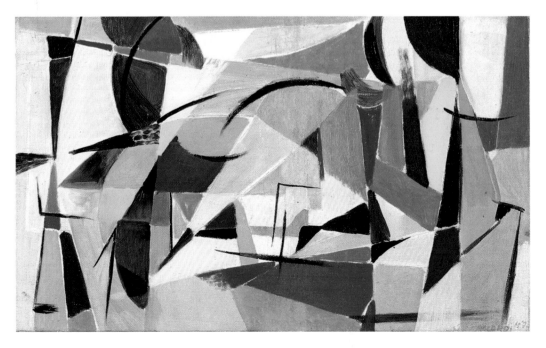

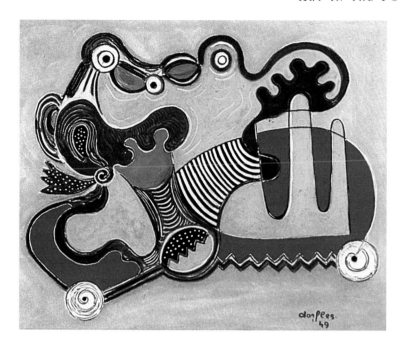

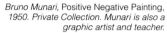

Gillo Dorfles, Composition, *1949. Dorfles later made a name as an art philosopher.*

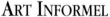

Bruno Munari, Positive Negative Painting, *1950. Private Collection. Munari is also a graphic artist and teacher.*

Consagra (b. 1920), Antonio Sanfilippo (b. 1923) , Piero Dorazio (b. 1927), Ugo Attardi (b. 1923), Giulio Turcato (1912–95), Achille Perilli (b. 1927), and Mino Guerrini – declared themselves "Formalists and Marxists." In order to placate those that were suspicious of Abstraction and associated its activities with bourgeois decadence, they emphasized that formal research did not necessarily rule out political commitment. As for their aesthetic aims, they declared that they were not interested in the figurative tradition ("the form of the lemon interests us, not the lemon"). They appeared to look to the French Neo-Cubist experience for inspiration and visited Paris frequently between 1947 and 1949. After three years, their collective activity gave way to individual work and led to the disbanding of the group in 1950.

CONCRETE ART

In 1948, the *Movimento Arte Concreta* ("Concrete Art Movement," or MAC) was founded in Milan to promote exploration into pure form.

Its objective was to ignore reality and create "art for art's sake," making "concrete" pictorial subject matter that would otherwise have remained in a mental sphere. Its argument was directed not only at the figurative art of the Neo-Realists but also at "lyrical abstraction" in general; they believed that it involved too much psychological analysis to be compatible with rigorous geometrical purism, as found in the work of the group's spiritual guides, Mondrian and van Doesburg.
Although they shared the same beliefs in purity and "concreteness," the founders of the movement – Gillo Dorfles (b. 1910), Gianni Monnet (1912–58), Bruno Munari (b. 1907), and Atanasio Soldati (1896–1953) – differed greatly in their choice of techniques. The paintings of Dorfles featured a dreamlike element, absent in the strictly formal work of Munari, whose tireless research was directed toward *Arte Programmata* ("Program Art"). In a decade of activity, the movement widened its horizons.
In 1953, MAC became associated with *Groupe Espace* – a society promoting the

fusion of architecture, sculpture, and decoration in order to give art a more active role in the social context. As a result, they worked closely with the architects of Studio B24 and showed much interest in industrial design. However, when Gianni Monnet passed away in 1958, the group recognized that it had failed in its original objectives.

MARK TOBEY

Mark Tobey (1890–1976) was attracted to the sign-painting direction of Art Informel and spent time studying Oriental calligraphy and brushwork in a Zen monastery. Following a trip to China and Japan, he produced his "white writing" – a form of sign-drawing in short brushstrokes that interlink and overlap in a tight rhythm, creating areas that are dense in spiritual and physical energy. The analogy with writing is merely formal, however, and the small signs depicted are not characters from any mysterious language. He said, "'Writing' the painting, whether in color or neutral tones, became a necessity for me."

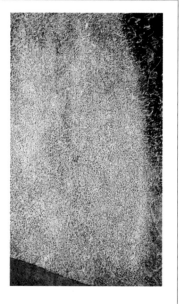

Mark Tobey, Edge of August, *1953. Museum of Modern Art, New York.*

ART INFORMEL

In the late 1940s and 1950s, Art Informel was a discernible trend in both America and Europe, particularly in France in the work of Jean Fautrier (1898–1964), Jean Dubuffet (1901–85), Georges Mathieu (b. 1921). Given such a wide geographical base, the results

JACKSON POLLOCK: "EYES IN THE HEAT"

1946; Oil on canvas, 54 x 44 in (137 x 110 cm); Peggy Guggenheim Foundation, Venice.

When Pollock painted this work, he was developing a new mode of expression – Art Informel using Action Painting. He was 34 and had already participated in various forms of artistic experimentation that characterized the 1930s and 1940s. In his work, he had remained faithful to the idea that the artistic process was the product of something within the artist, not just in the work, resulting from a mixture of religious, magical, and social

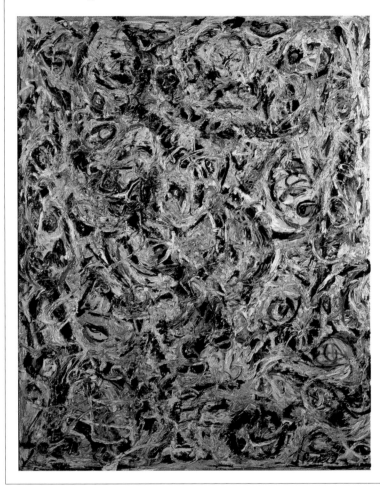

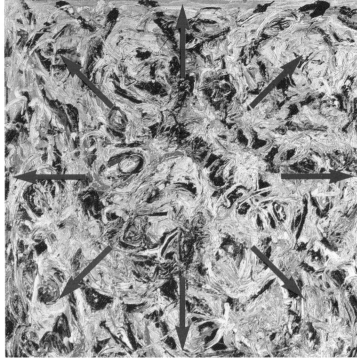

influences. He had formed this conviction through his studies of Native American artists, for whom the creation of art was a "shamanistic" act, and the work itself was considered a record and monument.

This picture was part of the personal collection of Peggy Guggenheim, who was one of the most important figures on the contemporary art scene on either side of the Atlantic at the time. While the work is to be considered in its own right, these details of its history help to set the context.

▲ *1. This rectangular, two-dimensional work does not appear to have a top or a bottom. In fact, it looks as if it should be part of a much larger work, rather like a photograph of a part of a distant galaxy. It appears so remote that it is hard to understand how the composition is structured and how the forms and colors can be understood. Pollock manipulates his surface by gestural strokes, strokes that contain a thought, a desire, or a force – he does not adapt to the expectations of the observer but liberates the work for its own intrinsic value. He does not reject all normal ideas of space and form but goes beyond them and makes himself the subject of the thick impasto.*

were varied, depending on the approach of individual artists and the particular cultural heritage that informed the works.

Art Informel soon abandoned figurative and geometric form and assumed various aspects that focused on gestural, material (matter-related), and calligraphic elements. In these three types of works, it exploited the energy of the gestures adopted in the execution of the painting; it extolled the values of the pictorial materials, not treating them in the traditional way as media, but giving them their own expressive force; and it used a sort of sign-writing derived from the "psychic automatism" of the *First Manifesto of Surrealism* (1924). While the styles that the artists adopted differed, one common denominator seemed to be the prevalently autobiographical nature of many of the works. They became symbolic visualizations of the artist's inner nature and a reflection of the artist's objection to the apparent lack of individuality in contemporary industrial society.

Among the most noted exponents of Art Informel in Spain were Antoni Tàpies (b. 1923), Rafael Canogar (b. 1935), and Antonio Saura (b. 1930); while in Germany, Emil Schumacher (b. 1912) and Georg Meistermann (1911–90) were the most important representatives. There was also some notable sculpture produced, particularly that by Asger Jorn

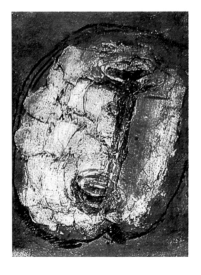

Jean Fautrier, Tête d'Otage No. 1, 1948. Giuseppe Panza di Biumo Collection, Varese. Fautrier used the haute pâte *technique, with superimposed layers of tempera and glue.*

▼ *2. In Action Painting, it is the gesture that both contains and manifests the concept. Attention is shifted away from the object being painted to the artist himself. The very act of painting lies at the root of the work and is more important than the subject that is depicted. Pollock is known for the "all-over" style, which leaves no points of emphasis. The passionate, assertive gesture creates a galaxy of lines, and in this maze of trails, spirals, and vortices we can see no depth but we can feel it. The painting seems to be in continuous movement, slipping and sliding, forming and dissolving, hiding and revealing. There is no pause in the work, no particular place on which to fix the eyes. The observer tends to follow with a mesmerized gaze the possible traces of how the work may have been constructed.*

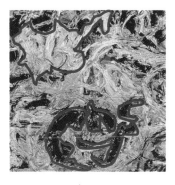

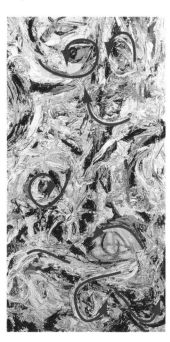

▲ *3. Like the work of a shaman, Jackson Pollock's paintings are not complete without the presence of light. It is not the light of chiaroscuro, of shadows or shading, however, for there is no identifiable source. Rather, it comes from the vibrancy of the gesture and is reflected in the color. The light is revealed in the application of whites and yellows, while the shadow lies in the blues and blacks. The whites stand out while the blacks sink into the background. This creates movement between the planes and makes the whole work palpitate. The colors seem to vibrate as the eyes follow them and traces the gesture. This way of understanding light breaks with the traditional concept of atmospheric space.*

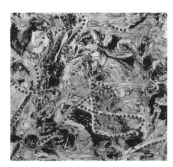

▼ *5. If we take the work and reproduce it in just black and white, it is hard to tell what the image could be. Is it a photograph of the surface of a planet? Is it a section of a piece of organic tissue? Anything that comes to mind seems to refer to a reality outside normal dimensions. This exercise does not seek to "understand" the subject of this painting by Pollock, which indeed has no subject above and beyond the act of painting. Its purpose is to appreciate the meaning of Action Painting. The intention is not to produce something attractive but to "create" in the strictest sense of the word.*

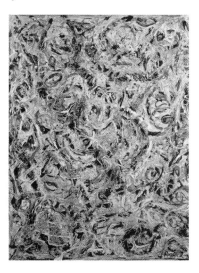

◄ *4. Pollock uses only a few colors in the work. Black and white dominate his palette. Black creates blots, vortices, and chasms in contrast to hints of shining yellow, stripes of red, or the occasional splash of blue. The colors gain in strength from powerful juxtaposition – for example, black and red, yellow and blue, and black and white. The brushwork becomes ever more entangled under the force of the gesture, which goes over and over the surface and displays the violent actions within the work.*

a particular place in the movement is reserved for Willem de Kooning (1904–97), who, while definitely a gestural artist, maintained an essentially realistic stance. His paintings are energetic abstractions that nonetheless display organic or biomorphic forms. The human figure is a central theme: for example, in his *Women* series, the shapes are just barely discernible, even though the brush has distorted their form in its construction – or destruction – of them. The figures seem close to disintegration and yet maintain a haunting presence within the whirl of color that engulfs them.

Franz Kline, Figure Eight, 1952. William S. Rubin Collection, New York. Displaying echoes of Pollock's aggressiveness in a maze of signs, Kline uses broad brushstrokes, like whiplashes, on the canvas.

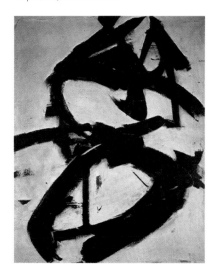

(1914–73), Corneille (b. 1922), Fontana (1899–1968), and the Pomodoro brothers Arnaldo (b. 1926) and Giò (b. 1930).

ACTION PAINTING

In the early 1940s, an art movement arose in New York that was inspired by the automatism theories of the Surrealists but at the same time driven by Expressionist tendencies. The work was very distant from figurative art, and its subject matter was the actual painting process itself. It became known as "Action Painting," a term coined in 1952 by American critic Harold Rosenberg. The works were produced with great speed to denote an urgency of communication. While the spontaneity of the gestures created the results, the general term "gestural painting" was used to describe them. Jackson Pollock (1912–56) worked in this vein, pouring, splashing, and dripping paint onto a canvas spread on the ground in an attempt to interact directly with it. Franz Kline (1910–62), on the other hand, used a decorator's flat brush to make sweeping black lines on a white background with a gestural vehemence of great visual impact. Sam Francis (1923–94) adopted similar methods to Pollock, using the drip technique on large canvases, but he achieved less convincing results. Outcomes such as these demonstrated how, in the absence of any real direction to the process, an artistic style based on the combination of colors in varying ways ran the risk of becoming reduced to decorative superficiality. However,

ACTION PAINTING IN ITALY

Action Painting found counterparts in Italy in the highly gestural work of the artists Emilio Vedova (b. 1919) and Mattia Moreni (b. 1920). In the early 1950s, Vedova began to handle the syncopated rhythm of his geometric shapes with more ebullience, creating tension on the canvas between contrasting elements. Moreni's style, on the other hand, featured large brushstrokes in bright colors that ran over the

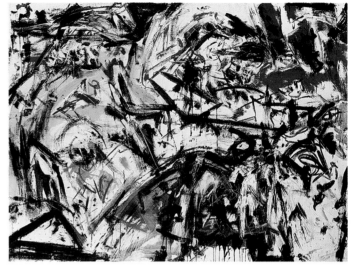

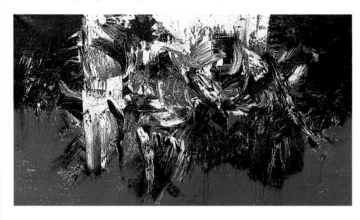

Emilio Vedova, Immagine del tempo '58 No. 3, *1958. Private Collection. Vedova is also a renowned set painter.*

Mattia Moreni, Situazione notturna, *1958. Private Collection.*

canvas in a rampant frenzy, representing in their size and thickness the psychological and physical energy that generated them.

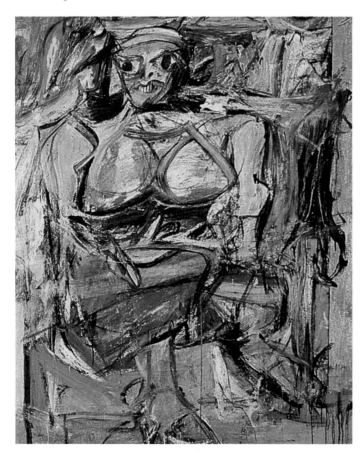

Willem de Kooning, Woman I, *1950–52. Museum of Modern Art, New York. The female nude is a recurrent motif in de Kooning's work.*

TACHISM

The term Tachism was adopted in 1954 by the French critic Charles Estienne to describe a way of painting characterized by *taches*, or stains of color, created by the splashing or spraying paint onto the canvas. Georges Mathieu (b. 1921) chose to express himself in this spontaneous way and developed a technique of composing tangles of abstract marks in a rapid semicalligraphic style. Mathieu carried out a number of his paintings in public with a sense of drama and panache that anticipated Performance Art. In 1959, in front of an audience at the Vienna meat market, he painted *Hommage au Connétable de Bourbon* on a large canvas in only 40 minutes. This instantaneous communication of a state of mind can also be seen in the random, chaotic drawings of the German artist Wols (*nom de guerre* of Alfred Otto Wolfgang Schultze, 1913–51), who arrived in Paris in 1932. Wols did not dedicate himself to Tachism until a few years before his death, turning to paintings of fibrous tangles mixed with patches and marks of color. Jean Fautrier (1898–1964) could also be counted among the tachistes. Fautrier gave his works a tactile consistency by building

Georges Mathieu, Les Capétiens partout, *1952. Musée National d'Art Moderne, Paris. Mathieu seems to stab at the canvas with the delicate thrust of a fencer.*

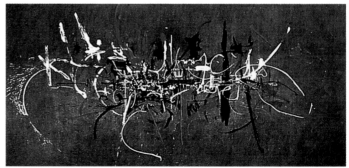

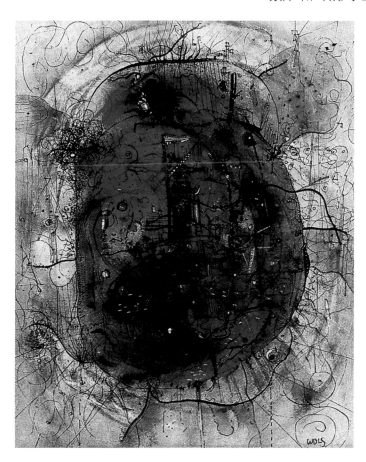

Wols, Composition V, *1946. Musée National d'Art Moderne, Paris. Wols's tangled threads suggest vibrant microcosms. The work has the echoes of the automatism of the Surrealists.*

uneven layers of tempera and glue, thickened with white, resulting in intensely dramatic impastoed surfaces. In his *Hostages* series, this medium brilliantly evoked Fautrier's reaction to the massacre of prisoners of war. His pictures often gave an impression of profundity and power.

"SPAZIALIZMO"

Spazializmo began with the "Manifesto Blanco," issued in 1946 in Buenos Aires by Lucio Fontana (1899–1968) at the Altamira Academy and became a movement a year later in Milan. Fontana wanted to open up artistic boundaries to the technical advances taking place. In his second manifesto (seven were published

between 1947 and 1953), he announced that new forms of artistic expression could be transmitted via the medium of television, and in 1952 he actually put forward a proposed artistic program for television, even though the medium was still in its early stages. Fontana was looking for a new artistic dimension that would allow him to escape from the confines of traditional tools, which would open up the skies with "artificial forms, rainbows of wonders, luminous sky writing." From this faith in technology came his use of ultraviolet light to create his "spatial atmosphere" at the Galleria del Naviglio in 1949 and for his neon decoration for the ninth Triennial in Milan in 1951. In his painting, he strove to go beyond the limited spheres of Neo-Realism and geometric Abstraction: hence his method of piercing the canvas in order to establish contact with the space

JEAN DUBUFFET

Influenced by the heavily impastoed painting of Fautrier and driven by a sort of Dada rebelliousness, Jean Dubuffet (1901–85) turned to the spontaneity of children's drawings in the years following the war. It was a subject that had previously fascinated Paul Klee. Despite their lack of formality, Dubuffet found more credibility in their simplicity than in any

other contemporary form of expression. In fact, naivete and an apparent lack of planning are inherent in his work, giving the impression that it was completed by the unsure hand of a child. Dubuffet valued creative intensity over the vagaries of composition. He found this quality in the works of psychotic artists and others outside the established art world, which he began to collect and gave the name Art Brut. He organized two shows – in 1947 and 1949 – at the René Drouin gallery in Paris and set up the *Compagnie de l'Art Brut* to gather and promote the art of the mentally ill. The numerous works assembled were then used to found the Musée de l'Art Brut in Lausanne.

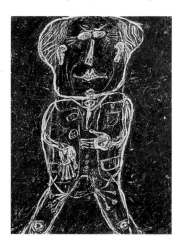

Jean Dubuffet, Monsieur Plume with Creases in his Trousers (Portrait of Henri Michaux), 1947. Tate Gallery, London. This work anticipates the graffito (scratched) technique.

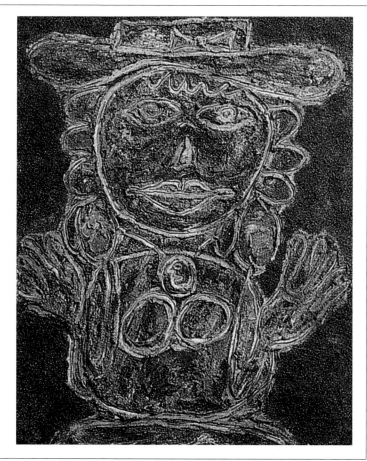

Jean Dubuffet, Noeud au chapeau, 1946. Moderna Museet, Stockholm. Children's drawings were the inspiration behind this composition.

BURRI

Originally trained as a doctor, Alberto Burri (1915–95) first began painting in a prisoner-of-war camp and subsequently made it his career. In 1949, together with Mario Ballocco (b.1913), Ettore Colla (1896–1968), and Giuseppe Capogrossi (1900–72), he founded the Origin group "as a liberation from multiple superstructures and as identification with the truth contained within ourselves" (1950 manifesto). His series of sacks, sheets, molds, cracks, and the like were often made from poor, degraded, or artificial materials. Using these methods, he expressed a world of splits, silence, decomposition, and aridity, albeit with classical elegance, great vigor, and a heightened sense of color. Among non-figurative artists, Burri most effectively transmitted the essence of the search for classical, vibrant, and vital form.

surrounding the painting. As well as the conceptual value of this action, the slashes in the canvas had a pictorial impact, creating protrusions and indentations with subtle chiaroscuro effects. The inevitable links with the working practices of Art Informel became more obvious when Fontana abandoned monochrome backgrounds. He took to making his canvases more elaborate with the additions of colored

materials – a technique that would lead to the *Stone* series (1951–56), followed in the 1960s by his "slashed" paintings. In fact, the experiments of the founder of Spazializmo far outlasted the active life of the group, which ended in 1954. During its life, it had involved personalities of various backgrounds, including Gianni Dova (b. 1925), Roberto Crippa (1921–72), and Cesare

Peverelli (b. 1922), and even artists inclined toward more informal styles, such as Parmigianni Tancredi, Giuseppe Capogrossi, and Alberto Burri. During the 1960s, Fontana continued his activities, when he produced works including *Ambienti spaziali* and *Teatrini,* which were forms of sculpture-paintings with irregularly molded projecting frames in lacquered wood.

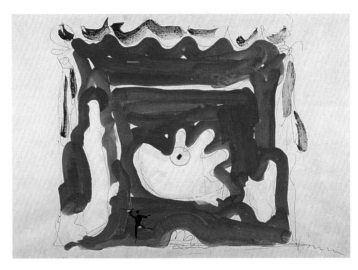

Lucio Fontana, curtain for the ballet Portrait of Don Quixote *by Goffredo Petrassi, 1976–77. Teatro alla Scala, Milan. This is one of Fontana's rare works for the theater.*

Lucio Fontana, Spatial Concept, 1951. *Civico Museo d'Arte Contemporanea, Milan. Fragments of colored material strewn over the canvas balance relief with the depth suggested by the holes in an interplay of convex and concave.*

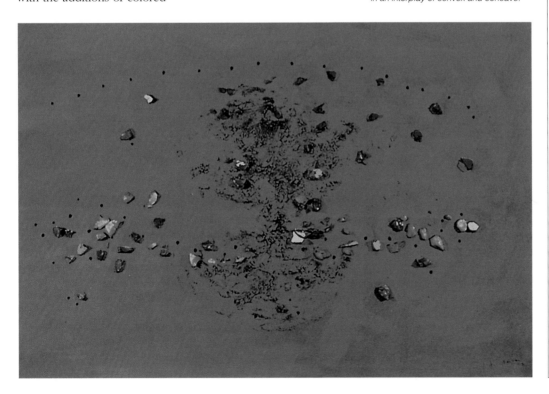

ALBERTO BURRI: "SACKING AND RED"

1954. Jute sackcloth sewn and glued to red background, 34 x 39 in (86 x 100 cm) Tate Gallery, London. The work has a bright, intense monochrome background, on which strips of sacking material are glued. On the lower edge of the horizontal motif, the material has been cut with scissors. In the central area, there are pieces that have been sewn or darned. At the top, the border is uneven and has been rolled like the edge of a handkerchief and stiffened with glue. On the natural jute, there are three colors. To the left, there is a gray insert with a mottled effect. A wide border of reddish brown sacking has its hem folded under and sewn with large stitches. A black background appears intermittently through the tears in the sacking. In this work, Burri reveals how important he considered the manual aspect of artistic production, its inherent imperfections loaded with expressive potential.

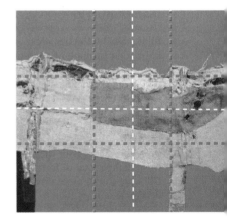

▲ *1. Initially, there appears to be no clear geometrical order to the work. The brown sacking starts about one-third of the way along the base on the left, and the jute border descending to the right is positioned about two-thirds along. The band of sacking that covers the canvas is split and sewn in a horizontal direction. This stitching continues in the bottom part of the brown sacking, and its line, uneven and broken, marks approximately the middle of the work. It is as if the artist had in mind classical rules of composition, imposing them lightly and subtly altering them, rather as a late 20th-century poet exploits metric scansion within seemingly irregular verse.*

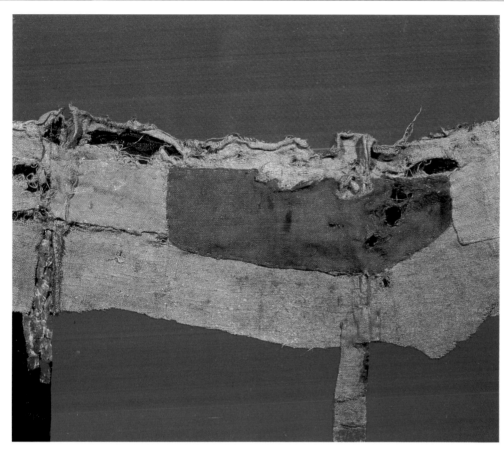

▼ 4. If the movement of the horizontal and vertical lines are considered separately, it is noticeable that the former are more prominent than the latter. All of them are relatively rigid, and there are no oblique lines. The dynamism of the work lies almost solely in the color. The material is presented flatly, without depth or perspective. There are no faster or slower moments in the steady flow of the wave crossing the picture from left to right. With the presence of stitching, tears, and variously colored points, it takes on meaning when juxtaposed with the red. From this wave, which becomes clearer after observing the work in detail, two strong vertical lines descend. To the left there is a black rectangle within the red, rich in gray; to the right is a strip of sacking, rich in red at its base. It is hard to say if the two elements act as a support to the band or as offshoots of material, shading, and color.

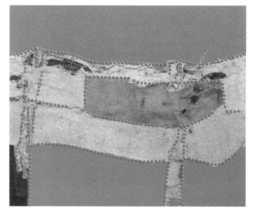

▶ 2. If one were to draw horizontal and vertical lines centrally onto the work, one would see that the sacking areas are not positioned casually at all. There is quite clearly an equilibrium between right and left. The large brown patch with the black parts on the right is counterbalanced by the area on the left, in which gray and black prevail. In the balance of colors, a dark surface "weighs" more than a light area of the same size. Through this sophisticated manipulation of dimensions, the artist has given an ordinary material like sacking the characteristics of painting. There are two main colors in the composition: red and the color of the jute. The other shades help bring out and balance these fundamental ones.

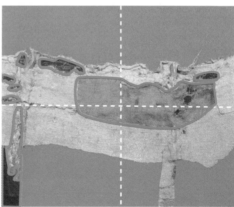

▼ 5. The tears in the sacking are of particular note. A modern artist who expresses himself through a specific material will often try out various adaptations of it to suit his or her needs. He can deform it, cut it, burn it, or tear it in order to give it the interpretation he desires. Sometimes, it is a case of realizing an impulsive idea through the medium, but at other times it is a way of revealing the violence of humankind. Burri was a doctor in the Italian army and a long-term prisoner of war in Texas; he treats the material in a way that reveals the violence of his era. The Italian writer Piero Bargellini once said that Burri's work revealed "a world at once wretched and refined, ephemeral and at the same time eternal." However, he remains an aesthetic artist, attached to the visual tradition and scenic values of central Italy. In its brilliant arrangement of red, sacking, and black, this work transcends its era and remains timeless.

◀ 3. As one looks at the work, no lines have been painted but have been achieved by juxtaposition, tears, and sewing, with some stronger than others. The contrast of the fabric with the red and black produces pronounced edges, while the stitching of strips of the same material gives movement to the surface. The tears create strong wrinkled lines, and where the material has been cut with scissors the line is slightly frayed, making it look softer. If we look at the movement of the horizontal lines, we can see that the most dramatic ones with the most relief are at the top, where they form a sort of horizon between the world of material and the sky of red paint. The contrast between the two different surfaces absorbs the tension created by the wrinkling and fraying. Above is the pure saturated color; below, the world of matter, with its earthy, natural colors.

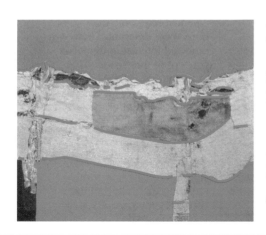

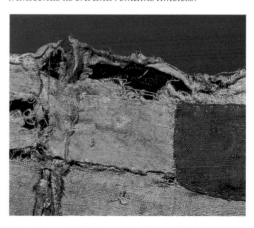

MARK ROTHKO

"I am interested only in expressing the basic human emotions – tragedy, ecstasy, doom, and so on – and the fact that lots of people break down and cry when confronted with my pictures shows that I communicated with those basic human emotions. The people who weep before my pictures are having the same religious experience I had when I painted them."

The work of Mark Rothko (1903–70) occupies a unique place in the field of American art of the 1950s. It cannot be

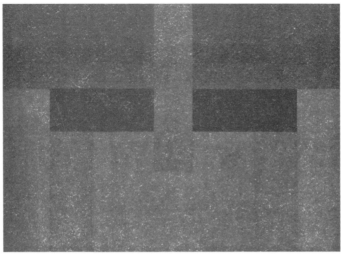

associated with the Action Painting of Pollock, de Kooning, or Kline, nor with the purist painting of Barnett Newman (1905–70) or Ad Reinhardt (1913–67), although it shared the use of color fields with the latter two. Rothko seems to fit halfway between the two extremes, sharing with both an interest in the Romantic notion of the sublime without using either gestural vigor or absolutely clean areas of color. Although Rothko worked on large canvases, he did not attack the surface with impetuous strokes in the manner of

Mark Rothko, Number 10, 1950. Museum of Modern Art, New York. The "color fields" – Rothko's trademark – are large areas of color set close to one another. The informal component of Rothko's mature work derives from the gestural freedom with which color is applied and from the irregular, superimposed outlines of juxtaposed color fields.

Barnett Newman, Onement VI, 1953. Weisman Collection, New York. Newman, too, worked with broad fields of color, but these were more strictly delineated. Unlike Rothko's works, these paintings did not invite emotional involvement but imposed themselves in terms of restrained abstraction.

gestural painting. On the contrary, he almost caressed the surface with soft brushstrokes, letting the color triumph without containing it within strict borders. The emotional intensity is revealed at the blurred edges, where one color yields to another with the fluidity characteristic of moods. The vast dimensions of the color fields are fundamental to the process of involving the viewer emotionally in the painting. The result of their scale is the prevention of a rational, controlled response in the views.

Ad Reinhardt, Red Painting, 1952, Metropolitan Museum of Art, New York. Like Newman, Reinhardt worked with bright color fields, but he contrasted chromatic tones in geometric compositions. His essentially formal works are identifiable with earlier Systemic Painting.

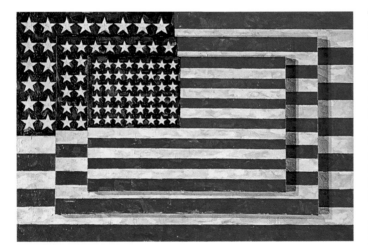

Jasper Johns, Three Flags, 1958. Mr. and Mrs. Burton Tremaine Collection, Connecticut.

NEO-DADA

At the end of the 1950s, the American art scene turned its attentions away from the interior world of the artist, valued so highly by the exponents of Action Painting, and began to concentrate on the nature of objects. This change of direction does not mean that the medium of painting was ignored, however. In the work

of Jasper Johns, it played an essential role; only the intentions were different. There was renewed interest in the Dada concept of the "ready-made," in the basic value of objects or in their mass-produced counterparts. Robert Rauschenberg (b. 1925) combined the gesture implicit in Action Painting with fragments of everyday life, used objects, stuffed animals – in short, anything that reflected the ways of contemporary society. Jasper Johns (b. 1930), on the other hand, used painting to

"NOUVEAU REALISME"

In the early 1960s, a parallel movement to American Neo-Dada was developing in Europe. Headed by the critic Pierre Restany (b. 1930), the French group of New Realists, including artists such as Arman (b. 1928), César (b. 1921), Daniel Spoerri (b. 1930), Jean Tinguely (1925–91), and Mimmo Rotella (b. 1918), took up the Dada concept of the "ready-made." They used objects in their raw state, advocating the use of real materials and existing artifacts. Arman used litter in his series of *Poubelles* ("Trashcans"), while Daniel Spoerri framed fragments of newspapers, like a memorial to past events. These works have clear echoes of the Dadaist artist Kurt Schwitters, who created collages with buttons, bus tickets, and various other paraphenalia. In Spoerri's work, however, the objects are given complete "roles" in which they seem to represent the tangible evidence of a scene from daily life. Therefore, the leftovers from a meal or an ashtray full of cigarette butts suspends actions that have been

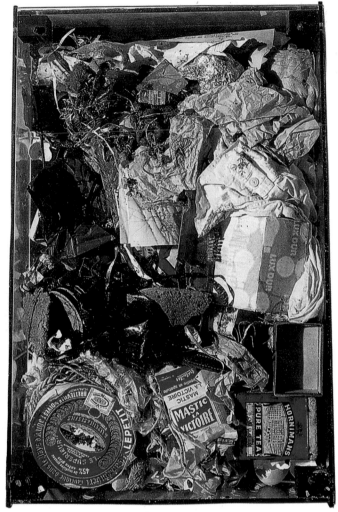

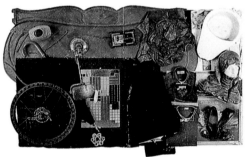

completed, remaining as a testimony for all time. Completely different results were achieved by the Bulgarian artist Christo (b. 1935), who was especially interested in the disorienting effects provoked by certain Dada works. For example, in Man Ray's *Enigma of Isidore Ducasse* (1920) the wrapping of a sewing machine in fabric completely changes the nature of this everyday object. All of a sudden it is

Fernandez Arman, Petits déchets bourgeois, *1959. Artist's Collection.*

Daniel Spoerri, Tableau-Piège, *1966. Galerie Mathias Fels, Paris.*

Christo, The Aurelian Wall, *1973. Rome.*

shrouded in an aura of mystery that really has nothing to do with the object. It is easy to understand, therefore, why Christo's most ambitious projects, such as the wrapping of the Aurelian Wall in Rome (1973) and the Reichstag in Berlin (1996), have reached the conceptual extremes of Land Art.

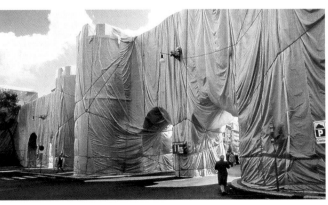

RAUSCHENBURG, JOHNS, AND DANCE

The activities of Rauschenberg and Johns were not confined to painting but extended to the experimental dance world of Merce Cunningham. Rauschenberg designed his costumes and sets and was responsible for the lighting of performances for ten years from 1955. Johns was the artistic consultant, bringing the rich variety of Neo-Dada to Cunningham's choreography. This union relied upon their shared interests. Cunningham's dance, in its conjunction of the most varied steps and positions, can be seen as almost a choreographic translation of the Neo-Dadaist assemblage of objects.

reproduce banal, commonplace objects. Exemplary of this is the series of *Flags* (1958), in which the pictures almost become objects themselves, though they never totally renounce their own intrinsic characteristics. In this mediation between a traditional concept of painting and the poetry of objects, Neo-Dada represents a moment in the passing from Abstract Expressionism to Pop Art.

Robert Rauschenberg, Untitled, *1963. Guggenheim Museum, New York.*

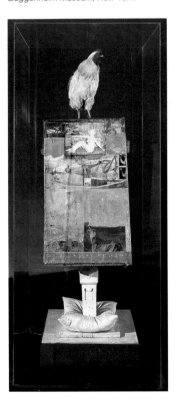

THE NEW AVANT-GARDE & POSTMODERNISM

Since the 1960s, artistic exploration has proceeded apace on a global scale. Among the many and varied developments witnessed in recent decades are the reworking of complex traditional styles, the introduction of new media, and a broadening of artistic horizons, characterized by a willingness to experiment and to push artistic expression to the limit.

The 1950s saw the triumph of Art Informel (Art without form), a type of expressive abstract painting that celebrated the artist's uniqueness and individuality in defiance of industrial mass-production and its dehumanizing effect on society. During the 1960s and 1970s, however, the creation and appreciation of art demanded less emotional involvement.

NEW DIRECTIONS

Of the prominent movements, Kinetic art favored mass-production, with materials and techniques borrowed from industrial science; meanwhile, Pop art took its inspiration from the iconographic reper-toire of the consumer world. However, neither of these new artistic tendencies wanted the viewer to be passive or alien-ated. Indeed, never before had the public been so encouraged to participate. While Art Informel had assimilated the experiences of Expressionism and Surrealism, the artists of the new avant-garde drew on the infinite inventions of Dadaism, which had attempted to break down all the barriers between art and life and to make them interchangeable. The "ready-made" (the mass-produced article elevated to the status of "art"), which had already surfaced in the art of Neo-Dada and Nouveau Réalisme, now appeared in a new guise under the banner of Pop art.

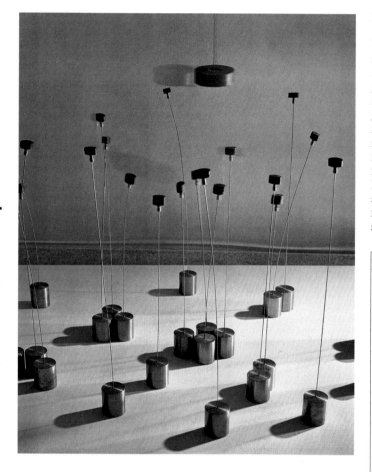

Takis, Magnetic Fields *(detail), 1969. Guggenheim Museum, New York. This Kinetic sculpture is based on the activation and deactivation of a magnet, which causes a reaction of the other negative and positive magnets, variously in states of repulsion or attraction. The composition created by the magnets changes in accordance with the variation of the magnetic field.*

Other revolutionary initiatives that were taken by the Dadaists emerged in the various forms of expression of Conceptual art. For the first time, art was to be found away from its usual location in a gallery and was presented in the open air, town squares, or remote, inaccessible parts of the world. It was seen on screen, for example, or in the street in the form of an artist pretending to be a sculpture. Towns and cities worldwide were becoming focal points for the new trends. In the early 1960s, the development of Pop art took place predomi-nantly in the US, while

Europe, previously the center of artistic change, lagged behind. A decade later, the art scene, as represented by its important events and leading groups, had become more international. However, by going down this road to total freedom and accessibility, many of these avant-garde movements paradoxically failed in their pursuit of the Dada connection between art and life. Art became distanced from the public, lost in intro-spection and experimentation.

OPTICAL ART

Optical art, or Op art, made its first official appearance in 1965 at the Museum of Modern Art in New York as part of "The Responsive Eye" show organized by William Seitz.

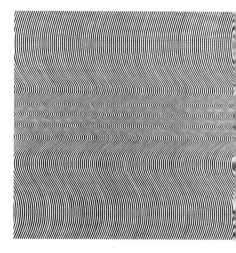

Bridget Riley, Current, *1964. Museum of Modern Art, New York.*

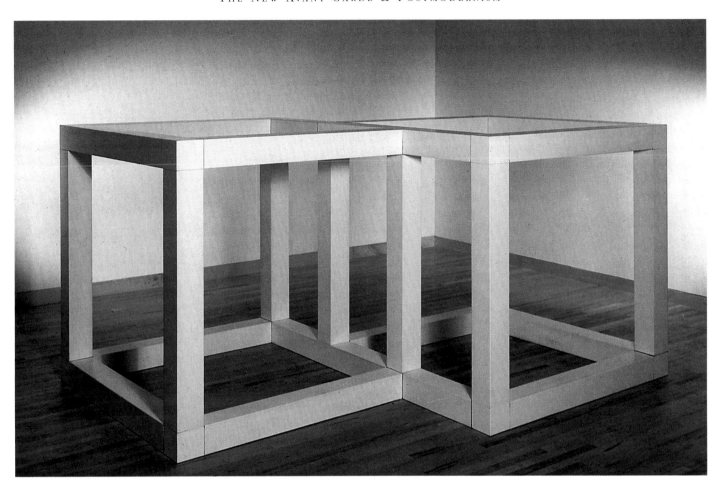

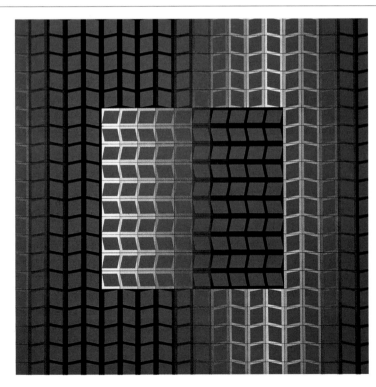

Participants included Victor Vasarely (1908–97), Jesús Rafael Soto (b. 1923), and Bridget Riley (b. 1931). The novelty of Op art works lay in the optical effects and illusions they contained, such as the illusion of movement or volume on a flat, static surface. For the effect to be successful, however, Op art required the participation of the spectator. This was not active participation as in some Kinetic art, nor audience participation as in certain happenings, but rather a psychological form of collaboration that would allow the illusions created by the artist to be experienced by the viewer. By concentrating on the picture or by moving to the best spot in order to view it, the spectator actually established contact with the work, often remaining transfixed by its hypnotic power. The images by British artist Bridget Riley capture the eye and invite it into a web of sinuous lines that look almost alive (*Current*, 1964).

Victor Vasarely, Zett-Kek, 1966. Sidney Janis Gallery, New York. The network structure and color variations create a three-dimensional illusion.

Sol Lewitt, Two Open Modular Cubes/Half Off, 1975. This large sculpture, or "structure," by the American Conceptual artist Sol Lewitt impresses both with its simplicity and its geometric forms. Its very construction invites intellectual curiosity and engagement rather than an emotional response.

KINETIC ART

The 1961 "Nouvelle Tendance" (New Tendency) show in Zagreb exhibited the diverse Constructivist tendencies that were coming to the fore in Western Europe. Participants included the GRAV (Groupe de Recherche d'Art Visuel) in Paris, Gruppo N in Padua, and Gruppo T in Milan, all of whom were motivated by the desire to make art more accessible by demonstrating the ways in which it is perceived. Their methods sought to bring art closer to a wider public by involving the viewer directly. The sculptures, or *assemblages,* which were devised with mathematical

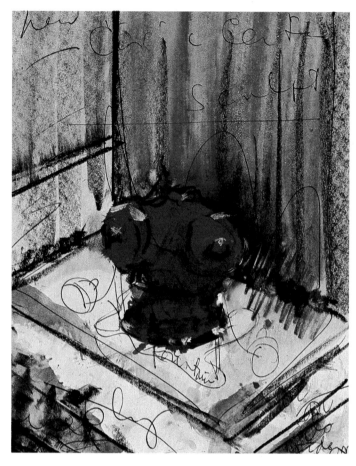

Claes Oldenburg, Giant Fireplug Sited in the Civic Center, Chicago, 1968. *Kimiko and John Powers Collection, Colorado.*

precision, did not bear the artist's stylistic mark or speak of any emotions but stood as basic demonstrations of themselves. Kinetic art incorporated actual moving parts (as opposed to Op art, which *implied* motion in its images).

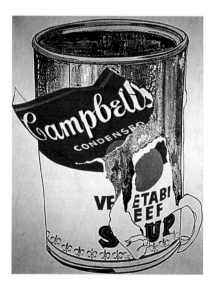

Andy Warhol, Big Torn Campbell's Soup Can (vegetable beef), 1962. *Bruno Bischofberger Gallery, Zurich.*

The movement was derived either from the intrinsic nature of the objects, such as mobiles, or from devices causing the motion. Sometimes the public was invited to intervene in the workings of the sculpture. This is the case with *Oggetto a composizione autocondotta* (Object with Self-Regulating Composition, 1959) by Enzo Mari (b. 1932), in which geometric shapes enclosed in a glass container change their arrangement according to alterations made by the spectator. Kinetic works were completely devoid of the sacred "do not touch" aura usually surrounding art and demanded more involvement than the passive acceptance usually associated with viewing art. The artists themselves wanted to avoid the narcissistic self-involvement of some Art Informel artists and

to lose their identity within the discipline of a more collective activity. However, these hopes were soon to be dashed by the rapid rise to fame of certain members of the group.

POP ART

In the early 1960s, an artistic trend developed in the US that was to represent a complete departure from Action painting, the dominant movement of the previous decade. While Action painting had given pride of place to the inner impulses of the artist and to autobiographical motivation and subjectivism, the new tendency was to accentuate the sheer neutrality of everyday consumer goods. But the images were not the actual objects, or "ready-mades," as found in Dadaism, but a reworking of them, greatly elaborated in dimension or color. Claes Oldenburg (b. 1929) blew up seemingly banal items into gigantic sizes, transforming trowels, tubes of toothpaste, and clothespins into huge sculptures. He also created brightly painted plaster sculptures of desserts, cakes, and pieces of meat and made models of hard, unyielding objects, such as light switches and typewriters, in soft, pliable materials. Andy Warhol (1928–87), on the other hand, took well-known images from popular culture such as cans of Campbell's Soup, Coca-Cola bottles, or photographs of stars who had become legends (Elvis Presley, Marilyn Monroe) and turned them into prints or paintings that shared the repetitive, mass-produced feel of commercial "art." The mechanical insistence of repetition also succeeded in removing meaning from images that were in themselves very dramatic. This is the case with the symbols of death and social struggle that Warhol depicts in *Orange Disaster* (1963) and *Race Riot* (1964); they are reduced to the status of decorative elements. If Warhol annihilated the

significance of an image by constant, unvarying repetition, then Roy Lichtenstein (1923–97) emphasized its importance, taking the image out of its context and reproducing it on a large scale. Thus a comic strip, usually a disposable piece of light reading, was suddenly elevated to the status of a work of art. Tom Wesselman (b. 1931) portrayed female nudes in commonplace environments as if they, too, were consumer objects, lacking facial expression and recognizable only by their

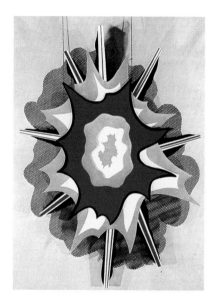

Roy Lichtenstein, Wall Explosion no. 1, 1964. *Wallraf-Richartz Museum (Ludwig Collection), Cologne.*

exaggerated erotic features. Striking a more existential note, American sculptor George Segal (b. 1924) made plaster-cast models, taken from life, of people frozen in varied poses or in the act of carrying out certain tasks. These figures, in their isolated stillness, seem to convey modern man's alienation from daily life.

CONCEPTUAL ART

Marcel Duchamp's *Bicycle Wheel* (1913) did more than transfer attention from the imitation of an object to the object itself: it opened up the way for the "ready-made,"

POP ART IN BRITAIN

At the "This is Tomorrow" exhibition of 1956 at the Whitechapel Art Gallery in London, a photographic collage by Richard Hamilton (b. 1922) marked the debut of British Pop art, later becoming a virtual manifesto of the movement. The collage's very title – *Just what is it that makes today's homes so different, so appealing?* – hinted at the satire to be found in the work. It contained in its interior setting various symbols of popular mass culture – from the body-builder in the foreground and the cover girl on the couch to the television and various electrical appliances, and the theater signs and posters glimpsed through the window. While these are all recognizable elements of daily life, they look unnatural, resembling items in a shop display.

A critical attitude toward the values of consumer society was an underlying theme of British Pop art, as opposed to the neutral stance that characterized American Pop art. Pop artists in Britain regarded contemporary life from a distance and depicted it with a critical eye, while those in the US seemed to

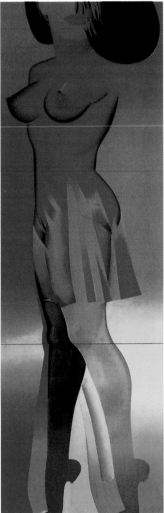

Allen Jones, Perfect Match, *1966–67. Wallraf-Richartz Museum, Cologne.*

restrict their work to live, "unedited" recordings of consumer society. Subtle irony permeates the work of Peter Blake (b. 1932), David Hockney (b. 1937), and Allen Jones (b. 1937). Jones reproduced the iconographic repertory of

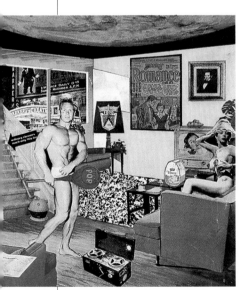

Richard Hamilton, Just what is it that makes today's homes so different, so appealing?, *1956. Private Collection, Thousand Oaks, California.*

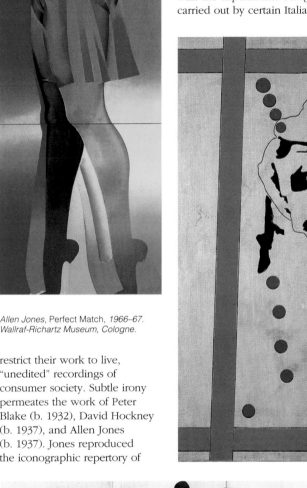

the female body as viewed in soft-porn magazines, with the pictorial synthesis of a billboard.

POP ART IN ITALY

When American Pop art was first seen in Italy at the Venice Biennial exhibition of 1964, it provoked a strong reaction from the authorities, and the President of the Republic refused to participate in the opening ceremony. However, the works included revealed clear links with the experiments being carried out by certain Italian

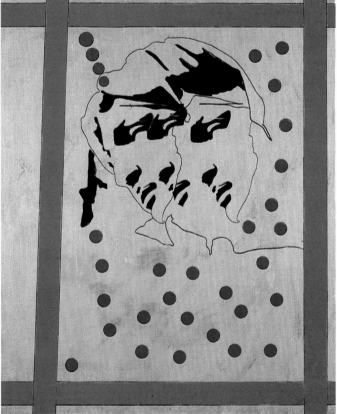

Tano Festa, Michelangelo according to, *1967. Comit Collection, Milan.*

Mario Schifano, Futurism Revisited, *1966. Private Collection.*

artists, such as Enrico Baj, Tano Festa, Mimmo Rotella, and Mario Schifano. The subject matter varied between the two currents, simply because of the differing economic and cultural backgrounds of the artists. The American artists favored consumer objects, whereas Italian Pop art was often based on a satirical observation of past art movements and masterpieces. In *Michelangelo according to* (1967) by Tano Festa (1938–88), the plasticity of Michelangelo's style is flattened into a polka-dot decoration, while

in *Futurism Revisited* (1966) by Mario Schifano (b. 1934), the historic photograph of the Futurist group led by Marinetti loses its original documentary value with the deletion of the subjects' faces.

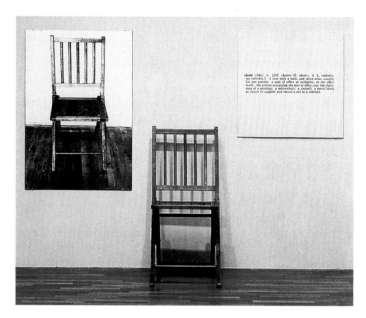

Joseph Kosuth, One and Three Chairs, *1965. Museum of Modern Art, New York. Kosuth's work operates on three levels: the chair is at once real, virtual (photographed), and described in words.*

exploited the potential of raising everyday objects to new levels of aesthetic worth. The Conceptual artists looked back to Duchamp and his principle of considering the concept more important than the artistic process. They devoted themselves to viewing the art object as only the inevitable visualization of the idea that generated it. In *One and Three Chairs* (1965), for example, American experimental artist Joseph Kosuth (b. 1945) displays an actual chair, a photograph of a chair, and a written definition of the word from a dictionary, drawing attention to the notion of appearances and concepts. In this rather cerebral artistic dimension, the power of the artist is accentuated despite his apparent absence, for even though the active presence of the artist is minimized, his role

which would prove so important in the second half of the century for the Neo-Dadaists and Nouveau Réalistes, and

as producer or director is in turn heightened. The work *Giovane che guarda Lorenzo Lotto* (Young Man looking at Lorenzo Lotto, 1967) by Giulio Paolini (b. 1940) is a simple photographic reproduction on canvas of a portrait by the Venetian painter Lorenzo

Giulio Paolini, Giovane che guarda Lorenzo Lotto, *1967. Private Collection.*

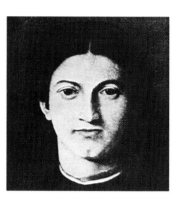

HAPPENINGS AND PERFORMANCE ART

Happenings were a hybrid form of art, taking their inspiration freely from theatrical, musical, literary, pictorial, and sculptural methods of expression. It was already an established trend in the 1950s, but only in the following decade did it receive serious widespread attention. More or less simultaneous experiments were carried out

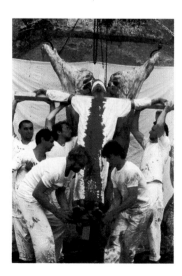

Herman Nitsch, Action. *The performance evokes pagan and Christian symbols.*

by the Japanese Gutai group, which was active in Osaka from 1954, and by the American artist Allan Kaprow (b. 1927). He was the first to use the term "happening" to define apparently improvised events that featured collaborators who had, in fact, been briefed beforehand. While these events were not totally spontaneous and were dictated by a plan, the final outcome was never intended to be predictable. Artists from other fields who dedicated their energies to happenings were the exponents of Pop art Jim Dine (*The Smiling Workman*, 1960) and Claes Oldenburg (*The Store*, 1961), and the Fluxus group. This included artists from various backgrounds, among them Daniel Spoerri (Nouveau Réaliste), George Brecht, Yoko Ono, Ben Vautier, and Joseph Beuys (working in Conceptual fields), and Nam June Paik and Wolf Vostell (founders of video art). Happenings exerted a strong influence on theater and contemporary dance, offering an alternative to more traditional forms of stage direction and

choreography. The expressive freedom of Performance art inspired the Off Broadway theater group and the Merce Cunningham Dance Company, whose collaboration with John Cage (avant-garde musician and member of Fluxus) led to a freer interpretation of the relationship between the body, music, and the stage. The exponents of

the Wiener Aktionismus were authors of particularly extreme happenings and performances, which were akin to behavioral research. The sequences performed by Herman Nitsch (b. 1938), founder of the Orgien Mysterien Theater in the late 1950s, were so gruesome that they verged on outright acts of sacrilege: in what appeared as

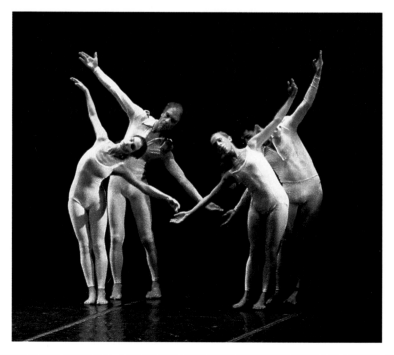

The Merce Cunningham Dance Company in Milan, 1980.

Lotto. The title, alluding to the original 16th-century work, is slightly odd and thought-provoking itself. If the young man in the portrait is looking at Lorenzo Lotto, then anyone in front of the picture can identify themselves with Lotto, i.e. the painter of the portrait Paolini's work, therefore, consists of an imaginary situation dictated by the title. Its impact rests on the possible momentary union of spectator and painter, based on the idea that Lorenzo Lotto could be transferred through time and space while painting his model. Conceptual art frequently posed such enigmas, often using the most simple of ideas to set off a chain of far wider questioning. More dramatic projects, however, were not ruled out. At the Venice Bienniale in

1972, Gino De Dominicis (b. 1947) exhibited a mentally ill young boy, who was seated on a chair to be viewed by the visitors. Meanwhile, Antonio Paradiso (b. 1936) organized a "Performance" that consisted of a bull mating with a mechanical cow.

BODY ART

When Duchamp dressed up as his feminine alter ego Rose Sélavy, covered himself with shaving foam to hide features of his body, or had his head shaved in the shape of a star to be recorded for posterity by the lens of Man Ray, he was giving artistic meaning to his body and transforming it into a work of art. The wit and irony found in Duchamp's work reemerged in the early 1960s in the creations of Piero Manzoni (1933–63), who in 1961 proposed turning people into living sculptures by keeping their bodies still and adorning them with certificates of authenticity. That same year, he also caused an uproar with his *Merda d'artista,* which consisted of 90 cans of the artist's excrement, for sale at the same price, weight for weight, as gold. However, the Body art that established itself in the later 1960s and 1970s was characterized by predominantly masochistic attitudes. It involves the misuse or abuse of the body and condemning

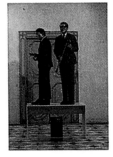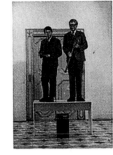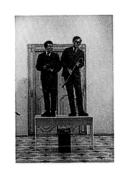
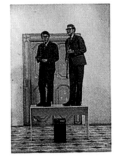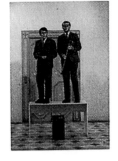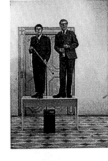
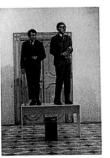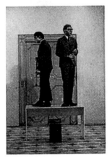

Gilbert & George, G & G at via del Paradiso, *1972. Attico Gallery, Rome. Exhibiting themselves in galleries as living sculptures is just one example of the art of British artists Gilbert and George. They regard their very days as works of art and their whole existence as a kind of artistic continuum.*

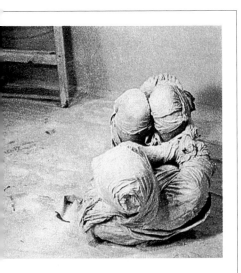

Günter Brus, Ana, 1964. Diagramma Gallery, Milan.

purging rituals, the participants were covered in the blood of sacrificial animals. Günter Brus (b. 1938), wrapped himself in bandages and simulated epileptic fits (*Ana,* 1964) or defecated in public (*Scheiss-Aktion,* 1967), while Rudolph Schwarzkogler (1949–69) would perform self-deprecating acts, such as smearing his body with blood and excrement. His suicide was interpreted by some as the final act of a performance of self-destruction.

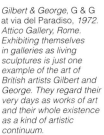

Piero Manzoni, Scultura vivente, 1961. La Tartaruga Gallery, Rome.

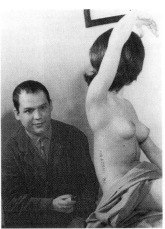

existential violence through a demonstration of self-inflicted suffering. Gina Pane (b. 1939), for example, wounded herself with a variety of instruments, assigning negative feelings to symbols usually viewed in the opposite context. The roses in *Azione sentimentale* (1974) were not embraced in an exaltation of romanticism but to show the physical suffering inflicted by the thorns. Even when not engaged in painful actions, the image of the human body was distorted and its vitality transformed into a brute force. The Austrian artist Arnulf Rainer (b. 1929) had himself photographed in unnatural poses and then accentuated the crudeness by painting violent brushstrokes on the results. Self-inflicted pain gave way to humorous narcissism in the work of Gilbert & George (b. 1943 and 1942 respectively), who united to proclaim themselves

"continuous sculptures" and to propose their very existence as an artistic continuum.

VISUAL POETRY

Visual poetry was a descendant of the Futurist free-word style, in which words were displayed in ways that contravened any of the traditional norms of order and arrangement on the page. However, whereas the free words of Futurist compositions were valued ultimately as icons, in visual poetry the actual *meaning* of the words was indispensable to our understanding of the work. The verbal content was not in the form of captions or as a support to the images it accompanied, but was present to introduce meaningful diversions with a provocative content. These verbal visualizations also took images and slogans from the mass media and employed them in an ironic context. Emilio Isgrò (b. 1937) achieved notable results in this field, although he opted for more personal interpretations than *assemblages* of words and images. In his work *Dio è un essere perfettissimo* (God is a Perfect Being, 1965) he parodies the link between religion, advertising, and mass-produced consumer goods. In another Conceptual manifestation, he deletes entire pages of books, leaving just a few words that gave evidence of unnecessary verbosity. More attention was given to the expressive potential of words by the protagonists of Concrete poetry, who came from literary, philosophical, and musical backgrounds. They conveyed their intent through patterns of words, letters, and symbols, rather than through a conventional arrangement of sentences. This

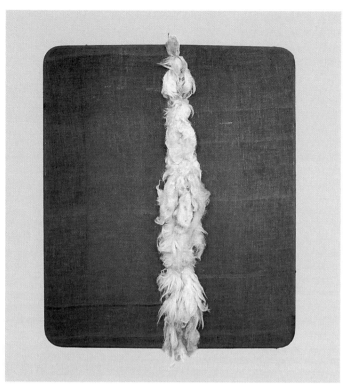

Jannis Kounellis, Untitled (Wool), 1968. Private Collection.

schweigen schweigen schweigen
schweigen schweigen schweigen
schweigen   schweigen
schweigen schweigen schweigen
schweigen schweigen schweigen

Eugen Gomringer, Schweigen, 1968. Celebrated example of Concrete Poetry.

LAND ART

Land artists distanced themselves from urban constraints in their search for open areas that inspired interaction. The nature of their work could best be described as a combination of the aspirations of a romantic traveler and the Dada rejection of traditional modes of artistic expression. In order to discover *Spiral Jetty* by Robert Smithson (1938–73), constructed in 1970 on Utah's Great Salt Lake, spectators had to follow in the footsteps of the artist, communing with nature in a dimension outside all normal experience. Alternatively, they would have had to accept its almost sacred inaccessibility and be content to examine plans and photographs. However, a work of art that exists but cannot be seen must be at the limits of abstraction. Although *Spiral Jetty* was supported by pictures that attested to its existence, the very fact that the spectator could not easily come into contact with it almost required an act of faith to believe it was there.

In a stand against the commercialization of art, the American artists Michael Heizer, Douglas Huebler, and Dennis Oppenheim worked in remote and desolate places. Sometimes, however, a piece of Land art can successfully be re-created within the confines of a gallery. The arrangement of natural materials in Richard Long's *Circle* (1972) seems to acquire added resonance when displayed within an artificial environment.

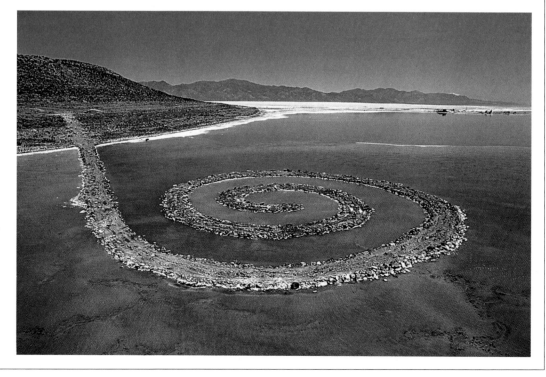

Robert Smithson, Spiral Jetty, 1970. Great Salt Lake, Utah.

644

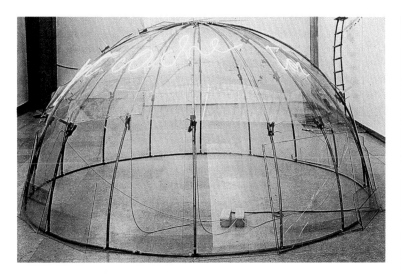

Mario Merz, Object cache-toi, *1968. Merz has for some years made his igloos out of a number of thought-provoking materials, both natural and artificial.*

was so with the Gruppo 70, formed in Florence in 1963 and involving poets and writers such as Eugenio Miccini and Lamberto Pignotti (also members of the literary Gruppo 63) and musicians like Giuseppe Chiari (in contact with the diverse artists of Fluxus). This experimentation in Italy, with contributions also from Vincenzo Accame, Carlo Belloli, Ugo Carrega, and Martino Oberto, had precedents in work that was carried out in the late 1950s in Brazil, Germany, and Switzerland. The style of the Concrete poets can clearly be seen in *Schweigen* (Silence, 1968) by Eugen Gomringer (b. 1925). The sudden interruption in the repetition of the word "*schweigen,*" and the void or visual gap that it creates, becomes a subtle visualization of the semantic value of the whole composition.

ARTE POVERA

In 1967, Germano Celant, inspired by the "poor theater" of Jerzy Grotowski, spoke of "poor art," referring to the work of certain Italian artists, including Alighiero Boetti, Luciano Fabro, Mario Merz, Pino Pascali, Michelangelo Pistoletto, and Jannis Kounellis (Greek, but resident in Italy since 1956). They wanted to make art out of rough, worthless materials found in everyday life and displayed in their

natural state. A similar approach had already been advocated in Nouveau Réalisme. This included scraps of discarded newspaper preserved in a frame, and, as in sculptor Daniel Spoerri's *tableaux pièges* (snare pictures) – existing artefacts used in a novel way to make crude and dramatic compositions. Arte Povera, on the other hand, gave reality a more intellectual and emotive treatment, bearing witness to its affinities with Conceptual art. In addition to materials that exhibited the banality of their nature, such as the colored wood of Alighiero Boetti (1940–94) or the woolly cotton used by Jannis Kounellis (b. 1936), there were the bright mirrorlike surfaces in the steel of Michelangelo Pistoletto (b. 1933), on which he printed photographs of objects, animals, and full-size figures. The effect of the latter's work is completed by the reflection in the "mirror" of the surroundings and the spectators themselves. The "conceptual" element of these works is to be found in their openness to all the changes that might occur in their environment, i.e. in the idea of a piece of art that is alters constantly and is the product of that perpetual state of flux. Mario Merz (b. 1925) combines the symbolic struc-

SYSTEMIC PAINTING

A branch of Minimal art that relied on the use of simple, standardized, nonrepresentational forms, "Systemic painting" was the title of a show organized by the British art critic Lawrence Alloway in 1966 at New York's Guggenheim Museum. Contributors included the American artists Frank Stella, Ellsworth Kelly, Agnes Martin, and Robert Ryman, as well as Barnett Newman and Ad Reinhardt, two leading exponents of Abstract Expressionism. Frank Stella (b. 1936) had already taken ideas from Reinhardt and Newman in the late 1950s as inspiration for his attempts to reduce painting to its fundamental essence; his work was to be read solely in terms of

Frank Stella, Six Mile Bottom, *1960. Tate Gallery, London.*

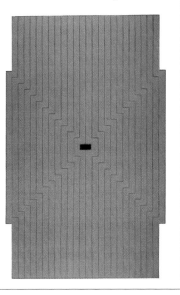

form and color, without any pretense that it revealed the artist's state of mind. In this respect, Systemic painting displayed similar intentions to the contemporary Minimal sculpture of artists such as Carl Andre and Don Judd.

ture of an igloo – shaped like a globe, but at the same time a shelter that protects people – with neon tubes (i.e. products of technology) often in the shape of Fibonacci numbers. This sequence forms the basis of the theory of dynamic symmetry as applied to art and living forms.

MINIMALISM

The term "Minimal art" was coined in 1965 by the critic Richard Wollheim and

encompassed a wide diversity of associated styles and concepts, among them ABC art, Object sculpture, Cool art, Primary structures, and Literalist art. The trend, which applied particularly to sculpture, arose in the 1950s, chiefly in the US. Its distinguishing characteristics were an extreme spareness of form and a minimal expressive content; this was in violent contrast to the flamboyant

Carl Andre, 64 Copper Squares, *1969. Virginia Dwan Collection, New York.*

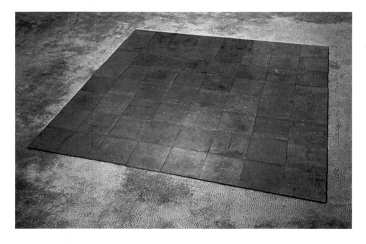

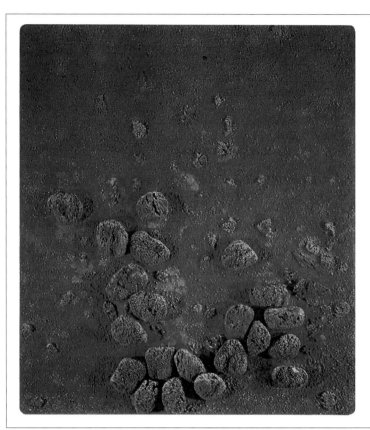

ANALYTICAL PAINTING

In Europe during the 1960s and 1970s, a period of experimentation took place comparable with that being carried out in the US in Minimalist painting. Two groups working in this area in France in the late 1970s were BMPT and Support-Surface, whose precedents could well have been the series of blue "monochromes" by Yves Klein (1928–62). A lack of pictorial content characterizes the work of Giorgio Griffa, Rodolfo Aricò, Claudio Olivieri, and Claudio Verna, while the work of Piero Manzoni and Giulio Paolini is full of Conceptual nuances. From 1958 to 1960 Manzoni was already producing his white monochrome *Achromes*, reducing the picture to a mere rough support

Yves Klein, Relief Eponge Bleu, 1958.
Wallraf-Richartz Museum, Cologne.

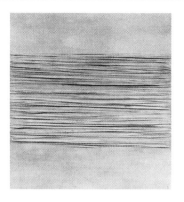

Piero Manzoni, Achrome, 1959.
Private Collection.

soaked in kaolin. Meanwhile, Paolini demonstrated the basic elements of painting in his *Geometric Design*, which was simply a square, unprimed, unadorned piece of canvas. With similar intentions in the 1970s, Morales (b. 1942) created diptychs composed of two canvases, one painted all over, the other left untouched.

Abstract expressionist style that preceded it. The term is applied in a precise way to the works of sculptors such as Donald Judd, Robert Morris, Carl Andre, Sol Lewitt, and Tony Smith, which display the same essentially cold, geometric forms in vast sizes. The sheer scale on which some were conceived meant that they had a strong relationship with their surroundings and often assumed an architectural nature, allowing the spectator to cross or walk along the structure. The square copper plates that Carl Andre (b. 1935) laid on the floor, or the smooth and anonymous parallelepipeds of Donald Judd (1928–94) did not appear so different in concept from the repetitive objects in the work of Warhol. However, Warhol took cultural icons and reproduced them flatly and without emotion, while the Minimalists wanted to draw people's attention to extreme formal simplicity, which they believed was yet to be fully appreciated.

POSTMODERNISM

In the 1980s, in contrast to the stark, cerebral experience of Conceptual art, there was a call for art to be more accessible and more immediately rewarding. There was nostalgia for traditional styles and techniques, and images that would express ideas in an intelligible way, at a time when very often the ideas had taken priority over the results. Artists seemed to want to turn back the clock to the artistic practices that prevailed prior to Conceptual art. In a way, that is what happened, except that the Conceptual experience had made too much of an impact not to have any influence on new developments. While painting again dominated the art scene, it bore the traits of Conceptualism and could never make a full return to former styles. In Postmodernism, there lingered a Conceptual taste for irony, as well as a freedom of choice that allowed artists to draw on any subject matter.

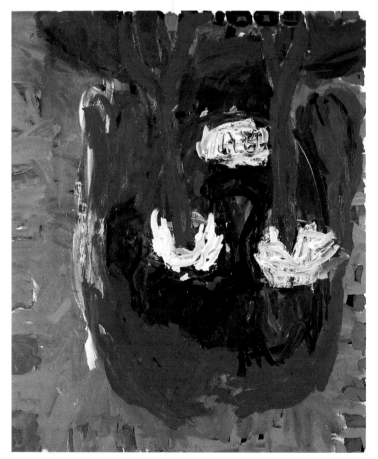

Georg Baselitz, Tränenkopf (Head of Tears), 1986. Private Collection.

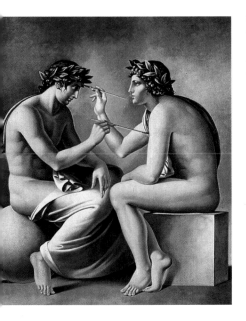

Carlo Maria Mariani, La mano ubbidisce all'intelletto, *1983. Private Collection, United States.*

TRANSAVANGUARDIA

The leading artists of the Italian Transavanguardia movement, defined by the critic Achille Bonito Oliva in 1979, were Sandro Chia, Enzo Cucchi, Francesco Clemente, Nicola De Maria, and Mimmo Paladino. However, the group soon became international, involving primarily the German artists Markus Lüperz, Anselm Kiefer, Georg Baselitz, Jorg Immendorf, and A.R. Penk. After many decades of Abstractionism in all its forms, followed by the Conceptualism of the 1970s, Transavanguardia took up figurative art again and reexamined the colors and tools of painting. Abandoning the search for intellectual reasons to modify or annul conventional artistic practices, these artists rediscovered the traditional skills of painting in works that were instantly recognizable in their form and content. This was not a return to certain figurative trends of the postwar period, however, and Transavanguardia differed from these both in style and ideology. The intention was to operate with the maximum of expressive freedom without relying on any particular cultural models, taking them all into consideration despite any eventual lack of consistency in content or form. The so-called "nomadism" of the Italian Transavanguardists led them to take inspiration from various artistic styles – Expressionism, Surrealism, Cubism – and excluded them from any cultural, or political, commit-

ment. The German artists had a different attitude, remaining more openly linked to their own avant-garde traditions and to Expressionism. Sensitive to their recent past, they also wanted to free German art from the process of subordination to American art that had occurred after World War II. An art form that made more precise stylistic references was Anachronistic painting, which looked to the examples of Mannerism and Neoclassicism. All the same, in the figurative purity that characterized the work of Carlo Maria Mariani (b. 1931), there are still echoes of Conceptual tautology. In *La Mano ubbidisce all'intelletto* (The Hand Obeying the Intellect, 1983), the painting is reflected in itself and is left to reflect on its own existence.

URBAN GRAFFITI

In many aspects the Graffiti art movement in America resembled the Transavanguardia experience in Italy, especially in that it saw a return to figurative art without highbrow artistic pretenses, yet with great communicative force. Graffiti art in America was the expression of a rebellious subculture and was to be found sprawled over the walls of the derelict districts and subway trains of New York. Consisting almost entirely of self-taught artists, the movement grew spontaneously amid the rhythms of rap and break-dance. The vibrancy of the art, which was not confined by the boundaries of a frame or limited by the size of a canvas, was enhanced by its sheer scale. The style adopted had clear associations with Pop art, but this time the artists were not looking cynically at mass popular culture and its habits but were the representatives of a culture that had emerged on the margins of urban society.

The Graffiti movement first received recognition when Stefan Eins, an artist originating from Austria, opened an alternative art gallery in the notoriously rough South Bronx district of New York. He entrusted its decoration to the Graffiti artist Crash and provided an outlet for the young Graffitists of the area. Before long, Graffiti art was being allocated space in the most prestigious New York galleries and was losing the aggressive image that had been its stamp on the walls of the dilapidated suburbs. Notable Graffitists include Jean-Michel Basquiat (1960–88), whose

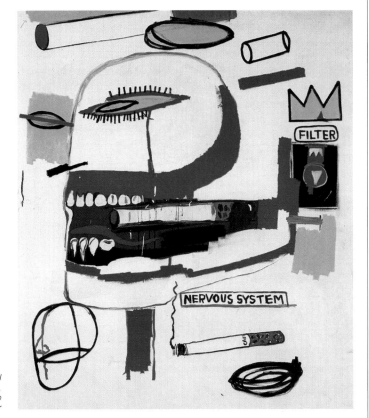

Jean-Michel Basquiat, Tabac, *1984. Bruno Bischofberger Collection, Zurich.*

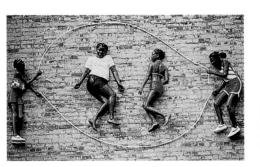

John Ahearn, Double Dutch, *double installation between Kelly Street and Interval Avenue, New York, 1982–83.*

untimely death only served to accentuate the aura of misadventure that surrounded him; Keith Haring (1958–90), known for his *Radiant Child*, whose vibrancy became the stylistic mark of the artist Justen Ladda, creator of a mural of extraordinary illusionism inside an old Bronx school next to the Fashion Moda gallery (*The Thing*, 1981); and John Ahearn, whose painted reliefs on Bronx walls recall the Pop plaster casts of sculptor George Segal.

ARCHITECTURE IN THE SECOND HALF OF THE 20TH CENTURY

An international architectural language developed in the second half of the 20th century, finding expression in many new types of buildings in ancient and modern cities throughout the world. While established architects discovered fresh inspiration, exciting new talents also began to make names for themselves.

The second half of the 20th century witnessed the gradual eclipse of the Modernist orthodoxy known as the International Style. In spite of this shift, the influence of the leading figures of the Modern Movement was felt well into the 1960s. Their design philosophy had to co-exist with new ideas, for which, ironically, they had paved the way through their own innovative approaches and willingness to change direction. The sinuous lines of Le Corbusier's design for the Chapel of Notre-Dame-du-Haut at Ronchamp (1950–56), for example, symbolized a departure from his earlier, more angular designs, and introduced a degree of artistic expression that went beyond functional demands. Walter Gropius also abandoned Rationalist rigour in his Pan American Skyscraper in New York (1958–63), when he enhanced the exterior of the building with a polygonal outline that relieved its

TOWARD POSTMODERNISM

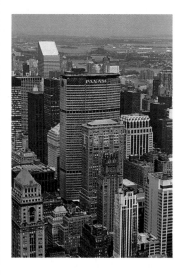

Walter Gropius, Pan American Skyscraper, New York, 1958–63.

The postwar buildings of the leading architects of the Modern Movement exemplified the Rationalist crisis that was to last for the next few decades. In the 1950s and 1960s Le Corbusier and Walter Gropius ventured beyond Rationalist austerity, aiming to enliven the exteriors of their buildings. In his chapel at Ronchamp (1950–56), Le Corbusier abandoned the neat outlines of his Villa Savoye at Poissy (1928–31), opting instead for a more flexible shape. Gropius moved away from the measured

clarity of his Bauhaus School Building in Dessau (1925–26) and introduced a polygonally faceted outline for the Pan American Skyscraper in New York (1958–63). Expressive values are even more strongly accentuated in the late works of Frank Lloyd Wright and Eero Saarinen. Saarinen, influenced by the architecture of Mies van der Rohe, especially by his modular grids, developed his own, more imaginative interpretation, introducing sinuous lines with a tremendous sense of movement. In his TWA Terminal for

New York's John F. Kennedy Airport (1956–62), the roof is shaped like the wings of a giant bird, accentuating the convexity and thereby emphasizing the contrast with the internal space. Frank Lloyd Wright had always been at more than a geographical distance from the European "Modern Masters." He was a great exponent of architecture that worked in harmony with natural shapes. His brilliantly executed Kaufmann House, also known as "Fallingwater," at Bear Run, Pennsylvania (1936–39), has superimposed terraces jutting out at right angles to one another over a stream at the point where it becomes a waterfall and

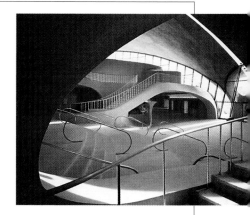

Eero Saarinen, TWA Terminal, John F. Kennedy Airport, New York, 1956–62.

reaching out toward the trees that surround the house. The Solomon R. Guggenheim Museum in New York (1943–59) was one of the last in a series of organic designs; here, Wright blended the complex natural features of the Grand Canyon with the native architecture of the Navajo. The arrangement of the internal ramps follows an upward spiral movement; visitors are taken to the top level by elevator and then make their way down the ramp on foot, looking at the pictures as they go.

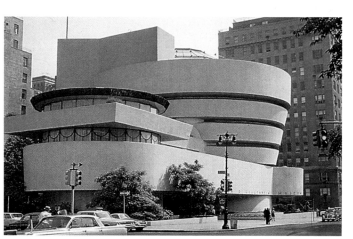

Frank Lloyd Wright, Solomon R. Guggenheim Museum, New York, 1943–59.

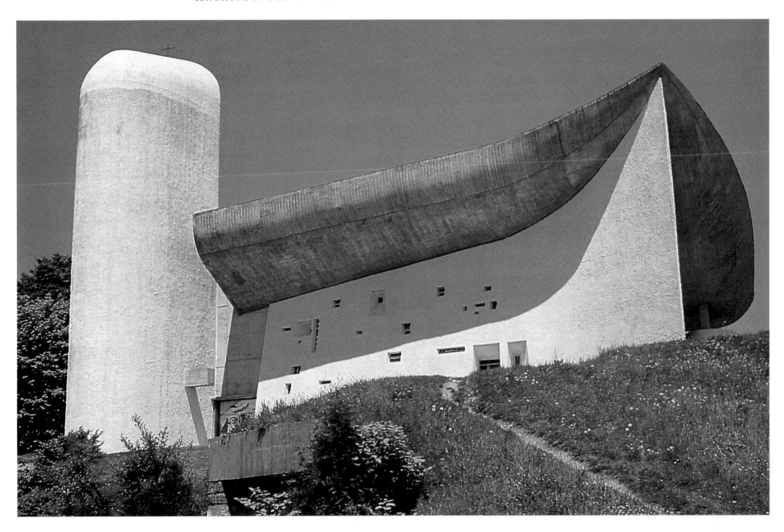

Le Corbusier, Chapel of Notre-Dame-du-Haut, Ronchamp, 1950–56. A late work that stems less from Modernist rigor than from a wish for greater formal freedom.

otherwise uncompromising verticality. A sober, austere architectural language, which tended to exclude any superfluous elements, was thus giving way to a freedom of interpretation that was to become the essence of Postmodern architecture. Spanning a wide spectrum, sources of inspiration for Postmodern design were many and varied. High-tech architects, for instance, created a hybrid Modernism, which took the notion of progress – embodied in the International Style – to its extreme by using state-of-the-art technology. Indeed, technology itself was often placed openly on display, becoming the most distinctive feature of the building, as in

the work of Richard Rogers, who collaborated with Renzo Piano on the Pompidou Center in Paris (1972–77). Here, the structural supports, escalators, and pipes are all exposed on the exterior of the building. They form a bulky metal skeleton that surrounds the interior, making available space that can be adapted to a wide variety of cultural events. Similar methods were adopted by I.M. Pei, although with a much lighter touch. His work relied on the transparency of glass, through which his elegant metallic structures are glimpsed, and culminated in the Louvre Pyramids, Paris (1985–93). Precedents for this concept include Buckminster Fuller's geodesic dome built for the United States Pavilion at the Montreal World's Fair (1966–67) and the steel cable-net roofs designed by Frei Otto for the Olympic Stadium

in Munich (1968–72). In the latter, the external structure of light supports emphasizes the internal space, avoiding any clutter and interruption of sight lines. Technology is often a secondary concern where the project is intended to serve a

specific purpose. In designing the Modena Cemetery in Italy (1971–78), Aldo Rossi displayed a simple functional approach inspired by the work of Adolf Loos, in which the buildings are fundamentally cubic in interpretation. Philip Johnson

I.M. Pei, Louvre Pyramids, Paris, 1985–93.

Richard Rogers and Renzo Piano, Pompidou Center, Paris, 1972–77.

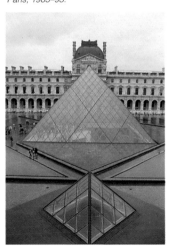

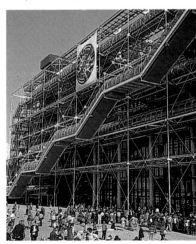

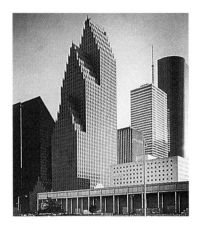

Philip Johnson, Republic Bank, Houston, 1984.

brilliantly exploited allusions to Gothic cathedrals in his Republic Bank in Houston (1984), with its stepped floors and lateral decoration suggestive of stylized pinnacles and spires. Ricardo Bofill reinterpreted the convex principle of the Baroque in his Le Palais d'Abraxas housing at Marne-la-Vallée, near Paris (1979–83). Past styles are recalled with obvious irony in American Postmodern architecture and are expressed with an emphasis on dimensions that sometimes acquire almost comic-strip proportions.

Robert Venturi transformed the wooden column of the Allen Art Museum of Oberlin College, Ohio (1976) into an entertainingly deformed caricature of an Ionic column, while Charles Moore fashioned the Piazza d'Italia in New Orleans (1975–79) in the shape of the Italian peninsula, flanked by pastiche classical buildings. He revamped Roman antiquity with marble and metal cladding and installed startlingly colored neon lights in the capitals of the columns, as well as plaques bearing his own portrait. Whereas

Venturi's work exhibits an almost Disneyesque interpretation, Moore's version of antiquity achieves its kitsch effect through the strident juxtaposition of materials. American Postmodernism modified the European architectural tradition, exaggerating it and sending it up in order to justify its repetition in a different context. The Japanese architect Arata Isozaki carried out a similar exercise by introducing Michelangelo's Piazza del Campidoglio, Rome, into the interior of the Tsukuba Civic

DECONSTRUCTION AND POP ARCHITECTURE

The irony implicit in much Postmodern architecture was to be expressed in a more dramatic fashion by the Deconstructivists – those artists who turned ostensibly impracticable designs into reality, creating something of a compromise between practical architecture and Utopian planning. The latter inspired the Viennese group Coop Himmelblau to produce an early design for a city constantly modified by the pulse rate, breathing, and movements of its inhabitants (*Feedback Vibration City*, 1971). Coop Himmelblau exploited the concept of unbalanced masses, exemplified by an apparently unstable exterior structural support system, as in their Funder Factory 3 at St. Veit-ander-Glan (1988), made to look

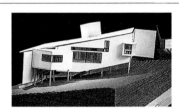

Frank O. Gehry, Wagner House, Malibu, Los Angeles, 1978. These images illustrate the ironic, seemingly unstable quality of the building. As the illustration (right) shows, the lines of the building closely follow the surface on which the house has been built. A sense of delicate simplicity underlines the apparent precariousness of the structure.

as if it were close to collapse. The notion of precariousness was also explored by Frank Gehry in the Wagner House at Malibu (1978): its sloping bulk seems to teeter on contrastingly fragile supporting columns. The menace of impending collapse

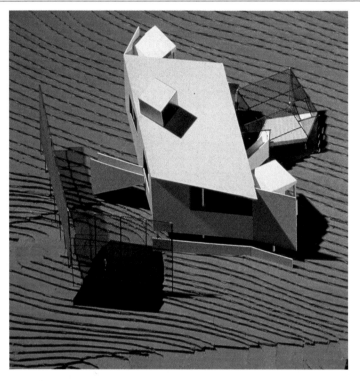

was also exploited by an American group, Site, whose approach to architecture was greatly influenced by the Pop art of the 1960s and 1970s. Their Best supermarkets, built in various locations across the US, are all individually designed: the Almeda-Genoa shopping center near Houston, Texas (1974–75), presents a semiruined exterior, while the entrance at Arden (1976–77) is formed by an angular breach. This is revealed

when an electrically controlled "slab" of masonry is moved aside during opening hours, sliding back when the store closes. As might be expected, the Deconstructivists' most daring ideas have so far been restricted to buildings on the outskirts of cities. By contrast, their buildings found in or near city centers are less extreme in design. Such is the case with Coop Himmelblau's smaller commercial premises in Vienna (Humanic Department Store, 1980–81), and their private studios (Studio Baumann, 1984) and cafés (Roter Engel, 1980–81).

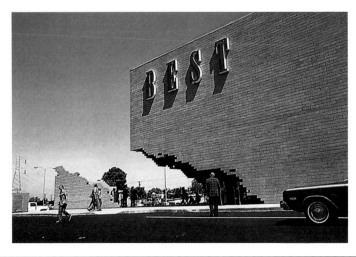

Site, Best Supermarket, Sacramento, 1977.

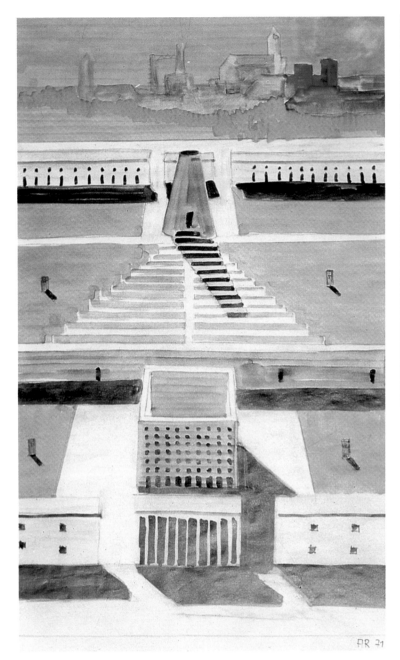

TOWARD AN ARCHITECTURAL UTOPIA

From the 1960s onward, architects were producing ever more fantastic designs for urban environments, inspired by the prevailing spirit of irreverence that called accepted concepts into question and was generally provocative and challenging. The targets of this subtle campaign were the clinically fastidious Modernist town-planning projects, with their meticulously theoretical approach; this was now parodied in fundamentally impractical projects and improbable environments. With a healthy sense of the ridiculous, the British group Archigram drew up a Utopian project called *Walking City* in 1964, with city districts constructed like enormous insects that could move from one site to another on long, mobile appendages. Equally unlikely was the Superstudio plan for glass buildings to fill the spaces between the skyscrapers of Manhattan, or to roof over empty areas in which young hippies would be free to wander around. These dissenting voices challenged the accepted conventions of city planning, reflecting widespread controversy as to how best to cope with rapid postwar urban growth and the consequent danger of alienation this posed within cities. As early as 1960, Hans Hollein had created the disquieting photomontage *Stadt*, in which closely packed skyscrapers loom over the city of Vienna like a sinister dark cloud.

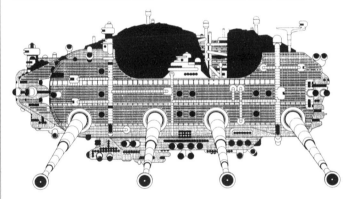

Archigram Group, Walking City, 1964.

Aldo Rossi, Modena Cemetery, 1971–78. Postmodernism refers to past styles and Aldo Rossi here echoes the regularity of Rationalism, its austerity underlining the function of the building complex.

Charles Moore, Piazza d'Italia, New Orleans, 1975–79. Typically for American Postmodernism, exaggeration in the choice and use of various materials here takes on almost comic-strip dimensions. It is significant that at the Venice Biennale exhibition of architecture in 1996, the United States Pavilion reflected the fantasy dream-environment of Disney World.

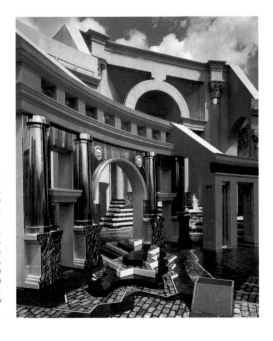

Center of Ibaragi (1983). The lack of balance, the unexpected disruption of apparent harmony, and the deliberate application of questionable taste were all typical of the Postmodern way of working. The distinctive use of the motif of battered surfaces and cracks that Robert Venturi introduced in the Vanna Venturi House, built for his mother in Chestnut Hill in Philadelphia (1963), is justified by its own rationale and fulfills the practical purpose of increasing the amount of natural light reaching the interior.

Elsewhere, this device has a more organic role, as in the entrance of the first Schullin Jewelry Store in Vienna (1972–74) by Hans Hollein, where the fissure resembles metal overheated to the point of fusion. Postmodernism's renewed interest in the outer skin of buildings was most effectively demonstrated at the Venice Biennale in 1980. On that occasion, the Strada Nuovissima ("Very New Street"), erected along the rope walk of the Arsenale, contained 20 different interpretations on the theme of "The Façade." This encouraged a "stage-design" approach, with outward appearance being given greater priority than practical organization or effective use of the interior space. Hollein designed an ironic version of the colonnade, demonstrating how the columns' supporting role had become redundant by suspending a broken pillar from the architrave. Venturi chose to tackle the project in pictorial terms, painting an exaggeratedly large Doric *pronaos* (vestibule) on a wooden billboard and inserting little skeletal statuettes on the pediment as caricatures of classical convention.

The Postmodern approach was not, however, confined to the display of stylistic virtuosity on the façade, which sometimes involved the introduction of elements likely to upset the linearity of the design – it could extend to every aspect of the building's design. Hollein achieved a

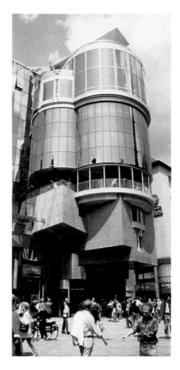

Hans Hollein, Haas Haus, Vienna, 1985–90.

striking interplay of volumes with his Haas Haus, Vienna (1985–90), which develops from an angular to a

semicircular shape, partially clad in mirror tiles that reflect the Gothic extravagance of St. Stephen's Cathedral. An even greater complexity is apparent in his proposed design for the Guggenheim Museum in Salzburg (1988–90), with its labyrinthine walkways, which ascend floor by floor around a central well or court. Interior space can also be organized by enclosing a succession of progressively smaller spaces. This solution was adopted by the German architect Oswald Mathias Ungers in his design for the German Museum of Architecture in Frankfurt (1979–84), built within the shell of an early 20th-century townhouse. Inside, there is a network of a series of spaces, the innermost – the display section– occupying several floors on a grid system. The element of visual surprise has also been exploited by the Deconstructivists, who practiced a sort of anti-architecture based on a total denial of the Rationalist principles of construction.

The second half of the 20th century produced a wide range of building types and equally varied architectural styles, reflecting the era's technological developments. Many new projects were modern versions of traditional public buildings, interpreted in an innovative manner and exploiting new construction techniques. The Sydney Opera House (1959–75), for example, designed by Jørn Utzon, is distinguished by its unusual series of shell-shaped roofs standing on a broad platform. In profile they resemble wind-filled sails ready to skim over the glistening waters of the harbor. In the Hong Kong and Shanghai Bank of Sir Norman Foster in Hong Kong (1979–84), the strength of the construction is emphasized; the structural elements displayed rather than hidden, as if to reassure the bank's customers. Styles during this period contrast starkly with one another: Foster's high-tech design of the Renault Distribution Centre at Swindon, Wiltshire (1981–83) is the absolute antithesis of Coop Himmelblau's Deconstructivist treatment of the Funder Factory 3 at St. Veit-an-der-Glan (1988). Similarly, the organic architecture of Frank Lloyd Wright's Solomon R. Guggenheim Museum, New York, commissioned in 1943 and completed in 1959, is a far cry from the formal Glass Museum at Weil-am-Rhein (1987–90), designed by Frank Gehry.

All these examples show how

Oswald Mathias Ungers, German Architecture Museum, Frankfurt, 1979–84. The interior spaces are locked into one another like boxes.

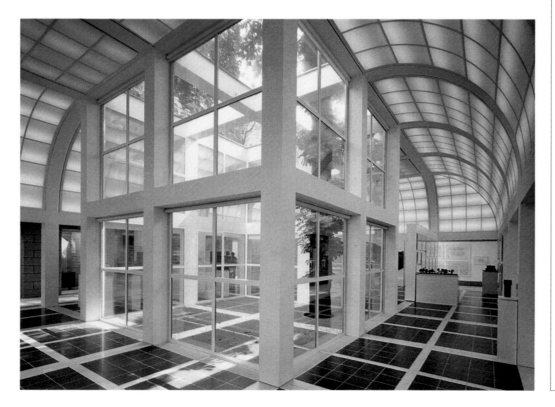

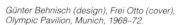

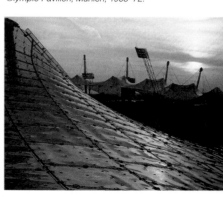

Günter Behnisch (design), Frei Otto (cover), Olympic Pavilion, Munich, 1968–72.

buildings, planned to fulfill a traditional function, need not be reliant on past concepts and can benefit from an architect's fresh and unexpected approach. Since the 1950s, many new types of buildings have emerged – evidence of fundamental changes in the economics, culture, and habits of society. Since World War II, the growth of air traffic has led to a proliferation of buildings to serve the industry, ranging from the monumental Lambert Airport at St. Louis, Missouri, designed in 1954 by Minoru Yamasaki, to Saarinen's TWA Terminal at John F. Kennedy Airport (1956–62), which looks like a bird about to take flight. Multifunctional complexes, such as arts venues or shopping centers, have been among the most popular building developments of the past few decades. Sidney Bregman and George Hamann's design for the Eaton Centre in downtown Toronto (1973–77) put high-tech

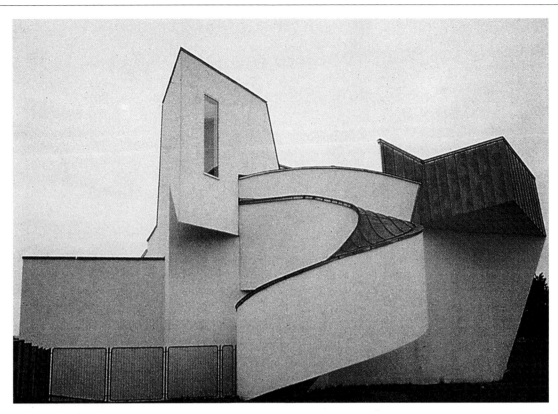

Frank Gehry, Glass Museum, 1987–90, Weil-am-Rhein.

solidity to practical use. High-tech was also the guiding principle for Richard Rogers and Renzo Piano in the Pompidou Center, Paris (1972–77), which contains a library, reading rooms, and exhibition space, while the futuristic pavilions of the Cultural Center in Sumida, Tokyo (1995), by Itsuko Hasegawa incorporate study areas, laboratories, a restaurant, a gallery, and even a planetarium inside a gigantic geodesic sphere.

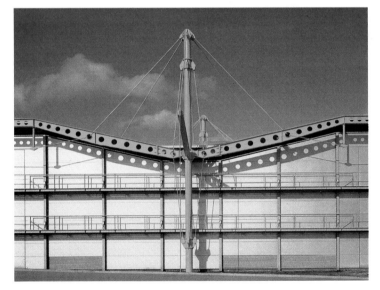

Norman Foster, Renault Distribution Centre, Swindon, 1981–83.

Jørn Utzon, Opera House, Sydney, 1959–75.

examples are the Olympic Palace of Sport by Kenzo Tange, Uichi Inoue, and Yoshikatsu Tsuboi in Tokyo (1963–64), and the Olympic Village designed by Günther Behnisch and Associates for the 1972 Olympic Games in Munich. Other notable innovations include the small translucent polycarbonate canopies that the design team of Giancarlo Ragazzi and Enrico Hoffer used for the San Siro Stadium in Milan (1989). Their lightness contrasts very effectively with the imposing supporting grid and the spiral progression of towers that mark out the perimeter. Another type of building that came to prominence in the second half of the 20th century is the

discotheque, which, with its precarious balance between fantasy and reality, offers architects a chance to put their more fantastic ideas into practice. Studio Nizzoli's Dihedron Discotheque at Santa Maria dei Sabbioni near Cremona, Italy (1970–72), had a playful and ironic exterior, partially buried underground and looking as if it were about to sink. (It has now been converted into a supermarket.) Outside Barcelona, Alfredo Arribas has created the enormous Gran Velvet Discotheque, which he invested with a suitably surreal subterranean atmosphere.

Sports stadiums have also provided excellent opportunities for the application of new building techniques, with the introduction of very strong, lightweight roofs that allow for a vast amount of free space inside the building. Among the most outstanding

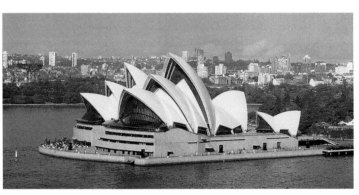

653

TOWARDS A NEW CENTURY

In recent years, art has become more accessible to the general public. The introduction of new media – including electronic and video art, assisted by the ever-growing versatility of computer technology – has led to fresh methods of artistic production and facilitated the emergence of the anonymous artist. In this vibrant atmosphere of cross-fertilization, once prevailing artistic hierarchies are slowly being eroded.

In the 1980s, the austerity of Conceptual art began to be replaced by works that required less intellectual effort to be appreciated. While paintings began to appear in galleries again, inevitably the new artistic trends did not take over completely from what had gone before. Even when the overall art scene appeared to have totally changed, the vestiges of past experiences continued to thrive in other forms. Conceptual art had not completely repressed the vitality of Pop art, for example, which reemerged in the spontaneity of American Graffiti art. Roy Lichtenstein made the comic strip the central focus of his art – taking it out of its normal context and presenting it on a vast scale – while the New York

Cindy Sherman, Untitled, *photograph, 1985.*

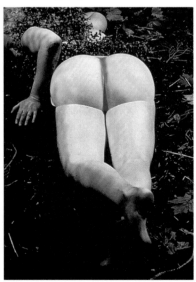

Graffiti artists, on the other hand, drew on its narrative simplicity and two-dimensionality. Their murals immortalized actual cartoon characters, such as Ronnie Cutrone's cheeky Woody Woodpecker with his classic orange crest. Another significant contribution to the genre was made by the American artist Jeff Koons (b. 1955), whose kitsch compositions of consumer objects often drew on favorite cartoon characters (*Pink Panther*, 1988) for their subject matter.

PHOTOGRAPHY AND TELEVISION

The artistic manifestations that formed the basis of Conceptual art were in no way suppressed in the 1980s, in the atmosphere of renewed interest in painting. A prime example of this is photography, which had played a fundamental role during the 1960s and 1970s, developing its own artistic genre and representing an invaluable tool for the recording of Performance art. From the ascetic intellectualism of American experimental artist Joseph Kosuth to the expressive violence of Barbara Kruger (b. 1945), photography had been variously associated with verbal expression, intensifying meanings in the representation of a concept or

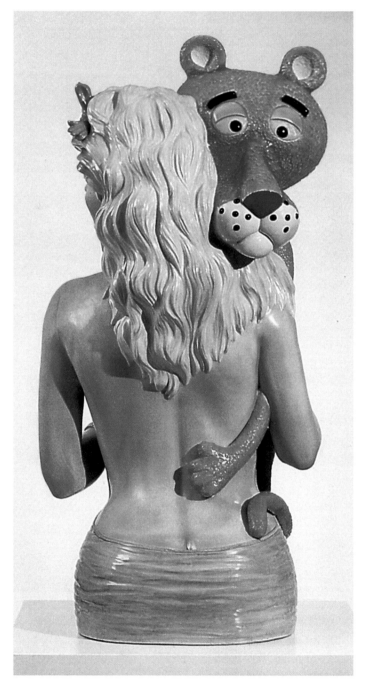

Jeff Koons, Pink Panther, *1988. Sonnabend Gallery, New York.*

DESIGNER WATCHES

The scope for artists and designers to make their mark on consumer goods is endless, so it is not surprising that they have also chosen to target that indispensable accessory of the modern world, the wristwatch. The digital watches known as Swatch (Swiss Watch) dominated the 1980s and left the old-fashioned models behind. Introduced in 1983, they were a true reflection of the Postmodern culture that produced them. The sophisticated technology involved in their manufacture is of almost secondary importance to the variety presented from season to season (new designs are launched every six months). Swatches change their appearance according to the fashion of the moment and reflect deeper and more wide-ranging changes in taste and fashion. When American underground culture began to make itself felt in Europe, Swatch produced its *Breakdance* watches (1985). Made of brightly colored plastic, these featured a fragmented decoration that alluded to the syncopated rhythm of the dance style. The fun, sometimes kitsch, aspect of the designs (the *Desert Puff* of 1988 was wrapped in colored fur) often mirrored the activity of the contemporary art scene. The 1986 collection was designed by the American Graffiti artist Keith Haring, who reproduced the *Radiant Child* of his murals in

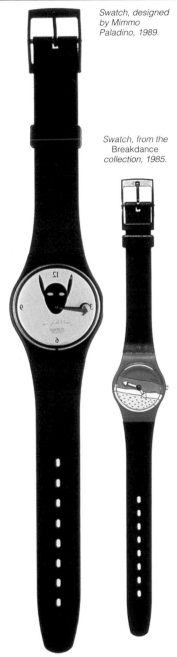

Swatch, designed by Mimmo Paladino, 1989.

Swatch, from the Breakdance collection, 1985.

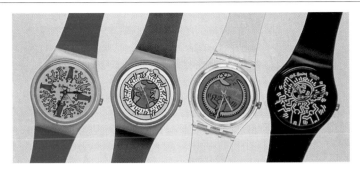

Swatches, from the 1986 collection, designed by Keith Haring.

Keith Haring, Untitled, 1984. Acrylic on muslin, Paul Maenz Gallery, Cologne. Haring was considered one of the most important exponents of Graffiti art.

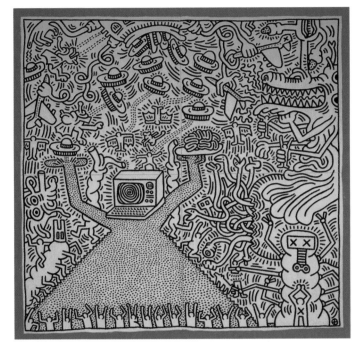

miniature on the watch face. In 1989, Mimmo Paladino, an artist of the Italian Transavanguardia movement, put his name to a limited number of watches that

featured a stylized human head, a recurring motif in his paintings. These series by artists have become highly sought-after collector's pieces.

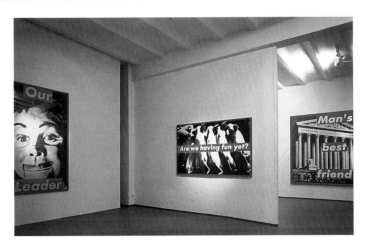

playing with words of no apparent significance to achieve a provocative effect. In the 1980s, photography was exploited for its explicitness and immediacy, as in the work of the American artist Cindy Sherman (b. 1954), whose distinctive images offer poignant interpretations of female stereotypes from popular culture.

Barbara Kruger, Installation, 1987. Monika Spruth Gallery, Cologne. This work is an expression of feminist art.

In 1963, in the Galerie Parnass in Wuppertal, Germany, Nam Jun Paik (b. 1932) and Wolf Vostell (b. 1932), both members of the Fluxus group, manipulated the medium of television by creating images of interference and distortion in a work called *13 Distorted TV Sets*. This marked the beginning of a new artistic medium as artists started to explore the electronic dimension to determine if they could make use of methods usually regarded as outside art.

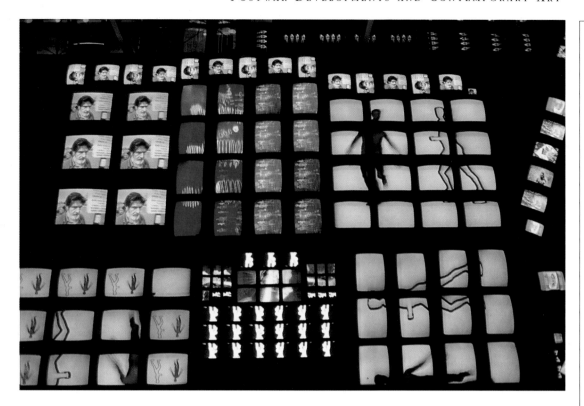

Video art production shared many of the techniques of television, but the results were not destined to be transmitted in the same way. Until at least the mid-1970s, artists preferred to exhibit their video art within the confines of the gallery. The process of filming with a fixed camera and capturing real-time action linked it with contemporary experimental cinema, which, in turn, recalled the avant-garde

Andy Warhol, Sleep, still, 1963–64.

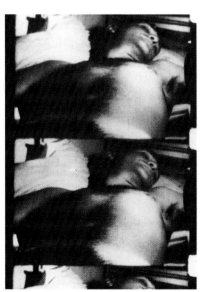

experimentation of the early 20th century. When Andy Warhol made his eight-hour-long film *Sleep* in 1964, containing shots of a man sleeping, he was employing the narrative neutrality that was a feature of his own Pop art style. At the same time, he heightened the dimension of time in a manner that had been explored 30 years earlier. In 1933, Fernand Léger conceived the film *24 Heures*, in which an anonymous couple were filmed for an entire day while carrying out their normal activities. Although video art was not limited to a sterile imitation of experimental cinema techniques and developed its own expressive forms, it could never hope to equal the superior quality of the cinematographic image. Rather, it explored the expressive potential of the medium, exploiting the new editing techniques and the possibilities of filming and transmitting images simultaneously using several cameras and monitors. One example of this was the video installation created by Nam June Paik at the Venice Biennale exhibition in 1993,

Nam Jun Paik, Video Installation at the Venice Biennale, 1993. Video installation is an art form that has evolved from television and retains its domination over the live image.

in which an entire wall was covered in screens transmitting different images and sounds. In the darkness of the room, the audience had to adjust continually to the rapid succession of audiovisual material, lost somewhere between the realistic fiction of the video and the black, dreamlike surroundings. In the 1980s, video artists overcame their initial hostility toward the world of television and opened up their work to a wider audience. Viewing time was then made available on channels in England (Channel 4), France (Antenne Deux), and Belgium (RTBF). In general, however, the time devoted to video art by the television networks was minimal compared to that reserved for other arts programs, which were undoubtedly less adventurous but able to attract far larger audiences. The cinema has enjoyed satirizing this phenomenon, particularly in Oliver Stone's film *Natural*

INDUSTRIAL DESIGN SINCE THE WAR

Since the 1950s, industrial designers have concentrated increasingly on household items, often pursuing an idea or style in tandem with the fields of art and architecture. This was an inevitable development, given the lively relationship design has with every other creative field. It is even possible to pick out similarities in the design of furniture, domestic appliances, and buildings from a particular period. The 1960s, for example, saw a frenzied boom in consumerism, which was celebrated in Pop art. At the same time, plastic and paper plates, cups, and cutlery came into fashion, to be used and discarded in keeping with the spirit of this disposable, consumer-led age.

The 1960s heralded an exciting new era in design with the appearance of products in strange shapes and bright colors. Italian design in particular came to the fore during these years, with articles such as the AM/FM TS 502 radio by Marco Zanuso for Brionvega and the automatic record player created in 1968 by Mario Bellini. Furniture, too, enjoyed a period of intense design creativity; the *Blow* armchair (1967) in clear, inflatable, and lightweight plastic by De Pas, D'Urbino, Lomazzi, and Scolari differed from traditional furniture in being potentially suitable for any kind of surroundings or decor.

Just as Postmodern painting and architecture had contributed to a

De Pas, Lomazzi, D'Urbino, Scolari, Blow armchair, Zanotta, 1967.

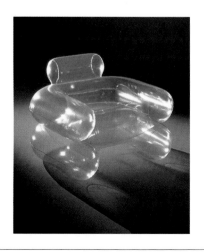

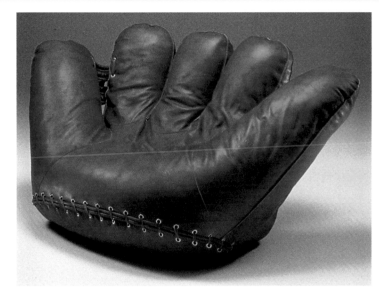

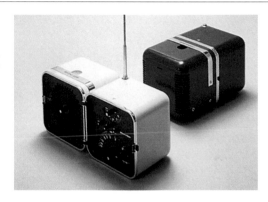

Marco Zanuso, AM/FM TS 502 radio, Brionvega, 1963. Input from innovative designers produced more refined industrial techniques and led to the emergence of more discerning and sophisticated tastes in design.

reevaluation of the expressive freedom of the architect and artist – as opposed to the rigidity of Rationalism and Conceptual art – so the design of furniture and ceramics turned toward more elaborate shapes. Designers often copied Pop art in their choice of complex shapes and unusual colors. The *Wink* chair (1980), designed by Toshiyuki Kita, is both multicolored and able to assume many different forms according to the user's requirements. The *Casablanca* unit (1981) by Ettore Sottsass – a mold-breaking piece of furniture covered with vibrant colored film – reveals affinities with the bold style of the American Graffiti artist Keith Haring. Sottsass, an Austrian-born Italian, was the driving force behind Memphis, a loosely affiliated group of young designers formed in 1981, whose designs for furniture

Lomazzi, D'Urbino, De Pas, Joe *chair, Poltronova, 1970.*

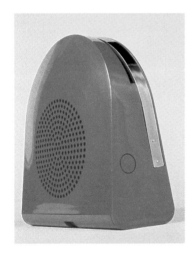

Mario Bellini, Pop portable automatic record-player, Brionvega, 1968.

and household accessories were characterized by a rebellious, anti-Establishment attitude. Their playful style manifested itself in brash colors and harsh, often kitsch forms that have great visual appeal. In later works, such as the *Casablanca* unit, Sottsass employed the highly personal and eccentric style that has been so influential in industrial design. In contrast, the high-tech style lent itself more to the design of electrical household appliances,

Toshiyuki Kita, Wink *chair, Cassina, 1980.*

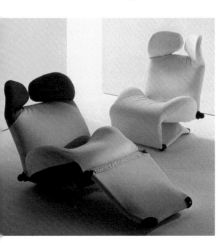

such as radios, tape recorders, and CD players, mainly in black metal, creating an effect of formal sobriety. The sleekness of the equipment was complemented by a dazzling quantity of buttons, controls, and lights, which served to show off its high technological standard. Conceptually, there is little difference between the design of a stereo system, with all its workings on show as proof of its scientific ingenuity and technological sophistication, and the design of a high-tech building such as the Pompidou Center in Paris, which flaunts its technically advanced structure by putting it on the outside.

Ettore Sottsass, Casablanca *unit, Memphis, 1981.*

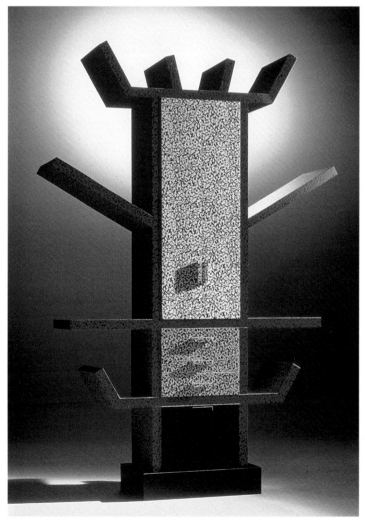

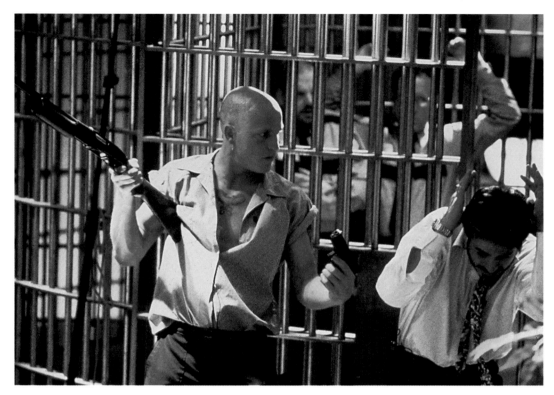

Born Killers (1994) in which the narrative is broken up by a variety of filming techniques. The first crime committed is featured on the sensationalist TV show "American Maniacs," which transforms the ruthless protagonists into heroes acclaimed by television audiences.

COMPUTER ART

Alongside video art, another medium that is becoming increasingly relevant in today's computer-literate culture is computer art, or computer graphics. Images can be created on screen in their entirety and three-dimensional reality can easily be simulated.

Oliver Stone, Natural Born Killers, still, 1994.

NOUVELLE CUISINE

In the late 1970s, Paul Bocuse created a new culinary style that was inspired by a desire for invention and an interest in the cuisine of other countries. This was nouvelle cuisine, a style of preparing and presenting food that sought to simplify the complicated methods typical of previous recipes.
Nouvelle cuisine, literally "new cooking," advocated a reduction in the size of portions and placed greater importance on the aesthetic appeal of the dish. Traditional recipes were reconsidered in an attempt to perfect the combination of flavors, adding just the right herb, spice, or sauce to bring out hidden tastes and aromas.
Great emphasis was placed not only on the combination of flavors but also on the formal appearance and color harmony of the individual components: the plate became a canvas on which to arrange the food with loving care. Intricate sculptures of *al dente* vegetables were carefully complemented by the shape of the plate or the colors of the china. Light sauces and

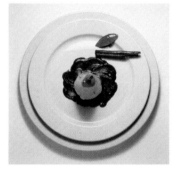

Caramel pears from the Vivolo Restaurant, New York.

A fan of asparagus with fondue sauce from the Hotel Hermitage Restaurant, Cervinia, Italy.

garnishes were now used to add further color and definition to the dish, rather than simply to enhance the flavor and texture of the food.
Food, once conceived as a mere source of nourishment, was now the star of a highly refined – and highly expensive – design production aimed at gratifying all the senses. Not surprisingly, given its immense visual and sensual appeal, nouvelle cuisine provided sumptuous material for the glossy pages of numerous magazines and books. In these, the skill of capturing a recipe in photographic form soon became as admired an art as the cuisine itself. The result was a further crossover between different creative disciplines, with a

culinary work of art coming to be regarded as a kind of still life from the contemporary world. Ironically, as food began to feature in magazine centrefolds, the fact that the subject of all this attention was actually designed to be *eaten* seemed of almost secondary importance.

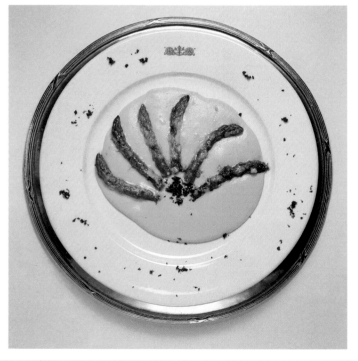

658

ELECTRONIC ART: BRIDGE BETWEEN EAST AND WEST

These outlines of a bridge, developed on a computer screen by the Japanese artist Katsuiro Yagamuchi, show how artists have now conquered a medium that is essentially the same for exponents all over the world. Paper, canvas, ink, tempera, and other traditional materials are, by their nature, different in the hands of different artists. An electronic screen, however, whether linked to a TV camera or a computer, is the same for everyone. As yet, the work

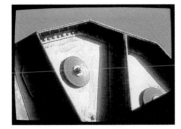

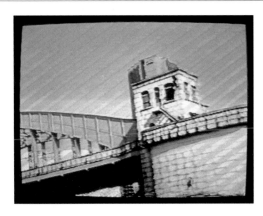

Katsuiro Yagamuchi, Bridge to Bridge, 1988. Bridge Museum, Kurashiki City. In "electronic" art, the absence of any tradition favors the birth of a language that expresses the artist's individuality. Barely even conditioned by the native culture of the artist, this art is capable of being even more of an international medium than the movies.

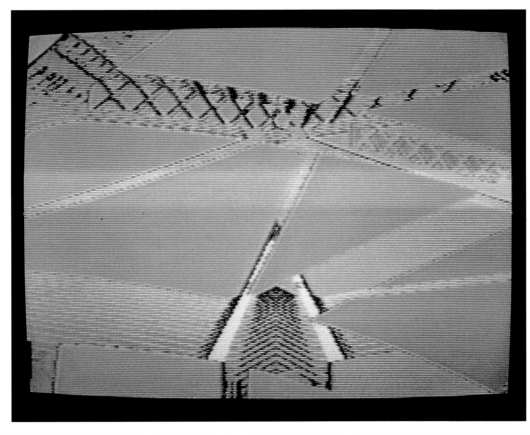

produced using electronic media has yet to be significantly influenced by local traditions or styles. Through a process of communication that allows information to be exchanged almost instantaneously from person to person across the world, artists have been able to contribute to the development of a truly worldwide art form. Electronic art is highly visual, and any piece of work can be modified at will by whomever accesses it on screen. The original work can be altered in any number of ways, with an ease and rapidity inconceivable in the past. The opportunities offered by existing computer programs – or by those currently being developed – tend to blot out the conventional link between manual dexterity and artistic skill. The role may be an anonymous one, but Yamaguchi and his fellow electronic artists could well develop bridges that link shores even farther apart than we can at present imagine.

This has had particular impact on the field of animation. For some time now Disney have been introducing computerized sequences into films – especially to heighten the drama of musical scenes (*The Lion King*, 1995) – and their blockbuster film *Toy Story* (1995) was made entirely in three-dimensional computer animation.

Virtual reality, which gives the illusion of being in a real, three-dimensional environment, is also gaining more and more popularity in the video-games industry. In the late 1980s, the British company W Industries launched a game called *Virtuality* on the international market. It is played with a display screen fitted to the head and a hand control that enables the player to manipulate the action. The success of this game lies in the illusion that one is actually participating in the events, confronting the enemy or personally piloting the plane. Developments in computer art have branched

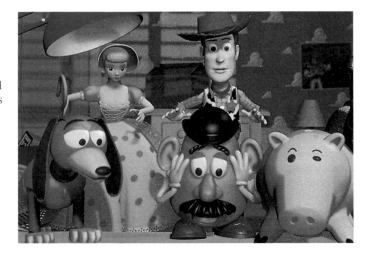

Still from Walt Disney's Toy Story, *1995.*

out from the world of art and overflowed into mass culture, too. Here it is not a case of representing a recognizable part of reality, as in American Pop art, but of producing parallel realities that can be shared by a wider public thanks to the accessibility of the medium. The borders between the artistic dimension and reality are, therefore, becoming more and more blurred, as if the impact of the early 20th-century avant-garde movements, intent on breaking with tradition, has gently been assimilated and finally found a natural successor.

systems, telephones, lighting – all carefully conceived with the aim of making our surroundings as comfortable, efficient, and *attractive* as possible. Aesthetic sensitivity has not only been limited to the confines of the home but has also spread to other consumer areas, such as transportation. Over the years, the motor industry has intensified its research into ever more-perfect designs, creating affordable vehicles with appealing, aerodynamic shapes that offer maximum comfort. With buses and trains, the ongoing process of streamlining has been

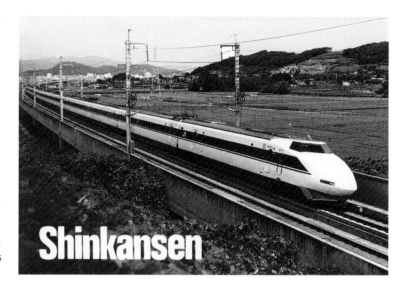

Shinkansen, *the Japanese bullet train, 1964. This design heralded an exciting new aesthetic dimension in the planning and design of public transportation.*

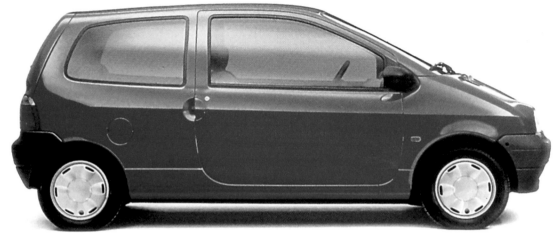

Twingo, *Renault's early 1990s design, which gave a new look to the small car. At the end of the 1950s another French car manufacturer, Citroën, unveiled its DS model, which very soon became a design classic.*

DESIGN IN DAILY LIFE

Over the course of the 20th century, there has been an increasing emphasis on the aesthetic side of every detail of daily life, from fashion to furnishing, gardening to cooking. Major contributions have been made by various aesthetic trends, such as those introduced by Hoffman's Wiener Werkstätte, Gropius's Bauhaus, and Marinetti's Italian Futurist movement. This drive toward increased aesthetic awareness culminated in the prolific activity, since World War II, of designers who have sought to combine aesthetics and practicality in mass-produced articles. A vast array of "designer" objects and appliances has appeared on the market – furniture, televisions, stereo

concurrent with improvements in passenger comfort. Examples of harmoniously combining elegance and speed can be found in Japan's Shinkansen, the "bullet" train built in 1964, and France's TGV. During recent decades, art, technology, and production methods have become

increasingly interwoven, allowing artistic expression to be shown in a far wider range of ways and, in turn, giving many technical processes an aesthetic as well as functional element. It was the new avant-garde movements of the 1970s that initiated this form of collaboration when they gave

up regarding industry as a nuisance and started working alongside it. Many of Andy Warhol's portraits, for example, were produced from his own photographs of famous people. Members of "The Factory" – his studio on 47th Street in New York – would then transfer and repeat the portrait images on canvas using the silk-screen process. Warhol began his career as a commercial artist, working in the fashion world, before moving on to graphic design and window dressing. He reserved the same neutral attitude toward art that had

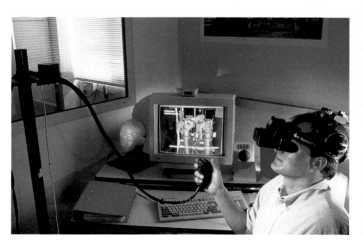

S. Aukstakdnis, D. Beatner, Electronic Mirages, *a virtual reality system produced for the French company EDF. Such systems have applications in a number of different fields, resulting in considerable savings in time and labor. In theatrical stage design, for example, a model of the set is no longer required.*

ART, MUSIC, AND FASHION

In the latter half of the 20th century, opera has enjoyed something of a revival, reaching far wider audiences than before and losing some of its elitist image. It is now, arguably, one of the most popular forms of theater. Directing an opera is a creative effort that requires immense artistic commitment and financial backing. In an age of increasingly creative approaches, set and costume designers, inspired by the original concepts of directors such as Jonathan Miller, Luchino Visconti, Giorgio Strehler, and Bob Wilson, have the freedom

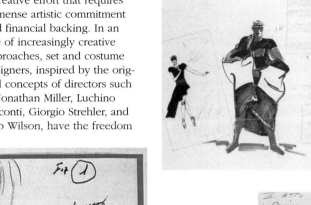

Costume design by Gianni Versace for Joseph-legende, Teatro alla Scala, Milan, 1982.

to devise ever more imaginative and dazzling designs. Inspiration has been drawn from an endless variety of sources, not least the world of art and fashion. While artists have been commisioned to create sets – David Hockney's designs for Mozart's *The Magic Flute* (Glyndebourne, 1978), for example – great fashion

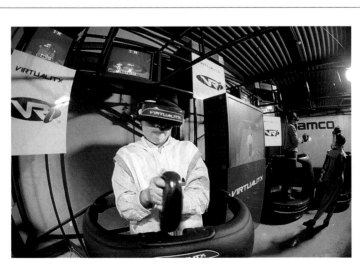

Costume designs by Karl Lagerfeld for Les Troyens by Berlioz, Teatro alla Scala, Milan, 1982.

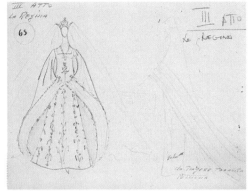

Costume design by Federico Forquet for Swan Lake, Teatro alla Scala, Milan, 1982.

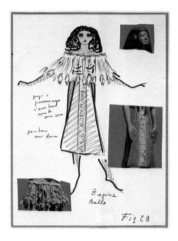

designers are also commissioned by directors and choreographers to create costumes for operas and ballets. For example, Jonathan Miller's 1997 production of Mozart's *Così Fan Tutte* for the Royal Opera House featured costumes by the Italian designer Giorgio Armani. The broad artistic talents of these designers and stylists have undoubtedly contributed to the renewed success of opera.

characterized his work as a contributor to the magazines *Vogue* and *Harper's Bazaar*. Other artists entered the world of ornamental art, designing jewelry or inspiring the creations of prestigious stylists. In the 1970s, fashion designers André Courrèges and Pierre Cardin presented collections dedicated to the space age, in which hats shaped like helmets seemed to turn models into astronauts.

From S. Aukstakdnis, D. Beatner, Electronic Mirages.

The Italian Lucio Fontana put forward his "space-age ideas" in the form of gold and silver rings and bracelets, and his printed fabrics were used for the garment designs of Mila Schön, while other materials reproduced the motifs found in the Op art paintings of Bridget Riley. Jesús Rafael Soto, on the other hand, transferred the optical illusions in his art to female faces with his dangling earrings (1968).

This type of exchange between one field and another is quite typical of the interdisciplinary

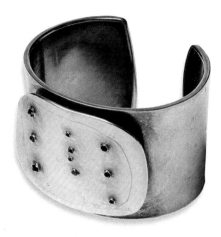

Lucio Fontana, bracelet, 1964–66, Pina Morini Collection, Milan.

evolution of the arts during this period. The boundaries are no longer rigidly defined, and each form of artistic expression can be applied to a wide range of fields. The film director Federico Fellini, for example, transferred the

surrealistic style he employed in his cinema films to highly successful television advertisements for Campari (1984) and Barilla (1986–87).

Ridley Scott introduced the glossy atmosphere of his commercials into the science-fiction films *Alien* (1979) and *Blade Runner* (1982). Meanwhile, actresses such as Juliette Binoche, the lead in Krzysztof Kieslowski's *Three Colors: Blue* (1993) and Louis Malle's *Damage* (1994), and Emmanuelle Béart, an acclaimed performer in Claude Sautet's *Un coeur en hiver* (1992) and Claude Chabrol's *L'enfer* (1994), have found success as endorsers of cosmetic brand names (Lancôme and Christian Dior respectively).

Mila Schön, dress inspired by Lucio Fontana.

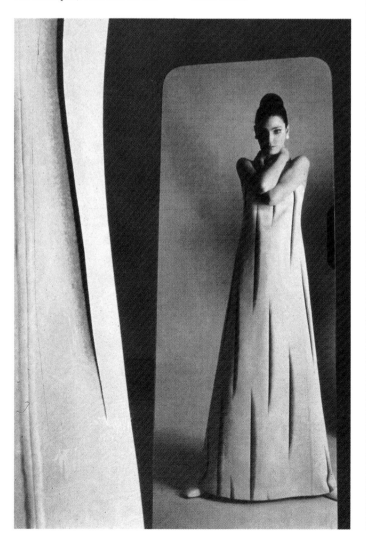

ART AND FASHION

Throughout the 20th century, art has frequently entered the world of fashion. Sonia Delaunay's fashion designs incorporated the color contrasts that characterized her paintings, and the bizarre clothes designed by the Futurists featured irregular shapes and clashing colors. The combination of the two disciplines led to successful collaborations between artists and fashion designers: Salvador Dalí, for example, created Surrealist-style accessories for fashion designer Elsa Schiaparelli, including the series of famous hats in the shape of an upturned shoe. For its part, the fashion world has chosen to celebrate leading artists of the early 20th-century

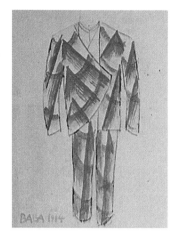

Giacomo Balla, Futurist suit, 1914. Private collection.

avant-garde and other art movements of the 19th and 20th centuries. In 1965, Yves Saint Laurent created clothes using the geometric designs of Mondrian, Gianni Versace used Futurist models for his 1989–90 fashion designs, and Valentino drew on the Vienna Secession for some of his creations. In the recent revival of 1960s and 1970s fashion, Op art designs have once again been revived and reproduced in dazzling black-and-white fabrics.

The relationship between art and fashion can, however, become more complex, when fashion designers become

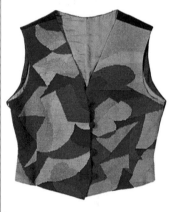

Giacomo Balla, vest, 1920. Private collection.

Sonia Delaunay, sketches for Vogue *magazine covers, 1916.*

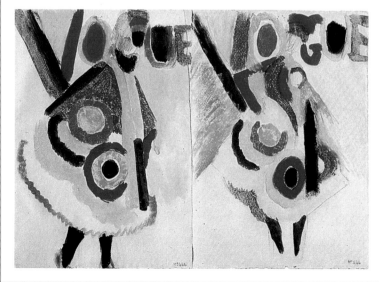

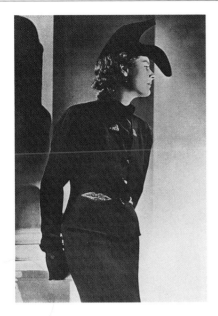

Elsa Schiaparelli, shoe-shaped hat designed by Salvador Dalí.

Richard Gere in Paul Schrader's American Gigolo, 1980.

aware of how creative values can go beyond the simple imitation of art. Except for the materials used, the work of Italian designer Roberto Capucci, for example, can be compared to that of an architect or a sculptor. He does not cut and stitch his fabrics according to the contours of the body, but gives them an independent structure; the shape of the garment therefore remains fixed and does not mold itself to the body when it is worn. Ignoring the force of gravity, Capucci turns fine materials into soft, spiraling shapes inspired by flowers and butterflies, or makes strict shapes that recall the work of the Geometric Abstractionists. Even his choice of venue for his fashion shows – usually grand settings such as the Italian Embassy in Paris (1984) and the Modern Art Gallery in Rome (1989) – reveal

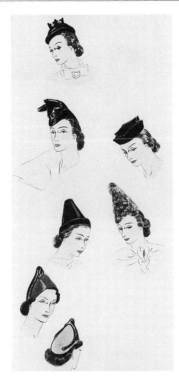

the collaboration between costume designers and film directors. The success lies not in designs that improve the actors' appearance, but in designs that – even though they retain the designer's unmistakable mark – contribute to the overall atmosphere of the film. Giorgio Armani's costumes for Richard Gere in Paul Schrader's *American Gigolo* (1980) and for Walter Hill's *Roads of Fire* (1984) illustrate this well. It is clear from such examples how the contribution of a fashion designer can establish a relationship between daily life and the cinematic realm: reality is mirrored in fiction and vice versa.

Salvador Dalí, hat sketches for Elsa Schiaparelli.

Gianni Versace, waistcoat inspired by Depero, 1989–90 collection.

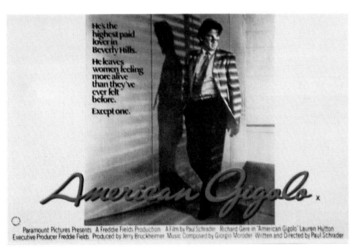

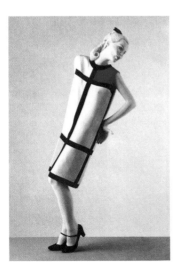

Yves Saint Laurent, cocktail dress inspired by Piet Mondrian, 1965.

his intention to replace the traditional catwalk fashion parade with a performance that is far more theatrical in style. The models are transformed, thanks to clever makeup that sculpts, rather than highlights, their features into the perfect extension of – or complement to – the garments they wear. The clothes are always the star of the show, and presented in this way they are given an even more prominent, theatrical role. A similar phenomenon occurs in

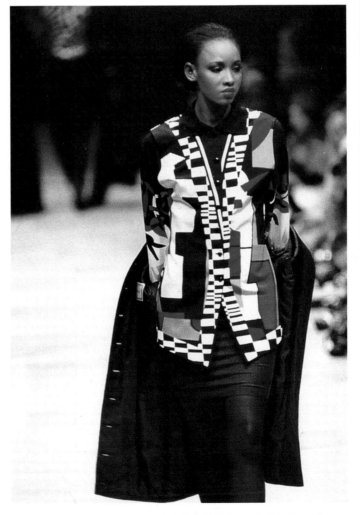

Top models such as Carol Alt and Cindy Crawford, on the other hand, took on film roles, demonstrating their acting potential and, above all, proving that it is possible to move freely between the various artistic professions. Highly popular and successful films have the power to influence trends in contemporary fashions, with the result that it can sometimes seem as if fashion shots are stills from movies and movies a continuous fashion show. Today, catwalks often feature more performance-style shows, frequently involving the collaboration of an artist, as in the Milan show of 1995 directed by Haim Steinbach for the Strenesse Group. The key to understanding such overlap-

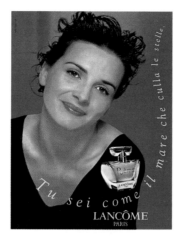

Lancôme advertisement for their perfume Poême. The intimate quality of this luxury product is conveyed by actress and film star Juliette Binoche.

Roberto Capucci, Column, 1989. This is one of several variations produced by the accomplished Italian fashion designer. He consciously presents his clothes designs as works of art. Column is a tribute to the caryatid, a pillar sculpted in the form of a draped female figure and used as an architectural support. The caryatid is the origin of Greek female statues.

ping roles is provided by Steinbach himself, who, when asked to define that experience, replied: "It is as much art as anything else I do, it was a piece of work in a situation characterized by its own way of life." Indeed, there is a strong similarity between the shelves on which artists display the *objets d'art* they

SCREAMS, LAUGHTER, AND FURY

The art of the 20th century is often cerebral and, far from restraining the artist's passions, has been the vehicle for tragic feelings in a most violently expressive way. Both intimate emotions and civil concerns have often been put forward in a vulgar spasm of feeling. In this respect, Edvard Munch's *Scream* (1893) can be seen as a kind of manifesto for a century of pain and conflict. Following the hopes and aspirations of its predecessor, the 20th century has been one of grief, in which artists' and intellectuals' social and political passions have been forcefully expressed. In the case of Picasso, there is an evident contempt for the bourgeoisie, its slavish attachment to convention, its prejudices, and its complacent sense of good taste. The Italian artist Piero Manzoni, in his labeled cans of human excreta, turns the

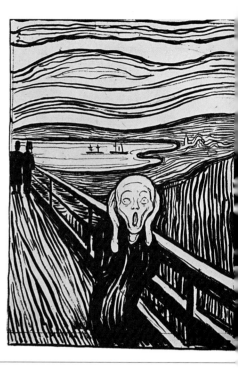

Edvard Munch, The Scream, 1895. Lithograph, Communal Museum of Art, Oslo. Munch painted themes of grief and pain in many of his works; the print below is the most famous of several versions of this subject.

have created and the catwalk with its fashion models: ultimately, the catwalk is one large display case. This mixing and matching of artistic disciplines effectively cancels out any hierarchy that may previously have prevailed. In this pursuit of a union between life and art – as promoted by Dadaism in the early part of the century – there is always the risk that it will turn into a meaningless, chaotic experiment in which each genre loses its own identity in the confusion of styles. However, the problem is not so much the blurring of demarcations between different branches of art, but

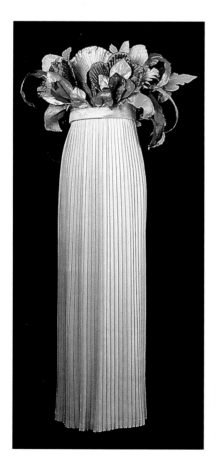

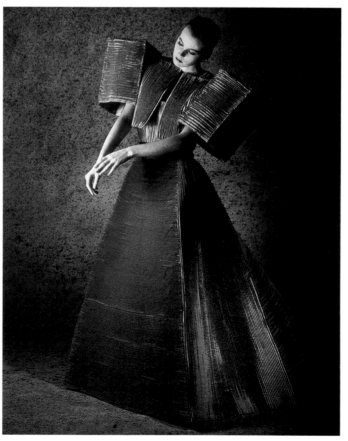

Roberto Capucci, Boxes, 1987. Capucci created this gown from a series of solid geometric shapes. As in Boxes, the expressive power of the color and the surface texture of the fabric is very strong, the folds creating a delicate play of shadows. Such garments, which have received great critical acclaim, are displayed as museum exhibits. They are worn not by models but by dummies, as they might appear in a shop window.

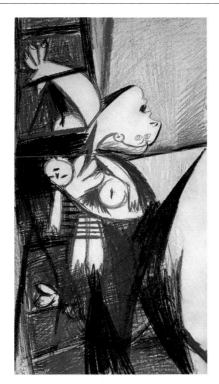

Pablo Picasso, Mother with Dead Child, *1973. Pencil and chalk on paper. For Picasso, the portrayal of death, the subject of many of his paintings, is an expression of his abhorrence of violence.*

scream into hysterical laughter in a kind of Rabelaisian protest. This raucous outburst expresses the tragic sarcasm of an artist who was spiraling inevitably toward suicide (Manzoni killed himself in 1963).

With the student revolts of 1968, the long season of postwar euphoria came to an end, and the conflicts in Asia showed the violent side of contemporary life. Some artists were, however, able to give aesthetic expression to the pain of hope betrayed. For example, the explosion in *Zabriskie Point,* one of Antonioni's most famous films, not only resolves the overall tension but also voices the impotent fury of the age.

The extreme, bloody performances of Body art were another manifestation of the artist's identification with the prevailing mood of pain and conflict. Vito Acconci (1970) bit his own body and marked out his wounds with ink; Chris Burden (*Shooting Piece,* 1971) had himself shot in the arm; and

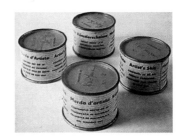

Piero Manzoni, cans of the artist's excreta, 1961. Private collection, Milan. In the same year, Manzoni adorned peeled boiled eggs with his fingerprints.

Marina Abramovich (*Rhythm,* 1974) invited the public to hurt her. Self-inflicted injury and masochism are in line with the art of the movies, one of continued violence in which an obscure humanity resolves the fury of mass powerlessness in a sea of fire and blood.

Michelangelo Antonioni, Zabriskie Point, still, 1970. This is not only an atomic explosion but also the frustrating banality of life making itself heard.

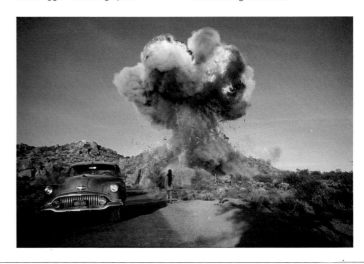

rather the potential loss of quality. Graffiti art, daubed over subway trains or on city walls, is a case in point. This simple, spontaneous form of expression falls outside classic artistic analysis, and its milieu is very different from conventional art settings. Where Graffiti art achieves good artistic and communicative results, it can contribute to the improvement of urban areas; what has less visual appeal is the gratuitous repetition of images or "tags" with no aesthetic value to them. If an artist shows an interest in several different fields, it can be because he or she has a fertile mind. Whether the results of the experimentation are any good, however, will depend on the level of skill the artist is able to attain. Lucio Fontana's jewelry, for example, was not just a bit of fun, a turning of his work on canvas into miniature objects: it was a re-creation of them in a different medium. In the

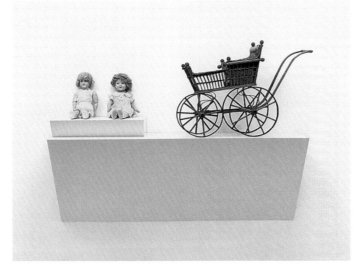

same way, the taffeta dresses designed by Roberto Capucci reveal an artistic worth that goes well beyond the transient world of fashion.

The Romanian poet Tristan Tzara, author of the 1918 Dada Manifesto, talked of how good he felt having repeated the word "scream" more than a hundred times. This irreverent

scream would inaugurate a century of artistic exploration, often giving rise to unorthodox experiments, and rarely bowing to any conventions. It was a cry that had wide repercussions and reverberated with all sorts of creative interpretations. Given the force behind it, its power to promote change is hardly surprising.

Haim Steinbach, Untitled, 1990. Two dolls and a carriage, banal objects from daily life, are set out like contemporary idols on an altar or as goods on a supermarket shelf. The observer is made to question whether there is any difference between idols and goods. Alienation as protest, confusion as condemnation, violence, and regression to the past as an escape from an unbearable present: these are all features common to much 20th-century art.

POSTWAR DEVELOPMENTS & CONTEMPORARY ART

1945: atomic bombs destroy Hiroshima and Nagasaki; international capital of art shifts from Paris to New York. **1947:** Treaty of Paris establishes conditions of peace between World War II victors and vanquished, deferred in the cases of Germany and Japan; W. F. Libby discovers carbon 14 and relative system of dating. **1948:** Movement for Concrete Art (MAC) is established in Milan; Vittorio de Sica's film *Bicycle Thieves* is an international success. **1949:** Atlantic Pact drawn up in Washington. **1950:** Albert Einstein publishes his *Significance of Relativity*, in which he asserts his theory of an expanding universe. **1951:** Lucio Fontana creates luminous spirals for the ceiling of Ninth Triennial of Milan. **1955:** the musical work of Luciano Berio is recognized. **1956–59:** building of Frank

1945   1950   1960

▼ JACKSON POLLOCK
(1912-56)
American painter, whose "drip and splash" technique ensured that the very act of painting became the subject of his art.

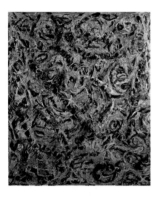

Jackson Pollock, Eyes in the Heat, *1946. Peggy Guggenheim Foundation, Venice.*

FRANCIS BACON
(1909-92)
This British painter aroused violent reactions at his London exhibition of *Three Studies for Figures at the Base of a Crucifixion*.

▼ JEAN DUBUFFET
(1901-85)
A precursor of *Art Informel*, this French painter's obsession with Art Brut ("raw art") was exemplified by a style consisting of almost infantile brushstrokes.

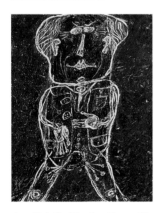

Jean Dubuffet, Monsieur Plume with Creases in his Trousers, *1947. Tate Gallery, London.*

▼ RENATO GUTTUSO
(1912-87)
Influenced by the work of Goya and Picasso, this Sicilian painter passionately tackled the issues of war and social injustice. In the course of a long career, he always remained true to the principles of expressive realism.

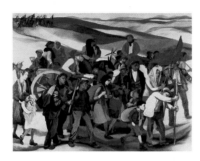

Renato Guttuso, L'occupazione delle terre incolte di Sicilia, *1949–50. Gemäldegalerie, Dresden.*

▼ MARK ROTHKO
(1903-70)
This Russo-American painter played a wholly individual role in the area of abstract art, creating a sense of pulsating space generated by superimposed fields of color.

Mark Rothko, Number 10, *1950. Museum of Modern Art, New York.*

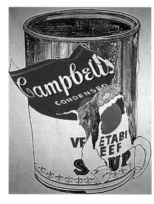

Andy Warhol, Big Torn Campbell's Soup Can (vegetable beef), *1962. Bruno Bischofberger Gallery, Zurich.*

▼ JOSEPH KOSUTH
(b. 1945)
This American experimental artist was an exponent of Conceptual Art. He took to extremes the ideas of Duchamp: art is not in the object but in its definition.

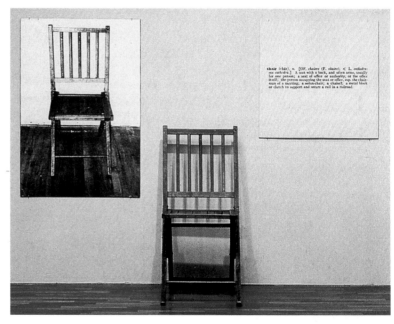

Joseph Kosuth, One and Three Chairs, *1965. Museum of Modern Art, New York.*

INDUSTRIAL MINIMALISM ►
This decade saw an increasing emphasis on minimal design, resulting in utilitarian objects and furniture in new shapes and colors. Among the most interesting artists were Ettore Sottsass, Marco Zanuso, Gae Aulenti, Joe Colombo, and Giorgio Giugiaro.

◄ ANDY WARHOL
(1928-87)
An American painter, graphic artist, and director, Warhol was a major representative of American Pop art. He was a bitter critic of the consumer society, using an effective style derived from the mass media.

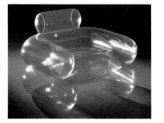

De Pas, Lomazzi, D'Urbino, Scolari, Blow armchair, *Zanotta, 1967.*

Lloyd Wright's Guggenheim Museum in New York. **1958:** Jasper Johns, representative of new Dadaism in the US, paints his series of American flags. **1961–62:** birth of the "Fluxus" movement, which conceives art as an interdisciplinary "event"; Piero Manzoni creates his "living" sculptures. **1965:** proclamation of Optical art at the New York Museum of Modern Art exhibition. **1967:** critic Germano Celant coins the term "arte povera." **1973:** death of Pablo Picasso. **1980:** deaths of Oskar Kokoschka and Graham Sutherland. **1986:** American artist Jean-Michel Basquiat dies at age 26. **1991:** after the failure of a Communist *coup d'état*, the Soviet Union is dissolved. **1997:** death of Willem de Kooning. **1998:** death of the Italian architect Alberto Sartoris.

1970　　　1980　　　1990

▼ CHRISTO
(CHRISTO JARACHEFF)
(b. 1935)

Initially an exponent of Land Art, this Bulgarian sculptor abandoned New Realism in favor of his spectacular "wrapping" enterprises.

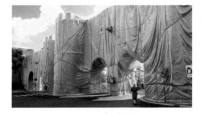

Christo, The Aurelian Wall, 1972. Rome.

▼ POSTMODERN ARCHITECTURE

With the support of the most advanced technology, Postmodern architecture sought to surpass previous rationalism and functionalism through the free interpretation of past styles. Technology was often openly displayed, becoming a characteristic feature of the building, as in the Pompidou Centre.

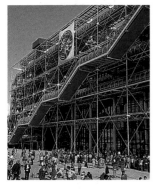

Richard Rogers and Renzo Piano, Pompidou Centre, Paris, 1972–77.

▼ TRANSAVANGUARDIA

The paintings produced by this group were inspired from various sources including Expressionism, Cubism, and Surrealism, as well as the figurative repertory of mythology and ancient art. The formal purity of Mariani's "anachronistic" painting creates a magical atmosphere reminiscent of the works of de Chirico.

Carlo Maria Mariani, La mano ubbidisce all'intelletto, 1983. Private Collection, US.

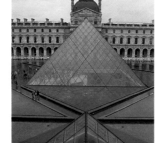

I.M. Pei, Louvre Pyramids, Paris. 1985–93.

CONSUMER GOODS ▼

The Swatch wristwatches were products of the Postmodern era. The variously colored collections were the work of international artists such as the American Graffiti artist Keith Haring and the Italian Transavanguardia representative Mimmo Paladino. These limited-edition Swatch "originals" are collector's items.

Swatch from the Breakdance collection, 1985.

◄ I.M. PEI
(b. 1917)

This Chinese-born American architect creates elegant structures that are strictly geometrical and predominantly angular in form.

▼ PUBLICITY

Famous faces from the worlds of movies, television, and fashion have become a part of our everyday life, often appearing in commercial advertisements.

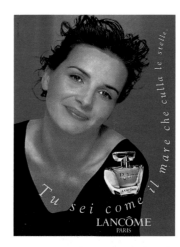

Publicity launch for Lancôme, featuring the French actress Juliette Binoche.

FASHION

The barrier between art and fashion has gradually become indefinable. Fashion designers have gone beyond simple imitation of art with their theatrical creations.

▼ COMPUTER GRAPHICS

Computer graphics now play a primary role in the making of animated films and video games for mass consumption.

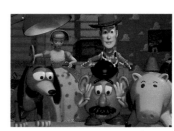

Still from Walt Disney's Toy Story, 1995.

Gillo Dorfles

THE FUTURE OF ART

LOOKING BACK BRIEFLY at the visual arts of the 20th century (not only painting, sculpture, and architecture, but also movies, photography, television, and comic strip), one important fact to recognize is that everything changed radically in the decade or so prior to World War I. The rise of the Avant-garde movements, the decline of figurative art, the trend toward abstract art, and the introduction of new architectural materials are only a few of the essential consequences of this revolution.

Another abrupt change of direction came in the aftermath of World War II, with the arrival of conceptualism, visual poetry, Land art, Body art, and, finally, video and computer art, television graphics, and electronic music.

The major advances in science that have characterized the latter part of the 20th century have stretched the arts to hitherto unthinkable dimensions. On the one hand, the new climate has pointed the way to untold novelties in ideas and achievements; on the other, it has stultified the

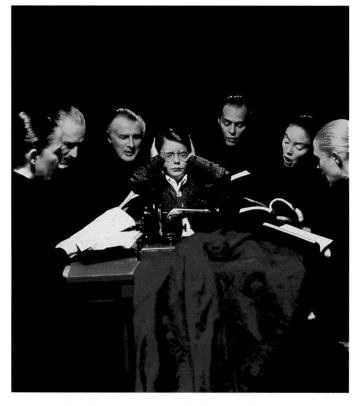

Pina Bausch, Kontakthof. *This photograph shows a scene from the 1983 Milan production of the celebrated stage show Kontakthof, first performed in 1978. Pina Bausch is one of the major figures in modern dance.*

Derek Jarman, Wittgenstein, *1993. The movie about the Austrian philosopher was one of the British artist and director's final works. Jarman is among the most innovative figures in the arts of recent decades. His other films include* Jubilee *and* Caravaggio.

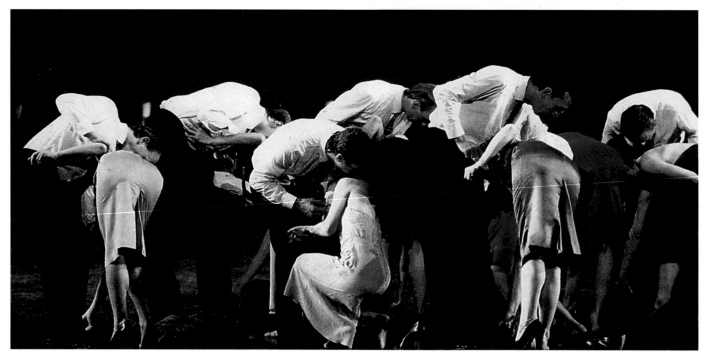

imagination, carrying to extremes the capacity for immediacy of sensation, as expressed, for example, in horror art, sado-masochistic Body art, recourse to practical objects, "disused" mechanisms, technocratic stimulations, and, in contrast, exaltation – obscene, scatological, mystical – of the body itself.

This is obviously not a complete overview, and it would be valid to argue that, despite such developments, we can still find traditional painting, drawing, engraving, sculpture, and architecture that is at least partially reliant on manual skills, not to mention a variety of craft activities.

Whatever lies in the future, it is more likely that this dichotomy between manual tradition and technological discovery will determine the path of the visual arts. In recent years, we have witnessed a rediscovery of the body: despite instances of deviation, there have been many positive examples, such as those of Theatertanz (Pina Bausch, Lucinda Childs, Carolyn Carlson), which demonstrate how the body can be used not only as an aesthetic but also a therapeutic instrument (as demonstrated by Rudolf Steiner's eurhythmics and many other forms of music therapy).

In addition to the discovery of the body as a component of art, we have a contemporary revival of interest in the "handmade": traditional crafts (ceramics, tapestry, alabaster, mosaic, wood, glass, etc.), which, because of their intrinsic value and relative cost, supplement and counteract the intrusion of industrially produced design objects. Indeed, in the design sector, where there was a powerful reaction against superfluous decoration, we are likely to see a revival of ornamental practice and a general rediscovery of manual expertise.

Examples of these new directions, therefore, are the celebration of the body, evident in much contemporary theater, including the work of Valdoca, Barba, Kantor, and Wilson; pride in craftsmanship; and greater expressivity in architecture. Notwithstanding the high-tech excesses of Foster, Piano, Rogers, and the like, the latter exhibits a more "humanized" approach, one that is organic rather than technological. This can be seen in the work, say, of Anders, Erskine, Asmussen, Makovezc, and, to some extent, of Ando, Hollein, and Gehry. In this sense, the visual arts, as well as architecture and the theater, appear to be reaching out toward interhuman relationships as a reaction against the excesses of electronic, cybernetic, and informational "communication."

Nevertheless, because the new media exist and cannot possibly be ignored, we have to recognize the unprecedented opportunities they afford for evolution in the world of art. In television, for example, although one may lament its all too frequent mediocrity and lack of cultural content (not to mention its stultifying effect on children's minds), there is no doubt that its potential as a medium of communication is immense and that it can be a positive influence to artistic invention in the spheres of the comic strip, the animated cartoon, publicity, and even education.

Marisa Bronzini, Filo 54, silk and cotton thread, 1994. Collection of the Artist. The explicitly manual technique gives perfect form to the creative concept expressed in the tapestry.

Marisa Bronzini, Filo 36, linen, silk, copper, cotton thread, stone. Collection of the Artist. In this hand-crafted work, the expressive pursuit has absorbed the natural subject matter.

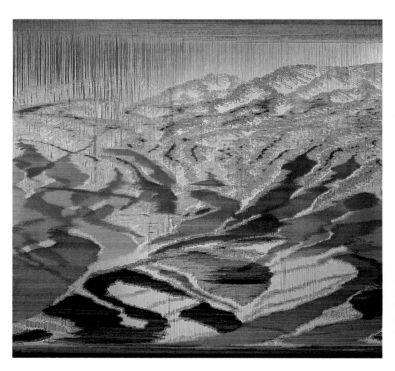

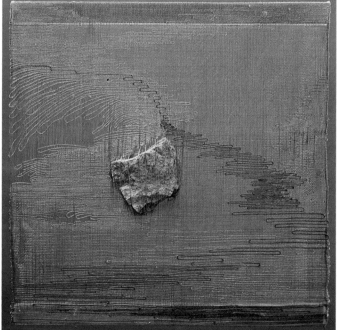

If television currently provides relatively little in terms of "reproducing" preexisting works of art, it can nevertheless be a determining factor in the conception of an entirely new approach to the integration of sound and color, to chromatic figuration, and to imaginative investigation into effects of space and time. Whereas the creation of a painting or a statue is often a slow, static process, television is capable of all manner of extraordinary experiments involving forms of art that are based on movement.

I am not convinced about the future evolution of a "computer art" in its own right, any more than I was about that of "video art," yet both can be extremely valuable in the service of already existing transmissions of other forms of artistic technique. In the same way as "electronic" music – initially regarded as a total substitute for traditional music – now constitutes only one of many "auxiliary" forms of instrumental music, so

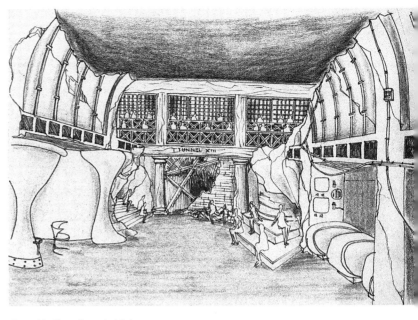

Frank O. Gehry, Loyola Law School, 1981–84. Los Angeles. In this project, the Canadian architect and designer has used the visual axes of the buildings to create a clear sense of tension.

Bruno Voglino, stage sketch for Tunnel, Rai, *1993–94. In this drawing for the Italian television magazine, Voglino creates an environment that assimilates audience and actors.*

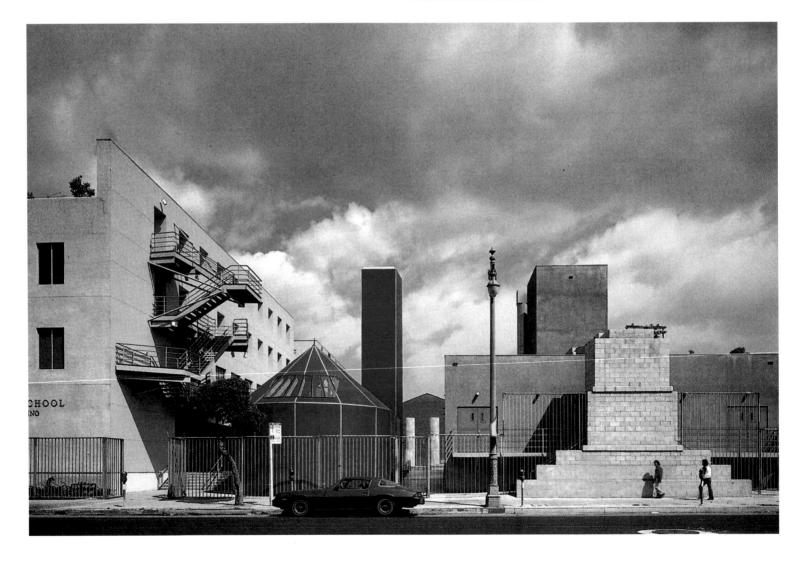

I believe that computer graphics can be a powerful aid to the traditional visual arts. In architecture, it already provides an almost total substitute for old-style design and is pointing the way toward easier and more adventurous planning procedures.

It is already evident today that these technological advances, not only in taking us beyond what is real but in truly "creating something from nothing" (as in the case of architectural design, computer art, and "virtual reality") can in theory lead to the development of highly interactive art forms, opening up new horizons, in terms of form and time, for the creative artist.

More explicitly, one can foresee a general revival of interest in the artist's autonomous and personalized creative activity, a reappraisal of works with a distinct individual signature. This applies also to dance and the theater, accompanied by sounds, colors, voices, etc., and to the manual production of objects, whether

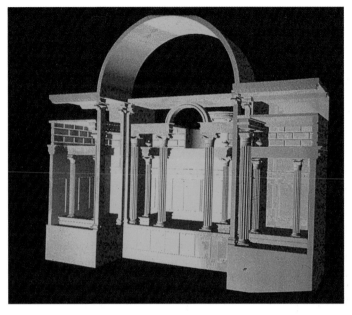

Photograph showing a scene from Outis *by Luigi Nono, Teatro alla Scala, Milan, 1996. Graham Vick and Timothy O'Brien employed various electronic devices in this production.*

IBM Foundation, Italy, computer development of a fresco from the Villa dei Misteri, Pompei. New computer applications now make it possible to create virtual works of art.

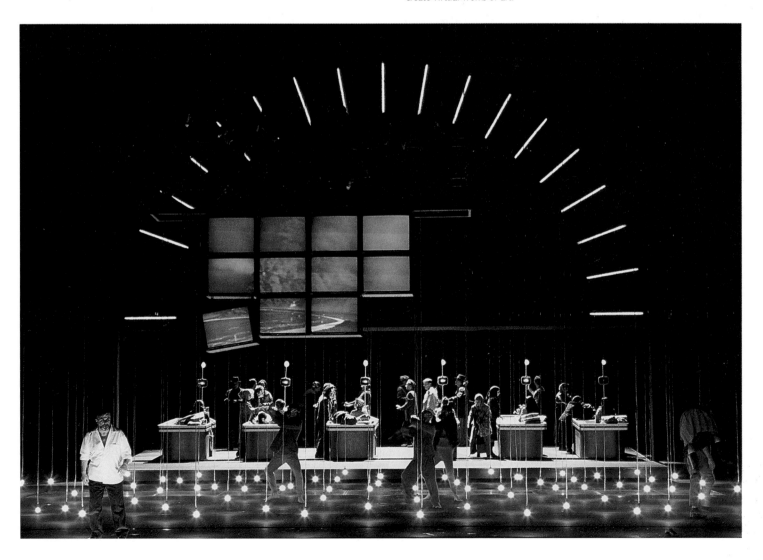

for decorative or more specifically symbolic purposes. Indeed, it is worth recalling that art, since its very origins, has always been founded on a symbolic component, without which it would not be able to communicate its message beyond the time of its creation. To attain, in fact, a kind of communication that transcends the threshold of intellectual understanding and historical definition, what is indispensable is the presence of that "transrational" thinking that we can identify in "visual thinking," inherent in the symbolic component of every artistic creation.

Photograph showing a scene from Kazou Ohno's Argentina, *1983. The Japanese artist blends several art forms in the on-stage presence of the actor.*

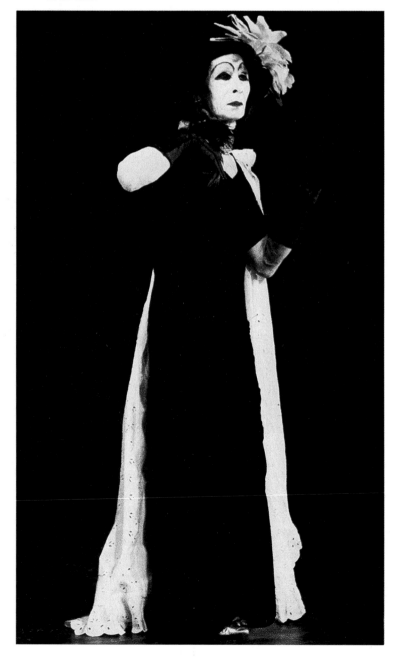

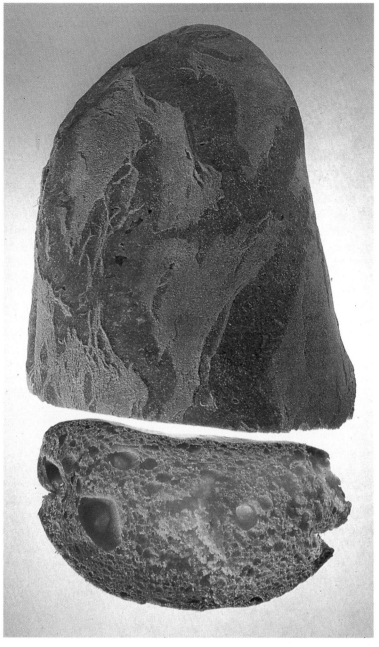

Image of a loaf of bread and slice of bread. The iconic value of this everyday item is here presented for aesthetic enjoyment, demonstrating an artistic urge to reinvent the commonplace.

In the arts of the near future we must verify the resurgence of this symbolic element – so often absent in many works of today – and we must aim to restore, in all art forms, the component capable of constituting the imaginative and reflective nucleus of every aesthetic activity. Not only that, but we need to bring about a greater "socialization" of art, or, if you will, a greater "aestheticization" of society, allowing every individual, even if lacking special scientific, historical, or philosophical knowledge, to be a participant in an art intended for all mankind.

Giorgio Taborelli

THE SEARCH FOR ART

OFF THE SOUTHWEST TIP OF Asia Minor lies the Greek island of Cos, home to the Mausoleum, and the ancient city of Halicarnassus. Here, one can still see the remains of the Asclepeion, once a magnificent temple of marble statues and reliefs, where pilgrims came to worship the god Asclepius. The island was the birthplace of Hippocrates who, in about the middle of the fifth century BC, began to practise medicine based on rational diagnosis and therapy. This was the age of Perikles and the age of the production on Cos of silk – a much prized commodity.

Cos boasts a remarkable concentration and wealth of culture, inquiry, and industry for an island of such modest size, yet throughout the world, wherever mankind has settled and stayed, marks have been made and lasting signs have been left. These cultural traces are often in the form of what we today call art, but to see them as such we must think about their context; the culture that has produced a well-drawn line, a carefully applied color, a skillfully delivered stroke of hammer or chisel, or the simple grace and beauty of form. Art is continuity, yet it is also part of a process of change and bound up within a culture.

Works of art can never be fully understood unless they are related to the circumstances in which they were created. The only way to glean any significance or meaning from a work is to set them within their general cultural ambience. In many cases, levels of meaning can never be fully recovered, and therefore our overall appreciation is something very different from the original.

Archaeological investigation and study informs us of a history and builds up a picture or a narrative of ancient cultures and their creations. Picking through the debris of a settlement, examining the fortifications of a castle, the rubble of a town, or the site of a marketplace, can provide valuable insights into the context of works of art.

History teaches us where to look for evidence of art. Wherever there was a flourishing civilization or abundant economic production, often manifested as a large, long-standing settlement, art tended to be produced and encouraged, and its traces often survive today. The emergence of urban cultures led to the importance of permanent records and therefore the birth of history. Art is akin to language in this way. It can control and interpret the natural and social universe that humanity inhabits. In every human society, art is part of the intrinsic and complex structure of beliefs, rituals, and moral and social codes. It is a system of signs and symbols that are intelligible to the members of the society that produces them.

History can also tell us of what we have lost. The magnificent African city of Great Zimbabwe, capital of the kingdom of Monomotapa in the 11th century, is now nothing but a ruin. The statues are gone, the marvelously adorned palaces and other monuments of the Zulu capital are gone; all that remains are its massive walls, the most impressive in sub-Saharan Africa. Everything was burned, ransacked, removed, dispersed, or melted down to make ingots of gold. There is also little evidence now of the ancient and medieval city structure of ancient Istanbul, with its buildings, fountains, statues, and colonnades – it was destroyed by the Crusaders in 1204 and later by the Ottomans in 1453. We know that one of the marvels of the world, the Porcelain Tower in China, was destroyed by the Taiping rebels after they had conquered Nanking in 1853. The art of southern and central America was almost totally wiped out, as were their cultures. The works and systems created over centuries can be destroyed in a remarkably short time. There are countless instances of such destruction, of cultural extermination throughout the world.

However, we still have our legacies. We have Venice – never taken by siege, never suffered terrible earthquakes like Santorini and Messina, never consumed by a disastrous fire, as was London, and never heavily bombarded during wartime. For these reasons, the art of the city of the lagoon has survived miraculously for some ten centuries.

673

There are layers and layers of forgotten culture throughout past civilizations. There is ample evidence of a succession of ancient cultures throughout the former Ottoman empire, which itself succeeded the Byzantine empire. The museums of modern Istanbul possess masterpieces of Mesopotamian, Hittite, Hellenic, and Byzantine art because the sultan was the overlord of all these territories. The Vatican State, which ruled Rome from the late Middle Ages to the Italian conquest of 1870, has inherited the remains of the many ransackings of the city, and also much of what gradually came to light in the course of archaeological excavations or site clearances for modern building operations. The American Museum in Madrid has inherited treasures of the Andean civilization and of pre-Columbian Mexico, due to the rule of the king of Spain over central-southern America. The Spanish museums, such as the Museo del Prado in Madrid and the Museo de Bellas Artes in Seville, chart the history of various lands: in addition to works by Spanish masters, they possess much Italian, Flemish, and German art. Art collections can reflect the shifting of peoples and the movement of empires. For example, when, in 1700, a prince of the house of Bourbon became king of Spain, French artists and craftsmen began to work in Madrid, while contacts with other regions weakened after the loss of the Spanish empire in Europe.

Art from the past can also be updated and improved. In Japan, parts of great, ancient temples are faithfully restored with modern materials, or entirely rebuilt in identical fashion. Elsewhere, entire buildings, or conspicuous parts, have been removed from their places of origin and reconstructed, sometimes with the consent of their countries of origin, or often as a result of pillage. There are numerous examples that enrich the museums and thoroughfares of many cities: in London, in New York, in Berlin, and in Rome, among others.

In the poor parts of Provence, where Crusaders once butchered the Albigensians, there are silent villages of stone where the simple harmony of the buildings is enhanced by the absence of ornament. In Castile, flocks now graze in fields once trampled by knights on horseback, and villages and walled cities impoverished during the European wars of the Hapsburgs remain empty but authentic in appearance, preserved to this day by the arid climate.

The economic history of a civilization also gives us clues to its particular art and culture. For example, the development of British capitalism during the reign of the Hanoverian kings led to the rich art collections of the Stuarts being imitated by the new nobility and aristocracy. Men of means, in addition to encouraging local artists, collected art from the cities of Europe, and, in due course, from the imperial possessions in Asia and Africa. Similarly, the development of capitalism in other European nations helps to explain the formation in the 19th century of large private collections, the contents of which sometimes found their way, often through patronage, into public and private museums. For example, the arms dealer Calouste Gulbenkian left a formidable museum to the city of Lisbon, while many objects from the rich collections of art housed by the great Vienna museum were donated by the Austrian branch of the Rothschild banking family. Today, many of the world's most important artistic items, whether acquired by private sale or by new discoveries, end up in the collections and museums of economically powerful nations and individuals.

The loss of great art treasures from the lands and cultures that created them is owing to a number of different factors. The fashionable Grand Tour that wealthy Europeans undertook in the 17th and 18th centuries, as well as the habit of many rich Americans and Russians during the 19th and 20th centuries of spending time in Paris, Deauville, Monte Carlo, Vichy, and the like, help explain the present whereabouts of paintings, sculptures, and items of fine porcelain and jewelry. These may have once been sold by desperate owners or professional art dealers to well-heeled foreign travelers.

Loss of works of art can be a sign of a gradual, eroding process, whereby a cultural identity slowly dissipates, often to the point of collapse. However, conversely, the shedding of a stagnant artistic style can lead to the renewal of a culture and of the assimilation of ideas and techniques of other cultures to produce a new and important form. A key example of this is the Europe of the Renaissance.

There are many places that are, in fact, museums in their own right, and have been recognized as such. Sacred buildings, even though long abandoned, merit respect as testaments to bygone faiths; so do palaces, even if their days of glory have faded. Monumental gardens, certain squares, and particular streets may contain a wealth of art. Temples, churches, and mosques open to visitors often house ornaments and works that testify to centuries of pious devotion and artistic expression. At Assisi, the city of St. Francis, the 16th-century church of Santa Maria, renovated in elegant Baroque style in the 17th century by Giacomo Giorgetti, is simply the elongated cella, still well preserved, of a Roman temple from the last years of the republic. In many areas of Rome, layer has built upon layer, and from the ruins emerge beautiful artifacts revealing a history of religion and power. The silent testimony of monarchs and their exploits, and the words of the patriarchs and the apostles, haunt the archaeological excavations and surviving monuments of Mesopotamia, Syria, Anatolia, and Egypt. Smells, colors, and sounds that remind us of a past world may pervade the cloister of an abbey or of a Spanish convent. Such emotional reverberations exalt the nostalgic value of a building or a work of art.

Great cities offer not only works in situ, but also important international collections. London has a wealth of treasures from all over the world in its museums and galleries, which are situated among the city's own historic buildings. Vienna boasts a huge number of museums holding collections from all periods of history and from a variety of cultures, many housed within the splendor of the city's Baroque architecture.

Full appreciation of a work of art requires sympathy and understanding. A work of art cannot be treated as a corpse awaiting an autopsy; it cannot always be dissected so we are left with only its constituent parts – it demands of the observer a reciprocal exchange of intelligence, empathy, and feeling. The genuine art enthusiast should be sensitive to its history, its values, and the culture that produces it.

For various reasons, climate and time count for much in the understanding and appreciation of art. A general consideration is that each climate has its own art. It is much more difficult to comprehend the meaning of a low, pale Norwegian sun by Munch when it is viewed in the tropics, or a colorful and exotic Venus by Gauguin when viewed thousands of miles from Tahiti. Heat and high humidity provide the ideal atmosphere in which to gaze on the stone figures that adorn the face of a tenth-century temple in Orissa. The ancient reliefs of the Acropolis cannot appear as beautiful in a London museum as they would in the sunlight of Athens. It may be impossible to see the faded frescoes of a Romanesque church on a winter evening in a Continental climate; electric light may provide excellent illumination, but for detailed study can only distort the images. Given a choice, the art lover will aim to see a work in the best possible conditions of natural lighting. Before an art market existed, virtually all works were made for a precise place and for a defined public, neither of which may any longer exist; this ideal setting can rarely be recreated, but sensitivity to this setting is essential.

The appearance of a building or work in its natural environment can be radically affected by the time of day. A city can sometimes reveal its beauties more effectively at the brief times of day when it is empty and quiet. The lines and details of an exposed surface are often best examined at dusk while the sun at its zenith flattens volume. Midday is not the most suitable time to look at a historic column or a Gothic tower, but it may be ideal for observing a square, a fountain, or the facade of an isolated building. The four sides of the exceptional Scamozzi villa, the Rocca Pisana at Longio near Vicenza, reveal the alchemy of color and nature. Though plastered in white, each face has a color slightly different to the others, according to how it is exposed. The north front reveals the thinnest covering of moss, while the one that faces a field of emerald green appears to be the purest white. Sculpture is one of the most imposing forms of art but also can be the most obscure. Rarely is it viewed in the best surroundings and lighting conditions; and often it is rather depressing to see in the gallery of a museum something that was designed for the top of a column or the triumphant freedom of an open-air space.

The diversity of art reflects the diversity of global culture, of place, and of history. We can see throughout the history of mankind the links and strands that form a continuous yet ever-changing artistic force, present throughout time and all around us.

The fact that modern art is apparently intent upon adopting a different perspective, often distancing itself from art history, leads us to wonder if we really know what art is and where it is going. Yet what currently may appear to us as historical discontinuity should perhaps be seen as yet another shift in values. No longer associated with Apollo or Dionysos, no longer religious by nature and function, art has become part of our everyday experiences. What is certain, however, is that art has always existed and will continue to exist, and that the quality of its future incarnations will depend largely upon social, moral, political, and technological changes. Whatever the future holds, artists, like writers and poets, are participants of the artistic tradition of reflecting what is around them, and making their creations accessible to all people for all time.

GLOSSARY

ABACUS
The square-shaped slab at the top of a *capital*, directly beneath the *architrave*.

ABBEY
A group of buildings occupied by a self-supporting community of Christian monks or clerics under the rule of an abbot or abbess. The buildings include the abbey church, library, scriptorium, living quarters, and working quarters.

ABSTRACT
A style of art where pure form and color, together with the materials and support used, constitute the subject matter of the work. Usually associated with 20th-century art, abstract work is also evident in Muslim and ancient art.

ACROPOLIS
The elevated part, or citadel, of an ancient Greek city, built to include temples and main public buildings.

ACROTERION
A small pedestal for a statue placed at the apex and ends of the *pediment*.

ALBARELLO
A cylindrical jar, originally with a plug or lid, often made of *majolica*, once used to contain medicines or ointments.

AMBO
A raised reading desk with steps at the side of an altar, for use during the service.

AMBULATORY
The circulation aisle around the east end of a church, especially the sanctuary.

AMPHITHEATER
An open-air theater such as those used in Ancient Rome for gladiatorial contests and public entertainment.

ANASTASIS
A Greek term covering any image of, or basilica or church consecrated to, the death and resurrection of Christ.

ANCONA
A large altarpiece made of painted panels set into a frame.

ANNUNCIATION
The depiction of Angel Gabriel telling Mary that she will bear a child and will call him Jesus.

ANTEFIX
Ornamental pieces that screen eaves or provide waterspouts in classical buildings.

ANTEPENDIUM
The cover on the front of an altar, usually of rich fabric.

APADANA
Audience chamber and central room within an ancient Persian palace.

APPLIQUE
Relief decoration or trimming sewn or otherwise attached to a surface, usually cloth.

APSE
A vaulted semicircular or polygonal area used as a termination, usually to *chancels* or *chapels*.

AQUAFORTIS
An archaic term for nitric acid, used in the etching process as a corroding agent.

AQUARELLE
A painting technique using Chinese ink and transparent water-based pigments. The term is also used for work made in this way.

AQUATINT
An engraving technique using resinous material with acid, producing areas of tonal quality. It is also the term used for the product of the technique.

ARABESQUE
A curvilinear motif in painting and decoration using intertwined foliage, animal, or geometric designs.

ARCH
A curved structure, usually composed of several wedge-shaped sections resting on supports at each end. Also called an archway.

ARCHITEKTON
The Greek term for the person responsible for the plans of a building; hence the modern term architect.

ARCHITRAVE
The lower molded part of the *entablature*, the horizontal band that caps a wall or row of columns.

ARCHIVOLT
The continuous ornamental molding that follows the contours of the *arch*.

ARCHOSOLIUM
A tomb niche in a catacomb.

ART INFORMEL
The term coined to describe the spontaneous *abstract* painting of European artists in the 1940s and 1950s; similar to *Tachism*.

ART NOUVEAU
A style of decorative innovation using organic motifs in late 19th-century France and, in related forms, throughout Europe and the US.

ASHCAN SCHOOL
A group of American realist artists whose name came from their interest in the sordid side of New York street life.

ATLANTES
A sculpted male figure used within a supporting *column*. The female version is the *Caryatid*.

ATTIC
A small order set above the main *entablature*, often as ornament, as in a triumphal arch; also, the enclosing space beneath the roof of a building.

AVANT-GARDE
A group or style that is at the forefront of artistic progress; generally describes work in a radical or experimental form.

AXIS

The center line of a work of art or building, usually implying symmetrical parts on each side.

B

BALLOON-FRAME

A method of wooden construction that uses light struts to make walls.

BANDKERAMIK

Prehistoric pottery from the sixth millenium BC, characterized by incised parallel lines and cross-hatching.

BARBARIAN

A term loosely defining a broad range of peoples and art styles that existed alongside "civilized" Mediterranean cultures. From "barbaros," the Greek word for "foreign."

BAROQUE

A period of European art mainly concurrent with the 17th century. Generally an exuberant union of all the arts that was intended to act on the emotions of the spectator.

BASCULE

A balanced lever that acts so that an object is lifted by a counterweight.

BASILICA

A Roman public hall that was adapted by Christians for congregational worship.

BAS-RELIEF

A sculptural carving that protrudes from the surface.

BELLE EPOQUE

The period at the end of the 19th century and preceding World War I (French for "beautiful epoch"). It was an era of great progress in the arts and technology.

BIGIN GA

Beautiful women, the portrayal of whom was very popular in the Japanese *Ukiyo-e* school.

BISCUIT

The initial unglazed firing of pottery before decoration is added.

DER BLAUE REITER

A loose association of German artists formed by Franz Marc and Wassily Kandinsky in Berlin in about 1910, embracing a philosophy of freedom of expression. It included music and literature as references in painting. The group split during World War I.

BONE CHINA

A type of china made by the process of adding bone meal or ash to allow lower temperature firing.

BURIN

A pointed steel tool used for engraving on wood or metal to produce the lines on the surface of the plate.

BYZANTINE

The style and culture of the eastern Roman Empire, between the 5th and 15th centuries, when the capital was Constantinople. Byzantine art had a distinctive linear and symbolic radiance.

C

CABOCHON

A smooth, domed gemstone, polished but not cut into facets.

CALOTYPE

The name given to a photographic printing process invented by William Henry Fox Talbot in about 1840.

CAMEO

A stone or shell composed of layers of different colors; one layer is carved in relief, revealing the under-layer as *ground.*

CAMERA OBSCURA

A viewing apparatus using a darkened box, in which images are received through a lens and shown on a glass screen from which they can then be traced.

CAPITAL

The decorated head or crowning feature of a *column.* Many different forms have been developed.

CARAVAGGISM

A style of painting reminiscent of that of the early 17th-century Italian painter Caravaggio; closely related to *tenebrism.*

CARICATURE

A portrait that exaggerates the physical characteristics of a well-known individual, usually for satirical effect.

CAROLINGIAN

The period of early European history named after Charles the Great.

CARTOON

A detailed working drawing for paintings or other large compositions such as frescoes or tapestries.

CARYATID

A carved draped, female figure, used in place of a *column* to support an *entablature.* The male version is the *Atlantes.*

CELADON

A pale sea green color; the name is used to refer to a *glaze* originating in China and popular in Europe in the 17th century.

CELLA

The central interior room of a classical *temple,* usually containing an image.

CERAMIC

The art of pottery or an object made with clay.

CHALCOGRAPHY

The technique of engraving on copper and brass.

CHANCEL

The part of the east end of a church in which the main altar is placed. It is reserved for the clergy and the choir.

CHANGLI

The Chinese concept of a separate, creative energy that is the constant principle inherent in all natural beings.

CHA NO YU

A Japanese tea ceremony seen to have particular spiritual and aesthetic qualities.

CHAPEL

A small place of worship, sometimes one of many in a large church building, usually in honor of a particular saint.

CHARTERHOUSE

A Carthusian monastery.

CHIAROSCURO

Italian for "light-dark," this term is normally used to refer to the skill of balancing contrast in a painting and to the management of shadows. The technique was first used to dramatic effect by Caravaggio at the beginning of the 17th century. It was later used with exceptional skill by Rembrandt.

CHIASMOS

The crossing-point of "force-lines" within the human body, as theorized by Polycleitos in about 450BC.

CHINGJONG SANSU
A genre of Korean painting developed in the 17th century, marking a transition to a more realistic and, later, nationalistic, style.

CHINOISERIE
A decorative style developed in the 18th century that revived Chinese details and motifs in furniture and decoration.

CHOIR
The arrangement of stalls or seating for the choir at the east end of a church.

CHROMOLITHOGRAPHY
Lithography that provided pictures printed in several colors; most often used for popular landscapes in the late 19th century.

CHRONOPHOTOGRAPHY
A form of sequential photography illustrating movement, sometimes with superimposed images.

CIBORIUM
A canopy over a high altar, sometimes a dome set over *columns.*

CLOISONNE
A technique of enameled decoration in which raised strips create a design on metal; the resulting areas are filled with colored enamels.

CLOISTER
An arcade or *colonnade* around an open courtyard, designed for quiet walking and reflection.

CODEX
Manuscript volume or loose leaves from the Middle Ages, often illuminated.

COEMETERIA
Tombs in early Christian Rome designed as "resting places"

where the dead were placed to await resurrection. These were later developed into catacombs.

COLLAGE
A method of building up a picture using pieces of a variety of materials – paper, fabric, plastic, etc. A technique much used in *Cubism, Surrealism,* and other *avant-garde* styles.

COLONNADE
A series of ornamental columns placed at regular intervals in a straight or curving line, supporting *architraves* or *arches,* sometimes with a pavement or roof.

COLORISTS
A loose grouping of French designers between 1900 and 1925 who rejected the craft element of *Art Nouveau* and combined bright ensembles with French Neoclassical revivals.

COLUMN
In architecture, a *pillar* composed of a base, shaft, and *capital,* usually supporting an *entablature*; sometimes standing alone as a monument.

COMMEDIA DELL'ARTE
The popular Italian theater of the 16th and 17th centuries that featured standard characters in a range of familiar plot situations.

CONSTRUCTIVISM
Begun during the first years of the new Communist regime in Russia by Kasimir Malevich and followers, this movement became involved in public art and architecture in Moscow. A variety of materials, including perspex and glass, were

built into abstract, free-standing or suspended sculptural works.

COPPERPLATE
A plate of polished copper on which a design is engraved or etched; a print made from such a plate.

COUNTERFORT
A buttress used to strengthen a wall or support a terrace.

CROSSING
The place in a cruciform church where the *transept* crosses the *nave.*

CRYPT
A *vault* or other underground chamber, as in a church, used as a *chapel* or burial place.

CUBISM
A movement initiated in about 1906 when artists such as Picasso and Braque examined ways of depicting several viewpoints of a subject in one painting, thus breaking down the apparent reality of an object into a semiabstract and geometrical creation.

CUBO-FUTURISM
Kasimir Malevich used this term for work he exhibited in about 1910, when he combined *Cubism* and folk art with machine parts to convey a sense of social progress and the excitement of machinery as a liberating entity.

CUPOLA
A small *dome,* often adorning the top of a roof; also, the inner ceiling of a dome.

D

DADA
A revolutionary movement begun in Zurich in about 1915 by a group of artists and

writers, including the poet Tristan Tzara and the artists Hans Arp and Marcel Janco. It was intended to force the viewer to reevaluate the meaning of visual art by challenging accepted views and giving emphasis to the absurd and illogical. Activities included public art as performance. Also known as Dadaism.

DAEDALIC
A Greek sculptural style synonymous with the early archaic style, named after the mythical inventor and architect Daedalus, who was said to have built the labyrinth for Minos on the island of Crete.

DAGUERREOTYPE
An early photographic process in which the silver image was fixed on a copper plate.

D'AL DI SOTTO IN SU
An Italian term used to describe illusionistic ceiling painting with dramatic upward perspective.

DEMIOURGOI
The Greek word for the public craftsmen who were responsible for the design, production, and decoration of functional objects.

DIASPORA
The dispersion or spreading of people originally belonging to one nation or having a common culture.

DIPTYCH
Painted images on two panels hinged together and closing like a book; often an altarpiece. The *Wilton Diptych* is the most celebrated example.

DIVISIONISM
A method of painting by which dots of unmixed pigment are juxtaposed on the canvas so that they fuse

"optically." Greater luminosity and brilliance of color is obtained in this way. Often referred to as *Pointillism.*

DOGE
The chief magistrate of the Venetian Republic in the medieval and *Renaissance* periods.

DOME
A curved roof or ceiling often raised over a central area.

DONOR
A person who commissions and finances a work of art for public use. Donors were often featured in paintings from the 14th century onward.

DRUM
The cylinder shape below a *dome,* usually having a circle of windows.

E

EARTHENWARE
A type of pottery made from low-fired clay, usually requiring colored *glazes.*

ECHINUS
The rounded molding of a *capital* below the *abacus,* varying in design according to the architectural order.

ECPHRASIS (or ECPHASIS)
A plain decoration.

ELEVATION
The external facade of a building, or a drawing of the same.

ENCAUSTIC
A painting produced with pigments melted with wax and fixed by heat.

ENGOBE
A coating of white pipe clay applied to *earthenware,* often to support *glaze* or enamel.

ENGRAVING
A design or picture made by cutting lines into a surface, usually metal or wood. If the surface is inked, a print is produced, which is also called an engraving.

ENTABLATURE
A large, projecting molding along the top of a classical building.

EPISTYLE
The Greek word for *architrave*; the horizontal band situated above *columns.*

ETCHING
A printing process in which lines are etched on a metal plate using acid through a wax coating. Also the name given to the image produced by this technique.

EXEDRA
The ancient Greek or Roman term for the *apse* opening into a larger room. This usually contained a continuous bench and was used for holding discussions and meetings.

EXPRESSIONISM
An early 20th-century style of painting originating in Germany that expresses an emotional experience through the use of violent color and distorted line. The earliest use of the term was to define those artists who were opposed to the *Impressionist* concept of imitating nature; the work of van Gogh is an example. Abstract Expressionism is a descendant, exemplified in the work of Mark Rothko and Jackson Pollock. The term also applies to the literary movement of the same period.

EXTRADOS
The exterior visible curve of an *arch* or a *vault.*

F

FAUVISM
The Fauves ("Wild Beasts") was a term of criticism used to label a group of artists, including Matisse, who showed paintings in violent colors and distorted shapes at the Paris salon in 1905.

FIGULINE
An object, usually a vessel, made of earthenware or clay.

FISH-EYE
The distorted circular image of a photographed subject. Also the lens of small focal length that achieves this distortion.

FLAMBOYANT
A late style of French Gothic architecture characterized by flamelike curves and other elaborately styled decoration.

FORESHORTENING
The depiction of parts in a painting that recede directly toward the background. A principal characteristic of perspective.

FRESCO
A rapid wall-painting technique in which pure pigments mixed in water are applied to a fresh lime-plaster *ground.*

FRIEZE
The middle section of a classical *entablature,* usually decorated with sculpture.

FROTTAGE
The practice of rubbing onto paper, revealing the texture of the hard surface beneath, such as wood, metal, or stone. Popularly used in *collages,* especially by the Surrealist Max Ernst.

FUNCTIONAL AESTHETICISM
The aesthetic emphasis given to the purpose and structure of components.

FUTURISM
An Italian movement begun in about 1910, in celebration of progress, machines in motion, war, and dynamic destruction. Painters such as Umberto Boccioni attempted to depict this glorification of violence, progress, and motion.

G

GABLE
The vertical extension of a wall into the roof. It is usually triangular, with a window for upper rooms.

GARGOYLE
A spout, often in the form of a grotesque animal or human figure, projecting from a roof gutter to carry rain water away from the walls.

GENRE
A category of art, literature, etc. Also the portrayal of domestic scenes, such as in 17th-century Dutch anecdotal paintings.

GLAZE
A transparent layer of paint applied as the first of many washes to build up a depth of color. In pottery, it is the glassy coating, either transparent or colored, applied before firing to give a water-resistant, lustrous surface to a *ceramic.*

GLYPTIC
Of engraving or carving, especially of gemstones; also a carved object.

GOLDEN SECTION
The harmonic ratio of proportion used in the *Renaissance,* established by dividing a line so that the ratio of the smaller to larger portion is the same as the larger to the entire length. It cannot be expressed as a finite number, but it is approximately 8:13.

H

GOTHIC
A style of late medieval art and architecture prevalent in western Europe from about 1150 to about 1500. Pointed arches, ribbed vaults, and flying buttresses are among the key characteristics. The style originally attracted criticism but gradually became an established and popular style.

GOUACHE
A painting medium in water-soluble, opaque colors. It differs from transparent watercolor in that it contains glue to bind the pigments. Also called body color.

GRAFFITO
A writing or drawing technique named after the Italian for "scratching," whereby a thin top layer of white plaster is scratched off to reveal a colored layer beneath. The method can be used on a variety of surfaces.

GRES
A type of stoneware in which the pottery shows through a transparent *glaze*.

GROTESQUE
Decoration composed of interweaved foliage, bands, and bizarre animals combined in intricate arrangements. Similar to *arabesque*.

GROUND
The surface on which a painting is made. On canvas or wood panel the ground is often white oil paint.

GUPTA
A fourth to sixth-century Indian dynasty. Under its rule, a distinctive and fine style of stone- and metalwork was produced. The period was also one of achievement in science.

HERM
A *pillar* surmounted by a bust, usually of Hermes.

HIEROGLYPHICS
A system of writing in which a symbol stands for a word. Particularly applied to Ancient Egyptian pictorial writing.

HIGH-RELIEF
Sculpture obtained by carving fairly deeply into a regular stone surface, achieving a modeled, rounded effect that projects wholly or partially from the surface.

HORIZONTAL LINE
An imaginary line across a picture that represents the viewer's eye level.

HYPOSTYLE
A large hall or space over which the roof is supported by rows of *columns*. Typically found in Egyptian architecture.

I

ICON
Greek word meaning image, this originally meant a picture of Christ, the Virgin and Child, or a saint on a portable panel. They were made for Greek and Russian Orthodox Christians from the sixth century onward. Later, the term was applied more generally to symbolic images.

ICONOCLAST ART
A Byzantine style of art devoid of religious images in the eighth and ninth centuries, when such images were prohibited.

ICONOGRAPHY
The study of the meaning of visual images in art and their symbolism and allegorical significance.

ICONOSTASIS
The wall screen defining the sacred area in a Byzantine church.

IDEOGRAM
A conceptual and simplified diagram.

ILLUMINATION
Pictorial and decorative illustrations to medieval (and later) manuscripts. This can be in color, gold, or silver.

IMBREX
A terracotta tile used on classical roofs. It was curved at the edges for overlapping.

IMPASTO
The thick application of oil paint. The paint stands up in lumps with clearly visible brushstrokes.

IMPOST
A molded block between wall pillar and ceiling vault, on which the end of an *arch* appears to rest.

IMPRESSIONISM
Begun in about 1870 in France, this painting style represented a new departure from traditional art. Exponents included Monet, Renoir, Manet, Sisley, Pissaro, and many others. Derided at first, these artists explored in their paintings the concept of the "fleeting impression," the phenomenon of changing light on a surface, and other experimental optical and colorist ideas.

INLAY
A decorative process in which contrasting materials are set into a surface.

INQUADRATURA
An illusionistic wall or ceiling painting, popular in the 16th and 17th centuries.

INTAGLIO
A printing process that uses engraved lines to hold the ink. The paper and metal plates are then run through a press, forcing the ink onto the paper.

IRONSTONE CHINA
Highly fired pottery, usually white.

IWAN
A large and deeply vaulted opening that acts as an entrance portico in later eastern Islamic architecture.

JK

JAPONAISERIE
The Japanese variant of *chinoiserie*.

JASPERWARE
A dense, hard stoneware invented by Josiah Wedgwood in 1775, capable of being stained with metallic oxides.

JUGENDSTIL
A late 19th-century German decorative style similar to *Art Nouveau*.

KARYATID
See *Caryatid*.

KORAI
Plural of *Kore*, below.

KORE
A sculpture of a standing, draped, female figure, typical of Greek art of the Archaic period.

KOUROI
Plural of *Kouros*, below.

KOUROS
A sculpture of a standing male nude figure, typical of Greek art of the archaic period.

KRATER
A Greek two-handled bowl, often inscribed or decorated.

KYLIX
An ancient Greek *ceramic* drinking cup of varying shape and size, with foot, handles, and various types of decoration. Its design was imitated throughout the Hellenic world.

L

LEKYTHOS
An oil flask in Greek and Roman antiquity, usually decorated and often buried with the dead.

LETTERING
The art of inscribing letters, often associated with calligraphy. Used in art works, such as illuminated manuscripts.

LIGHTWELL
An interior space lit from above.

LINTEL
The horizontal beam made of wood or stone across an opening such as a door.

LITHOGRAPHY
A printing process using oil-based ink on a flat stone or metal plate.

LOGGIA
An "outdoor" room with the open sides usually screened with *columns*. When set above ground, it is usually long and narrow and acts as a passageway.

LOST WAX
A molding technique for sculpture in which the wax model is cased in plaster. When molten metal is poured in, the melted wax escapes through a hole in the bottom. Only one cast can be made.

LUNETTE
A semicircular space, often with a window, above a door or below the vaults of a ceiling.

LUSTRE
A type of pottery *glaze* that uses metal to give a sheen to the surface.

M

MAJOLICA
The name for low-fired pottery with colored *glazes*, mainly used for Italian *Renaissance* pieces.

MANDALA
Symbolic representation of the universe and its origins, made up essentially of concentric circles and squares, used in Hindu and Buddhist tantrism. It can be woven, embroidered, painted, engraved, created in colored sand, or form the layout of a *temple*.

MANDORLA
An almond-shaped frame used for the depictions of Christ, suggesting radiating light.

MANNERISM
From the Italian word *maniera*, this was a virtuoso style of 16th-century art and architecture (principally in Italy) in which certain features were emphasized and even distorted.

MARTYRIUM
The site of a martyr's death, usually commemorated by a small central building.

MASTABA
An Egyptian solid tomb building with sloping sides and a flat roof.

MASTER OF
An anonymous artist whose style can be recognized in more than one painting. Such artists are therefore known as "the master of" their most characteristic work.

MEDERSA
An Islamic educational institution, particularly for religious and juridical subjects. Also, the buildings in which it is found, either standing alone or attached to a mosque. It is characterized by a courtyard, often with *colonnades* on at least one side and by a *minaret*, kitchens, and an infirmary. Also known as a *madrasa*.

MERLON
The raised section between the gaps of a castle parapet.

METOPE
In Greek architecture with Doric *columns*, the lower *entablature* is divided into projections and recesses known as metopes; these often carry relief carvings.

MINARET
The tower adjacent to a mosque that is used to call people to prayer. In later developments, additional ones would be added, often in pairs, for vertical contrast.

MINIATURE
A small and detailed piece of art, especially a portrait.

MODERNISM
In Europe, during the latter part of the 19th century, artists broke away from the tradition of focusing on the realistic representation of the subject; instead, the subject became subordinate to texture, shape, and color. In architecture, decoration became subordinate to function. The modernist movement dominated much of the 20th century in Europe and the US.

MONOTYPE
A single print made by taking one impression from a painted plate direct onto paper.

MONTAGE
The process of assembling a composition using fragments of objects, photographs, or other images.

MOSAIC
A picture made up of small pieces, usually glass or stone. Most spectacularly used in the Byzantine period.

MOSQUE
An Islamic prayer hall and place of worship, usually with one or more *minarets* and often decorated with texts from the Koran.

MYTHOGRAPH
A diagrammatic representation of a myth.

N

NARTHEX
An enclosed passage between the main entrance and the nave of early Christian or Byzantine church.

NATURALISTIC
Accurately representational of the forms found in nature, without using stylized or conceptual forms.

NAVE
The main congregational area of a church.

NEOCLASSICISM
The dominant movement in art and architecture in the late 18th century, which revived the forms of classical antiquity. This preference for the order and reason of ancient Greece

and Rome was a reaction to the frivolity and ornateness of the *Rococo* style. Jacques-Louis David was among the great Neoclassical painters.

NEO-PALLADIANISM

The revival of the *Renaissance* architecture of Andrea Palladio, notably in the domestic architecture of late 18th-century England.

NEO-PLASTICISM

An idea of painting as a new "plastic" reality developed by Piet Mondrian in about 1920. His philosophy of the dynamic tension between elements governed the movement.

NGANGA

An African initiated ritual expert or traditional healer.

NICHE

A decorated wall cavity, usually intended for a sculpted figure.

NKISI

Ritual objects and sculptures from the Congo basin, usually consisting of natural objects, wood, or shell. The plural is *minkisi*.

NYMPHAEUM

A small classical *temple*, usually colonnaded. It was developed into a pleasure pavilion in the Roman and Renaissance periods, with fountains and other diversions.

OBELISK

An Egyptian, four-sided, tapering pillar, topped with a pyramid and usually bearing hieroglyphic writing. Several were taken to Rome and set up as a focal points in the city squares.

OBI

A sash worn with a Japanese kimono, often ornately decorated.

OGIVE

The diagonal molding on a Gothic *vault*. The curved and pointed silhouette was also applied to arches.

OIL PAINTING

A painting technique in which the pigment is given fluidity by mixing with oil, usually linseed, and diluted with solvents. The paint dries rather than sets, allowing overpainting and translucent "glazing."

OLEOGRAPH

A *chromolithograph* printed to simulate oil painting, usually by using a textured surface.

OP ART

Optical art is based on pattern and color effects that create optical disturbance and illusions. It was exemplified in the 1960s by the English painter Bridget Riley.

ORDER

A system to categorize architecture in which the base, plinth, cap, and entabulature conform to prescribed proportion and decorative stylization. They are principally Doric, Ionic, Corinthian, Tuscan, and Composite.

OREJERA

Ear ornaments from the Inca culture of Peru.

ORPHISM

A term coined by the French poet Apollinaire with reference to an early 20th-century style of abstract art, of which Robert Delaunay was one of the main exponents.

ORTHOSTAT

A row of stone slabs set upright around the base of ancient Near Eastern buildings.

OVOLO

The architectural term applied to a convex molding forming a quarter of a circle.

P

PAGODA

A Buddhist commemorative building consisting of diminishing stories, each with its own projecting roof.

PALEOLITHIC

The term used to describe prehistoric Stone Age culture, roughly identified as the period before sharpened stone chips were used for cutting.

PALMETTE

A classical decoration of stylized leaves in a fan shape, usually used in rows with the stem downward.

PANOPTICAN

Late 18th-century "Enlightenment" proposal for a building design, in which all the parts of the interior are visible from a single point.

PANTOCRATOR

The representation of Christ, usually shown enthroned, as the ruler of the Universe. Common in icons and the domes of Byzantine churches.

PAPIER COLLE

A French term meaning "pasted paper," papier collé describes a technique, invented by Georges Braque, in which decorative pieces of paper are incorporated into a composition.

PAPIER MACHE

A material made of paper pulp mixed with glue, or sheets of paper stuck together.

PARALLELEPIPED

A prism with six faces, all of which are parallelograms.

PASTORAL

A landscape painting depicting idealized rural tranquility and innocence.

PEDIMENT

The gable over a classical *colonnade* or portico that serves as a decorative end to the sloping roof. Originally triangular, the shape was later transformed to surmount openings of all sorts and transferred to interior woodwork and furniture.

PENDENTIVE

The curved triangular surface formed between the base of a *dome* and the corners of its supporting structure.

PERISTYLE

A continuous *colonnade*, as in a courtyard or arcade.

PERSPECTIVE

A geometric system whereby three-dimensional objects, volume, or space, are portrayed on a flat surface to the correct scale as the distance recedes. Systematic perspective was developed in Italy by Brunelleschi in the early 15th century.

PHOTOGLYPH

An engraving produced by means of light exposure.

PHOTOMONTAGE

The use of photographic images in *montage* or *collage*.

PI

The ratio between the circumference and the diameter of a circle, calculated as approximately 3.141592.

PICTOGRAM
A sign or message made up of diagrams, a set of symbols, or other images.

PICTURESQUE
A term used to describe the aesthetic approach to the landscape in the late 18th century. Texture and irregularity were deemed visually intriguing.

PIER
A solid masonry support; also, the mass between *arches* or windows.

PILASTER
A shallow, flat *column* attached to a wall and usually with a *capital* of the classical order.

PILLAR
A slender structure equivalent to a square *column*.

PILOTIS
Pillars under a building that raise it above ground level – usually applied to modern buildings with steel column-piers.

PINNACLE
A thin decorative spire, used in such places as the top of outside *piers* or buttresses.

PLINTH
A solid base that carries a *column* or statue.

POINTILLISM
Another term for *Divisionism*, associated with the work of Georges Seurat and Paul Signac.

POLYCHROME
The term used to describe sculptures or artifacts painted in a variety of colors.

POLYPTYCH
An altar backdrop of painted or carved panels, usually hinged so that they can be folded together.

POMPADOUR
A term describing a range of features of delicate and affected decor named after the mistress of the French king in the early 18th century, Mme. de Pompadour.

POMPIERS
A description of a group of French painters in the second half of the 19th century. The term referred either to the ostentation and pomposity of the artists or to their habit of depicting nude subjects wearing plumed helmets that were jokingly compared to the headgear of French firemen, or *pompiers*.

POP ART
A movement that began in the late 1950s, employing imagery of consumerism and popular culture. Advertisements, cartoons, photographs, and images of cultural icons were the basis for the brightly colored, subversive, and often humorous works produced in Britain and the US.

PORCELAIN
A form of high-fired pottery, using pure clay, that is glasslike in quality. The clay is usually white, so the decoration can be applied directly to the object.

POSTMODERNISM
A style in art, design, and architecture that contrasts with Modernism and draws from the styles of several different periods, including classical, often in an ironic way.

PRE-COLUMBIAN
The indigenous art of the various cultures of the Americas prior to the arrival of Christopher Columbus.

PRE-HITTITE
The period and culture that preceded the Hittite civilizations of about 2000BC in the Near East.

PRE-RAPHAELITES
A group of mid-19th century English painters who intended to revive the direct simplicity of Italian art before Raphael.

PRESBYTERY
The area of the church reserved for the clergy, usually at the extreme end of the *choir*.

PRIMARY COLORS
Red, yellow, and blue, and defined as those colors not possible to obtain by mixing.

PRONAOS
A portico-vestibule with side walls and an open *colonnade* front.

PROSCENIUM
The area between the backdrop and the audience in the theater, reduced in European indoor theatres to the area between stage and orchestra.

PROTOHISTORICAL
Between prehistory and the earliest documented historical events.

PSALTER
A small devotional book usually containing the psalms.

PSYCHOGRAM
An image said to be produced by a spiritual being.

PULPIT
The interior platform in churches used for delivering the sermon.

PYLON
A massive sloping wall in front of Egyptian temples with a central ceremonial entrance.

R

RAYOGRAPH
The photographic print produced by the process of shining light on photographic paper with objects placed on it, used by Man Ray between 1920 and 1940.

READY-MADE
Man-made and commonplace objects that were taken out of context and redefined as art. The term was coined by Marcel Duchamp, whose first "ready-mades" were a bicycle wheel (1913), and a bottle-opener (1914).

REALISM
Ostensibly realistic depiction, generally contrasted with idealistic and Romantic art, which sought to improve on natural forms.

RELIEF
Sculptural or decorative arrangements projecting from and supported by a continuous surface.

RENAISSANCE
A period of European art beginning in 14th-century Italy and often using ideas of classical origin.

REPOUSSE
A form of relief decoration in metalwork.

RETABLE
A decorative structure at the back of an altar, framing a picture and often including a shelf.

ROCOCO
A style of French decor in the early 18th century that

combined small relief scrollwork with shell motifs. The definition was later extended to cover all art of the period.

ROMANESQUE
A style of European art and architecture between the 9th and the 12th centuries.

ROMANTICISM
A mainly northern European style of art and literature at the end of the 18th century. Its exponents set out to challenge rational thought with emotional feeling.

ROSETTE
A decorative component in a stylized flower shape.

ROSE WINDOW
A round window with radiating *tracery*, usually on the west facade of Gothic churches.

S

SANGUINE
A red-colored drawing crayon containing ferric oxide; also known as red chalk.

SCAGLIOLA
A type of plaster, with added components, that hardens and has a polished surface resembling marble.

SECESSION (OR SEZESSION)
The Post-Impressionist style of the several art movements in central Europe that broke away (seceded) from the official academies in about 1900.

SEPULCHRE
A burial monument or building; also, a separate alcove in some medieval churches.

SERIGRAPHY
A method of screen painting in which parts of a fine mesh screen are blocked out and paint is squeezed through onto prints.

SFUMATO
A drawing or painting process of blurring the line between different colors, avoiding sharp outlines to create the effect of rounded relief.

SIMA
A classical convex and partly concave molding.

SINOPIA
A layout drawing, originally made on a wall before the plaster was applied as a base for *fresco* painting.

SISTRUM
An ancient Egyptian musical instrument in the form of a metal rattle.

SITULA
An urn or bucket-shaped vessel made of metal or ivory, for religious or funerary use.

SKETCH
An initial or spontaneous drawing, giving a rough outline and no detail.

SPHRAGISTICS
The study of seals and signet rings.

SPIRE
A slender structure tapering to a point, usually on a tower.

SQUINCH
A corner arch that supports vaulting or a *dome*, and an alternative to the *pendentive*.

STALL
One of a row of seats in a church, fashioned from wood or stone and often with carved decoration.

STELA
A stone slab carrying ancient inscriptions or designs.

STOA
A Greek covered *colonnade*, commonly in public meeting places. In Byzantine architecture, a covered hall with a roof supported by a row of *columns*.

STONEWARE
A type of high-fired pottery with impure clay but more robust than low-fired *earthenware*.

STRING-COURSE
A simple horizontal band on walls, usually molded and projecting from the walls.

STUCCO
Reinforced plaster that can be used to cover buildings or molded for decoration.

STUPA
In Buddhist or Jain religious architecture, a hemispherical monument housing sacred relics, commemorating an important event, or marking a sacred spot. Of Indian origin, the shapes and sizes vary according to country and era.

SUBLIME
An aesthetic concept established in the romantic age of the mid-18th century; an attribute that inspires awe and spiritually heightens the emotions of the viewer.

SUPREMATISM
Kasimir Malevich gave this name to a totally pure form of geometric *abstract* art.

SURREALISM
An expression of the fantastic, the dreamlike, and the bizarre by artists of the modern movement interested in the subconscious and the

interpretation of dreams by Freud. The major exponents were Salvador Dalí, René Magritte, and Max Ernst.

SWASTIKA
A cross symbol, used since prehistoric times, with arms of equal length, each having a continuation at right angles.

SYMBOLISM
A movement begun by Gauguin and his followers in about 1890 in an attempt to express abstract or mystical concepts through the use of symbolic images, representing deep emotions and spirituality.

T

TACHISM
An instinctive style of painting using bold swirls or strokes, usually abstract, popular in the 1940s and 1950s. A similar term to *Art Informel*.

TAMBOUR
A variant of a drum, usually held vertically and beaten with the hand or a stick.

TAPESTRY
A large decorative textile wall hanging, first developed in the late medieval period.

TELAMON
A support *pillar* in the shape of a male figure.

TEMPERA
Paint pigments mixed in a binding agent that hardens, usually egg yolk. Generally associated with the developments of technique in the *Renaissance*.

TEMPIETTO
A small temple and monument.

TEMPLE
A religious building devoted to the worship of a deity or deities.

TENEBRISM
A style of painting in the early 17th century that used sharp lighting contrasts or low-lit figure groups, typified by Caravaggio.

TESSERAE
Small pieces of glass or marble used in mosaics. Often in cube shapes, they can also be irregularly shaped.

TOPOGRAPHY
The description or depiction of a particular geographical location.

TORC
A neckring from Celtic cultures, made of gold or other precious metals and worn as a status symbol. It became one of the characteristics of the Barbarians in Greek and Roman eyes.

TOTEM
The emblem of a clan or group of people that becomes the symbol for social beliefs and worship.

TOWN PLANNING
The layout of urban areas according to functional and/or aesthetic criteria.

TRABEATED
A type of construction using only horizontal and vertical components, or beam-and-post, rather than arches.

TRACERY
The narrow stone shafts in windows that hold the glass, usually ornamental and decorative. Many different forms of tracery are found in churches dating from the Middle Ages and Gothic

periods, such as plate tracery, bar tracery, and panel tracery.

TRANSEPT
The side or cross spaces in a cruciform church, usually between the nave and the chancel.

TRICLINIUM
The dining room of an ancient Roman house.

TRIFORIUM
The arched passageway in the interior of a church between the aisles and the clerestory.

TRIGLYPH
The projecting part of a Doric *entablature* with three vertical strips that separate the *metopes*.

TRIPTYCH
A set of three paintings or panels hinged together, with the central one larger than the other two.

TROMPE L'OEIL
A work of illusionist art with a convincing impression of reality. From the French meaning "deception of the eye."

TYMPANUM
Either the triangular panel in a *pediment* or the semi-circular panel above an entrance, usually carrying relief carving.

UV

UKIYO-E
Japanese term meaning "pictures of the floating world," covering Japanese art of the 18th and 19th centuries.

URUSHI
A form of lacquer used in Japanese art, usually mixed

with paint to obtain a thick, shiny medium.

VANISHING POINT
In *perspective,* the point at which a set of lines converge. The boundary lines of all surfaces running to the horizon meet (vanish) at one point directly opposite the eye of the viewer – or at two points to either side.

VARNISH
A protective surface applied over a finished painting, imparting a glossy or matte appearance.

VAULT
A masonry roof or ceiling designed in a curved shape to make it rigid. The groin vault, common in *Gothic* churches, is made by intersecting two continuous *arches* with weight-bearing *piers*.

VEDUTA
A depiction of a location – usually urban – either real or imagined.

VESTIBULE
An ante- or attending room, situated between the entrance and receiving room.

VIEWPOINT
The point from which an artist sees a scene. This determines the height of the horizon line and the nature of the composition.

VORTICISM
The name given to the work of a rebel group of English artists working in about 1913, led by Wyndham Lewis. They worked with sharp geometric forms in a discordant asymmetric style, with a whirling dynamic that appeared to create an engulfing vortex.

VOTIVE
A work of art offered with a vow, usually religious.

WXYZ

WESTWORK
A large square building at the entrance of a church, consisting of a low entrance hall and above it a room opening onto a nave. In the main upper room there was usually an altar, and the whole building was crowned with a broad tower.

XYLOGRAPHY
A printing process with wooden blocks, using relief to carry the ink, and therefore opposite in technique to *intaglio*.

YAMATO-E
The generic name for Japanese painting, describing a style based on outline and flat color. It was contrasted with Chinese styles after the tenth century.

ZIGGURAT
A stepped pyramid used in the ancient Near East for religious ceremonies.

BIBLIOGRAPHY

Ades, D., *Dada and Surrealism Reviewed*, Hayward Gallery and Arts Council of Great Britain, 1978

Akurgal E. and Hirmer M., *The Art of the Hittites*, Thames and Hudson, London, 1962

Antonova, I., Tolstikov, V., and Treister, M., *The Gold of Troy – Searching for Homer's Fabled City*, Thames and Hudson, London, 1996

Bahn, P. and Vertut, J., *Images of the Ice Age*, Windward, Leicester, 1988

Bazin, G., *Baroque and Rococo*, Thames and Hudson, London, 1964

Becker, V., *Art Nouveau Jewellery*, L.P. Dutton, 1985

Beckett, Sister Wendy, *The Story of Painting*, Dorling Kindersley, London, 1994

Blanck, H. and Proietti, G., *La tomba dei rilievi di Cerveteri*, De Luca, Rome, 1986

Boardman, J., *Greek Sculpture – The Classical Period*, London, 1985

Boardman, J., *Greek Sculpture – The Late Classical Period*, London, 1995

Boëthius, A., *Etruscan and Early Roman Architecture*, Pelican, Harmondswort, rev. ed. 1978

Bonfante, L. (ed.), *Etruscan Life and Afterlife*, Aris and Phillips, Warminster, 1986

Bordes, P., *Aux Armes et Aux Arts: les Arts de la Révolution, 1789–99*, Paris, 1988

Brendel, O., *Etruscan Art*, Yale University Press, 1996

Brett-Smith, S., *The Making of Bamana Sculpture: Art and Gender*, Cambridge University Press, 1996

Byars, M., *The Design Encyclopedia*, Laurence King, 1994

Cachin, F., *Manet*, Barrie and Jenkins, London 1991

Camfield, W., *Max Ernst, Dada and the Dawn of Surrealism*, Prestel-Verlag, Munich and Menil Collection, Houston, 1993

Clair, J. (ed.), *Les Réalismes Entre Révolution et Réaction*, Musée National d'Art Moderne, Centre Georges Pompidou, Paris, 1981

Clarke, D., *African Art*, Bison Books Ltd, 1995

Coen, E., *Umberto Boccioni*, Harry N. Abrams and the Metropolitan Museum of Art, New York, 1988

Cole, A., *Eyewitness Art: The Renaissance*, Dorling Kindersley, London, 1994

Collon, D., *Ancient Near Eastern Art*, British Museum Press, London, 1995

Coot, J. and Shelton, A., *Anthropology, Art and Aesthetics*, Clarendon, Oxford, 1992

Cowling, E. and Mundy, J. (eds.), *On Classic Ground, Picasso, Léger, de Chirico and the New Classicism 1910–1930*, Tate Gallery, London, 1990

Cristofani, M., transl. Phillips, B., *The Etruscans, a New Investigation*, Orbis, London, 1979

Crow, T.E., *Emulation: Making Artists for Revolutionary France*, New Haven and London, 1995

Crow, T.E., *Painters and Public Life in 18th-Century Paris*, New Haven and London, 1985

Curtis, J.E. and Reade, J.E. (eds.), *Art and Empire – Treasures from Assyria in the British Museum*, British Museum Press, London, 1995

Curtis, W.J.R., *Modern Architecture Since 1900*, Phaidon, rev. ed. 1996

d'Azevedo, W. (ed.), *The Traditional Artist in African Societies*, Bloomington, Indiana University Press, 1973

Elgar, F., *Mondrian*, Fernand Hazan, Paris, and Thames and Hudson, London, 1968

Elliot, D., *New Worlds: Russian Art and Society 1900–1937*, Thames and Hudson, London, 1986

Faunce, S. and Nochlin, L., *Courbet Reconsidered*, The Brooklyn Museum, New York, 1988

Fer, Briony et al., *Realism, Rationalism, Surrealism: Art Between the Wars*, Open University and Yale University Press, New Haven and London, 1993

Frankfort, H., *The Art and Architecture of the Ancient Orient*, London, 1954

Gamer, P. (ed.), *Phaidon Encyclopedia of Decorative Arts 1890–1940*, Phaidon, 1978

Garb, T., *Sisters of the Brush: Women's Artistic Culture in Late Nineteenth-Century Paris*, Yale University Press, New Haven and London, 1994

Gernsheim, H. and A., *The History of Photography: from the Camera Obscura to the Beginning of the Modern Era*, McGraw-Hill Book Company, 1969

Giedion, S., *The Eternal Present: the Beginnings of Art*, Bollingen Foundation, Washington, 1962

Golding, J., *Cubism: A History and Analysis, 1907–1914*, Faber and Faber, London, 1959

Green, C., *Cubism and its Enemies, Modern Movements and Reaction in French Art, 1916–1928*, Yale University Press, New Haven and London, 1987

Gudiol, J., *Goya*, Thames and Hudson, London, 1990

Hartt, F., *Italian Renaissance Art*, Thames and Hudson, rev. ed. 1987

Haynes, S., *Etruscan Bronzes*, Sotheby's, London, 1985

Henig, M. (ed.), *A Handbook of Roman Art*, Cornell University Press, Ithaca, New York, 1983

Herbert, R.L., *Impressionism: Art, Leisure, & Parisian Society*, Yale University Press

Honour, H. and Fleming, J. (eds.), *The Penguin Dictionary of Decorative Arts*, 1977

Hornblower, S. and Spawforth, A. (eds.), *The Oxford Classical Dictionary*, third edition, Oxford University Press, Oxford, 1996

Howard, M. (ed.), *The Impressionists by Themselves*, Conran Octopus, 1991

Huyghe, R. (ed.), *Larousse Encyclopedia of Prehistoric and Ancient Art*, Hamlyn, rev. ed. 1966

Huyghe, R. (ed.), *Larousse Encyclopedia of Byzantine and Medieval Art*, Hamlyn, rev. ed. 1968

Jeffery, I., *The Photography Book*, Phaidon, 1984

Julian, P., *The Triumph of Art Nouveau: Paris Exhibition, 1900*, Phaidon, 1974

Kostof, S., *A History of Architecture – Settings and Rituals*, Oxford University Press, 1985

Lancher, C., *Joan Miró*, Museum of Modern Art, New York, 1993

Layton, R., *The Anthropology of Art*, Granada, 1981

Lodder, C., *Russian Constructivism*, Yale University Press, New Haven and London, 1987

MacGaffey., *Complexity, Astonishment and Power: The Visual Vocabulary of Kongo Minkisi*, Journal of Southern African Studies, 14 (2) pp.188–203, 1988

Macnamara, E., *The Etruscans*, British Museum, London, 1996

Martindale, A., *Gothic Art*, Thames and Hudson, London, 1991

Matthiae, P., *Ebla – An Empire Rediscovered*, Hodder and Stoughton, London, 1977

Moortgat, A., *The Ancient Art of Mesopotamia*, Phaidon, London, 1969

Morosini, D., *L'Art Degli Anni Difficili 1928–1944*, Editori Riuniti, Rome, 1985

Moscati, S. (ed.), *The Phoenicians, Exhibition Catalog (Venice)*, Bompani, Milan, 1988

Nash, S.A. and Merkert, J., *Naum Gabo, Sixty Years of Constructivism*, Prestel-Verlag, Munich and Dallas Museum of Art, 1985

Novak, B., *Nineteenth Century American Painting*, Sotheby's, London, 1986

Pach, W., *Renoir*, Thames and Hudson, London, 1984

Parrot, A., *Mission Archéologique de Mari – Le Palais II: Peintures Murales*, Geuthner, Paris, 1958

Phillips, T. (ed.), *Africa: the Art of a Continent*, Royal Academy of Arts, Prestel, 1995

Pommier, E. (ed.), *Winkelmann: La Naissance de l'Histoire de l'art à l'Epoque des Lumières*, Paris, 1991

Pool, P., *Impressionism*, Thames and Hudson, London

Potts, A., *Flesh and the Ideal: Winkelmann and the Origins of Art History*, New Haven and London, 1994

Rewald, J., *The History of Impressionism*, Secker and Warburg

Richardson, J., *A Life of Picasso, 1907–1917: The Painter of Modern Life*, Jonathan Cape, London, 1996

Richardson, J., *A Life of Picasso, Vol 1: 1881–1906*, Jonathan Cape, London, 1991

Robertson, M., *A History of Greek Art*, Cambridge, 1975

Rosenblaum, N., *A World History of Photography*, Abbeville Press, 1984

Rosenblum, R. and Janson, H.W., *Art of the Nineteenth Century: Painting and Sculpture*, Thames and Hudson, 1984

Rubin, W., *Dada and Surrealist Art*, Harry N. Abrams, New York, 1968

Rubin, W., *Picasso and Braque: Pioneering Cubism*, Museum of Modern Art, New York, 1984

Rudenstine, A.Z., *The Peggy Guggenheim Collection, Venice*, Harry N. Abrams and Solomon R. Guggenheim Foundation, New York, 1985

Scharf, A., *Art and Photography*, Penguin Books, 1974

Schlieman, H., *Troja*, John Murray, London, 1884, reprinted P.P.B. Minet, Chicheley, 1972

Schmutzler, R., *Art Nouveau*, Thames and Hudson, 1964

Selz, P. and Constantine, M. (ed.), *Art Nouveau: Art and Design of the Turn of the Century*, The Museum of Modern Art, 1972

Sieveking, A., *The Cave Artists*, Thames and Hudson, London, 1979

Spate, V., *Orphism - The Evolution of Non-Figurative Painting in Paris 1910–1914*, Clarendon Press, Oxford, 1979

Steingräber, S. Ridgway, D. and F. (eds.), *Etruscan Painting*, New York, 1985

Stewart, A., *Greek Sculpture*, Yale and London, 1990

Stuckey, C.F., *Monet: A Retrospective*, Park Lane, New York, 1986

Summerson, J., *Architecture in Britain, 1530 to 1830*, seventh edition, London, 1989

Talbot Rice, D., *Art of the Byzantine Era*, Thames and Hudson, London, 1963

Talbot Rice, T., *A Concise History of Russian Art*, Thames and Hudson, London, 1963

Tempesti, F., *Arte dell'Italia Fascista*, Feltrinelli Editore, Milan, 1976

Thomas, A. (ed.), *Beauty of Another Order: Photography in Science*, Yale University Press, 1997

Thomson, *Camille Pissaro: Impressionism, Landscape and Rural Labour*, The Herbert Press and The South Bank Centre, London 1990

Tisdall, C. and Bozzolla, A., *Futurism*, Thames and Hudson, London, 1977

Tomlinson, J.A., *Francisco Goya – The Tapestry Cartoons and Early Career at the Court of Madrid*, Cambridge University Press, 1989

Turner, J. (ed.), *Dictionary of Art*, Grove/Macmillan, London, 1996

Valkenier, E.K., *Ilya Repin and the World of Russian Art*, Columbia University Press, 1990

Van Horne, J.C. and Formwalt, L.W. (eds.), *The Correspondence and Miscellaneous Papers of Benjamin Henry Latrobe*, New Haven and London, 1984

Vaughan, W., *Romantic Art*, Thames and Hudson, 1978

Verdi, R., *Cézanne*, Thames and Hudson, London, 1992

Watson, W. (ed.), *The Great Japan Exhibition – Art of the Edo Period 1600–1868*, Royal Academy of Arts, London, 1981

Welton, J., *Eyewitness Art: Monet*, Dorling Kindersley, London, 1992

Whitford, F., *Bauhaus*, Thames and Hudson, London, 1984

Wiggins, C., *Eyewitness Art: Post-Impressionism*, Dorling Kindersley, London, 1993

Wilson-Bareau, J. (ed.), *Manet by Himself*, Macdonald & Co. Ltd., 1991

Wilton, A., *Turner in his Time*, Thames and Hudson, London, 1987

Wright, P., *Eyewitness Art: Manet*, Dorling Kindersley, London, 1993

Art and Power: Europe Under the Dictators 1930–45, Hayward Gallery, 2 October 1995–January 1996

Art for the Nation, National Gallery of Art, Washington, 1991

Art Treasures of Turkey, Exhibition Catalog, Smithsonian Institution, Washington D.C., 1966

Diaghilev, Creator of the Ballets Russes, Art, Music, Dance, Lund Humphries and Barbican Art Gallery, London, 1996

Neue Sachlichkeit and German Realism of the Twenties, Hayward Gallery and Arts Council of Great Britain, 1978

Renato Guttuso, Whitechapel Art Gallery, London, 17 May–7 July 1996

The Anatolian Civilisations, I–I, Exhibition Catalog, Istanbul, 1983

Toulouse Lautrec, Exhibition Catalog, South Bank Centre

INDEX

Acknowledgments

Picture Credits

Agenzia Ricciarini, Milan
Amici dela Scala, Milan
Archivio Electa / Sergio Anelli, Milan
Archivio Fotografico Alinari / Giraudon / Bridgeman, Florence
Archivio Fotografico Mondadori, Segrate, Milan
Archivio Fotografico Scala, Antella, Florence
Archivio Grand Gourmet, Milan
Archivio Illisso, Photographs Alfredo Moreschi, Nuoro
Archivio Illisso, Photographs Massimo Arata, Nuoro
Archivio L. Pigorini, Rome
Archivio Michelangelo and Enrica Antonioni, Rome
Bardazzi Fotografia, Florence

Collezione Banca Commerciale Italiana, Milan
Diego Motto, Milan
Doubleís, Milan
Federico Borromeo, Milan
Fondazione IBM Italia, Segrate, Milan
Foto Musei Vaticani, Vatican City
Foto Studio Pollini, Sondrio
Foto Vasari, Rome
Franco Maria Ricci Editore, Milan
Grazia Neri, Milan
Istituto Lombardo Accademia di Scienze e Lettere, Milan
Luca Carrà, Milan
Luciano Pedicini, Naples
Mario Carrieri, Milan
Photo Mas, Barcelona
Raccolta delle Stampe Achille Bertarelli, Milan

Raimondo Santucci, Milan
Realy Easy Star, Turin

The publisher wishes to thank the photographic libraries of artists, museums, public and private organizations, and companies who have kindly supplied photographic material.

Dorling Kindersley would like to thank Chrissa Woodhouse for her assistance with the editing of the text and for compiling the index; Dennis Kelly and Ann Menpes for assistance with the glossary; Luci Collings, Jill Hamilton, Caroline Hunt, Irene Pavitt, Iris Rosoff, Jane Sarluis, Mary Sutherland, and Beth Sutinis for editorial assistance; and Tracy Hambleton Miles and Zirrinia Austin for design assistance.